BY

JONATHAN LEVY

Ages of American Capitalism

Freaks of Fortune

AGES OF
AMERICAN CAPITALISM

AGES *of* AMERICAN CAPITALISM

A HISTORY *of* the UNITED STATES

..

JONATHAN LEVY

RANDOM HOUSE • NEW YORK

Published in the United States by Random House,
an imprint and division of Penguin Random House LLC, New York.

RANDOM HOUSE and the HOUSE colophon are
registered trademarks of Penguin Random House LLC.

Grateful acknowledgment is made to Yale University Press for
permission to use the following maps: Figures 12, 40, 59, and 63
from *The Shaping of America: A Geographical Perspective on
500 Years of History: Volume 1, Atlantic America, 1492–1800* by D. W. Meinig,
copyright © 1986 by Yale University; Figures 39, 40, 46, and 77 from
*The Shaping of America: A Geographical Perspective on 500 Years of History:
Volume 2, Continental America, 1800–1867* by D. W. Meinig, copyright © 1993
by Yale University; and, figures 46, 48, and 51 from *The Shaping of America:
A Geographical Perspective on 500 Years of History: Volume 3, Transcontinental
America, 1850–1915* by D. W. Meinig, copyright © 1999 by Yale University.
Used by permission of Yale University Press.

Additional illustration credits are located on page 747.

ISBN 978-0-8129-9501-5
Ebook ISBN 978-0-8129-9502-2

Printed in the United States of America on acid-free paper.

randomhousebooks.com

246897531

First Edition

Book design by Barbara M. Bachman

To Chiara

CONTENTS

—

BOOK FOUR: THE AGE OF CHAOS, 1980–

INTRODUCTION

═══

ANY HISTORIAN CAN TELL YOU THAT ORIGINS ARE A VERY tricky subject. One beginning only reveals another. Still, I know the proximate origin for the writing of this book.

More than ten years ago I was walking in Princeton, New Jersey. It was Monday, September 15, 2008. The next day I was to make the short trip to New York City to meet a friend who worked on Wall Street for lunch.

But I received a message from my friend that obviously he would not be able to meet on Tuesday, given what was happening. What was happening? I had not been following the news. I had arrived at Princeton University one month before, a greenhorn assistant professor struggling to finish my doctoral dissertation. How lucky I was to be recently hired. The academic job market was about to collapse, too. So focused on completing my dissertation in order to keep my job, I was unaware that my chosen academic subject—capitalism—was then imploding in the most spectacular fashion. For on Monday, September 15, 2008, the New York investment bank Lehman Brothers declared bankruptcy. Fearful and panicked, bankers almost completely ceased trading with one another. Seizing up, the global financial system very nearly crashed. U.S. Treasury secretary Hank Paulson dry-heaved into an office trash can. The Great Recession had begun.

I finished my dissertation. In the spring of 2009, there were bank "stress tests," and the panic finally subsided. I taught a class on the history of American capitalism to a small group of enthusiastic undergraduates who were disappointed when the class ended not long after World War II, about as far as the existing historical literature was then able to take us.

The students wanted to know the whole story, how it all fit together. I did, too.

Since then I published my first book, a history of risk and finance in the nineteenth century. I kept teaching the class, eventually at the University of Chicago, where I earned my PhD, and where I am now currently employed. Every time I taught it, the endpoint of the class moved closer to the present, as 2008 moved further into the distance. I tried to tackle the whole story, how it all fit together. I wrote this book. Then, just as I finished it in 2020, the economy took another deep dive.

Writing this book has been an education. Since 2008, in the academic circles in which I travel, there has been talk of a "new history of capitalism." Whether I like the label or not, I am considered one of its practitioners. While much of this new scholarship is excellent, in my opinion what has been missing in it has been an engagement with economics. To write this book, I have learned and drawn from a tradition of thought in economics, sustained in the twentieth century by such thinkers as John Maynard Keynes, Thorstein Veblen, Joseph Schumpeter, John Hicks, Nicholas Kaldor, and Albert Hirschman. I have also drawn from the pre-twentieth-century, so-called classical political economists that many of them engaged with, above all Adam Smith but also Karl Marx. Learning from these writers, I worked to develop the economic framework that I have employed in this book.

Every single one of these individuals is dead, almost all for quite some time. Why go back to these men, all prominent in their day, but so long departed—their ideas so long dated? After all, over the years since, economics has made remarkable intellectual progress. But this progress has been in a particular direction, cutting a path of inquiry narrower than the one that economists once carved out for themselves. Today mainstream economics follows a path of great mathematical rigor that, precisely due to this virtue, does not make much room for other accounts of economic life—including historical accounts. I have attempted to make a place for economics in the study of history. That includes contemporary economics and its offshoot discipline of "economic history," an essential body of scholarship without which this book could not have been written. But I would argue for the rightful place of historical analysis in economics, and for a broader vision of what the economy is. Dormant traditions in economic thought once argued for this position. Seeking to revive them, I have tried to recut a wider path in order to make room for the inclusion of many subjects—spanning, say, politics and society, or environment and psyche—that once were but today are not typically seen as relevant to understanding the economy in which we live. My conviction is that these subjects and many others are relevant. The need to include them is my excuse for having written such a long book.

Therefore, in addition to an economic history, this book can be read as a new single-volume history of the United States. It is a chronicle of American economic life from the English colonial settlement of North America in the seventeenth century through the Great Recession. It is divided into four Ages of American Capitalism: Book One, "The Age of Commerce (1660–1860)"; Book Two, "The Age of Capital (1860–1932)"; Book Three, "The Age of Control (1932–1980)"; and Book Four, "The Age of Chaos (1980–)".

As the United States is often rightly taken to be the quintessential capitalist society, an economic perspective does afford a unique purchase upon its history. A history of the U.S. economy must encompass a great deal: demographic trends, trade patterns, growth rates, energy regimes, incentives, and productivity measurements. But it must also encompass Thomas Jefferson's disdain for the English. Henry David Thoreau's moral critique of commerce, and Herman Melville's response. The corruptions of the Lincoln administration. Labor violence. FDR's jokes. The persistence of white supremacy. The twentieth-century architecture of shopping malls. Second-wave feminists' critique of marriage. The erotic quality of much stock market speculation. Reagan's optimism about markets. Obama's ambivalence about bankers. And much more, in the pages ahead.

1. Capitalism, a Definition

To historians, there may be no worse sin than committing anachronism, which is to read the past too much through the lens of the present. Mindful of this danger, nonetheless I confess that I have written a "presentist" book, always with an eye on the extraordinary economic times in which we are living and on what might come next—in light of what has happened in the past. Before setting out, I would like to briefly introduce the economic vision that informs this book, its core concepts and themes, and the three overarching arguments about capitalism and its history in America that run through it.

It makes sense to begin with the term *capitalism*. The word has been in common use for over a century, but it has controversially lacked an agreed-on and precise meaning. For this reason, some scholars will not use it.

At the center of my understanding of capitalism, commonsensically enough, is capital. In my view, it is the centrality of capital to this form of economic life that makes the use of *capitalism* both necessary and illuminating. In the pages ahead, capital is the framework employed to make sense of economy and economic change, rather than any of the other guiding frameworks that scholars have often used to narrate the economic past, such as the market, growth, economic rationality, industrialization, or something else.

In the academy, debates over the meaning of *capital* are no less thorny than debates about capitalism. I have written about this topic elsewhere, which need not detain us too long here.[1] But after the industrial revolution, many economic thinkers began to define *capital* as a physical "factor of production." In this view, capital is a single material "stock." Eventually, many twentieth-century economists plugged capital into a "production function," alongside another productive input, "labor." Economists' treatments of capital have grown far more sophisticated over the years, but the notion of capital as a physical factor of production persists.

That is a far too narrow and restrictive a definition of *capital*. The first thesis of the book is:

Thesis #1: Rather than a physical factor of production, a thing, capital is a process. Specifically, capital is the process through which a legal asset is invested with pecuniary value, in light of its capacity to yield a future pecuniary profit.

Capital is an object of pecuniary investment in the first instance. Only then may it become an instrument of production, if it ever does. As an object of investment, capital is a legal form of property. A capitalized object is distinctive, given its capacity to yield a future pecuniary gain above the cost of its creation, purchase, and/or maintenance—thus becoming a capital "asset" of some kind or another.[2]

Capital is no inert thing, with an intrinsic value. The value of a capital investment, being in the flow of historical events, is always uncertain. Human agents, acting in concert, must capitalize, or instill pecuniary value in, an object.[3] Through investment and disinvestment, they create and destroy assets. In this way, over American history, capitalization has transformed various entities into assets: land, enslaved black persons, factories, real estate, or financial securities, to name prominent forms. A capitalist economy is one in which economic life is broadly geared around the habitual future expectation that capital assets will earn for their owners a pecuniary reward above their cost.

In this account, capital and capitalism are not defined exclusively in relation to production or market exchange. My position is that investment, the first mover, is the best perspective from which to watch capitalism at work. Without it, there simply cannot be wealth-generating labor and production, the market exchange of goods, and, what is ultimately the point of economic life, consumption.

Related to this primary focus on investment, this definition of capital has a number of key dimensions. They are: the significance of money, credit, and finance; the essential role of expectations; the need for capital assets to have a scarcity value; and the distinction between capital and income.

First, our definition considers money, credit, and finance as fundamental components of capital that cannot be abstracted away. In mainstream economics, commonly there has been a division between the "real economy" of the production, exchange, and consumption of goods, and the less tangible and less substantial realm of money, credit, and finance.[4] In this "real" guise, capital again takes the form of a factor of production—a factory, say—that then gets used up in production, generating wealth and pecuniary income. Such activity defined the industrial revolution, an epoch-making event at the heart of the story to come. But a factor of production is only one form that capital may take. A financial asset—a stock or bond, say—might simply appreciate in markets and thus yield a money income for its owners. As Keynes once put it, "It is much preferable to speak of capital as having a yield over the course of its life in excess of its original cost, than as being *productive.*"[5] Capital is a process of valuation, in which assets are expected to yield future pecuniary profits. That process might depend on labor and the production of wealth. But by not restricting capital to a factor of production, our working definition of capital is capacious enough to encompass money, credit, and finance as critical cogs in a capitalist economy.

Further, our definition of capital underscores the role of expectations.[6] What makes an asset a capital asset is the prospective yield attached to it.

If capital is considered only a physical thing, its origins by definition must come from the past. It must represent a past accumulation, often in the form of savings. By contrast, in our definition, an important relation is not only between the past and the present but also between the future and the present. As the American economist Irving Fisher long ago explained in his *The Nature of Capital and Income* (1906), with capital assets, "when values are considered, the causal relation is not from present to the future, but from future to present."[7] In the capitalist epoch, in addition to the heritage of the past, expectations of the future—unlike the past, always an uncertain business—determine the economic present to a remarkable degree. For example, credit, consisting of nothing but trust in a future expectation, can fund a capital investment as much as a past accumulation of material wealth—like, in an agricultural setting, stored up seeds carried over into the winter from the harvest. The present in a capitalist economy is thus determined by a mixture of past expectations, still working themselves out through actions, and present expectations that relate future horizons, of various durations, back to the present. If expectations rule, then individual and collective psychological projections of the future play a dynamic role in a capitalist economy.

If the definition of capital as process is capacious, it does have an important limit. Capital assets must have a scarcity value. The legal ownership and control of capital assets cannot be free and open to all. In a capitalist economy there must not only be capital. There must be capitalists—the owners of capital, who are charged with the critical task of investing their capital when and where they like and thus jump-starting the capitalist economic process. As Veblen argued, capitalists essentially corner the market in capital assets.[8] That, as Marx emphasized before him, is why the nonowners of capital must work for them to survive, let alone attempt to thrive. The owners of capital control investment decisions. More than anything, the investment power is what makes capitalists so powerful.

There are many ways to engineer and maintain the scarcity value of a capital asset. Land, say, may be ring-fenced. Law, for instance, especially property law, has been a foremost method.[9] In its primal money form, the scarcity value of capital is much determined by the rate of interest. What determines interest rates is a complicated matter. But for centuries, a metallic standard set a limit on the quantity of money, including on the availability of credit, as expressed in the going prices of interest rates. More recently, it is a state authority, the central bank—in the United States, the Federal Reserve—that through setting interest rates has the most power to expand and limit the quantity of money and credit. Periods of price inflation after moments when the state has reasserted the scarcity value of money—after three wars, and once in peacetime, the Volcker interest rate "shock" of 1979–82, named after Federal Reserve chair Paul Volcker—are thus all critical moments in the history of American capitalism. All else being equal, the less capital there is, the more one can get with it—if one has it.

Finally, there is the capital-income distinction. The value of a capital asset relates to its prospective pecuniary income. But the asset must be distinguished from its yield—capital from income. The distinction matters in tracing out important economic shifts. The capital-income distinction also helps organize change over time in the evolution of U.S. political economy. The United States was born with a political economy anchored in the widespread distribution of productive capital among white men— chiefly landed property but also enslaved black people. During the course of the industrial revolution, a higher concentration of private capital ownership among relatively fewer capitalists came about. And U.S. politics shifted toward a new focal point, toward the distribution not of capital but of the income yielded from capital. After the New Deal, during the twentieth century and into the twenty-first, what I call "income politics" has predominated, whether it has taken the form, variously, of income taxation, labor union collective bargaining, nonprofit philanthropy, or redistributive welfare policies. Thus the capital-income distinction offers a vantage point from which to understand the relationship between politics and economics under capitalism, especially as it relates to issues of equality and inequality. One of the fundamental arguments of the book will concern the distinction between "income politics" and a politics of capital.

2. The Profit Motive, Key but Not Enough

In the previous section, I argued that because of the future-based quality of capital, psychological projections of the future are important for understanding capitalism. If one common misconception is that capital is only a factor of production, then another is the belief in the purely rational psychology of all economic agents, including capitalists. Here the general picture is of capitalists who, like great calculating machines, are always sufficiently motivated to rationally invest their capital in pursuit of the highest possible pecuniary return, or profit. Economic efficiency results.

By contrast, this book argues:

Thesis #2: Capital is defined by the quest for a future pecuniary profit. Without capital's habitual quest for pecuniary gain, there is no capitalism. But the profit motive of capitalists has never been enough to drive economic history, not even the history of capitalism.

Consider this thesis a working rule of thumb rather than as a hard and fast rule. The issue is complicated, admittedly. At the extreme, there has been the pathological exception, the owner of capital who seeks only the highest pecuniary gain on capital and nothing more. Meanwhile capitalist economies have a number of devices—many legal contracts, especially debts, for instance—that impose binding duties on agents to seek pecuniary profit. Further, is not profit making at work in a deeply structural way in a capitalist economy? Do not the need and the motive for pecuniary gain constantly impinge on nearly everyone's lives? Must we not go to work, even to a job we dislike? Must we not consume? All so that capital gets its yield? It feels like the answer is—yes!

Yet the working assumption that even the greatest capitalists of all time have always been purely rationally motivated to maximize their profits at all costs and against all other considerations simply does not hold up on historical scrutiny. The ideological belief that a capitalist economy is governed by a rational economic calculus intrinsic to our natures and dedicated to the pursuit of moneymaking is so deep-seated in our culture that it can be difficult to shake. But the profit motive alone simply cannot explain what happened in the economy or why. As much as capital exerts pressure to pursue profit, it needs help. The help it gets, as well as resistance against its imperatives, matters decisively.

This is something of a paradox. The pull of profit expectations on economic life defines capitalism. However, the participants in a capitalist economy must be motivated to pursue its end—profit—by something other than that end. To be clear, that something is not necessarily disinterested, or laudatory, although it may be. So crucial to capitalism, technological innovation has very often resulted from the estimable cultivation of human ingenuity. Bold entrepreneurial risk-taking is also often worthy of high praise. But slave owners were entrepreneurial capitalists who eyed their bottom lines, even as they were motivated by, among other things, their quest for racial domination. Or in the era of industrialization, Andrew Carnegie left behind a profitable business as a financial speculator in railroad stocks and government bonds in the 1870s to become a steelmaker and make even greater profits, but only because in the first instance, he would recall, "I wished to make something tangible," as he had come to view his financial speculations as parasitical.[10] Henry Ford, another fabulous industrial profit maker, was an industrial tinkerer at heart, albeit with borderline totalitarian aspirations. The "automobile business," one of Ford's closest associates remarked, was a by-product of "his real business, which is the making of men."[11] I do not believe that my students have come to the University of Chicago, one of the world's great centers of learning, merely to earn a pecuniary return on their families' investments in their "human capital"—although it is well documented that the pecuniary return for higher education in labor markets has soared in recent decades. When, in the midst of the Great Recession, Goldman Sachs CEO Lloyd Blankfein remarked that his bank was busy "doing God's work," he likely believed it.[12] Self-deception, after all, is one of the great themes of capitalist moral psychology. Meanwhile, given the risks of climate change, is continued capitalist investment in fossil fuels profitable in the long term, or is it better interpreted as an expression of rather irrational, destructive human motivations?

In sum, capital's quest for pecuniary gain has always been complicated by a great variety of rational and irrational human motivations—sometimes energized by them and sometimes, as we shall see, enervated. Though it exists, the profit motive has always been entangled in complicated ways with larger individual and collective projects. For instance, what separates the ages of American capitalism, I will argue, are not strictly economic variables but rather political initiatives: the British Empire's mercantilist project of the 1660s, as it transformed its fledgling North American colonies; the electoral triumph of the antislavery Republican Party in 1860s, and the secession of southern slave states; the New Deal of the 1930s, responding to the Great Depression; and the beginning of the Volcker interest rate shock of 1979, followed by the election of Ronald Reagan in 1980.

And it is not just capitalists that matter. The expansion of commerce in the young American republic, for instance, does not make sense without the egalitarian yearning of many households for the sense of political independence and social autonomy provided by landownership. Industrialization does not make sense without understanding the nineteenth-century moral and psychological split between male entrepreneurial drive and female domestic affection. The generation and division of incomes in the twentieth century cannot be explained without charting the fate of labor unions, including their resistance to unrestrained capitalist profit making. The phenomenon of obsolescence behind consumerism, which accounts for the major part of the spending of incomes today, is often a matter of individual and collective fantasies about personal transformation through the purchase of goods. No account of American capitalism can afford to not grapple with the rise of "nonprofit" philanthropic wealth. Without attending to these projects and many more, we cannot fully understand the operating principles of the economy in which we live.

In brief, what propels capitalism is not any singular drive. There is no single essential quality of human nature, whether an economically rational profit motive or something else, that will unleash capitalism, if only obstacles against it are removed. The heart of the subject is this: dynamic amalgams, contradictory drives, and productive tensions account for the swirling motivations and factors, economic and not, that make for a capitalist economy at work.

To sum it up to this point:

Capitalism is an economy—an instrumental means of producing things for consumption—geared toward the achievement of capital's end, which is pecuniary gain. Capital is not an inert thing, a factor of production. It is a legal asset, property owned by a capitalist, that people and institutions instill with a peculiar kind of value that is related to a prospective pecuniary yield. Thus that property is capitalized. Capital may be invested in different objects, or forms of capital. Investment—not production, exchange, or consumption—is the first mover in a capitalist economy, though the relationship between investment and these other economic sites must be explored in great detail.

While profit is the end of the economic system, the rational profit motive of individuals or groups never shines independently and is not enough to drive capitalism. Attention must be paid to the many factors that motivate and sustain the capital process, and to those that push back against it, that account for the generation of pecuniary incomes, including profits and pay. This requires placing a capitalist economy in a variety of historical contexts. The critical role of putatively noneconomic issues is one of the principal reasons there is a need for a history of capitalism, and why the pages to come will consist not only of charts and statistics but also of political speeches and the diary entries of housewives, poems, and paintings.

If capital is the core economic process at stake in capitalism, the *ism* in capitalism also speaks to the significance of much that typically falls outside the purview of "the economy," when narrowly conceived. The focus must be widened, the depth of field increased. The history of capitalism must be economic history but also something more.

3. The Economic Problem

The book proposes a third overarching thesis about the part that investment plays as the critical actor on the economic scene, and that explains the distinctive characteristics of capitalism as an economic system. Since its arrival, capitalism has enjoyed long periods of economic development and growth. Economic growth, an increase in the value of production per head over time, is one of capitalism's distinguishing characteristics, and high rates of growth have long distinguished the American economy from others. But capitalist development has always been punctuated by repeating cycles of boom and bust.

In the long sweep of human history, capitalism has made a quite recent appearance. No matter which century any particular historian would date it to, its presence represents only a speck of time. Before capitalism, societies usually scraped along just above subsistence. The owners of material wealth rarely saw their wealth as capital. Nothing much induced them to orient their economic activities around investing it in light of profit expectations. In that sense, they lacked "ability to invest," as the economist Albert Hirschman once called it.[13] Any surplus wealth was more commonly hoarded, if only because the wealthy were invested in hoarding their social and political power. The worst off, for their part, hoped not to starve. Then something changed. Capitalism. The owners of wealth became owners of capital and, using their power in various ways, sought to invest their wealth for a future pecuniary profit. The emergence of capitalism must, in part, be explained by an historical oddity: the appearance of a new ability and willingness to invest that kick-started new kinds of wealth-generating labor and production.

But once capitalism was achieved, a propensity to hoard has always threatened to win out again.

> Thesis #3: The history of capitalism is a never-ending conflict between the short-term propensity to hoard and the long-term ability and inducement to invest. This conflict holds the key to explaining many of the dynamics of capitalism over time, including its periods of long-term economic development and growth, and its repeating booms and busts.

Building on thesis two, this thesis says that long-term committed investment will not just happen. When it does, the reasons why must be interrogated; no appeal to transhistorical economic rationality will work. Here putatively noneconomic factors matter greatly. The seventeenth-century New England Puritans, for instance, believed that commercial profits evidenced the salvation of their souls, and so they invested in commerce. A list of such reasons could go on and on. But the propensity to hoard may still win out over the ability and inducement to invest. It has many times in the past. In the current age, it has again.

The gist of thesis three was first suggested—only dashed off, really—by Keynes during the Great Depression. Buried in a paragraph near the end of *The General Theory of Employment, Interest, and Money* (1936), Keynes speculated:

> There has been a chronic tendency throughout human history for the propensity to save to be stronger than the inducement to invest. The weakness of the inducement to invest has been at all times the key to the economic problem.[14]

A thriving capitalist economy in which investment flows to its most efficient and profitable use is not a natural state of affairs. The reason the inducement to invest for the long term is weak, Keynes argued, is that the short-term "liquidity preference" of the owners of capital is usually stronger.[15]

Liquidity, an abstract concept and for that reason perhaps daunting, is a central theme of this book and so requires definition and explanation.[16] Liquidity is a relative quality of a commodity, including a subset of commodities—capital assets. First and foremost, a liquid asset is one that maintains its value over time.[17] For its owner, it acts as a safe warehouse of value, and thus a store of wealth—a lull from disquietude. For much of history, money was a hard metal, like gold, that stabilized its value due to its lack of physical deterioration. When money enjoys a stable value over time, it thus acquires one attribute of liquidity.

But a second attribute defines liquidity. Another reason money is typically a relatively liquid asset—in a well-functioning capitalist economy, the most liquid—is that there is always a ready buyer for it. In fact, one of money's functions is to be a means of transaction; money can readily be traded.[18] For this reason, in capitalist economies money is also a means of speculation, the rapid conversion of capital in and out of assets in pursuit of short-term pecuniary gain. A liquid asset thus offers its owner a precautionary lull from disquietude but also an energetic means of speculation, of rapid investment and disinvestment. Today, for instance, a stock market is organized around the principle of liquidity, or the idea that there should always be a willing bidder for every asset.

The two attributes of liquidity create a contradiction. One characteristic that makes an asset liquid—the fact that it is readily tradeable—can also be a reason why it is a store of value over time. When hoarded, a liquid store of value makes possible the next speculative strike but also a withdrawal from economic activity altogether, or the precautionary storing of wealth. If money credited can accelerate economic activity on the side of supply, money hoarded—not expended as purchasing power on investment or consumption—can sap demand and cripple economies from achieving their productive potential.

At this point, it makes sense to distinguish liquidity further, in order to grapple with the contradiction at hand. What I will call "transactional" liquidity speaks to one fundamental aspect of liquidity, the ready presence of buyers for goods in markets. Next, the second kind of liquidity is what I will refer to as "speculative," as liquidity makes possible the option of rapid trading in and out of various capital assets in pursuit of short-term speculative gain, even if it is never exercised. Finally, there is the preference for "precautionary" liquidity: an owner of wealth chooses to store value over time, seeking the psychic return of security, perhaps even at the expense of pecuniary profit. Speculation and precaution appear to be opposites. The former is busily energetic and active, while the latter is nervously cautious and inactive. But both are live options when capital is hoarded in a liquid form, and both differently express a short-term propensity to hoard, by contrast to the inducement to invest long term.

Indeed, the final link in this chain concerns the relationship between liquidity, in all its guises, and long-term investment. Money may serve as a means of transaction and a store of wealth. But money does not produce anything. If money is typically the most liquid good, then the purchase of relatively illiquid factors of production—money as a means of long-term investment—leads to the great leaps forward in wealth-generating enterprise and production. During the industrial revolution, for instance, the owners of capital parted with liquidity and invested in large-scale factories. These assets were illiquid. The industrial revolution required, to some extent, what may be called an "illiquidity preference." Henry Ford's River Rouge factory, outside Detroit, was hard to price, let alone sell. It also physically wore out through use, depreciating and losing pecuniary value. But it was responsible for epoch-making leaps in economic productivity. Ford, a great critic of speculation, was, however, a capitalist rarity.

Over the history of American capitalism, investment in wealth-generating production has typically come about through speculative investment booms. Confidence is the emotional fuel of these booms, and money credit the economic fuel. For instance, the speculative investment boom of the 1830s led to the capitalization of land and slaves and the extension of commerce across space into the Mississippi River Valley. It powered greater economic production. In comparison, the speculative investment boom of, say, the 1980s was far more speculative. It did not so much power greater economic production, although it did spawn new forms of employment in and related to financial services.[19] Short-term speculation can risk becoming an end in itself, merely a spin of capital's top in the money form.

At the same time, the liquidity of capital also makes possible sudden stops, reversals, and repetitions. If confidence in the future collapses, so does long-term investment. In financial panics, nervous actors particularly fear the risks of long-term investment. Horizons recede. Precautionary hoarding saps demand and through that channel supply as well, undermining economic activity and leading to slumps. For instance, in the wake of the twin financial panics of 1837 and 1839, credit retrenched, and economic development decelerated. After its repression during the post–New Deal Age of Control, the speculative investment boom of the

1980s inaugurated the return of the repeating capitalist credit cycle and its associated periodic slumps.

Liquidity and illiquidity are relative qualities, which must get attributed by actors to capital assets. They are not essential properties of them. Should trust ever collapse in a currency, its value may destabilize, and it ceases to be liquid. For centuries of U.S. history, an enslaved black person was relatively liquid—more easily convertible, in southern capital markets, than land, and a chosen store of value. Back then landed property could have been relatively more liquid. It was just that the slave economy of the South was not institutionally, legally, or psychologically organized that way by its rulers. But then, enslaved persons were also illiquid. They were persons, whose value depreciated over the life cycle, as their exploited labor yielded profits for their owners from production. Or much more recently, before 2007, another appreciating asset, the "mortgage-backed security," was considered by the largest banks that traded them to be very liquid—nearly as liquid as cash—until, due to rising home mortgage defaults, its value was questioned. Suddenly confidence collapsed, and they and nearly all other assets somehow tied to them became not tradable at all—illiquid. It is because the global financial system of today is premised on the principle of liquidity that it nearly collapsed—and likely would have completely without the Fed stepping into capital markets to backstop transactional liquidity. For a capitalist economy to function, some asset or another must enjoy the attributes of liquidity. Capitalist economies need a relatively liquid asset as a psychological anchor. If it is not money it will be something else.

Tracing the relative strength or weakness of the inducement to invest in light of liquidity preference makes it possible to see the overarching reasons for how and why, over time, capital has sometimes been invested in enterprise but sometimes not. It makes possible a history that can capture, on the supply side, the great long-term illiquid investment booms, and capitalism's restless transformation of productive methods: histories of labor, market expansion, technological innovation, entrepreneurship, and the growth, equitable or not, of wealth and money incomes. But it also makes it possible to capture the speculative convertibility of capital across assets, including money and money-like assets, and moments of demand-sapping hoarding: the repeating energetic upswings and panicked downswings of the capitalist cycle of boom and bust.

In sum, liquidity preference ties all three theses of the book together. It opens up to analysis the variety of factors at stake in the capital process that drive production but cannot be reduced to the productivity of capital; the liquidity of assets makes possible irrational forms of speculation and precaution that undermine any operative notion of a purely rational profit motive always at work behind economic processes; liquidity enables productive booms and enervating slumps. They are not oscillations around any "real" market equilibrium. They are all part of one eventful and sequential history of capitalism.

Within this general framework, the first half of the book tells the story of the emergence of American capitalism, focusing on the broad expansion of the ability to invest—chiefly in commerce, land, and enslaved black people. In economies where markets for goods are not ever-present—every single economy until quite recently, including in early America—the presence of transactional liquidity is doubtful. Over many centuries, the rise of commerce, through the slow buildup of market institutions, meant more transactional liquidity—a greater scope for sales, hence more commerce. The history of how and why this happened preoccupies much of Book One, "The Age of Commerce." Book Two, "The Age of Capital," begins after the Civil War and the abolition of slavery and thus slave capital. It explains how and why there were new long-term fixed investments in the high-energy, fossil-fuel-powered "factors of production" of the industrial revolution.

The first half of the book is a story of long-term economic development. It is a history of the enlargement of commercial opportunities for some, and the experience of domination for others, leading nonetheless to extraordinary achievements in wealth-generating production—first through the multiplying effects of commerce and finally through the multiplying effects of industrial investment. Development drew many resources, including people, into an emergent capitalist economy, in which economic lives and relationships took new shape. Sometime during the nineteenth century, the United States became the fastest-growing economy in the world, in terms of both the production of wealth and the augmentation of money incomes. By the end of the century, it was the largest and richest national economy on earth, even if, over the course of capitalist development, economic inequality increased. Arguably, there is no more extraordinary instance of economic development on record than the case of the eighteenth- and nineteenth-century United States. The high American inducement to invest in this period is a phenomenon that must be explained.

But with higher money incomes, the possibility of investment-undermining speculation and precaution appeared. Paradoxically, the higher money incomes were, the greater the risk that money could enable investment-undermining liquidity preference. During the 1920s the industrial revolution culminated with the arrival of electric-powered Fordist mass production, the greatest leap forward in productive capacity in world history. Yet it was accelerated by a great, credit-fueled speculative investment boom, the Great Bull Market of the 1920s, and followed by the greatest bust in the history of capitalism, the Great Depression of the 1930s.

The second half of the book follows the long arc from the Great Depression to the Great Recession. It begins with Book Three, "The Age of Control." During the 1930s, New Deal liberalism sought to control capital, by regulating it but also by inducing private investment in employment-giving production. Doing so, New Deal policies still shifted income away from capital and toward labor. But now a new reason to hoard emerged—capitalists' objections to political interventions in their investment power. A new kind of liquidity preference came into shape, in addition to the speculative and precautionary—what I will refer to as "political" liquidity preference, as the owners of capital threatened to not invest long term unless their political demands were met.[20] Regardless, during World War II, the state finally intervened and, through the fiscal multiplier of public investment in military production, ended the Great Depression. The United States ascended to hegemonic position in the world economy. The postwar period saw a private corporate investment boom in industry, the rise of consumerism, and the attempt of Cold War liberalism to stabilize the U.S. domestic and world economies.

But Cold War liberalism failed, and industrial society perished. A new age opened after 1980, examined in Book Four, "The Age of Chaos." Since then, I argue, there has been a relative shift to a capitalism defined by a very high speculative liquidity preference. Capital left fixed physical structures, to become more financial, intangible, leveraged, roving, and unsettled.

I call this the capitalism of asset price appreciation, which directs the bulk of fresh income gains not to labor earnings, or pay, but to the owners of capital, whether the era's financial capital, "human capital," or "social capital." This capitalism, which has so exacerbated inequality, has been fueled by the return of the capitalist credit cycle and speculative investment booms that, by historical standards, are very speculative indeed. In the new pattern of speculative investment lay the possibility for the panicked downswing of September 2008—the week after my Wall Street friend informed me that he could not meet for lunch—and the Great Recession that followed. After 2008, the same dynamics defined the economic recovery, which, strikingly, exhibited continuity with the pre–Great Recession economic pattern, until the U.S. economy experienced an even more vertiginous collapse in the spring of 2020. Once again, through the channel of liquid assets, speculative liquidity preference gave way to the fearful, precautionary variety and undermined economic production and employment.

Thus the propensity to hoard has triumphed again in our own times. The weakness of investment—in terms of quality and quantity—is the key economic problem. If there is one argument, quite prominent over the past decades, that this book argues against, it is that the free mobility of capital will accord with any rational or intelligent design when left to its own devices—that private investment will result in the greatest fulfillment of economic potential, with an allocation of goods that is reasonable, optimal, and just. I object to this argument.

Some of my moral and political sympathies will become apparent over the course of the book, but my primary motivation is to set the historical record straight. History does not confirm the belief in the existence of some economic mechanism through which the pattern of capital investment will simply lead to the best possible outcome so long as it is not interfered with. One likely outcome, among others, is that the propensity to hoard will win out, exacerbating inequality and crippling economic possibilities. As the profit motive is not enough, a high inducement to investment must come from somewhere outside the economic system, narrowly conceived. History shows that politics and collective action are usually where it comes from.

For good and for ill, and the historical record reveals many instances of both, it is possible for investment to win out over liquidity preference. The following pages present the history of how and why it has, when it has, and with what consequences over the ages of American capitalism.

BOOK ONE

———

THE AGE OF COMMERCE

1660—1860

COMMERCE

T HE PROFIT MOTIVE HAS NEVER BEEN ENOUGH TO PROMPT long-term capitalist development. For capitalism to emerge, more than obstacles against private initiative must be lifted—there must be inducements. The origins of American capitalism are to be found within the history of a particular political project that mixed varied impulses into a dynamic amalgam that created something new. The project was empire.

Not just any empire. American capitalism was first the result of the seventeenth-century English imperial effort to colonize the Caribbean and the Atlantic seaboard of the North American continent. The project, carried out by imperial statesmen, pious Christians, aristocratic lords, and gentlemen capitalists—often in the same figure, such as the first Earl of Shaftesbury, Lord Anthony Ashley Cooper (a leading character in Chapter I)—was motivated by many reasons. However strong or faint, commercial self-interest was one of them.

Commerce, the exchange of one unlike thing for another, has existed for time out of mind. Capitalist commerce, or exchange in expectation of a pecuniary profit, is more specific and recent. It is characterized by forward-looking investment in the generation of gain through trade. Episodically, capitalist commerce existed in Europe, as well as in many communities all over the world, long before the English colonization of North America. English colonizers, with their prayer books, farm animals, and sea-worn nerves, brought the habit of capitalist commerce to North America in the seventeenth century. They encountered indigenous nations, many of whom also desired to trade unlike things but who had different conceptions of economic life.

The efforts of the English, then the British Empire, led to the first North American political-economic settlement. It took some time to develop, but it lasted from the late seventeenth century to the outbreak of the American Revolution. It is the subject of Chapter 1, "Mercantilism." Mercantilism was a variety of imperialism in which rulers considered foreign commerce to be a critical source of state wealth and power and therefore an "affair of state." Mercantilist empires jostled and fought for a larger slice of the world's commerce. The state and the market, public and private, were fundamentally entangled and mixed from inside one another. British North American commerce was thus inseparable from an Atlantic geopolitical project, in the context of an interimperial European struggle over market access in the Atlantic world.

Empire kick-started the process of commercial growth, as described a century later by Adam Smith in *An Inquiry into the Nature and Causes of the Wealth of Nations* (1776). Introduced in Chapter 1, the concept of "Smithian growth," or the cumulative process resulting from the interactions of commercial self-interest, the division of labor, and the extent of markets, helps explain long-term commercial development throughout this age. By expanding market institutions, Smithian growth at once depended on and created greater transactional liquidity—as in, a greater scope for sales and more trade in goods. More commerce brought increasing returns. The effect of what may be termed a "Smithian commercial multiplier" is to generate ever more wealth for a community as a whole, regardless of its distribution.

Central to the process of Smithian growth, as it unfolded in early America, was the European enslavement of African and Afro-descendant people. Enslaved persons, as portable forms of productive capital, could be coerced against their will to move to places where they did not want to go, and to labor. While Smith was a critic of slavery, nonetheless in Smithian terms racial slavery increased both the extent of markets and the Atlantic division of labor. During the seventeenth and eighteenth centuries, there was a series of colonial slave-based commodity export booms to Europe, of sugar, tobacco, and later cotton, among other items. Thus the desire for imperial glory, racial domination, and pecuniary profit combined into violent tensions that fueled the British inducement to invest in America.

Commercial inducements in this age existed alongside stark restrictions on commerce. There were religious arguments for commercial empire, but also religious prohibitions on commercial "covetousness" and "self-love." There was commercial self-interest, but also a deep commitment to the maintenance of social hierarchy. And in a preindustrial era, before the tapping of fossil-fuel-energy supplies, ecology set a hard, organic limit on wealth production. In this setting, Chapter 2, "Organic Economy, Household Economy," introduces the dominant institution of American economic life until far into the nineteenth century—the household.

Households collectively organized labor and production. While some owned slaves, land was their dominant form of property and productive capital. Typically, until nearly the end of this age, most households directly consumed most of their output. But they also brought surplus goods to commercial markets, to exchange for that which they could not produce and perhaps also to increase their wealth. Typically, each household consisted of a "head," an adult man, who was the husband, father, and master. His dependents were his wife, children, servants, and slaves. Politically, the head of household was "independent," vested with a civic status to participate in the polity, as well as to rule in the household—a subsovereign of the empire. Landownership was widespread among households in British colonial North America. Despite the success of Atlantic commerce, property-owning white male heads of household emerged as the age's dominant figures. They set their eyes on the lands of the empires, nations, and communities that were indigenous to North America.

The Seven Years' War (1756–63), a global conflict in which the British Empire defeated the French Empire, implicated North America, and London imperial officials perceived that the colonists were not carrying their fair share of the empire's fiscal burden. Imperial taxes imposed on North American commerce, together with imperial limits set on the spread of western colonization, triggered a political crisis and ultimately led in 1776 to the War of American Independence.

After the American Revolution, there was a political struggle in the new republic over the postrevolutionary political-economic settlement, which is the subject of Chapter 3, "Republican Political Economy." The Caribbean-born revolutionary Alexander Hamilton led a party of national elites who, by mixing public and private authority, sought to emulate the British example and use the alchemical power of banking corporations and "pecuniary capital," as Hamilton called it, to trigger long-term economic development in commerce, agriculture, and manufacturing. Many of Hamilton's reforms proved lasting. They gave rise to a new monetary, financial, and credit system, although not immediately to industrialization. In the end, a different long-term republican vision for U.S. political economy won out, the Virginian Thomas Jefferson's Empire of Liberty. This settlement made a politics of property—widespread property ownership in land and slaves among white male heads of household—the anchor of U.S. political economy. To ensure that, it focused on the commercial and slave-based colonization of the agrarian West.

Following the Revolution, the new United States was not only a republic. It also joined the family of early modern empires. After the War of 1812, the Kentucky senator Henry Clay led a neo-Hamiltonian effort to legislate an "American system" to guide national commercial development from above—consisting of national transportation infrastructure, industrial tariffs, and a Bank of the United States. It failed, killed by the Democratic Party of President Andrew Jackson (the subject of Chapter 4, "Capitalism and the Democracy"). The rise of democracy in America fueled a popular, near-populist rage over participation in commerce. An anti-elitist politics of equality of commercial opportunity was born. Monarchical empires long ruled their colonies by accommodating local differences. Transformed, the script played out in the Empire of Liberty, too. In Jacksonian America, the individual states were largely left to politically guide their own economic development. Some states, not all, funded the public infrastructure of roads and canals to expand market access, which led to continental Smithian growth. Northern states carried out slave abolition. Southern states did not, as a series of cotton booms, and white fantasies of racial domination, spread slave-based commercial production west.

In the Age of Commerce, the dominant forms of productive capital were land and slaves. But at the same time, there first appeared the repeating capitalist credit cycle of confidence, credit, and speculative investment, followed by bouts of panic, hoarding, and commercial retrenchment. The contradictory drive of speculative investment called forth wealth-generating labor and enterprise. But two great democratic waves of imperial conquest and commercial expansion were punctuated by the financial panics of 1819 and 1837. The subject of Chapter 5, "Confidence Games," is the attempts by various figures—the showman P. T. Barnum, the transcendentalist Henry David Thoreau, and the novelist Herman Melville—to make moral sense of the increasing place of commerce in everyday American life. The chapter also clarifies concepts crucial for making sense of the relationship between long-term economic development and the repeating capitalist credit cycle, throughout the ages.

The Empire of Liberty was not to last, and the rise of democracy began its undoing. Jackson's Democratic Party insisted on sphering the political economy, or disentangling government from private market activity. In the Jacksonian politics of "antimonopoly," for instance, corporations—which had long been considered mixed public and private entities, chartered and brought to life by the state only for a "public purpose"—became increasingly stamped "private" by law. Commerce was increasingly marked private in the first instance, distinct from government, even if its consequences could still be politically regulated. The tense new relationship between politics and economics arose from a relationship without rather than a mixture from within. This vision of democracy hemmed in the capacities of the federal government, for fear it might bestow political "privileges" on elites rather than ensure commercial equality of opportunity. Almost by default, the ties of private commerce were left with the task of binding together a national political union.

Commerce alone was not up to the task. For by the 1840s, centuries of commercial development had resulted in the rise of two distinct American capitalisms in the North and South, the subject of Chapter 6, "Between Slavery and Freedom." In the South, following the same pattern as before, there was yet another western cotton boom. In the North, by contrast, far more novel changes accelerated. A "free labor" version of western colonization made conquests into the Great Lakes region. Before 1840, commerce had bound together the "Old Northwest" and the "Old Southeast" via the Mississippi River system, but afterward northwestern trade began to flow eastward—via the new railroads, in addition to the waterways. There it linked up with a new urban industrial society, where economic investment was shifting into the productive capital of the industrial revolution and where independence was defined by self-ownership, rather than by the ownership of land or slaves. Of equal importance, northern moral and affective investments were moving into the new breadwinner-homemaker family, different from the households of before. The breadwinner-homemaker family sphered not only private from public but also home from work—another stable tension, achieved through opposition rather than entanglement.

The greatest opposition to emerge was between the North and South. In many respects, the disparities between the northern and southern varieties of capitalism sharpened after 1840. But there was no definitive reason why the differences could not be accommodated politically. Rulers, in fact, designed early modern empires to incorporate different economies, societies, and cultures into the same composite political orders, the point being to facilitate the exchange of unlike things—more commerce.

What brought about the end of the Age of Commerce in America was precisely the issue that had initiated it—a geopolitical struggle over commerce, and over a particular kind. From the seventeenth century, enslaved capital had played a vital role in the extension of capitalist production across North American space. The free labor vision of the North now hoped to forbid its spread. The Republican Party, which arose during the national political crises of the 1850s over the extension of slavery in the West, desired a new political-economic settlement. No one was better at articulating the moral and economic reasons for it than the party's candidate for president in the election of 1860, Abraham Lincoln. Lincoln said slavery should exist only where it already stood and someday should die out altogether.

When Lincoln was elected president in 1860, Republicans announced that the slaveholders' western conquests were over. The rise and fall of American slavery frames the Age of Commerce.

CHAPTER I

MERCANTILISM

====

WEALTH IS POWER, AND POWER IS WEALTH. THE APHORISM commonly attributed to the Englishman Thomas Hobbes, author of the great political philosophical treatise *Leviathan* (1651), was later invoked by Adam Smith in the greatest treatise ever written on commerce, *An Inquiry into the Nature and Causes of the Wealth of Nations* (1776).[1] Smith was a Scot, not an American, but up until 1776, Scots and Americans shared something in common: both were subjects of the British Empire. In the Age of Commerce, empire and capitalism grew up together.

For centuries, empires had long assessed their control over land, population, and taxable resources. In Europe by the eighteenth century, commerce had become the most dynamic generator of imperial wealth and imperial power.[2] How states might best promote commerce was Smith's focus in *The Wealth of Nations*, published the year the thirteen North American colonies declared their independence from the British Empire.

Smith said Britain might let the colonies go, arguing that what he called the "mercantile system"—the imperial policies that defined the commercial relationship between Great Britain and its colonies, against which the North American colonists were then revolting—did not promote the wealth of nations. Smith admired the commercial character of British North America, and today many consider him to be something like a patron saint of capitalism, as, supposedly, he was critical of all government intervention into "the market."[3] That was not so.[4] Smith was a theorist of political economy, of the relationship between the ordering of power and the generation of wealth. He made no categorical separation between the political and the economic, or state and market. The question for him was their relationship and the consequences of their complicated overlap. The wealth of nations could be the result only of good policy making.

However, *The Wealth of Nations* does not begin with a policy analysis. Rather, book one lays out Smith's explanation of economic commercialization. To understand the dynamics of preindustrial capitalism, there is no better place to begin but here.[5] Book one of *The Wealth of Nations* holds the key to explaining the development of American capitalism from seventeenth-century English colonial settlement through the American Civil War, the era spanning the Age of Commerce.

Smith explained how the self-interested pursuit of commercial gain, breeding more commerce, tends toward an increasing division of labor. When the "extent of the market" for goods expands on the demand side, spurred on by self-interest under the pressures of competition, producers specialize, and on the supply side the division of labor increases. So then does labor productivity. The ongoing search for "gains from trade" induces more capital investment. In the cumulative process, economic activity brings increasing returns.[6] Everyone may gain from trade. The wealth of nations grows. This is what economists today call "Smithian growth," the combined and interactive result of self-interest, the division of labor, and the extent of markets.[7]

The analysis of commerce in book one of *The Wealth of Nations* is of great explanatory power, but it is incomplete. For the North American colonies, as well as their commercial character, were conscious political creations, in which politics and Smithian growth dynamically interacted. There was no capitalism in North America prior to the long-term British investment in imperial expansion. By force, states had to increase the "extent of the market."

The British project to do so was imperialist in character, of a mercantilist variety. Mercantilism had no fixed body of doctrine.[8] Smith named his own enemy when he spoke of the "mercantile system," as neither he nor anyone who came before him had used the term *mercantilism*. Nonetheless, during the seventeenth and eighteenth centuries, a common set of basic assumptions about the relationship between political and economic life held together that can usefully be labeled *mercantilist*.

Foremost, mercantilists promoted an understanding of political economy in which there was no categorical separation between state and market. Smith inherited this legacy. But unlike Smith, mercantilists defined national economic prosperity as the existence of a positive "balance of trade" with other nations. Greater market access and more commerce were the sources of imperial wealth, but only when a nation exported goods of a value greater than it imported, including in relation to its colonies. More coin flowed into the nation's coffers at the expense of its geopolitical competitors. "Foreign trade produces riches, riches power, power preserves our trade and religion," insisted East India Company governor Josiah Child in 1681.[9] Mercantilists took for granted a zero-sum global economy, occupied by warring states forever fighting over market access abroad.[10] Not all nations could gain from trade, not all at once.

In this economic combat—because so much commerce was seaborne, as goods, in this era, moved far more economically over water than overland—overseas colonies could be of decisive commercial importance. After the English Civil War, the Restoration English state moved to incorporate its wayward early North American colonies into its expanding imperial, mercantilist orbit. As it did, mercantilism transformed, and American capitalism was born.

1. The First Earl of Shaftesbury

The great pivot for British North American commercial development was the period after 1660, when Parliament restored Charles II to the British throne eleven years after the execution of his father in the English Civil War. Up until then, English colonization had been a haphazard affair, with early efforts leading to repeated failures—in terms of survival, let alone commercial gain.[11] A few ventures had "planted" lasting settlements in the Caribbean, the Chesapeake, and New England, but these colonies were still afterthoughts back home. Asia, the "East Indies," compelled much greater interest.

The Restoration English state reasserted authority over the Atlantic colonies. Legislation, including a series of parliamentary "Navigation Acts," sought to restrict much American colonial commerce to within the English Empire (and within the British Empire after the 1707 Act of Union between England and Scotland). The political-economic settlement was to last throughout the eighteenth century.[12] The British Empire strengthened in the Atlantic, commerce flourished, and the North American colonies prospered.

Among those who had crossed the English Channel to the Netherlands in order to persuade Charles II to return from exile was Sir Anthony Ashley Cooper, soon to be Lord Ashley. In 1672, serving as Charles II's lord chancellor, Ashley became the first Earl of Shaftesbury.[13] Shaftesbury was to be a leading figure in Restoration England. During the Civil War, he had played both sides, Crown and Parliament, before joining the victorious forces of Oliver Cromwell. After Cromwell's death, Shaftesbury then helped to restore Charles II to the throne. But he remained a vocal critic of royal absolutism, becoming a founder of the liberal-minded Whig Party. He opposed Charles II's wish for his Catholic brother James to follow him on the throne, and he fell out with the king in 1673. Eventually, in 1682, Shaftesbury fled England for his own Dutch exile. But he fell ill in Amsterdam and died in 1683.

By then, Shaftesbury's name had been dragged through the mud. When the king first broke with him, the earl's nemesis, the great French mercantilist Jean-Baptiste Colbert, had reveled in the political downfall of "the most knavish, unjust and dishonest man in England."[14] Meanwhile at home, Lord Ashley's political opponents accused him of tarnishing "Old Beloved Commonwealth Principles" for the sake of his own private commercial self-interest.

A public figure, Shaftesbury did have a great number of private commercial interests. He was a "gentlemen capitalist" of the rising English Empire.[15] As a member of the gentry class, Shaftesbury owned vast landholdings in Dorchester. Like many Whigs, and unlike many of their Tory political opponents, Shaftesbury was among the more enterprising of English lords. He sought to "improve" his lands and thereby increase their productivity and commercial yields. In that process, land became something more than the property and wealth that sustained gentry class rule. It also became a form of productive capital.

Shaftesbury was also involved in many commercial projects abroad, although he avoided established lines of commerce with Europe and Asia. He took little interest in New England. If Hobbes famously called the state of nature "nasty, brutish, and short," Cromwell called New England "poor, cold & useless."[16] Shaftesbury's private commercial interests concentrated on the West Indies.

Lord Ashley co-owned a 205-acre plantation in the British colony of Barbados, tended by white indentured servants and African slaves. He also co-owned a ship, *The Rose*, that participated in the African slave trade. Later investments included holdings in the islands of the Bahamas, Bermuda, and New Providence. Shaftesbury's private interests sprawled over the West Indies. Not surprisingly, an active concern for Atlantic colonial affairs distinguished his public career. One of Shaftesbury's biographers claims that after the Restoration, he was "better informed about colonial affairs" in America "than any man in England."[17] In 1672 Shaftesbury created the powerful Council of Trade and Plantations and became its president. For a time, the earl was the closest thing there was to an English minister for North American colonial affairs. In Shaftesbury, the entanglement of private interest and public power was nearly complete.

The result was a propulsive energy. It is difficult to appreciate, after the fact, what a fantastical project the quest for an Atlantic empire was at the time when Shaftesbury and other gentleman imperial capitalists embarked on it. Nothing quite like it had ever happened before. Convention offered only so much guidance. Shaftesbury may have been better informed about America than any man in England, but a thick fog of uncertainty remained.[18] At a minimum, any oceangoing commercial venture or empire-building endeavor took months, if not years, even to attempt to execute. No one, including Shaftesbury, could reasonably have expected fulfillment of the Atlantic imperial project within a single lifespan. Desire for power and glory, for piety and profit, and in individual cases who knows what else, all mixed together into the same cocktail of motivation to increase the reach of the English Empire across the Americas—and to make way for more commerce.

Shaftesbury held one project dearer than others, and that was the colony of Carolina—his "darling."[19] In 1663 he was one of the original eight lords proprietors of Carolina. He had grand designs for the imagined expanse stretching 350 miles from Virginia south to Spanish Florida and by pronouncement westward to "the South Seas." A decade later, before departing for exile, illness, and death in the Netherlands, the earl could be found frequenting London coffee shops, begging men to emigrate to the colony. The Ashley and Cooper rivers bear his name in South Carolina today.

As Shaftesbury rose to power, he formed a like-minded circle around him. In 1666, then chancellor of the exchequer, Shaftesbury traveled to Oxford suffering from a liver ailment. A young physician installed a silver tap to his abdomen and likely saved his life. The young physician was also a philosopher, John Locke. Locke joined his new patron's household in London, earning his keep as a secretary to the Council of Trade and Plantations. Locke even invested in the Bahamas projects, and together the two drafted the (never executed) *Fundamental Constitutions of Carolina* (1669).

Decades after his patron's death, Locke would go on to write the *Second Treatise of Government* (1690), a famous critique of royal absolutism that premised its philosophical argument on an archaic "state of nature" when "in the beginning all the world was America."[20]

Locke would later be considered a founder of modern liberalism. Indeed, Shaftesbury's intellectual circle advocated religious toleration and freedom of conscience. Before the Restoration, a few members of Shaftesbury's group had also been members of the Hartlib circle, followers of the philosopher and statesman Francis Bacon, and of the Prussian émigré polymath Samuel Hartlib, who believed in the possible infinite "improvement" of the world.[21] Eventually these sensibilities would crystallize, and the refractions would become the eighteenth-century British Enlightenment. But when it came to politics, Shaftesbury's circle was not against the exercise of state power. The Restoration was very much a state-building project.

Among public officials, Shaftesbury stands out because he sought to make colonial American commerce specifically an "affair of state." Benjamin Worsley, a Hartlibian before the Restoration and afterward a member of Shaftesbury's circle, explained that the state's interest in commerce was "widely different from the mercantile part of it."[22] For it was the duty of the merchant to consider not the public interest but rather only his "privatt profitt." Shaftesbury agreed. The state should promote commerce, an ever more critical source of imperial wealth. But the state must also regulate private self-interest so that commerce might lead to a desirable public end. The paradox that state authority should encourage the wealth-generating capacities of private commerce yet still restrain commercial self-interest— a dangerous impulse that threatened moral and political order—defined mercantilism. It would define the Age of Commerce. The "privatt profitt" motive was not enough. Even when it was active, a long-enduring English political-economic tradition said it must never run unchecked.

2. The Mercantilist Tradition

Tightening the imperial bonds between England and the North American colonies, Shaftesbury and his circle would transform mercantilist doctrines and jump-start a long era of North American commercial development. These men had inherited a worldview, however, that in its fundamentals could already be characterized as mercantilist.

English commerce was flourishing in the early seventeenth century, but in 1618 the Dutch rebellion against Spanish rule cut off the English cloth trade with the European continent, England's main source of exports, causing a sharp English commercial contraction.[23] The hard times encouraged early North American colonization, but at home debate about the causes of the bust focused the English mercantilist cast of mind. The result was three building blocks for Shaftesbury's generation to work with: the ethical ideal of "commonwealth"; the state theory of "political economy"; and the economic doctrine of "balance of trade."

Mercantilism was first a political translation of the religious impulse at work in the concept of commonwealth. The commonwealth was an ideal vision of a "body politic," consisting of interdependent and hierarchical ranks and orders. The dominant metaphor was anatomical. God was the head. Next came the nobility, down the chain of being. The poorest "sort" of commoners was at the bottom. Organically, the commonwealth functioned to achieve the collective interest of the common (or public) good. It had room for self-interested commerce, but individual acquisitiveness might upset it. The ultimate end of economic life was not private commercial gain. Rather, people should earn a proper share according to their function in the larger body politic. The commonwealth was not egalitarian. Nonetheless, it fulfilled an ethical-religious ideal of fairness.[24]

Commercial self-interest was understood to be a formidable adversary, as moralists recognized that it sprang from a source within human nature that was perhaps inexhaustible. In Christian theology, "self-love" was a manifestation of original sin. But medieval scholastics also followed Aristotle, who wrote in *The Politics* that the natural universe was finite. But in commerce men might seek to "to increase their money without limit," as human desire was "infinite."[25] Centuries later, in English commercial society, Hobbes noted in *Leviathan* "a perpetual and restless desire of power after power, that ceaseth only in death," among men, as if he were stating the obvious.[26] Altogether the commercial quest for profit might dangerously unleash infinite human desires. The limitless quest for something essentially finite would disrupt the natural harmony of the universe.

By the time English colonizers first came ashore in North America, the genie of commercial self-interest might already have been let out of the bottle. English colonizers saw the fish, fowl, and nature of America as "commodities."[27] Reasonably enough, many Native Americans desired to trade with Europeans for things they themselves did not have or could not produce. On this basis, long-distance Native exchange networks, linking the Caribbean to the continent, had long existed.[28] Nonetheless, some Indians noticed something different and strange about the English economic personality, and some Englishmen agreed. Thomas Morton, a New England fur trader, speculated that "[Indians] lead the more happy & freer life, being voyde of care, which torments the minds of so many Christians. They are not delighted in baubles, but in useful things."[29] The myth of the "primitive Indian," unspoiled by commercial interest, was born. In fact, for Indian nations, commerce was inseparable from relations of kinship and friendship, but also from captivity and war-making alliances. Some English colonists attempted to flee their settlements and join indigenous communities. Far more got down to business instead.

A historian once held that capitalism arrived from Europe in America with the "first ships" and that the entire project was little more than a commercial gambit.[30] But various means to check capital's quest for pecuniary gain also arrived that constricted that quest but also lent it validity. The ethical-religious notions at work in the commonwealth ideal traveled to colonial North America. The New England Puritan minister Thomas Shepard worried that commercial self-interest was a "raging Sea which would overwhelm all if [it] have not bankes."[31] The early-seventeenth-century Virginia colony, organized as a joint-stock company in 1606, was perhaps a near parody of commercial England, animated, according to one historian, by "the reckless and single minded pursuit of individual gain."[32] Nonetheless, seventeenth-century England and its colonies abounded with religious denunciations of unbridled individual "covetousness" and "greed."

The austere Calvinism of the early New England settlements was a response to the "covetousness" of commercializing England. John Winthrop, governor of the early Massachusetts Bay Colony, was a wealthy lawyer from Sussex, one of the most commercial regions in England. In 1630 he boarded the ship *Arbella* bound for America and sat down to write "A Model of Christian Charity." Winthrop's blueprint for a "city on a hill" was boilerplate commonwealth. God intended hierarchy: "in all times some must be rich, some poor, some high and eminent in power and dignity; others mean and in subjection." Winthrop asked, "What rule must we observe in lending?" Sometimes it was appropriate to engage men "by way of commerce," whereas other times it was not. Temptations of "pleasure" and "profit" could never secure moral order. But that did not mean there would not be commerce. There would definitely be commerce. The Massachusetts Bay Colony (1629), after all, was also chartered as a joint-stock corporation, with investors. The great problem would be to reconcile commercial self-interest with the "common good."[33]

New England Puritans tormented themselves about the proper balance. Robert Keayne was a London merchant and a member of the 1630s great migration of Puritans to America. In 1639 a fellow merchant accused him of selling six-penny nails for ten cents a pound, an exorbitant profit. Winthrop fined Keayne the extraordinary sum of £200, and Keayne was summoned before Boston's First Church, where he publicly bemoaned his own "covetousness" while Pastor John Cotton scolded him for trading according to the "false" principle that "a man might sell as dear as he can, and buy as cheap as he can." That was not "the just price."[34] What was the just price? Cotton alluded to communal norms and the intrinsic value of goods. No one could say exactly how much was too much, but one could have an anxious moral conscience about it.

These tensions fueled more commerce. Religious scruples might limit commercial self-interest, but in the Puritan economic personality, they also moralized commerce, paradoxically inducing a greater investment in commerce—comprising a contradictory drive. Commercial success, always a matter of great uncertainty, might signal the predestined salvation of the soul. The possibility spawned a Puritan commercial initiative that was anxious but an initiative nonetheless—in the argument of the German thinker Max Weber's *The Protestant Ethic and the Spirit of Capitalism* (1905).

At the time when Keayne was bemoaning his covetousness, in England a translation of commonwealth principles from religious moralizing into government policy making was well under way. Moral denunciation could do only so much. Good laws backed by the coercive apparatus of the state were necessary to harmonize commerce and commonwealth. In this spirit, mercantilist market regulations, regulating everything from prices and wages to the quality of goods, filled many volumes.[35] In this way, the state went about the work of "political economy."

In seventeenth-century thought, there was no such thing as "the economy" as a distinct sphere from other arenas of human experience, as it is known today.[36] In the late eighteenth century, Adam Smith still wrote of "political oeconomy." *Oeconomy*, which descended from the Greek root *oikos*, invoked the prudent management of a household's economic resources. Smith described political economy as "the science of a statesman," aimed at achieving "plentiful" resources for national consumption while supplying "the state or commonwealth with a revenue sufficient for the public services."[37] Political life and economic life were entangled. Emblematically, Shaftesbury, one biographer has stressed, was a man of "mixed character, acting from mixed motives" in his private and public lives, to the degree to which they could be separated.[38] Political economy would retain this core attribute—the refusal to separate states and markets, the joint pursuit of public good and private interest—throughout the Age of Commerce, far into the nineteenth century. Even if it has not been so dominant thereafter, this foundational mercantilist principle lives on, over the ages, to this day.

While inspired by the ethical need to maintain the domestic commonwealth, mercantilist political economy was born outward facing. Mercantilism was forged in the midst of a series of seemingly never-ending imperial wars among European empires, often over access to colonial commercial markets.[39] Child, of the East India Company, defined commerce not in terms of mutual exchange but rather as "a kind of warfare."[40] In the Atlantic, the Iberian powers had first claimed dominion over the Americas. The English settled Barbados in 1625 in part because Spain neglected it. The English had to fight to gain and keep their Atlantic colonies. At war with Spain, Cromwell sent a fleet to the Caribbean in 1654, with the goal of conquering Hispaniola, but England would settle for the violent colonization of Jamaica.[41] In the 1660s and '70s, England fought a series of wars against the Dutch, explicitly over global market access.[42] In 1664 Charles II dispatched a fleet to conquer New Netherland, which became the New York colony. English colonization in the Atlantic proceeded thus.

After the Restoration, in the wake of (yet another) bout of pan-European religious bloodletting between Catholics and Protestants, England's rulers shifted relatively toward thinking of empire in terms of commercial benefit much more than religious conquest.[43] Enough religious slaughter, thought Shaftesbury, and besides, the earl wrote to Charles II, considerations of "trade" were "of far greater import now than ever." The "Interest of Commerce," if formerly "neglected," had in "late years" become an "Express Affaire of State." For it was "Trade and Commerce alone that draweth store of wealth along with it and its Potency at sea by shipping which is not otherwise to be had."[44] European nations began to suffer from what Adam Smith's friend and fellow Scottish philosopher David Hume would call "jealousy of trade."[45] Without the wealth generated by Atlantic commerce, Shaftesbury told the king, the English would be powerless before the Dutch and the French (and maybe even the Swedes). It was a difficult and fraught balancing act to defend the commonwealth in the face of commercial expansion at home while promoting commerce abroad on behalf of the state's geopolitical interests.

In this context, the mercantilist economic concept of the "balance of trade" was a running scorecard tallying which imperial state was winning in the global zero-sum struggle over commerce. The doctrine had philosophical underpinnings, in the same neo-Aristotelian concept of a finite universe in which balance, not increase, was the natural state of affairs. Continuously over time, there could be no increasing returns to economic activity, of any kind—including commerce.[46]

As an accounting framework, balance was borrowed from the commercial Italian city-states, such as Florence, Venice, and Genoa, where double-entry bookkeeping enabled merchants to balance their credits and debts, and where Renaissance aesthetic ideals of balance and proportion were prominent. Mercantilists sought to increase national wealth, but they did not live in a capitalist world of exponential economic growth. No one ever had. The concept of a finite universe, with a finite stock of wealth and commerce, reflected what must have seemed an inevitable brute material fact in an economic world where most populations struggled to scrape above subsistence. A surplus must simply come at the expense of someone else—or from untapped riches from a so-called New World.

In its crudest formulation, a nation knew it was achieving a positive balance of trade when more bullion—gold and silver—flowed into it than was flowing out. The way to achieve that was for the home country to export more goods of a greater pecuniary value than it imported. In today's economics, this is called having a "current account surplus."

Adam Smith would caricature balance of trade doctrine as the ham-handed equation of national wealth with a stock of bullion, as if the goal of mercantilist policies were to stack up as much gold and silver as possible. That was not a complete mischaracterization. "Let the foundation of a profitable trade be thus laid," declared Francis Bacon, "that the exportation of home commodities be more in value than the importation of foreign; so we shall be sure that the stocks of the kingdom shall yearly increase, for then the balance of trade must be returned in money or bullion."[47] However, recent scholarship has emphasized that many seventeenth-century economic thinkers were far more sophisticated in their analysis of money—more sophisticated than some economists today, who believe money is but a "neutral" device for dispensing with barter, having no "real" effects.[48] The most incisive mercantilists recognized that money is a dynamic factor in economic development. For in addition to being a medium of transaction, as well as a unit of account, money may also be a form of credit—and thus a form of pecuniary capital. Credit, at the very nerve center of capitalism, may finance, and thus draw out, more commerce, labor, and wealth-generating enterprise. Increasing returns to economic activity are unlocked.

A quasi-myth, common in economic thought, has it that the origin of capital must be accumulation and savings, or abstinence from spending. The interest rate on loans is then the market price that equilibrates the supply of savings and the demand for investment. Savings can, of course, provide funds for investment. But credit—backed by trust, confidence, expectation, and imagination, if not outright sheer fantasy—can also fund capital investment in new enterprise. Enterprise then creates new wealth, resulting in more savings, and so investment is as likely to lead to savings as savings is to investment.[49] Some economic thinkers in the latter half of the seventeenth century very nearly stumbled on this idea.

Drawing from anatomical commonwealth metaphors, seventeenth-century mercantilists often lamented the scarcity of money by comparing it to a lack of "circulating blood."[50] In *Leviathan*, Hobbes, for instance, spoke of money as the "sanguification of the Commonwealth."[51] Drawing from prior European practices, English merchant-bankers were beginning to accept deposits of hard currency and issuing certificates in return against them. The certificates exchanged hands as money, thereby increasing money's circulation. Or merchant-bankers might even make investments in excess of their deposits in reserve, or issue commercial loans in excess of those same deposits.[52] Altogether, as if by some process of alchemy, the volume of "bank money," or "credit money," expanded. The quantity of money remained tied to the volume of minted, hard currency. But since coin backed the proliferation of bank money, more hard currency might lead to multiplying credits, more capital investment, and thus more enterprise and production for the community as a whole. Adam Smith well understood this process.[53] In the United States, after the American Revolution, Alexander Hamilton would preach it.

The pre-Restoration Hartlib circle of the 1650s, departing from neo-Aristotelian notions of a finite universe, became fascinated with credit money as a source of commercial expansion and civilizational "improvement." In this revision of classical mercantilist thought, the goal was not to stack up and hoard coin. It was precisely the opposite, to increase the circulation of money and credit so as to multiply commerce and generate new wealth. For this reason, the circle favored low interest rates, which required expanding the quantity, or supply, of money. But demand for money may also determine interest rates. Anxiety during slumps could lead merchants to distrust the future. Out of precaution, they might increase the demand for money, as a safe store of value—rather than lending it out, as commercial capital. The result would be to push interest rates up.[54] "High Interest decays Trade," wrote one English mercantilist in 1621. "The advantage from Interest is greater than the Profit from Trade, which makes the rich Merchants give over, and put out their Stock to Interest, and the lesser Merchants Break."[55] Decades later Child argued in his *Brief Observations Concerning Trade and Interest of Money* (1668) that "reducing the Interest of Money to a very Low Rate" was nothing short of the "CAUSA CAUSANS" of prosperity.[56] Since ancient times, the historical record does not contradict the thesis.[57]

In this context, laws banning usury—high, stifling interest rates— became mercantilist devices. The prohibitions expressed the religious origins of mercantilism. Excessive covetousness in the form of high interest was forbidden, as it threatened the ethical ideal of commonwealth. Yet usury caps also kept interest rates low, which prevented merchant-bankers from exploiting the scarcity value of coin. By undercutting mercantile precaution, the effect of state intervention was to induce greater commercial investment and risk taking. The legal rate of interest in England was 10 percent after 1571. In 1624 it was reduced to 8 percent. In 1651 it fell to 6 percent, where it stood until 1714. From what is known, in practice most English commercial loans hovered around 6 percent in the late seventeenth century.[58] Child advocated that government push the English rate down further to the going Dutch market rate of between 2 and 3 percent. Of course, if there were more investments in commerce, and more wealth production, there would be more fiscal resources for interimperial war making—including for Child's East India Company to fight for market access in Asia.

All told, the way to ensure that hard money did not drain from the community, halting the multiplication of credit and commerce, was to ensure that exports exceeded imports—to have a positive "balance of trade." But here again, if at times balance was fetishized, the mercantilists sensed important truths about economic development. The more states secured market access and demand for goods, the larger was the growth of specialized manufacturing. Then and since, manufacturing has been a more dynamic generator of wealth than agriculture. Thus export demand for industry may translate into what a later economist would call a "foreign trade multiplier," as the extra amount of demand may redound and encourage greater production and innovation on the side of supply.[59] Mercantilists supported those home industries that were capable of producing goods for export. Further, colonies could act as consumer markets of last resort, or "vents," for manufacturers. For even as commerce and manufacturing expanded in unison, urban industry posed risks for the commonwealth—namely, poverty and unemployment if home industry ever slumped. "Rebellions of the belly," Bacon chimed in, as if England's rulers needed reminding, and they did not, "are the worst."[60] Mercantilists generally promoted subsidies, taxes, and tariffs to protect employment-intensive as well as hard-currency-earning manufacturing exports.[61] They wanted more commercial investment, and they would also target its content—industry. Still today, policies that subsidize domestic manufacturers are called mercantilist.

3. Mercantilism Transformed

After the Restoration, Shaftesbury and his circle inherited this mercantilist tradition and transformed it. Policy doctrines, however, are not self-executing. States must build up the capacity to wield effective power. On its own terms, the extension of the English Empire in the Atlantic world was stunningly successful. It set the political and legal foundations for a century of North American commercial development and the first long American economic boom.

The task was daunting. To put it mildly, mercantilist theory, of whichever vintage, then sharply diverged from practice in England's North American colonies. No matter how absolutist the pretensions of the Crown were or were not, imperial sovereignty was more aspirational than accomplished. What historians call "composite" and "plural" rule, in which authority was dispersed to different institutions, was common, even inside England.[62] Tellingly, joint-stock corporations—subsovereigns of a composite empire—which were owned by private investors, were first

granted the task of colonizing North America and governing English subjects.[63] The great theorist of unitary and exclusive state sovereignty,
Hobbes, in a chapter of *Leviathan* on "Those Things That Weaken or Tend
to the Dissolution of a Commonwealth," referred to the "great number" of
corporations, so many "lesser Commonwealths in the bowels of a greater,
like worms in the entrails of a natural man." Hobbes, it turns out, was a
shareholder in the Virginia Company.[64]

Of necessity, at the edges of empires especially, sovereignty, the authority to rule, was contested and shared. For in North America, there were
indigenous powers. Early on, some European colonizers promoted the
myth that Native Americans were vanishing, in order to promote Euro-

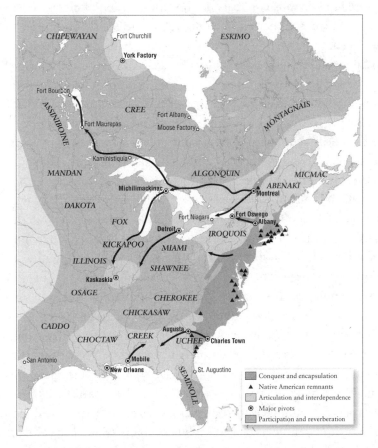

EUROPEAN ZONES OF ENCOUNTER WITH NATIVE AMERICANS
IN NORTH AMERICA, C. 1750
Despite European conquests, for centuries Native Americans controlled
the vast majority of the North American continent.

pean colonization.[65] In fact, Native American nations would long possess the vast interior of North America and would continue to rule the major part of the coastlines long after European contact. Upon arrival, Europeans could ceremoniously plant a flag, erect a cross, and read a proclamation, but none of it meant much on the ground.[66]

Only slowly did the English expand their enclaves. In 1636–38 the New England colonies, in alliance with the Narragansett and Mohegan nations, unleashed a devastating war against the Pequot, and in 1646 the Virginia Colony had conquered the Powhatan Confederacy.[67] Deadly pathogens began to ravage some Native populations, as European power started to fan out from coastal and riverine outposts, whereupon it encountered indigenous political communities, which often governed long-existing Native commercial circuits. By far the most organized Native power in contact with English North America was the Iroquois Confederacy, which had established trading alliances with various Indian nations. Through a trade in animal furs, the Iroquois absorbed early European settler-colonialists into their preexisting commercial networks.[68] The brute fact of Native power was one reason men like Shaftesbury focused on the Atlantic commercial relationship between the colonies and the home country. London imperial authorities imagined claiming dominion over the continental interior, but at first it was only a fantasy.[69]

In fact, London authorities exercised a rather weak dominion over their own Atlantic colonies.[70] In principle, colonial commerce existed to favor England's balance of trade. The colonies should not produce manufactures but instead should import them from England, stimulating English employment and exports. The colonists must not trade with England's enemies but must give the home country its commerce. Cromwell's Navigation Act of 1651 codified a long-standing rule that all colonial trade be conducted in English ships. Few of these laws held sway. Barbados colonists greeted the Navigation Act of 1651 by more or less declaring commercial independence—a right to trade with all European powers. Jamaican colonists commonly traded with the Spanish, and Spanish "pieces of eight" minted from the silver mines of Potosí provided the initial "sanguification" of nearly all of England's colonies. English colonists also sought out cheap Dutch credit and shipping.[71] The violations committed by New England were almost comical. Massachusetts blatantly pursued its own mercantilist policies. The colony encouraged its own manufacturers, regulated its own prices and wages, and minted its own silver coin.[72] New

England's commercial economy attempted to duplicate England's. For this reason, Caribbean planter Ferdinando Gorges complained in a 1674 memorial to Shaftesbury's council that New England was of limited value to the empire and more "Injurious" than "profitable to this Kingdome."[73]

Shaftesbury's first order of business was to reaffirm imperial laws and norms already on the books. He also supplemented them. The Navigation Act of 1660 confirmed the principle that English colonial trade must take place in English ships. The 1660 act also mandated that an English ship must be owned and captained by an English subject, with a crew three-quarters English. In a departure, the act specified "enumerated commodities" that could be exported from the colonies only to England. These staples raised the most revenue for the Crown—sugar and tobacco, chiefly. The subsequent 1663 Staple Act declared that all goods passing in and out of the colonies to Europe, not just enumerated ones, must land in England first, where they would be taxed before reshipment. The preamble to the 1663 ordinance made its purpose clear. It sought to create "a greater correspondence and kindnesse" between England and its colonies, which meant subjecting the colonies to a "firmer dependance." The new regulations would "farther imployment" in England, increase "English Shipping," and "vent" English "manufactures" to colonial buyers.[74]

The Navigation Acts established the imperial objectives. Shaftesbury had adversaries, in and out of government, who did not believe England should commit itself to the continued colonization of North America.[75] It would be a mistake to exaggerate the earl's influence. Yet until he fell out with Charles II in 1673, Shaftesbury was the driving force behind installing an effective American colonial policy. The touchstone was the mercantilist premise that the state must direct long-term commercial development for the good of the imperial commonwealth, however defined. Even when "the merchant trades for a great deale of Profit," Shaftesbury reminded the king in 1669, it may still be possible that "the nation loses."[76]

The Navigation Acts required new imperial administrative and legal capacities to implement them. The colonies were increasingly brought under Crown authority, typically granted a colonial assembly but also a royal governor. Shaftesbury's Council for Trade and Plantations began to meet twice a week.[77] The council reviewed colonial charters and acts passed by colonial legislation and also heard colonial complaints. It issued instructions to royal governors. It sought to ensure that colonial exports might be of "greater value, worth and repute."[78] It gathered information to ascertain the balance of trade. A 1668 memo demanded to know "how a due and exact account may be kept of all the commodities exported from or imported into any of the ports or custom houses of this nation to the end that a perfect balance of trade may be taken."[79]

At the same time, Shaftesbury practiced a light touch. The colonists' private commercial interests must not run free, but strategically they must be acknowledged. To ignore them completely would be to risk rendering English sovereignty a dead letter in the Atlantic. Shaftesbury was no absolutist. American commerce was all but left free of corporate trading monopolies (unlike in Asia, the East India Company's jurisdiction) and opened to all Englishmen. Relatively, the colonists were taxed little. Shaftesbury's advisers feared that New England was on "the very brink of renouncing any dependence of the crown." Some recommended sending at the very least a "menacing letter." In the end, Shaftesbury's council sent a toothless fact-finding mission.[80] He recognized that New England traded with other empires because commercially it had little choice. Probably, to get off the ground, Carolina would have to do the same. Shaftesbury never attempted to make the British imperial political economy a completely closed circuit. There would be "interlopers," smugglers, and pirates, and the strict enforcement of the Navigation Acts might actually hinder the growth of English colonization and trade.[81] Shaftesbury's governing disposition approximated what Edmund Burke, in the throes of the American Revolution, would later christen "a wise and salutary neglect."[82]

Meanwhile the mercantilist concept of balance began to change. Different colonies must have their commercial interests acknowledged. Properly regulated, they might each contribute something unique to the imperial whole. Commerce was still a zero-sum geopolitical struggle. The Dutch, for instance, must be pushed out of the Atlantic carrying trade. But within the English Empire, burgeoning colonial commerce properly channeled could increase the empire's economic pie. That was the benefit of "free trade," in the original meaning of that term: free trade within the empire. Within a well-ordered imperial political economy, everyone might gain from trade, even if the home country enjoyed the positive balance.[83]

If subtle, this idea was nonetheless a momentous shift in consciousness of economic possibility.[84] Shaftesbury's Whig circle was appropriating pre-Restoration Hartlibian, soon Enlightenment ideas about "improvement" and the possibility that an ever-expanding material abundance might transcend scarcity. Locke, secretary to Shaftesbury's Council for

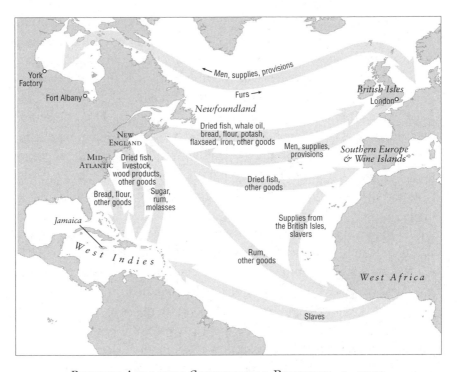

York
Factory

Fort Albany

Men, supplies, provisions

Furs →

British Isles
London

Newfoundland

NEW
ENGLAND

Dried fish, whale oil,
bread, flour, potash,
flaxseed, iron, other goods

Men, supplies,
provisions

Southern Europe
& Wine Islands

MID-
ATLANTIC

Dried fish,
livestock,
wood products,
other goods

Dried fish,
other goods

Bread, flour,
other goods

Sugar,
rum,
molasses

Jamaica

Supplies from
the British Isles,
slavers

West Indies

Rum,
other goods

West Africa

Slaves

BRITISH ATLANTIC COMMERCIAL PATTERNS, C. 1750
The British Empire created the necessary political conditions for colonial
North American commerce to flourish in the Atlantic Ocean. This is a
basic picture of the major commodity trades.

Trade and Plantations, would argue in the *Second Treatise of Government*
that human labor and ingenuity were the true source of value and wealth.
Thus Shaftesbury's circle moved English mercantilism even further away
from a strict equation of wealth with bullion. Glimpsed, if only glimpsed,
was the possibility that greater commercial investment could lead to increasing returns and multiply wealth—exponential capitalist economic
growth.

Shaftesbury's colonial agenda would reach full maturity only after his
exile in 1682 and quick death. In 1685 the Catholic James II ascended to
the English throne and attempted to reorganize the North American colonies into something more like his personal dominions. He promulgated
more absolutist enforcements of the Navigation Acts. Revolts in New England, New York, and Maryland accompanied the 1688 Glorious Revolution and Parliament's invitation of William and Mary of Orange to the
English throne.[85] The Whigs were back in power and favored the interests

of commerce at the expense of the landed Tory aristocracy. An expanding public debt underwrote imperial wars abroad. The new Bank of England (1694) provided funding while organizing money creation on new principles. The publicly chartered, privately owned bank held the exclusive privilege to issue paper "bank money" as legal tender. The value of coin remained anchored to a fixed metallic standard, but credit money could nonetheless expand in excess of bullion reserves and fuel commercial investment. The expansion of money capital now hinged on bankers' expectations of prospective commercial profit. Public and private power mixed, at once propelling long-term imperial expansion and commercial development.[86]

Meanwhile during the 1690s, negotiations between the North American colonists and Parliament ended with a reversion, more or less, back to Shaftesbury's status quo. British officers took up their posts in colonial customhouse offices. The Board of Trade—administrative inheritor of Shaftesbury's Council for Trade and Plantations—was established in 1696. Locke was a member. By now, nearly two-thirds of English revenue came from taxes and duties on overseas trade, funding a powerful English fiscal-military state erected on the basis of wealth-generating commerce. Political-economic debates in England remained contentious, and during the 1720s, the original Whig coalition fractured. But by then Great Britain was primed to become the major Atlantic commercial power. The War of the Spanish Succession concluded in 1714 on terms favorable to the British, and Dutch power in the Atlantic was in retreat. For the next century, the British Empire would square off against the French. But the eighteenth-century British mercantilist political economy was now settled in place in the North American colonies. Colonization proceeded and commerce prospered.

4. Roots of Smithian Growth

From the Glorious Revolution of 1688 until the outbreak of the Seven Years' War with France in 1756, the British Empire in the Atlantic enjoyed a remarkable institutional stability. The mercantile system induced a long commercial boom. The cumulative process was one of "Smithian growth."

When set in its proper imperial context, the concept of Smithian growth helps makes sense of colonial American commercial development. *The Wealth of Nations* best explains in theory how preindustrial economies might expand wealth production. It is a function of the "division of labor." Smith famously provided the example of a pin factory. The factory can produce more pins if workers divide the tasks of making a pin among themselves, each specializing at one task. The division of labor occasions an increase in the "powers of labor" in production.

What determines the division of labor? The answer is the "extent of the market," or the scope for sales. That is, there must be sufficient transactional liquidity—ready markets for goods on the demand side. When markets expand for goods, producers compete for them. They specialize and invest more capital in search of the gains from trade. They do this because of a natural human propensity to "truck, barter, and exchange one thing for another." It is commercial self-interest, or human nature, that is the mainspring of the division of labor. But the division of labor exists only in proportion to the "extent of the market."[87]

In sum, increasing returns to commerce are possible.[88] There is a "Smithian commercial multiplier," with respect to wealth production for a community as a whole. (The question of distribution within that community is another matter.) The requirements for Smithian growth are interactive and, as demand and supply interactively feed off of each other, self-sustaining. Unhindered, the circular process of Smithian growth would seem to take care of itself. Smith famously referred to an "invisible hand."[89] But how did Smithian growth in eighteenth-century North America first actually come about?

Shaftesbury's public and private interests lead directly to the slave plantations of England's West Indian colonies. The eighteenth-century North American colonies rode their backs to commercial prosperity first. In large measure, the Age of Commerce in North America began with the English imperial commitment to black slavery. Without it, early American commercial vitality would have been greatly diminished.[90]

Black slavery was not fated. It was a choice made by England's rulers. If commerce was a "kind of warfare," in essence the decision was tantamount to an act of continuous warfare against African and Afro-descendant people. At first, the American colonies were supposed to be a "vent" not only for manufactures but also for the excess population of England. The first waves of migrants were largely Englishmen, many indentured servants. But because of migration, plague, and civil war, the English population began to decrease. Many officials, Shaftesbury included, now argued that England should retain its population.[91]

Colonization thereafter proceeded through the embrace of slavery. Over time, for various reasons, not all the leading voices in London were for it. Racial slavery's advocates had to win an argument; there were different visions of empire at stake.[92] American colonists had tried Indian slave trafficking first, especially in the Southeast, where the absence of an organizing power like the northern Iroquois Confederacy in the seventeenth century meant political instability—an environment in which slave raiding flourished.[93] The joint-stock Royal African Company was reincorporated in 1672 with a trading monopoly on the west coast of Africa. Shaftesbury subscribed, a telltale sign of England's imperial intentions. By the middle of the eighteenth century, commodities produced by black slaves accounted for 80 percent of all colonial American commodities exported back to the home country.[94] Not only did commercial expansion depend on imperial expansion; the possibility of racial exploitation bolstered long-term expectations and spurred on the inducement to invest in North America.[95]

The first commercial jewel of the English Atlantic was Barbados. Seventeenth-century colonial Barbados must have been one of the worst human societies to have ever existed. Free migrants simply would not go there. The tropical island, twenty-one miles long, fourteen wide, became riddled with deadly pathogens. The labor of planting and refining sugar was dreadful. Barbados imported 130,000 African captives between 1640 and 1700, and by 1660 there were already more blacks than whites on the island. The Barbados slave code of 1661, which secured common law property rights in human chattel, and set a legal precedent for other English colonies, was draconian.[96] That was putting it nicely. Overseers hung disobedient slaves from trees in iron cages, leaving them to die of thirst as examples to others. By the 1710s, in not too dissimilar fashion, Jamaica—first a hub for English buccaneers—was producing more sugar than Barbados.[97]

Adam Smith abhorred slavery. Nonetheless, he might have chosen a Barbados slave plantation, not an English pin factory, to illustrate the division of labor. Almost all economic production in Barbados was destined for sale in Atlantic markets. The large capital investment necessary for a sugar plantation was often made on credit, which forced plantation owners to maximize pecuniary revenues. Barbados planters specialized in sugar. The governor noted that every "foot of land," up to the "seaside," was in sugarcane.[98] Plantations, each of which averaged 250 black laborers, maintained a detailed division of labor. Enslaved blacks were capital assets, priced competitively in Atlantic markets.[99] They could be replenished through purchase. All things considered, it was often more economical not to worry over their rapid depreciation—in other words, to work slaves to death.[100] The Enlightenment ideal of "improvement" took the form of racial domination.

Barbados, specializing in sugar, had to purchase many necessary economic inputs elsewhere. For pious New Englanders, the Barbados market was a godsend. A good mercantilist, Governor Winthrop had wanted Massachusetts to "exgot" more than it "ingot." But at first Massachusetts had little exgot besides animal furs bought from Native Americans. Winthrop worried that New England risked commercial collapse. But a Barbados planter wrote to him as early as 1647 requesting "trade for provisions for the belly." The boom in Barbados sugar production increased the "extent of the market," as Smith would put it, for New England fish, foodstuffs, timber, and livestock. Winthrop wrote in his diary, "It pleased the Lord to open to us a trade with Barbados."[101] Covetous Robert Keayne soon made his fortune in the West Indian trade. Whether brought about by the Lord or by the invisible hand of the market, both Barbados and New England gained from the trade. Commerce multiplied. West Indian trading credits assisted New England imports of English manufactures. The British Empire's multilateral Atlantic commercial system of triangular trades began to take shape. After the Glorious Revolution, Puritan leader Increase Mather traveled to London to negotiate a new Massachusetts charter. The English political economist William Petty still suggested that New Englanders give up on their "unprofitable" errand into the wilderness and all relocate to the West Indies.[102] But Mather lectured London officials that the West Indian colonies could not exist without New England provisions. Taxes on West Indian sugar flooded the English customs office with revenue. Mather's logic proved irrefutable to imperial officials.

British slavery continued to expand. In 1689 the Royal African Company's monopoly ended, and the slave trade, like all Atlantic commerce, was opened to all Englishmen. The Iberian powers had long dominated the slave trade, and in sheer numbers they would never be equaled. Still, British enslavers brought a total of 2.6 million African slaves to the Americas, the great majority during the eighteenth century. An estimated 391,060 landed in North America, while more than 2 million arrived in the West Indies.[103] Black slave labor capitalized a cascading series of export staple commodity booms in the Atlantic colonies.

The southernmost North American colonies followed the West Indian route to commercial success.[104] By 1700, Shaftesbury's "darling" Carolina exported 400,000 pounds of largely slave-cultivated rice. In 1708, Carolina became the first North American colony to have a black slave majority.[105] Echoing the 1661 Barbados slave code, Shaftesbury and Locke's *Fundamental Constitutions of Carolina* had declared, "Every freeman of Carolina shall have absolute power and authority over his negro slaves." As with the rule of subsovereign corporations, the authority of the white master was another aspect of "composite" imperial rule in the colonies. If empire always implied "governing different people differently," as leading historians of the subject have put it, racialized slavery became one possible mode of rule.[106]

In 1829 the English philosopher Jeremy Bentham would summarize Locke's *Second Treatise of Government:* "Property the only object of care to Government. Persons possessing it alone entitled to be represented. West Indies the meridian for these principles of this liberty-champion."[107] By 1740, Carolina was exporting 43 million pounds of rice. Indigo was a second export staple. To the west, the Indian slave trade declined, as the Creek Confederacy emerged as a formidable power, and Native Americans began to contribute another commercial export staple, deerskins, which were exchanged for guns, horses, and metals.[108] Rice and indigo stabilized sales at 75 percent of export earnings in Carolina and very soon in its neighboring colony of Georgia, as well.[109]

In Virginia, planters rode a seventeenth-century commodity boom in tobacco to eighteenth-century wealth and power.[110] Tobacco was indigenous to America, introduced to the English by Algonquians.[111] To cultivate it, planters first relied on white indentured servants. Smaller landholdings, some owned and operated by emancipated white indentured servants, were common. But by the 1670s, available land uncontrolled by Indian nations was dwindling, and the export market in tobacco collapsed. Price volatility in export markets was the scourge of the colonial commercial economy.[112] For a time, Virginia erupted into a triangular war among farmers, planters, and Indian nations.[113] The result was an outbreak of Indian hating, and by the time the tobacco market boomed again, large planters had further consolidated their power by importing enslaved Africans. Black slaves became cost effective, relative to paying white indentured servants.[114] By 1750 in Virginia, there were roughly 100,000 black slaves, about 40 percent of the population. An ideology of white racial domination hardened.[115] The Chesapeake colony of Maryland and parts of Delaware followed a similar path to colonial prosperity.

Slave plantations were thus the British Atlantic's first commercial centers of gravity. Because of slavery, the southern North American colonies remained the wealthiest, after the West Indies. Every British North American colony had slaves. However, over the course of the eighteenth century, the middle and northern colonies, if less wealthy, became considerable commercial players and in some respects were more dynamic than the southern colonies.

Northern and middle colonies developed more diversified commercial economies. Colonists "wove cloth, crafted furniture, etched silver, published newspapers, painted portraits, and built ships, barrels, houses and cities."[116] Coastal commerce among colonies was vigorous. On the land, barriers to the "extent of the market" remained high.[117] Even in the northern colonies, commerce was overwhelmingly Atlantic facing.[118] New England, consisting of the colonies of Connecticut, Massachusetts, New Hampshire, and Rhode Island, exported foodstuffs, livestock, fish, whale products, and rum. Its merchant class soon thrived in the Atlantic carrying trades, including the slave trade.[119] By the mid-eighteenth century, the middle colonies—New York, Pennsylvania, and New Jersey—were more prosperous. With fertile soils, the middle colonies had more success in the Atlantic grain trade. Philadelphia and New York City had their own merchant elites and eventually superseded Boston as commercial hubs.[120] In the northern colonies, over time, assemblies became more representative of the white male population. Relative to the South, greater political equality and a greater entrepreneurial dynamism appear to have emerged in tandem.[121] By 1750 the northern and middle colonies were importing more consumer goods than was the South, which passed, despite poor roads, through far more dense local markets. "Slaves spend but little," noted the Connecticut Reverend Jared Eliot in 1759.[122]

Adam Smith did more than explain the process of commercial growth. He also wrote about the coming of a "commercial society" in which commerce—not status, fear, or violence—defined relationships.[123] In such a society, every man would become "in some measure a merchant."[124] This was not a community of selfish egoists. Left alone, commerce would lead to an enlightened commonwealth, Smith argued. Eighteenth-century colonial North America, much more the North than the social disaster that was the early West Indies, began to reflect Smith's moral vision. Coffeehouses, libraries, and theaters appeared. Colonial elites rushed to participate in a British Atlantic consumer culture, sustaining, in good mercantilist fashion, considerable consumer markets for English manufacturers. By the 1750s, North America was the fastest-growing destination for British goods.[125] Commercial refinement became a marker of status.[126] Pastor Cotton Mather, son of Increase and grandson of John Cotton, donned fashionable London wigs.[127] Some religious leaders began to equate commercial gain with spiritual gain, during a wave of evangelical religious awakenings in the 1730s and '40s, called the First Great Awakening. "Covetousness," New Jersey reverend Joseph Morgan declared in *The Nature of Riches* (1732), "makes for the public good."[128] Only the commercial society that was colonial Philadelphia could have produced a character like Benjamin Franklin, the polymath and commercial moralist turned Atlantic celebrity. Franklin dined with Adam Smith in Scotland in 1759, urging him to write a book on commercial colonial policy and lecturing him on the benefits of "free trade" even outside the British Empire.[129]

London always remained the commercial entrepôt, financial hub, and center of imperial authority. American planters first sold colonial staples on their own accounts, or consigned them to English commission agents, before, in some instances, as in the Chesapeake, local merchants set up country stores. All told, British creditors willingly financed the North American trade.[130] The Bank of England oversaw the network of paper-money-issuing banks that funded the eighteenth-century Atlantic commodity booms. Price stability anchored an increasingly sophisticated English capital market for public and private debts. Low interest rates released credit to the colonies, as the 1732 Act for the More Easy Recovery of Debts in His Majesty's Plantations and Colonies in America made it easier for English creditors to recover "real" property, including slaves. That solidified confidence in English colonial investments.[131] Until the outbreak of the Seven Years' War with France in 1756, short- and long-term interest rates declined in the first British era of "cheap money." In 1714, the British legal rate of usury fell to 5 percent, but afterward reported market rates, including in the Atlantic trades, fell below that, indicating a willingness to part with money and thus confidence in the commercial future.

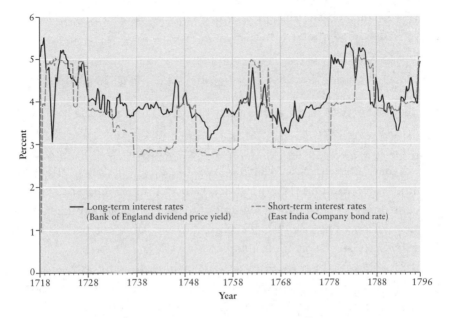

INTEREST RATES IN THE BRITISH EMPIRE

Low interest rates historically correlate with commercial prosperity.
In the eighteenth-century British Empire, they coincided with the
"golden age" of North American colonial commerce.

The commercial and financial sophistication of the British Atlantic, its
chains of credit, bills of exchange, flows of information, and policies of
insurance and reinsurance, was impressive. Because local changes in supply and demand reverberated across the ocean, some economic historians
characterize the empire as exhibiting equilibrium dynamics.[132] It could
seem that British Atlantic commerce coordinated itself.

The imperial economy was never a closed circuit. There was smuggling,
and trading with imperial rivals was frequent.[133] Nonetheless, trade within
the British Empire became so mutually beneficial that the Navigation Acts
became nearly self-enforcing. Colonists complained about the shortage of
coin (colonial legislatures experimented with paper currencies in violation of imperial law), the empire's refusal to support free immigration, and
imperial prohibitions on trade with Latin America. Politically, most colonists sided with the "Patriot" faction of English Whigs, who looked favorably on American commerce and lent less consideration to West Indian
sugar interests.[134] On the whole, many prospering white eighteenth-
century colonial Americans became proud British subjects. By its own

standards, the mercantilist project of Shaftesbury and his circle had proved a dazzling long-term success.

5. Mercantilism, on Balance

In the final analysis, what is the legacy of mercantilism for the history of American capitalism?

One legacy is the horror of chattel slavery and the birth of a modern racism that American capitalism has failed to rid itself of down to this day. In almost every human society in the seventeenth and eighteenth centuries, base forms of domination remained the norm. But slavery died out in western Europe. The rise of black slavery in the Americas was a choice made by European rulers and capitalists.

What about the balance of trade? The eighteenth-century balance of trade between Britain and the North American colonies favored the home country, as mercantilist doctrine said it should. The American colonies usually had a positive balance with the West Indies, while Britain had a negative balance with the West Indies. While figures are impossible to determine with precision, it more or less all came out in the imperial wash.[135]

Did it matter? The Smithian commercial multiplier triggered the expansion of wealth-generating enterprise. Flows of credit sustained commerce, drawing forth more production for markets. Adam Smith landed many body blows against balance of trade doctrine in *The Wealth of Nations*. He defined national wealth with respect to the "exchangeable value" of the goods that a nation produced, regardless of its trade balances. The standard later inspired more modern metrics, such as today's gross domestic product (GDP). By that criterion, the British North American colonists grew very wealthy under the British "mercantile system." The West Indies remained the wealthiest colonies, because of the market value and labor of their slaves. But North America closed the gap. In 1700, on a per capita basis, Barbados was 50 percent wealthier than the North American colonies. By 1800, it was only 20 percent wealthier than the new United States.[136] The best rough estimate is that American colonists achieved per capita income growth somewhere in the neighborhood of 0.5 percent per annum, which, in preindustrial times, was a lot. The presence of conquered land and natural resources meant American colonists enjoyed even greater advantages in living standards. By the eve of the American Revolution, "the average American colonist ate better, was taller, and lived longer than did the average Englishman" and probably the average person anywhere.[137]

Some historians pose a counterfactual, wondering if in the absence of mercantilist restrictions, the American colonies would have fared even better.[138] The question abstracts too much from what actually happened. Smithian growth in British North America took place within the long post–Glorious Revolution political-economic settlement. The colonies had limited internal commerce or access to overland markets. They grew rich selling overseas to British markets that provided them a critical source of effective demand. Parliamentary legislation constantly aided colonists. A 1705 law favored New England ship timber over Baltic imports. A parliamentary bounty of 1748 subsidized Carolina's production of indigo. At the same time, the imperial touch remained light. By 1750, without a murmur from Parliament, 80 percent of colonial grain exports were bound for southern Europe.[139] The British Empire promoted investment in colonial North American commerce. Finally, from the perspective of the home country, colonial America made great contributions to British wealth and, arguably, to the coming of the industrial revolution.[140]

Thus the imperial conquest of space instilled confident expectations over time. In the Age of Commerce, the Smithian "extent of the market" was largely a geopolitical phenomenon. In practice, preindustrial Smithian growth was spatial, achieved by the extension of commerce and production for markets across territory. What British mercantilism did was to transform the North Atlantic into a vast imperial trading zone. Expanding territory was what empires instinctively sought to do. Over history, empires have proved to be very effective extenders of commercial markets across space, thus ensuring market demand for their various subjects. Smithian dynamics appeared within all European empires, as well as in Mughal India, Tokugawa Japan, the Iroquois Confederacy, Qing China, the Ottoman and Persian empires, and the sub-Saharan Bornu Empire (and long before, it seems, in the Roman Empire).[141] The historical record is very clear. "Free trade" has always been an achievement of the legal infrastructure of state power.[142]

Adam Smith imagined what commerce would look like in the relative absence of the state, a rightly celebrated thought exercise but nonetheless only that. Smith himself knew that state policies mattered, and advocates of the "free market" today would do well to read past book one of *The Wealth of Nations*. Smith's critiques of a "mercantile system" that, at times, equated wealth with bullion and, to some degree, became corrupt over the eighteenth century resonate to this day. But in their most sophisticated forms, many mercantilist precepts deserve a more balanced assessment. Money and credit have been, and are, the nerve centers of capitalist economic development—hardly "neutral." In the course of economic development, manufacturing has proved to be a dynamic element. Barring the first industrializer, which was England, most every economy that would ever industrialize, including the United States, would do so under a protective tariff. For these reasons, in fact, while the British Empire triggered a long American commercial boom over the eighteenth century, by the end of that century it did limit North American economic development by proscribing the colonists from printing their own credit monies and encouraging their own manufactures. The colonists grew rich off what today would be called a global commodity "super cycle." The larger point, however, is this: for good and for ill, states have illustrated the capacity to orchestrate long-term economic development.

Lastly, we must consider the fundamental mercantilist assumption that denied the sphering of politics from economics, the public from the private, and the state from the markets.[143] The notion that private interest and the public good might productively entangle would persist into the American Revolutionary era, but so would a deeply moralized suspicion about the tensions between the two. Already in Shaftesbury's own lifetime, a familiar note sounded in the cynical uproar concerning less the results of his policies than anxiety about his motivations. The poet John Dryden's *Absalom and Achitophel* (1681–82) poked the first Earl of Shaftesbury:

> The next for interest sought t'embroil the state,
> To sell their duty at a dearer rate;
> And make their Jewish markets of the throne;
> Pretending public good, to serve their own.[144]

Was Shaftesbury a true commonwealth man or a conniving knave? Is it ever possible for individuals—especially those with immense power and considerable private interests—to really act disinterestedly on behalf of the public good? Or in the end, was Aristotle not right that once the genie of commercial self-interest is out of the bottle, we are all, the powerful and the powerless, slaves to our own limitless desires?

CHAPTER 2

ORGANIC ECONOMY, HOUSEHOLD ECONOMY

═══

BRITISH MERCANTILISM PLACED POLITICAL LIMITS ON CO-lonial American commerce. The greatest limit in the early American economy, however, came not from people but from nature.

The colonial American economy was, in the words of the historian E. A. Wrigley, an "advanced organic economy"—advanced because of its commercial character, organic because of the nature of the raw inputs of economic production.[1] Most manufactured goods were processed organic matter, whether wool, hides, straw, or fur. Water, wind, and human and animal muscle powered production. If a river dried up into a stream or froze for the winter, water-powered mills ceased to operate. (There was no steam power.) If arthritis debilitated a woman's joints, a spinning wheel ceased to spin, as there was no electricity. Animal muscle—the power at the human arm or at the hind legs of an ox—set productive limits.

Through photosynthesis, directly or indirectly, the sun was responsible for the vast majority of energy in economic production. The amount of sunlight set the pace of preindustrial economic life. Vegetation, whether by providing calories for human and animal muscle power, or by being burned for light and fuel, accounted for approximately 98 percent of the energy supply in colonial North America (wind and water the remaining 2 percent).[2] The flows of energy that powered preindustrial life indicate that nature is no inert "factor of production," merely a resource for human labor and ingenuity to exploit. Its processes are active agents in economic life. Energy and economy are closely linked, with relationships specific to historical epochs.

In an advanced organic economy, the dominant form of productive

capital was land. Ecology, not commerce, was the dominant factor in colonial economic life. From the land came food, fuel, clothing, and shelter.
Many animals required pasture to graze upon if humans were to have
meat, let alone wool and leather. In preindustrial economies, without extending the amount of land under cultivation or increasing its productivity, very little growth was possible. Otherwise, there would not be enough
food for everyone to eat, and not much labor could be shed from agriculture to manufacturing and commerce anyway. There could be no gains
from trade, no division of labor, and no Smithian growth. In the end, however, only so much of the earth's surface can be cultivated, and extending
cultivation onto poor soils does not increase productivity. If, in commerce,
the Smithian commercial multiplier is a possibility, allowing returns to
economic activity to increase over time, then in agriculture, because of
ecology, the specter of diminishing returns is ever present. Scarcity looms,
as a brute material fact.

The biosphere simply set limits on preindustrial economies. Some of
these limits were of the contingent, short-term variety. An Andean vol-
cano, say, might lead to a series of bad harvests in Europe.[3] The worst
checks, according to the Englishman Thomas Malthus, in his *Essay on the
Principle of Population* (1798), were cruel—famine, plague, and war. No political economist better appreciated the role of nature as an active agent in
economic life than Malthus. If, he held, all species of the "vegetable and
animal kingdom" were blessed with the capacity to reproduce in excess of
the demands of mere replacement, the growth of population would eventually meet with response from the "dreadful resources of nature." The
premature death of populations functioned, Malthus proposed in the second edition of the *Essay*, as one of many possible "positive checks" to bring
population back into balance with nature.[4]

No wonder the Scottish historian Thomas Carlyle in 1850 branded political economy the "dismal science."[5] For millennia, despite periodic bouts
of commercial efflorescence, material wealth expanded and contracted
like an accordion throughout the world.[6] There were simply limits. Adam
Smith acknowledged the possibility that everyone might gain from trade,
but even he spoke of the eventual arrival of any economic community at
a "stationary, or declining state."[7]

The productive limits of an organic economy would have to be transcended to enable modern, self-sustaining economic growth, a hallmark
of a capitalist economy and civilization. The industrial revolution allowed

economies to become exponentially more energy intensive by tapping inorganic stocks of fossil fuels rather than organic flows. Of course, nature would not cease to be an active agent, and given the emergence of climate change, the Malthusian trap may remain set and ready to spring. Nature may still have the last laugh.

1. Ecology and Economy in Early North America

By the seventeenth century, very little land in England was left to be brought under human cultivation and dominion. Land scarcity helped motivate Englishmen to colonize North America.[8] As they did, it was households that transformed North America into an advanced commercial society.

In the first centuries of the millennium, the climate had warmed, and English agricultural production had expanded in tandem with the population.[9] Already by 1300, no more than 10 percent of England was still forested. The seventeenth-century poet Henry Vaughan began his poem "The Timber" declaring "Sure thou didst flourish once!"[10] But then the climate cooled, inaugurating what archeologists call a five-hundred-year "Little Ice Age." Between the Great Famine (1315–22) and the Black Death (1347–53), the English population halved. Pressure on the organic economy relaxed.[11] Next came a commercial upswing, but the demographic cycle repeated. Malthus explained that while population growth was geometric, the expansion of wealth production, and thus food production, was only arithmetic.

A few early English arrivals to North America reported that they had stumbled on a lost Eden. Here was virgin soil populated by Indian peoples who, strangely enough, did not exploit it to the hilt. Some wondered if Adam's curse had not been lifted. In 1607 the Virginia Company brought roughly six thousand settlers to the Jamestown colony. When the first winters came, many starved to death. Some of the dead were cannibalized. By 1622, no more than twelve hundred were alive.[12] However, after the first wave of settlement, famine was largely absent from English colonies, in large part because the English could draw from Native ecological and environmental experience and knowledge. Indigenous populations soon began to suffer the brunt of hunger, plague, and war. In New England, epidemics in 1616 and 1633 killed vast numbers of Massachusett, Penacook, Wampanoag, and Narragansett Indians. However, in some instances in colonial America—the deerskin-selling Creek Confederacy of the eighteenth century, for instance—Native populations would actually increase.[13] European colonizers did not encounter a lost Eden, and Native Americans did not simply begin to vanish.

Nonetheless, British colonial North America provided what one economic historian has called ecological "ghost acreage" for resource-strapped Britain, easing ecological limits in the run-up to the industrial revolution.[14] Relative to England, land was abundant in colonial North America. The relative abundance of land, not its scarcity, was perhaps the chief economic fact of the Age of Commerce in North America. Because of it, colonial Americans grew up to be taller, stronger, and healthier than their European peers.[15] Malthus noted in the North America colonies a "rapidity of increase almost without parallel in history." It proved his general proposition that, unchecked, population "was found to double itself in 25 years." That remains an accurate enough description of colonial American demography.[16] Thus, simultaneous with the long eighteenth-century Atlantic commercial boom was the effort of a rapidly reproducing population of English colonizers to conquer territory.

The chief agents of this history, interacting with the organic economy, were households. The household was the central institution of early American economic life—the central institution of life, full stop.[17] Kinship, custom, law, and intimacy defined their character. Households carried out the task of "oeconomy," or the management of household wealth. Households were also governing institutions. In a world of "composite" and "plural" sovereignty, where imperial authority could be weak on its frontier, households, along with corporations, were the ruling sub-sovereigns of the British Empire. Individuals' relative position within the "little commonwealth" of the household, defined by sex, age, and race, determined their civic status. Men—husbands, fathers, and masters— were "independent" heads of household. Landed property was the anchor of their political "liberty." Wives, children, servants, and enslaved persons were their "dependents." A household was a social hierarchy where "reciprocal, not equal, rights prevailed." So did love, but also cruelty.[18]

All members of a household led substantive economic lives. Households collectively allocated resources, tasked labor, and transmitted property and wealth. The "household sector," as it is known today—with much of it not counted in contemporary calculations of a national economy's gross domestic product (GDP)—accounted for almost the entirety of early

American economic production, most of it destined for direct consumption, not commerce.[19] At this time, any distinction between the family and the market, home and work, would not have made much sense. Economy was no distinct sphere. Thus a mercantilist theme recurs. Much like mercantilist political economy, the household blended public and private into a tense, energetic mixture. Households' mixed character again illustrates the way commerce was furthered but still checked in early North America.

In early America, the household economy and the organic economy were deeply intertwined if only because the colonies were overwhelmingly rural societies. When the American Revolution broke out, at least 80 percent of the population still worked the land, and no more than 5 percent lived in cities, defined as urban settlements of 2,500 or more. An account of early American economy must attend to the interacting rhythms of organic economy and household economy, as commerce progressed in the midst of their cadences.

2. Property

American artistic expression has always reflected a sublime awe at the sheer immensity of the North American continent. In the Age of Commerce, the culmination would be the Hudson River School painters. Take Thomas Doughty's *In Nature's Wonderland* (1835).

THOMAS DOUGHTY, *IN NATURE'S WONDERLAND* (1835)
Sublime awe at nature and the myth of an untouched wilderness are both captured in this Hudson River School painting. Note the small individual dwarfed by the natural environment, a common motif of the school.

Seemingly, human domestication of the landscape makes no dent. But the continent was not *terra nullius*, empty space, an untamed wilderness awaiting human mastery.

Indigenous peoples collectively and individually exercised control over resources. Despite a long-enduring colonial myth that says otherwise, Native American nations had property. The first generations of English colonizers, if not future ones, recognized this, and the partial commensurability of Native and English property systems was a medium of early contact and diplomatic exchange—a medium through which some Native nations sought to incorporate European populations into their political worlds, and through which the British Empire sought to subordinate Native nations into its own composite imperial sovereignty.[20]

Nonetheless, colonizers brought with them to America a property regime that did not always make sense to Native Americans. It was a most peculiar English legal institution: private property. *Private* meant having the power and right to "exclude" others—even the state, if only to some extent—from the prerogative to enjoy the possession, use, or exchange of a particular object. The most consequential principle of English private property for the history of American capitalism was the Enlightenment doctrine of "improvement." Fittingly for this age, improvement warranted the simultaneous expansion of both British imperial power and private commerce in North America.[21]

What made landed property private was not only its possession but also its aggressive commercial cultivation, a lever, most colonizers believed, of material advance and civilizational progress. Consider the Hudson River School master Asher Brown Durand's *Progress—The Advance of Civilization* (1853). Sublime nature is still on the continental left, but cultivation and commerce are advancing on the right. Quickly, idle admiration of nature in early America was "swept aside in the rush for man's empire over nature."[22]

Capital is a form of property. Legally, the origin of contemporary private property rights—today including everything from intellectual property, to human genes, and to digital music streaming—is land. All the way back in ancient Rome, the legal concept of *dominium* was associated with landownership, in which "ownership was absolute: distinct, singular, and exclusive."[23] In early modern Europe, state formation and property formation grew in unison. European rulers appropriated the idea of *dominium* for their own use, as a principle through which to enforce their sovereignty

ASHER BROWN DURAND, *PROGRESS—THE ADVANCE OF CIVILIZATION* (1853)
Tellingly, in this Hudson River School painting intensive commercialization
encroaches upon the natural landscape from the east.

over "people and, increasingly, over a bounded territory."[24] Prior to the
colonization of North America, recognizably "private" rights to property,
distinct from public claims, had begun to emerge in Europe, and in England particularly.[25] But early modern property law still entangled private
"interests" with public *dominium,* in the ever-expanding European commercial domestication of the earth's surface. No clear separation between
public and private was possible.

For that reason, the Anglo-American history of landed property is at
times a bewildering subject. In England, before the Norman Conquest of
1066, land could be *alodial,* meaning it was not subject to the rule of any
feudal lord. *Alodial* land was the origin of what in the United States would
become the "public domain." After the Norman Conquest, the Crown
claimed title to all the land in England. In theory, the king's sovereignty
was not up for sale. Land could be "held" by a subject but not "owned." In
practice, English land became subject to a system of *tenures.* The monarchy released its grip, and landed estates fell into the grasp of the hereditary
nobility. Tenants-in-chief (*in capite*) were those who owed a service to the
Crown (often military service). Land held *in capite* became the basis of aristocratic lords' wealth and status. However, most medieval Englishmen
were commoners—peasants not noblemen—and held no legal *tenure.* To
meet their subsistence needs, peasants fought tooth and nail to maintain

customary use rights in land, a kind of extralegal possession. Lords extracted economic surpluses from peasants, but they also had obligations toward them to ensure their safety and subsistence. The point is that, except for the sovereign, in theory absolute and exclusive private property rights in land did not exist.

The fourteenth-century Black Death began to change this situation. Half the population perished, and the land-to-labor ratio soared. Peasants occupied vacated lands, and lords required new incentives to recruit peasant labor. A new land tenure emerged to compete with *in capite.* The doctrine of *ut de manore* restricted duties to the Crown, and lords had less scope to directly govern the occupants of their manors. Some peasants acquired legally enforceable and inheritable "copyholds." Lords struck back, commuting "copyholds" into "leaseholds." Peasants might now commercially lease lands. As England commercialized, the monarchy commuted *in capite* services to money (taxes). Slowly, layers of propertied claims unfurled, as more direct commercial relationships formed between English subjects and landed property, as an object. The ancient Roman legal notion of absolute *dominion,* in a private key, became newly prominent in property discourse.[26]

Lords increasingly became gentlemen capitalists, minding the commercial yields of their estates. In England, debates over the legal character of various land tenures raged in the first half of the seventeenth century. Ultimately, a series of parliamentary acts—culminating, in Shaftesbury's day, in the Statute of Tenures (1660)—reduced the complexity of English property law. The shift was toward exclusive and absolute legal titles. The ownership of land became more capitalistic. In the words of one historian:

> An absolute property right to land would mean a right to use and manage it; to derive income by letting others use it; to transfer it to another by gift or bequest; to capture the capital value of the land by sale; to claim immunity against expropriation of the property; and to operate without a term limiting the possession of these rights.[27]

Lords who pressed for commercial "improvement" prodded their tenants to "enclose" lands that were held subject to no title—including the "commons" and other plots of land in which multiple, communal use rights obtained—into the lords' exclusive private property. A differentiated agricultural population began to take shape, consisting of different classes, defined by different degrees of property ownership, in addition to differences of rank.[28]

There were landless, or almost landless, English "cottagers." Some shipped off to America. Between the lords and the landless, a new middle stratum of "husbandmen" emerged. Many were tenants, but some achieved the cherished commoner property claim, yet another tenure, of "fee simple" landownership. That meant they were "freeholders" and thus "independent" owners of property. They were autonomous "heads" capable of setting up their own households. The most commercially vigorous of the English freeholders were the "yeomen." For white male heads of household, colonial North American was to be a yeoman's paradise.[29]

On the eve of colonization, the English trend was toward more exclusive, individualized private property rights in land, which can be equated with the slow and steady transformation of English landed property and wealth into capital. However, the transformation was neither complete nor foreordained. English landed property remained a dizzying mix of tenures, titles, claims, counterclaims, rents, entitlements, fees, and dues. Even freeholding, fee simple ownership was encumbered, subject to taxation, eminent domain, or women's dowry rights. There was still no such thing as "exclusive personal control over land."[30] The English enclosure movement would not run its course until the nineteenth century, and nearly all the North American colonies carved out some form of communal "commons." Nonetheless, landed property, regardless of its commercial value, continued to earn its owner the cherished civic and political status of "independence."[31] To be under the thumb of no lord. To have no master. To have household dependents of one's own. In thought and experience, property has often been very much a matter of personality and self-validation—if also reciprocity and domination.

With respect to land tenure, colonial North America did not evade the feudal past. The Crown granted "proprietary" colonies to Catholic Lord Baltimore (Maryland, 1632), to Shaftesbury's circle of investors in Carolina (1663), to the founders of New Jersey (1664), and to the Quaker nobleman William Penn (Pennsylvania, 1681), all *in capite*. These proprietors parceled out lands, in theory, to colonizers who paid them quasi-feudal "quitrents," if they could be collected. In the Hudson River Valley, Dutch "patroons" erected large manorial estates and pretended to be feudal lords more than Dutch burghers. Elsewhere, the colonists resorted to a common fields system in which collective use rights to fish, forage, graze, and hunt in the open range prevailed.[32]

Nonetheless, colonial North America was—relative to the home country—a freeholding yeoman's dream. Colonial legislatures usually doled out land to all freeborn Englishmen according to "headright," or the number of members in one's household. In Virginia, the great planters gamed the system, claiming acres on the heads of their black slaves (an eerie premonition of the U.S. Constitution's three-fifths clause). Or households simply "squatted" on land, hoping for later legal imprimatur on their property claims. Legally, the vast majority of American colonists enjoyed the cherished land tenure of freeholding or fee simple ownership. Private property rights emerged in a stronger form in colonial America.[33]

White male heads of household enjoyed something of which their peasant ancestors had only dreamed. One Scotch-Irish immigrant in New York wrote home in 1737:

> Read this letter, Rev. Baptist Boyd, and look and tell all the poor folk of ye place that God has opened a door for their deliverance . . . for here all that a man works for is his own; and there are no revenue hounds to take it from us here . . . no one to take away yer Corn, yer Potatoes, yer Lint or yer Eggs.[34]

North America had more smallish landowners of capital than did Europe. "The hopes of having land of their own & becoming independent of Landlords is what chiefly induces people into America," noted a New York official.[35] As John Locke explained, without secure property rights in land that was free from arbitrary interference, there was no guarantee of republican liberty.

Before the American yeomanry could claim fee simple land tenure, colonizers had to wrest the land from Indian possession. Here was ultimate proof that private property and sovereign dominion marched hand in hand. For the conflict between English and Natives often took the form of strains between different and incompatible "commons," regimes that made property open to use by a community or public. Before the American Revolution, Natives "were dispossessed as much by the settler commons as by any sort of colonial version of the Enclosure movement."[36] Many northeastern American Indian communities were seasonally migratory, even if they often still engaged in horticulture, such as the Narragansett,

Massachusett, and Wampanoag, populous Algonquian-speaking nations of New England. In such indigenous polities, sovereignty and property did not commonly equate to permanent, fixed possession of land, in either its public or private guise.[37] Sovereignty flowed more from human relationships than from territorial possession, which then mapped onto control over resources, justifying multiple claims to them. Controlling land use made sense, as did acknowledging another nation's possession of a loosely bounded territory (although fencing in land was not common) and even in some instances the exchange of use rights. Roger Williams, the Puritan minister who was a founder of what became the colony of Rhode Island, remarked of the Narragansetts, "I have knowne them to make bargaine and sale among themselves for a small piece, or quantity of ground."[38] What did not make much sense to most Native American nations was to completely abstract land from the "life activity" of relationships in the human and spiritual worlds, and for individuals to assert exclusive claims to land backed by the coercive apparatus of law.[39] The commensurability of Native and English property systems had limits.

European legal traditions said land could not be dispossessed, even from "savages," without justification. Locke provided a justification, in the chapter entitled "Property" in his *Second Treatise of Government* (1690), that implicated the doctrine of improvement. Locke began with a fundamental assumption of man's common ownership in the natural bounty provided by God's munificence.[40] Property resulted when a self-owning claimant "mixed" his labor with what lay within common ownership. By *labor*, Locke did not mean only exertion; he meant the extension of personality into the external world. In doing so, the extender extracted from the pool of common ownership an exclusive right to control some portion of it. Thus, Locke wrote, the "wild Indian" who shoots a deer in "America" is entitled to its carcass and meat but not to the forest in which he killed it. That would require a conscious effort to clear, cultivate, and fence the land. The improvement that thus resulted excluded "the common right of other Men."[41] Locke chose the example of an Indian deer hunter even though he knew better—Indians in fact did improve the land, by his own standard.[42] But the insinuation of Locke's famous discussion of property was that Native Americans did not improve the land and that therefore all of America still lay in common ownership, ripe for dispossession.

Locke in fact recycled parts of colonists' own arguments. Massachusetts Bay governor John Winthrop, hailing from an enclosed agricultural region of England, argued "that which lies common, and that neuer been replenished or subdued[,] is free to any that possesse and improue it." The Indians, by having been there first, had a "natural" right to the land. But they forfeited their "civil" right, blowing it, by failing to "inclose" and "imprue" the land. John Cotton chimed in. In "a vacant soyle"—a description that did not pass the laugh test when applied to Native America—he that "taketh possession of it, and bestoweth culture and husbandry upon it, his right it is."[43] Faith in agricultural improvement went so deep that some colonists came to believe it might even improve the climate.[44] Regardless, improvement became an argument for why English public and private property—its commons and its independent plots—might justifiably dispossess Indian lands.

Locke made one exception: those who dispossessed land always had a duty to leave enough for everyone else should they want to mix their labor with it, improve it, and claim it as their own. It was truly the spirit of improvement and civilizational progress that a land grab must not leave anyone else worse off. Later, the doctrine became the inspiration for the "Lockean proviso" in the seminal twentieth-century text on natural property rights, Robert Nozick's *Anarchy, State, and Utopia* (1974).[45] At the time, it was another Lockean argument that could have been cribbed from the colonies. Was there not plenty of land left for the Indians to fall back on (and would heathens not be better off if civilized by Christians)?

Before, Locke wrote, many indigenous Americans had already surmised that given English land hunger, there might not in fact be plenty enough. The colonizers' foraging animals—their property—were often the first line of dispossession. Fed up, the Native leader Mattagund of the Piscataways complained to Maryland colonists in 1666, "Your cattle and hogs injure us you come too near us to live and drive us from place to place. We can fly no further let us know where to live and how to be secured for the future from the hogs and cattle."[46] In the end, "the conquest of the earth, which mostly means the taking it away from those who have a different complexion . . . is not a pretty thing when you look into it too much," the novelist Joseph Conrad would write more than two centuries later in *Heart of Darkness* (1899)—in the frenzy of yet another European imperial land grab.[47] It took a very long time for whites to dispossess Native Americans of their lands in North America.[48] It was still happening when Conrad was writing.

3. Capitalizing the Land

Improvement grounded property rights in the land. "Plantations in their beginings have work enough," noted Winthrop. Those arriving in America had "all things to do, as in the beginning of the world."[49] The labor of animals and humans domesticated the land into property, wealth, and an organic form of capital. Commerce required working credit, but more than anything, a massive investment of labor was the unavoidable means to capitalize a farm.

Many colonizers knew little about farming. A great number of English migrants were town or village people, not farmers.[50] The task of land clearing had been performed far back in the primeval English past. Some Europeans had migrated from places where land clearing was more recent, but many Englishmen had to rely on trial and error, learning from or relying on other Europeans, Indians, and enslaved African people. Colonial Americans developed a "mestizo agriculture."[51]

Land clearing was an awfully daunting task. Stones and boulders had to be removed, dragged on wooden sledges called stoneboats. The only mechanical instrument in use was the wooden lever, an ancient implement. Indians used controlled fires to clear ground for horticulture, while Europeans chopped down forests with axes.[52] Trees might also be "girdled," an Indian practice also introduced by Scandinavian settlers. To girdle was to "cut a notch in the barke a hand broad round about the tree," wrote Captain John Smith, then wait years for the tree to die.[53] Stump removal was almost impossible without an ox. Travelers commented on colonial American farms that were pockmarked with gray hulks of girdled trees and unremoved stumps. It took one man about thirty days to clear a single acre of land. The enslaved accomplished much of this work, which was one reason for the presence of slavery in the North. A horse could perform six times the workload of a man, oxen even more. Seventeenth-century colonizers brought domesticated animals across the Atlantic Ocean.

Mixing English and indigenous cultivation styles, colonial households rotated corn, squash, and beans along with European cereals and legumes across three fields. Early on, corn was the universal crop. Well before the arrival of Europeans, maize had spread north from Mexico through the Mississippi Valley. Everywhere, populations surged. (Many indigenous peoples began to live in cities.) As corn spread northeast, arriving in New England sometime between 1000 and 1300, various Natives began to combine it with beans and squash.[54] Corn could be planted almost everywhere, even on slopes and hills, and it was nearly impervious to weeds. It would grow in soil that had been prepared only by hand and hoe. In British North America, spades and plows were wooden (perhaps with iron sheaths). Corn required tending about fifty days a year. It yielded a far more abundant harvest than did the European cereals wheat, oats, and rye. An acre of good land could yield 30 to 50 bushels of corn. Colonists ate corn puddings, breads, meals, mushes, and mashes. Distilled corn became whiskey, dried husks stuffed mattresses, and dried stalks served as toilet paper. Two acres could feed the typical colonial household. Five acres was an uneatable abundance.[55]

Animals—horses and oxen, cows, pigs, sheep, and poultry—grazed off grassy meadows or ate corn, and their manure, along with legumes, fertilized and replenished the soils. They gave colonists access to energy and productive force.[56] Way back in ancient times, cattle were likely the first productive asset or "capital good"—the return or yield was that they gave birth and multiplied. Among the many roots of the word *capital* in Latin is the meaning "heads of cattle," while *pecus*, the Latin root of *pecuniary*, meant "flock." From the ancient world through the seventeenth century, exploitation of animal energies achieved the bulk of preindustrial gains in productivity.[57] Animals included human beings. In English North America, slave labor aided the colonial American project of agricultural "improvement."[58]

There was much work to be done beyond cultivation. New Englanders constructed clapboard houses. Elsewhere, log cabins were ubiquitous. Axes and frame saws fashioned logs. Chisel-edged broadaxes hewed them into square beams. Narrow-edged adzes cut notches. The saddle notch was round; the dovetail notch, from Sweden, was straight. Hatchets made shingles for roofs. Wooden mallets and iron claw hammers, another ancient tool, pounded wooden square-cut nails. Similarly constructed were outhouses, barns, smokehouses, pigsties, chicken coops, woodsheds, corncribs, and cider mills. The distinctively American postless, zigzagging worm fences kept animals out of fields and also established property lines.

Manufacturing and processing occupied many hours. After the harvest came the slaughter. Carcasses were dressed, hides scraped and stretched. Oak bark was the main source of tannin for treating hides. Households stretched leather and tanned their own shoes. Lard was rendered for cooking and stored in pig bladders. Ham and bacon were smoked for the winter.

Sheep were cleaned and shorn for wool. Households spun thread on wheels and wove cloth on looms. There were more tools to fashion—chisels, reaping hooks, bores, scythes, and hayforks. Most farm households had an orchard. For cider, bruised apples were mashed, placed between straw mats, and then pressed. The pomace rake made apple butter. Colonists drank milk in the summer, and in the winter cider and whiskey warmed their bodies alongside an ever-present fire. That meant having chopped firewood. "Lazy" households fueled winter fires with, what else, corn. In the spring, it was time again to sow. Planting corn required bending over six thousand times a day.

It took a household about fifty years to make a completely functioning farm. The average colonial farm probably was about 125 acres, an embarrassment of acres compared with the average English cottager. On a farm, time and the dominant motion of economic life were cyclical.[59] "As long as the earth endures, seedtime and harvest, cold and heat, summer and winter, day and night will never cease" (Gen. 8:22), promised the Bible. Plowing, sowing, and harvesting could be performed only about seventy-five days per year. Planting and harvesting bracketed the summer. Animal slaughter preoccupied the fall. Household manufacturing dominated the winter. Even conception had an annual rhythm, cresting in March and September.

During the seventeenth and eighteenth centuries, the shadow of the British Empire's frontier crept two to three hundred miles westward. To the west, Native power reordered itself but held strong. Though Smithian growth was largely a spatial phenomenon, increasing the extent of markets across territory, the pattern of North American settlement was remarkably sparse. Adam Smith, like many of his peers, associated commercialization with urbanization. Over the course of the long eighteenth-century commercial boom, the British North American colonies ruralized. While the absolute number of people in cities grew, after 1680 the urban share of the colonial population actually fell.[60] Why was colonial America not a more urban society? Why were colonial Americans so restless to move? The hunger of households for landed independence was strong. "No man who can have a piece of land of his own, sufficient by his labour to subsist his family in plenty," would remain in a city to risk poverty and "work for a master," speculated Benjamin Franklin.[61] Because it inflamed tensions with the French and a number of Native nations, London imperial authorities were not happy about the colonists' persistent western push. The Royal Proclamation of 1763 drew a line along the Appalachian Mountains, forbidding colonization west of it (undermining already existing claims) in a newly named Indian Reserve. Leading colonists quickly set out to lobby Parliament for revisions.

4. Independence and Dependence

Landownership, and a going farm, were not enough to make a man truly "independent." English liberty had relational properties as well. An independent man was a head of household—a husband, father, and perhaps also a master with dependents of his own. The social hierarchies and thick personal relationships of household government shaped the economic lives of all.

The household—like the corporation, whether a joint-stock trading company or a municipality—was a subsovereign of the British Empire. It was a "little commonwealth." The "head" of household ruled. The anatomical metaphor was no accident. The "head" made decisions on the household's behalf. He had voice in civic and public affairs. The head stood for election in assemblies, entered contracts, and served on juries. The head possessed the legal standing to own property. Because the ownership of property was necessary for voting in this era, on the eve of the Revolution two-thirds of male American colonials qualified to vote (compared to only a quarter in England).[62] In the colonies, political rights and property in land were distributed relatively equally among white men. There were many small owners of capital.

Early America also had a high "dependency rate." Because of land abundance, the marriage rate was elevated, and because of the high birth rate, colonial American households were large. In 1790 the median American household size was 5.7 free persons; including enslaved persons, it was 7.04.[63] This meant that on the eve of the Revolution, 50 percent of the colonial population were children.[64] Eighty percent of the colonial population were legal dependents of some kind, compared to less than 70 percent in England.[65]

British colonial North America was, demographically speaking, fertile ground for the strongest form of household governance, patriarchy, or the harsh and distant rule of the father. Patriarchy—absolute power over dependents, even life and limb—was an invented political tradition of the late seventeenth century. Sir Robert Filmer's political treatise *Patriarcha* (published posthumously in 1680) was the touchstone, arguing that the rule of the father was the basis of all sovereignty. Locke differed. In civil and political society, the right to rule continuously resulted from consent. Heads of households agreed to be governed so that their property rights would not be infringed. In addition to Lockean republicanism, the ideology of patriarchy circulated in the colonies, especially in the southern colonies among the great planters. The Virginian William Byrd II, a distant relation of Filmer and likely a serial rapist of his slaves, invoked the lives of biblical patriarchs:

> Like one of the patriarchs, I have my flocks and my herds, my bond-men and bond-women, and every soart of trade amongst my own servants, so that I live in a kind of independence of every one, but Providence. However tho' this soart of life is without expence yet it is attended with a great deal of trouble. I must take care to keep all my people to their duty, to set all the springs in motion, and to make every one draw his equal share to carry the machine forward. But then tis an amusement in this silent country, and a continual exercise of our patience and oeconomy.[66]

Capitalistic to be sure, the great planters' turn to black slavery in eighteenth-century Virginia oeconomy also became a self-consciously patriarchal project.

Marriage was a distinct oeconomical relationship. There was an aspect of patriarchy in the English legal principle of coverture, which defined wives as *femes coverts* whose legal personhood vanished into their husband's. The English jurist William Blackstone's *Commentaries on the Laws of England* (1765) included in the same legal zone "oeconomical relations" between master and servant, husband and wife, parent and child, guardian and ward, and corporations.[67] As for marriage, Blackstone explained:

> By marriage, the husband and wife are one person in law; that is, the very being or legal existence of the woman is suspended during the marriage, or at least is incorporated and consolidated into that of the husband: under whose wing, protection, and *cover*, she performs everything; and is called in our law-French a *feme-covert*. . . . Her condition during her marriage is called her *coverture*.[68]

Divorce was infrequent, sometimes impossible. Generally, once covered by marriage, wives could not own property, enter contracts, or enjoy legal standing in courts. Following Blackstone's chapter on husband and wife was one on parent and child, and the two often read alike. Children were under the dominion of the head of household until they reached the age of twenty and were fully "emancipated."[69]

The organic economy and the household oeconomy resonated with one another. Most colonists believed that sex difference was rooted in nature and justified men's authority. Nature determined men's and women's different oeconomical roles. Men plowed, sowed, reaped, hunted, and fished. Reproductive labor occupied women. The home and its surrounding yards, gardens, and outbuildings were the site of women's oeconomy. Women kept accounts, cooked, nursed, milked, scrubbed, reared, shopped, and spun. Selections from the diary of a prominent 1760s Salem, Massachusetts, housewife read:

> Washed . . .
> Ironed . . .
> Scowered rooms . . .
> Dressed a Calves Head turtle fashion . . .
> Sowed pease . . .
> Cut 36 asparagus . . .
> Bought 11 Ducks . . .
> Killed the pig, weighed 164 lb . . .
> Made two Barrels of Soap.[70]

Oeconomy was a common project, and women's contributions to economic life were critical. In this era, women's labors were visible and valued, placing them in the middle of early American economy.[71]

The authority of the male head of household had limits. According to law, wives, children, and servants could be subjected to "moderate" physical correction, but heads of household did not have patriarchal power over life and limb. Massachusetts banned the physical "correction" of wives. Further, heads had obligations to economically sustain and support their dependents. Women exercised power, often on the basis of their gender and sex. Meanwhile, there likely was genuine affection for many of a household's domestic animals that, nonetheless, were bound for slaughter. Probably most colonial household relations were less patriarchal and more paternal. So much in colonial life happened within households that economic and emotional lives were of necessity complicated and conflicted.

Marriage and parenthood were two of the four oeconomical relations of the household. The remaining two were master and servant, and master and slave. During the colonial period, roughly half of all willing migrants were indentured servants of some kind.[72] There were two waves of white indentures, a seventeenth-century migration to the Chesapeake, and a subsequent eighteenth-century one to the Delaware Valley. Indentures normally lasted between four and seven years, and young men usually traveled in hopes of bettering their conditions and setting up their own households. Many succeeded. But legally, white servants and black slaves alike became members of their masters' households.

William Moraley, an English indentured servant, sailed from London in 1729 and arrived in Burlington, Pennsylvania. Moraley joined a household consisting of "a Wife and two Daughters, with a Nephew, a Negro slave, a bought servant, and myself." There was also a "Gentlewoman."[73] He was indentured to his master for five years. For room, board, and clothes, he made nails and fixed clocks. He dined with the household's members. He shared a bed with his fellow servant. Moraley requested that he be sold to a household in Philadelphia, but his master refused, so he ran away, later to be captured, imprisoned, and beaten. Because of labor shortages, indentured servants had some leverage with their masters. The mayor of Philadelphia brokered a compromise, and Moraley returned to his master, but his indenture was reduced by two years.

Within the category of master and servant, there were two more subsets, in addition to indenture. One was wage work. Wages in America were by comparison with England high, but "hirling" was still a dependent legal status. Hirlings could not legally quit before ending their term of service. If they did, they could not claim wages for past services rendered. In these important respects, wage labor was not yet "free labor," in the later sense of the term.[74] In return, masters owed duties to wage workers. Hirlings could not be fired. If they became injured or sick in the course of their duties, their masters had to provide for them. Reciprocal, "not equal" rights prevailed.[75]

Another kind of servant was the orphaned member of another household. Colonies used household government to ameliorate pauperism and poverty. That is, instead of funding almshouses or conducting "poor relief," some colonies paid heads of household to take in orphans, as well as the elderly and the disabled.[76] The distinction between "servant" and "guardian," another of Blackstone's oeconomical relations, could be fuzzy.

The final oeconomical relation was that of master and slave. Slavery was distinguished by the marker of race, by its permanence, and by its inheritableness. Enslaved people had no legal right to exit the status. Colonial manumission was infrequent. Forty percent of all migrants to the colonies were African captives, and on the eve of the American Revolution, 20 percent of the British North American population was enslaved. Ninety-six percent of black people in the colonies were enslaved members of white households.[77] While the remaining 4 percent were not enslaved, they had no secure legal standing to set up households of their own.

Black slaves were human chattel. The colonial law of slavery, at first following the influential Barbados slave code of 1661, moved closer and closer to granting slaves the same attributes of private property as land.[78] Parliament's 1732 Act for the More Easy Recovery of Debts in His Majesty's Plantations and Colonies in America made it easier for English creditors to recover real property, including their slaves.[79] Enslaved people were the private property of their white masters.

Black slaves were commonly treated more harshly than white servants of any kind. In mid-eighteenth-century Pennsylvania—not the worst place, at the time, to be a black slave—Moraley noted that the lives of white indentures were "hard," but "the Condition of the Negroes" was "wretched." Moraley ran away, and his indenture was reduced. But a runaway "Negro" was "unmercifully whipped."[80] Moraley believed the ghost of a murdered black slave haunted his bedside. Surely, the presence of black slavery made Moraley look more favorably on his own indentured status.

Freedom is a moving target, and slavery, in this period, existed on the edge of a spectrum of oeconomical dependencies and unfreedoms. Across that spectrum, physical coercion was common. White indentured servants could even be sold. Slavery was no peculiar anomaly in a land of freedom, but black slavery was the basest and meanest of oeconomical relations. *Oeconomy* in this period remained closely associated with domesticity. *Domestic* might refer to the home, or to intimacies and affections, but it also evoked the process of domestication and dominion. The histories of animal domestication and human enslavement were long intertwined, and if cattle were the world's first productive assets under human dominion, so then were slaves. One historian has called enslavement an attempted "animalization" of humans."[81] William Byrd II spoke of his animal flocks and his bondsmen and bondswomen in the same patriarchal breath. The American slaveholder ideology of "paternalism" would be a nineteenth-century phenomenon. In the eighteenth century, according to one historian, enslaved persons were "part of the household and its possessions" but were "not often regarded as family members."[82] Masters commonly saw their slaves, according to another, as "luckless, unfortunate barbarians." They viewed them with suspicion, distance, and fear, and not infrequently masters referred to their slaves in their diaries as "devils."[83] Cruel and unusual punishments were common, including branding, mutilation, castration, ear cropping, burning alive, and dismemberment.

Some masters fantasized about transforming their slaves into capitalized labor and nothing more. But some aspects of enslaved lives were always fully outside capital's processes. Individually and collectively, African and Afro-descendant people commonly warred against their enslavement. African-American families and cultures formed.[84] Unlike in the West Indies, North American slave fertility was high, which granted black kinship a different quality. But at the same time, black sexual reproduction and reproductive labor represented for the white master a form of capital accumulation. The enslavement of black women represented a potential form of capital asset appreciation for the white master, as prospective biological increase meant prospective commercial increase. The biological increase of enslaved African and Afro-descendant people resonated with the origin of the concept of capital and its notions of multiplication and increase.[85]

Unfreedoms existed then that do not exist today, and therefore it is difficult to assess aspects of the colonial social order by today's standards. If we measure economic inequality with respect to household income and wealth, in 1774 the thirteen North American British colonies were economically the most equal society in the world (that can be measured) and also enjoyed the best standard of living in the world. American household incomes were on average 56 percent higher than those in England. Due to resource abundance, the relative cost of living in America must have been low. Wealth, property, and capital were much more widely dispersed. Without an aristocratic nobility, the colonies were more dominated by the "middling sort" of property-owning heads of household, with voice in political affairs. Many economic historians today believe that greater equality and fuller political participation led to economic benefits.[86] By these measurements, in 1774 the colonies were economically more equal than is the United States of the early twenty-first century. Back then, the top 1 percent of earners (including slave owners) earned 8.5 percent of total income. In the early twenty-first century, the top 1 percent earn more than double—20 percent of all total U.S. income.[87]

These numbers say something important and rather depressing about patterns of economic distribution in the early twenty-first century, but they do not capture everything. By the metric of household income, the economic living standards of American slaves were higher than those of the poorest free English commoners.[88] Something obviously important is missing from that comparison. Hierarchy was the norm in the colonial household, the central institution of colonial American life. Colonial North America might have been relatively equal, but the "dependency rate" was high. At the time, none of this was necessarily a contradiction. To enjoy liberty was precisely to live an economic life with personal dependents, whether ruling over them, loving them, or doing some combination of both.

Summing up, economically North America was overwhelmingly a very good place to be an adult white man, no matter how rich or poor, and it would consistently remain that way for a very long time.

5. Gambler and Peasant

Historians have long argued over the correct interpretation of the economic lives of early North American households.[89] Some have asked categorical questions: Was the household market-oriented or not? Were colonial Americans economically rational or not?

The problem is that the early American household was a mixed, ambivalent institution. Either-or questions are not much help. The right target of inquiry is the particular tension that both fueled and checked household commerce, legitimizing and limiting it at the same time.

The great economic historian William Parker once astutely proposed that the early American household had a split economic personality.[90] The conflict was between two ideal types that he called the "peasant" and the "gambler" mentalities. All colonial American households were peasants and gamblers to various degrees. The peasant desired landed property—political security of title, a home for the household, and noncommercial access to life's basic economic necessities. For the peasant, landed property, as wealth, secured a certain standard of living, but it was also something more than capital. By contrast, the gambler regarded landed property as capital. Desiring future pecuniary income, the gambler chased what Adam Smith called the "gains from trade."

Gambler and peasant alike desired secure land tenures and property rights, but they had different motivations. The gambler wanted property rights in order to secure his pecuniary investment in a capital asset. In colonial America, a speculative capitalist land market flourished. The system of "Indian land deeds," by which early colonizers had first negotiated with Indian nations through "ongoing, multipolar negotiations, involving a series of gifts, grants, agreements and amendments to those agreements," over time became instruments of coercion and deceit by which colonists dispossessed Indian lands—often to put them on the market for private sale.[91] By the end of the seventeenth century, even in Puritan New England, land speculation syndicates had formed to recruit profit-seeking funds from nonresident investors.[92] Parliament's 1732 debt recovery law made colonial land far more liquid and money-like than landed property was in other societies. A century later the noted American legal thinker Joseph Story, in his *Commentaries on the Constitution* (1833), underscored that land became "a substitute for money, by giving it all the facilities of transfer, and all the prompt applicability of personal property." Given land's marketability and the lack of coin, landownership was a means to store value—if only in preparation for the next speculative strike.

Speculation rewarded early colonizers, land hunters who "secured an interest." There were capital gains to be had—asset price appreciation—when the edge of colonization caught up. To read letters written by the founding generation of the United States is sometimes to feel as though one has inadvertently cracked a ring of savvy land speculators. The Virginia planter and land surveyor George Washington warned in 1767, "Any person . . . who neglects the present opportunity of hunting out good lands, and in some measure marking them for his own, in order to keep others from settling them, will never regain it."[93]

In colonial America, especially in Virginia, there was, according to one historian, "egregiously corrupt land speculation."[94] The colonies sometimes abetted it, parceling out territory to speculative "land companies," usually on the condition they would settle and fortify colonized lands. Most infamously Virginia in 1748 granted the insider Ohio Company two hundred thousand acres. London could not stop it. Colonists were not supposed to purchase lands directly from Indians, since only the sovereign had that right of "preemption." Regardless, colonists engaged in "direct dealings," a form of land speculation in itself, that led to a great many shameful swindles. The 1757 *Camden-Yorke* legal decision, undermining indigenous claims in India, legitimated many "direct dealings" in North America. For speculators, registering prospective land claims became a legal art form. Litigation would last into the next century.

Once a gambler acquired land, speculatively or not, commercial production was the main road to pecuniary income. Colonization first clung to lands nearest the coasts and navigable rivers that had the best market access. Roads were poor, limiting the extent of internal markets, but colonial farmers nonetheless drove wagons and herds over long distances and bad or nonexistent roads to sell their products.[95] Gamblers improved their land to make commercially viable farms as well as to increase its value as a transferable capital asset. They might specialize, putting more and more of their acreage into commodity production. Becoming more acquisitive, they might work longer and harder to make more money in order to be able to purchase more British consumer goods.[96] During the long eighteenth-century commercial boom, as interest rates declined across the Atlantic, gamblers also went into debt. Credit fueled the commercial settlement of the North American continent (and still does). Given the volatility of Atlantic commodity prices, the colonial gambler ran the great risk that he would not be able to repay his debts, which could mean forfeiting his property to creditors. To support investor confidence, the same 1732 Act of Parliament secured creditors' property rights.[97]

The peasant was no less hungry for land, and willing to grab it, but for different reasons. Lacking elite means to file land titles, peasants hoped "improving" land might be enough to ground a legally recognized claim. They wanted unimpeachable property rights because landed property and wealth—and only landed property and wealth—provided freedom from arbitrary interference over their lives. To get land from Indians, peasants did not so much subtly swindle them; they attacked them, violently, often bucking imperial authorities. This culminated, on the eve of the American

Revolution, in the series of land-grabbing backcountry "Regulator" insurgencies.[98]

Peasants also wanted land because landed wealth provided direct access to the basic necessities of life. Adam Smith had many ingenious things to say about the "gains from trade," but he had comparatively little to say about potential losses from trade.[99] For masterless American yeomen, landownership brought independence not only from arbitrary social and political power (the uncertainty Smith feared the most) but also from the vagaries of commercial markets. The extent of the market was not always assured. The peasant mentality intuited that market economies cannot always guarantee sufficient demand for all of the goods supplied by producers.

The Virginia planter, slave owner, and revolutionary Thomas Jefferson, as was so often the case with him, said it best even though he did not live it. In *Notes on the State of Virginia* (1785), Jefferson wrote, "Those who labour in the earth are the chosen people of God." Men who looked "to their own soil and industry" for "their subsistance" achieved independence, unlike those who "depend for it on the casualties and caprice of customers."[100] The colonial American yeomanry (especially the southern yeomanry) enjoyed high living standards for the day, due to commerce, resource abundance, and slavery. Subsistence production did not necessarily mean grinding poverty in the colonies, not with 125 acres. So why put all production at commercial risk? Why bet the farm? What Jefferson was saying was that an economic life of commerce alone was too unstable to adequately ground an "independent" household. The household had to be able to support itself. Only when it produced a surplus above what it consumed was it time to head to markets, in order to exchange for that which the household did not or could not produce, or to gamble on the gains from trade.

It was often possible to have it all. With a high "dependency rate," there was often labor on hand to capitalize a commercial farm while also producing basic necessities. One hundred and twenty-five acres was plenty enough both to cultivate the basic necessities and to produce for commercial exchange. Some regions had better market access, and some had better soil (unlike rocky New England), but very few regions were completely cut off from market access. Market engagements, and retrenchments, cycled. There was no one-off transition to capitalism but a cascading series of "market revolutions," and counterrevolutions, specific to geographical place.

By the end of the colonial period, great planters and middling yeomanry alike widely practiced a system of commercial "safety first" agriculture, or what households called achieving a "competency."[101] The average early American household directly consumed most household production. At the end of the colonial period, 9 to 13 percent of colonial economic production was destined for Atlantic markets. Coastal commerce among the colonists probably represented a similar figure.[102] Inland, due to poor transportation overland commerce was of a volume less than that. Altogether, in highly commercialized areas, between one-third and one-half of the product went to market.[103] But the sense of psychological security and the material subsistence that land provided induced as much as it checked economic investments in commerce.

Sometimes, however, conflict erupted, and the scales might tip. With the greater extent of markets, and more transactional liquidity, once the gains from trade appeared, might commercial self-interest spring the gambler mentality to life and finally overtake the peasant? Might Smithian growth accelerate, and might capital and its quest for pecuniary gain appropriate the production of wealth toward its ends?

From his position in Virginia, Thomas Jefferson became the most articulate defender and advocate of a popular oeconomical ideology that said commerce, while it must be promoted, must also be held in check. He would take this vision into revolutionary battle.

CHAPTER 3

REPUBLICAN POLITICAL ECONOMY

F OR DECADES, BRITISH MERCANTILISM TAXED NORTH AMERICAN commerce directly very little. After Britain's costly Seven Years' War with the French Empire, however, its Stamp Act of 1765 placed a new levy on American property to raise imperial revenue. More taxes, as well as London's repeated attempts to rein in colonizers' incursions onto Indian lands, brought about the antagonisms that led to the War of American Independence. The colonies declared their independence from the British Empire in 1776, and ultimately, in 1783, representatives of King George III signed the Treaty of Paris, recognizing a new republic, the United States of America.

A revolutionary epoch in the Atlantic world opened.[1] But the young U.S. republic remained precarious, threatened by European empires from without and by Native powers and separatist sentiments from within. Only a second war with Great Britain, the War of 1812, secured a lasting national independence. By then, the character of the republican political economy that emerged from what might be called the "long America Revolution" (1765–1815) was clear.

Old questions were raised in the new republic dedicated to popular sovereignty where "the people" reigned. What was the proper place of commerce in such a polity? What kind of political authority should encourage commerce, but also regulate it, and by what means? Toward what public ends exactly? The Revolution was in many respects a civil conflict, and Americans and their political leaders had a very difficult time getting together and answering fundamental questions about the character of their political economy.[2] Centuries later they still do.

1. A Massive Personal and Political Enmity

In 1815, at the close of the long revolutionary epoch, the Virginian Thomas Jefferson, having finished two terms as president six years earlier, was living in his Monticello plantation home surrounded by his French wine, books, black slaves, and gadgets. (The man held a legitimate claim as the inventor of the swivel chair.) Alexander Hamilton was eleven years in his grave, victim of a duel with Aaron Burr.

History is not just the recorded acts of great men, which Jefferson and Hamilton undoubtedly were. It is the lives and times of ordinary people, as well as the larger forces, such as capitalism, that are shaped by but also disappoint human projects and designs. Certainly the saga of the "massive personal and political enmity, classic in the annals of American history," that arose in the early 1790s between Jefferson and Hamilton has been told enough times.[3] Nonetheless, their mutual loathing was the flashpoint in the revolutionary conflict over a republican political-economic settlement. There is no other best place to begin to chart the significance of the American Revolution in the history of American capitalism.

The Revolution transformed American political life, from abstract ideas about sovereignty to everyday sensibilities.[4] But in the revolutionary era, the character of everyday economic life exhibited continuity—the household remained the central unit, its gender dynamics rather stable; and the republic continued to ruralize, with land, animals, and slaves dominating the productive capital stock. Further, after centuries of mercantilist imperial state building, most actors appreciated that the political and the economic were thoroughly entangled. The idea, in the words of the historian Gautham Rao, "that the state and the marketplace must be distinct simply did not exist."[5] And in this era, politicians—not men of business enterprise—were most responsible for charting the republic's long-term economic future. Who remembers, say, Elias Hasket Derby, a Salem merchant and one of the wealthiest men in postrevolutionary America who opened direct trade to China in 1787?[6] During the revolutionary epoch, contingent political events, not entrepreneurial innovation, most determined the trajectory of economic change.

The task for the revolutionary leadership was daunting. Economically, the colonists had done well under the British Empire, and the divorce from British mercantilism was risky. The war blocked Atlantic commerce, eliminating the overseas demand for goods that for more than a century had been the colonists' chief route to prosperity. Military campaigns ravaged farm households. One historian compares the period only to the Great Depression of the 1930s in terms of hardship.[7] Disorderly public finances and a period of monetary inflation imploded the credit system, followed by a postindependence moment of deflation and crippling debt, made all the worse because the British, remaining mercantilist, cut the Americans out from long-cherished West Indian markets. Between 1770 and 1800, according to estimates, per capita incomes probably declined by more than 20 percent.[8]

It was in this economic context, following the ratification of the Constitution in 1788, that the political conflict between Hamilton and Jefferson first broke out into the open. Both men were in government, and both were cabinet ministers under President George Washington. The moment for writing flashy preambles and fundamental laws had passed. Now it was time to govern.

Thus, 1789 was a particular kind of moment, one shared by all postrevolutionary societies. The Revolution being so recent, even the most mundane piece of legislation might seem to carry the gravest implications. The stakes being so high, politicians might interpret a personal slight as a challenge to their idea of the Revolution itself, and a genuine political challenge might be perceived as a direct personal affront.[9] The dynamic could, for instance, lead to rituals such as dueling—the way Hamilton (and his son) would die. Battles over the memory and meaning of the Revolution define politics for years, and the personalities of revolutionary leaders become objects of ideological projection reflecting the political fault lines of the Revolution itself.[10] During the 1790s, something like this happened with Hamilton and Jefferson.

The first disagreement between what would later become the Hamilton and Jefferson blocs appeared trifling: how much should Congress tax incoming British ships? From this disagreement erupted an epic conflict.

Foreign commercial policy was no trifling matter. Not only did export markets provide American commerce with its most critical source of demand, geopolitically the U.S. republic was born a minor power in a world of belligerent empires. In his approach, Hamilton chose commercial rapprochement with the British Empire. Meanwhile, emulating the British model, as secretary of the Treasury he launched an ambitious federal program to kick-start long-term national economic development. Finance, commerce, and manufacturing would prosper in unison—Enlightenment "improvement" on a grand scale. To initiate economic development, Hamilton would opportunistically reorganize the public finances. He would have the federal government capitalize a long-term public debt, a step toward fostering a dynamic private capital and credit market, as British experience proved. He would also charter a Bank of the United States in the image of the Bank of England. On behalf of his various projects, Hamilton always sought to energetically entangle private profit seeking and public power, market and state.

Jefferson objected. As secretary of state, he desired for the United States to break free, immediately, from all commercial dependence on the mercantilist British Empire. By opening up its ports to all nations, the U.S. republic would become a beacon of "free trade" to the world. Meanwhile, if Hamilton's sympathies were with urban, commercial elites, Jefferson's were with rural white heads of household, even with lesser yeomen. Hamilton looked east to the British model of long-term economic development. Jefferson looked west, eyeing the continental interior. The republic's long-term future, in his view, lay in more settler colonialism, including the slave-based variety. Not the economic development of finance, commerce, and manufactures in unison but widespread white male property ownership should be the aim of republican political economy.

During the 1790s, Hamilton's and Jefferson's different personalities, as well as their opposing republican ideologies, became the basis for the country's first two organized political factions: Hamilton and the Federalists, and Jefferson and the Democratic-Republicans. Budding democratic politics would decide between these two long-term visions for a postrevolutionary political-economic settlement. Given his nature, Hamilton spoiled for the fight. Jefferson was artfully circumspect, given his. But make no mistake: Thomas Jefferson hated Alexander Hamilton.

2. Hamilton and "Pecuniary Capital"

Jefferson's hatred took some time to grow.

Following the ratification of the Constitution in 1788, the two men arrived in the temporary capital of New York City as the two most important cabinet members of President Washington's administration. The first problem they faced was that the government could not finance the debts inherited from the Revolutionary War. Making matters worse, the British Empire had turned its mercantilist apparatus against its former colonies.

Stepping back, the republic's monetary and financial system—most critically, its public finances—was in complete disarray. In American politics, the so-called money question was an old one.[11] Before the Revolution, the colonists had long complained about the lack of coin. British mercantilism had long prohibited colonists from minting currency. Colonists experimented with issuing paper money anyway, backed by versions of land collateral, which colonial governments soaked up through taxation and retired (sometimes by burning) to tamp down inflation. Parliament's Currency Acts of 1751 and 1764 were further prohibitions.[12] The 1765 Stamp Act taxed colonials in pounds sterling, a form of currency that even the wealthy did not possess, which helped spark the political crisis.[13]

To fight the Revolution, Americans had borrowed money. Benefiting from the long eighteenth-century era of cheap money, they had sold public debt in Europe, at 5 to 6 percent interest, with promises to repay in hard currency. They also issued, essentially, promissory notes to domestic creditors, at the same rates. In 1790 Treasury secretary Hamilton estimated that the federal government still owed $29 million in principal. In addition, the individual states owed a collective $25 million in debts. But during the Revolution, Americans brought paper money back.

Both the Continental Congress and the individual states printed paper money, not backed by specie. The rebellious colonies thus asserted their new sovereign powers. Congress printed some $241.5 million in "continentals." Booming markets for farm produce to feed armies brought forward production.[14] Still, amid wartime disruption, much production was directly consumed, and the quantity of money outpaced the production of marketable goods. By 1781, $167 of continentals traded for $1 in specie. By destabilizing expectations of the commercial future, inflation began to undermine commercial confidence and participation in markets.

When Hamilton and Jefferson took office, the credit system was in no better shape. Consumer boycotts had been political weapons during the Revolution, but after the 1783 Treaty of Paris, postrevolutionary Americans leaped to purchase Britain's goods once again, and once again London extended them the credits necessary to purchase them. Parliamentary Navigation Acts cut the Americans out of the lucrative West Indian carrying trades with which, as colonists, they had earned the trading credits necessary to finance British imports. The British "robbed us of our trade with the West Indies," the Virginian James Madison complained.[15] During the mid-1780s, imports from Britain tripled American exports.[16] Debts filled the gap. The Articles of Confederation (written in 1777, ratified in 1781) rendered Congress hapless before British mercantilism. Nine individual states passed mercantilist restrictions against British imports but also against the individual states. During the 1780s, for instance, Connecticut imposed heavier duties on goods from Massachusetts than on those from Great Britain.[17] National trade policy was nonexistent.

In the late 1780s, the trade deficit with Britain contributed to a debt crisis and a sharp commercial contraction. In 1785 British creditors grew nervous and called in their debts, ceasing to issue new credits. Meanwhile most states had put away their printing presses, passing laws mandating that debtors pay back creditors in hard currency. States had raised taxes to service their Revolutionary War debts. With money absorbed by taxation, spending in markets of all kinds shrank. Urban wages and commodity prices plunged. But many debts were pegged to inflated prices. Households attempted to save to pay down their debts, but that only decreased spending, contributing to price deflation. What took hold was what the twentieth-century U.S. economist Irving Fisher would call, during the throes of the Great Depression of the 1930s, a vicious cycle of "debt-deflation," leading to economic depression.[18]

Heads of household sought political redress in the state legislatures. The Revolution had been fought against the perception of overweening executive authority, and the postrevolutionary state governments were relatively democratic institutions for their day.[19] Farmers in particular demanded debt and tax relief.[20] In 1784 a South Carolina deputy sheriff summoned farmer Hezekiah Maham to appear in court before his creditors. Maham not only refused, he shoved the writ in the deputy sheriff's mouth and made him swallow it.[21] Shays's Rebellion (1786–87), a tax revolt in rural Massachusetts, alarmed creditor elites everywhere. Debt-distressed farmers demanded the right to pay their debts in kind—such as in corn or cows, not scarce cash. Even more demanded that states begin again to print paper money, to help inflate away their debts. Some states obliged.

Creditors, most of them urban, cosmopolitan elites, were alarmed. Among those concerned were Hamilton and Madison. (Jefferson was then on a diplomatic mission to Paris.) A debt was a contract, the creditor's property right. The Revolution, after all, was fought because Great Britain taxed American property without their consent. Now overzealous democratic "majorities" trampled on private property rights. Hamilton also believed debts had to be paid in full, because rich Americans, not to mention

Europeans with capital to invest abroad, would not invest in the United States if men like Hezekiah Mahem could shove it down their throats. Hamilton worried over investor confidence. Those who possessed hard currency were too fearful to part with the liquid asset, and the paper credit system had nearly ground to a halt. By 1786, "credit at home and abroad was no longer available."[22]

What paved the road to the 1787 constitutional convention in Philadelphia was what today would be recognizably a politics of austerity.[23] After a surge in debt and consumption had come a credit crunch, deflation, and a slump. Debtors demanded relief. Creditors moralized about "laziness" and "extravagance" and demanded hard money. Creditors called for fiscal austerity, and higher taxes, to prevent any further profligacy. They and their advocates argued that such assurances from states would soothe the supply-side confidence of investors—including foreign investors (including British investors)—who threatened to sit on the sidelines and precautionarily hoard their money, credit, and capital until their political demands were met.[24] The same argument will repeat, over centuries.

On the money question, the Constitution of 1787 had much to say. It came down in favor of creditors. Article I, section 8 prohibited state governments from printing paper money and placed the power to coin money exclusively in the hands of the new federal government. So much for the state printing presses. Further, Article I, section 10 prohibited states from "impairing the obligations of contracts." That included the obligations of debtors to pay their creditors. Article III created a new system of federal courts, which Madison, at this point in agreement with Hamilton, believed was necessary, in part, because state courts were too friendly to farm debtors. Only about half the American population supported the Constitution, and Madison and Hamilton worked together for successful ratification, writing in haste, with some help from John Jay, the Federalist Papers in 1787–88.[25]

After ratification, when Madison and Hamilton, two ardent 1780s "nationalists," arrived in New York City to implement the new Constitution, they came as allies. At first, the two men, still young, went for walks in Lower Manhattan, talking and laughing, and an old woman would later remember that as a young girl she once saw the pair "play with a monkey that was climbing in a neighbor's yard."[26] Soon their relationship took a dramatic turn.

When the first Congress met in 1790, Hamilton proposed the Funding

Act, in which the new federal government would take fiscal responsibility for the Revolutionary War debts of the individual states—the policy called "assumption." Plus interest, he estimated it would come to a grand total of $79 million. (The real number was closer to $74 million.)[27] These sums were of great political significance. Arguably, public debt was the most explosive political issue of the revolutionary era on both sides of the Atlantic. British public debt had led to the 1765 Stamp Act and ultimately the American Revolution. French public debt had led King Louis XVI to convene the Estates-General, leading to the outbreak of the French Revolution in 1789. Conceivably, American public debts threatened to undermine the very existence of the young republic.

Sensing the stakes, and characteristically seeing opportunity in crisis, Hamilton had a bold plan to reorganize American finances, which he had announced in his January 1790 "Report on the Public Credit," the first in a series of brilliant state papers laying out Hamilton's grand vision of republican political economy.[28] He proposed the following. The United States would pay foreign creditors in full. The domestically held debt would be refinanced, at face value through the issue of bonds that, some technicalities aside, paid 4 percent interest—2 points less than originally promised, reducing the immediate need for federal revenue by a third. To all debtholders, foreign and domestic, Hamilton guaranteed interest payments in hard currency, which was a preview. (His 1791 "Report on the Establishment of a Mint" would establish a bimetallic gold and silver standard for the new American dollar.) Next, Hamilton proposed that the federal government assume all state debts. Finally, the federal debt would be permanent. The reissued U.S. bonds carried no maturity dates. The principal might never be repaid, but interest payments would extend into the infinite future. At present, Hamilton said, the federal government would service only interest payments. To do so, he calculated that the new federal government would need $2.8 million in annual revenue. There would be small internal taxes on property, such as an excise on the production of alcohol. Hamilton also proposed an "impost" on foreign commerce, a modest tariff on imports—by English manufactures mostly.

Congress first debated Hamilton's proposal refinancing the debt at full face value. During the war, many of the existing holders had purchased debts below face value. The notes had been issued broadly, including to soldiers in lieu of wages. Their farms suffering, given the heads of household's absent labor, soldiers turned around and sold the notes, at a discount, to merchants. This way, while wartime commercial stoppages leveled economic inequality, the notes slowly funneled into the hands of wealthy urban merchants. By 1790 less than 2 percent of Americans owned Revolutionary War debts.[29] Hamilton's measures granted these elites a windfall payout—face value, in hard currency, at reasonable rates of interest. In Congress, critics argued it was unfair that Hamilton did not "discriminate" between the original holders of the debt and those who had speculatively bought it up. Did not the original holders, who bled for the Revolution, deserve something? None other than Congressman James Madison organized the opposition. But he did not have the votes, and the measure passed.[30]

Madison's sympathies had by now turned toward his home state and away from his friend's policies. As for the federal government's "assumption" of the state debts, Madison believed Virginia, less in debt than other states, would pay more than its fair share under Hamilton's scheme. Madison had the votes in Congress to block the measure, and he did.

Soon after Madison's success, Jefferson encountered Hamilton pacing in a street, near President Washington's doorway. Jefferson would recall, "His look was somber, haggard and dejected beyond description. Even his dress was uncouth and neglected. He asked to speak with me. We stood in the street near the door." Hamilton explained to Jefferson the assumption bill's importance to "the general fiscal arrangement" of their administration and pleaded for help. Jefferson obliged, arranging for "Mr. Madison" and "Col. Hamilton" to join him for dinner at his lower Manhattan apartment for a "friendly discussion."[31]

For Hamilton, assumption was critical. It secured the power and legitimacy of the new federal government. Assumption would also increase the size of the national debt. Economically, that was something Hamilton actually wanted. He called a permanent debt a "national blessing." So soon after the Revolution, he cited British experience. After the Glorious Revolution of 1688, the publicly chartered but privately operated Bank of England (1694) had funded a permanent British national debt. Britain became what historians now call a "fiscal-military state," with the resources to win imperial wars.[32] Backed by public authority, a private capital market was formed with rates and terms anchored to the circulating public debt. British public debt had become a symbol of national and imperial strength and also a trigger of long-term capitalist development. In England, the industrial revolution was beginning.

Unlike Great Britain, in America "pecuniary capital," as Hamilton called it—or money and credit for private investment—was insufficient to capitalize what Hamilton believed was the country's extraordinary potential for long-term economic development, given the natural resources at its disposal as well as its commercial heritage. As Hamilton explained in "Report on the Public Credit," the right financial system was necessary to bring that economic potential forward into the present. The answer was "bank money" or "credit money," British style. With a permanent national debt, funded by earmarked future revenues, U.S. public debts would circulate in the hands of private investors and fulfill "most of the purposes of money." The public debt market would also set a foundation for a private capital market in securities. Hamilton would establish the hard-currency value of the dollar in his 1791 "Report on the Establishment of a Mint," and the Constitution had abolished the state paper printing presses. The scarcity value of money was secure. Hamilton could now vest the discretionary power to expand the money and credit supply in the hands of profit-seeking mercantile elites. From the supply side, an investor class of national elites would trigger wealth-generating investments in enterprise. This class Hamilton knew well.

Alexander Hamilton was born in 1757, most likely on the small British West Indian island of Nevis.[33] In 1772, at fifteen, he traveled to New York City under the sponsorship of St. Croix merchants. He attended King's College (later renamed Columbia University). At eighteen, he wrote a pamphlet in support of colonial revolt, "The Farmer Refuted" (1775). At nineteen, he became an army captain. By all accounts a brave and dashing figure, Hamilton became General George Washington's most trusted aide-de-camp. He married well, with a "face never to be forgotten," according to his sister-in-law.[34] After the war, Hamilton studied law, returned to New York City, and took a seat in the Continental Congress. Soon he wrote of the need for a "vigorous" and "energetic" national government.

Hamilton was not a mercantilist, in the sense that he did not believe in any variety of balance of trade doctrine.[35] But he had fully digested the lessons of political economy. There must be commerce, but there would be checks. "It is as easy to change human nature," Hamilton addressed the New York constitutional ratifying convention in 1788, "as to oppose the strong current of the selfish passions." But the "wise legislator will gently divert the channel, and direct it, if possible, to the public good."[36] The goal was to create the right combination—which sounded like the first Earl of

Shaftesbury. As Hamilton explained in Federalist no. 12, "*The prosperity of commerce* is now perceived and acknowledged by all enlightened statesmen to be the most useful as well as the most productive source of national wealth, and has accordingly become a primary object of their political cares."[37] Some of the Anti-Federalist critics of the Constitution had said commercial self-interest alone might act as "a bond of union."[38] Hamilton did not agree. In a republic, only state power could harmonize the tension between private self-interest and the public good. The private and public interest must, and would, entangle. The question was the right integration and how to achieve it.

Hamilton can claim originality as a political economic thinker. His thought can best be labeled "Hamiltonian."[39] He had read Adam Smith and commonly cited the benefits of the division of labor. His sharp financial acumen stands out above all.[40] He understood that capitalist economic development is led by financial investment. He gambled that the right application of state power might just conjure a U.S. financial system capable of capitalizing commerce, agriculture, and manufacturing all at once. Likewise, he judged from the contemporary British example that not just more commerce—as in the classical mercantilist's larger slice from the pie of world trade—but rather intensive national economic development was fast becoming the lever of power in international relations. Finally, state power was also something Hamilton wanted to wield, and he was fully prepared to do so with a remarkable audacity.

One more aspect of Hamilton's economic worldview deserves mention. Born low, illegitimately, and an immigrant, he was a self-made elitist. The new federal government, on the make as well, was ripe for his ambition. Hamilton was a revolutionary and a republican, but he believed in government of the wise, the rich, and the good. He was no friend to democracy. "The people," he announced to the Constitutional Convention, "are turbulent and changing; they seldom judge or determine right."[41] Hamilton admired the gentlemanly merchants of his own aspirational milieu. They were polite, refined, worldly men of affairs, who, as one critic put it, might have "snored through four years at Princeton."[42] At the time, this class could not have amounted to more than 5 percent of the U.S. population. The economic destruction of the Revolution and the democratic "excesses" of the 1780s had undermined their authority at the local and state levels. The Constitution was a chance to reconstitute at the national level, as the rightful ruling class of a representative republic.[43] Hamilton hoped to hitch elites' commercial self-interest to the project of building a strong national government. In turn, a strong national government would induce greater private investment among the mercantile elite.[44] It must be said, few of the constitutional framers were farmers.

In the summer of 1790, Hamilton joined Madison for dinner at Jefferson's Manhattan dinner table, and a compromise was reached. Madison accepted the federal assumption of debts. Hamilton agreed to support the eventual move of the capital from New York City to a miserable patch of swamp on the Potomac River, the future Washington, D.C.

Hamilton was not finished yet. Months later, in December 1790, he released his "Report on a National Bank," proposing a twenty-year federal corporate charter for a Bank of the United States (BUS). He quoted Adam Smith on the benefits of what is today called a "fractional reserve" banking system, in which bankers lend more money than they hold in specie reserves, in order to explain how private banks transformed specie, or "dead stock," into the "basis of paper circulation." That extended credits beyond hard reserves, creating more funds for pecuniary capital formation and the multiplication of commerce. The profit-seeking BUS would make private loans through branches opened throughout the United States. It would thereby increase both the "quantity of circulating medium and the quickening of circulation," keeping pecuniary capital in a state of "incessant activity."[45]

The BUS entangled private interest with public authority, mixing money and sovereignty. The BUS was like all chartered corporations of the revolutionary period, a subsovereign of the republican government, and this particular corporate subsovereign and its stockholders would have enormous power. Private stockholders would own $8 million of the bank's original $10 million capitalization (more than all existing U.S. bank capital), while the federal government would own $2 million. The BUS would enjoy a monopoly on the federal government's banking business. Inevitably, because of its behemoth size, the BUS would de facto enjoy the power to expand and contract the country's money and credit supply.

Once again Hamilton encountered resistance in Congress. In the British Empire, after the Bubble Act of 1720, only the Crown had had the authority to charter joint-stock corporations. Colonial North America had had no incorporated banks—none. After the Revolution, there was a flurry of state-level chartering of joint-stock corporations, all profit seeking, but each with a stated "public purpose"—marine insurance corporations, turnpike corporations, but also some banking corporations.[46] To critics, corporations were unrepublican, smacking of monarchical privilege and monopoly. Some did not want corporations chartered at even the state level.[47] Secretary of State Jefferson and Congressman Madison made constitutional objections to Hamilton's BUS, arguing that the federal chartering of corporations was not implicit in the Constitution's "necessary and proper clause." Hamilton made quick work of the Virginians' legal arguments. The charter passed, and the BUS opened its book for subscriptions on July 4, 1791. Within an hour, there was no more stock left to sell.

3. Jefferson's "Empire of Liberty"

James Madison watched the scene unfold with horror. He reported back to Thomas Jefferson, "Stock jobbing drowns every other subject. The Coffee House is in an eternal buzz with the Gamblers."[48] Investors did not have to put up $400 a share because with $25 they could buy "scrip," or the right to buy the stock at a future date. The scrip was negotiable and began to circulate. By sheer force of imagination and will, Alexander Hamilton was bringing to life a pecuniary capital market. To Jefferson, it was nothing short of the betrayal of the Revolution. The break from the British Empire was supposed to promote the interests of white rural heads of household, not those of finance capitalists.

Hamilton and Jefferson were both republicans, but not all republicans shared the same political beliefs.[49] American revolutionaries called themselves "Whigs," and both Hamilton and Jefferson identified with the Whig legacy of the Glorious Revolution of 1688. Both idealized the eighteenth-century British Empire, when the colonials had it good, and both argued that the Revolution had been necessary because George III's policies had strayed from the true principles of British liberty. But after the Revolution, Hamilton's republicanism moderated, while Jefferson's radicalized, or at least it became even more anti-British. Certainly, he believed, Hamilton's "scrippomania" was not in the spirit of '76.

Thomas Jefferson, like Alexander Hamilton, had grown up on an outer fringe of the British Empire to become a republican revolutionary.[50] There the similarities ended. Hamilton was handsome and dashing; Jefferson was tall, gangly, and shy. Hamilton was born low; Jefferson was born destined to become a member of the ruling Virginia gentry. After receiving his introduction to Enlightenment ideals at William and Mary College, Jefferson ascended quickly, joining the House of Burgesses at twenty-six. Construction began on his home, Monticello, in 1769, and in 1773, after inheriting his wife's estate, his property encompassed ten thousand acres and 180 slaves. At age thirty-two, he took a seat in the Continental Congress. During the Revolution, he became governor of Virginia. After the war, he departed for France on a trade mission. He was in Paris for the storming of the Bastille. Washington called him back, to become secretary of state.

Jefferson, unlike Hamilton (and also Madison), was not an original thinker. His greatest talent was for Enlightenment sloganeering, and it was a formidable one. The already-cited passage from *Notes on the State of Virginia* (1785) on political oeconomy must be quoted again, at full length:

> Those who labor in the earth are the chosen people of God, if ever He had a chosen people, whose breasts He has made his peculiar deposit for substantial and genuine virtue. . . . Corruption of morals in the mass of cultivators is a phaenomenon of which no age nor nation has furnished an example. It is the mark set on those, who not looking up to heaven, to their own soil and industry, as does the husbandman, for their subsistence, depend for it on the casualties and caprice of customers. Dependence begets subservience and venality, suffocates the germ of virtue, and prepares fit tools for the designs of ambition. . . . Generally speaking, the proportion which the aggregate of the other classes of citizens bears in any state to that of its husbandmen, is the proportion of its unsound to healthy parts, and is a good-enough barometer whereby to measure its degree of corruption. While we have land to labour then, let us never wish to see our citizens occupied at a work-bench, or twirling a distaff.[51]

The paragraph was a republican translation of the commercial safety-first strategy of rural American households. Liberty required independence—including from the caprice of customers, or from the vagaries of commercial demand, which no market-based economic system could ever ensure of its own accord. Any Virginia tobacco planter knew that from following the commodity's extraordinary price volatility over the years. In commerce, dependence thus always loomed.

Republicans believed in a system of political representation. For this reason, in politics the American revolutionary leadership was obsessed with personal "virtue." Republican leaders must act "disinterestedly," on behalf of the common good. Politics should not be a venue for self-interested ambition, as that would lead to "corruption." If a political representative were not "independent," if he did not own sufficient property, his "dependence" would make him corruptible and unfit for republican rule. Hamilton would have agreed with all this. But Jefferson went further. Not only republican leaders but also republican citizens must be "virtuous" and "independent." For that, they had to own a particular kind of property and wealth. Not financial "scrip," which represented the whims of finance and therefore the risk of dependency. Republican citizens should really own land.

Jefferson's ideology was another British inheritance. The entanglement of bank and state after the 1694 chartering of the Bank of England was subject to political debate. The "Old Whigs," "Radical Whigs," "Commonwealthmen," or "Country Party," as the faction was variously known, attacked the ruling ministry of Robert Walpole for being corrupt.[52] To secure power, Walpole had in fact passed out Bank of England stock to his political supporters.[53] Over the course of the eighteenth century, Walpole's adversaries, still howling against financial corruption, became increasingly irrelevant to British politics. But colonial Americans—who owned little bank stock and a lot of land—continued to lap up the ideology.[54] The leading English "Country" political theorist was Henry St. John, the first Viscount of Bolingbroke. George Washington literally plotted out his entire life to appear as if he had leaped directly from the pages of Bolingbroke's *The Idea of a Patriot King* (1738), and he basically pulled it off. Everyone agreed that President Washington had republican "character."

Jefferson democratized "Country" republicanism. Not the stolid gentleman farmer but rather the sturdy American yeoman was his ideal republican citizen. Does it need saying? Jefferson was no simple yeoman. He enslaved black people and exploited them physically, sexually, and emotionally. His own republican "character" hardly rated. Hamilton called him a "contemptible hypocrite," and contemptible or not, at minimum Jefferson was a hypocrite.[55] Instead of "character," he had, in the modern sense of the term, "personality," which is why he continues to fascinate us today—whereas Washington, if more admirable, can come across as boring. Jefferson was truly conflicted about nearly everything in his life. He hated cities but loved Paris. He celebrated commercial independence but died under a mountain of debt. Probably he thought he was in love with one of his slaves.[56]

But politically, Jefferson's commitment to white yeomen heads of household was genuine. Of course, white racial solidarity had been the first rule of Virginia politics ever since the late seventeenth-century turn to Indian hating and African slavery. During the war, Jefferson had proposed a massive redistribution of land to the Virginia yeomanry. He successfully supported abolishing primogeniture and entail in Virginia, which widened white landownership. Generally, the new state constitutions "swept away most remaining feudal restraints on inheritance, subdivision and alienation of land."[57] Meanwhile the war leveled tobacco markets, and Jefferson, among other Virginia planters reconsidering their views, even toyed with slave abolition.[58] He inspired the Northwest Ordinance of 1787, which banned slavery in the Old Northwest (the future states of Wisconsin, Michigan, Ohio, Illinois, and Indiana). After that, Jefferson stuck to merely being quotable on slavery's evils. That Alexander Hamilton combined disdain for democracy with antislavery while Thomas Jefferson became a slave-owning apostle of the widening of democracy is one of the great paradoxes of American history.

Jefferson's long-term political-economic program, no less fervently motivated than Hamilton's, was simple: Expand the agrarian white yeoman republic across space. Look West.[59] Above all, Americans needed *Lebensraum*. They must have property rights to secure their liberty. There would be commerce. Landed property was capital, but it was also something more. Land would ground a moralized republican political "independence" and "virtue." White gentry and yeomen would merge into a rural "middle landscape," an enlightened equipoise of commercial self-interest and rural republican simplicity. The virtuous subsovereign households of the republic would bask in "that happy mediocrity of condition."[60] Jefferson believed that slavery, someday, by someone else's doing, would die out. Blacks must return to Africa. Indians should civilize or be conquered. In 1780 Jefferson first called this vision an "Empire of Liberty." His vision of a postrevolutionary settlement was a politics of property, a political economy of widespread white male property ownership.

Jefferson believed Hamilton was far too committed to emulating British political economy. In January 1790 advance news of Hamilton's "Report on the Public Credit" leaked to the public through the assistant secretary of the Treasury, William Duer. The New York speculator Andrew Craige resided in a boardinghouse with six New England congressmen because he knew "no way of making safe speculations" other than by being privy to "public information."[61] Hearing rumors of assumption, speculators had snapped up $837,000 of Virginia debts and $3.51 million of South Carolina debts at far below face value and now stood to make a considerable profit.[62] Jefferson complained to Madison that speculators were trading in "federal filth."[63] Later, he would recall Hamilton as

> a singular character. Of acumen outstanding, disinterested, honest, and honorable in all transactions, amiable in society, and duly valuing virtue in private life, yet so bewitched and perverted by the British example, as to be under thorough conviction that corruption was essential to the government of a nation.[64]

The project of republican nation making should not, in his view, be hitched to financial profit seeking. After the creation of a permanent public debt and an incorporated national bank, Jefferson was sure a litany of British horrors would come next: financial oligarchy, government patronage, parasitical bureaucracy, heavy taxation, a standing army and navy, wars. Aristocracy by birth, perhaps even monarchy, might return.

Hamilton's policies posed for Jefferson a far more immediate problem: it was blocking Jefferson and Madison's own legislative agenda for economic development, and they did have one. Their first plank was the antimercantilist principle of "free trade," a radical Enlightenment ideal. During the Revolution, American ports were opened to the ships of the world. In 1784 Jefferson was dispatched to Paris to negotiate what he called "the total emancipation of commerce."[65] On pragmatic grounds, Hamilton believed rapprochement with British mercantilism was prudent, and he was less interested in abstract philosophies of free trade. Jefferson, however, sought complete emancipation from the British mercantilist system. Let America, extending across continental space, dispose of its agricultural surpluses in Europe, the land of the workbench, the distaff, the city, the bond market, and the corrupt. Jefferson saw Paris, but he did not accomplish much diplomatically. Mercantilist Europe was implacable.

The Virginians shifted their strategic objection to tactical uses of mercantilist restrictions on behalf of free trade ends. Tensions emerged between the two future blocs at the opening of first Congress, when

Congressman Madison proposed a Navigation Law against British imports—nearly a prohibitive ban. Wrongly, Madison believed the loss of the U.S. market would bring the British Empire to the negotiating table. But Jefferson agreed with him. Hamilton's Treasury reports are justly celebrated, but few read Secretary of State Jefferson's no less thorough "Report on the Privileges and Restrictions on the Commerce of the United States in Foreign Countries" (1793), a scathing assault on British mercantilism.

Hamilton could not abide a steep tariff against British imports, for 77 percent of U.S. imports were then British.[66] His proposed moderate duty was meant not to discourage British imports but rather to raise the fiscal revenue needed to fund assumption, and thus the permanent national debt, and therefore the entire Hamiltonian developmental project.

What finally brought Jefferson and Hamilton into open conflict was Hamilton's December 1791 "Report on the Subject of Manufactures." This was Hamilton's boldest strike of them all. The establishment of the BUS and circulating public debt had been first steps toward "the augmentation of Capital," Hamilton wrote. Next, the "incitement and patronage of government" would be required to inspire nervous private citizens to invest in manufacturing. In particular, Hamilton said governments must attend to the "confidence of cautious sagacious capitalists."[67] To induce industrial investment, he proposed that the government make direct subsidies to select U.S. manufacturers—today called the "industrial policy" of picking winners. Also, Hamilton approved the chartering of a manufacturing corporation in New Jersey, the Society for Establishing Useful Manufactures (SEUM). The governor of the corporation was the former assistant secretary of the Treasury, Hamilton's friend William Duer.

Duer was not a long-term investor in manufacturing enterprise, however. He was a financial speculator. The initial stock subscription in the SEUM sold out within days, and the price of scrip, opening at $19.91 a share, soon rose to $50.[68] Duer was quickly buying and dumping the stock for quick profits. His favored line of speculation, however, was U.S. public debt. In the spring of 1792 he formed a pool with other speculators. He borrowed cash from the SEUM, to acquire more collateral, in hopes of driving U.S. bond prices up. But prices fell. By early March, Duer's credit was exhausted. Hamilton's Treasury called in personal loans granted to Duer. Duer's creditors threatened to drag him from debtor's prison and disembowel him in the street. The short-lived financial panic of 1792 was the republic's first. Deftly, Hamilton used Treasury funds to buy assets—today called "open market operations"—in order to bring back transactional liquidity and stabilize prices in the capital market. The panic quickly lifted.[69]

Meanwhile Duer was too much for Jefferson. Whether Hamilton was personally corrupted or not, he was building a political economy in which a William Duer could happen—and that alone was bad enough.

Truly, Hamilton's reach had exceeded his grasp. To be sure, industrialization cannot be taken for granted. Hamilton was correct that many "cautious sagacious" capitalists preferred to hoard their wealth rather than risk their capital on long-term industrial enterprise. Something else was needed besides the profit motive to catalyze industrial development. Hamilton believed the promptings of the state could provide that outside component. But while the kind of capital market that Hamilton was using federal power to call into existence could induce such investment, its liquidity—the way assets can be instantaneously converted in the present—also makes possible short-term speculation. Duer proved that. Government could offer inducements, but entrepreneurs still had to possess the ability and desire to invest in corporate industry.

Finally, in a political error, Hamilton had snubbed existing U.S. manufacturers, the rising "mechanic interest." These men consisted of skilled artisanal craftsmen, household based, not corporate—property owners, but with low capital requirements. Incorrectly, Hamilton did not believe they could ever be a great source of industrialization, and so his industrial plan had largely bypassed them.

In the meantime, Duer went bankrupt. The "Report on Manufactures" was a dead letter in Congress. The Virginians saw a political opportunity to expand Jefferson's white yeoman ideology to encompass northern mechanics and even tradesmen who could not locate a scheduled federal Treasury auction. In 1792 Madison wrote an anonymous newspaper article accusing Hamilton of being "more partial to the opulent than to the other classes of society" and of believing that "mankind are incapable of governing themselves."[70] By the end of that year, Jefferson's "republican interest," or the Republicans, was publicly squaring off against "the Treasury" of Hamilton, or the Federalists.

Washington tried to patch it up. Hamilton took to writing anonymous newspaper tirades against Jefferson. Personally, he defended himself to the president:

> *I know* that: I have been an object of uniform opposition from Mr. Jefferson, from the first moment of his coming to the City of New York to enter upon his present office. I *know,* from the most authentic sources, that I have been the frequent subject of the most unkind whispers and insinuating from the same quarter. I have long seen a formed party in the Legislature, under his auspices, bent upon my subversion.[71]

Boxed out of Washington's administration by Hamilton, Jefferson chose to resign as secretary of state. In the meantime, he wrote to Washington:

> I will not suffer my retirement to be clouded by the slanders of a man whose history, from the moment at which history can stoop to notice him, is a tissue of machinations against the liberty of the country which has not only received and given him bread, but heaped it's honors on his head.[72]

There would be no patching it up, and Jefferson was not really retiring.

4. Federalists and Republicans

Now that the stakes had been established, the Hamiltonian and Jeffersonian projects could be put into motion and conflict. Hamilton had the first chance at power. His fiscal policies were startlingly successful.[73] U.S. commerce boomed. But somehow, politically, Hamilton still went down to defeat.

Initially, everything broke in the Federalists' direction. After Hamilton pushed through Congress a largely symbolic internal tax on the production of alcohol, a tax revolt broke out in southwestern Pennsylvania, where cash-poor farmers were using whiskey as a medium of exchange. In July 1794, Washington and Hamilton rode out on horseback and put down the Whiskey Rebellion without a fight.[74] A month later a U.S. army offensive defeated an Ohio Valley confederacy of thirty-five Indian nations in the Battle of Fallen Timbers. The Treaty of Greenville (1795) ceded the Ohio Valley to the United States.[75] By then, radical republicans in France had executed Louis XVI, and the Terror had begun. The French revolutionary wars opened fantastic trading opportunities for neutral American ships. In 1795 John Jay signed a treaty with mercantilist Great Britain that allowed Americans to make "broken voyages," transporting French and Spanish West Indian products to the United States first, before reexporting them to Europe. In light of Fallen Timbers, the British also agreed to comply with the Treaty of Paris and abandon their western military forts. Finally, Pinckney's Treaty (1795) with the Spanish Empire secured U.S. access to the Mississippi River, including the right to deposit goods in the port of New Orleans. The Federalists thus secured, and expanded, the American foothold in the trans-Mississippi West.

Meanwhile U.S. public finances were flush. Federal revenue from customs duties for 1789–91 combined was $4,399,000. In 1795 it was over $5,588,000.[76] Hamilton now claimed the federal government to be "in a most flourishing condition" and resigned from the Treasury. Having "contributed to place those of the Nation on a good footing," he wrote privately, "I go to take a little care of my own; which need my care not a little."[77]

Hamilton chose the right time. The United States enjoyed its first national commercial boom. The success of Hamilton's financial reforms deserves some credit. The BUS extended private loans, expanding the supply of money and credit. "Pecuniary capital" augmented. No less crucial were developments at the level of the states. During the 1790s, state governments chartered twenty-eight banks (after only three during the 1780s).[78] In 1791 the British Board of Trade noted with approval the foreign investor protections of the new Constitution, and European investor confidence returned.[79] Finance capital flowed into U.S. markets.[80] There was a great burst of Smithian commercialization.[81]

Yet more than anything, the immediate cause of the 1790s boom was the French revolutionary wars and the Atlantic commercial opportunities they made possible. Europeans demanded U.S. foodstuffs, which meant prosperity for the grain-growing mid-Atlantic states, as well as for U.S. shipping interests, which benefited the northeastern urban ports. While southern planters did not benefit so much, they found a new export staple— cotton. After having made peace with British mercantilism, economically the young U.S. republic was basically regressing to its colonial position, provisioning and trading with the West Indies, now under a neutral flag. Trading credits once again financed imports of British manufactures.[82] "The affairs of Europe," declared one American observer, "rain riches upon us; and it is as much as we can do to find dishes to catch the golden shower."[83]

Political scientists say good economic times normally benefit politicians in office, so the ease with which Jefferson and the Republicans politically dispatched the Federalists in 1800 is all the more remarkable.[84] Republicans proved far more skillful in the arts of partisan democratic politics.[85] Despite the 1790s Atlantic commercial boom, Federalism lacked a sufficient popular constituency among white heads of household, especially rural ones. The leading northeastern ports of Boston, New York, and Philadelphia benefited most from the golden shower.[86] Hamilton's reforms were settling in. But the yeomanry, the mechanic interest, aspiring middling urban tradesmen, and many southern slave owners wanted something different than Atlantic commerce with war-torn Europe.[87]

Politically, the administration of the Federalist John Adams confirmed the worst Democratic-Republican suspicions. After the Jay Treaty established peace with the British, the greatest threat to American commerce was French retaliations against neutral American shipping. By 1798, full-scale war with France was possible. The Federalists raised internal taxes, passing a stamp tax. Hamilton and others hinted at a permanent military establishment. To the Democratic-Republicans, it was one page after another pulled from the aristocratic and monarchical British playbook. There would be standing armies, internal taxation, incorporated banks, a national debt, ruling commercial elites, and after the Federalists pushed through the Alien and Sedition Act of 1798, the suppression of political dissent.

In the presidential election of 1800, Jefferson—the southern candidate, aided by the three-fifths clause of the Constitution, which increased southern electoral clout by counting slaves as three-fifths of persons for purposes of representation—prevailed.[88] Republicans trounced Federalists all the way down the ticket. Hamilton published an unhinged fifty-four-page letter disparaging Adams, effectively ending his political career.[89] Publicly, Jefferson came to power in a magnanimous spirit, but privately he wrote that "by the establishment of republican principles," he would "sink federalism into an abyss from which there shall be no resurrection for it."[90]

Downcast, Hamilton concluded in 1802, "What can I do better than withdraw from the Scene? Every day proves to me more and more, that this American world was not made for me."[91] America's "real disease," Hamilton declared two years later, hours before his fatal duel with Aaron Burr, was "Democracy."[92]

When Jefferson took office, he asked his Treasury secretary Albert Gallatin to uncover "the blunders and frauds of Hamilton." Gallatin reported back to the president: "Hamilton made no blunders, committed no frauds. He did nothing wrong."[93]

5. The Postrevolutionary Settlement

Jefferson had first invoked the "Empire of Liberty" in 1780, to evoke a political confederation to benefit rural white heads of household, the yeoman subsovereigns of the republic. There was no way to have it without the colonization of the trans-Mississippi West. The project also required diverting a "branch of commerce," as Jefferson put it, toward the Mississippi River.[94] Upon taking office in 1801, Jefferson set about putting the program in action. To succeed would be to end U.S. commercial dependence on Atlantic commerce. At stake was the same phenomenon that had given rise to the Age of Commerce in the era of mercantilism—the geopolitics of market access and trade.

The Mississippi River was the great commercial artery of the North American continent. The Treaty of Paris had ceded all British territory south of Canada and east of the Mississippi to the United States. But a number of Britain's Indian allies did not recognize the cession. West of the Mississippi was Spanish Louisiana, acquired from France after the Seven Years' War. It extended east across a narrow strip of Gulf coastland to Spanish Florida, which the Spanish used to control access to the great Mississippi port of New Orleans. The Spanish claimed territory east of Louisiana as far north as Tennessee. They sponsored Indian allies, including the Creek, Choctaw, and Cherokee nations. But the most active and hostile agents west of the Appalachians were neither European empires nor Indian nations. They were American colonizers. Some flirted with separation from the United States, but these men—white yeomen heads of household—were Jefferson's constituents. In 1780, the same year he announced the Empire of Liberty, Jefferson noted of the West that the national government could not hope to control colonization there. It was "necessary to give way to the torrent."[95]

Opportunity arose to clear the path. During the French revolutionary wars, the Spanish Empire had incurred heavy public debts. Napoleon reacquired Louisiana in a distressed sale in 1800. Next, he shocked U.S. diplomats by offering the territory to the United States for $15 million. The creditworthiness of the U.S. government in European capital markets—made possible by Hamilton's fiscal system—enabled Jefferson's administration to finance the Louisiana Purchase of 1803. The Louisiana territory was 820,000 square miles, forming a triangle with points at New Orleans and the future states of Minnesota and Idaho. Instantly the United States doubled in size, seemingly fulfilling Jefferson's inaugural boast that the yeoman republic had "room enough" to last "to the hundredth and thousandth generation."[96] In capital markets, confidence in the U.S. government financed the long-term U.S. imperial expansion across space.

The Louisiana Territory in 1803 was "less a place than a claim."[97] The Constitution had assigned the federal government the tasks of dispensing public lands and entering relations with Indian nations. The Federalists had originally hoped to control and slow the pace of settlement, much as prerevolutionary British imperial officials had done. They would acquire lands from Indian nations, by treaty, and sell off large blocs to wealthy speculators (maybe themselves) to help raise fiscal revenue. But after Jefferson came into office, Congress reduced the minimum purchase of federal land from 640-acre sections to 320 acres, at $2 an acre, with generous credit provisions. In 1804 60-acre lots went up for sale at $1.64 each.[98] A speculative market in western lands formed. The gambler arrived with the peasant. White colonizers, if not purchasing land, violated treaties and squatted and "improved" Indian lands, hoping to file recognized claims later. Thirty-three times, between 1800 and 1830, Congress would pass "preemption" laws legalizing squatting.[99] Before the Revolution, only the Crown enjoyed preemption rights. Now so did yeomen households. Such was the birth of popular sovereignty. In 1795 the American population west of the Appalachians was 150,000. By 1810, it already passed 1 million. The United States continued to ruralize.

Ironically enough, in some respects Jefferson's Empire of Liberty came to resemble the eighteenth-century British Empire.[100] Congress revoked all internal taxes. The military budget was cut in half.[101] A provision of the 1789 Constitution, the Commerce Clause, granted Congress the authority to regulate commerce "among the several states," forbidding interstate mercantilist discrimination. The result was to check state discrimination, opening up a unitary commercial space and increasing the extent of markets and thus the demand for goods. Empires, while forging common political jurisdiction, accommodate pluralism and difference in rule, often so that different elements in the empire might engage in commerce. In this respect, the Louisiana Purchase, in essence, handed the United States its own version of a West Indies in the lower Mississippi Valley.[102] By 1810 already 16 percent of the U.S. slave population lived in the trans-Appalachian West. New slave-based triangular trades appeared on the North American continent, in a great counterclockwise national wheel of commerce.

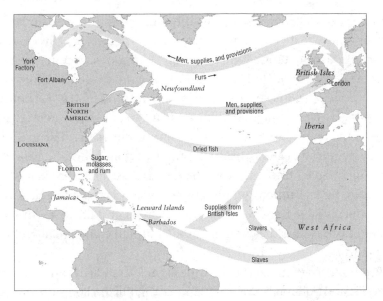

BRITISH ATLANTIC COMMERCIAL PATTERNS, C. 1750 /
EARLY NATIONAL AMERICAN WHEEL OF COMMERCE, C. 1820

Ironically, the commodity trades of the nineteenth-century U.S. Empire of
Liberty mirrored those of the eighteenth-century British Atlantic Empire,
as if the lower Mississippi Valley was the American version of
British Caribbean slave societies.

Rather than northeastern foodstuffs shipped to the West Indies, the Old Northwest floated foodstuffs and provisions down the Ohio and Mississippi rivers to budding southern cotton plantations. Cotton traveled up the coast.[103] With the closing of the Atlantic slave trade in 1808, slaves passed through a domestic instead of an Atlantic market, a "Second Middle Passage." Local, metropolitan, and intraregional commerce, especially in the Northeast and the mid-Atlantic states, was far greater in volume than transregional trade. Between 1793 and 1807, internal commerce increased fourfold.[104] Nonetheless, transregional ties helped bind the young federal union. As the Empire of Liberty conquered western lands, the invisible hand of the market held its grip firmly on the white master's lash. Across the continent, the Smithian commercial multiplier went to work.

"From one end of the continent to the other," remarked the disenchanted Federalist and Columbia professor Samuel Mitchill in 1800, "the universal roar is Commerce! Commerce! at all events Commerce!"[105] A distinctive U.S. "commercial society" began to appear.[106] It was rather rough-and-tumble, as well as crude. Adam Smith and many other eighteenth-century intellectuals had believed that commerce would pacify and refine society. In rural America especially, according to one English traveler, Americans were just as likely to brawl as they were to bargain—gouging out an eye, biting off a nose, tearing "out each other's testicles."[107] American vernacular culture was far from genteel. The culture was lowbrow, if democratic. Racy novels like Susanna Rowson's *Charlotte Temple* (1794), were best sellers. So was *The Autobiography of Benjamin Franklin* (1791), launching the career of the mythological "self-made man."

All the while, there was one form of commerce of which President Jefferson remained suspicious. He wanted the Empire of Liberty and its commerce to face west, but after 1803 the Napoleonic Wars heated up, and neutral shipping in the Atlantic once again flourished. From 1805 to 1807, freight charges alone exceeded U.S. domestic exports.

Fighting a war, in 1805 Britain passed numerous restrictions on neutral U.S. shipping.[108] On republican principle, the United States lacked the state capacity, including the naval power, to push back. So in December 1807 Congress followed Jefferson and passed an embargo forbidding all American vessels from sailing to foreign ports. Foreign ships were prohibited from exporting American goods. They could bring select imports but must then sail away empty, in ballast. Jefferson had, effectively, outlawed commercial prosperity. In 1808 U.S. exports plummeted dramatically, and so did customs revenue.[109] Unpopular at home, the embargo failed abroad. Free trade among European and American empires was not happening.

Jefferson retired to Monticello with his administration in tatters. But he had had enough of U.S. commercial dependence on Europe.[110] The embargo would redirect American economic life inward. A home market would provide demand. Jefferson now spoke of the American "manufacturer" and the American "husbandmen" working "side by side," both producers together in a perpetual struggle against parasitical, unrepublican merchant-speculators.[111] The embargo stimulated internal commerce and manufacturing—the small-scale, household variety, but also more innovative and lasting textile factories and machine shops.[112] It was a remarkable shift from the colonial era. Americans now defined themselves not by their old consumer identities as British subjects but by their republican "productive labor."

Congress ended the embargo in March 1809, the same month that James Madison was sworn into office as president. But war with the British lurched toward inevitability. When it did break out in 1812, the United States was not prepared. Madison had allowed the federal charter of the BUS to expire in 1811, so it could not assist the federal government in mobilizing resources. The United States entered arrears on the national debt. The military campaign was nearly farcical, and in the summer of 1814 the British invaded the Atlantic seaboard. British troops caught the Americans by surprise and set fire to Washington, D.C.

Washington was the capital that President Madison had acquired, a quarter of a century earlier, in negotiations with then–Treasury secretary Alexander Hamilton. Hamilton was dead, Jefferson retired. President Madison sat outside the capital, with U.S. troops, and watched the White House burn. The long-term strength of the U.S. republic, he believed, would come neither from executive state power, nor from the grandeur of its now-smoldering public buildings, but from the bottom-up republicanism of its white heads of household. It certainly would not come from the U.S. Army, with its 12 percent desertion rate. The Americans could not win the war, but neither could Great Britain hold the North American continent from the Atlantic Ocean to the Mississippi River. The Treaty of Ghent (1814) ended the War of 1812 and established almost the status quo antebellum. Napoleon was soon defeated, so neutral commercial rights in the Atlantic would no longer be much of an issue anyway.

If Jefferson's execution had been inadequate, his instincts had been correct. The Empire of Liberty was turning west. In declaring war, Madison had accused the British of rousing Indian "savages" in the West.[113] A composite British imperial geography, which had granted Native nations some room to maneuver, including commercially, gave way to something different.[114] The Empire of Liberty was not the same as European empires in this respect: it was less respectful of Indian sovereignty. It did not want to trade so much as to conquer. Popular violence was let loose against Indian peoples.[115]

The military hero of the War of 1812 was a popular major general of the Tennessee militia, Andrew Jackson. In the Southwest, General Jackson now waged total war.[116] In March 1814 he eliminated a Creek army at the Battle of Horseshoe Bend. We have conquered "the cream of the Creek country, opening a communication from Georgia to Mobile," he boasted.[117] No doubt, Native Americans east of the Mississippi were the biggest losers in the long American Revolution, while the biggest winners were rural heads of household. The United States was born with a politics of property, a political economy of widespread white male property ownership, that would last far into the nineteenth century.

The republican political economy born during the era of the long American Revolution led to the following settlement. Hamilton had laid the foundations for, as he put it, the augmentation of "pecuniary capital." The U.S. dollar was linked to hard currency, and the scarcity value of money capital was secured. Through paper note issues in excess of coin reserves, the BUS expanded the supply of money and credit—capitalizing economic development. Jefferson could not uproot this incipient capitalist financial system. By the time the BUS's federal charter expired in 1811, the state-level chartering of banks was well under way. Indeed, state governments energetically fostered economic development, in everything from chartering corporations, to creating infrastructure that increased the extent of markets, to, in the North, abolishing slavery.[118] But at the national level, a popular democratic mobilization of white heads of household dramatically overthrew not only monarchy but also any vestige of aristocracy or oligarchy.[119] The national party of elites, the Federalists, would not take charge over the union. National plans for economic development were abandoned. Jefferson's Empire of Liberty won out. Bottom-up, popular Republican nationalism, the colonization of Native American lands, household governance, the extension of slavery, and commercial self-interest would have to hold the union together.

Would it be enough? In 1815 President Madison called for the establishment of a national system of "roads and canals" for the purpose of "binding more closely together the various parts of our extended confederacy."[120] Senator John C. Calhoun of South Carolina agreed: "Let us conquer space."[121] But there was no agreement among Republicans about the constitutionality of a federal infrastructure program. There was, however, a final coda to the political-economic debates of the long Revolution. After the War of 1812, the Democratic-Republicans decided Hamilton had been right: a National Bank was both necessary and proper. On April 10, 1816, President Madison signed the charter of the Second Bank of the United States.

CHAPTER 4

CAPITALISM AND
THE DEMOCRACY

═══

THE UNITED STATES WAS NOT AT FIRST A DEMOCRACY. AFTER the Revolution, even among white men, voting was restricted according to property ownership. Alexander Hamilton and other revolutionaries regarded democracy as a suspect proposition. Democracy had to "rise" in the U.S. republic, and the crucial decades when it did were those after the War of 1812.[1] By 1828 property ownership was no longer a requirement for white male suffrage. In the presidential election that year, General Andrew Jackson roared into the White House on the back of a self-consciously democratic mobilization.

Electoral democracy, it must be stressed, was limited. Women could not vote. And it was not just limited: the logic of American white male enfranchisement meant the disenfranchisement of free blacks.[2] Nonetheless, the result of Jackson's two presidential administrations was a dramatic national political realignment. Jacksonians—self-styled inheritors of Jefferson's legacy—called themselves "the Democracy." Their opponents called themselves the Whigs. Our initial examination of the economic and political relationship between capitalism and democracy in America, arguably the first such contact in world history, necessarily concerns the relationship between capitalism and the Democracy.

At this moment in the history of American capitalism, politics remains the right register to inspect. In economic life, prominent continuities existed much as during the long Revolution. In production, the organic economy endured. The Empire of Liberty's greatest subsovereign, the household, remained the central economic institution. Smithian dynamics in commerce persisted, which meant that the geopolitical extension of markets across space was the engine of growth. Aggressive white land grabs of Indian possessions expanded the Empire of Liberty westward. The core postrevolutionary settlement, a politics of property, held firm.

What changed? First, there was more commerce. But it was also charged with new political meaning.[3] Alexis de Tocqueville's *Democracy in America* (1840) argued that democracy meant more than formal political institutions—it also included a nation's ethos. In the American instance, that ethos was commercial.[4] And Tocqueville was far from the only European travel writer to take that measure of Americans. The English novelist Fanny Trollope, in *Domestic Manners of the Americans* (1832), remarked that "every bee in the hive is actively employed in search of that honey of Hybla, vulgarly called money; neither art, science, learning, nor pleasure can seduce them from its pursuit."[5] Aristocratic European snobbery captured some degree of the truth.

The rise of American democracy accompanied two credit-led, speculative commercial investment booms. The first lasted from the conclusion of the War of 1812 until the Panic of 1819. The second began in the late 1820s and lasted until the Panics of 1837 and 1839. The Second Bank of the United States (BUS) extended money and credit beyond hard money reserves and capitalized wealth-generating labor and enterprise across the nation, much as Hamilton had said it would.[6] From a source deep within American democratic culture, a high inducement to invest in commerce positively raged. The Smithian commercial multiplier went to work, and the commercial economy expanded likely in excess of 1.5 percent GDP per capita, making the United States, where industrialization had but barely begun, already the fastest-growing economy in the world by that modern metric.[7]

Partisan democratic politics affected every single driver of the commercial dynamism. At the conclusion of the War of 1812, a number of national politicians who later became Whigs, led by the Kentucky congressman Henry Clay, put forward a long-term national plan for commercial development—the first since Hamilton. The federal government would manage land acquisition and sales, generating fiscal revenue. A steep tariff against foreign manufactures would protect young U.S. manufacturers and sponsor industrial production. The revenue from both would fund public investment in a coherent federal "system" of "internal improvements," or the public infrastructure of roads, turnpikes, and canals necessary to expand access to market demand. From above, the BUS would manage the scarcity value of money, extending private credit when appropriate. Clay called his plan the "American System."

Jackson's Democracy, like Jefferson and the Democratic-Republicans before him, balked at national economic planning. In the end, no positive system of national economic policy resulted from the rise of American democracy.

The Democracy saw to it that it would not. The American System violated the Jacksonian principle of "equal rights." In tandem with commercial growth—and in particular with the growth of the U.S. financial system—the period saw increasing economic inequality.[8] The Democracy blamed government, attributing the inequality to the federal government's favoring of elite economic interests. The publicly chartered and subsidized BUS, by allocating credit to its chosen favorites, was by definition a "corrupt" violator of equal rights. A tariff favoring northern manufacturers, at the expense of southern consumers of British manufactures, also played favorites. For the same reason, the Democracy was suspicious of public investment in federal infrastructure projects. Finally, Jacksonians argued that private initiative, at times violent, not calm federal management, should guide the colonization of Indian lands.

Altogether the Democracy's transformation of U.S. political economy would be a greater rupture than even the Revolution. President Jackson summed it up in his 1837 farewell address: "There is but one safe rule, and that is to confine the General Government rigidly within the sphere of its appropriate duties."[9] The Democracy demanded the disentanglement of state and market, public and private.[10] Such sphering gave birth to new political-economic tensions—over boundaries, not entanglements—and would prove critical to the unfolding of the Age of Commerce. Under the banner of equality, Jacksonianism at once crippled long-term federal government programs and gave birth to a popular democratic faith in the politically unhindered market.

One result in this period, in the words of one historian, was a great release of commercial "energy."[11] Another result was the emergence of a distinctively American, anti-elitist, proto-populist, and pro-commercial politics of "antimonopoly." Antimonopoly required equality of commercial opportunity and therefore prohibitions on "corrupt" government patronage and favoritism. Dramatically, Jackson killed off the BUS. In individual states, the Democracy led a social movement for democratic "open access" to incorporation. Corporations, long subsovereigns, began to shed their public status, migrating into the private economic sphere.[12] Finally, on democratic principle there would be no overarching plan for national commercial development.

Ironically, the assault on political privilege and government elites would soon enough smooth the path for the growth of economic privilege and corporate elites. Paradoxically or not, the rise of democracy in the United States gave rise to a popular suspicion of government authority. Meanwhile the United States became something like a natural experiment in Smithian economic growth.[13] The national market, emancipated from political direction and driven by the continued expansion of black slavery, would in future decades take the American republic down a perilous political path.

I. Cotton Boom, Bank Bust

After the final defeat of Napoleon at Waterloo in 1815, the British industrial revolution entered its most intensive phase. English textile manufacturers created demand for raw cotton, and southern slave production fueled a postwar speculative investment boom in commercial production. Cotton set a new pace.[14]

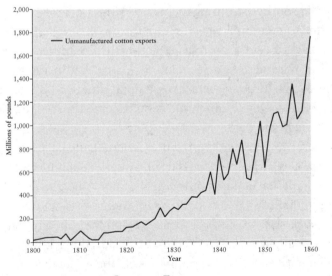

COTTON EXPORTS

Cotton was by far the leading U.S. export of the antebellum period, enriching white southern slave owners. Note that periods of increased export volumes coincided with speculative upswings in the credit cycle.

Even before Jefferson's embargo of 1807, cotton exports amounted to 22 percent of total U.S. exports.[15] In 1816 it was 39 percent.[16] By then the United States was growing more cotton than India, long the world's leading producer.[17]

South Carolina and Georgia, long dependent on rice and indigo production, quickly adopted the crop, growing a more productive "short staple" variety of cotton and taking advantage of more efficient "saw" cotton gins.[18] Meanwhile western colonization contributed greatly to the production surge.

There was more land grabbing and more land speculation. Land remained a relatively liquid asset in the United States—with more developed markets for it—compared to other countries. Congress tried to calm the colonization process, but to little avail.[19] The U.S. Supreme Court in *Fletcher v. Peck* (1810) and *Johnson v. M'Intosh* (1823), cases involving disputed land claims, abetted speculator and squatter rights under the doctrine of "improvement." Those rulings secured private property rights, which instilled popular expectations about the likely commercial benefits of future western colonization. In spirit, speculator and squatter sometimes joined hands in the same figure. A "level of westward migration unprecedented in the young nation's history" occurred.[20]

In the Old Southwest, during the War of 1812, General Andrew Jackson had wrested some 14 million acres from the Creek people. The "Creek Cession" was the crescent-shaped strip roughly three hundred miles long and twenty-five miles across, descending from the southwestern corner of Tennessee, down through central Mississippi (statehood, 1817) and across Alabama (1819). This region would soon become the most agriculturally valuable land in the world.

The federal government created the General Land Office in 1812. Soon public land sales surged.[21] In the Old Southwest, "Alabama fever" raged. In 1810 the population in the territory that became Alabama and Mississippi, excluding Indians, was 40,000. By 1820, there were 132,000 whites and 118,000 black slaves. The Chesapeake region had already sent 124,000 slaves westward. The positive fertility of enslaved black women assured the fulfillment of white expectations of their slave capital's future increase—and of future pecuniary profits. Black slaves, men and women, children and elders, cleared the lands and brought millions of acres under cotton cultivation.[22] Cotton was new, but by now white enslavers had honed for centuries the process of western conquest and colonization.

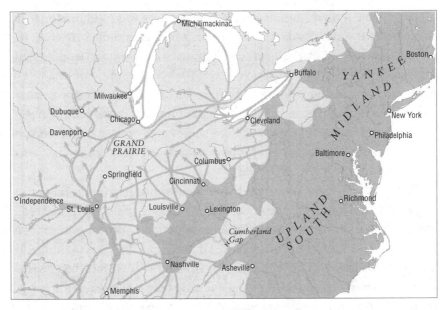

EARLY NATIONAL AMERICAN COLONIZATION, C. 1820
The arrows illustrate the main thrusts of American colonization
and settlement in the Old Northwest and Old Southwest.
Commercially and politically, the Ohio and Mississippi rivers
tied the two regions together.

Meanwhile settlers moved into the Old Northwest as well. North of the Ohio River, the new cities of Pittsburgh, Cincinnati, and Louisville expanded, as a corn and hog farm belt stretched across southern Ohio, Indiana (statehood, 1816), and Illinois (1818). In contravention of law, many northward-migrating southern "butternuts" brought with them black slaves to help break the soil.[23] Various Indian nations remained in rightful possession of lands hugging the Great Lakes, and west of the Mississippi Native power was strong. Southern-oriented, the Old Northwest faced south, toward the Mississippi River.

The great commercial artery, the Ohio-Mississippi river system, connected the Old Southwest and the Old Northwest. At this time, traffic largely flowed downriver. Commercial production was most viable forty miles or less from water transport. "Alabama fever" raged because Alabama had no fewer than five rivers—the Alabama, the Tombigbee, the Cahaba, the Tallapoosa, and the Coosa—to ship cotton to the tidewater port of Mobile. Bad or nonexistent roads limited the extent of markets. It was more cost efficient for a western Pennsylvania farm household to ship its goods down the Ohio and Mississippi rivers, more than one thousand miles, and then coastwise to Philadelphia, than it was to transport those same goods eastward overland across mountains. On average, thirty miles of overland transport approximated the cost of shipping goods across the Atlantic Ocean.[24]

Old Northwest provisions flowed downriver, for reexport or sometimes for feeding Old Southwest slave plantations with a high percentage of acreage in cotton production, so as to raise cash to pay debts—much like a seventeenth-century Barbados sugar plantation. Cotton sailed coastwise to the Northeast, often bound for transshipment to Europe. Still, by volume local and intraregional commerce was greater than the national and transregional.[25] Nonetheless, cotton did link a national, transregional trade and was an important source of economic demand as well as a political bond of national union.

Households moved west and increased the extent of commercial markets across space, triggering Smithian dynamics. Even squatters needed money and credit to capitalize new opportunities across the land. The Second BUS, chartered in 1816, headquartered in Philadelphia, led the way. The mixed public-private corporation was capitalized at $35 million—$25 million more than the First BUS. The Second BUS designated nineteen local branches in 1817. Branches in quite recent settlements, whether in

Lexington, Kentucky, or Chillicothe, Ohio, issued paper money in excess of the bank's specie money reserves. BUS credits backed further paper note issues by state-chartered banks.[26] Money and credit expanded, capitalizing labor and production, as the BUS network financed the reverberating cotton boom.[27]

In 1819 the boom turned to bust. Credit was backed by imagination and trust. The financial system needed to fulfill prior those expectations, by financing sufficient, but not too much, production. Regardless of whether U.S. supply overshot immediate British demand, or buyers simply began to expect it would, cotton prices in Liverpool declined by half. The BUS and its branches had been a conduit for British credit and capital. Banks in London pulled back, and a chain reaction followed. Everywhere creditors called in loans and demanded hard currency. That drained specie from the countryside. Commodity prices and land values plummeted together, making debts harder to repay. Reverberating, the collapse of demand in the countryside hit sellers in the cities. Confidence in the U.S. banking system evaporated. People panicked, hoarding money, which fueled the vicious cycle. Credit dried up. Prices fell. It was a spiraling cycle of debt-deflation, the first since the 1780s.

The BUS did not help. In 1818 it had withdrawn $2 million worth of hard currency for a scheduled debt payment to France for the Louisiana Purchase. The BUS's financial obligations at home and abroad had exceeded its hard metallic reserves by a factor of ten. During the panic, the BUS had called in loans from state-chartered banks, demanding hard money, which undermined the local extension of credit everywhere, putting a halt to commerce. During the Panic of 1792, Treasury secretary Alexander Hamilton had deftly entered financial markets to maintain transactional liquidity in money and credit markets and had snuffed out the panic. The Second BUS did not; its actions made the Panic of 1819 worse.

Speculative investment booms could turn to busts. Unlike in 1792, the panic rippled outward and created hard times in the commercial economy. The ongoing colonization of Michigan, for instance, halted. West of the Mississippi, the Indian fur trade suffered. Back east there were urban unemployment and bankruptcies. The cotton South, however, was hit the hardest. Cotton prices would never again climb so high as they did during the 1810s, and cotton would never be so important a driver of national commerce.

The gambler was stung. However, landed property, as wealth, was still something more than capital. The land still offered rural households the basic necessities. This financial panic did not matter as much as it would in future crises, when capital would command far more of economic life. After 1819, the peasant reappeared, retreating from the commercial economy to the household economy. The Philadelphia political economist Mathew Carey's *Essays on Political Economy* (1822) quoted an upstate New York cattle farmer who wondered if, so chastened, "our people will soon limit their exertions to the raising of food for their families" and forget about commerce altogether.[28] The bust did give some Americans pause. They had as yet no concepts of "the market," "the business cycle," or "the economy" with which to make sense of it conceptually on its own terms. How exactly did a pullback on credit in London translate into urban unemployment in Baltimore? By what mechanism did it all hang together?

Americans' rather uniform and consistent answer was that government was to blame. Recrimination fell on the BUS. It was true that the BUS's directors had run a loose operation, often granting loans to themselves without collateral. "Let every Shylock leave his hole, and in the open day boldly sharpen his knife, to take 'the pound of flesh' nearest the heart of his honest neighbor!" exclaimed the Baltimore journalist Hezekiah Niles after the BUS announced the suspension of notes among its many branches.[29] It made no sense to the large majority of Americans to think that economic events did not result, in the first instance, from politics and government.

The BUS suffered a political backlash.[30] Much as had happened during the last moment of debt-deflation, the postrevolutionary 1780s, class conflict arose between debtors and creditors. In response to popular pressure from debtors, state legislatures in Tennessee, Kentucky, Ohio, and also other western states passed stay laws that delayed debt prosecutions and also replevin laws that protected land from foreclosure.[31] The Federal Land Act of 1820 offered reprieves to past purchasers of land.[32] Debt forgiveness laws, by releasing households to spend in the present rather than save to repay their past debts in the future, helped sustain economic spending and benefited everyone. (These were precisely the kinds of laws that Congress failed to pass after the household debt crisis of 2008.)

Yet the BUS still had its defenders in Washington. At the U.S. Supreme Court, in *McCulloch v. Maryland* (1819), Chief Justice John Marshall held a hostile Maryland state tax against the BUS to be unconstitutional. That seemed to cement for good the BUS's fundamental constitutionality, an issue that went all the way back to Jefferson and Hamilton. Among the greatest defenders of the BUS in Washington was the Speaker of the House, the Kentucky congressman Henry Clay.

2. The American System

If there was a moment in the Age of Commerce when the federal government might have seized control over the long-term process of national commercial development, this was it—after the first genuine short-term cycle of speculative investment boom and bust in the nation's history.

In hard times, the public reflexively looked to the state. Slaveholders were suspicious of federal power, but a cotton boom and a bust had yet to make cotton lords into a self-conscious class. Rapid western migration meant a higher percentage of Americans than ever before or since lived in new settlements. Politically, the Federalists were finished. The Democratic-Republicans were in power, with no organized political factions or parties dividing them. Behind it, the federal government had at least the appearance of a unified public interest at work. The moment practically cried out for a state-led national consolidation, and confidently Henry Clay led the charge.

Clay, born in tidewater Virginia in 1777, studied law in Richmond in 1797 before joining the mass migration to Kentucky. He settled in Lexington, seventy miles east of Louisville and the Ohio River, to become a slave plantation owner, land speculator, and commercial lawyer. But he was not a cotton planter, did not think like one, and did not represent them in Congress. Louisville plantations grew hemp. A brilliant orator, Clay was elected to Congress in 1810 at the age of thirty-three—a piercing blue-eyed "hawk," spoiling for war with the British Empire. During his first term, remarkably, he became the Speaker of the House. He grew rich during the postwar boom but lost a lot of money during the bust after privately endorsing bad paper notes. He left Congress in 1821 to return to Kentucky and repair his finances. As a lawyer, he defended creditors, including the BUS, one of his consistent private clients. In Kentucky, for five years after the panic, a pro-debtor Relief Party dominated the legislature. Clay privately bemoaned "unfavorable laws to creditors."[33] In 1823, after his finances were restored, Kentucky, despite his pro-creditor stance, returned Clay to Congress.

He took back his position as Speaker of the House. In daylong orations on the House floor, he invoked the "general distress" that pervaded the "whole Union" after the Panic of 1819. He proposed his American System. He hit on old political-economic themes, as old as the commonwealth ideal of Shaftesbury's mercantilism:

> Commerce will regulate itself! Yes, and the extravagance of a spendthrift heir, who squanders the rich patrimony which has descended to him, will regulate itself ultimately. But it will be a regulation which will exhibit him in the end safely confined within the walls of a jail. Commerce will regulate itself! But is it not the duty of wise governments to watch its course, and, beforehand, to provide against even distant evils; by prudent legislation.[34]

There would and should be more commerce, but the state must guide and check commercial development so that it led to a desirable public end.

Clay argued, reasonably enough, that the chief problem at hand was that the United States remained commercially dependent on "foreign nations," especially the British Empire. No different from the eighteenth century, the United States was still an exporter of agricultural commodities to England and an importer of manufactures, capital, and credit from that same country. If Clay was wrong to bemoan debtor relief and blame overinvestment for the bust, it was true that the cotton boom had been led by misinvestment. Credit concentrated on cotton, at the expense of other enterprises, and the rapid expansion of western settlement had pushed ahead of political institutions, including transportation infrastructure. Instead, the United States needed a larger "home market" to ensure effective demand. Only it could be an adequate "vent for the surplus produce of our labor."[35] This was an old mercantilist principle, translated by Clay into a national setting. Likewise, such a national market would be the conscious creation of public policy. Policy would have to check private interests, in particular common white male heads of household, bent on colonizing Indian lands at a breakneck pace.

The American System was a federal program of national economic planning, and it consisted of four pillars. First, Clay offered unequivocal support for the BUS, which was now under the prudent charge of the Philadelphia banker Nicholas Biddle. The BUS remained Clay's private client, and in 1824 he successfully defended the institution before the U.S. Supreme Court in *Osborn v. Bank of the United States* (overturning another state tax against the BUS, this time in Ohio). The BUS was by charter a mixed public-private institution, a corporate subsovereign. Public and private interests inevitably entangled, hopefully in a harmonious tension. According to this view, there was nothing wrong if Congressman Clay benefited personally from representing the BUS so long as the BUS benefited the public interest.

Second, Clay advocated slowing down western colonization, if only so that national infrastructure could keep up. The federal government should raise the price of public lands, which would also raise more federal revenue.

Third, Clay advocated a higher tariff against foreign manufactures. This would help foster northeastern manufacturing and rid the United States of dependency on British imports. In 1816 he had pushed through a protectionist tariff, but it had not been steep enough. British manufactures of the industrial revolution flooded U.S. consumer markets anyway. The Tariff of 1824 was the most protectionist yet, raising duties on imports by 30 percent on average.

Fourth, revenues from land sales and the tariff would fund a national system of public investment in "internal improvements." Improvement was the old Enlightenment ideal, which defined private property rights in a reciprocal relationship to a larger public benefit. To make private property valuable, further improvements in public infrastructure were necessary. With the exception of the National Road—inaugurated at Cumberland, Maryland, on the Potomac River in 1811 and finally reaching the Ohio River in 1818—Congress had funded only one-off projects: a road from Athens, Georgia, to New Orleans (1806), say, or from Shawneetown, Ohio, to Kaskaskia, Illinois (1816). In 1816 Clay had tried to use the $1.5 million "bonus," which the Second BUS paid to the federal government in return for its charter, to invest in a national system of internal improvements, but Madison had vetoed it on constitutional grounds. "If Congress can make canals," a North Carolina congressman chimed in, "they can with more propriety emancipate" the enslaved.[36] In 1824 Clay, working with Secretary of War John C. Calhoun, passed the General Survey Act, to scope out potential infrastructure projects that would fit together into a comprehensive national plan.[37]

Clay's American System was a legislative program, but it was also a campaign promise for the presidential election of 1824. That year the

Democratic-Republicans were divided among a number of candidates, including Clay, Calhoun, and John Quincy Adams of Massachusetts. During the campaign, an antiestablishment constituency mobilized around a fourth candidate, the former general and current Tennessee senator Andrew Jackson.

Herman Melville was to write in *Moby-Dick* (1851) of a "great democratic God! . . . Thou who didst pick up Andrew Jackson from the pebbles; who didst hurl him upon a warhorse; who didst thunder him higher than a throne!"[38] Philosopher Ralph Waldo Emerson, not necessarily approvingly, referred to General Jackson as America's "representative man." Jackson, born into modest circumstances in 1767 in the Waxhaws, an isolated area of Scots-Irish settlement on the border of North and South Carolina, was orphaned at a young age. At thirteen, he fought in guerrilla campaigns in the Revolution, and he hated the British forever thereafter. Jackson studied law and at twenty-one migrated to Nashville. Soon, by force of will, he ascended to local wealth and leadership, making his fortune as a land speculator, then a slave plantation owner. He served an unremarkable term in Congress in 1796, siding with the Democratic-Republicans, but his true passion was for the military. He became a major general in the militia in 1802, and when the War of 1812 broke out he took a command, announcing that the national "hour of vengeance" was at hand. He attacked British and Indians alike. By all accounts, Andrew Jackson was a tempestuous, violent, vengeful man.

He was also a popular war hero. He belonged in the new mythical category of self-made American folk heroes, along with, say, the western frontiersman Daniel Boone: "My roots burrow down / to Col. Daniel Boone / and his frontier town / of Boonesborough, where / the brown-skinned dwellers / were his, bought and paid / for by the folk hero / of wild liberty, the bowie- / knifed fighter of Indians."[39]

But when the Panic of 1819 occurred the wealthy Jackson took the side of creditors—Clay's side. "Times are dreadfull here," he wrote from Nashville, bemoaning the hoarding of hard currency, with "confidence entirely destroyed, specie payments suspended, and no foreign notes to be got— and upward of six hundred [debtor] suits returnable to our last Country Court."[40] Jackson wondered aloud why "so much sympathy should be indulged for the *debtor,* and none for the *creditor.*"[41] In 1822 he considered running for governor of Tennessee but was advised against it due to his unpopular pro-creditor position.

The presidential election of 1824 was already a different political moment.[42] By then, the post-1819 debtors' revolt was finally defeated in state legislatures.[43] Jackson did not say much at all about creditors and debtors publicly. Gravitating to his dark horse candidacy were supporters of the national war hero, as well as squatters and speculators who eyed Indian and western lands. He also attracted elites who did not support Clay's American System—chiefly slaveholders who feared expansive federal governmental power and hated the tariff that taxed their consumption of British goods.[44] They wanted "free trade" and saw nothing wrong with the post-1815 cotton boom except for its bust. According to Virginia senator John Taylor's *Tyranny Unmasked* (1822), the national interest, invoked by Clay, was "imaginary." The "chymist" of commercial "*Self-Interest*" was enough to bring about all possible "mutual benefits."[45]

Finally, another constituency projected its views onto General Jackson, a group that shared in common a sense of grievance against cosmopolitan national elites, which Clay, Calhoun, and Adams undoubtedly were.[46] With roots in the Jeffersonian mobilization, the enduring, emotionally pitched American populist tradition first appeared.

In 1824 "Jacksonism was mixing in everything, and absorbing everything," as one Pennsylvania observer put it.[47] The Democracy's populist supporters included rural white heads of household who lived off the commercial grid and feared, probably correctly, that Clay's national program of internal improvements might connect urban mercantile elites but bypass them. His supporters also included the urban "mechanic interest," independent proprietors of small-scale manufacturing. If large-scale manufacturers thrived under Clay's proposed tariff, such men might find themselves as downwardly mobile "dependent" wage earners. Jackson's Democracy supporters also included critics of the Second BUS, who believed insider control of money and credit undermined their own aspirations for commercial greatness. And they included critics of the state-level incorporation process of banks and other joint-stock companies, who charged state lawmakers with bestowing corporate privileges upon themselves and their friends. What held them all together was a critique of the way private elites exclusively enjoyed government "privilege." Instead, they affirmed "equal rights" for all white men.

Jackson won a plurality of the vote in the presidential election of 1824, but insufficient votes in the Electoral College. The election was thrown to the House of Representatives. Strategically, Clay supported another losing candidate, John Quincy Adams, ignoring instructions from his Kentucky legislature back home, which favored Jackson. When President Adams named Clay secretary of state, Jackson's supporters denounced the "Corrupt Bargain." Clay had miscalculated—Adams's presidency was a dead letter. Eloquently Adams's ambitious first address to Congress pleaded for federal government action. He lectured congressmen that should his legislative proposals for all manner of internal improvements—roads, canals, an astronomical observatory, and a national university—be unpopular with their constituents, they should vote for them anyway. They did not. Adams's presidency yielded a more protective tariff, with rates now hovering around 60 percent, which was subsequently known in the South as the 1828 "Tariff of Abominations." But that was about all.

The election of 1828, partisan and even sordid, was no contest. Fifty-six percent of eligible voters cast a ballot, compared to only 25 percent in 1824.[48] General Jackson became president.

3. "The bank, Mr. Van Buren, is trying to kill me, but I will kill it!"

Jackson's inaugural address celebrated "the first principle of our system—*that the majority is to govern.*"[49] When Jackson set about translating his understanding of popular sovereignty into action, above all he sought to disentangle national public authority from corrupting private interests. Governmental and commercial spheres must be separate, with a hard boundary between them. That would ensure equal commercial opportunity for white heads of household, the owners of property, wealth, and capital in land and slaves.

One clearly constitutionally mandated sphere of federal government action, if not commerce, was the authority to engage Indian nations. Jackson's first task was Indian removal east of the Mississippi River. Removal was not foreordained. Between 1815 and 1830, the United States purchased 182 million acres of land from Indian nations, and popular white violence seized far more, but when Jackson took office, approximately 130,000 Indians still occupied 77 million acres east of the Mississippi. In the Old Southwest lived remnants of those whom white Americans called the "five civilized tribes"—Cherokee, Chickasaw, Choctaw, Creek, and Seminole. The Cherokees had signed treaties that explicitly acknowledged sovereign possession of their ancestral lands. They had adopted commercial agriculture, including black slavery, had written a tribal constitution, and in many cases had converted to Christianity. The citizens of Georgia were not placated. They attacked anyway. Jackson supported and signed the Removal Act of 1830. It appropriated half a million dollars for the War Department to remove all Indians east of the Mississippi, and it granted Jackson the authority to exchange lands east of the Mississippi for lands west. Indian removal was slow, violent, and tragic.[50]

The Indian Intercourse Act of 1834 established an Indian territory west of the Mississippi. Whites had arrived in the trans-Mississippi Valley for centuries, but now they came not to engage in commerce with Indian nations but to take their land.[51] The Preemption Act of 1841 finally granted squatters who occupied and improved federal lands the right to purchase between 80 and 160 acres at no more than $1.25 per acre. The Missouri painter George Caleb Bingham's painting *The Squatters* (1850) memorialized the white yeomanry's victory.

GEORGE CALEB BINGHAM, *THE SQUATTERS* (1850)
The Missouri-based Bingham, a political Whig, offered this explanation of his painting: "The Squatters as a class, are not fond of the toil of agriculture, but erect their rude cabins upon those remote portions of the national domain, when the abundant game supplies their phisical [sic] wants. When this source of subsistence becomes diminished in consequence of increasing settlements around they usually sell out their slight improvement, with their 'preemption title' to the land, and again follow the receding footsteps of the Savage."

Meanwhile, in May 1830, the day before Congress passed the Indian Removal Act, President Jackson vetoed a piece of congressional legislation. Congress had voted to invest in the stock of a Kentucky corporation, the Maysville, Washington, Paris, and Lexington Turnpike Company. The joint-stock corporation had been chartered in Kentucky for the "public purpose" of building a road to connect Henry Clay's hometown, Lexington, to a section of the National Road terminating on the Ohio River. The Maysville road was to run through one state, Kentucky, but the internal improvement extended an overland path from east to west and, via the Ohio and Mississippi rivers, from north to south. Jackson vetoed the Maysville Road Bill. His secretary of state, Martin Van Buren, along with James K. Polk, a Tennessee congressman, helped him draft the accompanying message. The president expressed support for public infrastructure projects in general but held the Maysville investment unconstitutional, because the proposed road ran only through Kentucky and was not a sufficiently national concern. Jackson would give no consideration of individual projects in light of what Clay called the national "system."

Specifically, Jackson objected to national public investment in a Kentucky-chartered corporation that benefited its private shareholders, some of them politicians. In 1828 the federal government had spent $401,183 to fund the direct public construction of internal improvements. It spent $1 million on stock subscriptions in state-chartered corporations.[52] But now the president declared federal public investment in corporate stock to be antirepublican and corrupt: "The Govt. of the United States owning half the capital in each state corporation will wield the state elections by corrupting and destroying the morales of your people."[53] Jackson did not disapprove of purely public infrastructure projects. Soon Congress sent him a $1.2 million package of appropriations bloated with the pet projects of various congressmen. The president did not use his veto pen. In fact, during Jackson's two administrations, Congress would spend more on internal improvements than it had during its entire history. Meanwhile the American Postal Service made critical contributions to the expansion of interregional commerce.[54] Jackson just would not budge from one simple principle. The Adams administration had made over $2 million in federal stock subscriptions in state-chartered joint-stock corporations, but the grand total under President Jackson was zero. Jackson would not stand for federal government patronage of private corporate stockowners.

Of course, one joint-stock corporation dwarfed them all. The Second BUS carried a federal charter. Four-fifths of its $35 million capital stock was in private hands, the rest owned by the federal government. Four-fifths of the BUS's directors were appointed by its private owners, the rest by the federal government. The BUS handled the federal government's finances in return for a $1.5 million annual fee. Led by Biddle, the bank's reputation had recovered after the Panic of 1819, and the BUS's 1816 charter would not expire for twenty years. Four years early, however, in the run-up to the presidential election of 1832, Clay, sensing a political advantage and working in concert with Biddle, decided that Congress would recharter the bank. "Should Jackson veto it," Clay proclaimed during floor debate, "I will veto him!" The charter passed in July, and Biddle hosted a celebration in his Washington lodgings. The noise was audible from Jackson's White House window. Days later Van Buren entered the White House to find Jackson, who suffered from numerous ailments and war wounds, reclining on a chaise longue. "The bank, Mr. Van Buren, is trying to kill me, but I will kill it!" he said.[55]

The Second BUS enjoyed extraordinary power over U.S. economic life. Money and sovereignty, public authority and private profit, mixed. The hard-currency value of the dollar maintained the scarcity value of money, but the BUS had the power, through issuing notes and loans, to expand the volume of paper currency and make profits for its stockholders. In 1830 BUS banknote issues accounted for some 40 percent of the U.S. circulating medium, typically issuing two dollars of paper currency for every one dollar in hard specie reserves. The BUS was responsible for between 15 and 20 percent of all American commercial loans—with much larger percentages in the Southwest and Northwest. At the same time, the BUS had the power to halt the expansion of money and credit. Its many local branches might purchase state-chartered banknotes and present them for "redemption" at their bank of origin for hard currency. The mere threat limited state banks' paper note issues. Altogether the widespread trust and confidence in the value of BUS notes backed the further extension of state-chartered banknotes and thus more money and credit. The credits capitalized more wealth-generating investment, enterprise, and production. Between 1830 and 1832, the BUS increased its own note and loan issues by 60 percent.[56] Liverpool cotton prices were rising again, and the BUS was issuing credits especially to the southwestern cotton frontier.[57]

All the while, Biddle demanded utter autonomy from government oversight. No "officer of the Government," he asserted, "from the President downward, has the least right, the least authority, the least pretense, for interference in the concerns of the bank."[58] At the same time, Biddle curried government favor. He used BUS funds to support the campaigns of politicians friendly to the bank. He made loans to editors of important newspapers. He granted loans to congressmen, on poor security, that sometimes went unpaid. He kept Massachusetts senator Daniel Webster, for instance, on a permanent legal retainer. Once, Webster wrote to Biddle, "my retainer has not been renewed, or *refreshed,* as usual. If it be wished that my relation to the Bank be continued, it may be well to send me the usual retainer."[59] Should such an arrangement appear "corrupt," it is because one is looking at it through the eyes of the Jacksonian Democracy. Biddle, Webster, and Clay saw nothing wrong with the BUS simultaneously benefiting both the public good and their private bottom lines, at once. That was the essence of political economy.

President Jackson disagreed. He vetoed the bank's new charter. Amos Kendall, a Treasury official, along with Roger B. Taney, the attorney general, assisted him in writing the accompanying statement, which surely ranks among the most explosive documents in all of American political history. Jackson's summary judgment was that the BUS's government-granted corporate "privileges" were "dangerous to the liberties of the people."[60]

Banking, the president declared, was "like farming, manufacturing, or any other occupation or profession." It was a "*business.*" Therefore, it should be open to all citizens on equal terms. Instead, private stockholders, "a few hundred of our own citizens, chiefly of the richest class"—in addition to foreign, worst of all British, stockholders—controlled the U.S. monetary and credit system, lining their pockets with government monopoly privileges. The bank was a "concentration of power in the hands of a few men irresponsible to the people." The president ended the bank veto with stirring words. "It is to be regretted," Jackson lamented, "that the rich and powerful too often bend the acts of government to their selfish purposes." For:

> In the full enjoyment of the gifts of Heaven and the fruits of superior industry, economy, and virtue, every man is equally entitled to protection by law; but when the laws undertake to add to these natural and just advantages artificial distinctions, to grant titles, gratuities, and exclusive privileges, to make the rich richer and the

potent more powerful, the humble members of society—the farmers, mechanics, and laborers—who have neither the time nor the means of securing like favors to themselves, have a right to com plain of the injustice of their Government.[61]

A democratic state simply could not grant privileges or favors to special economic interests. It must ensure "equal rights" and equal opportunity for all.

Clay and Biddle were delighted. Biddle said the bank veto reminded him of French revolutionary radicals Jean-Paul Marat and Maximilien Robespierre. "It has all the fury of a chained panther biting the bars of his cage," he wrote, then used BUS funds to distribute copies for Clay's presidential campaign.[62] Soon enough Biddle had to stop the presses: the bank veto was wildly popular. Jackson had proved to be a master of democratic political rhetoric and communication. At a time of great financial and commercial expansion but also rising economic inequality, Jackson brilliantly rallied populist resentment against banking and government elites, who were surprised. They had seen prosperity, not this, coming.

Clay's American System was in ruins. The BUS was now set to expire. There was no national plan for the public infrastructure of internal improvements. Congress was not slowing down popular western colonization. Next, Jackson signed the Tariff of 1832, which reduced rates on imports of foreign manufactures, undermining the protection of northern industry—another special interest, according to Jackson. The reduction was not enough for South Carolina, where Jackson's resigned vice president, John C. Calhoun, declared the law "null" in his state. South Carolina finally backed down before the president's enmity. However, tariff rates would keep trending downward, satisfying southern consumers of British goods—and keeping at least a portion of southern slaveholders in the Democracy's fold. In 1832 Jackson, officially running under the banner of the Democratic Party, defeated Clay in a landslide. "The Jackson cause," the pro-Jackson *Washington Globe* declared in 1832, "is the cause of democracy and the people, against a corrupt and abandoned aristocracy."[63] "After the destruction of the Bank," proclaimed one Democrat, "must come that of all monopolies, of all PRIVILEGE."[64]

The Democracy sought to circumscribe federal power in order to sphere public from private. It aimed to emancipate the private commercial sphere from government monopoly privilege and open it to all white heads of

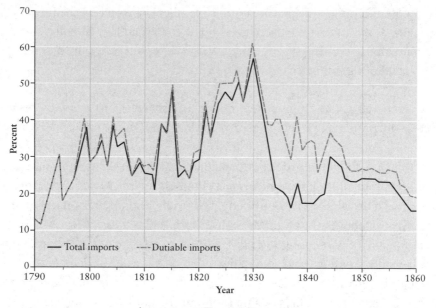

AMERICAN TRADE TARIFFS

Detested by southern consumers of British manufactures, the tariff
was a hotly contested political issue. President Jackson demurred
from the high tariffs of Clay's American System, but he
nonetheless enforced tariffs on the slave South.

household on equal terms. Dismantling privilege, however, meant more
than ensuring equal commercial opportunity. It also meant, in practice,
undermining the federal government's power to make any long-term plan
to guide national commercial development.

But the pro-commercial politics of "antimonopoly" was born. The New
York journalist and Democrat William Leggett, for one, called for the "total
separation of Bank and State" and for the complete removal of the state
from interference in the "natural economy." No private actor of any kind
should have the power to expand the money supply beyond its hard-
currency basis.[65] These men, Ralph Waldo Emerson proclaimed, "are fa-
natics in freedom; they hate tolls, taxes, turnpikes, banks, governors, yea,
almost all laws."[66]

In fact, rather than lawlessness, the sphering of public and private gave
birth to a new set of political economic tensions. In order to legally secure
open access to commerce, a Jacksonian jurisprudence developed that was
solicitous of private property rights but hostile to any "special" or "class"
legislation.[67] Sphering public from private did not mean that state power,

in its proper constitutionally limited domain, must be weak. Far from it. The Democratic Party built a more public and professional state bureaucracy.[68] Under the banner of "antimonopoly," New York and other cities deregulated their public food markets. But other utilities, like municipal waterworks, became exclusively public and state operated.[69] Jacksonians acknowledged public regulation and state "police power" at the local level. In all instances, Jacksonian political economy gave rise to a new concern for boundary policing between public governance and private commerce.

The Democracy's desire to define a private commercial sphere—and to open access to it for all white men on behalf of "equal rights"—had consequences. One immediate effect was to unleash a popular democratic drive for more commerce.

4. A Developing Economy

Continuities in economic life abounded. Urbanization had finally begun, especially in the Northeast. Nonetheless, even in that region, 81 percent of the population remained rural as late as 1840.[70] The political-economic settlement of the Empire of Liberty remained fundamentally grounded in a politics of property ownership among white heads of household, and Jackson was determined to keep it that way. Land improvements remained the largest category of productive investment.[71] The organic economy still set limits on production and on the extent of markets—with bad roads and nonnavigable rivers. A large number of households, most of which supported Jackson, remained nearly off the commercial grid.

Ever since the seventeenth century, the transition to a more market-based economy had consisted not of a one-off moment but rather of market engagements and retrenchments, market revolutions but also counterrevolutions, all specific to geographical place. Nonetheless, the trend was toward commercial development. And within it, a cycle was appearing: the repeating capitalist credit cycle of speculative investment booms followed by busts.

Indeed, Jackson's second term coincided with another credit-fueled boom of Smithian growth, made possible by government infrastructural projects that assisted the continued white colonization of Indian lands. But the expansion was guided by no overarching national political plan. It was much more driven by emotions and investor psychology—ambition, profit seeking, land hunger, desires for racial domination. Altogether expectations of future prosperity fueled the extraordinarily high American inducement to invest in land, commerce, and slaves. Then this boom too turned to bust.

The southern cotton economy, after its recovery from the Panic of 1819 slump, prospered. New Orleans cotton prices leaped from 9 cents per pound in 1831 to 15 cents in 1835. The Old Southwest's cotton frontier spread yet again. Cotton exports doubled between 1831 and 1836, reaching an all-time high of 63 percent of all U.S. exports. The corn and hog farmers of the Old Northwest once again sent goods to New Orleans for reexport or sometimes supplied the plantations of the Old Southwest. Ohio-Mississippi river traffic continued to supersede commerce between the Northeast and Northwest. At this time, a major innovation was new steam-powered riverboats, which made upriver traffic possible and opened up the Mississippi's tributaries. River steamboats clocked twenty miles per hour, reducing the upriver journey from New Orleans to the Ohio River from three months to eight days. New Orleans's population surpassed 100,000, and the city became the fifth largest in the United States, as its national commercial prominence peaked. The same was the case with its northern urban mirror, sixteen hundred miles upstream, Cincinnati, Ohio—the great "Porkopolis." Market prices began to converge between the two cities. St. Louis, long the center of the western Indian fur trade, began folding into the cotton-corn-hog commercial nexus.[72]

Nonetheless, in volume U.S. intraregional dwarfed interregional trade.[73] Coherent regional and metropolitan commercial economies emerged. New England farmers, for instance, shifted into "truck farming," supplying nearby cities with milk, meat, butter, cheese, fruits, and vegetables. Industrious farmers provided the bulk of consumer demand for local manufactures. Painter Jonathan Fisher's *A Morning View of Blue Hill Village* (1824) illustrates a diversified commercial landscape, picturing a series of towns in the background and the hillside fields that supply them in the foreground, divided by a property line.

Mid-Atlantic farmers enjoyed comparative advantages in grains but also supplied the region's expanding urban populations. In New York, Philadelphia, and Baltimore, small-scale manufactures sold largely in metropolitan and regional markets. Baltimore was a center of flour and paper milling. A Northeast urban core was emerging, and Smithian divisions of labor appeared. Boston and Providence became diversified manufacturing centers, while rural New England towns specialized in textiles, boots, and shoes. Connecticut towns manufactured tinware, buttons, spoons, plates, clocks, and hats. New York City became the "readymade" clothing center. The commercial economy of the Northeast, more dominated by local trade, enjoyed higher growth rates than even the cotton South.[74]

Smithian growth happened in part because of the dynamic source of demand provided by an increase in the extent of markets. Even as Jacksonianism gridlocked the federal government, a state-government-led "transportation revolution" in market infrastructure facilitated commerce. All told, between 1787 and 1860, the federal government would invest $54 million on transportation infrastructure, whereas the states collectively made public investments of $450 million.[75]

The history began as far back as the 1790s, when many states, northeastern ones especially, had chartered joint-stock turnpike corporations. Before, roads were commonly poor paths carved through forests, often by

PRINCIPAL ROADS, C. 1800

In the Age of Commerce, transportation infrastructure greatly determined the extent of markets and therefore the possibility of Smithian growth.

citizens laboring to "work off" their tax obligations. In 1804 Ohio passed a law stipulating that tree stumps in roadways could not be taller than one foot. Many farmers waited for winter to slide their crops on sleds over ice and snow. In the South, slaves hauled cotton on "mud boats" to the nearest river or creek bank. In swamps and wetlands, logs were laid next to one another to create "corduroy" roads. Bridges were wooden, only a few made of stone. Crossing a river usually meant locating a ford. The first large successful turnpike was the Lancaster Turnpike, between Lancaster and Philadelphia, which opened in the 1790s.

In the Northeast, turnpike corporations—joint-stock companies chartered because of their "public purpose"—fanned out from navigable waterways. The best were constructed from stone and were graded, with gravel dressings and drainage ditches. Between 1800 and 1830, the New England and Middle Atlantic states chartered almost one thousand turnpike corporations. They charged tolls, but few were profitable. Ordinary rural investors did not always invest to make a profit, it seems. Instead, they paid for a public good that was also of great private benefit: market access. In the Northeast, turnpike corporations increased the extent of metropolitan and regional commercial markets.[76]

Next came canal construction. In 1815 there were only one hundred miles of canals in the United States. In 1817 New York began public construction of the Erie Canal. The state, rebuffed after seeking funds from Congress, raised the necessary capital through a combination of state taxes and public debt sales. The Erie Canal connected Lake Erie, through Buffalo, to Albany on the Hudson River, across 363 miles. The canal's middle section opened in 1819, and tolls funded its completion by 1825. Upstate New York wheat production immediately prospered. Rochester, with 1,500 inhabitants in 1821, counted 10,000 a decade later.[77] New York City, which had captured the southern cotton transshipment trade, now expanded to include goods from its upstate agricultural hinterlands, becoming the Empire of Liberty's undoubted commercial colossus.

The geopolitics of trade was the great theme of the Age of Commerce. The Constitution's Commerce Clause forbade states to slap trade tariffs on one another, but it did not prohibit competition in public infrastructure projects to increase market access. The Erie Canal was a success in part because it ran through a single sovereign jurisdiction. Panicked by the canal's success, merchant elites elsewhere desperately sought routes to connect their Atlantic ports to the trans-Mississippi West. The construction of routes passing through multiple states often suffered political gridlock. Work on Pennsylvania's Main Line Canal, connecting Philadelphia to the Ohio River at Pittsburgh, began in 1826. State debt issues funded it. The canal had to climb the Alleghenies and opened only in 1833. Elsewhere states had even less success. Canals in different states were often redundant. There was no national system. Nonetheless, by 1830 some 1,277 miles of canals had been constructed nationally, mostly funded from states' public treasuries.[78] By 1841, there would be 3,326. In 1836 Illinois began construction on the Illinois and Michigan Canal to open a commercial waterway from the Mississippi River to the Great Lakes, via the new city of Chicago. The state of Ohio was the most prodigious canal builder.[79]

THE TRANSPORTATION REVOLUTION OF THE 1820S AND 1830S
The state-led construction of roads and canals made possible the commercial boom that coincided with the rise of democracy in America.

The federal government and the states moved in opposite directions. In public finance, states increasingly turned away from taxes and toward capital markets. Jackson, by contrast, paid down the entire federal debt in 1835. Altogether state debts increased from next to nothing in 1815 to $80 million by 1830, then to $200 million by 1841.[80] Jackson had put an end to federal investment in joint-stock corporations at the federal level, but when states did not directly construct infrastructure, they invested in their own state-chartered corporations, hoping to raise revenues from dividends. In the West, states sold bonds more commonly than investing in stock. Finally, states sold debt to foreign investors, especially British. In the Southwest, where public infrastructure lagged, state debt sales capitalized state-chartered joint-stock banking corporations. Often slave mortgages were the assets pledged as collateral for public debts, or as capital stock.[81] The United States was a fast-growing developing economy, absorbing funds from Britain, which was then undergoing industrial revolution and was the world center of capital accumulation. British capital chased expected gains from the extension of the North American commodity frontier, including in the slave South.

If public finance spurred growth, so did private capital. The United States was no longer poor in what Alexander Hamilton had once termed "pecuniary capital."[82] U.S. investment per capita surged from $14 in 1819 to $20 by 1835.[83] Jackson may have killed the Second BUS, but the United States was unique in the world for its great number of state-chartered banking corporations.[84] Bank chartering was concentrated in the Northeast.[85] As with public debt markets, the farther west, the more foreign capital mattered. In total, partly in response to the demands of more trade, between 1820 and 1836 the U.S. money supply increased by an annual rate of 7 percent.[86]

Debt has often compelled capitalist development. Altogether public and private debt instigated more labor and production, as it placed pressure on planters to maximize their pecuniary incomes. The exploitation of the enslaved was worse for it. All told, in the West, especially the Southwest, the 1830s boom was highly financially leveraged. The U.S. estimate of debt to GDP hit its highest point, over 60 percent, for the nineteenth century. Between 1832 and 1836, banknote issues had climbed from $119 million to $203 million, and wholesale commodity prices rose by 50 percent. As long as prices soared, there was no problem.

Instead, financial panics erupted in 1837 and 1839. After Jackson re-

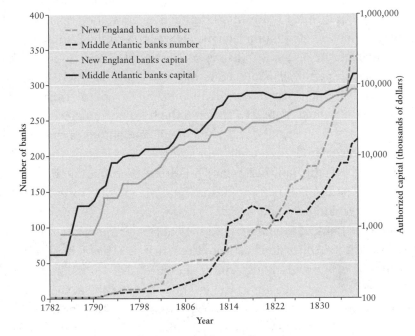

GROWTH OF STATE BANKS

State-chartered banks capitalized early American commercial development.

fused to recharter the BUS, the Bank War between him and his organized political opponents—who called themselves the Whig Party, referring to the revolutionary generation's opposition to unchecked monarchical power—dominated the late 1830s. At the time, many blamed one side or the other for the bust. For a long time thereafter, so did historians.[87] Jackson's administration had removed government deposits from the BUS and placed them in state-chartered "pet banks."[88] According to the Whigs, the pet banks expanded note issues beyond potential economic production. The BUS no longer had the power to chase bad notes from circulation. Credit was overextended, in excess of the potential supply of goods, leading to a necessary correction, which took the form of a panic, followed by a bust. There is some evidence this was true.[89] However, international events were paramount.

The chief cause of the expansion of money and credit in this period was that U.S. hard-currency reserves had increased, backing the multiplying banknote issues. In particular, silver mined in Mexico had swelled U.S. hard-currency reserves. Due to the British opium trade in Asia, this silver no longer flowed to China to finance Anglo-American transactions.

It stayed in the United States, backing further domestic credit issues.[90] In all this, however, the financial flywheel was the Bank of England. The prime interest rate on loans to its networks of banks—the "bank rate"— determined the permissible ratio of note-to-specie leverage, across oceans. In 1836 British gold reserves were dwindling, partly due to British capital exports to the United States. To preserve the hard-currency value of the pound, the Bank of England raised the bank rate, in hopes that paying a higher interest rate on deposits would attract specie back into British vaults. It did. But the Bank of England prioritized maintaining the scarcity value of the pound—its peg to a certain quantity of gold—over the credit needs of international trade.

When the Bank of England raised the bank rate, much capital swung out of the United States and back into Great Britain. The higher bank rate was attractive, and with money and credit more dear, across the chain of indebtedness creditors began to call in loans, to meet their payments. In the United States, money and credit began to tighten. Thus prices fell, including the price of cotton. Anglo-American mercantile houses that were invested in the cotton trade, carrying stocks, began to wobble. Some failed. The New Orleans and New York City banks that lent to them suffered from loans gone sour. Sensing trouble at the banks, depositors rushed to withdraw their deposits, and redeem their notes for hard currency. Hoarding hard currency only blocked the continued flow of credit and investment. Likely, the expiration of the BUS's charter contributed to diminishing confidence and trust in the entire banking system.[91] Further, Jackson's 1836 Specie Circular, which demanded that citizens purchase government lands with hard currency, drained specie from eastern banks westward, diminishing their reserves.[92] But the catching of the developing U.S. economy in the snares of capital markets governed by the British bank rate was the ultimate cause of the bust. Money and credit tightened, and spending dried up. It was the third debt-deflation slump in national history.

When the BUS lost its federal charter, Biddle quickly founded another bank in Pennsylvania. It speculated in the cotton trade and underwrote and marketed U.S. securities in Europe—especially American state debts. In 1839 Biddle's bank failed, in part due to cotton speculations gone wrong.[93] That triggered another negative chain reaction in the bank system and the Panic of 1839. In its wake, a state sovereign debt crisis broke out.

In 1841 U.S. state debts totaled $198 million, with more than half issued after 1837. Western land prices collapsed. Western banks failed. Public infrastructure construction in many cases halted. As foreign capital swung out of the United States, states could no longer raise tolls or taxes to repay their debts. In 1841–42 Louisiana, Maryland, Illinois, Arkansas, Pennsylvania, Michigan, Mississippi, Indiana, and the Florida Territory all entered default. Ohio and New York barely escaped.[94]

An international financial system premised on a currency pegged to a fixed hard-currency value can sufficiently anchor investor confidence and expectations to recruit scarce capital into a developing economy—in this case, the United States. But when the hegemonic center—in this case, London—raises the interest rate to maintain the hard-currency standard, given prior outflows to the periphery, capital can suddenly swing out, stopping credit and collapsing prices. A global credit cycle comes to an end.

Because of the many repetitions of the cycle since then, the general pattern is discernible. Back then, however, the vast majority of Americans could but dimly perceive the gravity of global economic interdependence under British hegemony. Nonetheless, ironies abounded. Jackson had decried British ownership of BUS capital stock. Clay had noted the U.S. commercial economy's dependence on British demand for cotton. In some sense, their assessments of U.S. foreign economic dependence on British capital and credit were more meaningful than their mutual political recriminations. By 1840, U.S. economic hard times were back.

5. Coda: Corporations

Political hard times were back as well. In 1840 Jackson's successor, Martin Van Buren, lost the presidency to the Whig candidate, William Henry Harrison, who had campaigned on a platform of general "improvement," supporting internal improvements, moral reform, and public education.[95] Nonetheless, politically, the economic slump played out most consequentially in the states.[96] The subject was corporations.

Before the financial panic, unlike the federal government, state governments had invested hundreds of millions of dollars in state-chartered joint-stock corporations, be they canal construction companies or banks. States also taxed corporate capital, which dispensed with the need for politically unpopular taxes on property—namely, land and slaves. Joint-stock corporations carried out public tasks, and public sovereignty and private profit entangled and mixed. States chartered corporations, to begin with, because they had a "public purpose." Legislatures voted on each "special" charter. In this sense, a joint-stock banking corporation was similar to a charity, hospital, or university. Because of their public purpose—to issue money for commerce or to provide higher education—corporations enjoyed legal privileges, such as legal personality, limited liability (in some cases), and sometimes monopoly. Corporations, like households, were subsovereigns of the Empire of Liberty.

The Democracy would have none of it. Corporate monopoly smacked of oligarchic if not aristocratic privilege. In *What Is a Monopoly?* (1835), Theodore Sedgwick wrote that the closed, special chartering of corporations was a "distribution of legislative favors." It was both "averse to the fundamental maxim of free trade" and incompatible with a "democracy of equal rights." But if incorporation "could be freely assumed by all," then corporations would "be perfectly compatible with equality of rights and freedom of trade."[97] Roger B. Taney, a former member of Jackson's cabinet and a co-drafter of the Bank Veto, now chief justice of the Supreme Court, struck down state-level corporate monopoly privileges in *Charles River Bridge v. Warren Bridge* (1837).[98] In 1838 New York State passed "free banking" legislation. Its advocates called it a "great and admirable improvement on the corrupting political monopoly it superseded."[99] Meeting universal reserve requirements, any citizen of New York State might charter a bank. During the 1840s many states began to pass "general incorporation" laws for banking, manufacturing, and sometimes all enterprise. Some states banned "special" chartering altogether. General incorporation would not triumph until the 1870s. But the trend was now afoot.[100] By 1860, eighteen states had passed free banking laws, inaugurating the "free banking era." Corporate charters proliferated in the tens of thousands, and corporations became uniquely American vehicles of association and enterprise.[101]

General incorporation was a momentous change and a blow against elites in favor of equal rights and equal opportunity. The oldest legal theory of corporate personality was "grant" or "concession" theory. Only the sovereign could grant corporate charters, thereby creating a new subsovereign.[102] In a democracy, however, where popular sovereignty reigned, grant theory was a contradiction. How could legislatures grant sovereignty back to "the people," where it resided in the first place? Why should the privileges of incorporation not be a democratic right, enjoyed equally by all?

General incorporation laws shoved joint-stock corporations into the emerging private commercial sphere, stripping them of some of their quid pro quo public obligations and of their role as governing subsovereigns. After the Panic of 1839 sovereign debt crisis came a Jacksonian revulsion against state-funded internal improvements. States ceased to invest in private corporate stock and began to tax property to raise revenue instead.[103] This was another instance of Jacksonian sphering in political economy, an attempt, at once ideological and legal, to delimit the private commercial sphere from state infringement.

Joint-stock corporations became more "private" with the rise of general incorporation, but a complete separation of public and private did not occur. Whether it was limited liability or perpetuity, corporations still enjoyed state-granted legal privileges, even if incorporation had been opened up. State authorities could still regulate private corporations. Further, democratic control (one vote per shareholder) as opposed to plutocratic control (one vote per share) often persisted.[104] No corporations, not even joint-stock corporations, were legally mandated to pursue commercial profits to the exclusion of all other projects.[105] The profit-maximizing corporation, familiar to the late-twentieth and early-twenty-first centuries, had not arrived yet on the scene, and there would first be much experimentation with the corporate form, which was still quite malleable.[106] But the attack on political privilege did, however unwittingly, open up the possibility of an unintended consequence, that corporations might become vehicles for the aggrandizement of private economic power.

In political economy, the Jacksonian project of sphering gave rise to new sets of tensions and contradictions, premised on borders from without rather than entanglements from within. The project to demarcate a private, market sphere had the effect of crippling any attempt to provide long-term political direction to the ongoing process of commercialization.

Instead, economic development rode the short-term credit cycle. Not until 1844 did prices finally begin to rise, and the U.S. commercial economy emerged from the latest debt-deflation slump. The downturn had been in the money and credit system, but regardless of market prices economic production and output had continued to expand. It remained to be seen where the burgeoning national market, newly liberated by the Democracy from the ossifying hands of political and economic elites, might take the republic. But the many wheels of American commerce were spinning once more. Confidence was back.

CHAPTER 5

CONFIDENCE GAMES

"LET US CONSIDER THE WAY IN WHICH WE SPEND OUR LIVES. This world is a place of business. What an infinite bustle!"[1] So exclaimed the American transcendentalist thinker Henry David Thoreau, in an 1854 public lecture. He was not talking about political economy. He knew little and cared less about corporate charters, tariff rates, or internal improvements. After all, "banks and tariffs," his mentor Ralph Waldo Emerson remarked in "The Transcendentalist" (1842), were "flat and dull" topics, for discussion by "dull people."[2] Thoreau wanted to talk about the "way in which we spend our lives."

Americans in Thoreau's day had lived through a series of credit-fueled commercial booms followed by financial panics and debt-deflation slumps. But soon after the twin Panics of 1837 and 1839, the commercial economy roared back to life, and many, not only Thoreau, felt that commerce was beginning to impinge on economic life, even just on life, in ways that it had not before. Commercial self-interest was jumping outside its age-old checks, be they moral disapprobation or a nonnavigable river, and conjuring a world of its own. The market extended indeed, boring into Americans' very beings. Not only political economy but social and cultural life, and even psychological and ethical life, appeared to be at stake. What kind of society was a "commercial society"? What kind of person succeeded or failed in it? What did ever more commerce do to the human soul?

These questions are perennial, of ancient vintage. But they sharpened in Thoreau's day, given the intensity of Smithian growth. Not long before,

Adam Smith had said that commercial dynamism should come not from the state but from the universal spring of "human nature." Smith had thought a lot about human nature in *The Wealth of Nations* (1776), and in his equally brilliant and edifying *The Theory of Moral Sentiments* (1759), he explained that a commercial society required of its members a particular kind of ethics in order to flourish: the bourgeois virtues of honesty, prudence, and respect.[3] Smith analogized them to friendship.[4] Commerce was premised on self-interest but required sympathy to function. There might be ethical tensions, but commerce presupposed a willingness to bargain, within agreed-on conventions of value and representation, without resorting to violence. That was why Smith and other thinkers of his day liked commerce so much. Religious authorities had long scorned commerce for being unholy. The nobility had sneered that commerce was inglorious. But after centuries of bloody religious warfare, many Enlightenment intellectuals began to see commerce as a civilizing influence.[5] It brought moral "improvement."[6] From Benjamin Franklin to Thomas Paine, a number of notable Americans were the inheritors and proponents of this intellectual tradition.

American "commercial society" ended up rather rough-and-tumble, but the Enlightenment's pro-commerce ethical argument received popular expression, for instance, in John Frost's *The Young Merchant* (1839), a primer for aspiring antebellum American merchants, not coincidentally published in the aftermath of the Panic of 1837. The genre was not new, dating back to Renaissance Italy. Benjamin Franklin's *Poor Richard's Almanack* (1732–58) had popularized it in eighteenth-century America.[7] *The Young Merchant*'s target audience was mercantile clerks, the shock troops of the recent commercial booms.[8] It pleaded above all for honesty and candor in commercial life. Perhaps the adequate regulation of commercial self-interest did not need a supervening state authority, as the mercantilists had believed, or even moral exhortation in the tradition of the "just price." All it needed was what we call proper "business ethics" today.

The Young Merchant lectured young merchants on "the immutable principles of right and wrong." But it also said that the appearance "of a high character among mercantile men" was "the best and most important element of credit."[9] *The Young Merchant*'s prescription contained an old metaphysical dualism, an inescapable tension between appearance and reality: the appearances of a commercial society, so often premised on credit and debt, and the professed reality of immutable moral principles. Commercial appearance required representations of the future, which is always to some degree uncertain territory. Therefore it opened a gap between the uncertainty of appearance and the alleged certainty of reality, including the moral certainty of right and wrong.

In business, is it not possible to appear to be one thing and in reality to be something different, and to still succeed? Certainly it is! What if human beings in a commercial society, instead of hacking each other to death, haggle with each other in order to live, but treat each other falsely, as instrumental means to their own future personal commercial ends? What if they are all artificial and inauthentic liars, merely trying to turn a buck?

With so much commerce buzzing in their ears, many antebellum American writers and artists were obsessed with this dilemma, worries that commercial appearances had swallowed reality and that life was becoming nothing more than a confidence game. Thoreau's *Walden* (1854) is a literary monument to the genre, which also, for instance, included Edgar Allan Poe's great detective story "The Purloined Letter" (1844). In the visual arts, there was Luminism, painting in which shining colors sought to brighten the reality of representation.[10] Everywhere in American culture, in other words, there was a fascination with "humbug."

Under the influence of ever more commerce, how was it possible to distinguish fact from fiction, or genuine entrepreneurial ingenuity from well-disguised fraud? And what kind of moral universe were Americans living in if they had to walk around all day asking themselves such questions?

In the opening scene of Herman Melville's novel *The Confidence-Man* (1857), a mute tacks a sign that reads "No Trust" to the wall of a Mississippi River steamship.[11] If the man or woman you are dealing with is a fraud running a confidence scheme, then you must pull back from investing in the scheme and hoard your confidence and trust. But if there is no confidence or trust, then there can be no commerce. Hoarding trust can be as dangerous as hoarding capital. The cost in both instances is an absence of investment in the future. Wisely, Hamilton had warned of the ill economic effects of "cautious sagacious capitalists."

Over the centuries, every single financial crisis there has ever been has been a crisis of confidence. Why is capitalism so dependent on interpersonal trust and the psychological state of confidence? When Americans panicked during the Panic of 1837, after all, they literally *panicked*.[12] Why is capitalism always a bit of a confidence game?

1. Humbug

Thoreau and Melville wrote during the period of literary history that scholars call the American Renaissance. A period of just seven years saw the publication of Emerson's *Nature; Addresses and Lectures* (1849), Nathaniel Hawthorne's *The Scarlet Letter* (1850), Melville's *Moby-Dick* (1851), Thoreau's *Walden* (1854), Frederick Douglass's *My Bondage and My Freedom* (1855), Walt Whitman's *Leaves of Grass* (1855), and Margaret Fuller's (posthumous) *At Home and Abroad* (1856). Poe was publishing short stories, and Emily Dickinson was writing poetry. It was thought to be the beginning of self-consciously democratic American literary expression, but in hindsight it was a peak.[13]

To this illustrious list, we must add another title: *The Life of P. T. Barnum, Written by Himself* (1855). Phineas Taylor Barnum, the great confidence man, was, according to himself, the "prince of Humbug."[14] Barnum made fraud into an art form as well as an honest living. Unlike Melville and Thoreau, he was also a bestselling author. *The Life of P. T. Barnum, Written by Himself* sold. So did his other autobiography, *Struggles and Triumphs* (1869), recounting mostly triumphs and updated frequently for the next twenty years. The *Life of P. T. Barnum, Written by Himself,* sold something like 160,000 copies. The prince of Humbug had invented a new genre, the popular entrepreneurial self-help book.

Barnum, born in Bethel, Connecticut, in 1810, was raised on a family farm. He plowed fields and milked cows. In a culture that celebrated the work ethic, "I never really liked to work," he admitted.[15] He was a clerk, then a shopkeeper, before he got into what he called the "showman" business. Today Barnum is most known for his final act, as the promoter of a traveling circus. But he first made his name in the museum business. The American Museum opened on lower Broadway in New York City in 1841. At this time, museums were not quite what they are today. They were cultural spectacles, more like theaters. With its Drummond Lights, its second-story orchestra, the American Museum dazzled onlookers. With 400,000 paying customers per year by the mid-1840s, it was said to be the most-visited place in the United States.

Its commercial success was due to the fact that Barnum ingeniously played with the distinction between appearance and reality. "Put on the *appearance* of business," he wrote in his autobiography, adding emphasis, "and generally the *reality* will follow."[16] Barnum's customers paid at the door to see something promised in advance by the showman. Perhaps it was Joice Heth, the delirious 160-year-old former slave of George Washington who was blessed with a golden singing voice. Barnum had purchased Heth for $1,000. Or perhaps it was Barnum's own fifth cousin twice removed, the child midget impersonator General Tom Thumb. Whatever it was, was it real, or was it humbug? Barnum was in the business of cultivating doubt. Everything, notes historian James Cook, was "plausible enough to be taken seriously and dubious enough to inspire uncertainty."[17] Barnum stepped back and let the audience members decide for themselves. He did not present himself as an authority. What was up for sale was the experience of incredulity.

Understanding what was going on inside Barnum's museum requires understanding what was going on outside it. New York City, having dethroned Boston and Philadelphia and fended off a challenge from New Orleans, had become the great national urban hub of trade. It was home to the southern cotton transshipment trade and also the entrepôt for the Erie Canal. Between 1840 and 1860, the city's population climbed from 312,710 to 813,669. Urbanization came late to America, but had finally begun. In 1840 the urban share of the U.S. population was 11 percent. By 1860, it had almost doubled to 20 percent, from 2 million to 6 million persons.[18]

Barnum catered to the new urban, commercial strata. The increasing extent of markets and the increasing division of labor were giving rise to a greater, differentiated class of commercial occupations. They were merchants, clerks, bankers, wholesalers, jobbers, dealers, plungers, retailers, grocers, peddlers, drummers, brokers, agents, auctioneers, and bookkeepers. Their chief task was to create transactional liquidity, in the trading sense—a greater scope for sales—by building the market institutions that connected so many producers and consumers. Ever since colonial times, the commercial "middling" sort had dominated America. In its inaugural 1839 edition, *The Merchant's Magazine and Commercial Review* labeled Americans as "essentially and practically a trading people."[19]

Even so, New York was different from minor trading towns and certainly from the countryside. The great metropolis was a world of strangers. Many new arrivals, crowding into the city's overflowing boardinghouses, sought public amusements outside the family circle. And commercially, one simply had to do business with strangers. Since customary relationships of accreditation were generally lacking, businessmen took steps to compensate. In 1841, to help reestablish trust in the wake of the Panics of 1837 and 1839, the New York merchant Lewis Tappan founded the Mercantile Agency, soon renamed R.G. Dun and Company, a credit-reporting agency.[20] Questions still arose: Was that price really the going price? Was that merchant's name really even his name? Or was it all a confidence game? The realm of commerce is flooded with interpersonal doubt.

Then, the money problem made matters more uncertain. What is called a "fractional reserve banking" system never has enough hard currency in reserve to back all the paper money and credit it issues. If all the holders of notes, because they lack confidence and trust, were to "redeem" them for hard money at once, all banks would fail. Such "bank runs" accompanied the Panics of 1819, 1837, and 1839. When Barnum opened his doors at the American Museum in 1841, the Second Bank of the United States—which had used its market power to chase bad notes from circulation—no longer existed. The era of "free banking," or open access to bank incorporation, in many individual states had begun. True, the states created banking commissions to regulate banknote issues and shore up confidence, but nonetheless banks issued paper notes of a value greater than their hard-currency reserves. It worked only if there was confidence and trust in their paper. Just as, shrewdly, Barnum did not claim to be an authority on his own humbugs, the world of paper money no longer had a central authority to tell anyone whether what they saw had authentic value.

After Jackson killed off the Second Bank of the United States, interpersonal trust and credit became even more a basis of what Hamilton had called "pecuniary capital." Farmers had their land; slave owners had their slaves. But tradesmen had trust, and without trust, instead of constant credit creation, a final reckoning would arrive—the moment when all debts came due. If it did arrive, the result would be bank runs and financial panics. By design, the system did not have enough hard currency to pay off all debt. Present truths were insufficient to compensate for the future fictions. Because a capitalist financial system is a perpetual leap of faith, over and over again, confidence becomes the emotional and psychological mainspring of economic activity.

No one understood this better than P. T. Barnum. His humbugs bore an uncanny resemblance to the interpersonal fictions of the paper credit economy. He trucked in the experience of doubt, playing on fears that appearance was not reality, and that reality was not appearance. The American Museum was located at the corner of Broadway and Ann Street, near

Wall Street, the heart of New York City's financial district. Most of the visitors were in the new middling, commercial class. They haggled with one another by day. By night, they joined arms and tried to figure out what exactly Barnum was selling them.

Barnum's greatest hit was the Feejee Mermaid, unveiled to the public in 1842. The Feejee Mermaid was a monkey and a fish smashed together that Barnum proposed was a rare species native to the Pacific island of Feejee. After you paid at the door, you got to see it, and then you decided for yourself. Was it real, or was it humbug? Barnum, a marketing genius, first advertised, "That the animal has lived, moved, and had its being, as it is . . . ADMITS NOT THE SHADOW OF A DOUBT, as all must acknowledge who see it." A few days later Barnum anonymously planted a story in a newspaper revealing that someone from within the museum had the "impression" that the mermaid was "humbug." The next day Barnum responded under his own name, outraged. The accusations were baseless! Next, he secretly set up another museum, with another Feejee Mermaid. He pocketed the profits from both. In one New York newspaper, two advertisements, one for the original Feejee Mermaid, the other for the knockoff, stood side by side, shouting baseless accusations at each other.[21]

In 1842, year of the Feejee Mermaid, commerce was recovering from the recent panics. In the repeating cycle, confidence was returning, and the credit system was projecting new fictions. Should they be trusted? Everyone had to decide for themselves.

What was there to limit or check the radical uncertainty of commerce? Tellingly, who was not inside the American Museum? What noncommercial forms of authority were absent from the scene? No king, no politician, and certainly no central banker was present to distinguish appearance from reality. The American Museum was no family farm—no father was there to decide, no slave master was present. And God? About a ten-minute walk from Broadway's American Museum stood the Chatham Street Chapel, just past City Hall. The same Lewis Tappan of the mercantile credit agency hired out the chapel to Charles Finney, the most popular evangelical preacher of the day, in the ongoing Second Great Awakening.

Finney himself was something of a showman. He said your soul's salvation was your own responsibility. You, not God, had to decide if you wanted to be saved, trusting in your own will—a stark departure from the Calvinist orthodoxy of Puritan New England, which insisted that only

God was truth, only God was real, only God knew and could be trusted to know the true state of your soul, including whether you would go to heaven after the final day of reckoning. Finney announced that you got to choose whether you were saved. The family resemblance between the leap-of-faith capitalist credit system and Finney's leap-of-faith theology is evident. Neither has a transcendent authority. If you did not take the leap and have confidence, you would not be saved spiritually. Also, the capitalist financial system might implode.[22]

Barnum was a Jacksonian Democrat who had grown up in Federalist Connecticut, and his humbug also had a democratic sensibility.[23] A democratization of truth was happening inside the American Museum, which placed on individuals the democratic duty of making judgments. In the American political economy, neither Henry Clay's American System, nor any other long-term political project of development, was directing commercial prosperity. The money and credit necessary to capitalize commerce and commercial production now bubbled up from below, in the form of democratic, interpersonal acts of trust, as well as a popular state of confidence and expectations. Arising from these excitements, doubts, and questions, emotional states and psychological drives fueled the speculative upswing in the credit cycle, which induced investment and pulled along commercial development.

The Feejee Mermaid was a smash commercial success. But not everyone approved. One review published in *The New York Herald* read, "Humbug—this Mermaid—and no mistake. We can swallow a reasonable dose, but we can't swallow this."[24] One has to wonder whether the prince of Humbug was behind this one, too.

2. *Walden*

Henry David Thoreau had zero appetite for humbug. In 1842, when the Feejee Mermaid was on display in Manhattan, Thoreau was living in Concord, Massachusetts, his hometown, in the household of his mentor, Ralph Waldo Emerson. Like Barnum, Thoreau's father had had commercial difficulty. For a short time, Henry worked for him making pencils. Emerson suggested to Thoreau that he keep a journal. In 1845 Thoreau spent some time living in a small, spartan cabin near Walden Pond, a striking contrast to Barnum's Bridgeport, Connecticut, mansion, the absurdly ornamented architectural monstrosity that he called "Iranistan." While Barnum worked on his autobiography, Thoreau assembled his reflections on his own experience into the transcendentalist masterpiece *Walden.*

Walden is a bitter indictment of capitalist commerce, not the exchange of one unlike thing for another, that is, but rather exchange in pursuit of pecuniary gain. Thoreau can be taken to task because he never lived in majestic solitude and self-sufficient simplicity at Walden Pond.[25] It turns out that he went to town quite often and left his laundry at his mother's house. *Walden* has no chapter about mothers doing laundry. It is less about a place, however, than about a state of mind and of being. Thoreau said that to find reality, even if just in your own conscious thoughts, you had to be able to leave behind the world of commercial squabbling. Ideally, you should seek nature, the world that leads to inner truths. The process should be organic. Keeping a journal helped, because that way you were in conversation with yourself and not with others. Or talk with good friends. Thoreau believed that his own experience of his independent thoughts, if he could only have them, was all that was real. Everything else was appearance and could not be trusted. *The Life of P. T. Barnum* makes no mention of nature—no forests, no rivers, no fields. Barnum left the organic economy behind.

Walden was a prime example of a shift in how intellectuals were coming to think about the moral worth of commerce. The old critique of commercial self-interest was more conservative—it was a religious critique, with aristocratic overtones. In the American political tradition, the Jeffersonian idiom was critical less of the market than of dependence on particular markets, whether stock markets or public debt markets. After all, Jefferson was a utopian about the geopolitical possibilities of "free trade." Jeffersonian republicanism had translated into a Jacksonian democratic rhetoric that was even more suspicious of privilege and oligarchy. Nevertheless, a large Jacksonian constituency was mostly critical of monopoly and positively yearned for equality of commercial opportunity. In contrast to time-worn religious counsels about the perils of too much commerce and also to the Jeffersonian critique of possible market dependence, *Walden* was part of a new, transatlantic intellectual movement, known as romanticism, that had grown suspicious of capitalist commercialization altogether.

The Romantics feared that the heartless world of commercial appearances was overtaking reality. Their intellectual master was the eighteenth-century Frenchman Jean-Jacques Rousseau, the Adam Smith of the anticommercialization Enlightenment, and their touchstone was Rousseau's *Discourse on the Origin and Basis of Inequality Among Men* (1754). Rousseau's speculative history of economic development granted the civilizational benefits of commerce and the division of labor. "No society can exist without exchange," Rousseau would write in *Emile, or on Education* (1762).[26] Unlike Smith (who wrote a disapproving review of the *Discourse*), Rousseau feared that commerce did not necessarily morally improve human relationships. Instead, commercial society bred bad dependencies—bad social relations, and bad self-relations. Commercial society was artificial and obsessed with inauthentic artifice. Freedom and independence and mankind's original nature were spoiled by individuals' "self-love," which filtered through their constant estimations of themselves through the eyes of others (like what happens on social media today, which Rousseau would have hated but undoubtedly would have used).[27] Rousseau's history of commercial society was a tragic narrative of moral decline, although later in life, in *The Social Contract* (1762), he heroically announced that he had discovered a solution: a small republic governed by a "general will" in a free community of equal citizens. Later, aging and outcast from gossipy Parisian society, Rousseau went on solitary walks in the countryside and wrote proto-transcendentalist reveries, mixed with recriminations against his old social enemies.[28]

The romantic critique of commerce traveled to Germany's Sturm und Drang generation, whereupon it filtered through the philosophies of Immanuel Kant and Georg Hegel to the young Karl Marx of the *Economic and Philosophic Manuscripts* (1844), who transformed Rousseau's concept of dependence into "alienation."[29] In England, for a time, commercial critique remained conservative. As for society, the conservative essayist Thomas Carlyle in 1843 bemoaned that "cash payment" alone was becoming the "nexus of man to man."[30] During the industrial revolution, a full-blown left intellectual critique emerged in England as well. For instance, the critical social commentary of Charles Dickens in his later novels such as *Hard Times* (1854) is far different from his comic but sympathetic depictions of commercial man in the early lighter novels like *The Pickwick Papers* (1836). The intellectual tide among the children of the rising bourgeoisie, by the 1850s, had begun to move against capitalist commerce. The critique of never-ending, all-consuming commodification was born. A century later, in *Capitalism, Socialism, and Democracy* (1942), the Austrian economist Joseph Schumpeter would note the tendency of capitalism to provide the material abundance necessary for intellectuals to have the time and leisure to criticize it.[31]

Like Dickens, Thoreau's mentor, Emerson, went through phases and stages. He first more or less agreed with Smith and Paine that commercial exchange had positive moral and political benefits. In "The Young American" (1844), published the same year that prices finally recovered from the Panic of 1839, Emerson wrote that "the new and anti-feudal power of Commerce, is the political fact of most significance to the American at this hour."[32] Soon, however, Emerson started to sound more romantic. After Dickens was critical of American culture in his travelogue *American Notes for General Circulation* (1842; the title was a pun on the recent U.S. financial panics), Emerson noted of industrializing England, in his *English Traits* (1856), that "a coarse logic rules throughout all English souls."[33] Emerson, and Thoreau with him, looked at the commercializing world around them and decided that something was being lost. Appearance, humbug, was corroding something more real, something deeper: feelings and sentiments within the human heart. From this perspective, Smith's celebration of the public benefits of commercial self-interest became a conservative defense of moral turpitude.[34] Like Smith, Emerson and Thoreau both celebrated friendship. Unlike Smith, following Kant, both underscored friendship's noncommercial, noninstrumental qualities. Commerce did not civilize, it did not tame the worst human passions. Rather, it coarsened the human heart and undermined the possibility of intimacy and trust.

Commercial society, Thoreau believed, was a hoax, and Americans had fallen for it hook, line, and sinker. Even the countryside was now under threat. Before Thoreau went to live at Walden Pond, he first thought about taking up farming. Characteristically, he walked around Concord's homesteads, inquiring as to how farmers lived. Concord's farms were then commercializing.[35] Industrious farmers were specializing, increasing the division of labor, working longer hours, demanding internal improvements (Irish workers built a railroad near Walden Pond), chopping down forests, enclosing the commons of the great meadows, mortgaging their farms, producing larger marketable surpluses, and purchasing more and more consumer goods from cities. Thoreau recognized—correctly, it turned out—that the delicate ecological balance of Concord's organic economy was at risk. In *Walden*'s scathing first chapter, "Economy," Thoreau addressed Concord's farmers.

> But men labor under a mistake. The better part of the man is soon plowed into the soil for compost. By a seeming fate, commonly called necessity, they are employed, as it says in an old book, laying up treasures which moth and rust will corrupt and thieves break through and steal. It is a fool's life, as they will find when they get to the end of it, if not before.[36]

The farm no longer offered escape from commerce.

Thoreau was not against work as a means to an end, only against work that became an end itself. Literary production, after all, was work, a craft, a means toward the end of democratic artistic expression. The right words flowed organically from the pen of the truly self-reliant author, who should live close to nature. From head to toe, Thoreau would physically bathe himself in Walden Pond leaves and mud. He tilled a few acres by his own hand, without the aid of any beast of burden. Mostly he raised a few beans, along with peas, corn, potatoes, and turnips. They could be exchanged for items he wanted that he could not produce—but not for a pecuniary profit. Considering the "importance of a man's soul," he was doing "better than any farmer in Concord." Thoreau learned at Walden

> that if one would live simply and eat only the crop which he raised, and raise no more than he ate, and not exchange it for an insufficient quantity of more luxurious and expensive things, he would need to cultivate only a few rods of ground, and that it would be cheaper to spade up that than to use oxen to plow it, and to select a fresh spot from time to time than to manure the old, and he could do all his necessary farm work as it were with his left hand at odd hours in the summer.

Thoreau did not believe in the commercializing farmer's limitless quest for more and more. Specialization and the division of labor, rather than increasing the wealth of nations, turned everyone into but "the ninth part of a man."[37]

The accusation gets to the heart of "transcendentalism." Thomas Jefferson had celebrated the republican virtue of independence, premised on the private ownership and control of landed property, wealth, and capital. Land had to be owned, and worked, for the feeling of independence to come about. For Thoreau, no private property outside one's own being could adequately ground independence and autonomy. He wanted to be independent in the worst of ways. He looked around and saw that land-ownership was no longer an adequate ground. Thus his counsel—you had to fall back on your own being, plumb its depths, to find the truth in the universal, your soul in the "over-soul," to achieve self-ownership, self-knowledge, self-reliance, self-confidence, and ultimately self-creation.[38] Thoreau, with nature, his thoughts, and his journal, was all that was. Only after having this experience could he rejoin society, and form friendships with those who had also discovered what was real and true within their own selves. Then and only then was it possible for all to live together democratically.

Commerce in pursuit of pecuniary gain did not help. You had to find your own personal Walden, if only because capitalist commerce wanted to distract you from what really matters. Thoreau threw down the gauntlet in his lecture "Life Without Principle" (1854). "The ways by which you may get money," he argued, "almost without exception lead downward." Thoreau complained about rampant "frivolity" and "falsity" among his neighbors.[39] An entire way of life was false—a striking philosophical indictment. What could it mean to lead a life that is not just frivolous, not just immoral, but somehow false? So false that nothing within it or about it could be trusted, because everyone in it was a confidence man and everything that happened was a confidence game? "No Trust," as the mute would tack to the wall in Melville's *The Confidence-Man.*

American democracy had become false because outward commercial appearances had triumphed over inner realities. The gap between the two had grown so great that reality could no longer even be represented by appearance. Americans

> do not worship truth, but the reflection of truth; because we are warped and narrowed by an exclusive devotion to trade and commerce and manufactures and agriculture and the like, which are but means, and not the end.

The Young Merchant's instrumental commercial values were corrupting youth. But Thoreau was not finished. His take on the internal improvements of the day, which increased the geographical extent of markets, read: "You may raise money enough to tunnel a mountain, but you cannot raise money enough to hire a man who is minding *his own* business." Thoreau bemoaned "improved means to an unimproved end." As for Adam Smith, there were "philosophers who are so blind as to think that progress and civilization depend on precisely this kind of interchange and activity—the activity of flies about a molasses-hogshead."[40] Thoreau simply could not believe that something so mundane as haggling over the price of a molasses-hogshead was all the world's first democracy had to offer to the world. While he complained, however, Barnum was off conquering Europe. Tom Thumb charmed Queen Victoria.

In the end, Thoreau's argument was that capitalist commerce was incompatible with democratic life. The freedom to choose whether the Feejee Mermaid was a humbug could not be freedom. There must be something deeper within us to democratically cultivate. After his trip to Europe, even Barnum remarked of Americans that "with the most universal diffusion of the means of happiness ever known among any people, we are unhappy." He came to believe that the problem was holidays from work—"we have none."[41] Thoreau, for his part, wrapped up his argument: "Even if we grant that the American has freed himself from a political tyrant, he is still the slave of an economic and moral tyrant."[42]

3. Friends

To Herman Melville, Thoreau's transcendentalism was a moral tyrant. Melville also recognized that many moral checks on commerce were fading fast, and he was worried, too, but he came to think differently from Thoreau about the morality of capitalist commerce. Rather than celebrating the market or pushing back against its always-corrosive effects, Melville wondered if commercial investment might be appropriated as a means toward a morally worthy end. He thought it might, but he had his doubts.

Herman Melville, born in New York City to an established family, was raised in high style in a house on Broadway. His father was bad with money and died at a young age. The family moved in with relatives in Albany. At age twenty, Melville began to travel, going as far west as the Mississippi River, then heading out to sea on a whaling ship, voyaging around the globe. Melville's first novels, *Typee* (1846) and *Omoo* (1847), about his travels to Polynesia, were commercial successes. They probably sold for the same reason people paid to see that other exotic Polynesian product, Barnum's Feejee Mermaid. Emerson took note of the young novelist's talent in his journal.

Soon Melville and his young family were living in a town house in Manhattan's Astor Square, across the street from Grace Church. His fiction became more serious, and he took long evening walks, often through Wall Street's financial district. He had only to walk one block west and hook a left on Broadway to look up at the American Museum. In 1847 he was likely the author of a *Yankee Doodle* newspaper scribbling "View of the Barnum Property."[43] Surely, Barnum fascinated Melville. That same year his series of short stories about the Mexican War, "Authentic Anecdotes of Old Zack," featured cameos from the prince of Humbug.

Possibly, Melville rubbed shoulders with the original confidence man. The cultural archetype of the trickster is nearly universal, and a version of it was a stock character in representations of commercial society at least as far back as the *commedia dell'arte* tradition in Renaissance Italy. The term *confidence man*, however, appears to be of American vintage. In 1849 a man named William Thompson was apprehended in Manhattan for larceny. Thompson's con was to stroll up alongside a passerby and ask, "Have you confidence in me to trust me with your watch until to-morrow?" Thompson collected more than a few watches in this way before he was arrested and sentenced to imprisonment in Sing Sing. Shortly after his arrest, a play, *The Confidence Man*, ran in New York. A writer in *The Knickerbocker* argued that Thompson was no worse than the typical Wall Street tradesman. Melville must have been aware of all this.[44]

Melville moved his family to the countryside to write a "metaphysical book" about whaling. With the financial assistance of two mortgages, money advanced by his father-in-law—the noted Massachusetts Supreme Court justice Lemuel Shaw—against his wife's future inheritance, and loans from friends, Melville purchased a farm in Pittsfield, Massachusetts, next to an old family estate. On the side, he became a working farmer, planting corn and potatoes. When *Moby-Dick*—arguably the greatest American novel—was published, it was a commercial flop. In 1856 Melville sold off part of the farm, but still only his father-in-law saved him from his father's ruined commercial fate.

Meanwhile the confidence man was back. Released from prison, William Thompson was caught in Albany passing under the name of Samuel

Willis. His new confidence game was to impersonate a Freemason. Whether Melville knew of the confidence man's return, and likely he did, he sat down to write *The Confidence-Man.* Initially intended for serialization, the novel is nothing more—as one reviewer at the time complained— than "forty-five conversations" among passengers aboard a Mississippi River steamship.[45] *The Confidence-Man* has very little plot or narrative direction. It somewhat resembles *The Life of P. T. Barnum,* which shares its dashed-off, anecdotal quality. In fact, *The Confidence-Man*'s chapters put before the reader forty-five distinct commercial transactions, many of which are nearly inscrutable, because Melville wanted the reader to ponder the relationship between appearance and reality in commerce. Another reviewer noted, fairly enough, that the chapters of the book might just as easily be read backward in sequence as forward. (I had my students do that once, and it worked.) Not surprisingly, unlike Barnum's autobiography, *The Confidence-Man* did not sell, and Melville's financial difficulties remained unsolved.

The novel is divided in two halves. The first is a procession of confidence games perpetrated by a number of different "operators," who may or may not be the same confidence man, dressed up in disguise. First, the Black Guinea, a black beggar, pleads for charity, providing his fellow passengers with a list of individuals who will attest to his truthfulness. Each passenger appears in later chapters, and each turns out to be a confidence man himself. Then a man "with a weed" solicits a loan from a trusting merchant, in return offering a stock tip for the Black Rapids Coal Company. A character named Pitch resists the overture of a scheming Herb Doctor, only to succumb to a representative of an employment agency from Philadelphia. Chapter 9 is titled "Two Business Men Transact a Little Business." Chapter 11 is titled "Only a Page or So," and so it is. There are allusions to Barnum, to the American Museum's "thin man" and its Siamese twins. A confidence man runs a scheme on a barber reminiscent of an episode from Barnum's autobiography. The second half of the novel, by comparison, settles down, following the "cosmopolitan" Frank Goodman's encounters with a variety of characters. At some point it becomes impossible to tell who exactly is conning whom. The novel ends. Like the American Museum, *The Confidence-Man* has no narrative voice to preside as an authority over the hoax or to adjudicate what is truth.

Historically, the best measure of capitalism's presence may not be the presence of its many defining features—capital, market activity, technological innovation, wage labor, or something else. All these things have existed to greater or lesser degrees for a long time, even if just at the margins. What defines capitalism's presence, rather, is not a presence but a relative absence. In the United States, the Age of Commerce had arrived at a point where it made sense for Melville to ask the following question, and to write an entire novel mulling over it: What would happen if economic life—nay, life itself—were nothing more than a running series of commercial transactions in pursuit of future pecuniary gain? Much like Barnum's American Museum, *The Confidence-Man*'s fictional steamship *Fidele* has no kings, aristocrats, peasants, or lords. There are no families, no households, no fathers, sons, or daughters. There are no masters, and there are no slaves. The characters have no histories. The state is absent, and so is legal authority. Even the stability of the land is absent. The entire novel takes place on the Mississippi River, as commerce then often followed the waterways. On the *Fidele*, nothing happens at all besides commercial bargaining. Commerce itself is the warp and woof of human relationships. When markets expand, Adam Smith had written, "Every man lives by exchanging, or becomes in some measure a merchant."[46] In *The Confidence-Man*, in every measure, all the passengers are "merchants on [ex]'change," and nothing else.[47]

Of course, no matter how wide, the latitude of capital is never complete. Only in fiction is it possible to attempt to imagine the absence of anything but commerce. Melville's reflections in this fictional register remain instructive.

On the *Fidele*, there is a pervasive sense of estrangement and distrust. The passengers, Melville never tires of telling us, are all "strangers." Melville used the word *stranger* no fewer than sixty times in *The Confidence-Man*. The novel begins when a man comes aboard. "He was unaccompanied by friends," Melville writes. "From the shrugged shoulders, titters, whispers, wonderings of the crowd, it was plain that he was, in the extremest sense of the word, a stranger."[48] The *Fidele* keeps taking on new passengers, "so that, though always full of strangers, she continually, in some degree, adds to, or replaces them with strangers still more strange." There are only questions and doubts. The Black Guinea pleads for charity. Is it humbug? Where is his master? It is hinted that the Black Guinea may in fact be white. Not even that most fundamental marker of American identity, race, is certain and can be trusted here. Perhaps the Black Guinea was in blackface? In 1836 Barnum had barnstormed through the South with a black minstrel singer and dancer. Nor is gender a stable marker of identity in the novel. Everything is potentially changeful, as if transactionally liquid. Every single character in *The Confidence-Man* is referred to as a stranger at least once, a figure that would not disappear from American artistic expression. (Think twentieth-century film noir.) If Adam Smith famously wrote that every man in some measure becomes a merchant in a commercial society, all the passengers on the *Fidele* were in some measure strangers from one another—and even to themselves.

At one point in the novel, a confidence man claims to know a man better than he knows himself. "Why," the man responds, "I hope I know myself." "And yet," the confidence man explains, "self-knowledge is thought by some not so easy. Who knows, my dear sir, but for a time you may have taken yourself for somebody else? Stranger things have happened." That sounds like Jean-Jacques Rousseau's fears about gossip and reputation undermining autonomy in a commercial society. Indeed, Rousseau makes an appearance in *The Confidence-Man*, in the title of Chapter 26. If we are strangers even to our own selves in a commercial society, then true self-knowledge and independence would seem impossible.[49]

It also sounds a lot like Thoreau, who pleaded for a retreat from commerce into more real and true private thoughts. But no such retreat is to be found on the *Fidele*. In one chapter, a confidence man attempts to engage in a serious conversation with himself but fails: "Society his stimulus, loneliness was his lethargy." On the *Fidele*, loneliness breeds not self-knowledge and independence but "melancholy" and "depression."[50] Individuals are too immersed in commercial transactions even to recognize themselves once they are removed from them. There is no longer any fixed point outside commerce, no law, no God, no self, no reality, no truth. Is it all humbug? We have no independent standpoint left from which to even tell! *The Confidence-Man* is a novel whose main protagonist is doubt. Doubts experienced by the characters; doubts experienced by the reader trying to unravel the layers of the seeming hoax. Melville wrote the greatest of all highbrow humbugs.

Such is Melville's description of commercial society. As to what he made of commercial society himself, he was unsure. Certainly, the moral universe presented in *The Confidence-Man* is somewhat terrifying. Everyone is a confidence man, and everything is a confidence game. It is all skin and no meat. A sense for truth succumbs to a deep skepticism. If full with-drawal from commerce breeds only lethargy and melancholy and no so-cial intercourse whatsoever, what is left beyond loneliness? What is left, it would seem, is an even more terrifying nothingness, a true existential "fal-sity," to return to Thoreau.

In this respect, the most terrifying figure in *The Confidence-Man* is the miser. Melville's other characters struggle to trust one another, but usu-ally in the end they do part with their confidence and enter into an ex-change. At a minimum, it keeps the game going. The miser is the one near exception. A merchant—a "stranger," of course—stumbles on the miser belowdecks at the end of a narrow corridor, a dark murky nook in the emigrant's quarters, a sort of "purgatory."

> The miser, a lean old man, whose flesh seemed salted cod-fish, dry as combustibles; head, like one whittled by an idiot out of a knot; flat, bony mouth, nipped between buzzard nose and chin; ex-pression, flitting between hunks and imbecile—now one, now the other.

The miser is in rough shape. Parched with thirst, he cries out to the stranger, "Ugh, ugh—water!" The stranger complies, bringing a glass of water. The miser asks, "How can I repay you?" The stranger responds, "By giving me your confidence." Not only that—"give me a hundred dollars." The miser panics. He clutches for something out of sight under his pillow and begins to speak gibberish: "Confidence? Cant, gammon! Confidence? hum, bubble!—Confidence? fetch, gouge!—Hundred dollars?—hundred devils?" The stranger promises to triple the miser's hundred dollars by in-vesting it, but he will not say where. The miser must trust him. Tortured, the miser proposes a ten-dollar investment. The confidence man takes the gold, bemoaning this "eleventh-hour confidence, a sick bed confidence." But when the stranger departs, the miser changes his mind. "Nay, back, back—receipt, my receipt! Ugh, ugh, ugh! Who are you? What have I done? Where go you? My gold, my gold! Ugh, ugh, ugh!"[51]

The miser's misery is a moral lesson. In a commercial society, anyone who hoards his confidence—refusing to trust others—is isolated and mis-erable. He is no wise transcendentalist, sitting peacefully and calmly at Walden Pond keeping a journal by himself. In fact, he is pathologically ill. Melville saw the transcendental retreat from commercial society as miserly, in a moral sense. He seems to have been saying that social appearances must sometimes be embraced for there even to be a reality. Perhaps commercial society had put the metaphysical cart before the horse. But there was no going back. The only thing left to do was grab the cart and pull it oneself, constructing ourselves moral values—uncertain ethical investments, but still ones that might bear fruit. By contrast, panicked and anxious, the miser has nearly lost his mind and can only speak gibberish. It is better to take the leap, and trust the confidence man, including our own inner confidence man. That way there is commerce, and also, Melville hints, life and meaning itself in a commercial society.

The miser's misery is also an economic lesson. The scene of nearly all *The Confidence-Man*'s chapters is not only a commercial exchange but also an exchange of a particular kind: a possible speculative investment. Money is not just a medium of transaction on the *Fidele*. It is also a potential means of investment. But only a potential means. One might also choose, like the miser, to cling to money as a safe store of value—due to some pathological need for a feeling of security, or to discomfort with the inevitable risk of a committed and irrevocable investment. But without such investments, capitalism simply dries up. Nothing happens economically. Would it not be the best of both worlds if one could make an investment without having to bear a long-term risk? To gain by only speculating, short term, keeping as many options alive as possible—with no opportunity cost? To speculate but always to be able, as the miser wishes, to get one's money back?

Melville's novel parses these contradictory desires and emotional states. His analysis was correct: the capitalist credit cycle of boom and bust, only just emerging in his day, is motivated by a contradictory drive of speculative investment. The contradiction consists in the fact that while credit-fueled and energetic speculation can lead to genuine capitalist investment booms, instigating wealth-generating enterprise, individuals can also succumb to the temptations of short-term speculation alone, in which, benefiting from the transactional liquidity of capital markets, they simply move their bets in and out of assets, confidently seeking only short-term gain. But speculations may not fix on objects of investment long enough for long-term economic development to happen. Capital just spins its top. And the speculative desire to leave all potential investment options open is only a fantasy. For if all options are kept open, but never exercised, nothing actually ever happens.

Next, should confidence collapse, the miser may reappear. Out of fear, the miser will not spend for any reason, let alone speculate short term—let alone invest. Thus the final contradiction is that the attributes of money capital make possible in equal measure both speculation and precaution, both confident booms and depressed slumps.

Melville illustrates how either obsessive speculation or obsessive precaution can undermine the kind of long-term committed investment necessary to create durable, worthy values—existential values, shared ethical values, economic values. Extreme short-term speculation, as depicted in Melville's novel, suffers from having no narrative, no overarching plot of development. Meanwhile Melville's miser, hoarding the hard currency of gold for precautionary rather than speculative reasons, is the most liquid. He keeps all future options, all desires, all possible future speculations, open and alive. Yet by continuing to hoard pathologically, the miser never exercises any of his options. Death will come to him before any enjoyment in life does. Hoarding and speculation are of the same complex.

During the 1780s, Alexander Hamilton warned about "cautious sagacious capitalists," but at that time so much household production was not geared toward commerce and pecuniary gain that the problem he feared was a lack of intensive economic development—not the lack of an economy altogether. Much household production remained decades later, when Melville wrote. But in the fictional universe of The Confidence-Man, extreme, investment-undermining hoarding poses the problem of economic nothingness.

Melville was not the only thinker to draw attention to the catastrophic economic consequences of the miser in a capitalist economy. An earlier, even more extended literary treatment was the French novelist Honoré de Balzac's Eugénie Grandet (1833). Marx was an avid reader of Balzac, and perhaps from this source the miser makes his appearance in Capital (1867): "This boundless drive for enrichment, this passionate chase after value, is common to the capitalist and the miser; but while the miser is merely a capitalist gone mad, the capitalist is a rational miser." Hoarding money is irrational, Marx wrote, for capitalist accumulation requires throwing "money again and again into circulation."[52] Later, in the twentieth century, the miser would reappear, taking center stage in the most incisive economic study of hoarding, the English economist John Maynard Keynes's The General Theory of Employment, Interest, and Money

(1936), written in the midst of the Great Depression.[53] Unlike Marx, Keynes thought about capital in terms not of past accumulation but of future "expectations." He coined the phrase *liquidity preference* to capture the propensities of the owners of capital to either in the short term speculate in liquid financial assets or cling to money with excessive precaution, both at the cost of long-term committed investment and economic development.[54]

In capitalist credit markets, the maintenance of transactional liquidity is an institutional problem. Today it is the preserve of central banks. In Melville's time, the Bank of England's power to set short-term interest rates affected liquidity on both sides of the Atlantic. Melville, a novelist, had a different set of concerns. Of course, in the fictional universe of *The Confidence-Man* there is no state, let alone a central bank. There is a moral antidote for "No Trust!," however, that pivots the analysis from the psychological back to the social register. The antidote is friendship.

Friendship was a central ethical theme of commercial society, discussed by all sides in the debate over the moral worth of commerce. Barnum, in his autobiography, spoke often of his friends; Smith celebrated friendship in *The Theory of Moral Sentiments;* Hegel viewed friendship as the quintessence of freedom; Emerson's great essay on friendship appeared in *Essays: First Series* (1841); the Hudson River School master Asher Brown Durand's painting *Kindred Spirits* (1849) pictured Durand with his friend and fellow painter Thomas Cole; Thoreau included a beautiful essay on friendship in his *A Week on the Concord and Merrimack Rivers* (1849); his poem "Friendship" (1838) spoke of "Two sturdy oaks." "Above they barely touch, but undermined / Down to their deepest source, / Admiring you shall find / Their roots are intertwined / Insep'rably"; and friendship is a great theme of many of the best slave narratives, including Douglass's *My Bondage and My Freedom.*[55]

Every character in *The Confidence-Man* is labeled a "stranger." But when confidence is granted to strangers, they instantaneously become "friends." The miser, for instance, in handing over his gold coins, declares, "I confide, I confide; help, friend, my distrust!"[56] *The Confidence-Man* takes up the topic of friendship explicitly in Chapter 39, "The Hypothetical Friends." The "stranger" who approaches the confidence man Frank Goodman is a cross between a "Yankee peddler" and a "Tartar priest" and turns out to be the mystic Mark Winsome, a thinly veiled Ralph Waldo Emerson, if only because tagging along with him is a disciple, Eggbert, who is even more obviously Thoreau. Goodman asks Eggbert to consider the following case:

> There are two friends, friends from childhood, bosom-friends; one of whom, for the first time, being in need, for the first time seeks a loan from the other, who, so far as fortune goes, is more than competent to grant it.

Would Winsome's philosophy permit Eggbert to grant such a loan? Eggbert says no, for it is wrong to treat a friend as a means to a commercial end: "The negotiation of a loan is a business transaction. And I will transact no business with a friend." True, there are "business friends," but a "true friend has nothing to do with loans; he should have a soul above loans." This must be a reference by Melville to the transcendentalist "oversoul." Loans should be had only from the "soulless corporation of a bank." Eggbert cites Winsome's "Essay on Friendship" to prove that loans between friends can lead only to their "estrangement."[57]

Disguising their names, Melville used Emerson and Thoreau to express the rising Victorian sentiment that commerce cannot be trusted. Unfeeling and heartless, it must be kept within its proper sphere. A hard wall must always separate the market from the warm sentiments of friendship and family. The market is always pushing against its own boundaries, threatening to corrode other spheres, and must be vigilantly walled off from them.

But must one oppose markets and morals?[58] Doing so, Melville suggested, lets markets off the moral hook while diminishing morality. There is another path, though one tinged with risk: to attempt to appropriate capital's pecuniary motion toward worthy, nonpecuniary ends. Of course, Melville had once taken loans from friends to settle on Arrowhead Farm to write *Moby-Dick*. The confidence man hopes the world will "postpone ratifying a philosophy that banishes help from the world." It is an "inhuman philosophy."[59] If transcendentalism forbids financial assistance among friends, it becomes a moral tyrant. Capitalism may be premised on uncertainty, warranting skepticism, but uncertainty need not undermine genuine moral values and commitments. A pragmatic ethical hope is possible.[60]

Furthermore, human beings are not self-sufficient, or at least stoic independence is a weak premise for true friendship. We are friends with one another because, as human beings, we are dependent on one another.

Thoreau, hoarding his confidence, is lampooned in *The Confidence-Man* as an ethical miser. A world without "confidence," Melville wrote, was both "solitary" and "dehumanized." Perhaps this was the reason so many of the American Museum's customers were all too willing to give Barnum, the prince of Humbug, the benefit of the doubt.[61]

One of Melville's best friends was the writer Nathaniel Hawthorne. They were neighbors in the western Massachusetts countryside, more than a hundred miles due west from Emerson's and Thoreau's beloved Concord. Melville, it seems, solicited a loan from his father-in-law in part so that he could continue to live at Arrowhead, if only to remain close to his good friend. Melville dedicated *Moby-Dick* to Hawthorne. After completing *The Confidence-Man*, strained from overwork, again with financial assistance from his in-law, Melville departed for a European vacation. In England, on a beach near Liverpool, Melville and Hawthorne went for a walk. Hawthorne recorded of the conversation in a notebook:

> Melville, as he always does, began to reason of Providence and futurity, and of everything that lies beyond human ken, and informed me that he had "pretty much made up his mind to be annihilated"; but still he does not seem to rest in that anticipation; and, I think will never rest until he gets hold of a definite belief. It is strange how he persists—and has persisted ever since I knew him, and probably long before. . . . He can neither believe, nor be comfortable in his unbelief; and he is too honest and courageous not to try to do one or the other.

Melville noted in his journal—"Good talk."[62]

CHAPTER 6

BETWEEN SLAVERY
AND FREEDOM

W ITH THE RETURN OF CONFIDENCE, ANOTHER SOUTHERN
U.S. cotton boom took place after the Panic of 1837. Cotton
planters moved west in pursuit of fresh soils, whether they were wrested
from Indian nations, gained during Texas annexation (1845), or conquered during the 1846–48 Mexican-American War. In Richard Caton
Woodville's widely reproduced painting *War News from Mexico* (1848), excited white men read aloud the news, while in the corner a black man and
a black child look tired and sad.

White masters coerced enslaved black people to move to places where
free migrants would not go, and to perform backbreaking labor that nobody would willingly do, all in order to produce goods that just about everybody did want to consume.

By now, the sight was familiar. The fundamental economic dynamic of
the Age of Commerce was geopolitical, involving investment in the extension of production for markets across space. Centuries ago the slave plantation was the cutting edge of seventeenth-century English mercantilism
in the Atlantic, and if a Barbados sugar planter from that time could have
been magically transported to the lower Mississippi Valley of the 1850s,
likely he would have marveled at the new steamboat technology and at
the great leaps forward in the biological "improvement" of crop seeds.[1]
The rest would have been recognizable. Much as in the eighteenth-century
British Empire, in the nineteenth-century Empire of Liberty, the owners of
capital confidently invested in the long-term expectation of racial slavery's future extension across space. A number of southern rulers, in fact,
harbored fantastical imperial visions of slavery's future.[2]

RICHARD CATON WOODVILLE, *WAR NEWS FROM MEXICO* (1848)
Woodville, an American-born painter based in Europe, was a popular artist
working in a new genre: the North American frontier scene. One figure
tosses his hat in the air, celebrating the news of war and potential conquest.
A black man and child in the lower right react differently.

There had been two previous U.S. cotton booms, each riding a speculative upswing in the capitalist credit cycle. What was different about the
third boom of the 1840s and '50s was how it ended: not in a financial
panic but in a Civil War. Why the cataclysmic outcome this time?

Nothing about the development of capitalism, per se, fated the end of
racial slavery. While in the abstract a pecuniary process of investment defines capitalism, at a more concrete level there are different possible capitalisms, in which capitalists, and the communities in which they live, may
prioritize investing in different forms of capital. In the American South, in
a strictly economic sense, enslaved African-Americans were "capitalized
labor," a "fixed-cost investment in potential labor," as the economic historian Gavin Wright has put it.[3] By the time of the third cotton boom, the
American South was home to a distinct, slave-based, or "slave racial,"
capitalism.[4]

In principle, multiple varieties of capitalism can coexist and prosper within the same imperial polity. In fact, the historic role of early modern empire had been to accommodate local differences and to create a composite political order, precisely so that commerce among different communities could flourish. One of the functions of empire, after all, was to guarantee market demand for different goods within the imperial hole. Only by the end of the nineteenth century, when modern nation-states insisted on far more definitive jurisdictions over their territories (including their imperial colonies), did the existence of multiple economic orders in the same nation-state come to appear potentially incompatible.

By the 1840s, the American South was commercially dependent on an industrializing capitalism elsewhere, in places where slavery did not exist. Meanwhile a budding industrial capitalism was no less dependent on the southern slave production of raw cotton. By 1860, cotton accounted for 54 percent of total value of all U.S. exports and 99 percent of British cotton imports.[5] Yet the cotton trade did not collapse meaningful distinctions between slave-based and non-slave-based capitalisms (much as the commerce in wheat during the 1970s between the United States and the Soviet Union would not collapse distinctions between capitalism and Communism). In the Age of Commerce, the cotton trade revealed the extent to which the American South remained dependent for demand on the British Empire, which had already carried out slave emancipation.[6] Meanwhile in the composite order of the Empire of Liberty, slavery existed in Louisiana but not in Massachusetts, where a novel industrial capitalism was emerging.

An American capitalism with more nationally uniform characteristics would be the result of the political history inaugurated by the Republican Party, a radical political agent born in 1854, which drew support from a rapidly changing northern economy and captured the federal government in 1860. It would make "freedom national," and the northern variety of capitalism national as well.

In the decades after the recovery from the Panic of 1837, far more path-breaking, with respect to economic life, than any developments in the South was the capitalism that was beginning to take shape in the North. It, too, had roots in the past, as ever since the eighteenth century, the North had been more commercially dense, entrepreneurial, and equal than the South.[7] Nonetheless, in a departure, only after 1840 was a U.S. industrial capitalism clearly on the horizon, defined by investment in fixed, industrial assets. Its further distinguishing characteristics emerged, too, and included: "free" waged male labor; the application of steam power to production; the sphering of home from work; the ideology of "separate spheres" for men and women; and the diversion of children from laboring to schooling. Altogether chattel slavery finally began to look peculiar. In the North, antislavery and abolitionist social movements also emerged, ultimately, giving rise to the Republican Party.

Some historians argue that the outbreak of Civil War had nothing to do with economics, that it was the result of a moral crusade, or was a mere political contingency brought about by bumbling politicians; in their view, it was hardly the result of what the New York Republican William Seward called, in an incendiary 1858 speech, an "irrepressible conflict."[8] But the regional conflict was in fact rooted in a sharp post-1840 economic divergence between southern rigidity and northern transformation. Most critically, one must return to the issue of the Age of Commerce that remained fundamental from the time of the first Earl Shaftesbury to the 1860 presidential candidacy of the Republican Abraham Lincoln: the imperial geopolitics of commerce.

That was the crucial issue that led the southern states to secede from the Union after Lincoln's 1860 presidential victory. Southern economic expectations, and white investments in enslaved capital, were rooted in the continued possibility of future western expansion, secured by the federal government. Lincoln and the Republicans said that in the future, slavery could exist only in the states where it already stood. Would any of the federal territories of the trans-Mississippi West continue to be open to slavery, or none at all? Once the mutually exclusive question was posed, it put the future of Jefferson's Empire of Liberty at risk.

1. Late Capitalism, Slave-Based

While we are focusing on the post–Panic of 1837 cotton boom, it is worth stepping back a bit to generally assess the capitalistic qualities of American slavery. In addition to taking the measure of American slavery as it developed through the final antebellum decades, our point here is to sharpen the comparison between the slave South and the North, where more novel economic change was taking place.

Historians disagree intensely about the relationship between capitalism and slavery. I have no room here to do justice to the debates.[9] This book's starting point is capital. Slavery is an ancient institution that has exhibited many common characteristics over centuries, but capitalization is not one of them.[10]

Throughout American history, however, enslaved black people were capital assets.[11] Certain matters were settled by the final cotton boom of the 1840s and '50s. As Karl Marx put it, in a passage from the posthumously published volume three of *Capital* (1894): "The price that is paid here for the slave . . . is no more than the anticipated and capitalized surplus-value or profit that is to be extracted from him."[12] Since the profit motive is never enough, however, many motivations combined to determine the going price of a slave.[13] Altogether, the white inducement to invest in black slaves was extraordinary.

In the well-developed southern capital market, enslaved persons, as property, were legally alienable, thus acquiring the attribute of transactional liquidity. At the same time, slaves were productive assets whose exploited labor generated wealth—the reason the owners of slave capital expected profits from their investments. Marx was right that the price of a slave corresponded to the expected pecuniary earnings of slave ownership.[14] And "the price of cotton[,] as is well known," the *Richmond Enquirer* explained in 1859, "pretty much regulates the price of slaves in the South, and a bale of cotton and a 'likely nigger' are about well-balanced in the scale of pecuniary appreciation."[15] The average price of a slave in 1850 was $300. In 1860 it was $800, while a "prime" field hand in New Orleans fetched $1,800. The nearly 4 million U.S. slaves at the time were worth a combined $3 billion. Southern slave property was far more valuable than southern lands—or even northern factories.[16] Three billion dollars was triple the value of the entire U.S. industrial capital stock in 1860.[17] Enslaved people represented highly exploited labor by any possible definition of the term. Nonetheless, they were not "cheap labor." Their cost was determined by their scarcity as a form of enslaved human capital, in light of their prospective pecuniary yield.

The bullish expectations priced into black slave capital markets say something about slavery's presumed fate as late as 1860. Tellingly, southern interest rates declined during the late-antebellum period.[18] The demand for money, even land, fell in the South, as slave owners preferred storing their wealth in slaves, in this sense the most liquid of all southern assets. "The Negro is here, and here forever; is our property, and ours forever," the *Richmond Examiner* boasted in 1854.[19]

Enslaved people acquired many of the qualities of other capital assets. They were the object of private property rights, and they had the attributes of alienability and expected future pecuniary gain. At the same time, as capital assets, they possessed a number of unique economic qualities. First and foremost, enslaved persons were "portable." Enslaved capital could be coerced to move across space, which was one reason why, during the Age of Commerce, slavery was such a dynamic factor in economic expansion.[20] Land cannot be physically moved, and industrial plant and machinery were far more cumbersome and fixed on the ground in place. Before the spread of railroad and telegraph after about 1840, money and credit could not move faster than people. In a preindustrial setting, the slave plantation, as a unit of production, could move across space relatively quickly.

First begun during the seventeenth century, the slave-based colonizing project continued during the post–Panic of 1837 cotton boom. But this final western push covered the best soils in the South, in the lower Mississippi Valley. Seen on a map, the region of the great cotton plantations forms an anvil shape. The horn was the Mississippi Delta, below Memphis, with one anchor in the alluvial-tributary bottomlands of the Mississippi,

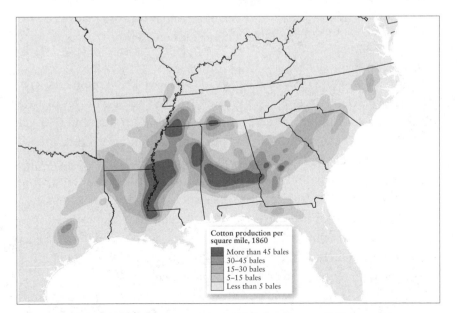

Cotton production per square mile, 1860

More than 45 bales
30–45 bales
15–30 bales
5–15 bales
Less than 5 bales

AMERICAN COTTON PRODUCTION PER SQUARE MILE, 1860
On the eve of the American Civil War, an anvil-shaped region east of the Mississippi River dominated slave-based cotton production.

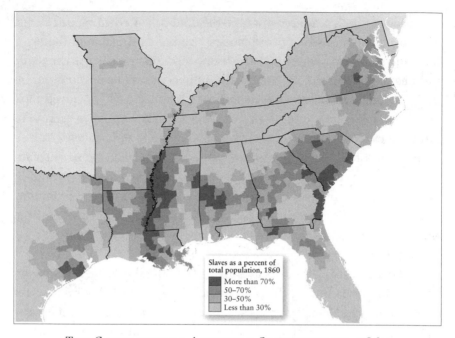

THE GEOGRAPHY OF AMERICAN SLAVEHOLDING, 1860
The high concentration of slaves along the Mississippi River was the result
of an extraordinary coerced western migration of black Americans.
As capital assets, slaves were valuable precisely because they were
highly portable factors of production.

down to Baton Rouge, and another in the rich-black-soil prairies of cen-
tral Alabama. Two streams of migrating planters settled in this district.
From the east came the cotton growers of South Carolina and Georgia.
From the south came growers from Louisiana, with their strong commercial ties to the Northeast. In the 1850s, cotton plantations edged onto the
Arkansas floodplains and the red soils of East Texas. By 1860 three-
quarters of the U.S. cotton crop was raised west of the Appalachians.[21]
Once again black slaves broke the land and made new plantations. Once
again, through a sophisticated financial system, with ties to northeastern
and European merchants and bankers, credit extended on the collateral of
slave property provided the necessary working capital.[22]

Between 1820 and 1860, about 875,000 slaves left the upper South for
the lower South in a massive forced migration.[23] That was twice the number of African slaves brought to North America before the closing of the
U.S. slave trade in 1808, and eight times as many as moved from the upper

to the lower South between 1790 and 1820. Probably 60 to 70 percent of the movement came from an internal slave trade.[24] Brazil and Cuba had domestic slave markets, but nowhere else in the Americas was there an interregional slave market like in the United States. Professional slave traders visited southern plantations and oversaw city slave markets, the largest being in New Orleans, where slaves on the auction block were poked, prodded, and examined.[25] A vast number of slave sales occurred locally. The former Kentucky slave Amelia Jones recalled of her enslavement:

> Master White was good to his slaves, he fed us well and had good places for us to sleep, and he didn't whip us only when it was necessary, but he didn't hesitate to sell any of his slaves. He said, "You all belong to me and if you don't like it, I'll put you in my pocket."[26]

After his enslavement, North Carolina slave Ben Johnson remembered:

> I was born in Orange County and I belonged to Mr. Gilbert Gregg near Hillsboro. I don't know nothing about my mammy and daddy, but I had a brother Jim who was sold to dress young missus for her wedding. The tree where I am still standing was where I sat under and watched them sell Jim. I sat there and I cry, and cry, especially when they put the chains on him and carried him off, and I ain't never felt so lonesome in my whole life. I ain't never heard from Jim since I wonder now sometimes if he's still living.[27]

That is what alienability, a common legal attribute of capital, meant to many enslaved black people.

Historians debate the sources of the productivity gains the planters achieved. In Smithian fashion, there were specialization and a complex division of labor on large cotton plantations that practiced the "gang labor" system.[28] In 1833 the *Southern Agriculturalist* might have been describing Henry Ford's twentieth-century industrial assembly line when it reported that a "plantation might be considered as a piece of machinery; to operate successfully, all its parts should be uniform and exact, and the impelling force regular and steady."[29] Planters developed a metric, "bales per hand," to track, assess, and improve slave effort. Thomas Affleck's *Plantation Record and Account Book* (1847) sold widely during the 1850s and helped planters keep numerical records.[30] The threat of sale coerced labor, as did the snap of the cat-o'-nine tails, the blunt force of the cowhide paddle, and the lacerating bullwhip. Violence was probably worse on the cotton frontier, where planters were more indebted and had more acreage in cotton. Last but not least, during the 1830s planters imported a new strain of cottonseed from Mexico, known as "Petit Gulf." The best statistical analysis attributes the largest share of productivity gains in the period thereafter to its spread and breeding—biological "improvement."[31]

The cotton economy was the most important and dynamic southern economic sector. Cotton was a year-round crop, and "unconstrained deployment of female labor in field work was one of the primary economic advantages of slavery in antebellum America."[32] From April to July, slaves planted seeds twelve inches apart in clean rows, then "thinned" the plants and cultivated them with a scraper plow and hoe to eliminate grasses and to keep the soil loose. Picking season ran from September to November, with tasks that required great effort, stamina, and dexterity. Cotton had to be ginned, removing "trash" from the lint. It was pressed into bales and hauled by slaves to landings and ports. By any criterion, late-antebellum cotton plantations were highly economically productive and efficient. Planters not only extended production across space, they successfully increased the intensity of economic production over time. During the 1830s, the average slave picked more than 150 pounds of cotton per day. In 1860, the year of an abnormal bumper crop, the rate reached 300 pounds.[33]

The cotton economy was not all there was. At the behest of masters, slaves planted other crops: rice in South Carolina, and sugar in Louisiana. New Orleans, Mobile, and Savannah handled and serviced the cotton trade, but cities like Richmond and Birmingham also had elaborate urban manufactures. Upper South plantations raised tobacco, hemp, and even wheat. The slave economy of Virginia produced the innovation of the McCormick reaper for grains.[34] This region was more diversified, with respect to commerce and manufacturing. The organized movement for greater southern diversification and agricultural "improvement," centered in Virginia, flourished during the 1850s.[35] But even if the upper South and the lower South were not shaped by the cotton, they were shaped by the internal slave trade. A Virginia writer explained it best: the price of a slave in Virginia was not "regulated by our profits, but by the profits of their labor in other states."[36]

In sum, through a series of successive upswings in the capitalist credit cycle after the War of 1812, the Panic of 1819, and the Panics of 1837 and 1839, southern white slave owners grew powerful and wealthy. They did so via three booms in staple production for foreign export—chiefly cotton. Commodity booms dependent upon foreign demand can make regions that are integrated well into global markets rich, but they do have stark developmental limits—lacking, for instance, the increasing returns born of either a local Smithian commercial multiplier or the knock-on effects of industrial investment.[37] The plantation economy, for instance, failed to commercially integrate the large group of white, upcountry yeoman farm households, many of them subsistence oriented.[38] The best way to understand the U.S. slave economy is this way: riding the upswings and the downswings of the speculative credit cycle, white slave owners progressively squeezed every productivity gain possible out of the scarce resources of an organic economy, whether that meant extracting kinetic energy from the bodies of enslaved men and women, colonizing the most ecologically fertile soils, or biologically innovating crop seeds. Likely diminishing returns—in the form, say, of broken black bodies or poor soils—loomed with respect to all these factors at some point in the future.

Nonetheless in 1860, on a GDP per capita basis—only one basis, to be sure—the South was wealthier than every country in Europe except England, and the existing economic trend appeared to be strong. In the 1850s southerners newly planted 3 million acres of cotton, and the average large planter that decade increased his wealth by 70 percent, both from selling cotton and from soaring slave asset price appreciation.[39] South Carolina senator James Henry Hammond spoke for many southern slave owners when he rose to the Senate floor in 1858 and famously taunted his northern colleagues. "No, you dare not make war on cotton. No power on earth dares to make war upon it. Cotton is king."[40]

The historian Eugene Genovese was probably too kind when he wrote that the very same James Henry Hammond was "an unfaithful husband, a less than supportive father, a lecherous uncle, and a demanding and often harsh slave master." The obsession with efficiency in the book of instructions that Hammond provided to his slave overseers would put a smile on the face of any early-twenty-first-century business consultant. But Hammond also wrote in his diary, "I love my family, and they love me. It is my only earthly tie. It embraces my slaves, and there to me the world ends. All beyond is blank."[41] Please, Hammond instructed his legitimate white son

Harry in 1856, "Do not let Louisa or any of my children or possible children be slaves of Strangers. Slavery *in the family* will be their happiest earthly condition."[42] No eighteenth-century U.S. slave master would likely have written such sentences to himself or his children. Hammond espoused a reconfigured, white supremacist slaveholding ideology, rooted in the familial intimacies of the plantation household—paternalism.[43] What most changed in the South after 1840 was not so much the economy. The dynamics of the post–Panic of 1837 cotton boom were quite similar to those before. What was new was the rise of a paternalistic slaveholding ideology that was professedly inimical to unchecked commerce. American slave capitalism transformed due to paternalism's triumph.

What historians call "paternalism" in this context was an unlikely nineteenth-century Christian "insurgency" to reform the most draconian aspects of slavery.[44] Paternalism had two core features. First, in a departure from common eighteenth-century beliefs that equated enslavement with attempted animalization, paternalism professed to acknowledge the "humanity" of enslaved blacks but nonetheless still considered them racially inferior. "Our slaves," insisted James Henley Thornwell, an important professor of theology in Columbia, South Carolina, "are moral beings."[45] Unlike many masters before, paternalists welcomed the religious conversion of their slaves to Christianity. They rejected the patriarchal slaveholding ideology—the harsh, distant rule of the father over his subjects—of colonial North America and instead promoted the "Abrahamic" kind, in which master-slave relations should be more intimate and affective. God's law checked the master's dominion.[46] Second, paternalism cast southern home life in the Victorian moral light of domestic sentiment. Black slaves were not just members of households, or economic units. They were members of families, emotionally speaking. William A. Smith, president of Randolph-Macon College, captured the essential idea in his *Lectures on the Philosophy and Practice of Slavery* (1856). "Domestic slavery," he proclaimed, "is made part of the family relation. The head of the family is the *master*, and the slave is subject . . . as the other members of the family."[47]

The paternalist movement, purposeful and concerted, took decades to achieve success and occurred in a shifting economic landscape. After the closing of the Atlantic slave trade in 1808, slave owners could no longer replenish their capital stock from abroad. Slave capital would have to reproduce itself sexually, as white masters grew ever more dependent on the reproductive labors of black women. Between 1790 and 1860, the U.S. slave population doubled every twenty-eight years, an increase of 2.5 percent per annum.[48] In addition to "portability," positive fertility was a second unique characteristic of enslaved human capital, compared to other forms of capital.

The blunt fact of the closing of the Atlantic slave trade opened a moral wedge for the paternalists, presenting them, so they thought, with a chance to improve slavery morally while salvaging its long-term economic viability. The aftermath of the Panic of 1837 was the next decisive economic event. Suffering from debt-deflation, many masters decided to make their plantations more economically self-sufficient and to rely less on commercial markets for foodstuffs. They would still rely on market demand for cotton, but would rely less on markets for the supply of some plantation necessities. The full-fledged U.S. "cotton and corn" system arose—distinct from the older, more cash-crop-oriented West Indian model—in which masters put sufficient acreage into corn to meet the plantation's basic subsistence needs. This new "safety first" strategy was thus a check on commercial risk.

There was a capitalist logic to this shift. For the final characteristic of enslaved capital is its "fixed" quality. If, on the one hand, slaves were relatively liquid, because they traded easily in markets and were objects of speculation, they were also illiquid, in the sense that over time their value depreciated, whether because of backbreaking labor or age.[49] In this strict sense, enslaved human capital was like a rusting, depreciating factory. Further, once a slave was owned, the cost of maintaining them—providing food, clothing, and care—continued to run, just as a factory might rust with age regardless of its use. For this reason, a market and a law for the renting of slave labor emerged.[50] In other words, the cost of slave ownership was what economists call "sunk."

Every idle hour for every slave was a carried cost. Cotton was a seasonal crop, with annual spring planting and fall harvesting seasons. Its cultivation could not occupy every single waking hour of every slave's life. Idle time became filled with subsistence production. In 1850, on U.S. cotton plantations, 38 percent of the average slave's labor time was devoted to cotton, but 31 percent went into corn and the care of livestock, with most production by far directly consumed on the plantation. Another 31 percent went into tending other subsistence items (like potatoes and peas), home manufacturing of clothing, land clearing, building construction, and an assortment of odd tasks that masters and overseers ingeniously invented to keep their slaves busy. Slave children entered the workforce at age three or four (becoming household servants or joining "trash gangs") and began producing a surplus above their own consumption for their masters by, on average, age nine. Boys might begin picking cotton at eleven. After a mid-thirties peak, on average slaves continued to yield surpluses for their masters until their late seventies.[51] The old, sick, and disabled could still watch children or tend the chicken coop. In 1860, with cotton prices soaring, only on plantations with fifteen or more slaves did cotton account for more than 50 percent of total plantation output.[52] Slaveholders granted their slaves "Negro plots" to cultivate on Sundays, their one day off. Slaves clung to them tenaciously, claiming informal property rights and transforming these plots into grounds of individual and communal autonomy.[53] In general, the slave plantations of the 1840s and '50s cotton boom were more self-sufficient than they had been before the Panic of 1837 and the bust that followed.[54]

Paradoxically, the post-1837 turn to "safety first" strategies, even if best interpreted as a capitalist hedge against risk and a way to squeeze all possible economic value from all the members of enslaved families, created an opportunity for paternalist ideologues to reinvent the plantation household as a site of domestic affection outside commerce. Rhetorically, paternalism was hostile to unchecked commerce. Indeed, paternalists lapped up the same transatlantic, romantic critique of commerce as did Emerson and Thoreau but spun something different of it.[55] Here, among the slave master's newly fashioned "domestic" Christian duties and burdens, none was more publicly celebrated than the need to provide for slaves' basic subsistence—apart from commerce. In paternalist ideology, the moral split between heartless commerce and domestic familial affection became sharp. Thus a particular economic logic of investment, given that slaves represented running and fixed costs, led to a large plantation household subsistence sector, which made it possible for paternalists to ideologically claim to themselves that southern economic life had set hard limits to the encroachments of commerce.

Perhaps the classic economic distillation of paternalism was made by E. N. Elliott, president of the Planters' College in Mississippi and editor of the monumental pro-slavery collection *Cotton Is King, and Pro-Slavery Arguments* (1860):

Slavery is the duty and obligation of the slave to labor for the mutual benefit of both master and slave, under a warrant to the slave of protection, and a comfortable subsistence, under all circumstances. . . . The master, as the head of the system, has a right to the obedience and labor of the slave, but the slave has also his mutual rights in the master; the right of protection, the right of counsel and guidance, the right of subsistence, the right of care and attention in sickness and old age.[56]

Paternalism, which seemed to evoke precapitalist tradition if not bygone feudalism, was in truth an invented tradition of late-antebellum slave capitalism. It was one more crack at the same old problem of the Age of Commerce: how might commerce be promoted, yet still checked and kept within its proper bounds? By the 1840s, commerce had made many advances over past centuries. As the best possible moral and social check on commerce, late-antebellum paternalism pointed to the "domestic" master-slave relation.

Just because paternalists invoked anti-commercial traditions does not mean that the South was any less capitalist. In fact, paternalist critiques of commerce only legitimized the white southern inducement to invest in black slaves—propelling, if in contradictory fashion, slave capitalism forward. As for the proper check on commerce, the late-antebellum North would have a different answer, prioritizing a different set of economic, moral, and psychological investments, with a different set of productive tensions. Meanwhile the paternalists really did moralize slavery, just in a morally repugnant way.[57] Who committed the greater moral crime, the master who simply wanted to physically extract the slave's labor, or the master who took an intimate interest in transforming the soul of the enslaved?

Nonetheless, on its own terms paternalism's achievements were not inconsiderable. In the late-antebellum period, the responsibility of masters to feed and care for their slaves entered many southern statute books. In a related departure, masters could no longer murder, let alone dismember, slaves for simple malice, without cause, and slaves slowly became a category of quasi-legal persons. Paternalism helped motivate and energize another economic boom, and it also transformed politics in the decades after Jackson's presidency. As masters claimed slaves as family members, and as public and private sphered, paternalists newly marked domestic slavery as

private. In 1857 President James Buchanan told Congress in his first annual message, "The relation between master and slave and a few others
are 'domestic institutions,' and are entirely distinct from institutions of a
political character."[58] That meant the federal government, in addition to
having no right to expropriate southern private property, had no right to
intervene in southern private family life. The shift, in fact, resonated with
the transformation of the corporation at the same time; both corporations
and slave households, long imperial subsovereigns, were newly being
marked as private.

In sum, late-antebellum southern slavery represented a significant departure from the postrevolutionary political-economic settlement. In the
early republic, landownership, not slavery, had been the bedrock of even
southern liberty and what the slave owner Thomas Jefferson branded "independence." But rising slave prices had led to the concentration of holdings and to an increased southern economic income inequality—perhaps
one reason why, by the 1840s, income growth in the North was outstrip-
ping that of the South.[59] Non-slave-owning southern whites became
vastly poorer than their northern counterparts. To maintain their political loyalty, southern elites stoked white racism and gender solidarity
among male heads of household.[60] In 1837 John C. Calhoun of South
Carolina, indicating the shift, championed the new pro-slavery ideology
from the floor of the U.S. Senate. Not widespread landownership but black
slavery and white racial solidarity, he bellowed, was "the most safe and
stable basis for free institutions in the world."[61] Paternalism justified both
the legacy of the older slaveholding capitalism and the prospect of a new
slaveholding democracy, distinct from northern democracy.[62] Powerful
white men in the South had invested nearly everything in the long-term
enslavement of black Americans.

2. Rise of Industrial Society

In the South, no matter what the paternalists said about commerce, the
household remained the basic unit of enterprise. By contrast, in the North
a rupture took place. There the romantic idealization of family life occurred in a different economic setting, creating a different kind of energy
and tension. Northern economic production began to sphere from the
home, as the male-breadwinner-female-homemaker family was emerging. The history of domesticity was fully implicated in the North's move-

ment of capital into productive assets with qualities similar to yet very different from those of enslaved persons: factories.

Quantitatively, the greatest two-decade spurt of growth in U.S. industrial history occurred between 1840 and 1860. In the Northeast, industrial production increased 7.5 percent per annum for a combined fivefold increase.[63]

For comparison, here is a brief picture of northern industrial life before 1840. The word *industry* might summon images of massive, hulking factories that belch out great billows of smoke, under whose iron archways armies of soot-faced, slump-shouldered men trudge—through factory gates where, inside, bulky machinery awaits them. That is a false picture of U.S. manufacturing before the late-antebellum surge. Before 1840, the limits of the organic economy were still in place; the dominant unit of production remained the household, and the Smithian commercial multiplier remained the dynamic factor.

It was still the Age of Commerce, in other words. In 1840 only 8.7 percent of the U.S. workforce was engaged in manufacturing.[64] The extent of commercial markets was what mattered most. Historian Thomas C. Cochran long ago explained:

> In early nineteenth-century America the machine spinning mill was of minor importance compared to the hard-surfaced road; the early steam engine was more significant for improvements in river transportation than in manufacturing; and iron puddling and rolling were far less vital to immediate progress than canals.[65]

The demand for goods, not changes in productive methods, was the driver of expansion. Given the Northeast's dense commercial geography, manufacturing growth was a response to local and regional urban and rural demand.[66] This was the case for, say, New England textiles and shoes, Connecticut clocks and brassware, upstate New York flour milling and cheesemaking, New York City ready-made clothing, Trenton, New Jersey, ironware, and Philadelphia machines and stoves. Transportation infrastructure was the key source of industrial expansion.[67] By 1840, because of improved transportation due to state-backed internal improvements, geographically a coherent northeastern industrial corridor was rounding into shape.

Contributing to continuity, human labor and water remained the pre-

JOHN NEAGLE, *PAT LYON AT THE FORGE* (1826–27)
Until 1840, small-scale household manufactures dominated U.S. industry.
This celebrated early American painting features a wealthy Boston
businessman and inventor who had first been a blacksmith. Lyon requested
the commission in these words: "I wish you, sir, to paint me at full length, the
size of life, representing me at the smithery, with a bellows-blower, hammers
and all the et-ceteras of the shop around me. I wish you to understand
clearly, Mr. Neagle, that I do not desire to be represented in this picture as
a gentleman—to which character I have no pretensions. . . ."
Note the young apprentice in the background.

dominant power source. Coal was used sparsely, for home heating. Manufacturing clung to the waterways, as waterwheels transferred power to
millstones by wooden shafts. Nearly everywhere in 1850, steam power cost
more per unit of horsepower than did water.[68] Large-scale manufacturing,
when it occurred, took place in dispersed rural mills.[69] Even iron making
was a rural industry, following veins of mineral deposits from Virginia,
through Pennsylvania and New York, as far north as Vermont.

Further, most U.S. manufacturing production by far involved the processing of organic materials—wheat, leather, wool, and cotton. Lumber

was important, too, as construction inevitably dominated manufacturing in growing cities. Western colonization required rural construction materials as well, for houses, mills, barns, carriages, wheels, and furniture. Due to its abundance, wood—not iron, let alone steel—remained the leading construction material.

In 1840 the average U.S. manufacturing establishment employed but four workers.[70] The household remained the dominant unit of industrial production. Small-scale proprietorships predominated. Productive capital requirements were low. Skilled labor was essential. In 1841 a resident of Cincinnati spoke for most of industrial America when he bragged, "Our manufacturing establishments, with the exception of a few, . . . are, in the literal sense, manufactures,—*works of the hand.*"[71] Inside the shops, employers and employees were "masters" and "servants." Master "mechanics" employed "apprentices" and "journeymen," former apprentices who aspired to be "independent" mechanics.[72] Servants were legally bound to fulfill the contractual terms of employment, subject to the disciplinary authority of their masters. Home and work were often the same place.

Before 1840, even when work did leave the home, the home often chased after it. In rural manufacturing, merchants commonly "put out" cloth for industrious women to weave at "piece rates" during slack periods on the farm. Next, in Rhode Island, Connecticut, and southern Massachusetts, a new generation of industrial capitalists—pulling their capital from Atlantic commerce after Jefferson's embargo—employed entire households in large-scale textile mills. Here greater productive capital inputs of labor-saving machinery were crucial. Unskilled women and children tended the water-powered spinning machines.

Then the corporate form of industry entered the picture. In Massachusetts in 1813, former Atlantic merchants chartered the Boston Manufacturing Company, benefiting from the protective tariffs after 1816.[73] They adopted English power looms that integrated spinning and weaving, though they were still driven by waterwheels. The first mill, in Waltham, Massachusetts, employed "principally the daughters of the adjacent farmers," reported Mathew Carey's *Essays on Political Economy* (1822).[74] So did the next, larger set of mills, in Lowell.[75] In 1832 no less than 40 percent of the remunerated U.S. manufacturing workforce was women or children. They were all paid less to perform the same work as adult men. The larger the manufacturing establishment, and the larger the capital requirements, the more firms relied on unskilled female and child labor. In textile firms with more than fifteen employees, 73.4 percent of employees were women or girls.[76] In large-scale cotton plantations and large-scale textile manufacturers alike, the labor of women and children was the key swing component.[77]

But then, after roughly 1840, in the Northeast a different kind of industrialization clearly had begun. In production, complementing the division of labor was the more intensive use of new forms of productive capital in industry. By increasing the extent of markets and the demand for goods in city and countryside alike, the Smithian commercial multiplier had set the foundation for the emergence of an industrial investment multiplier. Factories grew larger and more productive.

Later estimates of productivity growth point to the 1850s as the moment of rupture.[78] A new logic of greater fixed capital investment had appeared in industry.[79] The "intensity" of productive capital in manufacturing—the value of industrial structures and equipment—relative to labor increased. Taking advantage of Jacksonian general incorporation laws, entrepreneurs chartered corporations to raise the capital and credit necessary to increase the scale of economic production. Between 1840 and 1860, U.S. manufacturing employment tripled.[80] By 1860, the average number of employees per manufacturing establishment had more than doubled from 1840, up to nine laborers (which almost reached the average size of a slave plantation, which was ten).[81] Scale increased beyond the household, as larger factories required a physical space separate from the home. There was greater demand for unskilled labor relative to skilled labor. Increasingly, rather than women and children, the U.S. labor pool consisted of 3.3 million European immigrants—mostly from Ireland and Germany—who arrived between 1847 and 1857.[82] Finally, during the 1850s, northern manufacturing pushed at the productive limits of the organic economy. Coal-fired steam engines began to power many lines of production.[83] The British government survey *The American System of Manufactures* (1855) took note of U.S. industry's enduring distinctive features: the use of "standardized" components in manufacturing assembly; fast machine speeds; and greater work intensity. Altogether, in the Northeast in 1860, manufacturing labor productivity, or the amount of output wrested from the same input of labor, was likely higher than anywhere else in the world.[84]

Textiles were a case in point. In the Northeast, household manufactures were $9 million in 1840, but only $2.5 million in 1860, and even that was mostly because of their continued prominence in the South.[85] In the

North, textile production had left the home.[86] Machines and unskilled immigrant male labor replaced women and children. In one Lowell textile mill in 1836, immigrant male workers constituted only 4 percent of the labor force. By 1860, they accounted for 62 percent.

What did this look like even more up close? Consider the Boston "artisan-entrepreneur" Jonas Chickering. Born on a New Hampshire farm before the presidential election of Thomas Jefferson, Chickering became an apprentice cabinetmaker at age seventeen. Three years later he was a journeyman in Boston, then in 1819 he joined the small shop of a piano-making craftsman. Soon enough, he became a master-craftsman piano maker himself.

Chickering was ambitious, but he needed capital. New England's clannish banks were unwilling to fund him. In 1830 he went into business with a wealthy retired sea captain. When the captain disappeared on a wood-finding mission off the coast of Brazil, Chickering bought out his heirs. There was a pause following the Panic of 1837, but Chickering steadily increased his scale of operations. His firm built a new factory and increased the division of labor. It reduced the cost of high-quality, standardized pianos and developed a national marketing network. Chickering himself was an owner of capital but also a "tinkerer" who lived very close to the production process. Such artisan-entrepreneurs clustered in networks and learned from one another.[87] Chickering filed a number of industrial "improvements" with the U.S. patent office, and the great number of patents at the time indicated a rising democratic culture of innovation.[88]

In 1850 P. T. Barnum commissioned Chickering to build a piano for the "Swedish Nightingale" Jenny Lind's national concert tour. From forty-seven pianos in 1829, by 1850 Chickering was producing one thousand pianos a year, one-ninth of all U.S. production. He built another factory in 1853, at which time the company's fixed capital investment was $100,000, including a six-story factory, with over twenty separate specialized departments, employing more than one hundred wage workers. Chickering became wealthy, but by some reports he sometimes worked side by side with his employees on the shop floor. By all accounts, he was a nice fellow and a pleasant boss.[89]

The status of waged work was changing greatly in the North. Rather than a household dependency, it was becoming a variety of free labor. Ideologically, wage work was transforming from a dependency associated with femininity to a badge of male independence. Legally, it transformed masters and servants into employers and employees with different sets of legal obligations. Notably, the free labor doctrines emerging in the United States were quite "radical" compared to those of other countries.[90] They were not the foreordained endpoint of capitalist development.

The abolition of slavery in the North inaugurated the history of free labor there. New England abolished it first, in the midst of the Revolution or shortly thereafter.[91] Elsewhere it took more time.[92] A critical moment came when masters attempted to enroll emancipated slaves in long-term contracts as their servants. Northern legal decisions overturning these ruses undermined long-term contracts of all kinds, including even some forms of apprenticeship.[93] Free labor required more than the abolition of involuntary servitude; it would also require the outlawing of many kinds of coercion and unfreedom in the workplace.

What emerged, slowly, was an American right to quit work, a doctrine formalized legally decades later as "employment at will." Indentured servitude and legal punishments for "absconding from service" during the length of a labor contract fell by the wayside. Corporeal punishment of workers, even where and when it remained legal, was no longer practical, since workers, if beaten, often simply walked off the job—and demanded compensation for work already performed. English common law clearly stated that compensation was for the performance of a "whole" of a contract, and in the United States, labor contracts, if not otherwise specified, were annual, a principle upheld in Massachusetts as late as *Stark v. Parker* (1824). Soon enough, U.S. law recognized changes in practice. By roughly 1840, American wage workers enjoyed the legal right to quit at a moment's notice and nonetheless to receive "part compensation" for work already performed. A labor market with a "norm of high mobility" emerged.[94] The changes cut two ways. U.S. wage earners gained new rights but lost long-term job security as employer obligations thinned out. Southern pro-slavery ideologues, defending paternalism, harped on the latter.[95]

Chickering was a capitalist boss who had ascended from the ranks of wage-earning apprentices. Such upward mobility was not only aspirational but possible. The intensity of wage work in manufacturing resulted from the application of machines, but there is reason to believe many U.S. workers, young, if not immigrants, wanted to work and earn more so as to set up their own shops someday. Many wage workers aspired to be capitalist owners.

Meanwhile in the Northeast, in addition to sphering between market and state, and between home and work, a third, incipient sphering no less presaged industrial capitalism's future: the split between capitalist production and philanthropic wealth.[96] If Chickering lived out the Jacksonian ideal of equality of commercial opportunity, he was nonetheless a politically conservative Whig. He believed in the gospel of not only economic but also moral improvement, including in social reform. He withdrew profits from piano making, and instead of using them to augment his capital investments, they became charitable wealth. He placed this money in incorporated "voluntary associations" for the promotion of arts, education, and religion. Few such corporations existed in the South, and none on the slave plantations.

Further, Chickering was a manufacturer of pianos, instruments that were emblems of a rising middle-class urban gentility. They resided, in the North, in a new domestic space, the home parlor. Aiding the transformation of wage earning from a badge of dependence to an embodiment of free labor was the ability of northern domesticity, in the words of the historian Amy Dru Stanley, "to fence in the dependencies of the home."[97] In addition to being moral and ideological, that fencing was literally physical.

The comparison with the paternalist South, from which gushed forth no less Victorian domestic sentiment, is telling. In southern home architecture, the most pronounced physical boundary separated the plantation and all its grounds—big house, outbuildings, fields, gardens, and slave cabins—from the outside world. Inside the plantation gate, southern homes typically had wide and high porches, verandas, and piazzas—for cooling in the summer sun but also for plantation surveillance.[98] The northern landscape architect Frederick Law Olmsted noted in his travelogue The Cotton Kingdom (1861) that even poor southerners built a "small square log cabin, with a broad open shed or piazza in front."[99] The porches of the big houses of the wealthiest plantations were even grander. Commonly, slave cabins had no doors. On the plantation, there was no threshold—no physical boundary—between home and work.

The southern porch contrasts with the northern parlor. In the North, industrial economic production had left the site of the home, which then acquired new meanings.[100] Popular New York architect Andrew Jackson

"LACOSTE PLANTATION HOUSE,
ST. BERNARD PARISH, LOUISIANA" (1938)
By contrast to the northern domestic parlor encased from the outside world,
the porch in southern home architecture illustrated the still porous
boundary between home and work on the plantation. The porch might also
act as a venue for the surveillance of slaves. This house dates back to 1727.

Downing explained in *Cottage Residences* (1842) that the home must separate the family's inner and outer worlds. Set apart from commercial self-interest, it was a place for "inward good"—for economically disinterested love. In the romantic idiom, it was the "place dearest to our hearts," an "unfailing barrier" against the vices of the outside world.[101] Downing's architectural designs tucked the parlor deep into the home interior. There the "family circle" resided together in an intimate and affectionate space. In these years, folk art paintings depicting middle-class parlor domesticity proliferated. Erastus Salisbury Field's *Joseph Moore and His Family* (c. 1839) is one illustrative example.

In *A Treatise on Domestic Economy, for the Use of Young Ladies at Home and at School* (1841), the education reformer Catharine Beecher, sister of Harriet Beecher Stowe—the author of *Uncle Tom's Cabin* (1852)—would instruct that there be no "awkward porch on the outside of a house." The boundary between home life and the outside world was sacrosanct. The Beecher sisters renamed the parlor the "home room."[102] The home was "The Sphere of Woman," according to the title of a representative 1844

ERASTUS SALISBURY FIELD, *JOSEPH MOORE AND HIS FAMILY* (C. 1839)
The genre of domestic interiors traveled from the bourgeois seventeenth-century Dutch republic to the middle-class milieu of the nineteenth-century United States. Moore was a traveling dentist and the artist's neighbor. The "folk" qualities of this painting—its notably eccentric details—reflect the popularization of the middle-class norm of domesticity during this period.

middle-class magazine article. In the "home," wives and mothers were tasked with "developing the heart's best and holiest feeling." The "dominion of woman" was the "affections." Man's sphere was outside the home in the "seething marts of traffic, the devious though dazzling path of ambition."[103]

The gender ideology of "separate spheres" was yet another example of public and private sphering, giving rise to a new tension specific to an industrial society that was premised on borders from without rather than entanglements within. This was different from paternalism, which sought to draw oppositions by parsing the moral and economic morass of the plantation household.[104] Of course, middle-class women still labored in the home. A farm wife's labor in 1860 was still worth that of one hired male hand. Poor women worked both inside and outside the home.[105] Regardless of economic truths, the ideological shift was key. Women's affective labor became all the more estimable as their labors, in pecuniary

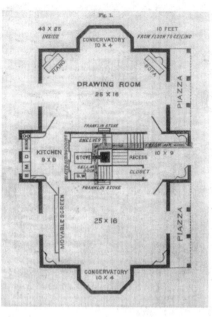

CATHARINE E. BEECHER AND HARRIET BEECHER STOWE,
"FLOOR PLAN OF FIRST FLOOR OF HOME" (1873)
The Beecher sisters' repositioning of domestic space to the interior of the
home is illustrated here, with spots assigned in the parlor for such middle-
class ornaments as the piano. The feminized domestic parlor was physically
and emotionally separated from male self-interested commercial life.
From the Beechers' *The New Housekeeper's Manual*.

terms, were devalued. This made it possible for men's industrial wage work
to become a new symbol of masculine independence and of "freedom,"
rather than dependence.[106]

Finally, northern home life saw associated changes in status concerning another household dependent—the child. Women's reproductive labors did not cease, but the modern "demographic transition," commonly
accompanying both urbanization and industrialization, had begun. Birth
rates dropped.[107] In the urban and industrial Northeast, especially among
the better off, child labor was becoming less important. Children went to
school, aided by the Whig Party's public school movement and bequests
from budding philanthropists like Chickering. Childrearing was recon-
ceived in more purely affectionate terms. In the relatively unschooled
South, where public education was less supported, "human capital" was
overwhelmingly slave capital.[108] By paying public school taxes, northern

families began to invest economically and affectively in their children's future economic lives. Meanwhile in the North, income from pay—a return on free, more highly educated human capital—was increasing in these years, relative to income from property. That was not true in the South, where slave asset price appreciation mostly increased property incomes but not wages.[109]

In sum, there were shifts in investment, in the broadest sense of that term—not only capital investments, but also emotional attachments and gender-defined aspirations. Critical changes were made in labor laws, new philanthropic associations were born, home architecture saw innovations, and a new emphasis was placed on childhood schooling. All this began to establish the many qualities of an industrial society. Economically, in the shift to industry the by-now-more-dynamic North had greater potential for increasing returns to economic activity over time than did the slave South, an agricultural society, premised on the rank extraction of black labor, where ultimately diminishing returns loomed. Industrial investment can potentially multiply the production of wealth more so than any other factor.

Over the next century, however, nothing, not even the new industrial factories, would be more central to the industrial order than the breadwinner-homemaker family, which arose as yet another late–Age of Commerce solution to the same old problem: how might commerce be promoted, yet still be checked and kept within its proper bounds? During the 1840s and '50s, the organization of family life made it clear that North and South gave two very different answers to this question. The growing distinction, which occurred in tandem with an economic divergence, contributed to the convulsion in politics.

3. Lincoln, Between Slavery and Freedom

But so what if the two regional capitalisms were becoming so different? The Empire of Liberty, like all early modern empires, had been designed to accommodate different forms of rule. Economically, empires ensured that different communities had export markets for their goods, while politically commercial ties helped hold empires together. Ever since the Revolution, transregional commerce, especially down the Mississippi River, had done much to bind the Empire of Liberty. However, after the recovery from the Panic of 1837, the invisible hand of the market began to fall down on the job of political union. The expansion of commerce began to sharpen rather than alleviate sectional differences.[110] The task of maintaining the Union was dropped into the hands of politicians. There may be no greater example of the power of democratic politics to determine capitalism's future than the sudden rise of the antislavery Republican Party after 1854.[111]

What happened in 1854 was the Kansas-Nebraska Act. The congressional legislation was so inflammatory because, first, it undermined a number of political compromises that the states had already reached over the status of slavery in the western federal territories. The Missouri Compromise of 1820 had admitted Missouri as a slave state, but had also barred slavery in the former Louisiana Purchase north of the 36°30' parallel. Then after the Treaty of Guadalupe Hidalgo, ending the Mexican-American War (1846–48), had "ceded" California and present-day Nevada, Utah, Arizona, and parts of Colorado, New Mexico, and Wyoming to the United States, an aging Henry Clay engineered the Compromise of 1850, which admitted California as a free state; granted the South a stronger fugitive slave law; and established the principle of "popular sover-

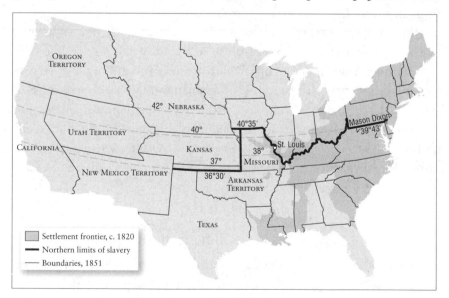

THE KANSAS-NEBRASKA ACT OF 1854

The politically explosive Kansas-Nebraska Act of 1854 overturned the Missouri Compromise of 1820, which had banned slavery north of the 36°30' parallel in lands acquired by the Louisiana Purchase. The 1854 law left the question of slavery in those territories open to the governments seeking admission as states.

eignty" to determine slavery's future in the New Mexico and Utah territories. There residents would vote, and the majority would decide slavery's existence.

After 1850, the powerful Democratic senator from Illinois Stephen Douglas meddled with this fragile state of affairs. Douglas wanted Congress to organize a new Nebraska territory, through which a transcontinental railroad would pass and from which Douglas stood to financially benefit. Southern representatives minded the balance of power in Congress. Already Minnesota and Oregon, whose northern boundary had been set by a treaty with the British Empire in 1846, were likely to request statehood (they would, in 1858 and 1859). Above the 36°30' parallel, more new free states would likely be carved out from any proposed Nebraska territory. That was too many new free states for southern comfort.

Douglas's 1854 Kansas-Nebraska Act overturned the Missouri Compromise. The 36°30' parallel banning slavery to its north would no longer apply in lands acquired through the Louisiana Purchase. Instead, "popular sovereignty" would also determine slavery's fate in the new territories of Kansas, which extended west into present-day Colorado, and Nebraska, which then extended north to Canada. In these territories, white male heads of household would vote on whether to have slavery.

Congressional voting on the Kansas-Nebraska Act broke almost completely along sectional and party lines. Ever since the rise of the Democracy and the Whigs in the 1830s, the two parties had cobbled together national, cross-sectional constituencies. The vote on the Kansas-Nebraska Act positively split the Whigs, and the party effectively ceased to exist. Douglas's Democratic Party, too, was in disarray.[112]

Meanwhile after 1854, in preparation for the vote on slavery in Kansas, northern and southern colonizers flocked into the territory. Antagonistic versions of empire—one free labor, another slave-based—violently crossed paths.

The West had not always been like this. The original settlement cluster of the Old Northwest had actually been southern "butternuts" who migrated north from Kentucky and in some instances brought black slaves with them in contravention of the Northwest Ordinance of 1787. For decades, the corn-and-hog complex of the Ohio River Valley was commercially connected to the slave plantations of the Old Southwest. In 1830 the Ohio-Mississippi river system took virtually the entirety of northwestern commercial traffic. In future decades, northwest commerce would shift from the southwest to the northeast. A contributing factor was the South's post–Panics of 1837 and 1839 retreat to "safety first" subsistence strategies, in the context of the shift to paternalism.[113] Northwestern foodstuffs were less in demand in the South. New interregional railroads linked the Northwest and the Northeast over the mountains. Altogether, by the 1850s, most northwestern goods were shipped by rail to the East rather than downriver to the South.[114]

Commercial expansion was no longer so binding in the West. Instead, the West was splitting between North and South. In the absence of a national economic program of development, state-backed public infrastruc-

AMERICAN RAILROADS, 1860

The construction of railroads in the Northwest commercially connected that region to the Northeast, diminishing southward commerce down the Ohio and Mississippi rivers. Rather than ameliorating north-south sectional political discord, after 1840 the growth of intersectional commerce contributed to it.

ture projects had routed commerce along paths that did not aid political union. Through the cotton trade, ties still bound the "lords of the lash" and the "lords of the loom," as the antislavery Massachusetts senator Charles Sumner put it in an 1848 speech. New York City's merchants and financiers had great economic interests in the South.[115] But in the trans-Mississippi West, where the sectional struggle over slavery was to play out, commerce could no longer help.

These shifting commercial patterns reflected a dynamic new Great Lakes thrust of colonization. A midwestern wheat belt had emerged north of the Old Northwest's corn-and-hog belt. In 1848 the Illinois and Michigan Canal linked the Mississippi River to the young city of Chicago, and by 1860 Illinois enjoyed the honor of being the top wheat-producing state. Northwestern wheat farmers, like southern cotton producers, were exporters. The British Empire's abolition of the Corn Laws in 1846 and the Crimean War (1853–56) created European demand. The Great Lakes region was fast becoming an international agricultural powerhouse.[116]

The Great Lakes thrust of settlement brought "free soil" settlers into the Kansas and Nebraska territories. While oriented toward agricultural exports, the contrast with southern colonization was sharp. Slave capital was portable, which was one reason why it was valuable, but in the Midwest, slave colonization was less rapid than free soil colonization. Slaves were not cheap. Instead, Americans and European immigrants absolutely flooded the Midwest. In 1850 the foreign-born share of the population in the Wisconsin and Minnesota territories was 44 percent.[117] The dominant form of capital was land that, relative to slaves, was cheap. A far more demographically and commercially dense pattern of colonization arose. Unlike migrating slave owners in the Old Southwest, settlements in the Northwest had to become places where free migrants actually might choose to live before they became wealthy.[118] Northwestern migrants quickly built schools, churches, and roads—the entire public infrastructure of civilizational "improvement." The Great Lakes basin largely voted Whig, in hopes of federal funding for lake harbor construction to increase market access. By contrast, one Texas settler boasted, "I am convinced that Texas must prosper. We pay no taxes . . . get our land at cost, and perform no public duties of any kind."[119] The Midwest took a different approach to achieving prosperity. Finally, unlike cotton, wheat is a seasonal crop, with only a two-week harvest period. The potential bottleneck at harvest time encouraged mechanization, while it released population to

cities such as Chicago where, by 1860, a great industrial future manufacturing farm implements such as mechanized reapers had already begun to
appear.[120]

In sum, the upper Northwest was developing a more diverse and dynamic economy, which began to resemble that of the Northeast. Newly
interlinked through trade, certainly the residents of both regions were far
more equal than those of the Southwest by any measure, even if in 1850,
because of slave wealth, per capita incomes in the Southwest were 25 percent higher than in the Midwest. That fact must have stoked the rancor of
recent migrants there.[121]

It was no accident that the antislavery Republican Party was founded
in the Great Lakes states of Wisconsin and Michigan in 1854, in the wake
of the Kansas-Nebraska Act. Among former Democrats and Whigs, the
Republicans quickly earned the loyalties of the Great Lakes wheat basin by
supporting a free soil Homestead Act, which southerners in the Senate,
hoping to slow down free soil colonization, had blocked, and also federally
subsidized internal improvements to expand market access. The Northeast was another story. There, the initial beneficiary of Kansas-Nebraska
was not the Republican Party but the Know-Nothing Party.

This was an extraordinary political moment. The two-party Whig-
Democratic system was in chaos, and the West was literally up for "squatter sovereignty" grabs. In the Northeast, meanwhile, industrial change
was posing new political questions. The industrial Northeast was likely the
fastest-growing and richest economic region on earth, but that is not the
entire story.[122] Northern urbanization was also rapid. Money incomes increased, but housing, water supply, and public sanitation suffered. Life ex-
pectancy actually declined, as did height and body mass indices.[123] Further,
the onset of urban industrialization had increased income inequality.[124]
Greater investment in industrial capital goods, in shaping labor demand,
widened the gap between skilled and unskilled pay. The continued growth
of the financial system, as it always does, showered income toward the
best-off.[125] Then in 1854 a sudden industrial downturn sharpened the
bite.[126] Jacksonian equality of opportunity had not necessarily led to
equality of outcome.

After the Kansas-Nebraska Act, the constituency of the Democratic
Party—the champions of white male equality—became more southern-
based, and the Whigs dissolved. But at first, in the Northeast, the Know-
Nothings benefited. This new party mixed anti-immigration appeals with

critiques of inequality. In New York City, foreign-born, largely unskilled industrial workers outnumbered native workers two to one.[127] While the Chickerings of the world continued to ascend, the "middle class" of skilled artisanal craft workers was hollowing out, a root cause of the rise of inequality.[128] The Know-Nothings charged the Republican Party with being in the grips of radical abolitionists, who cared more about the plight of southern slaves than about the sagging standard of living, if not the "wage slavery," suffered by northern industrial workers, many of whom were in competition with unskilled immigrants. The Republicans had to craft an appealing economic message.

So they did: "Free soil, free labor, free men."[129] The hollowing-out of the skilled artisanal middle had gone far, but it was not complete. Upward mobility still existed in male employment, even among immigrants.[130] Aspirations to proprietorship, to productive capital ownership, remained strong, as Republicans championed the hopes of "free labor." Every wage earner might still someday become an owner of capital himself. Wage earning need not undermine the independence of white heads of household. Rhetorically, however, the Republicans also had to convince a sizable northern working population that the "Slave Power" was as much if not more to blame for their economic grievances.

American abolitionists had tried economic arguments before, without much success. Joshua Levitt's The Financial Power of Slavery (1841) blamed the Panic of 1837 on the slave South, which Levitt said had drained money and credit from the North. Blows failed to land. The most successful abolitionist critique was the "outrage upon the family" committed by slavery, as Harriet Beecher Stowe charged.[131] In the early 1850s, American abolitionism was in transition, politically weak, fragmenting between radical and more moderate factions.[132] In 1852 the antislavery Free Soil Party had performed miserably in national elections.

In 1854 Republicans, to appeal to many northerners frustrated with the inequities of economic change, threw in a dash of Jacksonian antimonopoly, newly directed at slaveholders' ill-gotten gains. Before, antimonopoly had targeted the "Money Power." But with free banking, and with hard money from the California Gold Rush expanding the money supply, the money question during the 1850s was eerily absent from national politics. Ingeniously, Republicans directed antimonopoly politics against the "Slave Power." New York Tribune editor Horace Greeley was the deftest Republican rhetorician, charging the "Slave Power" with seeking to close access not to incorporation but to the western territories for free soil homesteaders. Yet the West was "the great regulator of the relations of Labor and Capital, the safety valve of our industrial social engine."[133] The "Slave Power" was to blame for sagging northern economic conditions. Probably, many northern workers found it easy to blame slaveholders for causing and benefiting from inequality and poor living standards, instead of their own bosses, since many of these workers still yearned to become bosses themselves someday.

It worked. The Republicans superseded the Know-Nothings swiftly, over the course of six months in 1855 and 1856. Timing and luck broke their way. European immigration had stalled in 1855, diminishing the Know-Nothings' appeal. Recovery from the 1854 industrial downturn was quick, injecting some hope back into free labor. Then in "Bleeding Kansas," free soil and slave colonizers had illegally grabbed Shawnee Indian lands, then turned against one another. In May 1856 a group led by the radical abolitionist John Brown murdered five pro-slavery men.[134] Meanwhile a rigged pro-slavery territorial legislature sent a pro-slavery state constitution to Washington, but Congress would not ratify it. Douglas's Kansas-Nebraska Act was a bloody disaster.

In 1858 Douglas was up for reelection to the Senate, and the Republicans ran Abraham Lincoln against him.[135] Lincoln, a former Whig, who had once declared Henry Clay his "beau ideal of a statesman," had served one term as a Whig Illinois congressman in the late 1840s, though without much distinction.[136] Afterward he returned to his law practice in Springfield, Illinois. Only the political crisis sparked by the Kansas-Nebraska Act prompted him to reenter national politics.

Lincoln was unusually tall, a gangly six foot four inches, with oversize ears, gray eyes, and a high-pitched squeaky voice. In the courtroom he had honed an engaging and folksy speaking style. People who knew him well commented on his ambition. He had not been a leading early architect of the Republican Party, but he was an eloquent spokesman for free labor, saying, "Free labor has the inspiration of hope; pure slavery has no hope." He saw no fundamental conflict between "capital" and "labor," as wage laborers could someday become property-owning producers.[137] Greater access to "education," he added, was key. In 1858, Lincoln squared off against Douglas in a series of celebrated political debates in which he put forward his position on the slave question.

Lincoln had always said that slavery was morally wrong. The founders had not intended it to last. But politically Lincoln was more moderate. In states where slavery was legal, slaveholders had property rights protected by their state governments, whereas the federal Constitution was silent.[138] In the western territories, the federal government had the authority to determine whether slavery should exist. There, he said, it must act, prohibiting slavery and thus bottling up the institution in the South where, eventually, it would perish. Lincoln believed that while blacks had moral and political rights, the races should not mix socially or, worse, sexually reproduce. He followed Clay in supporting black colonization to Africa.[139]

Lincoln's attack on Senator Douglas was simple. The "Slave Power" was conspiring to open not only the West but the entire United States to slavery. Douglas was aiding and abetting it. First, the Kansas-Nebraska Act had revoked the Missouri Compromise. Then in a monument to white supremacy, Chief Justice Roger Taney and the southern-controlled Supreme Court, in *Dred Scott v. Sandford* (1857), had erased the possibility of black citizenship rights and barred the federal government from regulating slavery in any federal territory that had been acquired after the signing of the Constitution. After *Dred Scott*, slave asset prices climbed in expectation of future profits from the spread of slavery.[140] Lincoln predicted the Supreme Court would declare slavery to be legal everywhere, including the North. Slavery would become national. "A house," Lincoln declared when he had announced for the Senate, "divided against itself cannot stand." The United States could not "endure, permanently half *slave* and half *free*."[141]

Douglas responded, on good authority, why not? That was what the federal government was for—to ensure that "each locality," as he put it, having "separate and distinct interests," could have those interests acknowledged and accommodated—in part, so commerce could prosper among them. What better way to ascertain those local interests, including the question of slavery, than "popular sovereignty," which allowed "the people in each State and each Territory to decide the slavery question for themselves"? Douglas did not shy from embracing white supremacy, attacking "Mr. Lincoln's conscientious belief that the negro was made his equal, and hence is his brother."[142]

Douglas won reelection to the Senate in 1858, sweeping downstate corn-and-hog Illinois. Tellingly, however, Lincoln carried the northern counties, the city of Chicago, and the Illinois wheat belt. Nevertheless, the Lincoln-Douglas debates made Lincoln a national political figure and while he was a dark horse candidate, in 1860 he would go on to win the

Republican Party's nomination for president. He learned of his nomination while sitting in his parlor in his home in Springfield. The house, fenced off from the public street, did not have a street-facing front porch. Lincoln had removed it in an 1855 home renovation.

The electoral map for the presidential election of 1860 looked like this: Despite the "lords of the loom," antislavery New England was Republican. Despite New York City, a Democratic Party stronghold, Republicans could still carry New York State. The Republicans bought off Pennsylvania with Whig-like tariff protection, especially for its ironmongers. The internal improvement hungry Great Lakes wheat belt was solid Republican. For Lincoln to win the White House, the Republican Party had to win enough votes in downstate Ohio, Indiana, and Illinois.

Among national Republican politicians, Lincoln was unique. He was born in Kentucky to a log-cabin farmer father, who had moved the family above the Ohio River, first to Indiana, then to Illinois. For decades, violating the Northwest Ordinance of 1787, masters had brought enslaved people north of the Ohio's banks, often through the subterfuge of long-term indentured servant contracts. In 1815 a Kentucky-born slave, Mary Clark, was brought to Indiana under such an indenture by her master, and she was liberated only after an Indiana Supreme Court decision in 1821.[143] Lincoln was different because he hailed from the land between slavery and freedom.

Lincoln knew slavery, had seen it with his own eyes, and despised it morally. By the 1850s, on a later estimate, the cost of hiring a wage laborer for the four-month corn harvest was roughly equivalent to the annualized cost of an adult male black slave.[144] Should the economic incentives tip, the racial views of downstate corn farmers would not exactly prohibit them from purchasing black slaves, should government allow it. After *Dred Scott*, Lincoln commonly made dire predictions about the spread of slavery into the North. Much if not most of it was calculated political rhetoric. One suspects, however, that Lincoln genuinely did fear the possible reintroduction of black slavery in such places as downstate Illinois. Did corn farmers north of the Ohio River want slaveholders using their slaves as collateral to buy up the best lands? Could they compete with slave labor on the other side of the river—or in Kansas and Nebraska? Lincoln spooked them. Between 1858 and 1860, Republican votes in a number of downstate Illinois, Indiana, and Ohio counties increased by just enough. He would carry Illinois and Indiana by a shade over 50 percent, Ohio by 52 percent. While he won only 40 percent of the national popular vote, it was enough in the Electoral College to put him in the White House.[145]

President Lincoln was determined to end slavery's geopolitical extension across space, that dominant theme of the Age of Commerce which, as we have seen, lay at the heart of the political-economic settlement of the Empire of Liberty. Moreover his proclamation that the United States could not forever exist half slave and half free meant that the Empire of Liberty was no more. Republican secretary of state William Seward glimpsed instead "the expansion of the empire of free white men"—an empire of free soil and free labor.[146]

Slave capital was valuable precisely because it was portable. The South still had plenty of land available for cultivation, but rationally or not, southerners now hitched their economic expectations to the continued geographic spread of slavery. As a Georgia congressman put it bluntly on the House floor in 1856, "There is not a slaveholder in the House or out of it, but who knows perfectly well that, whenever slavery is confined within

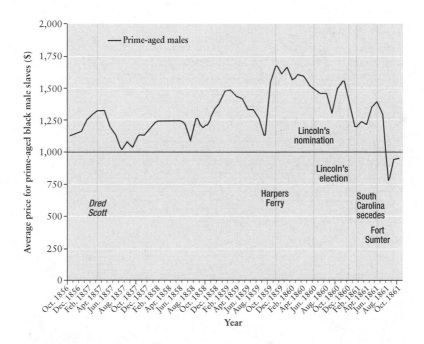

AVERAGE PRICE FOR PRIME-AGED BLACK MALE SLAVES

Black slave prices revealed white slave owners' long-term expectations of chattel slavery's future viability. Expectations radically shifted after Lincoln's triumph. Prime-aged males were aged eighteen to thirty years old.

certain specified limits its existence is doomed."[147] Lincoln agreed. No wonder that after his election, southern capital markets priced a different future expectation, and slave asset prices declined by a third.

The southern states seceded from the United States of America, and the war came.[148]

BOOK TWO

THE AGE
OF CAPITAL

1860–1932

CAPITAL

I N 1860 THE VALUE OF BLACK SLAVES EXCEEDED THE TOTAL
value of the U.S. industrial capital stock. The political destruction of
enslaved capital alone was bound to initiate a new age of American capitalism. That the most intensive period of industrial revolution in all of U.S.
history occurred in the decades after the Civil War was no coincidence.
The Age of Capital saw the emergence of an industrial capitalism.

The industrial revolution was exactly that—a revolution. In economic
history, only the permanent shift of hunting and gathering populations
into settled agriculture, the Neolithic Revolution of some 10,000 to 12,000
years ago, is of comparable significance. To many historians writing during the industrial epoch, which lasted from the 1870s through the 1970s,
a modern industrial economy appeared to be a natural state of affairs.
Their question was, what obstacles had for so long stood in the way, preventing industrialization from happening before? But industrialization
was not inevitable, nor did it play out everywhere in the same way. The
strangeness of the industrial revolution must be appreciated.

Chapter 7, "Civil War and the Reconstruction of Capital," covers the
Republican Party's creation of a new political economy in the wake of
slave abolition, which would greatly shape the future pattern of U.S. industrialization. The Jeffersonian Empire of Liberty was no more. Slavery
was abolished. The federal government asserted a more robust and uniform sovereignty, devolving relatively less rule than it had before to households, corporations, the individual states, and Indian sovereigns. Instead,
government offered inducements for private industrial development. It
granted subsidies to railroad corporations—no longer subsovereigns of

the Empire of Liberty, and more fully private, for-profit actors that, soon enough, had constitutionally protected rights as property owners. Indian lands west of the Mississippi, bought or wrested from their occupants by the federal government, were bisected by railroad corporations and possessed by white settlers. Republicans passed a tariff to protect incipient manufacturers in the Northeast. Federal legislation created a single uniform national currency and a national banking system that funneled money and credit from around the country into New York City's burgeoning capital and credit markets. Money capital and credit now concentrated on Wall Street. By contrast, in the South, former slaves fell prey to a sharecropping regime in which credit, for them, was scarce.

Not long after the war, the ruling twin dynamics of the Age of Capital appeared: a linear rise in productivity unleashed by the multiplying effects of greater industrial investment, and a repeating, speculative boom-and-bust credit cycle.

First, the industrial revolution transformed production. Capital moved into illiquid "capital goods," or intermediate means of greater production—the structures, machines, and equipment of factories. Capital goods generated gain by being used up, depreciating over time, and losing value, through labor and enterprise. The greater presence of capital goods in economic life alone justifies the name of this age. Critically, the capital goods of the industrial revolution were more energy intensive, tapping stocks of newly discovered fossil fuels, transcending the limits of the organic economy's flows of energy from the sun and from human and animal labor. Over time, productivity and growth increased exponentially. More wealth was generated, and even if more inequitably distributed, money incomes were higher. In practice, the Smithian growth during the Age of Commerce had worked by extending commercial activity across territory or space. The Age of Capital saw economic life harnessed to an additional cumulative process of prosperity, more temporal than spatial in its dynamic. In place, industrial producers began to systematically pursue gains in productivity over linear stretches of time, by investing in the new energy-intensive capital goods. In addition to the Smithian commercial multiplier, an industrial investment multiplier unlocked increasing returns to economic activity.

The era's second dynamic was the speculative cycle of boom and bust, dominated by confidence games—psychic energies, not fossil fuel energies. Its time signature was not linear. Rather, it repeated. Speculation, fueled by debt, was capable of accelerating long-term investment in the new capital goods that so transformed production. But whenever confidence collapsed, when a competitive panic broke out among the owners of capital, the cycle would reverse. Values and prices plummeted in the midst of the short-term hoarding of money and other liquid, money-like assets, offering a precautionary retreat from the hazards of investment. The multiplying effects of industrial investment diminished, and the result was not long-term growth. Industrial development decelerated. The economy slumped. In this way, the contradictory drive of speculative investment— the conflicts among speculation, investment, and hoarding—resulted in periodic booms and busts.

The arc of the Age of Capital followed the oscillations of the credit cycle over these most intensive decades of industrialization, from the late nineteenth century to the epic productive achievements of the Fordist electric assembly line during the 1910s and '20s, to the greatest capitalist bust of all time, the Great Depression. Over this age, the American inducement to invest was—by historic standards, and by comparison to other economies, even that of Great Britain, the first industrializer—unusually strong. We have no neat and tidy explanation for why this was the case. Many issues must be explored.

Chapter 8, "Industrialization," begins with Andrew Carnegie's conflicted departure from the field of Reconstruction-era financial speculation and follows his extraordinary industrial accomplishments in the manufacture of steel. It proceeds by analyzing the general characteristics of the industrial revolution, focusing on fossil fuels and the power revolution in manufacturing, then explores the geography of the northeastern-midwestern U.S. manufacturing belt—an industrial geography that would last a century. After examining the new industrial city of Chicago, the chapter pivots to the West and the industrialization of the countryside there. In this era, the United States became the world's agricultural powerhouse. The normally diminishing returns from working land over time appeared as if they might be transcended. Everywhere, capital touched more lives than commerce ever had. Land, which was long something more than capital—offering its occupants access to a noncommercial subsistence, or being the political anchor of republican citizenship—increasingly became just a capital asset. In the countryside, capital-intensive farms were sphered from, say, the pristine wilderness of national parks or the home life of families.

Chapter 9, "Class War and Home Life," covers industrial class formation. The proletarian migration of some 23.5 million eastern, central, and southern European "new immigrants" augmented the U.S. wage-earning labor force. From the Great Railroad Strike of 1877, through the Great Upheaval of 1886, to the infamous Homestead Strike of 1892 in Carnegie's steelworks, the record of U.S. industrial labor strife was extraordinarily contentious and violent. Pivoting from Adam Smith's *The Wealth of Nations* (1776), the chapter uses Karl Marx's *Capital* (1867) to explore the significance of wage labor in the new logic of industrial investment, as well as the persistence of class conflict in the industrial workplace over hours, working conditions, and wages. Founded in 1886, the American Federation of Labor's (AFL) politics of pay asserted an endemic class tension between industrial capitalists and wage earners, even as the AFL and its employer adversaries found agreement, in principle, on the need to split and protect affective, feminine home life from remunerated work of all kinds.

In this era, the Age of Commerce's political economy of property ownership gave way to a new political economy of income. Property ownership, of land and slaves, had been the anchor of U.S. political economy before the Civil War. Afterward a politics slowly emerged that politicized not so much the distribution of capital ownership as the division of the higher money incomes yielded from private investment of capital, in the midst of industrialization. The AFL adopted a politics of pay and male breadwinning. New schemes of income taxation replaced the taxation of property and foreign commerce. New ideas about regulating "rates of return" on private corporate capital investment arose. Finally, Carnegie blazed trails in philanthropy, a new practice that distributed profits through new nonprofit corporations, split from for-profit corporations, as philanthropic wealth—not as capital.

The outlines of the new political economy of income were on the scene by the 1890s, but they were hardly settled, especially in the western and southern countryside, where issues of property ownership, debt, and deflation continued to predominate. The Panic of 1893 and yet another cyclical downturn led to an agrarian political insurgency. Chapter 10, "The Populist Revolt," covers the struggles of a popular agrarian social movement in the West and the South to change the terms of the post–Civil War political economy. Populists attacked the gold standard—to which the United States had returned following the Civil War—for restricting the money and credit supply and for contributing to a grinding era of commodity price deflation. They attacked large, democratically unaccountable, and monopolistic railroad and banking corporations. Raising the Jacksonian banner of antimonopoly and equal commercial opportunity, Populists arrayed the interests of "the people" against those of industrial and financial elites. But William Jennings Bryan, at the head of the fused Populist-Democratic presidential ticket, lost the presidential election of 1896. The monetary stability of the gold standard was affirmed. After 1896 the northeastern-midwestern manufacturing belt saw the largest single moment of corporate mergers and consolidations in U.S. history. The Great Merger Movement redefined capital in corporate terms.

However, many Populist proposals lived on, feeding into the early-twentieth-century Progressive movement's attempts to expand the basis of government power to regulate the incomes yielded from corporate capital, on behalf of a reimagined public interest.

Chapter 11, "Fordism," pivots back to the industrial revolution, which was hardly over in 1913, when Henry Ford and his engineers installed the first electric-powered assembly line in the Detroit metropolitan area. The chapter covers the rise of both mass production and, in the figure of Ford, mass celebrity. Ford's River Rouge Complex—the largest factory in the world—became a fixed, monumental economic, social, and even aesthetic symbol of industrial modernity. With electric speed, Americans had entered the machine age.

In the 1920s, a great boom followed the rise of Fordism. But it, too, turned to bust during the subject of Chapter 12, "The Great Depression." The restoration of the gold standard following its suspension during World War I was followed by a moment of confident expectations in capital markets. During the 1920s the twin dynamics—the great industrial leap forward in labor productivity and the capitalist credit cycle—concentrated as never before. The industrial revolution had created significantly more wealth than trade ever had during the Age of Commerce. It led to higher, if unequally distributed, money incomes. But the cycles of boom and bust, exacerbated by policy makers' attachment to the gold standard, meant that the Age of Capital ended with the greatest bust in all history. Values plummeted, and factories, poised for mass production, idled. The Great Depression left millions of male breadwinners out of work, on the streets, and capital mired deep in a liquidity trap of precautionary hoarding from which the owners of capital could not escape. After generations of extraordinary economic vitality, their nerves were shot.

CIVIL WAR AND THE RECONSTRUCTION OF CAPITAL

═══

THE REPUBLIC THAT WAS BORN OF THE AMERICAN REVOLU-
tion ended in a colossal failure. The American Civil War (1861–65)
killed over 600,000 soldiers, maimed many more, and triggered a national
existential crisis.[1] Because of the scale of mobilization and the strategic
assaults on civilian populations, the war was arguably the world's first
"total war" and an awful portent of many industrial wars to come.[2]

The Civil War concluded with the abolition of black slavery.[3] The hor-
rible suffering meant something at least, as 4 million black Americans enjoyed a new birth of freedom.[4] Economically speaking, emancipation
destroyed $3 billion worth of enslaved property.[5] White masters could no
longer coerce black slaves to labor; they could not collateralize them in
credit markets; they could not sell black lives in appreciating capital markets. The "complete destruction" of slave property without any compensation was, as the historians Charles Beard and Mary Beard argued almost
a century ago, surely "the most stupendous act of sequestration in the
history of Anglo-Saxon Jurisprudence."[6] It made the Civil War into the
greatest turning point in the history of American capitalism, full stop.

After the war came the reconstruction of the nation but also of capital.
If not black slaves, what would be capitalized? On what terms would capital be invested in economic life?

Shaping the outcome was a new national political economy. After
southern secession and the creation of the Confederate States of America
(CSA), the Republican Party became a de facto one-party state, "the
Union." Republicans immediately pushed through legislation on behalf of

their constituencies. They provided for homesteads for white heads of household in the West. They passed an industrial tariff for the benefit of northeastern manufacturers, protecting them from cheaper British goods. The federal government lacked the economic capacity to muster the resources to wage the Civil War; instead, it drew resources from the dense northern commercial economy, and even as industrial output declined during the war, it mingled public authority and private self-interest, "patriotism and profit," into a dynamic amalgam.[7] Most dramatically, to win the war, it floated a massive public debt in international capital markets. By mixing bank and state, the Union, while defeating the slaveholders, brought to life a new class of New York City financiers, invested in and dependent on the federal government's future.[8] A new political economy settled, cutting a path for long-term economic development.

The Civil War also gave birth to a new national monetary system and credit network, based in New York. Its operations, and its operators, would determine the subsequent flow of money capital into enterprise and production. During the war the Union had resorted to using a paper currency, "greenbacks."[9] New York's financial rise requires that we give attention to the politics of "resumption," the name for the return to a metallic currency standard.

Though the on-the-ground Reconstruction of the South received far more attention, resumption could not help but determine its outcome. For resumption required fiscal austerity to secure a return to the gold standard, as the federal government, rather than spend on Reconstruction, had no choice but to hoard sufficient gold reserves to defend the prewar dollar-gold exchange rate in open markets. These steps could only drain resources from a meaningful transformation of the South. Further, given that Emancipation destroyed the asset basis of the prewar southern credit system—the enslaved—the politics of resumption implicated the economic future of the southern black freedpeople, who only continued to labor in the fields. Immediately after the war, the cotton South was starved for credit.

Northeastern financiers called for resumption and found allies in government. They wished for a metallic standard to guarantee the scarcity value of money capital and the place of New York bankers and financiers at the apex of the postwar monetary and credit system, where they would enjoy the power to direct the flow of investment. Further, postwar resumptionists hoped that by linking the dollar to gold, they could create a stable domestic investment environment and recruit fresh capital imports from Europe, especially Great Britain, the guardian of the international gold standard.

In the end, resumption, despite opposition, won out.[10] The South became trapped in an unjust and inefficient sharecropping system that blocked long-term southern economic development, even as it enabled a political reformulation of white supremacy. Meanwhile fresh capital investment flowed into the West. After all, the character of economic development in the West—would it have slavery or not?—was what the war had been fought over to begin with. Since the Empire of Liberty was no more, the federal government was far less accommodative of local rule and difference. Already during the war, as it was consigning the slaveholders to the dustbin of history, the Union Army attacked sovereign Indian nations west of the Mississippi.[11] After the war, reconstructed capital—flowing through joint-stock corporations, increasingly emancipated from public purposes—followed Union cavalry regiments into the West. Ultimately, reconstructed capital financed not black freedom but western railroads, not the overthrow of the southern planter class but the conquest of Native American lands west of the Mississippi.

Prosperity did follow. A great speculative investment boom in railroad construction led the first post–Civil War economic expansion, which kicked off in 1868. In the North, commitment to resumption led to a surge in confidence and expectations, and Wall Street transmitted capital into the fixed, illiquid investments of industrialization. But the rise of a Wall Street securities market in railroad stocks and bonds also made possible short-term liquid speculation. The Reconstruction-era political-economic settlement led immediately to an investment boom, which rode a speculative upswing in the credit cycle. It was followed by a reversal—the Panic of 1873, the first economic downturn of the Age of Capital. The hard times that followed helped bring about the final, sorry end of political Reconstruction in the South in 1877.

But make no mistake about it, in the words of a later poet, "After the Civil War, after the death of Lincoln, / That was a good time to own railroad stocks."[12] Capitalist fantasy displaced the difficult task of reckoning with the end of black slavery and realizing what Lincoln called for at Gettysburg, a new birth of freedom.

1. Union War Economy

In February 1861 Jefferson Davis became president of a republic, the Confederate States of America, dedicated to the principle that all men were not created equal. In March 1861 Abraham Lincoln was inaugurated the sixteenth president of the United States, and Republicans took nearly complete control of the thirty-seventh Congress. In April shots were fired at Fort Sumter in South Carolina, beginning a long, costly, and bloody war.[13]

The Union started the war with awesome advantages: in manpower of 2.3 to 1, in industrial production of 10 to 1, in incorporated bank capital of 4 to 1, and in the value of property of 3 to 1 (including slaves).[14] Confident, Republicans first pushed through unfinished business left over from before secession.[15]

Even before Lincoln's inauguration, Congress passed the Morrill Tariff of 1861 (named after a Vermont congressman) to fulfill a critical campaign promise, especially to Pennsylvania iron makers.[16] Republicans invoked nationalist planning, anti-British sentiment, and the Whig, neomercantilist, neo-Hamiltonian conception of a grand "harmony of interests." However, seemingly anyone who asked for tariff protection, including self-interested congressmen, received it.[17] By the standards of the Jacksonian Democracy, the Republican wartime Congress was hopelessly corrupt.

Next, the Republican Congress passed agricultural legislation. On May 20, 1862, Lincoln signed the Homestead Act into law, which offered loyal citizens and immigrants 160 acres of federal land from the public domain. After they paid a ten-dollar fee, then lived on and improved the land for five years, it would be theirs to keep. In the same year, the Morrill Act of 1862 granted public lands to create state agricultural colleges (free labor meant "education," Lincoln had said), and at Lincoln's suggestion, Congress created a Department of Agriculture. The Homestead Act fulfilled another campaign promise—"free soil"—and helped clear the way for white heads of household to settle the lands west of the Mississippi. The Homestead Act would eventually distribute 270 million acres of land. The last claim would be filed in Alaska in 1988.[18]

The final piece of economic legislation was a bill to authorize a transcontinental railroad. Government backing made the potential investment far more attractive. Congress passed two Pacific Railway Acts, in 1862 and

1864. The former created the first federally chartered corporation since the Second Bank of the United States, the Union Pacific, which built westward from Lincoln's chosen starting point of Omaha, Nebraska. Meanwhile the Central Pacific, a California-chartered corporation, approached from the west. Its backers were a band of Sacramento shopkeepers, "the associates," led by Collis P. Huntington. At first, investors did not flock to either the Central Pacific or the Union Pacific. But between the 1862 and 1864 acts, the Union Pacific acquired a federal land grant equal to the size of New Hampshire and New Jersey combined, and the Central Pacific got a grant equal to Maryland. By these and other future grants, railroad corporations would acquire 131 million acres of land. Furthermore, the Pacific Railway Acts loaned $100 million in U.S. bonds, for thirty years, to the Union Pacific and Central Pacific. The two companies returned the favor. Leading up to the 1864 act, the Union Pacific distributed $250,000 in bonds to members of government. Huntington himself traveled from California to D.C. to lobby Congress, granting undisclosed gifts to "friends of influence."[19]

Andrew Jackson might have rolled in his grave, and a transcontinental railroad would have no immediate wartime effect, but wars very often do create a productive tension between public authority and private economic initiative. A highly functional political economy of corruption helped the Union win the war. From a fighting force of 25,000 soldiers at the outbreak of conflict, the Union brought forth "the largest, best equipped, best fed and most powerful war machine ever assembled in the history of the world to that date."[20] The Union Army would peak at over 600,000 soldiers in 1863. It drew on public bakeries and public arsenals, and the Ordnance Department itself manufactured more than 60 percent of the Union's munitions. Most wartime Union expenditures, however, went to private contractors. The Quartermaster Department contracting system favored large corporations. For flour millers, meatpackers, ordnance manufacturers, and clothing makers, business was good.[21] Northern railroad corporations, critical cogs in the war infrastructure, profited handsomely. The Union had yet another prewar advantage over the Confederacy: 2 to 1 in track mileage, or 22,000 versus 9,500 miles.[22] To coordinate the flow of men and matériel, the federal government depended on private, state-chartered railroad corporations.[23]

A new kind of entrepreneur strode onto the stage. In 1861 President Lincoln appointed Thomas A. Scott, the brilliant superintendent and vice-president of the Pennsylvania Railroad, to serve as assistant secretary of war.[24] Scott worked under Secretary of War Simon Cameron, a friend of Scott's and the most corrupt government official in the Union. Scott did not even resign his post at the Penn Railroad when he went to Washington. He could set the terms, because the Union was in dire need of his expertise.

Eventually, in 1862, Lincoln banished Cameron, the "amiable scoundrel," from the War Department, and soon thereafter Scott was chased out on suspicions of corruption and returned full-time to the Penn Railroad. But he was always kept on call. In September 1863, during a critical military campaign, the War Department brought Scott back to coordinate rail movements. Different corporations owned different railroads. There was no uniform national rail network.[25] Scott traveled to Louisville, Kentucky, reporting personally to the president. While he was there, he scouted potential routes for the Penn Railroad to acquire after the war.[26] Scott's Penn Railroad would go on to make many postwar acquisitions, drawing from a Wall Street capital market transformed by the war effort.

The Civil War cost the Union $1.8 billion.[27] The U.S. funded 65 percent of expenditures by issuing public debt. Lincoln's first secretary of the Treasury was Salmon P. Chase of Ohio, the leading antislavery constitutional theorist of the Republican Party but a financial neophyte. In the fall of 1861, the Treasury Department sold a $150 million loan to a group of New York, Boston, and Philadelphia banks. The fall of 1862, however, brought a disappointing $13.6 million round of sales of federal debt. Sales abroad were insufficient. European capital and gold were in flight from the United States.[28] So Chase turned to "friends" of his from Ohio, the brothers and bankers Jay and Henry Cooke, now residing in Philadelphia, who promised to market small denominations of public debt to common citizens.[29]

In February 1862, Congress authorized the Treasury Department to issue $500 million in bonds bearing 6 percent interest, redeemable in five years, payable in twenty years; they became known as the "five-twenties." Chase named Jay Cooke as "general subscription agent" and granted him a commission of 0.5 percent on the first $10 million sold, and 0.25 percent on the rest. By January 1864, Cooke and his 2,500 subscription agents had sold all $500 million in denominations as low as fifty dollars. Chase believed Cooke was a financial patriot, but there were public outcries, and Chase had to reduce Cooke's commission.[30]

The national debt increased from $65 million to $2.7 billion and transformed the American financial system. The public bond market fueled the national accumulation of finance capital, just as Alexander Hamilton had once said it would. Bond holdings also began to nationalize a more uniform banking system. Before the war, despite the dollar's uniform metallic basis, in different localities and regions various banknotes circulated as money, trading at great discounts across distances. Cincinnati banknotes were worth less in Boston, for instance. Already by 1862, U.S. bonds deposited in New York City became the basis of a standardized system of payments among banks. Everywhere, smaller "country" banks made deposits in larger banks, successively "pyramiding" their reserves up to the largest banks in New York. Drafts on reserves held in New York became the means of payment across the North. Greater transactional liquidity assisted the integration of markets and the flows of commerce. Discounts on notes declined and converged.[31]

More changes came. Initial government purchases of war matériel had distributed gold to the public, but because of wartime uncertainty, precautionary liquidity preference—a preference for stores of value, passive stocks—increased. Much gold was privately hoarded. European gold holdings were repatriated. Due to credit expansion through bank money, there was not enough gold in the vaults to back note issues. In December 1861 the Union departed from a metallic standard. Thereafter the Treasury Department guaranteed interest payments on the public debt only in gold, and nothing else.

In February 1862, Congress passed the Legal Tender Act, which authorized the issue of an irredeemable paper currency and legal tender, called "greenbacks" because of their green ink. During the war, Congress printed $250 million in greenbacks.[32] Gold remained the currency of international transactions, while greenbacks, joining banknotes and U.S. bonds, became a currency of national commerce. Greenbacks began to trade against gold at a discount—the "gold premium"—and a gold market, formally organized as the New York Gold Exchange in October 1864, took shape. Paper money depreciated: while $1.00 in gold traded at $1.30 in paper in 1862, it traded at $2.33 in 1864. But the gold premium was volatile, depending on future expectations of the Union's military fortunes. Speculative short-sellers of greenbacks were known to whistle "Dixie" in the trading pit.[33] However, leaving the gold standard insulated the U.S. domestic supply of money and credit from international financial conditions. The issuing of greenbacks also overwhelmed the liquidity preference of precautionary hoarding due to wartime uncertainty and thereby induced greater commerce and production. The paper money, backed by nothing but government authority, announced a more robust national economic sovereignty.

The National Banking Acts of 1863 and 1864 created a new system of federally chartered banks.[34] Because the Jacksonian era of "free banking" had led to a regionally fragmented banking and payment system, coming into the war there were nearly fifteen hundred state-chartered banking corporations, issuing more than five thousand different paper notes under twenty-nine different state laws. The new national banks held federal corporate charters. As U.S. bonds replaced gold as the basis of the money supply, these banks were legally required to hold a third of their capital reserve in public debt. Against these reserves, the comptroller of the currency issued another national paper currency in the name of each bank— "national banknotes." Congress placed a prohibitive tax on state-issued banknotes, slowly chasing them out of circulation. Thus multiple monies gave way to a single national currency.

The National Banking Acts thus created an instant market for U.S. public debt. By law, confirming recent changes in banking practice, the acts required the national banks to pyramid their reserves. Small country banks held reserves in banks located in eighteen chosen cities, which in turn held their reserves in New York City banks. The effect was to concentrate money capital and credit on Wall Street. As the speculator Daniel Drew would say, "Along with ordinary happenings, we fellows in Wall Street had the fortunes of war to speculate about and that always makes great doings on a stock exchange. It's good fishing in troubled waters."[35] The Union's war fortune, and capitalist profit expectations, had become hitched.

Finally, the Union had to fund the debt. The tariff funded interest payments in gold but little of the principal. The Internal Revenue Act of 1862 (revised in 1864) introduced a system of national taxation that extracted 25 percent of Union revenues.[36] The new Bureau of Internal Revenue collected excise taxes on a long list of goods, and license taxes were placed on every occupation but the clergy. Stamp taxes extracted further revenue. Corporations paid taxes on profits. Congress passed a progressive tax on individual incomes, although it exempted most wage earners. Only 10 percent of Union households paid an income tax.[37] Taxes also soaked up greenback issues, tamping down wartime inflation. Prices did double during the war, but inflation did not run rampant. Northern civilian consumption probably did not even decline.[38]

The Union military economy could be characterized as follows. The federal government did not commandeer private economic activity but issued money and debt to further capitalize it. After a long period of northern Smithian growth—defined by a transportation revolution, the growth of banking, greater market density, and incipient industrialization—the government could draw from much private economic activity in order to assist the Union's military mobilization. The Union was happy to mingle its authority with powerful private economic interests, especially bankers and financiers. In this political economy, it might not have been clear who exactly was riding whom, but the fusion of public power and private interest called into being a productive Union war economy, even if its ultimate aim was destruction.

2. Southern Cannibalization

Confederate economic mobilization revealed important economic differences between the capitalism of the North and that of the South.[39] The CSA had no political parties, but former Democrats ran the Confederate Congress, and early government declarations promised restraints on central government. In the end, the CSA had little choice than to plunder southern economic life.

CSA war revenue alone makes for a striking contrast with that of the Union. In 1861 the Confederate Treasury successfully floated a $15 million bond issue, but further issues stalled at home and abroad.[40] As in the Union, the Confederate Congress suspended a specie standard and printed money. But it created no national, exclusive money. The $1.5 billion worth of CSA notes joined various private notes. Runaway inflation set in, as the issuing of paper money did not bring about greater economic production. The South's commercial geography was not dense, as in the North, but sparse, and it was geared toward long-distance exports. It could not be easily mobilized by simply printing more money. The notes had to somehow finance more production. As white manpower marched off to fight battles, the enslaved would not labor harder than in the past on behalf of their own continued enslavement. Thus, more money chased the same amount of goods, or even less. By 1863, prices in the Confederacy had climbed by a factor of thirteen.[41]

Taxation could have mopped up the paper notes and limited inflation. The CSA tried to tax. An April 1863 CSA tax bill looked somewhat like the Union's 1862 legislation, taxing everything except slaves. One distinctive Confederate tax was the 10 percent tax-in-kind on "wheat, corn, oats, rye, buckwheat, or rice" produced by households. The CSA could not feed its army, while in the North, midwestern foodstuffs poured into army depots. The Confederacy had no thriving internal market for foodstuffs, as southern slaveholders had practiced the cotton-and-corn system. Because of the South's large subsistence sector, it had little transportation infrastructure for foodstuffs. The CSA tried to build an internal rail network, but to little effect.[42] The southern planter class refused to switch from cotton cultivation to war production. Meanwhile southern planters had informally embargoed foreign cotton sales, hoping Britain would recognize the CSA, but that gambit failed when British cotton manufacturers tapped Indian imports.[43] The Confederate Army went hungry, while planters' bales of cotton rotted on docks due to the Union naval blockade. Then, as the tax-in-kind fell on yeoman households, massive tax resistance erupted. In 1863 mobs of women in Richmond promised "bread or blood."[44] In the South, patriotism and commercial self-interest conflicted rather than aligned, enervating rather than energizing the war effort. The South's internal market economy was simply not sufficiently developed for the CSA to induce a rapid wartime expansion.

Instead, the CSA made drastic and crippling interventions in southern economic life. A higher percentage of its war revenue came from direct "impressments" of private property. Such expropriations led southerners to withdraw from what little commerce existed, which led to even bolder acts of cannibalization. In industry, the CSA commandeered existing manufacturers, such as the Tredegar Iron Works of Richmond, Virginia, which produced almost all Confederate manufactured ordnance, even ironclad warships. The CSA erected manufacturers of its own, including gunpowder works in Selma, Alabama, and Augusta, Georgia.[45] Southern states had seceded from the United States because they feared central state power. But of necessity, central government power over the economy increased during the war. The irony was lost on no one.[46]

The CSA possessed one economic asset that the Union did not—slaves. While the immediate conduct of the war benefited northern capitalists like Tom Scott and Jay Cooke, there was not much in it for the slaveholders. Slaves were subject to state impressment, but masters did not want to give them up.[47] Slaves ran away in search of Union lines, believing what their masters told them—that the Republicans were fighting the war to end slavery.[48] Desperate, by 1864 the CSA was taxing slaves, but it was far too late. Still, the infringement on southern slave property undermined the very reason for the CSA's existence.

Superior northern economic mobilization did not translate immediately into military victory. At certain moments, the CSA might have achieved an independent peace.[49] The Union effort suffered from war fatigue, tax avoidance, draft riots, and labor strikes (price inflation burdened wage earners). Lincoln was unsure of his own reelection in 1864. Northern economic inequality continued its upward march.[50] But the Union did finally overwhelm the Confederacy, which surrendered at Appomattox on April 9, 1865, having collapsed from both without and within. The Union had destroyed slave capitalism.

3. Resumption over Reconstruction

The Civil War immediately brought about two great economic changes. Three billion dollars of enslaved capital no longer existed. For the Union, creating the military might necessary to destroy slavery had resulted in a $2.6 billion public debt.

The debt was capitalized by a new national banking system that concentrated capital and credit on Wall Street. After the war, northern economic interests focused above all on a return to a metallic standard, in order to safeguard the scarcity value of money capital. That would prevent possible inflation from eating into creditor's profits, thus ensuring past investments and encouraging new ones. Upon the Union victory, $1.00 in gold, at the prewar parity exchange rate, traded at $1.50 in paper currency. The policy of returning to par was called *resumption*. Since resumption would demand fiscal retrenchment and credit contraction, and the government's resources were limited, political will would be necessary to achieve a meaningful political and economic reconstruction of the South. In the economic reconstruction of the South, much would be up for grabs, and nothing would be more critical than control over land and labor.

On December 6, 1865, Congress ratified the Thirteenth Amendment to the Constitution abolishing slavery. By then Lincoln was dead—assassinated in April from a bullet shot by John Wilkes Booth. Andrew

Johnson, a former Tennessee Democrat and slaveholder, was the new president. Johnson's plan for Reconstruction had been to pardon most Confederates and readmit the former Confederate states to the Union after they ratified the Thirteenth Amendment.

Only a week after final ratification, however, on December 18, the leader of the Radical Republicans in the House, Thaddeus Stevens of Pennsylvania, rose to the floor. Abolition was not enough. Stevens demanded full civil and political rights for blacks, including enfranchisement. To ensure those rights, Stevens called for the confiscation of the plantations of former Confederate rebels and their subdivision into black homesteads.[51]

In the South, control over the land was crucial, inseparable from control over future black labor.[52] Land was the only capital asset the South had left—slavery was destroyed, and the region's monetary and financial system was in utter shambles. During the war, in the Union-occupied territories of the Confederacy, Yankee officers had lectured black people that they should enter wage labor contracts with landowners and marriage contracts with one another.[53] But the freedpeople wanted land: "Give us our own land and we take care of ourselves."[54] "We want homesteads."[55] In 1864, during his infamous and destructive march through South Carolina, General William Tecumseh Sherman's Field Order no. 15 had granted black families temporary titles to forty-acre plots. In 1865 President Johnson revoked them, demanding the restoration of southern lands to their former Confederate white owners.[56] Blacks howled in protest at "the man who tied me to a tree & gave me 39 lashes & who stripped and flogged my mother & my sister."[57] Meanwhile the wage labor contracts violated the Yankee free labor doctrine of "employment at will." Blacks could not quit employment in jobs governed by such contracts. Southern lawmakers passed the Black Codes, which promulgated outrageous unfreedoms. In the fall 1865 harvest, many planters failed to pay wages and instead offered workers slave rations.[58] Stevens's argument that abolition alone was not enough was looking convincing.

On the same day Stevens spoke, another Radical Republican, John B. Alley of Massachusetts, also rose to the House floor to much less future fanfare. He offered the following resolution:

> *Resolved,* That This House cordially concurs in the views of the Secretary of the Treasury in relation to the necessity of a contraction of the currency with a view to as early a resumption of specie

payments as the business interests of the country will permit; and we hereby pledge cooperative action to this end as speedily as practicable.[59]

To contract the currency would be to limit the supply of money and credit and potentially deflate values and prices.

"Free soil, free labor, free men"—the mantra that had brought the Republicans to power—had said nothing about money, banking corporations, or finance. These topics had been absent from the politics of the 1850s, when Republicans had transposed the Jacksonian critique of the "Money Power" onto the "Slave Power." But after the war, the money question came roaring back onto the national political stage.[60] It would split the Republican Party, throw the wrench of austerity into political Reconstruction, and both directly and indirectly undermine the black struggle for economic freedom.

As Congress debated the subject of black freedom, it simultaneously debated the "resumption of specie payments." Alley had asked for a congressional stamp of approval for the activities of Treasury secretary Hugh McCulloch. McCulloch was a former Indiana banker, an old Whig—decades earlier a critic of Jackson's Bank Veto. He had come to Washington in 1862 to contest Chase's proposed national bank system, then changed his mind and chartered a national bank instead. McCulloch became the first comptroller of the currency, the office in charge of issuing the new national banknotes. He became Treasury secretary in 1865, determined to retire the greenbacks from circulation and to put the dollar back on a metallic standard. He declared in an October 1865 address:

> Gold and silver are the only true measure of value. They are the necessary regulators of trade. I have myself no more doubt that these metals were prepared by the Almighty of this very purpose, than I have that iron and coal were prepared for the purposes for which they are being used. I favor a well-secured convertible paper currency—no other can to any extent be a proper substitute for coin.[61]

"Well-secured convertible paper currency" meant a metallic currency, whose quantity was not left to democratic politics to determine. It therefore secured the scarcity value of money capital while stabilizing the general price level. The discretionary expansion of bank money in excess of the hard-currency standard would remain the privilege of banking corporations, with the New York banks at the apex of the reserve and loan pyramids. All this required that the federal government retire greenbacks and deflate the value of the dollar, ultimately to repeg the currency to its prewar fixed exchange ratio to gold and silver. This was the policy of resumption.

Wall Street agreed.[62] In addition to support from the Almighty, it offered another argument in favor: Great Britain was on the gold standard. During the 1860s, the British industrial revolution had dramatically accelerated.[63] Higher money incomes, inequitably distributed, meant Britain had excess surplus capital, in the form of savings, to export.[64] The American northeastern banking and financial community hoped to seduce that capital and control where it went. To do so, the United States would have to credibly commit to resumption and to maintaining the scarcity value of capital on a consistent basis thereafter, so that foreign investments would never devalue on U.S. soil. For, as the New York Chamber of Commerce lectured Congress:

> Prudent men will not willingly embark their money . . . in ventures to *distant* markets, with gold at a premium of forty per cent., with the probability or even possibility of a fall of fifteen or twenty per cent., ere their returns can be brought to market.[65]

The war had proved that state-led, domestic credit creation—off gold— was up to the task of kick-starting greater economic production. Having been brought to life by that system, Wall Street financiers now turned against it, so as to secure their own interests and their own access to foreign capital.

In fact, the resumptionists had an entire political-economic program beyond gold. Intellectually, their leader was David A. Wells, a Pennsylvania Republican.[66] In 1865 McCulloch appointed him chairman of a special Revenue Commission. In the first of his annual reports (1866–69), Wells called for "contraction, pure and simple, without artifice or indirection."[67] To commit to an invariable metallic standard, the United States would have to devalue its currency and fiscally retrench. It must close budget deficits, signaling to investors that it would never help finance them by inflating away the value of the public debts, owned by the government's creditors.[68] Austerity would mean that wartime taxes could be rolled back, if not eliminated, also placating private investors fearful of taxation. The high tariff, while necessary to fund gold payments on the debt, could also be radically reduced. Federal revenue should be devoted to retiring greenbacks, bringing the "gold premium" closer to prewar parity, and extinguishing the U.S. public debt. Finally, the role of the South in all this would be to restore cotton production as quickly as possible, for cotton was the only real source of U.S. exports—and thus the hard, foreign exchange earnings necessary to support resumption of a specie standard. Men such as McCulloch did not like early reports that freedpeople, now possessing lands of their own, were employing safety-first strategies, as opposed to putting all acreage in cotton production.[69] In sum, the requirements of resumption must take precedence over southern Reconstruction. The argument that paying reparations to former slaves was not possible because government could not afford it has echoed over ages.

In December 1865, Congressman Alley's House resolution in favor of resumption passed. President Johnson approved, deploring the "evils of an irredeemable currency."[70] In February 1866 the Senate introduced a bill granting Treasury secretary McCulloch formal authority to contract the paper currency by retiring notes from circulation. The large majority of Republicans from the bank- and finance-rich districts of the Northeast supported the measure. But a bloc of Radical Republicans, largely from the Midwest, led by Congressman Stevens, broke ranks. Resumption had split the Radicals.[71]

The Stevens bloc of Radicals considered the greenback a symbol of national sovereignty. Surely, they believed, a genuine southern reconstruction demanded the federal fiscal resources that resumption would prohibit. The newfound "commercial freedom" of the freedpeople called for expanding currency in the cash- and credit-poor South. Congressman Benjamin F. Butler of Massachusetts, a prominent former Union general, declared:

> I propose a paper currency . . . its value based not only upon the gold in the country but upon every other source and element of the national prosperity. . . . It is the currency for a free people, strong enough to maintain every other of their institutions against the world, whose Governments they have antagonized; potent enough to sustain the measure of their business transactions with each

other independent of kings, the least, or bankers, now the most powerful sovereigns in the world.[72]

An expansion of currency and credit was necessary to sufficiently capitalize genuine black economic freedom.

Further, to the Stevens wing, greenbacks—unbacked by gold or silver—would make the domestic U.S. capital market freer from foreign dependency. Returning to gold would link the American and British money and capital markets. In 1866 a banking panic crashed London financial markets, and the Bank of England raised its interest rate in the short-term money market, which drained gold from the United States into Britain, in search of the higher yield. But because the greenback was not pegged to gold, the U.S. money market remained unstirred. The arch nationalist political economist Henry Carey boasted of American "monetary independence" from Britain. The United States "had no use for gold, and if it were needed abroad, we could say 'Why let it go!' "[73]

Finally, antiresumption Radicals represented districts of the Northeast and especially the Midwest that were poor in bank capital but were nonetheless rich with industry. During the war, inflation had boosted the profits of manufacturers. By contracting credit and spending, resumption would induce a manufacturing slump. "What we want" before resumption, said one Pennsylvania industrialist, "is *rest*, breathing time . . . to develop our resources—*dig out* our coal and *iron* and manufactured our iron into rails and machinery."[74] For similar reasons, the first national federation of industrial unions, the National Labor Union (1866), spoke out against resumption, too.[75]

Congress finally passed the Resumption Bill in March 1866, aided by northern Democratic support. President Johnson quickly signed it into law. At this point, resumption was the only matter on which the Congress and the president agreed, as weeks before Congress had overridden Johnson's veto of the Civil Rights Act of 1866. With resumption, the so-called McCulloch Contraction ensued. From 1865 through 1867, the U.S. money supply contracted and prices deflated. The "gold premium" narrowed.[76] Due to poor harvests in Europe, the prices of U.S. agricultural commodities were relatively stable, but industrial capital and industrial labor suffered the most, as prices fell. Thus the McCulloch Contraction became the economic backdrop for the opening of the political period known as Radical Reconstruction.[77]

In the congressional elections of 1866, President Johnson campaigned against Radical Republicans, at loggerheads over the South. Radical Republicans, promising to make good on the Civil War, swept the Congress, taking the reins of Reconstruction during the onset of the deflationary slump. Before ex–Confederate States could reenter the Union, the new Congress demanded passage of the Fourteenth Amendment, which enshrined the Civil Rights Act of 1866 into the Constitution. Congress divided the South into five districts of northern military occupation, and the U.S. Army oversaw state constitutional conventions, which began to sit in 1867. The South remained a chaotic and violent place.[78] Revenue Commissioner Wells estimated in 1868 that the annual cost of Reconstruction was rising to $63 million (likely a low estimate), which accounted for 25 percent of all federal expenditures, apart from debt servicing.[79] Radical Reconstruction would reach a high pitch of political drama, but due to resumption, the fiscal resources for a genuine reconstruction of the South were quite simply never made available.[80]

While the southern constitutional conventions debated, the Radical Republican Congress voted on other economic legislation. The protective industrial tariff survived the war. Rates actually increased. In 1870 the duty on finished steel rails was raised to twenty-eight dollars per ton, equivalent to the entire British selling price.[81] The tariff and continued fiscal retrenchment meant that wartime taxes could be reduced. Beginning in 1866, bills chipped away at, and finally eliminated, income taxation, as well as excise and license taxes (except on alcohol and patent medicines).[82] Postwar U.S. industrialization would occur in the context of a neomercantilist, protectionist tariff.[83] While pursuing resumption, the Republicans had taken good care of its manufacturing wing.

By 1867, however, the severe McCulloch Contraction broke the Democratic Party along regional lines. Opposed to northeastern Democrats, midwestern farmers, middling merchants, and small industrial proprietors raised the banner of Jacksonian antimonopoly against the concentration of money and credit on the East Coast. Detroit merchant Moses Field's *A Plea for Greenbacks* (1868) demanded that "the national banking act should be amended as to make it a Free banking law instead of a monopoly," which favored Wall Street.[84] Regardless of party ties, the Midwest called for more greenbacks, given the region's relative lack of note-issuing national banks. In December 1867, Congress, drawing support from disaffected Democrats and Republicans, passed a law slowing the Treasury de-

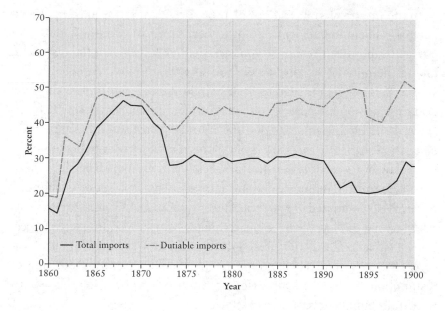

AMERICAN TRADE TARIFFS

Despite opposition from Democrats, during Reconstruction Republicans successfully maintained the high wartime tariff. The United States would industrialize under tariff protection.

partment's ability to retire the greenbacks from circulation. Privately Henry Cooke of Jay Cooke & Co. seethed, "Such men as Butler and Stevens must be put down."[85]

In 1868 the Republican nominee, General Ulysses Grant, won the presidential election. Grant was a resumptionist, and after his victory, with one-third of Democrats and three-quarters of Republicans in favor, Congress passed the Public Credit Act of 1869, which Grant signed. It pledged the federal government to pay back all U.S. public debt in gold, and promised to the world the eventual resumption of a metallic standard for the dollar at prewar parity.[86] Politically, resumption was settled.

The implications for the economic reconstruction of the South were significant. After 1866 the national McCulloch Contraction coincided with a devastating credit crunch in the South that was of decisive influence in the ongoing southern struggle over land and labor. The result was the rise of black sharecropping.

Before the war, enslaved capital had been the asset basis of the southern credit system. To capitalize a new asset class overnight, land being the obvious candidate, was not so easy.[87] In 1865 few southern banks were left standing in the war-ravaged South. Few national banknotes or greenbacks circulated. Of the 1,688 national banks incorporated between 1865 and 1868, only 20 were incorporated in the five leading cotton-growing states.[88] What emerged, quickly, was the crop lien—credit extended to planters on the promise of delivering future cotton.[89] Cotton cultivation still required labor, of course, so armed with the Black Codes, planters sought to reinstitute something like large-scale gang labor, now called "squads." But black resistance was massive.[90] In particular, black women, whether in the planters' fields, or in white homes—as cooks, washers, ironers, seamstresses, chambermaids—withdrew their labor. The old plantation household was dead, as black families demanded and won greater autonomy over their labor.[91] Meanwhile the withdrawal of black labor, in combination with bad weather, led to abysmal cotton harvests in 1865 and 1866.[92] It all contributed to planters' ongoing credit troubles.

By 1868 a regime of tenant sharecropping had rounded into shape—for freedpeople, it was better than slavery but hardly the best possible outcome.[93] With scarce cash on hand, planters began to commute black wages into crop shares. Planters divided estates into tenant plots—thirty to fifty acres—for individual black families to cultivate one year at a time. The landowner provided the tenant with seed, housing, fuel, stock, feed, and farm implements. The sharecropper, the black head of household, organized the labor. Planters had far less control over labor than they had under slavery. Sharecropping contracts listed the amount of land to be tilled for each crop, and soon enough the landowner-tenant split of the crop settled at 50-50. The final actor was the local furnishing merchant who, after first dealing with credit-strapped planters, began to deal directly with black sharecroppers. In the end neither white landowners nor black tenants got what they wanted. "Can't choose your system," one planter complained. "Have to do what negroes want. They control this matter entirely."[94]

By 1880, black landowners were tilling only 9.8 percent of southern acres under cultivation.[95] Still, compared to slavery, black economic gains were tangible. After slavery, black labor hours declined in the neighborhood of 30 percent. In 1859 slaves had consumed roughly 25 percent of the market value of the goods they produced. In 1879 black sharecroppers consumed 45 percent.[96] Accordingly, southern income inequality reduced.[97] But sharecropping was an abysmal institutional failure, and the

McCulloch Contraction did not help. Between 1865 and 1868, in the context of a national price deflation and credit contraction, the crop lien locked the southern agricultural economy into an unjust and economically inefficient credit regime.

The slave economy of the past had an economic rationality that the era of Jim Crow racism would lack.[98] Arguably, it was a more efficient capitalist economy, one that increased capital investment and labor productivity over time.[99] Sharecropping did not do that. It incentivized the immediate expansion of cotton production, to pay off debts, but not greater long-term capital investment.[100]

At the basis of sharecropping was the local, political exploitation of black families through debt. Without land, the freedpeople turned to democratic politics.[101] The Fifteenth Amendment, enshrining black suffrage rights, was ratified in 1870. In the face of white violence and property rights in the land, however, the ballot was not enough to stop the sharecropping regime from solidifying. Southern white elites did not appear to mind the lack of economic dynamism so much. Having lost political power at the federal level, white supremacy dug in at the local scale. The planter class successfully maintained its rule—racism transformed, now hampering economic development.[102] The black sharecropper Ned Cobb would later reflect on southern economic paralysis:

> Whenever the colored man prospered too fast in this country under the old rulins, they worked every figure to cut you down, cut your britches off you. So, it . . . weren't no use in climbin too fast; weren't' no use in climbin slow, neither, if they was goin to take everything you worked for when you got to high.[103]

Southern economic institutional failure would persist until the political intervention of the New Deal during the 1930s.[104] To their economic detriment, most southern blacks would remain tied to the rural plantation economy during the era of U.S. industrialization, which, unlike industrialization in any other country, would draw its pool of industrial laborers from abroad.

"Probably much more might have been done," the Freedmen's Bureau chief General Oliver Howard reflected, already in an 1869 report to Congress, "if I had been able to furnish each family with a small tract of land to till for themselves."[105] Not probably—definitely.

4. Entrepreneurial Two-Faces

In 1868 the McCulloch Contraction eased. Not for the last time in the Age of Capital, a postwar restoration of the scarcity value of capital led to a surge in investor confidence, and a speculative investment boom in the upswing of a credit cycle. (World War I and the 1920s would be next.) As it had not done before the war, the U.S. capital market pivoted westward.[106] Reconstructed capital rode the rails and eyed the West. A new generation of capitalist entrepreneurs enjoyed the fruits of Jacksonian equality of commercial opportunity as well as the overhang of wartime government largesse. They studied the levers of the new Wall Street monetary and credit system, as they took charge of giant railroad corporations that were increasingly emancipated from the public interest.

In 1868 Jay Gould was thirty-two years old. Starting from humble origins in New York's Catskill Mountains, by the time the Civil War broke out, he was living in New York City. On credit, he acquired a stake in a small railroad corporation. He was by all accounts a shy, wispy, and reserved man, but he soon enough became the greatest financial operator in U.S. history. He proved his mettle after the war when he outmaneuvered Cornelius Vanderbilt, then the richest man in America.

Commodore Vanderbilt, seventy-one when the war ended, had made his fortune in steamboats. In the fall of 1867, he was buying up stock of the New York Central, in hopes of taking control of the corporation. The New York Central was one of four national "trunk" lines connecting the Northeast to the trans-Mississippi West. Tom Scott's Pennsylvania Railroad was the largest, while the Baltimore and Ohio, and the Erie Railroad, ran alongside the New York Central for long stretches. Vanderbilt acted in secret, using proxies, since rumors, on the trading floor and over the new telegraph wires, could determine securities' prices.[107] Daniel Drew, a Wall Street speculator, happened to be treasurer of the Erie Railroad. He loaned himself Erie securities, using them as collateral for loans to purchase New York Central stock, making Vanderbilt's efforts to acquire the company more expensive. But then the two cut a deal. Now the stock prices of the New York Central and the Erie climbed in unison, benefiting both men.

Next Drew, acting with Gould and his partner James Fisk, Jr., double-crossed Vanderbilt and conducted what was called a "lock up." Using debt to acquire more corporate securities, for use as collateral to acquire more loans, they literally put all the money and credit they could get their hands on in a vault and "locked it up." Credit dried up on Wall Street, undermining stock prices, which was what they had wanted. The three shorted Erie stock in the market by borrowing shares, selling them, then hoping to buy them back at a lower price to make a profit. In January 1868 Erie stock plummeted, which harmed Vanderbilt's new position, given his deal with Fisk. The Erie War had begun.[108]

The National Bank Acts and postwar resumption made possible these complicated maneuverings. The reserves of the smallest country banks pyramided upward into New York banks, funding the liquid short-term Wall Street "call money" market, or short-term debt market for cash. Further, the pyramiding bank reserves consisted of U.S. public debt that the Treasury Department was retiring because of resumption.[109] That, even in the midst of the McCulloch Contraction, released hard currency onto Wall Street, which became the basis for the expansion of bank credit—but only on Wall Street.

Further, the new national bank system had a flaw. Bank reserves pyramided in New York City, but during the harvest, funds flowed out to the countryside to finance the movement of crops.[110] Thus speculators like Gould knew that the harvest period was the best time to attempt a "lock up," as transactional liquidity in the call money market dried up. During the Erie War, short-term borrowing rates soared from 3.5 to 17 percent.[111] Gould was the absolute master of the possibilities and vulnerabilities of the system, and he took great advantage of both.

During 1868 the Erie War competed in the headlines with news of Radical Reconstruction. Gould, Fisk, and Drew "watered" Erie stock, a dubious but not yet definitively illegal practice. They issued stock certificates in excess of the plausible value of the corporation's productive assets. (During his youth, Drew, a cattle driver, had fed salt to his cattle so they would drink more water and take on weight for the market—"watered stock.") A New York judge friendly to Vanderbilt issued an injunction against the watering. So Gould, Fisk, and Drew fled to Jersey City with millions of dollars of "locked up" bonds, stocks, and greenbacks in tow. At the same moment, many southern black sharecroppers were paying interest rates upward of 60 percent on their loans. Next, Gould decamped for Albany with a "suitcase full of greenbacks and a ready reserve of checkbooks," and lo and behold, the New York legislature passed a law undermining Vanderbilt's injunction. The final surprise was that Drew decided to crawl back to Vanderbilt and cut a deal. A general truce emerged. Vanderbilt swallowed a $1 million loss but secured control of the New York Central. Gould became president of the Erie.[112]

Drew and Fisk were rather clownish speculators, but Vanderbilt and Gould were not. They were entrepreneurial two-faces who had a hard time making up their minds about whether to speculate or invest.

There was money to be made manipulating the new national monetary and credit system, and placing short-term speculative bets on the appreciation of financial assets. Valuation in capital markets is prospective, a matter of expectations.[113] The game (and it was a game) was to competitively manipulate expectations and information, using credit and proxies to bid stock and bond prices up and down. It helped to buy off the occasional state legislator.

At the same time, a railroad was a going, long-term business concern, and both Vanderbilt and Gould were able chief executives. These men knew how to profit from taking a risk, parting with liquidity, and investing money capital in durable assets on the ground in the form of railroad tracks, steam engines, and railcars. At that point, the only way to make a business profit was to increase operating revenues over costs. In addition to the arts of financial speculation, the post–Civil War railroad corporations invented many of the methods of modern managerial bureaucracy, including accounting techniques, organizational hierarchies, and controlled technological innovation.[114]

Thus, the speculative credit cycle did induce long-term investment in wealth-generating enterprise and production. Combined railroad capitalization soared to $2.5 billion by 1870.[115] Vanderbilt's New York Central was the first railroad to complete a through line from New York to Chicago, in 1870. Between 1868 and 1873, railroad corporations constructed 24,589 miles of new rail, more than half in the trans-Mississippi West and the Far West.[116] In Smithian fashion, the railroads increased the extent of markets and the demand for goods across an expanding continental marketplace.[117]

However, the great railroad entrepreneurs always remained undecided, if not conflicted, about where to deploy their time, energy, and capital—whether in short-term speculation or in long-term durable investment.

Why go through the time, hassle, and uncertainty of actually building a railroad and running it on a profitable basis when credit was readily available (for these men at least)? If the right rumor gripped the trading floor, they could turn a fast buck through leveraged speculation on a financial asset, without ever having to part with liquidity, and put capital on the ground where it became a fixed, running cost. Long-term, high-grade railroad bond rates settled in the low 6 percent region after the war.[118] That was the hurdle for profit making from enterprise. Why do that, and of necessity divert resources to pay workers, when one could make profits from short-term financial speculations without paying anyone? Economic inequality increased in this era much because many of the owners of reconstructed capital sometimes could not find good answers to these questions. They manipulated finance to enrich themselves.[119]

Gould was a master at manipulating future expectations for his immediate personal benefit. He also bought up real estate on his own account, then sold it to the Erie Railroad, lining his own pockets through self-dealing. Infamously, in 1869 Gould attempted a failed corner of the gold market.[120] The business-friendly *Financier* branded Gould "the most accomplished of all modern criminals." Newspaperman Joseph Pulitzer called him "one of the most sinister figures that have ever flitted bat-like across the vision of the American people."[121] Nicknamed "the Spider," in visual culture Gould was commonly animalized, rendered something less (or more) than human. Or he was figured as a Jew. The great cartoonists and political satirists Joseph Keppler and Thomas Nast returned to Gould time and again.[122]

Henry Adams, the grandson of John Quincy Adams, contributed a scathing essay on Gould in a book published with his brother, Charles Francis Adams, Jr., called *Chapters of Erie* (1871). The brothers put their fingers on the main point. The issue was not private greed—unchecked commercial self-interest, after all, had been a moral problem time out of mind. Rather, corporations and the legal privileges that state legislatures bestowed on them in their charters were becoming vehicles of private acquisitiveness at a scale hitherto unimaginable. The Adams brothers wrote of Vanderbilt:

> [He] has combined the natural power of the individual with the factitious power of the corporation. The famous "L'etat, c'est moi" of Louis XIV represents Vanderbilt's position in regard to his railroads. Unconsciously he has introduced Caesarism into corporate life. He has, however, but pointed out the way which others will tread. . . . Vanderbilt is but the precursor of a class of men who will wield within the state a power created by the State, but too great for its control.

THOMAS NAST,
*JAY GOULD'S PRIVATE
BOWLING ALLEY* (1882)

German-born Nast was
arguably the greatest
American political cartoon-
ist. Of Nast's great Gilded
Age works, these are among
the crudest. Gould, nick-
named "the Spider" by the
press, was often illustrated
like this—in animalized
form, or as a Jew.

THOMAS NAST,
JUSTICE IN THE WEB
(1885)

"Already," they continued, in the era of slave emancipation, "our great corporations are fast emancipating themselves from the state, or rather subjecting the State to their own control."[123] Charles Adams first called Vanderbilt and Gould "robber barons" after the medieval warlords who charged extortive tolls on safe river passage.[124]

Gould was a man with little political ideology to speak of. By contrast, the elder Vanderbilt, during the 1830s and '40s, had been the representative Jacksonian businessman who believed in competition, open access, and antimonopoly.[125] The Democracy had called for an end to corrupt "special privilege," but something had gone wrong. Economically, given the reality of increasing returns to economic scale in railroading, the risk that first movers would capture a monopolistic share of the market loomed. Now powerful men, who competed over the buying of judges and legislators, were cynically manipulating the Jacksonian cry for equality of commercial opportunity to acquire such advantages politically, too.[126] Beyond the Erie War, in the construction of the Lincoln-mandated transcontinental railroads, the directors of the Union Pacific and the Central Pacific corrupted a host of legislators while chartering dummy construction corporations—Union Pacific's Crédit Mobilier being the most infamous—through which to enrich themselves by self-dealing.[127]

At the time, government was not passing regulations to prohibit this behavior. Rather, in addition to offering subsidies, it was creating protections for private economic actors. Another aging old Jacksonian Democrat was Stephen J. Field. Lincoln appointed this Unionist Democrat to the Supreme Court in 1863, and Field earnestly proceeded to carry out, in the words of one historian, a "crusade to fix a precise boundary between private rights and legitimate governmental interventions."[128] Government and market must be kept in their proper spheres, and even if there was scope for proper government regulation, the sphere of private economic rights was considerable. Under Field's influence, the Supreme Court would interpret the postwar Fourteenth Amendment to protect "freedom of contract," an expansive realm of private economic initiative, regulated by the state but distinct from it.[129]

The Supreme Court went further. A series of Supreme Court decisions that culminated in the *Civil Rights Cases* (1883) denied citizenship rights in practice to the emancipated blacks for whom the post–Civil War constitutional amendments were intended. The Court also withheld rights from women in *Bradwell v. Illinois* (1873), ruling that women had no right to practice a business profession. Meanwhile inspired by Field, *Santa Clara v. Southern Pacific Railroad Company* (1886) granted Fourteenth Amendment protections to corporate property. Another former Jacksonian, Michigan Supreme Court justice Thomas Cooley, author of a landmark 1868 constitutional treatise, clearly stated in 1870 that a railroad corporation consisted of nothing more than "exclusively private property, owned, controlled and operated by a private corporation for the benefit of its members."[130] The federal government would not enforce black civil rights. It would also not allow the states to infringe upon the property rights of corporations.

Originally, Jacksonian sphering had been about protecting commercial opportunity from government-sanctioned monopoly—even if it also meant stripping corporations of their duties to the public. After all, private corporations could still be regulated. At the opening of the Age of Capital, wittingly or not, Field and other jurists created rights protections for private economic actors, including corporations, that were so robust that the new risk was not that the state would deny equal access to commercial opportunity, but that private concentrated power might run roughshod over democratic government. Ringing the alarm, two American novels published at the time are especially worthy of mention, Henry Adams's *Democracy: An American Novel* (1880) and Mark Twain and Charles Dudley Warner's *The Gilded Age: A Tale of Today* (1873), which first named the age.

The Civil War had witnessed the massive buildup of central state capacity. Afterward, however, financiers had turned on the state and sought to shrink it through austerity, on the road to resumption, while the impulse of Jacksonian sphering returned. Once again, as in the antebellum era, there would be no national plan for building public transportation infrastructure—this time railroads, instead of turnpikes and canals. Better than *Democracy* or *The Gilded Age* was the Englishman Anthony Trollope's *The Way We Live Now* (1875), a novelization of fraudulent speculative British investment in North American railroads. Trollope was right to suggest in his novel that London drawing room intrigues and dinner party snubs could determine where roads were built in the United States. In fact, everywhere countless lines were duplicated; one railroad promoter admitted that this "needless paralleling of existing systems" was "unnecessary and uncalled for" by "public necessity."[131]

The nature of public interest would require some reimagination, and major political battles over the scope of private corporate power loomed in the future.[132] But first, during the post–Civil War boom, there would be still more railroad construction. A series of Granger railroads, funded by Boston and New York financial interests that were often the agents of European investors, spread out westward from Chicago, crossing the Missouri River in the late 1860s. In 1870 the first railroad reached Omaha, Nebraska, the Lincoln-mandated terminus of the Union Pacific.

The transcontinentals were built through lands that were occupied by, and often outright belonged to, indigenous nations. At the close of the Civil War, the U.S. government did not control the Great Plains, the territory west of the Missouri River, where approximately 65,000 Indians remained capable of violently resisting U.S. conquest.[133] As former Union general William Tecumseh Sherman, now commander of the U.S. Army, would reflect, "the *railroad* which used to follow in the rear now goes forward with the picket-line in the great battle of civilization with barbarism."[134] In 1867 Congress formed a peace commission to negotiate treaties with Plains Indians. More than a decade before, in 1851, the Treaty of Fort Laramie had acknowledged the sovereign possessions of the Great Plains tribes, while granting the United States the right to establish roads and build military forts. At an 1867 council in Medicine Lodge Creek, in Kansas, some members of Southern Plains peoples—Comanche, Kiowa, Apache, and southern Cheyenne and Arapaho—ceded tribal lands to the federal government. In 1868, at another council at Fort Laramie, some Crow, Lakota, northern Cheyenne, and Arapaho ceded their lands, too. These Native American peoples would thereafter live on government-policed reservations. The United States declared war against Indians who would not remove themselves to the reservations. This was called the "peace policy."[135]

U.S. colonial warfare had an economic dimension. Congress, committed to austerity on behalf of resumption, slashed the "peacetime" U.S. Army below fifty thousand troops. What was left of the army actively assaulted the economic basis of Indian political and military power. While southern white supremacists committed outrageous atrocities against black citizens, the army followed railroad corporations west into the Missouri Valley. In the winter of 1868, the army conducted devastating raids against Indian winter camps, while the Union Pacific and its southern branch, the Kansas Pacific, bisected the buffalo herds, cutting Plains Indians off from their food supplies. By the spring of 1869, the Plains Indians were economically ravaged and organized resistance was broken. Under the postwar Fourteenth Amendment, Indians were not citizens, and so—unlike the owners of railroad capital—they enjoyed no constitutional protections of their property. Indian nations had participated in the Age of

Commerce, forging trade ties with whites.[136] In the Age of Capital, Indian economic lives were devastatingly devalued and ultimately destroyed.

On May 10, 1869, at Ogden, Utah, Leland Stanford drove in the "golden spike" (technically it was iron) that connected the Central Pacific with the Union Pacific. In 1868 the insider Contract and Finance Company of Stanford and the "associates" billed the Central Pacific over $16 million for construction costs. They earned a profit of $10 million from Central Pacific construction.[137] The profits of the Crédit Mobilier were as high as $16 million. While the Union Pacific corporation was bloated with debt and had not yet made an operating business profit, nonetheless, through financial maneuverings and appreciation of the company stock, the original promoters of the corporation earned profits on their original investments in the company somewhere between 480 and 610 percent.[138]

Tom Scott of the Pennsylvania Railroad did not want to miss out, and he had the most audacious transcontinental dream of them all: he would build the first southern trunk line, connecting the Penn Railroad's Baltimore depot to New Orleans. From there, he would construct a road across Texas, then continue onward to southern California and the Pacific Ocean. It would be a true transcontinental through line from Atlantic to Pacific.[139]

Between 1868 and 1873, a railroad construction boom in the South accounted for 16 percent of national miles constructed.[140] Southern state legislatures, dominated by Republicans under Reconstruction, doled out land grants and state-subsidized bonds or sold state-controlled lines to private corporations at a discount. Scott's trunk line and associated spurs sliced through the southern piedmont, agricultural regions that before the war had been largely subsistence-oriented. Upcountry roads, even when northern owned, spread cotton cultivation, crop liens, and debt peonage with them. Cotton cultivation expanded by acreage if not by rate of productivity.[141] In 1870–71 the Ku Klux Klan, believing that the Pennsylvania Railroad brought with it Yankee influence, committed brazen assaults along some of Tom Scott's proxy lines. President Grant signed a law (his interior secretary was a friend of Scott), and the federal government intervened to put down the worst violence.

5. End of Reconstruction

After the Civil War, the sovereignty of the U.S. nation-state, within its expanding jurisdiction, was more uniform and robust. Yet the policy of resumption, and the desire to go back to a metallic standard, diminished national sovereignty, for resumption opened the U.S. financial system to the vicissitudes of international money capital. An Atlantic financial panic in 1873—the result of the interactions between a credit crunch in Europe and the vulnerable postwar Wall Street financial system—put an end to the post-1868 U.S. railroad boom. The economic slump that followed contributed to the end of political Reconstruction in the South.

The policy of resumption had harnessed the U.S. economy to the international gold standard and thus to the fortunes of international economic events. In 1873 gold began to drain from the United States to Britain. After the crash of the stock exchange in Vienna, shaky credit conditions in Europe led to a competitive panic among the owners of capital to hold safe, liquid assets.[142] As everyone sought to get their hands on gold, the Bank of England saw the British banking system's gold reserves dwindle. In response, it raised its short-term bank interest rate from 4 to 9 percent. Seeking the higher yield and fearful of a general panic, gold deposits swung into British banks from everywhere, including from the United States. Credit began to contract on Wall Street.[143]

Domestic conditions contributed to the credit crunch. In the summer of 1873, money and credit further tightened in the United States due to the annual harvest season. An additional problem was that, to fund their operations, U.S. railroad corporations had grown dependent on the short-term call money market to help roll over their prodigious debts. U.S. railroad corporate debt had climbed from $416 million in 1867 to $2.2 billon in 1870.[144] By 1873, interest rate yields on fresh railroad bonds remained at 6 percent. Yet rates in the short-term call money market soared from 3.8 percent to 61.23 percent.[145] Given those rates, another option for repayment was to generate earnings—business profit. But while corporations constructed thousands of miles of road, their business model was a confidence game. Postwar corporations built first and hoped for profits later.[146] Another debt repayment option was to take out more debt. If credit markets tightened, however, or even if there were rumors that they might, the entire house of cards could collapse.

The U.S. Panic of 1873 began with the failure of the Northern Pacific Railroad, which Congress had incorporated in 1864. In 1867 Congress bestowed on the corporation a land grant spanning Minnesota to the Pacific Ocean. But the road lacked the financial subsidies given to the Union Pacific. The Philadelphia banker Jay Cooke had made a fortune selling U.S.

debt, but given austerity, on the path to resumption, he needed new business. In 1870 he began to sell Northern Pacific bonds on commission. But the Northern Pacific did not make enough business profits carrying freight to meet its debt obligations. After general credit conditions tightened during the summer, Jay Cooke & Co. failed on September 18, 1873. The Northern Pacific declared bankruptcy.[147]

The failure of Jay Cooke & Co. set off a financial panic. Loans in the call money market hit 360 percent.[148] Depositors rushed to remove their deposits from New York banks, for fear that, caught out, they might fail as well. Creditors called in their loans. European investors, who had no less than £82.7 million invested in U.S. railroad securities in January 1873, repatriated their capital.[149] Confidence collapsed. Precautionary hoarding broke out. The collapse of credit and prices depressed spending and commercial activity. Railroad stocks lost 60 percent of their value. Half of all U.S. railroad corporations tumbled into bankruptcy.

Sensing an opportunity, Jay Gould swept in and took control of the tottering Union Pacific.[150] Not only had resumption channeled credit to Wall Street, at the expense of other regions (and people); the restoration of the scarcity value of money capital had led to a surge in expectations among

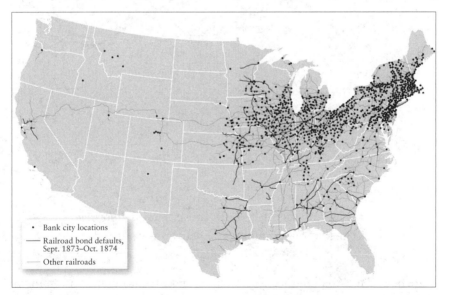

FINANCE AND THE AMERICAN RAILROAD NETWORK, 1873–74
The post–Civil War railroad construction boom followed the movement of
reconstructed finance capital—and vice versa—until the Panic of 1873
brought widespread bankruptcy.

the owners of capital, and thus to speculative lending, but at the high interest rates necessary to achieve resumption. Easy money, at high rates, often results in a particularly bad slump when the credit cycle reverses.

Americans had experienced the repeating credit cycle before, but the economic slump that followed the Panic of 1873 exhibited new characteristics specific to the burgeoning era of industrial capitalism. Industrial capital is fixed, sunk on the ground, and hence illiquid. Even as potential spenders hoard money, and demand for goods collapses, industrial capitalists may keep the machines running to recoup something of their prior investments. Goods still flood the market, and prices fall further.[151] The economic slump that followed the Panic of 1873 was not a slump in economic output.[152] Rather, it took the form of a grinding price deflation across the Atlantic. The "great depression" of prices, it was called.

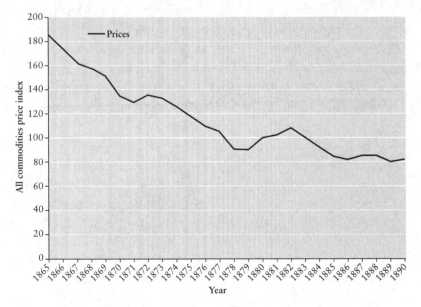

AMERICAN PRICE DEFLATION
In the late nineteenth century, the term *great depression*
referred to the era's grinding price deflation—initiated in the
United States by the policy of resumption.

In power in Washington, Republicans did little to help. The mantra "free soil, free labor, free men" provided little guidance for various emerging industrial predicaments: price deflation, poverty and inequality amid greater wealth generation, labor strikes.[153] Eight years after Lincoln's assassination, the "Slave Power" was no longer to blame. The Republican

Party fell back on the logic of resumption and called for greater government austerity—which together made the deflation even worse. "Confidence," President Grant's assistant Treasury secretary proclaimed, "was to be entirely restored only by the slow cautious process of gaining better knowledge of true values," and "by conducting business on a firmer basis, with less inflation and more regard to real soundness and intrinsic values."[154] More deflation was the solution to deflation, and more bankruptcy was the solution to bankruptcy—cries that would echo throughout the Age of Capital, through the Great Depression of the 1930s. During the 1870s, the U.S. Treasury did release $26 million in greenbacks, up to the legal limit. Beyond that, imminent resumption took priority.

In the 1874 midterm congressional elections, the Democrats pummeled the Republicans and for the first time since the Civil War took control of the House. The lame-duck Radical Republican Congress passed the Civil Rights Bill of 1875, which the U.S. Supreme Court would later annul in the *Civil Rights Cases* (1883). More troops were now stationed in the West to coerce Indians onto reservations than in the South to enforce black civil and political rights. In the fall of 1877, General Oliver Howard, once head of the Freedmen's Bureau, chased down a band of Nez Perce Indians, long a U.S. ally, forty miles from the Canadian border, concluding the "last Indian war."[155] The Great Plains were flung open to white capitalist development.

Far more immediately significant than the Civil Rights Bill of 1875 was the lame-duck Republican Congress's Resumption Act of 1875. In the midst of the economic slump, it announced the federal government's intention to return the dollar to a metallic standard at prewar parity, by January 1, 1879. In essence, the bill called for more price deflation, as the Treasury Department would have to hoard an adequate gold reserve to defend the peg by that date. Finally, in a parting shot, the outgoing Republican Congress raised rates on the protectionist industrial tariff.

Both candidates in the presidential election of 1876, the New York Democrat Samuel J. Tilden and the Ohio Republican Rutherford B. Hayes, were resumptionists. Tilden won the popular vote, but the balance in the Electoral College hinged on disputed returns in southern states. There was fear of a return to sectional violence.[156] Who stepped in to attempt to broker a compromise? Tom Scott.[157] The essence of the Scott plan was southern acceptance of Republican victory, in return for the full white "redemption" of the South, and federal subsidies for Scott's bankrupt southern transcontinental, the Texas & Pacific.[158]

Scott could not convince Republicans to promise Texas & Pacific subsidies in a Hayes presidency. More than future economic prosperity of any kind, let alone a northeastern- and European-owned railroad, southern congressional politicians were now invested, above all, in the restoration of local rule in pursuit of the maintenance of white supremacy.[159] Republicans acquiesced. In the Compromise of 1877, Hayes became president. U.S. troops left South Carolina, Louisiana, and Florida, and the military occupation of the South was formally over. Reconstruction was finished. In late 1877, while the debate over the presidential election still raged, the House actually passed a law to repeal the Resumption Act of 1875. The Senate defeated it by one vote. On January 1, 1879, the United States returned the dollar to the prewar specie standard.[160]

Of course, a lot had changed since the last time the dollar was pegged to gold and silver. Enslaved capital had been destroyed. Four million emancipated black Americans enjoyed a newfound freedom, but, as southern sharecropping continued the white exploitation of black labor, the monetary and financial system that arose during the war and its aftermath benefited Wall Street and the owners of private joint-stock corporations increasingly emancipated from public duties. During the war, the dynamic amalgam of wartime "patriotism and profit" had propelled economic activity. After the war, the contradictory drive of speculative investment energized economic life, as short-term speculation induced long-term investment in enterprise, before the reversal of the credit cycle led to another financial panic, precautionary hoarding, and a general economic slump. Meanwhile one response to the national trauma of the Civil War was a cynicism in political economy, in which the patriotism dropped out but the profit seeking remained. The neomercantilist, neo-Hamiltonian, and Jacksonian inheritances all acquired bad names.

In March 1879 prices finally began to rise, and the slump lifted. Confidence returned, and industrialization accelerated.[161]

CHAPTER 8

INDUSTRIALIZATION

GRANT'S ARMY WAS MARCHING ON RICHMOND IN 1865 when Andrew Carnegie, age twenty-nine, quit his job at the Pennsylvania Railroad Company. The corporation's president, J. Edgar Thomson, begged him to stay, promising a big promotion. But Carnegie left, "determined to make a fortune."[1]

Carnegie was born in Scotland to a handloom weaver father who had been displaced by the steam-powered looms of Britain's industrial revolution.[2] The family migrated to western Pennsylvania in 1848, near Pittsburgh. Teenage Carnegie did not attend school. In 1853 Tom Scott hired him as a telegraph operator, and by age twenty, Carnegie had become Scott's personal assistant.

Scott taught Carnegie everything he knew. The Penn Railroad deployed prodigious amounts of productive fixed capital, in rails, cars, and locomotives. Due to the running costs of using up that capital, the railroad had to run its cars as fast and as full as possible. To do so, the corporation became the first great modern managerial enterprise, probably the most efficient business bureaucracy in the world at that time.[3] Scott schooled Carnegie in the logic of industrial capital. Operating cost determined selling price. Profit in the face of fixed and running costs demanded high operating volume and velocity so as to achieve dynamic economies of scale.

But profiting from long-term investment in wealth-generating enterprise takes time, and Tom Scott could not always wait. Scott, an entrepreneurial two-face, also taught Carnegie the art of short-term speculation in liquid capital markets, as well as the art of corporate self-dealing. In 1856 Scott loaned Carnegie $600 to buy stock in the Adams Express Company, a freight handler for the Penn Railroad. The railroad sent Adams Express freight business, and soon enough the stock soared. From the rapid appreciation of the financial asset, Carnegie later received his first $10 dividend check. He recalled in his *Autobiography:*

> I shall remember that check as long as I live. . . . It gave me the first penny of revenue from capital—something that I had not worked for with the sweat of my brow. "Eureka!," I cried, "Here's the goose that lays the golden eggs."[4]

Money, Aristotle wrote long ago, was by nature sterile. As it could produce nothing itself, it was unnatural for it to breed.[5] But Carnegie had stumbled on a golden egg—the kind that tended to fall into the laps of the friends of Tom Scott. Soon enough, Carnegie's income from his speculations far outstripped his salary at the Penn Railroad.

Carnegie quit the railroad, announcing, "I'm rich. I'm rich."[6] A full-time speculator, he left Pittsburgh to take up a suite in a New York hotel with his mother. He traveled to Europe to recruit investments. "Big Business, Andy," Scott complimented him.[7] Back home, Carnegie, Scott, and Thomson maneuvered themselves onto the board of the Union Pacific. Scott yearned for the presidency, but much to Scott's dismay, Carnegie dumped his stock for a large profit. It was 1868, and Carnegie, at thirty-three, was weighed down by a guilty conscience. "Man must have an idol," he wrote to himself. But "the amassing of wealth is one of the worst species of idolatry. No idol more debasing than the worship of money."[8] Conflicted, he ceased his financial speculations.

What caused the change of heart? "In all of his speculative ventures," writes one Carnegie biographer, "he had felt like a parasite, a barnacle carried forward on the flank of the Scott-Thomson ship of fortune."[9] "I wished to make something tangible," Carnegie remembered. Perhaps recalling his father's labors, Carnegie also would say, "I had lived long enough in Pittsburgh to acquire the manufacturing, as distinguished from the speculative, spirit."[10] So Carnegie returned to Pittsburgh, determined to enter the business of steelmaking. U.S. railroad corporations were turning from iron to the more durable metal of steel—not only for rails but also for locomotives, cars, couplers, brakes, and wheels.[11] There was no question about the presence of demand for such goods.

Still, why do it? Why go through the effort and expense of fixing capital on the ground—erecting a steelworks, organizing production, hiring workers, manufacturing a product, and seeking a final market for steel, in hopes that the final sale price would ultimately exceed the cost of production—when one could, as Carnegie had, speculatively wheel-and-deal from a luxurious suite at the Windsor Hotel on New York's Fifth Avenue? Tom Scott had always played both games. Why abandon confidence games completely and drive only for industrial production?

Industrialization did not just happen. Carnegie's turn to manufacturing was contingent. By his own reckoning, he had a bad conscience and a guilt-ridden longing to produce something. It was also true that money could be made manufacturing steel. But that is only true in hindsight. Carnegie's project was only prospective at the time. He had to take a leap and he did.

First, in 1872, Carnegie formed a partnership, bringing in Thomson and Scott. During the Panic of 1873, Scott got in trouble at the Texas & Pacific Railway. The corporation's nervous creditors were calling in their loans. Scott summoned Carnegie to Philadelphia and practically begged his former protégé to endorse Texas & Pacific's notes. "You of all others should lend your helping hand," Thomson implored. Carnegie called it "one of the most trying moments in my life."[12] Nonetheless, he would not carry his old mentor. Feeling betrayed, Scott and Thomson made Carnegie buy them out of their investments in his steel manufacture. To raise capital, Carnegie set sail to London and sold bonds to the expatriate U.S. banker Junius S. Morgan.

By 1874, his falling-out with Thomson notwithstanding, Carnegie had named his first factory the Edgar Thomson Steelworks. The site was twelve miles south of Pittsburgh, a city with great industrial potential. Three rivers as well as two railroad trunk lines—the Penn Railroad and the Baltimore & Ohio—ran through it. Nearby lay abundant bituminous coal and coke, necessary energy inputs for the smelting of steel.

The Edgar Thomson Steelworks cost $1.25 million to build, an extraordinary fixed investment. Carnegie proceeded to apply to steelmaking the managerial principles he had learned at the Penn Railroad. "Big trains, loaded full, and running fast," became big factories, running at full capacity, and operating fast. Quickly, Carnegie realized that no one in steelmaking was calculating production costs:

I was greatly surprised to find that the cost of each of the various processes was unknown. Inquires made of the leading manufacturers of Pittsburgh proved this. It was a lump business, and until stock was taken and the books balanced at the end of the year, the manufacturers were in total ignorance of results. I heard of men who thought their business at the end of the year would show a loss and had found a profit, and *vice versa*.[13]

Carnegie stumbled upon a common issue in the Age of Capital. For centuries, in commerce, the goal had been to buy low and sell high, given competitive market prices. Early manufacturers knew the cost of their raw materials, or of labor, because market prices for them were available. But the larger the industrial enterprise, and the greater the fixed investment, the more difficult it became to tabulate the costs of manufacturing—using up capital by running a furnace, or moving around materials—because there were no markets, internal to a firm, to price these activities. The Pennsylvania Railroad, among other railroads, had led the way in developing new methods to account for such operating costs that could not be priced by markets. What was called the "operating ratio" among railroad accountants measured revenues in excess of production costs—per unit of output, over time.[14]

Ruthlessly, Carnegie applied product cost accounting to steelmaking. He once told his men:

Show me your cost sheets. It is more interesting to know how cheaply and how well you have done this thing than how much money you have made, because the one is a temporary result, due possibly to special conditions of trade, but the other means a permanency that will go on with the works as long as they last.[15]

"Carnegie never wanted to know the profits," his own protégé, Charles M. Schwab, recalled. "He always wanted to know the cost."[16] William P. Shinn, a talented former railroad executive and cost accountant, became Carnegie's chief of operations and introduced novel accounting practices in the bookkeeping department. He attached vouchers to goods and materials as they moved through the production process. The company calculated price-cost ratios in standardized units of time. "There goes that damn book-keeper. If I use a dozen bricks more than I did last month, he knows it and comes round to ask why!" one steelworker was reported to have said. Carnegie's plan was to "scoop the market," or to always undersell his nearest competitor. "Cut the prices; scoop the market; run the mills full."[17]

Carnegie also engaged in what economists call "capital deepening." More than increasing the division of labor, he put more productive capital in the hands of the same worker. That increased labor productivity over time. Whenever capital equipment became available, capable of producing more product at less unit cost, he invested in it—sometimes scrapping perfectly good existing structures and equipment. Like a seventeenth-century Barbados slave owner who worked his slaves to death, replenishing them from the African slave trade, Carnegie engaged in "hard driving," or running his steelworks into the ground at full capacity—unlike British steelmakers, whom Carnegie accused of coddling their factories. Bill Jones, a former machinist and Union Civil War captain, ran operations on the shop floor and became renowned for his expertise in production. Symbolically, Carnegie paid him the same salary as the president of the United States. He developed the "Jones mixer," a giant chest that received 250 tons of liquid iron directly from the blast furnace (eliminating the pig iron phase), holding it until ready for pouring into the Bessemer converter, named after Englishman Henry Bessemer—a giant vat into which the molten iron was poured at high temperatures where, oxidized further to remove impurities, iron became steel. Jones also developed a method of pouring steel directly into ingot molds that sat on moving flatcars, a premonition of mechanized assembly-line production, which would be, in Henry Ford's automobile factories, the productive culmination of the Age of Capital.

Meanwhile Carnegie increased the scale of his operations. "Cheapness is in proportion to the scale of production," he said. "To make ten tons of steel a day would cost many time[s] as much per ton as to make one hundred tons. Thus the larger the scale of operation the cheaper the product."[18] Larger scale demanded greater bureaucratic coordination from start to finish and the "vertical integration" of production. Carnegie himself could help sell the final product in final markets. "Sidney Dillon, of the Union Pacific, was a personal friend of mine. [Collis] Huntington [of the Central Pacific] was a friend. . . . Those and other men were presidents of railroads."[19] Pecuniary profits were continuously plowed back into the enterprise as reinvestments into fresh productive capital, and soon Carnegie was independent from bankers and external financiers, as well as from grumbling partners. Carnegie was still determined to make a fortune. But perhaps even more, he was now driven, obsessively so, to manufacture more steel at less cost.

The results were fantastical. In 1875 the Edgar Thomson works produced 21,674 tons of steel. In 1889 the same facility produced 536,838 tons. The production cost of steel rails plummeted from $58 to $25 per ton. Dramatic improvements in quality were attained as well. The average life of a rail increased from two to ten years. The bearing weight of a railcar leaped from 8 to 70 tons. Indeed, the profits took care of themselves. In its first month of operations, the Thomson works turned a profit of $11,000— a figure Carnegie believed was unprecedented in the history of U.S. manufacturing. In 1888 the annual profits of the Carnegie Steel Company were $2 million. In 1890, they reached $5.4 million.[20] In manufacturing nothing like this had ever happened in the history of the world.

Everything had clicked. The Civil War transformation of U.S. capital markets had made possible his early speculative fortune and initial start-up fund. Carnegie developed the entrepreneurial psyche of a committed industrialist. National demand for steel was elastic. Early on, the industrial tariff—passed during the war and increased after it—protected him from British steel imports.[21] Carnegie's productive capital also had new qualities, compared to that of his competitors anywhere in the world. His production process was not only more capital intensive, it was far more energy intensive. Coal powered his factories. Carnegie's factories had prodigious demand for wage labor at various skill levels. Immigration from eastern and southern Europe provided a sufficient supply of wage labor in Pittsburgh. Finally, Carnegie increased the scale of production to take advantage of managerial and technological economies. Altogether, over time labor productivity soared in his factories.

Indeed, Carnegie had created in his steelworks a new regimen of industrial time. The economic dynamic of the Age of Commerce had most involved space, as the extent of markets increased through the imperial conquest of territory. The post–Civil War spread of the railroads furthered the dynamic.[22] But to it, Carnegie added a new one. The result was a greater intensity of production in place, given standard units of time— more stuff, at less cost, per hour. As the resumptionist former U.S. Revenue commissioner David Wells noted in *Recent Economic Changes* (1889), "In the time of Adam Smith it was regarded as a wonderful achievement for ten men to make 48,000 pins in a day, but now three men can make 7,500,000 pins of a vastly superior character in the same time."[23] Something had changed.

The time signature of money capital was cyclical. The capitalist credit cycle—the eventfulness of boom and bust, the drama of speculative mania and precautionary panic—repeated. By contrast, the time signature of capital in the arena of industrial production was abstract, linear, and standardized. Carnegie accounted for costs and profits and paid his workers wages in such units. In the Age of Commerce, the economic life of production had been cyclical, too, as it conformed to patterns set by the sun, the seasons, and the particularities of place. The railroads, in addition to being the first large-scale fixed capital industry and the largest employers of hourly wage laborers, standardized time more generally. To coordinate rail traffic, railroad corporations first divided the North American continent into four "standard" time zones. Standard time went into effect on November 18, 1883. When it was noon in Philadelphia, it was noon in Pittsburgh.[24] Standard, abstract time coordinated national railroad traffic and would govern the life of productive capital when invested in industry.

A final issue to consider is the functioning of a new industrial investment multiplier, which now complemented the Smithian commercial multiplier, in the achievement of increasing returns to economic activity. A farmer might harvest wheat and, selling it in a competitive market, earn a higher money income, but that would be the end of it. By contrast, Carnegie manufactured steel. Steel, an "intermediate," or "capital good," multiplied a whole series of backward and forward linkages, fostering downstream demand for coal and coke, as well as for the components of his factories, while supplying, upstream, goods for railroad corporations or the construction industry.[25] Due to Carnegie's achievements, firms began to expect these activities to be profitable in the future, and so they were called forth in the present. Production in general expanded. Carnegie's singular drive to manufacture steel thus helped catalyze a larger, cumulative process of industrialization.

Carnegie had surmised that profits would take care of themselves if he dedicated his company to the production of ever more steel, while striving to reduce costs. He was right. By imagining an industrial economic future that was qualitatively different from the past, Andrew Carnegie became arguably the greatest American industrial revolutionary.

1. What Was the Industrial Revolution?

In all economic history, there have been but two great ruptures. The first was the Neolithic Revolution, roughly ten thousand to twelve thousand years ago, when many populations shifted into settled agriculture on a permanent basis, leaving hunting and gathering behind for good. The second was the industrial revolution, which began in eighteenth-century Great Britain. The United States joined its second wave.

The English historian Arnold Toynbee popularized the term *industrial revolution* in 1883, when U.S. industrialization had entered its most intensive phase.[26] Five years later the U.S. economist John Bates Clark popularized the term *capital good* to refer to a distinct kind of productive asset.[27] A capital good was a "factor of production," an already-produced, or "intermediate," means of even greater wealth production (unlike land, a natural given and first cause). Following Clark, many members of the economics profession for the next century would equate capital goods with capital itself, to the exclusion of other possible assets—like money, land, or slaves. However, given the period when he wrote, Clark's definitional restriction makes sense. Referring to capital goods, economic historians speak of such measurements as "capital deepening" and "capital intensity," all of which were increasing in Clark's day.

The best possible definition of *industrial revolution* in general is the process by which the pattern of investment definitively shifts into intermediate capital goods, breeding new economic habits. There is more productive capital in the hands of the same workers. Labor productivity increases, and over time enterprise generates more wealth, as money incomes, however distributed, multiply.[28] At a certain point in the process, a threshold is reached; there is no going back.

The economic rupture cannot be emphasized enough. By the numbers, the industrial revolution gave rise to what economists call "modern economic growth"—self-sustaining increases in per capita income growth over time. Smithian growth had initiated the phenomenon. Nonetheless, industrialization represented a quantitative break from the past. The rupture was qualitative as well: the industrial revolution was civilizational in scope. Industrial societies became the world's first urban societies. Culture, even aesthetic experience, changed, as color would now be dominated for a generation by the soot and cinder of industrial grays and blacks, by "the black boots, the black stove-pipe hat, the black coach or carriage, the black iron frame of the hearth, the black cooking pots and pans and stoves."[29]

Why did the industrial revolution happen?[30] No one factor was responsible—the causation was circular and cumulative.[31] To see it unfold, however, the best place to begin is with energy.

Fossil fuels were at the center of the productive feats of the industrial revolution.[32] The most remarkable quality of the new capital goods was their greater energy intensity. Many of the backward and forward linkages of industrialization were possible only given the use of new energy stocks. Further, energy stocks, as factors of production that deplete over time, themselves expressed the logic of "capital goods."[33] For it was not only the sheer amount of energy that made the difference. As one environmental historian has put it, "The logic of coal is fundamentally different from the logic of solar energy."[34]

The difference is between economies of energy flows and stocks. Coal is a geological accumulation that, as an intermediate economic input, has vastly more combustible power than wood, wind, or water. Coal, like a capital good, is a produced means of greater production—the resonance is striking. Further, being a stock, coal can be transported and concentrated in a particular place. Prior to widespread coal use, commercial economies remained rural economies, simply because energy flows were impossible to store or transport. Production necessarily dispersed to where there was waterpower. One reason economic development in the Age of Commerce was spatial was that populations, in order to tap into energy flows, had to move rather than concentrate. With industrialization, however, "specialization growth" across space was supplemented by "power growth" in place.[35] Concentrated stocks of energy could be brought to concentrated sites of production. Tellingly, in an organic economy, the only portable energy stock was enslaved people.[36] In 1885 the French demographer Émile Levasseur noted that in energy terms, existing steam power in France represented the equivalent of 98 million coerced laborers, "true slaves, the most sober, docile and tireless that could be imagined."[37] But no amassing of human laborers, even slaves, in one place could ever muster the equivalent power of coal-fired steam engines.

In eighteenth-century Britain, when coal was brought to production on a larger scale, cascades of positive feedback loops followed, harnessing all kinds of energies toward greater production. Men invented the steam engine in British coal mines, first using it to pump water from the mines. The steam engine liberated industrial activity from proximity to waterpower. It could cluster in cities, "industrial districts," as the late nineteenth-century English economist Alfred Marshall branded them, where capital, labor, commerce, and technical innovation agglomerated and networked, feeding off one another, increasing supply and demand, backward and forward.[38]

But how to transport coal from mines to cities? That was only possible with the steam-powered railroad, which ran along iron (later steel) tracks, made possible by new high-energy techniques in manufacturing—again made possible by the mining of coal, because of steam power. In the United States, the rise of the railroad prompted Carnegie to invest in steel manufacture, an instance that further added to the snowballing history. Finally, concentrating so much productive force in one place made it possible for the owners of capital to hire large pools of wage labor—should the supply be available. The industrial revolution resulted from the many dynamic complementarities of the new productive economy of coal, steam, iron, and steel.

In this way industrial capitalism opened up a new terrain of pecuniary profit making, as it blew past the productive limits of an organic economy. Long-term, exponential "modern economic growth" became possible. And yet unlike flows, stocks can be exhausted, and as it is now clear, industrialization has ecological and climatological consequences. But the many tightly spooled linkages of industrial production only make it that much harder to transform an industrial energy regime, once set in place.

In the United States, where, when, how, and why did the industrial economy of coal, steam, iron, and steel first emerge? Both the Pennsylvania Railroad and the Carnegie Steel Company were offshoots of the mid-century industrial transformation of eastern Pennsylvania, where the emergent properties of a new energy- and capital-intensive industrial economy first took root.[39]

In 1850 coal accounted for less than 10 percent of the U.S. energy supply.[40] Wood was abundant. Three-quarters of the earth's anthracite deposits once resided in a five-hundred-square-mile region that runs from the aptly named town of Carbondale, in northeastern Pennsylvania, southwest through the Lehigh River Valley to Pottsville, on the Schuylkill River. It became the first American coal mining region.[41]

Coal resulted from geological forces that were millions of years at work. Variously, North American coalfields began their formation as far back as the Carboniferous period, between 360 and 300 million years ago or, most recently, the Cretaceous period, 145 to 66 million years ago. Dead plants and animals decay in oxygen-poor environments, and after thousands of years a spongy biomass forms, called peat. Gravity, and heat from the earth's core, removes water and gases from peat, leaving behind high concentrations of carbon. After millions of years, peat bogs become coal. The more water and gases are removed from the peat, the higher the carbon concentration. Peat becomes lignite, then subbituminous, then bituminous coal. Pressure from the movement of tectonic plates produces anthracite coal, which is almost pure carbon. It burns longer, hotter, and cleaner than any other coal.[42]

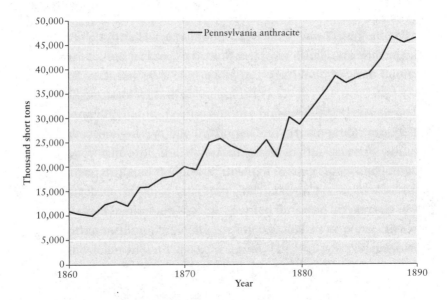

PENNSYLVANIA ANTHRACITE PRODUCTION
Due to the availability of the fossil fuel coal, the mid-Atlantic region was home to an energy-intensive American industrial revolution.

Anthracite mining was not economical until the public infrastructure of internal improvements brought down transportation costs. Until the 1850s, water was cheaper as an industrial power source. Because of their proximity to coal, Pennsylvania manufacturers first turned to coal. Philadelphia's cast-iron stove industry prospered as early as the 1830s, taking advantage of anthracite in metallurgy. By the outbreak of the Civil War, Pennsylvania produced a half-million tons of steel, consuming 1.5 million tons of coal per year. By then, the Pennsylvania Railroad was the largest industrial corporation in the world and a great consumer of coal. Between 1840 and 1870, the energy available for manufacture in the city of Philadelphia increased by a factor of twenty-five. Although the scale of enterprise remained small, Philadelphia claimed comparative advantage in heat-intensive industrial processes, like metalworking, dyeing, bleaching, glassworks, and papermaking. Philadelphia's foundries turned out many of the first steam locomotives.[43]

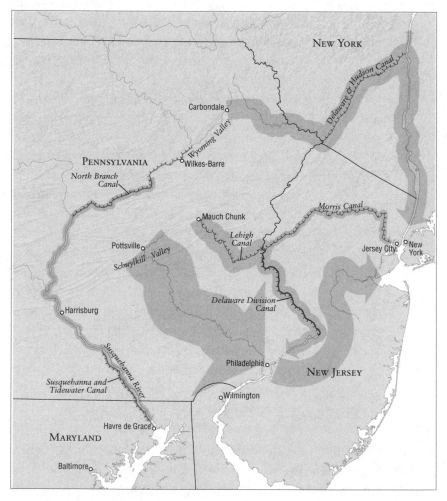

MID-ATLANTIC COAL FLOWS, C. 1855
As with other commodities, coal followed the paths set down by the prior transportation revolution. The Age of Commerce made possible the Age of Capital.

Thus the mid-Atlantic region industrialized differently from New England. It specialized in the production of intermediate capital goods, like metals and machines, rather than consumer goods such as textiles. In New England, waterpower drove the textile mills, so they flourished in small, rural villages.[44] But in the mid-Atlantic, the backward and forward linkages of coal, steam, iron, and steel first appeared in urban settings. By 1870 there were seven hundred steam engines in the anthracite coalfields of Pennsylvania.[45] Cheap coal made the stationary steam engine economical in manufacturing. Greater urban agglomerations of manufacturing became possible, which created network effects. Urban population growth strongly correlated with the adoption of the steam engine in manufacturing.[46] In the city factories, the coal-fired steam engine ran continuously, at command. Unlike waterwheel or windmill power, steam power was impervious to the natural rhythms of climate and weather. Carnegie ran his steelworks twenty-four hours a day, seven days a week. The man-made clock—another intermediate capital good—set the pace of work. Not only did industries link together upstream and downstream, they began to march in sequence and in unison. According to one observer, at all hours in the industrial districts of cities, there was "the hissing of steam, the clanking of chains, the jarring and grinding of wheels and other machinery, and the glow of melted glass and iron, and burning coal beneath."[47]

Urban demand for artificial light (as well as for machine lubricants) initiated the discovery and extraction of another fossil fuel, oil. The first U.S. oil rush occurred in Titusville, Pennsylvania, in the late 1850s. Steam engines powered the oil drills.[48]

Further distinguishing mid-Atlantic industrialization was the fact that it was both energy and capital intensive. That translated into heavy fixed capital costs. Coal mining itself was capital intensive, since accessing coal beds, veins running sometimes for miles far beneath the earth's surface, required prodigious capital investment. In manufacturing, the steam engine was the greatest capital good, the great "general-purpose technology" of the industrial revolution.[49] The continuous rotary motion of steam powered a great variety of industrial processes, spillovers of "innovational complementarities." The Rhode Island inventor George Corliss developed a new stationary steam engine that provided greater regularity of motion, as well as the ability, through the automatic "governor cutoff," to handle sudden changes in load (a special advantage in steel rolling mills). Cutoff mechanisms replaced the need for children to perform the same tasks. The Corliss engine increased energy transmission by 50 percent. In 1870, the year Corliss's patents expired, steam power in U.S. manufacturing finally exceeded waterpower. In New England's Lowell textile mills, steam power first supplemented waterpower in 1867 when the waterways froze, but soon the mills switched over to steam completely.[50] Coal-fired and steam-powered industrialization had triumphed.[51]

For the 1876 Philadelphia Centennial Exhibition, Corliss constructed the largest steam engine ever built. European visitors left the exhibition thunderstruck by American machinery. By then cables, gears, shafts, presses, and cranks had harnessed steam power to a variety of machines and industrial processes. The 1876 exhibition featured

> steam locomotives, steam fire engines, steam farm engines, steam road rollers, and engines for steamships. There were also steam pumps, steam air compressors, steam pile drivers, gargantuan steam forging hammers, and even larger steam blast-furnace-blowers.[52]

U.S. industry was catching up to British and would soon forge ahead.

Finally, the mid-Atlantic was also where a new industrial ecology and landscape of energy use first appeared. Urban industrial districts tapped hitherto unimaginable sources of energy and power. The transportation of energy stocks over the rails made industrial cities great net consumers of energy, while ravaging the locations of energy extraction. Such environmental "sacrifice zones," or "landscapes of intensification," left behind clouded and dusty atmospheres, stripped forests, scarred earth surfaces, and sludgy yellow green water.[53] As industrialization proceeded, "America would come to resemble the ravaged valleys of Pennsylvania much more than the model mill towns of New England."[54]

1870 was the year that coal surpassed all other energy sources in U.S. manufacturing, but it still accounted for only 25 percent of all energy use. 1885 was probably the year fossil fuels became the dominant energy source.[55] The transition to a fossil-fuel-based-energy- and capital-intensive manufacturing was in full swing and, in many places, like the Carnegie Steel Company, completed.

"THE SHOE & LEATHER PETROLEUM COMPANY AND THE
FOSTER FARM OIL COMPANY, ON LOWER PIONEER RUN, PA." (1895)
The ecological consequences of the new fossil-fuel-energy system so critical
to the industrial revolution immediately registered at the time in
photographs such as this one. Compare this image to the early
Hudson River School paintings of only decades before.

2. The U.S. Manufacturing Belt

The shift to a fossil-fuel-energy system in economic production would be
nearly total. For this and other reasons, Carnegie, although hardly a representative case, was emblematic of the distinctive characteristics of
industrialization. Different varieties of industrialism—especially smaller-
scale, "free labor" versions, with roots in the antebellum period—still
thrived in the second half of the nineteenth century. Which version won
out was a matter of politics as much as economics or the dictates of energy regimes. This struggle—over the property ownership of the new capital goods, the distribution of social power in the workplace, and the terms
of the post–Civil War monetary and credit system—will be discussed in
the next chapter. Nevertheless, during the 1880s, the decade of Carnegie's
triumphs, a geographically distinct "manufacturing belt" began to fill the
American map—"one large district."[56] It spanned the Northeast and Midwest, forming an "approximate parallelogram with corners at Green Bay,
St. Louis, Baltimore, and Portland (Maine)."[57]

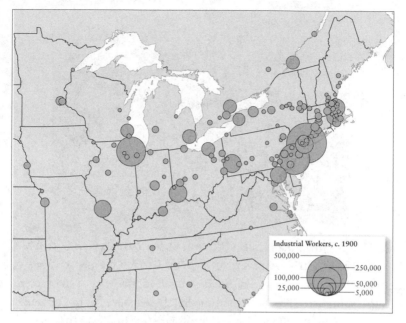

Industrial Workers, c. 1900

500,000
250,000
100,000
25,000
50,000
5,000

THE AMERICAN MANUFACTURING BELT, C. 1900

Due to expensive fixed capital investments, once in place many industrial firms warded off potential competitors. Notably, the presence of railroads decisively shaped industrial locations.

By 1900, this territory, one-sixth of the national landmass, would be responsible for 80 percent of U.S. industrial production.[58] Soon enough, by any criterion, it would be the most productive industrial region in the entire world.[59]

The sequence of industrial development was a matter of geography.[60] The extent of market access remained crucial. The paths cut by the transportation infrastructure during the era of "internal improvements" were great predictors of successful postbellum industrial location. In this respect, the Civil War proved decisive. Harmed by the conflict, the South fell back, as for decades Birmingham, Alabama, steelworks and piedmont textile mills would be the only significant southern dots on the national industrial map.[61] Meanwhile the war had sheltered the Midwest, giving the region's "free soil, free labor, free men" variety of industrialism a chance to develop, before the railroads delivered steam blasts of competition from the Northeast.[62] During the 1880s, when the post-1873 economic slump lifted and the credit cycle began again, railroad corporations completed a national rail network.[63]

The first movers in the Northeast and the Midwest—those who made the initial investments, were first in the economic field, and scaled up—warded off potential competitors and were rewarded. Many developed national marketing and distribution systems to capture markets for their goods.[64] Meanwhile, to recoup their fixed and running costs, railroads offered freight rebates and other subsidies to existing large producers who could guarantee them steady freight and thus revenue. That made it more difficult for new entrants in industrial production to sufficiently scale up their enterprises. For instance, the Ohioan John D. Rockefeller bargained with the railroads for such rebates, and by 1880 he controlled 90 percent of U.S. petroleum production capacity.[65] Having invested in the new capital goods, many of the larger firms in the manufacturing belt settled in place, determined to realize profits from their past sunk investments. Accordingly, smaller firms located around larger, successful firms. A lot of productive capital fixed on the ground, as an industrial geography that would last until World War II settled in place.[66]

New England remained a formidable industrial region. In 1870 its national share of value added to goods during the manufacturing process was 24 percent. In 1890 it was 17.5 percent.[67] By mechanizing production, New England dominated national markets in textiles. The Amoskeag Manufacturing Company in Manchester, New Hampshire, became the largest textile factory complex in the world. In shoes, Lynn, Massachusetts, remained the largest production complex. Connecticut continued to thrive as a light industrial district, home to the production of brassware, copperware, hats, and clocks. Providence, Rhode Island, home to the Corliss steam engine, became a diverse manufacturer with a specialization in jewelry.

As for the mid-Atlantic, it accounted for 42 percent of value added in manufacturing in 1870, and 40 percent in 1890. The region still specialized in energy-intensive lines of production, such as iron, steel, bleaching, dyeing, and paper products. New York, a diversified city, specialized in the garment and needle trades. Philadelphia, diverse as well, continued to dominate machine and machine tool production. New industrial districts appeared. Trenton, New Jersey, manufactured metal ropes and cables, as well as pottery and ceramics, benefiting from nearby deposits of feldspar, clay, and silica. Paterson, New Jersey—long ago the home of Hamilton's failed Society for Establishing Useful Manufactures—became "Silk City."

Connecting the Northeast and the Midwest was an industrial corridor that first arose along the Erie Canal. During the 1880s, Buffalo, with easy access to New York iron ore and Pennsylvania bituminous coal, surpassed Rochester and Albany in industrial might and was home to the state's largest iron and steel mills. Deindustrialization—a loss of competitive industries, leading to disinvestment and unemployment in some places that had once enjoyed manufacturing success—chased industrialization from the beginning.

Midwestern industry, hugging the Great Lakes, began in western Pennsylvania. By 1890, the Midwest had surpassed New England in manufacturing value added.[68] In western Pennsylvania, the opening of bituminous coalfields accelerated industrialization west of the Alleghenies. Carnegie's Pittsburgh and to a lesser extent Harrisburg developed iron and steel mills. Ohio, home to coal and iron deposits, crisscrossed with canals and railroads from the era of internal improvements, was dotted with urban industrial activity. Cleveland arose on Lake Erie as a site of diverse manufacture, home to Rockefeller and many oil refineries. In Michigan, Grand Rapids became a greater manufacturer of wood furniture. On Lake Michigan, Milwaukee became another small, diversified manufacturing center. At the southern tip of the lake, marking the western edge of the U.S. manufacturing belt, developed the astonishing industrial city of Chicago.

No one had ever seen anything like Chicago, the world's fastest-growing city during the Age of Capital.[69] Born a commercial hub of the Old Northwest, Chicago became something more, and something new, an industrial city of unprecedented spatial organization and scale. What made it possible were the combined emergent properties of the industrial economy of coal, steam, iron, and steel.

Chicago was founded by real estate speculators during the 1830s.[70] In 1848 the Illinois and Michigan Canal cleared an inland waterway between the Great Lakes and the Mississippi River, and as a result of this internal improvement, Chicago vied with St. Louis, long the hub of the Indian fur trade, to become the "gateway city" to the West. The processing of primary commodities—flour mills, lumber mills, breweries, and meatpackers—made Chicago a significant manufacturing center, although Cincinnati surpassed it for many years. The Civil War accelerated industrial production, especially for garment makers and meatpackers who benefited from army demand.[71]

Railroad traffic first made Chicago an economic center.[72] The city became the "break point" for eastern trunk lines and western Granger roads.

All east-west and west-east routes terminated in the city. By 1889 Chicago's switching district covered four hundred square miles. Roughly 15 percent of world railway mileage passed through the city, and the Chicago railyards were the greatest anywhere. The goods and people carried by the railroads terminated in Chicago as well. Farm products required handling and warehousing. In addition to western farm products, northeastern industrial products and northeastern and European finance capital arrived.[73] The railroad repair yards alone made Chicago's heavy industries formidable. Already by 1870, Chicago was exporting finished industrial products from the city.[74]

From its first settlement in the 1830s, Chicago's population reached 300,000 by 1870, but then the city almost burned down in the fire of 1871. It was rebuilt, not of wood but of stone, and also glass and brick (both, being heat intensive, became mass construction materials only after industrialization).[75] In 1880 Chicago had more than half a million residents. By 1890, through growth and annexation, the population was 1.1 million. Chicago passed Philadelphia to rank as the country's second-largest city after New York.

New York City was born during the Age of Commerce, and Lower Manhattan bears its traces. Commercial cities were walking cities, dense enough for commerce, where peoples and activities mixed. The scale was small. In industrial Chicago, the increased scale of manufacturing, as well the railroad and the urban streetcar, stretched the urban geography. During the daytime, Chicagoans traveled across long distances—first by horse, then by streetcar. Carnegie steel provided the structural supports for Chicago's elevated subway system. Different activities separated into different areas—an urban, architectural industrial sphering. The capital goods of industry had their own site of operations, physically separated from commercial and residential life.[76] Boulevards and other physical barriers separated the Loop, the central business district, where commercial, retail, and financial services concentrated, from the rail depots, the central manufacturing district, and the infamous Union Stockyards. More boundaries, in turn, separated these spaces from highly segregated residential areas—Chicago's Gold Coast, home to the lakeshore elite, and the Pilsen neighborhood, home to Czech stockyard workers. Working-class neighborhoods were, essentially, toxic industrial waste dumps.

Environmentally, Chicago was a "shock city." Visitors were quite literally shocked, as Chicago assaulted all the senses.[77] The city consumed pro-

"MAN STANDING ON CRUSTED SEWAGE IN BUBBLY CREEK" (1911)
Chicago was one of the world's first great industrial cities. Visitors in the late
nineteenth century were often shocked by the environmental consequences
of urban industrialization, especially after viewing the accumulated
industrial waste in the Chicago River and its branches.

digious amounts of coal, and giant piles of it clumped all over the city.[78]
Illinois bituminous coal, as James Macfarlane noted in *The Coal-Regions of
America* (1873), was "very inferior" to anthracite due to the "clinker, ashes,
soot, and smoke produced."[79] Chicago air was infamously dark and smoky.
In 1881 the city, employing "smell committees," passed the first U.S. ordinance banning "dense smoke."[80] Nonetheless, "its air is dirt," English
writer Rudyard Kipling said of Chicago during his travels there in the
1880s. He saw no "color in the street and no beauty."[81] The old "free soil,
free labor, free men" stalwart Horace Greeley countered that smoky black
was the color of progress and prosperity.[82] No one celebrated the Chicago
River, an open sewer topped with a "filthy froth" of industrial and animal
waste intermixed with "patches of oily scum."[83] Kipling reported seeing
"canals as black as ink" and "un-told abominations."[84] Cholera broke out
every year until the 1890s, when steam pumps reversed the river's flow. In
another positive feedback loop of industrialism, Chicago tackled ecological devastation with the very tools that had caused it.[85] Coal-fired steam
engines, iron and steel pipes, tubes, and wires were responsible for its
fledgling sewage system, waterworks, and gasification complex.

The U.S. urban population climbed from 6.2 million in 1860 to 30 million in 1900, and everywhere city life increasingly began to look more like

Chicago's. But Chicago still stood out. Kipling sensed that in the city he had seen, and smelled, something new. He left it musing about the American contribution to industrial civilization. "Having seen it," he remarked, "I urgently desire never to see it again. It is inhabited by savages."[86] By contrast, the Illinois-born poet Carl Sandburg, child of Swedish immigrants, saluted the city in the opening stanza to his poem "Chicago" (1914):

> Hog Butcher for the World,
> Tool Maker, Stacker of Wheat,
> Player with Railroads and the Nation's Freight Handler;
> Stormy, husky, brawling,
> City of the Big Shoulders.[87]

Could industrial civilization be made habitable, and its economic blessings—the production of ever more wealth—enjoyed? In downtown Chicago, Carnegie steel beams were the bones of the world's first skyscrapers. Home to the world's most imaginative modern architecture, the city would become one of the great laboratories of urban industrial society.

3. The Industrialization of the Countryside

Due to their potentially multiplying effects, commerce and manufacturing bring increasing returns to economic activity. In agriculture, however, diminishing returns always loom. There is only so much land on the face of the earth, and some parts of it are less capable of yielding a bounty than others. The new industrial energy regime always carried the potential for natural resource constraints, but they would hit in the 1970s, not in the 1870s. During the Age of Capital, when the industrial revolution swept across North America, diminishing returns were nowhere near in sight. Whether it was labor-saving machinery in manufacturing or land-saving techniques in the fields, productivity increased everywhere.

The birth of the manufacturing belt and rise of the industrial city were seamlessly joined with the industrial transformation of the countryside. Chicago, for instance, had a vast market hinterland. If the city's population hit one million by 1890, so did the population of the state of Nebraska.[88] Chicago anchored the western region of the manufacturing belt, but it was also the eastern terminus of a second economic geography, the

West—spanning Dakota wheat, Texas cattle, and Arizona copper. During the 1880s, due to the extension of white populations across space, the intensified land-saving cultivation methods, and the pressure on farm households to produce more for markets, the West, too, saw a great leap forward in economic output. It supplied and fed—literally, in the case of the supper tables of urban populations—industrialization. Greater money incomes in the countryside also provided a critical source of demand for the new urban manufactured goods.

During the nineteenth century, the U.S. agricultural sector remained equal to or greater than the U.S. industrial sector, by most any measure. In 1870 farmers and farm laborers were still 46 percent of the workforce.[89] But the logic of capital goods intensification began to appear in the countryside. There were steam-pump engines in mining camps, and steel-edged plows on the prairies and plains. The energy transition was again pivotal: coal powered the railroads, without which market access on the western prairies and plains could not have existed.[90] The same emergent properties of the new industrial economy—of coal, steam, iron, and steel—spread across the rural landscape.

There was one notable difference. U.S. agriculture was far more globalized and was subject to the competitive pressures of international markets and pricing. U.S. manufacturing was largely domestically financed, protected by the Republican tariff, and it relied on domestic sources of demand. Further, as Carnegie's system illustrated, costs determined pricing. By contrast, while the agricultural industry dominated U.S. exports, farmers at this time had no choice but to accept the international prices for their goods. Meanwhile the West (including its railroad corporations) imported capital and credit from Europe.[91] In agriculture, somewhat similar dynamics appeared elsewhere in the world. The Argentine Pampas, and the Canadian prairies and plains, were also export-oriented commodity frontiers, drawing capital from Britain, through the link of the gold standard. Melbourne, Australia, mirrored Chicago, if at a smaller scale. Twinning with industrialization, the white settler-colonialism of the Age of Capital saw a great land grab all over the globe, with the goal of extracting the resources necessary for industrialization. The U.S. West simply did it all at the greatest scale.[92]

"The world has never seen anything comparable" to the surge in agricultural production, Wells boasted in *Recent Economic Changes*, and he was right.[93] During the 1870s, U.S. farm acreage increased by 44 percent. Before 1880, wheat cultivation in the Dakota Territory was unknown. In 1887, after a sudden surge in white settlement, Dakota produced over 60 million bushels of wheat, one-seventh of the entire U.S. wheat crop (equal to the annual export of wheat from all of India).[94] In 1871 on the Great Plains, there were probably 3.63 million head of cattle, the vast majority aimlessly roaming. By 1885, there were 7.5 million, intended for industrial slaughter.[95] Except for Missouri lead, California gold, and Pennsylvania anthracite, "mineral development in the USA remained unimpressive during the first two-thirds of the nineteenth century." But "what European miners had done over the span of several centuries, the Americans accomplished in little more than in a single generation." The Comstock silver lode was discovered in Nevada in 1859; gold in Montana in 1862; silver in Utah, 1869; gold in the Black Hills of Dakota, 1874. Colorado's coalfields opened in the 1860s and '70s. During the 1880s, Colorado, Utah, and Nevada began to dominate lead mining. Michigan and Wisconsin ranges were the largest sources of iron ore, until the Mesabi range of northern Minnesota opened. Midwestern petroleum fields dominated until the discovery of oil at Spindletop, Texas, in 1901, soon followed by California exploration.[96] By 1900, the United States led the world in the extraction of industrial minerals—ranking first in coal, iron ore, copper, lead, zinc, silver, tungsten, molybdenum, petroleum, arsenic, phosphate, antimony, magnetite, mercury, and salt, as well as a close second place in gold and bauxite. After 1870 the increase in mineral output, like industrial output, doubled the rate of U.S. population growth. Corporations extracted the inputs necessary for the U.S. manufacturing belt to grow to world prominence.[97]

Nature, too, was thus newly capitalized. The greater application of energy-intensive capital goods—steam-powered drills, or more explosive blasting agents—increased the rate of extraction over time. Railroad corporations not only transported goods; raising the necessary capital, they organized large-scale extraction, hiring wage laborers. Meanwhile the Mining Laws of 1866 and 1872 barely structured the corporate orgy of mineral extraction. Prospectors enjoyed "apex" rights, which accorded ownership of a vein, no matter how deep and wide, to the owner of its apex, or highest point.[98] Environmental sacrifice zones emerged, in a "gigantic illustration of excessive resource depletion in a common-property setting."[99]

Similarities between western mining and farming are illuminating. The

Chicago-published western guidebook *Where to Go to Become Rich* (1880) featured chapters on gold prospecting and wheat farming.[100] Corporations entered the farming business, too. During the 1870s and '80s, highly capitalized corporations ran "bonanza" wheat farms that, in Dakota and also in California's Central Valley, ranged from 1,000 to 100,000 acres.[101] They introduced steam-powered plows and threshers into the fields. Yet in the West, wage labor remained seasonal, and between 1870 and 1890, its prevalence actually declined.[102] Corporations dominated mining, but in farming the household remained the dominant unit of enterprise. Typically in the West, holdings were between 150 and 200 acres. Nonetheless, industrialization transformed the farm household of the organic economy.[103]

In the Age of Commerce, farm households typically employed commercial safety-first strategies. Farming in the Age of Capital was a different project. West of the Mississippi, prairies gave way to plains. There was no timber on hand for construction, and fewer waterways. Without railroads, there was no market access. The bull-tongued, cast-iron sheathed wooden plow could not break plains sods. Of necessity, more farm inputs and outputs now passed through commercial markets. The farm household's split gambler-peasant economic personality passed from the scene.

Farming newly required a greater money investment in productive capital. *Where to Go to Become Rich* recommended arriving on the Great Plains with $1,000.[104] That purchased 160 acres on a six-year mortgage, paying $150 down. After 1870 a "western mortgage market" funneled European (mostly British) and northeastern finance capital westward. Banking corporations purchased western farm mortgages and sold them predominantly to northern life insurance corporations. Or they repackaged them into "debenture bonds"—what are today called mortgage-backed securities—for popular sale back east. During the 1880s, there was a western farm mortgage craze, in which U.S. farm mortgage debt increased by 42 percent. By 1890 farmers had mortgaged somewhere between 30 and 40 percent of farm acreage west of the Mississippi and east of the Rocky Mountains.[105]

Mortgage credit purchased land and many other necessary farm-making inputs. Chicago-based companies shipped ready-made balloon-frame farmhouses westward. A London traveler noted a prefabricated home could be "contracted in Chicago and put up anywhere within reasonable distance from the railroad in less than 30 days from the date of order."[106] Capital-intensive lumber corporations cut down Wisconsin's white pine north woods. The logs floated down Lake Michigan, and Chicago lumber mills shipped more than a billion feet of board in 1880.[107] When the north woods were stripped, during the 1890s new lumbering camps took shape in the Pacific Northwest and in the South.

In the cities, factories manufactured farm implements that, once shipped out, achieved the same result in the fields that factories had achieved by industrialization: greater productivity. Americans perfected steel-sheathed plows (including the John Deere "steep plow"), harrows, axes, and scythes. The Virginian Cyrus McCormick took out a patent on a mechanized reaper in 1834, with triangular knives, like sharks' teeth, that cut into stalks with serrated edges.[108] Sales exploded on the prairies in the 1850s, and McCormick wisely moved his factory to Chicago. The mechanized "self-raking reaper" appeared in 1875, a horse-drawn reaper with mechanized belts that brought grain up from the ground to a side table for binding. Borrowed from textile factories was the "automatic binder."[109] According to the U.S. labor commissioner writing in 1886, "six hundred men now do the work that, fifteen or twenty years ago, would have required 2,145 men."[110] Agricultural productivity was very likely higher in the American West than anywhere else in the world. The United States had more productive capital, fresh soils, labor (of dependent household members and passing wage hands), and biologically innovated crop seed.[111] "I have calculated that the produce of five acres of wheat can be brought from Chicago to Liverpool at less than the cost of manuring one acre for wheat in England," lamented a Devonshire, England, farmer in 1886.[112]

In the West, fixed running costs had another logic. A steel plow was a sunk cost, and mortgages demanded payment. To recoup costs and pay their debts, farmers produced regardless of the price offered for their products—just as railroad corporations ran their cars, no matter how full. Thus did the West unleash torrents of commodities onto world markets. For instance, by 1890 Minnesota was the largest wheat-producing state, and the Minneapolis flour miller Charles Pillsbury made heavy fixed capital investments in a new steel "roller process" that replaced water-powered millstones. "Minnesota fancy" flour took European markets by storm.[113] Undercut by U.S. foodstuffs, many central and southern European producers lost their domestic markets for good. Peasants shipped off to the United States—some to work in Carnegie's mills, which rolled the steel plates for the bottoms of the steamships that brought them to North America.[114] By 1900 some 20 percent of all U.S. manufacturing output was processed foods.[115] That included Pillsbury's flour, Campbell's soups (1869), Coca-Cola (1886), and Kellogg's cornflakes (1894).

U.S. foodstuffs sold in a highly competitive international marketplace. By 1890, wheat prices in Chicago, New York, and Liverpool—signaled instantaneously by telegraph—had all but converged.[116] An entire chain of mercantile houses and wholesalers connected producers and consumers across vast distances. Pricing farm products were new "futures" exchanges, the largest being the Chicago Board of Trade. The board used steam-powered grain elevator storage to develop a grading system ("Winter Wheat no. 2"), as merchants stored stocks of goods, depending on their expectation of which way future prices might move. Merchants began selling the elevator certificates as speculative objects, then created "futures" contracts, to price and trade commodities that did not yet exist. Futures enabled farmers to hedge their products in the fields against price fluctuations. No less, it allowed merchants and dealers, even the public at large, to speculate on futures prices in the "pits."[117]

Meanwhile, for many animal species, the industrialization of food systems was a horrific event.[118] During the Civil War, the Union Army cut off the cattle drive between the Texas southern plains and the New Orleans slaughterhouses. Three million head of cattle built up. Once railroad corporations crossed the High Plains, it made sense to drive cattle northward. In 1867 an Illinois livestock dealer, Joseph J. McCoy, bought 250 acres at a Kansas railhead, and the first cattle town—Abilene—sprang to life. From there cattle could be shipped to Chicago. After the conquest of the Plains Indians—a militant band of Comanche fell in the Texas Panhandle in 1875—the cattle trade boomed in the early 1880s.[119]

On the Great Plains, cattle replaced another animal species, bison.[120] The bison population, already in decline, probably stood at 15 million in the 1860s, sustaining Indians' economic lives. With the arrival of the railroads, the slaughter commenced. Between 1872 and 1874, more than 4 million bison died at the end of hunters' rifles. Bison meat fed railroad construction crews. Bison leather made stronger belts for machine equipment. Philadelphia tanners tanned the hides using new heat-intensive methods—European demand for leather goods was especially strong. In the early 1880s, the High Plains came under assault. In Montana, according to Granville Stuart, a gold prospector turned cattleman, writing in

Forty Years on the Frontier (1925), live buffalo once "darkened the rolling plains." By "the fall of 1883, there was not a buffalo remaining."[121]

The High Plains filled up with Texas longhorns. First, cattlemen drove herds northward across an open range. But farmers complained that cattle overran their crops and transmitted diseases. Cattlemen enclosed spaces, using a new industrial technology—the barbed-wire fence. In 1876 Washburn and Moen, a Massachusetts company, had bought the patent rights on an Illinois farmer's 1874 design of double-stranded wire, with barbs coiled around one end of each strand. By 1880 over fifty thousand miles of barbed wire, legally but just as often extralegally, fenced in the open ranges.[122] The train and the telegraph liberated human beings from space. Barbed wire locked animals in place. It also established clear property lines, which correlated with increases in agricultural production and land values.[123]

"Livestock," in the words of one historian, "became a form of capital."[124] James S. Brisbin, a Civil War general, wrote *The Beef Bonanza; or, How to Get Rich on the Plains* (1881). "The West! The mighty West!" he enthused. He included a sample balance sheet, "Estimate of Profits of a Cash Capital of $25,000 Invested in Cattle for Five Years," that would have made Andrew Carnegie smile.[125] As the federal government's *Report in Regard to the Range and Ranch Cattle Business of the United States* (1885) noted, "The average cost per head of the management of large herds is much less than that of small herds." Increasing in scale, corporations attempted to consolidate the cattle trade.[126] After cattle chewed through the grasslands, the largest outfits fed their cattle corn in feedlots for the final fattening-up before transshipment to Chicago.[127]

In Chicago, "death itself took a new form."[128] The Union Stockyards were capitalized in 1865 at a gargantuan $1 million fixed cost by the Chicago Pork Packers' Association and the city's nine largest railroad corporations. These stockyards could handle over 100,000 animals. In a premonition of Henry Ford's assembly line, workers struck hogs on the head with mallets, then hooked them onto a mechanized "disassembly line," feet first—cutting their jugulars to bleed out the animals to death. Cattle, by contrast, were simply bludgeoned until dead.[129] By 1900, Chicago received 14 million animals per year for slaughter.[130] Kipling noticed a young woman in the stockyards, "in a patch of sunlight, the red blood under her shoes, the vivid carcasses tacked around her, a bullock bleeding its life was not six feet away from her, and the death factory roaring all round her. She looked curiously, with hard, bold eye and was not ashamed."[131] Not much changed in the stockyards between Kipling's 1891 travelogue and the publication of Upton Sinclair's fictional exposé, *The Jungle*, in 1906.

Divisions of labor broke up the subsequent slaughtering and packing into minute steps. Sunk costs in fixed capital led firms to attempt to eke out every last penny from animal carcasses. Cow bones became buttons on the jackets of schoolchildren. Meanwhile meatpackers looked for ways to work year round. They harvested Wisconsin ice to cool rooms for packing. Soon enterprising packers refrigerated railroad cars. (The first patent was taken out in 1867.)[132] Chicago meat dominated the national beef market by the end of the 1880s. American beef conquered Europe, too. Fresh meat had first crossed the ocean in 1876 on the French steamship *Frigorifique*. Refrigerated American meat shipments to Britain, in competition with British-financed Buenos Aires products, reached nearly 2 million tons in 1876, and 11.8 million in 1886. Prices for prime beef declined 18 percent in that span.[133]

In the Age of Commerce, land had doubled as something more than capital. But the intermediate capital goods of the new age had a more exclusively instrumental logic. What was a Jones mixer good for if not making steel? A similar question could be applied to land: what was it good for, if not producing commodities for sale, to generate money income? To the degree to which the answer was nothing, economic life transformed. Farms became entrepreneurial endeavors and little, if anything, else. Geological deposits became nature's productive capital. Cattle became fleshy ledgers of prior investment, running costs, and prospective and realized profits. Mortgage debt forced farmers to value their lands as capital assets, to the exclusion of other attachments.[134] Barbed wire literally enclosed new frontiers, now dedicated to long-distance capital investments. Economic or otherwise, other modes of valuation dropped out. In 1887, after white colonization destroyed Indian economies, the Dawes Act attempted to "assimilate" Indians into capitalist farming methods.[135] When it failed, more Indian land was wrested away and hived off into the zone of white capitalist investment. Indian reservations became places of devastating economic devaluation.[136] Elsewhere, new "national parks" conserved nature, in the form of pristine wilderness, and thus protected it from any capitalist encroachment whatsoever. Yellowstone National Park (1872), spanning 3,500 square miles today, was the most ambitious project. To create such a space, the U.S. Army had to kick off, or arrest, white subsistence farmers, squatters, and hunters. National parks were not capital, so there must be no economic production inside them.[137] Industrial society was premised upon such stark boundaries and oppositions.

The point could be taken too far. Subsistence economies persisted, whether among white farm households in Appalachia—centuries of successive commodity booms had passed over them—or Hispanic villages in the Southwest, which mixed commerce and subsistence not far from corporate railroad and mining camps.[138] In New Mexico, the Navajo retained economic autonomy by combining horticulture and sheep herding.[139] Capital did not touch everything. But in addition to the extraordinary rise in wealth and output, what was different was how much capital did transform. Commerce had hardly ever left as much a mark on economic lives.

Another departure concerned what capital-intensive production left behind in its wake, as Enlightenment dreams of "improvement" and natural abundance translated into the economy of fossil-fuel-powered intensification. The result was not only more production and wealth but also vast destruction. In 1878 in Minnesota one of the first steel-rolling flour mills exploded, and the roof blew one hundred feet into the sky, killing eighteen persons.[140] Environmental "sacrifice zones" appeared across the continent. On the arid High Plains, farmers brought acres under cultivation in soils where capitalist farming was not sustainable. Rain did not "follow the plow," creating conditions for future "dust bowls." On the southern plains, cattle overgrazing led ranchers to drive herds northward. In the two unusually harsh winters of 1886 and 1887, as many as one million cattle perished in what came to be known as the "Great Die Up." Fleeing winter storms, cattle blindly piled into farmers' barbed-wire fences, where, trapped, they froze to death.

4. Homestead

In the winter of 1886–87, while the "Great Die Up" was in full swing, the Edgar Thomson Steelworks sat idle. Andrew Carnegie had continued to search for more costs to cut. But fixed costs were just that, fixed. So his eyes had fallen on a variable cost—labor.[141] But when he cut wages, his workers walked off the job. The willfulness of the human beings who tended the new capital goods was disrupting the implicit reason for their existence—to produce more, at less cost—and thus the logic of Carnegie's entire operation.

At first Carnegie got along well enough with his workers. Unlike many of his competitors, no matter the market conditions, he always ran his factories full, which meant his workforce never suffered from periodic bouts of unemployment. Also uncommonly, he was willing to negotiate with labor unions, including the Amalgamated Association of Iron and Steel Workers, formed in 1876. The Amalgamated was a "craft union," consisting of highly skilled, highly knowledgeable male laborers who combined to bargain with their employers over wages and working conditions.[142] In 1878 Carnegie had instructed Captain Bill Jones to cut wage expenditures, but Jones shot back, "Leave good enough alone." "Low wages," he lectured Carnegie, "does not always imply cheap labor. Good wages and good workmen I know to be cheapest labor." At Edgar Thomson, capital goods had only just begun to mechanize steel production and to shift company demand from skilled to unskilled laborers. Jones still needed committed skilled workers. He persuaded Carnegie to switch from the twelve-hour day to the eight-hour day. Then Carnegie changed his mind, because three shift turnovers a day were more expensive than two. Edgar Thomson went back on the twelve-hour day. Workers alternated between weeklong runs on the day and night shifts, with a periodic, grueling twenty-four-hour changeover shift.[143]

Carnegie also, in the winter of 1886, put Edgar Thomson wages on a sliding scale. When steel prices went down (as they did because Carnegie had cut costs), he thought it justified that wages fell proportionately. In response, the Edgar Thomson workers went on strike. Carnegie, hoping to appease them, chose not to hire replacements. Thomson remained shuttered for five months, until the workers caved. Carnegie had won.

In 1889 a blast furnace explosion at the Edgar Thomson works took Jones's life. But a new steelworks, one mile downriver in Homestead, Pennsylvania, had recently superseded Edgar Thomson anyway. At the Homestead plant, the process of making steel was almost thoroughly integrated. It was among the first U.S. steelworks to employ open-hearth processes, which reduced the need for the manual "puddling" of molten iron—"puddlers" had stood near the apex of Amalgamated's craft union hierarchy of skill. In 1889, the year of Jones's death, Carnegie Steel's 1886 contract with the Amalgamated expired. A strike broke out over Carnegie's insistence on the inclusion of a wage sliding scale in the new contract. Carnegie instructed his managers at Homestead to follow his model at Edgar Thomson two years before: there were to be no replacement workers, but also no negotiating. But a young executive who had been put in charge flinched and signed a three-year contract with the Amalgamated, which accepted a modified sliding scale in return for the company's recognition of the union as the sole collective bargaining agent for all Homestead workers. Carnegie, furious, scolded his underling for agreeing "under intimidation." For "men in other works now know that we will 'confer' with law breakers."[144]

By 1892, when the 1889 Homestead contract terminated, the cost of production and steel prices had slid further. His increased profits notwithstanding, Carnegie decided that wages must slide in tandem. By now, his leading business partner, Henry Frick, had changed his mind about unions. The two men decided that the Amalgamated should be eliminated. As another partner would recall, "It placed a tax on improvements, therefore the Amalgamated had to go."[145]

Carnegie did not have the stomach to do it, but Frick did. Carnegie set sail for Europe and his annual grouse-hunting trip. From England, he wrote to Frick, "We are with you to the end."[146] Before negotiations with the Amalgamated began, Frick had his men construct an eight-foot wall around the steelworks, dotted by twelve-foot-high platforms with floodlights, and slotted with holes large enough for the point of rifles. Strewn atop the four-mile wall that surrounded the steelworks was a blanket of barbed wire.

CHAPTER 9

CLASS WAR AND HOME LIFE

I N 1892, THE AMALGAMATED ASSOCIATION OF IRON, STEEL, and Tin Workers at the Carnegie Steel Company's Homestead steel-works, founded in 1876, counted 24,000 national members. It was the strongest union affiliated with the American Federation of Labor (AFL), a national association of craft unions founded in 1886. Homestead, Pennsylvania, was its best-organized local. A craft union organized workers by occupation and skill, unlike an industrial union, which organized entire workplaces regardless of occupation and skill. At Homestead, the Amalgamated had enlisted 800 of the 3,800 workers.[1]

Henry Frick believed the Amalgamated was preventing the Carnegie Steel Company from doing what Andrew Carnegie had obsessively designed it to do: increase steel output at a reduced cost. With Frick, the Amalgamated sought to negotiate a new contract with better wage rates and improved working conditions, including the pace of work. Since skilled labor in particular was a cost, Frick wanted the authority to replace skilled labor with machines and to assign tasks to unskilled workers. U.S. manufacturing was world-renowned for the speed of its production process, and new machines—the capital goods of the industrial revolution—would speed production even further, but the Amalgamated was hampering their introduction. A Carnegie manager complained that the company's "method of apportioning the work, of regulating the turns, of altering machinery, in short, every detail of working the great plant," was "subject to the interference of some busybody representing the Amalgamated Association."[2]

The Amalgamated had complaints, too. A number of its workers, for instance, were masters of the highly skilled and physically onerous craft of "puddling" steel. Their accumulated knowledge about production processes had long been the basis not only of their bargaining position but of a masculine pride in their physical labor.[3] Representatively, Thomas Pollock Anshutz's painting *The Ironworkers' Noontime* (1880) depicts the physical prowess of the kind of metalworkers who only a decade later, at Carnegie's steelworks, were in danger of becoming obsolete. But the pro-

THOMAS POLLOCK ANSHUTZ, *THE IRONWORKERS' NOONTIME* (1880)
Anshutz painted this scene near Wheeling, West Virginia. The naturalistic style places emphasis on the physical prowess of ironworkers, as well as on the homosocial qualities of the industrial workplace (where gay subcultures were present at the time). The bleakness of the scene alarmed the painting's first viewers, fearful of what it foretold of industrialization. Note that many of the poses evoke classical forms; the man rubbing his bicep suggesting a pose from the Parthenon.

cess of capital deepening—putting more productive capital in the hands of the same worker—made management less dependent on these workers. At Homestead, for instance, the new open-hearth process of rolling steel dispensed with the "puddling" of steel.

Falling steel prices were the fruits of the company's productivity gains, delivered to its owners. Carnegie believed that workers' wages should fall accordingly. But sliding wages threatened the aspirations of young, transient, single male wage earners, who perhaps hoped to earn and then quickly move on (if not migrate back to Europe). For married men, lower pay threatened their breadwinning ability—another common aspiration of working people, who sought to prevent their wives from leaving the home and entering the sphere of remunerative labor that according to middle-class prescription was supposed to be only for men. If husbands could not earn a breadwinning wage, wives, perhaps even children, might need to endure the middle-class indignity of working for wages. In 1890 over 90 percent of women over the age of thirty-five were married, and only 3.3 percent of them engaged in paid labor outside the home.[4] The company thus threatened Homestead workers' "manly bearing."

In 1892, when Carnegie Steel made an estimated $4 million in profit, Frick proposed that Homestead workers take at least a 12 percent wage cut. The Amalgamated countered with 4 percent. Frick refused and fired a number of Amalgamated-affiliated workers. In sympathy, the rest walked out. On July 29, Frick shut down the factory, locking out its entire work-force.[5] The national Amalgamated had forbidden locals to include unskilled workers, but the Homestead local, mostly American-born Prot-estants, had welcomed unskilled Slovak and Hungarian Catholic immi-grants, which now granted the strike a broader worker basis. They were among the 23.5 million central, southern, and eastern Europeans—Poles, Slavs, Hungarians, Czechs, Jews, and Italians—who came to the United States during the proletarian migration of 1880 to 1920, a great number of whom planned to return and subsequently did.[6] Meanwhile they trans-formed U.S. labor markets, and their supply of waged labor made possible industrialization, including Carnegie's steelworks. Frick blamed "Huns" for the discord.[7]

The town of Homestead—eight thousand people all directly or indi-rectly bound to the United States' largest rolling mill—sympathized with the workers. The mayor, "Honest" John McLuckie, a Union veteran and a former steelworker, sat on the Amalgamated's advisory committee, which was led by the Irish-immigrant steel roller Hugh O'Donnell. When O'Donnell saw Carnegie Steel construct its eight-foot wall around the steelworks and string it with barbed wire—complete with lookout towers, shooting posts, and floodlights—he knew Frick was planning to bring in nonunion, replacement workers. O'Donnell instructed the Amalgamated to organize on "a truly military basis."[8]

Nine days after the lockout began, two barges appeared on the Monon-gahela River, bearing three hundred uniformed guards armed with Win-chester rifles. Frick had hired them from the Pinkerton Detective Agency and was paying them to protect the coming replacement workers. When the Pinkertons tried to land on the riverbank, thousands of Homestead workers and local sympathizers greeted them from behind makeshift steel barricades. They, too, were armed with rifles, some carried home from the Civil War; with dynamite left over from Fourth of July fireworks; and with two artillery pieces, including a Union Army cannon, reputedly from the Battle of Antietam. The Pinkertons landed, and shots were fired, although from which direction first it remains unclear. For fourteen hours, the two sides traded gunfire. Homesteaders launched handcarts doused with flaming oil down the embankment. The beleaguered Pinkertons finally surrendered, in return for safe passage to the local train station to depart from the city. But the path to the station became a six-hundred-yard gauntlet. Men stripped the Pinkertons' uniforms off their backs, women swung umbrellas and whips, and children shouted insults. In the "Battle of Homestead," two Pinkertons and seven Homesteaders died.

On July 12, Frick persuaded the governor of Pennsylvania to send 8,500 members of the National Guard to Homestead under the guise of protecting the company's property. Replacement workers, mostly eastern European immigrants and blacks, entered the steelworks. Based on a dubious interpretation of a Civil War statute, members of the Amalgamated's advisory committee were sent to jail on charges of treason. Meanwhile an anarchist Russian émigré, Alexander Berkman—at the time running an ice cream parlor in Worcester, Massachusetts, with his lover, Emma Goldman, another anarchist Russian émigré—boarded a train for Homestead, with his pistol. He barged into Frick's office, yelled, "Murderer," and shot Frick, who yelled "Murderer" back. Berkman pulled out a dagger and stabbed Frick multiple times, then was finally subdued. It was not enough; Frick was back at his work desk that afternoon. Berkman spent fourteen years in prison.[9]

Homestead workers grew desperate. Some directed their animosity toward black replacement workers, who they called Frick's "nigger black sheep."[10] Nearly four months after Frick's lockout, the Amalgamated relented and voted to return to work on Frick's terms. But Frick reinstated only a few of them. He had won. Nationally, the Amalgamated reeled. Carnegie returned home from his hunting excursion in Europe and was genuinely sad, he said, about what had happened in his absence. Carnegie and Frick's relationship never recovered. Late in life, Carnegie reached out to

Frick in hopes of reconciliation. Frick rebuffed Carnegie's messenger, allegedly replying, "Tell him I'll see him in Hell, where we both are going."[11]

1. Class War

The Battle of Homestead was an unusually violent instance of industrial labor conflict in the Age of Capital, but it was no aberration. In 1892 alone state militias intervened to put down strikes on twenty-three separate occasions.[12] The Homestead strike followed nearly two decades of labor strife, which had begun, no less dramatically, in the aftermath of the Panic of 1873 with the Great Railroad Strike of 1877.

Carnegie's mentor, the Pennsylvania Railroad executive Tom Scott, precipitated the strike. After the Panic of 1873, the Penn Railroad suffered from lack of business, and to maintain dividends for his restless stockholders, Scott slashed wages by 20 percent. The cost of capital goods was fixed, but the cost of labor was variable. Other railroad corporations, colluding with the Pennsylvania Railroad in a "pool" to coordinate rates and wages (a practice not yet outlawed), followed. One of them was the Baltimore & Ohio.[13]

"THE GREAT STRIKE— THE SIXTH MARYLAND REGIMENT FIGHTING ITS WAY THROUGH BALTIMORE" (1877) The Civil War was in the recent past when the Great Railroad Strike of 1877 took place. Labor violence led many Americans to wonder if another "irrepressible conflict" loomed.

The Great Railroad Strike of 1877 began in July at the Baltimore & Ohio, erupting in Camden, Maryland, and spreading to Martinsburg, West Virginia. In response to wage cuts, workers went on strike and set up physical barricades to block traffic. The West Virginia governor sent in the state militia to restore freight passage, but many members of the militia sympathized with the strikers. A rolling series of strikes, on the Baltimore & Ohio and beyond, broke out in Baltimore, Pittsburgh, Chicago, and St. Louis. The only regions spared were the Deep South and New England.

New industrial cities were the chief arenas of conflict, and municipal authorities struggled to contain the violence.[14] In Pittsburgh, a crowd of workers and sympathizers, many women and children, blockaded the Pennsylvania Railroad's freight yard. The Pittsburgh police, in solidarity with the strikers, would not act. State militiamen arrived, bayoneted a few protesters, and fired on the crowd, killing twenty. Angry mobs, in the thousands, chased the six hundred militiamen into a roundhouse, where they barricaded themselves, clinging to a Gatling gun. The mob destroyed more than two thousand railcars, one hundred locomotives, and nearly forty buildings, and they tore up the tracks of a three-mile stretch of the Pennsylvania Railroad. More militia arrived from Philadelphia and re-

"DAMAGED TRACK, RAILROAD RIOTS— PENNSYLVANIA RAILROAD" (1877) The Pennsylvania Railroad was among the largest corporations in the world when the Great Railroad Strike of 1877 broke out. Afterward, because of the loss of property due to the destruction pictured here, the company successfully sued Allegheny County for compensation, after claiming the state had failed to provide the railroad's private property adequate police protection.

stored order. Scott and the Pennsylvania Railroad would later successfully sue the city of Pittsburgh for loss of property.[15]

Meanwhile in St. Louis, railroad workers led a general strike. For several days, the Workingmen's Party of the United States, led by émigré German socialists, controlled the city. Strikers did not always blame the bosses. In San Francisco, a Worker's Party–led strike deteriorated into a pogrom against Chinese immigrants.[16] The worst violence, however, occurred in Chicago.

The Chicago Workingmen's Party organized demonstrations. Large banners proclaimed "Down with wages-slavery." Leaflets taunted workers, "Have you no rights?—No ambition? No manhood?" The Workingmen's Party demanded public ownership of the railroads, a 20 percent wage increase, and an eight-hour workday. An Irish Union Army veteran of the Battle of Shiloh addressed a crowd: "I was through the war. I fought for the big bugs—the capitalists—and many of you have done the same. And what is our reward now? What have the capitalists done for us?" Chicago's owners of capital, recently organized in a "citizens association," began to drill their own private "businessmen's militias." Chicago quickly became engulfed in violence. The working-class neighborhoods of Pilsen (home to Czech Bohemian immigrants) and Bridgeport (home to Irish immigrants) were in open revolt. On sight, Chicago police arrested women who were wearing a single stocking, on the assumption that the second was filled with stones to be swung as a weapon. Police and two companies of the U.S. Army, fresh from fighting the Sioux in Dakota, killed thirty men and boys, burying many anonymously in lime pits.[17]

In the summer of 1877, the Great Railroad Strike finally exhausted itself. New U.S. president Rutherford B. Hayes, lately withdrawing troops from the Redeemed South, declared the strikes "unlawful and insurrectionary proceedings" and sent in the federal troops to restore municipal order. Tom Scott made the request—but he never recovered from the trauma of the strike and soon suffered the first of a series of debilitating strokes.[18]

Had sectional conflict given way to an equally irrepressible class war? One popular account of the Great Railroad Strike of 1877 was a novel by Abraham Lincoln's former personal secretary, John Hay. *The Bread-Winners: A Social Study* (1883) predicted that the country would see unending industrial strife.[19] Make no mistake, by any possible criterion, in the Age of Capital the United States had the most contentious and violent labor relations of any country in the world.[20]

2. Marx's Theory of Industrial Capital

For the Age of Commerce, it made sense for us to begin with a look at Adam Smith's *The Wealth of Nations* (1776). For the labor strife of the Age of Capital, we must turn to Karl Marx's *Capital* (1867).[21] *Capital* was a "critique" of Smith's political economy but also, like it, a thought experiment that sought to capture the logic of a competitive economic system unhindered by outside interference. To Marx, capitalism, left to its own devices, would lead to endemic class struggle.

Capital is rich with various arguments, but the core of Marx's economic argument was very simple. Capital was, for him, not a factor of production but rather the premise and result of a production process that ended in the creation of "surplus value." Under capitalism, Marx argued, one single commodity, "labor power," was the source of all economic value—including surplus value. That was because labor power, and only labor power, was a good capable of producing more value than the cost of its own production. For assuming a competitive labor market, capitalists paid labor only the cost of its reproduction, or workers' minimum subsistence needs. Capitalists pocketed the excess value produced by labor power above the cost of its reproduction as surplus value—or, in pecuniary terms, their profits.

If Smith believed economic growth and development occurred through a commercial multiplier, Marx argued that the only way to unlock increasing returns to economic activity was through what might be called a labor exploitation multiplier. Thus, Marx concluded, "capital is not a thing, but a social relation between persons, established by the instrumentality of things."[22]

Capitalists, he wrote, could extract surplus value from labor power in two ways. First, they could make wage earners work more hours while paying them the same wage. This "absolute surplus value," as Marx called it, was, and is still today, a well-documented method of capitalist profit making and exploitation. Absolute surplus value has a strict limit, however, as there are only twenty-four hours in a day. Second, capitalists could invest in capital goods, which produced more goods for sale in the same increment of time—thereby increasing labor productivity. This Marx called "relative surplus value."

For the sake of this theory, Marx generally assumed that capitalists would always invest in capital goods, that industrial investment would never be lacking. Liquidity preference—money acting as a safe haven store of value, for either precautionary or speculative motives, rather than as an investable means of achieving more surplus value—is excluded by assumption. Capitalists yearn to invest, produce, and exploit. Further, assuming competitive markets, if one capitalist increases relative surplus value to stay in business, other capitalists must do so, too. The owners of capital are locked into the system, no less than are workers. The book is called *Capital*, after all, not *Capitalists*.

Marx believed that capital forced capitalists to invest in fixed capital goods and to be technologically innovative. By increasing the productive powers of an economy, capital was a progressive force. The production of ever more wealth made possible greater human emancipation. However, putting wealth aside, there was a problem with relative surplus value. Under competitive pressure, capitalists become smitten with labor-saving capital goods. But labor power is the only true source of surplus value and thus profits. By shedding labor, capitalists ultimately shed their profits as well. If not in wealth generation, there would be diminishing returns in profit making. The long-term tendency of the rate of profit, Marx argued, was therefore to fall—so dooming capitalism to crisis.

Further, from a moral point of view, did not workers deserve the fruits of their labor, including the fruits of its capacity to yield surplus value? Capitalism, Marx believed, was an economic system of unjust labor exploitation and economic inequality. But he also predicted that the proletarian working class would become politically conscious of its unjust exploitation. It would demand shorter working hours and a larger share of the wealth-generating capital goods. Ultimately, it would demand collective ownership. Marx further prophesied that capitalism pointed beyond itself, beyond class, to a future of material abundance and emancipation from drudgery and domination, where everyone would be free to develop their full human potential.[23]

Note that, whereas the Smithian dynamics of the Age of Commerce were spatial, the dynamics of Marx's economic system were of time alone. He was concerned with the rate of exploitation over time, the systemic urge toward the constant increase of productivity over time, and ultimately an economic future—Communism—that would be qualitatively different from the present.

To a fault, the Marx of *Capital* was a philosophical determinist. His historical writings, by contrast, have a wonderful feel for historical contingency, like *The Eighteenth Brumaire of Louis Napoleon* (1852). By contrast, capital's contingent dynamics—the repeating credit cycle, the eventful histories of money, liquidity, speculation, panic, and hoarding—were not a subject of *Capital*, although Marx treated them, at times insightfully, at times not, in writings posthumously published.[24] *Capital* presents a theory of a specific kind of productive asset, industrial capital goods. The time signature is linear and rather fated. Nonetheless, the book is full of insights about the kind of capital that, after all, was at the heart of the industrial revolution.

Time is indeed a crucial dimension of fixed productive capital. Assuming the owners of capital do part with liquidity and invest long-term in illiquid capital goods—and the late nineteenth century was an era, more so than any other perhaps, when they did—the cost of their investment becomes fixed over time. It becomes sunk, or irrecoverable. To industrial capitalists under conditions of market competition—which the consolidation of the national railroad network heightened during the 1880s—the variable cost of labor, no matter what percentage of total costs, loomed large. It was fungible, neither fixed nor sunk. Marx predicted capitalists would substitute machines for labor, but late-nineteenth-century American industrialists found ways to complement capital goods and labor; labor was deskilled more than it was shed.[25] Still, industrial capitalists were stuck with their capital goods, whereas to increase profits, labor could always be paid less, to the lowest point borne by labor markets.

Notwithstanding any lawlike long-term tendency in the profit rate, the profit rate in the late-nineteenth-century United States suffered for more contingent reasons. Resumption and the return to the gold standard restricted the supply of money. Industrialization produced more goods, chased by, relatively, a quantity of money that was expanding at a lesser rate.[26] But capitalist producers had to keep producing to recoup their fixed costs. More goods kept coming onto the market, driving prices downward. This deflation put a squeeze on profits. During the era's periodic financial panics, money and credit were hoarded, diminishing demand for goods. Altogether production threatened to run out ahead of demand. To increase their profits, industrial capitalists could, however, attempt to cut their labor costs, and they did.

Setting aside the ultimate validity of Marx's theory, the late-nineteenth-century U.S. industrial economy was something like a caricature of *Capital*. Much as Marx predicted, industrialization led to a system-wide drive to produce more wealth. But many U.S. industrial capitalists kept complaining about their profit margins. The United States had the world's longest workday, ten hours in 1880, and capitalists and workers fought over its length (absolute surplus value).[27] The implementation of the new capital goods in the workplace brought no less tension (relative surplus value). It all culminated in dramatic strikes and periodic violence. There was a lot of class conflict.

Finally, while U.S. wages were high by international comparison, the living standards of working people in industrial cities did not at first improve. Inequality increased. More income flowed to the owners of capital and the top 1 percent of the income distribution.[28] During the 1880s, a number of writings noted the trend toward greater inequality. Henry George's *Progress and Poverty* (1879), which blamed land rents, sold millions.[29] Further, regardless of their distribution, the rising incomes brought about by economic growth did not immediately improve human welfare. After all, the cumulative process of industrialization was catalyzed by investment in the production of "intermediate" capital goods. For instance, Andrew Carnegie produced steel ingots but not life-saving medicines or clean drinking water. Much of the fresh income generated by his heroic productive feats flowed first to him, for Scottish mansions and grouse-hunting trips, while most households still spent the vast majority of their incomes on food, clothing, and shelter.[30] In the aggregate, total output and money incomes increased, but so what? By many indices, the first generation of industrial Americans fared worse than their more rural forebears. They were shorter in height and sicker, ate less nutritious foods, lived in crowded unsanitary homes, and died younger. Infant mortality increased (probably because of bad milk).[31] The trends did not reverse until 1890 at the earliest.[32] For this generation of proletarians, Marx's "immiseration" thesis did not look so bad.

3. The Fate of Free Labor

Marx's analysis in *Capital* pointed to the workings of a large, abstract system that assigned restricted roles to capital and labor. By contrast, Americans of Marx's generation who were critical of the direction of industrial change more often looked to politics. If something was wrong with economic life, they believed, it was politics that was fundamentally to blame, not an abstract economic system. During the course of U.S. industralization, a political rallying cry—"free labor"—functioned both as a benchmark to assess the worth of economic life and as a plausible ideal worth striving for.

In contradistinction to chattel slavery, "free labor," as it emerged during the Republican mobilization of the 1850s, contained a core principle of aspirational upward mobility—hope. In 1870, 27 percent of the U.S. labor force were industrial wage earners.[33] Lincoln himself had said that wage labor was supposed to be a temporary status. The goal was ownership of productive property. This was a politics of property. In the United States, ever since the seventeenth century, white male heads of household had enjoyed, relative to those in other societies, widespread property ownership in land. Would such a distribution continue in the new era of industrial capital goods? Or would some men, the capitalists, corner the market in the ownership of capital goods and force others to permanently work for wages?

Andrew Carnegie's steelworks demonstrated the economic incentives to increase the scale of industrial enterprise. Scale reduced costs, brought increasing returns, and had first-mover advantages, warding off potential competitors. But it also meant hiring many wage laborers—who would never ascend to the ranks of business ownership or compete with Carnegie. Increasingly, unskilled operatives in factories were European immigrants, whose preference was for long hours of work and the highest possible wage, regardless of working conditions, because their aspiration was not to own and operate their own businesses, as proprietors, but rather to return to Europe with money in their pockets.[34] Their outlook and preferences disrupted U.S. labor-organizing efforts. The immigrant return rate was 10 percent in the 1870s, but it would approach 70 percent in the early twentieth century.[35] However, while the average scale of industry and the prevalence of wage labor were increasing during the late nineteenth century, a small-scale and owner-operated variety of U.S. industrialization persisted with less capital-intensity, a larger role for skilled labor, and more specialization in the particular goods produced. Because of this economic basis, the politics of property ownership was not doomed to obsolescence.[36]

Still, change was afoot. In 1870, despite new demand for them, highly skilled white-collar workers accounted for just 4.8 percent of the industrial workforce. Industry also created demand for unskilled wage-earning operatives at the bottom of the distribution, who in 1870 were already

63.4 percent of the manufacturing workforce. Immigrants would increasingly fill these ranks. Much like the service economy of the twenty-first century, industrialization threatened to hollow out the middle strata. Nonetheless, in 1870, 31.8 percent of the manufacturing workforce—not white collar—was still "skilled."[37] This group included the middling artisan or craftsman—the modest, small-scale owner of capital who employed but few men in his shop.

The Great Railroad Strike of 1877 scared men like Tom Scott so much because it represented the possibility of a class-based alliance among middling artisan-proprietors, skilled craftsmen, and unskilled, often immigrant industrial operatives. The landscape was fluid. The Great Strike was a largely spontaneous action that did not ideologically discriminate. It was carried out in the streets, by Democrats and by Republicans, by members of the Greenback-Labor Party and the Workingmen's Party, by socialists and anarchists. Thus the recurring motif of the Great Strike's visual representations was the depiction of workers together with sympathetic middling folk, including finely dressed ladies and innocent children, all participating in the demonstration.[38]

The question raised by the Great Railroad Strike of 1877 was whether this heterogeneous mix of producers, ranging in skill and in native-or-

"THE GREAT STRIKE—BLOCKADE OF ENGINES AT
MARTINSBURG, WEST VIRGINIA" (1877)
The Great Railroad Strike of 1877 was a mass action. Middle-class
sympathizers, women and children among them, participated,
as seen here. The American class structure at the time was fluid.

immigrant status, could politically organize to shape the course of American industrialization. Firms like Carnegie's, because they took advantage of greater capital-intensity, scale, and operational efficiency, were highly competitive economically speaking. However, the political question of which variety of industrialization, and in which proportion, would triumph still hung in the air.

Surely, familiarity with Marx was not necessary to develop a critique of the inequities of industrial change. American critics were more likely to look backward—to the revolutionary inheritance of Thomas Jefferson's "labor republicanism," and to the politics of widespread white male property ownership—than to look forward to any socialist, communist, or anarchist utopia. They believed that the new capital goods should be treated as the land was previously. First, capital goods should be widely distributed. Second, while they were capital, a means of production, they should also be something more: property that guaranteed equal democratic citizenship. Desire for the "manly" ownership of property—regardless of any rate of pecuniary profit—mingled with the profit motive and was a critical component of a popular inducement to invest in industry, different from Carnegie's.

In this "free labor" vision, the issue of pay—the wage, no matter how high—was simply not enough. This politics of property sought to politicize the ownership of industrial capital itself. After the Great Railroad Strike of 1877, the Noble and Holy Order of the Knights of Labor was the most successful labor union promoting this vision. Unlike Marx, the Knights of Labor did not believe in endemic economic class conflict. They opened their tent to all producers, even to middling owners of capital.[39]

Labor unions were not new in the United States. Before the Civil War, workers—"servants," in light of their dependent legal household status—organized to bargain with their "masters." The Massachusetts case *Commonwealth v. Hunt* (1842) recognized union membership, although the legality of various union tactics—including strikes—remained dubious until as late as the New Deal legislation of the 1930s. Relative to those of other industrializing countries, nineteenth-century American labor unions operated in a uniquely inhospitable legal environment.[40] Long-term membership loyalty, paid professional leadership, and employee-recognized collective bargaining were rare. The first national federation of American labor unions, the National Labor Union (NLU), was organized in 1866. Spontaneous strikes defined the bulk of union activity. After the Civil

War, the NLU leadership campaigned against the policy of resumption and the return to the gold standard. The hard times that followed the Panic of 1873 were not good for organizing. The NLU dissolved. Then came the Great Railroad Strike of 1877 and the rapid rise of the Knights of Labor.[41]

The Knights of Labor formed in Philadelphia in 1869.[42] At first, it was more of a society for male fraternization and mutual aid. But soon it transformed into an industrial union open to all "producers." Anyone who was not a banker, doctor, lawyer, or liquor manufacturer counted as a "producer." In 1879 the Knights counted ten thousand members. That year Terence Powderly, mayor of Scranton, Pennsylvania, and a member of the International Union of Machinists and Blacksmiths, became president. By 1886, the Knights had 729,000 "official" national members and counted 610 locals. In the South, the Knights opened lodges for black "producers," who tended to be agricultural laborers of some kind.[43] The Knights opened women's lodges. A plank of its national constitution promised "to secure for both sexes equal pay for equal work." In 1885 probably 10 percent of the Knights were women.[44] They were ideologically and politically diverse: Powderly was a disappointed Republican, elected mayor of Scranton on the Greenback-Labor Party ticket, while Albert Parsons, leader of the Chicago Workingmen's Party, was a socialist anarchist. The Knights hoped to organize the fluid American industrial social order.

Ideologically, the Knights raised the banner of antimonopoly. Before the Civil War, the Republican Party, in cobbling together "free labor" ideology, had transferred the antimonopoly critique of the "Money Power" onto the "Slave Power." Among Democrats, the party of Jackson, antimonopoly remained powerful.[45] Many members of both parties wondered, with economic life newly subject to sharp competition, and with profits squeezed, how the Goulds, Scotts, and Rockefellers of the world could have amassed great fortunes without somehow corrupting politics. They also raised questions of money and credit.[46] The post–Civil War national bank system pyramided bank reserves onto Wall Street. On Wall Street, going interest rates during the 1870s and '80s declined, but not everyone had access to capital at such rates. Middling to small-scale owners complained both about unfair competitive business practices by large corporations and also about small-scale proprietors' lack of access to money and credit to fund and operate their businesses.

Symbolizing both problems, the great nemesis of the Knights was Jay Gould. Membership in Knights' lodges across the country exploded in

1884–85, when local lodges successfully struck Gould's "Southwest System," which covered more than four thousand miles of railroad track, spanning five states and Indian territory. It included Tom Scott's Texas & Pacific, which Gould had snapped up from Scott in 1879, after yet another of his crippling strokes.

An essential element of the Knights' antimonopoly appeal in the West was its virulent racism against Chinese immigrants.[47] Chinese immigrants might otherwise have been natural allies of the Knights. Many were railroad wage laborers, brought to the United States on long-term labor contracts, but were highly entrepreneurial, with recognizably "free labor" aspirations toward business-owning proprietorship.[48] Instead, the Knights viewed the Chinese as low-wage tools of railroad monopolies, hired on contract conditions unacceptable to the "white race." Anti-Chinese racism was most prevalent in the West, but even the Boston Knight George McNeill warned of the "yellow peril."[49] Powderly lobbied in favor of the Chinese Exclusion Law of 1882, which barred "skilled and unskilled Chinese laborers and Chinese employed in mining," the first explicitly racist immigration ban in U.S. history.[50]

In addition to antimonopoly, the Knights criticized the industrial "wage system," or the necessity of working for wages to survive when one did not own a business oneself.[51] The Knights called for practical measures clearly meant to appeal to unskilled operatives. They demanded that employers pay their employees weekly, in full, for work performed the previous week. They called for the abolition of convict labor. Sometimes the critique of wage earning was grandiose. McNeill foresaw "an inevitable and irresistible conflict between the wage-system of labor and the republican system of government," in a callback to Jeffersonian "labor republicanism."[52] Wage earning was unmanly, unrepublican dependency. The message targeted the middling owners of capital, as well as skilled wage-earning artisans, both dreading downward social mobility. The Knights called for the "abolition of the wage system," which appealed to radical anarchists and socialists of European origins, too. The Knights thus combined, in the words of one historian, "entrepreneurial hopes and anti-capitalist despair."[53]

The Knights had more than a critique: they had a solution, calling for worker-owned cooperatives. The advantage of the "co-operative plan" over the "wage system," according to one Knight, was that "each man can feel that he is as proprietor. . . . He can feel that he is working for himself and not for a master. . . . He can feel and know that his brain and muscle weighs equally in the scale."[54] It must have been unnerving, in a culture dominated by the work ethic, to see the sheer productive force unleashed by the new energy-intensive capital goods. To own them—even in common with fellow workers rather than on terms of sole proprietorship— was one way to "feel" like one's own labor counted for something. Cooperation had broad ideological appeal. The leading liberal intellectual E. L. Godkin supported cooperatives, while the first avowedly socialist exposition of Marxist thought for an American audience was Laurence Gronlund's *The Cooperative Commonwealth* (1884).[55]

During the 1880s, the Knights of Labor founded thousands of cooperatives, including grocery stores, iron manufacturers, and home mortgage credit societies. Many were legally chartered corporations. The problem was always to obtain sufficient capital and credit, which was where the Knight's antimonopoly position and its critique of the industrial wage system overlapped. The national federation organized a capital fund to sponsor local cooperatives. Local funding mechanisms for small-scale industry, including cooperatives, ranged from hand-to-hand stock sales to formalized exchanges in small towns far from Wall Street.[56] But not much scarce capital and credit was available to meet start-up cooperative demand.

An instigator of cooperative enterprise among the Knights was its Department of Women's Work.[57] Many women were industrial wage earners—overwhelmingly young, unmarried, and segregated by sex in particular trades, like sewing, typesetting, and garment making.[58] The Knights called for equal pay regardless of sex, in an era when women earned on average half as much as men. Women formed labor unions, but they were admitted by only two national male craft unions, the printers and the garment makers.[59] Female unions commonly organized cooperatives. Kate Mullany was the young president of the Troy, New York, "Laundry Union and Co-operative Collar Co.," founded in 1869. An 1870 woman suffrage journal published the following letter from Mullany:

> I wrote to know what the ladies are doing in the way of taking the stock for our company. We are getting started now. We have enough subscribed to begin with, and we are starting up with a good prospect of getting a quick sale for our goods as soon as we have got them ready for the market. Of course, we depend altogether on the working people of the country, and on the people who are able and willing to help working girls and wish to see them get along.

The price of a debt security in the cooperative was five dollars. The "working girls" would eventually use the income from the cooperative to convert the debt into their own equity ownership. They raised enough capital. But men refused to give them laundry orders, so the business failed. The Troy, New York, union cooperative nonetheless became the model for the Knights of Labor's Department of Women's Work.[60]

Irish-born hosiery seamstress Leonara Barry was the Knights' national organizer. Widowed at a young age, she entered factory employment to support her children. By 1886, she was the president of a local Knights women's assembly in upstate New York. To organize women's assemblies nationally, she sent one of her children to a convent and another to live with a sister-in-law. She made "many unsuccessful attempts," in her own words, to found cooperatives and replace sweatshops. She complained that among male Knights, the principle of "equal pay for equal work" was "but a mockery." But even Barry believed that ideally "it was intended that man should be the breadwinner." She married a fellow Knight in 1890 and quit her organizing job. Powderly sent a letter to Knights locals comparing Barry's marriage to death. "Sister Barry's days are numbered," as she was being called "across the dark river." Upon her marriage, the Department of Women's Work collapsed.[61]

By then, the entire Knights' momentum had gone in reverse. Powderly and the national leadership had not been able to control the local unions; they kept going on strike. Powderly did not believe in strikes, as he feared they antagonized workers' potential allies among property owners. "Opposing strikes and always striking," he lamented.[62] The strikes were spontaneous and the demand was almost always the same: not the abolition of the wage system—rather, disgruntled workers wanted shorter hours and higher pay.

In the end, it was Jay Gould who turned the tide against the Knights. Knights lodges had successfully struck his Southwest System in 1884–85, but Gould quickly backtracked on wage agreements. After he fired a Knights of Labor foreman in Marshall, Texas, the state's District 101 Lodge called a strike. The strike spread, as 200,000 southwestern railroad workers walked off the job. Gould declared the Texas & Pacific bankrupt and placed parts of the corporation into temporary federal receivership. That entitled the corporation to U.S. Army protection of its property.[63]

The Great Southwest Strike against Gould sparked the nationwide Great Upheaval of 1886. That year at least 600,000 workers went on strike

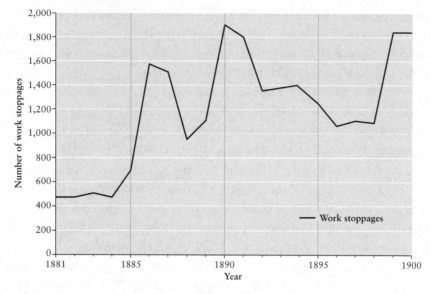

AMERICAN WORK STOPPAGES

No industrializing country had a more contentious labor history than the
United States. Spontaneous worker strikes undermined the Knights of
Labor's preferred strategy of a broad-based producers' alliance.

in at least fourteen hundred different actions, disrupting 11,562 businesses.[64] The strike wave caught Powderly and the national Knights leadership off guard. It had come from below. The leading demand was not for
the abolition of the wage system, or for better credit terms for cooperative
enterprise. It was for the eight-hour day—a simpler rallying cry, for a more
immediate and attainable demand.

Once again Chicago witnessed the worst violence. Strikes broke out first
at the Union Iron and Steel Company in the Irish neighborhood of Bridgeport.[65] Meanwhile a recently founded national craft labor union, which
was open to skilled workers only, called for a nationwide general strike on
May 1, 1886. The leader of this craft union was a former English immigrant cigar maker and union representative named Samuel Gompers.

In Chicago, workers of all loyalties rallied. On May 1, Albert and Lucy
Parsons and their two children led a march of 80,000 down Chicago's
Michigan Avenue. Across the United States more than 300,000 workers
went on strike for the eight-hour day, closing more than a thousand factories. On May 3, Chicago police shot and killed six striking workers outside
the McCormick reaper works. Chicago anarchists called a rally at Haymar-

ket Square, and 3,000 showed up. After most of the crowd dispersed, some-one (no one knows who) threw a homemade bomb into the police phalanx. Confused firing erupted. Seven police and five demonstrators were killed, and more than a hundred casualties lay in the open square. Having spoken early at the rally and departed for a nearby anarchist saloon before the vio-lence, Albert Parsons was among the eight anarchists arrested. He was among the seven sentenced to death and the four executed (one committed suicide in his cell). His final words from the gallows, "Will I be allowed to speak, oh men of America? Let me speak, Sheriff Matson! Let the voice of the people be heard! Oh . . ." Parsons was cut off by the opening of a trap door beneath his feet. He strangled to death slowly.[66]

The Great Upheaval ended at Haymarket Square. In Chicago, a red scare broke out, and police cracked down on labor organizers for months. In the Southwest, Gould had triumphed against the Knights. His lawyers found a U.S. court that issued an "injunction" against the strike on grounds that the strikers were violating nonstriking workers' constitu-tionally protected "freedom of contract," or their right to freely engage in commerce, through employment.[67] That was one appropriation of the equal commercial opportunity legacy of Jacksonian antimonopoly.

The Knights would never recover. An 1887 massacre of hundreds of black Knights sugar workers in Thibodaux, Louisiana, left the Knights reeling in the South as well.[68] By 1890, its membership had dwindled. The Knights left several legacies: industrial unionism; the possibility that labor might cross the black-white color line as well as the sex line; a politics of property and capital rather than pay and income; and the institutional project of cooperation. Virulent anti-Chinese racism figured no less. Step-ping into the vacuum left behind by the Knights would be a national labor federation of a very different kind.

In December 1886 a national federation of craft unions organized as the American Federation of Labor (AFL), with Samuel Gompers as its president. He would go to work on a far narrower, more class-based vision of labor solidarity and organizing than the Knights. The Knights had failed to cobble together a producers' alliance of middling and lower classes—modest owners of capital, skilled workers, and unskilled, commonly im-migrant, operatives. Far more successful during these years was class formation from above, at the top of the U.S. income and wealth distribu-tion. The U.S. working class fractured as it formed. Fearing the rabble, a U.S. bourgeoisie consolidated.

4. Class Consciousness, from Above

In periods of rising economic inequality when there are new ways to make money, elites commonly self-remove from their fellow citizens. In Gilded Age America, distancing of different kinds was the rule, in addition to class conflict. "Free labor" and the gender ideology of "separate spheres" arose together, and while the fate of the former hung in the balance, the latter kept its potency among the best-off. As if barbed with wire, the hard fence between the sphere of home life and that of industry made possible a newly merciless understanding of competition: Social Darwinism.

When the Great Upheaval of 1886 broke out, Upper Manhattan was the scene of national capitalist class-consciousness.[69] There the richest men in the country built faux French castle monstrosities in the day's Beaux-Arts architectural style. Their homes had steam-powered central heating and plunger flush toilets (invented in 1875). Some also had artificial illumination once Thomas Edison's 1882 Pearl Street electric power station came online (three years after his invention of the filament for the electric light bulb). But each day, of necessity, house servants still hauled water, coal, and wood in and out. Elites consorted in the Union League Club (c. 1863), the Knickerbocker Club (c. 1871), or later the Metropolitan Club (c. 1891)—all far cries, in the newly spatially separated industrial city, from working-class saloons and beer halls. Carnegie had kept a residence in New York City since 1870. John D. Rockefeller purchased a residence at 54th Street and Fifth Avenue in 1884. In 1889 Collis Huntington of the Central Pacific built a mansion at 57th Street and Fifth Avenue, across the street from the largest mansion of all, belonging to Cornelius Vanderbilt II. An even larger complex, William Vanderbilt's Triple Palace, occupied an entire city block. When Henry Frick finally decamped from Pittsburgh, he rented one of the three palaces.[70]

In an 1886 lecture on the "Labor Question," Edward Atkinson, a leading Boston intellectual, said of Commodore Vanderbilt's mansion, "Such a dwelling is not capital" because "it produces nothing." For "capital is a tool, an instrument, to be applied to production, to increase the abundance of things."[71] Such was the restrictive new definition of capital as a factor of production, a thing—even as, financially, Gilded Age mansions were capital, since they were real estate assets that appreciated in markets. Further, the many social hours that occurred within them translated into capital and credit—converted "social capital," as we would call it today.[72] But the Victorian sensibility so crucial to capitalist class-consciousness at this time was one of binaries and opposites. A series of splittings, sharper than spherings, organized consciousness.

Atkinson's answer to the "Labor Question" was that industrial capital and industrial labor must compete with each other in the sphere of private commerce between isolated individuals. When they did, each would earn its just reward—what economists today call their "marginal product." But capitalist competition must not be all consuming. It took place in one sphere. No less essential were others, split off from it.

Outside the sphere of economic competition, home life was the great focal point.[73] Prescriptively, the home was a feminized, affective space removed from commercial calculus. Nothing upset elites more than to discover, in point of fact, how much economic production still remained inside the home for many working people.[74] Jacob Riis's photographic exposé *How the Other Half Lives* (1890) provided stunning visual evidence.

JACOB RIIS, *KNEE-PANTS AT FORTY-FIVE CENTS A DOZEN—
A LUDLOW STREET SWEATER'S SHOP* (C. 1890)
A pioneering photojournalist, Riis took photographs of tenements and sweatshops in New York City's working-class neighborhoods. Nothing shocked middle-class and well-to-do viewers of the photographic series more than scenes of industrial labor performed in the home, which violated the putative domestic sanctity from commerce.

To elites, the breadwinner-homemaker family economy was sacrosanct. Industrial capitalists took this moral division of labor seriously. For many men, it made their business dealings palatable, if not desirable. It at once checked commerce, keeping it in its proper sphere, yet validated their inducement to invest in enterprise, on behalf of their families. At home, even Jay Gould was a gushing sentimentalist, a "homebody," according to his biographer, whose emotional life was organized by a sharp splitting between the "fierce extremes" of capitalist competition and the domesticity of the home.[75] In affection, Frick favored his daughter Helen over his son Childs, and upon his death he bequeathed most of his fortune to her. He had artists paint portraits of her flooded in angelic light.

THÉOBALD CHARTRAN, *PORTRAIT OF HELEN CLAY FRICK* (1905) The strong separation many Gilded Age American industrialists felt to exist between the male world of work and female domesticity is depicted here, in the maudlin and light-flooded painting Henry Frick commissioned of his daughter Helen Clay Frick—who would be a notable philanthropist and art collector in her adult life.

Tellingly, the visual focus of the portraits of upper-class women was usually the heart. Of the painted portraits at the time, the most intelligent were those by John Singer Sargent—the best and strangest being that of the Bostonian Isabella Stewart Gardner.

JOHN SINGER SARGENT,
ISABELLA STEWART GARDNER
(1888)
Gardner, the "millionaire bohemian," as she was known, was born into a wealthy New York family and was the wife of Boston shipping and railroad financier Jack Gardner. Both were important philanthropists and art collectors. At this time, the focal point of many female portraits was the heart. Sargent's portrait of Gardner is a visually arresting play on the genre.

The Cult of True Womanhood increasingly became a class project, in which elite women participated.[76] In the public square, middle- and upper-class women often leveraged the moral power of their private femininity. In 1879, Francis Willard became president of the Woman's Christian Temperance Union—a mass women's movement for "home protection" against commercial encroachments, including the intoxications of the working-class saloon.[77] Willard was also a suffragist. Competing national suffragist "women's rights" movements consolidated in 1890, but by then the movement had become disconnected from the plight of workingwomen. "This association is useless and a sham, and has never done anything for working women," angry women's typographical union members once chided the suffragist Susan B. Anthony.[78] Most wage-earning women in this era were young and not yet married. If they had to work, elites hoped they might at least be separated from men in the workplace. "Wherever the sexes work indiscriminately together," warned the Bureau of Labor Statistics report *Working Women in Large Cities* (1889), "great laxity obtains."[79] What followed laxity and pleasure would surely be the ultimate working girl commercial vice of prostitution.[80]

Elite women thus gained a form of class power. But many paid a price. Arguably, Sargent's greatest painting was *The Daughters of Edward Darley Boit* (1882). The four daughters are painted in domestic space. The youngest smiles in the foreground, while the oldest is removed to the background and looks away; with age she has become more isolated and sullen. In their parlors, many idle upper-class daughters, wives, and mothers became anxious wrecks, suffering from "neurasthenia," according to neu-

JOHN SINGER SARGENT, *THE DAUGHTERS OF EDWARD DARLEY BOIT* (1882)
Sargent's painting illustrates the psychic costs of the middle-class
ideal of domesticity.

rologist George Beard, author of *American Nervousness* (1881).[81] The intellectual Charlotte Perkins Gilman's "The Yellow Wallpaper" (1892), a short story about the psychic torments of a woman who is suffering from postpartum depression but is forbidden to perform physical activity, including work, memorialized the condition.[82]

Home life served a crucial function for the male owners of capital, providing them with the sharp moral counterpoint that they required. In stark contrast to saintly portraits of women, portraits of the great Gilded Age capitalists focused not on the heart but on the piercing eye—a tunneled, entrepreneurial vision, conveying a singular focus and drive. A 1903 photograph of banker J. P. Morgan epitomizes the genre. The shadows fall on the armchair as if Morgan were holding a knife, ready to pounce.

Many capitalists found an idealized justification for relentless economic

EDWARD STEICHEN, *J. PIERPONT MORGAN, ESQ.* (1903)
In contrast to the era's female portraiture, so often visually focusing on the heart to convey domestic sentiment, male portraiture often focused upon the piercing eye of the entrepreneur.

competition in the doctrines of so-called Social Darwinism. Charles Darwin's *On the Origin of Species* (1859) was the intellectual bombshell of the century, and in the decades after its publication, the United States became the "Darwinian country," and not because it had a great number of internationally renowned evolutionary biologists.[83] Instead, a garbled translation of Darwin gripped the imagination of the U.S. bourgeoisie. Darwin himself was not responsible, once writing to a friend, "I have received in a Manchester newspaper rather a good squib, showing that I have proved 'might is right,' and therefore that Napoleon is right, and every cheating tradesman is also right."[84]

In Upper Manhattan, the Darwinian expression "survival of the fittest" perked up some ears. "Struggle for Existence" was the title of Chapter 3 of *On the Origin of Species.* The next chapter was called "Natural Selection," but in the fifth edition Darwin changed it to "Natural Selection; The Survival of the Fittest." Not Darwin, but the English philosopher Herbert Spencer, had coined that term.[85] Spencer's writings popularized pop-Darwinian social-biological metaphors in the United States. In the struggle for the survival of the fittest, Spencer explained, the individual motive of "egoism" reigns, and society is barbarous and militant. However, in an evolving industrial society, a second basic psychological human motive—"altruism"—wins out, bringing voluntary cooperation and industrial peace. Industrialization would have a happy ending, if evolution were only left to its own course.

The U.S. owners of capital and their favored intellectuals forgot to read Spencer's book through to the end.[86] They got stuck on the stage of egotistical industrial rapaciousness. "Egoism" was a far crueler concept than Adam Smith's notion of commercial "self-interest."[87] It was abstract and antisocial, and it need not be peaceful, whereas Smith had believed that commercial discourse refined sociability and was a blow to hierarchy. Julian West, protagonist of Edward Bellamy's bestselling utopian science fiction novel *Looking Backward: 2000–1887* (1888), looks back from the fictional year 2000 and recalls that for capitalists during the 1880s, "selfishness was their only science."[88] Indeed, "the fortunes of railroad companies," proclaimed James J. Hill, who consolidated the Great Northern Railway system during the 1880s, "are determined by the law of the survival of the fittest."[89] Of this law, Carnegie remarked, "It is here; we cannot evade it." Further, "while the law may be sometimes hard for the individual; it is best for the race, because it insures the survival of the fittest in every department."[90]

Andrew Carnegie adored Spencer.[91] When he first read Spencer's books, he later recalled, "I remember that light came in as a flood and all was clear. Not only had I got rid of theology and the super-natural, but I had found the truth of evolution. 'All is well since all grows better' became my motto, my true source of comfort."[92] When Spencer arrived in New York for a triumphant U.S. tour in 1882, Carnegie took him to see his steelworks, but Spencer saw no evidence of evolutionary progress, remarking, "Six months' stay here would justify suicide."[93] Back in Manhattan for a farewell steak dinner at Delmonico's restaurant, Spencer gave a speech. "My address," he recalled in his autobiography, "was mainly devoted to a criticism of American life as characterized by over-devotion to work."[94] We have no record of the speech's reception among the very likely stunned audience.

Spencer's 1882 tour came at the height of his American popularity. By then, even the Protestant clergy had converted to a version of Social Darwinism, with divine purpose its first cause. The new religious inflection enabled these doctrines to appeal to religious businessmen. Perhaps the most important American advocate of evolution was a former Congregationalist preacher who went on to become a founding father of American sociology. William Graham Sumner, who became a professor of political and social science at Yale in 1872, wrote in *What Social Classes Owe to Each Other* (1883) that the law of competition "can no more be done away with than gravitation" and that "millionaires are a product of natural selection."[95] What the social classes owed to each other was, essentially, nothing: "Poverty was the best policy."[96] There was no exploitation—only "freedom of contract." Men who by their supposedly voluntary unemployment refused to be breadwinners were borderline criminals. Elites implored state and municipal authorities to criminalize unemployment through "involuntary pauper labor laws."[97]

The political implications of this line of thinking were deeply conservative. *Popular Science Monthly* editor Edward Youmans once debated Henry George, author of the redistributionist *Progress and Poverty*. Sure, Youmans admitted, "New York City is corrupt and the rich are selfish and do nothing to help the poor." "What do you propose to do about it?" George pressed. Youmans answered, "Nothing! You and I can do no thing at all.

It's all a matter of evolution. We can only wait for evolution. Perhaps in four or five thousand years evolution may have carried men beyond this state of things."[98] Sumner called democracy "the pet superstition of the age."[99] Charles Eliot Perkins, president of the Chicago, Burlington, & Quincy Railroad, expressed the antidemocratic tendencies of elite thought:

> When we have two or three times as many voters as now and few owners of property in proportion to the whole, there may be troubles which will upset the whole scheme and make it necessary to establish one or more strong governments with large standing armies.[100]

Broad support emerged among upper-class New Yorkers for limiting suffrage according to property ownership in municipal government, to limit the "excesses of democracy."[101]

Labor violence sharpened capitalists' sense of distance from their fellow citizens, which often took overtly racist form. After the Great Railroad Strike of 1877, Joseph Medill—who decades earlier had championed "free labor" and Abraham Lincoln's first presidential nomination—published an editorial in his *Chicago Tribune* titled "The Dangerous Classes." Typically, the most dangerous included the "new immigrants" who arrived not from England or Germany but other parts of Europe. The notion of "white ethnics" did not yet exist. (There were as many as sixty-three distinct "races" among the working population of the United States, declared one 1888 study of the subject.)[102] At its birth, the American republic had been among the more economically equal places in the world. By 1877, industrial class formation had made it possible for the former abolitionist Medill to write that "dangerous classes" were "governed by their passions; they are coarse in tastes and vicious in habits; they are ignorant and revengeful; they are readily influenced by the worst class of demagogues and revolutionists, and are easily maddened by liquor." The best solution? "A little powder, used to teach the dangerous classes a needful lesson, is well burned, provided there are bullets in front of it."[103]

5. Birth of a Politics of Income

Many of the class tensions of the 1870s and '80s were rooted in a distributive politics—the question of who got how much of what—of property and capital. During the 1880s, however, the outlines of a new distributive politics were already emerging: the distributive politics of income rather than property, the division of the spoils of capital between profits and pay. As the right of where and whether to invest is an element of property ownership, the politics of income, while full of redistributive potential, ceded the prerogative of investment to the owners of capital.

In the twentieth century, the politics of industrial income would be the leading site of distributive conflict. In the late nineteenth century, it emerged from two separate locations. One was the Samuel Gompers–led labor union, the AFL, which focused on pay (labor income). The other was a new "nonprofit" corporate philanthropy that focused on what to do with profits (capital income). Both social movements accepted, grudgingly in one instance, happily in the other, that the ownership of capital would not exist on an equitable basis. The AFL sought a more equitable distribution between profits and pay, or labor earnings. Meanwhile, from above, "nonprofit" corporations transformed profits from industrial capital into redistributive, philanthropic wealth—not capital.

After the collapse of the Knights of Labor following the Great Upheaval of 1886, the AFL quickly became the dominant national labor federation.[104] The AFL was a nationwide association of craft unions, of skilled workers. It was thoroughly class conscious but focused on a single issue of distributive justice, as it sought to increase its members' pay and reduce capitalists' exploitation of labor. Between 1870 and 1920, the number of hours worked per person each day nudged up ever so slightly.[105] The ten-hour workday was the norm; the eight-hour workday remained an aspiration. The AFL also advocated an "economy of high wages." The union operated in a hostile workplace and legal environment, and it took employer-employee antagonism for granted. But the AFL agreed with employers on issues of sex difference. Seeking to tame the bachelor culture of transient young male industrial wage earners, the AFL's economy of high wages was an economy of aspirational male breadwinning, to support female homemaking.

Gompers was born in 1850 in London, the grandson of Dutch Jews, into a family of cigar makers.[106] The family migrated to New York in 1863, and Gompers learned the craft of cigar rolling while working in his father's Lower East Side tenement shop. The craft was then in flux. In some shops, female Czech and Jewish immigrants were replacing skilled male craftsmen, as were new capital goods such as cigar-rolling machinery.[107] In

1873 Gompers joined the craftsmen shop of a skilled German émigré who preferred to hire "fellow Socialist exiles."[108] Gompers learned German and read Marx in working-class beer halls. In 1876 he became president of Local 144 of the Cigarmakers' International Union. Gompers, however, was most taken with another German text. Carl Hillman's "Practical Suggestions for Emancipation" (1873) called for disciplined trade unionism instead of uncoordinated mass action. Gompers became critical of labor radicalism, asking what came of it? He believed workers should demand less of political action in the electoral arena, and more economic spoils from their unions in their everyday lives.

Gompers called it "pure and simple unionism." Union members would do more than spontaneously strike. They would pay regular dues. The union would have a strike fund and would also offer unemployment, sick, and death benefits. Union officers would be paid regular salaries. They would decide when workers went out on strike. The role of the union was to bargain with employers for better pay and working conditions, including shorter hours. When and where capitalists invested capital and sought profits, the AFL sought a more just wage bargain.

Gompers had a brush with the state that proved consequential for his worldview. The Cigarmakers' Union had at first supported legislation to ban "unsanitary home-work" from tenement houses. Sweatshop labor brought down skilled male wages. In 1884 New York State passed a statute that abolished cigar making in tenements. But in *In re Jacobs* (1885), the New York court of appeals struck it down, holding that it infringed on workers' "personal liberty." In 1885, Gompers later recalled, "We found our work was nullified."[109] So began a two-decade streak of decisions striking down "protective labor legislation," culminating in the U.S. Supreme Court's decision in *Lochner v. New York* (1905), which—carrying forward the old Jacksonian ideal of equal commercial opportunity through U.S. Supreme Court Justice Stephen Field—declared that a New York ten-hour law for bakers was an unconstitutional infringement on the Fourteenth Amendment's protection of "liberty to contract." In a hostile legal environment where past Jacksonian critiques of government privilege now served to protect the economic privileges of private capitalists, unions had no recourse but their own devices.

Gompers distrusted the state, for good reason, so he shied away from political action. An astute political tactician, he sensed that most spontaneous strikes were mounted over issues of wages and hours—practical, not utopian, issues. Gompers and the AFL announced full support for the eight-hour day. To achieve greater discipline, he drew a line around skilled craft labor, a homogenous group. The AFL was distant from, if not hostile to, small-scale owners of capital and to "new immigrants"—unskilled central and eastern Europeans who continued to arrive by the millions. As the president of the Amalgamated had put it in 1883 to a Senate committee, these "Hungarians, Poles, Italians, Bohemians" didn't "know the difference . . . between light work and heavy work, or good and bad wages."[110] Following the path set by Chinese exclusion, the AFL supported the legal restriction of immigration from Europe. AFL locals also commonly excluded blacks.

The AFL counted a national membership of 50,000 in 1886. In 1890 its membership reached 200,000.[111] Gompers continued to hone the message. In its politics of pay, the AFL supported industrial male breadwinning. Gompers's Cigarmakers' Union 1867 constitution had opened membership to women, but as large-scale cigar-making factories replaced skilled male laborers with machines tended by unskilled female operators, Gompers had bowed to the wishes of his membership. The same happened at the AFL. By 1904, as one AFL member put it:

> We stand for the principle that it is wrong to permit any of the female sex of our country to be forced to work, as we believe that the man should be provided with a fair wage in order to keep his female relatives from going to work. The man is the provider and should receive enough for his labor to give his family a respectable living.[112]

In 1886, correctly or not, Gompers told Congress that more than anything union members simply wanted to eat "meat." They wanted "leisure," to wear a "clean shirt," to have "time to read," and to have "a pretty picture on the wall, or perhaps a piano or organ in his parlor."[113] The evocation of separate spheres was highly strategic in its appeal to elite mores. Eight hours for work, eight hours for rest, and eight hours for "what we will" was the mantra.[114] Meanwhile, to protect male wages, the AFL supported "protective legislation" for women. In *Ritchie v. People* (1895), the Illinois Supreme Court held that an eight-hour law for women was an unconstitutional infringement on women's "liberty of contract," but the U.S. Supreme Court upheld protective labor legislation for women in *Muller v. Oregon* (1908).[115] Aspirational male breadwinning also meshed with the AFL's exclusion of "new immigrants"—many of them young men without families yet to support. In cities such as Carnegie's Pittsburgh, the AFL's labor aristocracy might earn twice the wages of unskilled operatives.[116]

The blind spot in the AFL's vision was that it took for granted the private inducement to invest. What if liquidity preference triumphed instead, and the owners of capital chose not to invest in employment-intensive enterprise? The AFL had no means to make them. Meanwhile the owners of capital continued to resist unionization of any kind, armed with legal injunctions from sympathetic courts. "Government by injunction" was a unique aspect of the U.S. landscape. Other common-law nations took different paths, developing, say, systems of arbitration (which had been the Knights' preference).[117] Between 1880 and 1930, according to one estimate, U.S. courts would issue no less than 4,300 injunctions against labor union activity.[118] The AFL's "pure and simple unionism," although it had superseded the Knights in labor organizing, struggled to operate in what little space government by injunction left to the embattled labor movement.

Meanwhile another politics of income arose: nonprofit corporate philanthropy. In March 1881, two months before his death, Tom Scott sent a letter to the chairman of the trustee committee of the University of Pennsylvania (a month before he would sell all his holdings in the Texas & Pacific to Jay Gould for $2.4 million).[119] It read: "I want to present to the University of Pennsylvania fifty thousand dollars of 6% Bonds to endow a chair of Mathematics in the Arts Department as I understand help is needed for a chair of this character."[120] The Thomas A. Scott Professor of Mathematics still exists. Nonprofit corporate philanthropy was yet another Gilded Age innovation that Tom Scott had some hand in creating and that his former protégé Andrew Carnegie took to new heights and perfected.

Charity was not new, but what was new was its institutional home. In the Age of Commerce, all corporations, including charitable corporations, had been subsovereigns, chartered for a distinct "public purpose" that limited their activities. A corporation that was chartered to be a university could not become an orphanage, just as a joint-stock corporation that was

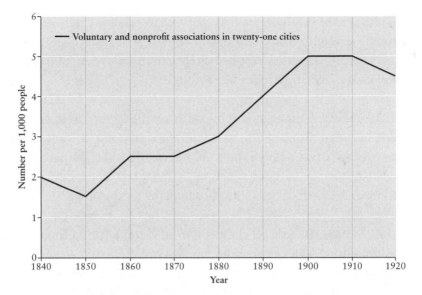

VOLUNTARY AND NONPROFIT ASSOCIATIONS PER CAPITA
Paralleling the rise of the for-profit business corporation was the
proliferation of its putative mirror opposite, the nonprofit corporation,
whose tasks were to embody nonmarket altruism and redistribute
philanthropic wealth.

chartered to build a bridge could not turn around and sell insurance.
Jacksonian-era general incorporation laws opened access to incorporation and marked corporations newly private.

Some chartered restrictions remained.[121] In 1873 the Commonwealth
of Pennsylvania held a constitutional convention, in large part because
many members of the legislature hoped to curb the Pennsylvania Railroad's purchasing of mines and other property, arguably in excess of the
corporation's 1846 charter, as well as its influence on legislation. The
new constitution that emerged from it ultimately led to a 1874 General
Incorporation Law that introduced a binary corporate classification—
"corporations for profit" and "corporations not for profit."[122] This institutional split of capital from its opposite mirrored the era's psychological
sphering. Egoism and altruism, commonly marked masculine and feminine, would be located in corporations that were either for profit or not.[123]

Carnegie appropriated that split and scaled it up far beyond the endowment of a single math professorship. In 1889 he published an essay in the
Boston literary magazine *North American Review* called "Wealth." "The
problem of our age," he opened, "is the proper administration of wealth,

so that the ties of brotherhood may still bind together the rich and poor in harmonious relationship." He acknowledged industrial class tensions, which, he freely admitted, resulted directly from his variety of large-scale capital- and energy-intensive industrialization:

> We assemble thousands of operatives in the factory, in the mine, and in the counting-house, of whom the employer can know little or nothing, and to whom the employer is little better than a myth. All intercourse between them is at an end. Rigid castes are formed. . . . Each caste is without sympathy for the other.

Further, "under the law of competition, the employer of thousands is forced into the strictest economies, among which the rates paid to labor figure prominently." That sounded like Marx. Capitalists had no choice but to compete, systematically driving down the cost of labor. Of necessity, Carnegie argued, "there is friction between the employer and the employed, between capital and labor."[124] Gompers, too, could not have agreed more. Carnegie just had a different plan for what to do about it than either Marx's Communism or Gompers's pure-and-simple unionism.

The problem of "wealth" was actually the problem of what Carnegie called "surplus revenues" (what Marx called "surplus value"). The capitalist had a number of options. Profits could become capital again. The capitalist could reinvest long term in more productive capital. Profits could remain money capital, for purposes of short-term speculation or precautionary hoarding. Carnegie did not believe in speculation; he was too bold to hoard; and his own profits were so large that his business enterprise could not possibly absorb them as new investments. Consumption was another option. Carnegie bought a yacht named *Seabreeze* and a Scottish castle he called Skibo. But as money incomes rose with industrialization and were unequally distributed, the propensity to consume among the rich could not keep up. Carnegie could not spend it all. And conspicuous consumption did little to repair the ties of brotherhood sundered by industrialization. Another option was to pay workers higher wages, but that would not do, for "the law of accumulation of wealth, and the law of competition" could not be challenged. That was a matter of evolution.[125]

According to Carnegie, what was left were "three modes in which surplus wealth can be disposed of." First, there was inheritance to family members. Second, "it can be bequeathed for public purposes" upon death.

Finally, "it can be administered during their lives by its possessors." Carnegie advocated the final option. It was "the duty of the man of wealth" to consider "all surplus revenues . . . simply as trust funds, which he is called upon to administer" in order "to produce the most beneficial results for the community." The "man of wealth thus becoming the mere agent and trustee for his poorer brethren, bringing to their service his superior wisdom, experience, and ability to administer, doing for them better than they would or could do for themselves." "The man who dies rich thus dies disgraced." The owner of capital who wisely gave away surplus revenues during his lifetime was practicing philanthropy.[126]

Philanthropy was not charity, which smacked of dependency.[127] Distributing "small quantities among the people" for short-term reasons, like quelling hunger, Carnegie argued, would lead only to "indulgence of appetite" and "excess" (read: alcohol and sex).[128] Philanthropists had to think big and long term. Carnegie's own long-term industrial investments had prepared him for that. Rockefeller said, "The best philanthropy is constantly in search of finalities—a search for cause, an attempt to cure evils at their source."[129] In "Wealth," Carnegie listed the best targets of philanthropic giving: libraries, universities, concert halls, public baths, parks, conservatories, and astronomical observatories. All these cultural institutions benefited the "race," and Carnegie would go on to endow many of them.

Philanthropy's first mission, rather explicitly, was to balm class conflict through cultural and civilizational uplift. "All classes of our people," explained Boston mayor Samuel C. Cobb at the dedication of a building for Boston's Museum of Fine Arts in 1876, "will derive benefit and pleasure from barely looking upon objects that appeal to the sense of the beautiful." Boston's MFA was founded in 1870, the same year as the Metropolitan Museum of Art in New York. The Philadelphia Museum of Art (1876) and the Art Institute of Chicago (1879) soon followed.[130] It was yet another industrial-era splitting, between capital and its opposite, between economic production and idealized aesthetic appreciation.[131] There were critics. Walt Whitman, the greatest American "producerist" artist, lamented that "immense capital and capitalists" were funding a new form of aristocratic cultural production that was an "anti-democratic disease and monstrosity."[132] In the arts, a backlash would set in quickly against distancing Culture with a capital C from the nitty-gritty of economic life. This backlash, called "realism," was led in the United States by the Boston Brahmin

William Dean Howells, author of a breakthrough social realist novel, much about class conflict, titled *A Hazard of New Fortunes* (1890).[133]

Carnegie had split redistributed philanthropic wealth from profit-seeking capital. Of course, he, as the owner of capital, had the power to decide how much of his profits were "surplus" and could therefore become philanthropic wealth. Like a pair of scissors, the emerging for-profit-nonprofit split cut out institutions, such as cooperatives, that explicitly mixed capitalist production with other values besides profit maximization. Consciously, egoistic and altruistic drives became more singularly expressed. At the same time, philanthropy promised some kind of engagement with the working class. The effort, as well as the for-profit-nonprofit corporate split, and the building of so many libraries, universities, and museums, began to lend U.S. industrial society its institutional, ethical, and architectural structure.

In their lifetimes, Carnegie and Rockefeller gave away hundreds of millions of dollars. Rockefeller helped endow many universities, including rechartering the University of Chicago in 1889. Both nonprofit philanthropy and pure-and-simple unionism, born in the fires of the class conflicts of the 1880s, would prove to be lasting. But by shunning partisan democratic politics, both philanthropists and pure-and-simple unionists would be on the sidelines during the political crisis of the 1890s, which was initiated not by industrial class conflict but by a farmers' revolt.

CHAPTER 10

THE POPULIST REVOLT

I N THE SUMMER OF 1896, THE DEMOCRATIC PARTY GATHERED
in Chicago to nominate a new candidate for president. The party had
been born in the Age of Commerce, in the days of Andrew Jackson, with
an antimonopoly critique of government privilege, on behalf of a commitment to equal commercial opportunity. Now many in the party had come
to believe that concentrated private corporate power, rather than central
government, posed the greater risk to democracy. Using the tools of government, the idea went, the people must wrest back power and fight economic, not political, privilege, and plutocracy, not aristocracy.

In 1896, the sitting president, New York Democrat Grover Cleveland,
was unpopular due to the economic slump that had followed the Panic of
1893, which was made worse by U.S. adherence to the British-backed gold
standard, given its deflationary bias. Cleveland believed in the sanctity of
the gold standard as the visible anchor of international investor confidence and expectations. He would do nothing to reinflate prices. But he
would also not run for the presidency again.

The Constitution granted the federal government the right to coin
money, and Hamilton had established a gold and silver metallic basis to the
dollar. But the Coinage Act of 1873—passed in preparation for resumption, the 1879 return to dollar-gold convertibility at pre–Civil War parity—
had eliminated the free minting of silver and effectively demonetized the
metal.[1] Critics of the gold standard noted that the Coinage Act of 1834 had
mandated gold-to-silver convertibility at a ratio of 16 to 1. In the early
1890s, in the absence of major recent world gold discoveries and in the
wake of a surge in silver mining in the U.S. West, the market ratio of gold

to silver hovered near 30 to 1. "Silverites" decrying the "Crime of '73" demanded that the U.S. Mint freely coin silver at 16 to 1. That would enrich silver producers but also increase the U.S. hard money supply, reflate prices, prompt credit expansion, and ease the economic depression.

Ever since the Civil War, the Democratic Party had been divided regionally on the money question.[2] Cleveland's northeastern wing was pro-gold. Western silver miners and western indebted farmers were not. One leader of the anti-gold bloc was a thirty-six-year-old congressman from Nebraska, William Jennings Bryan, who in 1896 decided on an improbable run for president. His long-shot strategy was to secure the nomination in Chicago by delivering a convention speech so rousing that delegates could not help but vote for him.

Bryan, a former lawyer, took the podium in Chicago on July 9, 1896, and proceeded to give arguably the most electrifying speech in all U.S. political history.[3] The first passage to draw significant applause was the definition of a "business man."

> We say to you that you have made the definition of a business man too limited in its application. The man who is employed for wages is as much a business man as his employer; the attorney in a country town is as much a business man as the corporation counsel in a great metropolis; the merchant at the cross-roads store is as much a business man as the merchant of New York; the farmer who goes forth in the morning and toils all day, who begins in spring and toils all summer, and who by the application of brain and muscle to the natural resources of the country creates wealth, is as much a business man as the man who goes upon the Board of Trade and bets upon the price of grain; the miners who go down a thousand feet into the earth, or climb two thousand feet upon the cliffs, and bring forth from their hiding places the precious metals to be poured into the channels of trade are as much business men as the few financial magnates who, in a back room, corner the money of the world. We come to speak of this broader class of business men.[4]

This populist rhetoric pitted "the people" against a sinister, illegitimate power that was outside the true polity.[5] A powerful economic elite was choking off economic opportunity for a "broader class," Bryan argued, hearkening back to the party's roots in the Jacksonian rhetoric of equality of commercial opportunity. But when he referred specifically to "the farmer," the convention hall began to rumble. "My God! My God! My God!" one delegate shouted, throwing his hat into the air, beating the empty chair in front of him, as if a politician were directly acknowledging his plight for the first time.[6]

The gold standard was only "the issue of 1776 all over again," Bryan remarked. Should the American republic have a "gold standard because England has?" No, he answered:

> Having behind us the producing masses of this nation and the world, supported by the commercial interests, the laboring interests, and the toilers everywhere, we will answer their demand for a gold standard by saying to them: You shall not press down upon the brow of labor this crown of thorns; you shall not crucify mankind upon a cross of gold.[7]

Bryan laced his fingers over his forehead in the shape of a crown, then stepped back from the podium and extended his arms from his sides, posing in the shape of a cross. He held the stance for five seconds. The audience stood in hushed silence. Finally he descended from the stage and walked back to the Nebraska delegation.

"When I finished my speech," Bryan would remember, "I went to my seat in a silence that was really painful. When I neared my seat, somebody near me raised a shout, and the next thing I was picked up—and bedlam broke loose."[8] All of a sudden "the floor of the convention seemed to heave up," the *New York World* reported, and "everybody seemed to go mad at once." There were "hills and valleys of shrieking men and women." Two delegates were "crying bitterly, great tears rolling from their eyes into their bearded cheeks."[9] The pandemonium lasted twenty-five minutes. The next day, in a stunning repudiation of the party's sitting president and the party elites, the Democrats nominated Bryan.

A few weeks later the People's Party, an insurgent, agrarian-based third party founded in 1891, met at their convention in St. Louis. The Populists (as they were also known) voted to nominate Bryan for president, too, and thereby "fuse" with the Democratic campaign. The Republicans had already nominated a gold supporter, Ohioan William McKinley. From the Republican convention came this report: "There is no life in it. The applause is hollow; the enthusiasm dreary and the delegates sit like hogs in a

car and know nothing about anything."[10] The 1896 "battle of the standards" had begun.

1. The Populist Cause

Bryan went on to lose the presidential election by a comfortable margin.
Having merged its fate with Bryan's candidacy, the People's Party collapsed and quickly passed from the scene. President McKinley signed the
Gold Standard Act of 1900, which officially demonetized silver. What,
then, was the significance of the Populist Revolt, beyond a great political
speech and an electoral repudiation?

For one thing, it kept alive the Populist current that has always run
through U.S. politics. It is often rural and distrustful of elite and urban
power. It is nationalist and antiglobalist but also ideologically indeterminate. Above all, it has a distinctively emotional pitch (that has often been
religious in substance and tone). It is critical of economic inequality but
commonly succumbs to racist, and sometimes also anti-Semitic, scape-
goating. In the 1890s, for instance, after making a short-lived attempt at
cross-race solidarity, the Populist Revolt ended in the South with an orgy
of racist violence that secured white supremacy there for another generation.[11] Populism, however, did contribute to a turn-of-the-twentieth-
century political-economic project that was larger than itself. No matter
how sophisticated they may be, economic elites may abuse their power
and deserve criticism, even of the uncultured kind. The only democratic
recourse may be the state. "We believe that the power of government—in
other words, of the people—shall be expanded," the People's Party platform stated.[12] By contributing to a reimagining of national public authority in the midst of a globalizing economy, the Populists helped set an
agenda that would last long after the Age of Capital.[13]

Bryan and his 1896 supporters were not all clodhopping farmers, destined for the dustbin of history.[14] The U.S. agricultural sector was hardly
backward: in the era of industrialization, it was more economically productive than that of any other country in the world. What the agrarian
revolt of the 1890s did was to further politicize the course of industrial
economic change. Industrial proprietors and wage earners had struggled
to do that in the 1880s, but that industrial class war did not overlap with
the Populist Revolt. No alliance between disgruntled industrial wage earners and farm households ever materialized. By 1896 the violent class wars

of the 1880s were over, and the AFL's "pure and simple unionism," shunning electoral politics and committed to a politics of male pay, was on the rise. But in the large agricultural sector, property-owning farm households rallied to the Populist critique of unchecked private corporate power. Their critique would prove consequential for the entire political economy.

For one thing, critics of the British-backed gold standard were not wrong on the details. While the gold standard created international confidence and a stable environment of expectations, it is not clear that the United States needed European capital, and the gold standard also transmitted financial volatility and a strong deflationary bias. Only the international gold standard would make the Great Depression of the 1930s truly great—putting an end to the Age of Capital altogether. Arguably, the 1896 U.S. presidential election was the first democratic election in history that explicitly put the issue of economic globalization on the table. Not for the last time did globalization—so seemingly abstract a process—filter through national politics at such a high emotional pitch.

Further, Populism, resonating with some urban constituencies, kept alive antimonopoly ideology. That meant the economic drift toward large-scale, corporate industry remained squarely in the political arena, even after 1896.[15] Bryan, who ran as the Democratic nominee again in 1900, and lost again by an even greater margin, evoked more than agrarianism; he also stood for the possibility of small-scale industrial economic life, defending the American value of market competition, which was why his invocation of the "business man" stirred such deep emotions.

None of these issues were going away anytime soon. The defeat of Bryan affirmed the gold standard, but the founding of the decentralized Federal Reserve System in 1913 reformed the U.S. monetary system—with the approval of Bryan, who was by then a member of the progressive Democratic president Woodrow Wilson's cabinet. Meanwhile scale continued to increase dramatically in the industrial corporate sector. The Great Merger Movement, from 1895 until 1904, was the greatest moment of industrial corporate consolidation in U.S. history, recapitalizing in a short span a significant share of industry. That the merger movement went into high gear after the defeat of Bryan was surely no coincidence. Capital was becoming ever more corporate, in both its money and its productive forms, consisting of corporate stocks and bonds, as well as the productive assets of the factories.

Industrial corporations aggrandized power. In 1901 the Wall Street banker J. P. Morgan consolidated Andrew Carnegie's steel companies into the largest corporation in the world, U.S. Steel. Meanwhile the Populist Revolt was superseded by the more urban Progressive movement. In the early twentieth century, Progressives, focusing on the industrial corporation and on cities, began to reconceive the relationship between private corporate power and the public interest, fashioning such concepts as "natural monopoly" and "public utility." By politicizing capital's pecuniary gains, the Progressives would make great contributions to twentieth-century income politics.

For all the drama of the Populist Revolt, American political economy, a step at a time, kept shifting from targeting the ownership of capital to targeting the regulation and distribution of the gains realized from capital investment—away from a distributive politics of property, toward one of income. The public interest was reimagined, but investment was left to corporations. In this sense, too, the Populists, and their increasingly anachronistic politics of property—in defense of farmers, small-scale businessmen, and the business project of cooperatives—lost once again.

2. The Farmers' Alliance and the People's Party

In the era of industrialization, the household remained the central unit of U.S. farm enterprise. In 1880, 43.8 percent of Americans—22 million people—lived on farms. Between 1860 and 1900, there were 3.75 million new U.S. farms, the vast majority west of the Mississippi.[16] The American farm sector was the great agricultural powerhouse of world markets, which were both globalized and highly competitive.

As the gold standard held prices down and more commodities flooded the world market, urban industry benefited greatly from ever cheaper inputs due to increased agricultural productivity. After a harvest, farmers were forced to accept a competitive world market price for their crops. Farmers in this era grew wealthier in absolute terms. But relatively, industry captured a larger share of the newfound productivity gains, due to increasing returns in commerce and manufacturing.[17] While many farmers were in debt, the great railroad corporations, which farmers depended on to take their crops to market—and which set prices for their customers based on their own costs rather than being forced to take a competitive market price, as farmers were—grew rich. Bankers, who controlled farmers' access to credit, increased their own incomes.

During the late 1880s, crying out against "monopoly," many farmers organized a series of Alliances, whose chief goal was to create farmer-owned business cooperatives. These cooperatives would allow farmers to store their own crops and thereby increase their market power—maybe even transform them from price takers to price givers. Credit cooperatives would expand farmers' access to finance on better terms. But the cooperative movement failed. Many disgruntled agrarians then turned to electoral politics, and the Populist Revolt—which would later join Bryan's upstart 1896 Democratic presidential campaign—was born.

The Farmers' Alliance, founded in 1877, was first, basically, a farmers' mutual aid society and a periodic forum for rural socialization. In 1886—the year of industrial labor's Great Upheaval—the Alliance became something else, and membership exploded. It began in the Cross Timbers region of central Texas, where the cotton farms of the South met the wheat farms of the Great Plains.[18]

The issue in Cross Timbers was the terms under which farmers would become commercial, as they undoubtedly would. In 1883 Jay Gould's Texas & Pacific Railway bisected the region, expanding possibilities for commercial production of both cotton and wheat. Farmers complained of land titles stolen by large landowners and cattlemen, discriminatory railroad rates, an insufficient money supply, and high levels of debt. Because of Gould's Texas & Pacific, the Knights of Labor had arrived. When the Knights carried out their fateful strike against Gould in 1886, the Cross Timbers Farmers' Alliance supported it. The Great Upheaval of 1886 was a turning point for urban labor. After Gould's triumph, the Knights entered their demise, urban labor radicalism flagged, and Gompers's AFL and its politics of pay, or white male breadwinning, surged. But in the rural United States, the Farmers' Alliance grew after 1886, picking up the banner of antimonopoly and the politics of property.

In 1886 members of the growing statewide Farmers' Alliance met in the Cross Timbers town of Cleburne, Texas, and issued its fifteen Cleburne Demands, all but four of which evoked the Knights of Labor's 1878 platform:

> We demand: The recognition by incorporation of trade unions, cooperative stores and such other associations as may be organized by the industrial classes to improve their financial condition, or to promote their general welfare . . . [and] the substitution of legal tender Treasury notes for the issue of the national banks; that the

Congress of the U.S. regulate the amount of such issue, by giving to
the country a per capita circulation that shall increase as the population and business interests of the country expand.[19]

The Texas Farmers' Alliance called for the federal government to issue not
only silver coinage but greenbacks. Further, it called for more favorable
laws of incorporation for labor unions and cooperatives. This was not an
anticorporate demand *tout court*. At a time when state law was splitting
the corporate form between for-profit and nonprofit, Texas farmers hoped
to incorporate organizations that fell somewhere in the cooperative, entrepreneurial middle.

After 1886 the Farmers' Alliance became a genuine social movement,
sustained by the political ideology of antimonopoly and rooted in the ambitious entrepreneurial project of forming economic cooperatives. In
1887–88 its "lecturers," many of them women, rode circuit, all preaching
the gospel (the evangelical Christian tone was inescapable) of cooperative
enterprise. Local chapters of the Farmers' Alliance spread like wildfire
across the South and the West.[20]

The majority of U.S. farmers did not become members of a Farmers'
Alliance. Nonetheless, due to the interactions of the gold standard, high
debt loads, railroad pricing strategies, and competitive world market
prices, the grievances of many small-scale commercial farmers were real.
In the South, the unjust and inefficient crop lien system, which crowded
black and white sharecroppers into producing cotton, was to blame. Cotton was an international commodity, but the South remained cut off from
national labor markets and, to a lesser degree, from international capital
markets. With the entry of Egyptian and Indian cotton onto the world
market, demand proved insufficient, and the price of cotton fell, which exacerbated southern debt burdens. Chapters of the Farmers' Alliance and
of the segregated Colored Farmers' Alliance appeared across the South in
great numbers in 1887–88.[21] Unlike the South, the Great Plains was fully
integrated into the Atlantic capital market. U.S. farm mortgage debt increased by 42 percent in the 1880s, and by 1890 farmers had mortgaged
somewhere between 30 and 40 percent of farm acreage west of the Mississippi and east of the Rocky Mountains.[22] More commodities came onto
market, threatening to overwhelm it. Further, due to the gold standard,
the quantity of hard money did not keep pace with the surge in commodity production. Price deflation set in, increasing existing debt burdens.

Many western farmers complained of debt, worsened by a restricted money supply and falling prices.

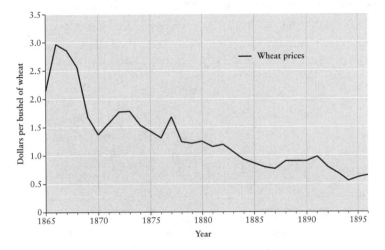

DOLLARS PER BUSHEL OF WHEAT

In the Age of Capital, the United States was a world agricultural powerhouse, exporting great volumes of many commodities. But in tandem with U.S. commitment to the deflationary gold standard, greater production contributed to falling prices, which exacerbated the debt burdens of many farmers.

The railroad corporations contributed to the farmers' troubles. The Farmers' Alliance charged the railroads with discriminating against small, rural customers, a violation of property owners' equality of commercial opportunity. The antimonopoly charge evoked Jacksonian Democracy but also the post–Civil War Granger movement. Granger laws, which had passed in many midwestern states, forbade railroad rate discrimination.[23] The U.S. Supreme Court had upheld such laws in *Munn v. Illinois* (1877), holding that the railroads, being "common carriers," "affect[ed] the public interest."

Railroad rate setting thus became the critical issue in rethinking the scope of democratic public authority in light of private corporate power. The 1886 Cleburne Demands endorsed the creation of a federal Interstate Commerce Commission (ICC), charged with scrutinizing the justness of railroad rates. The ICC was modeled after state-based railroad commissions, including the first, the Massachusetts Board of Railroad Commissioners (1869), and the most powerful, the Illinois Railroad Commission (1870).

The Farmers' Alliance politicized railroad rate setting. During the

Age of Capital, there was no farming—no life at all, including social connection—in the West without the market access provided by railroad corporations (just as in the early twenty-first century for many people, there is no social life without the Internet). For farmers, the railroads'

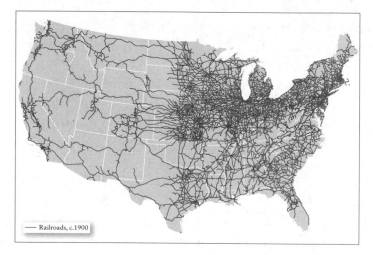

AMERICAN RAILROADS, C. 1900

In the West, given the absence of waterways, there was no market access without the railroads. Illustrated here is the American railroad network by century's end, but also the extraordinary power that the great railroad corporations exercised over commercial farmers in the Plains states, the hotbed of the Populist Revolt.

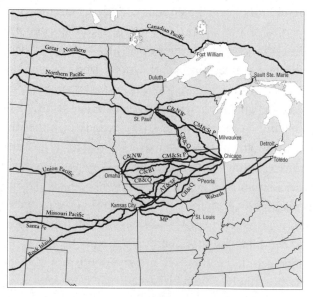

power to set rates truly was extraordinary. In many farming communities, one single railroad corporation provided market access. For a railroad, being the first to enter a particular territory and establish a line there warded off potential future competition. In the absence of market competition, it could set rates.

On economic grounds, the railroads were what the University of Michigan professor of political economy Henry Carter Adams, in an influential essay, "Relation of the State to Industrial Action" (1887), branded a "natural monopoly."[24] Given increasing returns to scale in railroading, first movers always threatened to capture a monopolistic share of a market. Rather than receiving market prices, the railroads—just like many large industrial producers—set prices according to their own costs. As they had large, fixed, and running costs, they preferred large customers who could guarantee them freight. Thus they commonly offered them lower rates, relative to smaller farmers, who suffered commercially from such "discrimination."

Adams's analysis of natural monopoly would prove highly influential. But the Farmers' Alliance did not lack for intellectual leadership of its own. Charles Macune, born in Wisconsin, was by age twenty a North Texas cowboy. For a short time, he worked as a clown. By 1886, he was practicing medicine in the Cross Timbers region. He joined the Knights' struggle against Gould, then the Farmers' Alliance. He ascended to a leadership role in the Texas Alliance, which began to merge with other state alliances. He became president of the newly formed National Farmers' Alliance and Co-operative Union. On its behalf, he proclaimed:

> Co-operation, properly understood and properly applied, will place a limit to the encroachments of organized monopoly, and will be the means by which the mortgage burdened farmers can assert their freedom from the tyranny of organized capital.[25]

By "organized capital," he meant the national bank system, which pyramided bank reserves on Wall Street and, together with the gold standard, enforced the scarcity value of money capital and credit. "Organized monopoly" referred to the rate-setting power of railroad corporations, as well as the price-setting power of the organized commodities futures exchanges, like the Chicago Board of Trade and the New York Cotton Exchange. In 1886 Macune set to work laying the business foundations for a new "Cooperative Commonwealth."

The national cooperative movement never really got off the ground, for lack of funding capital and working credit. In 1887 the Dakota Alliance incorporated a joint-stock company to cooperatively bargain and purchase farm machinery for Alliance members. But most cooperatives were intended for marketing farm products. The idea was that if farmers could collectively hold their crops off the market, they might bargain for a higher price.

The most ambitious cooperative was Macune's Texas Exchange. The Exchange would purchase farm supplies, whether seed, machinery, or fertilizer, at wholesale prices. Then in exchange for the crops its farmer members raised, the Exchange would issue them notes, which presumably local bankers would accept as money. The Exchange would then negotiate the sale of the entire crop on international markets. Macune assessed each member of the Texas Farmers' Alliance two dollars. With a quarter-million members, he hoped to capitalize the Exchange at $500,000. But only $20,000 materialized. In 1889 farmer cooperative start-ups were everywhere.[26] But by the end of that year, even the most audacious experiment, the Texas Alliance, had failed. The cooperative movement burned out quickly for want of sufficient capitalization.

The Farmers' Alliance had no choice; rather than support bottom-up cooperative initiatives, it now had to look to the regulatory powers of the state. In December 1889 the National Farmers' Alliance and Industrial Union formed, banding Macune's Texas-based organization with the Dakota and Kansas alliances. Its platform demanded outright government ownership of the railroads, and implementation of Macune's "subtreasury plan."[27] According to his plan, instead of farmer-owned cooperatives, the federal government would own and operate warehouses, issuing federal notes to farmers in return for their crops, which would be held in storage until farmers chose to sell them. Farmers would cease to be price takers. More like the railroads, they would have some ability to set prices. Thus would the federal government subsidize the market power of small-scale producers.

The National Farmers' Alliance could not avoid entering democratic politics now. But would it work within the existing two-party system, or would it form a third party? Most Alliance members on the northern Great Plains leaned Republican. Southern members, like Macune, leaned heavily Democratic. The two parties themselves were highly organized, using tactics ranging from picnics and parades, to bribes and corruption, to "beatings" and "killings."[28] "Ethnocultural" and wedge issues, such as Prohibition, divided the electorate.[29] Republicans held their coalition together by providing generous Civil War pensions and the spoils of the nationalist protective tariff.[30] Especially given the winner-take-all electoral system, the odds against third-party success were considerable.

Further, support for issues dear to the Farmers' Alliance to some degree transcended party lines. In Iowa and Minnesota in 1889, Republican legislatures passed antimonopoly measures against rate discrimination. In Congress in 1887, Democrats supported the creation of the ICC, to regulate railroad rate discrimination. "Fair and reasonable competition is a public benefit," ICC chairman Thomas Cooley, a Michigan jurist, declared on behalf of farmers, middling tradesmen, and small-scale producers everywhere.[31] In 1890 Democratic votes pushed through the Sherman Silver Purchase Act, which mandated that the federal government purchase and mint a greater quantity of silver—pushing back somewhat against silver's postwar demonetization. That same year Democrats also pushed through the Sherman Antitrust Act, which granted the Department of Justice legal authority to quash contracts or combinations "in restraint of trade or commerce." The U.S. Supreme Court would have the final say on the scope of the ICC's authority, as well as the meaning of the Sherman Antitrust Act. Nonetheless, neither of the two parties were deaf to agrarian demands.[32]

In the end, the money question was responsible for the birth of the Populist Party. In 1892, when the Democrats nominated former president Cleveland on a strong pro-gold platform, it was the last straw for many southern Alliance members. In July they traveled to Omaha, where the People's Party came into being. The preamble to the Populists' Omaha Platform began, "We believe that the powers of government—in other words, of the people—should be expanded." The platform called for the abolition of the national bank system and the free coinage of silver at 16 to 1. It also demanded that no less than fifty dollars per capita should ever be in circulation—if necessary, fiat money, not backed by metal, should fill the gap. The greater money supply would relieve debt burdens and expand the supply of credit for farm enterprise. Likewise, the Omaha Platform called for Macune's subtreasury system. Among its other demands were a progressive income tax and government ownership of railroads, telegraphs, and telephones: "We believe the time has come when the railroad corporations will either own the people or the people must own the railroads."[33] The antimonopoly position required government ownership, but not for its own sake. It was to ensure fair market access and thus equal commercial opportunity. A final plank in the platform in favor of women's suffrage was struck in the final drafting.

In the presidential election of 1892, the Republican Benjamin Harrison was the sitting president, and the Populists nominated James B. Weaver of Iowa, a former member of the Iowa Greenback-Labor Party. The Populists ran well in the Plains states but nowhere else. Northeastern farmers, in their more diversified rural economy, were less vulnerable to international market prices and the rates of single railroad corporations. They did not break Populist. Populists also failed to appeal to small-scale proprietors in the northeastern-midwestern manufacturing belt.[34] In the South, white supremacy doomed Populist success. In Georgia, where Populists appealed to the votes of both white and "colored" Farmers' Alliances, the young Populist firebrand Tom Watson explained that the Democratic argument against the Populists "may be boiled down to one word—nigger."[35] In 1892 Populists carried only Kansas, Colorado, Idaho, and Nevada, earning only 8.5 percent of the national popular presidential vote. The party picked up but a smattering of congressional seats. Grover Cleveland, who had served a presidential term from 1884 to 1888, returned to the White House, as the pro-gold Democrats swept the Congress. The future of the Populist Party looked bleak.

3. Globalization and the Election of 1896

If not for the Panic of 1893, the Populist Revolt might have died out in 1892. It was the international panic and the general slump that followed that made possible the fusion between the Populists and Bryan's insurgency in the Democratic Party in 1896. At issue in the presidential election that year were the benefits and dissatisfactions of economic globalization.

The cause of the Panic of 1893 was nothing other than the normal operations of the international gold standard, as presided over by Great Britain. Between 1865 and 1914, Great Britain, by far the world's largest creditor, exported £4 billion in capital overseas.[36] The United States, despite its prodigious agricultural exports, remained a net debtor in a globalizing economy. Adherence to the gold standard was the price of entry into the world capital market.[37] The gold standard transmitted capital but also financial volatility and fragility. The Panic of 1893—the result of international credit linkages—led to yet another deflationary economic slump.

The late nineteenth century was an era of both empire and globalization.[38] Through mass migration, labor markets integrated, and through international trade, so did product markets. When countries, or colonies, adopted the gold standard, confidence increased among potential foreign investors that the value of their investments would never be inflated away in the future.[39] Interest rates fell, and capital moved across borders into wealth-generating enterprise, which increased output.

The problem was that if for any reason gold began to flee their country, states had no choice but to raise interest rates to attract hard currency to defend their gold-currency peg. Capital moved around the world to take advantage of opportunities, but by the same logic, at the first, small sign of trouble, when liquidity preference among the owners of capital increased, the capital movements could destabilize the system. The only possible state response to crises, which was to raise interest rates, then choked off credit, only contributing to the gold standard's normal deflationary bias, and causing generalized slumps that halted economic development.

For instance, Argentina was a darling of English bankers, who hoped to make the Argentine Pampas another U.S. West.[40] In 1890, however, the Argentine investments made by the great British merchant bank Baring Brothers went sour. The Bank of England and the House of Rothschild organized a bailout. Nonetheless, the aftershock depressed British credit markets. British investors, in the competitive flight to cash and security, sought to get their hands on the safest store of value—gold. But given the integration of Atlantic capital markets, panic and recession spread across national borders.[41]

British capital fled from the United States, too. British capital had helped finance the extractive economy of the West, as well as the U.S. merchandise trade deficit. But now British investors called in their investments and stopped making new ones. Credit became scarcer. Railroad construction paused. With less spending, international commodity prices began to fall. On April 30, 1893, the U.S. Treasury's gold reserve dipped below the symbolic threshold of $100 million. On May 5 the New York Stock Exchange crashed. In July the Erie Railroad declared bankruptcy. Panic broke out, as nervous depositors pulled their money out of banks. Atop the pyramid of the national bank system, New York City banks suspended conversions, and depositors could not withdraw their funds. Banks called in old loans and ceased to make new ones. Credit dried up, investment and spending of all kinds declined, the commercial economy shrank, and economic output and employment fell.[42]

The depth of the resulting depression is difficult to know. Later estimates of unemployment in 1894 range from 12.3 percent to 18.4 percent.[43] U.S. farmers suffered the brunt of the slump. Between 1893 and 1896, farm incomes fell 22 percent. No U.S. public authority existed to raise interest rates or attempt to draw gold back into the country. Doing that, however, would have only choked off credit and commercial activity and made the slump worse. That was the negative consequence of the gold standard. For his part, President Cleveland believed that more deflation and depression were the right medicine. U.S. price deflation would increase American international competitiveness and thus export earnings, drawing gold back into the country. Depression would purge the economic system of rot and excess and prepare the ground for recovery. Such beliefs only made matters worse. Meanwhile in the 1894 congressional elections, the Republicans retook the House, in the largest single swing—120 seats—in U.S. electoral history.

In February 1895, U.S. Treasury gold reserves dipped to $9 million. The New York banker J. P. Morgan met with President Cleveland at the White House. Morgan had recently sent a cable to London saying the United States was on "the brink of the abyss of financial chaos." Morgan told the president that from his private contacts he knew that $10 million in gold drafts were about to be presented to the U.S. Mint. "What suggestions have you to make, Mr. Morgan?" asked the president. Morgan offered to syndicate a loan to the federal government that would bring 3.5 million ounces of European gold to the U.S. Treasury in exchange for $65 million worth of thirty-year bonds. Morgan wired London, "We consider situation critical, politicians appear to have absolute control. If fail & European negotiations abandoned, it is impossible overestimate what will be result U.S." Congress failed to act, but Cleveland accepted the loan. From the brokerage fees and their own investments, the Morgan- and Rothschild-led syndicate booked profits between $6 and $7 million. The gold standard was saved in the United States, but the grinding depression continued. Populist firebrand Mary Elizabeth Lease accused President Cleveland of being a tool of "Jewish bankers and British Gold," while Congressman William Jennings Bryan had the clerk of the House of Representatives read out loud passages incriminating the Jewish moneylender Shylock from William Shakespeare's *Merchant of Venice*.[44]

Interactions between the gold standard and liquidity preference were a fundamental design flaw in the global economy. The Populists, attempting to pin down and locate human agency in a rather abstract and impersonal global financial system, simply blamed elites, especially international elites, who existed outside "the people." Populism reached a fevered emotional pitch. Sarah E. V. Emery's *Seven Financial Conspiracies Which Have Enslaved the American People* (1892) was a representative title. Meanwhile Bryan became the most vocal advocate in the Democratic Party of a bimetallic standard. Many Populists believed a pro-gold Democrat would earn the nomination in Chicago, whereupon Bryan and his constituency in the Democratic Party would flock to the Populist convention that summer. But surprisingly Bryan won the Democratic nomination. The cooperative movement and the Alliance Exchanges were in tatters, economically. The Populists had not fared well at the polls in 1894 and now really had no choice.[45] They nominated Bryan for president and fused with the Democrats.

Bryan appropriated one Populist issue—silver—and adopted their evangelicalism, barnstorming across the country for six months.[46] The "Great Commoner" could have run a much more intelligent campaign. Bourbon Democracy was at no risk in the white supremacist South, and the Republicans would win the industrial and finance-capital-rich Northeast. Bryan should have focused more on the Midwest, appealing to the industrial wage-earning class. But Gompers was taking the AFL and skilled labor in a different direction. In 1895 he placed a statement in the AFL constitution that "party politics shall have no place in the conventions of the American Federation of Labor."[47] In 1896, he would later recall, "Mr. Bryan sent a number of messages that he was anxious to meet me to which I made no reply."[48] Meanwhile Bryan's overt Protestant evangelism alienated many unskilled, Catholic immigrants.

A second possible midwestern constituency for him would have been small- and medium-size industrial firms—small industrial property owners. But many existed because they already had, one way or another, access to capital and credit—even if it came from local sources rather than Wall

Street.[49] The Republican tariff appealed to them much more than silver. This stratum did not cohere politically, let alone rally to the Democrats.

Meanwhile the Cleveland industrialist Mark Hanna ran the McKinley campaign, with a war chest of at least $3.5 million, benefiting from large contributions from wealthy individuals ($250,000 each from John D. Rockefeller and J. P. Morgan). Bryan's entire campaign fund was $300,000.[50] Bryan had handed the Republicans an opportunity to bring together Republican industrialists and Democratic financiers.[51] McKinley promoted the economic benefits of the protective tariff among industrial wage earners and proprietors. As for the money question, the northeastern intellectual class promised that a Bryan victory would lead to anarchy. Edward Atkinson's "The Money of the Nation: Shall It Be Good or Bad?" (1896) proclaimed that "money made out of gold is good money; money made out of silver is bad money."[52] Bryan, an advocate of market competition and small enterprise, was tarnished with accusations of anarchism, socialism, and Communism. George Perkins, a partner in J. P Morgan & Co., called Bryan's speech in Chicago "anachronistic" and "wicked."[53] In London, the *Times* spoke of "lawlessness, of warfare on property on public and private rights."[54]

In 1896 the gold standard emerged victorious. While both were nationalist positions, the Republican-sponsored protectionist tariff against British manufactures in the northeastern-midwestern manufacturing belt captured as much support as, if not more than, the anti-British gold standard position in the South and West. Further, in the summer of 1896, prices began to reflate, with more gold coming onto world markets from recent strikes in South Africa, Australia, and the Canadian Klondike. Bryan carried the agricultural West, but he won no state east of the Mississippi or north of the Mason-Dixon line. He lost the popular vote by more than half a million.[55]

The failure of the Populist Revolt in 1896 had two dramatic, immediate consequences. In the agricultural South, a wave of popular white racist violence broke out. A new southern commodity entered markets: photographs of mutilated black bodies, victims of lynching.[56] Coincidentally or not, violent consolidation of Jim Crow in the South coincided with a surge of investor confidence and expectations on Wall Street. For in the manufacturing belt, what followed the election of 1896 was the greatest large-scale corporate consolidation in U.S. industrial history, the Great Merger Movement.

4. The Great Recapitalization

What soon earned the name the Great Merger Movement occurred between 1895 to 1904. The slump that followed the Panic of 1893 triggered it, but then it paused during the election campaign year of 1896. After Bryan's defeat seemingly secured the future of the gold standard, the mergers accelerated. In all, no less than 20 percent of U.S. gross domestic product consolidated into new manufacturing corporations, as 1,800 industrial firms became 157 corporations.[57] In the history of capitalization, the Great Merger Movement was the greatest rupture since the abolition of black slavery. As the Populists' politics of property fell by the wayside, property transformed.

The Great Merger Movement began with the "Morganization" of the railroad industry. J. P. Morgan—his friends called him Pierpont—took control of the London-focused banking partnership Drexel, Morgan, & Co. in 1890, upon the death of his father, J. S. Morgan. By 1895, the firm had become J. P. Morgan & Co., its operations centered in New York City.

At first, Morgan focused on reorganizing the post–Panic of 1893 U.S. railroad sector, which had become heavily indebted but was not very profitable. Many corporations had loaded up on debt, to rapidly scale up and secure first-mover advantages, only to overshoot demand for their services. To salvage them, the method of "Morganization" was born.[58]

Essentially, Morgan strong-armed railroad corporations' creditors and reduced their claims. First, Morgan bankers placed the railroad corporations in preemptive bankruptcies called "friendly receiverships"—perfecting a legal technique employed by Jay Gould during the 1880s.[59] Next, the House of Morgan studied each railroad's earnings, interest rate charges, and operating and maintenance costs and estimated its prospective future profits. That became the basis of the new value of the firm—as well as what the firm could afford to pay its creditors. Before, corporate valuation had hinged on already "paid in" capital—the "par" value on the face of stock certificates—representing the "intrinsic" value of the corporation's productive capital, or its engines, cars, tracks, and other equipment. This was the standard "trust fund" theory of corporate value, stated as recently as William C. Cook's *A Treatise on the Law of Stock and Stockholders* (1887).[60] In Morgan's new style of valuation, present value hinged not on the certitude of past investments but on expected future earnings—a matter of uncertainty, by definition, but also a matter of the House of Morgan's expertise.

Based on the new valuation, Morgan's bankers slashed railroad corporations' debt obligations, by on average one-third. Instantly, fixed costs—the great business problem of the Age of Capital—were reduced. Bondholders contested the "haircuts" in the courts, but the House of Morgan's redefinition of the value of a corporation ultimately prevailed. Morgan further changed corporations' capital structures, often replacing debt with equity. He reissued debts as "income bonds," which paid out only on future, realized profits. Prospective profits, rather than paid-in investments, thus became the new basis of both corporate capitalization and corporate property rights.

During the 1890s, no less than one-third of the U.S. railroad sector was placed in bankruptcy. Railroad corporations positively lined up to be "Morganized." The managers or owners of failing railroad corporations came to Morgan personally, hat in hand, among them the owners of the Southern Railway (legacy of Tom Scott's southern strategy), the Erie (of Gould and Vanderbilt's famed machinations), and the Northern Pacific (of Jay Cooke's infamy). Wall Street investment bankers followed Morgan's lead, be they Kuhn and Loeb, August Belmont, or Kidder, Peabody. By bringing railroad corporations under their control investment bankers consolidated the industry. By the turn of the twentieth century, the U.S. railroad sector was dominated, essentially, by six intercontinental systems.[61]

Outside the railroad sector, investment bankers were to play a crucial role in the Great Merger Movement. Nonetheless, another impulse behind the Great Merger Movement was more specific to industry itself.

On the eve of the merger movement, U.S. industry could be categorized into three distinct types, along a spectrum of size and scale. First, a significant stratum of small- to medium-size firms remained, often legally organized as proprietorships or partnerships. On average less capital- and energy-intensive, they relied on skilled labor and made specialized goods. They financed themselves from retained earnings, or they accessed still-thriving local capital and credit markets.[62] The Great Merger Movement did not much touch these firms, and they would thrive until the Great Depression of the 1930s.[63] Second, at the opposite end of the spectrum were large-scale capital- and energy-intensive firms that employed unskilled, often immigrant labor. They ruthlessly cut costs to undersell competitors in continental markets and thus contributed to price deflation. Carnegie Steel Company was one such firm. Finally, there was a third category of industrial firms, somewhat between the two extremes. Their sudden turn toward consolidation was what made the Great Merger Movement so great between 1895 and 1904.

These firms—some already incorporated, some not—ended up suffering from the same general problem that large-scale, fixed-cost producers faced. During the late 1880s and early '90s, they made ill-timed large fixed capital investments. After the Panic of 1893, sales slumped. To recoup their fixed costs, these producers kept on producing—much like farmers during the late 1880s and early '90s. Competition only made matters worse, as firms engaged in brutal pricing wars to gain market share. It was difficult to limit competition between firms. Voluntary or "gentlemen" price agreements ultimately failed. Next, the U.S. Supreme Court, interpreting the 1890 Sherman Antitrust Act, outlawed cross-firm price agreements as an antimonopoly "restraint of trade."[64] However, in *United States v. E.C. Knight Co.* (1895), the Court ruled that large manufacturing consolidations were not in violation of the Sherman Act, for manufacturing was distinct from trade. Firms rushed to legally consolidate, to ensure that they would limit their production volumes and thus put a floor under market prices for their goods.[65] The strategy was not much different from what the Farmers' Alliance had tried to do—cooperate—in order to raise prices for its members' crops. Except, through mergers and acquisitions, manufacturing firms succeeded.

In order to merge, manufacturing firms needed to raise funds in the capital market. Furthermore, the new corporations that resulted, no different from "Morganized" railroad corporations, required a new capital value and a new capital structure—combinations of stocks, bonds, and various ownership instruments. In short, the new corporations had to be recapitalized. This was where investment banks figured in.

Ever since the post–Civil War resumption of the gold standard, Wall Street financiers had remained committed to it. After Bryan's defeat in 1896, confidence and expectations surged in the Wall Street capital markets. One specific market burgeoned—the market in corporate stock. As a result of the postwar national bank system, the reserves of small country banks pyramided into New York, the basis of the short-term, "call money" loan market. There were large bond markets on Wall Street, especially for railroad corporate debt. However, the market in corporate equities (stocks) was not large. In fact, until the Great Merger Movement, the largest stock market for industrial corporations was the Boston Stock Exchange. Throughout the country, there were many securities exchanges.[66]

In yet another consolidation during the Great Merger Movement, the New York Stock Exchange became the largest transactionally liquid market in corporate securities. Investment banks tapped it, to raise the capital necessary for mergers and acquisitions. The consolidation of a liquid securities market in corporate stock made corporate industrial investment newly subject to the contradictory drive of speculative investment—which made possible new forms of credit-fueled short-term speculation but also long-term investment in enterprise.

Upon consolidation, the value of each small firm had to be estimated, then added into the grand total. Next, to merit the valuation, the capital markets had to absorb the new issues of that corporation's securities, thus capitalizing the enterprise. Commonly, merger and acquisition negotiations among firms went more smoothly if a third party, an investment banker, conducted the estimates.[67] In capitalization, following the "Morganization" example, the drift was toward prospective future earning capacity.[68] In 1899 *American Banker* claimed that 25 percent of the "aggregated capital" through the new mergers was "nothing more than bags of hope."[69] But as the standard post–Great Merger Movement text, William Lough and Frederick Field's *Corporation Finance* (1909), would put it, "Capitalization should be based upon the corporation's [future] earning power, regardless of the [past] capital investment." Finally, in 1912 New York State passed a law allowing stock issues "without the dollar mark"; that is, with no stated par value. By law, corporate stock valuation was now explicitly a confidence game.

The great U.S. economist Irving Fisher explained the new post–Great Merger Movement logic, in his *The Nature of Capital and Income* (1906). With capital, "when values are considered, the causal relation is not from present to the future, but from future to present."[70] So neatly expressed in the merger movement, this reversal of time in economic life counts among capitalism's greatest transformations.[71] Outside even Morgan's control, the confidence game would be increasingly played at the New York Stock Exchange. The year 1896, when Bryan lost the election, was the same year more stocks than bonds were issued on Wall Street. Soon the NYSE would declare a new political philosophy—that stock ownership, like landownership long before, could be the property anchor of democratic citizenship.[72]

The capstone event of the Great Merger Movement was the creation of the United States Steel Corporation. One night at dinner in Manhattan's University Club, in December 1900, the Carnegie executive Charles M.

Schwab floated aloud the possibility of a merger in the steel industry—within earshot of J. P. Morgan.[73] Recently, the House of Morgan had consolidated two new corporations, Federal Steel and National Tube. They competed with Carnegie Steel. Schwab's and Morgan's partners met in Morgan's library to hash out a proposed merger of the three firms, as well as eight other steel manufacturers, as well as Lake Superior Consolidated Mines. When Schwab played golf with Andrew Carnegie at the St. Andrew Golf Club in Westchester County, New York, Carnegie wrote his price on a piece of paper—$480 million. Morgan agreed. Carnegie said, "Pierpont feels that he can do anything because he always got the best of the Jews in Wall Street. . . . It takes a Yankee to beat a Jew, and it takes a Scot to take a Yankee." Carnegie later admitted to Morgan that he had sold out for too little, probably by $100 million. "Very likely, Andrew," Morgan responded.[74]

Carnegie retired as the richest man in the world and dedicated himself to philanthropy. The House of Morgan capitalized the new corporation at an astounding $1.4 billion, valued according to the projected future earnings of U.S. Steel, or "The Corporation," as it became known. The creation of U.S. Steel required an initial public offering of $500 million in stock. The Morgan-led syndicate consisted of no fewer than three hundred stock underwriters to release the stock onto the NYSE and stabilize its initial value. U.S. Steel was nothing short of a big bang for the Wall Street capital market in industrial securities, accounting for one-tenth of the total capitalized value ($5 billion) of all industrial combinations created between 1898 and 1903.[75]

The productive capital wielded by, and organizational scale of, U.S. Steel were extraordinary. The Corporation controlled 213 separate factories, 41 mines, and over one thousand miles of railroad, spread out across the entire northeastern-midwestern manufacturing belt. It employed 162,000 individuals. Its capitalization included another expectation—projected labor costs. It crushed a recognition strike by steelworkers in 1901, and another by the United Mine Workers in 1902. *McClure's Magazine* said of U.S. Steel, "It receives and expends more money every year than any but the very greatest of the world's national governments; its debt is larger than that of many of the lesser nations of Europe; it absolutely controls the destines of a population nearly as large as that of Maryland or Nebraska, and indirectly influences twice that number."[76] By 1905, industrial corporations in manufacturing—23.6 percent of all manufacturing establishments—owned 82.8 percent of total U.S. industrial capital. They hired 70.6 percent of all wage earners.[77] *The Wall Street Journal* confessed to "uneasiness over the magnitude of the affair."[78]

Perhaps in principle stock ownership could be widely distributed, much as landed property had been before, among white heads of farm households in the Empire of Liberty during the Age of Commerce. But in fact in the Age of Capital, the ownership of productive capital was concentrated—in the name of legal persons, industrial corporations. If the capital side was corporatized and no longer so politicized, perhaps the income yielded from corporate capital could be made subject to distributive politics.

5. Progressive Income Politics

The creation of U.S. Steel established the large, joint-stock industrial corporation as a fact. In the first decades of the twentieth century, the urban-based Progressive movement set its sights on fashioning new regulations for this kind of corporation. Many of the Progressives were cosmopolitans, influenced by transatlantic intellectual currents (even if they had strikingly little to say about transatlantic capital markets).[79] But corporations like U.S. Steel were relatively specific to the United States. To regulate them, Progressives appropriated a number of Populist ideas.[80] However, they accepted the corporate reconstruction of property and capital. They focused on the regulation of corporate behavior. Above all, they sought to politicize corporate incomes—to forge a new distributive politics. Through income politics, the goal was to alleviate poverty, and more broadly to spread the benefits of economic development to urban populations that had not benefited so much from industrialization in the late nineteenth century.

To this end, Progressives reconceptualized the public interest. It was not necessarily pretty, as racist eugenics counts among Progressive political-economic thinkers' legacy.[81] Progressives recognized the industrial corporation as a powerful "social" entity that had superseded commercial markets, demanding new forms of public regulation. "When the market is viewed as a social mechanism rather than a private one," argued the future New Dealer Rexford Tugwell in *The Economic Basis of Public Interest* (1922), there was a wedge for public "control" in the "general interest of the public."[82] The Progressive political imagination consigned the politics of widespread landownership by white male heads of household to the rural past. It politicized instead the income yielded from private, corporate capital, arguing for various supports for male breadwinning, income taxation (as opposed to property taxation), and the enforcement of reasonable "rates of return" on corporations that affected the "public interest."

After a period of political agitation and policy innovation, the Progressive legislative breakthrough occurred, at both the state and federal levels, in the arenas of tax policy, antitrust, public utilities, welfare, and banking, all during the first administration of the southern Democrat Woodrow Wilson, which began in early 1913.

In the nineteenth century, except during the Civil War, it was property and commerce that had been taxed, not income. At the turn of twentieth century, northeastern progressive intellectuals and university professors began to reconceive the corporation as a "real" legal person, independent of its stockowners.[83] Taxing corporate income would be no different from taxing the incomes of flesh-and-blood individuals. Further, the principle of progressive income taxation was premised on the "ability to pay" and the "marginal" rate of taxation that would not inhibit private spending and investment. Proposals for a new income tax had drawn strong populist favor during the 1880s and '90s.[84] In 1913 states, with agrarian and Progressive support, ratified the Sixteenth Amendment, which constitutionalized income taxation. The Democratic Congress dramatically slashed the tariff and introduced corporate and personal taxes on high incomes.[85] Corporations paid a large bulk of the first income tax. They also aided personal income tax collection "at the source," by withholding income from employee paychecks. Finally, the new income tax included exemptions for philanthropic giving to nonprofit corporations.[86] Taxation and tax-exemption became a matter of income politics.

Like income taxation, antimonopoly underwent a Populist-to-Progressive translation. "Antitrust," as it became known, was the central issue of the presidential election of 1912. The first so-called trust had been John D. Rockefeller's 1882 Standard Oil Company, in which forty different oil companies had turned over their capital, and control of their enterprises, in exchange for "trust certificates" in Standard Oil. Rockefeller thus consolidated the oil industry—controlling production volumes, stabilizing prices, and ensuring profits.[87] In popular discourse, "trusts" became synonymous with large consolidated firms, though the Standard Oil Company would reincorporate as a New Jersey holding company in 1899. By that time, Rockefeller's corporation was vertically integrated, encompassing the activities of oil exploration, through processing, to marketing and final sale all in the same company. It was also horizontally integrated, meaning it had largely eliminated market competition in each specific activity. In 1911 the U.S. Supreme Court in *Standard Oil Co. of New Jersey v. United States* broke up Rockefeller's New Jersey holding company. Its decision declared the "rule of reason," distinguishing between "reasonable," lawful restraints of trade and "unreasonable," unlawful restraints. An unreasonable restraint was anything an already existing firm in a particular line of trade did to prevent new entrants into their field of competition. Vertical integration was largely protected. Bryan complained, "The Trusts Have Won."[88] But horizontal combinations that restrained market competition came under new scrutiny. Wilson and the Democrats followed with the Clayton Antitrust Act of 1914 and the creation of the Federal Trade Commission. Hearkening back to long-ago calls for equality of commercial opportunity, its mandate was to rid enterprise of "unfair methods of competition." In the end, not even U.S. Steel would be able to ward off competition.[89]

On behalf of small-scale, household-based enterprise, Populists had called for public ownership of the railroads. Taking up the Populist cause, although more in cities than in the West, Progressives transformed the concept of "natural monopoly" into the associated notion of a "public utility" corporation.[90] In 1905–7 they largely lost the battle for municipal ownership of streetcars and subways, but the capital of privately owned "utilities"—the municipal infrastructure of transportation, gas, waterworks, and sewage—became newly affected with the "public interest."[91] Rather than targeting rate discrimination, the new focus was on a "reasonable" rate of return—or profit—on privately owned corporate capital.[92] Public utility commissions began to determine "fair" rates of return. It was not so easy to do, either technically in accounting terms or legally. The Supreme Court had ruled in *Munn v. Illinois* (1877) that railroads were affected with a "public interest," but *Smyth v. Ames* (1898) held that corporations had a Fourteenth Amendment due process right to realize a "fair return" on their capital investments. In sum, corporations could decide when and where to invest, but the rate of return on capital was newly politicized. Many future New Dealers cut their teeth on public utility rate regulation.

Further, in urban industrial life, Progressives attended to the male-breadwinner-female-homemaker family, lending it new public supports at the state level.[93] Feminism was one face of Progressivism, and 1920 saw the passage of the Nineteenth Amendment to the Constitution establishing female suffrage.[94] Incipient American social policy acquired both "maternalist" and "paternalist" variants. Progressives created a Children's Bureau in 1912 and passed laws barring child labor in 1918 and 1922.[95] For male breadwinners, states passed a series of workmen's compensation laws in the period 1910–13. Further, states also passed "mothers' pension" laws between 1911 and 1919—income subsidies for women without breadwinners in the home.[96] The new taxation of corporate incomes funded these building blocks of the U.S. welfare state, including redistributive supports for male wage earners—the income politics of male pay.

Finally, Progressives worked to regulate finance, credit, and money.[97] Upon securing the gold standard in 1896, Wall Street financiers, at the conclusion of the Great Merger Movement, began to see the need for an American central bank. The post–Civil War national bank system had always suffered from the periodic tightening of money and credit in New York City during the annual harvest season, when money and credit drained back to the countryside to finance the sale of crops. After the Great Merger Movement, the short-term-loan "call money" market, fueled by the pyramiding of the reserves of small, country banks in New York, became the credit nexus that sustained prices and maintained transactional liquidity at the NYSE—adding an extra potential strain on the money market. In the autumn of 1907, as reserves flowed to the countryside, a financial panic broke out on Wall Street. Only a private syndicate led by J. P. Morgan to backstop markets restored confidence and prevented a worse credit crunch and perhaps a general economic slump.[98]

As a number of homegrown U.S. monetary theorists argued, a truly central bank would have the public authority to be the "lender of last resort" in such crises. Further, by setting a short-term interest rate in the money market, if need be, it could raise rates and draw sufficient gold into the country to defend the dollar-gold exchange rate. Last, within the limit set by the quantity of gold, by accepting a variety of bills and notes as collateral for loans, a central bank would have the power to issue credit and thus to expand the money supply, to prevent any reversal in the credit cycle that risked panic and precautionary hoarding.[99]

The Federal Reserve Act of 1913, passed because of agrarian political power in Congress, created something different from what either monetary theorists or Wall Street bankers had wanted—twelve regional reserve banks. These "banker's banks" accepted the deposits and discounted the notes of other banks. By law, the national banks had to purchase stock in the twelve reserve banks and hold their reserves in them. Ownership came with voting rights to determine the board members and governors of the regional reserve banks. The regional banks printed federal reserve notes, which replaced the national banknotes and became the sole U.S. currency. The Federal Reserve was required to have 40 percent of the currency backed by gold reserves. Each regional bank had the discretion to set its own interest rates on loans to its members. Immediately, given the importance of the Wall Street capital market, the Federal Reserve Bank of New York became the most powerful of the twelve banks. The president appointed and the Senate confirmed a seven-member board to oversee the Federal Reserve.[100]

In the creation of the Federal Reserve System, the agrarian interest in the Democratic Party flexed some muscle. According to the 1913 act, the regional banks could discount a category of banknote backed by crops—in the spirit of Charles Macune's "subtreasury" system. Congress's Warehouse Act of 1916 subsequently enabled regional reserve banks to grant farmers credit upon the collateral of certificates issued to them for the storage of their crops in government warehouses. The 1913 act licensed national banks to issue farm mortgages, while the Federal Farm Loan Act of 1916 created twelve federal land banks, with the capitalization of each guaranteed by the Treasury at $750,000. Credit flowed to many farmer-owned cooperatives.[101] The new Federal Farm Loan Board was granted powers to regulate private farm lending.[102] Without these provisions, which bolstered farmers' market power and were thus friendly to the Democrats' agrarian base, the Federal Reserve Act of 1913 would likely not have passed Congress, and Wilson would likely not have won reelection in 1916. A note from William Jennings Bryan himself to Democratic congressmen representing agrarian districts— "I am with [Wilson] on all the details"—had secured the final votes.[103]

Meanwhile the same year, 1913, was an industrial annus mirabilis. Twenty-two days before Congress passed the Federal Reserve Act, the Detroit automobile manufacturer Henry Ford installed the very first continuous assembly line. In the Age of Capital, industrial revolution was not over yet.

CHAPTER 11

FORDISM

====

THE GREATEST ACHIEVEMENT IN THE ANNALS OF THE industrial revolution took place just outside Detroit, Michigan, during the 1910s. There the Ford Motor Company manufactured more than 20,000 Model T automobiles in 1910. The number was 585,000 in 1916. During that period, the price of a Model T fell by more than half, from $780 to $360.[1]

"Mass production" made founder Henry Ford an international celebrity. In 1922, when automobile production at the Ford Motor Company approached 2 million, he published the widely translated international sensation *My Life and Work*.[2] Ford did not like books, once saying, "I don't like to read." Why not? "They muss up my mind."[3] But Ford read at least one author, dear to him, whom he called the "Concord philosopher," Ralph Waldo Emerson.[4] The business journalist Samuel Crowther wrote Ford's *My Life and Work* on the basis of their conversations. Ford's autobiography begins not with an account of the modest childhood of a Michigan farm boy but with a question: "What is the Idea?"[5]

The idea was that machines should do more work. In 1920 the U.S. census announced that for the first time, the majority of Americans were city dwellers, a product of industrial urbanization, but with mass production, Ford proposed that humans would have more time for "the trees, the birds, the flowers, and the green fields." With greater wealth at hand, human beings might have more time to be more human, as Emerson might have said. *My Life and Work* continued: How come "when one speaks of increasing power, machinery, and industry," one usually pictured "a cold, metallic sort of world"? Did industrial civilization have to be that way? Did the coming of the "great factories" mean there have to be only "metal machines and human machines"? No—with a better understanding of the "mechanical portion of life," Ford promised something nearly biblical, "a new world, a new heaven, and a new earth."[6]

Henry Ford was many things. "I'm going to see that no man comes to know me," he once jotted in an introspective note to himself.[7] He was an eccentric, surely, but also a pacifist and a suffragist. For health reasons, he attacked the pasteurization of milk. He was an anti-Semite, publisher of *The International Jew* (1920), which, soon enough, sat dog-eared on the bookshelf of Adolf Hitler.[8] Ford was also an industrial genius and one of the great modern visionaries. Along with Hitler, Benito Mussolini, and Vladimir Lenin, all of whom grudgingly or enthusiastically admired mass production methods, Ford belongs in that rare company of twentieth-century figures who, by force of their personal charisma, succeeded in casting modern industrial mass society in the form of their totalizing visions—only in the end to fail.[9]

Ford was not a mass politician (although without him campaigning much, Michigan almost elected him a Democratic senator in 1918). But he was a mass capitalist. He was a capitalist of a very particular kind who became very, very rich, but did not care so much about making profits in the first instance.[10] Profit was far too narrow an aim for Ford's massive, homespun ego. A far more grandiose motivation fired his extraordinary dedication to investing in mass production. He was not conflicted about short-term speculation versus long-term investment—let alone hoarding. He associated short-term profit making in liquid financial markets with the "International Jew" and never participated in it, even during the 1920s as the New York Stock Exchange enjoyed the spectacle of the Great Bull Market.[11] Ford, in the beginning an industrial tinkerer in the small-scale-producer tradition, was enamored with production and nothing else. In this respect, he had a singular, focused drive and was committed—like no capitalist before or since, not even Andrew Carnegie—to putting productive capital on the ground, over the long term, in order to produce, produce, and produce. In doing so, he himself concluded, "I invented the modern age."[12]

Ford left distinctive marks on productive capital. First, he accelerated the energy revolution in production and increased the speed at which goods passed through the manufacturing process. In 1913 he and his engineers introduced the first electric-powered assembly lines. Coal-fired electric power stations mechanized them. Other manufactures quickly followed him. The electrification of assembly in the 1910s and '20s gave rise to even greater capital deepening, and stupendous gains in productivity occurred.[13] From negligible amounts in 1900, electricity powered 78 percent of U.S. industry by 1929.[14] During the 1920s, U.S. manufacturing productivity increased at an annual rate in excess of 5 percent—the fastest rate of growth of any decade on record.[15]

Second, by focusing on continuous speed, the Ford Motor Company reconceptualized the architecture of the factory. Ford and his "industrial architect" Albert Kahn imagined the factory as a machine itself—a mechanism of self-contained motion.[16] "Capital goods" were mechanized. The new electric speed notwithstanding, Ford amassed fixed, illiquid capital at hitherto unheard-of scales. Ford and Kahn's River Rouge Complex was the largest factory ever seen—a giant machine, which attempted to internalize the many backward and forward, intermediate linkages of industry under Ford's personal dominion. Much of the "mass" in mass industrial society was the new architectural massing of capital in place at a scale far greater than before. Industrial society acquired greater "structure."

No less significant, Ford's product was the automobile. In the dawning Machine Age, the automobile caught the public imagination more than any other item. Cars liberated individuals from place and rapidly changed the character of everyday life.[17] "You can't go into town in a bathtub," said one Indiana farm housewife in 1919. "Every time a woman learns to drive—and thousands do every year—it is a threat at yesterday's order of things," noted *Motor* magazine in 1927.[18] From 468,000 in 1910, there were 9 million automobiles in the United States by 1920. By 1929, there were 23 million—nearly one per U.S. household, accounting for nearly 80 percent of the world's cars.[19] Auto-industrial society, powered by coal-fired electricity but also gasoline, accelerated fossil-fuel-energy consumption.[20]

An automobile was a consumer good. The industrial revolution had first brought about the manufacture of intermediate "capital goods"—like Carnegie's steel, which became railroad tracks. Carnegie's investments had multiplying effects on wealth creation, as they induced fresh enterprise backward and forward, from mining to railroad service, all linked to steel manufacture. Similarly, Ford's automobile initiated an industrial investment multiplier. But he manufactured a consumer good, so in addition to his productive achievements on the supply side, he also triggered, on the demand side, another dynamic variable in economic development with multiplying effects—consumerism.

Indeed, the electric machine age saw the introduction of many new consumer goods. In garages, there were automobiles. In homes, there were electric-powered vacuum cleaners, irons, and refrigerators. Electric radio set sales increased from $60 million in 1922 to $843 million in 1929, by which time 30 million Americans were tuning in every evening.[21] Electric-powered mass communication instantaneously connected Americans to mass society and mass consumer culture—cars, radios, the newest fashions.

One final new mass product arrived: the Ford man. The Reverend Samuel Marquis, Ford's pastor, who became the first head of the Ford Motor Company's "sociological department," would say that the idea that Ford was "in the automobile business" was not "true." Automobiles were "by-products of his real business." Ford's "real" business was "the making of men."[22] Carnegie had endowed libraries but viewed his labor force as nothing more than a running cost. Ford had a grander design, as he announced in a company newspaper bearing the name *Ford Man.* Ford spent the 1910s perfecting mass production, but he soon sensed that the stakes were civilizational. Beginning with 1922's *My Life and Work,* he leveraged his mass celebrity to become an industrial prophet.

Ford's vision was total. The mass production assembly line, he saw, would run and wind through economy and society but also politics and culture, body and mind, soul and spirit. In 1934 the Italian prisoner of fascism Antonio Gramsci, in an influential fragment titled "Americanismo e Fordismo," called Ford's project the "biggest collective effort to date to create, with unprecedented speed, and with a consciousness of purpose unmatched in history, a new type of worker and of man."[23] This type of worker, like a good soldier, stood at an assembly line. In return for his obedience and consent, he earned a breadwinning wage—after work, he could buy the new consumer goods of the Machine Age. Ford was as hostile to labor unions as he was anti-Semitic. As he massed so much capital, he instituted his own politics of pay—the vaunted 1914 five-dollar day—in return for which breadwinners' families might be subjected to company home visits. American Fordism, said Gramsci, was as totalizing as Italian fascism, or German Nazism, or Soviet Communism. The comparisons were apt. For in the wake of Europe's self-immolation during World War I, the history of American capitalism was clearly no longer, as the historian Adam Tooze has put it, a "domestic drama."[24]

By any quantitative measure, global economic supremacy had been shifting toward the United States, even before the birth of the assembly line. Fordism put American capitalism over the top. The greatest prize in the modern age, however, was for the very definition of the good life. Industrial society proliferated many modern "isms": fascisms, communisms, capitalisms. They borrowed from one another, but they would also war with one another in a global struggle to the death for what Gramsci called "hegemony."

I. Mass Production

"Mass production," Ford announced in an entry of that title to the *Encyclopaedia Britannica* (1926), yet another ghostwritten piece, "is the focusing upon a manufacturing project of the principles of power, accuracy, economy, system, continuity, and speed."[25] The Ford Motor Company was incorporated in the state of Michigan on June 16, 1903, when Henry Ford was forty years old.

Ford grew up on a farm near Dearborn, Michigan. His father, an Irish immigrant, hoped his son might take over the family farm, but Ford did not like farming. Like many successful industrial innovators, especially in the nineteenth century—before university-trained scientists and engineers inside the walls of big industrial corporations became responsible for innovation—Ford was a mechanical tinkerer.[26] He "learned by doing," as economists would later put it.[27]

When Henry was in his teens, his father gave him a pocket watch, and Ford was enraptured. He took it apart and put it back together, over and over again. Here the theme of abstract time in industrial capitalism arises, in a moment that must be considered one point of origin for mass production. The best book ever written about capitalism and the machine is Lewis Mumford's *Technics and Civilization* (1934). While economic historians would later debate whether there was a "general purpose technology" of the second industrial revolution, Mumford was already correct that the clock was the "key-machine of the modern industrial age." A tool and a machine were different, he explained, since "the tool lends itself to manipulation," whereas "the machine to automatic action."[28] The mechanical precision of the clock would be visible in the "accuracy" of Ford's mass production methods. More generally, from the clock sprang the abstract industrial time of linear, standard duration. It had been the time signature of Carnegie's factories, but Ford and his men took it to new levels, using, for instance, stopwatches to coordinate and time assembly. Before the assembly line, it had been difficult to know why and how time passed in the factory. Mass production pulled time itself into the project of production. "Time is the Most Valuable Thing in the World," Ford's factory newspaper, *Ford Man,* would declare.[29]

When he was sixteen, Ford migrated to Detroit to become an apprentice to a skilled machinist. Most Detroit machinists were American-born, or perhaps German, skilled producers—not the unskilled European "new immigrants" who were increasingly present in large-scale capital- and energy-intensive industries such as steelmaking. The master machinist stood at his workbench wearing his work apron and tending his "lathe"—a general-purpose machine tool that rotated pieces of metal on an axis, where the machinist, depending on his particular skill, might cut, drill, knurl, sand, or finish them. Detroit was home to a significant agglomeration of machine shops but also an energetic entrepreneurial culture, committed to the arts of craftsmanship. Small-scale urban industry, financed by local networks of capital and credit, thrived. Ford lapped up the midwesterners' "producerist" entrepreneurial ethos, born of the "free labor, free soil, free men" Republican Party a generation earlier, which had, however indirectly, filtered through Populism.[30] It was distant from the East Coast financial establishment. The New York–financed Great Merger Movement had not so much as touched Detroit industry.[31]

Ford had had another job before he turned to automobile manufacture. In 1891 he became an engineer at the Edison Illuminating Company. There in 1896 Ford met his hero, the company's namesake, Thomas Edison. The electric dynamo, a mechanism for producing electric current, had been developed during the 1860s, but it was Edison who designed the first central power station in 1882, New York's Pearl Street Station.[32] When they met, Edison encouraged Ford to continue with Ford's side experiments on gasoline-powered self-propelled "horseless carriages."

Germans, not Americans, invented the internal combustion engine: Karl Benz first began to manufacture gas-powered automobiles in 1885. Detroit became one home to the early U.S. automobile industry, as it had the right kind of local agglomeration of industry. At first, small start-ups and associated spin-offs predominated. Invention spilled across firms, through cooperative networks. Funding was informal, by local investors, not by distant capital markets. The number of automobile-manufacturing firms peaked in 1909, at 272. By then, however, Ford was already established, having introduced the Model T in 1908. An auto-industrial district had formed. Detroit absolutely dominated car production.[33]

Ford resigned from Edison in 1899 and, backed by a local Detroit investor, formed the Detroit Automobile Company—which quickly failed. Ford and fellow tinkerer Harold Wills then designed a new car, and local investors put $35,000 into the Henry Ford Company in 1901. But the owners soon pushed Ford out, renaming the company Cadillac, which was bought up for more than $4 million in 1909 during the formation of a new holding company, called General Motors. Ford now formed a partnership with the local coal dealer Alexander Malcomson to lease a machine shop from the brothers John and Horace Dodge, in order to assemble automobiles. The Dodges manufactured the engine, transmission, and axles. Ford and Malcomson could not pay them, so the brothers asked for a piece of the ownership. The Ford Motor Company was incorporated in 1903. The original twelve investors put up $28,000 (somewhere in the neighborhood of $350,000 today). The corporation was capitalized at $100,000.[34]

Malcomson wanted Ford to build a luxury car, but Ford had decided to build an affordable automobile and bought out Malcomson. The Model N was introduced in 1906. A remarkable team formed at Ford's company. James J. Couzens was an initial investor (a future Republican mayor of Detroit and U.S. senator) and managed the business side, including accounts. The rest were like Ford, tinkerer-engineers lacking formal college and university education. They believed "work was play"—as "Cast-Iron Charlie" Sorensen later put it in his revealing memoir *My Forty Years with Ford* (1956).[35] There were personal rivalries, but no job titles. The process of innovation was social and cooperative. Sorensen had a background in new methods to punch, press, and stamp steel. Among others, Walter Flanders was a New England machinist, familiar with the Yankee practice of interchangeable parts. Carl Emde designed special-purpose machine tools. In 1905 the Ford Motor Company bought its first factory on Piquette Avenue.

In 1909 Ford announced that the company would produce only one model of car, the Model T, painted black. Factory methods so far had been rather traditional. The building, a shell made of iron, stone, and brick, was long, narrow, and cluttered. Much of the clutter was because the factory was powered by a steam engine. A power train of leather belts, shafts, and cranks hung from the ceiling, and machines had to be clustered near the power train, or power loss was considerable. Skill also organized production and factory space. Machinists built individually "fitted" parts, whether engine block, cylinder, or chassis, which were then subsequently assembled, one at a time, into automobiles. The final "fit" to every part bore the imprint of a skilled machinist. Around the workbench of skilled machinists, teams of unskilled common laborers, "operatives," or "helpers"—truckmen, pushers, and shovers—scurried about. Wheelbarrows, hand trucks, and lifts brought working materials to the machinists' bench. When finished, products moved farther along, eventually to final assembly.[36] "When we cast our first Model T cylinders in 1910, everything in the place was done by hand," Ford recalled. On the floor, "shovels and wheelbarrows abounded." "The work was skilled."[37]

In a short span of years, everything had changed. Ford and his engineers had designed precision, special-purpose machine tools outfitted with company-designed jigs, fixtures, and gauges. This achieved standardization and the interchangeability of parts. It also increased the division of labor. Ford bragged that he did not read books, but he might have still realized he was evoking Adam Smith when he declared, as early as 1903, "The way to make automobiles is to make one automobile just like another automobile, to make them all alike . . . like one pin is like another pin when it comes from a pin factory."[38] The use of interchangeable parts was long common to U.S. manufacturing. Ford's engineers went further, however, and developed, for instance, a special machine for drilling holes in the Model T's engine cylinder. In one motion, it drilled forty-five holes in the same precise positions. An unskilled laborer could operate it. By 1914 Ford would employ fifteen thousand machine tools, numerically more than his thirteen thousand workers. That year in fixed capital—illiquid, productive capital goods—the company invested $3.6 million on "plant, buildings, tanks and fixtures," but almost as much, $2.8 million, on "machine-tool equipment."[39]

Meanwhile the company began to rearrange machine groups. Ford and his team designed factory space so that each part required only one treatment at each particular workstation. The completion of one treatment prepared the material for the next. They also began to group machines uncommonly close together. "Our factory buildings are not intended to be used as strolling parks," he said.[40]

Ford also systemically eliminated "wasted motion" from the labor process. Historians still debate whether Ford consciously employed so-called scientific management, whose founder was Frederick Winslow Taylor. First at the Midvale Steel Company and later at Bethlehem Steel, Taylor developed "time-motion studies" to eliminate wasteful physical movements. Workers resisted. Exhausted from trying, Taylor retired. He would go on to publish *On the Art of Cutting Metals* (1907) and *The Principles of Scientific Management* (1911), among other books, to promote his views. In 1911 the Society to Promote the Science of Management formed. Taylor's ideas were generally in the air.[41] Christine Frederick's *The New Housekeeping: Efficiency Studies in Home Management* (1913), for instance, applied them to housework at the same time Ford was rationalizing the labor process. Consciously or not, the Ford Motor Company "Taylorized" its labor force.

In rational steps, automobile parts progressed from one workstation to another. Assembly gangs rotated in circles, performing distinct tasks, while work teams brought parts to the assembly spot. Using stopwatches, Ford's engineers choreographed every sequence. There was a right way to hand a fellow worker a nut or a bolt. Special timekeepers oversaw production schedules, and the Ford Motor Company would soon have an entire time study department.[42] Production of Model Ts surged forward, their quality improved, their price declined, and their sales increased.

The automobile was a durable consumer good, but many of the backward linkages, typical of the cumulative process of industrial revolution, unfolded. The Model T had uniquely high power (22 horsepower) relative to its weight (1,200 pounds) because it was made from vanadium alloy steel. Thus upstream demand for vanadium alloy steel to build Model Ts drove greater innovations in steelmaking.[43] The engine block was cast in a single block. It had a four-cylinder motor and planetary transmission with foot pedals that made it easier to rock the automobile out of muddy roads. The car sold particularly well in rural areas because, unlike other automobiles, it could travel over poor or nonexistent roads. To sell Model Ts, Ford developed a vast network of commercial dealers—another example of the multiplying effects of his fixed industrial investments. And he still looked to expand production.

Ford turned to local architect Albert Kahn, the son of a German rabbi. Kahn lacked a formal education, but he was to become as influential in the field of modern industrial architecture as Ford would be in modern mass production.[44] In 1903 Kahn designed the factory for Detroit's Packard

Motor Company, which caught Ford's eye. Rather than brick, Kahn used steel-reinforced concrete—a revolutionary new construction material, for which the Ford Motor Company increased demand. Kahn's brother Julius, a structural engineer, had patented the Kahn System of Reinforced Concrete, a steel skeleton with soldered wings pointing upward and concrete poured over it. It combined the elasticity of steel with the compression strength of concrete. Construction began in 1908 at Ford's new Highland Park factory, nicknamed the Crystal Palace for the glass-paneled exterior that hung on the brick-and-reinforced-concrete walls.[45] Reinforced concrete construction opened up room for continuous open production space, since fewer load-bearing columns were structurally necessary. Interior dividing walls could go. Also, Ford's engineers had more room to experiment with the arrangement of machine groups. Kahn's factory designs eliminated wasteful ornamentation, long the external symbol of the work of the craftsmanship taking place inside. His architecture featured rational straight lines—mere "planes surrounding a volume," as the modernist architectural mantra would go. Natural light flooded into much larger enclosed spaces, granting the buildings a nearly temple-like quality. In 1919 *Architectural Forum* published a glowing article, "The Concrete Factory," with photographs of Kahn's work.[46] Concrete had the advantage that it better absorbed vibration, reducing machine wear and tear as well as the need for constant machine realignments. Kahn designed the Highland Park factory, although he claimed its first principles came from Ford. The factory was no longer a shell for production. Ford considered his factory part of the continuous production process.

The Highland Park plant, completed in 1910, immediately became the largest factory in the world. In late 1913, Fred Colvin of the *American Machinist* visited and left stupefied. Ford then manufactured half of all U.S. automobiles. "We think of 200,000 automobiles," Colvin gasped. "We lose all sense of proportion." It meant "a million lamps; eight hundred thousand wheels and tires; ninety thousand tons of steel . . . 2 million square feet of glass." What more, Colvin wondered, could Ford, "the greatest high priest of efficiency," accomplish?[47]

He would accomplish much more. The crown jewel of the Highland Park factory was its massive electric power station. The station was powered by Ford-designed hybrid gasoline-powered internal combustion and coal-fired steam engines. It produced half the wattage necessary for the entire city of Detroit. Visitors came just to see it. Mass production required electrification. Electric power was more efficient and less costly than steam. It transmitted power over longer distances without loss. Electric wires replaced leather belts and bulky shafts, which freed up factory space for rational reorganization. Rather than relying on a single power source, many different electric motors made possible the "group drive" of machines and soon enough the "unit drive" of single machines. Industrial production was no longer dependent on immediate physical proximity to a power source. Liberated, production could operate according to fresh principles.

Those were the principles of the clock but also of electricity itself. Ford's time as an engineer at the Edison Illuminating Company had left a mark. After 1900, with the development of alternating current by inventor Nikola Tesla and entrepreneur George Westinghouse, power could travel over great distances without loss. But electricity could not be stored. It did not sit still. It kept moving. It required continuous flow. Electric utility system builders like Edison integrated networks of electric generators, transformers, and power lines, keeping electric currents flowing until final consumption.[48] Ford's mechanization of capital was not only powered by electricity. It captured the essence of electric power transmission—the abhorrence of idleness, the yearning for continuous motion. The culmination was the electric-powered moving assembly line.

It, too, had industrial precedents.[49] In the late nineteenth century, moving-line production had been used in the manufacture of tin cans, and iron foundries had employed moving lines to eliminate human labor. Animal slaughterhouses used "disassembly lines": the socialist writer Upton Sinclair had written about their use in Chicago slaughterhouses in *The Jungle* (1906), where animal carcasses, hung from hooks, circulated slowly, their parts chopped, scraped, and lopped off. Sinclair would later write about Ford's automobile assembly lines in the much-less-read but also excellent novel *The Flivver King* (1937). Ford himself cited animal disassembly as an influence. In 1913 he was hoping to produce 200,000 Model Ts; the machine groups were already arranged in sequence, set as close as possible next to one another. Somehow Ford, Sorensen, Wills, and two other engineers—who exactly is not clear, although Sorensen would claim the credit—got the idea to replace the series of workbenches with a waist-high line of pipe frames and conveyor chains.

On April 1, 1913, the production of magnetos—small electric generators whose magnets ignited the Model T's engine—was put on such a line. Before, magnetos had been assembled on workbenches. Now foremen told workers to perform one task—whether it was to start a screw, tighten a nut, or fasten a magnet clamp—and then push the magneto down the line. Next they had to repeat the same task, over and over again, for nine hours. The workers complained of sore backs, so the line was raised six inches. Some worked too fast, others too slow. The engineers realized if they moved the magnetos along with a chain, they could set, and regiment, the tempo.

"MAGNETO ASSEMBLY AT THE FORD
HIGHLAND PARK PLANT" (1913)
A photograph of what is reputed to be the first assembly
line at the Ford Motor Company.

Eureka! After eight months of study, everything, all the way to chassis assembly, followed. Soon enough electricity would power the line. After the introduction of the assembly line, the company-published *Ford Methods and the Ford Shops* claimed that the production time for a single Model T had been reduced from 12.5 hours to 93 minutes.[50]

Sorensen declared the Ford Motor Company a "perfectly synchronized operation."[51] Since its introduction, the price of the Model T halved. Company profits soared. To give a sense of just how much more productive Ford's methods were, in 1913 Ford manufactured almost half of all U.S. automobiles, 261,000 Model Ts versus the rest of the industry's 287,000. Ford had 13,000 employees. The others employed 66,000.[52] Mass production arrived with an awfully big bang.

Ford had eliminated much human labor, especially truckmen, pushers, and drovers, but he did need men to stand at the assembly line. The work demanded repetition and regimentation. The "psychology of the new industrial order," Mumford wrote in *Technics and Civilization*, "appeared upon the [military] parade ground before it came, full fledged, into the workshop."[53] The time signature of the battle march, regimentation by drumbeat, augured the regimented tempo of the mechanized assembly line. Human labor was dragooned by mechanization into greater feats of industrial productivity. The initial response was commonly a stupefying disorientation. John Dos Passos's novel *The Big Money* (1933) sought to capture the feeling, as if the speed of electric-powered mechanization eliminated the spaces between words:

> At Ford's production was improvising all the time; less waste, more spotters, straw bosses, stool-pigeons (fifteen minutes for lunch, three minutes to go to the toilet) the Taylorized speedup everywhere, reachunder, adjust washer, screw down bolt, reach-underadjustscrewdownreachunderadjust, until every ounce of life was sucked off into production and at night the workmen went home gray, shaking husks.[54]

Nonsensicalness, humor, as well as the looming prospect of insanity were common responses to the mechanization of labor. In the opening frames of Charlie Chaplin's film *Modern Times* (1936), the Tramp finds himself inside the factory's gears and cogs. The scene is funny, but the Tramp ends up in a straitjacket.

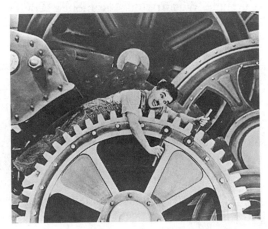

MODERN TIMES (1936) Perhaps no work of art has better pondered the relationship between man and machine than Chaplin's great film. No scene is more iconic than this one.

There were other reactions. The craft-based Detroit Metal Trades Council, affiliated with Gompers's AFL, noted in 1914 that Ford was eliminating "the necessity of skilled labor." Ford workers would "become mere slaves." Not by accident, organizing labor at Ford encountered obstacles. Ford barred labor unions, by firing anyone who joined one. As the company mechanized production, it ceased to employ skilled machinists, and turned to unskilled male "new immigrants" (Ford would not employ married women on principle), which complemented his productive capital goods.[55] In 1914 U.S.-born workers accounted for only 29 percent of Ford's labor force. The remaining 71 percent was represented by more than twenty-two nationalities, the most common being Poles, Russians, Romanians, Italians, and Hungarians. The language barrier alone made organizing difficult, but there was "No talking!" on the line anyway. There was a reason Chaplin's *Modern Times* was a silent film. (Talkies had been common for some time.) Ford foremen learned to say one expression in almost every European language: "Hurry up."[56]

Ford's workers were not slaves—they were employed at will. Ever since the rise of U.S. "free labor" norms before the Civil War, the U.S. labor market had featured a high rate of mobility and turnover for young, male, especially immigrant workers. Turnover at Ford was shockingly high. Every day in 1913 between 1,300 and 1,400 workers did not show up to work—about 10 percent of the entire workforce. Labor turnover was a staggering 370 percent. The American economist John R. Commons called it a "continuous, unorganized strike." Meanwhile the radical Industrial Workers of the World attempted to unionize Ford workers by marching to the Highland Park factory gates and holding rallies. Another industrial union, the Carriage, Wagon, and Automobile Workers Union, was also present. As for what skilled labor was left—machinists, molders, platers, and polishers—the AFL attempted to organize them. All efforts foundered, however, on the final cog in Ford's assembly line, the five-dollar day.[57]

Basically, to keep the line moving, Ford bought off his workforce. He preempted the AFL's politics of pay with his own brand of income politics. Unlike Carnegie, he would hand over a portion of his expanding profits. To great public fanfare, he announced the five-dollar day on January 5, 1914. Work was reduced from nine hours a day to eight. Daily pay for unskilled workers doubled from $2.50 to $5. Job application lines quickly ran out the door of the Ford employment department, and by 1915 labor turnover was down to 16 percent.[58]

Why did Ford do it? *My Life and Work* declared the motivation had been "social justice."[59] In another line of thought, Ford realized that if he did not pay his workers high enough wages, they would not be able to afford to buy his cars. That Ford was manufacturing a consumer good as opposed to an intermediate capital good was of great significance. Mass production would usher in an era of mass consumption, in which consumerism joined commerce and industrial investment among dynamic economic factors. It would have been absurd for Andrew Carnegie to wonder if his workers could afford to buy his steel ingots. Nonetheless, recall that in 1913 Ford manufactured 261,000 Model Ts with 13,000 employees. Ford's workforce hardly constituted adequate demand.

Another motivation behind the five-dollar day was that mass production was vulnerable to mass labor action. The assembly line demanded productivity, but it also demanded machine-like cooperation. It only took one worker, no matter how unskilled, to hold up the line. Mass production would indeed prove quite vulnerable to industrial unionism and mass strikes. At this point, Ford was willing to pay for peace. When he doubled wages, some of his fellow capitalists grumbled that he was breaking the "iron law" of wages, interfering with the natural workings of supply and demand in the labor market. Taking his pronouncements on social justice seriously, *The Wall Street Journal* complained that Ford had in his "social endeavors committed economic blunders, if not crimes."[60] A disillusioned former Ford employee, E. G. Pipp, saw it another way, claiming in 1927 that Ford once told him personally that "machinery was playing such an important part in production that if men could be induced to speed up the machinery, there would be more profit at the higher wage than at the low wage."[61] Later economic studies of the Ford Motor Company conclude that the five-dollar day was in fact an "efficiency wage."[62] It made economic sense for Ford to pay.

However, how much did Ford really care about the bottom line? What motivated him was not so much profit making as the potential awesomeness of achievement in production. His most likely single motivation for the five-dollar day was that he had just built himself a new machine—not the Model T but rather the Highland Park factory assembly line. He wanted to run it, to race it, to see how fast it could go, to see what it could accomplish if the workers stopped gumming up the works. Let it rip! If the workers were holding back production, pay them to stop.

Ford had a final motivation: he was also in the business of producing men. The five dollars were not a daily wage. A portion was called a profit share, granted only under certain conditions. The worker had to live the right way, as the company's "sociology department" administered the five-dollar-day program. As one Ford manager explained, an unskilled worker received "$2.34 per day for working" and "another $2.66 for living as the company wanted him to live." "Drinking" and "riotous living" were forbidden, as were "lack of thrift," "domestic trouble," and "indebtedness." The sociology department conducted home inspections, such that "there was nothing to keep from them." "This man lives in a dirty unsanitary hut," Ford records read. Or "Polish wedding, Drunk." "My wife told them everything," one worker lamented. Ford's vision was total.[63]

It was as if the assembly line extended outside the factory gates and into working-class homes, even into working-class saloons, where it yanked the beer right out of Ford employees' hands. That was assuming they could walk to the saloon to begin with. As the wife of one Ford assembly-line worker wrote to Ford, only weeks after the introduction of the five-dollar day:

> The chain system you have is a *slave driver! My God!*, Mr. Ford. My husband has come home & thrown himself down & won't eat his supper—so done out! Can't it be remedied? . . . That $5 a day is a blessing—a bigger one than you know but *oh* they earn it.[64]

For five dollars a day, Ford asked that his workers show up to work, every day, on time, be sober (in 1920, not long after the birth of mass production, a constitutional amendment achieved Prohibition), and be ready to submit to being a mindless cog in his great machine. At home, they had to live the right way. High wages bought consent, but this was hardly liberation from drudgery.

And what about the trees, the flowers, the birds, and the green fields?

2. The Rouge

Ford wrote in *My Life and Work*, "Power and machinery, money and goods, are useful only as they set us free to live. They are but means to an end."[65] Ford had accomplished the electric mechanization of productive capital and achieved a standard of industrial efficiency never before seen. Mechanization, however, could not answer the most fundamental question that it posed: efficiency at doing what, besides making more cars?

Among others, the twentieth century was to provide one awful end: efficiency at total war and mass death. During World War II, the architectural firm Albert Kahn Associates would design more than two hundred factories, including the mammoth Willow Run plant in Ypsilanti, Michigan. Mass production and total war developed a strong affinity, as twentieth-century warfare states proved adept at mobilizing the mechanization of capital, bringing factory discipline onto the battlefields (or was it the other way around?).

To his credit, Ford had doubts about the merits of war. He opposed U.S. entry into World War I, which had broken out in the autumn of 1914 among the Great Powers of Europe. In December 1915, Ford financed the Peace Ship and personally traveled to Europe on a publicity campaign to talk soldiers out of the trenches. That did not work. The U.S. economy boomed, exporting raw materials to Great Britain and France. Wall Street financed their war debts. German militarists judged that U.S. economic power, even under a neutral flag, might eventually tip the balance, and so Germany announced unrestricted submarine warfare against U.S. ships. Congress voted to enter the war in April 1917. The United States did help tip the balance, and an armistice was declared in November 1918. Peace brought a dramatic worldwide postwar economic cycle of inflation and deflation, as nations had departed from but now returned to the gold standard.[66] In the United States, a sharp recession in 1920–21 threatened Ford's efforts to build another factory, the great industrial colossus, the River Rouge Complex.

The Rouge was an end in itself, and when successfully completed at the end of the 1920s, it became one of the great modern symbols of the Machine Age.

Ford chose the Rouge River site, some 1,110 acres ten miles south of Detroit, in 1915. He announced in the fall of 1916:

> My ambition is to employ still more men, to spread the benefits of this industrial system to the greatest possible number, to help them build up their lives and their homes. To do this we are putting the greatest share of our profits back in the business.[67]

He planned to finance construction out of retained earnings. Wall Street was not an option. "Mr. Ford didn't like Wall Street because there were

Jews in it," recalled one employee.[68] But two of Ford's original investors, the Dodge brothers, owned 10 percent of the company and did not want all profits reinvested in the construction of the Rouge. They wanted Ford to pay them dividends on their stock. In fact, the Dodge brothers needed capital to finance their own car company. In November 1916 the Dodges had sued Ford in a Michigan court demanding that he pay out 74 percent of the company's existing cash surplus in dividends, a reasonable figure given standard corporate practices at the time.

Ford objected. "The primary object of a manufacturing business," he would declare in *My Life and Work,* was not to make a pecuniary profit for the company's owners but "to produce."[69] That was Ford's politics of capital. If the Dodge brothers did not like it, they could sell their shares, and he would buy them. In the case of *Dodge v. Ford Motor Co.* (1919), the Michigan Supreme Court found in favor of the Dodges, declaring, "A business corporation is organized and carried on primarily for the profit of the stockholders."[70] The Michigan court ordered Ford to pay $19 million in back dividends to his investors.

Ford then needed capital himself, to build the Rouge. When the United States entered World War I, he had called Washington, offering to build antisubmarine Eagle boats at cost, taking no profits. The war ended before U.S. mass production was fully brought to bear, but military contracts brought money into the company, and the Army Corps of Engineers widened the Detroit River from 98 to 295 feet, dredging its bottom and opening port access. Ford handed the federal government a bill to install roads, a railroad, and a sewage system at the Rouge. During the war, the Kahn-designed "Building B," the Rouge complex's first manufacturing building, was constructed for Eagle boat assembly. But the war contracts were not enough. Desperate to be rid of meddling, profit-seeking stockholders, Ford hired stockbrokers to feel out the minority owners of the company. He wanted to buy them all out.

For $106 million, the Ford family bought 100 percent ownership of the Ford Motor Company. Including Ford's shares, the company was now valued at $255 million. To complete the purchase, Ford had to secure a $75 million credit from a syndicate of New York and Boston banks.[71] Despite the debt, not even Rockefeller or Carnegie had ever enjoyed complete equity ownership and control of their firms. By now, mass production was clearly the future of industry. The Great Bull Market of the 1920s at the New York Stock Exchange began, and Ford's chief competitor, General

Motors, was among its darlings. The Ford Motor Company was an anomaly. Ford had secured complete control.

Between 1917 and 1920, Ford invested $60 million in the Rouge.[72] Arguably, this was the greatest single outlay of fixed capital investment in all of history. Given economic conditions, it nearly broke the company. During World War I, Great Britain and France, in addition to borrowing heavily from U.S. financiers—J. P. Morgan & Co. above all—had gone off the gold standard to expand their domestic money and credit supplies in order to finance the war. Upon its conclusion, as economic production converted back to peacetime ends, and as workers demanded more from the economy in recompense for having bled in the trenches, demand ran ahead of supply for many goods. Uncertainty over the future postwar monetary system destabilized expectations. Altogether there was inflation. The convulsions shook the United States. In 1919 as many as 4 million workers went on strike for the eight-hour day and higher wages.[73] Anarchists bombed J. P. Morgan & Co.'s headquarters, killing thirty-eight people.[74] Ford shut down the sociological department in 1919: his workers, it turned out, would not stand for home visits or similar intrusions.

In 1920, in unison with the Bank of England's effort to restore the pre–World War I gold standard, pillar of the British Empire, the Federal Reserve sharply raised interest rates. To return currencies to their prewar levels of exchange parity with gold, everywhere the money and credit supply would have to shrink. The scarcity value of money capital would be enforced. It was the post–Civil War policy of resumption all over again. A punishing deflation set in. Money, credit, and economic activity constricted. Unemployment neared 9 percent.[75] In Detroit, the Ford Motor Company helped organize the violent breaking of a number of strikes among many of its suppliers—in ports, mines, and steelworks. Elsewhere, U.S. Steel defeated the largest steelworkers strike since Homestead. In the wake of the Russian Revolution, an anti-Bolshevik red scare broke out. Everywhere in the world, including in the United States, organized labor was beaten back.

Ford would call the post–World War I recession his "black winter."[76] During the deflation, his instinct was to cut prices further and to increase car sales, even if it meant maintaining production at a loss. But there was one thing that not even Ford could control—effective demand in the economy as a whole. There simply were not enough buyers for automobiles. On December 24, 1920, the Ford Motor Company halted production. In September, Detroit automakers had employed 176,000 workers. By December, the number was 24,000. Ford owed $25 million to the creditors who had enabled him to buy his company. He also owed the federal government a hefty tax bill, somewhere between $18 million and $30 million (given income tax rate hikes during World War I). At this point, Wall Street bankers literally appeared on Ford's doorstep, offering their services.[77]

A vice president of the Liberty National Bank of New York, which was part of the J. P. Morgan & Co. network, was among them. Recently, Liberty had taken a large financial interest in General Motors, acquiring seats on its board of directors. "I don't need to borrow money," Ford told the banker. "I think not," the man responded. "We know your obligations, we know your cash reserves, and we know you need money. . . . Who is going to be the new treasurer of your company?" "That makes no difference to you, does it?" Ford responded. "Oh, yes, it does," said the banker. "We'll have to have some say as to who the new treasurer shall be." Ford picked up the man's hat and showed him the door.[78] He was not going to be "Morganized." The company forced thousands of its car dealerships to "advance" it cash for future delivery of stock. The Highland Park plant reopened on February 23, 1921. Soon the deflation bottomed out, with the price level one-third below the 1920 price level. The recession lifted, and demand for automobiles returned. The peak year of Model T production would be 1923—1.8 million automobiles.[79] The same year the company's share of the market peaked at 66 percent.[80]

Ford paid off his creditors and plowed profits back into factory construction. The "High Rouge" strategy of the early 1920s, pushed by Ford—and by Sorensen, with a "demoniac energy"—was for the company to integrate everything from raw materials to the final product into one seamless flow of production.[81] For decades now, investment in intermediate capital goods had catalyzed industrial revolution, creating supply and demand in markets upstream and downstream, from production to consumption. Everywhere output increased; due to an investment multiplier, one firm's investments stoked business for others, and vice versa. Like no one before him, Ford hoped to internalize the multiplying effects of his investments under the single roof of his own company. The Ford Motor Company now tried to encompass all the many backward and forward linkages of automobile production into one, single working unit.

By the completion of construction in 1928, there would be ninety-three separate buildings at the River Rouge Complex. Among them were an integrated steelworks, a foundry, a glass plant, a cement plant, a textile mill,

"FORD MOTOR COMPANY RIVER ROUGE PLANT,
DEARBORN, MICHIGAN" (1927)
An aerial view of perhaps the most famous factory in world history,
a year before its 1928 completion.

a leather plant, a hospital, a motion picture laboratory (Ford issued pro-
motional films), an airport, and more than 15 million square feet of factory floor space. There was a 100,000-horsepower coal-fired electric power
plant, capable of powering a city of more than 1 million. The Rouge's pay-
rolls climbed past 100,000. Ford bought the Detroit, Toledo & Ironton Railroad to secure railroad access, and the company owned its own fleet of
ships, led by the 611-foot steamship the *Henry Ford II*. To supply the Rouge,
Ford bought up—among other territorial possessions—Michigan forests
and ore mines, Kentucky and West Virginia coal mines, and, most infamously, a failed rubber plantation in Brazil.[82] A farm tractor, the Fordson,
was assembled at the Rouge, but the Rouge was mostly for the production
of component parts. Assembly still occurred at Highland Park. Yet to be
closer to markets by 1924, there were Model T assembly plants as far and
wide as Antwerp, Bordeaux, Buenos Aires, Copenhagen, Cork, Manchester, Montevideo, Santiago, São Paulo, Stockholm, and Trieste.[83] The Ford
Motor Company's supply chain was becoming a global empire unto itself.

The Rouge was built of newly standardized structural components.
Kahn had designed a series of one-story buildings held up with reinforced
concrete columns forty feet apart. This was a new factory design. Ford had

requested one-story buildings to simplify "the flow of materials." (By contrast, Highland Park was six stories tall.) Raw materials entered the Rouge complex by canal or train. The major innovation at the Rouge was a "high line," a concrete structure, forty feet high, stretching three-quarters of a mile, with five sets of railroad tracks, from which cranes automatically distributed material to moving cars below. Kahn boasted in *Architectural Forum* of the incorporation into his design of the "process of manufacture so that there may be continuous and direct flow from the receiving of the raw material to shipping of the finished product."[84] Everything was in synchronous motion.

No less remarkable was the sheer physical massing of productive capital. Ford had fixed, and settled, prodigious amounts of illiquid capital goods in place. There would be no pulling out of the investment anytime soon. The Rouge was truly monumental, by far and by any measure the largest factory in the world. It inspired awe, soon attracting over 100,000 tourists a year—166,000 as late as 1940.[85] *Industrial Management* argued that the Rouge challenged the "time-honored law of Supply and Demand." Through integration, Ford had eliminated commercial markets from his supply chain. The idea behind the Rouge was "complete control."[86] When the American literary critic Edmund Wilson—a great critic of Ford, whom he called a "despot"—visited the Rouge, he spoke of Detroit as one "huge organism." From the Rouge, Wilson argued, arose "the whole structure of an industrial society."[87]

With so much massing of durable, industrial capital, "structure" increasingly became a metaphor for industrial society itself. The first generation to live through industrialization often experienced it as uprootedness—perhaps from rural life and the stolidity of the land. Many of Ford's workers were European peasants. Nonetheless, when gazing up at the Rouge, it was hard not to think that, after the rupture of industrial revolution, the time horizon was now extending, and that economic life was at last settling down into a long-term structure.

Quickly, in addition to being a symbol of economic modernism, the Rouge became an aesthetic symbol of cultural modernism. The Swiss-French modernist architect Le Corbusier, who learned a lot about concrete construction from Kahn, visited the Rouge and left "plunged into a kind of stupor," he later wrote, mesmerized by the "totality of thought and action."[88] Kahn's industrial architecture, stripped of all waste and ornament, ruled by the efficient straight line, would find high artistic expression.

The American fiction writer Sherwood Anderson, after touring a number of mass production factories, noted that "the machine dominates American life." He continued:

> I have felt the poetry of all this. I have felt the terror of it. After having written no verse of several years and after visiting the factories of the towns I have again the hunger. In some moods I want to be the poetry of industry, of the machine. For the machine, as the American has developed it, I feel only admiration and love.[89]

New York's 1927 Machine-Age Exposition was organized by the feminist Jane Heap, to illustrate the "inter-relation-inter-influence of architecture, engineering, industrial arts, and modern art."[90] Much was in fact interrelated, from the design of factories, office buildings, and skyscrapers, to consumer products like automobiles and electric toaster ovens. Photographs of machine cranks became art objects, as with Paul Outerbridge's *Marmon Crankshaft* (1923). The machine conjured more associations and connections, more totality. "Prose is architecture," proclaimed

KATHERINE DREIER, "MACHINE-AGE EXPOSITION" (1927) Feminist Jane Heap organized this exposition—an early sign of modern artists' widespread appropriation of the aesthetic principles of the machine.

MAY 16 — 119 WEST — MAY 28
FIFTY-SEVENTH STREET

NEW YORK 1927

MACHINE-AGE EXPOSITION

ARCHITECTURE
ENGINEERING
INDUSTRIAL ARTS
MODERN ART

PRESENTED TOGETHER FOR THE FIRST TIME IN SUCH A MANNER THAT THE INTER-RELATION-INTER-INFLUENCE WILL BE SHOWN AND EMPHASIZED

GLASS SKYSCRAPER

DESIGNED BY HUGH FERRISS WILL BE A SENSATIONAL FEATURE

DAILY AND SUNDAY
1 P.M.-10 P.M.

TICKETS 50 CENTS

PAUL OUTERBRIDGE, JR.,
MARMON CRANKSHAFT
(1923)
Outerbridge was an advertising photographer, associated with the precisionist movement in visual arts. This photograph of an automobile crankshaft, depicting the sculptural qualities of machine engineering, was made for a Marmon Motor Car Company advertisement.

Ernest Hemingway, who developed his precise, economical writing style at this moment. According to the modernist William Carlos Williams, a poem should be a "small (or large) machine made out of words," that is "pruned to perfect economy."[91]

Modernists like Williams expressed fascination with the electric speed-up of life across multiple cultural media. Rather than perspective, motion became the "pictorial language to express psychic content," observed Siegfried Giedion in *Mechanization Takes Command* (1948).[92] In Gerald Murphy's *Watch* (1925), it is as if Ford's boyhood watch exploded out of his pocket and across an entire canvas. Meanwhile the synchronicity of Ford's assembly line exploded through popular mass culture. If Sorensen considered the Ford Motor Company one "perfectly synchronized operation," the German culture critic Siegfried Kracauer identified the "mass ornament" in new consumer entertainments, whether it was "synchronized dancing" or even "synchronized swimming."[93] Elsewhere, if the patented Kahn reinforced concrete system uniformly absorbed vibrations, similar engineering systems in music halls and recording studios began to standardize a "modern" soundscape.[94]

GERALD MURPHY, *WATCH* (1925)
No industrial technology was more significant than timekeeping. Reputedly,
this painting was inspired by a railroad watch designed for Murphy's family
business, the Mark Cross Company, a maker of leather goods. Murphy was
an American expatriate in France and a member of the post–World War I
"Lost Generation." He painted for only a short period of time during the
1920s. Notably, the painting is large, seven by seven feet.

The Rouge itself directly inspired great works of art. The photographer
and painter Charles Sheeler spent six weeks there in 1927 and called the
complex "incomparably the most thrilling I have had to work with."[95]
Sheeler's art, soon called "precisionist," homed in on the clarity of the
Rouge's structural lines. But it also conveyed sheer physical mass—
productive capital electrified and mechanized but also fixed, settled, and
ordered. Sheeler's great painting of the factory was called, tellingly, *American Landscape* (1930). The industrial landscape conveys stillness and quiet.
The smoke emitted from the Rouge's smokestacks blends seamlessly with
clouds in the sky—as if the Rouge were a given, natural fact. Was industrial capital now as much of a given as the land had been before? Was this
a new organic economy, or a longing for the past one? In the painting, the
scale of the factory dwarfs the one barely visible human figure. "Every
age," Sheeler wrote, "manifests the nature of its content by some external
form of evidence." *American Landscape* makes for an interesting comparison with the frescoes of the Rouge painted by the Mexican artist Diego

CHARLES SHEELER, *CRISS-CROSSED CONVEYORS, RIVER ROUGE PLANT, FORD MOTOR COMPANY* (1927) Sheeler, commissioned by the Ford Motor Company with advertising in mind, took many photographs of the River Rouge Complex. The conveyer belts pictured here illustrate the company's desire for continuous motion, yet the image also conveys the monumental stability and structure of the Rouge.

CHARLES SHEELER, *AMERICAN LANDSCAPE* (1930)
Early-nineteenth-century Hudson River School painters often featured
a solitary individual dwarfed by nature. A century later, just barely
visible in Sheeler's industrial landscape is a sole individual,
running along the railroad track.

Rivera. *Detroit Industry Murals,* installed at the Detroit Institute of Arts in 1932–33, were commissioned by Ford's son Edsel. Rivera, like many Marxists, reverently respected production and was inspired by the Rouge, yet human labor is foregrounded in his murals, which are mythic in their themes. Was the Rouge not only natural but also supernatural in its powers? In 1928 *Vanity Fair* published one of Sheeler's photographs of the Rouge with the caption "an American altar of the God-objective of Mass Production."[96] Large truths lurked in the new mechanization and massing of industrial capital.

3. Fordism After Ford

The Rouge was the apogee of Henry Ford's industrial ambitions. During the 1920s, his grandiose visions began to border on megalomania. There were limits to his celebrity, charisma, and initiative, even as electric mechanization spread across industrial society. The future of mass production began to slip beyond his control.

For one thing, the labor policies of the Ford Motor Company became ever more reactionary. Infamously, Ford's legendary anti-union enforcer Harry Bennett began to stroll around the Rouge with a gun. In U.S. manufacturing, union membership declined from 19 percent of the workforce in 1921 to 10 percent by 1929.[97] The 1920s saw many experiments in "corporate welfare" schemes, but a policy of "militant anti-unionism" took hold at the Ford Motor Company.[98] If wages remained high, the five-dollar-day program in all its guises was phased out. With the closing of European immigration due to World War I, followed by the exclusionary Immigration Act of 1924, Ford began to hire thousands of black workers of the great migration out of the South. Blacks became 10 percent of Ford's workforce.[99] He expected them to reward the opportunity with loyalty, only to be disappointed when black residents of Detroit did not support his own chosen political candidates for city government. Meanwhile by the early 1920s, the Detroit-based industrial United Automobile, Aircraft, and Vehicle Workers' Union, with at least forty thousand members, threatened to organize the Rouge.[100] The company employed spies to ferret out union sympathizers so that they could be fired.

Ford had imagined pastoral harmony for his employees. During construction of the Rouge, he had also constructed satellite plants in the countryside. "There is something about a city of a million people which is untamed and threatening," Ford wrote. "A great city is really a helpless mass."[101] Kahn designed a number of industrial hamlets, but the greatest effort was Ford's bid to develop Muscle Shoals, an economically depressed rural area in northwestern Alabama on the Tennessee River. During the war, the federal government had begun construction on hydroelectric dams and nitrate factories but had left them unfinished. Ford promised Congress he would complete the project "along unselfish lines," without taking any company profits. "I am consecrated to the principle of freeing American industry," he declared, promising a "new Eden of our Mississippi Valley."[102] Architect Frank Lloyd Wright enthused at Kahn's combined residential and industrial designs for Muscle Shoals, pictured in *Scientific American* in 1922, calling it "one of the best" examples of an industrial pastoralism to which he, too, aspired. But Congress refused Ford the concession. Instead Ford would build "Fordlandia" at the company's rubber tree plantation in the Brazilian Amazon.[103] Fordlandia would fail, and the development of Muscle Shoals would have to wait for the Tennessee Valley Authority of the New Deal.

In business, despite the completion of the Rouge, during the 1920s the Ford Motor Company's market share declined.[104] Ford's competitors adopted his mass production methods and in some respects improved on them. After 1921, General Motors was under the controlling interest of a Delaware explosives manufacturer, the DuPont Company. GM's Chevrolet model began to compete with the Model T. GM's mass production methods were more flexible. It built more lines of cars, catering to different consumer market niches. Grudgingly, Ford began to paint the Model T different colors. GM also encouraged its customers to buy on credit. The General Motors Acceptance Corporation (GMAC) launched in 1919. Ford was against debt on principle, although his son Edsel quietly opened a credit agency, the Guaranty Trust Company, on a different set of books.

Ford realized the Model T's days were over, and in 1927 the fifteen-millionth Model T to be produced was the last. He had to completely shut down production to retool for the new Model A (a great car, by all accounts)—his assembly line was fast but not as adaptable as GM's. The U.S. economy experienced a short recession while the company reconfigured its 45,000 machine tools. The "High Rouge" strategy slowly gave way, as Ford began to rely on a more flexible commercial network of suppliers. By 1929, Ford and GM each had 35 percent of the automobile market. Production was Ford's metric of industrial success, but Ford's pecuniary revenues were half those of GM. GM was a much more profitable corporation.[105]

The Ford Motor Company had lost the initiative in mass production methods.[106] Ford thought he could internalize every step of the automobile production process into his firm. Instead, his mass production methods spread to other automakers. They were reproducible and could even be improved—made nimbler and more profitable. Given his personality, Ford was not well equipped to take these next steps.

Politically, the Ford Motor Company remained under the personal whim of its founder. By contrast, GM invested in bureaucracy. Ford's method of accounting was: "Put all the money we take in in a big barrel and when a shipment of material comes in, reach into the barrel and take out enough money to pay for it."[107] GM took a different approach, separating management and ownership.[108] The DuPont stockowners developed new bureaucratic methods to keep the Detroit managers accountable.[109] In 1923 MIT graduate Alfred Sloan became the Detroit-based president of GM. The corporation developed a sophisticated hierarchy, with power and authority vested in impersonal titles and offices—which was the ongoing corporate trend.[110] Mechanization created great demand for skilled, white-collar workers.[111] Vice presidents, managers, middle managers, and associates piled into head offices, sitting in standardized chairs, at standardized desks, in standardized office cubicles.[112] In a mass society, paradoxically faceless bureaucracy and the cultural celebrity of a figure like Ford arose in tandem. Corporations hired new "industrial psychologists" to administer standardized personality tests to job applicants.[113] Industrial corporations internalized "research and development" in their own labs.[114] Unlike Ford and his early producerist tinkerers and engineers, many had attended university. Franklin Bobbitt's *The Curriculum* (1918) celebrated new "standardized" tests. Corporate accountants employed new accounting techniques, in light of the companies' long-term investments in productive capital—"cost accounting," "capital budgeting," and "sales forecasting."[115] They read professional trade journals, such as *Management and Administration,* published by the American Management Association. Personalities with a taste for order and control were judged best suited for these jobs (although in Elmer Rice's popular play *The Adding Machine* [1923] a corporate accountant snaps and murders his boss). Regardless, next to a corporate manager like the MIT-trained Alfred Sloan, Henry Ford increasingly appeared an idiosyncratic crank.

The new corporate values of bureaucracy, efficiency, and professionalism entered electoral politics. During the 1910s, Progressives advocated them. It was no coincidence, surely, that in 1928 Machine Age Americans elected for their president a former engineer, Herbert Hoover. During the

1920s, as secretary of commerce, Hoover had organized the Committee on the Elimination of Waste in Industry, which pleaded for applying the virtues of "standardization" and "efficiency" toward industry's "only real objective—maximum production."[116] In 1928 Samuel Crowther, only six years past ghostwriting Ford's *My Life and Work*, wrote another book, *The Presidency vs. Hoover*, that lavishly praised the Republican presidential nominee. Ford even granted Crowther an interview to publicize his support for the Great Engineer.

Modernity and progress evoked efficient, linear, straight-line time—the path of Ford's sped-up electric-powered assembly line, capable of such great production. But while Ford kept complete financial control of his company, the great leap forward in the rest of U.S. industrial production during the 1920s was sustained by yet another upswing in the repeating capitalist credit cycle, another speculative boom. On the NYSE, it was the decade of the Great Bull Market, which followed a surge in investor confidence after the post–World War I restoration of the gold standard.

Hoover could champion efficiency, and Ford could bray against Wall Street and Jews all they wanted, but by now the United States was at the center of global finance. After World War I, the world owed the country $12 billion. The United States sat on most of the world's gold reserves, and the Federal Reserve was newly burdened by the responsibility of maintaining the worldwide gold standard. Hoover the Great Engineer would be at the wheel when the international financial system would implode, and the lights, so recently electrified, would go out on capitalism.

CHAPTER 12

THE GREAT DEPRESSION

THE GREATEST INTERPRETIVE CHALLENGE POSED BY THE AGE of Capital is to connect two of its central economic narratives, both of which speak to the increasing centrality of capital in economic life.

First, industrial revolution took place. Due to fixed investment in production, capital settled into more energy-intensive, illiquid capital goods. Over time, labor productivity increased on the supply side, and through long-term industrial economic development, wealth and money incomes grew—even though they were more inequitably distributed, relative to the past. Second, the capitalist credit cycle repeated. Here the timing was not linear. Periods of short-term speculative investment booms motivated industrial economic development, accelerating industrial revolution, but these episodes were followed by moments of panic and the competitive flight to safe liquid assets. Precautionary hoarding prevailed, demand collapsed, and development decelerated. Entrepreneurial energy enervated, as long-term investment in productive capital halted. Economic life was nervously pulled into the present, before confidence returned.

The dynamic appeared at the opening of the Age of Capital. Following the post–Civil War restoration of a metallic currency, expectations and confidence surged, propelling the post-1868 railroad construction boom. But the Panic of 1873 followed, and a debt-deflation slump. Recovery brought the most intensive period of industrialization on record, punctuated nonetheless by periodic booms and busts. The post–World War I repetition of a similar sequence, culminating in the speculative investment boom of the Great Bull Market of the 1920s and the Great Depression of the 1930s, was, in every respect, the most extraordinary yet.

Once again, in 1920, a postwar return to the gold standard led to a price deflation, which fueled a surge in psychological confidence among the owners of capital—who guarded the scarcity value of their money capital. During the 1920s, a great speculative upswing unfolded across all sectors. Due to Fordist mass production, expectations of future gains in industrial production were brighter than ever before: in hindsight, the 1920s spread of the electric assembly line beyond the Ford Motor Company brought about the largest surge in labor productivity ever recorded. In commodities, worldwide agricultural production boomed. But then in 1929 the credit cycle dramatically reversed. Expectations shifted. The New York Stock Exchange (NYSE) busted. Agricultural prices plummeted. Soon a vicious spiral ensued, and the economy of production collapsed. Confidence did not return. The Great Depression had begun.

No bottom was apparent, above the limits of human endurance. The U.S. unemployment rate, 2.9 percent in 1929, would soon surpass 15 percent. Virtually every known economic indicator went into free fall. Most worrisome was the crippling price deflation, the ongoing Depression's most singular symptom.[1] In the summer of 1931, the British central banker Montagu Norman wrote to the head of the Banque de France, "Unless drastic measures are taken to save it, the capitalist system throughout the civilized world will be wrecked within a year."[2]

What caused the Great Depression? A still-celebrated scholarly interpretation, Milton Friedman and Anna Schwartz's *A Monetary History of the United States* (1963), argues that it was the result of a series of outside monetary and financial shocks on the real economy of production, exchange, and consumption, made worse by terrible policy blunders by the Federal Reserve, without which the real economy would have autocorrected to its natural market equilibrium soon enough.[3] Surely, policy blunders were committed, and they made the Great Depression much worse than it needed to be. But a hard and fast division between the "real" and the "financial-monetary" will not do. Any plausible account must integrate them and cannot place the dynamics of speculative investment outside the real economy of timeless market equilibrium.

The initiating cause of the Great Depression was governments' insistence on restoring the pre–World War I gold standard, which necessitated very high central bank interest rates. Thus what drove the great investment boom of the 1920s was borrowing on very high interest rates. High rates created a high bar for future expected profits. But expectations during the 1920s were sufficiently high to bring about an unusual moment in capital and credit markets—a moment of abundant but expensive credit. (There had been a moment like this after the Civil War, and there would be another moment in the 1980s.)[4]

During the 1920s, debt-fueled borrowing and speculation did lead to long-term Machine Age investments. The cumulative, multiplying process of industrial investment in capital goods increased productivity and growth. But with money borrowed at such high rates, if the credit cycle reversed, the aftermath was likely to be ugly: the calling in of expensive loans, panic, a flight to security, and the kind of liquidity preference—precautionary—that does not lead to fixed investment in production and that undermines the use of existing capital equipment.[5] Demand for goods would evaporate, as spending of all kinds—and thus production, output, and employment—would go into reverse.

That was what happened: when expectations of future profits dampened, the credit cycle did reverse. U.S. fixed investment started declining in February 1929, months before the Great Crash of the NYSE in October. As expectations shifted, agricultural prices collapsed, and the drop in farm incomes further diminished demand for manufactured goods. The industrial and agricultural sectors strained against each other. As countries struggled to maintain the gold standard, a series of reverberating international financial panics made matters far worse. Incredibly, by later estimates, gross private U.S. domestic investment, $16.2 billion in 1929, would fall to a paltry $300 million by 1933.[6]

A fearful, precautionary liquidity preference among the owners of capital broke out. They would not part with money to invest capital in employment-giving production. Economic life suffered from a lack of psychic energy. Existing factories and willing workers sat by, idle and unoccupied. Something would have to come from outside the economic system to bring back demand and prompt a full-fledged recovery in production.

Paradoxically, the Great Depression could not have happened a century earlier. Only generations of industrial revolution had sufficiently increased money incomes, while pulling so many people into the commercial economy, to the extent that the propensity of rich investors and even poor consumers to hoard money could so halt economic activity. Only in an economy with so much of its wealth denominated in money—in contradictory fashion, both a potential means of investment in production and a potential store of value that saps production—could a crash have such collapsing economic effects. The repeating capitalist credit cycle had made possible long-term economic development and greater riches, but in doing so had also led to the possibility of greater busts and—in a society with so little access to sustenance outside capitalism anymore—perhaps even greater suffering.

How remarkable that the Great Depression took place so soon after the advent of mass production. Electric energy could not be unleashed on production without a corresponding psychic energy. What "an extraordinary imbecility," remarked the British economist John Maynard Keynes in 1930, in a lecture at the University of Chicago, not far from the recent midwestern birthplace of mass production, "that this wonderful outburst of productive energy should be the prelude to impoverishment and depression."[7]

An anonymous October 30, 1930, letter to President Herbert Hoover from the anthracite coal region of Pottstown, Pennsylvania, well diagnosed the problem: "Money tied up hoarded up Is a crime."[8]

1. Golden Fetters

Any account of the origins of the Great Depression must begin with the ill-fated restoration of the international gold standard in the aftermath of World War I.[9] Powerful statesmen and financiers believed gold was the linchpin of the fragile postwar peace in Europe, as well as the recovery of international investor confidence and, with it, national economic health. At first, they seemed to be right, but then the return to orthodoxy led to ruin.[10]

A great post–World War I cycle of price inflation and deflation extended during the early 1920s. Everywhere peace first brought inflation. The European states had financed the war largely by printing money, fully suspending the gold standard so as to issue credit in hopes of compelling maximum production. Meanwhile Wall Street replaced the City of London as the world's great lender. In the United States, because of wartime exports and nervous European capital flight, gold bullion reserves doubled during the war, from $2 billion to $4 billion. That was more than one-third of the world's gold reserves.[11] The swelling of the U.S. monetary base only contributed to U.S. inflation, as production transitioned to peacetime. But the greater cause of inflation was that everywhere peace unleashed popular demands for better living standards, which further pushed upward the prices of goods.

As a matter of principle, statesmen and financiers desired a return to gold.[12] Thomas Lamont, after 1922 lead partner at J. P. Morgan & Co., now the world's most powerful bank, called it the "old-fashioned religion."[13] Only the certainty of fixed gold-currency pegs could ensure the future value of investments, and restore cross-border global capital movements, a given fact of pre–World War I economic development, which after all had been an era of both historically unprecedented low interest rates and capital mobility.

The Federal Reserve, dominated by the regional New York Federal Reserve Bank and its privately appointed governor Benjamin Strong, formerly a member of the Morgan banking network, took the lead in asserting the scarcity value of money and credit. Since demand for money can determine its quantity in addition to its supply (banks can create credit money), central banks best control prices by setting interest rates, not by directly controlling the issue of money. In 1920 the New York Fed raised interest rates (the short-term rate it charged its member banks to borrow funds) to 7 percent, to initiate the global march toward deflation and what post–Civil War Americans, in their own wrenching path back to the gold standard, had called resumption. In a private 1925 letter to his British counterpart Montagu Norman, Strong wrote that the absence of the gold standard

> would mean violent fluctuations in the exchanges, with probably progressive determination of the values of foreign currencies vis-à-vis the dollar; it would provide an incentive to all of those who were advancing novel ideas for nostrums and expedients other than the gold standard to sell their wares; and incentive to governments at times to undertake various types of paper money expedients and inflation.[14]

European central bankers followed, raising rates, and as national economies began the slog back to the gold standard, a punishing bout of deflation and depression coursed through them.

However, economies quickly recovered from the postwar cycle of inflation and deflation, catalyzed by a speculative investment boom in the

United States, which spilled over into the channels of international lending. The United States was responsible for 60 percent of all international loans between 1924 and 1931.[15] U.S. capital financed European reconstruction. Such confidence may be attributed, in part, to the restoration of the gold standard and its assurance of future price stability for lenders. Thus in 1920s capital markets, the combination was price stability, high borrowing rates, and abundant available financing.

Republican Warren G. Harding had called for the return to gold during his successful 1920 presidential campaign—a "return to normalcy." It took some time to restore anything resembling a normal state of affairs. The punitive Treaty of Versailles (1919) had burdened Germany with $33 billion in war reparations but Britain and France owed prodigious war debts to the United States—$5 billion and $4 billion respectively. Famously, after massive international capital flight, Germany suffered hyperinflation from 1921 to 1923.[16] In 1923, after a currency devaluation, Germany repegged its currency to gold. That same year, to extract reparations payments, France occupied Germany's coal-rich Ruhr Valley. The Chicago banker Charles Dawes brokered an agreement, and France evacuated in 1925. The Dawes Plan revised Germany's immediate reparations payments downward (leaving the final number open), and the German Reichsbank came under foreign supervision. Wall Street granted a $200 million loan to Germany, floated by a Morgan syndicate. Ultimately, Britain returned to the gold standard in 1925 at the pound's prewar gold parity—restoring the sine qua non of the prewar British Empire at the expense of the British working class. (British unemployment remained high.) France finally pegged the franc to gold in 1926. In return for a balanced budget pledge, J. P. Morgan floated the French government a stabilizing loan of $100 million.

In sum, U.S. loans to Germany began to be recycled into reparations payments to Britain and France, which then traveled back across the Atlantic to pay down British and French war debts. In 1925 Charles Dawes was awarded the Nobel Peace Prize and became vice president in the administration of Republican Calvin Coolidge. The hope was that sound finance might keep a tight leash on any return of German militarism and preserve the peace. Not international diplomacy but Wall Street financiers would have to do the job.[17] The United States, after all, had failed to join President Woodrow Wilson's proposed League of Nations, which had begun meeting in 1920.

By 1926, officials everywhere believed the postwar crisis was over. The gold standard and international lending appeared to be restored. An extraordinary boom commenced. The $1.5 billion in gold bullion in the vaults underneath the New York Federal Reserve Bank, at the corner of Broad and Wall streets, seemed to act like some great giant magnet, attracting capital and credit to the trading floor of the New York Stock Exchange.

2. The Great Bull Market

Ever since the Great Bull Market of the 1920s, commentary has focused on the question of whether the country's underlying economic "fundamentals" justified the run-up in U.S. stock prices. John Kenneth Galbraith's influential 1954 book *The Great Crash, 1929* said they did not. More recently, a number of economic historians have disagreed.[18] But the contradictory drive of speculative investment is not so easy to parse.[19] Why did the NYSE soar so high during the 1920s, and why, in the fall of 1929, did the sudden reversal propagate a broader collapse of long-term fixed investment?

The NYSE during the 1920s was something new. Its prominence in capital markets had increased during the Great Merger Movement, but on the eve of World War I, less than 1 percent of Americans owned corporate stock. Capital markets still remained highly regional, sometimes local.[20] Only during the 1920s did the NYSE begin to command the nationwide stock market. Organized on the basis of transactional liquidity—a willing buyer for each listing—the NYSE mobilized long-term investment in wealth-generating enterprise for corporations. No less, it made possible short-term speculation. Meanwhile during the 1920s, the number of U.S. households owning stock increased by a factor of sixteen. By 1929, one-quarter of all U.S. households had money in the NYSE.[21] The Great Bull Market of the 1920s was a product of mass communications and mass psychology, and was nothing short of a mass cultural spectacle.

Once again World War I loomed large as a cause: the United States had financed it by selling $20 billion worth of Liberty Bonds to some 30 million American citizens.[22] The Civil War had been financed in a similar way, but it had not led to a new mass investment market in corporate securities. By the 1920s, Americans were wealthier, with higher incomes and money to invest. And after the Great Merger Movement, they had many more large manufacturing corporations in which to invest. In the early 1920s, many corporations, wary of the wartime nationalization of particular indus-

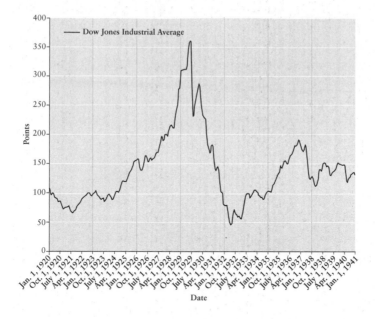

Date

DOW JONES INDUSTRIAL AVERAGE

With the American industrial sector on the precipice of a Fordist great leap forward, rising stock prices reflected reasonable expectations of future prosperity. But the speculative boom became a highly leveraged house of cards.

tries, such as the railroads, for political reasons promoted corporate stock ownership as an emblem of democratic citizenship, as Liberty Bonds had been. By 1928, almost 800,000 employees at 315 companies held $1 billion worth of stock.[23]

The NYSE did not truly begin its upward march until 1925. An important factor was a new kind of financial corporation, the publicly listed "investment trust." To increase profits, trusts—like brokerage firms—often leveraged their investments by going into debt. Short-term credits were available in the Wall Street "call money" market. In the call market, investment trusts as well as stockbrokers could take out loans "on margin," meaning that some of the collateral for the loan to purchase a stock was that stock itself. If its value ever plummeted, the collateral would be worth less—the loan might be called in. As long as the value of the stock went up, however, there would be no problems. In principle, because of the gold standard, the quantity of gold restricted the expansion of credit of this or any other kind. Further, during the 1920s, as European gold kept washing up on U.S. shores, New York Fed governor Benjamin Strong "sterilized" gold inflows—effectively withdrawing them from circulation.[24] Nonetheless, credit kept expanding. Central banks may restrict the supply of money and credit, but when expectations are high, demand may also create bank credit. On this basis, the NYSE roared.

For a short time, the new prices were plausibly warranted. Typically, the price of a stock has been linked, naturally enough, to the dividend paid on it to its owner—due to past corporate profits earned. That relationship remained stable until 1927.[25] Furthermore, expectations of future industrial profitability were optimistic—not unreasonably, given the recent birth of Fordism and the electric assembly line. Many investors seem to have been pricing into their purchases the expected results of ongoing innovations in mass production.[26] Meanwhile stock market darlings such as General Motors (GM) and the Radio Corporation of America (RCA) were already highly profitable. GM—the most profitable U.S. corporation—saw its profits more than double between 1925 and 1927. Its stock price quadrupled. Still, its stock-price-to-business-earnings ratio, given historical averages, was sensible (less than 9).[27] Most corporations did not rely on the NYSE to raise capital, relying instead on flush retained earnings. Nonetheless, the birth of Fordism, and the new mass production methods, genuinely merited a long-term investment boom. A liquid securities market like the NYSE can be a channel for directing savings and credit into long-term investment in wealth-generating enterprise.

But not always.[28] The Great Bull Market of the late 1920s unquestionably evolved into a short-term speculative market. In fact, the first sign that something was amiss in capital and credit markets came in the agricultural sector. There commodity prices, high during the war due to European demand, had plummeted in 1920 during the deflationary down phase of the postwar crisis. After that they had stabilized, even as supply kept overshooting immediate demand. But prices did not drop. Instead dealers began to accumulate large inventories of crops—expecting, in the midst of the general boom mentality, that prices would increase.[29] Meanwhile in 1928 the NYSE's upward march detached from realized profits. Investment trusts, brokerage firms, and individuals were purchasing stocks and hoping to gain, short term, from the immediate appreciation of the stock price, with no apparent heed for the dividends the stocks might pay over the long term because of business profits earned. By 1929, some 2 million Americans had bought stock in some 770 different investment trusts; 3.5 million had opened a brokerage account.[30] As Keynes would write, "When the capital development of a country becomes a by-product of the activities of a casino, the job is likely to be ill-done."[31]

Historians have not yet convincingly answered the question of why, by 1928, the Great Bull Market succumbed to short-term speculation, apart from referring to delusional popular "mania."[32]

One possible explanation is the affinity between the logic of financial speculation and changing cultural norms. The Machine Age routinized production and repressed human bodies at work, but the new mass consumer culture of pleasure and play made available many compensating stimulations—in department stores, jazz music, gin joints, Model T "pleasure rides," but also stock market speculation. John B. Watson, a founder of the twentieth-century psychology of behaviorism, noted in April 1929 that "even sex has become so free and abundant in recent years that it no longer provides the thrill that it once did, and gambling in Wall Street is about the only real excitement that we have left."[33] Moments of stock market speculation and sexual liberation have gone together—after the 1920s, the next great bull market would occur in another era of sexual liberation, the 1960s (the next during another, the 1990s). Sherwood Anderson's Freud-inspired novel *Many Marriages* (1923), whose title says it all, was arguably the most acute American account of changing sexual mores published during the 1920s. For men and for women (said to be a third of all new stock investors in 1929) stock speculation does seem to have become a highly energized activity, in which the desires of speculators slipped on and off one liquid security after another. Stockbrokers advertised nationally over the radio, to which an estimated 30 million Americans listened every evening in 1929.[34] In mass communications, the radio competed with the booming 1920s motion picture industry, in an era before the Hollywood "Code" banned overtly sexual content.[35] The mass celebrity sex symbol of the 1920s was actress Clara Bow, who starred as a romantically frivolous shopgirl in the silent film *It* (1927)—she was the original "It Girl." Bow was the top box-office draw in both 1928 and 1929, by which time 50 million Americans were buying movie admission tickets per week. For centuries, in fact, men had equated the whimsical prices of financial securities with female promiscuity.[36]

During the 1920s, Strong and the New York Fed tried to damp down speculation by "sterilizing" gold inflows, preventing them from loosening credit. Secretary of Commerce Herbert Hoover, among many others, bemoaned the ongoing "orgy of speculation."[37] In fact, after 1928 the phrase "orgy of speculation," or "speculative orgy," became, according to one historian's sober analysis, "so commonplace over the next few years as to lose all meaning."[38]

New York Fed governor Strong, who had called the "speculative orgy" a shame as early as 1925, came around to the view that something beyond sterilizing gold had to be done about it.[39] In 1927 he had actually cut the New York Fed's short-term interest rate to 3.5 percent—to make the British pound more attractive to investors and thus push gold back to Britain to help its return to the gold standard. This was one way the gold standard forced officials to privilege the international over the national. If Strong raised interest rates to cool U.S. credit markets, it would make the British march back to gold, which Strong believed was of great symbolic significance for even the U.S. economy, more difficult. Meanwhile banks were borrowing money from the Fed at 3.5 percent and then turning around and lending it on the short-term call money market at 10 percent, which was feeding NYSE stock speculation, in what Galbraith would call in *The Great Crash* "the most profitable arbitrage operation of all time."[40]

In February 1928, however, Strong began a series of interest hikes from 3.5 percent up to 5 percent. At this moment, long suffering from tuberculosis, he became seriously ill and died. The Fed plunged into bureaucratic confusion. In 1929 his successor, George Harrison, raised the New York Fed's interest rate to 6 percent. The Fed also intervened to limit the ability of investment trusts to borrow in the call money market and buy on margin. The Great Bull Market rushed ahead anyway.

With so much gold in U.S. vaults, the New York Fed was at the apex of the international monetary system. Yet the Fed had lost control of the situation. Even at high borrowing rates, investors kept borrowing for purposes of speculative investment, and lenders were willing to lend.

Furthermore, after 1928 two new players entered the NYSE: U.S. manufacturing corporations and European capital. Corporations began to divert their excess business profits to the NYSE. Initially, at the birth of mass production, industrial corporate profits ran far ahead of wages.[41] Working people did not participate in the 1920s speculative investment boom.[42] Increasing economic inequality put more money in the hands of the wealthy, who kept bidding up stock prices—increasing their incomes from asset price appreciation, leveraged by credit, while labor incomes at the bottom of the distribution stagnated. Meanwhile European capital was fleeing Europe to join the party on Wall Street. German capital flight, for instance, led to another negotiated settlement of its reparations debt—the 1929 Young Plan. The general result was that European central banks had no choice but to continue to raise rates to attract capital to their national banking systems, in order to defend the so recently restored gold standard. But gold kept rushing to the United States anyway. In sum, the gold standard was at once failing to restrain credit expansion (which it was supposed to do) and forcing central banks to prioritize international obligations (to maintain currency-gold pegs) over any national economic objective.

The credit cycle began to reverse in early 1929. A number of factors explain the drop in fixed industrial investment that February. U.S. manufacturing corporations' orgy of stock market speculation was one; also, corporate profits began to disappoint. The Fed, seeking to temper speculation, raised its short-term interest rate on money above 10 percent. The hurdle rate for speculative investment had become exceedingly high, and finally the credit markets broke. Money and credit became tight, as expectations shifted. In agriculture, dealers who had speculatively accumulated large inventories of crops, confident that future prices would rise, now changed their minds and dumped commodities on the market. By March 1928, dealers had accumulated 48.2 million bushels of corn. By July 1929, they had dumped more than 30 million bushels on the market. Prices fell. Farm incomes dropped, sapping consumer demand for manufactures. In July industrial production began to fall.[43] In August total economic output began to drop.

The NYSE held out for a month. The Dow-Jones industrial stock average, which paused at 191 in early 1928, peaked at 381 in September 1929. The stock market began to slip in early October. Then came October 24, Black Thursday. October 28 was Black Monday. Panic broke out, concentrated especially in public utilities stocks, which investment trusts had recently bid up using leverage and debt.[44] In total, $14 billion in stock market value was quickly shed. Crowds gathered on the street outside the NYSE. News traveled over the radio. Sellers placed sell orders to brokers on telephones. A pool privately organized to stop losses on the trading floor dramatically failed. Credit had bid up the market, but now banks that had loaned funds accepting stocks as collateral placed margin calls, calling in their loans, which borrowers could not repay because the value of the stocks that had been the collateral for the original loan was plummeting. Excessive leverage led to a vicious downward spiral of distressed sales and

"29TH OCTOBER 1929: WORKERS FLOOD THE STREETS IN A
PANIC FOLLOWING THE BLACK TUESDAY STOCK MARKET CRASH
ON WALL STREET, NEW YORK CITY" (1929)
The Great Bull Market was among the new "mass" phenomena
of the 1920s. Capturing that quality were photographs of
the crowds that gathered when it crashed.

cascading paper losses in the competitive struggle to get liquid. That European banks had recently raised interest rates to compete with the NYSE for funds only assisted the massive sell-off. Capital fled in reverse, back to Europe. The Dow-Jones finally would pause at 198 on November 13, after $26 billion in losses. The comedian Eddie Cantor was among those who lost his personal savings in the crash. He would write in *Caught Short! A Saga of Wailing Wall Street* (1929) that during the crash he checked into "one of the larger hotels in New York City." Asked the man at the front desk, "What for? Sleeping or jumping?"[45]

On paper, the Great Crash wiped out 10 percent of U.S. national wealth. That, and the seizing up of credit markets in the panicked selling, inevitably depressed all kinds of spending, both investment and consumption.[46] As the release of stockpiles led commodity prices into free fall, rural demand for manufactures went into free fall as well, further depressing spending. Automobile production plunged from 319,000 in October to 92,500 in December.[47] Many consumer durable purchases had been financed by credit, as well, which had run up to a staggering 140 percent of GDP—a level not reached again until the 2000s.[48] No matter the going rate, credit was now rationed.[49] A dynamic of debt-deflation set in, as the economist Irving Fischer named it in real time, in which distressed sales to raise cash to meet debt payments drove prices down further, only to increase the real value of debts.[50] The Fed reduced interest rates to 2.5 percent in early 1930 and injected $500 million in cash into the banking system. But it was too little too late. Due to mass investor flight to and thus demand for safe bonds, long-term real interest rates remained stubbornly high, a hurdle rate that further suppressed risky long-term investment, given collapsing profit expectations in enterprise.[51]

Evidently, the slump was serious. As economic activity constricted, between 1929 and 1930 unemployment climbed from 2.9 percent to 8.9 percent. Many observers compared what was happening to the prior downturn of 1920–21. That was a plausible assertion through the middle of 1930, when purchases of the expensive consumer durables of the mass production industries began to decline sharply, dragging economic activity down further.[52] Nonetheless, in June 1930 President Hoover confidently declared, "The depression is over."[53]

3. The Great Engineer

"No American president," according to the historian William J. Barber, "has come into office with a more detailed conception of what he wanted to accomplish in economic policy and of the way to go about it than did Herbert Hoover in 1929."[54] In the Age of Commerce, many Americans had believed that it was politics that determined economic booms and busts. In the Age of Capital, whether it was industrialization, Darwinian evolution, or some other process, the economy seemed to become more autonomous from human agency. But in 1929, a failing capitalist economy seemingly fell into the hands of one person, Hoover. In the White House, the president did a lot to try to stem the economic collapse. But it was not enough.

Hoover, born an Iowa Quaker in 1874 and orphaned at age nine, was raised by a stern schoolmaster uncle in Oregon. He graduated in the first class of Stanford University in 1895, with a degree in geology. Soon he made a fortune overseeing mining operations across the globe. *Principles of Mining* (1909) was Hoover's first book. In 1914, at forty, he retired from business and entered public life without a party affiliation.[55]

Hoover was a progressive dynamo. Reserved in temperament and moved by his wife's religious devotion, he worshipped technocratic expertise. During World War I, he organized private relief efforts in Europe to wide public acclaim. Assistant Secretary of the Navy Franklin Delano Roosevelt called him "a wonder," exclaiming, "I wish we could make him President of the United States. There could not be a better one."[56] The era's great admiration for energy in machines and in power utilities carried over to the vigorous figure of Hoover. In 1920 he supported Republican Warren Harding's candidacy for president, and upon his election he became secretary of commerce—"and Undersecretary of all other Departments," as one official put it.[57] After Harding's death, he continued to actively serve under President Coolidge, who by contrast was a taker of prodigious White House naps.

In economic policy, Hoover sponsored what 1920s academic and policy circles called the "new economics."[58] According to this view, during World War I, military urgency and paper credit had ramped up production so much as to prove that nations had greater economic capacities than previously thought. Intelligent human action could transcend dismal economic laws. Empirical economic investigation and statistical analysis, leading to greater efficiency, could raise economic output. In 1921, as president of the Federated American Engineering Societies, Hoover had commissioned a study called *Waste in Industry* (1921), the subject of which he considered bad and preventable. Even business cycles could be evened out with better information. During slumps, for instance, government might spend more on commercially viable public works that employed people. Hoover called for a politics of "administrative intelligence."[59]

Government should aid private industry, Hoover believed, but never coerce it. In his short book *American Individualism* (1922), he argued that the growth of government coercion in industrial societies, especially the Russian Bolshevik menace, threatened the "divine spark" within every individual. Individualism must not come to mean "selfish snatching," which was incompatible with "capitalism," allowing a "few men through unrestrained control of property determine the welfare of great numbers." Rather, self-interest must be checked. Hoover advocated "mutual cooperation" among businessmen through trade associations. Government could facilitate. In 1923, Secretary Hoover even cajoled U.S. Steel, which had recently crushed the steelworkers union in 1919, to abandon the twelve-hour day. He championed "the vast multiplication of voluntary organizations for altruistic purposes." Government should support nonprofit corporations. Helped by a Rockefeller Foundation grant, Hoover coordinated private relief efforts to the victims of the Great Flood of 1927 in the lower Mississippi Valley. In *American Individualism*, he advocated a political philosophy of government-enabled "neighborly helpfulness."[60]

In his 1928 presidential campaign, Hoover declared that "government must be a constructive force."[61] He took office in March 1929 armed with a NBER study, *Recent Economic Changes in the United States* (1929). Characteristically, one of his first moves was to instruct the Census Bureau to gather better unemployment statistics. But the most pressing issue that he had to address—in addition to what Hoover called the ongoing "orgy of speculation" at the NYSE—was a farm debt crisis.

Even though farm commodity prices had fallen in the years after World War I, many U.S. farmers had continued to borrow at the high rates, necessitated by the government assault on postwar inflation. They did so either to expand production or to mechanize production, hoping that prices would stabilize, if not rise. When commodity prices plummeted in 1929, farm debts remained on the books. Debt-deflation was the same dynamic that had led to the Populist Revolt, except in this instance it was much worse and more sudden due to the high-interest-rate environment of the 1920s and the depths of the rapid price collapse. In April 1929, Hoover called Congress into special session, and in June he signed the Agricultural Marketing Act. The U.S. Treasury would inject $500 million of capital into a new Federal Farm Board to finance agricultural cooperatives (an old Populist demand) that might buy and store farm products, to counter price deflation. The Farm Board realized Hoover's vision of a mixed public and private "associational state."[62]

When the NYSE crashed in October 1929, Hoover did not share the infamous austerity view of his Treasury secretary, the Pittsburgh banker Andrew Mellon, who (as Hoover would later recall) "had only one formula." It was to

> liquidate labor, liquidate stocks, liquidate the farmers, liquidate real estate. It will purge the rottenness out of the system. High costs of living and high living will come down. People will work harder, live a more moral life. Values will be adjusted, and enterprising people will pick up the wrecks from less competent people.[63]

Agreeing in principle with Mellon, a number of other economic thinkers proposed, too, that only from widespread bankruptcy could general prosperity ever return. For on this account, the cause of the crisis was overin-vestment in an inflationary boom, which called for less investment after the bust. The purge of the system would re-equilibrate savings and invest-ment at a higher rate of interest and at lower prices, including wages. But it would restore economic health and prompt a natural recovery. Among economists, the Austrian Friedrich Hayek's *Prices and Production* (1931), the Englishman Arthur Pigou's *The Theory of Unemployment* (1933), and the Englishman Lionel Robbins's *The Great Depression* (1934) all generally diagnosed the slump this way. Most important, the market autocorrection of the "real" economy must occur without government interference. These were very sophisticated logical arguments, made by very intelligent economists, in defense of economic suffering.

They were wrong. The problem was not profligate excess. What they diagnosed as overinvestment is better characterized as speculative misin-vestment. In a monetary economy, when a credit-fueled speculative in-vestment boom gives way to the precautionary hoarding of liquid assets, the problem in the bust then becomes underinvestment. Out of fear, the owners of capital refuse to invest. Liquid assets lock up purchasing power. Demand suffers, and so does output and employment. Not only are fresh investments not made. Existing capacity—perfectly good factories, per-fectly willing workers—needlessly idles. Unemployed workers with no in-comes spend less. The general problem was not that something outside the real economy was preventing markets from autocorrecting. Something within capitalist enterprise itself was stuck, and required a jolt.

Hoover did not agree with Mellon and pledged he would "use the pow-ers of government to cushion the situation."[64] On the telephone and at two White House conferences, the president personally pleaded with the corporate executives of the largest, most regulated industries to increase capital investment expenditures. In 1930 railroads and utilities obliged.[65] Yet everywhere else, especially in residential construction, fixed invest-ment kept falling. Hoover recognized that during the 1920s, corporate profits had run ahead of wages, and he believed that high wages would stabilize spending, a good thing. "The first shock," he declared, "must fall on profits and not on wages."[66] Whether because of Hoover's promptings or not, the nation's largest employers agreed to not slash wages, even as they continued to fire their less desirable employees, a pattern that would persist.[67] Proudly, Hoover said the agreements were "not a dictation or in-terference by the government with business." Rather, they were the result

of a "request from the government that you co-operate in prudent measure to solve a national problem."[68] The president boasted, "This is a far
cry from the arbitrary and dog-eat-dog attitude of the business world of
some thirty or forty years ago."[69] Hoover believed his "associational state"
transcended the Jacksonian sphering of public and private, state and market, which, under the banner of equal commercial opportunity, had with-
ered state action throughout the Age of Capital. But he drew one line in
the sand: he would not coerce capitalists to invest.

President Hoover also mobilized the federal budget. In 1930 Treasury
and Congress reduced corporate and personal income tax, as planned.
Hoover was tempted by an investment tax credit, but Treasury Department
officials balked.[70] Congress passed a special appropriation that doubled
spending on highway construction and released funds for the Army Corps
of Engineers. This was not charity or "relief" but public investment in commercially viable projects that would at a minimum break even. In 1931 the
federal government began to run budget deficits.[71] The problem was that
the volume of expenditure was still very little. The tax cut was $160 million.
From less than 1.8 percent of GDP, federal government spending only
climbed to 2.2 percent in 1930, as GDP shrank. Hoover also dispatched tele-
grams to governors saying it would "be helpful if road, street, public building and other construction of this type could be speeded up and adjusted in
such fashion to further employment."[72] Between 1929 and 1930, state and
local expenditures as shares of GDP climbed from 7.4 percent to 9.0 percent, but many states had Progressive reform-era balanced-budget laws
and eroding tax bases. They could not take on debt. There was no notion yet
of a potential "fiscal multiplier" in the midst of the Depression—the idea
that increased government spending might actually increase private expenditures and tax receipts, not only compensate for them.

Under Hoover, the federal government did little more. Grudgingly, the
president had signed the protectionist Smoot-Hawley Tariff in 1930. World
trade was collapsing, but that was because everywhere incomes were collapsing, as much as it was because of a protectionist trade war.[73] True to
form, Hoover further implored private nonprofit corporations to provide
relief to the growing ranks of the unemployed. With capital failing, perhaps philanthropic wealth could fill the breach. The Rockefellers kicked in
$1 million in New York. When Henry Ford was approached in Detroit, he
refused, with the bizarre response, "Endowment is an opiate of the imagination, a drug to initiative."[74]

Given existing government capacities and the president's ideology, there was not much more to do. Then again, there was not much more that Herbert Hoover believed needed doing.

4. The Depression Becomes Great

In 1930 policy makers everywhere remained committed to the gold standard. But where its restoration after World War I had led to a surge in confidence and increased international lending, it now transmitted financial volatility and fragility. Golden fetters made national economies easy targets in the plunge further into the economic deep.

The free convertibility at pegged rates of all national currencies for gold made it easy for capital to swing in and out of national economies at a whim. It now did, due to a cascading series of political and economic crises. If too much gold decamped from one country, that country lost its ability to freely convert its currency into gold at its stated exchange rate. Its only choice was to raise rates, to recruit opportunistic but fickle money capital back into the country. In the early 1930s, short-term capital movements among countries became, in the words of President Hoover, a "loose cannon on the deck of the world in a tempest-tossed era."[75] Nonetheless, Hoover's own commitment to the gold standard destroyed the U.S. economy and with it his presidency.

In 1931 the United States and Germany—the former the strongest and the latter the most fragile of the largest economies—became especially fatefully intertwined. During the late 1920s, capital whipsawed between them. In September 1930, after Hitler won 6.4 million votes, $380 million fled Germany.[76] In 1931 a right-leaning German government opened secret negotiations with Austria concerning a customs union, in violation of a number of postwar treaties. When news of their deal broke that March, more capital fled Germany. Next, in May 1931 the Rothschild-run bank Credit Anstalt, based in Vienna, with $250 million in assets and 50 percent of all Austrian bank deposits, announced staggering losses.[77] The bank had borrowed heavily in short-term international credit and money markets. France, with its undervalued franc, sitting on 25 percent of world gold reserves, offered to bail out Austria, but only if it abandoned the Austro-German customs union. Bank runs now coursed throughout central Europe. Whether out of sheer panic or a belief that Germany was now following a renegade path, half of Germany's gold reserves now left the country. It could not make its outstanding reparations payments. In June, Hoover announced a plan to delay all political debt payments, including German reparations. France balked, but by July, when it finally agreed to suspend a portion of Germany's political debts, the German financial system had already collapsed.[78]

Financial contagion now caught the world in its grip. People did not trust banks to hold their money deposits and rushed to withdraw them, in a nervous flight to security. Without deposits, banks could not meet their obligations, let alone lend. The Hungarian banking system shut down. Runs occurred on German bank branches in the Middle East. In Latin America, falling prices for world exports led countries to default on international loans, and numerous countries between 1930 and 1932 fell to military dictatorships.[79] Anyone who could convert their currency to gold at the stated exchange rate tried to do so before the vaults ran dry. For that reason, in a vicious cycle, governments could no longer maintain free convertibility. Countries everywhere began to leave the gold standard, impose capital and foreign exchange controls, and devalue their currencies.[80] Japan had just adopted the gold standard, with the aid of a J. P. Morgan & Co. syndicated loan, in 1930, but it departed from it in December 1931. But now all eyes were on London—the historic home, and until World War I the guardian, of the international gold standard.[81]

In the last two weeks of July, the Bank of England lost half of its gold reserves—$250 billion—to capital flight. Nervously, investors shifted their gold to other countries. Without gold in British bank vaults, the fixed convertibility of the pound was at risk. To recruit gold back, the Bank of England raised interest rates from 2.5 percent to 4.25 percent. That only tightened credit and spending and further weakened the already-depressed British economy. On August 28 a J. P. Morgan & Co.–led syndicate and French banks granted two $200 million loans to the British government. In three weeks it was all gone. In late September, fully spent, Britain suspended gold convertibility for the pound.

The British departure from the gold standard was an event of historic proportions. The international gold standard was a British imperial institution and an anchor of pre–World War I globalization—an era of low interest rates and much international investment. For British central banker Montagu Norman, as one friend put it, "Going off the gold standard was for him as though a daughter should lose her virginity."[82] The British pound declined in value from $4.86 to $3.25 by December 1931.

What happened next, though, was telling. British prices began to rise, and the Depression became less severe. As the British socialist Sidney Webb reportedly exclaimed, "No one told us we could do that!"[83] Expectations of rising prices, and thus profits, began to induce greater spending on investment. Of the forty-one countries that began the year 1931 on the gold standard, by the opening of 1932 the only ones left were South Africa, France, Belgium, Luxembourg, the Netherlands, Italy, Switzerland, Poland—and the United States.[84]

Might the United States be next to suffer capital flight? The day after the Britain left the gold standard, the French central bank sold $50 million for gold bullion. The French wanted gold now, should the United States, like Britain, break its gold-to-currency peg, and $50 million would instantly buy far less gold. In other words, international monetary cooperation had utterly broken down. In the next month, "gold bloc" European central bankers and European investors depleted U.S. gold reserves by $750 million.[85] But U.S. reserves still had plenty of gold bullion. Nonetheless, if destabilized by short-term capital flight, the U.S. banking system now collapsed from a source within.

U.S. banks were known to fail all the time.[86] In 1929 alone, 659 banks had shut their doors, but that was not an unusually high figure for the decade: between 1920 and 1929, an average of 630 banks failed each year. Ever since Jackson killed the Second Bank of the United States, U.S. politics had long forbidden centralized banking power, which was why the Federal Reserve System consisted of twelve reserve banks. "Unit" banking generally prevailed, meaning banks had no separate branches—most banks consisted of only one unit. If a bank made bad loans, if there was a run on its deposits, it did not have multiple branches to fall back on. In 1930 there were 25,000 U.S. banks. Only one-third were members of the Federal Reserve System, and only 751 operated branches.[87]

The plummet in world commodity prices hit banks in agricultural regions hard. In the autumn of 1930, a rash of bank failures broke out in Nashville, Tennessee. Then in December 1930 the largest bank failure in U.S. history occurred. New York's Bank of the United States was a private institution that largely catered to small and middling Jewish depositors; it had $286 million in assets and 400,000 depositors (double the number of any other bank in the country). It had been involved in the short-term call money market and leveraged NYSE speculations.[88] In 1930 it suspended operations.

That was only a dress rehearsal. In the spring of 1931, bank runs began in Chicago. In the months after the European financial meltdown, 522 U.S. banks failed. The 2,294 total bank failures of 1931 would set an annual record (doubling those of 1930). That was one out of every ten U.S. banks and 4.5 percent ($1.7 billion) of all deposits.[89] Meanwhile by the summer of 1931, the Farm Board had given up. It stopped accumulating stocks, waiting for prices to rise. Instead, it threw stored farm products onto the market, further deflating commodity prices and thus jeopardizing rural banks. Now the U.S. banking system crashed in a massive popular flight to security. Banks that survived stopped lending and hoarded reserves.[90] Credit was rationed regardless of the going rate.[91] Economic historians debate whether illiquidity or insolvency was most to blame for the rash of bank failures—did banks with ample reserves and good loan books suffer unwarranted bank runs, or were they really broke?[92] In regions where reserve banks offered greater cash lifelines to hold them over during the panic, banks survived at a greater rate.[93] However, depositors did not wait to find out whether banks were insolvent because of the general collapse, or were simply illiquid because the general mass psychology of panic was leading depositors to pull out their cash. In 1931 Americans removed $500 million in cash—and took it to "holes in the ground, privies, linings of coats, horse collars, coal piles, hollow trees."[94] The ratio of cash held by the public to bank deposits rose significantly.[95] It was not just weak-willed capitalist investors. Among ordinary people, a moment of mass, popular precaution had broken out as had never been seen before.

At this stage, the Fed committed its worst blunder. There was still plenty of gold in U.S. reserves, but by law, for every ten dollars in Federal Reserve notes (the U.S. currency), four dollars required backing in gold reserves and another six dollars in so-called real bills, or paper backed by traded commodities. There was by now little commodity trade, so few real bills. This created a need for more gold reserves in the system. While the Fed had been lowering interest rates, now in October 1931 it raised interest rates from 1.5 to 3.5 percent. This was a grave error, as the restricted supply of credit and money was another blow to spending of all kinds.[96] In the midst of the general panic and collapse, the demand for fresh loans had dried up, which contributed to the ongoing deflationary contraction. The Fed could have done more, such as lend freely at low rates. But even if it orchestrated that brilliantly, it could only do so much to induce economic activity.

Deflation piled on deflation. Economic life entered a dark place. In September 1931, U.S. Steel, the largest U.S. employer, slashed wages by 10 percent, and other employers followed. The Ford Motor Company, which had employed 120,000 workers in 1929, by the end of 1931 employed but 37,000. General Electric, in an attempt to prop up prices and production, proposed the suspension of all antitrust laws to allow corporations to collude. President Hoover said no, calling it "an attempt to smuggle fascism into America through the back door." In 1931, further undermining future expectations, the average U.S. profit rate tipped into negative territory.[97] The Depression had become Great.

In the Age of Capital, the gold standard was the leading mechanism of control. President Hoover simply could not imagine any other way forward. He believed Great Britain had acted unconscionably. The United States must assert international leadership and save the gold standard, a basis of cooperation between countries. Meanwhile, without a certain anchor in gold, business would break down. Without gold, the president would say, "no merchant could know what he might receive in payment by the time his goods were delivered."[98] There would be no confidence, only more fear. In late 1931, to set an example for the world, Hoover drafted the Revenue Act of 1932, calling for higher taxes to balance the federal budget—long the good housekeeping seal of approval for global capital under the gold standard, but exactly the wrong medicine to combat deflation.

Then in classic style, Hoover invited a group of U.S. financiers to the White House for a conference. For capitalism to work, capitalists must invest capital. The president implored the bankers to voluntarily pool their resources and stave off the banking panics. Instead, nervous bankers "constantly reverted to a proposal that the government do it."[99] Finally in January 1932, Congress created the Hoover-approved Reconstruction Finance Corporation (RFC), which had authority to lend up to $1.5 billion but only on a commercially viable basis—it was not "relief." Congress passed a 1932 law authorizing the Fed to use a wider variety of paper bills as reserves for its own note issues. But the law still declared faith in the gold standard.[100]

The RFC and the Fed now injected more money and credit into the financial system, but it was too little too late.[101] In 1932 the economy entered a short-term "liquidity trap"—there was no short-term interest rate, not even zero, that would induce the owners of capital to part with liquidity.[102] In November 1932, the return on three-month U.S. Treasury bonds hit 0.05 percent, around which it would hover throughout the 1930s. The

Fed's cautious open market operations—purchasing short-term, near-cash-equivalent securities to prop up their prices and lower their rates—had lost power as early as 1931. By 1932, no increase in the supply of money could make the owners of capital willing to part with it and spend. Nor could it prompt inflation. Precautionary liquidity preference—the demand for cash and other safe liquid assets—was simply that high. Investors invested in assets with near-zero pecuniary returns. The profit motive had disappeared—or at least, no one believed there were any future profits on offer. Meanwhile long-term interest rates remained stuck, with few willing lenders. Corporate bond rates were upward of 10 percent.[103] In prevailing conditions, for business to borrow at that rate and hope to profit at a greater rate was sheer madness of a different kind.

Thus, as long-term investment utterly collapsed, the economy was pulled into a fearful present and trapped inside it. If anything, firms ran existing plants at less than capacity. If capitalists accumulated assets with no return, ordinary Americans stuffed cash under mattresses. Hoarders sought the psychological return of immediate safety and little else, while a mass psychological dynamic of deflation gripped economic life, in which potential investors and consumers alike forwent spending, waiting for prices to fall further. That only made prices fall even further.

In the history of American capitalism, one may isolate this moment: the liquidity trap of the fall of 1932. From it would issue a long historical arc, into the twenty-first century, from the Great Depression to the Great Recession. Along its path an escape from the liquidity trap would be achieved during World War II, which induced—by public investment—a long-term industrial investment boom in productive capital assets. Decades after that, the arc would follow the next era of high speculative liquidity preference beginning in the 1980s, then end in the next precautionary liquidity trap, in the fall of 2008, after the bankruptcy of the investment bank Lehman Brothers. Capitalism would but barely climb out of the trap in the late 2010s, before it fell back again in 2020.

As for the Great Depression, the numbers from the beginning of the slump in August 1929 until it hit the very bottom in March 1933 are staggering. U.S. consumer expenditures fell from $79 billion to $64.6 billion.[104] The value of world trade was down 65 percent.[105] U.S. prices dropped 30 percent. U.S. industrial production declined 37 percent. Of the workforce, 22.9 percent were unemployed, and of those employed, one-third worked less than full time. Industrial unemployment hit 37.6 percent. Economic output fell 52 percent. Farm prices declined by a staggering 65 percent. U.S. corporations, profiting by $10 billion in 1929, suffered losses of $3 billion in 1932. The Dow stock index for the NYSE hit 41, a total loss of 90 percent since the 1929 peak. No fewer than 600,000 homeowners defaulted on mortgages, and $7 billion in deposits were lost. *Fortune* estimated that 34 million Americans—out of a population of 120 million—had no money income on which to live.[106]

5. Dumb with Misery

Recollections of what it was like to live during such a vertiginous economic descent convey a range of emotions, from fear, to desperation, and sometimes to anger. In 1931 Charlie Chaplin made his greatest film, *City Lights*, a romantic comedy, about his homeless tramp, his friend a suicidal millionaire, and his romance with a blind flower girl who could not pay her rent. What most comes across from the historical record, however, is a sense of disorientation, even bewilderment. It had all happened so fast. Edward Hopper's *Early Sunday Morning* (1930) captures this sense of a full stop, a complete cessation of activity. Many were unable to adequately

EDWARD HOPPER, *EARLY SUNDAY MORNING* (1930)
The Great Depression was a sudden halt of economic activity. The dark shadows cast on business fronts indicate the operation of mysterious forces. Some critics see the large structure on the right representing the threat of large corporations to small enterprise.

communicate their experience. Historical memory normally works like this in the aftermath of wars or natural disasters. The Great Depression, too, left behind much unprocessed trauma.[107]

Metaphors of natural disaster and economic calamity rang especially true in the countryside, where the two actually went hand in hand.[108] In the southern plains, a region of terrible hardship, drought conditions in 1930–31 cracked the earth. Weather and climate were responsible, but so was the overextension of cultivation during the credit-fueled 1920s.[109] Then came windstorms, "black blizzards" that swept away hundreds of millions of acres of topsoil in the Dust Bowl of Kansas, Colorado, New Mexico, and Oklahoma. After the overproduction of the late 1920s, the land became unworkable. The warped, curved landscape paintings of these years, such as John Steuart Curry's *Tornado over Kansas* (1929), capture the emotional tone of the disaster.

JOHN STEUART CURRY, *TORNADO OVER KANSAS* (1929)
Curry was known as a regionalist painter. Bad weather was a
proximate cause of rural Midwestern depression. Mostly, it was due to
drought, but a tornado better captures the general sense of dislocation.

By car, rail, or foot, millions abandoned their homesteads. The largest percentage of rural migrants headed for California. Elsewhere, the countryside—much of it still lacking electricity and indoor plumbing—fared little better. It is hard to believe, but rural money incomes declined from $6 billion in 1929 to $2 billion in 1932.[110]

In the past, collapsing money incomes had mattered less. Before the Age of Capital, market depressions had not necessarily had the same effect. In the wake of the Panic of 1837, the economic depression deflated prices but did not restrict total output. Back then, markets aside, the land still offered access to subsistence. Land was capital but also a more expansive category of wealth. But by the 1920s, the remarkable productive achievements of industrial revolution during the Age of Capital had generated high money incomes, while integrating people into the market economy. Americans were wealthier, to be sure, but more dependent on the "causalities and caprice," as Thomas Jefferson had long ago put it, of the commercial economy. The dramatic drop in effective demand, largely due to the collapsed "confidence of cautious sagacious capitalists," as Alexander Hamilton had described it, now constricted the market economy from which most Americans sustained their economic lives. Economic productivity was greater, but so was the risk of devastation. Higher money incomes meant greater purchasing power, but only when spent. This was the paradox of poverty in the midst of plenty.

Cities fared little better. In the winter of 1932, unemployment in Detroit and Chicago reached as high as 50 percent. The most vulnerable—women, children, the elderly, the disabled, minorities—suffered the most. The rate of black unemployment doubled that of white unemployment. Men, women, and children lined up for bread, foraged in streets, rummaged in trash cans, and lived in "rusted-out car bodies" or "shacks made of orange crates." Single men, men who had abandoned their families, and sometimes women as well became "hoboes," hopping trains, traveling from city to city, searching for work, living in makeshift "Hoovervilles." They put chalk marks on the porches of houses that gave them food: "It was beggary on a grand scale," one man recalled. Theft dominated arrest rolls: "Stole clothes off lines, stole milk off back porches, you stole bread. . . . You were a predator. You had to be."[111]

For male breadwinners, self-blame was especially prominent.[112] The sectors of the labor market where women tended to work in fact did do better in these years. A Chicago psychoanalyst with middle-class male patients said, "Everybody, more or less, blamed himself for his delinquency or lack of talent or bad luck."[113] For a commissioned article on "the social revolt," collected in his *Puzzled America* (1935), the writer Sherwood Anderson reported back on "how all the jobless people" he saw "blame themselves for being down and out rather than 'blaming capitalism, the machine, our American overlords.'"[114] Many people appeared to be in numb shock. Mirra Komarovsky's *The Unemployed Man and His Family* (1940) remarked on the high incidence of impotence among unemployed men during the 1930s.[115] The unemployed were "apathetic," the journalist Lorena Hickok observed, "dumb with misery."[116] A Houston mechanic committed suicide in 1930, writing, "I can't accept charity and I am too proud to appeal to my kin or friends, and I am too honest to steal. So I see no other course."[117] Shame at seeking charity was widespread. "I simply had to murder my pride," said one engineer before requesting relief.[118] Men commonly walked past relief stations, then circled back again, for days before finally mustering the courage to walk inside. The black blues singer Victoria Spivey sang in the popular song "Detroit Moan" (1936), "Detroit's a cold hard place / And I ain't got a dime to my name / I would go to the poor house / But Lord you know I'm ashamed."

Not everybody blamed themselves. But then who? "Who do I shoot?" wondered the "Okie" Muley Graves, in John Steinbeck's novel *The Grapes of Wrath* (1939). Some blamed bankers. "I hope the guilty gang will be punished before they die," an anonymous citizen wrote to President Hoover.[119] It baffled many people how, so suddenly, in a "land flowing with milk and honey," as the Houston suicide had lamented, there could be so much poverty and want. How, when so many people lacked work and food, could factories sit idle, animals die on the hoof, and farm produce rot on the vine?

It was possible to blame political institutions and the president. An unsigned letter to President Hoover from Vineland, New Jersey, dated November 18, 1930, read:

> Could we not have employment and food to Eat. and this for our Children Why Should we hafto [illegible] now and Have foodless days . . . and our children have Schoolless days and Shoeless days and the land fully of plenty and Banks bursting with money. Why does Every Thing have Exceptional Value. Except the Human being—why are we reduced to poverty and starving and anxiety and Sorrow So quickly under your administration as Chief Executor Can not you find a quicker way of Executing us than to Starve us to death. . . . Why not End the Depression have you not a Heart. . . . Yet we are served from the Source of Life by setch an un-

just System. . . . Why Isn't there an limitation to you people planning to get It all and Starve the rest of use. . . . Yet you have cut us of with plenty before our eyes—for your Selves. Yet You Can not use it. The people are desperate and this I have written, only typical of the masses of your Subjects. how can we be Law abiding citizens and Educate our children and be Happy Content with nothing to do nothing to Eat. when your System has Every Thing under control and cant use It. nor will you give any thing a way. why take more than you need. why make Laws. and allow Industry to take It all. why Isnt the Law fixed so Its Just as Just for one or the others then Industry couldnt take it all. and make us all victims of your Special arrangement. of things. . . . I am an Ignorant man and you are Supposed to have great Brains yet I appeal to you In behalf of thousands In your dominion who would be good americans Citizins If you would make It Possible.

A woman from Los Angeles taunted Hoover, "Engineers may be intelligent but poor Presidents."[120]

Hoover's political philosophy of "neighborly helpfulness" was stretched beyond its economic limit. Neighborly helpfulness could still go a long way, however. The primal need for human community, its endurance under unspeakable hardship, was, in fact, at the heart of Steinbeck's two great Depression-era novels, *The Grapes of Wrath* and the earlier *Tortilla Flat* (1935). In the most impoverished agricultural regions, such as the Appalachian South, farmers were indeed able to retreat to the subsistence of the household economy. "We were largely self-sufficient," one rural Virginia resident would recall. "We cooperated and helped each other."[121] In the cities, one unemployed person remembered that everybody "was evil to each other" and that there "was no friendships." But another would later yearn nostalgically for the "camaraderie" of the Depression. "You were in trouble . . . damn it, if they could help ya, they would help ya."[122]

Empathy did not die with hard times, but empathy was simply not up to the task economically. The most popular song of the time, "Brother Can You Spare a Dime?" (1932), resonated widely—most likely because Brother in fact could not. One of the great tragedies of the Great Depression was that it wiped out large swaths of civil society, the voluntary associations that President Hoover continued to champion.[123] Hoover vetoed a 1931 congressional relief bill, partly because he thought relief was not the business of government and partly because fiscal discipline protected the gold standard. He would allow the RFC to loan only small sums to states for unemployment relief. By the end of 1931, the American Red Cross alone had come to the aid of 2.7 million rural drought sufferers.[124] Soup kitchens, local charities, churches, philanthropic foundations, immigrant fraternal orders, and ethnic savings societies all together lacked adequate funding and institutional capacity to provide services. The scale of hardship was too vast. By 1933, at least thirteen hundred cities, counties, towns, and school districts were effectively bankrupt.[125] An AFL leader warned Congress, "If something is not done and starvation is going to continue," then the "doors of revolt in this country are going to be thrown open."[126]

Political agitation in 1931–32 was widespread. In the Iowa-Nebraska corn belt of the northern plains, farmers more decimated by debt than by drought rioted against foreclosures. The National Guard was called in.[127] Industrial strike activity focused on the mines. In cities, organized protests halted evictions in St. Louis, Chicago, and New York. In March 1932, workers at Henry Ford's River Rouge complex mounted a "hunger march"; Dearborn police shot and killed four of them.[128] Elsewhere, the jobless organized in unemployed councils and unemployed leagues. In July 1932, most dramatically, 25,000 unemployed World War I veterans marched on Washington, pleading with the federal government to pay them the bonuses they said the government owed them for military service. The "Bonus Army" camped out across the Potomac River in Anacostia, Virginia. General Douglas MacArthur sent in tanks and bayonets, and the Bonus Army disintegrated.[129]

An Iowa farm boy would later say that he was struck by the "helpless despair and submission" he saw. "There was anger and rebellion among a few, but by and large, that quiet desperation and submission." Decades later a wealthy Chicago banker would reflect that the American people

> just sat there and took it. . . . In retrospect, it's amazing, just amazing. Either they were in shock, or they thought something would happen to turn it around. . . . My wife has often discussed this with me. She thinks it's astonishing, the lack of violent protest, especially in 1932 and 1933.[130]

6. FDR

Political revolution was not afoot, but the United States was a democracy, and in the congressional elections of 1930, Republicans suffered heavy losses. In 1932 there would be a presidential election, and Hoover's administration was spent. Even a Wall Street banker who supported the president confessed that "a monkey could have been elected against him."[131] Hoover, a journalist recorded, now sat "crouching behind his desk," shouting random insults at foreign governments.[132]

The Democratic presidential candidate was the governor of New York, Franklin Delano Roosevelt. Born into privilege, raised on his family's wealthy Hudson River Valley estate in the company of Vanderbilts and Astors, FDR was nevertheless something Hoover was not—a gifted politician. In 1921 FDR had contracted polio and lost the full use of his legs. Recovery from the disease changed him and granted him his political gift for empathy. Historian David M. Kennedy observed that FDR's "shallow, supercilious youth" gave way to "the precious gift of a purposeful manhood." In 1931 Governor Roosevelt created the Temporary Emergency Relief Administration to provide $20 million in direct aid to suffering New Yorkers. In 1932 he went to Chicago to accept the Democratic presidential nomination in person. "I pledge myself," he called, "to a new deal for the American people."[133]

That FDR was going to win was crystal clear. As for how exactly a Roosevelt administration might grapple with the Depression, the picture was dark mud. FDR's campaign staff had no overarching consensus about what to do. But one of the candidate's great political assets was his ideological flexibility. Unlike Hoover, he was not a technocrat. Nor was he an intellectual; hence he was free from the problem that plagues most intellectuals in politics, their almost aesthetic desire for a grand ideological system, in which all the different parts must fit together into a unified whole. When asked during the campaign what his "philosophy" was, FDR responded, "Philosophy? Philosophy? I am a Christian and a Democrat—that's all."[134] If intellectually he had no grand design, nonetheless FDR had memorized the voting tendencies of every congressional district.

On the campaign trail, like all good Democrats, FDR called for lower tariffs and support for agriculture. He criticized Hoover for not balancing the federal budget. That was about all. Around himself he assembled many advisers, who made different, sometimes contradictory suggestions. Much to their amazement, the candidate would agree with them all. "Yes! Yes! Yes!" "Fine! Fine! Fine!" Thus intellectuals thoroughly underestimated FDR. Supreme Court justice Oliver Wendell Holmes, Jr., once said of FDR that he had a "second-class intellect" but a "first-class temperament." Journalist Walter Lippmann referred to the incoming president as "a kind of amiable boy scout," without "a firm grasp of public affairs and without very strong convictions." Hoover thought the Democratic nominee a hopeless lightweight. Upon FDR's landslide victory over him in 1932, he predicted disaster.[135]

The interregnum between FDR's election in November 1932 and his inauguration in March 1933 stretched long. A week after FDR's victory, the outgoing and incoming presidents met in the White House. When they met again in January 1933, Hoover said he found Roosevelt "very ignorant."[136] In February, he sent FDR a telegram. Yet another banking panic had begun in the West, then arrived in Detroit. Edsel Ford's Guardian Trust Company, which had financed automobile purchases, failed; the RFC refused it a loan, and Henry Ford, who believed credit was immoral, refused to bail out his son. That led to further panic. The Michigan governor had to close all 550 Michigan banks for eight days.[137] Implausibly, Hoover blamed this latest round of banking panics on the specter of Roosevelt-induced inflation.

Before FDR entered the White House, Hoover badgered him to publicly commit himself to maintaining the gold standard. If we "should inflate our currency, [and] consequently abandon the gold standard," the outgoing president warned the American public, the consequence would be "complete destruction." FDR, however, would commit to nothing. Hoover then tried to get FDR to publicly approve a delegation that Hoover was sending to a World Economic Conference, to be held in London later in 1933. Again FDR demurred—he would wait until he was president to act. The economy kept tanking. On March 2, 1933, the New York Fed fell below its minimum gold reserve. On March 3 it lost $350 million—$200 million to foreign wire transfers, and $150 million in hard currency withdrawn.[138] Steel factories were then operating at 12 percent of their capacity.[139] As panic still rippled across the banking system, it is no exaggeration to say that American capitalism was very nearly grinding to a halt when, on March 4, FDR was finally inaugurated as president.

Among FDR's widely commented-upon personal qualities was his bottomless reserve of self-confidence and his almost preternatural sense of calm. In contrast to so many nerve-shot capitalists, according to one of his closest advisers, FDR "had no nerves at all." In the most memorable line of his inaugural address, he declared that Americans had "nothing to fear but fear itself."[140] Days after taking office in March, FDR declared a week-long national bank holiday, to calm popular panic and fear. Then, to the surprise of many—including his own Treasury Department—FDR indicated he would support a provision in Congress's Emergency Banking Act, enabling the executive to control international and domestic gold movements. The new law granted to the president the power to take the United States off the gold standard. On April 5, 1933, FDR signed an executive order "forbidding the hoarding of gold coin, gold bullion, and gold certificates within the continental United States."[141]

On April 20, FDR suspended the gold standard. At the time, U.S. gold reserves had recovered and were ample. After Hitler became chancellor of Germany in January 1933, much gold had fled to the United States. The free convertibility of dollars to gold at the rate of $20.67 per ounce—the rate, attacked by the Populists, that had been mandated ever since post–Civil War resumption—was not at risk. Going off gold was intended to stoke the reflation of national prices and assert political control over the U.S. economy.[142] FDR announced a new policy of "definitely controlled inflation."[143] The price of the dollar, now allowed to float in currency and gold markets, quickly devalued with respect to gold and other currencies (against the British pound by 30 percent). U.S. prices across the board began to reflate. Finally a bottom had been reached.

In an act of great political courage, FDR broke America's golden fetters. The New Deal was begun.

BOOK THREE

THE AGE OF
CONTROL

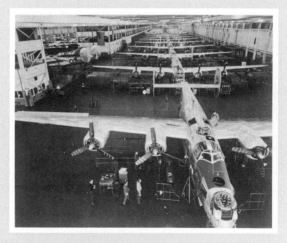

1932–1980

CONTROL

B Y THE TIME FRANKLIN DELANO ROOSEVELT WAS INAUGURATED as president on March 4, 1933, every known economic indicator, already in perilous territory, was still moving in the wrong direction. Making objective economic matters worse, a narrative of fear and depression was hardening and was fast becoming self-fulfilling. "The only thing we have to fear is . . . fear itself, nameless, unreasoning, unjustified terror which paralyzes needed efforts to convert retreat into advance," the new president declared.

A mass psychology of deflation had set in. Capitalism was not going to lift itself out of the slump—it was stuck in the short-term present. Fear was so intense that the owners of capital favored the psychological return of security over seeking pecuniary profit—to wait it all out instead of investing. Many other people with money to spend joined them. Not just capitalists but ordinary Americans were running on banks and removing deposits, then putting the money perhaps under a mattress, if not in a hole dug in the ground. Due to fear, much economic activity simply ceased.

Something from outside the system had to come to the rescue. The only real candidate was the federal government. The United States still had considerable economic resources. The Fordist revolution in energy-intensive mass production was still new. Rarely if ever before had an industrial economy been so poised on the brink of a great leap forward in wealth-generating enterprise. But it had stalled in mid-leap. FDR was right: there was nothing to fear but fear itself.

Chapter 13, "New Deal Capitalism," recounts how FDR's New Deal began to reverse the tide. When FDR took the United States off the gold standard, prices began to climb. Expectations shifted, and economic spending returned. Next, the New Deal attempted a dizzying variety of policy experiments. The overarching keyword that motivated them all was *security*. The primary goal was control: to de-volatize capitalism and to employ breadwinning men. The New Deal's regulatory arm transformed banking and finance, as well as the conduct of industry and agriculture. The politics of income now blossomed. Multiple programs lifted commodity prices and shored up farm incomes. The Social Security Act of 1935 provided new income security. The Wagner Act, of the same year, legally institutionalized union collective bargaining over pay.

The New Deal state also had a developmental arm, on the side of capital. New federal agencies granted credit to the agricultural and real estate industries. They made public investments in the infrastructure of the still-dawning energy-intensive, auto-industrial economy, including dams, roads, and power utilities. Developmental policies offered inducements, but investment remained largely in private hands. With a strong regulatory arm and a weaker developmental one, the "liberalism" of the Democratic Party was born.

Despite the strong post-1933 recovery, private investment remained insufficient to end the scourge of mass male industrial unemployment. The New Deal hit a political and economic wall in 1937–38, after FDR's administration attempted to balance the federal budget, reducing government expenditure. It gave rise to a recession in the Depression. Meanwhile a new kind of liquidity preference appeared, in addition to the speculative and the precautionary motivated by economic-psychological considerations. Capitalists politicized liquidity preference. Decrying liberal regulations and taxation, the owners of capital once again pulled back their investments, demanding their desired economic policies. Politically, the New Deal sat stymied, as the unemployment rate, having never fallen below 10 percent, rose to 20 percent.

It was not the New Deal but World War II—the subject of Chapter 14, "New World Hegemon"—that finally pulled the United States out of the Great Depression. The "total energy" of total war did the trick, even if the war economy was good only at producing bombs, tanks, and airplanes. Very likely, energy-intensive war economies everywhere definitively tipped geological history into the era of human-made climate change, the Anthropocene. But World War II eliminated U.S. unemployment through massive public investment in war factories, operated by private contractors. Public debt and progressive taxation propelled the economic war effort, rather than private speculative investment. The U.S. war economy positively boomed, as liberalism, big government, and private initiative together amounted to a dynamic amalgam. When the war ended, much of the world lay in economic ruins, but the United States enjoyed a worldwide economic supremacy never before seen in all of history.

The final settlement of the Age of Control's political economy was not determined until the postwar era, however. Chapter 15, "Postwar Hinge," covers the struggle over its fate, in the context of the U.S. effort to rebuild the postwar capitalist world economy. The Bretton Woods agreements of 1944 established the U.S. dollar, pegged to gold, as the chief world currency. While the new international political economy restored world trade, Bretton Woods granted states the right to enforce cross-border capital controls so as to ensure autonomy for national economic policy making, independent of the cross-border capital movements that had been a cause of the Great Depression. In the U.S. national economy, President Harry Truman's attempt to revive some of the New Deal's most ambitious developmental efforts was defeated in the context of the outbreak of the Cold War with Soviet Communism. By 1948, a rising anti-Communist ideology had set a hard left edge on Cold War–era liberalism. Wartime government controls on economic life were lifted. The owners of capital regained control over investment. The United States was the hegemon of the capitalist world economy. Postwar U.S. industrial society took shape.

What we can call a new political "illiquidity preference" prevailed. Industrial capital settled on the ground long term for a generation after the war. Because of union power, and postwar fears that depression and male unemployment might return, many postwar industrial capitalists decided they must invest in employment-giving enterprise. They did, as government restored a politics of income—union bargaining over pay, progressive and redistributive income taxation, and various forms of regulation—as the central aim of U.S. political economy. But in a new departure, the federal government took responsibility for countercyclical spending in times of recession. Austerity was out. In fiscal policy, the government accepted that budget deficits in times of recession were necessary to achieve the "economic growth" of the "macroeconomy." A new multiplier was born: the Keynesian "fiscal multiplier."

Postwar capitalism came to be defined by high growth and economic "abundance." Chapter 16, "Consumerism," explores how consumption began to matter to economic life more than ever before. A postwar real estate boom, in the suburbs, saw the construction of single-family homes, highways, shopping malls, and strip malls. The spread of a consumerist auto-suburbia across space was built into this age, the way the spread of the plantation had been built into the Age of Commerce, or the construction of the northeastern-midwestern manufacturing belt had been built into the Age of Capital. No less central to consumerism, during the 1950s, was the mental dreamscape, as the postwar corporate advertisement industry set about finding ways to get Americans to buy new versions of what they already owned—cars, television sets, washing machines, clothes, and entertainments. Consumerism was not new to the postwar era, but its cultural significance and economic implications intensified, as "consumer confidence" and planned obsolescence became new dynamic factors in economic expectations.

In the postwar period, the U.S. economy, having recovered from the Great Depression and won the war, achieved consumer abundance. It was a "golden age" of capitalism, when, by historic standards, rates of growth, productivity, profits, and wages remained high, and income and wealth inequality were compressed. Chapter 17, "Ordeal of a Golden Age," explores the many structures of postwar industrial society, including the cultural, the social-psychological, and the aesthetic. In political economy, a fiscal triangle—consisting of the federal government, industrial corporations, and nonprofits—was charged with the production, distribution, and redistribution of industrial income. Industrial corporate managers invested in fixed, illiquid capital. Income politics expanded, for instance in the 1965 Social Security amendments, which created the public health care programs Medicare and Medicaid. The voluntaristic "nonprofit" sector became the latest chapter in the history of philanthropy, and in the sphering and splitting of public and private. The boundaries dividing the postwar spheres of "free enterprise," the "nonprofit" sector of civil society, and the fiscal state of the government were hard and tense.

The fiscal state took responsibility for the performance of the macro-economy of "aggregates"—aggregate demand, aggregate investment, aggregate consumption, aggregate output, and aggregate employment. For the first time, professional economists became important policy advisers, ensconced in the President's Council of Economic Advisors, created in 1946. National economic growth, the most important aggregate of all, was robust in this period, but the aggregates did not address the fabric of everyday economic institutions and relationships. Inside the aggregates were many details. Aggregates said nothing about the specific geography of investment and disinvestment, or about the economic lives of the individuals, groups, and places that investment and disinvestment decisions shaped. The 1964 Tax Reduction Act, first proposed by President John F. Kennedy, attempted to use tax cuts to boost an ongoing economic expansion. Many liberals hoped it would stimulate private investment so as to meet a rising sense of economic expectations among people—blacks in inner cities, poor rural whites, and working women—who had hitherto been excluded from an economy designed to deliver a high white-male-breadwinning wage. By now, with World War II in the past, liberalism's only developmental vehicle was the income tax code. Otherwise, President Lyndon B. Johnson's "War on Poverty" was insufficiently funded. Together with the Vietnam War, the 1964 tax cut left behind a national macroeconomy that was booming, to be sure, but overstimulated in some places and underresourced in others. Massive political protests erupted against the dissatisfactions and inequities of postwar society, and liberalism began to crack up.

As liberalism encountered political troubles in the late 1960s and '70s, its economic foundation began to crumble. Industrial society became enervated. Chapter 18, "Crisis of Industrial Capital," describes how industrial society and liberalism alike suffered from a number of destabilizing shocks. Profits flagged first, after 1965. Average male labor compensation flatlined after 1972. Commodity prices climbed too high, straining the relationship between the industrial and the agricultural sectors. In 1973 the Nixon administration announced the end of the Bretton Woods dollar-gold peg, and soon the United States lifted controls on cross-border capital movement. The same year, the Organization of Petroleum Exporting Countries announced an embargo on oil. The rate of productivity growth, especially in the most energy-intensive lines of production, declined. The subsequent recession of 1973–75 was the worst since the Great Depression. The standard corrective measures—a stimulating tax cut, counter-cyclical budget deficits—brought the U.S. macroeconomy out of recession, and national economic growth returned. But something ill was now at work inside that aggregate. By now, high rates of inflation and unemployment were endemic—"stagflation."

Meanwhile economic life on the ground was changing, unsettling. It was losing its industrial structure. The historic northeastern-midwestern manufacturing belt began to rust. In Sunbelt cities like Houston, Texas, economic life revolved less around capital used up in long-term industrial production, or the male breadwinning wage, than around real estate appreciation and the more labor-intensive, historically feminized service economy. Back in Washington, liberalism lost its nerve. An era of deregulation began, as high rates of inflation destabilized long-term expectations, which had the effect of pulling economic horizons toward the present, crippling political control. After an internationally coordinated Keynesian stimulus was perceived to fail, due to speculative cross-border attacks on the U.S. dollar, the administration of President Jimmy Carter announced a policy of fiscal austerity and general economic "decontrol."

The Age of Control began with a deflationary crisis, at a time when nation-states around the world were erecting barriers to many international economic forces—especially fickle cross-border capital movements. It ended in a double-digit inflationary crisis, when U.S. policy makers announced the need for "decontrol" in a new era of "global interdependence," when walls between national economies were coming down. Control worked by inducing, but never coercing, capital to fix and settle in place on the ground, long term, within national territories. In the last analysis, the project was a developmental failure. The Age of Control ended as capital became ever more roving, short term, and undecided.

CHAPTER 13

NEW DEAL CAPITALISM

T HE GREAT DEPRESSION DROPPED THE FATE OF ECONOMIES directly onto the laps of national governments. The crisis of confidence in capitalism was profound, but the crisis of confidence in liberal democracy was even greater.[1] The "liberal state is destined to perish," Mussolini predicted in 1934, and Hitler and Stalin too claimed that unified mass, democratic publics stood behind their illiberal governments.[2] Dictatorships seized power across Latin America. Militarists did the same in Japan. The journalist Walter Lippmann advised FDR, "The situation is critical, Franklin. You might have no alternative but to assume dictatorial powers."[3]

FDR would invoke emergency powers, and a number of the New Deal's features would harmonize with those of thoroughly illiberal polities abroad, including, say, its monumental government architecture—a sharp visual contrast to so much recent economic volatility.[4] No less, the New Deal would draw from America's homegrown illiberal traditions. The white supremacy that maintained its grip on the South was no monument to liberty, and FDR was willing to cooperate with southern racists, as he needed Democratic votes in Congress. Nevertheless, many liberal democratic institutions—periodic elections, an independent judiciary, greater or lesser freedom of assembly and conscience—survived in the United States.[5] FDR believed in democracy, for Groton and Harvard had drilled schoolboy American truths into him. The president also simply loved the art of democratic politics. The New Deal always had an electoral political logic.[6] FDR relished, in the words of one historian, cobbling together "big-city bosses, the white South, farmers and workers, Jews and Irish Catholics, ethnic minorities, and African Americans" into the lasting electoral bloc behind New Deal liberalism.[7] *Liberalism* was the moniker FDR adopted, in a departure from the classical or "laissez-faire" liberalism of the nineteenth century. Now Republicans became "conservatives." At a moment when politics, across the globe, newly asserted control over economic life, FDR was the right mass democratic politician. He did not assume dictatorial powers, but it nonetheless was the Age of Control.

Policy-wise, here and there, FDR winged it. Raymond Moley, a Barnard professor, and an important early economic adviser to the president, was to write that to attribute coherence to the New Deal "was to believe that the accumulation of stuffed snakes, baseball pictures, school flags, old tennis shoes, carpenter's tools, geometry books, and chemistry sets in a boy's bedroom could have been put there by an interior decorator."[8] A number of historians of the New Deal have agreed.[9] "Take a method and try it. If it fails admit it frankly and try another. But above all, try something," FDR proclaimed publicly in 1932.[10]

In that spirit, FDR got the most important immediate economic policy call right: he took the United States off the gold standard. At an April 19, 1933, press conference, the president announced a policy of "definitely controlled inflation." Privately, he quipped, "my banker friends may be horrified," and a great number of them were.[11] Regardless, he did break the mass psychology of deflationary future expectations. Going off gold was what economic historians have called a "regime change." As money devalued, prices began to go up. Consumers began to spend in the present. Rising prices portended rising profits. Investment and its multiplying effects began to recover, and a broader economic recovery ensued.[12]

The New Deal's first impulse was to reflate prices, and in this effort it was a success. Four decades later the inflationary bias of New Deal liberalism would dig its own grave. But in 1933 it was what the doctor ordered.

After that, perhaps stuffed snakes lay next to school flags, but at least a pile of stuff existed—policy options. That distinguished 1933 from a later moment, 2008, when there were would be precious few novel initiatives. By contrast, when FDR took office in 1933, a generation of Populist and Progressive policy proposals were already on the shelf, ready for someone to pick them up.[13] After all, going off gold was precisely what William Jennings Bryan had demanded in 1896, at the helm of the fused Populist-Democratic ticket. FDR's first two administrations would draw from old Populist demands for agrarian credit and price supports, and the income politics and banking regulations of Progressivism. As they did, some new and enduring patterns took shape.

Ideologically, the New Deal was committed to "security."[14] To hoard money and forgo spending of all kinds had become a respite from anxiety and fear. During the 1930s, interest rates remained low, stuck in liquidity-trap territory.[15] Interest rates approached zero, and no further reductions were capable of calling forth present spending. Not enough people wanted to part with liquid assets as safe haven stores of value, which meant purchasing power and demand for goods dried up. If government found new ways to make people feel secure, however, economic initiative—including spending on both investment and consumption—might resume. At the same time, speculation in the run-up of the 1920s credit cycle had created so much of the trouble to begin with. New Deal policies ran counter to short-term financial speculation. Profit making shifted away from finance and toward production. Relatedly, the New Deal had the general effect of distributing income away from capital and toward labor earnings.[16] The new policy preference was for a political economy of less financial volatility and therefore greater economic security and equality.

The way to achieve it was to anchor economic life in the illiquidity of industrial capital, which had the great political advantage of offering male employment. In politics, the most broadly shared expectation of New Deal capitalism was that factories would provide male breadwinners jobs—presupposing, no less, female homemaking. In this respect, while the ultimate end was newfound economic security, nevertheless the New Deal was conservative, or at least restorative.

Against this backdrop, New Deal policy initiatives can be distinguished from one another into two categories, the regulatory and the developmental. In the end, the New Deal's regulatory arm proved far more robust.

Regulation can further be divided into two subsets: regulations of the conduct of business, and regulations aimed at income politics. First, new agencies, such as the Securities Exchange Commission (SEC), promulgated many new rules regulating banking practices. By the end of the 1930s, there was a revival of antimonopoly in industry. Second, as enterprise recovered, incomes were newly regulated, in the form of new personal and corporate income taxes, while new legislation intensified "fair rate of return" regulations on public utilities. Meanwhile new laws supported liberalism's robust politics of male pay. Immediately, the New Deal provided relief measures for the many unemployed. Enduringly, male pay

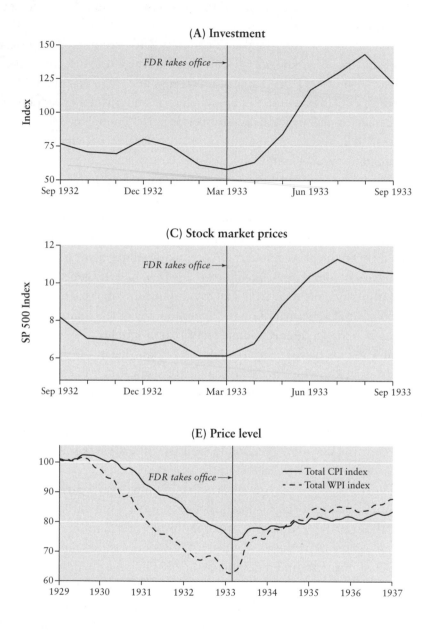

RECOVERY FROM THE GREAT DEPRESSION

Upon the election of FDR, many forward-looking economic indicators reversed direction, and following the change in expectations a broad-based economic recovery ensued. The recovery began even before FDR made the fateful choice of going off the gold standard.

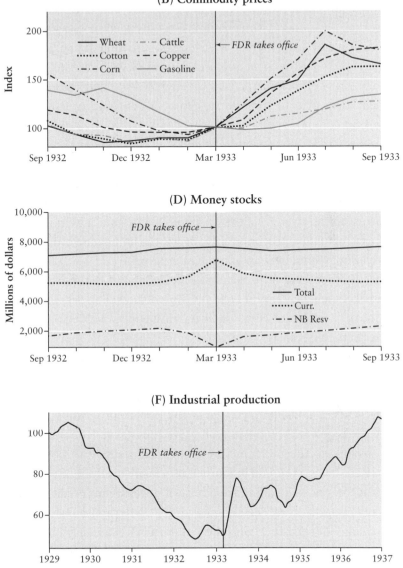

(B) Commodity prices

Index

— Wheat   —·— Cattle
······· Cotton   — — Copper
—·—· Corn   —— Gasoline

← *FDR takes office*

Sep 1932   Dec 1932   Mar 1933   Jun 1933   Sep 1933

(D) Money stocks

Millions of dollars

FDR takes office →

— Total
······· Curr.
—·—· NB Resv

Sep 1932   Dec 1932   Mar 1933   Jun 1933   Sep 1933

(F) Industrial production

FDR takes office →

1929   1930   1931   1932   1933   1934   1935   1936   1937

Key: CPI = consumer price index; WPI = wholesale price index; Curr. = currency;
NB Resv = national bank reserves

became twentieth-century liberalism's chief currency of distributive justice—both its aim and its great imaginative limit. Next, the Wagner Act of 1935 legally institutionalized union collective bargaining over wages and working conditions. Once capital was invested in industry, unions could struggle over the income it yielded. Meanwhile the Social Security Act of 1935 became the cornerstone of a new U.S. welfare state, which created new forms of income security through old-age pensions and unemployment insurance. In agriculture, a host of new government programs propped up commodity prices so as to ensure farm incomes. New Deal regulations would shape economic life for decades to come, down to the present day.

The New Deal's developmental arm was more directly concerned with issues of long-term planning and the *ex ante* politics of capital investment, in contrast to the *ex post* politics of income.[17] Despite the dramatic post-1933 price reflation and economic recovery, the immediate problem of the 1930s was not so much the regulation of enterprise and the distribution of incomes. Rather, long-term economic development remained disrupted because so much capital remained on the sidelines. The dearth of investment meant a dearth of employment-giving enterprise to generate labor incomes in the first place.

Developmental policies had two subsets as well: state-funded public corporations that placed capital and credit in private hands, and federal programs that made direct public investment outside any private channel. Through the organizational vehicle of the public corporation, a number of New Deal policies sought to reenergize long-term economic development. In banking, the government-owned Reconstruction Finance Corporation (RFC) invested capital in many financial institutions, if only to keep them solvent, and helped finance a host of government credit programs, especially in agriculture. Federal government programs subsidized credit in the collapsed real estate construction industry. State-subsidized credit, if unequally enjoyed, became an enduring entitlement of U.S. citizenship.[18] Meanwhile there were New Deal public investment programs. The Tennessee Valley Authority (TVA) was a massive state developmental agency. Through the Works Progress Administration (WPA) and the Public Works Administration (PWA), federal government projects made long-term public investments in the infrastructure of the auto-industrial economy—roads, power utilities, dams, and more, especially west of the Mississippi.[19] The effect of these programs was to induce greater private investment and kick-start development down the Fordist capital- and energy-intensive path. The more economic recovery there was, the more that a fossil fuel energy system entrenched.

New Deal capitalism was a variety of capitalism because the discretionary power of when and where to invest remained in the hands of the owners of capital. During the 1930s, whether the investment was private (incentivized or not) or public, its combined magnitude was simply insufficient to draw out sufficient economic activity to end the Great Depression. A general lack of initiative and spending remained.

In 1937, four years into the recovery, on behalf of fiscal rectitude FDR's administration sought to balance the budget, while the Fed took measures to prevent possible inflation. The recovery stalled. In 1937–38 there was a "recession in the Depression." Now for the first time, FDR's administration changed course and turned to the possibility of government deficit spending to fund public investment—and bring about a "fiscal multiplier." The owners of capital, fearful not of financial panic but of the real possibility of government intervention into capital investment, re-retrenched. A new kind of liquidity preference appeared on the scene: the political.[20] Decrying government-caused "uncertainty," demanding policy changes friendly to their interests, capitalists pulled back on their fixed industrial investments, parked their money on the sidelines, and accelerated the new dropoff in spending.

By the time Hitler invaded Poland in 1939, industrial unemployment in Nazi Germany—due to the fascist mobilization of mass energies, including a massive public investment campaign in the tools of war—stood at 3.2 percent.[21] At the end of the decade, the New Deal sat stymied, with many accomplishments but with the total volume of investment insufficient; the Depression was groaning on, and mass white male unemployment, the New Deal's stated enemy, was not yet licked.

The political economy of New Deal liberalism would not be settled until after World War II. Back in March 1933, however, FDR first had to save capitalists' skins, entering the political psychology of uncertainty and "fear itself."[22]

1. Back from the Brink

By the time of FDR's inauguration on March 4, 1933, the latest round of panic had led to the withdrawal of millions of dollars of deposits, and more than $500 million in currency was being hoarded in such places as "holes in the ground, privies, linings of coats, horse collars, coal piles, hollow trees."[23] Prices deflated, in a mass psychological dynamic: expectations that prices would decline became self-fulfilling, as individuals did not spend, expecting lower future prices. Taking office, FDR had no choice but to play confidence games with the American public. "Capitalism," Moley would say, "was saved in eight days."[24]

FDR was a quick study of the new mass political psychology. Mussolini, Hitler, and Stalin preferred mass open-air rallies, but FDR's chosen political instrument was the radio. Sixty percent of all U.S. households owned a radio in 1933.[25] In his upper-class but distinctive intonation, FDR addressed his "fellow citizens." Journalist Lorena Hickok reported to Harry Hopkins from New Orleans in 1934, "People down here all seem to think they know the President personally. . . . They feel he is talking to each one of them."[26]

Arguably, in the first eight days, much hinged on the timbre of FDR's voice. On March 12, 1933, the president delivered his first fireside chat on "The Banking Crisis," explaining that the Emergency Banking Act retroactively authorized a six-day national bank holiday. Among other provisions, the act banned the private export of gold and let the federally chartered and Treasury-funded RFC invest in banks' preferred stocks. FDR calmly explained that banks would begin to open the next day: "You people must have faith. . . . Let us unite in banishing fear."[27] Lo and behold, nearly $200 million in withdrawn gold coin now began to reenter bank vaults.[28] The banking panic was over. Hoarded currency began to move back into the banking system.

As for deflation, on April 19, FDR announced the policy of a "definitely controlled inflation." The administration let the dollar trade freely against gold. It began to devalue, and the general price level began to rise. If there was any doubt about FDR's intentions, in the summer he scuttled negotiations at the World Economic Conference in London when he wired his "bombshell" message. The maintenance of the gold standard had required that countries privilege an international obligation—to defend their currencies' fixed exchange rate with gold—over any domestic economic priority. Defending the gold standard periodically required raising interest rates to recruit foreign gold, which restricted the supply of domestic credit and caused deflation. From now on, FDR declared, the "old fetishes of so-called international bankers" would have no hearing at the White House.[29]

Meanwhile the RFC began to inject public capital into banks. The public corporation, having important precedents during World War I, became a significant developmental mechanism.[30] FDR appointed RFC board member Jesse H. Jones its new chairman. Jones hailed from Houston, a city Jones believed, rightly, was destined to become the "Chicago of the South." After FDR, Jones was arguably the second most powerful man in the country during the 1930s. He was a banker, a Democratic Party operative, and an old Bryanite who believed Wall Street had monopolized capital and credit. "Most of the country lies west of the Hudson River and none of it east of the Atlantic Ocean," he once remarked. Characteristically, he granted loans to railroad corporations but forced their directors to move their headquarters away from New York: "You live too far from your tracks."[31] FDR would commonly bemoan Jones's power, calling him "Jesus H. Jones." The president had to put up with Jones's racist "nigger stories." Yet the two shared an animosity for "No. 23"—that is, 23 Wall Street, headquarters of J. P. Morgan & Co. Once, a number of bankers confronted FDR in the White House and demanded Jones's removal from office. FDR placed a cigarette in its holder. "Boys, I am going back to Jess."[32]

Jones's RFC closed down 5 percent of all U.S. banks and funded many of the rest by purchasing their preferred stock. By 1935, the RFC owned one-third of all U.S. bank capital.[33] It would also become home to a host of New Deal credit agencies. Jones maintained that the RFC's public investments should be commercially viable—they should not bear losses. This was not debt-financed "relief." The public capital and credit of the RFC accomplished its aims. The RFC halted bank panics, capitalized various New Deal agencies, and helped reflate prices.[34]

If the western state capitalist Jones was a new breed, so was New Dealer Tommy Corcoran—"Tommy the Cork." FDR enjoyed giving nicknames and telling jokes, which, if clubby and male, could soothe nerves. (By contrast, President Hoover had been tense and humorless in office.) Tommy the Cork was an Irish Catholic New Englander and a favorite former student of the Viennese émigré Harvard Law professor Felix Frankfurter. Frankfurter cut his teeth on Progressive public utility regulation and was generally inimical to Wall Street. Many of Frankfurter's "boys" would swarm New Deal administrative agencies.[35] Corcoran had practiced corporate law in New York before becoming an RFC lawyer in 1932. He worked closely with Benjamin Cohen, another Frankfurter student turned disillusioned Wall Street corporate lawyer.[36] The Cork was the legislative fixer, corralling votes in Congress, while Cohen was the master legislative draftsman.

A new working coalition emerged. Anti–Wall Street Harvard and Yale corporate lawyers entered into alliance with non–Wall Street bankers, such as Jones, and disgruntled western farmers and southern white planters, long the Democratic Party's constituency, in order to put adversarial regulations of Wall Street on the books. More regulated, Wall Street suffered. Cohen was the brains behind the Securities Act of 1933, which began to chip away at the NYSE's self-regulation, prohibiting deceitful securities issues. However, even as Wall Street fell under new regulations, laws such as this had the unintended consequence of further concentrating U.S. capital markets on Wall Street. Local securities markets, especially in the Midwest, so critical to late-nineteenth-century small-scale industrialization—its fleeting politics of property—already weakened by the Depression, faced the high costs of new regulations and perished.

The New Deal's regulatory arm thus began to move into action. More consequential than the Securities Act was the Banking Act of 1933, commonly named after its southern Democratic sponsors, Carter Glass of Virginia and Henry B. Steagall of Alabama. Glass-Steagall separated deposit-taking and loan-granting commercial banking from securities-underwriting investment banking. J. P. Morgan was thus forced to spin off a separate investment bank—Morgan Stanley. Glass-Steagall also created the Federal Deposit Insurance Corporation (FDIC), a public corporation like the RFC. Its aim was to prop up "unit" banking, or small country banks without branches. The creation of the FDIC was an old Populist demand. Rather than letting banks consolidate so that during bank runs they could draw on a larger, more diversified pool of resources, the FDIC insured deposits up to $2,500. The FDIC's actions worked, as bank runs ceased. Finally, Glass-Steagall's "Regulation Q" granted the federal government the power to cap interest rates on deposits. If banks could compete for deposits by raising interest rates, of necessity they would have to search for higher speculative yields to pay for them. Regulation Q created a cartel-like structure among commercial banks, limiting, but ensuring profits.[37]

Economists and historians debate the merits of Glass-Steagall. Surely over the years it would have many unintended consequences, and according to one standard of economic efficiency in which capital must be allowed to move anywhere in order to achieve its best possible use, the legislation was disruptive.[38] But disrupting was precisely the point. Uninhibited capital mobility had been a source of the bust. The explicit regulatory goal was to slow capital down, to create walls and pockets, blocking and controlling the free convertibility of assets—in other words, to make the financial system less dependent on transactional liquidity and less vulnerable to leverage and volatility.[39] The Glass-Steagall wall between investment and commercial banking was an instrument, and a symbol, of the effort. As for Regulation Q, the high-interest-rate environment of the 1920s, which had created incentives to speculate and had accelerated the credit cycle, was a reasonable target of financial reform.

Glass-Steagall was one of the more significant of the banking and financial reforms of the New Deal's vaunted First Hundred Days.

2. Overproduction and the First Hundred Days

In the First Hundred Days, a single economic idea animated both agricultural and industrial policy: that the reason for falling prices was "overproduction." Therefore, to limit the supply of goods would be to make them more scarce and thus increase going market prices for them. On the basis of price reflation, economic activity, including employment, would recover. True, anything that broke the deflationary spiral would be of benefit—even if the real problem was unused capacity, and underinvestment, rather than overproduction. In the spirit of trying something, during the First Hundred Days, congressional legislation made quite dramatic interventions in commercial markets, to restrict supply and thereby reflate the economy. Some, if not all, of the interventions proved lasting.

On May 12, 1933, Congress passed the Agricultural Adjustment Act, creating a new federal agency, the Agricultural Adjustment Administration (AAA). Its stated goal was to reflate commodity prices and thus farm incomes. Another aim was debt relief. FDR cited the "human impossibility of deflation," but more deflation was also politically impossible.[40] In April, indebted Iowa farmers nearly lynched a judge in protest of farm foreclosures. Milo Reno's Farmers' Holiday Association called for the government to guarantee farm incomes above the "cost of production."[41] That phrase evoked industry, where large, nearly monopolistic producers gave prices rather than taking them from competitive markets. In the highly competitive agricultural sector, farmers aspired to be price givers themselves, with guaranteed incomes above their cost of production—regardless of the intersection of supply and demand. This version of income politics required government intervention.

The "domestic allotment" programs of the AAA worked to restrict supply by paying farmers not to produce. The cost of production did not prevail politically. Instead, the stated target was commodity price "parity," using a World War I–era commodity price benchmark, before supply had run far out ahead of demand during the speculative investment boom of the 1920s. Under domestic allotment, production was banned beyond the volume that threatened price parity. To fund the program, Congress passed a tax on agricultural processing, which fell heavily on northeastern and midwestern industrial states.[42] By the time the AAA was created in the spring of 1933, most farmers had already planted their fields. In the South, tenants plowed up 10 million acres of cotton—for which landlords (not tenants) received checks for $100 million. Infamously, Secretary of Agriculture Henry Wallace ordered the slaughter of millions of piglets and hundreds of thousands of sows. Milk was poured onto roadsides. But prices did rise. Cotton climbed from 6.5 cents in 1932 to over 10 cents in 1933.[43] In 1934 the federal government restricted supply by paying farmers not to plant and sow in the first instance. By then, thousands of county-level production "control committees" existed in rural America to monitor production. If at times the methods were inelegant, restricting agricultural supply reflated prices and finally undermined deflationary expectations. Increased farm incomes also became a fresh source of consumer demand for manufactures and services, aiding recovery.

Meanwhile the administration's continued devaluation of the currency helped raise farm commodity prices. In 1933 the dollar was not linked to gold, but the gold-dollar exchange rate was still important for determining the currency's relative value and thus the general price level. In his October 22, 1933, fireside chat, FDR explained that "ever since last March the definite policy of the Government has been to restore commodity price levels." To that end, "the United States must take firmly in its own hands the control of the gold value of our dollar."[44] FDR and his new Treasury secretary, Henry Morgenthau, began to meet over breakfast at the White House to set the gold-dollar exchange. One morning FDR recommended a twenty-one-cent increase. Why? "It's a lucky number because it's three times seven."[45] The Gold Reserve Act of 1934 would repeg the dollar to gold at $35 an ounce. The devaluation against gold since FDR's inauguration was 60 percent. Rather than repegging it for all time, FDR announced that if need be, there would be more adjustment. "I reserve the right," he declared, "to alter this proclamation as the interest of the United States may seem to require."[46]

The AAA also created programs to inject credit into the agricultural sector. The Farm Credit Administration absorbed Hoover's Federal Farm Board and appropriated $200 million to refinance farm mortgages. The Farm Credit Act of 1933 created and funded a series of government-supported public corporations and farm credit cooperatives.[47] Jones's RFC was also everywhere, providing hundreds of millions of dollars in loans to AAA-created credit agencies.[48]

Extending Populist-inspired Progressive-era programs, the Commodity Credit Corporation (CCC), for instance, granted "nonrecourse" loans of up to 60 to 70 percent of the parity price of their commodities—then stored them. Now government—rather than speculative dealers, who had dumped so many crops on the market in 1929 during the bust, destroying prices—carried over stocks of commodities. If prices rose above parity, farmers sold their crops, paid the loans, and pocketed the difference. If not, the CCC swallowed the loans and took possession of the crops. Only farmers who obeyed production controls received such supports. Upon its completion in 1936, the Department of Agriculture's sprawling bureaucratic headquarters in Washington became the largest office building in the world.

The farm bloc was long the electoral backbone of the Democratic Party, and many New Dealers felt at home with agrarian policy. "Back to the land" movements, tinged with nationalist, if not fascist nostalgia, were common across depressed industrialized economies.[49] Not coincidentally, it was FDR who signed off on the construction of the Jefferson Memorial in 1934. In industrial policy, the New Deal was more hesitant but began similarly, hoping to restrict output and thereby reflate prices. Here, in contrast to the competitive agricultural sector, handfuls of large industrial firms already often set prices. Government interventions to prop up prices were less necessary. Yet once again anything that worked against price deflation at this early stage of the recovery was helpful.

In industry, the FDR administration's initial preoccupation during the First Hundred Days was with unemployment relief.

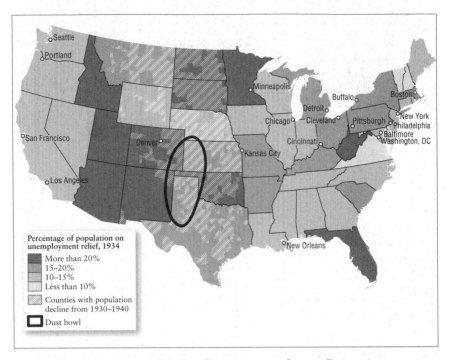

UNEMPLOYMENT RELIEF DURING THE GREAT DEPRESSION

This map of unemployment relief illustrates a geography of economic
suffering. It also indicates where the New Deal was able to
provide relief assistance.

In March 1933, Congress created the Federal Emergency Relief Administration (FERA), led by FDR's former New York head of relief, Harry Hopkins. FERA set a precedent of funneling federal welfare funds through
state governments, which did most of the administering. Municipal governments lost out.[50] Tellingly, rather than disbursing cash—charity, or the
"dole" as FDR called it—FERA paid state governments to pay men wages
for work, essentially simulating male breadwinning. Ellen Woodward,
who headed FERA's women's division, complained to Eleanor Roosevelt
that Hopkins's goal was only "to put men to work."[51] That also meant that,
as Grace Abbott of the U.S. Children's Bureau put it in her *The Child and the
State* (1938), "Employment of mothers with dependent children . . . is to
be deplored."[52]

The final act of the First Hundred Days was the National Industrial Recovery Act (NIRA) of 1933, which created the National Recovery Administration (NRA).[53] The act aimed to raise prices, wages, and profits—if

necessary, by restraining production through government-sanctioned monopolies. Monopolistic tendencies among firms would be welcomed, even embraced. It was a bold step for the Democratic Party, long home to antimonopoly, illustrating the early New Deal's intellectual critique of unrestricted market competition. "The jig us up," New Deal policy adviser and Columbia University economist Rexford Tugwell declared in a June 1933 address. "The cat is out of the bag. There is no invisible hand."[54] FDR named former War Industries Board official Hugh Johnson as head of the NRA. The NRA suspended antitrust law. The plan was that all the firms in every industrial sector would cooperatively agree on "industry codes"—binding agreements to limit production volumes, prices, and wages. The NRA was modeled after the short-lived War Industries Board of World War I, but government intervention of this kind outside wartime was unprecedented in U.S. history. Johnson hung a portrait of Mussolini in his office and passed out to his staff copies of the Fascist state theorist Raffaello Viglione's *Lo stato corporativo* (1927).

The NRA's industry codes applied to labor standards. In a dramatic legal departure, Section 7(a) of the NIRA established the rights of industrial workers to "organize and bargain collectively through representatives of their own choosing"—at a time when unions represented only 5 percent of U.S. industrial workers. The NIRA also called for maximum hour and minimum wage standards.

Finally, two more First Hundred Days agencies—in addition to Jones's RFC shop—rolled out the New Deal's developmental arm. They were tasked with making public investments. In May 1933, Congress chartered a public corporation, the Tennessee Valley Authority (TVA), to take over Henry Ford's failed bid to develop the Tennessee River valley at an abandoned World War I munitions site near Muscle Shoals, Alabama.[55] The TVA would expand electric power generation to an impoverished rural region, which private power utilities had deemed unprofitable. David Lilienthal, another of Frankfurter's "boys" and most recently a Wisconsin utility regulator, would take charge of the TVA.

The other developmental agency was the Public Works Administration (PWA), created by Title 2 of the NIRA. FDR handed the PWA to Secretary of the Interior Harold Ickes, a Chicago political reformer. On the basis of a $1 billion bond issue, the PWA was granted authority to issue up to $3.6 billion in public investments in, essentially, infrastructure—"internal improvements," to call back the Age of Commerce.[56] A Progressive Republican, Ickes proceeded cautiously, believing that public investments should be commercially viable, at a minimum carrying no cost to taxpayers.

Far more dominant than public investment in the First Hundred Days was the adversarial regulation of banking and finance, the tackling of male unemployment through relief, and the effort to reflate prices by ending "overproduction" in agriculture and industry.

3. Fate of the All-Class Alliance

As for politics, in the spirit of emergency upon taking office, FDR had wished to marry the Democratic Party with Progressive Republicans into a single grand "all-class alliance." But in 1934, as the administration passed further transformative legislation in finance and banking, politics began to polarize. Social movements erupted, on the left and the right. Industrialists rejected workers' bargaining rights, and a massive strike wave in protest threatened the National Recovery Administration. FDR risked losing control of the political situation.

Washington's assault on Wall Street continued, as Benjamin Cohen drafted the Securities Exchange Act of 1934. Publicly traded corporations now had to issue yearly and quarterly financial reports. The act banned "insider trading" and was full of antifraud provisions. To enforce the act, a new regulatory agency was created, the Securities and Exchange Commission (SEC). FDR adviser Adolf Berle and Gardiner Means's *The Modern Corporation and Private Property* (1932) had surveyed the growing division of ownership and management in large industrial corporations since the Great Merger Movement. The Securities Exchange Act codified many of their recommendations on behalf of shareholder rights and interests. Wall Street had vigorously opposed the bill, but Tommy the Cork, garnering the support of anti–Wall Street southern and western Democrats, orchestrated its passage through the Congress.

In 1934 Congress also passed the National Housing Act, bringing about massive changes in the market for residential investment. If the SEC focused on regulation of securities trading, the National Housing Act's goals were developmental—to use public authority to reduce uncertainty and induce profitable long-term investment in real estate construction. It succeeded. Fixed residential investment had collapsed from over $4 billion in 1929 to only $724 million by 1933 and was a major cause of the Depression. The National Housing Act created the Federal Housing Administration (FHA), which pushed private residential investment onto a longer-term time horizon. Before, most private mortgages had had terms of three to five years, not amortized, with large "balloon" payments in the final year. The FHA standardized the terms of home improvement loans (Title I) and home mortgage loans (Title 2). It also extended amortized payment schedules, typically between twenty and thirty years. Soon 1938 legislation would create the Federal National Mortgage Association (FNMA, or "Fannie Mae") to sponsor a secondary national market in FHA-approved mortgages. The FHA also insured approved loans. Long-term real estate investment, if a tad boring, became nearly risk free, with guaranteed profits. Government guaranteed transactional liquidity—a willing buyer—for bonds. In this case, the fusion of public authority and private initiative was fruitful. With these inducements, in 1935 private residential investment climbed back to $1.4 billion. This would prove to be a lasting long-term developmental mechanism, even if it was not tried much outside housing during the New Deal. It was not direct public investment. Government supports coaxed private capital off the sidelines.[57]

The regulatory SEC and the developmental FHA, both created in the spring of 1934, would prove to be of lasting significance. By that summer, however, the NRA was in trouble.[58] The agency had begun its work with great fanfare in September 1933, when 1.5 million New Yorkers lined up on Fifth Avenue to watch a quarter-million people parade in celebration of the writing of NRA industry codes, many brandishing the NRA's quasi-fascist "Blue Eagle" symbol. Hugh Johnson's task of writing one industry code after another was daunting. In July 1933 the first code—"Code of Fair Competition No. 1"—with the Cotton-Textile Institute trade association was struck. It sought to reflate prices by limiting textile production. Other codes were frustratingly slow in coming so FDR finally announced a "blanket code." Among other provisions, it mandated a thirty-five-hour workweek and a forty-cent minimum wage. The blanket code, with slight modifications, immediately applied to 450 industries and 90 percent of all industrial workers. It included the language of the NIRA's Section 7(a), recognizing workers' rights to "organize and bargain collectively through representatives of their own choosing."

But the NRA did not have sufficient administrative capacity to execute its ends. Regardless, employer objections to Section 7(a) sunk it. The cotton textile industry had 440,000 workers in July 1933, a growing number, overwhelmingly in New England and the low-wage southern piedmont. The bumbling, AFL-affiliated United Textile Workers of America (UTW) had represented only 27,500 in 1932—all in New England. By 1934, inspired by Section 7(a), membership in the UTW surged to a union-reported figure of 270,000, but textile manufacturers would not recognize the union. In September 1934, just when the NRA approved a reduction in working hours to limit overproduction, a massive general strike over the issue of union recognition—in other words, following the letter of the law—broke out from Maine to Georgia.

In all of U.S. labor history, few years rival 1934 for drama.[59] There had been rumblings in 1933, as rubber plant workers unionized in Akron, Ohio, and prepared a large strike, and Mexican, Japanese, and Filipino fruit pickers struck in California. However, 1934 was an eruption: in 1,856 work stoppages, 1.5 million workers demanded the upholding of Section 7(a). In Toledo, Ohio, auto parts workers won recognition, despite a violent clash that brought out the National Guard. In San Francisco, the Communist-influenced longshoremen won recognition. In October, under pressure, Hugh Johnson succumbed to mental illness, resigning from the NRA after delivering a farewell address to baffled and demoralized staffers comparing himself to Madame Butterfly.[60]

In the White House, FDR equivocated, as the left continued to agitate. In January 1934, the California doctor Francis Townsend called for monthly pensions of $200 for persons over age sixty, and 2 million joined Townsend "clubs." Twenty-five million signed Townsend petitions. Louisiana senator Huey P. Long announced his "Share the Wealth" campaign, proposing a basic income of $5,000 for all families.[61] In his diary, PWA boss Harold Ickes noted that the president "would have to move further to the left in order to hold the country."[62]

At the same time, organized opposition to the New Deal from the right first visibly broke out into the open. One of FDR's "banker friends," James P. Warburg, resigned from the administration in protest and wrote the critical *The Money Muddle* (1934). The president sent Warburg a letter recommending that he buy a car and tour the country, witness the poverty and widespread suffering firsthand, then write the book all over again.[63] August 1934 saw the founding of the conservative American Liberty League—to "teach the necessity of respect for the rights of persons and property."[64] The Du Pont family, owners of the explosives manufacturer and a controlling stake in General Motors, were important early funders of the league. Even two former Democratic presidential nominees, Al Smith and John W. Davis, joined. Frankfurter met with FDR and warned him, invoking William Seward's incendiary speech in the buildup to the Civil War, of an "irrepressible conflict" between his administration and many, if not all, of the owners of capital.[65]

Republicans expected gains from the midterm congressional elections of 1934. Instead, Democrats increased their overwhelming majorities in both the House and Senate by nine seats in each chamber. FDR was now a celebrity, and his charisma remained a potent weapon.[66] The president's mastery of political communication mattered especially at a time when many working people, from textile workers in the Carolina Piedmont, to "white ethnics" in Chicago, to Mexican communities in Los Angeles, were first experiencing mass culture—including FDR's fireside chats.[67] Meanwhile prices were rising in general, and an economic recovery had begun.

Nonetheless, in 1934 U.S. unemployment remained at 16.2 percent. In industry, the figure was 32.6 percent.[68] Something more had to be done, and there was political support for it. "Boys," Hopkins told his staff (a number of whom were women), "this is our hour. We've got to get everything we want—a works program, social security, wages and hours, everything—now or never."[69] FDR himself, attempting to read the political winds, was not sure of the next step.

4. "I welcome their hatred"

FDR vacillated politically during the winter of 1935.

Legislative activity did not cease. The president's January 4, 1935, annual message harped on two themes, the need for economic security and the fact that "work must be found for able-bodied but destitute workers."[70] May 1935 saw the creation of the Works Progress Administration (WPA), which FDR handed to Hopkins, of the now-superseded FERA. The WPA became the largest New Deal agency, for which Congress appropriated nearly $5 billion. Individuals seeking employment could apply to a local WPA agency and take a means test. The WPA directly employed its beneficiaries. Employment was limited to one person per household, with overwhelming preference for able-bodied male breadwinners. Women made up roughly 15 percent of the WPA's work rolls, as did African-Americans. The WPA could not officially discriminate according to race. Approximately 75 percent of WPA employment was on the public infrastructure projects of "highways, streets, public buildings, airports, public utilities, and recreational facilities."[71] One-quarter of WPA employees were in its "service" division—white collar and clerical work, even university research assignments. The WPA was not "relief." Rather than simply lessen as much human suffering as possible, or stimulate spending, government continued to focus on simulating the capitalist wage bargain.[72]

In the spring, the president vacationed on an Astor yacht, and rumor had it that he was seeking a rapprochement with business elites. He vetoed PWA proposals to invest in public housing, thereby satisfying the Realtors' lobby. On grounds of sound public finance, he vetoed Congress's "Bonus Act" to distribute $1.7 billion in bonds to World War I veterans. Nonetheless, the U.S. Chamber of Commerce—an association including many small-scale businesses, by contrast to the more heavy-industry National Association of Manufactures (NAM)—announced opposition to the New Deal. "The President expressed amazement that capitalists did not understand that he was their savior," recalled economic adviser Raymond Moley.[73]

As the president waffled politically, the U.S. Supreme Court acted. In May 1935 the Court handed down its decision in *Schechter Poultry Corp. v. United States,* striking down NRA codes, ruling them unconstitutional delegations of legislative power.[74] FDR could not believe the decision was 9–0. "And what about old Isaiah?" he asked, referring to Jewish justice Louis Brandeis. Old Isaiah—long a champion of regulated competition and a critic of monopoly—summoned Tommy the Cork to his chambers for a lecture. "This is the end of this business of centralization, and I want you to go back and tell the President that we're not going to let this government centralize everything. It's come to an end."[75] The NRA was dead.

It was at this juncture that FDR made up his mind politically. He decided to tack left, especially rhetorically. Populist rhetoric, arraying "the people" against elites, was not new to the Democratic Party. The "more I learn about Old Andy Jackson the more I love him," FDR now quipped.[76] Energized, on June 4, 1935, he called on Congress to remain in Washington for a sweltering special summer session. He requested that four bills be passed: the Social Security Act; the National Labor Relations Act; the Banking Act; and the Public Utility Holding Company Act. A few days later, he added to the list a Revenue Act, including a new progressive income tax bill. This period became known as the "Second Hundred Days." The Jacksonian Democracy had supported a politics of property; "security" now became the new rallying cry, as income politics now moved to center stage, both in the New Deal and in the Democratic Party.

FDR's June 19, 1935, speech on income taxation—written by Frankfurter, Corcoran, and Cohen—was a point of no return. The president lambasted "vast fortunes" and "vast concentrations of capital." When the bill was read on the Senate floor, Huey P. Long, who would fall to an assassin's bullet one year later, said, "I just wish to say 'Amen.'" The new revenue tax targeted the top 1 percent of income earners, and the top tax rate climbed from 63 to 79 percent. (Until 1938, only John D. Rockefeller, Sr., was rich enough to pay it.) Only the top 5 percent saw their taxes raised. Estate taxes increased, and so did the progressive corporate income tax.[77] Among large industrial economies, the U.S. corporate income tax emerged from this moment as particularly progressive.[78] New Deal liberals believed in "corporate personality." If a corporation was a legal person, then its income could be taxed no differently from that of any other legal person, including flesh-and-blood individuals.[79]

Much New Deal economic policy still aided large-scale business interests, from credit subsidies to wage-earning supports for workers.[80] But the change in rhetoric at the White House had effects. Returning the acrimony, business interests pivoted hard against FDR and the New Deal.[81] The Chamber of Commerce and NAM lobbied vigorously against the "soak the rich" bill. *Business Week* reported that the rift between FDR and business "seems complete and permanent."[82] A new pattern emerged, in which the federal government acted to facilitate capitalist enterprise even while many businessmen railed against its tax and regulatory policies. Politically, FDR stopped trying to explain to capitalists that he might well be "their savior."

The Public Utility Holding Company Act of 1935 was perhaps the most direct assault against the owners of capital of any piece of New Deal legislation. It was another Frankfurter, Cohen, Corcoran job, working in alliance with southern Democrats, led by Texan Sam Rayburn in the House. When he was governor of New York, FDR had been an advocate of public electric utilities. In 1932 most power was generated by privately owned utilities, and 40 percent of private power was generated by three sprawling national holding companies—the greatest being Samuel Insull's of Chicago—that had bought up smaller companies through debt and stock issues. The collapse of utility stocks in particular had helped trigger the

Great Crash of 1929. Insull fled the United States on charges of fraud, only to be extradited from Turkey (and found not guilty).[83]

If soak-the-rich income taxation was a Populist ideal, public utility regulation was a Progressive staple.[84] To Frankfurter, the parallel between nineteenth-century railroad corporations and early twentieth-century power utilities was perfect. The preamble to the Public Utility Holding Company Act declared, "Public-utility holding companies and their subsidiary companies are affected with a national public interest."[85] The purpose of utilities was to provide a public service in return for a "reasonable" rate of return above cost and nothing more—a politicization of capital income. The act's infamous "death penalty" granted the SEC the authority to break up holding companies if the ownership of noncontiguous systems under the same financial umbrella could not be demonstrated to benefit the "public interest." Meanwhile, through its public investments, the TVA was beginning to generate public power, charging and publicizing a "yardstick" for electricity against which to measure the reasonableness of private rates and profits.

Next, the Social Security Act of 1935 concerned the politics of income, with respect to pay, or labor earnings. Social insurance, perhaps the ultimate emblem of the New Deal's commitment to security, was another culmination of Progressive reform. It was shaped by FDR's demand—according to Barbara Armstrong, a UC Berkeley professor and member of the President's Committee for Economic Security—that American social insurance be no "dole."[86] The final bill, complex if only because of intense private insurance lobbying, added new citizenship entitlements to old-age pensions and unemployment insurance.[87] Benefits were "contributory." If relief simulated the capitalist wage bargain, Social Security simulated a private insurance contract. The act levied payroll taxes on pay for employees of sufficiently large enterprises. Reserves accumulated in a "trust fund," kept separate from general revenue, and paid out benefits that were scaled to contributions. Means-tested benefits for women and children— Aid to Dependent Children, it was called—were a second welfare track. Despite the fact that women wage earners represented 25 percent of the U.S. workforce, the founding principle of Social Security was the male-breadwinner-female-homemaker ideal.[88] Architects of Social Security, including Grace Abbott—although Labor Secretary Frances Perkins demurred—explicitly sought to salvage male breadwinning. Abraham Epstein of the Council on Economic Security said:

> The American standard assumes a normal family of man, wife, and two or three children, with the father fully able to provide for them out of his own income. This standard presupposes no supplementary earnings from either the wife or young children. . . . The wife is a homemaker rather than wage-earner.[89]

The New Deal state also would make heterosexuality an explicit criterion of what Epstein called "normal."[90] Social Security catered to industrial, male wage earners, working in large corporations where payroll taxes could be easily collected. The program excluded rural and domestic workers, many of whom were members of minority racial and ethnic groups. Initially, only 15 percent of all wage-earning black women were entitled to Social Security benefits.

The Banking Act of 1935 reformed the Federal Reserve System.[91] It increased the powers of the system's Washington-based board of governors. The board, its chairman, and its vice-chairman were now to be nominated by the president and confirmed by the Senate and were independent of the regional banks. Furthering the downgrading of the power of the New York Fed, five of the twelve regional bank presidents joined the governors on a rotating basis on the new Federal Open Market Committee, which enjoyed the power to set short-term interest rates in the money market and to determine member bank reserve requirements. The effect was to dilute the power of private bankers in monetary policy.

Finally, in the Second Hundred Days, Congress passed the National Labor Relations Act, otherwise known as the Wagner Act after its chief legislative sponsor, New York senator Robert F. Wagner.[92] Wagner's bill to legally enforce workers' collective bargaining rights had sat on the Senate's dockets for fifteen months, while FDR equivocated. When the Supreme Court killed the NRA and Section 7(a), FDR declared the Wagner Act "must" legislation. The act salvaged 7(a) and created a new administrative court, the National Labor Relations Board (NLRB). The NLRB would enforce workers' newfound rights in the workplace: to organize; to elect unions by majority votes certified by the NLRB; to have those unions recognized as their exclusive bargaining representatives over wages, hours, and working conditions; and to go on strike. The Wagner Act further outlawed "unfair labor practices," which barred employers from interfering with the exercise of workers' bargaining rights. Finally, the NLRB would determine the appropriate "bargaining unit," opening the possibility of industrial rather than AFL-style craft-based labor organizing. The American Liberty League declared the act "more than six times as dead as the Supreme Court could kill it."[93]

Instantly, a social movement for industrial unionism erupted. The AFL, dominated by skilled craft unions outside the mechanized mass production industries, did not take the initiative. Instead, it was a national affiliation of industrial unions, led by John L. Lewis of the United Mine Workers. At the AFL's 1935 annual convention in Atlantic City, Lewis and a number of mass production unions formed the Congress of Industrial Organization (CIO), which then set about organizing the mass production industries.[94]

At this time, FDR accepted the Democratic Party's 1936 nomination in Philadelphia, lashing out against "economic royalists." His campaign crested with an October 31, 1936, rally at Madison Square Garden. The president told speechwriters Tommy the Cork and Ben Cohen to "take off all gloves."[95] They did. "Organized money," FDR roared, is "unanimous in their hate for me—and I welcome their hatred." The "selfishness and lust for power" had "met their match" in FDR's first term; in a second term, he promised they would meet their "master."[96]

The presidential election of 1936 was a historic landslide, securing the New Deal. FDR drubbed the Republican candidate, Alf Landon, winning every single state except Maine and Vermont. In 1932 FDR had swept the South and West. Now, he made even greater inroads into the northeastern-midwestern manufacturing belt—reaching industrial workers that William Jennings Bryan had failed to capture in 1896. The AFL's Gompers-style "pure and simple" unionism had restrained itself from entering mass politics, but Lewis, though long a Republican, had no such misgivings. The CIO contributed somewhere between 10 and 15 percent of the Democratic Party's 1936 expenditures.[97] Organized labor's seat at the table of New Deal liberalism was bought and paid for with money and votes.

FDR's winning 1936 coalition encompassed the labor left in nearly all its varieties. Many Communists had supported FDR since 1934, after the Soviet Union called for a "popular front" against fascism. Now a "cultural front" also aligned itself with the New Deal.[98] The WPA would perhaps most be remembered for Federal Project Number One, which spent $27 million to hire unemployed American artists. The WPA-funded art of the 1930s—plays, folklore collections, murals—had one ever-present theme, and that was the dignity of human labor, especially of physical labor, whether it was fruit picking, harvesting, railroad track laying, construction, or machine welding.[99]

In the arts, a new "social documentary" aesthetic took hold. Painters, writers, poets, filmmakers, and photographers all attempted to move "in the direction of reality," to capture the "extraordinary actuality" of the Depression, as the greatest twentieth-century poet, Wallace Stevens, put

SEYMOUR FOGEL, *INDUSTRIAL LIFE (MURAL STUDY, OLD SOCIAL SECURITY BUILDING, WASHINGTON, DC)* (1941)

A great theme of 1930s art, especially much of the public art sponsored by the WPA, was the dignity of human labor. Notably, the mural was designed for a Social Security Building. Social Security was premised upon wage earning—no "dole," as FDR put it.

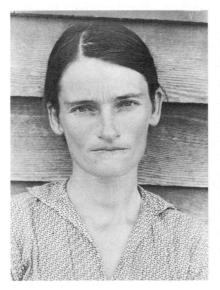

WALKER EVANS, *ALABAMA TENANT FARMER WIFE (ALLIE MAE BURROUGHS)* (1936)

An iconic Evans photograph from his and James Agee's *Let Us Now Praise Famous Men*. Burroughs was a Hale County, Alabama, sharecropper. "Realist" artists like Agee and Evans during the Great Depression made great efforts to empathize with and depict the poor.

it.[100] Arguably the greatest American work of art created during the 1930s was in this sprit: that was James Agee and Walker Evans's *Let Us Now Praise Famous Men* (1939), a blend of creative and empathic nonfiction that featured photographs of impoverished southern sharecroppers.

Not coincidentally, FDR's historic 1936 electoral triumph coincided with the CIO's historic union organizing drives at U.S. Steel and General Motors.[101] A week after FDR's reelection, the AFL ejected the ten CIO unions, which now became an independent national affiliation. Lewis had already hijacked the formerly AFL-affiliated steelworkers union, which was focusing on U.S. Steel's massive plants south of Chicago, which alone produced almost as much steel as Germany, the world's number-two producer. By January 1937, by organizing unskilled white ethnic workers long shunned by craft unions, the CIO claimed to have enlisted 125,000 workers. U.S. Steel blinked. With heavy order volumes, and having returned to profitability in 1935 despite operating at only 39 percent capacity, the corporation did not want to disrupt production. Lewis agreed to a 20 percent wage hike. The Wagner Act had shifted the politics of pay in the direction of labor earnings. The workweek was reduced from forty-eight hours to forty, with time and a half for overtime. When union and company officials met on March 17, 1937, to sign the agreement, a union negotiator noticed that a portrait had been removed from the day before. "Whose picture was there yesterday?" The answer was "Old H. C. Frick. They took him out. Didn't think he could stand it."[102]

No less extraordinary were organizing drives by the CIO-affiliated United Auto Workers (UAW) at General Motors and the Ford Motor Company.[103] The UAW's membership surged from 30,000 to 375,000 between April 1936 and August 1937. Since mass production depended on a continuous mechanized flow, it was vulnerable to choke points—to just one worker stopping the line. The UAW employed a new tactic of dubious legality, the sit-down strike.[104] Workers seized the GM "Fisher One" plant and occupied it for six weeks. Neither the Michigan governor nor FDR would intervene on the company's behalf. GM relented and released a one-page document recognizing the UAW as the sole bargaining unit at GM. Elsewhere in Detroit, "We will never recognize the United Automobile Workers Association," declared Henry Ford.[105] When UAW organizers distributed handbills on a pedestrian overpass outside the River Rouge factory, Ford "security" physically assaulted them, while reporters snapped photographs.[106] The UAW stalled at the Rouge.

JAMES KILPATRICK, *BATTLE OF THE OVERPASS, FORD MOTOR CO., U.A.W.* (1937)
In the wake of FDR's labor-backed 1936 electoral triumph, the wave of New
Deal–backed unionization hit one wall at the Ford Motor Company in 1937.
A staged United Auto Worker photo-op led to the "Battle of the Overpass," in
which Ford's security guards assaulted Dick Frankensteen (seen here) and
Walter Reuther of the union. The fallout in publicity hurt Ford's image.
The company would finally unionize during World War II.

But if there is one reason why, in the United States, a left-leaning liberalism emerged from the Great Depression as opposed to a right-wing populist, if not fascist, nationalism as in other polities (and the UAW's union
drive in Detroit took place near the home of the right-wing anti-Semite
Father Charles Coughlin), it was because of the presence of a left-leaning
organized labor in the New Deal's winning political coalition—and not
only its presence but its assertion.[107]

5. Economic Consequences of the New Deal

The beginning of FDR's second term is a good moment to step back and
assess. The New Deal had reflated prices, passed adversarial regulations of
banking and finance, mingled public and private in agriculture to increase
farmers' market power, made economic security and male breadwinning

the overriding concerns of political economy, and made forays into developmental policies. The regulatory arm was stronger than the developmental, and income politics was the rule. Since 1933, U.S. economic life had enjoyed a broad-based recovery. By 1936, a number of lasting post-1933 economic trends for which New Deal policies were responsible, both intentionally and unintentionally, had become visible. The economic consequence of the New Deal was to advantage large-scale enterprise and to support high productivity, high male wages, and high-energy auto-industrial society.[108] Further, New Deal policies reconfigured the relationship between the agricultural and industrial sectors, creating a long period of balance between them.

By 1936 many measures of economic activity—prices, production, and incomes—had recovered to 1929 levels. What was initially responsible for that? It was not a fiscal policy of government deficit spending, which had not been tried on principle. It was not the Fed, or monetary policy, whose discretionary supply of credit remained at more or less constant levels, as short-term interest hovered above zero in the midst of the liquidity trap.[109] The main early pivot of recovery was, rather, the devaluation of the currency upon the departure from the gold standard in 1933, which broke deflationary expectations and led to a recovery of spending of all kinds, including the most dynamic factor of investment.[110] Meanwhile, after Hitler's rise to power in 1933, as many feared a Nazi-induced inflation, much gold departed from Europe and fled into the U.S. banking system, which helped expand credit and raise prices.[111] The American maintenance of the liberal dimensions of its democracy was, quite literally, worth its weight in gold. By 1940, the United States possessed an astonishing 80 percent of world gold reserves.[112] Meanwhile the AAA's supply-side program also helped reflate prices, while it increased rural demand for manufactures and thus spurred recovery. Even if they were short-lived, NRA's price-fixing "industry codes" contributed to the price reflation.[113]

If we peek inside the dynamics of this recovery, a number of qualities stand out. In manufacturing, many large capital-intensive corporations had returned to profitability by 1935. The Fordist mechanization of existing industrial capital had proceeded. Manufacturers continued to adopt and extend new high-productivity, large-scale mass production methods. Industrial scale steadily increased, as the New Deal did little to help what became known as "small business" ride out the Depression. Yet if fixed investment in capital equipment recovered to nearly its 1929 peak, investment in the construction of new factories recovered only to half of its pre-Depression level. Basically, firms retooled existing factories to take advantage of mass production methods. For instance, factory electricity generation surged at a greater rate than during the 1920s.[114] In fact, the 1930s were a particularly innovative decade for industry. Given the emphasis on technology, the pre-Depression expansion of white-collar work continued. Tellingly, employment in industrial "research and development" nearly tripled. Patent applications were up. In chemicals and plastics, new products, such as polyethylene (1935) and Teflon (1938), arrived. Productivity growth in manufacturing continued to surge, as it had during the 1920s.[115]

That helps explain another 1930s trend: the persistence of male unemployment. The growth of white-collar jobs meant that many women entered white-collar employment. (Faith Baldwin's 1933 *White Collar Girl* was a best-selling novel of the decade.) That increased female labor incomes, although it did not so much as budge the gender gap in pay.[116] As productivity increased, many firms produced the same level of output by employing less labor. The labor that was employed tended to be relatively skilled. Despite persistent unemployment, manufacturing wages rose during the Great Depression.[117] Perhaps employers had kept on their most productive workers, who tended to be more highly paid. Meanwhile the AFL's craft unions protected skilled, high-wage laborers. For those with jobs, the Wagner Act guaranteed industrial unions' collective bargaining rights over pay and hours.[118] Altogether the 1930s featured what is called today a "jobless recovery."

Outside the manufacturing core, in the cotton South and west of the Mississippi, similar dynamics were at work. Productivity surged through mechanization, and the scale of enterprise increased. The number of small farms decreased, as a corporate farm bloc emerged.[119] At the same time, AAA regulations ensured that the growth of commodity production, commodity prices, and farm incomes would stay in line with the needs of industry, whether for inputs into production or for demand for its finished goods. After all, the misalignment of industry and agriculture during the 1920s speculative boom had contributed to the general bust after 1929. Meanwhile, in the South and West, the New Deal's developmental arm made more decisive contributions to the pattern of future economic life.

During FDR's first term, farm incomes increased 50 percent.[120] New

Deal policies also began to induce people to leave the land. Before, under-employment in the U.S. agricultural sector had acted as an economic drag, especially in the South, given the toxic marriage of sharecropping and white supremacy. Mechanization had failed to take command during the Age of Capital. At first, New Deal legislation remained locked in its "south-ern cage," dependent on the votes of Jim Crow Democrats.[121] But after 1935, New Deal agricultural programs increasingly supported sharecrop-pers' rights.[122] The absolute number of farm tenants decreased by 25 per-cent between 1935 and 1940.[123] Planters used federal credit subsidies to mechanize pre-harvest labor, then employ wage labor at harvest time. To-gether with national minimum wage decrees, the New Deal state finally began to undermine the regional separation of the South's low-wage labor market from the higher-wage North—a blow to the economics of Jim Crow. In favoring mechanization over agricultural labor, the New Deal also primed southern economic life for the mass black out-migration of World War II.[124]

As for developmental initiatives, New Deal policies affected residential investment everywhere. By 1939, banks originated $4 billion in FHA-insured loans, and the residential construction industry had nearly recov-ered.[125] West of the Mississippi, however, the impact of the New Deal's developmental hand was most visible.[126] There, public investment was the most consequential.

By March 1939, the PWA had deployed billions of dollars through pri-vate contractors and government agencies.[127] Fixed "street and highway" capital increased by two-thirds through the 1930s. A large share of the economy-wide productivity gains during the 1930s have been attributed to the building of roads, tunnels, and bridges. Schools, post offices, train stations, and airports were also built. The "PWA Moderne" architectural style featured solid massing, evoking stability, and lines that swerved, as if they were electric.[128] What had been called "internal improvements" in the Age of Commerce increased the national extent of markets, bringing about an Age of Control wave of Smithian economic growth.[129] The over-whelming bias toward spending on infrastructure of the more sparsely populated West created political support for the New Deal. "We shall tax and tax, spend and spend, and elect and elect," intoned WPA head Harry Hopkins.[130]

The largest, most capital-intensive projects were electric power genera-tion plants. In the South, David Lilienthal's TVA generated electricity at the public "yardstick" rate of kilowatt-hour, to a new network of municipal and cooperative utilities. Meanwhile Jesse Jones's RFC state capitalist empire offered cheap consumer loans for farmers, especially in the South, to buy electric appliances—say, General Electric refrigerators—and to thereby become consistent electric utility customers. The RFC supplied $246 million to the Rural Electrification Administration.[131] The PWA's largest individual projects were the completion of the great western hydroelectric power dams, the largest concrete dams in the world—Bonneville, Shasta, and Grand Coulee. Congress had appropriated funds for the Hoover Dam in 1932. Folksinger Woody Guthrie wrote no fewer than twenty Columbia River ballads while on the Bonneville Power Administration's payroll.[132] In the West, New Deal public investments set the foundation for a future high-energy, high-productivity, mass production and mass consumption auto-industrial society.

Harold Ickes explained that PWA public investments were needed "because of the timidity of private capital to come out from under the bed."[133] Relative to the pre-1929 "trend," the recovery of economic activity still had a long way to go. Above all, unemployment remained high—still 10 percent in 1936.

6. Capital Strike

In 1937–38 came a sharp economic downturn, the so-called "recession within the Depression," particularly in the industrial sector. Many New Dealers finally began to make the correct diagnosis: the economic problem had been not overproduction but rather underinvestment and underconsumption. They began to consider using government deficit spending to kick-start private economic initiative through a fiscal multiplier.

However, by now a bitter enmity between many liberals and many industrial capitalists had broken out into the open. Industrial capitalists threatened not to invest unless their political demands were met, especially for lower taxation on their incomes. Precautionary liquidity preference, born of panic and fear at the beginning of the decade, had transformed by the decade's end into a political weapon wielded by the New Deal's capitalist critics. Economic possibility became subject to a dynamic of political psychology. Liberalism had spent much energy on income politics, professing an illiquidity preference for long-term fixed capital investment that provided employment to men. But its chief weakness was that it had no effective politics of capital investment to ensure its stated aims, in the face of unwillingness by the owners of capital to invest in the first instance. Here the New Deal hit a wall, as did the economic recovery.

The trouble began after FDR's 1936 electoral triumph, when the president overplayed his political hand. Following the U.S. Supreme Court decisions in *Schechter*, which overturned the NRA, and in *United States v. Butler* (1936), which overturned the AAA, FDR feared more New Deal legislation was in legal jeopardy. He threatened to "pack" the Supreme Court by appointing new members. Congress balked, and the president suffered politically for the overreaching suggestion. Nonetheless, the Court changed its tack. *NLRB v. Jones and Laughlin Steel Corp.* (1937) accepted the constitutionality of the Wagner Act under the Commerce Clause, while Congress quickly repassed AAA policies under the Soil Conservation and Domestic Allotment Act. As cooperative relationships fused between the federal government and agricultural interests, a "corporatist" political economy, rid from industry by the death of the NRA, survived in agricultural policy.[134] Such corporatism never took root in U.S. industry.

Meanwhile Jim Crow Democrats sensed that the New Deal might threaten the economic basis of white supremacy. Matters came to a head in the debate over the administration's proposed Fair Labor Standards Act, which set maximum hours and minimum wage laws.[135] In 1938 Congress passed a bill that, while mandating a maximum forty-hour workweek and a forty-cent-per-hour minimum wage, included gaping exemptions for agricultural and domestic workers—namely, many southern black workers. After the publication of the administration's critical *Report on Economic Conditions in the South*, FDR unsuccessfully campaigned against a number of conservative Democrats in the 1938 primary.[136] Soon the CIO attempted to organize black workers in the South. Jim Crow racists successfully pushed back. Southern Democrats joined anti-labor Republicans in advocating a rollback of the Wagner Act.[137]

In the 1938 congressional elections, Republicans made gains for the first time since the Depression. One reason was that in 1937 the Depression was back. The 1937–38 slump was a uniquely industrial event. Unemployment climbed from 9.2 percent in 1937 to 12.5 percent in 1938. In industry, the numbers were 21.3 percent to 27.9 percent.[138] The reasons for the downturn were many. FDR's administration sent deflationary signals, worrying publicly over inflation and committing itself in 1936 to fu-

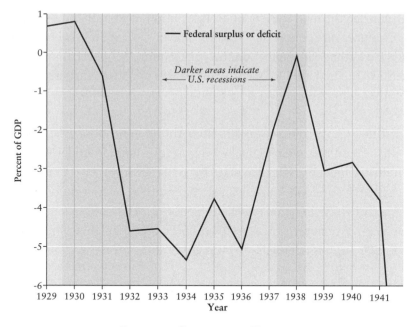

Federal surplus or deficit

Darker areas indicate
← U.S. recessions →

FEDERAL SURPLUS OR DEFICIT

The federal government never attempted deliberate deficit spending in order to aid economic recovery; FDR's second administration's attempt to balance the budget contributed to the 1937 recession within the Depression. The cause of the post-1939 deficit was federal spending on military preparedness.

ture balanced budgets. While in 1936 Congress had passed a one-time $1.8 billion "Bonus Bill" to World War I veterans over FDR's veto, in 1937 the federal government began to collect Social Security payroll taxes, which withdrew potential spending from economic activity.[139] During the sit-down strike at GM, many consumers expected that future wage gains would be passed on to them in higher prices, so they immediately purchased cars. After the strike, automobile purchases plummeted by 600,000 units in 1938.[140] The Fed, still working in liquidity-trap territory, mistakenly doubled commercial bank reserve requirements, which limited the flow of credit money. Finally, fearing inflation, the Treasury Department began to "sterilize" gold—effectively removing it from circulation, so that it would not lead to the expansion of credit—from Europe in December 1936.[141] Altogether private investment depressed. As it failed to return, it became clear that a confidence game between the federal government and the owners of capital had begun.

Organized through the National Association of Manufactures and the U.S. Chamber of Commerce, a leading bloc of U.S. capitalists blamed the lack of investor "confidence" on the "uncertainty" of government policy. The New Deal had brought security to farmers and wage earners only, apparently. Lammot du Pont II sang capital's grievances:

> Uncertainty rules the tax situation, the labor situation, the monetary situation, and practically every legal condition under which industry must operate. Are taxes to go higher, lower or stay where they are? We don't know. Is labor to be union or non-union? . . . Are we to have inflation or deflation, more government spending or less? . . . Are new restrictions to be placed on capital, new limits on profits? . . . It is impossible to even guess at the answers.[142]

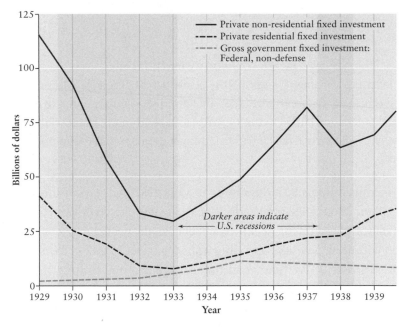

FIXED INVESTMENT

Public investment was not a main driver of economic recovery from the Great Depression. A collapse in private nonresidential fixed investment (investment in industry) was a major cause of the 1929 and 1937 downturns; subsidized by New Deal programs, the recovery in private residential fixed investment (investment in housing) was strong over the 1930s, contributing to recovery.

To this day, the owners of capital level the same charges against government. Back then capitalists complained especially about the 1936 "undistributed profits tax," which taxed profits that companies did not immediately invest or distribute through wages or dividends—a direct policy assault on the precautionary hoarding of corporate cash.

In the winter of 1938, Treasury secretary Morgenthau pleaded with the president to abolish the undistributed profits tax in order to alleviate "uncertainty" and spark investor "confidence." New Dealer Adolf Berle worked in concert with Thomas Lamont of J. P. Morgan to broker a grand truce between FDR and the business community. Business "cannot be spanked into prosperity," Lamont instructed the president.[143] Confidence, expectations, uncertainty—all were politicized. FDR believed there was a "capital strike," parallel to the CIO sit-down strikes. Corcoran, Cohen, and Frankfurter (in one year nominated by the president to sit on the Supreme Court) convinced FDR that no truce was possible. Concentrated economic power was responsible for the slump, against which the New Deal state must square off, in adversarial style.

The federal government's confrontational stance did little to induce investment. But this late New Deal impulse quickly translated into a lasting liberal politics of adversarial business regulation. The Justice Department's head lawyer Thurman Arnold's *The Folklore of Capitalism* (1937) called on this new "religion of government" to police bad business behavior, such as various anticompetitive practices.[144] Indeed, in a complete reversal of the abolished NRA, FDR now approved the reinvigoration of the Democratic Party's old cry of "antimonopoly" on behalf of equality of commercial opportunity.[145] The 1938 Temporary National Economic Committee (TNEC) opened public investigations on "monopoly," and the Justice Department antitrust division let suits fly. In industry, this activated the New Deal's regulatory arm that had been present in banking and financial regulation since 1933.

Meanwhile, as the business-branded "Roosevelt recession" wore on, another New Dealer faction coalesced with a new developmental agenda, distinct from adversarial business regulation. The loose group formed around WPA director Harry Hopkins, who now believed that private business activity would never recover to levels sufficient to end unemployment. These men included New Dealers such as the presidential adviser Leon Henderson, Jerome Frank (purged from the AAA, now at the SEC), Marriner Eccles, head of the Federal Reserve, and his staff economist Lauchlin Currie, among others.[146] They all, at some point, had argued that "under-consumption," not "overproduction," was the economic problem stunting development. Now they argued that with the 1937 withdrawal of private industrial investment, compensatory government spending—including deficit-financed public investment—must fill the gap.

The British economist John Maynard Keynes had just published *The General Theory of Employment, Interest, and Money* (1936), making a very simple economic argument. Say's Law (named after the early-nineteenth-century French economist Jean-Baptiste Say) stated that supply creates its own demand, or that for every seller there must be a buyer. That is because in a given period of time in the process of production, what individuals are paid to produce provides them with the money income sufficient to pur-chase the goods they have produced. Paid as incomes, production costs translate into necessary purchasing power. This is true, Keynes said, only if money is considered a means of payment. But money is also a store of wealth, over periods of time. For a variety of motives—what Keynes origi-nally branded "liquidity preference"—given uncertainty, individuals will store their wealth in money and money-like assets rather than spending their entire incomes. When capitalist economies grow fast, consumption may not increase at the same rate as money incomes. For their part, the owners of capital will not spend on investment unless they expect future pecuniary profits. If they do not, and if they prefer the security of storing their wealth in liquid assets over the risk of an investment, they will not spend all of their incomes on investment. Altogether not all money in-comes earned will be expended to purchase the volume of goods that must be produced in order to employ all willing workers. Capitalist economies may therefore be demand-constrained, stuck in a state of semi-slump below their full present and future supply-side potential.

Paradoxically, the greater the growth of money incomes—running out ahead of consumer spending, while making investment-sapping liquidity preference possible—the more likely a below-potential state of economic affairs might exist. A fresh source of demand from outside the system is required, to kick-start supply, which then, as Say's Law premised, creates more demand. Keynes referred to this process of demand leading to supply leading back to demand as the theory of the "multiplier."[147]

In *The General Theory*, Keynes argued that in a state of semi-slump, with the economy in a liquidity trap, monetary policy—government's discretionary setting of interest rates—may become impotent. Thus only government expenditure can kick-start investment—the kind of spending with the biggest bang for the buck. That is because investment generates expenditure on capital goods, often leading to the production of consumer goods, thus redounding in the largest possible stream of spending. Investment is therefore the best outside source of fresh demand—the best multiplier. When government spending does the trick, there is a fiscal multiplier.

In the late 1930s, it was needed. Capitalists themselves still suffered from disquietude and were falling down on the job of investment, hoarding out of precaution instead. Keynes proposed in *The General Theory* that a volume of investment sufficient to end mass unemployment would likely "prove impossible without a far-reaching change in the psychology of investment markets such as there is no reason to expect." Keynes wrote, "I conclude that the duty of ordering the current volume of investment cannot safely be left in private hands." *The General Theory* recommended "a somewhat comprehensive socialization of investment . . . though this need not exclude all manner of compromises and devices by which public authority will co-operate with private initiative."[148]

But cooperation between FDR's administration and the private initiative of industrial capitalists had broken down. *The General Theory* had yet to make an impact as a book, but Keynes's ideas were in circulation.[149] And he clearly saw the political bind posed by his theory. He attributed the 1937–38 recession to a "peculiar kind of new crisis of confidence," leading to the "failure of durable investment to develop."[150] In February 1938 he wrote to FDR, "You must either give more encouragement to business or take over more of their functions yourself." If "public opinion" was not "yet ripe" for a greater role for public investment in, say, electric utilities, then "what is the object of chasing the utilities round the lot every other week?" In light of political liquidity preference, FDR's administration had only two options: to socialize investment or to coddle capitalists. As for the owners of great wealth, "If you work them into the surly, obstinate, terrified mood, of which domestic animals, wrongly handled, are so capable, the nation's burdens will not get carried to market."[151]

In March, Hopkins cornered the president while vacationing in Warm Springs, Georgia. He was accompanied by, among others, Beardsley Ruml, a member of the PWA's National Resources Planning Board who was familiar with Keynes's ideas. He also drew from the work of the Commerce Department, charged by Congress in 1932 with developing a statistical measure of the "national income." U.S. economist Simon Kuznets had just published his pathbreaking *National Income, 1929–1932* (1934), which computed the annual national income, an aggregate of all money incomes that flowed from production in a given year—a progenitor of the gross domestic product (GDP) statistic.[152] Ruml and Henderson estimated that the U.S. national income was $56 billion. That would be a prospective $32 billion, they approximated, short of the economic output necessary to bring employment up to full potential. Citing the concept of a multiplier, when targeting $32 billion, Ruml advocated government expenditure of somewhere between $7 billion and $10 billion in "*additional* investment or spending, public or private, to get reasonable full employment." Ruml projected $4 billion in forthcoming private investment. Therefore he recommended to FDR a program of $3 billion in direct public investment—a new kind of jolt to economic development.[153]

FDR accepted the argument that the need for public investment was greater than the need for a reduction in government budget deficits. In April 1938 the president proposed to Congress a "new" federal expenditure of $1.5 billion for public works. It would raise the "national income" from $56 billion to $80 billion (the numbers kept shifting), which was necessary, FDR argued, to end the scourge of mass unemployment.[154] Congress went along. But first it slashed the capital gains taxes and killed off the undistributed profits taxes. Government spending went up, and taxes went down—something of a truce. The federal budget, $89 million in deficit in 1937, was $2.85 billion in deficit in 1938. Meanwhile the Treasury Department ended the "sterilization" of gold inflows, which helped expand the money supply. Altogether in 1938, the mini-slump began to lift somewhat.

Some historians have argued that the New Deal's turn toward budget deficits in 1938 represented the "end of reform," since New Deal liberalism became preoccupied with adjusting macroeconomic aggregates rather than transforming the core institutions of capitalism through political and legal interventions.[155] The attempt to induce greater private investment by slashing taxes on the owners of capital—a core policy staple of New Deal liberalism over the decades, persisting to this day—confirms such an analysis. However, the owners of capital rightly hold no prerogative so dear as control over investment. The struggle over it would dominate the Age of Control.

Ruml and his allies in favor of robust public investment programs remained on the attack in 1939. They cobbled together the Works Financing

Act to create twelve regional public "investment trusts." The business lobby raised massive opposition. That, and the lack of Jesse Jones's support at the RFC—he believed the proposed act went too far in the direction of public authority—killed the legislation in Congress.

In September 1939, Hitler invaded Poland, and the subject of FDR's fireside chats became war in Europe. U.S. unemployment was still stuck in the double digits, as the New Deal had failed to achieve its great goal of reemploying white male breadwinners. Much more, it left open the question of employing them to do what exactly? Keynes believed increased government expenditure in the right dosage could end the slump (end all slumps). But he also drew a troubling conclusion: "It is, it seems, politically impossible for a capitalistic democracy to organize expenditure on the scale necessary to make the grand experiment which would prove my case—except in war conditions."[156]

CHAPTER 14

NEW WORLD HEGEMON

—

URING THE GREAT DEPRESSION, THE LIGHTS WENT OUT on capitalism. Economic activity ceased, as if a power station failed and electric currents ceased to flow. That is not just a metaphor but quite literally what happened. For despite the recent electrification of industry, many of the new mechanized mass production assembly lines idled throughout the 1930s, their power shut off.

What capitalism lacked was energy from a human source, the ability to pull people and resources back into the industrial economy and get the line moving again. The profit motive was not enough, nowhere near enough. The owners of capital could not be induced to part with their money and money-like assets. Entrepreneurial energy was lacking. Nor was mere electricity, available in greater abundance due to the New Deal state's developmental public investments, enough either. Capitalism suffered from a general lack of social and psychic energy. During the 1937–38 recession within the Depression, political enmity between New Deal and organized business interests had become yet another source of economic enervation.

What finally provided the necessary jolt was an all-consuming "total war." World War II was the most total of all wars, fought not only between armies but also "with, for and against peoples."[1] The lead character in the popular war film *Mrs. Miniver* (1942), directed by William Wyler, said:

> This is not only a war of soldiers in uniform. It is a war of the people, *all* the people, and it must be fought not only on the battlefield but in the cites and the villages, in the factories and on the

farms, in the home and in the heart of every man, woman, and child who loves freedom.[2]

World War II did not just "mobilize" polities and economies—it veritably stormed mass psyches. During the Depression, capitalism required a kick start from outside the system. During the war, very little fell outside the effort. (Along with Joseph Heller's 1961 *Catch-22*, James Jones's 1962 *The Thin Red Line* was one of the two truly great American novels written about World War II, because its characters in the Pacific theater, even if just for moments, do successfully step outside the sheer magnetism of the conflict.) By pulling people and resources into its maelstrom, total war generated the "dynamic fields of violent energy," as the historians Michael Geyer and Adam Tooze have put it, necessary to shock national economies back to life.[3] In doing so, it took mass production to previously unimaginably prolific and destructive heights.

Public investment in the tools of war making was responsible. In Europe, Hitler's militarization of the German economy during the 1930s had sparked a rapid industrial recovery, curing mass unemployment. But in the United States, military spending was meager, and mass white male industrial unemployment was not yet licked. Of course, the Nazi Wehrmacht and the Luftwaffe were good for only one thing, invading and bombing other countries.[4] To defeat fascism on the battlefields, U.S. factories had to run full. Ships, tanks, guns, and bombs poured off the assembly lines. "Excess capacity" was no longer a problem. The U.S. warfare state allocated capital directly into the production of war matériel. The factory lights were finally switched back on, and many new factories were built. Liquidity preference, of any kind—speculative, precautionary, or political—was thrown out the window. For political reasons, fixed investment in production ruled.

Energy became a great theme of capitalism's twentieth-century history, a theme as old as the organic economy, certainly, but now with many new dimensions. During the 1920s Great Bull Market, speculative investment had placed psychic energies, and money capital, into liquid securities markets—just when, on the ground, electric energy began powering illiquid, productive fixed capital. The Depression depressed everything. Then during the war, through public investment, the "dynamic fields of violent energy" brought a high-energy industrial capitalism back on line. Everywhere war energized mass popular expectations for long-term development and greater abundance. Afterward a generation of long-term private, illiquid investment in wealth-generating industrial production throughout the world would follow, settling down industrial society. Meanwhile, during World War II, fossil fuel industrialism further became entrenched. During the war, oil was a great strategic prize, after all. If it had not already begun, the Anthropocene, or the geological era of man-made climate change, now became fated.[5]

The New Deal's western-focused developmental arm beefed up, and after Japan bombed Pearl Harbor in 1941, U.S. economic expansion was nothing short of stupefying. If depressed, the U.S. economy was still the world's largest in the 1930s. Mass production and "Americanism" had remained synonymous. Once the United States entered the war, by the end of 1942—the fateful year of the so-called war of the factories—U.S. unemployment no longer existed.[6] The remunerated workforce gained 11.25 million persons.[7] In the war economy, the government did not nationalize existing industries. Recalling the U.S. Civil War, a wartime blend of patriotism and profit blended into a dynamic amalgam, a propulsive force. Prodigious public investments in newly constructed "government-owned, [private] contractor-operated" (GOCO) enterprises drove war production forward.[8] The public allocation of capital induced private industry back to life. By the opening of 1943, in the Grand Alliance against the Axis powers, the Soviet Union was still doing most of the fighting, and the dying, by far, but the awesome potential of U.S. mass production began to be unleashed, and soon it would overwhelm its enemies. The job was finished in 1945 when the most horrifying weapon in history, the atomic bomb, was dropped on the civilian populations of the Japanese cities of Hiroshima and Nagasaki.

By then, the U.S. strategic achievement was spectacular. Most warfare states had ruthlessly shifted their resources from consumption to military production. Soviet starvation became a badge of patriotic honor; despite a starving population, the Japanese army appropriated the entire potato supply to process gasoline. While economic historians debate whether World War II even constrained American civilian consumption, the United States built the first fighting force in the history of the world that was capable of strategically commanding two oceans.[9] American GIs arrived on foreign soils bearing cornucopias of Spam, cigarettes, and chewing gum. In 1945 the Soviet Union's Red Army was the largest, occupying Europe as far west as Berlin. But much of the world's industrial capacity lay in a smoldering ruin. Apart from one failed Long Island German U-boat landing and a few Japanese balloons carrying flammable materials that harmlessly peppered American shores, the U.S. economy emerged without a scratch.

One must risk hyperbole: the United States enjoyed global economic preeminence on a scale unmatched in history. Meanwhile another total war was fought over nothing short of the very way that life should be lived. Stalin said victory brought not only the occupation of territory but also the right to declare a "social system."[10] U.S. capitalism held out one such vision of the good life, and behind it was the obliterating apocalyptic nuclear capacity of U.S. state power. At this point, the history of American capitalism inescapably becomes global history.

At home, wartime Americanism brought about an overriding public interest in political economy on a scale never before seen in American history. Would it last, and would it aid postwar New Deal liberalism's project of control? During the war, the New Deal state's regulatory arm supercharged in unison with its developmental arm, slapping numerous controls on economic life, including price and wage controls as well as income taxes. As the economy approached the frontier of its productive capacity, such policies also tamped down inflation—New Deal liberalism's great future nemesis.[11] During 1944, as the outcome of the war looked increasingly secure, planning began for peacetime. Battle lines had already begun to appear in preparation for the great postwar political struggle over the size and purpose of the New Deal state. The final political-economic settlement of the Age of Control, the mix of regulatory and developmental policies, waited for the war to end. But "big government" was here to stay.

1. Arsenal of Democracy

When Germany invaded Poland on September 1, 1939, the United States had an army of 175,000 soldiers. That barely edged out Bulgaria for sixteenth place in the world.[12] FDR reaffirmed the U.S. policy of "neutrality," even as, in important ways, American engagement with the world was shifting and widening. Soon the president would announce the creation of an economic "arsenal of democracy" to aid the Allied powers. Already, in the autumn of 1939, the U.S. war economy was roaring to life, and the Depression began to lift.[13] By aiming public investments at military targets, it might not be that hard to end the slump after all.

Hitler's invasion of Poland revealed beyond doubt his bid for Nazi domination of continental Europe. The Führer wrote down some chilling reflections on American economic history.[14] Germany's European rivals, he said, had enjoyed far-flung overseas empires that granted their economies access to menial labor, raw materials, and export markets. Hitler's *Second Book* (1928) noted that the United States had developed differently. Americans conquered the North American landmass, removing, by violence, a putatively racially inferior native population. Hitler compared eastern Europe's Slavs to America's "Red Indians." He was sorry that the American Civil War destroyed "the beginnings of a great new social order based on the principle of slavery and inequality."[15] The film *Gone with the Wind* (1939) was a favorite of both the Führer and the Nazi minister of propaganda, Joseph Goebbels. The aim of the Third Reich's twentieth-century version of a continent-wide settler-colonialism was to create *Lebensraum* for Germans and to absorb crucial raw inputs, especially oil, into the German economy. Germany might then even rival the United States in economic might.

Decades before Hitler celebrated Americans' nineteenth-century imperial past, the United States had made its own bid for a European-style overseas empire. The Spanish-American War (1898) was the largest U.S. land grab since the Mexican-American War (1846–48). The United States acquired overseas colonial possessions in Puerto Rico, Guam, and the Philippines, and in 1898 it annexed Hawaii. In the Philippines, the U.S. troops waged a brutal racial war of occupation that lasted until 1902 and was responsible for no less than 200,000 Filipino deaths.[16] In the Americas, U.S. troops landed in Nicaragua and Cuba. They occupied Haiti and the Dominican Republic. U.S. financiers and monetary reformers tethered the banking systems of the Philippines and many Caribbean and Latin American nations to a U.S. dollar standard—in part, to ensure the interests of U.S. creditors abroad, who wanted their loans repaid in dollars.[17] Hitler was not wrong: the continental United States still provided the lion's share of raw inputs into U.S. economic production. But the "Greater United States," as the historian Daniel Immerwahr has put it, was expanding.[18] Certain raw materials that the continental United States did not possess— bauxite, for instance, a mineralogical source of aluminum, a new construction material of the Machine Age, with large deposits in South America—were critical to new mass production industries.

The New Deal altered the U.S. imperial trajectory.[19] The Depression undermined foreign banking and effectively shut off many international financial relationships, imperial or not. At the 1933 Pan-American Conference in Uruguay, FDR's secretary of state, Cordell Hull, voted in favor of a resolution that "no state has the right to intervene in the internal or external affairs of another." The United States ended all occupations of Latin American and Caribbean countries by 1934—apart from a naval base in Guantánamo, Cuba, and a military base at the Panama Canal Zone. The Philippines Independence Act of 1934 held out Filipino independence after a ten-year transition period. Internally, New Deal legislation revived the possibility of federal acknowledgment of Indian sovereignties. So while Hitler was attempting to colonize continental Europe, the United States was rethinking the basis of its colonial holdings. An imperialism that seeks out new territorial and colonial possessions is, after all, only one possible mode of hegemony.

During the 1930s, a different form of U.S. economic engagement with the world was emerging, focused less on ensuring the mobility of finance capital than on reviving world trade. The "Open Door" policy toward China of the late 1890s was an important precedent. The United States acknowledged Chinese territorial sovereignty but demanded that China allow unhindered economic access to its markets.[20] In this vision, the United States leveraged state power to ensure foreign market access, and thus demand, for U.S. goods, more than it put U.S. boots on the ground to oversee "nonwhite" populations. With an Open Door flavor, the 1934 Reciprocal Tariff announced U.S. commitment to trade liberalization throughout the world and granted the president the authority to negotiate bilateral trade agreements in order to slowly chip away at ever-tightening European imperial trading blocs. Further, many New Dealers supported national programs of economic "development," which meant industrialization, throughout the world.[21] In 1940, for instance, the United States provided capital, credit, and technical assistance to Brazil for the construction of its Volta Redonda steelworks.

Meanwhile the United States had withdrawn from engagement with European affairs. After World War I, despite its sheer economic clout, the country had not attempted to seize the mantle of hegemony. Even as the Great Depression unraveled the peace, and Hitler plunged Europe into a gray zone of semi-war, a mass American social movement supported "neutrality."[22] In 1936, fully 95 percent of polled Americans said the United States should stay out of foreign wars. Congress passed three Neu-

trality Acts that embargoed U.S. sales of "arms, ammunition, or implements of war" to belligerents.[23] The Neutrality Acts did not restrict U.S.
arms sales to countries that were not at war. Through this channel, the
U.S. war economy began to take shape.

The foreign buying spree began in the summer of 1938, after a group of
British officials toured Lockheed Aircraft's California facilities. By April
1940, Britain and France ordered nearly six thousand planes, injecting
$573 million into fledgling firms such as Douglas, Lockheed, North Ameri-
can, the Glenn L. Martin Company, and the Curtiss-Wright Corporation.
After Great Britain and France declared war on Germany following its
1939 invasion of Poland, Congress revised the Neutrality Acts so that the
United States could still export arms to the Allies. Over the objections of
more isolationist midwestern representatives, southern Democrats provided the votes. Czechoslovakia, say, had been an important U.S. cotton
importer—but not after it fell to Germany in 1938. The South balked at
federal programs of public investment generally, for fear that the federal
government might undermine the southern racial order. But it did support
FDR's May 1938 request for a $1.1 billion naval appropriation to expand
the U.S. fleet by 20 percent. The 1938 Air Corps Expansion Act called for
almost tripling the size of the U.S. fleet. Total U.S. military spending for fiscal year 1939 was $650 million, surpassing all nonmilitary federal expen-
ditures.[24]

When the German blitzkrieg rolled out of the Ardennes forest in the
spring of 1940, and France surrendered, Congress authorized $6.5 billion
in military spending. FDR proclaimed that the United States would build
the world's first "two-ocean navy" and strive to produce what at the time
seemed a staggering "50,000 planes a year."[25] U.S. rearmament was fully
under way in July 1940 when the German Luftwaffe flew over the English
Channel and the Battle of Britain began.

U.S. rearmament was massive.[26] In the last half of 1940 alone, the federal government invested $1.4 billion in fresh manufacturing construction
(compared to $1 billion in private investment that year).[27] The mechanism
was public investment in what was called "government-owned" but private "contractor-operated" facilities, or GOCO. Jesse Jones's state capitalist
RFC empire was the largest umbrella for many new public corporations,
charged with the task of allocating fixed investment, the largest being the
Defense Plant Corporation (DPC). Under the guise of military necessity,
private industry now welcomed public investments. For instance, in June

1940, the War Department contracted with DuPont—the great political nemesis of the New Deal—to run a five-thousand-acre smokeless powder facility in southern Indiana. Meanwhile the U.S. Army invested in the famed Chrysler Corporation–operated 690,000-square-foot Detroit Tank Arsenal. The GOCO agreement guaranteed the reimbursement of all production costs as well as the allowance of a predetermined profit—"cost plus." This became the GOCO norm. Chrysler's Detroit Tank Arsenal would go on to manufacture twenty thousand tanks, including the M3 "Grant" and M4 "Sherman" models.

Economic production and employment began to lift. Undoubtedly, the jolt aided FDR's historic reelection in 1940 over the Republican Wendell Willkie, the former head of the Commonwealth & Southern electric utility, a great nemesis of the TVA. "These foreign orders mean prosperity in this country and we can't elect a Democratic Party unless we get prosperity and these foreign orders are of the greatest importance," FDR noted in private.[28]

As U.S. assembly lines were rolling, Britain began to buy war matériel for which it could not possibly pay. In December 1940, FDR announced that America "must be the great arsenal of democracy." A Lend-Lease Bill passed Congress by large majorities. The United States would loan war matériel, food, and critical raw materials—especially oil—to Allies, who, in principle, would return it after the conclusion of hostilities (which they mostly did not). Between March 1941 and September 1946, the United States would expend $50 billion on Lend-Lease items.[29] That alone was more than the $40 billion in total expenditures by New Deal agencies between 1933 and 1943. The large bulk of Lend-Lease would go to Britain. The next greatest recipient would be the Soviet Union, which FDR had recognized in 1933; when Hitler reneged on his 1939 agreement with Stalin and invaded the Soviet Union in June 1941, the USSR had joined the Grand Alliance against the Axis powers. That invasion was Hitler's greatest error.

In 1941 FDR asked Congress for $7 billion in Lend-Lease appropriations, but also another $13.7 billion for U.S. rearmament. Total military spending for fiscal year 1941 would be $12 billion—a tenfold increase since 1938. The DPC funded the construction of the largest factory in the world, Ford's Willow Run facility, in Ypsilanti, Michigan. Albert Kahn, Henry Ford's old industrial architect, designed both Chrysler's Detroit Tank Arsenal and Willow Run. With 3.5 million square feet of space, Kahn's design called for more than 1.5 million square yards of concrete.

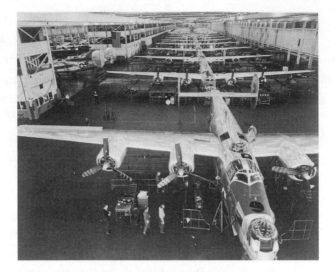

"B-24 LIBERATOR ASSEMBLY LINE AT
FORD WILLOW RUN BOMBER PLANT" (C. 1944)
A great symbol of the American victory in World War II's "Battle of
the Factories," Ford Motor Company's Willow Run B-24 bomber production
facility was said to be the largest one-roof factory in the world. On the
production line, there was room enough for 110-foot winged airplanes
to make full ninety-degree turns.

In the summer of 1941, Willow Run began building B-24 bombers.
Bombers were made from aluminum—an industry that up until then had
been dominated by one corporation, Alcoa. Refining aluminum takes
twelve times as much energy as refining steel. DPC capital helped the
Reynolds Metal Company develop facilities in both Alabama and Washington, near cheap sources of public hydropower. World War II would help
launch both the airplane and the aluminum industries.[30]

Meanwhile, as German forces poured into the Soviet Union, Japan,
which became Germany's formal ally in September 1940, was stymied in
China, where hostilities had broken out in 1937. The United States would
not acknowledge Japan's claim to govern resource-rich Manchuria, but it
was far from providing the Republic of China the kind of support it was
providing Great Britain. Japan eyed the resource-rich European colonial
possessions in Southeast Asia, including British Burma and Malaya,
French Indochina, and above all the oil-rich Dutch East Indies.[31] In the
summer of 1941, Japanese forces moved south into Indochina. In re-

sponse, the United States embargoed oil and froze all Japanese assets. Japan had imported most of its fuel from the United States, but now watched Lend-Lease American oil tankers cruise to the Soviet Union while its own supply diminished. On December 7, 1941, Japan bombed a number of American military bases in the Pacific, including the large naval base at Pearl Harbor in the U.S. colonial territory of Hawaii. The United States declared war on Japan. Germany and Italy declared war on the United States.

2. The Battle of the Factories

Total war mobilizations were not all the same. At first, Japan and Germany had advantages because of their prior 1930s militarization. The German logic of blitzkrieg was to strike and conquer before larger, more potentially productive enemy war economies could be brought to bear against it.

Other mobilizations were more labor intensive, squeezing the energies of their populations more ruthlessly than those in the United States. Germany, in fact, hoping for a colonial *Lebensraum* windfall, did not engage in all-out mobilization until mid-1943, by which time it was too late—U.S. military production was peaking, and the tide had turned.[32] Truly nothing compares to the Soviet experience.[33] In the European theater, the epic Soviet victory in the Battle of Stalingrad (August 1942–February 1943), where combined military and civilian casualties ran around 2 million, was the decisive battle of the war. Compare the 419,000 U.S. wartime dead to the estimated 27 million Soviet. Only the grotesque final death throes of the Japanese and German regimes in 1944–45 matched the enormity of Soviet suffering. By contrast, in a February 1945 Gallup poll, almost two-thirds of U.S. civilians admitted they had not made "any real sacrifice for the war."[34]

U.S. economic mobilization was of the capital-intensive and thus the labor-saving variety, relative to the Axis powers' labor-intensive strategy.[35] New Deal supply management policies, for instance, with their "parity" farm commodity price floors, continued to foster land-saving agricultural mechanization.[36] Military mobilization brought many existing factories back on line and paid for new ones. At the same time, productivity soared. In industry, the war reformatted business expectations of what would be possible after the war. Meanwhile, pulling labor into the factories, wartime production ended mass unemployment, the greatest scourge of the Great

Depression. Quickly, a new social expectation of government was born, that unemployment would never return.

After Pearl Harbor, the United States began its all-out industrial mobilization for war. 1942 was a year of construction; 1943, production; 1944, fighting. Industrial production peaked in October 1943, at which time manufacturing, in value-added terms, reached its highest share in all of U.S. economic history.[37] In January 1942, FDR created the War Production Board (WPB), naming the affable Sears corporate executive Donald Nelson its head. FDR also announced fantastic production targets, including 60,000 planes and 45,000 tanks in 1942 alone. That led to the "feasibility debate" in Washington, in which the WPB and military departments disputed national economic capacities and priorities.[38]

Assisting the deliberations were new kinds of statistics. In the Commerce Department, a group led by Milton Gilbert, a former student of Simon Kuznets (who in the 1930s had developed the construct "national income"), developed the construct "gross national product" (GNP). GNP was a yearly measure of the income flow of total output, including war matériel. The Commerce Department first published a GNP figure in 1942. GNP was 25 percent higher than Kuznets's national income. Kuznets dissented from GNP accounting in his *National Product in Wartime* (1945), pleading for a more welfare-sensitive measurement of growth than how many bombs were built.[39] Regardless, the Commerce Department announced that, given the available supply of economic resources, the U.S. economy was massively below its productive frontier. FDR's prodigious 1942 requests were only slightly scaled back. The attitude was, let mass production rip.[40] If FDR has asked for 60,000 planes in 1942, then over the course of the war, the United States would manufacture 300,000.

For Keynes's *The General Theory of Employment, Interest, and Money* (1936), World War II would be a vindication. Between 1942 and 1945, net private investment was negative. Public investment however was $99.4 billion.[41] A fiscal multiplier went to work, as public investment pulled unused resources and capacities off the sidelines, while adding, through new factory construction, a fresh source of demand from outside the economic system. Spending redounded, and economic activity brought increasing returns, with a cumulative effect. Economic output multiplied by a factor greater than public investment, and unemployment nearly disappeared. During the war, Keynes's economics of total national output and employment—branded "macroeconomics"—spread across government bureaucracies and statistical agencies.[42]

During the war, GNP rose 58 percent. Americans built military bases, ammunition depots, airplanes, tanks, warships, guns, and bombs. If Keynes was right that there was no good reason for the Great Depression to have persisted, then Kuznets was also correct that the content of GNP "growth" raised a larger issue: total output and employment increased, for sure, but on behalf of mass destruction and millions of deaths.

In orchestrating the war effort, the WPB had final authority. In practice, the RFC and DFC placed public investments, and the army and navy handled procurements. Responsibility was so divided that in 1943 FDR created another supra-agency, the Office of War Mobilization, headed by the conservative U.S. Supreme Court justice South Carolinian James Byrne. Despite confused lines of authority, public and private productively mixed, and the war machine began to hum.

In war production, GOCO "cost plus" with large industrial corporations continued to be the preferred arrangement. The Northeast remained a significant home to shipbuilding, but the Midwest, more impervious to potential foreign attack, fared better. The largest new factory of the war would be the $175 million Chrysler-Dodge plant on the South Side of Chicago, to manufacture engines for Boeing B-29 bombers. The plant's main assembly room—this was Albert Kahn's last industrial factory design—featured 3.5 million square feet of space, and the thirty thousand employees parked their cars in the world's largest parking lot. (Today the plant is a shopping mall.) Still, the greatest economic transformation of the war occurred outside the now historic northeastern-midwestern manufacturing belt.

The argument has been made that World War II, while increasing aggregate demand sufficient to cure mass unemployment, distorted the economy by too narrowly diverting economic activity into war production, stunting supply-side economic development.[43] The case has merit but fails to fully appreciate the geographical transformation of U.S. economic life. For during World War II, a third, western industrialization took place, with far-reaching consequences.[44] After the iron-, wood-, and textile-based industrialization of the Northeast during the Age of Commerce; and the steel-, coal-, and eventually mass production–based industrialization of the Northeast and Midwest in the Age of Capital; now, in the Age of Control, industrialization was based on aluminum, hydro-power, and electronics. It took place in the South but above all in the Pacific West.[45] This time the driver was not a speculative investment boom, which was up to this point the most dynamic impulse of American capitalism. It was the federal government, which stamped one factory onto the ground after another. In but three short years, U.S. economic geography radically changed.

The New Deal had set the stage. The Grand Coulee and Bonneville dams supplied the electric power necessary for war production in the Pacific Northwest. But if the New Deal had delivered $7.5 billion in spending to the West, World War II brought no less than $70 billion, accounting for 90 percent of all wartime western investment capital.[46] In Fontana, California, forty-five miles inland in case of Japanese attack, the RFC loaned the industrialist Henry Kaiser $100 million to construct the first integrated steelworks west of the Mississippi.[47] Nationally, the capacity-use rate in steel production reached 97 percent in 1941. Steel, along with oil production, was one of two major industries where private investment, funded by tax incentives, remained robust.[48]

Henry Kaiser was a western New Deal entrepreneur who had joined with Warren Bechtel, founder of the privately owned (and still privately owned) San Francisco–based Bechtel construction company to become one of the six companies that built New Deal–era dams in the West.[49] After Pearl Harbor, Kaiser constructed "Liberty ships," the Model T of the seas, in Portland, Oregon, and Vancouver, Washington, although his largest yard, funded with DPC capital, was in Richmond, California, north of his Oakland home. "Pop" Kaiser joined the ranks of the great industrial paternalists. He paid high wages and welcomed black workers, women workers, and unions to Richmond. Paycheck deductions financed the Permanente Health Plan. The Richmond yards would build 20 percent of all Liberty ships, and Kaiser shipyards constructed 30 percent of all U.S. wartime ships, employing 200,000 workers. The RFC and DPC combined invested $364 million in Bay Area industrial facilities, and the region received $4 billion in contracts.[50] FDR's two-ocean navy was built.

At the center of the wartime Pacific transformation, however, was the city of Los Angeles. At the beginning of the war, only 5 percent of the Los Angeles County labor force was in industry. The region was dominated instead by motion pictures, oil, and fruit canning. Soon the Pacific West manufactured nearly half of all U.S. warplanes, and the big-six aircraft manufacturers—Douglas, Lockheed, Vultee (called Consolidated after 1943), North American, Vega, and Northrop—located themselves along a corridor running near Los Angeles Airport that was built by the Works Progress Administration. By 1944 no fewer than four thousand war factories were operating in Los Angeles, in all lines of industry. By 1945, Los Angeles County surpassed prewar Detroit in total value of war production (and in 1945 was second only to Detroit).[51] The California population grew by 3.5 million persons between 1940 and 1950.[52] California was now "the great world of the future."[53]

Pacific industrialization created demand for labor and coincided with the greatest moment of internal migration in U.S. history. Nationally, 57 percent of Americans changed residences, 21 percent crossing state lines—in addition to the 16 million mobilized by the military.[54] The federal government's War Manpower Commission oversaw migration.[55] The largest migration was the 8 million Americans who moved west of the Mississippi. Los Angeles had been a "Jim Crow town," but the great migration of more than one million blacks from the South finally began to undermine the regional segregation of southern labor markets from the rest of the country—a great economic blow to Jim Crow in the South.[56] One southern sharecropper who migrated to Pop Kaiser's Liberty shipyards recalled, "It looked like just about everybody was going into the army or doing war work [so] I sold my tools and mules and come out to Richmond."[57] California's population bulged by 3 million. Wartime industrialization pulled southern labor off the land, while in 1942 the Braccro Program oversaw the immigration of hundreds of thousands of "guest workers" from Mexico to work California's farm fields.[58] Nationally, the countryside was a large contributor of labor to wartime industry. Pacific industrialization helped finally eliminate underemployment on American farms, aiding rural mechanization, yet another capital-goods-intensive feature of U.S. war mobilization.

Rapidly, the Pacific West ended any semblance of dependence on the East, whether for "Pittsburgh-plus"-priced steel ingots or Wall Street finance. Its leading industries, especially aerospace, were militarily funded but also technologically innovative. The war saw new innovations in electronics, computing, the mass production of penicillin, and jet propulsion.[59] Professors at California Institute of Technology's famed Jet Propulsion Laboratory moonlighted for aerospace companies, and Stanford University in particular was hospitable to government-funded industry.

The top secret Manhattan Project for building the atomic bomb was led by the University of California Berkeley physicist J. Robert Oppenheimer. In GNP terms, bombs were good only for dropping. But wartime public investment planted a strong foundation for the western base of the future postwar "military-industrial" complex, as well as the end-of-the-twentieth-century new economy of Silicon Valley.

Stepping back, all warfare states spread industrial capacity into new regions, whether it was German-occupied eastern Silesia, or Japan's Pacific Belt. When Germany conquered 75 percent of Soviet industrial capacity, the Red Army, in the "great evacuation," relocated 2,600 factories and 12 million workers east of the Urals and stamped new war factories out of the frozen ground.[60] German, Japanese, and Soviet industry increased productivity by dragooning labor. Many of the Axis powers' absolute advances came on the backs of coerced labor. That was the basis of Albert Speer's production "miracle" of 1945. Japan most ruthlessly coerced labor in its Southeast Asian colonies. (The British Empire did that, too.)[61] There was no Pop Kaiser in Germany and Japan, but there were slave labor camps. Indeed, the Third Reich's colonization of eastern Europe looked more like the slave economy of Louisiana in Jefferson's Empire of Liberty than it did the high-tech industrialization of the wartime U.S. Pacific West, whose factories were filled with the descendants of southern slaves. There is a reason Bill Gates of Microsoft Corporation would hail from Seattle and not Silesia.

The Axis powers fought a relatively labor-intensive war compared to the capital-goods-intensive U.S. variety. Hitler's bloody drive for direct colonial control over eastern European raw materials and coerced, unskilled labor appeared ever more anachronistic as U.S. state capital financed one technologically innovative mass production industry after another from Seattle to San Diego. Meanwhile, the new expanding U.S. economy brought idling resources and people back into the fold; Fordist productivity gains continued to spread.[62] War necessity induced more efficient labor-saving methods in production. At Willow Run, production volumes of the B-24 Liberator bomber leaped from 75 per month to 432. In Kaiser's Liberty shipyards, prefabrication and replacing riveting with welding famously cut mass production times from eight months to a few weeks—in one instance, to four days.[63]

All these techniques would not be forgotten after the war, and they would energize business and mass expectations alike.[64] Further, the U.S.

military's vast networks of procurement, contracting, and delivery became a truly global effort.[65] The United States possessed vast internal reserves of necessary raw materials, including critical fossil fuels. During
the war, it produced half the world's coal and two-thirds of its oil. State
capital built the Big Inch and Little Inch oil pipelines from Texas to New
Jersey. Among the only necessary materials the United States ever was in
danger of lacking was bauxite for aluminum, which it acquired from British colonial holdings, and copper, which it acquired from Chile. Meanwhile Germany failed to logistically integrate much-needed Ukrainian
coal and iron ore and Baku oil supplies into its war economy. The Japanese, unable to control the necessary shipping lanes due to U.S. submarine
attacks, failed to incorporate much-needed oil, coal, and iron from its
newfound imperial possessions. By contrast, the United States transported
132 million freight tons across the seas during World War II.[66] It fed its
Pacific army largely from supply lines to Australia. The U.S. war effort was
a marvel of global logistics.

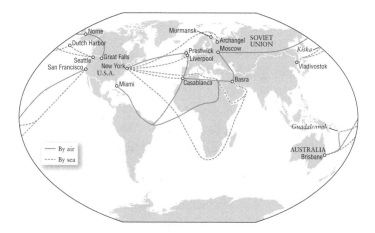

U.S. LEND-LEASE SUPPLY ROUTE DURING WORLD WAR II
The U.S. military's wartime global logistics network set a foundation
for postwar U.S. world political and economic hegemony.

By flipping the lights back on in the northeastern-midwestern manufacturing belt, constructing a new industrial corridor in the Pacific West,
and fashioning global supply chains, the Americans won the "war of
the factories." The pivotal year was 1942, when the United States produced $20 billion worth of munitions, compared to Germany's $8.5 bil-

lion and Japan's $3 billion.[67] Economic disparity reached the point of "overkill."

The war still had to be won. In the Pacific, the decisive campaign was the Battle of Guadalcanal, fought from August 1942 to February 1943. Given the disproportionate burden of suffering by the Russian people, Stalin fumed while FDR and Churchill kept American and British forces on the sidelines, as they deliberated over how to bring the superior U.S. economic might to the European continent. Churchill favored operations in the Mediterranean, to shore up the British Empire, while engaging in "strategic bombing" of civilians on the European continent. The United States, with better-armed airplanes, capable of flying higher and conducting daytime sorties, preferred to bomb military targets. But eventually the Americans gave way to the British strategy. The British incendiary bombing campaign of Hamburg, Germany's second-largest city and a major industrial producer, commenced in July 1943. It did not harm industry much, but it did engulf the city in fire, killing over 40,000 civilians. In November 1943, the Allies commenced the bombing of Berlin.

Over the course of 1944, Allied planes dropped more than a million bombs over Europe. Estimates vary, but in February 1945 a British strategic bombing campaign killed approximately 135,000 civilians in the German city of Dresden. In June 1944, Rome was liberated, and the Allies finally landed in Normandy, France. The Soviets advanced across German territory, discovering the death camps of the Nazi Judeocide. In April, Soviet troops reached Berlin. Italian partisans shot Mussolini and strung him up by his heels for public viewing. In his underground Berlin bunker, Hitler committed suicide. On May 8, 1945, Germany surrendered to the Allies.[68]

In the Pacific, U.S. forces bogged down. In March 1945 a strategic bombing campaign killed almost 90,000 civilians in Tokyo and burned down much of the ancient wooden city. The incendiary material was magnesium dust "goop," a by-product of a Kaiser San Francisco magnesium ingot plant.[69] Then in April 1945 FDR died from a stroke. The new president, Harry S. Truman, decided to drop atomic bombs on Japan to end the war.

The atomic program used the three largest public investments of the war to produce metals that had existed before only in microscopic quantities. That included prodigious state capital investments in two Oak Ridge, Tennessee, enriched-uranium plants, run by Union Carbide and Eastman

Kodak. TVA substations powered them. The top-secret Hanford, Washington, "site," for producing plutonium, covered 586 square miles along the Columbia River and cost $339.7 million.[70] Grand Coulee provided the extraordinary amounts of electricity necessary. DuPont ran the site, at no profit. At Hanford, eight water-cooled reactors cooked plutonium in aluminum tubes. Italian physicist Enrico Fermi arrived in Hanford in late 1944 to supervise the reactor. Convoys of ambulances then brought the first atomic bomb plutonium cores to Oppenheimer's Los Alamos Laboratory. The first experimental bomb exploded at Alamogordo on July 16, 1945.[71]

The big bang of American global supremacy was an atomic one. The United States bombed Japanese cities of Hiroshima and Nagasaki on August 6 and August 9, 1945, killing at least 139,000 people and likely tens of thousands more. Later, Truman said there had never been serious doubts about whether to drop the bombs. The plan had always been to build them, then to use them.[72] Japan unconditionally surrendered on August 15, 1945.

3. Big Government

It was World War II and not the New Deal that brought about the birth of American "big government."[73] Under the banner of a unitary national public interest, the federal government expanded prodigiously in sheer size and scope. On the side of capital, the New Deal's developmental arm had sprung to life through public investments. In the national emergency, its regulatory arm moved no less into action. In income taxation, in price, wage, and profit controls, and in monetary policy, the central state made dramatic interventions in American economic life. The economy would convert back to a peacetime basis, but there would be no putting the genie of big government back into the bottle.

The question became what big government should do exactly, or not, given its new capacities as well as what was desirable politically. The struggle over the answer to this question began to emerge during the war, certainly by 1943. As public investment expanded, the hostility of many business elites to the New Deal did not diminish. They began to agitate politically for government to return investment back to the private owners of capital after the war. Meanwhile New Deal income politics acquired momentum and took greater shape. Organized labor asserted itself. And as the total energy of World War II broke the back of the Depression's mass psychological pessimism, wartime Americanism contributed to a new mass expectation of capitalism. "Freedom," the war's great ideological rallying cry, must mean not only greater economic security but also abundance for all—including groups, such as women and blacks, excluded from the New Deal's prime income benefits. In the end, however, the war only solidified the New Deal's commitment to shoring up white male breadwinning.

The war granted legitimacy to national authority as never before in U.S. history. There was blatant coercion. J. Edgar Hoover's FBI prosecuted a number of dissenters.[74] The federal government interned 120,000 residents of Japanese ancestry, including at least 60,000 American citizens.[75] At first, in 1941–42, Americans' rather placid consent to big government and "war mindedness" was notable. Americanism seeped into and through workplaces, shopping markets, tax offices, and bedrooms. The great medium of wartime propaganda was film, which was handled by the Office of War Information's Bureau of Motion Pictures. New enlistees into the army were greeted by Frank Capra's *Why We Fight* series (1942–45) (some episodes of which were quite good). As the leader of the Motion Pictures Producers' Association explained, "We'll have no more *Grapes of Wrath*. . . . We'll have no more films that treat the banker as a villain."[76] Many members of the 1930s leftist "cultural front" joined the Grand Alliance against fascism. The film genre of "conversion narrative," in which class animosity and racial and ethnic tensions gave way to patriotism, had many entrants. The best was *Lifeboat* (1944), directed by Alfred Hitchcock, using a screenplay written by *Grapes of Wrath* author John Steinbeck based on his novella, in which the characters struggle to unite, despite their differences, against a Nazi threat, while at the same time warding off their own instincts to submit to authoritarianism. Hitchcock was of course one of the greatest of all filmmakers. During the war, more commonly corporate advertising directors, for now government employed, sharpened their tools in preparation for postwar consumerism.

The federal government made good on the immediate window of popular patriotic support. Congress's First and Second War Powers Acts of 1941 and 1942 granted the executive a sweeping mandate to intervene in private American economic activity, of the likes not seen in North America since the Confederate States of America. The 1941 Office of Price Administration (OPA), first headed by New Dealer Leon Henderson, was given a broad mandate to control prices and thus prevent inflation. In February 1942 government halted all civilian automobile production in favor of war production, and it restricted the production of many consumer durables, like furniture and refrigerators. In response, the OPA began to ration consumer items like gasoline and coffee. To enforce price caps, it enlisted as many as 300,000 volunteers, both men and women.[77]

Public investment and military expenditure required financing, in addition to managing consumption. To raise the funds, there were two possible mechanisms—taxation and debt. The war utterly transformed the U.S. fiscal state, bringing a mass but nonetheless redistributive income tax into the center of fiscal policy. Not the Great Depression but the war gave rise to a politics of "fiscal fairness," combating pretax economic inequality—one of the war's great contributions to income politics. Of the $413.7 billion in war expenditures, 49 percent came from tax revenue, overwhelmingly from the income tax.[78] It included a series of corporate "excess profits taxes," topping out at 90 percent. The effective wartime corporate income tax was between 50 and 70 percent.[79]

The U.S. national debt was $50.7 billion in 1940. By the end of the war, it was $251 billion. U.S. public debt reached 112 percent of gross domestic product (GDP). Through tax receipts and public debt sales, the federal government had no difficulty financing the national debt. U.S. economists inspired by Keynes's *General Theory*, a growing group, whose chief academic bases were at Harvard and MIT, claimed yet another wartime vindication. Abba Lerner's "Functional Finance and the Federal Debt" (1943), for instance, argued that in an economy that was producing under capacity, the issuance of debt could trigger the fiscal multiplier. The expansion of output and money incomes led to higher tax receipts, funding the debt issues.[80] Since the United States issued debt in dollars (not in a foreign currency it did not control), if need be it could always inflate away accumulated public debt. But an even better option would be to expand the production of goods. No inflation would occur or be necessary.

In public finance, in addition to the fiscal policies of public taxation, expenditure, and debt, there was monetary policy in the hands of the Federal Reserve. The Fed's tools included its capacity to expand the quantity of money through its discretionary power, as a lender, to set interest rates on credit, and to enter credit markets and purchase assets, including public debts (called "open market" operations). During the war, the Federal Reserve, led by Chairman Marriner Eccles, prioritized assisting the Treasury Department with its public debt issues. Through open market purchases, the Fed financed an estimated 23 percent of war expenditures.[81] Intervening in the public debt market, it sought to stabilize a rate of return of 2 percent for all bondholders (today a policy called "yield control"). It was "the 2-per-cent war," said Paul Samuelson, a wunderkind Keynesian economist at MIT.[82] The Fed kept interest rates low. It did not raise them in order to tamp down possible wartime inflation. (Price management was left to the OPA.) Unlike during private-led speculative investment booms, the interest rate played a very minor role in the allocation of capital during the war. The Fed was a servant, sponsoring the larger political project of fixed investment in all-out production. These were wartime policies, but there was no reason why they could not be used in peace, as well.

Mass production boomed, and unlike inflation during World War I, which had been 20 percent, inflation during World War II remained in check. Keynes, more fearful of inflation than many of his American followers, in *How to Pay for the War* (1940) had proposed forced workers' savings accounts, in part because forced savings would remove money from circulation and prevent demand from running out ahead of supply, a cause of inflation. Instead of forced savings, the Treasury Department embarked on a successful propaganda campaign to induce savings through popular investment in U.S. war bonds. Bugs Bunny, Elmer Fudd, Porky Pig, and Daffy Duck hit the screen to peddle U.S. government debt, insisting that the sacrifices of American soldiers abroad for freedom demanded financial sacrifices at home.[83] Additionally, by removing money from circulation, higher rates of income taxation tamped down inflation.

Meanwhile FDR announced the Leon Henderson–led OPA's "general max" policy in April 1942, which presented firms with a general target for restraining prices. Over the next year, the annual rate of inflation was somewhere between 5.1 and 7.8 percent. By April 1943, the OPA began to set specific targets, and until February 1946, inflation subsequently held at a paltry 1.4 percent.[84]

From price, wage, and profit controls, to high rates of income taxation, the extraordinary interventions taken by the federal government to restrain the price level and halt inflation are worthy of note—given their implications for the long-term fate of New Deal liberalism in the Age of Control. When the state held down interest rates on short- and long-term loans in order to induce private fixed investment, and issued debt to finance budget deficits and public investment, it pulled in untapped resources: labor, machines, and technological know-how. That led to the growth of total output and employment. But there were limits. Should there be no more resources left to draw from, should the "macroeconomy" reach its productive limit, monetary and fiscal expansion might lead to inflation—more money chasing a limited amount of goods. There is nothing wrong with inflation per se. Some inflation, by undermining the incomes of creditors, who tend to be bankers and financiers, fulfilled the distributional aspirations of New Deal liberalism. But high inflation might undermine expectations by creating future uncertainty about prices. For fear of future price increases, it might also encourage present consumption to the detriment of long-term investment. Meanwhile mass expectations of continued abundance—the expected payoff for wartime sacrifice—might lead demand to overshoot supply and become another potential source of inflation. During the war, the New Deal state managed inflation largely because of the OPA's price controls. Would such drastic interventions into the market price mechanism—into private activity—be politically palatable during peacetime? As the war wore on, OPA price controls became among the most unpopular measures of the U.S. warfare state. The New Deal was born to fight price deflation. The liberalism it gave birth to was potentially inflationary.

In 1943 inflation was held in check, yet cracks in the war-minded consensus broke out. Politically, conservative hostility to the New Deal reappeared. In the 1942 midterm elections, the Republican Party gained forty-seven seats in the House of Representatives and nine seats in the Senate. When the new Congress sat in 1943, Republicans acting in unison with southern Democrats, who before the war had already turned against the New Deal's most ambitious economic programs, shut down a host of New Deal developmental agencies. They included the National Resources Planning Board (NRPB), which had just published *Security, Work, and Relief Policies* (1942), which included a series of blueprints for postwar public investment programs. Then over FDR's veto, Congress passed the Revenue Act of 1943 that, while maintaining the sharp progressivity of the income tax, transformed it for the first time into a truly mass tax. In 1939 only 7 percent of U.S. households had paid a personal income tax. By 1945, almost two-thirds would. Revenue from the personal income tax finally superseded corporate income taxation.[85]

Outside Congress, the owners of capital counted their wartime profits, many guaranteed by the state through GOCO "cost plus" agreements, but they also began to assess the merits of big government for their long-term interests. A new business group, the Committee for Economic Development—led by Beardsley Ruml, a former member of FDR's administration, who had first persuaded FDR to turn to debt-financed public investment in 1939—sought greater government and business, public and private, cooperation. Far more vocally, the pro-business lobbies, the National Association of Manufactures (NAM) and the U.S. Chamber of Commerce, began to complain about government red tape and the assault on "private enterprise."[86] Government intervention, in their view, must not override the sphere of private economic activity. In particular, these lobbies sought to guarantee that after the war, responsibility for investment would be returned to private hands. In 1943, representing this faction, GM chairman Alfred P. Sloan asked NAM, "Is it not as essential to win the peace, in an economic sense, as it is to win the war, in a military sense?" Sloan warned of the ongoing "socialization of enterprise." If that happened, "private industry is finished."[87]

Also outside Congress, the wartime consensus broke down in the ranks of labor. Labor leaders made various demands. Some imagined the possibilities opened up by the war economy and articulated a new platform—"industrial democracy." Two steelworkers leaders, Clinton Golden and Harold J. Ruttenberg, in *The Dynamics of Industrial Democracy* (1942) argued that democracy in the workplace must mean that labor unions would have direct participation in production and investment decisions—which could lead to even greater productivity increases. Unions and management would collectively bargain over more than what ended up in workers' pay packets. But far more prominently, over the course of the war, the rank and file—expanding in numbers prodigiously—focused their demands on just that: pay. Further, groups that were marginalized and excluded from the economic benefits of the New Deal and collective bargaining thus far began to agitate for more.

At the outset of the war, labor had been calm. Leadership of both the AFL and the CIO had supported a "working-class Americanism" that patriotically submerged class conflict. Unions signed no-strike pledges. Sidney Hillman, a CIO leader from the Amalgamated Clothing Workers, agreed to chair the labor division of one of FDR's war boards. The National War Labor Board promulgated the "little steel formula," which limited pay increases to hold down inflation and set the workweek at forty-eight hours. It also proclaimed the labor-friendly "maintenance of membership" rule, whereby workers newly employed in a plant under a union contract automatically became dues-paying members unless they opted out in the first fifteen days of employment. Dramatically, in April 1941 the Ford Motor Company finally agreed to recognize the UAW. That year the CIO also organized Westinghouse, International Harvester, Goodyear, a number of West Coast aircraft manufacturers, and even a few southern textile companies. During the war, CIO membership climbed from 1.8 million to 3.9 million. In 1943 the CIO formed the first political action committee (PAC) to funnel donations to Democratic campaigns. By 1945, much because of the CIO's expansion, 35 percent of U.S. nonagricultural workers were unionized.[88]

However, CIO leadership could not enforce the no-strike pledge. In 1943 a wave of wildcat strikes broke out from the rank and file.[89] Between 1942 and 1945, more than 7 million workers joined no fewer than fourteen thousand strikes.[90] Most dramatically, John L. Lewis, leading the United Mine Workers out of the CIO in 1942, directed a number of contentious strikes over the "little steel formula." Complaining about the mild inflation, strikers demanded greater pay. In response, Congress passed, over FDR's veto, the War Labor Disputes Act of 1943, which granted the executive the power to seize and operate critical war production industries that were threatened by strikes.

Meanwhile, despite blemishes, the CIO was by far the most racially integrated of the more important national institutions. The war economy opened up significant opportunities for black workers. In 1941 A. Philip Randolph, head of the all-black AFL auxiliary Brotherhood of Sleeping Car Porters, visited FDR in the Oval Office and threatened a mass march on Washington. The president relented, issuing the executive order that "there shall be no discrimination in the employment of workers in defense industries or government because of race, creed, color, or national origin." The federal government created the Fair Employment Practices Committee (FEPC) to investigate complaints, the origins of New Deal liberalism's legal approach to handling workplace discrimination. By 1945, African-Americans accounted for 8 percent of war industry jobs, about the same percentage of the total population.[91] No executive order, however, prevented a number of spontaneous "hate strikes" against black workers in the summer of 1943. In Detroit, 25,000 Packard Motor Company workers went on strike when two black workers were promoted to nonmenial positions.[92] During the war, black intellectuals couched sharp critiques of racism in patriotic appeals, including in the compendium *What the Negro Wants* (1944). Simply, black Americans wanted the end of white supremacy. Leveraging wartime sacrifice, many African-Americans demanded a "double V" against oppression abroad and at home.[93]

Blacks were not the only group disadvantaged by New Deal income politics and its overriding commitment to white male breadwinning. In April 1943 the War Department issued a pamphlet to employers bluntly titled *You're Going to Employ Women*. Already, as men shipped off to battle, more and more women had entered a workplace sharply segregated according to gender and sex difference. In 1939 women's median annual income was $568, compared to $962 for men. Black women, long the most disadvantaged group in the labor market, earned a median income of $246.[94] Before the war, the female labor participation rate was already climbing, and it rose from 26 percent in 1940 to 36 percent by 1944.[95] The War Manpower Commission's propaganda campaign for "Rosie the Riveter" symbolized the scale of total mobilization. Nonetheless, by contrast, in Great Britain and the Soviet Union, female labor force participation doubled the U.S. rate. The war did foster a new cohort of American labor feminists. The black labor feminist Addie Wyatt, for instance, found a job in 1941 at a Chicago Armour meatpacking plant, and went on to lead a local.[96] However, after World War II, by choice or not, most American women would leave the factories.[97] By 1947, female labor force participation would slip back to 28 percent. The breadwinner-homemaker family ideal held strong during the war, as it had during the Great Depression.[98]

In this context, the most consequential piece of social and economic legislation that Congress passed during the war was the June 1944 GI Bill.[99] The legislation guaranteed World War II veterans a range of federal government entitlements, from a year of backstop unemployment insurance to residential mortgage assistance, education subsidies, and business loans. Economic entitlements thus flowed through male citizenship, explicitly defined by the GI Bill as heterosexual citizenship.[100] The principle that male pay was the chief currency of distributive justice was by now deeply rooted in the political economy of the Age of Control. In this respect, the war economy did what the New Deal did not do: in creating 11.25 million new jobs, it ended mass male unemployment. In his final, January 1944 State of the Union address, FDR called for an ambitious "Second Bill of Rights," of economic rights, guaranteeing jobs, housing, medical care, education, and living wages. All these rights, FDR noted—

hitting the central New Deal keyword—spelled "security." But in an increasingly conservative Congress, FDR's request fell on deaf ears. The Second Bill of Rights dropped like a dud. The narrower GI Bill passed instead. In 1944 *Fortune* conducted an informal poll, asking if the federal government "should provide jobs for everyone able and willing to work, but who cannot get a job in private employment?" Two-thirds answered yes.[101] In the 1944 electoral campaign, both political parties promised that government should guarantee "full employment," a new political and economic catchphrase.[102]

Upon the Allies' final victory in 1945, the federal government had an extraordinary number of economic regulations on the books, of both the regulatory and the developmental kind. Future control over investment still hung in the balance. Investment was no longer insufficient in volume (as it had been during the Depression), but its wartime content—bombs, tanks, and guns—would require peacetime conversion. Investment in what exactly? Keynes had written in 1933 that "decadent international but individualistic capitalism . . . is not a success. . . . But when we wonder what to put in its place, we are extremely perplexed."[103] In the United States, big government had at least one clear postwar rule of thumb. "The Government has a mandate from the people," *Public Opinion Quarterly* proclaimed in 1945. "The public wants jobs."[104]

The urgency to employ male breadwinners would dominate the dramatic postwar hinge, when the political economy of New Deal liberalism finally settled in place. The issue would be inseparable from the question of on what terms and by what principles the federal government would attempt to rebuild the war-torn world economy, given both the blunt power of U.S. economic and military might and the hegemonic aspirations of a triumphant cultural Americanism abroad.

CHAPTER 15

POSTWAR HINGE

"AMERICAN JAZZ, HOLLYWOOD MOVIES, AMERICAN SLANG, American machines and patented products," the entrepreneurial journalist Henry Luce promised the world in his 1941 declaration of a dawning "American Century" in *Life* magazine.[1] Now that the war was over, 1945 was a global "Year Zero"—a moment, though mixed with exhaustion and mourning, nonetheless of regeneration and possibility.[2] But the slate was not blank. However distantly, the world's peoples faced the brute fact of American power and influence.

Global domination of this order had not existed before. In 1945 the United States possessed roughly 70 percent of all gold reserves and half the entire world's manufacturing capacity. It had, by far, the largest food stores in the winter of 1945–46, when many populations around the world suffered from hunger, if not starvation. At the war's close, Americans owned three-quarters of all invested capital in the world, and the U.S. economy accounted for nearly 35 percent of world GDP—tripling its nearest rival, the Soviet Union.[3] In military terms, the Soviet Red Army, an unmovable force, occupied much of Europe, but the United States was the only atomic power, and the U.S. military boasted the only globe-spanning, high-tech logistical supply chain in the world. By contrast, the Red Army, bound within the Eurasian landmass, transported no less than half of its materials by horse-drawn wagons. Finally, implicated with anti-imperial postwar decolonization movements the world over was an Americanism aspiring to universal cultural hegemony, whether through the allure of mass consumption or through the new liberal imagination of "human rights."[4]

"WWII, Hiroshima, Aftermath of Atomic Bomb" (1945)
Hiroshima after the American dropping of an atomic bomb. An image of
hitherto unimaginable destruction, it also conveys the "Year Zero" quality of
1945, as a war-torn world embarked upon reconstruction in the context of
an unsurpassed American global might.

American statesmen seized the mantle of global hegemony. As early as
1941, FDR had promoted a new forum for international cooperation, the
United Nations. In U.S. policy-making circles, postwar planning was in full
swing by 1943. War Department and State Department officials drafted
plans for a global network of overseas bases and air rights privileges that
crisscrossed every ocean and every continent, touching down at Green-
land, the Aleutians, Karachi, Manila, and Curaçao.[5] At a minimum, the
United States would have access to crucial raw economic inputs, especially in Latin America and the Middle East, secured by the threat of violence if not by boots-on-the-ground formal occupation. In 1944 the United
States, Great Britain, the Soviet Union, and China began to deliberate over
the creation of the United Nations. The same year, 730 delegates from 44
Allied nations met at the United Nations Monetary and Financial Conference in Bretton Woods, New Hampshire, to negotiate working principles
for the postwar reconstruction of the world economy.

In 1945 much was up for grabs around the globe, and the United States
would have the power to shape what happened next. At the same time,
much was at stake at home. The war had energized both arms of the New

Deal state, the regulatory and the developmental. Only public investment in war-making industries had ended the Depression. The U.S. economy would undergo a peacetime "reconversion," as military spending reduced from 36 percent of GDP in 1944 to 3.5 percent by 1948.[6] But toward what ends? Americans had "grand expectations" for the economy but no less fear that the Depression might come back.[7] A government that could not ensure the employment of white male breadwinners could not expect to enjoy broad political support. Upon the conclusion of the war, various plans for "full employment" circulated as the final political struggle over the contours of New Deal liberalism came to its conclusion.[8]

In this critical conjuncture—the dramatic post-1945 hinge—international and domestic politics cannot be disentangled. Perhaps no other moment in the history of American capitalism is more worthy of detailed narration.

By 1948, the moment had closed. The Cold War between the United States and the Soviet Union had begun, and the world was splitting into capitalist and Communist blocs. The structure of the postwar capitalist world economy solidified. Bretton Woods named the U.S. dollar, newly pegged to gold, as the world's currency of reserve—against which to peg the world's other currencies. By exporting capital, commodities, and consumer culture, the United States sat at the capitalist world economy's hegemonic center. Meanwhile, as Coca-Cola sales increased abroad, the Cold War "containment" of Communism would lead to some brutal interventions throughout the world.

Also in the postwar decades, in order to employ men and foster economic growth, governments everywhere tried, one way or another, to induce or force fixed, illiquid investment in factories. Toward that end, Bretton Woods, while attempting to revive world trade, explicitly granted states the right to block cross-border, short-term speculative capital movements that might undermine their national economic objectives. But those objectives were not everywhere achieved in the same way.[9]

In the United States, the 1945–48 hinge saw a great industrial strike wave, contests over full employment legislation, the appearance of inflation, the reappearance of threats of capital strike, and a red scare. But by the time it was over, the U.S. owners of capital had seized back control over capital investment. In politics, large industrial corporations reasserted their prerogative over where and when to invest. Nonetheless, pressed by popular demands, they would invest in employment-giving production.

For that political reason, liquidity preference of any kind remained low. The postwar economic boom would be driven more by capitalists' sense of political necessity than by the credit cycle and private speculative investment. Political illiquidity preference ruled.

The events of the postwar hinge, however, severely stunted the New Deal's developmental arm, especially its capacity for public investment—a capacity that would never recover. The liberalism of the Age of Control (or after it) would never advance a successful politics of capital investment.

In the presidential election of 1948, in a surprise result, President Truman, who had ascended to the White House upon FDR's death in 1945, emerged victorious. Truman's instinct was to revive the New Deal's ambitions, but that was no longer politically feasible. In regulation, the adversarial monitoring of private business conduct remained on the books. And the U.S. welfare state had expanded through income politics, as U.S. income tax rates remained high and progressive. Meanwhile, in the greatest departure, the federal government acquired a new macroeconomic target: the "growth" of the national income. To foster and control the national macroeconomy, countercyclical fiscal policy was born. Austerity was no longer the cure for slumps. In times of recession—1948–49 being the first—federal government budget deficits propped up incomes and stabilized gross domestic product (GDP). But as private investment again became the first mover, the interest rate on money capital again played a leading role in the allocation of capital. Here, monetary policy reasserted itself. In 1951, for the first time since before the Great Depression, in monetary policy, the executive branch granted the Federal Reserve independence to again use its discretionary power over interest rates—raising them if necessary, even if that halted private investment—to control inflation, the postwar economy's great malady. These were the core economic policies of Cold War liberalism.

The federal government might tax and redistribute incomes, and it might regulate specific industries, but it remained incapable of acting autonomously and creatively in furtherance of a recognized public interest beyond "national security." Cold War military spending was the most legitimate form of government expenditure to sustain economic growth. What emerged in tandem with the new national security establishment was a "broker state," where competing "interest groups" jostled in Congress: organized labor, the farm bloc, the U.S. Chamber of Commerce, Social Security pensioners, and so on. That the government enjoyed an autonomous arena of action only when targeting benefits toward white male breadwinners, or invoking national security, warped state action at home and abroad. Breadwinning remained liberalism's currency of distributive justice, while macroeconomic policy focused on the abstract aggregate of national economic income growth, lacking the institutional tools to target specific places or to right more concrete relational economic wrongs—for instance, those rooted in racial domination or sex difference. Surely, government planning for long-term economic development on behalf of the public interest was off the table.

The Depression did not return, and a long postwar period of economic growth commenced. Given capitalism's recent post-1929 implosion, this must be counted a great success. The problem was that as industrial capitalism entered its postwar "golden age," the New Deal state had limited capacities to address the future fault lines of the fatefully intertwined U.S. and world economies.

1. Bretton Woods

During the Great Depression, both fascism and Communism had undeniably bested liberal democracies in eliminating mass unemployment while, not coincidentally, shunning the capitalist world economy. In 1945 statesmen and capitalists alike in the United States, let alone in those war-torn countries tasked with reconstituting democracy, shuddered at the possibility that mass unemployment might return. As the converted Keynesian economist Alvin Hansen had put it in a postwar planning document written as early as 1942, "If the victorious democracies muddle through another decade of economic frustration and mass unemployment, we may expect social disintegration and, sooner or later, another international conflagration."[10]

In 1944, with this in mind, Bretton Woods negotiators designed an international monetary system that—unlike the gold standard of the Age of Capital, a cause of the Depression—granted national economic policy makers some room to privilege domestic concerns over international economic obligations.

The negotiations at Bretton Woods over the postwar international monetary system began in July 1944.[11] The two leading figures were a U.S. Treasury official, Harry Dexter White, and the representative of the British Empire, John Maynard Keynes. White was a New Dealer who had written about the problem of international capital flight under the gold standard. Backed by U.S. power, he dominated the negotiations. He and Keynes agreed that the postwar monetary order should bring about a revival of international trade in goods. The United States favored free trade, already the focus of New Deal foreign policy during the 1930s, while Britain favored a system of trading preferences within its old empire. Nonetheless, they broadly agreed that a revival of global commerce in goods stood to benefit national economies.

White and Keynes also agreed that international finance was another matter. In order to secure national economic policy making, states must be able to limit short-term capital movements. White explained that cross-border capital controls "would give each government much greater measure of control in carrying out its monetary and tax policies," by inhibiting "flights of capital, motivated either by prospect of speculative exchange gain, or desire to avoid inflation, or evade taxes" that might undermine democratically determined national economic policies.[12] Keynes added,

> In the post-war years there is hardly a country in which we ought not to expect keen political discussions affecting the position of the wealthier classes and the treatment of private property. If so, there will be a number of people constantly taking fright because they think the degree of leftism in one country looks for the time being likely to be greater than somewhere else.

To White and Keynes, short-term speculative capital movements (what today are called short-term "portfolio" or "hot money" investments) were suspect and demanded regulation. International finance had only two proper functions. The first was to act as a servant to production by financing world trade in goods. That would trigger the old commercial multiplier, as trade would beget more trade. Economic activity would have increasing returns, and the cumulative effect would trigger economic development. The second function, long-term committed investment (what is now called "foreign direct investment"), could finance productive economic activity that might, as Keynes put it, "satisfy practical needs"—and trigger an industrial investment multiplier.[13] To sponsor long-term fixed investments, the Bretton Woods agreements created the International Bank for Reconstruction and Development, progenitor of the World Bank.

Few international bankers agreed with these doctrines. As before the

Depression, they hoped to be at liberty to place their money and pull it out anywhere they liked, at a whim. But the U.S. delegation agreed with White and Keynes. By inclination, many New Dealers were hostile to Wall Street. Further, at Bretton Woods, delegates from Latin American, Asian, and African countries hoping to industrialize their national economies gravitated toward a vision of the postwar world economy that favored long-term investment in production, even at the expense of globe-spanning private capital mobility.[14]

Where negotiations broke down at Bretton Woods was over the status of the U.S. dollar as the world's reserve currency. To finance world trade, any international financial system would require the expansion of credit money, in the context of bilateral national trading relationships in which, very likely, one country was a net creditor, another a debtor. Keynes saw that should creditor countries build up large credits, the resulting pools of cash might become a source of short-term hot money. To prevent this outcome, he had the brilliant idea of a new global currency. He called it the "bancor." The bancor would be an international "unit of account" only—fiat money issued by some new international institution. It would exist only for countries to clear their bilateral trading transactions, their credits and debts, with one another. It would be a money of transaction only—not a store of value, subject to liquidity preference of any kind. That is, the international arrangement would be for a "clearing union," to assist trade, as opposed to a liquid global capital market, to enable casino-like speculation. Finally, should large trade imbalances build up between countries, Keynes called for rules whereby creditors and debtors would share the burden of adjusting the value of their currencies. Once again, this mechanism was different from the gold standard, which had placed all the pressure on debtors to repair their balance of payments by deflating their economies—by raising interest rates and slashing wages. That mechanism had spelled disaster for national economies at the outbreak of the Great Depression.[15]

Ingenious though Keynes's bancor currency proposal was, the U.S. delegation balked. It wanted the U.S. dollar to be the world's reserve currency. Why should the dollar not express and reinforce U.S. world economic hegemony, as the British pound had in the era of the gold standard? Wall Street certainly wanted it to. Mindful of U.S. geopolitical power, even New Deal critics of Wall Street found bancors a bridge too far.

The final Bretton Woods agreement pegged the U.S. dollar to gold at the

convertible exchange rate of $35 to the ounce. This peg was never sup-
posed to budge. In turn, other national currencies would be pegged to the
U.S. dollar, at freely convertible rates with it and one another. At the same
time, the competitive devaluation of currencies—a strategic cheapening,
to gain a trade advantage—was forbidden. However, according to the
Bretton Woods agreements, currencies could be revalued in light of extreme international trade imbalances or reasonable national economic
needs. State capital controls could prevent cross-border speculation on
interest rate differentials and potential currency valuations. Altogether it
meant scope for national monetary and fiscal policy. National interest
rates could be set according to domestic priorities—not raised, deflating
prices, chocking off credit, and possibly halting expansion, all simply to
defend a fixed currency peg, as had been the case with the gold standard.
The risk that expansionary fiscal policy might provoke crippling capital
flight was less.

The Bretton Woods agreements called for the creation of the International Monetary Fund (IMF) in order to manage potential trade imbalances. Member countries would pay, in capital "subscriptions" of gold or
U.S. dollars, into the $8.8 billion fund based on "quotas," given their rela-
tive economic might. By far, the United States had the largest quota and
the most power at the fund. If member countries had difficulty managing
their international payments, the IMF had the discretion to grant them
loans in order to provide their currency exchange rate with "stability."[16]
The IMF was also granted discretionary authority to enforce the Bretton
Woods agreements, which were to go into effect in December 1945.

The Bretton Woods agreements had two fatal flaws. First, over time,
precisely as Keynes predicted and feared, due to trade imbalances, large
pools of U.S. dollars would build up in the international monetary system,
overwhelming the IMF. Due to speculative liquidity preference, the cash
would become the basis of short-term hot money rather than long-term
committed investment in productive activities to support national economic development and world trade—the point of Bretton Woods. Second, the U.S. dollar was the anchor of the Bretton Woods system, but
should the dollar-gold peg, at $35 to the ounce, ever be threatened—and it
would be—the entire international monetary system was at great risk. To
run a world economy on the basis of a single national currency was risky.

Keynes did not get his way at Bretton Woods.[17] Still, he left the meeting
in good spirits. Back in Britain, before his peers in the House of Lords,

Keynes bragged that Bretton Woods "accords to every member government the explicit right to control all capital movements. What used to be a heresy is now endorsed as orthodox." Across the Atlantic, a Wall Street banker invoked the legacy of Nazi capital controls and complained of the new "Hitlerian monetary system."[18]

2. Full Employment

In 1945 the United States sat on 70 percent of the world's gold supply. For Americans ever to become unable to defend the $35-per-ounce peg to gold was at that time inconceivable. Within the international context, no country had as much room to maneuver in its domestic economic policy as the United States (and it was not even close). In the immediate postwar conversion to a peacetime economy, American politics boiled down to one catchphrase: "full employment."

In January 1945 the left-liberal Montana senator James E. Murray introduced to Congress the Full Employment Bill.[19] The idea of full employment was a legacy of the war, when the wartime economy had eliminated voluntary unemployment. Inspired by Keynes, new "macroeconomists," inside and outside the government, had found new economic concepts, like "effective demand," and new statistical tools, like gross domestic product (GDP), to determine just how close the national economy was to operating at full capacity, using all available resources, including labor. Or not—that it was possible to still increase production and ratchet employment up further. During the presidential campaign of 1944, the Democrats had included a "guarantee" of "full employment" in their party platform. The Bureau of the Budget, an ever more powerful executive agency, circulated reports with titles such as *National Budgets for Full Employment* (1945) and *Fiscal Policy for Full Employment* (1945).

The policy idea was simple. Public investment had achieved full employment during the war. Why could it not guarantee the same afterward?

Not everyone agreed. Before he died, FDR had expressed very little interest in carrying public ownership of GOCO ("government-owned, contractor-operated") factories into peacetime. In preparation for the "conversion" of the war economy, he put the financier and pro-business New Dealer Bernard Baruch in charge of planning. In October 1944, following Baruch's advice, Congress passed the Surplus Property Act, which mandated that reconversion "give maximum aid in the reestablishment of a peacetime economy of free independent private enterprise."[20] If "full employment" was a powerful ideological rallying cry, "free enterprise" and "private enterprise," meaning government should leave all investment decisions to the private owners of capital, were phrases now commonly uttered by NAM, the Chamber of Commerce, and conservative congressmen.

Coming from left liberals, the Full Employment Bill, introduced in January 1945, was a rejoinder to the drift that FDR had established before his death. It evoked the spirit of the prewar Works Financing Act of 1939, which had called for regional public "investment trusts." In 1945 most left Keynesians retreated to agricultural bureaus, or farm labor unions, although they had allies. Interior Secretary Harold Ickes proposed that war factories be transformed into public corporations in which war veterans owned shares.[21] The United Auto Workers (UAW) announced support for such an idea.

The first draft of the Full Employment Bill declared the federal government's responsibility to provide "sufficient employment opportunities" for those "able to work and seeking to work." The proposed legislation called for the president to submit an annual budget to Congress that forecast the "aggregate volume of investment and other expenditure." If prospective private investment and expenditure were expected to fall short of that mark, then the "president shall include, in the Budget transmitted . . . a general program of such Federal investment and other expenditure as will be sufficient to bring the aggregate volume of investment" up to a level commensurate with full employment.[22] This was one vision of the postwar relationship between capitalism and democracy: a democratic politics of public investment. In good Keynesian fashion, it spoke of investment as a statistical aggregate, or volume, but it evoked the possibility that the content and composition of investment might be politicized as well. For the New Deal developmental state, the proposed Full Employment Bill was high tide.

The bill was introduced in January 1945, but the two houses of the U.S. Congress would not produce their final version for Truman's signature for over a year. The legislation that ultimately passed in February 1946, known as the Employment Act, would be very different from the original Full Employment Bill that Senator Murray introduced. NAM, with its annual budget of $5 million, in unison with the Chamber of Commerce, representing two thousand business associations and fifteen thousand companies, had mobilized against the original bill.[23] Such "peak" business lobbies, as political scientists call them, very rarely just dictate legislative possibilities, but this time they did.[24] To them, what was at issue was their own power to make investment decisions, as well as the long American political-economic tradition of sphering. The arena of private capital investment, in their view, should remain free of state encroachment, and state control over investment was nothing short of Soviet Communism.

As in 1937–38, when the New Deal state announced it might experiment with robust public investment programs, business lobbies threatened a capital strike. In response to legislation they did not like, capitalists might just lose "confidence," exercise a political liquidity preference, and park their potential private investment on the sideline. It was not good, one NAM representative said in congressional hearings on the Full Employment Bill, for the state to do "thinking and financing," for that would undermine "confidence" among the owners of capital and diminish employment-giving private investment.[25] A representative NAM publication, *Competitive Enterprise versus Planned Economy* (1945), explicitly equated the Full Employment Bill with Communism. In November 1945, Frank Donaldson Brown, a member of NAM's board of directors and vice president of GM (the largest, most powerful, and most politically important U.S. corporation), took charge of NAM's Washington strategy, as the Full Employment Bill sat in congressional committee.

GM was at the center of the postwar hinge. In November 1945, while still fighting the Full Employment Bill, the corporation encountered other problems. That month 180,000 UAW members went on strike. The GM strike was the central labor action in a massive national strike wave that erupted in autumn 1945 and lasted into 1946.[26] In the last four months of 1945, strikes accounted for more than 28 million lost workdays, more than any previously recorded peak. The CIO, representing 5 million of the nearly 15 million organized U.S. workers, accounted for two-thirds of the striking workers, focused in the capital-intensive, male-employment-intensive mass production industries.[27] Labor feminists too fought for postwar gains.[28] The national telephone workers strike, for instance, was the largest female strike in history.[29] In the general strike wave, labor leadership, including CIO president Philip Murray, of the steelworkers, could not control events. In September 1946 ninety unauthorized strikes broke out in Detroit alone. The strikes were orderly. Usually, when workers walked out, they demanded recognition of their collective bargaining rights and more pay.

During the war, government caps had limited wages, while profits had surged, bolstered in 1945 by postwar peacetime tax rebates. Not even NAM denied that industrial workers were due a pay increase. Still, GM management chose to make the strike about much more than pay. With an eye on the proposed Full Employment Bill, it chose to reframe the issue as the "right to manage."

For GM management, it was a three-way struggle. Congress was threatening to encroach on their investment decisions. The workers were on strike. And the corporation's stockowners, the Du Pont family, great enemies of the New Deal who owned a controlling financial interest in the corporation, were nervous about postwar conversion and preferred liquidity.[30] Self-undermining, they thought it best to hoard corporate cash out of precaution and wait to see if the Depression would return. They also wanted GM's wartime profits distributed to them immediately as stock dividends. GM management, led by Alfred Sloan, had a different vision. As managers, they wanted to manage. They planned prodigious fixed investments in production. Wanting to manage production, by inclination, they preferred illiquidity. Further, politically, they knew they must provide employment, or the public investment provisions of the Full Employment Bill loomed. GM management would invest. But in public they defended a "right to manage" free from meddling labor unions and congressmen. In private, this also meant free from meddling stockowners.

When the strike wave broke out, GM management announced it would bargain over "wages, hours, and working conditions"—it would pay its workers more, in a distributive politics of income, or the division of spoils between profits and pay—but over absolutely nothing else. In the days leading up the strike, President Truman had convened a Labor Management Conference, where CIO president Murray raised the issue of a broader "industrial democracy," in which union representatives might meaningfully participate in production and investment decisions. The conference deadlocked when GM insisted that labor unions must have no say over investment and production decisions that would encroach on the corporate "right to manage," which was synonymous with the "public interest."[31] During the strike, Walter Reuther—the UAW's lead negotiator with GM—called for a 30 percent pay increase. But management said that was too much—such a pay increase would eliminate all GM profits. Reuther said GM should "open the books" and prove it.[32] No, said GM, that would be "the day when union bosses, under the threat of strike, will seek to tell us what we can make, when we can make it, where we can make it, and how much we can charge."[33]

As the strike continued, in January 1946 the renamed Employment and Production Act of 1946 was brought before the House floor. Earlier, President Truman had announced his public support for "the right to work for every American citizen able and willing to work." But for the revised bill, he had cut a deal with stubborn conservative, white supremacist southern Democrats.[34] Any government declaration of a "right to employment"— the original purpose of Senator Murray's proposed bill—was gone. Removed, too, was any pledge of government resources, including public investment if necessary, to achieve full employment.

Instead, the final act pledged government promotion of "maximum employment, production, and purchasing power." Purchasing power was a nod to private consumption, Keynes's second macroeconomic variable after investment—second in the economic sequence, second in importance. If investment would remain in private hands, the government might ensure sufficient consumer incomes, and thus sufficient consumer demand for what businesses produced after they chose to invest— assuming they would. In a private communication, one business lobbyist bragged, "To the extent that the goal is achieved by stimulating business investment it will in fact be a 'business bill.' " Further, the 1946 act called for the creation of a new executive agency, the Council of Economic Advisers (CEA), to advise the president on how to "promote employment, production, and purchasing power," but only in a system of "free competitive enterprise."[35] In February, President Truman signed into law the Employment Act of 1946.

Meanwhile the strike wave rolled on. In January 1946 half a million steelworkers went out on strike. Joining them were 200,000 electrical workers and 150,000 packinghouse workers, roughly a third of them women.[36] Truman appointed a board to mediate the strike, which, following Reuther's demands, asked to see GM's books. Sloan refused. Regardless, federal mediators declared that without raising prices on cars, GM could afford a 17.5 percent wage increase. Reuther and the UAW held out.

However, representing the steelworkers, CIO president Murray leaped at an industry offer for a 17.5 percent pay raise. Murray knew the steel industry was less productive and efficient than GM and likely could not afford more. If Reuther's UAW received a higher wage hike from GM, Murray would be in an awkward spot with his union. Instead, the steel agreement put Reuther in the bind. The UAW relented in March 1946, and the 113-day strike at GM ended, with a pay raise less than Reuther's demanded 30 percent.[37] There had been no bargaining over "industrial democracy."[38] There had been only the politics of pay, a version of income politics. That political arena was where the relationship between capitalism and democracy would still be defined.

Now the assembly lines at the most profitable factories in the world began to roll. GM successfully lobbied the Office of Price Administration (OPA) and passed on the wage increases through higher car prices. Finally, GM's largest stockowner relented, and management projected what ownership called a "staggering" $600 million in investment in physical plant for 1947—perhaps the greatest single private capital investment of all time.[39]

In Congress, on the shop floor, and in its private conflict with its stockowners, GM managers had won the "right to manage"—on behalf of all businesses. By 1948, the vast majority of government-owned plant and equipment with any postwar value was back in private hands.

But the political and economic precondition of this victory was known. GM management accepted that it would commit to long-term fixed investment in production: the factories. Capital would employ male breadwinners and pay them a larger slice of the income generated from investment in production than had been the case before in the Age of Capital. By all accounts, working people, asserting their interests during the postwar strike wave, most wanted better pay.

3. Cold War

Immediately after the war, U.S. unemployment peaked at 4 percent. Capitalists too cautious to invest had not triumphed. The mindset of Sloan and GM management had. What they were willing to invest, they earned back in a higher rate of profit. In 1950 GM would make a record 69.5 percent return on net capital investment and sign a generous five-year contract with the UAW—the so-called Treaty of Detroit.[40] Gainfully employed, workers spent what they earned on the consumer goods that replaced the materials of war. The Depression did not come back.

Only one portentous macroeconomic strain remained: inflation. From January 1946 until August 1948, U.S. prices rose at an annual rate of 16.4 percent.[41] Inflation is a complicated phenomenon, and this postwar inflation had many causes. Popular demands for abundance operated in tandem with supply strains, due to reconversion and the strike wave, to push up prices. Popular war bond purchases fell off, freeing up cash to add to demand. The Fed maintained its commitment to support bond sales at low rates, abstaining from raising interest rates to tamp down inflation. Finally, one source of the inflation was international: before it was even tried, the Bretton Woods system did not work.

In 1945–47, outside the United States, the world economic situation was critical.[42] American statesmen had hoped that by pegging national currencies to the U.S. dollar, private investment would sufficiently kick-start European economies—and create demand for U.S. imports, in particular farm products. But that did not just happen. "It is now obvious that we grossly underestimated the destruction to the European economy by the war," admitted Will Clayton, the U.S. undersecretary of state for economic affairs, in a 1947 memo on "The European Crisis."[43] In the harsh winter of 1946, European populations were destitute. The great Italian filmmaker Roberto Rossellini's telling neorealist *Germany Year Zero* (1948) presented a bleak picture that hardly presaged any postwar economic boom. U.S. officials feared famine, a humanitarian crisis, and perhaps even revolution, as western Europe's Communist parties, which had resisted the fascists, had considerable popular support. In 1946 U.S. occupiers feared a French Communist coup, and many U.S. officials all but wrote Italy north of the Po River off to Communism. Even the Japanese Communist Party was on the rise. As so many economies struggled to recover, even more gold decamped for U.S. borders. The free convertibility of European currencies to the U.S. dollar and the Bretton Woods–mandated exchange rates was not going to happen anytime soon. There was a "dollar gap"—European economies could not earn enough dollars either to pay for U.S. imports or to defend their currency pegs. As gold arrived, the contribution to the U.S. monetary base was one cause of postwar U.S. inflation.

What happened next was that the onset of the Cold War between the United States and the Soviet Union overwhelmed the initial attempt to constitute the Bretton Woods system. Now in the United States, the political consequences of inflation joined together with the ideological consequences of the Cold War. As foreign affairs ramified in domestic politics, the combination pushed the final terms of New Deal liberalism a step further to the right, as the global war against fascism was displaced by the global war against Communism.[44]

The United States had the bomb, controlled the skies and the seas, and was a military occupying force in the defeated Axis powers. Europe was not only in economic ruins but was also riven by two very different political and economic systems, American capitalism and Soviet Communism. But the two powers had been allies in the war against fascism. Another global struggle to the death—between them—was not fated. But Stalin would not withdraw the Red Army from where it stood in eastern Europe, period. If Stalin thought little about western Europe's Communist parties, the Chinese Communist Party, or the Workers' Party of North Korea, he would not forbid their fomenting revolution—assuming he even could have. Stalin further refused to withdraw troops from Iran and pushed for Soviet bases in the Dardanelles, among other provocations.[45] Truman griped that Stalin had reneged on a wartime promise to FDR to grant free elections in eastern Europe. Diplomatic engagements began to sour.

Meanwhile the appearance of inflation did not benefit Democrats at the polls. In the 1946 congressional elections, Republicans—far more likely to see the Soviet Union as a mortal ideological enemy, and to brand American left liberals as near Communists—swept back into power in both the House of Representatives and the Senate for the first time since FDR was elected president in 1932. Little more than a month after the sitting of the new Congress, on February 21, 1947, a telegram from London confessed British imperial insolvency and asked Washington to grant aid in support of the royalist forces against Communists in the ongoing Greek Civil War (1946–49). U.S. undersecretary of state Dean Acheson, perhaps the leading architect of the Cold War, told a friend at lunch, "There are only two powers in the world now."[46] Over the spring and into the summer, Truman would explain to the American people the need to "contain" the growing totalitarian threat. The May 1947 request to Congress for $400 million to shore up anti-Communist (not necessarily democratic) governments in Greece and Turkey was approved. No rump of liberals fearful of a "garrison state" together with isolationist Republicans could resist the Truman Doctrine—the strategy of containment.[47] American statesmen talked themselves into waging a Cold War against a foe that, while in principle ideologically committed to capitalism's destruction, was nonetheless a far lesser power.[48]

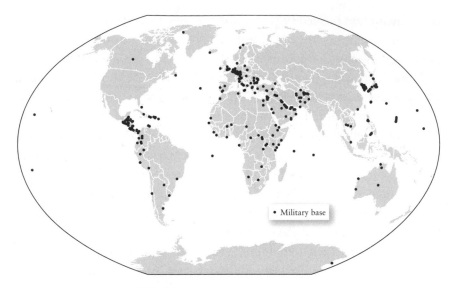

KNOWN U.S. MILITARY BASES ABROAD, C. 2019

During World War II, American military planners began to design a global network of military bases that, extending previous footholds, would secure U.S. world hegemony. The Cold War gave rise to an American national security state that justified a global archipelago of U.S. military bases that has lasted into the twenty-first century.

Cold War geopolitics shaped economic recovery in Europe, while at home it called into being something that had never before existed in U.S. history, a peacetime "national security" state.

The National Security Act of 1947 created the Department of Defense (superseding War), the National Security Council, and the Central Intelligence Agency (CIA). After a Communist coup in Czechoslovakia, the 1948 Marshall Plan sent $13 billion in U.S. economic aid to rebuild western European economies. The Soviet Union and its eastern European satellites refused the aid, as they had by now also refused to join the IMF and World Bank. The Marshall Plan circulated much-needed U.S. aid into Europe but also much-needed dollars.[49] Together with European currency devaluations, the "dollar gap" began to close. U.S. producers began to export. In particular, the farm bloc hoped to export commodities abroad, to help support commodity prices. Earlier, in 1945, occupying U.S. officials had openly considered the complete annihilation of German and Japanese industrial capacity, but now U.S. officials decided to sponsor the industrial reconstruction of West Germany and Japan, if only because industrial economic revival would be a bulwark of Communist containment. At last, western European economies began to climb out of the depths, and western European elections in 1948 brought to power broadly social democratic rather than Communist governments. The first Cold War military frontier hardened at Berlin's Brandenburg Gate in 1949, the year the Federal Republic of Germany (West Germany) was founded.

The onset of the Cold War contributed to an ideological context at home, with consequences not friendly to even Truman's preferred policies. In May 1947, in addition to appropriating military expenditures to contain Communism, the Republican-dominated Congress dissolved the OPA—an enemy to "free enterprise." In June 1947, over President Truman's veto, Congress passed the Taft-Hartley Act. The labor law was not a complete rollback of the 1935 Wagner Act, but it chipped away at union bargaining power. Among its provisions, it mandated that union officials sign anti-Communist affidavits. Labor leaders, including Reuther, proceeded to purge their left flanks. Taft-Hartley allowed states to pass right-to-work laws, which forbade closed union shops. The law also outlawed "secondary" labor actions, such as boycotts and sympathy strikes. Further provisions forbade industry-wide and economy-wide bargaining, which the CIO favored. Instead, Taft-Hartley demanded that collective bargaining proceed business unit by business unit, which both balkanized and bureaucratized the labor movement. Taft-Hartley also banned "supervisory unionism," among foremen and white-collar workers. "Where will unionization end?" wondered GM's Charlie Wilson. "With the vice presidents?"[50] Contributing to southern, white supremacist Democratic conservative support for Taft-Hartley was the CIO's failed 1946 "Operation Dixie," which had sought to unionize white and black southern textile, tobacco, and furniture workers.[51] The 1947 Taft-Hartley Act effectively contained unionization to the blue-collar workers of the existing mass production industries of the nearly one-century-old northeastern-midwestern manufacturing belt. Soon afterward the Republican-sponsored Revenue Act of 1948 reduced individual income taxes across income brackets by 5 to 13 percent.

By now, the capitalist world economy of the "free world" had acquired many enduring characteristics. Capital controls on hot money were the rule, under Bretton Woods. The United States sought to open the world economy to everything else. Like world economic hegemons of the past, the United States, controlling the world's reserve currency, was an ex-

porter of capital and goods. Unlike any hegemon before, the United States'
ambitions were truly global. Disfavoring old imperial-European-style
trade blocs, the United States aspired, instead, to break open the entire
world to long-term U.S. investment, commodities, consumer culture, and
liberal democracy, without explicit coercion, as if it was a world with, to
quote from Elizabeth Bishop's postwar poetry of travel, "Everything only
connected by 'and' and 'and.' "[52]

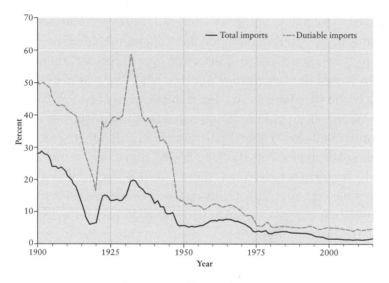

AMERICAN TRADE TARIFFS
After World War II, the United States was generally in favor of lowering
trade barriers at home and abroad. Many manufacturing countries,
including those under the U.S. security umbrella in Europe and
Asia, would not return the favor to the United States.

The United States sponsored free trade in the talks leading up to the
1948 General Agreement on Tariffs and Trade (GATT), which chipped
away at prewar systems of trading preferences, even if American farmers
undermined the creation of the International Trade Organization in 1947
for fear it would forbid New Deal "supply management" agricultural subsidies.[53] Imperial European trading preferences held strong during the decades of decolonization.[54] And European and Asian economies passed an
assortment of protectionist measures to subsidize home industries. But
offenders were allies in the struggle to contain Communism. For geopolitical reasons, the United States looked away.

The same logic carried over into the relationship between the United States and its allies' domestic political economies. Imperial sovereignty is always composite and plural by nature. Empire had always implied "governing people differently," and in that spirit now there emerged different "varieties of capitalism"—even as the world's consumers would not be able to resist American soft drinks, blue jeans, and rock-and-roll music.[55] A hard-left edge had been set on New Deal liberalism, a line drawn at income politics. In the "mixed economies" of western Europe and Japan, states were far more interventionist, often practicing long-range planning and public investment—justified by appeals to democracy.[56] In West Germany, for instance, the return of democracy meant greater worker representation in firms' investment and production decisions. Should these measures have been proposed in the United States, nearly all Republicans and many Democrats would have branded them far too close to Communism if not Communism itself—even when these policies actually favored stable capitalist development.[57] Not only did U.S. officials acquiesce to such policies in European countries, the Marshall Plan and military aid helped launch them. That the United States sponsored the long-term economic development of its defeated enemies was laudable. The revival of world trade lifted up all national economies. But soon these countries would become the U.S. economy's chief industrial competitors. The problem would be a "dollar glut" abroad, from export earnings—German cars, Japanese electronics—in the open, unprotected U.S. consumer market, which would one day threaten the functioning of the Bretton Woods system.

At the same time, American statesmen began to misread national politics around the world through the binary lens of Cold War. Some officials pushed for "rollback," beyond containment. If a perceived Communist threat jeopardized a U.S. corporate economic interest, covert military intervention was possible. The CIA backed a coup in Guatemala in 1954, overthrowing a democratically elected government that had meddled with the United Fruit Company. Far more important than bananas was oil. Postwar economic growth and the postfascist return of liberal democracy would not be possible if the available supply and going price of fossil fuel did not keep in line with the demands of industrial production.[58] A 1953 CIA-backed coup would restore a monarchy in Iran, after British petroleum company interests were threatened.[59]

Certainly, there were limits to U.S. economic power, and even when the world's peoples were seduced by Americanism, they would appropriate it for their own ends, globalizing U.S. culture. Often thick-headed Americans did not get it. Graham Greene's novel *The Quiet American* (1955), about U.S. support for France's attempt to recolonize Indochina, remains the best on this subject. A new kind of global hegemon, an "irresistible empire," an empire "by invitation," capable of destructive violence nonetheless, had come into existence.[60] From this point on, no history of American capitalism can be told without attending to its fate.

4. Cold War Liberalism

The polls said President Truman was going to lose the election of 1948. Instead, despite a number of southern Electoral College votes going to the arch-white-supremacist and third-party "Dixiecrat" Strom Thurmond, Truman beat the Republican candidate Thomas Dewey, and the Democrats also retook control of Congress. Truman had run against Republican "obstructionism," and upon victory he announced an ambitious revival of New Deal programs that he called the Fair Deal.

But the postwar hinge was shut, and the Fair Deal hit a wall—the hard-left edge of postwar U.S. politics. To be sure, New Deal regulations remained on the books. Income politics expanded. In the greatest departure, countercyclical fiscal policy to manage the "growth" of the national income became a new macroeconomic tool. But Cold War liberalism, if still the liberalism first brought to power by FDR, was distinct from the New Deal version. The New Deal had tried to rally the public interest around an urgent national economic crisis. After 1948, its keyword of "economic security," and FDR's promise that there was nothing to fear but fear itself, gave way to the general climate of anti-Communist fear in the nuclear age—and the need for "national security."[61] Big government discovered that its greatest source of popular support, beyond income politics, was a war footing.

Truman's proposed Fair Deal included, among other regulatory and developmental measures, a program of universal public health care; the promotion of public power utilities and public infrastructure through TVA-style public corporations; public housing programs; public education subsidies; a large-scale extension of Social Security; a minimum wage increase; and an agricultural bill that would remove income subsidies for agribusiness and promote "family farming." At the Justice Department, it proposed a revival of antitrust in industry. In 1949 the Justice Department brought suit against the Du Pont family's controlling interest in GM. President Truman, a failed former small businessman in Missouri, was an antimonopoly champion of the "little guy" and equality of commercial opportunity. Further, his Council of Economic Advisers also discussed the possibility of a "guaranteed annual wage" and various other "wage policies," to help tackle possible inflation, should incomes run ahead of the ability of the economy to produce. The council's first annual report remarked that "economic disturbances *originate* in maladjustments, not of the aggregates, but of economic relationships."[62]

Congressional lobbies proceeded to maul the Fair Deal beyond all recognition. Truman expressed surprise at just how much private interest lobbying now shaped congressional policy making. Rather than overturning farm subsidies, the Agricultural Act of 1949 maintained price supports at a maximum of 90 percent "parity"—a backward-looking price index that guaranteed commodity price levels and thus farmer incomes. That year one southern supporter proclaimed, "We as farmers look to God for seasons to grow our crops. We also look to our national Congress for laws to assure us a fair price for our crops."[63] Truman had hoped that the greater sense of national unity and purpose from the war might carry over to his presidency. In his memoirs, he explained the Fair Deal's failure:

> The American Farm Bureau Federation, which represented the special-interest farmers . . . attacked the price-support programs on the same grounds that the private utilities companies fought every attempt of the government to make public power available to the people, and as the American Medical Association fought the health program which would benefit all the people.

If the multitude of interest groups had not been "so greedy for gold," the Fair Deal might have succeeded, Truman concluded.[64] In 1951 Columbia University's David Truman (no relation to the president) published the canonical political science study of postwar policy making, as the result of a clash of private interest groups. In *The Governmental Process: Political Interests and Public Opinion* (1951), what President Truman bemoaned as "greedy," Professor Truman influentially branded "pluralism," announcing to the world that it was the very substance of liberal democracy.[65]

The elements of the Fair Deal that succeeded can be classified as income politics, adversarial regulation, or developmental policies that blatantly subsidized private investment. The Social Security Amendment of 1950 expanded coverage to millions of workers, shoring up labor incomes. The regulatory 1950 Celler-Kefauver Act made vertical integration in industry more difficult.

As for development, most telling was the fate of the 1945 Taft-Ellender-Wagner housing bill. This piece of postwar public housing legislation met the same fate as the Full Employment Bill.[66] During the war, private home construction had been scant, although the New Deal agency the Federal Housing Administration (FHA) funded a number of public housing projects.[67] After the war, the need for housing, especially given the extraordinary internal migration under way, was acute. Six million families lived with relatives or friends.[68] The Taft-Ellender-Wagner bill, introduced in 1945, included robust public housing provisions. Wisconsin senator Joseph McCarthy, who dominated the 1947–48 housing hearings, branded "public housing" a Communist plot. The National Association of Realtors (NAR, founded c. 1908) and the National Association of Home Builders (NAHB, c. 1942), two powerful rising Washington interest groups, went to work. NAHB put up $5 million to fight the Taft-Ellender-Wagner bill. NAM threw its weight against public housing. Multifamily public housing was "red." Single-family home ownership was the essence of American individualism and freedom, and women, leaving the war factories, must return to them to become homemakers and mothers. Nuclear families too contained Communism.[69]

The Taft-Ellender-Wagner bill stalled. After his victory in 1948, Truman revived a housing bill, but what passed was the Housing Act of 1949, which focused on government supports for private investment in construction. Title I called for "slum clearance" and "urban renewal," which, underfunded, would subsequently become "Negro removal," as the black writer James Baldwin would put it.[70] Title II expanded the government credit subsidy programs of the FHA, joining the veterans' mortgage subsidy programs of the 1944 GI Bill.[71] Title III called for the construction of 810,000 units, over ten years, of "low-rent public housing." The U.S. Chamber of Commerce called it "creeping socialism."[72]

Tellingly, residential fixed investment helped carry the U.S. macroeconomy out of the mild recession of 1948–49. Among the recession's contributing factors was the satiation of the postwar demand that had been bottled up during the war, as department store sales fell by 22 percent. Retiring the public debt, the Treasury and the Fed tightened the money supply. The Fed also enforced congressionally mandated controls on consumer credit, while maintaining bank reserve requirements to slow down loan growth, as well as margin requirements in the stock market. Meanwhile the post-1948 recovery of European economies dented demand for U.S. exports. More than anything, however, upon Truman's victory and proposals for a Fair Deal, there was a corresponding upturn in liquidity preference and downturn in nonresidential fixed investment.[73]

At least in the private residential construction market, government and business struck an accord. Between 1945 and 1950, the share of gross residential fixed investment in GDP climbed from 0.8 percent to 6.9 percent, reaching its all-time high. By 1952, the FHA was indirectly responsible for injecting $50 billion into the economy, some 14 percent of GDP, at the cost of less than 1 percent of the federal budget. Further, new home construction meant fresh demand for consumer durables to fill garages, living rooms, and kitchens. As a share of GDP, personal consumption, 48.4 percent in 1944, peaked in 1949 at 66.7 percent—a share not reached again in the twentieth century. Postwar consumerism was born.

At the same time, the 1948–49 recession saw the birth of countercyclical fiscal policy.[74] By 1949, the economist Leon Keyserling had become acting chair of the Council of Economic Advisers. Putting aside "economic relationships" in favor of macroeconomic "aggregates," Keyserling's council argued for "economic growth" as the organizing principle of U.S. political economy. Achieving that goal meant sustaining the two macro-aggregates that, as Keynes wrote in *The General Theory,* flowed into total output—investment and consumption. If private investment and consumption flagged, and recession occurred, countercyclical government spending, debt-financed if need be, would kick in to compensate and thus automatically stabilize GDP.[75] Keyserling would later recall that by 1950 the Truman administration had dropped its antimonopoly rallying cries, "guaranteed income" studies, and anti-inflation "wage policies," in order to concentrate on a single target: national macroeconomic growth.[76] Austerity in times of recession was out, as the government adjusted abstract national aggregates to ensure the steady growth of the national income. But that meant acting at a remove from the nitty-gritty of economic relationships and institutions, or the specifics of place.

Contributing to countercyclical fiscal policy was Cold War military spending. Here the turning point was the outbreak of the Korean War in 1950.[77] Secretary of State Dean Acheson reflected that Korea "came along and saved us," solidifying the policy of containment and the federal military budgets necessary to sustain it.[78] CEA chair Keyserling noted that the Truman administration's post-1950 decision to "go for a program of very large economic expansion" coincided with greater Cold War military spending.[79] In 1950 the Columbia University historian Richard Hofstadter surmised, "We are living under a curious kind of military Keynesianism, in which Mars has rushed in to fill the gap left by the decline of the market economy."[80] Conservative southern Democrats who had set the left legislative limit to the New Deal were happy to funnel military spending toward their districts. Stoking the Communist menace continued to have consequences. In February 1950, Senator McCarthy denounced the presence of Communists in the federal government and launched a red scare.[81] Nonetheless, by 1953, when Korean War spending peaked at the top of the post-1949 business cycle, total federal government expenditures accounted for nearly a quarter of GDP—nearly two-thirds of which was military spending. Thus, rather than an upturn in the capitalist credit cycle and a speculative investment boom, as during the Age of Capital, during the Age of Control military spending and government-subsidized private residential construction drove the first postwar macroeconomic recovery from a recession.

During the Korean War, Congress again granted the president extraordinary authority to intervene in economic life on behalf of national defense. Income taxes increased. The corporate income tax rate reached an all-time high. Still, the political economy of this war was very different from that of World War II. Rather than public investment, the federal government financed war production by granting income tax incentives to private business.[82] Congress had stumbled on an enduring policy for inducing private investment: income tax breaks for the owners of capital. Again, federal economic policy acted at a remove—inducing private investment but with limited powers to direct its content and location.

Finally, during the Korean War, inflation reappeared. Mostly this occurred through the mechanism of a shift in forward-looking expectations that the return of war might lead demand to run out ahead of supply, especially in commodities. Truman had signed a wartime executive order creating the Economic Stabilization Agency, which performed many of the functions of the Office of Price Administration. But now, unlike during World War II, the Federal Reserve refused to support public debt sales at low interest rates to fund a war effort. In the Treasury–Federal Reserve Accord of 1951, the Fed, led by New York Fed president Allan Sproul, reasserted its right to use its discretionary power to set interest rates—monetary policy—as a tool to fight inflation. In banking and finance, many New Deal regulatory tools remained on the books, including credit controls, reserve and margin requirements, and Regulation Q, which granted the Fed the authority to set interest rate caps on deposits.[83] But as the rest of the federal government looked to abstain from the kinds of interventions in economic institutions and relationships—such as the wage bargain—that might control inflation, the Fed was handed back final government responsibility for maintaining the price level. At the same time, the Fed's interest rate policies—pricing credit and setting the bar over which expected profit making from enterprise needed to climb—would once again be a major determinant of the volume and flow of private investment.

The pattern of private investment would determine the fate of liberalism during the Age of Control. By the early 1950s, the U.S. economy had climbed out of the Depression's liquidity trap. The owners and managers of capital, energized by total war, pressed by the popular postwar demand for full employment, eyeing expected profits, and satisfied that "creeping socialism" in the United States had been turned back, took up the task of committed long-term investment. During the 1950s and '60s, a postwar long-term investment boom in productive capital would trigger a wave of productivity growth and wealth-generating enterprise to last a generation. In the era of postwar abundance, consumers reaped the harvest.

CHAPTER 16

CONSUMERISM

S AMUEL FEINBERG WAS THE AUTHOR OF THE BOOK *WHAT Makes Shopping Centers Tick* (1960), a collection of reports published in *Women's Wear Daily* that described the expansion of suburban shopping centers in the United States in the decades after World War II. Feinberg recalled that the American journalist Lincoln Steffens, upon returning from a trip to the Soviet Union during the 1920s, had said, "I have seen the future, and it works." No, Feinberg insisted, it was he himself, who had just returned from touring American suburbia, who had seen the future. It was the suburban shopping center, and it worked.[1]

Feinberg's future was an entire civilization devoted to mass consumption. First and foremost, it was premised on the automobile, as it featured low-density, detached single-family homes in suburbs, where new shopping malls lined newly paved roads, highways, and parkways. There would be credit cards in wallets and purses, advertisements in magazines, and commercials on television sets. In fact, by 1960 Feinberg's future had basically become the American present. For in 1950, there were 40.3 million cars registered to 39.9 million families, and in 1955 two-thirds of homes boasted televisions sets.[2] The physical landscape of mass consumption, the suburbs, single-family homes, car dealerships, and shopping centers had settled on the ground.

Consumerism was far from new in the postwar decades. Historians have recorded too many "consumer revolutions" in the past to count. Some economic historians argue that household consumer demand had triggered the Age of Commerce, setting the stage for industrial revolution.[3] An eighteenth-century British North American consumer revolution is well documented.[4] Later, in the antebellum South, black slaves, especially women, were objects of conspicuous consumption.[5] The Age of Capital witnessed the rise of standardized consumer products and, through national mail ordering, the creation of national "consumption communities."[6] By the turn of the twentieth century, cities had downtown department stores, like John A. Wanamaker's and R. H. Macy's, movie palaces, and many other forms of urban leisure and "cheap amusements."[7] Corporate advertising had been a billion-dollar industry during World War I, and it exploded during the Fordist consumer durables boom of the 1920s, when company and store installment credit began to proliferate.[8] That decade the city of Los Angeles practically invented automobile suburbia.[9] Even during the hardships of the Depression and war, many working-class and ethnic communities—Mexicans in Los Angeles, Poles in Chicago, Jews in New York—encountered mass consumer culture.[10] Aided by the new mass communication of radio, a national consuming culture was forming.

Nonetheless, postwar consumerism was a break from the past in important respects. First, mass consumption became a truly national phenomenon, as television, the "selling machine in every room," slowly replaced radio as the dominant medium of communication.[11] By 1960, the so-called average American watched twenty-five hours of television per week.[12] It was no longer possible to escape a national, homogenizing mass consumer culture—especially as immigration dramatically slowed down in the decades after the Immigration Act of 1924.

Second, the political significance of consumption changed after World War II, as the very ground of civic identity shifted. It became more consumerist. Once again, consumption had long been politicized. American revolutionary patriots had passed nonimportation laws against the British.[13] Nineteenth-century Americans associated citizenship with the consumption of "luxuries."[14] Progressive-era consumer league and union boycotts had publicized deplorable factory conditions, and civil rights consumer boycotts had their origins in the nineteenth century.[15]

But postwar America opened up a new frontier, so to speak, in the commodification of politics, as civic identity became entangled with consumption in ways that it had not been before. "Abundance" became an entitlement of economic citizenship.[16] The line between citizen and customer, rights and gratifications, blurred. Even democratic politics increasingly became yet another form of consumer entertainment, although that did not necessarily mean citizenship became less dignified. That blacks "couldn't even get a hamburger and a Coke at a soda fountain" became one of the political indignities of racial oppression, as the civil rights leader John Lewis once put it.[17] The civil rights movement of the 1950s and '60s had long roots in past labor organizing on the side of production. But that the movement made significant breakthroughs in venues of consumption, through boycotts and sit-ins, was no coincidence, reflecting just how charged consumption had become with political meaning.[18]

During the Depression and the war, consumption had been first depressed, then subsequently repressed.[19] In 1941 FDR's famous "Four Freedoms" speech promised there would be "freedom from want." After the war, decades of pent-up demand exploded. Europe and Japan first had to focus on rebuilding their productive capital, sacrificing consumption for investment in capital goods. That was also the economic logic of Soviet Communism. Cold War liberalism, of course, left capital investment to the capitalists. But U.S. income politics redistributed earnings away from the top and toward the middle of the income distribution. As the less wealthy are more likely to immediately spend, that increased the aggregate volume of consumption—a strategic factor in the maintenance of national income growth. In *The General Theory*, Keynes had assumed that for psychological reasons, personal consumption was a rather stable aggregate, even when personal incomes grew; investment, he thought, was more dynamic. Perhaps Keynes was wrong, many American Keynesians began to think. Not investment but private consumption could both drive and stabilize growth. In part, postwar consumerism was new because of its newly anointed "macroeconomic" significance.

It was true that after the war, more than before, the stabilization of growth resulted from expanding personal consumption. Paradoxically, control over the economy demanded a moral revaluation of prior controls on consumer desire. Benjamin Franklin in the eighteenth century, and William Graham Sumner in the nineteenth, both moralized an economy dedicated to savings and rectitude, asceticism and thrift, salvation and piety, and thus physical capital accumulation in a world of economic scarcity. The dominant Protestant white male economic culture emphasized virtue, character, and the repression of desire. Now new values competed with the old. For consumer capitalism was about fun and play, pleasure and gratification, personality and self-realization, publicity and celebrity, entertainment, and sex. The birth control pill Enovid (1960) was yet another postwar consumer product.[20]

Samuel Feinberg's nod to Lincoln Steffens was telling. For one thing, consumer booms and red scares have tended to accompany one another, as they did in both Steffens's 1920s and Feinberg's 1950s. While Feinberg was touring the suburbs, Vice President Richard M. Nixon was debating the merits of capitalism and Communism with Soviet premier Nikita Khrushchev in Moscow, as the two stood in the middle of a model U.S. suburban kitchen. Communism to Steffens was a utopian project. But by the 1950s, the U.S. consumer economy featured kitchen appliances, Coca-Cola, blue jeans, baseball games, hamburgers, rock and roll, Hollywood films, and getaway vacations to sunny beaches, along with so many other entertainments available for purchase. If not a Communist universal brotherhood of man, it was a universal dream world, sustained by a seemingly bottomless well of consumer desire. A new contradictory drive of capitalism arrived on the scene: the perpetual quest for satisfaction through unending consumption.[21] What could one become tomorrow, discarding obsolescent identities over and over again, in repeated acts of consumption?

Postwar U.S. capitalism set its sights on a new terrain: the dreams and fantasies of the world's peoples. As one French critic of American consumerism would say, "Whatever happens, and whatever one thinks of the arrogance of the dollar or the multinationals, it is this culture which, the world over, fascinates those very people who suffer most at its hands, and it does so through the deep, insane conviction that it has made all their dreams come true."[22] American consumerism was a utopian project no less audacious than Soviet Communism. That was why the shopping centers ticked, and why, in the twenty-first century, online shoppers click.

1. The Consumer Landscape

During the postwar hinge, the original 1945 Taft-Ellender-Wagner housing bill raised the possibility of public housing programs, including supports for urban apartment building construction. By contrast, the final Housing Act of 1949 focused on urban "slum clearance" and inducements for private residential home building, in the form of income tax breaks and credit subsidies. Title II expanded the FHA's government credit subsidy programs and further established the amortized thirty-year home mortgage as the industry standard.[23] The income tax code handed out deductions for mortgage interest. The federal government extended and guaranteed home mortgage payments over time, to induce private investment to build out, across space, and meet the critical demand for housing, given the Depression and wartime halt in residential construction.

What followed was a postwar housing construction boom, an important dimension of the larger postwar surge in fixed investment. In 1950 residential fixed investment reached a GDP share of 7.3 percent, its all-time high. (It would cross 6 percent again only during the 2000s housing boom.) Residential investment pulled the U.S. macroeconomy out of the 1948–49 recession, before Korean War (1950–53) military spending came on line. By 1960, one out of every four homes standing had been built after World War II. By then, 62 percent of U.S. households were homeowners, compared to 42 percent in 1940.[24] The percentage of households that owned their own homes has not dropped below 50 percent since. Single-family homes, and the ideal typical breadwinner-homemaker families who lived in them, became the physical and affective anchors of postwar consumer suburbia. New highways and expressways connected them to the new suburban shopping malls. Stepping back, we can see that this was another defining moment in the geographical extension of economic activity across space, rivaling, say, the geographical movement of plantations during the Age of Commerce, and the construction of the northeastern-midwestern manufacturing belt during the Age of Capital. Now the purpose was not commerce or manufacturing but consumption.

Why suburbs? For one thing, postwar real estate developers preferred to build on suburban "greenfield" sites—land free from any prior commercial development.[25] Such land was cheap, with no existing structures, let alone people, to build around. In all, bulldozed farmland was more easily and cheaply converted into mass-produced subdivisions. Of the 13 million homes built between 1948 and 1958, 11 million qualified as suburban. The suburban population surged by over 40 percent, and the share of suburbanites among all residents peaked during the 1960s at 35 percent.[26] Further, the FHA's *Underwriting Manual* channeled capital and credit into suburban development. In the conduct of appraisals, the determination of "neighborhood quality," and the assessment of lending risks, the FHA was notoriously biased against urban property. Accommodating the racist preference for the white suburbs was a conscious government policy.[27]

William Levitt, of the suburban homebuilders Levitt & Sons, which benefited from hundreds of millions of dollars of FHA-insured financing, once remarked, "Utopia in this business would be to get rid of the government, except in its proper function of an insurance agency."[28]

In the 1950s, Levitt & Sons was for the home what Henry Ford had been for the automobile during the 1920s. To be sure, suburbs had precedents. In the early twentieth century, the Sears, Roebuck catalog, for instance, had sold single-family homes for delivery to "streetcar suburbs."[29] But postwar builder-developers such as Levitt & Sons in New York and Pennsylvania, or Fritz Burns in the San Fernando Valley of Los Angeles, or William G. Farrington in Houston, were the first to integrate the entire process, from land purchase, to home construction, to final sale. New synthetic materials developed during the war, whether plywood or particleboard, along with other factory-produced parts, were standardized. A four-room Levitt house rolled off the assembly line every sixteen minutes. On site, Levitt & Sons broke down the home construction process into twenty-seven separate steps. New power tools replaced skilled, unionized labor. The "Cape Cod Cottage" was the Model T of homes, priced at $6,990, with a free Bendix washing machine, a General Electric stove, and an Admiral television. In some instances, a down payment of $90 with a monthly payment of $58 purchased a Cape Cod. Financially, often, an FHA mortgage made it more affordable to own in a suburb than to rent in a city. Home ownership increased household wealth. A home was a financial investment. But in this era most households expected to better their economic lives through continued income gains—not through the financial appreciation of their homes (a factor that distinguishes the housing boom of the 1950s from that of the 2000s).

The psychological investment in the postwar single-family home is as worthy of comment as the financial. The postwar divorce rate, after a 1945–46 uptick, declined, and the marriage rate increased.[30] Some couples waited in line for days to purchase a "dream home" in Levittown, Long Island.[31] New York–based art critics such as Lewis Mumford would mock the suburbs; New Left children of affluence would give them a bad name as "conformist"; and liberal feminist Betty Friedan's *The Feminine Mystique* (1963) would call them "comfortable concentration camps."[32] But for those who lost their homes during the Depression, or who had once made their beds in European or Pacific theaters of war, ownership of a single-family home, long the preserve of the upper middle class if not the affluent, was an understandable desire. Working-class people had long kept boarders in multifamily housing units to support their incomes. Finally, demand for single-family homes was intensified by the postwar baby boom. After declining during the Depression, the American birth rate dramatically increased after the war, by the tens of millions.[33]

Inside the typical postwar suburban home, there were two new rooms: the "utility room," for home appliances, and the even more ideologically charged "family room." Suburban homemakers presided over both rooms and more generally the postwar "domestic ideal." The kitchen was moved to the front of the house, next to the garage, so that the living area opened up, through double-glazed patio doors, to another new postwar space, the backyard lawn.[34]

"1960S FAMILY OF FOUR SEEN FROM BEHIND STANDING
IN FRONT OF NEW SUBURBAN HOUSE HOLDING HANDS" (1960)
Postwar American society made no larger investment than
in the single-family suburban home.

The architecture of the postwar suburban home embodied the affective investment in the nuclear family. So did it embody the themes of industrial modernism. Los Angeles, with pristine "Case Study Houses" sponsored by *Art & Architecture,* enjoyed a postwar wave of exquisite flat-roofed, steel-framed glass houses in the manner of the great modernist architect Ludwig Mies van der Rohe, this time with Mumford's approval. In Houston, as elsewhere, it was the "ranch house" that became ubiquitous.[35] Regional house styles, from the New England colonial to the New Orleans plantation, converged into this one homogenous postwar product.

California architects developed the style during the 1930s, drawing

ROBERT ADAMS, *COLORADO SPRINGS, CO* (1968)
The dominant horizontal line of the popular ranch-style single-family
suburban home conveys the flattening of household economic inequality
during the postwar decades. No less, the photograph depicts the potential
alienation of the female suburban homemaker.

from Spanish colonial architecture in the Southwest, as well as Frank
Lloyd Wright's Prairie modernism. Levitt & Sons installed Wright's three-
way fireplaces as the focal point of their ranches. The suburban ranch
house is "rambling"—spread out over one story, with maximum facade
width to convey the sparseness of low-density living. The FHA's *Underwriting Manual* established lot size at no less than one quarter-acre, 40 by 100
feet, far larger than previous suburban lots. Following the Prairie style, the
ranch features horizontal lines, most prominently its long horizontal
roofline. The ranch roofline, as much as any line on a graph or chart, conveys the political-economic values of the Age of Control—stability, structure, and the compression of postwar household income inequality.

Meanwhile postwar subdivisions accomplished a terrific trick, breeding
both conformity and exclusion. The FHA's *Underwriting Manual* has become infamous for its racism. Frank Lloyd Wright's ingenious design for
prefabricated "Usonian" homes was rejected because of a low rating in the
"adjustment for conformity" category.[36] That was the least of the FHA's
sins. White male breadwinners were good mortgage risks, but female

heads of household were not. In 1955 the Columbia professor and noted urban planner Charles Abrams remarked that the "FHA adopted a racial policy that could well have been culled from the Nuremberg laws."[37] In 1960 there were 82,000 residents in Levittown, New York; of them, 82,000 were white.[38] The same was true for many white subdivisions, at first regulated by formal "restricted covenants" among property owners that banned sales to nonwhites. When the U.S. Supreme Court in *Shelley v. Kraemer* (1948) struck down the judicial enforcement of overtly racist restricted covenants, white property owners used more insidious methods. By 1960, less than 2 percent of FHA-sponsored mortgage lending financed home construction for minorities.[39]

Much of this was because suburban developers themselves had written much of the FHA *Underwriting Manual.* The real estate lobby even succeeded in passing a law that prohibited the FHA from hiring its own civil servants to conduct ratings and appraisals, an emblematic example of the postwar "broker state" in which competing "interest groups" jostled for handouts from Congress—one consequence of development through tax subsidy, without an overriding sense of a unified public interest. The FHA hired real estate agents and brokers. Planning was left to developers and property owners, and so property interests determined real estate patterns. This meant many postwar urban real estate markets, especially for poor people, were governed through alliances of white and black property owners and landlords who together sought to extract profits from segregated black housing.[40]

The new construction required more than state subsidy. After the homes went up on the lots, public infrastructure was often left to local governments, if not to homeowners themselves. For instance, Levitt & Sons installed septic tanks rather than sewage systems. During the 1960s, the federal government finally had to step in and provide funds for local governments to install sewers in many of the subdivisions built during the 1950s. Local and state governments built water and sewage systems, gas and electric utilities, and school systems to serve suburban communities. Many developers built roads in subdivisions only to transport the construction materials—they did not link up with existing transportation systems. As the suburbs sprawled, the need for roads in particular was pressing. Eisenhower's 1956 Interstate Highway Act underwrote a federal system of over 41,000 miles of highway, built with suburbs and their residents, more than with cities and their inhabitants, in mind.[41] The highway

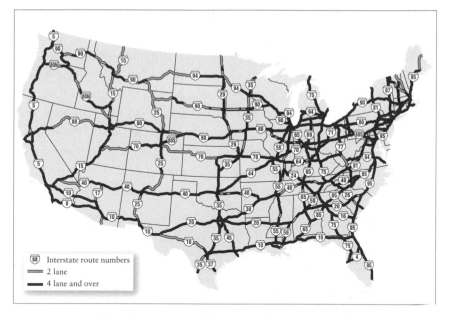

THE INTERSTATE HIGHWAY SYSTEM, 1958
The Federal Aid Highway Act of 1956 marked another chapter
in the long American history of "internal improvements."

act, justified in terms of the national security interest, funneled more government subsidies toward the private builders of the postwar suburban
consumer landscape.

Investment in the physical infrastructure of suburbia did not stop at
single-family home construction or highway construction. The shopping
centers came next. In 1946 only eight recognizably suburban "shopping
centers" were operating in the United States.[42] Shopping strips that catered to car rather than foot traffic had arisen in the 1920s and '30s. During the suburban housing boom, urban department stores began to chase
their customers to the suburbs. Retail trade fled urban downtowns.[43]
These "anchor stores" worked in concert with developers and investors to
hire architects and secure commercial mortgages. Given that the postwar
income politics included benefits such as health insurance and pensions,
private insurance corporations began to accumulate capital that had to be
invested somewhere. These "institutional investors" became the largest
investors in suburban shopping centers. They required that shopping centers seek long-term leases with national retail chains instead of local store-
owners.[44] The 1950s were the golden age of suburban shopping mall

construction. By 1960, there would be 3,840 shopping malls, and most retail shopping would take place in the suburbs.[45]

The greatest architect and designer of shopping malls was Victor Gruen, who had cut his teeth in Vienna with the famed modernist Adolf Loos. Gruen had designed public housing projects for Vienna's Socialist municipal government, then fled Hitler's Europe in 1938. In New York, he found work designing Fifth Avenue storefront windows. Soon he was drawing up plans for concrete ramps leading up to rooftop shopping center parking lots, a contribution to the emerging field of parking lot design.

VICTOR GRUEN ASSOCIATES, "AN ARCHITECTURAL
MODEL OF GRUEN'S NORTHLAND CENTER" (1954)
Gruen's Northland Center shopping mall in Southfield, Michigan,
a Detroit suburban, was a landmark in mall design and
modernist architectural planning.

In 1952 Victor Gruen Associates broke ground on Northland Center, an outdoor shopping center in booming suburban Detroit, anchored and financed by J. L. Hudson's department store. When it opened in 1954, Northland was the largest shopping center in the world, the result of a $30 million fixed investment. It sat on 163 acres, providing 2 million square feet of retail floor area for its one hundred stores, which included a grocery "supermarket."[46]

Gruen's design was boldly horizontal and spread out, with visible structural components—emblematic architecturally of the postwar International Style of high modernism. He conceived of Northland as a self-enclosed and fully designed city. It had its own private road system, power plant, police force, and water tower. It had ten thousand parking spaces. The project, according to Gruen, involved "planning, architecture, transportation engineering, mechanical engineering on a large scale, electrical engineering, interior work, landscape architecture, graphic design."[47] *Time, Life, Newsweek, Business Week,* and *U.S. News and World Report* all sent reporters to cover Northland's grand opening.

"INTERIOR VIEW OF GRUEN'S NORTHLAND CENTER" (1957)
Gruen's planning vision demanded a controlled consumer environment.

Edina, Minnesota's, Southdale Shopping Center (1956) was Gruen's true masterwork. Just outside the Twin Cities, off federal highway I-294, Southdale was the world's first fully enclosed climate-controlled shopping mall. Its exterior décor was consciously dull and neutral. The glass, color, and light were all on the inside. The shopping center was two stories tall, with escalators and a two-story parking garage. The "center court" was meant to dazzle, landscaped as it was with trees, flowers, fishponds, and a thirty-foot cage with exotic birds.

Gruen's design was intended to achieve nearly complete control of the shopping environment. Stores led a "double life," he philosophized: they were "show places" that must "arouse interest," but they were also "factories." Southdale's great design innovation was to move the "machinery" of the mall "behind the scenes."[48] Gruen built underground tunnels for stores to take delivery of goods, so the merchandise would appear on the shelves, as if by magic. Wires, pipes, and everything else that was not for sale were hidden from view.

Gruen himself did not like to shop. Fin-de-siècle Vienna had been a hotbed of modernist architecture and urban planning, and Gruen had similar civic ambitions for postwar U.S. shopping centers.[49] American suburbs, he lamented, were "communities without hearts," but shopping malls could change that. He believed Southdale would become a "community center," the anchor of a new planned community that would rationally integrate apartment buildings, streets, parks, schools, lakes, and office towers. In *Shopping Towns USA* (1960), invoking the sidewalk café culture of Vienna, he congratulated himself on designing a new "urban space."[50]

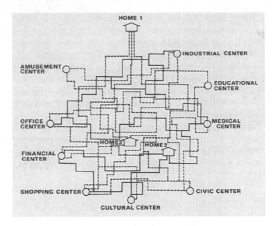

VICTOR GRUEN, "THE SUBURBAN LABYRINTH" (1973)
This cybernetics-like visual of the principles of postwar American suburban design is from Gruen's *Centers for the Urban Environment: Survival of the Cities* (1973). By the 1970s, Gruen had become disillusioned with American suburbia.

Throughout the postwar world, often urban planning took the form of mass public housing projects, including some in the United States.[51] Gruen's most ambitious plan was a complete redesign of the city of Kalamazoo, Michigan, *Kalamazoo: 1980!* (1958). It was never tried, but after Southdale, a wave of enclosed malls swept the nation. Almost none, not even Southdale, became planned multiuse suburban communities.

Instead, Southdale, to Gruen's horror, conformed to the common pattern of suburban land use: the uncontrolled sprawl of the mall, single-family subdivisions, and roadside commercial strips. It was not master architect-planners like Victor Gruen but rather the veiled planning device of the income tax code—accelerated depreciation schedules for commercial real estate, or tax breaks on new construction, for instance—that explained much of the emerging pattern. During the late 1950s, fixed commercial real estate investment construction boomed. The late 1950s also saw the construction of suburban fast food restaurants, gas stations, motels, and eventually office spaces and industrial parks. The first Holiday Inn opened in 1952, and by 1960 it was a successful national chain. Ray Kroc opened his first McDonald's in Des Plaines, Illinois, in 1955. By 1960, there were 228 McDonald's franchises. Eventually, strip malls and massive regional shopping centers would extend the suburban fringe, giving birth to the "edge city," a suburban or "exurban" space of rapid obsolescence.[52]

FRANK GOHLKE, *LANDSCAPE, LOS ANGELES* (1974)
Gohlke's photography during the 1970s was associated with a new
emphasis on landscape in the medium. Postwar consumer sprawl,
ultimately postindustrial exurban sprawl, led to a new built environment.
Consider this landscape in comparison to the Hudson River School
paintings, or to Charles Sheeler's renderings of River Rouge.

The novelist Thomas Pynchon aptly described these emerging landscapes in *The Crying of Lot 49* (1965). "Like many named places in California it was less an identifiable city than a grouping of concepts—census tracts, special purpose bond-issue distracts, shopping nuclei, all overlaid with access roads to its own freeway."[53]

Gruen was appalled. Disenchanted with American suburbia, he fled back to Vienna, only to find an American-style (Gruen-style?) shopping center going up in his backyard. Instead of providing the "need, place and opportunity for participation in modern community life that the ancient

Greek Agora, the Medieval Market and Place, and our own Town Squares provided in the past," as Gruen had once predicted, his shopping centers had become "bastard developments," narrow private spaces solely dedicated to mass consumption.[54] Retired, Gruen wrote a science fiction novel in which a character named Victor Gruen discusses the environmental impact of suburban sprawl with a space alien; Gruen convinces the alien that American suburbs were destroying planet Earth. This utopian vision of consumer society had turned dystopian.[55]

2. The Consumer Dreamscape

Detached single-family homes, highways, shopping malls, and strip centers accounted for the material landscape of consumerism. No less important was the American mental landscape, as consumers must be motivated to consume. Cold War liberalism directed income growth to the average U.S. household, which increased mass purchasing power. But could investors and producers reasonably expect consumers to continue to buy more and more stuff? The answer concerns Americans' relationships to these new objects, to themselves, and to one another.

There have been a number of approaches to explaining consumption. Economists have often taken individual consumer preferences as givens in their analysis—simply revealed, putting to the side the question of how they are first generated, and why consumers desire what they do in the first instance. Other interpretations of consumerism are more sociological. Thorstein Veblen, in *The Theory of the Leisure Class* (1899), coined the term *conspicuous consumption*.[56] Perhaps consumers purchase not so much goods as status. Keynes's *The General Theory* focused more on the "inducement to invest" rather than the "propensity to consume" as a dynamic economic factor, but his brief analysis of consumer motivations approximated a status explanation. Influentially, David Riesman and Nathan Glazer's *The Lonely Crowd* (1950), a postwar sociological classic, argued that Americans, who had been "inner-directed" during the nineteenth century, were becoming "outer-directed" in the twentieth. Americans consumed to conform—in other words, to acquire the "standard-package."[57] When "society" updates the package, status-conscious consumers spring into action.

In the wake of the 1953–54 recession, *Time* explained the rebound. Consumers "realized that they could increase economic growth by replacing their fans with air conditioners. They *ensured the boom* of 1954 by purchasing five million miniaturized television sets."[58] Air-conditioning, entering the market after 1951, had entered the standard package, as had color television sets. The consultancy Social Research (1946), founded by a social anthropologist turned business school professor, promoted this view. Social Research was an important advocate of sociologically "segmenting" the mass consumer market into groups, within which individuals could emulate one another. Janet Wolff's *What Makes Women Buy: A Guide to Understanding and Influencing the New Woman of Today* (1958) and D. Parke Gibson's *The $30 Billion Negro* (1969) were important works in this advertising genre.[59]

What neither economics nor sociology could account for so well was the defining feature of consumer capitalism, which is obsolescence. Perhaps it is "rational" to purchase an automobile, but what explains the desire to junk a perfectly good car for a new one? It might be status anxiety. But in a consumer society, purchasing "the new" never stops. This phenomenon most demands explanation.[60] "Basic utility cannot be the foundation of a prosperous apparel industry," announced a leading apparel executive in 1950. "We must accelerate obsolescence." At a moment during the recession of 1957–58, corporations realized that Americans would soon have no new necessities to purchase.[61] True, many people abroad still needed the things that Americans had already acquired. U.S. multinationals were expanding rapidly into the now fast-growing industrial economies of Europe, where Bretton Woods–mandated currency convertibility finally arrived in 1958. In postwar reconstruction, European production had focused on capital goods, not consumer goods. As national incomes around the world climbed, American consumer culture became more powerful everywhere.[62] Nonetheless, if U.S. consumers were to sit on the sidelines until their things broke, U.S. producers might suffer from a lack of effective demand.

The most pressing problem that the postwar advertising industry faced was how to make people want what they already had. No fresh start on the problem was required. By now, commerce had cultivated human desires for quite some time; long ago Aristotle had taught that once the genie of commercial desire was let out of the bottle, there would be no putting it back, as human desire was potentially "unlimited."[63] In the postwar era, however, marketers found new ways to tap into human desires. They appealed to the fantasy and dream lives of the individuals and households that benefited from rapidly rising money incomes and new purchasing power.[64] For instance, in James Thurber's short story "The Secret Life of Walter Mitty" (1939), Mitty is so bored on a shopping trip to Main Street that he cannot help but daydream. "Walter Mitty, the Undefeated, inscrutable to the last," goes the famous last line.[65] As consumption moved from Main Street to the suburban shopping center, the postwar advertising industry set for itself the task of scrutinizing the mind of Mitty. They had to get Mitty to daydream about consumption, not about escaping consumption.

In tapping into the fantasy life of consumers, advertisers began with the goods themselves, planting fantasies about what consumers could become if they bought them. But then advertisers stumbled on a far more effective strategy, one still in use: instead of selling the goods, they began to sell the psychological qualities of the consumer experience itself. This opened up an entire new field of possibilities.

As for dream life, Sigmund Freud launched the discipline of psychoanalysis with *The Interpretation of Dreams* (1899). Many postwar U.S. advertisers were pop Freudians who hoped to induce consumption—much as many post–Civil War Americans had been pop Darwinians, hoping to induce competition. Here was one postwar Chicago adman on cigarettes, quoted in Vance Packard's best-selling *The Hidden Persuaders* (1957):

> All cultures have expressed basic needs for oral comfort by some form of smoking or sucking. In the South Sea Island they suck betel nuts. Gum chewing is common to both males and females and the same is true of cigarette smoking. Both offer oral comfort. The deeply ingrained need for intake through the mouth arose originally as a reaction to hunger and tension in the infant, who was pacified at the breast or with a bottle. This need became modified but remains as a primary impulse and need all through adult life.[66]

Probably, if Freud had come across this drivel, he would have spit out his cigar. Certainly, we should not exaggerate the influence of postwar psychoanalysis on postwar advertising. Nonetheless, Pierre Martineau, a leading postwar advertising theorist, kept a copy of the Austrian-born Abraham Brill's *Basic Principles of Psychoanalysis* (1949) on his desk. Ernest Dichter, author of *The Strategy of Desire* (1960), director of the influential Institute for Motivational Research—yet another Viennese émigré—championed psychoanalytic principles to advertisers.[67] It was in *Formulations on the Two Principles of Mental Functioning* (1911) that Freud proposed the "pleasure-unpleasure principle, or more shortly the pleasure principle," as a motivating force in mental life, in irresoluble tension with the "reality principle."[68] Postwar advertisers turned to themes of pleasure, fantasy, and dissatisfaction, positioning consumption less as an escape from reality than as a means—back to P. T. Barnum—of making reality follow the form of appearance, in the mode of fantasy.

The feeling that there is something new and better to purchase, and that I will not be satisfied until I buy it, although of course if I do, I will not be satisfied, because I will want to buy something new, repeat, is the contradictory drive of consumer capitalism. The contradictory drive in speculative investment is the tension that money makes possible both short-term liquidity preference and long-term committed investment. In consumerism, the desire to consume something new over and again in the present may increase effective demand and also become a driver of long-term economic development, but the contradiction is that consumers must keep buying, even knowing that what they buy can never satisfy their wants. Consumer desire must gnaw at the psyche, never to be satiated. Dichter's mantra at the Institute for Motivational Research was "Don't sell shoes—sell lovely feet!"[69] That is, sell people not goods but the person they want to be, which is not someone with shoes so much as someone who can find happiness in the experience of having lovely feet. It will require always having to purchase new shoes, long before the soles wear out on the old ones.

In 1959, in the wake of recession, *Popular Mechanics* sat down to interview a handful of American automotive "stylists." Robert H. Maguire, chief interior stylist at Ford, explained:

> You buy a car more because you want it than because you need it. The old car probably didn't wear out. You have a desire to acquire a new car. You don't have this feeling about a refrigerator. You get excited about a car.

As an object of desire, cars were like women:

> A car gets into a face symbol very easily with its headlights that look like eyes and a grille that looks like a mouth.

Other stylists explained:

> The stylist must create demand. What is good design? "Excitement" is the word for it. It must excite your desire to own it.

Maguire added:

> We design a car, and the minute it's done we hate it—we've got to do another one. . . . We design a car to make a man unhappy with his 1957 Ford along about the end of 1958, so he'll buy another one. Planned obsolescence, I guess. It's a nasty word nowadays, isn't it?

Popular Mechanics asked, "Is it really necessary—this planned obsolescence?" Maguire answered, "It is, if the country is to keep on doing what it's doing."[70]

In the wake of the recession of 1957–58, themes of pleasure, fantasy, and newness began to predominate in advertising. The same January 1959 issue of *Popular Mechanics* featured the following advertisements. One spot promised to show "How to Get Double Pleasure from your OutBoard Motor and Boat." Harley-Davidson boasted of the "extra measure of riding pleasure" brought by its new duo-glide seat. A move away from the goods themselves and to abstract qualities of the consumer experience was evident:

> Play Any Instrument. Imagine! Even if you never dreamed you could play. . . . Popularity! New friends. Gay parties. . . . Relax! Banish worries and frustrations. Satisfy self-expression. Creative urge. Gain Self-confidence.

A muscle-bound Charles Atlas claimed: "I'll show how you can be a new man in just 15 minutes a day." Not to be outdone, muscle-bound Billy Van promised *Popular Mechanics* readers, "You can have a new body at any age. . . . With New Health—New Strength!"[71] At this same moment, banks began to offer local consumer credit charge accounts, so that future desires could be pulled into the present. Bank of America and Chase Manhattan, the largest U.S. banks, introduced credit cards in 1958.[72]

Obsolescence would no longer have to be "planned" if the consumer experience could occupy a particular mental space—the gap between dissatisfaction with the present reality and the dream and fantasy about the future. That human desires are fundamentally ambivalent and contradictory, as Freud taught, only helped. More than the consumption of a good, it was the experience, the pursuit of pleasure in the abstract, that came to motivate purchasing. At the most extreme, life itself could become an object of consumption, with the goods themselves merely what are purchased and discarded along the way. It is extraordinary how consumerism promotes dissatisfaction with consuming without undermining fantasies about the pleasures of consuming again.

The consumer experience began to cut deep, not only in the postwar American economy but also in its psyche and culture. Fantasy genres achieved prominent places in consumer culture; in the 1950s, the so-called silver age of comic books, Spider-Man, Batman, and the Fantastic Four furthered their careers. More than any other industry, of course, Hollywood film, with its romantic heterosexual love plots, wheedled itself within the fantasy lives of Americans.[73]

Meanwhile consumption became one of the great themes of postwar artistic expression. Andy Warhol was a successful 1950s commercial illustrator, once known for shoe design in advertising. *100 Cans* (1962) inaugurated Warhol's "pop" style, becoming an iconic image of serial mass production and consumption. In *Eight Elvises* (1963), Warhol said much more, having turned to the photo-silkscreen process, commonly used by corporate advertisers. Each repeating Elvis Presley blurs and fades, ultimately deteriorating. A new pop song comes out, and one listens to it over and over again, before the desire to hear it again eventually dissipates. Perpetually turning the dial, hoping to hear the "new" song, was a model consumer experience. The object, the song, changes, but the experience is the same.

As the logic of planned obsolescence worked its way through the mental landscape of postwar consumer capitalism, it blew back on the physical landscape, too. Americans discarded their automobiles, refrigerators, toasters, sweaters, and shoes with dramatic consequences, as Vance Packard wrote in *The Waste Makers* (1960). Between 1940 and 1968, solid waste per capita doubled from two to four pounds a day. Most likely it went to new landfills, if not down the drain, through the new consumer product, the garbage disposal. By 1969 New York City alone was burdened by 57,000 junked automobiles, not to mention the used tire dumps. Plastics,

ANDY WARHOL,
100 CANS (1962)
Warhol was a
commercial illustrator
before he became a
celebrity pop artist.
The Campbell's Soup
cans are an iconic image
of the serial nature of
mass consumption.

ANDY WARHOL, *EIGHT ELVISES* [FERUS TYPE] (1963)
The fading of Elvis captures an important quality of the consumer
experience—the diminishing returns to repeated acts of consuming the
same thing, leading to the unending search for new goods and experiences.

a petroleum by-product, were another postwar phenomenon, and by 1964
Americans were discarding about two thousand plastic packages a year.
Paper was by far the largest waste product, and paper towel use between
1947 and 1963 exploded from 183,000 tons per year to 629,000 tons.[74]
Finally, automobile-based suburbia was a fossil-fuel-intensive way of life.

During the 1960s, energy use per household increased 30 percent.[75] Even as consumption became newly aligned with fantasy, the original meaning of the term *consume*, to "use up," or to "exhaust," remained no less relevant. As consumerism obsessively discarded the present, environmentally precarious futures loomed on the horizon.

3. "Think Small"

At a certain moment—when exactly cannot be said—American dream life became so crowded with consumer fantasies that corporations and advertisers could stop worrying about manufacturing consumer desire. Enough Walter Mittys were now dreaming about consumption, instead of escaping consumption. Advertisers could focus simply on listening more closely to consumer fantasies—even to their own fantasies. This became clear by just how well advertisers and marketers listened to the 1960s counterculture. A most striking feature of consumer capitalism became its ability to assimilate critiques of consumer capitalism.

The business of postwar corporate advertising did not want for critics—whose fears still resonate in the early twenty-first century, amid concerns that great technology and social media companies deviously manipulate consumer preferences.[76] Packard's *Hidden Persuaders* (1957) was downright creepy. He quoted the president of the Public Relations Society of America: "The stuff with which we work is the fabric of men's minds." "We move from the genial world of James Thurber," Packard mused, "into the chilling world of George Orwell and his Big Brother."[77] John Kenneth Galbraith's *The Affluent Society* (1958) coined the term *dependence effect*, which referred to the fact that "independently determined desires" were a chimera, as the purpose of Madison Avenue was to "create desires" that "previously did not exist."[78] Advertising expenditures surged threefold, reaching $11 billion, between 1945 and 1960. Galbraith called for more public investment—long-term developmental policies—to fulfill genuine human needs that corporations could not meet in their pursuit of consumers. Galbraith and Packard joined a larger chorus. Advertising's conscious cultivation of a commercial "youth culture," a new market segment of the 1960s, created particular unease. In 1959 *Life* magazine counted the 10 million phonographs, 1 million televisions, and 13 million cameras of baby-boom teenagers: together they spent $10 billion a year.[79] Fredric Wertham's best-selling *The Seduction of the Innocent*

(1954) took comic books to task for promoting juvenile delinquency, and cultural conservatives, in particular, wrung their hands about the teenage pursuit of consumer pleasures, from rock-and-roll music to automobile "pleasure rides."

By attacking consumer culture, postwar intellectual elites, from left to right, were to some extent lamenting the loss of their own cultural authority. Consumers swim in a vast sea of symbols and images that conspire to make them consume, so as to sustain "aggregate demand" for the macroeconomy. But there is air in which to maneuver.[80] Roy Lichtenstein's pop art reproduced clichéd consumer images, such as in his comic book paintings from the 1960s. Yet Lichtenstein subtly altered and manipulated the images with his own hand. He did not mind consumerism, he once said, as long as it left him "something to do."[81] The equivocation was revealing, as consumerism was by then so inescapable that, in its constant cultivation of desire, it had become at once emancipatory and enslaving.[82] In this respect, the pop style of Ed Ruscha was arguably more revealing than Warhol's. Like Warhol, Ruscha began with images of goods, producing black-and-white photographs of advertisements for, say, Oxydol soap or Sun-Maid raisins. Soon, however, his paintings replaced objects with pop-stylized words, conveying feelings. Ruscha produced three "Hope" paintings in 1972–73. In Ruscha's paintings, emotions and aspirations were submerged—co-opted?—into the cultural vortex of consumerism. Did *hope* still mean hope, even if it was being marketed? Ruscha posed the question for the viewer of the art—the consumer?—to ponder.[83]

ED RUSCHA, *HOPE* (1972) Ruscha's art commonly plays on the incorporation of words and speech into the consumer maelstrom.

Corporate advertisers knew all this. They themselves were consumers, after all. Enter Bill Bernbach, the creative genius behind the legendary ad agency Doyle Dane Bernbach. The counterculture of the 1960s produced a fresh critique of mass consumerism; Paul Goodman's New Left classic *Growing Up Absurd* (1960) called advertisers "confidence men."[84] Bernbach, himself an instinctive critic of the inauthenticity of mass consumption, absorbed the critique and ironically mirrored it back to consumers. The consumer's psyche was no longer a Fordist-Freudian engineering problem. Rather than manipulate it, Bernbach sought to connect with it. That meant he trusted his own creativity and imagination and left some of the dreaming for advertisers to do.[85]

A Bernbach ad was "hip"—smart, detached, and often ironic. His greatest campaign, arguably the most celebrated in the history of corporate advertising, was "Think small," inaugurated in 1959 on behalf of the Volkswagen Beetle.

"THINK SMALL" (1959) Advertisers learned how to sell to consumers by playing on consumer critiques of advertising. This iconic advertising campaign mocked planned obsolescence. The opening line of the text reads, "Our little car isn't much of a novelty anymore."

Think small.

The Beetle had an image problem: "Brought to You by Hitler," as it first had been, was never going to be a winning slogan. Bernbach's ad campaign transformed the Beetle from a symbol of totalitarianism into a symbol of the 1960s counterculture. "Think small" mocked the stylistic pretensions of the big U.S. automakers. Bernbach's firm launched the campaign with a sparse black-and-white reproduction of a tiny black car, framed by empty gray-white space, with the caption at the bottom, "Think small." The copy argued with the reader. It did not tell the consumer what to think. Adman Jerry Della Femina, cut very much in the mold of Bernbach, who shunned what he called the "assembly-line method" of advertising, called the Volkswagen ads "the first time the advertiser ever talked to the consumer as though he was a grownup instead of a baby." Bernbach even mocked planned obsolescence. "The '51 '52 '53 '54 '55 '56 '57 '58 '59 '60 '61 Volkswagen" read one caption.[86]

By the end of the 1960s, Madison Avenue was crawling with Bernbachians. Advertising became more aligned with art and creativity rather than psychiatry and science. Advertisements became more imaginative and intelligent. They sought to represent youthfulness (Oldsmobile introduced the "Youngsmobile"), authenticity, and even rebellion. In 1966 the president of J. Walter Thompson announced, "We are dedicated to constant discontent with the status quo."[87] Dodge spoke of the "Dodge rebellion," imploring car buyers to move away from the "crowd." In 1968 a clothing advertisement declared:

> Men of the world, arise! The revolution has begun and fashion is at the barricades. Charge into Chapman's shops for men and lead the way to this new found freedom in men's clothes.

By that time, a disillusioned Gruen had fled for Vienna, but the Viennese Dr. Dichter of the Institute for Motivational Research had embraced the counterculture. In 1967 he argued that admen might learn from LSD, appreciating "psychedelic colors and motions" and striving to "bring the product alive with new, more exciting meaning."[88] Pop art, which had already made the equivocations of consumerism into an artistic theme, became absorbed by consumerism, as consumerism began to exploit equivocation through ironic winks and nods. Warhol appeared in commercials and even directed a few. The foment of the 1960s eased the path from a "planned" to a "hip" obsolescence, which turned over not so much by model years as by the passing of rebellious generations. Every generation would get its crack at dreaming up something new.

4. Consumer Capitalism

Some historians have successfully narrated nothing short of the entire history of capitalism from the point of view of consumption.[89] Capitalism did not exist for most of human history, and for it to exist, a dynamic factor had to appear that past economic systems had not mobilized—desire for more, consumer demand. Consumption has thus always been a vigorous impulse. In the broad sweep of time, notwithstanding inequality, if there is one thing that capitalism has been good at it in absolute terms it is delivering consumers more material goods—in this strict sense something that has translated into better living standards and greater human welfare.[90]

Still, the postwar period was in some respects a departure. Nineteenth-century industrial revolution increased money incomes but not so much living standards, which only began to improve in the twentieth century—an improvement that arguably crested in the decades after World War II.[91] Furthermore, in the Age of Control, when speculative investment remained offstage (it would return), planned obsolescence increasingly took center stage as a dynamic economic factor. Keynes taught that investment was a more volatile macroeconomic variable than consumption, as the owners of capital had the option to hoard their wealth rather than invest, while most consumers, to live, needed to consume at least some base amount. In high-growth economies, where income growth exceeded the marginal propensity to consume, he also proposed that investment became ever more necessary for an economy to meet its productive potential. Perhaps, but was it at least possible to expand the propensity to consume more than Keynes thought, and achieve growth that way? Yes, it was.

A new dimension of expectations, related to consumption, not investment, became more prevalent: the issue of "consumer confidence." George Katona, a Hungarian gestalt psychologist who fled Germany in 1933, became an economist at the University of Michigan, where, in 1952, his team collected survey data measuring "consumer expectations" and "consumer sentiments"—the origins of contemporary "consumer confidence," a new confidence game.[92] Katona summarized his research in *The Powerful Consumer: Psychological Studies of the American Economy* (1960).[93] For consumption to drive long-term economic growth, in the absence of expanding long-term investment, in the short term consumers must always desire more, even as they learn that the final satiation of consumer desire is not possible. In the postwar period, it was a new long-term way of life, a new structure at once economic and psychological. As consumerism became culturally hegemonic, the short-time mindset of consumerism might even bleed into the investment function—undermining

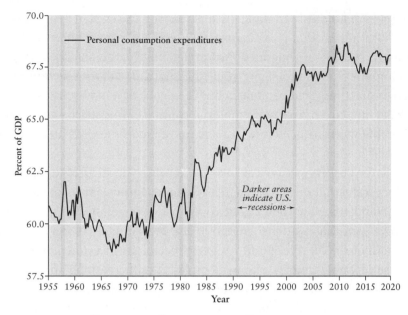

PERSONAL CONSUMPTION EXPENDITURES

Ever since the birth of consumer society in the postwar decades, personal
consumer expenditures have accounted for a larger share of GDP.

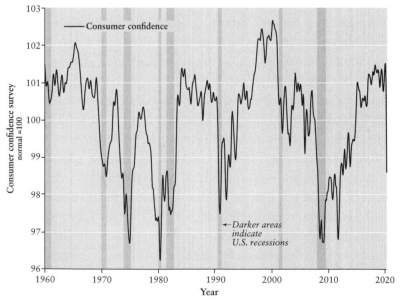

CONSUMER CONFIDENCE

Given the rising share of consumer expenditures in GDP,
consumer confidence became an ever more critical factor
in American economic development.

long-term investment, compelling even more consumption to sustain the macroeconomy.

Of all the aspects of the Age of Control, nothing has persisted more than the logic of postwar consumerism. What are we to make of the possibility that human beings may actually find genuine satisfaction and the fulfillment of their desires through consumption in a capitalist economy?[94] Consumer confidence was a mass phenomenon, broader than the mere confidence of an investor class. Its increasing importance reflected the democratization of abundance, but also a democratization of capitalism's core economic dynamics. But the flip side of material abundance was that it became increasingly difficult to step outside consumer culture, if only to reflectively recalibrate one's desires autonomously. The welfare metric becomes not more stuff, but something more intangible: our freedom.

The French historical memoirist Annie Ernaux reported from a postwar life never lived outside the American-infused consumerist stream: "the old brands, short-lived, the memories of which delighted you more than those of better-known brands, Dulsol shampoo, Cardon chocolate, Nadi coffee—like an intimate memory, impossible to share. . . . The world is suffering from lack of faith in a transcendental truth."[95] In 1998 after many decades pop artist Ed Ruscha would return to his "Hope" series. The word in his images remained the same, if much grainier that it had been thirty years before.

ED RUSCHA, *HOPE* (1998)
Hope has blurred, but nonetheless remains.

CHAPTER 17

ORDEAL OF A GOLDEN AGE

C APITALISM DEMANDS AN ORIENTATION OF ECONOMIC LIFE toward the future, and so the constant urge to look back, and nostalgically stamp past ages "golden," is probably some kind of psychic compensation for the unremittingness of that demand, especially in moments when, to many, it feels difficult to muster a positive vision about the future.

How many golden ages have there been in the American economic past? One may need both hands to count them. In the eighteenth century alone, there was the golden age of colonial commerce, followed by what observers literally called the 1790s "golden shower" of the neutral trade of the French Revolutionary Wars. Today the most recent golden moment is the industrial economy of the post–World War II decades. In the early twenty-first century, whether it is because of income equality or family values, for this moment there is no shortage of nostalgia.

Surely what explains much of the backward-looking fondness is that postwar industrial society had what early twenty-first-century economic life lacks, which is structure. The postwar era was one of containment, borders, and walls. Income inequality was "compressed."[1] Nuclear families contained husbands, wives, and children.[2] When world trade revived, state controls restrained cross-border speculative capital investment. Immigration was limited. The high modernist straight line ruled in the International Style of corporate architecture. One of its greatest practitioners, Ludwig Mies van der Rohe, carried out the principle, according to critics, that "the task of art is to impose order on the existing chaos."[3] In corporate offices, white-collar office cubicles were laid out in five-by-five-foot squares. Glass-Steagall and other regulations segregated the financial industry into different "geographically confined" silos that forbade the sale of assets across the classes of lending and investment.[4] Racist segregation continued, homosexual activity was policed as "deviant," bureaucracies experienced existential tedium, and an anti-Communist *Manchurian Candidate* (1962) level of creepiness and anxiety prevailed.[5] But even if the walls were closing in, there was at least structure.

In postwar social thought, *structure*, a term with physical connotations, was a broad metaphor for social stability.[6] Quite literally, however, much of the structure of mass industrial society resulted from the physical structure and mass of long-term investment in illiquid, productive capital—the plant, machines, and walls of the factories, within which labor and production yielded pecuniary incomes. Men marched off to work, passing through factory gates, to return home to nuclear families and live in the many postwar communities that formed around the factories. This was "social structure."

In the postwar political economy, corporate managers' long-term investment in industrial capital anchored what could be called a "fiscal triangle."[7] The fiscal triangle—the federal government, for-profit corporations, and nonprofit corporations; big government, big business, and big philanthropy—was the dominant political-economic coordinating mechanism of Cold War liberalism. Its task was the production, distribution, and redistribution of industrial income.

Industrial capital was the fiscal triangle's anchor. By the 1950s, the task of investment was comfortably back in the hands of large scale private corporations. White-collar managers, styled as bureaucrats, deployed capital. Bureaucracy, not credit-fueled cycles of speculative investment, was in the driver's seat. Even postwar finance was boring—the lead character in Walker Percy's *The Moviegoer* (1961), one of the best postwar existentialist novels, remarked that there was "much to be said for giving up such grand ambitions and living the most ordinary life imaginable, a life without the old longings," and an ordinary life in this era could be lived by "selling stocks and bonds and mutual funds."[8] The route to making profits was not through volatile financial asset appreciation—the value of stocks, or bonds, momentarily soaring. Rather, it was through depreciating the value of productive capital—stamping it on the ground, employing labor, and using it up, thus maxing out the energy-intensive productivity gains of mass production Fordism. By historic standards, rates of productivity, profits, and median wage growth in the postwar era were high. It seemed to work.

Another corner of the fiscal triangle was the federal government. High rates of progressive income taxation—relative to other postwar societies, and to the U.S. past or future—sustained fiscal revenues. There was more security, the New Deal's great ideological keyword, both in the sense of greater macroeconomic stability than during the Age of Capital and in the sense of "income security," given the expansion of Social Security and other entitlements (some based on citizenship, others employment), under both Democratic and Republican administrations. Between 1960 and 1970, for instance, federal "income security" disbursements climbed from $2.2 billion to $7.9 billion. Fiscal policy evened out the periodic recessions of the business cycle through countercyclical spending. There was no great slump.

Completing the fiscal triangle, income-tax-exempt donations flowed to postwar nonprofit corporations and foundations, the keepers of philanthropic wealth—be they the Ford Foundation or the United Way. Universities, the great nonprofit corporations of the postwar era, engaged in the mass education of the future workforce, as well as intellectually producing the economic and normative standards of assessment applied to the national economy. Rates of national "economic growth" were measured and defined in university economics departments. To guide income politics, the postwar liberal principle of "distributive justice" was first and most famously codified in the moral and political philosopher John Rawls's *A Theory of Justice* (1971).[9]

The fiscal triangle's institutional structure was the culmination of the U.S. politics of income. It differentiated U.S. political economy from others around the world, where, say, income taxes were less progressive, or where the developmental policies of "mixed economies" activated government on the capital side in ways the U.S. fiscal triangle did not. Further, the fiscal triangle expressed a postwar ideology of three sharply separated spheres— government, economy, and civil society—which distinguished the United States from the specter of the all-consuming state of Soviet totalitarianism.

By the standards it prescribed for itself—security, structure, white male breadwinning, a shared abundance—the postwar U.S. political-economic settlement functioned rather well. Its achievements cannot be dismissed. Yet it had limits and fault lines.

The postwar decades were also an era of decolonization, "economic development," and greater aspiration among all the world's peoples.[10] U.S.

income politics had always been discriminatory, privileging white male heterosexual breadwinners. Meanwhile U.S. macroeconomic variables and measurements, such as GDP, or "aggregate demand," were not well suited for addressing the concrete wrongs of many economic relationships or the festering disadvantages suffered by many groups. By definition, no national statistic could capture the place-based, geographical dynamics of postwar U.S. economic change, in which, due to the dynamics of private capital investment, economic growth and development in some cities and regions coupled with persistent want in others. The central piece of postwar liberal economic policy—the 1964 Tax Reduction Act, proposed by JFK, passed by LBJ—channeled macroeconomic stimulus through already-existing channels, rather than bringing underappreciated places and peoples into the project of long-term economic development.

An extraordinary conjuncture opened during the 1960s. A decade-long economic boom began, furthered by the 1964 tax cut. Economic growth increased in the aggregate. Nonetheless, liberalism began to crack up, as a result of urban uprisings, sexual liberation, feminism, political assassinations, university student protests, capital flight, the Vietnam War, inflation, and speculative attacks by London-based currency traders on the dollar-gold peg. The golden age of capitalism in the end proved to be quite the ordeal, and we have few good reasons to be nostalgic for it.

1. The Fiscal Triangle

In the United States, the postwar era, often treated by historians as a single period, a golden age, was far more eventful economically than such treatments may suggest. During the 1950s a business cycle—because of fluctuations in industrial investment (usually related to how firms accumulated and released inventories) rather than because of a credit cycle—led to multiple American recessions. If structure and stability were conspicuous, due to the fiscal triangle, nonetheless the U.S. macroeconomy ended the decade suffering from tensions among economic growth, unemployment, and inflation.[11]

In the elections of 1952, Dwight D. Eisenhower won the presidency and Republicans took control of both houses of Congress. That meant a defense of "free enterprise," a fight against what even the mild-mannered Eisenhower called the "creeping socialism" of the New Deal, and a "never-ending" war against inflation and federal budget deficits.[12] Cold War liberalism lurched to the right, while Eisenhower—former supreme commander of Allied forces in Europe during World War II—became the next president to come to office hoping to appeal to the "national interest," only to be disappointed.

Months after Eisenhower's inauguration in 1953, there was a mild recession largely due to a slump in industrial investment. Further, fearing inflation during the Korean War, the Federal Reserve, following its liberation from Treasury control in 1951—and under the leadership of a new chairman, William McChesney Martin—had raised its short-term interest rate target in money and credit markets. When recession broke out, despite the fall in military spending after the Korean armistice in 1953, the federal budget entered deficit territory.

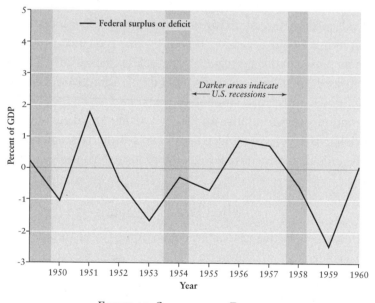

FEDERAL SURPLUS OR DEFICIT

Unlike in the Age of Capital, in the Age of Control fiscal austerity
was no longer a policy response to economic slumps. Instead, the
federal government practiced compensatory federal deficit
spending to stoke macroeconomic recoveries.

Deficit spending helped the macroeconomic recovery. So did the Federal Reserve lowering its targeted short-term interest rate target. (The Fed announced it no would longer seek to directly intervene in long-term interest rates and thus in the long-term allocation of capital.)[13] But the 1953–54 recession proved that even a Republican administration, despite grave fears of deficits and inflation, was willing to engage in countercyclical fiscal policy.

As macroeconomic stimulus, in 1954 Congress proposed a large income tax cut, meant to encourage private investment. Eisenhower's head of the Council of Economic Advisers (CEA), Columbia University economist Arthur Burns, believed that "confidence" among the owners of capital was the crucial driver of investment.[14] A tax break would bolster businessmen's expectations of future profits and thereby induce investment. The 1954 act, in the end, cut personal income taxes only slightly, by 2 percent in most brackets.[15] The action was not in the rate; it was in the rebates.

The Internal Revenue Act of 1954 was a major piece of legislation for two reasons. It solidified a fiscal triangle in political economy, and it favored a novel form of income politics: income tax credits and rebates. Congressional staff spent 300,000 hours working up the 907-page bill. After "interest-group pluralism" did its work, the final bill offered a total of $1.5 billion in tax breaks—on the personal income side ranging from fringe corporate employee benefits, including employer-based health insurance, to continued home mortgage interest payment deductions. The act even granted income tax deductions for childcare-related expenses for employed mothers if their husbands were physically or mentally "defective." On the investment side, the federal government offered a variety of inducements to increase the rate of fixed residential and nonresidential investment.[16] In the immediate wake of the 1954 act, the postwar housing construction boom enjoyed its last phase, while in 1955 nonresidential fixed investment picked up, reaching a peacetime share of GDP not seen since 1929. The federal budget existed as a countercyclical stabilizer of the macroeconomy. To promote national economic growth, the tax code offered a host of interest-group-specific inducements to invest.

The 1954 act also established the "501(c)" categorization for nonprofit corporations, and other unincorporated entities, exempt from the federal income tax. This anchored another corner of the postwar fiscal triangle—what would soon be branded the "nonprofit sector" of American civil society, no less than for-profit "free enterprise" an ideological bulwark of "voluntarism" against big government. The largest postwar nonprofit was the Ford Foundation, established by Edsel Ford in 1936, which upon father Henry Ford's death in 1947 received $321 million in Ford Motor Company stock. The Ford family thus avoided paying the inheritance tax. By 1960 the Ford Foundation had an endowment two-thirds the size of all U.S. university endowments combined. It was the largest player in "big philanthropy." Soon the most populated 501(c) category would be 501(c)(3), whose main subcategories were "religious," "charitable," and "educational" entities. An amendment proposed by the Texas senator Lyndon B. Johnson banned 501(c)(3)s from engaging in political activity. The 501(c)(4) category, mainly "social welfare organizations," would soon enough become the conduit for philanthropy to enter politics. By 1954, the Ford Foundation already had a public affairs program that employed many liberal Democrats exiled from Republican-controlled Washington.[17]

Income politics continued as Eisenhower oversaw the 1954 expansion of Social Security to 10 million more beneficiaries, including citizens with disabilities, a newly organized interest group lobby.[18] The 1954 Farm Bill barely dented price supports for agribusiness and added export subsidies through the guise of third world "food aid," since western Europe had thrown up tariff barriers against many U.S. farm products.[19] President Eisenhower summed it up to his brother: "Should any political party attempt to abolish Social Security, unemployment insurance, and eliminate labor laws and farm programs, you would not hear of that party again in our political history."[20]

A Republican-controlled Congress and a Republican president sealed the legitimacy of the U.S. welfare state, which, relative to other such states, uniquely funneled benefits through employment rather than universal citizenship rights. The United States had no "mixed" economy of public and private enterprise, as many postwar social democratic states did. Rather, private interest groups jostled for big government benefits. In 1956, for instance, Congress passed Eisenhower's National Interstate and Defense Highways Act. Through private contracting, the federal government funded 90 percent of a federal system of over forty thousand miles of highway, to build out the auto-suburbia of the consumer landscape.[21] The bill was pushed through the Congress on behalf of "national security." It satisfied a plurality of interest groups—automobile manufacturers, suburban commuters, truckers, construction industries, and the oil lobby. However, in application it exhibited no overarching national plan—it was Age of Commerce–style "internal improvements" all over again. A complicated network of federal and state government relationships with private contractors built the federal highway system.

Balancing growth and inflation became the Eisenhower administration's self-imposed mandate, yet by the end of Eisenhower's presidency, troubling macroeconomic dynamics had appeared. In 1956 the nonprofit Rockefeller Brothers Fund hired a panel of leading economists from universities—501(c)(3) tax-exempt nonprofits—to pronounce on "national purposes and objectives." They reported back, "We must accelerate our rate of growth."[22] In 1956, in the midst of a business cycle expansion, led by a surge in fixed industrial investment, the U.S. budget entered surplus, and Eisenhower claimed success. But in 1957–58 the U.S. economy plunged back into recession, again. The Fed had tightened money, worrying over inflation. Private investment dropped. Economic commentators spoke of a possible "recession psyche"—after short periods of growth, capitalists for some reason recoiled from investment. Personal consumption led the U.S. macroeconomy out of this recession.

Worryingly, if ever so slightly, inflation and unemployment climbed in unison in 1957. Inflation topped 3 percent in 1957–58, and the unemployment rate hit a distressingly high 7.4 percent. The administration blamed labor unions, especially the steelworkers, for demanding unwarranted pay increases, and corporations for passing wage hikes on to consumers, through higher prices. Focusing on macrotargets alone, for fear of government meddling with "free enterprise," the Eisenhower administration had no effective policy to intervene in economic institutions or relationships to control inflation. In fiscal policy, during the recession, the Eisenhower administration again dutifully let the federal budget enter deficit.

The problem of inflation was passed along to monetary policy and the Fed. The Fed believed it was in a bind. It had raised its short-term interest rate to 3.5 percent in the fall of 1957 in the first months of the recession to stave off inflation. But the rate was below 1 percent in 1958, as the Fed sought to loosen credit and release money in order to induce more spending. When national economic growth returned in the summer of 1958, Eisenhower committed his remaining years in office to building up large enough budget surpluses to combat inflation. Worried about inflation, Martin and the Fed brought rates up to 4 percent. In 1959 inflation was less than 1 percent. However, unemployment remained above 5 percent.

Despite the nagging reappearance of recessions, the macrofluctuations were quite moderate. But with every business cycle, unemployment now cycled around a higher rate. Despite the high and stable economic growth trend of the 1950s, something ill appeared to be at work inside the U.S. national macroeconomic aggregates.

Meanwhile Eisenhower had hoped for a harmonious "corporate commonwealth" that hemmed big government in its proper public sphere, next to the private sphere of "free enterprise." But by now many private interests could not be disentangled from big government, and public action in the spirit of the public interest remained elusive. In particular, Eisenhower's letters and diaries during his presidency were "filled with angry denunciations of military self-interest."[23] Eisenhower had brought national defense spending down to 11 percent of GDP, but Congress still legislated defense budgets as much as $3 billion more than the president, a five-star general, requested. In Washington, military contractor lobbyists and congressmen together diverted defense dollars to private corporations in the expanding southern and western "gunbelt" economy. In his 1961 farewell address, Eisenhower lashed out at what he called the rising "military-industrial complex," controlled by a "scientific-technological elite."[24] On the way out, Eisenhower hit old, classical republican, nearly populist themes—a presidential plea for the little guy, in an era of bigness.

In 1960 the federal budget went back into surplus, but upon another tightening of money by the Fed for fear of inflation, yet another recession struck, and unemployment passed 6 percent. Inflation remained muted. But in the midst of disappointment about U.S. macroeconomic performance, the Democratic presidential candidate John F. Kennedy sent a delegation to France to study the country's state-directed economic planning methods.[25] U.S. big government now accounted for 15.9 percent of GDP. It helped stabilize total national output when private economic activity, especially investment, slackened. It did so, however, at a distance and a remove. By design, big government did not touch so much the fabric of everyday economic life. Big government left that to big business.

2. Corporate Managerialism

The victory of white-collar industrial corporate managers during the postwar hinge was dramatic. The managers of industry, salaried employees, had wrested or maintained the prerogative to run their businesses, whether it was from government, union-organized workers, or even their own stockholders. During the 1950s, the victory was widely remarked upon.[26] Coauthored by four prominent university economists, *The American Business Creed* (1956) noted that corporate managers had a vast "sphere of unhampered discretion and authority." "Stockholders" were entitled to a "fair return on their investment" but no more. Surely they had no say in day-to-day operations.[27] The law agreed—jurists' "business judgment rule" granted corporate managers wide discretion to deploy corporate funds as they saw fit.[28] In 1954 the old New Dealer and corporate law professor Adolf A. Berle, Jr., surveyed the situation and declared, "The capital is there; and so is capitalism. The waning factor is the capitalist."[29] The profit motive appeared nowhere to be found. Agreeing, another scholar of the postwar corporation declared that "profit maximization" was a "vestigial remnant from an earlier full-blooded capitalism."[30]

Who were these postwar corporate managers, and what did they do during their brief postwar moment under the sun? Credit-fueled speculative investment was not what they were about. Postwar corporate industry had no overriding short-term profit motive. For a short time, the managerial inducement to invest long-term in illiquid productive capital, in order to produce, won out over liquidity preference—the precautionary, the speculative, or the political. As capitalists as a group tend to earn more when they are willing to spend more, the high rate of investment on behalf of a commitment to production, rather than profit, paradoxically resulted in high profits. Meanwhile managerial investments anchored postwar industrial structures that were at once economic, architectural, organizational, and psychic.

This was not an era of entrepreneurial swashbuckling or heroic technological invention. Unlike Andrew Carnegie in the past or Steve Jobs in the future, few postwar corporate executives ever became household names. As New Deal banking reforms blocked the convertibility of assets across different sectors of the financial system, there was little financial wheeling and dealing. The Bank Holding Company Act (1956), for instance, which Eisenhower signed into law, limited banks headquartered in one state from acquiring financial institutions in another state.[31] Many industrial corporations reinvested their profits and thus funded themselves through retained earnings, rather than through commercial loans or the stock market. Most simply wanted to produce; managers wanted to manage. Doing so, they sought to perfect Fordist mass production by rationally squeezing out every last possible productivity gain from existing energy-intensive methods.

Capitalism became rather boring, as corporate management took on the character of an educated and trained bureaucracy. A representative example of postwar industrial innovation would be the 1952 founding of the Operations Research Society of America, which published the mind-numbing journal *Operations Research.* The Ford Foundation–commissioned study *Higher Education for Business* (1959) surveyed the era's proliferation of undergraduate and professional business degrees.[32] Profit seeking itself, even if profits were high by historic standards, became a highly bureaucratic phenomenon.[33] GM executive Frank Donaldson Brown, while working for DuPont until 1921, had invented a new bureaucratic benchmark for corporate profit making called Rate of Return on Capital Invested (ROI). ROI was a metric fit for measuring profits realized from the past deployment of productive fixed capital.[34] The critical variable was the rate of depreciation of the physical capital stock, the value lost from using productive capital up. Only highly trained corporate accountants, white-collar bureaucrats, even had the technical competence to know whether industrial corporations were making profits.

As a profit metric, ROI had many corporate uses. Its bureaucratic character made possible the new managerial practices of long-range "profit planning," "profit control," "profit smoothing," and "capital budgeting."[35] GM, for instance, announced that it sought to run its physical plant at 80 percent capacity and make a 20 percent ROI. This was not Andrew Carnegie "hard driving" his factories into the ground, running them at full capacity, using the more momentary railroad profit metric of the "operating ratio." ROI also assisted head offices in allocating capital among different product lines and divisions. GM had introduced the multidivisional, or M-form, organizational structure during the 1920s. Chevrolet and Oldsmobile were different operating divisions, with different sets of books.[36] For all divisions, what ROI did was to help corporate managers stretch out the time horizon of capital investment. Tellingly, in postwar accounting departments, "straight line" forty-year depreciation schedules became standard. By the end of the 1950s, the large, diversified M-form industrial corporation with a putatively predictable long-term future had become textbook.[37]

This had consequences for labor policies. In 1950 GM and the UAW signed a historic five-year collective bargaining agreement—the "Treaty of Detroit," as Daniel Bell called it in *Fortune,* setting a "pattern" followed by many postwar industries. The mere length of the agreement was notable. The contract factored in continued productivity gains and also "cost of living adjustments" (COLA), which tracked inflation. It also provided for "fringe" private welfare benefits, including corporate pensions and health insurance, stretching far into the future.[38]

Profit was still the light at the end of the corporate tunnel, but the tunnel stretched out for years. In addition to labor policies, corporations had what was called "organizational slack" to pursue a variety of goals besides immediate profit making.[39] Many courts upheld the legality of corporate managers' philanthropic donations to nonprofits, making possible the new field of "corporate social responsibility."[40] Might productive capital double again, valued as something more than capital—as the land had, long ago? The "great happy paradox of the profit motive," *Fortune* magazine explained in 1959, was that "management, precisely because it is in business to make money years on end, cannot concentrate exclusively on making money here and now."[41] Taking the cue, one group of white-collar corporate employees—academics—began to imagine postcapitalist futures.[42] Another group set out to study the managerial mindset.[43] The economist and polyglot social scientist Herbert Simon described corporate managers in 1955 as profit "satisficers," not maximizers.[44] Scholars of postwar corporate management noted that managers were committed to "growth" in market share, more than to profit margins.[45] In 1957 the Harvard economist Carl Kaysen summed up the new view:

> No longer the agent of proprietorship seeking to maximize return on investment, management sees itself as responsible to stockholders, employees, customers, the general public, and, perhaps most important the firm itself as an institution. . . . Responsibilities to the general public are widespread: leadership in local charitable enterprises, concern with factory architecture and landscaping, provision of support for higher education, and even research in pure science, to name a few.

Kaysen concluded, "The modern corporation is a soulful corporation."[46] So long as profits, however measured, remained high, profits did not need to matter so much.

In essence, postwar corporate managers were high modernists. They believed in rationality, efficiency, and the straight line.[47] Consider their commissioned architecture—the design aesthetic of their coveted fixed capital investments. In production, factories were still low-flung reinforced concrete buildings containing electric-powered assembly lines. Postwar corporations focused on the fresh construction of buildings specifically for the white-collar managerial class. Wartime technical and engineering advances in steel, concrete, glass, and plastic made possible a truly machine-style architecture, premised on the aesthetic principles of a rational purism. The so-called International Style became the "architecture of bureaucracy."[48] Its master, German émigré Ludwig Mies van der Rohe, who worked out of Chicago, proposed the single module as the ideal "unit of control."[49] He designed buildings with glass curtains draped over exposed metal structures. Among them, his celebrated Seagram Building (1954–58), a skyscraper corporate headquarters in midtown Manhattan, most achieved a formal beauty. But the obsessive proliferation of right angles often led to a rigidity and near "neurosis of forms" in postwar corporate architecture.[50]

Once more GM took the lead. "Modern science is the real source of economic progress," said executive Alfred Sloan, when GM invested $125 million in the GM Technical Center, the grandest postwar "corporate campus," which opened in 1956 in suburban Warren, Michigan. The Finnish architect Eero Saarinen drew from GM's manufacturing principle of "standardization with precision" and mechanical repetition. Saarinen designed the entire corporate campus out of interchangeable standardized prefabricated five-foot-two-inch modules, applying it "not only to steel construction but also to . . . furniture, storage units, wall partitions and so on."[51]

EERO SAARINEN, "GENERAL MOTORS TECHNICAL CENTER, WARREN, MICHIGAN" (C. 1946–56) / EERO SAARINEN, "DEERE & COMPANY HEADQUARTERS, MOLINE, ILLINOIS" (C. 1956–64)
Postwar industrial corporations made heavy fixed capital investments in white-collar corporate campuses. In postwar corporate architecture, the standardization of goods resonated with the standardization of building and design—and, some worried, the standardization of people, too. American-Finnish architect Eero Saarinen designed both the GM Technical Center and the Deere & Company Headquarters.

In these years, following their employees, many corporate headquarters moved to the suburbs, which granted corporate architects opportunities to "integrate" design with the landscape—a callback to the organizing structure of nature, in the organic economy. In this genre, Saarinen's 1964 Moline, Illinois, corporate campus for John Deere would be the great masterpiece, the culmination of postwar corporate architecture.

EERO SAARINEN, "DEERE & COMPANY HEADQUARTERS, MOLINE, ILLINOIS" (C. 1956–64)

Modernist corporate architecture turned to natural motifs, as if to recall the organic economy of the preindustrial past, and to evoke the seeming stability of postwar industrial society (which would not last).

Inside the buildings, how far could the logic of standardization go? Might corporate rationalization include "interchangeable" white-collar human beings—homogenous, one-dimensional men? The great postwar managerial keyword was *integration*. The task was to "integrate" divisions and product lines, "integrate" flows of material, and "integrate" individual psyches into larger corporate social wholes.[52] Hierarchy—the "big chains of authority," breeding a bland social conformity, as the Columbia sociologist C. Wright Mills complained in *White Collar* (1951)—was the prevailing organizational principle.[53] Individuals occupied titles, offices, and statuses stripped of contingent individual characteristics. The specter of an individual's overidentification with corporations got the widest hearing in *Fortune* writer William Whyte's *The Organization Man* (1956).[54] Organization man passed through a series of "integrating" environments:

the nuclear family, a nonprofit university education, and then finally, "human resource" offices in for-profit corporations where managers conducted "personality tests" to determine appropriate job roles and career paths. Corporate managers used organizational slack to pay "industrial psychologists" salaries to monitor employees' integration in the workplace.[55] Notes from one corporate group therapy session:

> At the fifth meeting the group's feelings about its own progress became the initial focus of discussion. The "talkers" participated as usual. . . . Dissatisfaction was mounting. . . . George Franklin appeared particularly disturbed. Finally pounding the table, he exclaimed, "I don't know what is going on here! I should be paid for listening to this drivel!" . . . Some members of the group applauded loudly, but others showed obvious disapproval. . . . George Franklin became the focus of discussion. . . . "How does it feel, George, to have people disagree with you when you thought you had them behind you?" . . . Finally Bob said, "Why don't you leave George alone and stop picking on him?" . . . With the help of the leaders, the group focused on Bob. "What do you mean, 'picking' on him?" "Why, Bob, have you tried to change the discussion?" "Why are you so protective of George?" . . . Now Bob was learning something about how people saw him, while gaining some insight into his own behavior.[56]

Oedipal complex struggles appeared more prominent than the class struggle.[57]

There was bureaucratic tedium but also plenty of drama inside the rationalized white-collar workplaces. For heterosexuals and homosexuals alike, the corporate workplace was erotically charged. The white-collar workplace was feminizing, as the number of secretaries quadrupled during the 1950s, and the growth of typically feminized "service workers" far outstripped blue-collar manufacturing jobs everywhere.[58] In 1959 the journal *Modern Office Procedures* published the article "Love-in-the-Office," telling corporations to "face up to the facts of life" that many of their workers engaged in romantic and sexual relationships.[59] Helen Gurley Brown's chapter "The Office Affair" in her book *Sex and the Office* (1964) argued that offices were "sexier than Turkish harems, fraternity house weekends . . . or the *Playboy* center-fold."[60] Maybe, as the assembly lines took care of themselves, many midlevel white-collar managers did much of nothing at work all day, pocketing breadwinning salaries nonetheless—with ample time to harass female subordinates? Answering yes, Billy Wilder's great film, *The Apartment* (1960), portrayed male sexual exploitation of women in a corporate insurance office. But it was also a romance, in which a low-level male executive and a female elevator operator fall in love—in the end, over a game of cards. It was as if Wilder were saying that no matter how much rationality and efficiency, room for chance always remained.

THE APARTMENT (1960)
Scenes from life inside the postwar world of work. If the first image captured the bureaucratic tedium of the era's corporate white-collar jobs, the second—"Shut up and deal," Shirley MacLaine's character says to Jack Lemmon's in the concluding scene of the film—indicated that love and chance could not be expunged from the corporate workplace.

Postwar culture continually posed the question of what was left of individuality, given so much integration into larger corporate bureaucratic structures. Arthur Miller's play *Death of a Salesman* (1949) was one of many works with a little-guy antihero. The greatest postwar novel was Ralph Ellison's *Invisible Man* (1952), in which the protagonist spoke of the struggle against the "passion toward conformity," pressing on "the mind, the *mind*."[61] In response, artistic expression pivoted from 1930s popular front social-documentary realism to postwar existentialist abstraction.[62] In painting, the very term *abstract expressionism* said it all. Bureaucratic corporations hung Mark Rothko paintings from the walls of their headquarters. When a 501(c)(3) nonprofit corporation, the New York Metropolitan Museum of Art, paid $30,000 for Jackson Pollock's *Autumn Rhythm*

(Number 30) (1950), the postwar art market took off, as other nonprofits sought to corner the market in creativity. Among the artists funded by 1950s Ford Foundation grants were Josef Albers, James Baldwin, Saul Bellow, Jacob Lawrence, and Flannery O'Connor. Ralph Ellison settled into a nonprofit corporate teaching job at New York University. Bellow wrote the defensive essay, "The University as Villain," before taking a position at the University of Chicago in 1962, where he wrote *Humboldt's Gift* (1975), the greatest novel about the postwar corporatization of American culture. He described one nonprofit setting, Princeton University, where he had finished his breakout novel *The Adventures of Augie March* (1953):

> [Princeton] was a sanctuary, a zoo, a spa, with its own choochoo and elms and lovely green cages. . . . But maybe what Princeton was not counted for more. It was not the factory or department store, not the great corporation office or bureaucratic civil service, it was not the routine-job world. If you could arrange to avoid that routine job-world, you were an intellectual or an artist. Too restless, tremorous, agitated, too mad to sit at a desk eight hours a day, you needed an institution—a higher institution.[63]

In the era of postwar abundance, for white, heterosexual men like Bellow, the danger appeared to be that big business, with all its structures, integrating powers, and demands for conformity, might put a stifling squeeze on them as individuals—even as it diverted the lion's share of the era's economic benefits toward them. For many others, the problem was not so much identification and repression as oppression, exclusion, and the persistence of poverty in the midst of an era of long-term economic growth—with corporate managers having put so much fixed capital on the ground.

3. Liberalism Triumphant, "Chased on All Sides"

Bellow left New York for the sticks in Chicago, at the edge of the century-old northeastern-midwestern manufacturing belt. The postwar production of "national" culture was centered in New York—the largest dot in the urban "megalopolis," a continuous I-95 urban corridor running from Harvard University to Washington, D.C.[64] Postwar "public intellectuals," fewer and fewer of them religious leaders, universalized their experience for the nation itself, speaking for "The Establishment."[65] By contrast, the great American photojournalist Robert Frank's slyly titled *The Americans* (1958) was a book of grimy photographs of people living in inner cities or in unheard-of southern and western outposts. In principle, these Americans did live in the national economy of macroeconomic aggregates. Frank's lens captured the specificity of their lives. Could a national statistic like GDP, or a liberal policy goal such as national economic growth, do the same?

Not so much. For one thing, the keepers of postwar "American life" were remarkably inattentive to geography. GDP growth captured time only, not space. It assumed a homogenous national economy, growing over standardized chunks of time. The leading postwar economic theory of growth, for instance, fleshed out in MIT economist Robert Solow's "A Contribution to the Theory of Economic Growth" (1956), modeled capital as a single homogenous productive stock, or thing, called "K." K excluded money capital, and thus liquidity, by definition. It abstracted from space completely. "All theory depends on assumptions which are not quite true," Solow began.[66] True enough, but to refer to "national economy," or "K," was to say nothing about the spatial patterns of capital investment and disinvestment within either K or the national economy. The federal government had acquired the means to stimulate the macroeconomy, but it had relatively less ability to get inside the macroeconomic variables in order to change the fabric of economic life. This was one reason why during the presidential administration of Lyndon B. Johnson, liberalism could so spectacularly succeed macroeconomically and nonetheless fail politically.

The recession of 1960–61, the fourth since World War II, helped make Massachusetts senator John F. Kennedy president. On the campaign trail, JFK promised 5 percent national economic growth. When he arrived at the White House, national unemployment was near 7 percent. The president lamented that the United States had "the lowest rate of economic growth of any major industrialized society in the world."[67] A number of prominent Keynesian public intellectuals, including MIT's Paul Samuelson, Yale's James Tobin, and Harvard's John Kenneth Galbraith, pointed to the dearth of private investment since 1957. Galbraith's *The Affluent Society* (1958) argued that private investment had tipped too far toward the production of consumer goods, rather than much-needed public goods, which explained the persistence of poverty in so many geographical pockets, whether in northern inner cities or in Appalachia. Even as household income inequality remained at historically low levels during the postwar decades, "poverty" emerged as an issue of public debate, prompted by books such as *The Affluent Society* and Michael Harrington's *The Other America* (1962), as well as liberals ensconced at the Ford Foundation.[68] Galbraith, Samuelson, and Tobin all advised JFK that he should increase targeted public investments. The man JFK dispatched to Europe to study French methods of state economic planning, Walter Heller, became chair of his Council of Economic Advisers.[69]

In the end, Heller recommended an income tax cut. His critique of the Eisenhower macroeconomy was that the booms had been cut short by a "fiscal drag"—income tax intakes that had spoiled investor "confidence." In 1961, amid recession, budget deficit spending had kicked in, and the macroeconomy climbed out of recession in 1962. To forestall a fiscal drag, the Revenue Act of 1962 legislated a 7 percent investment tax credit. Committed to tax cuts on capital, JFK's administration believed that, politically, taxes on personal incomes must come down as well. JFK presented the broader tax cut bill to Congress in the summer of 1962. The president, according to one economic adviser, believed "that there were unmet social needs much more important than private needs that would be satisfied by tax reduction." The 1961 Area Redevelopment Act had allotted $507 million for loans and grants to "alleviate conditions of substantial and persistent unemployment in certain economically distressed areas."[70] Much greater was the $17 billion JFK pumped into the military-industrial complex.[71] But JFK fretted over "the lack of confidence of business in the administration." In other words, the threat of political liquidity preference loomed. The owners of capital won this round of confidence games, as "Kennedy offered what business had wanted in 1937–8 and still wanted in 1962—tax reduction."[72]

Kennedy's tax bill would not pass until February 1964: in the intervening eighteen months, as the bill slowly wound through Congress and was picked at by special interests, events of epic consequence occurred. In the fall of 1962, the Cuban Missile Crisis brought the world to the brink of nuclear war; in the spring of 1963, civil rights protests in Birmingham, Alabama, led to white police offers violently assaulting black children on television; in the summer of 1963, Martin Luther King, Jr., led the March on Washington for Jobs and Freedom, and white supremacists bombed a Birmingham church, killing four black children; in the fall of 1963, in California's Salinas Valley, a freight train crashed into a bus of Mexican agricultural laborers, killing thirty-one and calling national attention to the exploitation of braceros under national immigration laws. Then in November 1963, Lee Harvey Oswald, a little guy in the era of bigness, as if on loan from some film noir central casting agency, assassinated Kennedy, and the vice president, Lyndon Baines Johnson, became president.

LBJ hailed from the Hill Country of central Texas, decades before his birth the hotbed of the Populist Revolt. LBJ won a congressional seat in 1937, at age twenty-nine, and kept it, delivering dollars to his district and then, after becoming a senator in 1949, to the state of Texas. LBJ was a master parliamentarian but also recognizably a new political type, the southern elected representative, desperate to attract federal dollars for roads, hospitals, power utilities, airports, military bases, and prime military contracts—and hoping that after these inducements, private capital might follow. While LBJ was a senator, the South's share of military dollars increased from 7 percent to 15 percent of the national total.[73] Among pro-business liberals, what made LBJ unique was his general empathy for the poor and, compared to many of his southern legislative peers, his relative distaste for white supremacy.

In January 1964, LBJ's first State of the Union address called for an "allout war on human poverty and unemployment in these United States."[74] His first two legislative priorities, he declared, would be to pass JFK's proposed tax cut and civil rights legislation. LBJ invited a group of business executives to the White House and faulted "uncertainty" for stunted past economic expansions. He pleaded for business "confidence," explaining that "this administration wants to help you and work with you." The Revenue Act of 1964 was a $10 billion tax cut, one-tenth of the federal budget. Corporate income taxes came down only slightly, from 52 percent to 48 percent, but the legislation offered many tax incentives for private investment. Personal income tax rates came down from 91 percent to 70 percent in the top marginal bracket, and from 20 percent to 14 percent in the bottom bracket.[75] Meanwhile, after a dramatic filibuster, the 1964 Civil Rights Act passed. Among its more controversial provisions was Title VII, which prohibited employment discrimination on the basis of race, color, religion, sex, and national origin and created the Equal Employment Opportunity Commission (EEOC) to enforce it. JFK also created the President's Commission on the Status of Women, led by postwar labor feminists, including its chairwoman, Esther Peterson, to grapple with the rising rate of female labor force participation.[76] But the inclusion of "sex" in Title VII had been an eleventh-hour legislative decision.[77]

The table was now set for an extraordinary conjuncture. The Revenue Act of 1964 was something new in the history of U.S. fiscal policy. It was not a countercyclical tax cut to compensate for a recession; it was a reduction in revenue to fuel a continued macroeconomic expansion. A long macroeconomic boom did commence. Private investment did surge. Capacity utilization in industry reached 90 percent. The stock market reached an all-time peak in 1965. For the first quarter of 1965, GM announced the largest profit—$636 million—in U.S. history.[78] GDP grew nearly 6 percent. Profits and wages climbed in unison. Unemployment moved below 4 percent. At first, inflation remained moderate. If inequality did increase a bit, the poverty rate declined. Noting the happy harmonization of every macroeconomic variable, the annual reports of the CEA began to read like self-congratulatory victory laps. In the election of 1964, LBJ trounced Barry Goldwater, and the Democrats won large majorities in both houses of Congress. After the moderately disappointing 1950s, the very notion of an American postwar golden age of capitalism might well have been invented in a liberal MIT economics department seminar room in the opening months of 1965.

And yet somehow, by the end of 1965, despite the macroeconomic boom, the United States found itself embroiled in a social and political crisis. The moment of triumph for postwar liberalism did not so much contain the seeds of its later demise; it was its demise. How was this possible?

For one thing, liberalism paid dearly for its original sins and limitations. FDR had cut a deal with southern white supremacists because he needed their votes. The postwar political economy of pay successfully channeled wages and "income security" into the hands of white male breadwinners, expanding a consumerist middle class of nuclear families.[79] But the distribution of incomes did not address relational wrongs, and with white male breadwinning being the currency of distributive justice, when other groups made claims on the economy, it threatened zero-sum struggle and political trouble, rather than a more equitable division of the spoils of growth. For when long marginalized and oppressed groups demanded more from the economy, liberalism had few politically legitimate mechanisms available. The new "rights consciousness" of civil rights movements simply did not align with the existing grooves of macroeconomic stimulus.[80] The macroeconomic expansion that followed the post-1964 tax cut, no matter how good the aggregate numbers looked, was not capable of delivering.

Furthermore, by the mid-1960s, the composition and geography of capital investment were shifting. The illiquid, productive capital of the historic northeastern-midwestern manufacturing belt, which had so settled the postwar political economy of income, was beginning to unsettle. Capital mobility, including resurgent global capital mobility, undermined the ability of the federal government to control the economy toward any end whatsoever.

The most pressing manifestation of these problems was the "urban crisis."[81] Since the New Deal, the federal government had not invested resources in cities, least of all in northern cities, leaving them, politically, to Democratic Party city bosses. Cold War liberalism had instead induced residential investment in suburbia, which undermined urban economies. Postwar "urban renewal" meant public authorities razed many a city block, but just as the rain had never followed the plow on the post–Civil War western plains, private investment did not follow the postwar bulldozer.[82] Instead, private capital fled. Capital dispersed to the suburbs, the South, and the West. At the national and local levels, liberal policies had little capacity to address the phenomenon.[83]

Capital dispersion happened slowly at first. In 1947 GM opened a Chevrolet plant in Doraville, Georgia, outside Atlanta, and GM's postwar capital expansion increasingly put capital on southern ground.[84] According to the labor law of adversarial collective bargaining, unions had no say over corporate investment decisions. Southern states passed laws granting tax credits for industrial relocation, and new business consultancies recommended that corporations move.[85] Taft-Hartley-blessed right-to-work legislation kept both southern unionization rates and wages low. Agricultural labor accounted for 73 percent of the southern workforce in 1940, but with mechanization and the rise of southern industry, only 6.8 percent by 1970.[86] So began the deindustrialization of the northeastern-midwestern manufacturing belt.[87]

While intellectuals complained about bureaucratic white-collar "conformity," the brief investment surge after the 1957–58 recession, then the even larger spurt after the 1964 tax cut, saw accelerated capital mobility. Firms reinvested profits in different locations, first in the South. In 1958, a recession year, national fixed investment dipped by 17 percent, but the South experienced no such contraction.[88] Northern urban blacks had recently fled the South for northern manufacturing jobs—which now disappeared.[89] Whiplashed, their communities now suffered the most. Because of white racism, blacks could not so easily decamp, yet again, to follow capital investment, for either the suburbs or back to the South.[90]

The post-1964 tax cut focused private investment in what political commentator Kevin Phillips branded the "Sunbelt," in *The Emerging Republican Majority* (1969), a region roughly below the thirty-sixth parallel, extending from North Carolina to Southern California. Electronics and aerospace firms built new capacity in central Florida near an array of military contractors that benefited from JFK's increased military spending. U.S. Steel opened a plant in Houston in 1963, a city that benefited from public dollars first bestowed by LBJ, including to the National Aeronautics and Space Administration (NASA), which opened in 1958. After the space program built a facility in Huntsville, Alabama, IBM erected a new facility there in 1965.[91] In 1967 the average white unemployment rate in Chicago might have been 3.4 percent, but that year, among the white ethnic communities of the Chicago stockyards district, long an electoral backbone of New Deal liberalism, unemployment hit 20 percent.[92] The dynamics of place in the pattern of private capital investment began to undermine the relevance of aggregate national economic statistics.

Peeking inside the aggregate national capital stock—what MIT economist Solow, a member of JFK's Council of Economic Advisers and an early drafter of what became the 1964 tax cut, simply called "K" in his growth model—reveals two more consequential qualities. First, automation was eliminating many low-skilled, commonly unionized blue-collar jobs. Congress even held hearings in 1963 on "the marriage of the assembly line and the computer." In 1964, in Birmingham, Alabama, where civil rights protests had recently raged and the Democratic commissioner of public safety Bull Connor sicced attack dogs on black children, U.S. Steel, taking advantage of a Revenue Act of 1964 "modernization" investment tax credit, was automating steel production processes through computer systems—eliminating relatively high-paying black jobs.[93]

Second, the post-1964 investment boom also pushed U.S. capital overseas. Europe's mixed economies had focused on heavy industries but left consumer markets untapped, so multinational U.S. consumer goods corporations now rushed fixed investment to Europe.[94] By 1970 U.S. foreign corporate manufacturing investment was nearly 25 percent of its domestic volume (up from 9 percent in 1957).[95] In addition to U.S. multinational investment, as European economies grew, European firms began to sell goods into the U.S. market, earning dollars. When dollars accumulated overseas, that threatened the basis of the Bretton Woods international monetary system.

Another golden age ordeal: the Bretton Woods system never quite worked. The mandated convertibility of European currencies to other currencies had returned only in the late 1950s. By the mid-1960s, hoarded overseas dollars were piling up in Europe—due to the export earnings of European economies, or the transactional needs of overseas U.S. multinational corporations—creating an "offshore" crevice in the capitalist world economy.[96] Further, many U.S. banks, chafing against New Deal–era regulations—especially the Regulation Q cap on interest—opened in the relatively unregulated London-based Eurodollar market, or Euromarkets, which the British government actively cultivated. In London, Eurodollars became pools for cross-border currency speculation, which threatened to overwhelm state capital controls on the movement of cross-border hot money. Under Bretton Woods, the United States had a legal obligation to exchange one ounce of gold for $35. The presence of too many dollars abroad threatened the maintenance of that peg. London-based currency speculators first attacked the dollar in 1960. In 1963 the Kennedy administration declared a tax on short-term capital outflows, to keep more U.S. dollars at home. LBJ would slap on greater capital controls. After the dangerous "dollar gap" of 1947–48 abroad, the "dollar glut" overseas was more threatening now.

LBJ's ambitious legislative program of a "Great Society," to extend economic opportunities to the disadvantaged, ran up against these constraints. The U.S. welfare state expanded through more income politics.[97] The Social Security Act of 1965 extended benefits and created Medicare, a federal entitlement to hospital and medical insurance for citizens over age sixty-five. Medicaid provided federal grants for states to fund means-tested health insurance. The centerpiece of the Great Society, however, was the "War on Poverty" and the Economic Opportunity Act of 1964. War on Poverty programs did reduce poverty, by as much as 26 percent.[98] But the War on Poverty was a political failure, as, unlike FDR's New Deal, it did not build an adequate electoral constituency, for reasons that say much about the economic limits of liberalism by the 1960s.

In 1964 LBJ's administration allotted $750 million to the Office of Economic Opportunity and another $1.5 billion in 1965. That simply was not enough. But with the macroeconomy booming after the tax cut, the administration did not necessarily believe the problem was structural, economically speaking. What was needed was only "equality of opportunity." Conservatives identified the problems in black communities as stemming not from economic adversity but from corrupt city political machines, and not from racial discrimination but from a black cultural "pathology" that allegedly undermined the black family and the black work ethic, leading to the ongoing wave of violence and crime. During the China shock of the 2000s, when capital flight would eliminate white manufacturing jobs at the same scale, and poor whites would be incarcerated at a mass scale, few would be so quick to blame a pathological "white culture" instead of the root cause, which was a profound social and economic dislocation resulting from sudden capital disinvestment.

Institutionally, to achieve its ends, the Great Society tapped nonprofit corporations. Big government did not have the legitimacy, either fiscally or politically, to do the job itself. The fiscal triangle went into motion and transformed. The federal government leaned on the Ford Foundation, especially, and on smaller local nonprofits. It also created new entities, such as community development corporations, to act as conduits for federal funds and tax breaks. Tellingly, LBJ's secretary of health, education, and welfare, was John W. Gardner, a former president of the Carnegie Foundation, who had sat on the boards of the Metropolitan Museum of Art and the Shell Oil Company—an "in and outer" all around the fiscal triangle. Medicare, Medicaid, and the Economic Opportunity Act for the first time sanctioned federal government contracting with nonprofit corporations, which still drew funds from philanthropic foundations.[99] The institutional structures and ideological boundaries of the fiscal triangle began to blur. Nonprofit corporations increasingly became absorbed into the state. Philanthropy increasingly appeared politicized by liberals, and soon enough, conservatives would respond in kind.

Poverty was reduced, but the politics did not work. Republican conservatives would not support any war on poverty, period. Meanwhile oppressed and marginalized peoples, through bottom-up social movements for welfare rights and public housing, expected to enjoy the "maximum feasible participation" that the Economic Opportunity Act promised. In August 1965 congressional members held outdoor hearings in Los Angeles to discuss "community action" in the implementation of War on Poverty programs, which mostly included youth job skill training programs.

Instead, they heard black and Mexican-American residents of East and South Central Los Angeles demand more participation, a political voice, and jobs.[100] Days later an uprising, prompted by police violence, broke out in Watts, where the black unemployment rate was 33 percent. GM, Chrysler, and Firestone had shuttered their postwar factories in the Los Angeles area, and the local aerospace industry, still militarily funded and ever more high-tech, was shedding the kinds of unskilled jobs that commonly went to blacks—who, because of white racism, were disproportionately neither engineering graduates of Caltech nor members of local unions, which had national reputations for racist exclusion. During the Watts uprising, thirty-four people died, and $40 million worth of property was destroyed.[101]

Not surprisingly, in inner cities that suffered from capital disinvestment and therefore unemployment, rates of violence and crime of all kinds surged, initiating a nationwide crime wave.[102] Blacks in impoverished urban areas were disproportionately offenders and victims. In September 1965, LBJ signed the Law Enforcement Assistance Act, and the strapped local and state governments, which had nowhere near the fiscal capacity to even attempt economic development policies of their own, began to shift their funds toward policing. Historically blacks had been five times more likely to be imprisoned than whites, so when incarceration increased, in turn blacks would be more likely to go to jail. (The ratio of five to one has proved persistent.) Soon enough, the building of prisons would become a new kind of economic development. The failure of twentieth-century liberalism's economic development agenda has no more telling statistic than that black men born between 1965 and 1969 were more likely on average to end up in prison than to graduate from college.[103]

Two years later, in 1967, came the "long hot summer" of urban uprisings. Liberals reached for the standard political economic measures. Credit subsidies extended to farmers were now indirectly offered to urban residents. The Housing and Urban Development Act of 1968 moved Fannie Mae off the federal budget and created the Government National Mortgage Association (Ginnie Mae) to securitize home mortgages, in the hope of luring investment into low-income housing.[104] Using military Keynesianism to defend the Cold War military frontier in Vietnam, LBJ escalated U.S. military support for the proxy South Vietnamese government. The draft conscripted 112,386 American youths in 1964, and 230,991 in 1965.[105] In 1965 military spending ticked up greatly, which in tandem with the 1964 tax cut, further stimulated the ongoing national macroeconomic boom.

If fiscal stimulus did not draw resources into the productive economy that had been excluded—places and people, forgone economic capacity, forgone economic possibility—it risked bringing existing lines of production up to full capacity. At that point, more stimulus threatened inflation, as it either threw more dollars at the same amount of goods or encouraged demands that the economy could not satisfy. In 1966 inflation began to climb again, in a national economy overstimulated in some geographical places but still vastly underresourced in others. Meanwhile the war in Vietnam pushed more dollars overseas, as the U.S. military supply chain wrapped around Southeast Asia. In 1966 the Fed raised interest rates—above 4 percent for the first time in the postwar era—both to halt inflation and to attract foreign capital into the United States, in order to help defend the dollar-gold peg against London-based currency speculators. The "offshore" London money market in dollars was something new, but competitive central bank interest rate adjustments recalled the old gold standard mechanism of national economic adjustment, before the birth of liberalism in the Age of Control.

LBJ, the most dexterous national politician since FDR, would recall:

> I felt that I was being chased on all sides by a giant stampede coming at me from all directions. On one side, the American people were stampeding me to do something about Vietnam. On another side, the inflationary economy was booming out of control. Up ahead were dozens of danger signs pointing to another summer of riots in the cities. I was being forced over the edge by rioting blacks, demonstrating students, marching welfare mothers, squawking professors, and hysterical reporters.[106]

During the so-called golden age of capitalism, big government, for all its power at home and abroad—and it did sit on a nuclear arsenal capable of ending all civilization—nonetheless enjoyed a rather weak mandate to act in the name of the public interest when moving outside the orbits of either national security (Vietnam even threatened that) or shoring up the incomes of white male breadwinners. All the postwar presidents learned these lessons, and so did LBJ.

The postwar period was a golden age of aggregate productivity, profit, wage, and GDP growth, and relative household income equality. Nonetheless, the U.S. postwar project of economic development failed politically, both at home and abroad.[107] To contain the possible spread of Communism in the midst of world decolonization, LBJ marched liberalism off to Vietnam, but at the end of the path lay only death, military defeat, more inflation, a greater "dollar gap," and a broader crisis of industrial capitalism, which would spell the end of the Age of Control altogether.

CHAPTER 18

CRISIS OF
INDUSTRIAL CAPITAL

ORE THAN A CENTURY OLD, THE LONG INDUSTRIAL EPOCH
of American capitalism came to a close during the 1970s. Actually, the share of total U.S. employment in manufacturing peaked during World War II at 38 percent, at which time there were already more employees in the "service-providing industries." After the war, in raw totals, service employment expanded while manufacturing held steady, but during the 1970s evidence abounded of a structural shift. For instance, "the increase in employment in eating and drinking places since 1973," noted Emma Rothschild in 1981, became "greater than the total employment in the automobile and steel industries combined."[1]

After 1973, not just industrial employment but industrial productivity, profits, and wages, by various measurements, all sagged. Manufacturing would hardly disappear—roughly, it would retain its share of "value added" (the amount of value added to goods during the relevant stage of production) to the economy. However, as opposed to the era of industrialization, from this period forward in U.S. history, the recomposition rather than the expansion of manufacturing better captures the process at hand.[2] Meanwhile the 1970s crisis of industrial capital was broader than anything captured in any economic statistic. Across all industrial societies, the decade saw one crisis of legitimacy after another—economic but also social, cultural, environmental, and political.[3]

For generations, the productive capital of factories had anchored the generation of profits, pay, and fiscal revenue, as it had also anchored communities and families, inner lives and identities. In the 1970s, that base failed. Emblematically, the artist Gordon Matta-Clark's *Day's End* (1975) was an abandoned industrial structure in deindustrializing Lower Manhattan, designed in the manner of one of Albert Kahn's Detroit mass production factories. Matta-Clark, to great visual effect, "cut" the floor, foundation, and ceiling while punching holes in the windows.[4] Having been so important to civilization for so long, industrial structures were worthy of such artistic treatment. Matta-Clark depicted old structures hollowing out, as if the foundations of industrial society had begun to crack. They had. The many fault lines of the Age of Control set off a series of shocks—a very 1970s term, when there was "future shock," the "Nixon shock," "oil shocks," and finally the "Volcker Shock" in monetary policy—that brought the decade to an end. The total transformation would be tectonic.[5]

GORDON MATTA-CLARK, *DAYS END PIER 52.3 (DOCUMENTATION OF THE ACTION "DAY'S END" MADE IN 1975 IN NEW YORK, UNITED STATES)*
As industrial structures crumbled during the 1970s, Matta-Clark audaciously (and dangerously) "cut" buildings further. This site is part of Manhattan's Pier 52, which has roots in nineteenth-century industry. With industry gone, the artist hoped the public might be inspired by his "anarchitecture" to use the space creatively. Instead, the police closed the building on the day it opened to the public. Tragically, it sat empty until it was demolished two years later.

Given the total nature of the crisis of industrial capital, we might plausibly chart a number of pathways into discussing it. Economically, the sequence was clear. First came a profit squeeze. Between 1965 and 1970, despite macroeconomic expansion, the net corporate profit rate dropped from 16 percent to under 10 percent, and U.S. manufacturers, many suffering under international trade competition, saw their profits cut in half.[6] The profit rate remained low throughout the 1970s relative to the postwar standard. However, as if from habit, on average, industrial corporate managers kept investing and producing. It became a decade of profitless prosperity, with high rates of corporate investment and production but flagging profits.

Swiftly, problems compounded. In 1971, for the first time in the twentieth century, the United States ran a trade deficit in goods with the world. For several reasons—foreign countries' export earnings by selling into the U.S. market, U.S. multinational investment, and U.S. military commitments abroad—U.S. dollars kept accumulating in the London Eurodollar market. They became the basis of currency speculators' attacks on the free convertibility of the Bretton Woods–mandated peg of the dollar to gold at $35 an ounce. After decades of world economic recovery and growth, the dollar was now overvalued relative to other currencies. That hurt U.S. manufacturers at home and abroad. With them in mind, in 1973 President Richard Nixon's administration broke the dollar-gold peg. The Bretton Woods international monetary system was over. Soon the United States lifted all cross-border capital controls. Now the value of the dollar would be determined in global currency trading markets—subject to the momentary whims of trade and speculative expectations.

Meanwhile another dislocation emerged in the world economy, in the relationship between manufacturers and raw materials. The worldwide postwar industrial expansion—the multiplying effects of industrial investment and global commerce—had been possible only because of the continuing availability of the needed primary products. In agriculture across the world, there was a land-saving "green revolution." Further, government stockpiling of inventories and commodity price support programs in the United States and elsewhere adjusted the available quantities of goods and smoothed prices. Nonetheless, in agriculture and raw materials, the threat of decreasing returns always loomed due to ecological limits (there is only so much land), by contrast to manufacturing activity, so often subject to increasing returns.[7]

In 1973 came the first global "oil shock," as the Organization of the Petroleum Exporting Countries (OPEC) raised the price of the fossil fuel, the most crucial of all industrial inputs. Unrelatedly, bad harvests in the Soviet Union and China had led to the exhaustion of government stockpiles of grains. Inventories could not adjust, so prices did. Interacting with speculative expectations in the post–Bretton Woods currency markets, commodity prices surged. Commodity price inflation broke out. The cost of primary inputs increased. Immediately, the U.S. rate of productivity growth was bumped onto a lower track.[8] It would never recover.[9] Given the immediate shock, economic production declined. In 1973 the United States entered into the deepest recession since the Great Depression—except now in the midst of price inflation, rather than deflation, as was the case in the 1930s.

The federal government rolled out the standard corrective measures, all fashioned since the 1930s. Government welfare payments—more than doubling between 1970 and 1975, nearly equaling military expenditures—stabilized incomes and thus spending. In 1975, in countercyclical fashion, the federal budget entered a deficit. Congress passed tax rebates to induce private investment. Altogether the macroeconomy climbed out of reces-

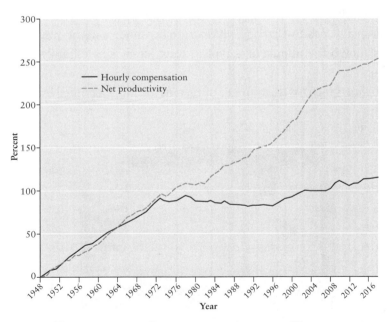

PRODUCTIVITY GROWTH AND AVERAGE HOURLY
COMPENSATION GROWTH
The New Deal shifted income from capital to labor. The tight link
between productivity growth and average labor compensation in
the decades after World War II contributed to the phenomenon.
After 1970, the link was broken.

sion by the end of 1975 and began an expansion that would last until 1980, making it the second longest of the postwar period.

Nonetheless, when the Age of Control's two chief economic maladies, inflation and unemployment, began to worsen, they worsened in unison. Postwar Keynesian macroeconomists had suggested that government could buy more employment with inflation. In the recessionary year of 1975, however, the unemployment and inflation rates both topped 8 percent. The combination was called "stagflation."

U.S. political economy still funneled income and welfare entitlements largely through the white-male-breadwinning wage. Without high rates of male employment and pay, there would be trouble. Average male pay flatlined after 1972. Troublingly, it delinked from the growth, however meager, of productivity, with which it had roughly correlated since World War II. Meanwhile the male workforce participation rate declined steadily.

Ideologically backdated since the beginning of the industrial epoch in the nineteenth century, the male-breadwinner-female-homemaker family entered crisis, too.[10] In 1973 the divorce rate hit 50 percent. No less emblematically, Matta-Clark's *Splitting* (1974) made one of his sculptural "cuts" down the middle of a typical New Jersey single-family suburban home.

During the 1970s the number of men living alone climbed from 3.5 mil-

GORDON MATTA-CLARK, *SPLITTING 2 (DOCUMENTATION OF THE ACTION "SPLITTING" MADE IN 1974 IN NEW JERSEY, UNITED STATES).*
More so than the factory, the home was the anchor of industrial
society. Matta-Clark applied another of his daring sculptural
"cuts" to this Englewood, New Jersey, suburban home.
The artist died from cancer at age thirty-five.

CIVILIAN LABOR FORCE PARTICIPATION RATE, MEN
The steady decline in the percentage of working-age men in the remunerated
workforce over the twentieth century indicates how tenuous one foundation
of the Age of Control—the male breadwinning wage—in fact was.

lion to 6.8 million.[11] Male identity crisis became a, if not the, great theme
of popular cultural expression.[12] Meanwhile, without productivity gains,
including access to the cheap oil necessary for energy-intensive industries, industry could not deliver ever-rising profits and wages (to any gender). It could not produce an ever-expanding consumer abundance. There
would be inflation.

The economic debate over the causes of inflation during the 1970s continues to this day.[13] To release bank credit and help lift the macroeconomy
out of recession, the Fed, pressured by elected politicians, lowered its targeted short-term interest rate. More credit and money chased the same
amount of goods—especially given flagging productivity and a reduced
trendline in the expansion of economic output. Thus monetary policy
threatened inflation. But inflation can rarely be reduced to the mere supply of money—and surely not in this instance.[14] After 1973 fiscal and
monetary policy stoked an expansion that only exacerbated the strains
between the manufacturing and primary product sectors. The latter had
hit supply limits. Accordingly, commodity prices inflated. Meanwhile, as
productivity and profits declined in industry, a distributional conflict between capital and labor, over the division of the spoils from an economic

pie expanding at a lesser rate, was inevitable. However, wage and price inflation could paper that over by delaying an answer to the question of who, in the end, would pay for the economy-wide productivity slowdown. Finally, that productivity slowdown was exacerbated by the prodigious growth of the relatively low-productivity service sector: the new economy of eating and drinking places, which dominated the decade's fastest-growing urban areas, which were in the Sunbelt.

Inflation is not always a bad thing. Some inflation may chip away at rentier profits, encourage present spending, support expectations of future profits, and discourage the hoarding of cash and other liquid assets. But persistent, volatile, and high inflation may destabilize expectations and, by creating uncertainty, pull economies into the short-term present. That undermines long-term development. Thus the inflationary 1970s became, in the words of the historian Jefferson Cowie, a decade of "wholesale transformation without a narrative."[15]

To end inflation, an authority must arbitrate discord, adjudicate distributional conflicts between economic sectors and groups, and rechart a viable long-term economic path. Deflationary spirals require that, too, and during the Great Depression the New Deal, if far from perfectly, had proved up to the task. During the 1970s inflation, the prime candidate for the job was once again the U.S. federal government—the government of the world economic hegemon.

Federal economic policy making was active during the 1970s. In addition to fiscal policy, liberalism's regulatory arm beefed up. At the behest of white middle-class liberals, new consumer and environmental regulations went on the books, which only ate into profits and contributed to the inflation. The federal government simply did not have the mechanisms at hand to master inflation. There was no notion of a unified public interest on the basis of which to act anyway. Instead, the polity was splintering into Nixon's Silent Majority, black nationalists, "back to the land" farmers, white ethnic revivalists (including neo-Confederates), Friends of the Earth, pro-life evangelical "family values" Christians, radical lesbians, international bankers, advocates of Indian sovereignties, Business Round-table CEOs, black women activists of the National Welfare Rights Organization, white nationalist Vietnam veterans, and last but not least, individual practitioners of narcissism. For the 1970s was also the "Me Decade," when "enchantment of self with self," to quote the poet John Ashbery's "Self-Portrait in a Convex Mirror" (1975), became a major cultural preoccupation. "I am on a lonely road and I am traveling / traveling, traveling, traveling," sang Joni Mitchell in 1971's "All I Want," inaugurating the confessional songwriter genre of the decade.[16]

Every single American alive in the 1970s had grown up in an industrial society. Even if they had experienced the Great Depression and World War II, they had also experienced the postwar commitment to security. It was natural to think that control was the default state of affairs, and that somehow things would muddle through. Perhaps for this reason alone, following convention, corporate managers maintained the rate of investment, despite flagging profits. By contrast, William Gaddis's *J R* (1975), the most inscrutable novel about capitalism, and perhaps the best since Melville's *The Confidence Man*, said it was a mistake

> to assume that organization is an inherent property . . . and that disorder and chaos are simply irrelevant forces that threaten it from outside. In fact it's exactly the opposite. Order is simply a thin, perilous condition we try to impose on the basic reality of chaos.[17]

The Age of Control was a perilous condition, and it would come to an end.

Already during this crisis decade, a new capitalism was being born. Leaving fixed structures on the ground, capital was becoming ever more roving, convertible, and global. New economic ways of life were appearing, especially in the Sunbelt. A new condition of generalized uncertainty arose, corrosive but also productive. Postwar industrial society had had its virtues—structure, stability, and the channeling of income growth to the middle of the distribution. Yet premised as it was on the white male heterosexual breadwinning wage, on social conformism, on an energy regime capable of threatening the planet's future, and on dangerous, at times stultifying factory work, regret over its death was and is unwarranted. After all, Matta-Clark made his sculptural "cuts" at industrial and suburban structures in order to let in the light.

1. Nixon Shock

In the presidential election of 1968, LBJ declined to run, the Democratic Party imploded over Vietnam, and the victor was Republican Richard Milhous Nixon. With representative hubris, LBJ's chairman of the Council of Economic Advisers (CEA), Arthur Okun, bragged in *The Political Economy of Prosperity* (1970) of the "unparalleled, unprecedented, and uninter-rupted economic expansion" that had occurred on LBJ's watch.[18] But the truth was that Nixon inherited a political economy under serious strain. The most pressing problem was the inability of the United States to main-tain its international obligations under the Bretton Woods international monetary system, while also stimulating the U.S. macroeconomy. Nixon's administration never squared the circle. The consequences of its restor-ative attempts would be momentous.

The dollar policy that LBJ bequeathed Nixon was bankrupt. Because of federal government spending abroad (if only to fight the Vietnam War), U.S. multinational foreign investment, and the U.S. trade deficit, too many dollars were abroad. They accumulated, chiefly in the London Eurodollar market, which financed long-term U.S. multinational corporate invest-ment in enterprise but also financiers' short-term international currency speculation. The contradictory drive of speculative investment was back. London speculators bid up the value of gold, questioning how long the United States could maintain the dollar's $35-per-ounce peg to gold. JFK's and LBJ's policies had been ad hoc. But in 1968, when domestic inflation hit 4.2 percent, LBJ, on the way out, acted decisively. His administration slapped on firm capital controls, to stanch dollars' movement overseas. The United States announced it would no longer exchange dollars for gold with private parties, only with foreign central banks. "Free convertibility" under Bretton Woods had lasted no more than a decade.[19] LBJ also stood down while the Fed raised interest rates to over 6 percent to recruit "hot," short-term money arrivals from London, which eased the strain on the dollar in foreign exchange markets. After Nixon took office, the Fed raised the short-term rate to over 9 percent. The dollar crisis appeared averted. But tight money and credit meant the U.S. macroeconomy entered into recession in 1969, for the first time since 1961, ending the longest postwar expansion. That year inflation reached 5.4 percent.

Nixon had been vice president to the inflation-obsessed Eisenhower, but he also blamed the Fed for tightening money and credit during the 1960–61 recession, which he believed was responsible for his narrow loss to JFK. At first, President Nixon supported the Fed's tight money policy to bring down inflation and reduced federal spending by happily slashing LBJ's War on Poverty programs. But he feared the political consequences of recession and of unemployment in particular—one adviser said he had a "phobia."[20] This was a president who once instructed his staff that he needed "everybody here now to start thinking politically, instead of worrying about running things well."[21] In economic policy, Nixon was a political cynic but not an inflexible ideologue. He was consistently only one thing, an economic nationalist—the last Keynesian, the first Trumpist.

Even before the 1970 midterm elections, in which Republicans performed poorly, Nixon had changed course. He turned to fiscal stimulus to bring down unemployment, and in 1971 the federal budget neared its postwar high. With inflation still hovering near 5 percent, Nixon appointed the inflation hawk Arthur Burns, a chairman of the Council of Economic Advisers under Eisenhower, the new chairman of the Fed. Burns nonetheless obliged the president, and eased credit conditions, after Nixon threatened to aides that if he did not, "he'll get it right in the chops."[22] In 1971 the Fed brought the short-term rate below 4 percent, and the U.S. macroeconomy emerged from recession.

The problem was that such macroeconomic stimulus was by now incompatible with the dollar-gold peg. With a lower U.S. interest rate, liquid short-term capital decamped for London and converted into other currencies. Further, because the international monetary system was on a dollar basis, when more dollars headed overseas, foreign countries accumulated greater bank reserves, which translated into inflation. Cold War allies France and West Germany complained the loudest about the American "export of inflation," though such Cold War allies, Japan as well, did not want to revalue their currencies since so much of the international success of their manufacturing sectors had come from exporting to the U.S. market, aided by their weak currencies, relative to the dollar. In 1971, for the first time in the twentieth century, the United States ran a trade deficit.[23]

Nixon's message to the world was clear. The United States would prioritize domestic concerns over international obligations. Thus the "Nixon Shock" of 1971, or the "new economic policy" as Nixon called it. Nixon's Treasury secretary was the Democrat John Connally, a former governor of Texas and a nationalist who believed, "The foreigners are out to screw us. It's our job to screw them first." Both men deeply desired to restore U.S. manufacturing's international prowess, which Nixon believed was the basis of postwar U.S. geopolitical power.[24] As for domestic politics, "we'll take inflation if necessary," Nixon said, but "we can't take unemployment."[25]

Nixon shocked U.S. allies when on August 15, 1971, the United States announced it was closing the "gold window" and would no longer exchange gold for dollars at any price. It was also slapping a 10 percent tariff on all imports. Treasury undersecretary Paul Volcker was dispatched abroad to negotiate, and by November 1971 an agreement was announced at Washington's Smithsonian Institution. In the end, the United States waived away the 10 percent tariff. The dollar was repegged to gold at $38 an ounce, not $35. All told, against European currencies, the dollar was devalued by approximately 8 percent, and against the Japanese yen by 17 percent. Finally, the new economic policy included a 10 percent income tax investment credit and a number of excise taxes; to fight inflation, Nixon announced wage and price freezes. To increase U.S. exports earnings and reverse the trade deficit, he mildly relaxed agricultural supply management policies. Commodity inventories reduced.[26] With that, the president believed economic policy was solved, and he pivoted to his chief policy interest, international diplomacy, including the opening of China, détente with the Soviet Union, and his cynical "peace with honor" policy in Vietnam.[27]

When announcing the new economic policy, the president had instructed speechwriter William Safire to avoid the "gobbledygook about crisis of international monetary affairs" and to focus on "emotional feel, lift."[28] This spoke to the president's electoral dream of a "new majority"— his populist appeal to white blue-collar workers, in an effort to divide and conquer the old New Deal liberal political coalition. The idea was to drive a wedge between blue-collar whites and the New Left, which AFL-CIO political director Al Barkan described as "kids, kooks, Communists, and other far-out 'kinky' left-liberals." The way to do this was to ignite the already existing tensions among liberalism's disparate interest groups. Always blunt, Nixon remarked, "we need to build our own new coalition based on Silent Majority, blue-collar Catholics, Poles, Italians, Irish. No promise with Jews and Negroes."[29] In practice, the president's political strategy was far more sophisticated.

Nixon had a talent for setting traps for "liberal elites." Often they walked right into them. True, from Birmingham to Boston, white backlash against black civil rights took care of itself, while the Republican Party reaped the benefit. But Nixon was happy to sign into law a raft of new social regulations advocated by middle-class white liberals: the New Left sprang the New Deal's anti-big-business regulatory arm back into action. It began with the politicization of consumerism and shifted to environmentalism.

The breakthrough piece of legislation was the National Traffic and Motor Vehicle Safety Act of 1966, passed after the publication of Ralph Nader's *Unsafe at Any Speed* (1965). Nader, Princeton class of '55, represented a new kind of liberal, whose constituency was largely middle- and upper-class whites—not blue-collar workers, whose loyalty Nixon now eyed. A new generation of 501(c)(3) and allied 501(c)(4) nonprofits established headquarters in Washington—Common Cause, the National Resources Defense Council, Public Citizen—sustained by revelations of corporate malfeasance, as well as galvanizing public spectacles, whether it was the prone-to-exploding Chevrolet Corvair or the Santa Barbara oil spill of 1969. Between 1968 and 1977, the percentage of Americans who agreed that "business tries to strike a fair balance between profits and the interests of the public" plummeted from 70 to 15 percent.[30] Nixon signed the National Environmental Policy Act of 1969 and by executive order created the Environmental Protection Agency (EPA) in 1970, the same year he signed the Consumer Product Safety Act. The new "rights conscious" social regulation took consumerist, middle-class abundance for granted. It had nothing much to say about the dollar crisis, corporate investment and disinvestment at home or abroad, or inflation. Emboldened, liberalism's regulatory arm had by now completely lost touch with its enfeebled developmental arm. As for social regulation, however laudatory it was, it cut further into the already declining U.S. corporate profit rate. Lower profits threatened lower wages for blue-collar workers.

Profits dropped after 1965, especially in industries, such as steel and auto, that were exposed to international trade competition from lower-cost European and Japanese producers, benefiting from lesser-valued currencies. World trade volumes had accelerated after 1965, aided by JFK's Trade Expansion Act of 1962, which promoted world economic growth but at various rates for various countries. The "manufacturing import penetration ratio," a measure of the penetration of foreign producers into the U.S. home market, climbed from 6.9 percent in the period 1959–66 to 15.8 percent in the period 1969–73.[31] Manufacturing profits suffered from trade competition. Some industries hoped for dollar depreciation to help in export markets, which Nixon provided in 1971, and they also began to lobby for trade protection.

Industry sought other remedies. One response was to shift production to the lower-wage South or overseas. But another response was, as if from habit, to keep investing, and keep producing, in the same places—the old northeastern-midwestern manufacturing belt. But then the "possibility of further technological improvement in our business is not as great as in the past," admitted Edward N. Cole, president of GM. The potential productivity gains of the manned, electric-powered assembly line were all but tapped out—even if unmanned automation still held out promise. Another option was simply to speed up the line and reduce "idle time," Cole added.[32] Tellingly, the industrial accident rate increased by 20 percent in the second half of the 1960s, indicating the speed-up, which prompted Nixon to sign legislation creating the Occupational Safety and Health Administration (1970). The greatest attempted speed-up of the line occurred at GM's computer-monitored Lordstown, Ohio, Chevy Vega facility, which suffered a three-week strike in 1972—the "Industrial Woodstock," as the workforce, on average twenty-five years old, would not stand for it.[33] In response, GM redoubled multinational investments in production abroad. Then a final way to squeeze more profits from existing lines of production was simply to shift earnings from labor to capital—away from wages to profits. In the early 1970s, accounting for continued price and wage inflation, "real" labor compensation began to stall.[34]

In many instances, when squeezed, the union rank and file rebelled, including against an increasingly sclerotic labor leadership. The seventy-four-year-old plumbers union representative, AFL-CIO president George Meany, was an able representative of organized industrial labor's steady transformation since the New Deal from a social movement to, nearly, just another liberal interest group. Wildcat strikes broke out. Members voted down leadership-approved contracts. Insurgents campaigned for union offices.[35] Unions had more troubles still. By 1971 the Equal Employment Opportunity Commission was investigating thousands of complaints by individuals from minority groups against union work rules, which had led, on average, to nonwhite, nonmale union members being paid less, enjoying less security, and having fewer chances for advancement. Politically liberal civil rights lawyers filed Title VII class action suits in the courts under the 1964 Civil Rights Act. The U.S. Supreme Court held in *Griggs v. Duke Power Co.* (1971) that seemingly race-neutral union rules—like those favoring seniority, for instance—had "adverse impacts" on minorities and violated Title VII. Financial fines forced unions to integrate, as did pressure from below. In 1972 black workers gathered in Chicago to protest their discriminatory treatment by the leadership of the AFL-CIO, forming the Coalition of Black Trade Unionists. Legally, the drive for civil rights was now on a different track from collective bargaining or larger economic policy making.[36] Meanwhile, in 1972, the EEOC won a sex discrimination case against AT&T Corporation, extracting a $50 million settlement, and soon Title VII class action suits followed against a number of corporations. In *Williams v. Saxbe* (1976), the U.S. Supreme Court would rule that Title VII forbade what would soon be termed "sexual harassment" in the workplace.

The table was being set for Nixon's "hard hat" strategy. In 1970 the Nixon Labor Department produced a research document, "The Problem of Blue Collar Workers," inspired by a *New York Magazine* article written by journalist Pete Hamill, "The Revolt of the White Lower Middle Class," which had caught Nixon's eye. In May 1970, New York construction workers, members of a particularly racist and corrupt union, assaulted "hippie" antiwar protestors, culminating in a 100,000-large hard hat rally of Nixon supporters. An aide noted to the president "their admiration for your masculinity."[37] The Nixon administration would commission a serious study, *Work in America* (1973), of the fact that "millions of Americans are dissatisfied with . . . dull—repetitive jobs that stifle autonomy and initiative."[38] Nixon sensed that the combination of white blue-collar dissatisfaction, civil rights challenges to the privileges of white male breadwinning, and liberal consumerist and environmentalist challenges to business interests and blue-collar wages provided him a political opening. He began to maneuver. Cynically, for instance, he announced support for a federal "basic income" program, to replace all welfare "dependency." Conservative Republicans called it a handout, the National Welfare Rights Organization complained the income floor was too low, and the bill failed. But Nixon was happy, for the debate alone incensed working-class whites fed up with liberal elites "who want to take their money, and give it to people who don't work."[39] When the Comprehensive Development Act then passed to federally fund childcare facilities, Nixon vetoed it, calling it "family-weakening."[40] Nixon had a political genius for drawing liberal proposals out into the open, where they triggered white conservative grievance.

The presidential election of 1972 marked the birth of what the historian Robert O. Self has called "breadwinner conservatism." Nixon absolutely trounced the New Left darling, South Dakota senator George McGovern. The AFL-CIO did not even endorse McGovern, declaring itself neutral. Nixon won over 60 percent of the popular vote, including 57 percent of manual workers, 54 percent of the union vote, and 60 percent of white union members. A conservative, populist white male identity politics thus appeared.[41] It was a long road traveled from FDR's labor-backed 1936 electoral triumph, which had brought about the New Deal political coalition.

However politically effective the "new majority" program was, it did not change the character of U.S. macroeconomic expansions, which were inflationary, ballooned U.S. trade deficits that needed financing somehow, and led to speculative attacks on the dollar-gold peg, even at $38 per ounce. In January 1973, Nixon triumphantly announced the end of wage and price controls. Instantly, inflation climbed.[42] Now everything unraveled quickly. With the announcement of a $6.4 billion trade deficit, in the first quarter of 1973 the United States suffered a net short-term capital-out movement of $6 billion. By now, Connally had been replaced as Treasury secretary by the former University of Chicago economics professor George Shultz. Inspired by his colleague Milton Friedman, Shultz had a new plan: the elimination of currency pegs and capital controls altogether, to encourage the "flow of capital to the places where it can contribute most to growth."[43]

In truth, "flow" is often a bad metaphor for global capital: when liquid stocks in some bank account somewhere move across borders, it is due to speculative expectations as much as to the needs of growth-inducing enterprise somewhere else in the world. For his part, Nixon, assuming he even cared, was by this time becoming preoccupied with the Watergate scandal. He was simply over it. When told that currency speculators were attacking the Italian lira, the president snapped, "I don't give a shit about the lira."[44]

The United States ended Bretton Woods. In March 1973, the dollar-gold peg ended for all time. Within a year, the United States abolished all capital controls on short-term "hot money." Chicago futures traders began selling "currency options," to help traders hedge risk. Newfangled financial products thus replaced state controls. Once the U.S. dollar was floating, it depreciated fast, 20 percent against the West German mark, 12 percent against the Japanese yen. The competitiveness of U.S. manufacturing exports improved, which was what Nixon had always wanted, and in 1973 the U.S. balance of trade recovered, soon achieving a surplus.

On behalf of a nationalist economic agenda, seeking a restoration of world U.S. manufacturing supremacy, Nixon had in fact brought forth a new day without precedent in world economic history: an international monetary system of fiat money—state-issued currencies backed only by the imprimatur of governments, whose relative values were determined by open market trading.

At this point, the United States had not had to do this. As its European allies pleaded, the United States still had the power and resources, acting in unison with other states, to maintain an international monetary system, of some kind, featuring capital controls.[45] Even Arthur Burns, chairman of the Fed, "feared" the breakdown of fixed exchange rates with "a passion." But when he shared that fear with Treasury undersecretary Paul Volcker over lunch, Volcker responded, "[Arthur,] you better go home right away and tighten money."[46] Only the high interest rates necessary to tighten the money supply would recruit enough hot money into the United States, to save the gold-dollar peg. But Burns did not want to raise interest rates, for fear that that would choke off the supply of credit, reduce growth, and increase unemployment. Then he might get it right in the chops from the president.

In 1973, however, the most immediate issue was inflation. In the second quarter of that year, inflation was 8.6 percent; in the fourth quarter, 9.8 percent. Already during the 1960s, inflation had begun to appear during macroeconomic expansions. A host of new factors now contributed: new consumer and environmental regulations, the cost of which were passed on to consumers; and the profit squeeze, amid expectations among workers of continued wage gains. But in 1973, the largest contributor by far was the sudden surge in commodity prices.

OPEC announced an oil embargo against the United States during the October 1973 Yom Kippur War in Israel.[47] Oil prices surged by 400 percent. The United States, still the largest world oil producer, was by now an even greater consumer. The U.S. auto-industrial society was the most energy-intensive economy in the world. The oil shock raised the cost of the most critical energy input. Immediately productivity flagged in the most energy-intensive industries, and U.S. economic activity instantly dropped.[48]

Meanwhile, in a disconnected event, there were bad grain harvests around the world, especially in the Soviet Union and China. Sales of U.S. commodities filled the gap but further depleted farm inventories. Stocks of inventory could not adjust to stabilize prices. Instead, commodity prices began to rise. This was even the case for commodities like coffee, which were then under no supply constraints. Likely, inflationary expectations on account of the recent end of the dollar-gold peg were the culprit.

Nixon finally did what Johnson had been forced to do in 1968: to cool inflation, he trimmed federal expenditures. He stood back as the Fed raised short-term interest rates to record-high postwar levels—above 12 percent. By the time Nixon resigned from the presidency in August 1974 due to the Watergate scandal, the U.S. economy had plunged into the worst recession since the Great Depression. Inflation kept climbing, surpassing 10 percent, while GDP turned negative, and unemployment surged, reaching 9 percent by May 1975. The decade's defining economic malady had appeared: "stagflation."

2. Houston, the Liquid City

The U.S. macroeconomic recession that began in the final months of 1973 was steep. At the bottom of the slump, in late 1974, inflation was nevertheless 11.1 percent. Yet in the middle of 1975, the U.S. macroeconomy climbed out of recession. Complete macroeconomic control was not lost.

The standard corrective measures worked, to some degree. In March 1975, with a Democrat-dominated post-Watergate Congress, President Gerald Ford grudgingly signed a tax-cut bill to stimulate the macroeconomy. National macroeconomic growth returned, and the resulting expansion lasted until the end of the decade. Inflation fell to 5.7 percent in 1976. Nonetheless, unemployment never dipped below 5.5 percent. In 1977 inflation began to tick up again. Still, the post-1975 surge in private investment, a last industrial gasp, was particularly notable, although it crested by 1978.

Even as profits sagged, inflation had reduced the real cost of capital. Capital was free, or nearly free, should industrial corporations want to invest, and many chose to do so. However, during this expansion, once again the U.S. trade deficit ballooned. Once again London-based international currency speculators—owners of liquid capital in its primal money form—attacked the U.S. dollar. And once again inflation and unemployment remained worrisomely high. Obviously, stagflation was now endemic to the U.S. macroeconomy.

But we must put the macroeconomy aside for a moment, as its aggregates tell only so much of the story, if only because they veil striking geographical discrepancies in the experience and trajectory of American economic life. During the 1970s, virtually every single already-industrialized economy around the world, even Communist ones, experienced some variety of macroeconomic "malaise." What was different about the United

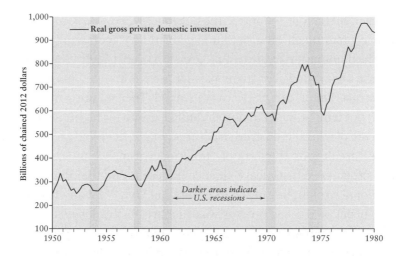

REAL GROSS PRIVATE DOMESTIC INVESTMENT
In the face of falling profits, many corporate managers, as if by habit,
continued to invest in old lines of industry. In tandem with the fresh
expansion of investment in the Sunbelt, the 1970s witnessed a last gasp
surge in industrial investment.

States was, first, the extreme degrees of economic deprivation in the most
devastated urban spaces of the now-deindustrializing historic northeastern-
midwestern manufacturing belt. Second, the United States, unlike other industrial economies, featured a region of striking postindustrial economic
regeneration. This place was the Sunbelt, stretching from Carolina to California, whose so-called golden buckle was the city of Houston.

During the post-1975 macroexpansion, Houston experienced arguably
the greatest moment of peacetime urban expansion of any city in all of
U.S. history. But its growth happened according to a novel economic logic.
While the macro numbers say stagflation was groaning on, in Houston
the outlines of a new economy for a new age of capitalism were sketched.
In 1976 the New York intellectual Daniel Bell published *The Coming of Post-
Industrial Society*.[49] In Houston, it already existed.[50]

A modern industrial economy was an economy of unidirectional, linear time. It was an economy of long-term investment in productive fixed
capital, from which it took time—literally—to use up capital and generate
wealth and profits from labor and enterprise. The best way to do that was
to increase productivity, or the amount of physical output wrested from
the same input. Doing that required settling illiquid capital in place, for the

long term. In the Age of Control, the U.S. macroeconomy, bound in territorial space, had taken on a similar logic of time. "Economic growth" became the dominant narrative of progression over straight-line time.

By the 1970s, however, many past long-term investments were beginning to rust. Flight, not fixity, was the mood. The emerging dynamic was spatial, not temporal. An almost dreamlike desire for flight, a yearning to escape the old, fixed industrial structures, was both visible and audible. In architecture, it took the form of "postmodernism," or an exhaustion of linear, progressive historical sequence in design and the obsolescence of the rational straight line of the International Style.[51] Meanwhile the best-selling novel of the early 1970s was Richard Bach's *Jonathan Livingston Seagull* (1970), about an outcast seagull that loved to fly, yearning for a "higher purpose for life."[52] In music, postindustrial flight songs, all individualistic, competed with older, industrial train songs in which collectivities were bound for common destinations. The rise of country music may have reflected the "southernization" of the U.S. economy, but in 1974 the southern rock band Lynyrd Skynyrd, draped in Confederate flags, released the song "Free Bird"—in which a man just takes off.[53] "Won't you fly high, free bird, yeah!" 1970s culture registered many individual yearnings for transcendence from old structures, including economic ones, and in some places economic life obliged.

The century-old northeastern-midwestern manufacturing belt suffered. What was first called the "snow belt" or the "frost belt" soon enough became the rust belt.[54] Parts of the Midwest were hit the worst, the most dramatic case involving the 1977 closing of the Campbell Works of Youngstown Sheet and Tube, which employed five thousand workers. This was the first in a series of highly publicly visible "factory closings." Unions rediscovered that they had no voice in corporate investment decisions, or now disinvestment decisions.[55] Smaller industrial towns and large industrial cities all suffered. During the 1970s, Chicago lost 12 percent of its population, Baltimore 14 percent, Cleveland 24 percent, and St. Louis 28 percent. People were on the move, headed to the South and the West. In the same period, Houston bulged by 24 percent, San Diego by 25 percent, and Phoenix by 33 percent.[56]

Not everyone could fly away. In northern cities, black political power increased, but capital investment decreased. Between 1970 and 1977, black net urban outmigration amounted to a not inconsiderable 653,000, but black unemployment rates continued to approximately double white rates.[57] At this moment in northern cities, black men especially were expelled from the labor force, or dropped out, at alarming rates. By 1980, at Chicago's largest public housing project, the Robert Taylor Homes, the unemployment rate among the twenty thousand official residents was a shocking 47 percent.[58] Due to white racism, black residents found it difficult to move to the more prosperous suburbs and exurbs. The U.S. Supreme Court, in a case concerning a Chicago suburb, *Village of Arlington Heights v. Metropolitan Housing Development Corp.* (1977), held that municipalities could zone against low-income housing. In northern cities, "poverty traps" emerged and, in the second half of the 1970s, the joblessness and hopelessness of a postindustrial black urban "underclass."[59] Arguably, nowhere in the world was the 1970s industrial "malaise" worse than in the inner-city United States, where increased violence and crime, which began during the 1960s, continued to fester. In response, black urban leaders, requesting resources both for economic development and law enforcement, had the first request rebuffed by the Nixon administration. Local and state fiscal resources increasingly flowed into mass incarceration.[60]

Meanwhile economic activity shifted to the South and the West, the

REGIONAL CHANGES IN POPULATION AND
MANUFACTURING JOBS, 1970–80
The crisis of industrial capital was a crisis for the century-old
northeastern-midwestern manufacturing belt. Population and
manufacturing shifted to the Sunbelt.

site of the post-1975 Sunbelt boom. At the time, many public intellectuals missed it, since economic development looked different in the postindustrial Sunbelt than it had in the industrial Northeast and Midwest. New York City tottered on bankruptcy, as its industrial base, and its tax base, shrank.[61] Regardless, most New York intellectuals found it inconceivable that a place like Houston might be the harbinger of the nation's economic future. Or that, just maybe, economic life was better in Houston, as the Philadelphia migrants Douglas and Virginia Caesar explained to *The New York Times* in 1978. "Much better," the Caesars added.[62] In fairness, the Houston economic model had some difficulty narrating itself.

Houston was a liquid city.[63] Built on coastal marshlands that once lay at the bottom of the ocean in the geological past, the city, ever since its founding as a real estate speculation in the 1830s, had always flooded. The banker and New Deal capitalist Jesse H. Jones was the true founding father of the city, and after a 1935 flood, Jones's government agencies committed resources to help the city with flood control. By then, after the 1901 discovery of oil at Spindletop near Beaumont, Texas, Houston had become home to a number of oil exploration and refining corporations. And after a 1900 hurricane destroyed the port of Galveston Island, the government had dredged the Houston Ship Channel, and Houston had become Texas's chief seaport. Jones, who called Chicago the "miracle in growth in modern cities," prophesied that Houston would be the next Chicago.[64] In 1980 the Port of Houston ranked first in foreign tonnage among all U.S. ports.[65] Many Chicagoans migrated to Houston, in search of economic opportunity. "My brain is tired of the wind / Chicago winters, just do me in," sang punk rocker Iggy Pop in "Houston Is Hot Tonight" (1981).

Scientists debate the moment of origin for anthropogenic climate change. However, the rapid expansion of Houston during the 1970s undoubtedly represents an anthropogenic form of urban economic growth.[66] Between 1975 and 1981, because of the cluster of refineries and petrochemical plants that lined the Ship Channel on the city's working-class East End, Houston enjoyed the highest rate of manufacturing growth in the United States. By the end of that period, Houston ranked fourth as a city in manufacturing value added, behind Chicago, Detroit, and Los Angeles. Houston's "oil service" companies, such as Halliburton, all dating from the 1920s, were global, with operations in Europe, the Middle East, and Latin America. The continued centrality of fossil fuels to the U.S. and world economy was the reason for Houston's existence and, during the 1970s, an era of high oil prices, its extraordinary growth. Furthermore, sprawling as it was, Houston was also dependent for its existence on the automobile and, given the city's heat and humidity, on energy-consuming air-conditioning. In 1973 because of air pollution, the EPA instructed Houstonians that they must drive 10 percent fewer miles, but Houstonians refused. The EPA backed down. In 1982, Houston had exceeded its pre-scribed daily EPA ozone limit on 181 separate occasions.[67] During the 1970s, with the continued growth of automobile- and air-conditioning-based cities such as Houston, U.S. national energy consumption climbed.

Oil and petrochemicals were Houston's manufacturing base. Remark-ably, during the later era of scientific confirmation of anthropogenic cli-mate change, the most economically dynamic American city would continue to be automobile-based Houston—a city premised on oil, the great fossil-fuel-energy input of industrial society. So what then made the city "post" industrial exactly? Part of the answer concerns space.

The city of Houston generated incomes by growing rapidly across space, rather than by increasing productivity over time. Spatially, it would one day encompass the areas of Philadelphia, Chicago, Detroit, and Balti-more combined. Its built environment shifted without any urban plan whatsoever. Its metropolitan population reached 2.75 million in 1980, an increase of 45 percent since 1970, but its population density remained half that of Los Angeles. Its downtown actually lost population during the 1970s, as other urban "nodes" popped up. Urban geographers called what emerged a "multi-nodal city," "an edge city," maybe an "edgeless city," or a "limitless city."[68] An industrial city like Chicago, with its zoned and marked-off commercial, industrial, and residential spheres radiating out from a central business district, was no guide. To migrants and visitors, Houston did not offer much structure. It had no long-term plan. Its pat-tern was indeterminate and uncertain. It was a city, according to one mi-grant, "three-fourths of which sometimes gives the impression of being at the edge of town." To others, it was "elusive," a "conundrum," a "chame-leon," "hard to pin down," "hard even to perceive."[69]

Famously, Houston had no zoning ordinances. The city planning com-mission did no planning; it merely tried to keep adequate records and failed. Did the sprawl result in a discernible pattern? Not even the city government had the capacity to know. Real estate developers determined what was built and where. "You better watch your step if you're just standing around / Because the buildings ain't constructed, they erupt from the ground," sang the Amarillo native Joe Ely in "Imagine Houston" (1984).[70] Brown & Root, a commercial construction company, was Houston's biggest employer during the 1970s, when the city added no less than 66.6 million square feet of office space.[71] Gerald Hines, a native of Gary, Indiana, and soon the largest private developer in the United States, built the Galleria, an indoor shopping mall, modeled—in the postmodern architectural style of historical reuse—after its 1877 namesake in Milan. Hines also developed one of the greatest postmodern skyscrapers, the Philip Johnson–designed Pennzoil Place (1976), which, like Matta-Clark's *Day's End*, featured a sculptural cut—as if to mark a great divide, separating epochs.

PHILIP JOHNSON, "PENNZOIL PLACE" (1976)
Johnson was one of the era's most important postmodern architects.
He designed a number of buildings in Houston. Here, from the exterior of
Pennzoil Place, is another 1970s sculptural cut at one of the pillars of
industrial modernism, this time the skyscraper. A visual break in space,
connoting a divide in time between the industrial and postindustrial, in the
emblematic city of Houston. Given the collapse or absence of industrial
structures, disorientation was a quality of the initial experience of the
postindustrial. As seen from this interior view of Pennzoil Place, it was
also a common theme of the art and architecture of the 1970s and '80s.

The cultural critic Fredric Jameson, in his landmark essay on postmodernism, would note the ability of new architectural spaces to transcend "the capacities of the individual human body to locate itself, to organize its immediate surroundings, perceptually."[72] Disoriented or not, if Houstonians were to locate themselves, it was likely to be in a shopping mall. The postindustrial model was if anything more committed than the industrial to consumerism, and in the absence of factory communities, spaces of consumption became venues for social life. By 1980, Houston had a staggering two hundred shopping malls of more than 750,000 square feet of space.[73]

Real estate, residential and commercial, rather than industry, was the city's true economic engine. Houston led the country in residential housing starts between 1975 and 1980.[74] Moreover, Texas was a right-to-work state, and Houston manufacturing was not unionized. The AFL-CIO did not even attempt an organizing drive in Houston until 1981 (which would fail).[75] Manufacturing was also highly automated, meaning it employed a smaller percentage of the population than did manufacturing in other industrial cities.[76] This led to another disorienting feature of the city's economic life: in contrast to previous industrial economies, the male breadwinning wage was not the anchor of Houston's economy. Leading a national trend, Houston had a very high rate of female labor force participation in the middle and bottom ranges of the income and wealth distribution—one reason why, even with the halt in real labor compensation among men, income inequality, measured at the household level, actually declined during the 1970s.

A postindustrial positive feedback loop appeared in the labor market. The more women entered the workforce—as the result of flagging male wages, or divorce, or both—the greater the market demand for labor that had been traditionally performed by unremunerated housewives, whether it was food preparation, childcare, or cleaning. Home and work, breadwinning and homemaking, converged. Joining real estate were the dynamic "service industries," comprising an economy of oil exploration "services," real estate speculation and construction, hamburger stands, and health care. The city's large medical center was another of its urban "nodes."

The following features of Houston's urban economy were all great premonitions of an age of capitalism soon to come. It had little structure, in the industrial sense. Rather than ever-rising unionized male breadwinning wages, fresh incomes were often generated from the appreciation of real estate values, as the city shifted across space so rapidly as to be imperceptible. The centrality of real estate, commercial and residential, meant high levels of debt, in the form of mortgages.

The level of inequality was also high. For if income generation through property ownership—not labor earnings—is the game, the rich will always do better at it, since, by definition, they own most of the property. Houston had both economic opportunity and inequality; in the labor market, the high- and low-wage regions of the service economy expanded in unison, whether it was well-paid real estate developers, corporate lawyers, and doctors at the top of the distribution, or nurses, nannies, and fast-food workers in historically feminized occupations at the bottom. Finally, the increasing prominence of services, always a low-productivity sector of the economy, explains the disappointing trend of productivity growth in the 1970s economy at large—one of the causes of inflation.

A final quality of Houston is no less worthy of mention: it was born a "privatized" city. To lure entrepreneurs, it kept taxes low. In turn, its municipal public services were scarce, from parks and public spaces to state-funded and state-administered welfare or public housing. Retail and service economy venues—shopping malls, strip centers, restaurants, and hospitals—stood in for public and civic spaces. New York's municipal debt, as the city attempted to maintain welfare services, achieved junk status, while Houston, rated AAA, floated few issues of debt. Public and private blurred, and converted, too. Federal resources—Jesse Jones's beneficence, and NASA's Manned Spacecraft Center, brought by LBJ in 1963—were once important to Houston's growth. The government credit subsidies of the Federal Housing Administration (FHA) would always be important to the residential mortgage market. But Houston became the self-styled "free enterprise city."[77] The city actually had to pause real estate development in 1973 because of inadequate sewage systems. But soon it began sprawling again by incorporating and absorbing the debts of "special districts," through which real estate developers offloaded the cost of roads, sewage systems, and power utilities.[78] Many utilities were private, or quasi-private, anyway. Houston had weak municipal services and high concentrations of poverty, especially in its black and Mexican-American neighborhoods. But it also had fewer urban "poverty traps" than a city like Chicago, as the post-civil-rights South became a better place for blacks, economically speaking, than the North.[79] Blacks migrated to cities like Houston and Atlanta. For the poor, private charity, through religious nonprofit corporations, replaced public welfare. Or nonprofit intermediaries might sell "tax credits" to for-profit real estate developers of public housing. The fiscal triangle corroded and lost its structure. Actually, Houston had never had a fiscal triangle—state infrastructure was weak in the city because it had never existed.

Thus in Houston was born a new political economy defined by corruption—not in the sense of nefarious deeds, but in the sense that institutions and identities became shape shifting, amphibious, and androgynous. What was thought to be public became private or never was public. Private spaces, like shopping malls, had to be appropriated as public spaces. Women flooded the workplace, while the home became a new site of remunerated work. For-profit and nonprofit lost their margins and blended with the state. It could all be disorienting. At first, many of those who lived through these changes experienced them as uncertainty and lack of direction. The city had no blueprint, no long-term plan. Houston was a liquid city because it sat on wetlands and always flooded, and also because of its great economic premise, oil. But its pattern of development uncannily embodied some of the themes of speculative liquidity preference: an energetic restlessness, the convertibility of once seemingly unlike things, markets for everything, and a busy present with no heed for the long term.

Nonetheless, nothing was more important than the declining economic status of the male-breadwinner-female-homemaker family, anchor of industrial economic life and U.S. political economy for over a century. The male labor force participation rate declined, as the average real male wage flatlined. By 1976, more than 50 percent of married women with school-aged children were in the labor force, as sex discrimination complaints continued to backlog at the Equal Employment Opportunity Commission (EEOC).[80] But at the opening of the decade, in the words of the historian Alison Lefkovitz, "wives owed their husbands household labor including child care, housework, work in a family business, and any improvements they made to household property."[81] Legally, women had a right to divorce husbands that could not or would not economically support them. Should the male wage no longer support families, the legal institution of marriage, as it existed on the books, was destined to become an anachronism. Many men joined political advocacy groups demanding that state legislatures release them from their breadwinning obligations. In 1970 Texas was among the first states to pass no-fault divorce legislation, and during the decade no fewer than forty-five states passed laws chipping away at men's legal obligations to economically support their wives. In 1975 Texas became the ninth state to pass a "homemaker entitlement" law mandating that divorced women receive property to compensate for past household labor.[82] Ruth Bader Ginsburg successfully argued *Weinberger v. Wiesenfeld* (1975) before the U.S. Supreme Court, securing Social Security survivor benefits for male widowers, advancing the principle of gender neutrality. That the male wage would no longer be the linchpin of economic and legal entitlements was an epoch-making event. But what exactly would replace the male-breadwinner-female-homemaker family was uncertain. Politically, the issues all came to a head in Houston.

In November 1977 the congressionally funded National Women's Conference—inspired by the United Nations' International Women's Year gathering of 1975 in Mexico City—met in Houston.[83] Two thousand delegates appointed by state-level assemblies arrived in the city to vote on a "plan of action" for Congress, called "What Women Want." In Houston, feminists squared off against a pro-family conservatism that was increasingly on the march.

The main subject of the conference was the status of the Equal Rights Amendment (ERA) to the Constitution, long a liberal feminist aim, which had finally passed the House in 1971 and the Senate in 1972. The amendment declared, "Equality of rights under the law shall not be denied or abridged by the United States or by any State on account of sex." Delegates at the Houston conference voted in favor of the ERA and another twenty-five resolutions, including those calling for the end of sex discrimination in the workplace and in the provision of credit. Another measure demanded government support for "displaced homemakers" in the labor market. There was a request for a "homemaker entitlement" upon divorce. A resolution demanded marriage reforms "on the principle that marriage is a partnership in which the contributions of each spouse is of equal importance and value."[84]

Meanwhile, across town, conservative anti-ERA groups organized a pro-family counterconvention to protest the conference. The industrial breadwinner-homemaker family may have been crumbling, but, if anything, the family and the home were becoming more important. Houston may have had the highest divorce rate in the Sunbelt, but it also had the highest marriage and remarriage rates.[85] As asset price appreciation replaced labor earnings from using up, or depreciating, industrial capital, in the new era, home ownership would become more economically significant than in the past. The home—a sphere putatively outside the economy in the industrial epoch—would be burdened with an ever greater economic investment. At the same time, because of the sprawl and the sheer newness of Houston, many institutions—labor unions, parent-teacher organizations, Elks Clubs—were either nonexistent, unfinished, or thin. So the home became even more of what the firebrand pro-family activist Phyllis Schlafly wanted it to be, "the basic unit of society."[86] Prominent conservative intellectuals, from George Gilder in *Sexual Suicide* (1973) to Daniel Bell in *The Cultural Contradictions of Capitalism* (1976), wondered if it was a good idea for society to unleash men from family bonds.[87] Yet on the ground, given the nature of life in a city like Houston, there was fresh demand for "family values." Finally, the basic unit of society in Houston, if not the family or the shopping mall, was the evangelical Christian church.[88] The Texas legislature had ratified the ERA in 1972. The lead organizer of the 1977 Houston counterconvention was Lottie Beth Hobbs, a Texas Church of Christ member who was the founder of the anti-ERA group Women Who Want to Be Women. It was Hobbs who brought Schlafly to Houston.

Schlafly would later call the 1977 Houston conference and counterconvention a turning point, where "the ERAers, the abortionists, and the lesbians made the decision to march in unison for their common goals."[89] Abortion was Schlafly's wedge issue. But the most dramatic moment of the National Women's Conference was the broad support for a measure written by a minority caucus that included a demand for "equal rights" for lesbians. By 1977, homosexuality had become an explosive national political issue. That same year James Dobson founded Focus on the Family, and he, Schlafly, and other Christian conservatives would organize a powerful social movement to push the Republican Party to embrace antifeminism.[90] The next decisive gathering held in Houston would be the 1979 Southern Baptist Convention—its so-called Houston meeting—when politically conservative fundamentalists took control of the denomination.[91]

Congress continued to pass piecemeal legislation barring sexual discrimination in economic life, but under pro-family pressure in 1980, the Republican Party would remove support for the ERA from its national platform. After the 1977 Houston Women's Conference, not another state would ratify the ERA, which has to date never become a constitutional amendment.[92]

3. Twilight of Liberalism

The New Right came from the Sunbelt. At this writing, the last time the state of Texas, home of LBJ, voted for a Democrat in a presidential election was 1976, when it voted for the Georgia governor Jimmy Carter. Post-Watergate, Democrats retained control of both houses of Congress. In power during this final inflationary expansion of the Age of Control, liberalism completely lost the political initiative. Exhausted, liberalism nonetheless mustered its last reserves of energy for the leap headlong into its grave. What happened?

The obvious answer was inflation, which in 1979 unnervingly climbed into double-digit territory. Despite its transformations over the course of the century, liberalism had been born during the 1930s to master a deflationary event, the Great Depression. If anything—as it had always sought to prop up commodity prices, industrial profits, and breadwinning incomes—it had had an inflationary bias. By now, the causes of inflation were compounding. The rate of productivity growth had been low since 1973 (without which unemployment likely would have been even higher). Economic growth was still geographically uneven, which wasted much untapped economic potential. In monetary policy, the Fed's nominal short-term interest rate, below 5 percent well into 1977, was below the rate of inflation—thus not fighting inflation. In 1978 there was another oil shock. The larger question is why the federal government could not do anything about any of this and act deliberately to break the mass psychology of inflationary expectations. It was not just liberalism that failed; democracy suffered blows to its legitimacy as well.

Carter was elected president as a political outsider. A southern evangelical Christian and by all accounts a morally decent man, Carter was cast in the opposite mold of Richard Nixon. But the country's problems ran deeper than presidential ethics—they were institutional in nature.[93] Carter tried to compensate for liberalism's dire lack of political-economic imagination with moralism, but his "antipolitics" was inadequate to the task at hand.[94]

The different ideological impulses and interest groups within the Democratic Party did not add up to effective economic policy making. Litigious liberal lawyers filing class action lawsuits to extend adversarial rights-based claims did not address stagflation. Neither did well-meaning support for community action programs, such as the many "grassroots" responses to factory closures. New Left critiques of "regulatory capture" sparked renewed interest in an antitrust program, but that did not go very far. The labor movement, with its ossifying leadership, became all but cut adrift from congressional liberals. There was one ambitious liberal initiative, which recalled the New Deal's developmental origin. In 1974, Senator Hubert Humphrey and Representative Augustus Hawkins introduced the Humphrey-Hawkins Full Employment Act, which guaranteed all citizens the right to a job. It had no chance to pass in Congress. On the campaign trail and in office, Carter paid it only lip service. He signed a version of it in 1978, which symbolically called for full employment. But it contained no provisions to achieve its goals. What liberalism lacked in 1978 was what it had lacked ever since World War II: an institutional mechanism to control not only the volume but also the location and composition of investment.

By Carter's presidency, Democrats were facing a far more formidable and unified adversary. If 1978 was a pivotal year for the gathering pro-family social movement, so it was for a much-reinvigorated "pro-business lobby." Profitless prosperity defined the post-1975 macroexpansion, as many corporate managers tried to invest their way out of trouble. But at least some of the owners of capital realized change was afoot. As the productivity trend declined, and as consumerist and environmental "social regulations" cut further into profit rates, they looked to Congress to pass laws that would help them restore their profits. The Business Roundtable, a group of corporate executives from the leading 150 U.S. corporations, formed in 1972, became the new, aggressive "peak" business lobby.[95] Irving Shapiro, the politically active CEO of DuPont, noted that business executives had newly become "personally involved in the government process," for knowledge of that process was becoming "as important as being skilled in knowing how to manufacture a product."[96] In particular, many capitalists believed that labor unions' continued strength in bargaining for higher money wages—even if "real" compensation was flat—was the great driver of inflation. Now many corporations decided that labor earnings, not profits on capital, must bear the burden of the productivity slowdown. That meant an assault on the very legitimacy of collective bargaining.

The corporate business offensive began to count many successes in 1978, and there is little wonder why. During the 1970s, the number of corporate lobbyists in Washington skyrocketed. In 1975 the Federal Election Commission sanctioned corporate political action committees, or PACs.

In 1976 the U.S. Supreme Court ruled in *Buckley v. Valeo* that political donations were constitutionally protected speech. In the 1976 election, corporate spending, organized through PACs, exceeded election spending by unions.[97] In 1978 business lobbying helped scuttle the creation of a Consumer Protection Agency, long the dream of Ralph Nader's Public Interest Research Group movement, and it also killed a bill enabling "common-situs picketing," or the ability of unions to picket entire construction work sites, which Democratic Congresses had recently passed twice, though never overcoming President Ford's vetoes. The defeat was highly symbolic—the common-situs bill had been intended to prepare the ground for a raft of labor reform legislation, which now never happened. In 1978, responding to the business lobby's complaint that taxation inhibited private capital formation, Congress reduced the capital gains tax from 35 to 28 percent and made permanent a 10 percent tax credit for investment. In 1980 the number of lobbyists and other professionals employed by private businesses to influence policy making in Washington finally exceeded the number of federal employees. A Democratic Congress, with a Democratic president in the White House, could no longer pass "social regulation" or union-friendly labor laws. It passed tax cuts instead.

The shift to the right appeared not only in policy details but also in the intellectual tide. In the late 1970s, public opinion polls that a few years earlier had reported negative popular opinions about business began to shift in favor of business. Promoting the ideas were new conservative, allied networks of 501(c)(3)s, 501(c)(4)s, and PACs, such as the Heritage Foundation (1973), the Cato Institute (1977), and the John Olin Foundation (1953), led by William Simon, former Treasury secretary under Nixon and Ford and author of the 1978 best seller *Time for Truth*. The truth, he argued, was that capital must be liberated from all taxation. The Olin Foundation began to endow professorships in "free enterprise." Liberals would gripe about the nefarious influence of right-wing money, but in fairness the liberal-minded Ford Foundation had generously funded postwar higher education.[98] This was only different ideologically.

Regardless, the Carter administration was actually open to new "pro-market" ideas. Like many governors, Carter was a fiscal moderate. He also came from the "free enterprise"–friendly Sunbelt. On the campaign trail, he promised to balance the federal budget. He was only a "reluctant Keynesian," according to Charles Schultze, Carter's chairman of the Council of Economic Advisers. Schultze had run the Bureau of the Budget for LBJ, and his macroeconomics consisted of investment-inducing tax cuts. Upon Schultze's advice, when Carter took office, he passed a tax cut in hopes of stimulating investment, a "Kennedy rerun."[99] Tellingly, Schultze's council was more excited about microeconomic than macroeconomic policy. Schultze had recently written a book about regulation that recommended "injecting the discipline of the market into regulatory policy."[100] Schultze's *The Public Use of Private Interest* (1977) argued:

> Relationships in the market are a form of unanimous-consent arrangement. When dealing with each other in a buy-sell transaction, individuals can act voluntarily on the basis of mutual advantage. Organizing large-scale social activity through the alternative open to a free society—democratic majoritarian politics—necessarily implies some minority who disapprove of each particular decision.[101]

Carter read this book and liked it. He agreed that instead of macroeconomic development, his administration should push for regulatory reforms, which would restore more efficient market dynamics to microeconomic relationships.

For the dyspepsia of stagflation, "the market" was the proposed tonic. In an era of institutional paralysis, perhaps the market was the cure-all. The year Carter took office, 1976, was also the year the Nobel Prize in economics (first awarded in 1969) was given to the University of Chicago economist Milton Friedman.[102] What Schultze said about the market being a form of "unanimous-consent arrangement," more compatible with freedom than "democratic majoritarian politics," Friedman had been saying for many years.

Friedman was a longtime critic of Keynesian macroeconomic policy. After he had toiled for decades, this was his moment. Intellectually, his project was to resurrect the "quantity theory of money," or the idea, as he put it, that inflation was "always and everywhere a monetary phenomenon," a matter of more money chasing the same amount of goods.[103] Friedman called it "monetarism." He used his Nobel Prize address to attack the "Phillips curve," the notion that there was a smooth trade-off between inflation and unemployment, and that governments could buy employment before worrisome inflation appeared. Friedman said there was a "natural rate of unemployment."[104] "Natural," because markets, including labor markets, functioned efficiently independent of money.

Money was "neutral" and should be kept neutral. If only the government would always everywhere ensure a stable, predictable increase of the money supply—Friedman preferred 3 to 5 percent—the market itself would ensure efficiency, justice, and the maximum use of all available scarce resources. Supply creates its own demand; economies cannot suffer from demand constraints. When during the 1970s the Phillips curve ceased to be smooth and ran jagged because of stagflation, Friedman claimed vindication in the economics profession.[105]

By then, Friedman was well on his way to being a gifted libertarian rhetorician more than a working academic economist.[106] At any opportunity, he spoke out in favor of the broad benefits of "the market." His popular *Capitalism and Freedom* (1962) had contributed to the reclamation of the word *capitalism* on the political right.[107] He would go on to say that politically the market, premised on consent and mutual benefit through commercial exchange, was more legitimate than the state, premised on legal coercion. That meant any state, including a democratic state. Friedman was suspicious of democracy, which might overload the state with more popular demands, leading to more taxation, more spending, more black welfare recipients, weakened families, and inflation.

Friedman was by far the most ideological member of the influential Chicago school of economics, but he was not the only one. Of his generation, George Stigler worked on regulation, attacking the liberal ideas of "public utility" and "natural monopoly."[108] The Law and Economics movement was born in Chicago. Its most influential (if often misinterpreted) member, the British economist Ronald Coase, arrived at the University of Chicago Law School in 1964. Emblematically, Law School faculty member Richard Posner's *Economic Analysis of Law* (1973) argued that the "economist's idea of efficiency" was a ready proxy for "justice."[109] Law School professor Robert H. Bork argued that the "only goal that should guide interpretation of the antitrust laws is the welfare of consumers," which was best served by the efficient market allocation of goods free of government regulation. Low consumer prices, not general market structure or barriers to entry in enterprise, were the only proper standards for the application of antitrust laws. Besides, market competition would always blow down any barrier to entry worth blowing down.[110] Among the post-Friedman generation, Eugene Fama helped spawn the "efficient markets hypothesis" in finance, which argued that asset prices efficiently incorporated all possible information.[111] Gary Becker's *The Economic Approach to Human Behavior* (1976) concerned all behavior, including in the family.[112] Becker clarified the economic idea that human beings, whether they knew it or not, possessed a form of capital, "human capital." How could there be distributive conflict between capital and labor, the thought went, when labor itself was a form of capital? Conflicting groups became consenting individuals.[113]

Finally, in the field of macroeconomics, Robert Lucas helped found the "rational expectations" school. Lucas, unlike Friedman, was no ideologue. The "Lucas critique" of postwar Keynesian macroeconomics, as it had developed (as opposed to what Keynes actually said), was utterly devastating. Keynesians had not much considered, when constructing macroeconomic models and policies, that individuals themselves took note of those same macroeconomic models and policies. Individuals, Lucas suggested, made choices in light of the likely consequences of what governments did and could be expected to do. Governments could not outsmart them. For instance, if governments lowered interest rates, because of loose money individuals might expect inflation, and so interest rates would rise.[114] Reasoning in various ways like this, Lucas drew the conclusion that all macroeconomics required "microfoundations" in individual decisions. In fact, macro was really only a version of a market-based microeconomics of choice. Given the feedback loop, the effect was to narrow the scope for effective discretionary policy making.[115]

The Chicago school produced a body of economic thought of great formal complexity and mathematical rigor. Politically, however, the upshot was often simple. In the abstract, markets were efficient and just—which just happened to agree with what the CEOs of the Business Roundtable already knew in their guts rather than from any mathematical model. Such simplicity and certainty, at a moment when Keynesian macroeconomics was in "total chaos," as Lucas put it, was of great advantage.[116] Arthur Okun's posthumously published *Prices and Quantities* (1981) was the greatest Keynesian attempt to design policies to deal with stagflation.[117] It was nearly four hundred pages long—intricate, ornate, and very difficult to summarize to a twenty-something congressional staffer. By contrast, how simplifying and soothing it was, to assume in one's economic model that individual knowledge of the future was perfectly rational and certain, a mere set of mathematical probabilities, when in reality everything was becoming so uncertain, because long-term industrial structures were evaporating. Institutions could be shunted to the side. Whatever they might be, Lucas recommended invariable policy "rules," immune both from democratic politics and from presidential economic advisers.[118] Then everyone could step back, politicians and their congressional staffers, too, and watch markets harmonize the macroeconomy. "Real" business cycles, as one branch of Lucas's followers branded them, would be rather calm affairs. State interventions would only be self-defeating anyway, as individuals took them into account, being rational agents. There was nothing in the world except individual choice and the logical precision of mathematical rigor. With its emphasis on stripped-down individual choice, the economic thought of the 1970s, later branded "neoliberal ideology," was really just "Me Decade" economics.[119]

In policy making, one cannot give Chicago school economists that much credit, however.[120] Not Friedman but council chairman Schultze's *The Public Use of Private Interest* had said that markets "not only minimize the need for coercion as a means of organizing society; they also reduce the need for compassion, patriotism, brotherly love, and cultural solidarity as motivating forces behind social improvement."[121] Let the market discipline when democratic politics could not. Let the market do what the state should not.

The Carter administration's recommended economic therapy for stagflation was market "deregulation." After 1978 Alfred Kahn—a liberal Cornell economics professor, who was made chair of the Civil Aeronautics Board to oversee the Senator Edward Kennedy–sponsored 1978 Airline Deregulation Act, which abolished airline price regulations—quipped that deregulation bills were "being put forward in the name of anti-inflation efforts, energy conservation, competition, regulatory reform and free enterprise. 'Motherhood' and 'apple pie' are being taken care of in other legislation."[122]

From past decades a number of ill-considered New Deal price regulations definitely remained on the books. For instance, price caps on natural gas to protect consumers from monopolies were actually causing shortages, creating pressure for higher prices. The deregulatory National Gas Policy Act of 1978 was, at first, a success. But the drift now was not to write better market regulations: even among liberals, it was to throw in the towel on market regulation altogether. When Carter sent trucking deregulation legislation to Congress in 1979, he promoted "increasing reliance upon the competitive marketplace." He signed an executive order mandating that all federal agencies cease to "impose unnecessary burdens on the economy, individuals, public or private organizations, or State and local governments."[123] The Staggers Rail Act of 1980 deregulated railroad rate setting in the industry that had given rise to "public utility" rate regulation a century earlier. The Interstate Commerce Commission would limp along until 1995. The 1935 Public Utility Holding Company Act was chipped away at and would finally be repealed in 2005. Banking deregulations removed regulatory walls, which had blocked the liquid convertibility of assets. The 1980 Depository Institutions Deregulation and Monetary Control Act phased out Regulation Q interest rate caps on deposits.

By one estimate, in 1977, 17 percent of the country's GNP was subject to some kind of price regulation. By 1988, the number was down to 6.6 percent.[124] But the administration of Ronald Reagan would only finish the job begun by Carter. Forget about developmental policies—liberals now gutted regulatory ones.

In economic policy, Carter, once a Georgia peanut farmer, felt at home in microeconomics, at the scale of markets, firms, and individuals. The national macroeconomy was not his favored scale, nor was the region or the city. The Carter administration said nothing about the wave of Ohio and Pennsylvania steel plant closures in 1977 and 1978.[125] Carter's favorite subject was foreign policy, where he sought to achieve what he called a new "world order" in an era of greater "global interdependence." He supported the new transnational politics of human rights, in which the sanctity of the individual contrasted to the state, yet again.[126] But Carter's attention to the global scale was the reason the only novel macroeconomic initiative of his presidency played out there—in a coordinated attempt of states at "International Keynesianism." Foiling it was another transnational constraint on national sovereignty: not human rights but short-term speculative movements of liquid global capital.

It was called the "locomotive strategy," agreed on by the Group of 7 (G7) nations, which began to meet in unannounced summits in 1976. Inflation was a problem everywhere. The United States, Japanese, and West German economies were growing the fastest, however, by contrast to the French, Italian, Canadian, and British. The locomotive strategy was that the United States, West Germany, and Japan would stimulate their national economies. Their combined demand then would stimulate the weaker economies, which would focus on holding down prices and becoming more competitive, to sell in the American, West German, and Japanese markets. The problem was that the West German and Japanese economies were themselves export-driven, reliant on U.S. consumer demand. The locomotive strategy required that the West Germans and Japanese stimulate domestic demand, which they were not in the habit of doing.

Nonetheless, in 1978 in Bonn, Germany, the G7 struck a deal. Carter agreed to eliminate U.S. subsidies for the domestic price of oil, as the G7 countries believed high U.S. energy consumption was a driver of world inflation. West Germany and Japan agreed to stimulate their economies, which would help close the ever-widening U.S. trade deficit, and put a floor under the value of the dollar in international currency markets. The remaining countries agreed to hold down prices and be pulled along by the American, West German, and Japanese demand-led locomotive.[127]

International Keynesianism might have worked. But the first blow to it was the second oil shock of the decade, in the wake of the Iranian Revolution. OPEC, concerned about the declining dollar, as global oil sales were denominated in dollars, was raising oil prices anyway, but oil prices doubled in 1979, accelerating the existing inflationary macroeconomic dynamic to politically disastrous heights. Having pledged to reduce oil subsidies, the Carter administration had no effective strategy besides voluntary wage and price guidelines, which were brazenly ignored.[128] The oil shock dominated the headlines. Americans lined up at gas stations, and there was the occasional riot.[129]

But it was global currency speculators who leveled the deathblow to International Keynesianism. By now, capital—in its most primal, liquid money form—had already been pooling in the London Eurodollar markets for decades. From the two oil shocks, "petrodollars" earned by the oil-producing states from sales abroad became dollar deposits in the lightly regulated London Euromarket. They did not just "flow" to the place where they could contribute most to growth. They became hoarded in London banks—rather than spent—adding to demand. Or they became the basis of short-term speculations that did not always contribute to long-term investment in enterprise. With exchange rates floating and capital controls lifted, the sheer volume in movements of cross-border hot money exploded.

In the United States, according to the historian Daniel Sargent, "with more than a half-trillion dollars of dollar-denominated assets now owned by foreigners, financial interdependence defined the terms of domestic policy choice."[130] In ending Bretton Woods, Nixon had sought a shortcut toward restoring the postwar moment of U.S. hegemony. Instead, the result was a regression to an even earlier moment, which had seemingly ended with the Great Depression. Global liquidity preference, and international capital mobility, once again acted as constraints on national economic policy making. The locomotive strategy could not even go into effect before capital fled the dollar, which plummeted. Carter blinked: he announced a new policy of budget balancing, fiscal restraint, and monetary tightening. He brought the G7 along with him. When the G7 met in Tokyo in May 1979, the communiqué promised "tight monetary measures and tight and prudent fiscal measures." The Tokyo G7 communiqué declared that tackling inflation was the "immediate top priority."[131] For the first time since the early 1930s, austerity was back in economic policy making.

When Carter returned to Washington from Tokyo, his approval ratings were dipping into the 20s—Nixon Watergate territory. In addition to austerity, Carter turned to moral exhortation. Polling documented widespread "long-term pessimism" and a national "psychic crisis." In July the president departed for Camp David for a week of reflection and deliberation with politicians, ministers, and academics, and even the historian Christopher Lasch, author of the best-selling *The Culture of Narcissism: American Life in an Age of Diminishing Expectations* (1979).[132] Carter asked Lasch what he should do. "I don't know," the historian said, true to his calling. At Camp David, Vice President Walter Mondale nearly suffered a nervous breakdown. Carter scribbled notes to himself: "The Great Society days are over. The problems of the nation can't be solved with massive spending programs, public works, et cetera."[133]

Upon returning to the White House, Carter addressed a national television audience on the "crisis of confidence." "All the legislation in the world can't fix what's wrong with America. . . . The erosion of our confidence in the future is threatening to destroy the social and political fabric of America." Carter bemoaned that citizens "worship self-indulgence and consumption" and that the national polity suffered from "fragmentation and self-interest." He reached for the language of war. World War II, which Carter invoked, had after all provided the total energy, as well as the overriding public interest in political economy, necessary to kick-start a depressed economy and society. The overhang of Vietnam surely explains why the federal government's crisis of legitimacy during the 1970s was so severe.[134] But the 1970s "energy crisis" had many manifestations. The oil shocks made that crucial input more expensive and contributed to a productivity slowdown in the most energy-intensive industries, all of them together triggering inflation. At the same time, as the sun set on industrial society, Carter sensed a broader enervation of the polity that undermined long-term expectations and stuck the U.S. economy into the inflationary present.

Carter's administration was dead in the water even before Iranian students stormed the U.S. embassy in Tehran in November 1979, bringing on the subsequent hostage crisis. Carter had fired his Treasury secretary and replaced him with G. William Miller, who had been chairman of the Federal Reserve. The president now needed to appoint a new chairman of the Fed. He appointed the current New York Fed president Paul Volcker. Carter's chief domestic policy adviser Stuart Eizenstat explained, "Volcker was selected because he was the candidate of Wall Street." Undoubtedly, Wall Street was fed up with inflation eating into the value of investments. Eizenstat added, "What was known about [Volcker]? That he was able and bright and it was also known that he was conservative. What wasn't known was that he was going to impose some very dramatic changes."[135]

Volcker turned to Milton Friedman's monetarist policies, which produced the final shock of the decade, the "Volcker Shock." Up till then, normal practice for the Fed had been to target an interest rate in the short-term money market, which indirectly loosened or tightened the money supply. But now Volcker would attempt to use the Fed's powers to directly target the growth of the quantity of money. He would leave interest rates alone, to set themselves freely in the market. Volcker was not a monetarist, but he liked the optics of it, saying, "More focus on the money supply also would be a way of telling the public that we meant business."[136] At the same time, the Carter administration also mandated credit controls. Altogether interest rates spiked, above 17 percent in April 1980.

Dramatically, the Fed had reasserted the scarcity value of money capital. The high interest rates that resulted from monetarist policy recruited short-term capital into the United States and halted the dollar's decline. Meanwhile the reduced money supply and high cost of credit finally assaulted inflation and inflationary expectations. No less significantly, left to the markets, interest rates began to experience extreme volatility. Volcker had attacked inflation but had also exacerbated uncertainty. The predictable consequence of all this was to halt all kinds of spending. In the second quarter of 1980, GDP contracted by 7.9 percent.

Meanwhile Carter announced a new general national economic policy, what he called "decontrol."[137]

Liberalism had been born in the 1930s, in a moment of economic crisis, when FDR wrested control over the dollar, at a time when nation-states, through capital controls and trade protection, were erecting walls around their national economies so as to better control them. The 1970s crisis of industrial capital, which was a crisis for liberalism, too, ended very differently. Walls would come down. Global interdependence would increase. Trade in goods and services would accelerate, as would cross-border movements of liquid, undecided capital in its primal money form. The Age of Control was over, and the stage was set for a new age of American capitalism.

BOOK FOUR

THE AGE
OF CHAOS

1980–

CHAOS

NEARLY ALL COMMENTATORS AGREE THAT A "NEW" CAPITAL-ism emerged in the last decades of the twentieth century. However, a difficulty in characterizing, let alone naming, this new capitalism is one of its distinctive features. Perhaps it is "postindustrial" or "post-Fordist," but those labels say what it is not, as opposed to what it is. Is it a "Second Gilded Age," or a period of "neoliberalism," in some sense a mere repetition of the late nineteenth century? Surely aspects of this capitalism, like its pattern of inequality and its dependence on debt, resonate with past eras. But there were no computers during the late-nineteenth-century Gilded Age, and today few people ride horses. Much has changed. The new capitalism born after 1980 is hardly young anymore. It should be portrayed with respect to its own defining qualities.

What most distinguishes the Age of Chaos is a shift in what has always been capitalism's core dynamic: the logic of investment, as it works through production, exchange, and consumption. Since 1980, a preference for liquidity over long-term commitment has dominated capital investment as never before. Fast-moving money, rapid investment and disinvestment, across various asset classes, as well as in and out of various companies, has not only overturned old methods of production—its logic has often threatened to overwhelm other economic patterns. In short, the liquidity of capital has made for a chaotic age dominated by the vagaries of appreciating assets.

In Chapter 19, "Magic of the Market," the new age opens with a familiar sight: the state reasserting the scarcity value of money and credit. During the years 1979–82, to attack inflation, without being able to resort to any metal standard, given the 1973 monetary departure from gold, the Federal Reserve under the new chairmanship of Paul Volcker rolled out the weapon of the high interest rate. Double-digit interest rates and the sharp double-dip recession that followed the tightening of credit during the "Volcker Shock" finally mastered inflation. The Fed thus ascended to a preeminence in global economic policy making that lasts to this day. In 1982 with the job done and the macroeconomy still in recession, the Fed relented and lowered rates. Newfound price stability brought a surge in confidence and expectations. A new macroeconomic expansion began, led by a speculative investment boom.

What happened after 1982 was not something policy makers expected. Not Volcker, and not President Ronald Reagan. After his inauguration in 1980, Reagan left Volcker alone. His administration, ideologues chiefly, celebrated "the magic of the marketplace," lambasted "big government" regulations, and decried black "welfare dependency." In general, their policies were friendly to the owners of wealth. Important "deregulations" did occur. But not one of Reagan's economic promises—a manufacturing employment revival, a surge in national savings and investment, a reduced budget deficit, a great slash in welfare spending—was fulfilled. Instead, the new capitalism was born.

The Volcker Shock transformed the character of capital investment at home and abroad. In the world economy, high U.S. interest rates brought about a worldwide credit crunch and worldwide economic depression. Seeking high interest rates, global capital moved into the U.S. capital market in prodigious amounts. The value of the dollar soared. Accordingly, the U.S. trade deficit expanded. This new pattern would ultimately stick. It was an utter reconfiguration of U.S. global economic hegemony. After World War II, like other hegemons of the past, the United States was an exporter of capital and goods. After the Volcker Shock, it became a net importer of global capital and the consumer market of last resort for the world's manufacturing export-led economies, including Japan, West Germany, and eventually, China.

At home, due to capital imports and financial deregulations, money and credit were more available. There was greater convertibility among assets, and more transactional liquidity. At the same time, still fearful of inflation after 1982, the Fed kept interest rates relatively high. Not since after the restoration of the gold standard following World War I had there been an era like this in capital markets, when credit was so newly and freely available—but at high rates. Just as in the 1920s, there was a great speculative investment boom during the 1980s. Confidence high, to hurdle over the high interest rate, investors resorted to debt to leverage up short-term speculative profits in stocks, bonds, and commercial real estate especially. Speculative investment was back as the dynamic factor in economic life, joining hands with an insatiable American consumerism.

There had long been a contradiction between short-term speculation for its own sake and long-term investment in enterprise. Unlike the 1920s, which saw the birth of industrial Fordism, the 1980s speculative boom did not lead to a great surge of investment in productive activity. Rather, using new access to capital and credit through "leveraged buyouts," financiers blew up the postwar industrial corporation and dethroned the postwar managerial class. There was a purge of fixed capital stock, especially in the historic northeastern-midwestern manufacturing belt. Male manufacturing employment, and unions, suffered devastating blows from corporate disinvestments. As profit making shifted toward short-term finance, tellingly the macroexpansion of the 1980s remains the only one on record in which there was a declining share of fixed investment in GDP.

Capital was more roving, and so the new capitalism became chaotic. In the industrial epoch, fixed investment had put enough capital on the ground long enough for many of the stabilizing structures of industrial society to arise around it and settle down—the factory communities, the fiscal triangle, the male-breadwinner-female-homemaker family. Following these investments, incomes, whether in the form of profits, pay, or fiscal revenues, were made from using up industrial capital goods. In the Age of Chaos, of course, there was still labor, production, and wealth-generating enterprise. But a different logic of valuation took precedence. The generation of incomes shifted away from the depreciation of a capital asset through its use and toward its price appreciation. What did that mean? Regardless of whether a corporate stock was connected to a wealth-generating or profit-making enterprise, its value might still go up. Or the value of another asset class—such as bonds, or real estate, or synthetic "financial derivatives," an asset class newly created for the purpose—went up. The financial appreciation of the asset—through its sale (capital gains) or its capacity to be leveraged in credit markets—generated the pecuniary income.

Income growth thus shifted from labor to the owners of property, or those who owned the appreciating assets. Accordingly, income inequality increased. The incomes of the owners of capital and labor incomes related to capital asset price appreciation in the "financial" and "business" services soared. That created fresh employment demand, in the places where the best-off lived, for jobs in the low-wage and historically feminized and racialized occupations of the service sector—in, say, food preparation or home health care. In the wake of the Volcker Shock, much of the world economy remained depressed during the 1980s, as finance capital kept pouring into the United States. Thus the new capitalism was born in the United States.

Asset appreciation depended on what Reagan called "the magic of the marketplace." Speculation on short-term asset price run-ups depended on the presence of transactional liquidity—that there would always be a willing buyer in the upswing. For if a capital asset is not used to produce yet another good for sale, it must be sold itself in order to yield a profit. The general expansion of credit during this era fueled this behavior. If an asset could not be easily sold, then it at least could be funded through debt. In this process, market participants' beliefs in the presence of transactional liquidity became critical. For without such beliefs, confidence might collapse. Transactions would halt, and the nervous calling in of debts could lead to a reversal in the credit cycle and a shift from speculative to precautionary liquidity preference. In the resulting slump, macroeconomic expansions led by speculative investment booms in asset prices would come to an end.

In the Age of Chaos, in times of stress more than ever before the new guarantor of transactional liquidity in financial markets was the Fed, the "lender of last resort." So long as the Fed could maintain confidence in the belief that asset values would continue to appreciate, as if by magical thinking, they could continue to appreciate. On that basis macroeconomic expansions could carry on. The post-1982 expansion might have seen a dearth in long-term investment, but it was a very long business expansion nonetheless.

By the end of the 1980s, the new capitalism had arrived for good. Having left behind 1970s industrial malaise, after the fall of the Berlin Wall and the death of its twentieth-century ideological other, Soviet Communism, capitalism enjoyed a remarkably optimistic moment, as discussed in Chapter 20, "The New Economy." During the 1990s, by contrast with the more improvisational Reagan administration, the "New Democrats" of President Bill Clinton articulated a coherent political-economic settlement for the new age. Clinton went all in on a finance- and technology-driven, center-left vision of "globalization." This was a global economy, still dominated by the United States, of newfound fluidity, flow, energy, and risk. There was movement of global capital, of goods across borders due to new free trade agreements, and if to a lesser degree also of immigrants—legal and illegal. Structures and walls that were long charged with the task of ensuring stability—national borders, the divide between public and profit, profit and nonprofit—weakened and blurred. The era of "Big Government," Clinton declared, was over. So long as overtly racist or sexist discrimination was checked to ensure equality of opportunity, capital, left to its own devices, would flow to its best possible use and to the benefit of all.

The Fed, now under the chairmanship of Alan Greenspan, became a believer in the new economy, too. The late 1990s were the only moment in this age when the rate of fixed investment increased—in the new infrastructure of information technology (IT)—and the rate of productivity increased, as well. As they did, the relationship between investment and enterprise changed. Often, the valuation of Silicon Valley–based technology companies hinged on the prospective value of the innovative "ideas" of entrepreneurs—rather than the past generation of business profits. New, intangible forms of capital, like "human capital" and the "social capital" that connected Silicon Valley's recombinant networks of relationships, appreciated. Everywhere, online and off, the "network" became the new organizing principle of business for increasingly multinational U.S. corporations, but also in social life more generally. Meanwhile global capital, ever more liquid and roving, began to rush into the U.S. capital market, bidding U.S. technology stocks up during the early commercialization of the Internet. In the wake of the Asian financial crisis of 1997–98, when a global credit cycle reversed and capital flight shook markets and economies around the world, Greenspan's Fed came to the rescue and lowered interest rates. The action soothed the nerves of the owners of capital. Cheap funding, however, only bid U.S. technology stocks further up into the stratosphere.

In 2000 the credit cycle nonetheless reversed. Investors posed unanswerable questions about the ultimate value of technology stocks. The U.S. stock market suffered massive losses. Chapter 21, "The Great Moderation," covers the next economic expansion of the 2000s. A historically low short-term interest rate from the Fed supported a genuine worldwide economic boom, centered on the rise of China as a world manufacturing power after its admission to the World Trade Organization in 2001. Regions of China became ever more linked to U.S. multinational supply chains, as Chinese producers exported such things as flat-screen televisions and, beginning in 2007, Apple's iPhone, into the great U.S. consumer market. To help finance U.S. consumption and to accumulate dollar-denominated assets— the world's safest, most risk-free, liquid investment—China also began to export prodigious amounts of its savings into the U.S. capital market. That helped hold down long-term interest rates as well. In 2004, Fed governor Ben Bernanke, noting that since the Volcker Shock macroeconomic expansions, relative to the past, had become elongated and, in GDP terms, less volatile, spoke of the era's "Great Moderation."

Bernanke was correct that in addition to price stability and low inflation, the 2000s expansion shared many qualities with those since 1982. What he did not emphasize was that the pattern of economic development continued to be asset-led and therefore new income gains flowed largely to the best-off, who by now increasingly tended to be highly educated, and lived in those cities where the new economy thrived. In those places where it did not, economic life suffered.

In the 2000s, stock market prices rebounded. Led by Google, a number of IT companies found ways to make actual business profits by creating a new class of synthetic capital assets. These assets were digital constructs of data, made from personal information scraped off company websites, which could then be sold to marketers hoping to learn more about, and perhaps influence, consumer preferences. Google and Facebook led the way, both buying up other social media companies, which granted them more access to raw personal "data exhaust" and enabling them to become "first movers" in a new industry, warding off competition. Yet another sector that saw conglomeration during this decade was Wall Street, which began to engineer another new appreciating, synthetic capital asset, another mere construct of information: the mortgage-backed security.

In 2003 President George W. Bush advocated a new "ownership society." Arguably, not since Jefferson's Empire of Liberty had there been a vigorous politics of property ownership in the United States. Ever since late nineteenth-century industrialization, income politics had largely ruled. In the Age of Chaos, income politics fast became anachronistic. In the 2000s, however, there was a genuine attempt to fling open the economy of asset price appreciation to a broader constituency, through the vehicle of home ownership. It was the economic apogee of "family values." Aided by the low global interest rates of the 2000s and favorable government policies encouraging home ownership, residential real estate prices began to soar nationwide—although, as in Jefferson's time, white households disproportionately benefited from the surge in wealth. No matter their race, many households whose labor earnings were stagnant used debt to purchase or refinance homes, hoping to sustain consumption through asset price appreciation. Debt thus replaced income growth through pay. So long as home prices went up, the Great Moderation continued. On Wall Street, by employing mathematical models to securitize home mortgages banks believed they had discovered gold at the end of a rainbow: a perfectly mathematically hedged, riskless way to make fabulous profits. But they had not; it was only a fantasy.

In Chapter 22, the Great Moderation becomes "The Great Recession." Many indebted homeowners did not have sufficient incomes to pay their mortgages. Mortgage defaults increased, and national home prices began to decline in 2006. Many banks were bound to book heavy losses. Instead, confidence utterly collapsed, and the global financial system very nearly unraveled after the September 2008 bankruptcy of the investment bank Lehman Brothers. Suspicious of the entire system's solvency, banks stopped trading and funding one another. Capital markets dependent on transactional liquidity seized up when trading evaporated. The magical belief that there would always be a market to sell an asset, or at least a willing creditor to fund it, went up in smoke. A panicked flight to security ensued, an extreme desire to convert assets for cash—or the most cashlike asset in the global economy, U.S. Treasury bills—if only to meet nervous creditors' demands. To end the panic, the Fed dramatically entered the capital markets. It became not only the lender of last resort but the buyer of last resort for a host of "troubled assets." Meanwhile the Treasury Department, through the Troubled Asset Relief Program (TARP), injected public capital into the largest U.S. banks. Panic subsided. But for the first time since the Great Depression, the U.S. economy was stuck in a liquidity trap. The demand for cash was extreme. Though short-term interest rates were at or near zero, the owners of wealth still hoarded their liquid assets. Accordingly, economic output declined and unemployment increased.

What happened next was no less remarkable. The administration of President Barack Obama successfully put the capitalism of asset price appreciation back together. Obama's first years in office were filled with political drama: the inauguration of the country's first black president; the 2009 fiscal stimulus; the 2010 health care reform; the rise of the antigovernment and anti-immigrant Tea Party; financial regulatory reforms; the extraordinary departure in monetary policy, when the Fed began to purchase trillions of dollars of assets to lower long-term interest rates (inelegantly called quantitative easing) in an attempt to stimulate investment; the no less extraordinary pivot in fiscal policy to austerity. But the story of the Great Recession is one of economic continuity. Many people suffered, losing their homes and jobs, but capitalism continued to bestow most of its benefits upon the best off, whose interests politicians protected. In this crisis, politics failed to chart a viable new long-term vision of economic life, as had been the case after the Great Depression. Instead, the Great Recession slowly began to show signs of lifting, as another new asset-led macroeconomic expansion, to last over the 2010s, began to exhibit many of the same qualities as every single one since the 1980s.

Amazingly, in the wake of such a dramatic slump, the Great Moderation reappeared. Democracy began to look more vulnerable than capitalism.

CHAPTER 19

MAGIC OF THE MARKET

═══

THE UNITED STATES WAS SUFFERING FROM AN "ECONOMIC affliction of great proportions," remarked Ronald Reagan in his 1981 inaugural address. In a rejection of FDR's 1933 first inaugural, the new president declared that "in this present crisis, government is not the solution to our problem, government is the problem."[1] The solution was the market or, more specifically, what Reagan would soon call "the magic of the marketplace."[2]

Market advocacy was not new. In the American past, markets had been celebrated in at least three ways: as arenas for a positive vision of individualism, as engines of economic betterment, and as just arbiters of social and political conflict. In the 1970s crisis of industrial capital, market advocacy had appeared in all these forms. However, the 1980s saw an absolute "contagion" of market metaphors.[3]

Pro-market, "neoliberal" ideology, as some scholars call it, mattered, but it cannot explain everything. Just because a market advocate such as Friedrich Hayek or Milton Friedman once said something about the market does not mean that when Reagan became president, something in particular came to pass. In reactive mode after Reagan's election, much of the intellectual left fell prey to assuming it did, hauling out a neo-Victorian, romantic critique of the corrosively greedy "market."[4] But to debate the appropriate moral limits of the market—a salutary debate, to be sure—is not to say all that much about how and why capitalist enterprise since Reagan has changed.

In this period, much of the devil was in the details of economic life—not in grand ideological pronouncements about the market, which Reagan, as well as his advocates and his critics, had a great proclivity to espouse. After all, Reagan's invocation of the "magic" of the marketplace expressed the former Hollywood actor's belief that "politics is just like show business."[5] In a 1980 campaign commercial, an unemployed white, blue-collar-looking man had stood in the middle of an idling factory just waiting for the magic of the market to put it right after Reagan's election. How nice if a magic wand could instantly solve the "crisis of confidence" that President Carter had declared in 1979. Reagan's election did help augur in a new age of capitalism, but the transformation cannot be easily attributed to the conscious intentions of his administration, as it rolled into office.

On the campaign trail, Reagan and his advisers predicted that letting the market decide (whatever that meant) would lead to a surge in private savings, fixed investment, productivity growth, and profits. Altogether the combined result would be a national revival in manufacturing employment and output, and also in manufacturing exports, which would reverse the U.S. trade deficit. Reduced federal spending, especially on welfare, would lead to a balanced federal budget and a lower national debt.

The day after Reagan's inauguration, stock prices at the New York Stock Exchange (NYSE) began to climb. Against surprisingly little resistance from Democrats, Reagan was able to push through much if not all of his agenda. Basically, what happened next was that none of what Reagan had promised came to pass. Reagan delivered on but one economic campaign promise, a military buildup, in line with his early confrontational stance toward the Soviet Union. Based on high-tech weapons, it was a version of the old military Keynesianism but far less employment intensive.[6] It was also financed by budget deficits. Dogged to the end, Reagan never stopped putting faith in what his favorite supply-side economics intellectual, George Gilder, called the "metaphysical capital of human freedom and creativity."[7] But of Reagan, the Federal Reserve chairman Paul Volcker judged, "I speculate that he was not a highly sophisticated economist." Of the president's economic advisers, Volcker concluded, "They had monetarist doctrine, supply-side doctrine, libertarian doctrine all mixed together." It "wasn't terribly coherent."[8]

All the same, by the end of Reagan's first term, a new age of capitalism had already been born. Reaganite supply-siders argued that liberal, demand-focused Keynesians had put the cart before the horse. In capitalism, the supply-side decisions of entrepreneurial capitalists were where all the magic happened. There is some truth to that (as Keynes himself had long ago recognized). But the Reaganites bet on a supply-side horse that turned around and ran the wrong way, or at least in an unexpected direction. As capital was liberated on the supply side, the pattern of capital investment was transformed. There was no going back to postwar industrial society. During the Reagan years, not only did a "postindustrial" economy continue to materialize, but something new and distinctive emerged that has persisted down to this day: a capitalism dominated by asset price appreciation.

The new capitalism would feature some durable new patterns: a surge in service employment, a shift in the share of income from labor to capital and therefore an increase in inequality, a spread of the Houston model of Sunbelt development, a reconfiguration of global U.S. economic hegemony, a commitment to low inflation and price stability, an expansion of debt and leveraged profit making, and more. All, as well as their interrelationships, require elucidation. But all of it revolved around one key new characteristic of the rising economic order, which was a high degree of liquidity preference among the owners of capital. It injected a new quality of uncertainty into economic life, as the short term triumphed over the long.

But the first question is how exactly the new age of capitalism first came about. When Reagan took office, the inaugurating event had already begun, down the street from the White House at the Federal Reserve.

1. Volcker Shock

President Carter had appointed Paul Volcker chairman of the Fed in 1979. Thus Reagan became president in the middle of the Volcker interest rate "shock." Not since after World War I, when, in the context of postwar inflation, the victorious Allies made the decision to return their currencies to the gold standard, had state power so overtly enforced the scarcity value of money capital in an attempt to attack inflation.

The difference was that now currencies were no longer backed by metal. The discretionary authority of the Fed controlled the money supply of the dollar—still the global currency of transaction and reserve. The Volcker Shock successfully slew the inflationary dragon, in a broad reboot for the U.S. and global economy.

Inflation, said Volcker, "was a dragon that was eating at our innards, or more than our innards."[9] The Fed's experiment with monetarism was an example of letting the market decide. Since the postwar period, the Fed had sought to adjust the quantity of money on the supply side, indirectly, by using its powers to set a target short-term interest rate in the credit market, or the market for short-term U.S. Treasury bills, the nearest equivalent to cash. Monetarism said that the Fed must intervene more directly, targeting the actual quantity of money. Less money would mean less inflation. Interest rates on credit would then set themselves in the market, free from government intervention. However, as the quantity of money was restricted, the cost of credit—interest rates—would increase accordingly. Short-term interest rates surpassed 19 percent in 1981.

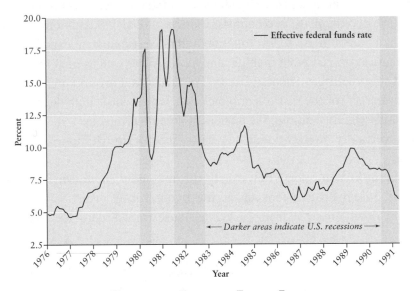

EFFECTIVE FEDERAL FUNDS RATE

The Volcker Shock brought about both high and (less expectedly) volatile interest rates. Historically, rates remained elevated over the 1980s.

With money and credit so tight, spending decreased, and the U.S. macroeconomy plunged into the double-dip recession of 1980 and 1981–82, the worst since the Great Depression. The initial downturn contributed to Reagan's election. Once in office, Reagan largely left Volcker to his job. "I think he had some kind of a feeling that the Federal Reserve was trying to deal with inflation," Volcker remembered.[10] Unemployment reached 10.8 percent. The Fed ended the monetarist experiment in October 1982. A macroeconomic recovery ensued in the midst of newfound price stability. The shock worked. The dragon of inflation was slain.

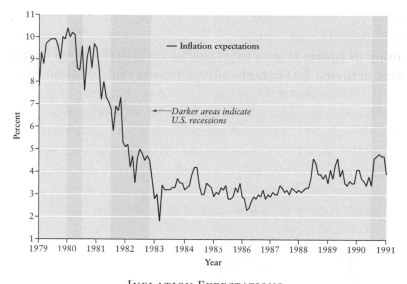

INFLATION EXPECTATIONS

The Volcker Shock dramatically quelled both inflation and
expectations of future inflation.

The Volcker Shock was a reboot for both politics and economics. In
politics, it brought about a policy regime change not seen since the days
of FDR (when FDR had relaxed the scarcity value of money). Surely no
government since the Great Depression had believed that government-
induced double-digit unemployment, on behalf of deflation, was a legitimate policy option. Volcker was not a very popular public figure during
the 1980–82 recession, and he was hauled before Congress for the occasional tongue-lashing. Nonetheless, he judged correctly that he had room
to maneuver. Both Congress and the public sensed that "something had
to be done," he surmised.[11] Volcker was not a complete believer in Milton
Friedman's monetarism, which argued that economic growth always
followed, after a lag, from an increase of the money supply, and that inflation was always and everywhere a result of the money supply increasing too much. The Fed, Friedman thus argued, should always target a
steady increase in the money supply that approximated the capacity of
the "real" economy to grow—"real" meaning independent of money.
Strangely enough, monetarists thought the underlying "real" economy
had nothing much to do with money. Volcker surmised that the monetarist targeting of the quantity of money would provide good political cover
for the job that needed to be done. By targeting the money supply, the Fed

was not responsible for setting punishingly high interest rates. The market was deciding.

In fact, the Federal Open Market Committee (FOMC) retained broad discretionary power. Further, the actual quantity of money and credit, a matter of both supply and demand, is not so easy to know or even to define, and may respond to upsurges in economic activity as much as it may initiate them. Monetarism in use was emblematic of what market deregulation in this period actually looked like. After Reagan's election, policy makers in general increasingly expressed a preference for market prices over government regulations. But regulation is not always a zero-sum game—with there being either more of it or less of it.[12] In this period, power in economic policy making was shifting from the Congress and the presidency to administrative agencies that, by their very design, were less democratically accountable.[13] Above all, the Fed ascended to regulatory preeminence.

The mantra in monetary policy soon became "central bank independence."[14] Even if Volcker's Fed would scrap monetarism, Friedman's basic argument prevailed. This meant the Fed had to follow a simple and transparent "rule." It should target a noninflationary and thus "neutral" interest rate, neutral in that it kept the growth of the money supply in line with the growth of the real economy. The Fed had only to set the right interest rate and it could sit back and watch the market economy optimize itself. Inflation could take priority over unemployment, since with low inflation and a stable general price level, employment would find equilibrium at its "natural" market level. As democratic politics were not likely to facilitate a neutral interest rate, which the inflationary 1970s so well illustrated, the central bank had to be independent from elected politicians.

The triumph of "independent" monetary policy was one long-lasting result of the Volcker Shock. Another was an utter transformation of American hegemony in the global economy. Inflation had threatened the primacy of the dollar as the global currency of transaction and reserve. This had spooked Carter and also had frightened Volcker. "I was certainly worried about the future of the United States in terms of its place in the world," Volcker later said. "I grew up in a generation where you naturally look upon the United States as being the last great hope of mankind."[15] The high interest rate of the Volcker Shock recruited short-term, speculative hot money into the United States, in search of the generous rate of return on offer. The consequence was to bid up the dollar,

TRADE WEIGHTED U.S. DOLLAR INDEX AGAINST MAJOR CURRENCIES
The high interest rates of the Volcker Shock contributed to a rapid increase
in the value of the dollar, securing its continued hegemony as the global
currency of transaction and reserve.

securing its role as the hegemonic global currency of transaction and
reserve.

Meanwhile the high dollar led to a surge in U.S. imports, while undermining the competitiveness abroad of American manufacturing exporters. The opposite side of the same coin was that capital inflows financed
the bulging U.S. trade deficit. In a new global trend, capital ran "uphill"
into American capital markets.[16]

In short, the Volcker Shock launched a second, far more novel U.S.
global hegemony. After World War II, the United States, like many world
hegemons before, was an exporter of both capital and goods to the world.[17]
After the Volcker Shock, these movements reversed. Now the United States
imported global capital and became the consumer market of last resort for
the world's producers.[18] Likely the Fed neither intended nor expected to
trigger such a momentous shift. True, relative to many other national
economies, the United States remained rather "closed," with world trade
comprising a very small percentage of GDP. But that small percentage
could matter very much—in the way new trade patterns affected some
localities, as well as in the increasing prominence of global finance—and
the new global configuration would, at specific moments, have great consequence in this new age.

Meanwhile the consequences of the Volcker Shock were no less signifi-

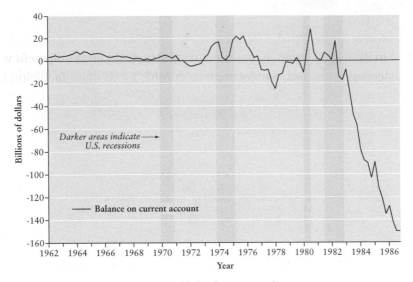

BALANCE ON U.S. CURRENT ACCOUNT

As the owners of wealth sought security in safe-haven dollar assets,
the export of capital to the United States financed the critical role of the
American consumer in the global economy—as foreign capital inflows
closed the U.S. current account deficit, or its balance of transactions
with the world, excluding financial items. In the Age of Chaos,
global capital movements would ultimately supersede trade
patterns in macroeconomic importance.

cant, or surprising at the time, for the U.S. national macroeconomy. By
tightening the money supply, the Volcker Shock brazenly restored the
scarcity value of money capital. Just as with foreign hot money, high and
volatile interest rates recruited capital into the money form, in search of
income from interest rate accrual, in the midst of a sudden corporate
purge of not-very-profitable industrial fixed capital. Deindustrialization
surged in the northeastern-midwestern manufacturing belt.[19] The new
emphasis was on short-term, financial profit making. The Volcker Shock
thus induced a greater liquidity preference. This was all the opposite of
Reagan's promised manufacturing revival.

In some sense, the fixed capital purge had been a long time coming. The
U.S. profit rate, especially for industrial corporations, had been in decline
ever since 1965.[20] Capital moved toward the low-wage Sunbelt South, as
well as abroad through corporate multinational investment. Despite the
1977 wave of steel plant closures in Ohio and Pennsylvania, many indus-

trial corporate managers, as if by habit, had tried to invest their way out of the profitability crisis. No more. Between 1979 and 1983, the percentage drop in fixed investment in manufacturing structures and equipment was the steepest on record. Employment in durable goods manufacturing fell by 15.9 percent, with the loss of more than 2 million jobs—overwhelmingly male jobs.[21] Prime-age (25–54) male employment fell from 91 percent to 86 percent.

The origins of this transformation preceded the Volcker Shock. Among industrial corporations, a new conception of capital investment had been developing for some time. Business consultancies and finance-trained corporate managers drew from financial economics, whether it was "portfolio theory" or the "capital asset pricing model."[22] Postwar managers had been committed to growth in production and market share as well as a long-term rate of return on investment (ROI) on fixed capital. As profits flagged, time finally ran out on the industrial managerial class. The new goal was to maximize an immediate, risk-weighted "return on equity," or paid-in capital. Thomas E. Copeland and J. Fred Weston's *Financial Theory and Corporate Policy* (1979), for instance, distilled the new thinking.[23] The basic point was clear, however: pull capital from less profitable lines of production and deploy them wherever more immediate profits can be made.

That sounds obvious—maximize profits. But the profit motive, over the short or long term, had not been the only postwar managerial consideration, and managers, many of whom lived near production facilities, including factories, were often committed to specific localities. Some were committed to particular production processes. They therefore did not see their investments as always convertible and liquid, or the entire globe, and all economic sectors, as open fields of potential investment. But financial economics had no concern for physical process or human frictions. It assumed transactional liquidity, or the potential convertibility of all investments, with no physical sources of friction. No less, it assumed capital would always seek the highest profit. It assumed an economic rationality in which the owners of capital would not hoard money but would always invest in the most profitable asset class, adjusting for risk.

Here the Volcker Shock came into play, as it led to a dramatic pause in long-term fixed capital investment among corporate managers. High interest rates made credit for investment of any kind scarce, while recession only undermined profits for reinvestment. Furthermore, as the Fed relinquished control over interest rates during the monetarist experiment, rates not only climbed but became far more volatile than usual. The turn to the market made things more unpredictable and uncertain. In response, the owners of capital hoarded what cash they had, sapping long-term investment. Why not simply park corporate cash in a bank account, and earn profits through interest rate accrual, as the Fed enforced the scarcity value of capital? Between 1979 and 1982, the percentage of manufacturing firms' total revenues resulting from "portfolio income," whether dividends, capital gains, or interest accrual, climbed from 20 percent to 40 percent. As a share of portfolio income, interest accrual, which stood at 40 percent in 1965, climbed to over 70 percent.[24] In the shift from profit making on productive capital to more liquid, money-like assets, this was the first Volcker Shock–induced step. The pursuit of rentier profits on money capital was a trigger for the recession. Every dollar that sat in a bank account, seeking high interest rates, did not fund employment-giving or output-expanding investments.

Meanwhile deindustrialization in the northeastern-midwestern manufacturing belt accelerated, with the Midwest suffering the most. Many working people experienced the new "profit orientation" as something like a shock. In 1980 a round of steel closures hit the Calumet region, south of Chicago and in northwestern Indiana, eliminating ninety thousand manufacturing jobs. Local communities met the closures with "bewilderment" and "disbelief" because many of the factories were profitable. But they were not profitable enough by the new criteria, applied by executives at an ever-increasing distance from the "physical process."[25] The new CEO of U.S. Steel, David Roderick, declared that the corporation was "no longer in the business of making steel." It was "in the business of making profits." U.S. Steel announced major layoffs in Pittsburgh, shut down the old Carnegie Homestead works, and built a new, highly automated facility in Houston. By 1984, having bought Marathon Oil, U.S. Steel counted steel as only one-third of its assets.[26] Emblematically, Richard Serra's Pittsburgh sculpture *Carnegie* (1985), a monument to the U.S. industrial past, was of course made of steel.

In 1982, capping the Volcker Shock deindustrialization cycle, Bethlehem Steel closed its sprawling Lackawanna, New York, steelworks outside Buffalo. As steelworker Benjamin Boofer recalled, "Things got to booming pretty good, then all three plants'd be going like crazy, then things fell apart completely one day." Kenneth Sion added, "Everything was booming, and all of a sudden it stopped, just like that."[27] That was not true—

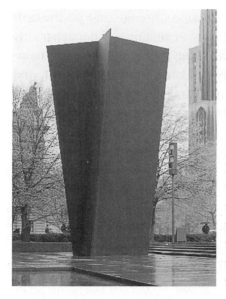

RICHARD SERRA, *CARNEGIE* (1985)
Many industrial structures, including
steel factories, were swept away by the
1980s' turn to finance and the
triumph of the ideology of
"shareholder value" in corporate
governance. In this monument to
Pittsburgh's industrial past, it is as if
the effect was to turn the industrial
upside down. Visually the top appears
to be heavier than the bottom. Recall
that Carnegie himself had once
turned from finance to industry; in
the 1980s the direction reversed.

things had not been booming. But the sense of a sudden "shock" in economic life was real enough. One day the factory closed, and, as their union had no say in corporate investment and disinvestment decisions (a limit to adversarial postwar collective bargaining over pay), neither Boofer nor Sion could do anything about it.[28] Workers had a "concern for physical process." The metaphor of body and plant appeared time and again. Lackawanna steelworker Dick Hughes said, "You feel it's a part of your life, it's a part of your body. . . . It's like getting a part of your stomach cut off, if the plant closes."[29]

More shock was to come for organized labor in manufacturing. In 1980, 42 percent of union households voted for Reagan. In 1981–82, the AFL-CIO, still the largest labor organization in the world, lost a staggering 739,000 members.[30] In August 1981 the Professional Aircraft Traffic Controllers Organization (PATCO) voted to go on strike over pay. Reagan granted PATCO a forty-eight-hour deadline for its members to return to work, and when they did not, the president replaced them. That step was technically legal, but few employers had been willing to take it since the New Deal.[31] Emboldened now, private employers followed. The number of strikes plummeted.[32] In the United States, male-employment-intensive industry was fast becoming a dead end for organized labor.[33]

The Fed finally ended the monetarist experiment in October 1982. But first, it began to perform a new function in capital markets. Not only did it help to usher in a greater liquidity preference through high and volatile interest rates, it also took new steps to ensure that transactional liquidity always existed for the owners of appreciating assets.

The convertibility of assets, including debts, was becoming the new functioning norm. In 1984 Continental Illinois National Bank, the sixth largest bank by assets in the United States, was on the brink of failure.[34] Taking advantage of new sources of funding in the money markets, the bank had increased leverage and made a number of risky loans to domestic oil producers. They went bad after the Volcker Shock depressed commodity prices. High interest rates made it more difficult for Continental to roll over its debts. A Japanese investor sell-off, in the wake of an unfounded rumor, led to a run on Continental's stock. But a Continental failure threatened contagion, as due to financial deregulations, capital and credit markets were becoming more fluid and transactionally interlinked. A single bank failure thus threatened a broader panic. In 1983 John Shad, the Reagan-appointed chairman of the SEC, informed Congress about the "unprecedented movement of capital" across financial institutions. Money and credit were jumping across "traditional gaps," overwhelming "regulation by industry categories." According to Shad, capital was "thundering over, under, and around Glass-Steagall," the New Deal wall separating commercial from investment banking—such as in new "over-the-counter" markets, for instruments such as interest rate "swaps."[35] Because of the Volcker Shock, bankers had new access to money and credit, even if at higher rates. But if confidence departed, capital could just as easily engage in flight, crippling financial institutions, solvent and insolvent alike.

The Fed decided to try to bail out Continental. It granted the bank credit through its "discount window," accepting collateral that no private actor would accept. The Fed thus granted funding, and transactional liquidity, so that Continental might remain solvent—if only for a time. In 1984 the bank went into FDIC receivership. At that time Continental was judged "too big to fail," but it was much too interconnected to fail. Acting as lender of last resort, the Fed had come to the rescue of the system. To observers, it was seen as an extraordinary intervention, a departure from the past, which it was.

Meanwhile the Fed's new responsibilities became global. On June 30, 1982, the FOMC met to discuss the "saga of Mexico." During the inflationary 1970s, Mexico, like many Latin American countries, had taken advantage of the low real cost of capital and high world commodity prices to borrow heavily in public debt markets. U.S. commercial banks had recycled petrodollars from oil-producing economies into Latin American public debt.[36] The high interest rates of the Volcker Shock undermined commodity prices and plunged the world into recession. The price of oil thus fell—one reason the Volcker Shock so diminished inflation in the United States. However, high U.S. interest rates made it more difficult for Latin American sovereigns to roll over their debts. Mexico was the most exposed country, and Citibank was the most exposed U.S. commercial bank. Chairman Walter Wriston had once quipped, "Countries don't go bankrupt."[37] But foreign investors were questioning that belief. Mexico was suffering from short-term capital flight. In June 1982 the Fed was debating whether to grant Mexico a $600 million credit line, an injection of funding that would be only a bridge loan to a much larger International Monetary Fund (IMF) bailout.

During the deliberations, Fed governor William F. Ford from Atlanta remarked that "$600 million is peanuts." The Fed must address the crucial issue, he said: "the flight of capital." In the wake of the demise of Bretton Woods, there were no longer cross-border capital controls. Volcker responded, "I don't know what is going to happen with regard to the flight of capital." Who did know? We "can speculate about everything" when it came to capital flight, Volcker informed his colleagues. It seemed that the unintended consequence of the Volcker Shock was to foil even Volcker's expectations. If any one person was responsible for the global economy at this moment, it was Paul Volcker, and if he could not answer the question, that said something about the fundamental indeterminacy that was being wired into the new political economy. FDR once knew how much gold was fleeing U.S. borders: none, because he had passed an executive order banning it.

How much money did Mexico owe to American commercial banks? Volcker asked. Vice Chairman Anthony Solomon from New York answered, "Twenty-odd billion." "Well," Volcker responded, "that's big." With capital moving across borders so quickly, a Mexican default could lead to large losses among U.S. banks and raise suspicions about the solvency of other sovereigns, threatening more capital flight and a rolling international financial panic. So the Fed approved the bridge loan, to get to a nearly $4 billion IMF bailout. U.S. banks booked losses, though not crippling ones. This would not be the IMF's last "structural adjustment" of the

Mexican economy.[38] For the Fed, global financial crisis management was to become the new normal.

An epoch was opening, much defined by short-term and potentially fickle global capital movements across space, as time horizons compressed. For that reason, global economic events became not so easy to narrate over time. Even from Volcker's chair, they were not looking very purposeful. *Volcker Shock* has another meaning. Volcker, no different from a laid-off Lackawanna steelworker, was surprised by the course of global economic events that had followed from his actions, as well as their seeming unpredictability. If capital is kept undecided, then Volcker was right: we "can speculate about everything." It was a fitting epigram for the new age.

Nonetheless, the Volcker Shock had finally brought inflation to heel. The stability of the general price level did aid predictability. This achievement was considerable, not to be dismissed. A monetary tightening had mattered this much before, during the post–World War I restoration of the gold standard. But then there were also moments, like during World War II, when monetary policy played little role whatsoever in the allocation of capital. Arguably, in no era has monetary policy ever mattered so much as the era after 1980. For as capital became more liquid and convertible, the Fed's targeted interest rate became ever more a global benchmark for the flow of global investment, as the Fed—if belief in the presence of a market for a debt ever waned—became responsible for ensuring the transactional liquidity upon which the smooth functioning of one big global capital market was more and more premised.[39]

The Fed ended the monetarist experiment in 1982, returning to targeting short-term interest rates rather than the money supply—lowering interest rates if just a bit, to help ease the recession. A credit-fueled speculative investment boom now commenced, focused on asset price appreciation. But before that, first the Reagan administration made its own contributions to the new political economy.

2. Reagonomics

The Volcker Shock's consequences concentrated in capital markets. On ideological grounds, the incoming Reagan administration's policies were capital friendly and aligned with the interests of property owners. But as Republicans focused on transforming existing policies on the books, they made forays into income politics—both income security policies, and rates of income taxation. The Economic Recovery Tax Act of 1981 was the centerpiece, as the Reagan administration hoped to liberate capital on the supply side.[40]

Upon coming into office, Reagan's top policy priority had been a tax cut. Candidate Reagan's pollsters discovered that tax cuts were broadly popular, and the Reagan administration had found common cause with a new pop economic theory, supply-side economics, promoted by New York congressman Jack Kemp, in tandem with *The Wall Street Journal*'s Jude Wanniski and an academic economist named Arthur Laffer. First drawn on a cocktail napkin, the "Laffer curve" claimed to illustrate that high rates of income taxation at some threshold led to lower tax revenue, because it disincentivized economic activity, whereas lower taxes, unleashing the supply-side forces of self-interest and entrepreneurial ingenuity, led to more economic growth. By this reasoning, lowering income taxes, up to a

"LAFFER CURVE NAPKIN" (1974)

Legend has it that the "Laffer curve," or the idea that tax cuts pay for themselves through higher revenues, was invented in 1974 at a restaurant meeting of Laffer, journalist Jude Wanniski, and politicians Dick Cheney and Donald Rumsfeld. The napkin reads: "If you tax a product less results, if you subsidize it more results. We've been taxing work, output and income and subsidizing non-work, leisure and un-employment. The consequences are obvious!"

point, should lead to greater investment, more economic growth, and thus increased fiscal revenues.[41]

Kemp sponsored the Economic Recovery Tax Act of 1981 in Congress. President Reagan rolled out the plan in a February 18, 1981, speech, which polled well. Congressional Democrats, having lost the Senate in 1980 but controlling the House, responded by advocating a more "responsible" tax cut. In the end, personal income tax rates came down across the board. The top rate was slashed from 70 percent to 50 percent. The bottom rate declined from 14 percent to 11 percent. The capital gains rate fell from 28 percent to 20 percent. The corporate tax rate remained roughly level, at 46 percent. But through a new formula—10-5-3, ten years for buildings, five years for machines, three years for trucks and automobiles—capital depreciation rates for tax purposes accelerated. The tax rebate was supposed to induce greater investment, growth, and government revenue. Still, the administration projected that the tax cut would lead to a $480.6 billion loss of revenue.[42]

Would the numbers ever add up, according to the Laffer curve? George Shultz, the former Nixon Treasury secretary, then a Bechtel executive, and soon to be Reagan's secretary of state, promised the bill would have an "electric effect on expectations."[43] The 1981 tax cut was a supply-side elixir for capital. Down the entrepreneurial hatch it went—let the market take care of the federal budget. But its immediate costs were so steep that the next year Reagan and Congress had to slip in a tax increase for businesses, to the dismay of the business lobby.

Meanwhile, on the spending side, Reagan's proposed 1981 budget called for $30 billion in cuts. For instance, the last Carter budget allotted $30 billion to farm income supports through supply management farm policies. The first Reagan budget targeted reductions of $20 billion, but they did not make it through Congress. Farm income politics proved hard to budge. When Congress was finished, after increasing military spending, the rate of federal spending growth was just barely restrained. What was cut steeply was means-tested welfare programs catering to women and children—but not Social Security. The 1981 budget slashed Aid to Families with Dependent Children (AFDC) by 14.3 percent, food stamps programs by 13.8 percent, and Medicaid by 2.8 percent. Federal eligibility criteria were also restricted, eliminating an estimated 442,000 cases from the AFDC program.[44] Employment training was cut to the bone, but states were allowed to enforce "workfare" requirements for recipients, as Reagan had when he was governor of California and had targeted phantom "black welfare queens."[45] In the midst of the Volcker Shock–induced recession, the federal government punished the poor.[46]

The federal budget aside, programmatic changes in governance accelerated some already-existing trends. Reagan's 1981 Task Force on Private Sector Initiatives promoted the privatization of public functions such as welfare delivery.[47] Government contracting with nonprofit and for-profit corporations was encouraged. For-profit and nonprofit corporations increasingly partnered up with one another and also with the state.[48] In the blending of public and private, state and market, for-profit and nonprofit, it is possible to see how the theme of transactional liquidity in enterprise— fluidity, convertibility—resonated more broadly at this time, here in the venue of governance.

3. Shareholder Value

A new macroeconomic expansion began. In many respects, it was different from those that had come before. Since the post-1982 macroeconomic expansion was the first in a new series, it is worth exploring in some detail.

This business expansion is the only one on record, before or since, in

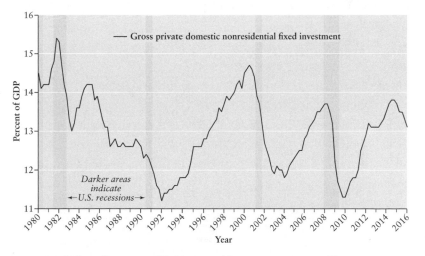

GROSS PRIVATE DOMESTIC NONRESIDENTIAL FIXED
INVESTMENT AS SHARE OF GDP
Typically, macroeconomic expansions have been led by a rising
share of nonresidential fixed investment in GDP. Tellingly,
the 1980s expansion featured a declining share.

which fixed investment as a share of GDP declined. Unlike what the Reagan administration promised, there was no domestic investment boom in manufacturing. Meanwhile U.S. multinational corporate investment continued to flow abroad, except now at an ever-higher rate.[49] At home, tellingly, the value of new U.S. "industrial structures" declined by one-third between 1981 and 1986.[50] Relatively, there was more speculative investment in financial and real estate assets. The post-1982 boom focused in particular on American stocks and bonds and also on commercial real estate. Notably, even for nonfinancial American firms, the ratio of net acquisitions of financial to durable assets climbed.[51] This had consequences for labor markets. As asset prices climbed, the owners of financial assets, and professionals in the business and financial services classes directly or indirectly employed by them—bankers, accountants, commercial real estate appraisers—saw their incomes swell.[52] These incomes then created fresh demand for service and care labor in the lower regions of the income distribution—say, retail, childcare, nurses, and nannies.[53] The middle began to hollow out.

Related to the declining share of investment in GDP, personal consumption accounted for a greater share. But what sustained personal consumption, if median pay growth remained flat, as it had during the 1970s, but now severed from a lower trend line in productivity growth (in part a consequence of the lower rate of investment)? There were tax cuts. However,

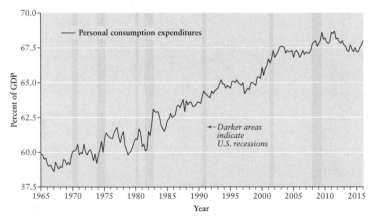

PERSONAL CONSUMPTION EXPENDITURE AS SHARE OF GDP
The greatest economic continuity between the Age of Control and the Age of Chaos was the increasing importance of consumerism. Indeed, in the global macroeconomy after 1980 the United States became even more so the world's most important consumer market.

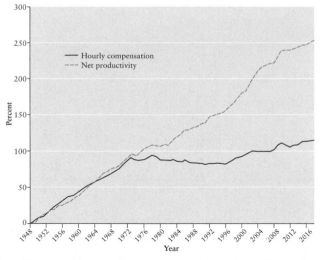

PRODUCTIVITY GROWTH AND AVERAGE HOURLY
COMPENSATION GROWTH

In the Age of Chaos, productivity growth continued to disappoint, and it
remained severed from average compensation growth. The benefits of
productivity gains flowed to the best-off; for many working Americans
to sustain consumption, debt growth replaced income growth.

unlike what Reagan had promised, a surge in the household saving rates
failed to materialize. Instead, household debt increased. Effectively, household debt replaced inflation, papering over flat pay.[54] For instance, outstanding consumer credit loans, mostly credit cards, sold by commercial
banks, doubled during the 1980s.[55] Conforming to the post–Volcker Shock
pattern, indebted American consumers purchased the manufacturing imports of the world, financed by U.S. capital imports—in this decade, especially manufactures from Japan.[56]

Finally, another great driver of the expansion was federal budget deficits. Supply-side economics failed—the national debt expanded. Snapping
up U.S. debt, however, would be a lot of foreign capital.[57]

American households and the federal government both turned to debt,
but so did American corporations. Why? For one thing, credit was available in the United States—not everywhere, as much of the world economy
remained mired in post–Volcker Shock public debt crises and national economic recessions. But for fear that inflation might return, the Fed kept its
short-term-interest-rate target relatively high. It fell below 8 percent only
in December 1984. The unusual combination of abundant available fi-

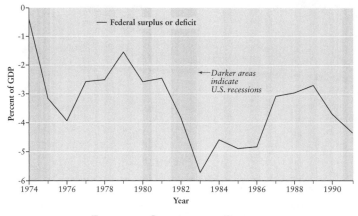

FEDERAL SURPLUS OR DEFICIT

By increasing budget deficits, Reagonomics accomplished the opposite of what it promised. But the expansion of U.S. debt would create more dollar-denominated safe assets for the global owners of capital to purchase.

nancing, but at high rates, was not seen since the 1920s, after the restoration of the gold standard. Credit booms at high rates demand quite confident expectations, and here Reagan's capital-friendly policies surely mattered. Yet, borrowing at 8 percent required a rate of return greater than 8 percent in order to turn a profit. One way to juice profits was to increase leverage, or to use more borrowed money, rather than one's own, for the investment at hand. Therefore, paradoxically enough, a credit-fueled investment boom at high rates meant snowballing debt.

U.S. corporate debt doubled during the 1980s. If step one during the Volcker Shock was the decision among the owners of capital to hoard cash and earn short-term profits through interest rate accrual, during the post-1982 expansion, step two was indebted speculative investments, to hurdle over high borrowing rates through leverage. Thus the great "discipline of the market," promised by Carter, Reagan, and Volcker alike, failed.[58] Instead, a rather undisciplined upswing in the capitalist credit cycle occurred. Its premise was the belief that transactional liquidity—a funder, if not a buyer for all assets—would always be present in what was fast becoming one big interconnected capital and credit market.

An emblematic pictorial representation was the painter Bernard Frize's *Drexel, Burnham, Lambert* (1987), named after the decade's great corporate junk bond firm.

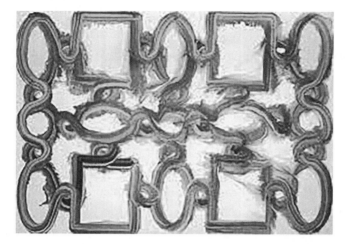

BERNARD FRIZE, *DREXEL, BURNHAM, LAMBERT* (1987)
Named after the greatest junk bond firm of the 1980s, the painting
symbolizes the increasing interconnection of capital markets
during the decade.

The painting consists of one continuous line, as if there were one single market. The surface is busy, with active spatial movement, but no narrative; the line does not go in any particular direction. But different classes of objects are connected. Frize also painted the canvas with different brushes, as if to stitch together different classes of assets into a single energetic flow of credit.

The investment bank Drexel Burnham Lambert is a good place to begin to dig into the character of the post-1982 business expansion. In enterprise, the turn to leveraged asset appreciation required nothing short of a revolution in U.S. corporate governance, in which financiers, including investment bankers, continued to wrest ever more power from an already-floundering managerial class.

The weapon was the new gospel of "shareholder value," which demanded that managers act in the pecuniary interests of shareholders. That often meant slashing wages, foregoing long-term investments, or selling off assets, all in order to benefit the immediate bottom line. There was and is no hard law that says that U.S. corporations must be motivated to maximize short-term profit.[59] Most postwar industrial corporations, focused on long-term growth metrics and the maintenance of "organizational slack," had not even tried. With the shareholder value revolution of the 1980s, the present stock market price of corporate shares newly became the metric of corporate success.

What enthroned shareholder value was a wave of sometimes hostile corporate takeovers. The movement began in the late 1970s, when oilmen flush with cash from the high prices of the oil shock came to believe that the stocks of large, diversified energy companies were trading below the value of their physical assets. During his 1983 bid to take over Gulf Oil, the Texas oilman T. Boone Pickens declared in *The Wall Street Journal*, "We are dedicated to the goal of enhancing shareholder value."[60] That was one of the earliest uses of the phrase. Pickens tried to convince the majority of Gulf Oil shareholders to convey the corporation into Pickens's "royalty trust." Then he would sell off assets unrelated to the oil business, returning cash to the owners. After that, he would offer the stripped-down oil company back to the public, hoping it would fetch a high value. Pickens never acquired majority control of Gulf Oil, but management paid him "greenmail." That is, they bought back the shares that Pickens and his allies had accumulated at a price above the going market rate—far above what Pickens's group had originally paid. Boone, Houston oilman Oscar Wyatt, Jr., and New Yorker Carl Icahn, among other corporate "raiders," followed this strategy successfully. Icahn even "greenmailed" U.S. Steel.[61]

Corporate raiders could never have pulled off the shareholder revolution by themselves. They needed help in the capital markets. Joining corporate raiders were institutional investors, especially public and private pension funds. In other words, accumulations of capital that were the result of the postwar politics of pay funded changes in corporate governance that, ironically enough, undermined the politics of pay. The critical economic site shifted from income to property. If working people began to use debt to compensate for flagging pay and to sustain consumption, then leveraged buyouts demonstrated how property owners could use debt to leverage up their profits from their investments. In all, relative income growth shifted away from labor to capital.

During the 1970s, inflation had cut into pension funds' investment returns, and new state and federal laws enabled them to seek riskier investments.[62] In 1975 pension funds owned $113 million worth of stocks. In 1980 they owned $220 million. In 1985 they owned $440 million. This was a perfect example of how capital began to newly traverse asset classes in this period. The fund managers in charge of these investments believed they could hedge the risk of stock market investments through new financial products. For instance, pension funds bought "portfolio insurance," in which computers automatically sold off stocks from their portfolios if stock prices declined. The academic theory behind portfolio insurance assumed transactional liquidity, "that continuous trading was possible"— that there would always be two sides for a trade, and not everybody would always be on the sell side. Furthermore, in 1982 the Chicago Mercantile Exchange began selling stock index futures contracts—essentially, an asset that tracked the price of the Standard & Poor 500 (called the "spooze"). Institutional investors, with regulators approving, bought them to hedge their stock market positions.[63]

Hedges in hand, institutional investors followed the raiders. In 1984 Texaco paid $55 million in "greenmail" to the Texas Bass family, at $55 a share when the market price was $35. The trustees of the California Public Employees' Retirement System (CalPERS), the largest U.S. public pension fund and one of the largest shareholders of Texaco, wondered why CalPERS got nothing. CalPERS led the Council of Institutional Investors (1985) and joined the chorus demanding greater corporate focus on shareholder value.[64] At all costs, the managers must focus on company stock price.

"Shareholder value" was the rallying cry for a wave of leveraged corporate buyouts and associated mergers and acquisitions. In 1982, in the midst of a revolution in antitrust law, Reagan's Justice Department changed its "merger guidelines." No longer was the goal, as stated in 1968, to "preserve and promote market structures conducive to competition." The new standard in assessing a merger was only whether its outcome would or would not "maintain prices above competitive levels."[65] This reflected the spreading influence of the Chicago Law and Economics movement, which argued that the only relevant standard for antitrust enforcement was "consumer welfare," or lower prices—not market structure or barriers to entry. Judges stripped antitrust prescriptions against vertical and horizontal mergers out of the law.[66] Between 1985 and 1989, there were thousands of leveraged buyouts, valued in excess of $250 billion.[67]

Assuming that adequate greenmail was not paid, the art of the leveraged buyout was this. Raiders and also new "private equity firms"—the largest at the time was Kohlberg Kravis Roberts (KKR, founded in 1976)—bought a portion of the target company's shares, usually between 5 and 10 percent.[68] The game had begun. Other shareholders, especially the large institutional investors, had to be willing to sell out to the acquiring interest. Management could even choose to participate, and often business consultants encouraged them to do so.[69] A company was far more likely to engage in a buyout transaction when executives from the finance rather than production or sales side of the corporation were in leadership.[70] If managers resisted, the buyout would be "hostile." To raise cash for the purchase of the shares, buyers secured credit lines from banks, or issued junk bonds—risky corporate bonds paying high yields. This was the final ingredient: the newly burgeoning debt market in junk bonds. They were what made the buyout leveraged. Investment bankers, above all Michael Milken of Drexel Burnham Lambert, made this market.[71] Finally, after investor groups built up a large stock position, it offered corporate boards a bid—a named share price—to buy out the company and take possession and ownership of it.

Thus publicly traded companies became privately owned. But the company then had to raise cash to meet the debt payments. That normally meant selling physical assets, as well as cutting operating costs—including labor costs. Spectacularly, employee pension funds, to compensate for their employees' flat compensation growth, sought yields by participating in leveraged buyouts, which then led newly indebted corporations to slash wages and eliminate jobs—so they could meet their debt obligations. Commonly, conglomerates were broken into parts, with many divisions sold off. It was a vertical and horizontal disintegration of the postwar multidivisional industrial corporation—more purging of fixed capital, more hemorrhaging of blue-collar jobs. After that, the corporation was sold back to public capital markets, hoping that the new share price had warranted the original purchase. If the stock prices kept going up, generally it had. Even if the stock price rose, did that necessarily mean that the underlying company was more valuable than it had been before the leveraged buyout? If the stock price rose, did it matter?

The last great leveraged buyout of the 1980s was Kohlberg Kravis Roberts's $31.1 billion takeover of RJR Nabisco. The CEO of RJR Nabisco was F. Ross Johnson. For a corporate manager, Johnson had long been an instinctive critic of white-collar bureaucracy. His managerial style belonged to the college frat house. Postwar managerial industrial capitalism, he decided, was boring. He put his own company "in play"—a telling term for putting together a group to tap debt markets and buy out a corporation. The ensuing saga was immortalized in the business journalists Bryan Burrough and John Helyar's *Barbarians at the Gate: The Fall of RJR Nabisco*

(1989), which launched a new literary genre—the gripping and eventful nonfiction business narrative.[72] *Barbarians at the Gate* could not have been written about postwar managerialism, as the commissioning of efficiency studies and long-term capital depreciation budgeting does not make for a page-turner. A leveraged buyout does.

In one scene in *Barbarians at the Gate*, Chicago investment banker Jeffrey Beck, the "Mad Dog," loses out to a higher bid for the midwestern conglomerate Esmark Corporation. But the LBO was his idea. That entitles him to a fee. As a joke, the managers on the deal tell the Mad Dog he will not receive a fee. Beck opens a window from a Chicago skyscraper and shouts, "That's it! I'm going to jump out the window! I'm going to kill myself!" Beck ends up with a $7.5 million fee for the role he played in the deal.

Johnson lost out to KKR in the bid for RJR Nabisco, but he still took home $53 million.[73] These monies counted as labor earnings. But the income resulted from the economic activity of leveraged asset price appreciation—the fees were hived off from the gigantic sums raised in debt markets. With such giant corporations in play, and so few individuals wheeling and dealing, with access to bank credit, enormous sums were at stake. It is hard to argue that Johnson was a better manager because of his education or talent—his "human capital." He was simply in a powerful position because of his job title and his social network, which he had leveraged as much as his own company.[74]

Probably the fate of RJR Nabisco was sealed when CEO Johnson decamped from corporate headquarters in Atlanta to live and play in New York City, which had reversed its postindustrial fortunes and was no longer a 1970s punch line. Wall Street quickly became an object of cultural fascination. Oliver Stone's *Wall Street* (1987) stands out among films. It tells the story of the fictional corporate raider Gordon Gekko, a combination of real-life raider Asher Edelman and the stock market speculator on buyouts Ivan Boesky, author of *Merger Mania* (1985), who told a graduating class of the UC Berkeley business school that greed is "healthy."[75] "Greed, for lack of a better word, is good," Gekko says in the film. Stone wanted *Wall Street* to be a critique of Wall Street, but the film made Gekko too likable, in part because it so well captured the obvious eroticism of the new financial dealing. Gekko passes along stock trading tips and his girlfriend to his protégé, Bud Fox. A worthy complement in the novel category was Bret Easton Ellis's *American Psycho* (1991), a satire about an investment banker misogynist serial killer.[76] Ellis raised the suspicion that there was something deeply antisocial about this financial activity, which compensated for, but did not solve, male identity crises.

Stepping back, no doubt many old industrial corporations deserved to be shut down, one way or another. And in their drudgery and danger, many blue-collar jobs, so quickly shed, had hardly been worth saving. The liquidity of capital made it possible. But where was the creation in this destruction? What did it create exactly, besides the enrichment of a narrow group of people, on one patch of the earth?

Regardless, by the mid-1980s a new "common sense" of what a corporation was had taken shape.[77] In 1976 two Chicago-trained University of Rochester business school professors, Michael Jensen and William Meckling, had published what was to be one of the most widely cited of all academic economics papers, "Theory of the Firm: Managerial Behavior, Agency Costs, and Ownership Structure."[78] A firm, they argued, was a spot market, a "nexus of contracts." The most important contract was that between a principal (the equity owner) and his agent (the manager). The manager's job was to maximize shareholder value. Now. The standard postwar managerial profit target had been twenty years; by the mid-1980s, the industry standard for a successful leveraged buyout "payback" was two years.[79] Jensen and Meckling's model assumed transactional liquidity among all assets.[80] In 1985 Jensen left Rochester for the Harvard Business School, cheering on the shareholder value revolution, as this "agency theory" of corporations began to seep into business schools, consultancy recommendations, and popular consciousness.[81]

As for shareholder value, buoyed by debt and computer automation, NYSE trading volumes exploded during the 1980s. So did U.S. stock market prices. Stock market capitalization climbed, even though the corporate profit rate—actual business earnings—remained below that of the bear market 1970s.[82] Corporate boards, buying their shareholders' loyalty, increasingly tied managerial compensation to stock options instead of pay. Managers, in turn, began to buy back company shares, to keep the stock price up.[83] Discussions of "fundamentals"—what a business actually did—still mattered in valuation, but asset prices, throwing off capital gains, might delink from what was supposed to be their anchor in the "underlying" business profit of the firm, made from using up capital in wealth-generating enterprise and labor.[84]

But then why did the "underlying" business profit have to be founda-

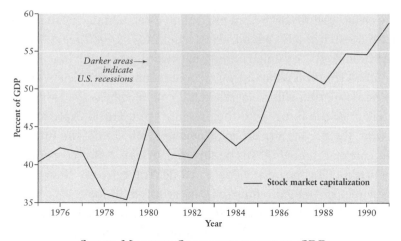

STOCK MARKET CAPITALIZATION TO GDP

Over the 1980s the new political economy of asset price
appreciation contributed to a rise in corporate stock prices.

tional? In the early 1980s, profits from the FIRE sector (finance, insurance,
and real estate) surpassed those from manufacturing. In 1978, for manufacturing firms, portfolio income (from interest accrual, dividends, and
realized capital gains) was 18 percent of total profits. By 1990 it was 60
percent.[85] Why bother parting with liquidity—bearing a risk of loss by investing in enterprise, employing labor, making a product, and selling it at
a profit above cost—when one could lean back and buy and sell assets in
markets fueled by debt (if not threaten to jump out of a window for a hefty
fee)? At least, the line between what was thought to be reality and representation in the economy was blurring, and the latter was perhaps getting
out ahead of the former—back to P. T. Barnum and confidence games.

The blurring of appearance and reality was a great preoccupation of
1980s cultural "postmodernism."[86] Take what might be considered one of
the great postmodern literary genres, "mark-to-market" accounting.[87]
Postwar managerialism's "historical cost" accounting had computed
profit in relation to the past use of productive capital, or its long-term depreciation. In mark-to-market accounting, the present market value of
assets, foretelling future incomes, is what matters. The horizon is perpetually short-term. Future "return on equity," or the trajectory of the stock,
replaces "return on investment," or the return on the company's past out-
lay of resources, in order to produce something and sell it above its cost of
production. The distant past is wiped out. So is the distant future, as the

future collapses into the present price of an asset, updated by the millisecond. (In novels from this period, like Martin Amis's 1991 *Time's Arrow*, "reverse chronology," or time running backward, was a popular narrative technique.) That was what Chicago school economists' "efficient markets" hypothesis theorized: financial markets do not recognize the past, they accurately price the future into the present.[88] In cultural expression, that was what the decade's neon color palette symbolized—the intense but fleeting present moment.[89] In the sartorial style of 1980s corporate raiders, a bright color meant the power red tie. The celebrity New York real estate developer Donald Trump self-caricaturized the look.

In style, like the 1880s, the 1980s also saw the renewed prominence of the color black, made especially popular by the pop artist Madonna. Black was the color of mourning, back then arguably for the agrarian past, now arguably for postwar industrial society. Surely 1980s capital markets left postwar industrial corporate managerialism dead in the dust.

4. "Truthful Hyperbole"

The new macroeconomic pattern of the 1980s was capable of creating a sustained economic expansion. It also sponsored forms of economic life far from Wall Street. This boom looked a lot like the growth of cities such as Houston, where the economy did not revolve around the male breadwinning wage, or on long-term fixed investment and productivity growth, but rather on the spread of real estate across space, and on high- and low-wage service employment—and where the principle of liquidity spread outside capital markets and into everyday life. There was only one Wall Street. The post-1982 expansion saw the extension of the previous Sunbelt pattern of economic development across the United States.

During the 1980s, employment in the service sector grew prodigiously. Between 1980 and 1988, of the 12 million new jobs created, 2 million were in the "business services" subcategories toward the top end of the income distribution. That included everything from bankers to sales representatives, insurance adjusters, and real estate managers. Toward the middle to low end were 3 million less-skilled, lower-paying jobs in such things as food preparation, retail work, education, and health services.[90] All of these jobs, regardless of their pay, were in low-productivity regions of the economy, as commonly measured: the kind of productivity gains Henry Ford made in turning out more Model Ts per minute are not so easy to achieve when flipping burgers, cleaning bedpans, teaching aerobics, or prescribing drugs. The 1980s saw no trendline increase in productivity growth.[91] If the general price level was held steady after Volcker, there was inflation in asset prices, especially commercial real estate.

Commercial real estate was another unintended consequence of the Volcker Shock story that combined with the unforeseen results of Reagan's tax policy. Prices had bottomed out during the 1973–74 recession but had begun to recover during the late 1970s, as commercial rents, unlike many streams of income, could be updated to account for inflation. After the Volcker Shock, funding abounded. For instance, Japanese capital poured into Los Angeles real estate.[92] Latin American capital, fleeing debt crises, arrived in Houston.[93] It was at this moment that Trump arrived in Manhattan bankrolled by his Queens-real-estate-developer father, as well as friendly government tax credits. Trump, leveraging his real estate assets and no less his celebrity, built his Manhattan real estate and Atlantic City casino empire on debt, funded by a "sprawling network of seventy-two banks," including Citibank, Chase, and Bankers Trust, as well as British, German, and Japanese banks.[94] Trump was emblematic of a larger trend. He was a business concern with very little underlying income generation, relative to his assets, which he purchased through bank debt. When his assets increased in price, he used them as collateral for more loans, which became his income, given that his actual businesses usually lost money in the end. "Truthful hyperbole" was what Trump branded the business model in his ghostwritten autobiography *The Art of the Deal* (1987).[95]

Trump was the clownish though savvy extreme. But real estate was no different from the stock market. Tapping new sources of credit, commercial real estate saw its asset values during the 1980s surge far beyond what had long been considered the sector's so-called fundamentals—the construction and actual use of commercial buildings.[96] The decade's national real estate construction boom did create 1.5 million new jobs, mostly for men, in construction, although focused on cities such as Dallas or Phoenix, not Pittsburgh or Cleveland. Nonetheless, in terms of values, appearance was everywhere running out ahead of reality.

Commercial real estate was a sector where grand ideological pronouncements about the market mean very little, in comparison to some of the nitty-gritty details of the ongoing transformation. Reagan's 1981 tax cut had created a new accelerated depreciation credit for "structures." Manufacturing was the intended target, but the law also applied to commercial real estate. Companies could sell tax credits to one another.[97] The paperwork meant more jobs in "business services" for tax lawyers. Rather than building factories, even industrial corporations such as General Motors began to invest in office building construction, if only for the tax credit. Lawyers began to charter a host of new kinds of legal partnerships and shell companies. Income shifted to them, especially when the 1986 tax reform bill benefited such entities by granting them lower tax rates than corporations.[98] Liberalism had long used the tax code to attempt to induce private investment in industry, to mixed effect. The technique now became a near parody of itself, as capital moved—in this instance into leveraged commercial real estate, not industry—through mind-numbingly complex tax-friendly intermediaries.[99]

A similar story can be told about the new sources of funding. In 1982 the Garn–St. Germain Depository Institutions Act changed the financial regulation of "thrifts" in the savings and loan industry. New Deal–era regulations had highly limited thrifts' loan portfolios. In real estate, savings banks were limited largely to the residential market within fifty miles of their location. The pattern begins to look familiar. Here again, 1970s inflation undermined the industry, in this case mostly because so many thrifts' assets were old home mortgage loans with low, fixed interest rates. The 1982 law let thrifts invest up to 40 percent of their assets in commercial real estate. It increased the federal insurance limit of deposits from $40,000 to $100,000. It also allowed individuals to own thrifts. Finally, it let savings banks accept "brokered deposits" from the unregulated shadow banking sector. Money managers thus cobbled together $100,000 CDs, deposited with thrifts. There was no risk, only gain, as they were government insured.[100]

Thrifts' commercial real estate loans climbed from 7 percent of their total assets in 1982 to 20 percent by 1989.[101] Credit flowed, mostly, to the fringes of expanding Sunbelt cities and suburbs, like office parks in California and Texas. Many real estate developers chartered or acquired thrifts themselves. They might funnel federally insured brokered deposits through thrifts, into their own "pass-through" real estate subsidiaries. In this period, many commercial buildings earned the nickname "see-through" because they had so few occupants. In Houston, Gene Phillips used a shell company called Southmark Corporation to buy a thrift, San Jacinto Savings and Loan. San Jacinto exchanged $246 million worth of commercial real estate mortgages back and forth with entities of a New

York real estate developer and thrift owner, Charles Keating. Such deals were now possible. These people simply traded the same asset among themselves over and over again, each time booking profits by assigning a higher price. From these swaps, the two booked $12 million in mark-to-market accounting profits, which Keating used to fund leveraged purchases of leveraged buyout junk bonds from Drexel Burnham Lambert.[102]

Aghast, a Florida state regulator noted that "money availability" had become "more of a reason for real estate development than economics."[103] Funding was available, but interest rates were high, so debt and leverage were needed for profits to hurdle over the cost of the loan. But this was economics, or at least one way to have an economy. Commercial real estate was no frothy market on top of an underlying business expansion. Maybe, increasingly this was it: capital rushing into an asset class, throwing off income and creating jobs—for bankers, developers, construction workers, and self-employed building inspectors, appraisers, assessors, accountants, and fraudsters. Meanwhile, as median male wages flatlined and more women entered the labor force, their absence from the home and their newfound incomes created demand for more service jobs in the care sector. Someone had to cut the hair, cook the dinners, watch the kids, and tend to the elderly parents of members of the financial and business services class.

Of course, capital did not rush everywhere. As for real estate values, northern black urban property prices continued to fall, as they had been doing since the late 1960s urban uprisings.[104] Black migration back to the South advanced. But many northern urban black people—increasingly trapped in jobless ghettos, devalued by capital, and with unemployment and means-tested welfare benefits declining—had no choice but to become entrepreneurial, in the spirit of the times. The informal and criminal economies expanded.[105] The nationwide increase in violence and crime that began during the 1960s had not yet reversed.[106] In 1982 Reagan doubled down on Nixon's "War on Drugs." Rates of black male incarceration for nonviolent drug offenses surged in particular, but in general white incarceration increased at the same rate as black. The U.S. prison population climbed from around 300,000 to over 1 million by 1996. The United States became by far the most punitive state in the world. Spending on incarceration increased as means-tested welfare benefits and public housing expenditures fell. And here were some new walls—prison walls. Capital might invest in them. The first for-profit prison since the 1920s was contracted in

Tennessee in 1983: "Incarceration for profit concerned 1,345 inmates in 1985; ten years later, it covered 49,154 beds."[107] Likewise, for public housing, the Reagan administration offered tax credits to for-profit developers who built a minimum number of "low income" units.[108] Both rates of incarceration and for-profit "public" housing surged in the Sunbelt. In cities following the Houston model of economic development, it was easy to privatize—with so much new development, "public" prisons, hospitals, and other service deliverers never existed to begin with. This was the new political economy. When public infrastructure crumbled in the North, it would replace it.

From the point of view of the worst-off, economic life began to look bleak. Increasingly, incarceration was the solution to the exclusion of people from the postindustrial labor market.[109] The "overdevelopment of American penal policy" corresponded to "the underdevelopment of American social policy."[110] However, the expanding service economy did offer new possibilities.

In Buffalo, New York—to return to the site of the 1983 steel closures—the macroeconomic expansion did bring jobs. Doris McKinney, a black single mother and a former steelworker who lost a high-paying, secure unionized job, found a new job in a New York state hospital working with geriatric patients. The pay and benefits were worse, but the activity was better. "I work with geriatric patients. And I do various crafts and arts. . . . Oh I love it, I love it. I can't tell you how happy I am to be doing it. . . . This is what I would want to do for the rest of my life."[111] Health and education services added 3.1 million jobs during the Reagan years, a nearly 40 percent increase. At first, the Reagan administration had reduced the number of disability recipients and benefits, but by the mid-1980s levels were soaring again, and due to an aging population, welfare transfers during the Reagan years increased as a percentage of total incomes.[112] The public welfare state and the private welfare economy expanded in unison. In many rustbelt cities, health care replaced industry, as in households the incomes of female nurses caring for aging male manufacturing workers, paid indirectly by union health insurance plans, replaced the lost incomes of male breadwinners.[113]

A new world of service work was taking shape. It was socially interactive, consisting of affective, emotional, and care labor.[114] These kinds of service labor were still marked feminine. Few laid-off male steelworkers applied for jobs as home health care aides. Men were more likely to find jobs in "self-employment," often precarious and with low benefits. But one former GM worker at the streamlined Linden, New Jersey, plant reported that in his new job, "the relationship is better." He had hated his boss. A new self-employed operator of a laundromat noted, "It's so different now. People who come in to have their clothes [washed] are usually in a good mood, and if I'm in a good mood, too, things are rosy."[115] Because of the social content of the new service jobs, some people appreciated them, valuing them relationally. But as workers, they were not appreciated so much in distributive, pecuniary terms. A willingness to care for others did not count as appreciable "human capital," but an accounting degree from a university did. Soon economists developed a name for this phenomenon: "skill-biased technical change."[116]

Exploitation was also common in service labor markets. Acknowledging the collapsed boundary between home and work, labor unions tried to find ways to root it out. Home health care workers in New York, Chicago, and San Diego, overwhelmingly black women, fought to organize. For-profit firms could now contract to provide Medicare-funded home health care services, so workers might have to bargain with states, nonprofits, and for-profits.[117] The Service Employees International Union (SEIU), led by John Sweeney, supported such organizing efforts. The International Ladies' Garment Workers' Union created a childcare center in New York in 1983 and in 1988 won parental leave for its 135,000 members. Nonetheless, organizing workers in precarious positions, employed by contractors, subcontractors, and numerous "vendors," was not easy. From this moment onward, however, American women began to join unions at higher rates than men.[118]

5. Politics of Nostalgia

In 1984 Reagan was reelected by 59 percent of the popular vote—a triumphant landslide. It had been a remarkable number of years of dizzying economic transformation. Too dizzying? Even the Reagan administration stopped to assess and, walking pro-market ideology back a bit, participated in a new politics of nostalgia for the bygone economic order. Released months after Reagan's second inauguration, the highest-grossing film of 1985 was bathed in nostalgia for the postwar period—*Back to the Future.* In the late 1980s, even the cultural avant-garde shifted from postmodern obsession with representation to the theme of trauma from loss.[119]

Then the credit cycle finally closed, and the long business expansion came to an end.

While glad that capital imports paid for its budget deficits, the second Reagan administration began to question the post-Volcker global economic configuration. The value of the dollar was awfully high. The Plaza Accord of 1985, struck at New York's Plaza Hotel, announced to the world the commitment of the United States, Japan, West Germany, France, and Britain to intervene in foreign currency markets and bring down the relative value of the dollar. Between 1985 and 1987, compared to other currencies, the dollar declined by 40 percent—taking it about back to where it had been in 1980.[120]

Why the Plaza Accord? Japanese and European finance ministers had not liked watching their countries' savings flow abroad to purchase dollars and dollar-denominated assets. Because of the high dollar, American manufacturers' goods were more expensive abroad, while in the domestic market, the imports they competed against were cheaper. They began to lobby Congress. Moreover blue-collar job loss had become difficult for the entire political culture to stomach. Something must be wrong in an economy where female employment in health services surged, while male manufacturing employment declined. After a lag following the Plaza Accord, the U.S. trade deficit dramatically narrowed. An interregnum opened in which the post-Volcker pattern reversed. (It would come back, with a vengeance.) In the late 1980s, benefiting from the reversal in terms of trade and also from the continued halt of average real wage growth, U.S. manufacturing profits began climb.[121]

Nowhere did the politics of nostalgia play a greater role than in farm policy. Like many third-world commodity producers, many American farmers had gone into debt during the 1970s to expand production, only to be punished by higher funding charges due to the Volcker Shock. U.S. farm debt reached $215 billion by 1983. The "farm crisis" became a national story in 1984–85 and also a postindustrial media spectacle. The small family farm did not exist anymore. On free market principles, Reagan vetoed a congressional bailout. Farm lobby Democrats rolled out celebrity actresses before their committees as "expert witnesses." Jessica Lange, who starred in *Country* (1984), about an Iowa family farm foreclosure, pleaded with Congress not "to allow the last remnants of our heritage [to] disappear." *Field of Dreams* (1989), the best film about the Iowa farm crisis, had no politics, just a yearning for the past that could only be brought back, truly, by magic. In 1985 Reagan backed down and signed an expanded farm bill that distributed 80 percent of its welfare to overwhelmingly white farm proprietors or corporations that earned more than $100,000 a year. The white yeoman Jeffersonian farmer was no less mythical than the black welfare queen.[122]

Neither yeomen farming nor male industrial breadwinning was coming back. But with the return of the credit cycle, something repressed did. On a single day of trading, October 9, 1987, the NYSE's Dow Jones Industrial Average fell 22.6 percent, a historic drop. Unheard-of levels of volatility began to appear in the NYSE in 1986. Given the rise of one big, interconnected capital market, money was rushing in and out of the NYSE at unprecedented speed. "Moves like this used to take ten days to make. Now they take ten minutes. You can't get a handle on it," said one market participant.[123] When Chicago "spooze" contracts—a stock index derivative, or a synthetic asset, whose value derived from price movements in other assets—soared, money managers sold them and bought underlying stocks, driving up the NYSE. The reverse trade brought the price of stocks down. Would someone buy them, to bid them back up? Would transactional liquidity in the market be sufficient? Regulatory agencies saw no problem with the financial innovation. In 1985 a Treasury, Federal Reserve, SEC, and Commodity Futures Trading Commission report noted that a host of new complex financial derivatives fulfilled "a useful economic purpose," since "firms and individuals less willing to bear [risks]" could trade them to firms and individuals who were willing to do so. The report noted the "rationality" and "efficiency" of financial markets and concluded that derivatives "appear to have no measurable negative implications for the formation of capital."[124]

In October 1987 institutional sell orders through portfolio insurance and stock index trades leveled prices at the NYSE. At the bottom of the market, there were no buyers—no transactional liquidity. Stock markets in Tokyo, Hong Kong, and London suffered routs. On Monday, October 9, the NYSE lost 508 points. Confidence collapsed, in a massive flight to cash—now precautionary liquidity preference broke out. That undermined short-term speculation, let alone any long-term investment. The next day trading all but halted in the Chicago and New York pits. Traders wore DON'T PANIC buttons. The Fed, under the chairmanship of Alan Greenspan since August, announced, "The Federal Reserve, consistent with its responsibilities as the nation's central bank, affirmed today its readiness to serve as a source of liquidity to support the economic and financial system." Panic subsided, and confidence returned. The NYSE clawed back value.[125] The sudden crash did not lead to an immediate economic recession.

Over the decade, it had become obvious that the Fed was willing to support the new political economy of asset price appreciation. So long as markets believed in the continued presence of transactional liquidity for assets, or just for the debts that funded them, then confidence was maintained, and asset prices might continue to climb. Long, credit-fueled macroexpansions could continue. But the only agent with the ultimate power to guarantee liquidity was a state institution, the Fed. Greenspan could not have been clearer that the Fed was willing to embrace this role.

Lasting until 1990, the post-1982 expansion was the longest peacetime expansion on record since World War II, second only to the one that lasted from 1961 to 1969. Not Reagan but President George H. W. Bush oversaw the brief downturn of 1990–91. Still wary of inflation, Greenspan's Fed raised short-term rates from under 6 percent to nearly 10 percent between 1986 and 1989. The action closed the credit cycle. Leveraged commercial real estate values dropped. As a business model, truthful hyperbole perhaps had its limits. Trump went bankrupt. Leveraging his personal celebrity and not much else would soon become his business. In real estate, the fraudulent savings and loan industry imploded, ending in an approximately $150 billion government bailout.[126] Access to credit had enabled criminality. In 1990 the junk bond maven Michael Milken was sentenced to ten years in jail for insider trading. The junk bond market tanked. The leveraged buyout wave of corporations ended. Finally, in a leading cause of the recession, personal consumption decreased. Having accumulated debts, in part to compensate for weak pay growth, many households now decided to halt the rise in their indebtedness and spent less, undermining economic activity. That mattered a lot, since, after all, the business expansion had been led much more by consumption than by investment.[127]

Stepping back, let us assess the economic changes over the decade. During the 1970s crisis of industrial capitalism, almost every single national economy had experienced a malaise of some sort. Many states had turned to the capital markets, accumulating public debt, looking for salvation of one kind or another, but usually they sought to revive their industrial economies. When the Volcker Shock hit and a worldwide economic recession broke out, interest rates on funding shot up, resulting in crippling public debt crises—in Latin America and Africa especially. But even some eastern European Communist countries, Poland being the most dramatic case, had gone to the capital markets to attempt to borrow their way out of the industrial doldrums. These regimes doubled down on their investments in capital goods industrialism, in a gamble that failed. Communism would perish.[128]

For its part, capitalism transformed. Aided by the liquidity of capital, the United States, still the global hegemon, led the way. Due to the dollar's status as the world's reserve currency, the United States uniquely benefited from capital imports during the 1980s, while much of the world suffered economically. The Volcker Shock had contributed to that by raising interest rates, thus making holding dollars more attractive, and even more important, it broke the back of inflationary expectations—bolstering the confidence of the owners of capital. The United States experienced an economic boom during the 1980s, while other countries did not. (There are no Houstons in, say, France.) What an extraordinary and unique opportunity the United States had to capitalize and chart a postindustrial future.

The Reagan economy can count a number of achievements. It consigned postwar industrial society to the past. Job growth in services was prodigious. Perhaps its greatest achievement was the narrowing pay gaps between men and women.[129] Related, the post-civil-rights entry of women and minorities into jobs that white male discrimination had previously excluded them from became a significant driver of productivity growth.[130] But in general the rate of productivity growth still disappointed—in that sense, the 1980s was the worst decade on record since the industrial revolution.[131] This was much because long-term investment, private and public, was so weak (outside military investments in such things as an interstellar missile system that did not work to fight a Cold War enemy that was collapsing anyway). With money and credit so abundantly available both at home and abroad, most of what the U.S. owners of capital did during this decade hardly deserves praise: in particular, their fostering of a bloated financial sector focused on short-term speculation that was of questionable social value. It was of questionable economic value, too—finance's contributions to productivity since 1980 have been hard to find in the statistics.[132] Meanwhile, as income gains began to flow to the owners of appreciating assets more than to workers, economic inequality widened.[133] Many of the new jobs created to service the better-off were low paying, and some were exploitative. Finally, even as during this decade science confirmed the existence of anthropogenic climate change, the high-energy fossil-fuel- and automobile-based economy of the Sunbelt only entrenched and expanded.

Various economic policies had encouraged the shift, but the new capitalism was hardly the conscious result of any long-term political or economic vision. Instead, a new, persistent pattern of expectations arose, defined by a new preference for liquidity—more transactional liquidity, as in more convertibility across assets, often to aid busy eventful speculation that had no particular purpose or end beyond itself. Paradoxically, a liquidity preference for money or money-like assets generates speculative uncertainty and also offers a potential response to it—the precautionary hoarding of liquid, safe-haven stores of value, as a lull from any moment of disquietude, which have the added advantage of providing the opportunity to instantly jump back into the speculative game. Thus whether seemingly busy or literally inactive, a high liquidity preference may trap economies in some version of a short-term horizon. Meanwhile, in lieu of taking a long view, the politics of nostalgia directed gazes backward, to a past that was not coming back and did not deserve to anyway. Outside the movies, there was no going back to the future.

Altogether American society saw a loss of control, and of a capacity to deliberately create economic outcomes. One "can speculate about everything," Volcker had surmised off-record in 1982, after becoming arguably the world's most important economic policy maker. "I don't know what is going to happen with regard to the flight of capital," he confessed in private to his colleagues. American workers who lost their factory jobs during the 1980s but landed on their feet, finding new work in services or self-employment, were often quick to qualify it: "I got lucky," "I lucked up," "I lucked out."[134] "I guess there's good opportunity if you can get a good education," said former steelworker Benjamin Boofer, who now cut firewood. "But it looks a little bit to me that everybody is going to have to be smart and then the ones that get it are going to be lucky."[135]

CHAPTER 20

THE NEW ECONOMY

P ERHAPS CAPITALISM HAS NEVER BEEN MORE CELEBRATED than during the 1990s. The recession of 1990–91, if mild in GDP terms, was followed by a "jobless recovery," especially for young men, a troubling portent for future business cycles. For a short time in the early 1990s, both grunge music and slacker films—the best being the Houston-based *Reality Bites* (1994)—were popular. But soon, fueled by a speculative upswing in the credit cycle, the next macroeconomic expansion began, and what a heady economic decade it turned out to be.

In the new economy, capital, having left many fixed industrial structures during the 1980s, surged into the infrastructure of information technology (IT), often via the financial securities of dot-com corporations associated with the birth of the commercial Internet, such as Yahoo! and Google. By contrast, after its own version of 1970s industrial malaise, the Soviet Union failed to chart a postindustrial economic future and perished. Following the destruction of the Berlin Wall in 1989 and the collapse of the Soviet Union in 1991, political scientist Francis Fukuyama announced to great fanfare "the end of history" in 1992. No alternative to liberal capitalist democracy was visible on the horizon.[1] Moreover, the past no longer mattered so much. Nostalgia for industrial society temporarily all but vanished from discourse. Corporate management guru James Champy wrote in *Reengineering Management* (1995):

> Nothing is stable. The business environment is changing before our eyes, rapidly, radically, perplexingly.
> *Now, whatever we do is not enough.* Incremental change is what

we're used to: the kind we could manage gradually, with careful planning, broad consensus-building, and controlled execution. Now we must not only manage change, we must create change— big change—and fast.[2]

By 1998, with capitalism triumphant and recent U.S. macroeconomic performance strong, Fed chairman Alan Greenspan, in testimony before the U.S. Congress, openly considered (despite personal skepticism) whether it was "possible that we have, in a sense, moved 'beyond history.' "[3]

The Fed continued its climb toward regulatory preeminence, begun during the Volcker Shock. Greenspan, the celebrity "Maestro" of monetary policy, was not the only politician in Washington who embraced the new mobility of capital. In 1999 the Harvard economist and deputy Treasury secretary Larry Summers (a decade later the chief economic adviser to President Barack Obama) summed up the "lessons from the 1990s." The most notable was that the world had "entered a new age of markets: one that rewards openness, flexibility, and innovation." That meant that states must "accelerate the pace of creating an environment in which resources, especially capital, will flow to their highest-return use."[4] Postwar liberalism's commitment to "equality of opportunity," back in an era when cross-border capital movements were controlled, was now updated. President Bill Clinton—a Democrat elected in 1992, in the wake of the 1990–91 recession—promised to transcend the old ideological division between left and right politics and move toward a "third way," a meritocratic commitment to equality of opportunity. In this brand of liberalism, individuals and states alike would have both the freedom and the necessity to seduce global capital investment or suffer the consequences.

Continuing the trend well under way during the 1980s, borders and walls were coming down, and institutional boundaries were blurring. Trade barriers fell. The wall between investment and commercial banking collapsed. In April 2000, President Clinton told a computer trade show, "Over and over again over the last 7 years, I have found, in some of our most important endeavors, the only thing that really works is the right kind of public-private partnership."[5] The only wall Clinton ever defended was the one between his life as a public official and his private sex life, but in the spirit of the times, it fell, too. The 1990s "slowly chipped away at the division between private and public," remarked the White House intern Monica Lewinsky.[6]

In a popular film of the decade, *Terminator 2* (1991), a robot made of liquid metal constantly reliquefies and reforms, reliquefies and reforms. Many once-distinct institutional spheres in political economy and social life became increasingly related, like an ever-shifting Venn diagram. What was public, and what was private? What was personal, and what was political? What was the difference between male and female identities? Were not race and gender mere "social fictions"? Was national affiliation outdated? Boundaries were transgressed, the solid became liquid, seemingly everything was becoming "networked," so much that it all left little independent standpoint from which to stand back and assess, or to draw new boundaries. Certainly, the standpoint of an independent public interest became very difficult to find.[7]

Twenty-seven years would pass from the fall of the Berlin Wall to the campaign rally cry "Build that wall!" But the end of the millennium was a moment of positive celebration of "flow" by ruling elites. Why worry about stability, structure, or sphering? The great keyword of the decade, *globalization*, expressed the sentiment best. Goods and culture flowed across borders. To a lesser extent, people did, too—legal and illegal immigrants.[8] Above all, globalization meant letting capital rove, embracing change. It would all work out to the benefit of everyone somehow.

It would not, in the end. But statistics from the 1990s make a plausible case that the American economy was then working out quite nicely at that time. In 1998 Greenspan boasted before Congress that the performance of the macroeconomy was "as impressive as any I have witnessed."[9] Because of investment in IT, the total rate of fixed investment, or the purchasing of new productive assets, was up, over what it had been in the 1980s. During the late 1990s, productivity rates increased to levels not seen since before the 1970s.[10] Likewise, unemployment fell below 5 percent for the first time since 1973. Labor markets were tightening, and median wages, for the first time since the 1970s, climbed. General price inflation remained low. Even rates of violence and crime fell to levels not seen since before the 1960s.[11]

Asset price appreciation, however, was even more extraordinary. In 1996 Greenspan warned of "irrational exuberance" in stock market valuations.[12] Stock prices began to climb far beyond their historical relationships to underlying business profits or GDP.

Was history no longer a guide to the economic future? Greenspan shared the belief that stock market values were justified because expecta-

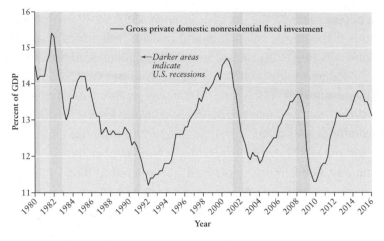

GROSS PRIVATE DOMESTIC NONRESIDENTIAL
FIXED INVESTMENT AS SHARE OF GDP

A genuine investment boom and a consequent surge in productivity
growth fueled the new economy of the 1990s. In the Age of Chaos,
this brief moment represents an exception to the rule.

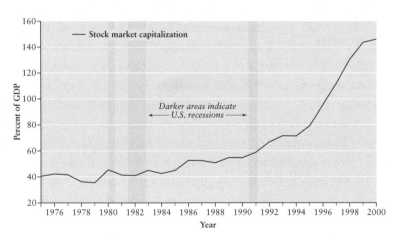

STOCK MARKET CAPITALIZATION TO GDP

In terms of asset price appreciation, the 1980s run-up in stock
prices was nothing compared to the new economy of the 1990s.

tions were justified. The rate of productivity growth, given innovative
ideas and prodigious investments in IT, would someday lead to future business profits—thus validating present high stock prices. Reality would follow appearance. The cart could pull the horse, until the horse woke up.

Or was the dot-com stock market bubble of 1997–2000 only an instance of "truthful hyperbole," if not magical market thinking—yet another iteration of the capitalism of asset price appreciation, born during the 1980s? The dot-com boom did result in fresh long-term investments in IT infrastructure, but it also rode a great speculative upswing in the credit cycle, which levered up asset prices—yielding capital income for the best-off. In capital markets, the contradictory drive of speculative investment ruled, and perhaps never has its ambivalent character been more apparent. Fixed investment in new forms of enterprise and productivity surged. Yet a constant, fickle convertibility meant that speculation also became a short-term end in and of itself. With so much energy and flow, everything could seem to be happening even if nothing much was happening at all. Speculative capital spun its top, converting at a new, digital speed in one big, global capital market. However, if confidence and belief ever faltered, the speculative investment boom might turn to bust—no short-term speculation, no long-term investment. The flight to hoarding cash, the plummet in asset values, and the blow to economic activity in general would then reveal the contradictory character of the credit cycle.

Indeed, Greenspan's speculation that history itself might be left behind was in the wake of the 1997–98 Asian financial crisis, a moment that would prove to be of great global economic significance. The Fed had to intervene in order to guarantee global transactional liquidity.

The political economy of asset appreciation that had first appeared during the 1980s solidified. Still, the new economy proved to be about something more than a single upturn in the credit cycle, a single stock market boom. Something else, new and lasting, was born during the 1990s. If only because of the Internet, the new economy began to transform the character of economic life. Taking its full measure requires traveling to the place of its birth, Silicon Valley, California.

1. Silicon Valley, the Idea

By the turn of the millennium, the world's most vibrant economic region was the Transpacific West—specifically, the vast region under the pledged security protection of the U.S. military, including California and Washington but also Japan, South Korea, Hong Kong, and Thailand.[13] In particular, capital focused on a location where U.S. military contracts, university scientists, Japanese-design-obsessed engineers, Buddhism-curious hippie entrepreneurs, and venture capital all mixed. That was Silicon Valley, a roughly forty-square-mile area of peninsular land in Santa Clara Valley, south of San Francisco. There, during the 1990s the Internet was first commercialized. Amid extraordinary technological innovation, a new style of entrepreneurship and a new logic of financial valuation arose.

"Silicon Valley" was first branded in 1971, the year local industry began to shift from its first great product, the silicon semiconductor, to its next, the silicon microprocessor, or the "computer on the chip." The microprocessor was at the heart of the digital electronics revolution. It was a "general purpose technology," as economists call it, meaning it could be put to use in a variety of ways, like the steam engine in the first industrial revolution.

What made Silicon Valley into Silicon Valley?[14] Several prerequisites are commonly cited. During World War II, the U.S. warfare state industrialized California, and afterward Pentagon research funds fertilized the valley. Stanford University was a hub for faculty and graduate students to contribute academic knowledge to enterprise. The area's culturally left libertarianism celebrated creativity and collaboration, and shunned stodgy white-collar dress and bureaucracy. When local entrepreneurs became rich, many became venture capitalists, admirably taking risks by making long-term equity investments in young companies. Silicon Valley entrepreneurs proved adept at working the corridors of power in Washington. Also, the weather in northern California is nice.

But many if not all of these elements were present in other places. (The Soviet Union had a military-industrial complex but no Google.) Some of them succeeded at a smaller scale, such as Boston's Route 128, benefiting from MIT and Harvard. But Houston, with its sprawling university-based medical center, never developed a successful biotech industry. During the 1980s, its entrepreneurial oilmen funded leveraged buyouts of existing corporations instead of placing venture capital in humanity-changing technologies.

Silicon Valley became what it was not so much because of the elements it possessed but because of the way it combined and ceaselessly recombined them all. According to the best account, the region featured "the active presence of for-profit, nonprofit, and public science organizations in three robust clusters," which "enabled cross-network transposition, where experience, status, and legitimacy in one domain were converted into 'fresh' action in another realm." After that, "cross-domain contact became routinized and interorganizational mobility channeled the flow of people, ideas, and resources."[15] Networked industrial districts have a long historical lineage. In Silicon Valley, institutions overlapped and shape-shifted creatively, while networks of people and capital were articulated in more creative ways than anywhere else.

The very world that Silicon Valley capitalized into existence is one in which what makes for success is the qualities that made Silicon Valley successful in the first place. To succeed would mean to be creatively networked and well-funded. Think of the rise of Silicon Valley as a cascading history caused by a never-ending game of "Six Degrees of Separation from Kevin Bacon"—fittingly, a popular parlor game of the late 1990s. If anyone in Silicon Valley played the role of Bacon, it would be Stanford University, with so many spokes jutting out from its Office of Technology Licensing (OTL), first established in 1970.

Silicon Valley first truly coalesced during an eleven-year period, starting in 1969, when UCLA made its first transmission to Stanford University over the Advanced Research Projects Agency Network (ARPANET). In 1971 Intel commercially introduced the first "microprocessor," and in 1980 the biotechnology firm and maker of recombinant DNA Genentech made its first initial public offering (IPO), as did the personal computer manufacturer Apple.[16] By then, a new business model of valuation had clearly been born in the valley. In the 1990s, it would appropriate the Internet and then, arguably, the end-of-the-millennium global economy.

The U.S. Defense Department created the Internet in the late 1960s, the brainchild of Texan Robert Taylor, an aerospace engineer who ran the Information Processing Techniques Office at the Pentagon's Advanced Research Projects Agency (ARPA). Taylor was particularly taken with a recent report he had read on the possibility of man-computer symbiosis, which speculated, "The hope is that, in not too many years, human brains and computing machines will be coupled together very tightly, and that the resulting partnership will think as no human brain has ever thought." Taylor told his boss, "I want to build a network."[17]

In 1968 ARPA funded the construction of a network through grants to the first four "network nodes" at the University of Utah, Stanford, UCLA, and UC–Santa Barbara.[18] By the time the first ARPANET transmission was sent in 1969, Taylor had quit the Pentagon in protest of the Vietnam War.

In 1970 he landed in Silicon Valley to run the Xerox Corporation's Palo Alto Research Center (PARC). Xerox PARC's lab was on land leased from Stanford University, the Stanford Research Park, established in 1951. Stanford professors and their graduate students frequently stopped by to chat with Taylor's scientists and engineers.[19]

When Taylor arrived in Palo Alto in 1970, the area was still dominated by the semiconductor industry. As early as the 1920s, the region had been known for contributions to electronics. In 1939 William Hewlett and David Packard, two electrical engineering graduates of Stanford, formed Hewlett-Packard, a company famous for its organizational culture, the "HP way"—which meant informal dress, first names, no hierarchy. In 1956 physicist William Shockley had decamped from AT&T's Bell Labs in New Jersey and arrived in Palo Alto to live closer to his sick mother and develop transistors. Shockley hired eight young PhDs. In a bizarre turn, following his 1956 Nobel Prize, he started advocating eugenics and founded his own sperm bank. The "traitorous eight" departed and, bankrolled by Sherman Fairchild, son of the first chairman of IBM, founded Fairchild Semiconductor. They used silicon, which amplifies and insulates electricity and possesses extraordinary durability. In 1968 Fairchild begat Intel Corporation, founded by two Fairchild founders, Gordon E. Moore and Robert Noyce.[20]

The Intel 4004 (1971) was the first commercially available silicon-chip, integrated circuit microprocessor. It was a "computer on a chip," with programmable software, computational power, and memory. Most microprocessors were still sold in the "sheltered market" to the military. But the microprocessor would end up in everything from computers to coffee makers, factory automation systems, smartphones, and drone aircraft. Moore proposed in 1965 that the number of transistors packed into an integrated circuit would double every two years—"Moore's Law." In the decades ahead, the exponential rate of growth would be even faster.[21]

Meanwhile, at Xerox PARC, Robert Taylor oversaw the development of a personal computer. Mainframe and "minicomputers" already existed for office use in business. But Xerox PARC's Alto personal computer had an operating system of pop-up windows, icons, word processing, a mouse, email, and an Ethernet connection. Xerox had no interest in bringing it to a commercial market, but by then many individuals in Silicon Valley were building personal computers.[22] Steve Jobs and Steve Wozniak founded Apple in 1976. Wozniak was a tinkerer in the small-scale industrial tradition of Henry Ford—early twentieth-century Detroit had itself been a networked industrial district. Just as Ford had built automobiles as a hobby while working for Edison, Wozniak kept his day job at Hewlett-Packard. Jobs, for his part, had worked as a line assembly engineer at Atari, Silicon Valley's greatest video game company. Atari was funded by Sequoia Capital, the first "Sand Hill Road" venture capital firm, founded in 1972 by Don Valentine, a former employee of Fairchild Semiconductor. Valentine declined to fund Apple at first, but he alerted Mike Markkula, a thirty-three-year-old former employee of Fairchild and Intel who had cashed out his stock options and was bored. Markkula bankrolled Apple $92,000, and later arranged for further investments from Sequoia and then a $1.05 million injection from Xerox.[23]

Jobs went to Xerox PARC to study the Alto, believing that Xerox's investment entitled him to sample its technology. What he and his engineers saw—a windows-based graphical user interface—led Apple to quickly rethink its designs. That same year, 1979, in Seattle, Bill Gates purchased an operating system called 86-DOS from Seattle Computer Products for $50,000 and sold it as MS-DOS to IBM, for use in its own personal computer, introduced in 1981, a competitor of the elegant, Wozniak-designed Apple II—no less a marvel in its own right than the Alto. Gates's operating system was windows-based, too, and would be branded Microsoft Windows in 1983. Jobs confronted Gates, who reportedly responded to the accusation of theft, "Well, Steve, I think there's more than one way of looking at it. I think it's more like we both had this rich neighbor named Xerox and I broke into his house to steal the TV set only to find that you had already stolen it."[24]

Apple became a public company in a December 12, 1980, initial public offering of stock. Back in 1977 Markkula valued Apple at $5,309. During the Volcker Shock–induced double-dip macroeconomic recession, Apple shares opened at $22. By the end of December 1980, they closed at $29, for a market value of more than $1.79 billion.[25] Jobs's personal stock was worth hundreds of millions. In October the biotech company Genentech opened at $35 per share and closed at $71.25. Large institutional investors, including pension funds, purchased stocks, newly funneling capital to the valley. These were early versions of new-economy-style valuation—sudden large injections of capital into budding businesses. "Every time I drive down and think about what's happening in this valley," one San Francisco venture capitalist remarked in 1980, "I have an orgasm."[26]

Apple was a profitable company by any possible criterion, but capital valuation was changing. Investors were considering more than operating profits. They were capitalizing into the value of companies, speculatively, the possible results of the innovative ideas of Silicon Valley's recombinant networks of relationships. Expectations had long figured into capitalization, of course, but the focus was changing, from the prospective profits to be yielded by the use and thus depreciation of fixed capital (building something somewhere) to the more intangible capital of ideas, or "human capital," and social networks, or "social capital." As much as wires and hardwire, these forms of capital proved very important to the rise of the new economy.

In Genentech, as in other biotechnology or pharmaceutical companies, the costliest part of the business was intellectually finding the right molecular structure for a drug. Next came the legal process of ensuring the scarcity value of the idea as a new income-generating asset. In 1980 the U.S. Supreme Court, in a 5–4 decision in *Diamond v. Chakrabarty,* ruled that man-made genetically engineered organisms could be patented. Congress's Bayh-Dole Act of 1980 let universities patent inventions that had been funded by the federal government. The new economy would be a boon for the labor incomes of intellectual property (IP) lawyers. Once the right molecular structure was discovered and patented, the actual manufacture of Genentech's products—including employing unskilled labor— was relatively cheap. Similarly, in 1981 at Apple, after engineering, design, and marketing were completed, labor assembly accounted for exactly 1 percent of the corporation's costs.[27] Brook Byers, of the early leading Silicon Valley venture capital firm Kleiner Perkins, noted, "What was so different about Genentech was the astonishing amount of capital required." Further, "it was science, it was hardly profitable, and it had essentially no revenue."[28] The capital required meant a heavy fixed investment in biomedical labs. It also meant employing a highly educated, if small, workforce. The manufacture of the product was cheap, but given the prior cost of innovation the company was not profitable. Nonetheless, its stock might value not present profits but rather the prospective significance of the idea—in capital markets.

By the 1980s, something new was brewing in Silicon Valley. Apple introduced the Macintosh in 1984, yet another elegant and landmark personal computer. Gates's Microsoft went public in 1986. At the time, Wall Street was focusing on the leveraged buyouts of aging industrial corporations, more than on funding technology start-ups. When that game was up after the 1990–91 recession, Wall Street moved on, and Silicon Valley high tech would lead the next surge in Wall Street stock prices. By decade's end, the focus would be on the commercialization of the Internet.

The Pentagon funded ARPANET through the 1980s. In Geneva, Switzerland, the British computer scientist Tim Berners-Lee designed software to enable any computer to add and access information to and from any computer connected to the Internet. Berners-Lee, committed to the open-source movement, released the program to the public for free in 1991. The World Wide Web was born. That year online portal America Online (AOL) launched an interface for Windows. In 1993 a twenty-one-year-old University of Illinois student at a National Science Foundation–funded supercomputing center, Marc Andreessen, led a team that wrote a software program for a more user-friendly version of the World Wide Web and called it Mosaic, the first Internet browser.[29]

Jim Clark, another Texan and a Stanford University computer scientist, resigned in 1982 to found Silicon Graphics, a maker of a 3D graphics chip. Clark noticed Mosaic and recruited Andreessen to Silicon Valley, where he then led the rewriting of the code. This Internet browser was called Netscape. Clark instantly valued Netscape at $18 million. The company had only a handful of employees and no revenues to speak of. Eight months after releasing the browser on August 9, 1995, Netscape went public. Shares in the IPO first priced at $18 and closed at $58.26, for an end-of-day market capitalization of . . . $3 billion. Clark's stock was worth $500 million. The company had yet to record a single dollar of operating profit.[30] While something similar had happened with Apple and Genentech—the capitalization of an idea—this was different. Netscape had made no profits whatsoever. Many dated the arrival of a new economy to Netscape's IPO.

From Benjamin Franklin to Donald Trump, the self-congratulatory business autobiography is a tested American literary genre. Clark's *Netscape Time* (1999) outdid even Trump's *The Art of the Deal* in self-regard. "I had some specific victories at crucial points along the way, and I savored them," Clark reflected on Netscape's IPO. Also, "I had the pleasure of knowing that whatever else others had done, none of this could have happened without me. This feeling, of having been absolutely essential to something extraordinary, is the kind of pleasure that doesn't come often in life," although it had for Clark. What about Andreessen, the guy who wrote the code? "Of course, Netscape couldn't have happened without Marc, either, but if I hadn't recognized the special quality of that subdued, sleepy kid at our first meeting . . ."[31]

Though Clark's self-regard was ridiculous, it captured the emphasis on talent in new economy valuation, which seemingly justified his putatively merit-based enrichment. Average labor incomes did increase over the 1990s, for virtually all groups. But the new economy valued the big ideas of Stanford graduate students and Clark-style promoters. The extreme valuation of some happened in tandem with the extreme devaluation of others—if not their outright exclusion, or even incarceration. In 1994 the California state assembly voted on punitive "three strikes and you're out" laws, and soon the Corrections Corporation of America, the country's largest for-profit incarceration company, would raise $400 million in capital through a Wall Street IPO. Even in booming California, the prison population surged over the decade.[32]

In 1995 Stanford graduate students Jerry Chih-Yang and David Filo created Yahoo!, first as a list of hyperlinks to their favorite websites. They raised venture capital from Sequoia. For its April 1996 IPO, underwritten by Goldman Sachs, the company dutifully warned prospective investors that Yahoo! would "incur significant losses on a quarterly and annual basis for the foreseeable future."[33] Yahoo!'s opening market capitalization was $848 million. That was a good opening day "pop," as it became known. One stock analyst noted, "The market is somehow justifying these ridiculous capitalizations."[34] But Yahoo!'s stock price never stopped popping during the decade. By 1999, the company's market capitalization would approach $120 billion. Capital, having become more liquid and convertible in this new economy, rapidly rushed into the equity ownership of dot-com companies. To be clear, such extremes had never been seen before in the history of capitalism.

Next up, two National Science Foundation–funded Stanford graduate students, Larry Page and Sergey Brin, developed a search engine, Back-Rub, that first went online in 1997 on Stanford University's website. It used algorithms to "crawl" and rank websites based on their density of citations. Ingeniously, the search engine "scaled," meaning it became even better whenever more information was added to the Internet. The domain name Google.com was registered in September 1997. At the time, Ethernet connections were then replacing dial-up connections. In 1999 venture capital arrived for Google both from Sequoia and from Kleiner Perkins. In exchange for the license rights to the search algorithm, Google granted Stanford 1.8 million shares. Google possessed the best Internet search algorithms—another highly capitalized idea that was not embodied in any physical capital equipment. Google was soon worth billions.[35]

Profitable or not, Google had created something of value—an utterly new human relationship to information. Further, "when a really difficult thing is being worked on and you get synergy from the small team in just the right way, you can't describe it. It's like love. It is love," reflected Alan Kay, a computer scientist at Xerox PARC and later Apple.[36] Human creativity and cooperation are valuable in their own right, regardless of business profits or stock market valuations. Stock market valuations were responding to something that was ineffable but undeniably real and significant.

Google would crack the code on how to make actual business profits from the Internet. The company began to sell advertisements—"banners," introduced in 2000, rather than the previous, annoying "pop-up" windows. It would mine and extract the "data exhaust" left behind on its search engines, for aggregation, manipulation, and then sale to marketers. But that business model was just consumerism, hardly anything revolutionary. (The dreamlike quality of Silicon Valley–style valuations evokes the fantasy life of consumerism.) Google's IPO waited until 2004. People, especially investors, just sensed the Internet was big—it had to be worth something in pecuniary terms. Capital followed the hunch. Asset values first. Profits later?

It is still too soon to take the full measure of just how new these aspects of the new economy truly were. Given its 1990s acceleration by the capitalist credit cycle, aspects of it surely resonate with past speculative investment booms, like the stock market craze of the 1920s. Back then, at the dawning auto-industrial society, financial activity sponsored new long-term fixed investments, just as the 1990s saw new long-term investments at the dawning of an Internet-based economy. (By contrast, the 1980s had been a moment of speculative disinvestment, with little creation.) At the same time, something truly new was arguably at work during the 1990s. The hypervaluations of many new economy firms that made no business profits whatsoever opened up the possibility that financial asset appreciation might delink altogether from business profit making, demanding the establishment of new (nonprofit?) criteria for what should be valued in economic life. Would that be "postcapitalism"? If not, at a minimum, perhaps financial appreciation could be appropriated toward other ends—

"social investment," as it now goes—rather than merely enriching the owners of capital. Something like that had happened after the 1920s speculative investment boom, when the New Deal and the labor unions successfully redistributed industrial incomes away from capital.

Meanwhile what was the early Internet actually used for? E-commerce companies were a spring 1997 IPO fad, including the Seattle-based Internet retailer Amazon.com, which was founded in 1994. None were anywhere near profitable by decade's end. In the late 1990s, however, the co-owner of the website Image.net once visited the company's physical server site and noticed the biggest box of servers of all. "It was going nuts. The lights were flashing. It sounded like it was alive—sort of buzzing, like it was steaming." What was it? It was the server for the "porn industry," he was told.[37] Amazon.com, already by far the leading online merchandiser, saw its net sales climb to an annual $1.6 billion by the end of century; at that time there were half a million sex-dedicated websites, and online pornography was estimated to be a $2 billion industry.[38]

When Google went online in 1998, according to Michael Wolff, the journalist, failed Internet entrepreneur, and author of *Net Guide: Your Complete Guide to the Internet and Online Services* (1995), "the biggest search word was just 'sex.'"[39] This was the decade that saw the AOL sex chat room, the online sex tape, the sexual encounter aptly called "the hookup," the birth of "cybersex," *Sex and the City* (1998–2004), the artist Matthew Barney's *The Cremaster Cycle* (1994–2002), Stanley Kubrick's *Eyes Wide Shut* (1999), and the medical diagnoses of "sex addiction" and "hyperactive desire disorder." Moments of energetic stock market speculation and sexual liberation commonly appear together—another resonance between the 1990s and the 1920s, when the new medium was film. Coincidentally, on the same day in November 1995 that Bill Clinton and Monica Lewinsky began their White House affair, the Dow Jones Industrial Average tied the record of fifty-nine new highs reached in one year, reached only twice before in 1925 and 1964. In February 1996, in the midst of the birth of Internet pornography and cybersex chat rooms, the Silicon Valley–based online stock trading company E*Trade went online. The Internet quickly became a forum for sex and stock market speculation.

Regardless of what first drew people to use and invest in the Internet, it was astonishing how much capital so quickly routed into Nasdaq listings. Between 1995 and 2000, the Nasdaq climbed 400 percent, achieving the astounding "stock price to earnings ratio," or stock market valuation relative to actual business profits, of 175—the historical ratio was typically between 10 and 20. By 2000 the market capitalization of publicly traded corporations in Silicon Valley was nearly $750 billion, while the market capitalization of the entire American auto industry was $136 billion. Capital had never before moved so quickly into a new asset class. By 2000 the state of California had the ninth-largest GDP of any national economy in the world.

2. The Network

The Internet was not only a story of human invention and new frontiers of entrepreneurship and capital valuation. It also changed the conduct of enterprise. At the end of the millennium, Jack Welch, CEO of old economy General Electric and an apostle of shareholder value, gushed over "this elixir, this tonic, this e-business." A new principle of social organization moved to the center of economic life—the network. Welch predicted that GE would become a "boundaryless" entity, nothing more than a "business laboratory" with "ideas everywhere."[40]

In particular, the corporation transformed. During the 1980s, capital markets had assaulted the large multidivisional form, or M-form, industrial corporation, dethroning if not co-opting the managerial class. Fixed capital stock was purged, and factory walls came down. During the 1990s, what began to emerge was a new organizational logic, defined not so much by industrial structure, bureaucracy, hierarchy, or even one-off market exchange, but rather by networks. A network is a group or system, defined by repeated interactions and a force-multiplying connectivity.[41] Networks, compared to one-shot market exchanges or bureaucratic hierarchies, were not new to U.S. business.[42] But during the 1990s the Internet and globalization made them more prominent.

In 2000 the most valuable corporation by market capitalization in the world was Silicon Valley–based Cisco Systems—at a stunning $569 billion in March 2000, after being but $15.9 billion in 1995. Cisco, founded in 1984 by a married Stanford couple, well represented the new economy business model. The corporation was the largest manufacturer of modems and routers, the physical plumbing that organized and directed Internet traffic. The Cisco Aironet 1200 router—the Model T of routers—was introduced in 1997. Such IT infrastructure was a large component of the late-1990s increase in private fixed capital investment, and Cisco was responsible for a significant portion.

Cisco was also representative because of the nature of its business model, not simply because of what it produced.[43] The network was its model: it was a "platform company." During the 1980s, many corporations used computers to create electronic data interchange (EDI) systems to coordinate information in real time between suppliers and customers. Cisco took this practice online. Its website, Connection Online, was a platform that matched suppliers to customers; Cisco was merely the node. In 2000, Cisco received $40 million a day in online orders. Sixty percent of them were automated by the website. Cisco then subcontracted the vast majority of production to an ever-shifting, low-wage "global supply chain." The company formally employed 34,000 people (sitting on an average of $250,000 in stock options, smartly appreciating), mostly in design and logistics. Subcontractors manufactured products and shipped them directly to customers, with the brand "Cisco" stamped on the resulting bricolage. For this reason, through the globalization of supply chains, world trade in manufactures shifted during the 1990s—from between economies, like Japan and the United States, at relative parity, to the export of manufactures from the low-wage regions of the world to high-wage regions.

While hierarchies plan in advance, networks adapt in real time. Corporate supply chains began to straddle the globe, as time shrank in logistics. Due to these methods, the prices of goods such as personal computers appear to have fallen precipitously.[44] Corporations used new information technology, for instance, to gather information about consumer preferences. White-collar bureaucrats once sat in offices and planned long-term mass production schedules; now multinational corporations gathered and analyzed enormous amounts of "Big Data," which then triggered short-term product cycles. One new-economy Spanish clothing firm exhibited wonderful "scalability." Zara was the first retailer to give to all its sellers handheld optical scanners that instantaneously transmitted consumer purchases to its designers in the Arteixo industrial district of northwestern Spain. Zara's chief global competitor, the Gap, computerized its inventory system and shortened its design-production-distribution cycle to two months. Zara achieved two weeks. If teenage girls in America were "trending" yellow, a supplier in some low-wage region of the world would dash off more yellow blouses.[45]

The M-form corporation was a global entity.[46] National trade statistics began to conceal the vast global trade in intermediate inputs. Corporations became dependent on rapidly mutating global archipelagos of ever-shifting supply chains. For instance, the Taiwanese electronics manufacturer Hon Hai Precision Industry, known as Foxconn, began operations in 1974. Foxconn's big break was a 1980 order to manufacture joysticks for the Atari 2600 video game system. It opened its first factory in mainland China in 1988. The corporation could rapidly scale labor and production up and down upon request.[47] In the twenty-first century, Foxconn would manufacture the Apple iPhone. Global and regional economic scales, above and below the national level, interacted. Sometimes the assembly end of the global supply chain did land in the United States. To be closer to final consumers, for instance, Japanese or European car manufacturers set up assembly facilities in the low-wage, more lightly unionized American South.

Networked multinational corporations did not completely float free in the air. They still retained strong roots in particular places, but usually cultural roots. Apple's corporate culture was and is Silicon Valley through and through, but good luck mapping its Asian-focused global supply chain, let alone the complex tax avoidance network of its corporate subsidiaries in Switzerland, Ireland, and the Cayman Islands. During the 1990s, the mass retailer Wal-Mart emerged as another corporate exemplar. Headquartered in Bentonville, Arkansas, it never relinquished its locally forged Christian service ethos.[48] Wal-Mart had another kind of new economy cost structure. "Asset light" in fixed capital, forcing its suppliers to warehouse and carry its goods, its profitability hinged on cheap service labor and on hard-driving what little fixed capital was on its own books.[49] But Wal-Mart was also one of the great global IT companies, featuring a sophisticated computerized warehousing system and the just-in-time delivery to its many stores in rapid response to shifts in consumer preferences. Wal-Mart, which became the largest U.S. employer in 2002, replacing General Motors, was a retailer.[50] In one estimate, a third of the increase in productivity in the second half of the 1990s came from the retail sector, with Wal-Mart, and its low prices—benefiting low-wage consumers—taking the lead.[51] If there was one thing not new about the new economy, it was consumerism.

Individuals employed by networked firms had a parallel need for flexibility and suppleness. Temp work and self-employment became employment growth industries.[52] In 1999 in California, only 33 percent of all workers had a single, full-time, year-round, permanent job at a company that paid them for the work they did on its premises, and not working from home or as self-employed "independent contractors." Add the condition of three or more years of tenure at work, and the number dropped to 22 percent. Those employees still formally employed by corporations had to become "self-programmable."[53] They must always adapt and scale their talents and abilities to each particular one-shot "project." In 1993 GE's home appliance division removed assembly lines from the factory floor, replacing them with smaller and nimbler project-based "work teams." James Meadows, vice president for human resources at AT&T, advised in 1996:

> People need to look at themselves as self-employed, as vendors who come to this company to sell their skills. In AT&T we have to promote the whole concept of the work force being contingent [i.e., on short-term contract, no promises], though most of the contingent workers are inside our walls. "Jobs" are being replaced by "projects" and "fields of work," giving rise to a society that is increasingly "jobless but not workless."[54]

Google would declare of its talent-focused and human-capital-based corporate culture, "We favor ability over experience."[55]

Projects are ad hoc, with intense bouts of work broken up by periodic bouts of idleness. If idleness becomes sustained, layoffs loom. The fortunate get rehired on a short-term contract basis. This happened in the 1990s at IBM, which had mistakenly staked its future on selling and servicing mainframes. IBM reoriented to "business IT" and downsized its workforce from 405,000 to 225,000 employees. Then it turned around and rehired one-fifth of those it had let go as "consultants," with no permanent status, and with fewer or no benefits. Kodak Corporation, like IBM, was another paragon of postwar industrial capitalism that was rocked by white-collar downsizing during the 1990s. "We've got to recognize that the Great Yellow Father can't take care of all of us any longer. We've got to grow up and take care of ourselves," declared the Rochester *Democrat & Chronicle.* Jim Sharlow, a Rochester native, began work at

Kodak when he was twenty-three, a machinist eventually promoted to a manager. He got laid off. His daughter Karen got the message:

> We've been taught our whole lives that if you give your loyalty to someone or something, it gives you something back. In our house, we didn't even use anything that wasn't Kodak, Kodak film, Kodak cameras. No one will take care of you. We know.

No longer employable, Jim Sharlow joined the ranks of those day-trading stocks online from their homes.[56]

In this era, when capital did settle and fix on the ground, its architecture embodied the new themes. In the 1990s the high modernist, reinforced concrete factories of the Machine Age were replaced by more malleable, portable, and cheaper factory "sheds." In office design, long corridors and boxy executive office suites yielded to cubicles and shared desks.[57] Breakout spaces replaced conference rooms. When sales flagged at Apple in 1985 and Steve Jobs was pushed out, he made a large investment in Pixar Animation Studios. In 1999 Jobs helped design its headquarters, which featured a large, open-air central atrium where workers might informally bump into one another and spontaneously innovate. Apple's Cupertino headquarters, opened in 2016 after Jobs's death, had been designed by Jobs with Foster + Partners, the global architectural firm that introduced a new style of office design. Stairways and building services were pushed to the exterior so that work spaces could remain open and fluid. The walls that still existed were increasingly made of glass. Did such architecture represent the designed democratization of the workplace and evidence of flattening corporate hierarchies? Or did it mean that the only place left to hide from the boss's glare was the bathroom? The iron cage of industrialism gave way to the open-air cubicle.[58]

For working people, to build a career and a life from the inside of an institution that was now designed to have no inside was no longer a recipe for success. Business self-help books in the 1990s began to advise individuals to think of themselves as consultants, "employable" rather than "employed"—as human capital that was capable of appreciating in the future, rather than as labor employed to help a business realize a past investment. John Kotter, a Harvard Business School professor, advised individuals to exist "on the outside rather than on the inside of organizations." "Move toward the small and entrepreneurial and away from the big and bureaucratic!" Do not get "entangled."[59] One's social network was one's unemployment insurance. Literally, the advice to people was to go to more "parties."[60]

Corporations, for all their new interconnectivity and adaptability, lost their structure, their accumulated solid mass—in many instances even their reinforced concrete walls. Enterprise became so liquid that it became more difficult for individuals to recognize corporations as collective agents responsible for their fates. Instead, individuals internalized both their successes and failures. This new economic personality has been called the "entrepreneurial self" or the "human capital self," living in a constant and unending search for publicity and appreciation—the kind of person who in the twenty-first century would be obsessed with their social media "likes," or even become a well-compensated "influencer."[61] This individual is future-oriented to the extreme, often discounting the past. For when improvisation is constantly called for, one's past attachments—loyalties to people, places, and companies—can render one inflexible.

To what degree do people want economic life to provide them with long-term attachments and loyalties, as opposed to constant change, disruption, energy, and fun?

The director David Fincher's *The Social Network* (2010), a fictional account of the real-life 1990s origins of Facebook, remains perhaps the best treatment of the question in popular culture. Focused on the future, the fictional Mark Zuckerberg runs roughshod over friends, foes, and women alike, with no interest in looking backward unless a multibillion-dollar intellectual property lawsuit is at stake. If Fincher had made a film about postwar industrial society, it would have been called *The Social Structure* and might have featured the adult malady of depressive dread at marching off to work every day to perform the same task. "How are you gonna get excited pullin' steel," lamented steelworker Mike Lefevre in Studs Terkel's *Working* (1974).[62] In the new economy workplace, more youthful, energetic, and fun, if there was a new problem, it was How you gonna stop checking your email?

Silicon Valley firms of the 1990s, famous for being nonhierarchical and juvenile, quickly also became infamous for being male and sexist. "I'm CEO—Bitch," read Zuckerberg's early business card.[63] Nationally, during the 1990s, the female workforce-participation rate, that is, the percentage of adult women in the remunerated workforce, long on the ascent, leveled off at 60 percent. By contrast, during the same decade, the male workforce participation rate kept declining, falling below 75 percent. The rapid closing of the gender gap in earnings that had begun during the 1980s now slowed as well. Most significant was the entry of highly educated, high "human capital," married women with children into the labor force. It helped increase incomes at the top of the household distribution. Less educated and less skilled men and women began to marry less, widening household income inequality from the bottom of the income distribution.

As highly educated women of the "global north" increasingly entered the workforce, women from the "global south" arrived to become housekeepers, nannies, or babysitters in their households or to care for their elderly family members. In 1999 between 14 and 18 percent of American households employed a home cleaning service. The wall separating home and work corroded, with "emotional labor" newly becoming paid labor. In 2000 the U.S. multinational corporation Kelly Services, a temp agency, employed 750,000 individuals, just edging out Wal-Mart as the nation's largest employer.[64] Kelly Services could dispatch a highly trained technician to an office, or a nanny or maid, who often was an immigrant, to a home. Quite strict immigration restrictions remained. But what did globalized labor markets often look like? Picture a Filipino nanny raising the child of a highly educated female Silicon Valley executive. That executive earns less money to perform the same task as her male peers at a start-up funded by a Saudi Arabian sovereign wealth fund. She also employs a Mexican gardener, who wires money back home on a computer assembled in a Mexican maquiladora, from parts manufactured in a Taiwanese free trade zone.

The kind of workers whom Kelly Services provided were referred to, in new economy management-speak, as "peripheral." The practice of subcontracting extended beyond manufacturing. Back-office work, whether clerical duties or customer service, was outsourced to nondescript exurban office parks. Certainly the "core competency" of Cisco Systems was not to clean its own toilets. It subcontracted out janitorial services. "Self-employed" janitors did not receive stock options. The new economy neither dignified nor remunerated manual labor.

California was again at the cutting edge, this time in low-wage labor organizing. The Service Employees International Union (SEIU) responded to the new realities of the new economy, recognizing that "self-employment" was often a legal excuse to undermine collective bargaining rights.[65] The SEIU sought to organize entire labor markets and engaged in confrontational, symbolic actions, like blocking traffic or crashing shareholders meetings. The Justice for Janitors movement swept California in the early 1990s, after L.A. police assaulted a peaceful protest of immigrant janitors seeking to organize in Century City in 1990. They later won certification of their union and doubled their pay. In 1991, after protesting a shareholders meeting, SEIU Local 1877 convinced Apple to force its janitorial service subcontractor, Shine Building Maintenance, to collectively bargain. In 1996, in the midst of the dot-com boom, Justice for Janitors held a large rally in Silicon Valley. During the decade, it won a number of contracts for its members from valley firms, including a contract with the company subcontracted to clean Hewlett-Packard. Before that moment, unionization had never been part of the "HP way."[66]

3. Rubinomics

It is difficult to imagine a fuller embrace of the new economy than the one made by the Democratic administration of President Bill Clinton. The Reagan administration had come into office with a pro-market, antistate ideology that was, beyond a few guiding principles—regulation bad, tax cuts good—inchoate if not incoherent. Despite his "New Democrat" rhetoric, Clinton had arrived with a rather standard liberal agenda, including labor law reform and the expansion of health care entitlements, a project tasked to his wife, Hillary Rodham Clinton. Both measures failed politically. In 1994 Republicans won the Congress, and Clinton tacked right.[67] In economic policy making, a group of advisers led by the director of the National Economic Council (NEC), Robert Rubin, a former CEO of Goldman Sachs, became the dominant force within the administration.

It was at this moment that a coherent Age of Chaos political-economic settlement—as ideology, call it Rubinomics, or "neoliberalism" if one must—fully rounded into shape. Clinton Democrats went all in on Rubin's version of a private-capital-markets-led globalization that was enabled, at crucial junctures, by administrative state power.

Proximately, "Rubinomics" emerged from a critique of federal budget defecits.[68] Clinton had inherited high budget deficits from Reagan. As the government would have to borrow money in the future to meet its obligations, Rubin believed the national deficit pushed up benchmark long-term interest rates on public debt. For the long-term rate had remained stubbornly high even when, to stoke the "jobless" post 1990–91 recession recovery, the Fed brought short-term rates down to 3 percent in 1993. Even if inflation was not yet presently appearing, Rubin speculated that bond traders were pricing inflation into the long-term rate. What the federal government had to do was balance the federal budget, signaling fiscal rectitude. Rubin could not read bond traders' minds, but his reasonable analysis was that the high long-term interest rates of the 1980s had created a high hurdle rate for profit making, inducing leveraged speculation. Lower rates would free up capital for long-term fixed investment. Rubin thus recommended catering economic policy to the whims, real or perceived, of capital markets. Clinton political adviser James Carville summed it up: "I used to think if there was reincarnation, I wanted to come back as the president or the pope or a .400 baseball hitter. But now I would want to come back as the bond market."[69]

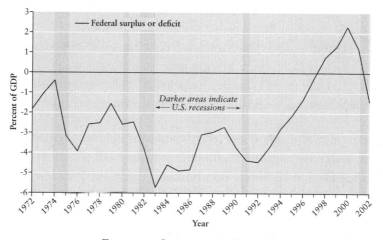

FEDERAL SURPLUS OR DEFICIT

Reversing the Reagan trend, the Clinton administration closed the federal budget deficit. The idea was that lower deficits would free up capital for private investment in the new economy.

Rubin's group convinced Clinton that he must close the budget deficit. The administration did so by increasing taxes on the wealthy and by slightly slowing the growth of federal expenditures—achieved by a reduction of military expenditures, in light of the end of the Cold War. Long-term bond prices did fall.

To be of assistance, given the jobless recovery, Greenspan's Fed lowered the rate of interest in the short-term money market for federal funds through the end of 1993. Further, after the savings and loan crisis of the

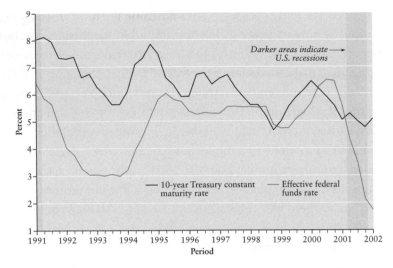

TEN-YEAR U.S. TREASURY CONSTANT MATURITY RATE
AND EFFECTIVE FEDERAL FUNDS RATE

As the Clinton administration intended, bond rates fell. As U.S. monetary
policy became increasingly more prominent in the global allocation of
capital, short-term rates came down in tandem. Policy makers believed that
capital, freed up, would naturally flow to its best possible global use.

late 1980s, new legislation had forced banks to hold more "risk-free" capital. The Fed, enforcing the regulation, included U.S. Treasury bonds in
that category, and so banks accumulated them. As long-term interest
rates declined, the value of existing bonds, paying higher rates, increased.
Flush with profits, banks parted with liquidity and made new loans, expanding credit.[70] Altogether a new upswing in the credit cycle and allied
macroeconomic expansion commenced.

By now, two administrative agencies had become the preeminent economic policy-making vehicles, with the U.S. Treasury Department joining
the post–Volcker Shock Fed. For one thing, the dollar remained the global
currency of transaction and reserve. The Fed controlled its supply, and as
global capital markets and interest rates converged across borders, the
Fed's short-term interest rate increasingly shaped the global flow of investment.[71] Despite the fact that the Fed was a quite large bureaucratic
institution, and that many members of the Federal Open Market Committee (FOMC) voted on interest rate policies, Greenspan's personal fame
reached nothing short of mythic proportions.[72]

By 1995 the Clinton administration had set the tone of its national economic agenda for good. In January, Rubin became the new Treasury secretary. The Netscape IPO launched the dot-com stock market boom. Capital began to flood into Silicon Valley IT companies. The Fed continued to lower its rate, as Greenspan became a believer in the new economy. However, 1995 was a year of great global macroeconomic significance for other reasons as well.

The Fed was lowering its short-term interest rate target in response to yet another bout of capital flight south of the U.S. border. Since the last IMF bailout of Mexico in 1982, the government of Mexico had liberalized its capital account. In 1994 it had signed the Clinton-promoted North American Free Trade Agreement (NAFTA) with the United States and Canada.[73] Following the IMF's advice on how to recruit capital, the Mexican government had slashed public expenditures and pegged the peso to the dollar to guarantee foreign investors that it would not devalue their investments. Mexico, the model citizen, was rewarded with capital inflows.

Yet, more manufacturing began to locate in even-lower-wage parts of Asia than expected, undermining the promise that NAFTA would induce U.S. multinational investment in Mexico. Meanwhile Mexican farmers were overwhelmed by lower-cost U.S. agricultural producers. Millions of Mexicans began to illegally immigrate to the United States—some becoming Silicon Valley gardeners and janitors.[74] After the Fed had raised its short-term rate in 1994 for fear of U.S. inflation, which made holding dollars more attractive, and after the assassination of Mexican presidential candidate Luis Donaldo Colosio, global capital suddenly changed its mind and decamped Mexico for the United States. The Mexican government did not have access to enough dollars to defend the dollar-peso peg in open markets. So the Mexican central bank raised its short-term interest rate to seduce capital back, which only tightened domestic credit and plunged the Mexican economy into a deep recession. American banks and institutional investors held Mexican investments. The investment bank Lehman Brothers was especially caught out. Rubin worried that a panic might bring down "economies around the world."[75] The U.S. Treasury organized a $52 billion credit line to Mexico.[76]

In 1995, in a supporting action, the U.S. Fed lowered interest rates. Access to cheap dollar funding soothed the nerves of the owners of capital. Any panic subsided. It worked. Mexico used only $13 billion in Treasury credit, and the Mexican economy, benefiting from a weaker currency in export markets, quickly recovered. Rubin and his inner circle at the Treasury, including a young Timothy Geithner, learned that they could use the overwhelming force of government authority to provide transactional liquidity to credit markets and overpower any hint of panic. All that remained was to restore confidence in global capital markets.

In 1995, in another event of global macroeconomic consequence, Rubin negotiated the Reverse Plaza Accord with Japan and Germany.[77] These governments agreed to intervene and increase the relative value of the dollar in global currency markets. American consumers could buy more of the exports of U.S. allies (which were hardly enjoying new economy booms themselves).[78] Blessed with new economy productivity advantages and globalized supply chains, U.S. producers could weather the competition, or so American policy makers figured. In his memoir, Rubin claimed little credit for the currency shift. "My experience with foreign exchange markets at Goldman Sachs led me to believe that trading flows were simply too vast for [government] interventions to have more than a momentary effect."[79] Regardless, in hindsight, the period 1985–95 was an interregnum for the global economy. Following the 1985 Plaza Accord, the dollar had declined in value until 1990. U.S. manufacturing exports increased accordingly. Capital imports reduced, now less necessary to balance the U.S.'s external account. In 1995 the dollar began to rise in value. U.S. trade deficits reap-

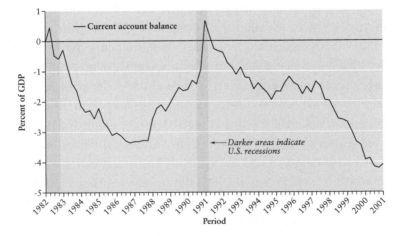

U.S. CURRENT ACCOUNT BALANCE
1995 was a hinge year for the U.S.-anchored global economy. The U.S. capital and consumer markets again became magnets for the world—represented here by the return of a U.S. current account deficit, or the balance of U.S. transactions with the world, excluding financial items.

peared. So did capital imports from abroad, which helped finance American consumers' purchases of the world's goods. The post–Volcker Shock configuration of U.S. global economic hegemony was back.

After Clinton's 1996 reelection, Congress descended into the politics of the Clinton-Lewinsky sex scandal. But in economic policy making, the Clinton administration's program won more victories. The new political-economic settlement was that government must facilitate the mobility of capital, which, by assumption, would automatically flow to its best possible use, benefiting consumer welfare, so long as there was market competition. If the speculative upturn in the credit cycle rained capital down on Silicon Valley dot-com companies, they must, by assumption, have earned it. The Fed had the most important task, to manage the short-term interest rate in credit markets, lowering them in support of the new economy, while raising them, if need be, to guard against inflationary pressures. In a pinch, it could lower rates or intervene in open markets to guarantee transactional liquidity in capital markets. In the meantime, the federal government could continue to deregulate.

At least the Democrats tried to "feel" the pain of the worst-off, as Clinton put it, unlike Republicans who, in Democrats' view, were simply callous. For Clinton, greater empathy granted him license to agree with Republican-inspired policy and legislation. The "era of big government is over," he declared twice in his 1996 State of the Union address, the year he would sign into law the Personal Responsibility and Work Opportunity Reconciliation Act.[80] The act was everything Ronald Reagan had ever wanted. It ended a New Deal entitlement—federal-government-guaranteed support for indigent citizens. Aid to Families with Dependent Children became Temporary Assistance for Needy Families. By instituting block grants, it devolved much responsibility to states for determining eligibility criteria and benefits. It also let states contract welfare to for-profit corporations or to religious nonprofits (called "charitable choice"). It capped benefits at five years, lifetime. But the bill had no jobs program. The new economy would provide enough jobs. Social scientists debate to what degree the poverty rate fell during the 1990s, or not. Regardless, the poor became more so the working poor.[81]

On behalf of deregulation and market competition, the Telecommunications Act of 1996 overturned New Deal–era regulations that had worked by maintaining silos within the industry to prevent monopolistic cross-ownership and conglomeration. Now telephone, cable, satellite, cellular, and Internet service providers could all compete with one another.[82] Published in 1996, an influential study by two economists concluded that rates of productivity growth increased "after deregulation," primarily as a "result of a reallocation of capital toward more productive establishments."[83] Regulatory walls had to go. Clinton asked philanthropists to donate money for Internet-wired computers in schools to eliminate the "digital divide." The Telecommunications Act proclaimed, "The Internet and other interactive computer services have flourished, to the benefit of all Americans, with a minimum of government regulation." The old Progressive regulatory concept of a "public utility" was basically dead. In antitrust law, the new gospel among jurists, heavily influenced by the Law and Economics movement, was that the only relevant standard for antitrust law was consumer welfare, meaning short-term consumer prices—not market structure or barriers to entry in enterprise.[84] The blithe assumption was that the market would maintain competition by itself, if left alone, without much state oversight or legal coercion. Monopolistic tendencies would not naturally arise. In this spirit, the Telecommunications Act promised that deregulation would promote "vigorous economic competition," which always stood to benefit consumers. That alone was equivalent to the "public interest."[85] The Clinton administration noted the high level of telecommunications investment after 1996 and patted itself on the back.

The next great regulatory wall to fall was highly symbolic. For decades, capital had been thundering over the barrier between commercial and investment banking, set by the Glass-Steagall Act of 1933. Through a series of administrative decisions, the Fed and Treasury had weakened the wall. Congress's 1999 Gramm-Leach-Bliley Act overturned Glass-Steagall altogether. What had instigated the repeal was the ongoing conglomeration of Citigroup during the 1990s, with various commercial and investment bank subsidiaries. Citigroup began to pivot in and out of various financial asset classes, in an era when finance was fast becoming one big global capital market.[86]

In this spirit, in 1997, the IMF economist and deputy managing director Stanley Fischer, speaking in Hong Kong, defended a proposed amendment to IMF's charter that would for the first time enshrine "the liberalization of international capital movements" as a "central purpose of the Fund."[87] Fischer, however, spoke in the midst of an Asian financial crisis, which would prove to be of great global significance. A cause of the global crisis was nothing other than the liberalization of international capital movements.

4. Globalization

Globalization, however the word is defined, was not new. But during the 1990s a new global, cosmopolitan consciousness was born. During the twentieth century, by choice or by necessity, industrial capitalists had tied their fates to nation-states.[88] Now many owners of wealth were not so sure. New York, London, and Tokyo, all centers of finance, became recognized as "global cities," where trends in food, fashion, and design began to move in unison.[89] There new forms of private "global governance" emerged, in lieu of state regulation, whether arbitration agreements among multinational corporations, or entities such as the International Swaps and Derivatives Association (ISDA), with its offices in New York, London, and Tokyo, among other cities, and through which banks created uniform contract language for very lightly state-regulated global financial derivatives markets.[90] To some extent, sharing much in common with one another, global cities appeared to detach from their national locations.

Economically, end-of-the-millennium globalization consisted of greater world trade in goods, combined with closer financial linkages. Compared to previous chapters of globalization, like during the late nineteenth and early twentieth centuries, the immigration of labor was not as prominent. Trade and finance closely correlate, as international trade requires international financing, at a minimum an international payments system for goods, which at this time remained overwhelmingly dollar-based. The spread of global commerce and global supply chains during the 1990s, inducing greater specialization in production and increasing the extent of the market, unquestionably led to the multiplication of commerce, wealth, and economic growth—just as, long ago, Adam Smith had described. Due to increasing returns to economic activity, global poverty was reduced, even if income gains were not evenly spread.[91] A surge in cross-border long-term "foreign direct investment" in productive activity also aided growth. Finally, as many manufacturing-led export economies throughout the world, especially in Asia, gained greater access to foreign markets—including to the great, booming U.S. consumer market—an investment multiplier went to work, absorbing into production untapped resources, including labor—just as, not too long ago, Keynes had described.

However, during the 1990s, the growth of "financial openness" vastly outpaced the growth of "trade openness." That is, movements of hot money, often speculative—in the form of financial investments in foreign currencies, stocks, debts, and derivatives—expanded at a rate disproportionate to the needs of fixed investment or trade. Financial globalization simply dwarfed other kinds. In 1997 IMF managing director Fischer argued that "put abstractly, free capital movements facilitate a more efficient allocation of savings, and help channel resources into the more productive uses, thus increasing economic growth and welfare." That was the late-1990s gospel. But the actual concrete evidence since then for a link between financial openness and greater economic growth is not very good.[92] What global capital did do during the 1990s was, due to the new IT, move at a new lightning, digital speed. In these years, the German artist Andreas Gursky took photographs of the world's financial exchanges—frenetic nerve centers, though at the same time abstract and contained, as if to demonstrate the decoupling between finance and other parts of the economy.

ANDREAS GURSKY, *TOKYO, STOCK EXCHANGE* (1990)
Gursky's great series of photographs of financial exchanges from around the world during the 1990s captures the frenetic energy of end-of-the-millennium financial globalization—just before much trading moved out of the physical pits and online. Tokyo is seen here; the unraveling of speculative dollar trades financed by yen borrowing was an instigator of the 1997–98 Asian financial crisis, which redounded upon the U.S. capital market.

Pulsating global financial movements are quite difficult to narrate historically, which says something about the degree to which they are difficult to put under political control. At the same time, global finance capital, unlike what Fischer predicted, can undermine the more slow-moving global economy of physical production and trade. In the late 1990s, as capital markets globalized, the most important global link to emerge was between the U.S. dollar and the Japanese yen. From this linkage, a series of contingent events unfolded that threatened to bring down the entire global economy.

In 1995 the Japanese central bank lowered its short-term interest rate target to 0.5 percent. Japanese asset price appreciation in real estate and the stock market had climbed after 1985, cresting in 1989. In 1991–92 Japanese asset prices collapsed. The Japanese economy entered a liquidity trap and would experience a "lost decade" of deflation and low growth.[93] The goal of the 0.5 short-term interest rate was to encourage lending, spending, and investment, and thereby to restart growth.

Given the low rate, global borrowing in yen surged. Japanese firms borrowed low and invested in the expansion of low-wage, export-oriented manufacturing throughout Asia. In auto production, for instance, Thailand became "the Detroit of Asia." Many U.S. multinational corporations were offshoring production to Asia as well, including Apple, Wal-Mart, and Cisco. In credit markets, the yen "carrying trade" developed. Banks and various investment funds borrowed yen at the low rate. They then placed short-term hot money in U.S. markets, where short-term rates hovered around 5 percent—or, seeking a greater, though riskier profit differential, into Southeast Asian capital markets, growing on the basis of manufacturing exports. By 1997, the yen carrying trade was estimated at $200 to $350 billion.[94]

In May 1997 events suddenly shifted. Global currency speculators attacked the Thai baht's peg to the U.S. dollar. The Thai currency had been pegged to the dollar to increase the confidence of foreigners that their investments would not be devalued, but the dollar's post-1995 appreciation after the Reverse Plaza Accord had weakened the competitiveness of Thai exports. A May 1997 Goldman Sachs research note speculated that Thailand might soon devalue in order to spur greater export competitiveness. That sparked rumors. Foreign investors sold Thai bahts. Lacking enough dollars to defend its currency peg in open markets, in July 1997 Thailand broke the peg and floated the baht in open currency markets.

The Thai stock market plunged in value, and so did Thai output and employment.[95]

"No one anticipated how quickly contagion could spread," remarked one Hong Kong regulator. By October the Filipino, Malaysian, Indonesian, and Hong Kong currencies were under attack. In December, South Korea began negotiations with the IMF and the Fed's International Finance Division. The IMF coordinated a $57 billion line of credit to South Korea alone and other lifelines to other East Asian economies. In return, it mandated that these economies must remain open to global capital flows and imposed state budget austerity ("structural adjustments") to assist in the re-recruitment of foreign investment. Countries where U.S. troops were stationed, such as South Korea, often received better terms.[96]

Still, panic spread rapidly across the interconnected global capital market. Brazil tottered. In August 1998, despite a Rubin-coordinated IMF bailout of $22.6 billion a month before, Russia defaulted on its state debt. In its post-Communist "market transition," Russia had experienced in living conditions something far worse than a lost decade.[97] The IMF bailouts only lined the pockets of a rising Russian class of oligarchs, which had fleeced state assets. Meanwhile Russian default frightened global capital markets further. "The most basic thing," the Japanese minister of finance announced, "is not to panic."[98]

As asset prices everywhere shed value, a large U.S. investment fund, Long-Term Capital Management (LTCM), tottered on bankruptcy. LTCM, founded in 1994, was a hedge fund—or a lightly regulated banking partnership that charged rich investors fees to invest their money. LTCM never had more than one hundred investors, but they included institutions such as Hong Kong and Singapore sovereign wealth funds, a Japanese bank, the University of Pittsburgh, and the Italian central bank.[99] A founding partner of LTCM was John Meriwether, a former bond trader who specialized in arbitrage, or trades on price differentials between different assets. Two more LTCM founders were the economists Robert Merton and Myron Scholes, both of whom were awarded the Nobel Prize in economics in 1997 for creating a mathematical formula for pricing "options," a kind of financial derivative.[100] The formula assumed the magic of the market. It assumed transactional liquidity, that there would always be a buyer present for any of its assets, or at least a creditor willing to fund its debts. Yet another assumption was that prices followed "normal" statistical distributions, like life insurance actuarial tables.

LTCM traders sat at Sun Microsystems (a Silicon Valley firm) workstations linked to new global digital trading platforms, which synchronized in real time one big global capital market.[101] They plugged historical price data into their models and at first made enormous returns, upward of 40 percent, accumulating more than $100 billion in assets, greater than the investment banks Lehman Brothers and Morgan Stanley. Usually, LTCM bet that prices between assets would converge to their historic norms. Traders then hedged the risk of that trade by making counterbets, by writing derivatives contracts with investment banks, using the same models. Confident in their models, LTCM made greater profits by using debt to leverage up their trades. By using less of their own money to trade, that is, profits on their own money increased. Greenspan complimented hedge fund trading simply because it brought more trading to capital markets. That meant more efficiency, as it brought reality closer to economic theory, which assumed transactional liquidity.[102]

LTCM had two problems. First, the global capital market was increasingly interconnected, precisely because there was more trading. But historical data came from a moment when markets were more separate. After the Russian default, prices that available historical data said should never correlate began to move together. When they did, LTCM's sophisticated models became worthless. They did not consider the degree to which the future might not resemble the past. As one Wall Street trader critical of LTCM put it, "You take Monica Lewinsky, who walks into Clinton's office with a pizza. You have no idea where that's going to go. Yet if you apply math to it, you come up with a thirty-eight percent chance she's going to go down on him. It looks great, but it's all a guess."[103] Second, because the models assumed transactional liquidity, they assumed, mathematically speaking, "continuous time"—ever-present buyers to price all assets. But price declines in 1998 were discontinuous and jumpy, and for many assets there were no buyers. LTCM was in a lot of debt and needed to sell its assets for cash to meet its creditors' demands. If it could not sell its assets, because there were no buyers, illiquidity in the markets meant insolvency for the hedge fund. Realizing that, banks stopped lending to LTCM. For it, the magic of the market had gone up in smoke.

On September 23, 1998, at the New York Fed, chiefs of the largest Wall Street banks—Bear Stearns, Chase Manhattan, Goldman Sachs, JP Morgan, Lehman Brothers, Merrill Lynch, and Morgan Stanley among them—met to consider LTCM's fate. Markets might "cease to function" in the event of an LTCM default, warned the New York Fed president William J. McDonough. LTCM's derivative hedges had interconnected it with seemingly every financial institution. The banks organized a private $3.6 billion bailout. Bear Stearns balked at contributing. Dick Fuld, chairman of Lehman, batting away rumors that LTCM's demise threatened Lehman's solvency, kicked in less than others. Many of the same principals would be back in the room a decade later, after they applied many of the essentials of LTCM's trading strategy to the U.S. residential mortgage market—ending in a similar result. They would remember Fuld's lack of generosity.[104]

The New York Fed announced LTCM's private bailout. Less than a week before, Greenspan gathered the Federal Open Market Committee, charged with setting interest rate policy, on a conference call. U.S. stock prices were volatile. Nervous, global capital was seeking safe haven in U.S. Treasury bonds, the closet asset in capital markets to cash. Liquidity preference threatened to veer from speculative to precautionary, which would sap investment. On September 29, 1998, the FOMC cut its short-term interest rate target from 5.5 to 5.25 percent. On October 15 there was another cut, down to 5 percent. A November 17 cut brought it down to 4.75 percent. A Lehman Brothers economist said, "Without actually saying it, Greenspan is saying: 'We're going to supply liquidity to the system, and we're going to keep the U.S. economy out of recession in 1999.' "[105] It seemed to work. Asian economies moderated. Bank bailouts, IMF structural adjustments, and cheap funding from the Fed appeared to be enough to keep the global economy on track. The U.S. Treasury Department had worked in conjunction with the Fed and the IMF during the crisis. The February 1999 cover of *Time* magazine announced that Greenspan, Rubin, and Summers (soon the new Treasury secretary) were "The Committee to Save the World."

The three had certainly prevented a worse calamity. Nonetheless, the IMF's proposed charter amendment to enshrine open capital mobility failed to pass—1997 represents a high tide of the push for this kind of globalization.[106] And there were lessons to be drawn. It is worth revisiting the original link in the chain: the Japanese yen. Somehow a contingent break in a speculative multibillion-dollar currency carrying trade in the yen had, after triggering a financial panic from Thailand, to Brazil, to Russia, threatened to cut a hole in the entire global economy. Furthermore, that was even possible because the Japanese central bank had lowered its interest rate so much, to try to induce spending in its domestic economy. That was what had freed up the cheap yen-based global credit. But Japan lowered rates because its national economy was in the midst of a devastating debt-deflation, which had followed a drastic financial crash in its stock and real estate markets. Greenspan, Rubin, and Summers might have saved the global economy in 1998, but despite all the supply of mobile capital the world had to offer, Japan remained stuck in a liquidity trap.[107] Low rates could not budge precautionary liquidity preference at home, even as those same low rates aided a global speculative liquidity preference abroad— neither led to the spending, especially in long-term investment, necessary for Japan to emerge from its low-interest-rate liquidity trap. The Japanese economy was simply demand constrained. Japan was a premonition. It would take a decade, but much of the global economy, including the U.S. economy, would end up in the exact same place after the financial crash of 2007–8—and then again in 2020.

Regardless, for now the supply of late-1990s global capital kept pouring into U.S. capital markets, seeking both safety and profit in dollar-denominated assets. The more uncertain the global economy became, in other words, the more it relied on one certain anchor: the dollar. U.S. hegemony facilitated economic globalization; economic globalization needed U.S. hegemony. U.S. capital inflows soared. Because Rubinomics was moving the federal budget into balance, the supply of U.S. public debt was down. Rather than purchasing freshly minted U.S. Treasury bonds, foreign investors bought up U.S. stocks, corporate debt, and agency debt (like the bonds of Fannie Mae and Freddie Mac). Foreign net financial investment in U.S. assets climbed from $145.5 billion in 1998 to $444 billion in 2000. In particular, foreign purchases of American corporate stocks climbed from $42 billion in 1998 to $193.8 billion in 2000. At this stage, global capital went all in on the new economy.[108]

1999 was the year U.S. stocks absolutely soared into the stratosphere. Historically, there had never been valuations like this. Yet "history can also become tyranny," declared a book titled *Dow 36,000* (1999).[109] In 1999 *The Wall Street Journal* critiqued the "quaint idea" of business profits.[110] By now, more than a million Americans had opened online stock day-trading accounts. An industry convention met. "It's strictly a confidence game," said one trader. The founder of one day-trading brokerage said, "Liquidity. That's why the stock market is the best place in the world to invest. You can buy at 50 and sell at 49 and ⅞. Where else can you do that? Is your car liquid? No. If you had to sell it, it could take three hours or three months to get fair value."[111]

In August 1999, while noting the possibility of "ruptured confidence," Greenspan declared it was best for regulators to do little. After all, stock prices were nothing more than the "judgments of millions of investors, many of whom are highly knowledgeable about the prospects for the specific companies that make up our broad stock price indexes."[112] Meanwhile in 1999, U.S. GDP growth clocked 4.7 percent. Inflation was low. Unemployment dropped below 4 percent. Average real wages were increasing for the first time in decades.

But could stock prices be justified? In a string of appearances before Congress in 1998 and 1999, Greenspan proposed yes. The stock market surge, he argued, was an asset-led "virtuous cycle." For expectations of future IT-led productivity and profit bonanzas warranted high present stock market prices. The "increases in equity values," Greenspan explained, raised fresh funds for "productivity-enhancing capital investment." One passage from Greenspan's congressional testimony in 1999 must be quoted at length:

> Something special has happened to the American economy. . . . The synergies that have developed, especially among the microprocessor, the laser, fiber-optics, and satellite technologies, have dramatically raised the potential rates of return on all types of equipment that embody or utilize these newer technologies. But beyond that, innovations in information technology—so-called IT—have begun to alter the manner in which we do business and create value, often in ways that were not readily foreseeable even five years ago.[113]

There were so many good ideas! With a high dollar, global capital inflows, and a balanced federal budget, capital could bid up the stock market. The "virtuous cycle" was that U.S. corporations, tapping wealth from equity gains, could invest in further IT, the reason stock prices were so high to begin with. Add to this the broader "wealth effect" of the stock market, as rising stock prices threw off fresh wealth to their owners, thus sustaining incomes and creating fresh consumer demand. American consumers could even more afford to buy imported goods from export-dependent countries beleaguered by the global financial crisis of 1997–98. Everybody won. The new economy had put the global economy on its back.

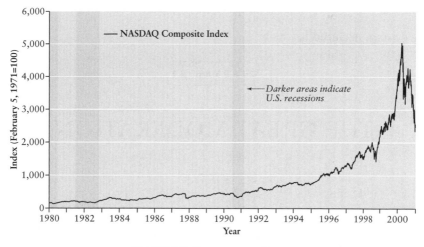

NASDAQ COMPOSITE INDEX
The new economy stock market boom concentrated on information technology and Internet companies, which were heavily represented in the Nasdaq stock exchange.

As the millennium approached, the U.S. macroeconomy enjoyed its longest sustained business expansion ever, surpassing even that of the 1980s. Every leading macroeconomic indicator was moving in the right direction. Had the Maestro drunk the Silicon Valley Kool-Aid? In the new economy, short-term speculation would become long-term profitable and productive investment. Probably, Greenspan equally calculated that some truthful hyperbole in the gravity-defying U.S. stock market was simply the necessary price to pay for global economic crisis management. And so the global economy glided along the knife-edge of confidence games into the twenty-first century.

CHAPTER 21

THE GREAT MODERATION

I N A February 2004 speech before a gathering of academic economists, Ben Bernanke, then a governor of the Federal Reserve, formerly a Princeton macroeconomist and economic historian of the Great Depression, spoke of a "Great Moderation."

Bernanke coined the phrase in light of the genuine reduction of macroeconomic volatility since Volcker had slain the inflationary dragon in 1982. He speculated that monetary policy was most likely most responsible for the era of stability. For the so-called real economy, or the market economy of the production, exchange, and consumption of things, naturally tends toward stability. Therefore, so long as monetary policy maintained a stable general price level—through interest rate policies guarding against inflation, transparent so that individuals could anchor their expectations around the Fed's predictable actions—there was no good reason why the real economy should experience much volatility. In this model, by definition the dynamics of money, credit, and finance were largely excluded from "real" economic activity.[1]

But in reality, finance and credit are not so easy to exclude. Bernanke confidently spoke of the Great Moderation only years after the last U.S. recession of 2001. The finance-led new economy stock market boom of the late 1990s had stabilized the global economy in the wake of the Asian financial crisis of 1997–98, but in 2000 the U.S. stock market had collapsed. In response to recession, in 2003 the Fed slashed rates in the short-term money market to below 2 percent before the end of 2001. Thus the Fed not only transparently guarded the stability of the general price level. In times of stress, the Fed also provided the cheap funding necessary to keep financial values aloft when confidence in financial markets waned, threatening to bring down asset prices. The Fed was not averse to inflation of a specific kind: asset price inflation.

Confident belief in the Fed's supportive actions helped sustain the suc-

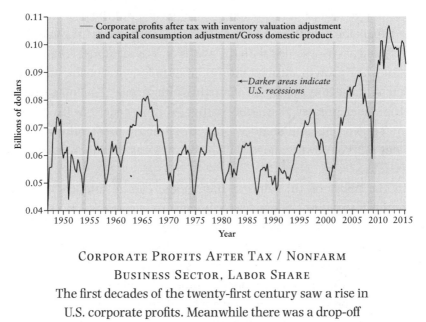

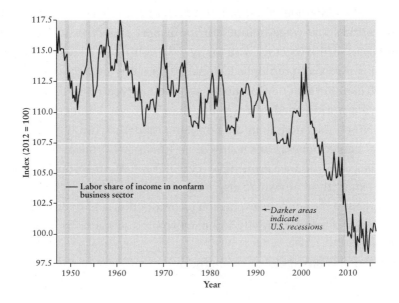

CORPORATE PROFITS AFTER TAX / NONFARM
BUSINESS SECTOR, LABOR SHARE
The first decades of the twenty-first century saw a rise in
U.S. corporate profits. Meanwhile there was a drop-off
in the labor share of income.

cessively longer credit-fueled and asset-price-led expansions of the age, which distributed, logically enough, more money to the property owners of assets, rather than to working people.[2] Between November 1982 and Bernanke's 2004 address, the macroeconomy experienced but sixteen months of recession. The recession of 2001 lasted but eight months. So it was indeed a Great Moderation, in GDP terms. But the post-2001 business expansion that Bernanke spoke within would prove to be even more credit- and asset-price-led than the 1980s or '90s versions. Trend lines in productivity growth, disappointing for decades, except for one happy moment in the late 1990s, fell off further after 2000.[3] The fall correlated with an ever greater post-2000 plunge in nonresidential fixed investment.[4] But profits still climbed—due to climbing asset values and the greater market power enjoyed by large firms—as the labor share of income fell.

In the midst of this, during the 2000s, capital and credit moved smoothly into a new U.S. asset class: homes. To see how this worked, some distinctive characteristics of this, the first speculative investment boom of the twenty-first century, must be appreciated. In particular, the global scale became more important.[5] This was a genuine worldwide economic boom. With the spread of global commerce, trade cumulatively begat more trade, production cumulatively begat more production, and economic activity brought increasing returns. Throughout the world, millions of people escaped economic deprivation.[6] In particular, China, which joined the World Trade Organization (WTO) in 2001, led the rapid growth of the world's low-wage manufacturing export economies. Chinese regions began to link together with many U.S. multinational corporate supply chains. As wealth multiplied, global commodity prices boomed, given the fresh demand that new economic production created for commodities all over the world, whether it was Brazilian iron ore, Indonesian rubber, or Russian oil. Meanwhile in the Eurozone monetary union, introduced in 1999, banks binged on cheap dollar funding. European economies "financialized"—finance growing at a greater rate than production—to a greater extent than anywhere else, even the United States.[7] The question is, how did the tremendous expansion of production and the tremendous expansion of financial activity unlinked to production both increase so prodigiously?

In the dollar-based global economy, one great lever of the boom was

Fed-mandated low U.S. interest rates, which loosened credit conditions. An upswing in the global credit cycle meant that money capital financed long-term investment in wealth-generating trade, enterprise, and employment. Prosperity boomeranged. Gross fixed capital formation as a percentage of world GDP, depressed relative to the postwar past ever since the 1980s, now even began to rise after 2002.[8] But the upswing in the credit cycle also meant that money capital could fund short-term speculation for its own sake in liquid assets. Liquid assets, furthermore, potentially enabled a precautionary propensity to hoard, at the expense of either short-term speculation or long-term investment.

During the 2000s the financial dynamics of speculative investment and precautionary hoarding played out through one particularly crucial global link, between the United States and China.[9] Chinese economic development had followed a familiar historical pattern. Labor, enterprise, and the production of more wealth lifted millions from poverty. But inequality increased, and the greater money incomes that were the result of economic growth did not at first lead to a surge in Chinese consumer spending. Instead, the American consumer market remained the great magnet. The Chinese Communist Party did not direct its manufacturing export earnings to domestic investment, which was far more state-directed than dependent on the global financial system. Instead, China chose to invest much of the savings earned from its exports in the U.S. capital market, especially in U.S. public debt. These Chinese investments helped finance the U.S. trade deficit, which helped sustain American consumption of Chinese-produced goods. This was the post–Volcker Shock configuration of American global hegemony, on steroids.

But the Chinese state also wanted to hoard dollars, should something like the Asian financial crisis of 1997–98 ever happen again: during that panic, which had brought down a number of governments, everyone had wanted to hold dollars, the world's reserve currency and most liquid asset. The Chinese state did not want its legitimacy dependent on the whims of global capital. Altogether, a year after he branded the Great Moderation, Bernanke referred to a China-backed global "saving glut" in 2005.[10]

But it was no less a global "liquidity glut," buoyed by the Fed's low interest rates.[11] The world economy boomed, much through the U.S.-China link. Investment increased, even though China practiced a new kind of political liquidity preference—hoarding prodigious amounts of U.S. debt

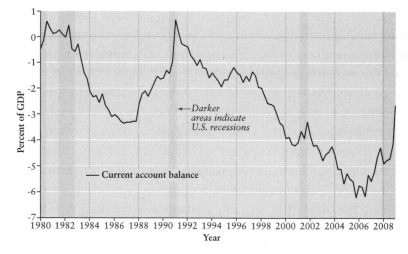

Percent of GDP

←Darker areas indicate U.S. recessions

— Current account balance

1980 1982 1984 1986 1988 1990 1992 1994 1996 1998 2000 2002 2004 2006 2008
Year

U.S. CURRENT ACCOUNT BALANCE

In the balance of U.S. transactions with the world, the 2000s represented an extraordinary amplification of the existing Age of Chaos trend. By now, global financial dynamics—especially the export of wealth into U.S. capital markets in pursuit of safe assets and profits—were in the global macroeconomic driver's seat much more so than trade.

out of precaution. But the liquidity glut also made possible credit-fueled stock speculation, concentrated in the American residential housing market.

The global liquidity glut funded Wall Street speculation in U.S. residential mortgages, and a host of related financial derivatives, such as mortgage-backed securities, all somehow bets or counterbets on whether American residential housing prices would rise in the future. That they would rise became ever more important, for the post-2001 business expansion featured a historically abysmal labor market, a "jobless" recovery. The labor force participation rate actually declined (the male rate falling, female rate holding steady). Meanwhile average household incomes did not recover their pre-2001-recession level until late in 2005. So how could American consumers, who were not saving, afford to buy the flat-screen TVs of U.S. multinational corporations that assembled them using Chinese labor? Especially since, in some regions of the United States, a "China trade shock" had absolutely gutted U.S. manufacturing employment?

One reason was that the well-off kept doing well. The new economy was not a sham. Well-educated and well-compensated Americans lived in cities, where high-tech jobs and related business services clustered, creating consumer demand for goods and services, as well as employment demand in the persistently low-wage regions of the care services sector. Further, under the pressure of the dot-com bust, a number of Silicon Valley–based IT companies finally found ways to make actual business profits from the Internet. They did so by blazing new trails in the field of consumerism. The online retailer Amazon.com saw its sales climb. Some companies, such as Apple, made new luxury consumer products, such as the iPod and the iPhone. Others, such as Google and Facebook, hired engineers and mathematicians to mine personal data from their users, which was then aggregated and mathematically manipulated and sold to marketers as new synthetic constructs of data that were predictive of consumer preferences—an entirely new synthetically engineered asset class.

But in the end, what most compensated for a bad labor market and weak labor earnings was a popular extension debt, specifically mortgage debt. U.S. investment and commercial banks hired PhDs in math and physics who mined past data concerning home prices and mortgage defaults to construct predictive models, which generated more novel synthetic asset classes—including the mortgage-backed security. They were funded by cheap credit in the short-term money market due to the Fed's interest rate policies. Even when the Fed increased its short-term rate target in 2004, long-term U.S. interest rates, including on mortgages, remained low—in part because of the investment of Chinese savings. Credit rushed around. U.S. housing prices shot up. Through a "wealth effect," capital gains on leveraged property ownership could translate into new incomes for American homeowners. The housing stock thus became a new personal income flow. The age's capitalism of asset price appreciation had found a new asset class to concentrate on, as many ordinary homeowners were given the chance to participate in the game of credit-fueled asset price appreciation. As in credit cycles before, it only worked so long as confidence was maintained, and prices kept going up. That was what the Great Moderation had come to depend upon.

Watching it all, the Bush administration celebrated the rise of an "ownership society." Perhaps U.S. political economy could shift from policies designed to redistribute income to policies designed to fling open asset price appreciation to a broader constituency. Every American homeowner could make a living as a savvy financier.

In hindsight, the Great Moderation named a broad-based political-economic settlement of the 2000s, which gave the finance-led globalization of the 1990s—so strongly supported by the Clinton administration—a particular shape. It was a settlement of global expectations. The Fed expected macroeconomic stability, so long as there was inflation only in asset values, not in the baseline price level. The Chinese Communist Party settled on the prospect of high growth, by selling manufacturing exports to the world, while it hoarded U.S. dollar–denominated debt as a backstop just in case. Silicon Valley firms expected free access to their users' personal data. Banks expected the Fed would continue to provide cheap funding and transactional liquidity, so that they could ramp up leverage and profits. U.S. homeowners expected that housing prices would go up and up, sustaining their consumer lifestyles despite flat average pay and a declining share of labor earnings in total income. How long could it all last?

1. The Greenspan Put

The 2000s business expansion began with a sluggish, jobless rebound from the short 2001 recession.[12] To stoke the torpid recovery, the Federal Reserve lowered its targeted short-term interest rate in the federal funds money market to historically low levels. Worldwide, the expansion finally gained momentum in 2003, but not before the downturn exposed the downside of the capitalism of asset price appreciation.

Traders in financial markets coined the phrase *Greenspan put* after the 1987 stock market crash, when, in its wake, Greenspan reduced interest rates, releasing cheap credit to help the market claw back value. In finance, a *put option* gives its buyer a right to sell an asset at a specified price at a future date, even if the price in the meantime falls below the put price—thus protecting its owner from a loss due to a market downturn. The Fed always lowering interest rates when asset prices declined had the same effect—downside protection, which encouraged more risk-taking. The term *Greenspan put* became even more prominent when, in response to the Asian financial crisis of 1997–98, the Fed lowered its interest rate target to soothe jittery global capital markets.

Powerful people had invested their hopes in the U.S. stock market, and Fed chairman Greenspan was among them, speaking of a "virtuous cycle." Stock market asset price appreciation would generate capital gains, he argued, which would then become fixed investments in new information technology, warranting the high stock market valuations to begin

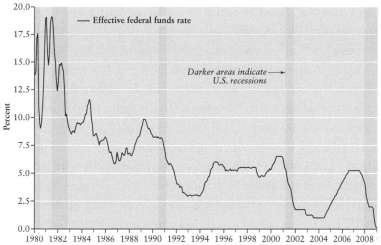

EFFECTIVE FEDERAL FUNDS RATE

The "Greenspan put": in response to any turbulence in financial
markets, to sustain asset prices under chairman Alan Greenspan
the Fed kept lowering interest rates.

with. But what if the virtuous cycle was a vicious cycle? What if the only
way the U.S. macroeconomy could grow was through run-ups in asset
prices, which inequitably threw off income to the owners of capital and
high-wage employees in related financial and business services? What if
asset price appreciation was a confidence game, in which the owners of
capital used leverage to bid up values and book profits on the way up, while
hoping not to be the last to hit the exits on the way down?

Could stock prices soar without actual business earnings? After a negative series of corporate earnings reports in July 2000, stock analysts, journalists, and institutional investors began to question the earnings potential
of many dot-com companies. A sell-off commenced. The Nasdaq lost half
of its value by the end of 2000. In March 2001, the U.S. macroeconomy
entered recession. By the time stock prices bottomed out in the fall of
2002, the Fed's targeted rate was down to 1.75 percent. Fixed investment
in new plant and equipment, increasing at an annual clip of 10.1 percent
between 1995 and 2000, clocked minus 4.4 percent between 2000 and
mid-2003.[13] The macroeconomic recovery was weak.

The late-1990s speculative upswing in the credit cycle had not always
led to prudent investments and had enabled some financial shenanigans.
After 2000 some fly-by-night dot-com companies—Pets.com, "because

pets can't drive"—passed from the scene. In particular, the dot-com bust concentrated on one industry, telecommunications.[14] Late-1990s telecom corporations had made prodigious fixed investments. The Telecommunications Act of 1996 had overturned New Deal regulations and opened up the industry—telephone, cable, satellite, cellular, and Internet—to cross-ownership and competition. Mergers and acquisitions followed. Between 1995 and 2000, U.S. investment banks organized no fewer than 1,670 mergers and acquisitions valued at $1.3 trillion in telecommunications, earning $13 billion in fees. The banks raised capital for telecom fixed investments, then pushed shares on the public. Citigroup analyst Jack Grubman told *Business Week*, "What used to be a conflict of interest is now a synergy."[15] But in 2001 one utilization rate for the U.S. telecommunications industry—the percentage of broadband being actually used—was a paltry 2.5 to 3 percent.[16] Much of it would get used in the future, but presently, excess capacity eliminated any profits to be made by selling a scarce resource. To create the illusion of profitability, the telecom firms WorldCom, Adelphia, and Global Crossing engaged in accounting frauds worthy of the Crédit Mobilier scandal of 1873.[17] At this point, Enron entered the picture.

The origins of Houston-based Enron were in the successful deregulation of the natural gas market during the 1980s, when the company, under the leadership of Ken Lay, bought up natural gas pipeline.[18] Since deregulation was Enron's business, Lay was politically connected. The goal was to eliminate the 1935 Public Utility Holding Company Act, which, like Glass-Steagall, suffered death by a thousand administrative rulings; it was finally repealed by Congress in the Energy Policy Act of 2005. In 1990 Lay hired McKinsey & Company consultant Jeffrey Skilling, another midwestern transplant to Houston, to run a new financial division of the company. By 1997, Skilling was second in command, and financial services were dwarfing the company's other divisions.

Skilling's Enron created new liquid markets to trade energy, including "synthetic" energy derivatives—tradable constructs of data that allowed traders to bet on various movements in prices in markets, or even combinations of movements. Following the new economy platform model, Enron created Enron Online for trading "energy commodities" in November 1999. In January 2000, Enron announced Enron Broadband, an online platform for trading fiber-optic telecommunications cable capacity.

Nobody needed capacity, since most of it was not used, but Enron would still make a market and trade it—if only to swap excess capacity among itself and telecom companies, which could be booked as profits. The corporation also rebranded itself a tech company and began to speak of its "flexibility," "networks," "innovation," "creativity," and "optionality."[19] It worked at first, as Enron's stock price soared.

When dot-com stocks tumbled, public sentiment turned against Enron. The corporation made a major public relations mistake when its traders manipulated California's deregulated spot electricity markets in 2000 and 2001. Then *Fortune* journalist Bethany McLean asked, "Is Enron Overpriced?"[20] That depended on what happened next.

Investors began to ask: how exactly did Enron make profits? The answer was accounting gimmicks and, given the blessings of the era's commitment to transactional liquidity, trading with itself. If a seller finds no buyer for an asset at a profitable price, the seller could find a way to become the buyer, too—truly, the magic of the market. This kind of fraud had appeared in the savings and loan industry during the 1980s, when some individuals used credit to trade the same piece of real estate with themselves over and over again at a higher price, each time booking a profit. Basically, Enron CFO Andrew Fastow and Enron's corporate lawyers created a series of "off-balance" shell corporations, called "special purpose entities," so that the company could carry out such trades internally, creating the illusion of profit. Critically, the SEC had let the company use mark-to-market accounting standards, which meant that the values of its assets were determined by present market price—not by the price when purchased, or the running cost. Since many of Enron's assets were derivatives, dependent on future price swings, the company could infer future profits from present market prices and book them. That impressed investors and secured access to funding. In debt markets, Enron used its own stock as collateral. When investors and journalists began to question how all this worked, and if Enron actually made profits by selling products to customers or by actually booking trading profits (not just expecting to book them), publicity turned against the company. Stock analysts and credit rating agencies "downgraded" it. When Enron stock plummeted, it unraveled the company's finances. The company was in a lot of debt, which it could not pay back when its collateral, its own stock, was in freefall. Enron filed for bankruptcy on December 2, 2001.

Lay and Skilling blamed the media, short sellers, a "liquidity problem," and Fastow. Fastow cooperated with federal prosecutors, and Lay, who sold his own Enron stock while publicly defending the company, was convicted of fraud. He died of a heart attack before sentencing. Skilling would go to jail, lamenting that "the market did not like [me]."[21] Enron's long-respected accounting firm, Arthur Andersen, suffered devastating blows to its reputation and would ultimately collapse. Citigroup, JP Morgan, Merrill Lynch, and a number of other banks would pay billions of dollars in fines for helping Enron cook the books. Enron was the largest corporate bankruptcy in American history but held the title only for a year, until the telecommunications firm WorldCom, led by "telecom cowboy" Bernie Ebbers, followed Enron into accounting fraud and bankruptcy infamy.

President Bush said he worried about "confidence" in U.S. financial markets. But global investors were not worried. Capital was still pouring into the United States. Astutely, Greenspan noted of Enron that any firm was "inherently fragile" if its market value rested on "capitalized reputation," or public confidence in its business model, rather than on "physical assets," which could produce a product to be sold, above the cost of its production, for a pecuniary profit. But had not the market ferreted out the fraud? Enron had manipulated complicated derivative contracts relating various financial price swings to hide losses and create the illusion of profit, but had not "credit default swaps"—another kind of derivative, one that allowed companies to bet against Enron, either as a stand-alone gamble or to effectively insure themselves against Enron's failure—spread losses, preventing any broader carnage?[22] Such derivatives, traded over the counter among the investment banks that engineered them, were not regulated after the Greenspan-supported, Clinton-era 2000 Commodity Futures Modernization Act. Financial industry "self-regulation" was the rule. The Bush administration was hardly about to revisit the issue. President Bush signed the 2002 Sarbanes-Oxley Act, which forced executives to endorse their companies' accounting statements at risk of their personal liability. That framed the issue as a matter of personal malfeasance and responsibility and nothing more—certainly nothing systemically wrong about U.S. capital markets. The law enraged corporate executives, who subsequently mobilized, effectively, to lobby against their prosecution.[23]

Corporate accounting scandals hovered over the sluggish U.S. macro-economic recovery. Not even the 2001 Bush tax cuts budged activity so much. The law slashed marginal income tax rates across the board between 3 and 5 percent. The Bush administration came back for more tax cuts in 2003, and the budget was back in deficit, after Bush had inherited a budget surplus from Clinton. "Reagan proved deficits don't matter," Bush's vice president, Dick Cheney, declared.[24] True, foreign capital—from Japan especially in the 1980s, from China especially in the 2000s—had proved willing to finance U.S. budget deficits. They purchased U.S. Treasury bills, depressing long-term interest rates, because they wanted assets denominated in the currency of the global hegemon, and they were happy to finance the U.S. trade deficit, if only to fund U.S. consumption of their goods.

As for that hegemony, Cheney was among the architects of the Bush administration's spring 2003 invasion of Iraq, an unmitigated disaster. It was imperial invasion privatization style.[25] A network of for-profit firms followed the invading army, maintaining its supply lines and even providing security. If the goal of the Iraqi invasion was "military Keynesianism," the war was no great success. In 2003 national defense spending jumped to 0.36 percent of GDP, after which it declined. By one estimate, the war's direct and indirect costs would total $3 trillion.[26] If the goal had been cheap oil, the invasion was an even greater failure. Oil prices surged during the 2000s because of high global economic growth and thus demand for the crucial energy input. Surely, the fact that the more general commodity price boom of the 2000s did not result in inflation had something to do with the incorporation of new commodity frontiers into the global economy, staving off the looming threat of diminishing returns in agricultural and primary production. But the Fed also deserved credit for anchoring noninflationary expectations—while still providing cheap funding. Meanwhile the Iraq war might have raised doubts among foreign powers about U.S. global hegemony. But the world kept investing in U.S. dollar–denominated assets, including its public debt, regardless of the imperialist fiasco. The global economy needed a hegemon, however humbled and bumbling.

By the time American troops poured into Iraq, the Fed had reduced the federal funds target to 1 percent, where it remained until the summer of 2004. The Age of Chaos had opened with the high interest rates of the Volcker Shock, which reestablished the scarcity value of money capital. Now the historically low short-term interest rate of the Greenspan put induced a most extraordinary speculative upswing in the global credit cycle.

2. First Movers and Born Losers

Easily, the economy of asset price appreciation moved on from 1990s dot-com corporate stocks to the 2000s residential mortgage market. But 2000s economic life had other qualities. At the time the expert view was that as globalization was irrevocably proceeding, everyone, on net, was gaining. *New York Times* journalist Thomas Friedman's *The World Is Flat: A Brief History of the Twenty-First Century* (2005) was a typical title.[27] Yet, despite globalization, the dynamics of geography and place mattered as much as ever. In the United States, a distance emerged—at once economic but also social, cultural, and political—between places that remained the most economically dynamic in the world and those that did not benefit so much from globalization and suffered for it greatly.

Despite the dot-com bust, the new economy expanded. The "Internet sector alone is responsible for about one-fifth of the growth of the American economy between 2004 and 2008." Silicon Valley and other places surged forward, creating high-paying jobs for highly educated and well-networked people, whose high incomes created fresh demand for typically lower-wage service employment—in retail and in restaurants, for yoga teachers, and for life coaches. Two-thirds of all U.S. jobs by now were in the "nontradable" sector—and thus more subject to local conditions. Internet platform companies such as Twitter (founded in 2006) formally employed few people and made no business profits. But Twitter created jobs outside its walls—for lawyers, investment bankers, and subcontracted janitors.[28] Still, these companies, racing to the top of corporate valuations, employed fewer people and stimulated surrounding businesses less than high-valued firms had done in previous eras. They had smaller footprints, compared to, say, General Motors in the 1950s. In 2010, 79.5 percent of all high-tech jobs were in the hundred largest metro areas.[29] Not surprisingly, San Francisco, Boston, and Seattle did well. So did, say, Austin, Texas, and Rochester, New York, specializing in optical technology, or Dayton, Ohio, with its research cluster in radio frequency identification.

Nonetheless, Silicon Valley remained the hotbed for the new economy. At last, in the 2000s, a number of its companies, though not all, found ways to realize profits from operating a business enterprise. Two strategies stand out. One was new: the extraction of data for sale to marketers. The other was quite old: the anticompetitive drive for monopoly. Both strategies, however, used the same means—prodigious long-term capital investments—to achieve the same desired end of being the first mover in a new IT business so as to become impervious to market competition.

Growth at all costs, heedless of losses, let alone profits, remained a corporate strategy during this decade. This led to some aggressive investment strategies and monopolistic tendencies—defying the governing Law and Economics movement, which had stripped the law of many antitrust enforcements on the assumption that short-term, rational profit maximization among firms would always increase competition to the benefit of all consumers.

One corporation that practiced this strategy to great effect was Amazon. When Amazon did finally post a profit in 2002, it was deemed newsworthy. But then the company dipped back into the red. Amazon's CEO, Jeff Bezos, prioritized expansion and "market leadership." Its website became a marketing platform, as it slowly developed its own independent logistics, warehousing, and delivery infrastructure. It offered users free shipping, at a loss to the company, aspiring to dominate the market. Sales revenues climbed, which were reinvested, as outside investors poured money into the company. Unlike Wal-Mart in the 1990s, Amazon in the 2000s was not responsible for lowering retail prices—that new economy effect, cheaper goods, now trailed off. Amazon most benefited "busy, high earning households."[30] For these high-earnings households, increasingly, were two-income households, with less time for shopping. Amazon offered not lower prices so much as time savings. Because of Amazon, at the opening of the twenty-first century, the average well-off American consumer could, lying in bed, order with a click on the laptop or a swipe on the phone, various products from around the world and reasonably expect their rapid arrival on their doorstep in two days. But Amazon's rise to market dominance through below-cost pricing meant it began to acquire the power to prevent market competition—as well as place demands on its suppliers. Further, when profits arrived at Amazon, they would come not from consumer retail but rather from Amazon Web Services, which offered data storage and "cloud" computing for businesses.[31]

Meanwhile it was not Amazon but Google—fearful of its future in the midst of the dot-com stock market meltdown—that during this decade first stumbled on a new business model to actually make profits from providing Internet services to consumers, not businesses.[32]

The way to do it was to mine and manipulate personal data. The "data exhaust" left behind by so many Google Internet searches was personal information that, if extracted and aggregated at sufficient scale, then smartly manipulated by sophisticated algorithms, could be sold to companies and marketers as predictive guides of consumer preference—another synthetic construct of data, a "behavioral" rather than a financial asset. Google's Gmail, introduced in 2004, the same year of Google's IPO, allowed Google to scan (private?) correspondence and scrape it for marketing purposes so that Google could sell "banner" ads on its websites, with companies paying for "click-through" rates. Google's revenues leaped from $347 million in 2002 to $3.5 billion in 2004, from selling ads.[33] Google bought up one company after another—YouTube in 2006, for instance—that would grant it access to even more personalized data or a better ability to interpret it. The jury is still out on the degree to which having large companies like Google always buying up smaller ones is good or bad for innovation.[34] But unlike the 1990s, during the 2000s investment in the "intangible assets" of new economy innovation did not climb.[35] Amazon made many fixed investments in its logistics and delivery networks, which better facilitated commerce—like investments in canals and railroads more than a century ago. But productivity growth in general disappointed because few potentially productivity-enhancing innovations appeared, given the overriding emphasis on finding ways to gather and use data to predict or even modify consumer behavior. In that endeavor, there were rewards to scale, a "network effects" multiplier. Data became "Big Data." The social network company Facebook would follow the same strategy after its CEO and founder Mark Zuckerberg hired Google employee Sheryl Sandberg in 2008.[36] Soon the line between attempted consumer preference prediction and attempted consumer behavior modification would blur.

In the late 1990s capital had valued the proprietary "ideas" of new economy firms. Google and Facebook hired armies of lawyers, and lobbied government, to protect their access to everyone's personal information and their proprietary algorithms. But there was nothing much "new" about how the new economy ended up making business profits. It was just consumerism—even if, as the American consumer market absorbed so many of the world's exports during the 2000s, it reflected the fresh nudge of Silicon Valley behavior modification.

Other 2000s first-mover business strategies were hardly as novel as data mining. In the telecom industry, the wave of consolidation that had begun during the late-1990s mergers and acquisitions moment continued. In a regulatory era that professed the blessings of market competition, industry consolidation was conspicuous. AT&T, which had been broken up in 1984 into "Baby Bells," swooped in after the telecom bust and reconglomerated a budding media empire. In Silicon Valley, Apple made IT breakthroughs of its own, introducing the iPod in 2001, then the iPhone in 2007. The company made profits by selling beautifully designed luxury products manufactured at scale. It did not harvest personal data, but it did resort to an old, monopolistic strategy, known in the nineteenth century as the tie-in. Google was an open platform in constant search of personal data. Apple closed its platform, hoping to lock in consumer loyalty. Meanwhile the American antimonopoly tradition remained largely dormant. A federal district court ruled in *United States v. Microsoft Corp.* (2001) that the corporation had violated the 1890 Sherman Antitrust Act by "tying in" Windows and Internet Explorer, but in a 2002 settlement the Bush administration merely slapped Microsoft on the wrist.[37] When Apple introduced the iPhone in 2007, it announced an exclusive carrier partnership with AT&T—a classic tie-in strategy.[38] Meanwhile, without benefiting from an antitrust law jurisprudence that emphasized short-term consumer welfare over long-term market structure, Amazon likely could not have done what it did in retail.[39]

Altogether in the twenty-first century, much because of mergers and consolidation, "competition . . . declined in most sectors of the U.S. economy."[40] For large firms offering no better services but operating in markets with little competition—telecommunications, airlines, and health care stand out—profits climbed. Thus one reason the labor share fell so precipitously after the 2000s was that consolidated, large corporations enjoyed monopsony power in labor markets—workers could not so easily bargain for higher wages, as there were so few firms with which to bargain.[41] It was the same old story: the reality of increasing returns to economic activity came with the risk that first movers would acquire a monopoly share of a market. On top of that, firms used politics to acquire and reinforce such advantages.[42] Any student of the nineteenth-century U.S. economy— think of the railroads—could have foreseen this possibility.

The dynamics of commerce and market competition transformed, and so did labor and production. The first Apple iPhone was assembled in Shenzhen, China. Between 1990 and 2011, China's share of world manufacturing exports climbed from 2 percent to 16 percent. From 2001 to 2011, the Chinese share of U.S. manufacturing imports climbed from 10.9 percent to 23.1 percent.[43] After 2000, the "China trade shock" was a great contributor to the starkly diverging economic fates of American economic regions.

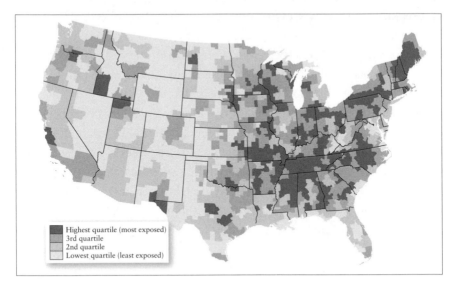

CHINA TRADE SHOCK EXPOSURE, 1990–2007

China became a member of the World Trade Organization in 2001. Shown here are regions of the United States that were most negatively exposed economically to the surge of Chinese manufacturing imports that followed.

Regions where white male manufacturing jobs had once been economically important suffered the most. After the Volcker Shock, the total number of U.S. manufacturing jobs had held steady at 17 million. Between 2001 and 2003, however, the United States lost 3 million manufacturing jobs. Exposed to international competition, U.S. manufacturing was one sector where concentration and market power did not increase.[44] In addition to facing continued automation, any job was at risk of loss if a low-wage alternative was available overseas. Asia and eastern Europe had hundreds of millions of new wage earners, many newly lifted from economic deprivation even if by other criteria—poor working conditions, breached employment contracts, and unpaid wages—exploitation was rife.[45] According to one estimate, "import growth from China between 1999 and 2011 led to an employment reduction of 2.4 million workers" in the United States. The above map of 2000s U.S. "trade exposure" reveals that cities such as Detroit, Buffalo, and Providence were hit hard. So were rural areas of Tennessee, Missouri, Arkansas, Mississippi, Alabama, Georgia, North Carolina, and Indiana.[46] Decades earlier, U.S. trade with industrialized economies like those of Germany and Japan, which might have enjoyed some advantages but not so many, could not have had such an effect. The China "shock" did.

For decades, U.S. manufacturing jobs had been shifting to the low-wage low-unionized South. By 2000 southern migration had played out, and jobs now went overseas.[47] There was zero political management of the process. According to economic theory, displaced workers should migrate, and some of them did. Houston's population boomed, and metropolitan Detroit experienced a population loss of 25 percent (nearly what New Orleans suffered after the 2005 Hurricane Katrina). But not everybody wants to or can move as much as economists' models imply they should.

The jobless recovery in the labor market was gloomy. Between 2000 and 2005, average pay remained flat, as it had at the beginning of every jobless postrecession recovery since 1982. Prime-age U.S. labor force participation declined, as the share of women in the remunerated labor market finally stalled at about 60 percent in 2000. The male labor force participation rate kept falling. For those lacking education credentials at very young ages, lifetime earnings prospects had turned bleak.[48]

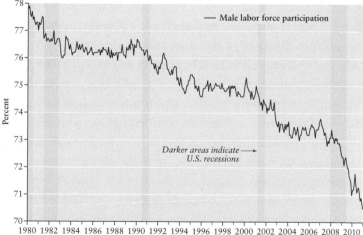

CIVILIAN LABOR FORCE PARTICIPATION RATE, MEN
The declining share of the male population in the remunerated workforce was another long-term trend that accelerated in the twenty-first century.

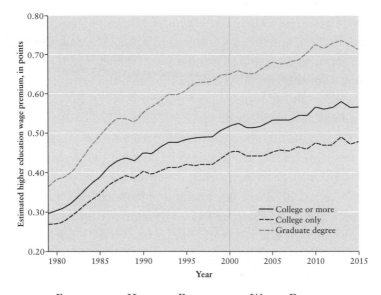

ESTIMATED HIGHER EDUCATION WAGE PREMIUM

Returns on higher education, or on "human capital," have been a major determinant of the growing inequality of labor incomes in the Age of Chaos.

If one did not graduate from college, one had better become a celebrity. Appropriately, education was the major theme of the decade's greatest popular artist, Kanye West, a college dropout, who released the albums *The College Dropout* (2004), *Late Registration* (2005), and *Graduation* (2007).

The population shut out of the labor market altogether fared worse—drastically worse. Data reveal that beginning in 1999 there were marked increases among white men aged 45 to 54 without college degrees in deaths due to drug overdose, suicide, and alcohol-related liver mortality. Such "deaths of despair," responsible in the first two decades of the twenty-first century for an estimated "600,000 deaths of midlife Americans," disproportionately took place in regions where the jobless recovery festered. The phenomenon did not appear in other countries. Due to the persistence of historic disadvantages, black morality rates were still higher than white rates.[49] But class dynamics rooted in education became prominent. Despite the well-documented racist biases of the American penal system, by 2017 "a white high school dropout was about fifteen times more likely to be in prison than a black college graduate."[50]

Meanwhile, if premature death was one theme of the 2000s labor market, another was delayed male adolescence. Not since the 1970s was male identity crisis so prominent a cultural theme: arrested male development was a preoccupation in films, especially comedies—*The Forty-Year Old Virgin* (2005) being the best.[51] On television, in *The Sopranos* (1999–2007), the fragile New Jersey mob boss Tony Soprano suffered from panic attacks and worried about the economic future of his son, A.J.[52] To compensate, *The Apprentice* (2004–17) featured the power-red-tie braggadocio of Donald Trump, childish in its own way. *The Apprentice* was less critically acclaimed but far more popular than *The Sopranos.*

Having social and economic life increasingly organized by networks had consequences: they not only "scale" and fluidly mutate, as recognized in the 1990s, but also have the capacity, it turned out, to rigidly exclude. Inequality increased, with respect to income and wealth, in the realm of abstract numbers. But more concretely, in a parallel dynamic of social exclusion, many individuals and groups were simply ejected from the production side of the new economy. Ironically, the best remedy at hand for exclusion and isolation was greater connectivity through social media— "likes," "selfies," and "memes" were all phenomena of the decade. But then social media companies scraped the data left behind by such activities so that more stuff could be sold to American consumers. And while genuine and meaningful social connection through social media cannot be discounted, the new venues brought with them well-documented pathologies, including—to complete the circle—negative feelings of exclusion and isolation. Soon enough Google and Facebook's algorithms would sell to marketers the information that online users, given inferences from their online presence, were likely feeling lonely and hence susceptible to advertisements that might tempt them to buy something in order to soothe the feeling. The question lingered: if many American consumers were not new economy first movers—particularly well educated or talented, living in thriving cities, and well compensated—how could they afford to buy?

All these social and economic trends manifested geographically. In the cities, elites self-removed by marrying only each other or finding common cultural tastes with respect to, say, cuisine. Political polarization surged in tandem.[53] Even estimations of human worth sharpened. Mark Zuckerberg's warped conception was that "someone who is exceptional in their role is not just a little better than someone who is pretty good. They are 100 times better."[54] So corporations should hire only the exceptionally talented—and pay them well, due to their "human capital"—not the born losers.

During the 1980s and '90s, many Americans were cut free from employment by business corporations and told by experts to construct economic lives outside them. Corporations were not loyal to persons, so why should persons be loyal to corporations? It was better to float free and be opportunistically entrepreneurial on a short-term basis. A countertrend emerged in the 2000s: the talented, educated, and fortunate entered protected new spaces and were embraced. Born losers, not so much.

Facebook, for instance, built a giant corporate campus, an island unto itself, an almost perfect miniature of the high-salary-low-wage service economy, with on-site dentists, nannies, and sushi chefs, as well as automated dry cleaners. It provided places to work, eat, have fun, and sleep. The boundary between home and work continued to blur.[55] Of all the great Internet companies, Facebook has had the fewest spillover effects. It does not stimulate greater economic activity, having almost no backward and forward linkages to other firms—it buys almost nothing from them, for instance. In George Saunders's 2003 short story "Jon," life is totally encased, but secure, inside a dystopian future corporation—the Facility— obsessed with consumer product assessment.[56] Corporations have a long history of exhibiting traits of sovereignty, and twenty-first-century corporations like Facebook, and their allied arms of philanthropy, may well reflect a new chapter.

3. Home

In 2003 President George W. Bush began to invoke the term *ownership society*, first in defense of income tax cuts. But income politics were fast becoming anachronistic. Naturally enough, an economy oriented around property asset ownership benefits the rich, since by definition they tend to own most of the property. But there was an option to expand the ranks of ownership—if not through the actual redistribution of assets, then through access to credit, to purchase them. During the 2000s, politicians and financiers alike engaged in a genuine attempt to execute this strategy, through the vehicle of home ownership.

The federal government could not have been more supportive. Many laws on the books were intended to prevent the extension of mortgage credit on questionable terms. In a 2003 photo op, the same year President Bush waxed eloquently about home ownership, two regulators, John Reich, vice-chairman of the Federal Deposit Insurance Corporation (FDIC), and James Gilleran, director of the Office of Thrift Supervision, together with three banking industry representatives ritualistically took a chain saw and pruning shears to ribbons of red tape wrapped around a stack of government lending regulations.[57]

In finance, the largest investment and commercial banks raced to provide mortgage loans to existing and aspiring homeowners. They believed that they had discovered the end of the capitalist rainbow—a way to make guaranteed profits, without incurring risk or sacrificing liquidity. The way to do it was to buy and sell liquid mortgage-related assets that they had synthetically engineered among themselves, and that they traded for a profit among themselves, funded by short-term interbank money markets among themselves, with everything then insured in the event of any loss, by another set of derivatives trades conducted among themselves. Corporate consolidation during the 1990s and 2000s had swept not only through the telecom, media, and high-tech sectors: a Wall Street funding, rating, and trading cartel had emerged.[58] The principal players were: the five great investment banks, Goldman Sachs, Morgan Stanley, Merrill Lynch, Lehman Brothers, and Bear Stearns; three mega-

"Cutting Regulations with a Chain Saw" (2003)
Increased residential mortgage lending was one route to President George W. Bush's promised "ownership society." Here, a number of federal regulators and banking representatives take a chain saw and pruning shears to the "red tape" of government-lending regulations. Lax government oversight contributed to fraudulent lending practices during the 2000s. From left to right: Office of Thrift Supervision director James Gilleran, Jim McLaughlin of the American Bankers Association, Harry Doherty of America's Community Bankers, Federal Deposit Insurance Corporation vice chairman John Reich, and Ken Guenther of the Independent Community Bankers of America.

commercial banks with their own investment arms, Citigroup, JP Morgan, and Bank of America; the three ratings agencies that stamped mortgage-related assets "investment grade," Moody's, Fitch's, and S&P; and large, mortgage-originating savings banks (thrifts), led by Washington Mutual and Countrywide. The giant insurance company AIG backstopped it all. In previous decades, all these firms had grown larger, merging with and acquiring other institutions, while consolidating their sectors. During the 2000s, they became larger still and even more profitable.

Internationally, the 2000s U.S. housing boom was not unique.[59] Because of the Fed's policies, low global interest rates and cheap dollar money markets fueled a synchronized boom in many countries.[60] Nonetheless, the mechanics and consequences of the U.S. boom were distinct because of the precise way the banks funded and profited from mortgage lending, as well as the role that the generation of fresh money incomes through continued home price increases played in sustaining American consumer demand, despite weak average American pay growth, for the booming global economy.

Mostly because of mortgage lending, U.S. household debt service payments as a percent of disposable personal income climbed from an already high 12 percent in 2004 to a historic high of 13.2 percent in 2007. The climb was supported by historically low interest rates. For the banks, the carrying trade was easy—borrow short at low rates and lend long at higher rates. The interest rate on a standard thirty-year fixed mortgage had fallen from above 7 to below 6 percent. Greenspan noted the "powerful stabilizing force over the past two years of economic distress" due to "the extraction of some of the equity that homebuilders had built up."[61] That meant Americans were not flocking to buy new homes yet, so much as pulling cash out of their homes by either refinancing their mortgages or going into debt through home equity loans—in which the home's present value, and not the past value at which the owner purchased it, is the basis and collateral for a loan at a lower rate than the existing mortgage.

In this way, rising home prices translated into fresh funds to sustain the personal consumption that pulled the U.S. and global economy out of the early-2000s doldrums. In 2003 one in four American homeowners refinanced their mortgages at lower rates, some 15 million homes, cashing out $427 billion. Homeowners extracted another $430 billion through home equity loans. The Fed estimated 45 percent of extracted home equity went toward "medical bills, taxes, electronics, vacations, or to consolidate debt." Another 31 percent went for "home improvements." The remaining purchased "more real estate, cars, investments, clothing, or jewelry."[62] Then after 2003 the boom moved on to the purchase of new homes.

Geographically, the housing boom exhibited variation. In high-income cities, such as New York and San Francisco, prices soared because real estate markets were tight. In steady urban markets, such as Chicago and Houston, prices rose, but at nowhere near so fast a clip. And in the regions of the born losers, no so-called fundamentals were at work—just the capitalism of leveraged asset price appreciation, dangerously democratized. Many of these regions were among those gutted by globalization and the China trade shock. Notably, as manufacturing employment declined, jobs in residential real estate construction surged. In the west side of Detroit and inner-city Cleveland, both longtime black neighborhoods, the expansion of "subprime" mortgage debt—loans extended to borrowers with bad or risky credit—strongly correlated with households' negative income growth.

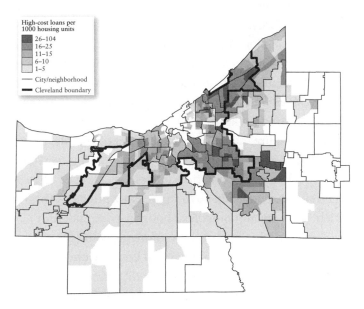

CONCENTRATION OF HIGH-COST LOANS MADE BY
INDEPENDENT MORTGAGE COMPANIES, CLEVELAND, 2006
During the 2000s, residential lending geographically correlated with regions where labor incomes had flatlined for decades. Debt compensated for income growth. Cleveland was a city with a high volume of subprime mortgage lending, often predatory. Lending concentrated in the relatively poor east side, including in predominately black neighborhoods.

People with flagging pay and labor earnings prospects tapped their homes to maintain—not increase, but simply maintain—their level of personal consumption.[63] Many homeowners were not making new home purchases, just leveraging what they already had. Then in the final years of the boom, 2004–6, both lending and speculative construction surged in the four so-called sand states of Nevada, Arizona, California, and Florida, led by the metropolitan areas of Las Vegas, Phoenix, Riverside–San Bernardino, Miami, and Tampa. Here new homes were purchased, and property values soared. White homeowners in these largely white neighborhoods saw their home values increase at a rate much greater than those of nonwhite homeowners. In the sand states, it all got out of hand.[64] But the leveraged boom in U.S. housing prices during the 2000s unquestionably served to paper over the absolutely abysmal decade in U.S. labor markets.[65]

Here is how it worked.[66] Mortgage brokers were closest to the ground in contact with borrowers. Savings banks, or thrifts, whose business model had long been in home mortgage lending, also originated mortgages. Since the savings and loan deregulations of the late 1970s and early '80s, thrifts no longer originated mortgages locally, holding the investments on their books or selling them to the government-sponsored enterprises (GSEs) Fannie Mae and Freddie Mac for packaging into mortgage-backed securities. Now the goal was to "originate and distribute"—to make loans and, instead of holding them on the books as investments, to sell them as quickly as possible in a competitive national and ultimately international market. In 2003 the largest subprime lender was Long Beach, California–based Ameriquest (founded in 1979 to take advantage of thrift deregulations, which also ended limits on subprime lending).[67] But California's Countrywide would soon become even more aggressive.

Wall Street banks, especially investment banks, were eager to purchase mortgages. They granted "warehouse" credit lines to thrifts to originate fresh loans. Ameriquest, for instance, had a $3.5 billion open line of credit with Citigroup. Over time, commercial and investment banks began to simply buy up originators. Lehman Brothers, for instance, bought six mortgage lenders between 1998 and 2004.[68] If homeowners were desperate for loans to compensate for flagging pay, investment banks were no less eager to fund and buy those same loans.

The banks packaged the loans into mortgage-backed securities (MBSs). They cobbled together individual loans, then resliced them into different

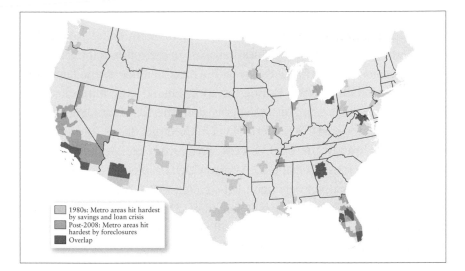

1980s: Metro areas hit hardest by savings and loan crisis
Post-2008: Metro areas hit hardest by foreclosures
Overlap

GEOGRAPHIES OF THE SAVINGS AND LOAN CRISIS
OF THE 1980S AND THE GREAT RECESSION OF 2008
The highly leveraged and often fraudulent lending practices of the savings
and loan crisis were a premonition of the later U.S. residential lending boom.

"tranches" of bonds, with different levels of risk and thus interest payments. They paid fees to rating agencies, Moody's especially, to rate the MBSs according to their risk of default. Moody's, a publicly traded company after 2000, used mathematical models, just like the banks, to predict default risk by plugging in historical price data that hailed from a time when the market was different, because it was vastly more geographically disconnected. (The late-1990s hedge fund Long-Term Capital Management had previously made this mistake.) They did not inspect actual mortgage loans. The SEC signed off on the "value at risk" models. Moody's stamped the safest, lowest-paying tranches with an AAA rating, and then the ratings descended, down to AA, A, BBB. Banks sold the tranches in over-the-counter markets to investors, including pension funds, insurance companies, and university endowments. Or they held on to them as their own investments. In 2004 banks' "private label" securitization surged past Fannie Mae and Freddie Mac, which had long offered government subsidies to the mortgage market. With confidence in risk management due to MBS diversification high, banks believed they could profitably offer loans to riskier, subprime borrowers. Between 2003 and 2007, there was $4 trillion in new MBSs.[69]

That was not the end of it. Next, banks took A- or BBB-level tranches and repackaged them into another interest-paying bond, a "collateralized debt obligation," or CDO. These securities first arose in the 1980s in the junk bond department of Michael Milken's Drexel Burnham Lambert, and later at JP Morgan during the 1990s.[70] During the 2000s, banks and ratings agencies used the same models and historical price data they used for MBSs to engineer mortgage-backed CDOs. Merrill Lynch, Goldman Sachs, and Citigroup specialized. Through the CDO process, 80 percent of A- and BBB-rated mortgage MBSs newly became AAA-rated CDOs. Banks even created CDOs out of CDOs, bets upon bets upon bets, called CDOs "squared." Between 2003 and 2007 there was $700 billion in new CDOs that referenced MBSs.[71]

The final link, was the "credit-default swap," or CDS. A CDS was effectively an insurance contract that paid out if a CDO defaulted, using the same models and the same data. Here the London-operations-based financial products division of AIG took the lead. AIG wrote $20 billion in CDS contracts in 2003 and $379 billion in 2007. It collected 0.12 percent of the notional value of the swap per year, effectively an insurance premium. Its largest customer was Goldman Sachs. Since a CDS was an over-the-counter derivatives contract—it did not exchange in a public market, like the New York Stock Exchange—it was not regulated much. Between 2004 and 2007, the value of CDS-referenced assets in the world increased from $6.4 billion to $58.2 trillion.[72] Bankers charged fees for generating such synthetic assets, so securitization rained down service fees on them. But to increase profits, the banks increased their leverage, posting AAA-rated mortgage-related assets as collateral to raise funds in liquid short-term money markets to engineer and buy more bonds. They turned to short-term money markets that were not regulated—the so-called shadow money markets, which included the London market in Eurodollars but also short-term markets between banks, or short-term markets in the "commercial paper" of businesses, through which they sometimes raised cash. In the funding of business enterprise, this "shadow" money market was slowly replacing commercial banks, which had traditionally accepted deposits from businesses and on that basis extended loans. Finally, to mask leverage, the banks used off-balance-sheet "structured investment vehicles" (SIVs) or accounting gimmicks—both practices recalling Enron. Between 2003 and 2006, the five largest investment banks doubled their pretax-realized profits from $20 billion to $43 billion.[73]

As if they had the Midas touch, the banks believed they had discovered a magical new way to make guaranteed profits without parting with liquidity and therefore taking a risk. Financial engineers—the PhDs in math, physics, and engineering hired by the banks—could create synthetic assets out of thin air. It was a new kind of capital asset—the predictive construct of information and data, dependent on computing power. Here the banks' efforts resonated with Google's and Facebook's contemporaneous attempts to engineer synthetic predictive assets, using personal data mined from the Internet—mathematically certain predictions of future consumer preference. The banks, however, believed they could generate a certain profit from assets that were also money-like and liquid, because they were always tradable in an over-the-counter (OTC) market among the same banks that created them. With cheap dollar funding available given the Fed's benchmark rate, and in short-term money markets among the banks, they could be financed through debt, leveraging up profits. The fantastical financial universe of acronymic abstraction—MBS, OTC, CDS, SIV, and CDO—sprang to life.

Their assembly line had only one constraint. It needed fresh material, actual people who bought—and even sometimes lived in—homes. So mortgage originators lowered their standards, even as home prices surged by another 36 percent between 2004 and the peak of the lending boom, April 2006. In July 2005 the AMC television show *Flip This House* (2005–9) first aired. The show was about real estate speculation, but it was also about the fraught relationships among home, home equity, and the emotional dramas and conflicts of family life, as the boundary between capitalism and home life utterly collapsed. The 2000s housing boom was the economic apogee of an era of "family values."[74] The home had to generate family income, since male breadwinner wages were flat, and yet the home was . . . home. Striking these ambivalent notes, in a revealing 2004 episode of *The Sopranos*, Tony reunites with his wife, Carmella, after he agrees to front her $600,000 for a down payment on a "spec house." In the sand states, entire local economies gave way to housing speculation, as in the Central Valley of northern California. Outside Tampa, "boombergs" of McMansions and Wal-Marts sprouted up in a parody of Sunbelt development. In some instances, the children of former autoworkers migrated from Detroit to Florida to work for mortgage lenders.[75] The stench of moral rot was unmistakable.

Between 2000 and 2007 in Florida, there were 4,065 new mortgage brokers who had previously been convicted of "fraud, bank robbery, racketeer-

"LAS VEGAS AREA SUBDIVISION BECOMES GHOST TOWN" (2010)
The aftermath of the 2000s residential housing boom, as seen from the
Las Vegas metropolitan area in one of the "sand states" where the boom
concentrated. What was built with the cheap capital and credit of the era—
much of it supported by an influx of foreign capital seeking safe assets?
The desolation speaks for itself.

ing, or extortion."[76] But in 2004 President Bush addressed the National
Association of Home Builders noting that "good policies" were creating an
"ownership society," in which "more Americans than ever will be able to
open up their door where they live and say, 'Welcome to my house. Welcome to my piece of property.'" The president added, "We're going after the
terrorists," and stated that in Iraq, "Freedom is on the march."[77]

There was at least some truth to the ownership society claim. During
the 2000s many people, not just the rich, were finally able to play the
asset-price-appreciation game. Even as wealth inequality soared, the rate
of increase in household wealth more than doubled—for now.[78]

By 2005 the United States was in the midst of yet another asset-led
macroexpansion with enough momentum that, just as during the late
1980s and '90s, labor markets tightened and average wages began to crawl
up. That year the Fed held its annual conference in Jackson Hole, Wyoming, which doubled as a retirement party to celebrate the outgoing
chairman Greenspan's accomplishments. The University of Chicago
economist Raghuram Rajan gave the one paper critiquing the economic
value of "financial innovation" and wondering if it was systematically increasing risk rather than reducing it. In response, Harvard University
president Lawrence Summers called Rajan's premise "slightly Luddite."[79]

Greenspan was far more of a free market ideologue than Summers. But Greenspan—always an astute and highly informed observer—was more cautious than his celebrators. In 2005 he would alert Congress to a "conundrum."[80] Setting short-term interest rate targets, the Fed had nonetheless lost control of benchmark long-term U.S. interest rates, including mortgage rates. In an era when so much faith was put into the Fed (Bernanke credited it with achieving the Great Moderation, after all), monetary policy could only control so much, it turned out.

Short-term interest rate hikes by the Fed beginning in 2004 did not cause a dent in long-term rates. The global demand for long-term U.S. debt—whether safe-haven U.S. Treasuries, government-sponsored enterprise debt, or even banks' "private label" MBSs and CDOs—was simply extraordinary.[81] Between 2000 and 2006, led by China, foreign owners of U.S. Treasury debt climbed from $0.6 trillion to $1.43 trillion, from 18.2 percent to 28.8 percent of all U.S. debt. Foreign ownership of Fannie and Freddie bonds increased from $348 billion in 2000 to $875 billion in 2004.[82] European banks especially were buying up extraordinary amounts of American MBSs and mortgage-referenced assets.[83]

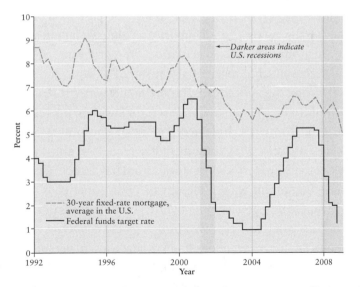

LONG-TERM AND SHORT-TERM INTEREST RATES IN THE UNITED STATES
While monetary policy rose to regulatory preeminence during the Age of Chaos, it turned out there were limits to what central banks could accomplish. During the mid-2000s, for instance, the Fed lost control over long-term interest rates.

What was happening? It was a decade of high global economic growth, lifting millions from pecuniary poverty.[84] Money incomes were higher, though more inequitably distributed at the national scale. But as incomes increased, the propensity to consume did not keep up. Growth did not immediately convert into consumption. Instead, in the aggregate, the global owners of capital were hoarding safe, risk-free assets—some of which, like MBSs, now had the added advantage that they offered handsome profits. In China, the state was forcing stupendous fixed investments in manufacturing and urbanization. Nonetheless, the global hoarding of safe haven U.S. bonds depressed U.S. long-term interest rates and funded both American consumption of the world's goods and Wall Street banks' financial engineering of new synthetic assets for them to speculate in. Hoarding and speculation paired, diverting investment into American housing. Indirectly, the Chinese hoarding of its export earnings in safe dollar assets made possible the extraordinary speculative investment boom in residential American real estate.

Summers saw the efficiency of U.S. capital markets at work and declared that "the overwhelming preponderance of what has taken place has been positive."[85] But studies since then have failed to find evidence that the financial innovation of this era led to any increase in economic efficiency.[86] Back in the 1980s, capital imports were largely Japanese, not Chinese, and they funded U.S. speculation in corporate equities and commercial real estate, not residential housing. The same question posed then echoed during the 2000s, except more loudly: what got built with all this capital and credit? The answer, in this round, was: many McMansions and gas-guzzling Humvees. Indebted American consumers bought the world's goods—iPhones, PlayStations, flat-screen TVs, and sneakers. In another of George Saunders's short stories from the decade, a disgruntled old man, objecting to this way of life, says, "What America is, to me, is a guy doesn't want to buy, you let him not buy, you respect his not buying."[87] But that was not what America was in this global economy, as Google's and Facebook's engineers set about finding new ways to persuade Americans to buy. "I shop so much I can speak Italian," rapped Kanye West in 2007, which was more like it. Meanwhile, Wall Street enriched itself by trading with itself. It was a new frontier for the magic of the market: as an SEC lawyer explained the cartel-like business model, "You buy my BBB tranche, and I'll buy yours."[88]

The problem was not debt per se. Used wisely, credit may expand economic possibility, unleashing underutilized or unknown capacity and potential. The United States, simply because of its position as the global economic hegemon and the status of the dollar as the world's reserve currency, had abundant access to credit, deservedly or not. What a wasted opportunity to make broad-based investments in economic life. During the 2000s, for instance, the alarm kept sounding that man-made climate change required long-term fixed investments in a new energy system to capture and reduce carbon emissions.

By 2006 the mortgage game was clearly up. The rate of home ownership had peaked at 69.2 percent in 2004. The rapid ascent of housing prices stopped in April 2006, with the absolute peak occurring no later than January 2007. But the banks could not quit. At this stage, the GSEs, Fannie Mae and Freddie Mac, fearful of having lost 20 percent of market share between 2003 and 2006, tried to win it back. They ramped up leverage 75 to 1 and also bought riskier loans. Origination standards degraded. In 2006, 27 percent of all new mortgages had no or low documentation proving income, and in the summer the number of mortgages defaulting within months of their issue doubled. In the spring of 2006, residential investment declined, and mortgage defaults began to arrive. AIG stopped writing CDS contracts. An AIG consultant, after listening to a Bear Stearns analyst's pitch for why AIG should write it more CDS contracts, concluded he "was out of his mind" and "must be on drugs or something."[89] The hyperbole had gone far beyond truthfulness, bordering on insanity.

In early 2007 subprime delinquencies hit 20 percent. Still, the banks kept securitizing. After the summer of 2006, banks led by Citigroup, Merrill Lynch, and Lehman engineered another $1.3 trillion in MBSs and another $350 billion in CDOs that referenced mortgages. Citigroup was among the many banks that were holding most of their mortgage assets as investments. Finally on July 10, 2007, Moody's downgraded 399 mortgage-backed securities that had been issued in 2006.[90] Only a day earlier Citigroup CEO Charles Prince had remarked, "When the music stops, in terms of liquidity, things will be complicated. But as long as the music is playing, you've got to get up and dance."[91]

CHAPTER 22

THE GREAT RECESSION

"W E ARE FIGHTING FOR LIQUIDITY"—IT'S A PERFECT insider description of the slow-burning financial panic of 2007–8. After more than a year of "stress" in capital markets, on September 15, 2008, the investment bank Lehman Brothers filed for bankruptcy. The short-term funding of debts in global capital markets evaporated. Fearful, banks stopped trading and lending with one another. The magic of the market, the belief that there would always be liquidity in the form of a willing buyer for any asset, went up in smoke.

Dick Fuld, CEO of Lehman, would later say his bank did not "have enough liquidity to ride out the storm." It had too many "illiquid assets." These included Lehman-engineered mortgage-backed securities, for which there were no longer any buyers, and which the bank could not sell to raise cash to meet its creditors' demands. Illiquid assets are a critical problem if their owner is in debt. Lehman was leveraged as high as 40 to 1.[1] That meant that for every $40 it borrowed, it had $1 as a cushion in the event that its creditors all suddenly came calling. Every night, as a matter of its business model, Lehman borrowed $200 billion from overnight interbank money markets. When nobody would lend to Lehman anymore, the bank went under. If no one would trade with Fuld's bank anymore, at least, he quipped, "my mother still loves me."[2]

"We are fighting for liquidity" would be a fitting epitaph for the Panic of 2007–8, except no banker during that event ever uttered these words. Instead, Linda Lay did, following the collapse of Enron, the Houston-based firm led by her husband, Ken Lay, in a 2002 NBC interview.[3] Ken Lay was another ex-CEO of another bankrupt financial corporation whose balance sheet was weighed down with complex financial derivatives, and that had used debt and dicey accounting gimmicks to create the public appearance of profitability and access more credit in order to keep the confidence game going. The business model was the hope that reality might follow appearance, and for a time it had worked. But whether it was an astute reporter, an unimpressed hedge fund manager, or merely market rumors, appearances were questioned. Beliefs shifted. The confidence game blew back.

Fuld, like Lay before him, watched his company's share price plummet on CNBC stock market entertainment news shows. Fuld, like Lay before him, blamed the short sellers—traders who borrow shares, sell them, then hope to buy them back at a lower price to make a profit—who ruthlessly attacked his company's stock. Lay's right-hand man, Jeffrey Skilling, told congressional investigators in 2002, just as Fuld would seven years later, that Enron suffered only from a "liquidity problem."[4] Skilling had a point. Just about any company can remain a going enterprise if it can maintain access to funding and perpetually roll over its debts into the infinite future.

In fairness to Fuld, Enron was much more of a criminal operation than was Lehman. But by 2007, aspects of Enron's business had become so normalized within capital markets that to question them meant to question the entire global financial system—the trillions of dollars of short-term bets, speculations, hedges, and counterhedges that comprised a single interconnected global capital market. In the Age of Chaos, nothing is more fundamental to sustaining this global market than market participants' confidence in it.

But that meant that something like Lehman could happen, and it did. The Panic of 2007–8 was not an "exogenous shock"—an unpredictable factor unexplained by economic forces—as many blindsided economists would categorize it. Neither was it a natural disaster—a "perfect storm," as Fuld called it, or a "once-in-a-century credit tsunami," as former Fed chairman Alan Greenspan told Congress in 2008—whose causes were outside human control.[5] No, the possibility of Lehman Brothers had been baked into the cake of the post-1982 capitalism of asset price appreciation, dependent as it was on the dynamics of money, credit, and finance.

Many intelligent experts who omitted money, credit, and finance from their understanding of the "real" economy therefore did not see it coming. In 2003 the Nobel Prize–winning University of Chicago economist Robert Lucas, in his presidential address to the American Economic Association, noted that the "problem of depression prevention has been solved, for all practical purposes, and has been solved for many decades."[6] His address, titled "Macroeconomic Priorities," mentioned the word *credit* a single time, and *finance* not once.

Leading the macroeconomic expansion of the 2000s was a surge in housing prices made possible by Wall Street's provision of debt to many homeowners who lacked sufficient income from employment to pay their mortgage loans. If housing prices only went up forever, or if at a minimum beliefs in the prospect could be sustained, there would have been no problem. However, housing prices did not, beginning in mid-2006. Residential investment fell off, and mortgage defaults increased. Consumption declined in late 2007. The macroeconomy entered recession in December 2007.

The decline in housing prices and mortgage-related assets that followed then led to one of the greatest financial collapses in the history of capitalism, threatening the destruction of the dollar-based global financial system both inside and outside the United States. To some degree, capitalism is always credit-led. Capitalism always depends on someone rolling over someone else's obligations into the future. Arguably, in September 2008, after the collapse of Lehman, capitalism came as close as it ever did to a singular moment of reckoning with its fundamental dependence on the future, making for a close brush with death.[7] Nervous, precautionary hoarding among the global owners of capital broke out on a massive scale. Capitalism regressed back to where it was during the Great Depression of the 1930s—mired in a liquidity trap. Across the board, spending of all kinds, whether for investment or for consumption, dropped off. Employment collapsed.

No less remarkable was what happened next. After a presidential election of extraordinary historical significance, in which Barack Obama won the White House, officials at the Treasury Department and especially the Fed invented new policies on the fly to halt the collapse. Administrative state power successfully brought transactional liquidity back to global capital markets and ended the panic. This was a genuine policy achievement. In the end, there was a hint of truth in Lucas's comment that the problem of "depression prevention" had been solved. Due to creative government intervention, the Great Recession did not become the Great Depression.

A new macroeconomic expansion began in June 2009. The problem was that the Treasury and the Fed had only put the capitalism of asset price appreciation back together. Economically, the post-2009 expansion would exhibit many of the same qualities as every single one since 1982. Starting from a deeper bottom of unemployment, it was yet another of the era's jobless recoveries. As asset values climbed, especially stocks, income flowed to the best-off.

The Great Recession was a dramatic story of financial panic, economic suffering, and rancorous politics, but in the end it was also largely a story of continuity. Almost all the banks survived, most of them larger than before. Tellingly, many of the most popular television shows of the 2010s—*The Walking Dead* (2010–) and *Game of Thrones* (2011–19)—were about zombies. Unlike the Great Depression of the 1930s, no new age of capitalism issued forth from this crisis, even as so many economic dissatisfactions persisted. As in the 1930s, however, a crisis in capitalism would spell trouble for liberal democracy.

1. Panic

"Who owns residential credit risk?" asked two Lehman analysts in September 2007.[8] When national home prices declined after April 2006, and when in early 2007 subprime mortgage delinquencies surpassed 20 percent, the U.S. commercial and investment banks heavily invested in mortgage-related assets were bound to book losses. Something much worse happened because of the way the global capital market and U.S. dollar money markets had become fatefully intertwined and dependent on the presence of transactional liquidity—a willing buyer for all assets. When even the prospect of illiquidity appeared, beliefs shifted. Confidence evaporated, and panic ensued. During the slow-burning Panic of 2007–8, capitalism survived because the Fed crossed new frontiers in the history of "unconventional" central banking and kept the dollar-based global financial system alive, barely.

The Age of Chaos had begun with the Volcker Shock, when the Fed reasserted the scarcity value of money capital by raising interest rates. In the decades of price stability that followed, the massive expansion of credit fueled the new capitalism of leveraged asset price appreciation. It all came crashing down at the end of 2008, and to salvage the system, the Fed followed the reverse policy that had brought it to global economic policy-making preeminence under Volcker—not scarce credit but loose credit, and for the largest banks nearly free money. Meanwhile Wall Street's instinctive response to the crisis was to further consolidate the financial industry.

The trouble began in July 2007, as the ratings agencies kept downgrading mortgage-related assets. That summer a number of investment funds in mortgage-related assets went belly up, and transactional liquidity in the $1.2 trillion worth of asset-backed commercial paper dried up. The banks had commandeered the market in short-term commercial paper, which nonfinancial companies for decades had used to raise cash for their day-to-day operations. The asset-backed-commercial-paper market shed $800 billion in volume, indicating a slowdown in one of the mortgage-related-asset market's most important funding engines. Meanwhile Goldman Sachs and a number of hedge funds had begun to short mortgage-related assets. For this reason, Goldman demanded that banks "mark down" the value of the assets to reflect real-time values. That, said Ralph Cioffi, who ran Bear Stearns's mortgage investment subsidiaries, meant "doomsday," since the fund could not wait for market values to reclimb. It had to mark the bad losses.[9]

The commercial paper market aside, two short-term money markets, where banks posted collateral, still remained: the London-based Eurodollar market, and the interbank short-term "repo" market, in which banks sold assets for cash, then "repurchased" them soon thereafter. As banks began to doubt the value of mortgage-related assets, funding costs shot up in all credit markets. "It was as if your entire life you had turned the spigot and water came out. And now there was no water," recalled one bank executive.[10]

On August 10, 2008, the Fed announced it was "providing liquidity to facilitate the orderly functioning of financial markets."[11] To ease funding conditions, the Fed cut its short-term-interest-rate target from 6.25 percent to 5.75. As always, it did so by intervening in the money market for "federal funds" where banks lend to one another the reserves they must legally hold at the Fed. Typically this money market, not backed by collateral, set a rough benchmark for other collateral-backed money markets. But as banks lost faith in collateral, rates diverged. In a vicious circle, higher funding costs in collateral-based money markets meant less funding for the assets posted as collateral—the assets, declining in value, that the banks were caught holding on their books.

At this moment, the banks began to announce large losses after mark-

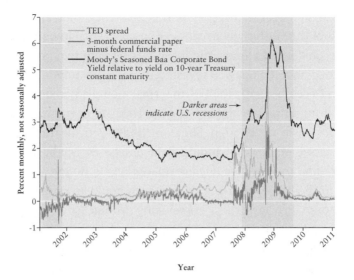

U.S. CREDIT SPREADS

Widening credit spreads indicated the scale of the 2008 financial panic.
Each line represents a spread between private and public sources of credit,
as private credit during the panic became more costly. The "TED spread"
represents the spread between rates in the interbank money market
and on three-month U.S. Treasury bills.

ing down their mortgage-related assets. The surprise was that banks held
so many of these assets on their own books. At Citigroup, CEO Charles
Prince held "DEFCON calls" with senior management, including former
Clinton Treasury secretary Robert Rubin, whom Citigroup paid $115 mil-
lion between 2000 and 2009 for an advisory position with "no operational
responsibilities." Prince resigned in November when Citigroup announced
$8 billion to $11 billion in losses. His parting compensation was $11.9 mil-
lion in cash and $24 million in stock.[12]

On December 12, 2007, the Fed announced the formation of the Term
Auction Facility (TAF).[13] To remove the stigma of commercial banks using
the Fed's normal discount window—in which banks borrowed directly
from the Fed—under TAF, the Fed held regular auctions for loans against
a broader range of collateral than what it accepted at the discount window. Within three weeks, the Fed had lent $40 billion, including to many
foreign banks.[14] The same day the Fed also announced $24 billion in credit
"swap lines" with foreign banks.[15] In the brewing crisis, everyone wanted

access to U.S. dollars, the currency of the global hegemon and the operational basis of the one big global capital market.[16] Then in January the Fed cut the targeted federal funds rate from 4.25 percent to 3 percent. Credit still tightened nonetheless, and investment and consumption declined in tandem. In December 2007 the U.S. macroeconomy entered recession.

Easy Fed funding—cheap loans in the short-term money market for federal funds—was not enough. Someone had to provide transactional liquidity in asset markets, including debt assets. Especially, some agent somewhere had to accept mortgage-related assets no longer trading as collateral in the money markets so that cash could be raised to pay nervous creditors.[17] Private actors were refusing to do so, for mortgage-related assets that had once been rated AAA had not only lost value, they could not be valued. The banks' predictive models had failed since home prices across the United States had—departing from historical price movements—declined in unison. A risk to the previous decade's consolidation of finance had emerged, as the great banks all threatened, essentially, bank runs on one another.[18]

On March 11, 2008, the Fed announced the new Term Securities Lending Facility (TSLF).[19] In return for GSE or even AAA-rated "private label" MBSs, the Fed would lend out U.S. Treasury bills, which hopefully would reliquefy the interbank money market. The Fed claimed authority under Section 13(3) of the Federal Reserve Act, which allowed the Fed, in "unusual and exigent circumstances," to lend unlimited amounts of money to individuals, partnerships, and corporations against collateral it deemed sufficient—upon Treasury Department approval. Legal scholars still debate whether, during the 2008 crisis, the Fed acted within the bounds of its legal mandate.[20] Regardless of the law, in practice the Fed asserted new powers, hitherto unthinkable, to purchase assets and lend money.

Although TSLF was announced March 11, it did not go into effect until March 27. In the meantime, Bear Stearns failed. Bear Stearns had mortgage-related assets stuck on its books. Leveraged 38 to 1, it had survived by funding itself through the overnight repo market to the tune of $50 billion to $70 billion every night. But ratings agencies kept downgrading its assets, as its stock price crumbled. No one wanted to trade with the firm. Creditors demanded cash. "It was like having a beautiful child and they have a disease of some sort that you never expect to happen and it did," lamented CEO Jimmy Cayne. On March 12 a false market rumor circulated in the media that Goldman Sachs had refused to transact with Bear Stearns. Bear Stearns ran down its $18 billion cash cushion.[21]

JP Morgan bought Bear Stearns for $10 a share, with government subsidy. Treasury secretary Hank Paulson, former CEO of Goldman Sachs, and New York Fed president Timothy Geithner, a career civil servant and 1990s protégé of Rubin, organized a $12.9 billion loan to aid the acquisition. Invoking Section 13(3), the Fed also purchased nearly $30 billion in toxic mortgage-related assets from Bear Stearns, which JP Morgan would not touch.[22] This was the beginning of government by deal making, leading to further industry consolidation.[23] Among bankers, Geithner's bank matchmaking earned him the nickname "eHarmony."[24]

Sunday, March 16, two days after Bear Stearns ceased to operate, invoking Section 13(3) yet again, the Fed announced the Primary Dealer Credit Facility (PDCF).[25] Now in return for AAA-rated MBSs, the Fed would provide not just Treasuries but cash. The Fed was now "lender" and, for the first time ever, the "dealer" of last resort—announcing it would stand ready as the buyer of last resort for sellers of assets.[26] In the week after Bear, the PDCF provided $340 billion in cash. But then the banks stepped back from Fed supports, fearful of signaling distress to their private creditors. "Who's next?" asked the scroll at the bottom of CNBC. Lehman Brothers CEO Dick Fuld met privately with CNBC's Jim Cramer and pleaded with him to use his television program *Mad Money with Jim Cramer* (2005–) to rebut market rumors. At this point, AIG discovered that it, too, might have a "liquidity problem," according to its head of strategy, who alerted AIG's CEO in a late-night conversation. "You scared the shit out of me last night," he would remark the next day, before reaching out to Geithner, saying, "No reason to panic," but "what's the likelihood, if AIG had a crisis, that we could come to the Fed for liquidity?"[27]

The GSEs Fannie Mae and Freddie Mac were next.[28] Neither was the proximate cause of the mortgage-securitization fiasco, but both—benefiting from government subsidies—had rushed in near the end, as the music kept playing. Now, stuffed with mortgage-related assets, they struggled to borrow in short-term money markets. Congress passed the Housing and Economic Recovery Act of 2008, which granted the Treasury Department the ability to take over the GSEs. When Treasury estimated gigantic imminent losses, the boards of Freddie and Fannie voted to accept government conservatorship. Paulson hoped that taking over the GSEs would halt the ongoing panic and "provide confidence to the market."[29]

Instead, "Lehman started to go." Lehman suffered from the same problems as Bear Stearns and was relying on the same solution—short-term repo funding, but to the tune of $197 billion. Mortgage-related investments remained stuck on Lehman's books. Lehman's stock kept going down. On September 4, 2008, Lehman alerted its largest repo broker, JP Morgan, that it would soon announce a $3.9 billion loss. JP Morgan, Citigroup, and Bank of America began to demand more collateral from Lehman to roll over its repo loans.[30] A Morgan Stanley banker left a Lehman meeting saying, "We just watched guys who are staring into the abyss."[31]

Lehman could not fund itself. So on Friday, September 12, Paulson assembled the CEOs of the biggest banks—the "heads of family"—for the first time since the Long-Term Capital Management crisis of 1998. He hoped for a "LTCM-like solution."[32]

Many in the room recalled Fuld's previous unwillingness to kick in Lehman's full share to save LTCM. Regardless, even more than had been the case with LTCM, the value of Lehman's mortgage-related assets was too uncertain. The mathematical models had failed. There was almost no more trading in such assets. The magic of the market—the belief that there would always be a willing party to buy, or at least price, an asset, or at a minimum a creditor to accept it as collateral—had simply evaporated.

Sensing his bank might be next, Merrill Lynch CEO John Thain sold the firm to Bank of America, at $29 per share. British-based Barclays Bank cobbled together an offer for Lehman but on Sunday, September 14, the British financial regulator refused to endorse it. Geithner, Paulson, and Bernanke informed Lehman's board that it should file for bankruptcy before markets opened Monday morning. Lehman filed.[33]

Why was Lehman allowed to fail? Lehman's bankruptcy lawyer predicted it would "take liquidity out of the market. The markets are going to collapse. This will be Armageddon!"[34] At the time, Bernanke said markets were prepared for Lehman's bankruptcy, but he later questioned whether the Fed would have had adequate legal authority to bail out Lehman. But the Fed had already made most unconventional use of Section 13(3), so why not keeping pushing it? Bernanke also said Lehman was not only suffering from a liquidity crisis—he thought it was insolvent. Even if trading came back, the new market prices set on Lehman's assets would prove it to be bankrupt. There were mumblings about "moral hazard," that bailing out Lehman would prove that banks "too big to fail" could always engage in egregious behavior and expect to be bailed out by government in the end. But the Fed was now propping up the entire money market—worries about moral hazard had not stopped it. In truth, Bernanke, Paulson, and Geithner braced for the worst. As Bernanke would say, "there was never any doubt in our minds that it would be a calamity, catastrophe, and that, you know, we should do everything we could to save it."[35] Officials tried to find a way to save Lehman. They simply failed.[36]

On Monday, September 15, 2008, the U.S. stock market lost $700 billion in value. There was panic and a massive flight to cash or the closet equivalent—short-term U.S. Treasury bills. Still, JP Morgan CEO Jamie Dimon would say, "I didn't think it was so bad. I hate to say that. . . . But I [thought] it was almost the same if on Monday morning the government had saved Lehman. . . . You still would have terrible things happen."[37] Dimon was right, for it was not Lehman that triggered "Armageddon." It was AIG.

AIG had $1 trillion in assets, many of which, however, were locked up in state-regulated insurance subsidiaries. They were illiquid. But AIG needed cash to post as collateral for its insurance-like CDS contracts. Its options in short-term money markets were drying up. "We've got a big problem. I mean, *fucking* big," said the JP Morgan banker hired by AIG to examine its books on Sunday, September 14. "We need $60 billion!"[38]

AIG informed the Fed it could not raise the cash. Once again the Fed invoked Section 13(3). On Tuesday, September 16, it issued an $85 billion loan to AIG to meet its immediate obligations, in exchange for ownership warrants in 79.9 percent of the corporation.[39] AIG was not too big to fail. It was too interconnected with one big global capital market—"$1 trillion of exposures concentrated with 12 major financial institutions," AIG's CEO confessed in a memo to Geithner.[40]

Not sufficiently appreciated at the time was how much the money markets depended on confidence in AIG's CDSs. Because of AIG's portfolio of $2.7 trillion in over-the-counter derivatives, dealers in money markets believed that their trading books were adequately hedged. They could confidently keep dealing. When AIG's CDS contracts were thrown into doubt, fresh anxieties arose. All the money markets seized up. Even trading in the market for federal funds, regardless of the interest rate, which the Fed kept lowering, slowed down. Without fresh credit provided from the money market, old debts could not be rolled over. That truly would mean financial collapse.

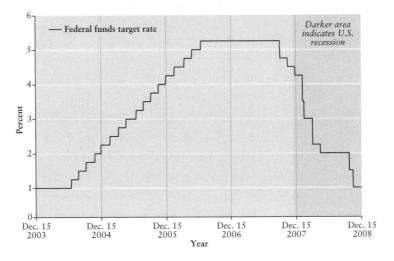

FEDERAL FUNDS TARGET RATE

Not long after attempting to raise its targeted short-term interest rate from a historically low peacetime level, in response to the financial panic the Fed slashed rates once more and found itself right back where it started—and soon enough, in a liquidity trap.

"The failure of AIG," Bernanke said, "would have been basically the end." Now banks nearly stopped trading assets of any kind whatsoever with one another. In a financial system premised on transactional liquidity, illiquidity threatened insolvency for everyone—no matter what assets really were, or should have been, worth. Furthermore, there were consequences for nonfinancial corporations, dependent on these markets. For instance, the original purpose of the commercial paper market was for corporations to raise cash to finance their day-to-day business operations. Now, as the commercial paper market came to a halt, industrial corporations, such as General Electric, feared they might not be able to fund their day-to-day payroll obligations. Meanwhile "prime" money market funds (prime because they do not invest in U.S. Treasury securities) "broke the buck," no longer guaranteeing a one-dollar redemption for every dollar of deposits. Americans had approximately $3 trillion in such funds—more than a third of all bank deposits. In one week there were $349 billion of withdrawals from them. Recalled one Fed economist, "It was overwhelmingly clear that we were staring into the abyss."[41]

Precautionary hoarding ruled. There was a massive flight to cash and to the most money-like asset, U.S. Treasury bills. In the three weeks after Lehman-AIG, institutional investors in money market funds withdrew $434 billion.[42] Mostly it was placed into the U.S. Treasury bills market. On Friday, September 12, the secondary market yield for four-week U.S. Treasuries was 1.35 percent. On September 17, the return was 0.07 percent. It would not climb over 1 percent again until 2017. The long arc from the liquidity trap of November 1932 to the liquidity trap of September 2008 closed, as panic and fear had once again triumphed.[43] Once again the owners of capital exercised a strong preference to hoard, even when holding U.S. Treasuries earned them no gain besides the psychological return of safety. That psychological return offered only a false hope. For if everyone clung to cash or its nearest equivalent, and no one traded or lent, let alone invested, economic spending of all kinds would plummet, and the economy as a whole would tank. That was what happened.

At this moment, only the federal government had the capacity to shift beliefs and restore liquidity—if the political goal was only to repair the dollar-based global financial system, not transform its structure fundamentally, which it was. The Fed kept stepping into the breach, purchasing assets and lending money, trying to cajole financial markets back to life. The week after Lehman and AIG failed, Morgan Stanley, one of the two remaining U.S. investment banks along with Goldman Sachs, borrowed $75.3 billion from the Fed. On Thursday, September 19, the Fed expanded foreign currency swaps to $180 billion—so that foreign central banks could provision their banks with dollars. In the global financial system, all parties still wanted to get their hands on dollars in a crisis. Finally, on Friday, September 20, Treasury announced it would guarantee the one-dollar net value of money market funds. On Sunday, September 22, Morgan Stanley and Goldman Sachs applied to be reclassified for regulatory purposes from independent investment banks to "bank holding companies." That granted the Fed new regulatory oversight over them, so that the Fed could now grant them greater access to funding. The survival of the two corporations was not ensured, however, until Warren Buffett invested $5 billion in Goldman Sachs, and Japan-based Mitsubishi UFJ invested $9 billion in Morgan Stanley. Government authority only midwifed more industry consolidation. For instance, the FDIC seized Washington Mutual, the largest U.S. thrift, which was facing $16.7 billion in depositor withdrawals, but it then quickly sold it to JP Morgan for $1.9 billion.[44]

On Friday, September 19, Paulson announced a new government program to buy "these illiquid assets that are weighing down our financial institutions and threatening our economy."[45] The Treasury Department sent Congress draft legislation for a Troubled Asset Relief Program (TARP). It was three pages long and requested blanket authority for Treasury to buy up to $700 billion in toxic assets. Paulson and Bernanke traveled to Capitol Hill to lobby Congress. Bernanke told twenty congressmen, "I spent my career as an academic studying great depressions. I can tell you from history that if we don't act in a big way, you can expect another great depression, and this time it is going to be far, far worse."[46] Soon Paulson's staff overheard him vomiting in his office.

The next week brought more dramatic events, though the scene of action shifted to Washington. Republican presidential candidate John McCain announced he was suspending his campaign to return to the capital to participate in congressional deliberations. A staged televised September 24 White House meeting failed. Afterward Paulson walked into the next room and fell on one knee and begged Democratic House leader Nancy Pelosi to continue to negotiate with Republicans.[47] Later he visited Democratic Senate leader Harry Reid in his office, and Reid asked Paulson if he should call a doctor as Paulson dry-heaved into Reid's office trash can.

On Monday, September 29, the House voted TARP down 228 to 205: a great number of Republican congressmen voted no, on the belief that the discipline of the market was the solution to the crisis—a solution that, understandably enough, Paulson did not have the stomach for. The stock market kept tanking. But then a revised 169-page bill passed the Senate. Finally, on Friday, October 3, after raising FDIC deposit insurance from $100,000 to $250,000 and granting Republican-requested tax cuts, the House assented 263 to 171 to a now-450-page bill. President Bush signed the legislation into law the same day.

The Fed remained ever creative. On October 7 it announced the Commercial Paper Funding Facility.[48] The Fed would now accept commercial paper, including from nonfinancial corporations, such as Verizon and McDonald's, that needed access to cash to make immediate payments. On October 8 the Fed and a number of foreign central banks announced the first-ever internationally coordinated reduction of short-term interest rates.

By then, the Treasury Department had changed its mind about TARP. Instead of buying toxic assets, Treasury would inject capital into the banks. On October 13 Paulson called a meeting with the chief executives of the nine leading financial institutions, holders of 75 percent of all U.S. bank assets. Through the Capital Purchase Program, in return for non-voting stock—no policy-making voice in the companies, that is—Treasury invested $25 billion in Citigroup, JP Morgan, and Wells Fargo; another $15 billion in Bank of America; $10 billion in Merrill, Morgan Stanley, and Goldman; $3 billion in BNY Mellon; and $2 billion in State Street. Treasury also announced it would guarantee the financial institutions' senior debt. Treasury invested $188 billion in TARP funds in financial institutions by the end of 2008. That included another $40 billion into AIG (which paid out its CDS contracts dollar for dollar) and another $20 billion each into Citigroup and Bank of America. On December 19, $81 billion in TARP money was invested in General Motors, GMAC, Chrysler, and Chrysler Financial. TARP expenditures would reach $395 billion by September 2010.[49]

Meanwhile, the Fed's balance sheet had doubled in size. The Fed's emergency role as a dealer of last resort peaked in January 2009. TSLF hit $483 billion. PDCF hit $156 billion. Money market funding reached $350 billion. Commercial paper peaked at $365 billion. In November 2008 the Fed announced a plan to buy as much as $500 billion in GSE mortgage-related securities. The Fed also wrote credit risk insurance for $306 billion in mortgage-related assets for Citigroup and $138 billion for Bank of America.[50] Thus far the total ran to nearly $2.3 trillion. Foreign banks had benefited from Fed lending, including UBS of Switzerland ($77 billion), Royal Bank of Scotland ($85 billion), Japan's Norinchukin ($22 billion), and the Franco-Belgian bank Dexia ($59 billion). The central banks of foreign countries had borrowed $580 billion from the Fed.[51] The Fed became lender and dealer of last resort for the global economy.[52] A new day had dawned in global economic governance. There was no going back.

By January 2009, some credit spreads were closing and the state of acute panic was over. But the financial crisis was not over, and the world economy had entered into a deep slump. Politics, however, were about to shift. For on January 20, a new American president was inaugurated.

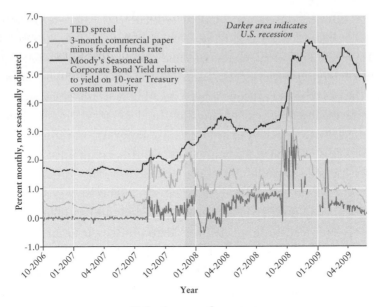

U.S. CREDIT SPREADS

Closing credit spreads indicate the end of acute financial panic by the spring of 2009. The "TED spread" represents the spread between rates in the interbank money market and on three-month U.S. Treasury bills.

2. The Ordeal of Barack Obama

The economic downturn that followed the financial panic was quickly named the "Great Recession." The initial descent was of a depth not seen since the opening months of the Great Depression. If government action prevented a repeat of the 1930s, and positive economic growth returned in June 2009, the tag *Great Recession* stuck nonetheless because of a widespread belief that something was still not right with the economy. Economic problems that had accumulated during the 2000s—especially a poor labor market, riven by inequality—and been papered over by the credit-fueled rise in residential housing prices now broke out into the open and festered. The attempt to let ordinary Americans play the asset-appreciation game, through mortgaging their homes, had stunningly failed. Due to collapsed housing prices, between 2007 and 2010 median wealth declined 44 percent—back, adjusted for inflation, to where it had been in 1969.[53] If the Fed's actions averted a worse economic disaster, capital markets nonetheless remained in liquidity-trap conditions, as the precautionary propensity to hoard undermined long-term investment. What was needed was for democratic politics and the state to chart a new direction, a new, viable long-term economic path, by changing the logic of investment.

That did not happen. Surely the period from the presidential inauguration of Barack Obama on January 20, 2009, until the midterm 2010 congressional elections was one of the more dramatic in all of U.S. political history.[54] Obama won 52.9 percent of the presidential vote, and after 2008 the Democratic Party controlled the House of Representatives and enjoyed a filibuster-proof Senate majority of sixty. In Obama's administration, Clinton-era Democrats returned to power. The restoration of the capitalism of asset price appreciation proved to be the limit of their imagination.[55] Meanwhile by 2010 the populist, conservative Tea Party movement had arisen and was pushing politics to the right. In the end, despite the largest fiscal stimulus in the nation's history, significant legislative reforms, and an unconventional monetary policy called "quantitative easing," no major transformation of the U.S. economy occurred. If from a deeper recessionary hole, another macroeconomic expansion began, repeating many of the same economic patterns that occurred in every such expansion since the 1980s.

Until Lehman failed, Obama's electoral race against Arizona senator John McCain had been close. Post-Lehman, Obama projected calmness and a greater sense of mastery, which translated into success in the polls. It was no accident. Obama was in back-channel communication with a number of prominent and well-informed Wall Street bankers, inside the belly of the crisis, who were backing his campaign.[56] Long ago FDR had refused to pronounce on Hoover's policies, so as to enter office without being boxed in politically. By contrast, candidate Obama announced support for TARP.[57] Still, Obama did campaign against what he called the "Bush economy." He said the government must play an active role in ending the financial crisis but that afterward there would need to be a turn toward greater "responsibility."[58] *Responsibility* was a keyword in Obama's politics of bipartisan blue-state-red-state moralism, evoking for liberals the need for economic regulation and for moderates and conservatives fiscal rectitude. While Obama did depart from Clinton's New Democrats by explicitly embracing redistributive policies, he also spoke out, in moral tones, against debt. He promised to reduce federal expenditures and public debt by cutting benefits for the best-off while still investing in public goods such as education and infrastructure.[59] His first budget, *A New Era of Re-*

sponsibility (2009), was a forceful presentation of such principles.[60] In sum, Obama had an expansive vision for federal economic policy, but he also openly campaigned on a pivot to austerity.[61]

Once in office, Obama chose for his economic policy-making team experienced members of the Democratic establishment who had worked for Clinton, under Robert Rubin.[62] Timothy Geithner became Treasury secretary; Lawrence Summers became director of the National Economic Council, as well as one of the president's chief economic advisers. Other policy advisers came from outside this circle. Christina Romer, a UC Berkeley macroeconomist and a scholar of the Great Depression, became the head of the Council of Economic Advisers. Paul Volcker—who had become an outspoken critic of financial innovation—had an advisory role. One may question Obama for appointing so many members of the 1990s Clinton-Rubin circle, some of whom, like Summers, had moderated their views since the heady 1990s, while others, like Geithner, had not.

However, what was most remarkable about this moment was something that cannot be placed at Obama's feet, and that was the sheer lack of economic imagination on the part of the left in 2008. No left-wing ideologue himself, FDR had benefited from generations of Populist and Progressive proposals, which were ready on the shelf when he entered office. Obama was recommended mostly old ideas. Some were good, like Volcker's recommendation for a new Reconstruction Finance Corporation, the great New Deal and World War II public-financing vehicle. But what would a twenty-first-century version look like exactly? Romer advocated tax credits for hiring and investment, as if she were directing the Council of Economic Advisers of President Lyndon B. Johnson. Were there not any new ideas? The truth was that the Democratic Party under Clinton had embraced finance-driven globalized capitalism and so was not adequately prepared to think or act creatively when that capitalism self-destructed. Therefore, nor was the Obama administration. In fairness to Obama, he had set out on a career in politics intending to transcend racial disharmony and regional blue-state-red-state discord—not the capitalism of the Age of Chaos. After all, in 2008, finance had made greater campaign donations to Obama than to McCain.[63]

And yet in the first half of 2009, the capitalism of asset appreciation was awfully vulnerable. Perhaps too vulnerable—too near collapse for officials to worry about anything but preventing a collapse. Still, policy makers had an extraordinary opportunity at hand, should they choose to take action. When Obama took office, the economic status quo had little popular support. Economic output was declining, and unemployment in 2009 would reach 10 percent. Consumption was in free fall.[64] The sand states were hit worst. But even if housing prices did not fall as sharply elsewhere, say in Michigan and Tennessee, the fall in national demand for durables nonetheless led to idling Michigan and Tennessee automobile factories.

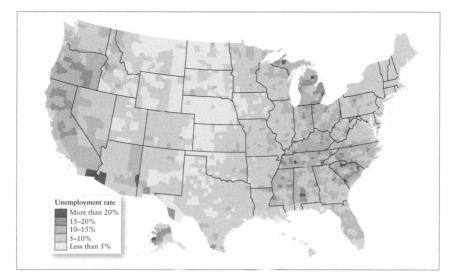

U.S. UNEMPLOYMENT, 2009 / U.S. HOME FORECLOSURES, 2009
These maps illustrate the overlapping geographies of unemployment
and home foreclosure in the wake of the Great Recession.

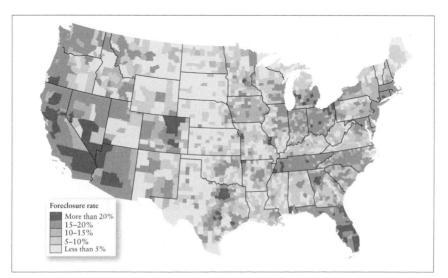

Further, the overhang of debt built up during the 2000s meant that, as incomes dropped, consumers repaid their loans, spending even less.[65] It was a textbook debt-deflation recession. By Obama's inauguration, because of the Fed's munificence, bank reserve balances with Federal Reserve banks sat at roughly $843 billion—compared to $11.6 billion one year before. But money in circulation remained roughly the same, while the volume of loans declined.

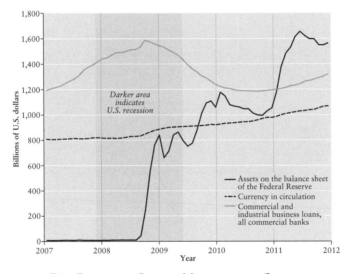

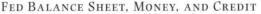

FED BALANCE SHEET, MONEY, AND CREDIT

A surge in precautionary liquidity preference after 2008 meant that the dramatic provision of credit by the Fed to banks did not translate into the extension of credit by those same banks to fund enterprise and employment (nor did it lead to inflation). This was one reason why recovery from the Great Recession was so weak.

Political conservatives and many pro-market economists predicted that the Fed's wall of money would lead to inflation.[66] It did not. With returns on short-term Treasury bills nearly zero, the banks were nervously hoarding cash instead of lending or investing. But such low interest rates also meant the federal government could borrow in its own currency nearly for free. Meanwhile, while the worst of the panic had subsided, the banking system remained dependent on the life supports of the Fed's various lending and asset purchase programs.

In hindsight, GDP growth in the final quarter of 2008 was an annualized negative 8.2 percent. At the time, however, government statisticians

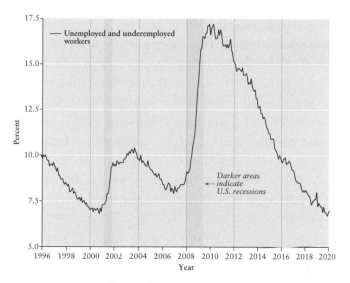

TOTAL UNEMPLOYMENT

In the series of Age of Chaos "jobless recoveries," the Great Recession was
the worst (up to that point). In time, after 2008 another asset-led
macroeconomic recovery tightened job markets during the 2010s.

estimated only a negative 4 percent decline, so Obama's team did not
know how bad the situation actually was.[67] In early 2009, Romer's CEA
macroeconomic calculation called for a stimulus of $1.8 trillion to close
the "output gap" and prevent mass unemployment. Summers decided
that anything above $1 trillion was politically impossible, due to Repub-
lican critics of big government and Democrats far more fiscally hawkish
than Obama. Still, given the cheap financing available, deficit-financed
fiscal stimulus had many potentially productive outlets. Given the collapse
of spending of all kinds, the economy was demand-constrained, so virtually any kind of public spending would have had multiplying effects—the
fiscal multiplier. But should one want to emphasize the supply side, to get
a bigger bang for the buck, many productive opportunities for spending
cried out: to repair public infrastructure on dilapidated roads and bridges,
to lay the foundations of a "green" energy grid, to invest in productivity-
enhancing technology, or to support early childhood education to reverse
the drastic effects of education gaps in the future labor market, to name
some obvious candidates. Obama had come into office demanding some
kind of symbolic "moonshot" from his economic policy team.

Public investment requires at a minimum two things—a compelling concept of a public interest and state capacity to achieve developmental ends. In 2009 neither existed. Had either ever? In U.S. history, large-scale public investment had enjoyed political legitimacy only in times of war—not even during the Great Depression. The last time public investment had been on the table was in the immediate aftermath of World War II, but the postwar hinge in political economy had soon shut the door on it. The Great Recession reopened the question, but the answer would still be the same. In times of peace, in the United States the owners of capital have maintained the prerogative to decide where, when, and in what to invest. Peacetime American democratic politics have always worked within this hard constraint—so far.

That does not mean that the $800 billion American Recovery and Reinvestment Act, passed in February 2009, if barely, was inconsiderable. It was the largest fiscal stimulus in American history. The act included $350 billion in tax cuts, which meant that even if it was spent rather than saved—and the well-off do not typically spend the full percentage of a tax break—nearly half the stimulus increased spending only in existing channels.[68] Another $145 billion went to fiscally strapped states—stopping the gap, not reworking the foundations—where spending and employment still on average retrenched.[69] What was left of the stimulus did fund a number of "shovel-ready" infrastructure projects and targeted government research programs.[70] The Obama administration hoped it would right the macroeconomy by the end of 2009 and, with high political stakes, promised that it would.

The passage of the stimulus coincided with the rise of the Tea Party. On February 19, 2009, CNBC's Rick Santelli ranted from the floor of the Chicago Board of Trade against possible government programs to forgive mortgage debt for "losers."[71] Santelli called for a new "tea party," and a genuine democratic social movement was born—although Republican donors and party officials appropriated it, and the entertainment television news channel Fox News fueled it.[72] Tea Party members were on average conservative, white, old, and relatively well-off citizens who feared the federal government. The Great Recession had taken a giant cut into the wealth of this demographic. Many of its members continued to work instead of retire, resentfully. Others, if they could not find employment, prematurely drew Social Security.[73] Tea Partiers said the stimulus had given away money to "freeloaders" and thus sacrificed "entitlements" of their own that they had "earned" through a lifetime of work. Freeloaders included especially young people, welfare recipients, and illegal immigrants.[74] True, the Supplemental Nutrition Assistance Program (Food Stamps), especially for children, expanded by 18 percent during the Great Recession.[75] Other claims were factually questionable at best. Santelli's fear of a massive government-funded mortgage-loan-forgiveness program (which would have helped, since the debt overhang depressed consumer spending) never came even close to materializing.[76] Actually, the young fared even worse than the elderly in the Great Recession labor market.[77] Welfare spending during the Great Recession under the Clinton-era Temporary Assistance for Needy Families (TANF) declined and was no more than 1 percent of the federal budget anyway.[78] Finally, after an early-to-mid-2000s increase, by 2009 illegal immigration from Mexico, on net, was negative.[79]

Regardless of the facts, the Tea Party, in common with many populist movements of the American past, was bound together by an emotional logic. "I want my country back," the feeling went. Tellingly, Fox News trafficked rumors that the stimulus proposal to research a "smart" electric grid was a ruse for government officials to manipulate citizens' thermostats, which some viewers believed, because they fundamentally did not trust the federal government to act in their interests.[80] Decades of privatization meant that many citizens no longer interacted with the government when exercising their rights as citizens—they interacted with nonprofit and for-profit "service providers."[81] Thus the statement "Keep your government hands off my Medicare!" actually made some degree of sense.[82] As a matter of fact, the fall 2008 bank bailouts and the Fed's "unconventional" policies had acted directly in Wall Street's interest, but had it acted in theirs? If so, it was only indirectly, by offering free loans to bankers, who then rarely turned around and loaned to them. Why the stimulus would be any different was a reasonable question for citizens to ask.

Meanwhile the personal figure of Obama loomed large. He was black, which conjured for many white Americans false racist myths of black welfare dependency. He was an Ivy League graduate, which evoked for many the snobbish well-educated coastal elite that benefited the most from the Great Moderation and had suffered the least during the Great Recession. By raising taxes, he advocated greater government redistribution, so he might also represent some warped notion of "socialism." Obama's father was born in another country, and immigrants were the main focus of Tea Partiers' ire. Some even suspected Obama was Muslim and not born in the United States, that he was an illegitimate president. The reality television celebrity Donald Trump entered politics fanning the false flames of this "birther movement" and quickly mastered the insidious brand of political rhetoric. "Our current president came out of nowhere. Came out of nowhere," Trump insisted. "In fact, I'll go a step further: the people that went to school with him, they never saw him, they don't know who he is. It's crazy."[83] When Trump later became president, to a number of his opponents Trump became the impossible outsider, the illegitimate president sent from a foreign agent, in this case Russia. Obama was not born in Kenya. In 2016 the Russian state did favor Trump, who welcomed the favor. But legitimate state action in a democracy is difficult when so many citizens believe that their political opponent could not possibly be a member of the same polity as themselves.

Meanwhile, for all the venom directed at Obama, for all the unpopularity of the bailouts and the stimulus, the absence of political mobilization outside Washington against the banks—after what they had done to the economy and what the government had done for them—was remarkable. "Who owns residential credit risk?" asked two Lehman analysts in September 2007.[84] In the end, while the Fed and Treasury subsidized the banks' recovery, that risk was passed down to 10 million foreclosed homeowners—4.6 percent of all homeowners. In the end, they, not their creditors, bore the downside risk. Undoubtedly, many distressed homeowners would have loved access to zero-interest loans from the Fed.[85] Very few bankers were prosecuted, and fewer convicted.[86] For its part, the left mostly basked in Obama's extraordinary electoral accomplishment. (Occupy Wall Street would not emerge until September 2011.) In general, survey opinions about citizen's ideological beliefs on economic policy matters barely budged.[87] Those who economically suffered the most never rounded into a political movement. It was not clear where or how to exert popular pressure on the capitalism of asset price appreciation. The millions of foreclosed, otherwise demographically ordinary Americans became renters, often moving down the street. They could not find one another, let alone politically organize, and perhaps, marked with shame, they did not want anyone to find them anyway.[88] At least, they did not resort to the new connectivity of social media to organize. Tea Party meetups were at first rather traditional, face-to-face affairs. The Obama political team's attempts to translate electoral euphoria into an online social movement fizzled. Not until Trump would social media be effectively politically weaponized.

In American culture, the economic downturn barely registered.[89] There was no parallel to the 1930s "cultural front." No great novel was written about the Great Recession.[90] There was at least one great film, *Margin Call* (2011), but it made precisely this point: nearly every scene was shot inside a fictional Wall Street investment bank's skyscraper, fully encasing all the action, with little visible relation to the outside world.

Ironically enough, many large banks—including Citigroup and Bank of America—remained dependent on public funds for their continued survival. In March 2009 the Fed announced the Term Asset-Backed Securities Loan Facility (TALF). The Fed, already with $1.75 trillion in U.S. Treasury debt, bank debt, and mortgage-backed securities on its balance sheet, would have to subsidize the return of debt securitization, including mortgage-related assets.[91] Bernanke went on television and spoke of recovery as "green shoots."[92]

Popular outrage was expressed only in momentary flickers. In March 2009, as Tea Party meetups gathered locally across the country, AIG announced—despite a $61.7 billion loss for the fourth quarter, the largest on record ever, for any company—that it would still pay $28 million in bonuses that it had contracted prior to its government bailout. Geithner's New York Fed signed off, saying contracts were sacrosanct—recalling the political debate, long ago, between Alexander Hamilton (who would have agreed) and James Madison. Obama called thirteen leading bankers to the White House. "My administration," he scolded, "is the only thing between you and the pitchforks." But Obama demanded only that banks voluntarily limit compensation, for now. That was all. Congress stepped in and passed a 90 percent tax on bonuses issued by banks with TARP funds.[93]

At this time, the Obama administration was conducting its most important deliberations over what to do with the banks. The debate was whether banks suffered from illiquidity (meaning that they had no willing buyers for assets, which would likely be of great value, should market trading and prices return) or insolvency (meaning that when trading came back, they would likely prove to be bankrupt). Summers led the insolvency faction, pleading for the nationalization of Citigroup at a minimum. In some accounts, Obama approved Citigroup's nationalization, indicating his desire for a broader reconstruction of the financial system. But his political aides feared the fiscal cost. Geithner, of the illiquidity faction, kept pressing: How exactly would this reconstruction be carried out? What was the plan? What if the nationalization of Citigroup induced another round of panic?

Geithner won, and his plan moved forward. The Treasury Department used the remaining TARP money to subsidize private investment in mortgage-related assets, in the Public-Private Investment Program. Treasury announced a trial of "stress tests" to determine, in the event of further financial stresses, whether the banks still needed to raise more capital to ensure their continued solvency. In 2007 and 2008, the Fed became the primary dealer in money markets, stepping in for the banks to keep the system alive; in 2009, through the stress tests, Treasury temporarily replaced the private ratings agencies such as Moody's and Fitch's. This was a simulation of how the capitalism of asset appreciation was supposed to work, with government playing the part of a private actor. Government would stamp the banks solvent and thus restore confidence in capital markets back to what it had been before the Panic of 2007–8. Geithner had come of age at Treasury's international desk during the 1990s, and to him the Panic of 2007–8, while grander, was little different from the Mexican currency crisis of 1994 or the Asian financial crisis of 1997–98. Restore confidence, restore capital markets, honor all private contracts, and presto—behold Humpty-Dumpty put back together.[94] In May 2009, Geithner announced the results of the stress tests, which were an inexact science to say the least. Treasury demanded that banks raise $75 billion in additional private capital. But the banks received friendly government loans, with few strings attached. Government did not take voting ownership stakes, through which it might have compelled a fundamental change in the relationship between the financial system and the economy.

Whether it was the stress tests or something else—perhaps the government's forced recapitalization of the banks, perhaps finally a waning of fear in the markets—the fog of disquietude began to lift. Transactional liquidity among banks began to return. By June 2009, nearly all credit spreads had returned to pre-crisis levels. Most of the banks had begun to redeem TARP funds from the government. The federal government would actually profit from the program. The nearly two-year financial crisis was over. That same month, in GDP terms, the recession ended. Remarkably enough, the Obama administration had skillfully cobbled the financial system back together.

In technical GDP terms, the next macroeconomic expansion began. But few who stopped to look around were ready to declare that the Great Recession was over. Restoring transactional liquidity to the financial system might have ended the crisis, but it did nothing whatsoever to reshape the character of economic life. Many of the troublesome trends of the Age of Chaos persisted. If rates of productive investment declined, the Fed's provisions to restore transactional liquidity in money and credit markets aided the reflation of asset prices in 2010—years before average labor incomes began to climb again. Profits recovered first and quickly reached high levels. Thus, the incomes and the wealth positions of the best-off were restored first.[95] The pattern of the recovery aggravated economic inequality.[96] That household debt radically declined after 2008 indicates how much expansions had become dependent on consumer debt, and why recovery in this instance was so weak. Meanwhile many worrisome trends that had first appeared in the early twenty-first-century persisted. Geographical disparities in economic life outcomes worsened.[97] The waning of market competition and the rise of corporate monopoly and monopsony power continued to exacerbate.[98] Finally, the frequency of "deaths of despair" from alcoholism, drug overdose, and suicide in regions where the labor market was most ravaged only became worse.[99]

In particular, the post-2008 labor market was in abysmal shape. It was another jobless recovery, especially in those regions and places passed over by the new economy. The number of long-term unemployed increased.[100] Notably, the historic ascent of the percentage of women engaged in the remunerative labor force halted. Much worse were the Great Recession's effects on men—it was called a "mancession." Perhaps the best fictional account of economic life in the Great Recession was *Magic Mike* (2012), set in Florida, ground zero of the housing crisis. A housing construction worker (construction being a booming sector of male employment, as male manufacturing collapsed), played by Channing Tatum, is laid off and has to do the women's work of exotic dancing. His female love interest, a nurse—that is, a member of an expanding service employment category—is the breadwinner. That was film. In reality, after 2008 male applications for disability insurance soared.[101]

What held back the recovery, and especially employment? Some companies took advantage of the recession by firing their least productive workers and not hiring new ones, while automation proceeded—as in the Great Depression. No doubt, the labor supply suffered from structural deficiencies, including many inadequately educated and trained workers. Still, as in the Great Depression, the bigger problem was an immediate demand constraint. Spending, whether for investment or for consumption, was simply insufficient to bring about employment-giving enterprise. When many corporations made profits, rather than invest in new capacity, they distributed the profits as dividends, bought back their shares to increase their values, or simply sat on giant piles of hoarded cash. Given their access to nearly free short-term funding, banks returned to profitability by way of various new carrying trades, including in U.S. Treasury bills. Often, instead of investing or lending, they hoarded cash, too. Seamlessly switching from speculation to precaution, the television channel A&E replaced *Flip This House* with *Hoarders* (2009–), a show about how hoarding pathology afflicted middle-to-lower-class homeowners, to the point of threatening the loss of their home, in a barely veiled symbol of foreclosure. As the housing bust pushed risk down from the banks to homeowners, *Hoarders* displaced an aggregate macroeconomic pathology onto individual family dramas.

In fairness, the Obama administration counted hard-won political achievements. The chief policy priority of the president was health care reform, and his administration invested all its political capital in it, shelving any possibility of, say, labor law reform or a "green energy" bill. A significant health insurance reform bill did emerge, which included an expansion of Medicaid and a "mandate" to tax citizens who did not purchase health insurance to expand the risk pool and increase coverage. To fund it, the bill also included an increase in redistributive taxes, as Obama had promised on the campaign trail.[102] But in a political sign of what was to come, the Tea Party–backed Republican candidate Scott Brown won a special election in January 2010 to replace deceased Massachusetts Democratic senator Edward Kennedy, and the bill hung in the balance. The Democrats had to push the law through with no Republican votes.[103]

In addition to the Patient Protection and Affordable Care Act of 2010, which gave rise to what became known as "Obamacare," Congress passed the Dodd-Frank Wall Street Reform and Consumer Protection Act of 2010—first pushed by the White House's political arm in the wake of the AIG bonus scandals. Dodd-Frank worked in important ways around the edges. It granted the Fed new regulatory powers to oversee "systemic risk" and to more orderly resolve failed financial institutions, even as it curtailed the Fed's freewheeling mandate to act under Section 13(3) in the future. Ratings agencies fell under more stringent regulation. Popular backlash against the banks helped pass the so-called Volcker rule, which prohibited banks from using government-insured bank deposits to engage in "proprietary trading" on their own accounts. That, and new regulations that forced banks to decrease leverage, cut into trading profits—especially among investment banks. However, the legislation would be open to administrative interpretation and discretion. The new Consumer Financial Protection Bureau was placed under the regulatory umbrella of the Fed. The consequences of Dodd-Frank would be left to regulators, continuing the now-decades-long trend in which Congress devolved economic regulation to administrative agencies—above all, the Treasury Department and the Fed.[104]

With Dodd-Frank signed into law in July 2010, the Obama administration was largely politically spent. Undoubtedly, without the 2009 stimulus, the Great Recession would have been worse economically.[105] Politically, the stimulus was nonetheless a great failure. In the aggregate, it was simply not enough to close the gap in demand. At the same time, if only because of its reliance on tax cuts—given the dearth of public investment plans, and the lack of political will or capacity to carry them out anyway—the stimulus lacked the facility to push economic life in any particular, better direction. Republicans reaped great political benefits from these shortcomings.

In this context, the Fed embarked on a new venture. Bernanke, reappointed by Obama in 2010, convinced members of the policy-making Federal Open Market Committee to again double the Fed's balance sheet. The demand for safe assets among owners of wealth was insatiable. The Fed had lost control of the long-term interest rate before the crisis, when raising short-term interest rates in 2004 did nothing to raise long-term rates. Now, with short-term rates at zero, long-term rates remained stuck high. So in another unconventional monetary policy, the Fed purchased billions of dollars of long-term bonds, mostly U.S. Treasury bills and U.S. mortgage bonds, hoping to bring down long-term rates. The goal of lowering the pecuniary return for parking cash on the sidelines was to induce greater immediate private investment and spending. The strange name for this policy was "quantitative easing."[106] In November 2010, to try to bring down long-term rates, the Fed announced it would purchase $600 billion

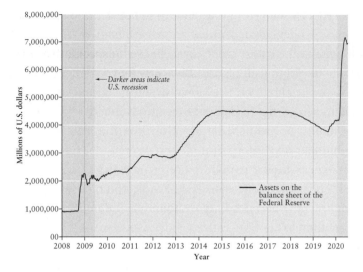

FED BALANCE SHEET

In the new "unconventional" monetary policy of quantitative easing,
the Fed expanded its balance sheet by purchasing long-term bonds, hoping
it would bring down interest rates and thereby induce private spending,
especially on investment. The policy worked, but through the channel
of more asset price appreciation.

in Treasuries through mid-2011. Critics kept promising runaway inflation, which did not occur, even as, by 2014, the Fed's balance sheet was at
$4.5 trillion, vastly dwarfing the 2009 stimulus. The Fed had seized the
reins of macroeconomic stimulus. Monetary policy kept winning out—
another continuity during the Great Recession.

In the arena of fiscal policy, in 2010 a global movement for austerity
tempted the Obama administration. On February 6, a G7 summit held in
Canada announced countries' joint intention to "move to a more sustainable fiscal track."[107] That year austerity's advocates were many. Moralizers
decried debt of all kinds and counseled saving and suffering. Conservatives
noticed bulging government deficits and debt loads and saw an opportunity to advocate slashing social expenditures. Bankers feared inflation,
which might cut into the profits made from their cheap money carrying
trades, including in public debt. Some said the problem was not overcau-
tious capitalists but government's failure to create hospitable enough
environments in which capitalists might choose to invest—recalling the
"capital strike" of the 1937–38 recession within the Great Depression.
However, the best-off were literally reaping all income gains from the still-

young macroeconomic recovery. What else could the owners of capital want?

Moral revulsion against the character of the speculative investment boom of the 2000s is well placed. But profligacy in one period does not necessitate compensatory austerity in the next. Bad investments simply demand better investments. Anything worth doing that can be done can be financed. The Fed experimented with quantitative easing because—despite profitable opportunities and urgent necessities abounding—the private owners of capital would not do it. An administrative agency, the Fed, which prided itself on "independence," standing outside democratic politics by its very design, could attempt to induce private investment only indirectly. Quantitative easing could depress long-term interest rates and assist the reflation of asset values, fueling inequality, but it did very little to reshape the kind of economic investments made. There was no democratic politics of capital investment, inspired by a shared long-term vision of the future, adequate to the challenge at hand.

By the close of 2010, economic sluggishness weighed down the Obama administration. The publicity attempt to brand a "recovery summer" failed. Geithner published one of the more tone-deaf statements in American political history, an op-ed in *The New York Times* titled "Welcome to the Recovery," announcing that the macroeconomy had turned a corner for all (it had not) and that it was time to turn to austerity.[108] In the fall, Tea Party activists, incensed by the passage of Obamacare, helped carry the Republicans to resounding victories in the congressional midterm elections. Tellingly, in states hardest hit by the Great Recession, such as Florida, Ohio, Michigan, and Nevada, Republicans swept into power. It was undoubtedly a resounding rejection of the Democrats' handling of the Great Recession, as well as the Democratic Party's decades-long contributions to the creation of an economy whose restoration was, so far, mostly benefiting elites. In December 2010, Citigroup, having returned to profitability, was the last of the major banks to pay back its TARP funds, thereby freeing itself to pay larger bonuses.[109]

When Obama lost the midterms, he decided to negotiate austerity measures with Republican House leaders. Austerity did not work in the 1930s, when it had brought liberal democracy under great strain, and it would not work in the 2010s either. The Great Recession groaned on.

AFTERWORD

—

I TURNED IN THE FINAL MANUSCRIPT OF THIS BOOK IN THE FIRST week of March 2020, when the possibility of the global COVID-19 pandemic was first dawning. Now months later, after a deep economic dive, and with unemployment numbers not seen since the Great Depression, I write this afterword during the outbreak of a national uprising after the murder of George Floyd. A moment like this one—marked by spasms of anxiety and anger, but also determination and hope—is a risky one from which to perceive the future course of events. But I cannot help but wonder, will it mark a break in time and the beginning of a new age of American capitalism?

It is impossible to know. Historians have no special advantage in predicting the future. But knowledge of the past does make it possible to assess which moments are more or less ripe with potential for change. These times are an excellent candidate.

Paradoxically, if a new age does soon issue forth, one reason why will be the many continuities that have marked economic life since the Great Recession—which then looked like it might be a significant historical rupture, but in the end was not. The Age of Chaos continued. The change to come will be more consequential if only because for a long time not all that much has changed.

Nonetheless, we can glimpse latent possibilities that have appeared in the last decade, as particular trends have become more pronounced, clarifying the stakes of the transformation that surely will happen someday. No age of anything lasts forever.

In this afterword, I want to briefly examine the characteristics of the post–Great Recession economic expansion before COVID-19 hit. They look a lot like those of every single one since the opening of the Age of Chaos in

1980. Given that, I conclude with some reflections about the relevance of history to capitalism—an economic system defined by its dependence upon future expectations—during a time such as this, when conventional beliefs about the likely course of events have been thrown into so much doubt.

1. The Great Repetition

Much like all expansions since the 1980s, the post-2008 economic expansion that ended in 2020 was asset-led. The political economy of asset price appreciation, put back together by the Obama administration, held. During the 2010s, many of the same patterns repeated, even if some did so differently in their details.

In another of the age's jobless recoveries, after 2008 the owners of capital watched their liquid assets appreciate first—before the recovery of ordinary labor incomes. This time, the asset class was not homes, but largely corporate equities, much like during the 1990s. Conforming to the post-1980 trend, the rally was supported by the extension of debt. Not household debt—households deleveraged after 2008, one reason why weak household spending and demand for goods hobbled recovery. Public debt as a percentage of GDP rose until 2014, before stabilizing until 2020. But after 2014 a massive extension of corporate debt took place. Through the mechanism of company stock buybacks, the debt directly contributed to the surge in stock prices. New corporate loans included securitized "leveraged loans," a lot like mortgage-backed securities in their synthetic construction.

An important cause of the surge in debt was that the price of credit remained low for those with access to it. The Federal Reserve, hoping to stoke recovery, engaged in multiple rounds of quantitative easing through 2012, and kept interest rates on credit low. This is perhaps the most important Age of Chaos continuity: the Fed, an administrative agency outside democratic politics by design, is the most powerful economic policy-making institution.

When in March 2020 financial markets collapsed after the outbreak of COVID-19, the Fed, like in 2008, came to the rescue, cutting new paths in the arena of post-2008 "unconventional" and "accommodative" monetary policy. In fact, the Great Recession already appears to have only been a dress rehearsal for 2020. In March 2020, immediately the Fed stepped in to prop up asset prices, including supporting the troubled corporate debt market, something it did not do in 2008, because the corporate debt market was not then so distressed, but also because officials believed that to do so would have been a dangerous public encroachment upon private markets. This river has now been crossed.

The wall of money the Fed has thrown at the economy only moves dollars into existing economic channels. Therefore, monetary policy does not transform the economic system. A liquidity preference among the owners of capital that oscillates between speculation and precaution remains strong. Capital remains flighty and fickle, and the Fed backstops its whims. If confidence ever falters, the central bank bails out asset owners, and brings back the same game.

Thus, many pre-2008 trends carried over into the 2010s. Investment and productivity growth remained weak. Infrastructure dilapidated. A fossil fuel–based energy system persisted—entrenched further by a 2010s domestic oil fracking boom, capitalized by the decade's cheap credit. Large corporations, especially the great technology companies, accumulated more market power and profits. The greatest departure from 2008 arguably occurred in finance, with the rise over the decade of the great asset managers. Led by BlackRock, among others, they have threatened to surpass even the great banks, whose scope for wheeling and dealing, and profits, suffered from post-2008 financial regulations. Meanwhile as asset prices recovered first, delivering gains to their owners, economic inequality continued its upward march until 2014. Although, during this decade inequality finally became a matter of public debate and concern. Job creation focused in the high-paying and low-paying services, still exhibiting pronounced geographical disparities, as well as disparities concerning educational attainment. White male "deaths of despair" continued, while the most historically disadvantaged groups, as always, continued to fare the worst.

In 2008 capitalism nearly collapsed, but it did not. Instead, the same economy was brought back to life. The elites who benefited from the recovery most were the quickest to declare success. True, the United States, relative to other national economies, has much to boast about. It has a dynamic entrepreneurial culture; a labor market of great diversity that attracts talent from all parts of the globe; some of the world's leading universities, in a time when education matters so much economically; world leadership in technology; the exorbitant privilege of the dollar, still the world currency of transaction and reserve; a labor market capable of generating many new jobs, especially in the services; the glimmers of a potential manufacturing revival; and, finally, a large pool of young, disadvantaged peoples whose untapped talents may yet translate into future economic development. But in the Age of Chaos, economic benefits have flowed, largely, only to the best-off—and increasingly to the largest firms.

After 2008, as has been the case with every recovery during this age, eventually the expansion began to tighten labor markets, and income gains occurred at the middle to the bottom of the distribution, in this instance beginning in 2014. At this point, the expansion was led by a rising share of personal consumption in GDP, in another continuity: the enduring significance of the American consumer for the global economy. Further, as these expansions hinge on the maintenance of the credit cycle and the confidence of the owners of capital, which the Fed ensures, they have, historically, been long expansions. The 2010s expansion was the longest on record in the U.S. The problem is that no matter how long, the briefest of downturns wipe out much of the gains from the expansion. That is how meager the gains have been for most people, despite the business cycle's elongation. The collapse of March 2020 took many households right back to where they were in 2008.

In sum, to say that the 2010s American economy was roaring—maximizing its potential, distributing its deserts justly—is to engage in nothing short of "truthful hyperbole," as Donald Trump memorably branded his business strategy in 1987's *The Art of the Deal*. It is something that plays "to people's fantasies." "People want to believe that something is the biggest and the greatest and the most spectacular."[1]

It is too early to say what the historical significance of the presidency of Donald Trump will be. No one factor, including economic anxiety, was clearly responsible for his victory. But it is not too early to take the measure of the significance of the fact that Trump, and his style of politics, could even have come *close* to winning the American presidency.

In American public discourse, there was never an honest discussion about the benefits and the costs of the capitalism sewn back together in 2008, and the economic suffering many ordinary people endured to achieve it, only to benefit from it last and least. Leaders dodged those facts. That Trump went further, often making up facts when speaking about economic issues—including his signature issue, trade—must be placed in this context. The stories the financial and political elite told about the economic recovery over the 2010s did not ring true. The political and economic establishment's characterizations of the post-2008 economic recovery was post-truth politics before Trump.

To this file, one can add Obama's outgoing quip about Trump's appeal to such a large part of the American electorate: "I've got the economy set up well for him. No facts. No consequences. They can just have a cartoon."[2] But the Fed was at the wheel over Obama's presidency, struggling to return to "conventional" monetary policy, when it would wind down quantitative easing by selling off the assets it had acquired since 2008, to then merely focus on targeting a "neutral" interest rate that would enable the economy to smoothly function of its own accord. It did not make it. The Fed never emerged from Great Recession recovery mode before the economic collapse precipitated by the outbreak of COVID-19 in March 2020—when the unconventional policies inaugurated in 2008 were put on steroids. That the economic downturn, unlike 2008, was initiated by a pandemic and not a financial panic does not change the fact that the economy, being so vulnerable, required the Fed's outsized supports.

The numbers tell the story. Having purchased $4.5 trillion of assets through quantitative easing by 2014, the Fed only trimmed that number to $3.75 billion in 2019. By the end of May 2020, the number topped $7 trillion (and is still climbing as I write). Meanwhile the Fed raised its short-term interest rate target from 0.12 percent near the end of 2015 to 2.4 percent in March 2020. By April 2020, it was down to 0.05 percent. That final number indicates the technical conditions of an economy that is in a "liquidity trap," in which fear and the desire for safety are so strong that many will not part with money and money-like assets, even if the rate of return on hoarding them is next to nothing.

In fact, the American economy has been stuck in a liquidity trap of a broader kind, and for decades now. The Great Moderation, as Ben Bernanke branded the era in 2004, turns out to be a Great Repetition. For we are trapped in a recurring economic pattern dependent upon converting leveraged asset price appreciation into fresh incomes, a process not dependent in the first instance upon rising labor incomes, but upon the credit cycle and the magic of the market—beliefs and confidence among the owners of capital that there will always be liquidity in capital markets. What is now abundantly clear is that that liquidity is a product of state power, lodged inside the U.S. central bank. The situation resembles a confidence game, in which American government authority strains to make economic fictions reality.

This is not a capitalism that works in the interests of a large part of the American citizenry, who do not rely on appreciating assets for their incomes. To the extent that Trump's victory was driven by economics, it was not so much the Great Recession that was responsible. It was the nature of the recovery. Since 2008, the same old asset-led capitalism slowly but steadily wore down the political establishment's reserves of legitimacy. When Donald Trump said, cynically to be sure, that the game is rigged, and that ruling elites were not themselves capable of reforming existing institutions, many believed him because their experience told them as much.

In spite of Trump's pronouncements about a rigged system, between 2016 and 2020 the Trump administration did little to alter the direction of the economy. Its legislative centerpiece, the Reagan-style tax cut of 2017, failed to increase investment and growth, as promised, and increased budget deficits. A trade war was more about bluster, although bluster of rhetorical significance. "Build that wall!" "Lock her up!" Targeting immigrants and women, Trump's 2016 campaign rallying cries meant something very specific. But they also expressed the general tenor of the moment. The values of the Age of Chaos—flow, fluidity, risk, individual choice, the blurring of boundaries, the collapse of walls, globalization—have been losing their luster. Since 2008, in many respects economic life has begun to harden. Elites hoard wealth and privilege, living in different social networks, inhabiting different cultural worlds, and enjoying higher life expectancies. Because of inequality, there was a version of social distancing before COVID-19. Meanwhile national affiliation has proven to be a more durable identity than prophets of cosmopolitan globalization once proclaimed. Nor, despite what many of these same commentators claimed, did institutional power evaporate into the networked global ether. It exists, residing in the hands of the nation-state and of large corporations, especially technology corporations—and above all, the Fed.

One bet seems safe. Politics stands to assert more authority over economics. But an authority wielded by whom, on what basis, and toward what ends? Giant technology corporations, promising greater ease of life? Authoritarian states, sustained by a politics of anxiety, recrimination, and fear? Reconstituted democratic publics? Institutions of global cooperation and governance? All of this remains to be seen, but the answers to these questions are likely to constitute the defining qualities of a new age. It is possible, unfortunately, that the next age of capitalism will be something far worse.

In American history, what has always brought about new ages of capitalism—whether it was the British Empire's commercial colonization of North America, the rise of the Republican Party and Civil War, the election of FDR and the coming of the New Deal, or the Volcker Shock and the presidency of Ronald Reagan—has been state action. In the Age of Chaos, vast sums of capital and credit have rushed around the world in digitized bits every millisecond. Capital moves fast, but politics, in turn, have remained always at least one step behind, chasing events. State action lags; it is responsive, not generative. The vexed American history of state action and its impact on capital has had many chapters in this book. Likely, another will soon have to be written. Projected federal spending in 2020 is 25 percent of GDP—a figure not seen since World War II, when public investment lifted the U.S. economy out of the Great Depression.

The New Deal state that emerged from the Great Depression and World War II shifted income generation, in distributive terms, away from the owners of capital to labor. Largely, it did so through income politics, the central aim of American political economy for over a century now. But the capitalism of the Age of Chaos has not been controlled through such means; given the fickle character of capital in this era it likely cannot be. The key is to transform the structure of investment. For that, income politics, which redistribute the spoils of capital at the end of the economic process, cannot do the trick. Nor can cheap money and credit. A democratic politics of capital is called for. In order to repair the broken link between capitalism and democracy, what politics must do is get out in front of capital at the beginning of the economic process, in order to reshape its end.

Keynes wrote in a 1933 essay, "National Self-Sufficiency," that "decadent international but individualistic capitalism . . . is not a success. . . . But when we wonder what to put in its place, we are extremely perplexed."[3] Keynes himself fell back on the idea that any investment was better than no investment—in our day, this is the veiled social philosophy of the Fed's quantitative easing, which induces investment into already existing channels. How could Keynes's perplexment still ring so true so long after he wrote? Is there not another economic future worth investing in?

2. Reckoning

Throughout this book, I have emphasized that American capitalism is an especially forward-looking economic system, in which expectations of the future play a prominent role in determining the present—whether it was seventeenth-century British rulers' fantasies of Atlantic empire, white Americans' dreams of racial domination and of conquering the continent, the innovations of industrial revolutionaries, mass expectations of abundance and employment after World War II, Silicon Valley techno-utopians, and on. But somehow after all of these centuries of evolution and change, the American economy has reached a point of repetition. By relying on the Fed to keep the music playing, we have turned the economy into a broken record.

Capitalism's future orientation is a complex issue. It grants the owners of capital, charged with the task of when and where to invest, power over others. But investment is a broad phenomenon. At stake is not only ledgers of profit and loss. Investment concerns to what end and on what terms a community as a whole decides to direct its energies, capacities, and aspirations. Ethically, capitalism's dependence upon projections of the future is its greatest *potential* virtue, as it urges us to imagine the possibility of a future that is qualitatively different from and better than the past—that includes post-capitalist futures. But none of this means that the past should be ignored. Nor can it be.

Not coincidentally, the United States, perhaps the most capitalist of all countries, has long been distinguished from other countries for its pronounced historical amnesia. In American capitalism, the urge to dispense with the past has led to many flights of economic fancy. Most recently, this happened with the new economy of the 1990s, when it was believed by many powerful figures that the U.S. economy had somehow moved "beyond history." End-of-millennium faith in a finance-led vision of globalization, which persisted, incredibly enough, after the panic of 2008 and over the Obama years, may have been consigned to the dustbin of history by Trump's 2016 election and then COVID-19. But we still live in the aftermath of that project. Recall that following the single most important event in U.S. history—the Civil War—instead of reckoning with the crime of black slavery, it became a good time to own railroad stocks. We still live in the aftermath of that project, too, and others as well. The past simply cannot be swept under by capitalist fantasy. Misplaced nostalgia for bygone eras will not do either. However uncomfortably, history must be faced.

One reason why is that history unreckoned only sustains repetition. What would it mean for American economic life to break free from the patterns of the Age of Chaos, and to capitalize and chart a different and better economic future? The question demands economic imagination. It calls for moral and political courage. And it cannot be answered without reckoning with the history I have attempted to tell in these pages.

—Jonathan Levy, June 14, 2020

ACKNOWLEDGMENTS

═══

S EAN WILENTZ CAME UP WITH THE IDEA FOR THIS BOOK during a casual lunch conversation in the spring of 2012, and I thank him for the suggestion. I took the leap after encouragement from Tom Holt and Amy Stanley, my former PhD advisers, both of whom thankfully have continued to offer their counsel and support over the past years.

To begin the project, the Department of History at Princeton University provided a year of research leave from teaching in 2012–13. I was fortunate to spend that year at the Center for Advanced Study in the Behavioral Sciences at Stanford University. The book finally came together in 2017 during a visit at the École des hautes études en sciences sociales in Paris, thanks to the invitation of Nicolas Barreyre. The Department of History at the University of Chicago provided another year of research leave in 2017–18, and this time I was fortunate to spend it at the Center for History and Economics at Harvard University, thanks to its co-directors Sunil Amrith and Emma Rothschild. I finished a complete draft of the manuscript during the summer of 2018 as a visitor at the Scuola Normale Superiore, thanks to Donatella della Porta and Mario Pianta. The final corrections of the proofs would not have been possible without the gracious hospitality of Duccio Cordelli and his family in Bologna.

This book grew out of an undergraduate course I taught first at Princeton and later at Chicago. Students' reactions greatly assisted the development of the book. I also want to express my gratitude to those who have helped me teach the course, especially Matt Backes, who first came up with the idea of "Ages," and Caley Horan. Thanks also to Ben Schmidt, Sean Vanatta, Andrew Edwards, Jonathan Quann, Chris Florio, Rosina Lozano, Matt Karp, and Margot Canaday at Princeton, and Robert Kaminski, Trish Kahle, Julia Dufosse, and Evelyn Atkinson at Chicago. In the final stages, I assigned a number of draft chapters to a combined under-graduate and graduate student course I taught at Chicago on global economic history from the Great Depression through the Great Recession. I thank the members of that class for their criticisms and feedback.

A number of individuals generously offered trenchant readings of the manuscript. I thank John Clegg, Chiara Cordelli, Katrina Forrester, Eric Hilt, Matt Karp, Thomas Kleven, Alison Lefkovitz, Jennifer Ratner-Rosenhagen, Sean Vanatta, Wendy Warren, and Gavin Wright for their feedback.

This book has benefited from interactions with too many people, and from presentations at too many university workshops and seminars, to attempt to name. But conversations with a number of individuals have in particular provided inspiration and reassurance, while also checking my worst tendencies, as much as they can be checked. Thanks to Aaron Benanav, James Campbell, Michel Feher, Kimberly Hoang, Naomi Lamoreaux, Marty Levy, James Livingston, Greg Kaplan, Sarah Milov, Gautham Rao, James Robinson, Emma Rothschild, Bill Sewell, Richard White, Tara Zahra, and Michael Zakim.

Joining the John U. Nef Committee on Social Thought at Chicago in 2019 and having the opportunity to discuss a number of the book's themes with Joel Isaac and Jonathan Lear provided the extra jolt that pushed it over the finish line. Thanks to a gift that Lois and Jerry Beznos made to the Committee, the inclusion of images, maps, and figures in the book was possible. I thank Anne Gamboa and Robert Pippin for their help and support in that process.

I have been aided by a number of excellent research assistants. I thank Sean Vanatta at the beginning and Nick Foster and Chris Hong at the end for going above and beyond the call of duty. I am also grateful to Solomon Dworkin, Raymond Hyser, Christian Payne, Lillian Weaver, and Tina Wei. Kat Edmiston and Ethan Hsi provided essential help with the final preparation of the manuscript.

During the writing process, many friends have provided crucial support. In particular, I want to thank Garrett Long.

I am grateful to Andrew Wylie and Jacqueline Ko at the Wylie Agency for their confidence in the book and for their efforts on behalf of it. At Random House, Molly Turpin took on the project and edited two long drafts with remarkable skill and insight. I thank her for the extraordinary amount of work she had to do to get this book in order, as well as for her unflagging enthusiasm for it. Likewise, Craig Adams at Random House expertly moved the book through production. I thank Janet Biehl, whose copyedits improved the final manuscript beyond measure.

Finally, what a joy it is to dedicate this book to Chiara Cordelli, and to recall the arrival of our daughter Giulia Levy-Cordelli at the time of its completion.

ILLUSTRATION CREDITS

═══

272: "The Great Strike—Blockade of Engines at Martinsburg, West Virginia" (1877), Library of Congress, Prints & Photographs Division, [LC-USZ62-125624]

281: Jacob Riis, *Knee-Pants at Forty-Five Cents a Dozen—A Ludlow Street Sweater's Shop* (1890), Jacob A. (Jacob August) Riis (1849–1914); Museum of the City of New York, 90.13.1.151

282: Théobald Chartran, *Portrait of Helen Clay Frick* (1905), Frick Art & Historical Center, Pittsburgh

283: John Singer Sargent, *Isabella Stewart Gardner* (1888), Isabella Stewart Gardner Museum, Boston

284: John Singer Sargent, *The Daughters of Edward Darley Boit* (1882), photograph © [2021] Museum of Fine Arts, Boston

285: Edward Steichen, *J. Pierpont Morgan, Esq.* (1903), image copyright © The Metropolitan Museum of Art; © 2020 The Estate of Edward Steichen/Artists Rights Society (ARS), New York: Art Resource, NY

336: "Magneto Assembly at the Ford Highland Park Plant" (1913), from the Collections of The Henry Ford

337: *Modern Times* (1936), Modern Times Copyright © Roy Export S.A.S.

345: "Ford Motor Company River Rouge Plant, Dearborn, Michigan" (1927), Library of Congress, Prints & Photographs Division, [LC-DIG-det-4a25915]

347: Katherine Dreier, "Machine-Age Exposition" (1927), Beinecke Rare Book and Manuscript Library, Yale University

348: Paul Outerbridge, Jr., *Marmon Crankshaft* (1923), Paul Outerbridge, Jr. © 2020 G. Ray Hawkins Gallery, Beverly Hills, CA; The Art Institute of Chicago/Art Resource, NY

349: Gerald Murphy, *Watch* (1925) © Estate of Honoria Murphy Donnelly/Licensed by VAGA at Artists Rights Society (ARS), NY; Gerald Murphy, *Watch,* 1925; oil on canvas; canvas dimensions: 78½ x 78⅞ in.; Dallas Museum of Art, Foundation for the Arts Collection, gift of the artist, 1963.75.FA

350: Charles Sheeler, *Criss-Crossed Conveyors, River Rouge Plant, Ford Motor Company* (1927), from the Collections of The Henry Ford

350: Charles Sheeler, *American Landscape* (1930), digital image © The Museum of Modern Art/ Licensed by SCALA/Art Resource, NY

367: "29th October 1929.: Workers flood the streets in a panic following the Black Tuesday stock market crash on Wall Street, New York City" (1929), photo by Hulton Archive/Getty Images

379: Edward Hopper, *Early Sunday Morning* (1930) © 2020 Heirs of Josephine N. Hopper/licensed by Artists Rights Society (ARS), NY; digital image © Whitney Museum of American Art/licensed by Scala/Art Resource, NY

380: John Steuart Curry, *Tornado Over Kansas* (1929), Hackley Picture Fund purchase, Muskegon Museum of Art, Muskegon, Michigan

421: Seymour Fogel, *Industrial Life (mural study, old Social Security Building, Washington, DC)* (1941) © 2020 Estate of Seymour Fogel/licensed by VAGA at Artists Rights Society (ARS), NY; Smithsonian American Art Museum; transfer from the General Services Administration

421: Walker Evans, *Alabama Tenant Farmer Wife (Allie Mae Burroughs)* (1936), The Metropolitan Museum of Art, Purchase, 2000 Benefit Fund, 2001 (2001.415); © Walker Evans Archive, The Metropolitan Museum of Art

423: James Kilpatrick, *Battle of the Overpass, Ford Motor Co., U.A.W.* (1937), Detroit Institute of Arts, USA; gift of *The Detroit News*/Photo: © Detroit Institute of Arts, USA/Bridgeman Images

444: "B-24 Liberator Assembly Line at Ford Willow Run Bomber Plant" (c. 1944), from the Collections of The Henry Ford

463: "WWII, Hiroshima, Aftermath of Atomic Bomb" (1945), USAF/Science Source

494: "1960s Family of Four Seen from Behind Standing in Front of New Suburban House Holding Hands" (1960), photo by Camerique/ClassicStock/Getty Images

495: Robert Adams, *Colorado Springs, CO* (1968) © Robert Adams, courtesy Fraenkel Gallery, San Francisco

498: Victor Gruen Associates, "An architectural model of Gruen's Northland Center" (1954), © Gruen Associates

499: "Interior view of Gruen's Northland Center" (1957), © Gruen Associates

500: Victor Gruen, "The Suburban Labyrinth" (1973), © Gruen Associates

501: Frank Gohlke, *Landscape, Los Angeles* (1974), Minneapolis Institute of Arts, MN, USA, Minneapolis Institute of Art/Gift of the Artist/Bridgeman Images

508: Andy Warhol, *100 Cans* (1962) © 2020 The Andy Warhol Foundation for the Visual Arts, Inc./licensed by Artists Rights Society (ARS), New York

508: Andy Warhol, *Eight Elvises* [Ferus Type] (1963) © 2020 The Andy Warhol Foundation for the Visual Arts, Inc./licensed by Artists Rights Society (ARS), New York

510: Ed Ruscha, *Hope* (1972) © Ed Ruscha, courtesy of the artist and Gagosian

511: "Think Small" (1959), © Volkswagen Aktiengesellschaft/Estate of Wingate Paine

515: Ed Ruscha, *Hope* (1998), Edward Ruscha, photo © Tate

528: Eero Saarinen, General Motors Technical Center, Warren, Michigan (c. 1946–56), Library of Congress, Prints & Photographs Division, Balthazar Korab Archive at the Library of Congress, [LC-DIG-krb-00107]

528: Eero Saarinen, Deere & Company Headquarters, Moline, Illinois (c. 1956–64), Library of Congress, Prints & Photographs Division, Balthazar Korab Archive at the Library of Congress, [LC-DIG-krb-00664]

529: Eero Saarinen, Deere & Company Headquarters, Moline, Illinois (c.1956–64), Library of Congress, Prints & Photographs Division, Balthazar Korab Archive at the Library of Congress, [LC-DIG-krb-00627]

531: *The Apartment* (1960), *The Apartment* © 1960 Metro-Goldwyn-Mayer Studios Inc. All Rights Reserved; courtesy of MGM Media Licensing

545: Gordon Matta-Clark, *Days End Pier 52.3 (Documentation of the action "Day's End" made in 1975 in New York, United States)* © 2020 Estate of Gordon Matta-Clark/Artists Rights Society (ARS), New York

548: Gordon Matta-Clark, *Splitting 2 (Documentation of the action "Splitting" made in 1974 in New Jersey, United States). 1974, printed 1977* © 2020 Estate of Gordon Matta-Clark / Artists Rights Society (ARS), New York

566: Philip Johnson, "Pennzoil Place" (1976), © Richard Payne, FAIA

605: Richard Serra, *Carnegie* (1985) © 2020 Richard Serra / Artists Rights Society (ARS), New York

609: "Laffer Curve Napkin" (1974), Division of Work and Industry, National Museum of American History, Smithsonian Institution

615: Bernard Frize, *Drexel, Burnham, Lambert* (1987) © 2020 Artists Rights Society (ARS), New York / ADAGP, Paris

662: Andreas Gursky, *Tokyo, Stock Exchange* (1990) © Andreas Gursky/courtesy Sprüth Magers/Artists Rights Society (ARS), New York

691: "Cutting Regulations with a Chain Saw" (2003), Federal Deposit Insurance Incorporation 2003 Annual Report

698: "Las Vegas Area Subdivision Becomes Ghost Town" (2010) © David Becker/ZUMA Press

FIGURE CREDITS

23: D. W. Meinig, *The Shaping of America: A Geographical Perspective on 500 Years of History*, vol. 1: *Atlantic America, 1492–1800* (New Haven, Conn.: Yale University Press, 1986), 209, figure 40.

27: Stephen John Hornsby and Michael Hermann, *British Atlantic, American Frontier: Spaces of Power in Early Modern British America* (Lebanon, N.H.: University Press of New England, 2005), 69, figure 2.20; 136, figure 4.6; 156, figure 4.18.

35: Kenneth J. Weiller and Philip Mirowski, "Rates of Interest in 18th Century England," *Explorations in Economic History* 27, no. 1 (1990): 6, figure 1.

97: Douglas A. Irwin, "Exports of Selected Commodities: 1790–1989," in Susan B. Carter, Scott Sigmund Gartner, Michael R. Haines, Alan L. Olmstead, Richard Sutch, and Gavin Wright, eds., *Historical Statistics of the United States, Earliest Times to the Present: Millennial Edition* (New York: Cambridge University Press, 2006), table Ee569-589.

99: Meinig, *Shaping of America*, vol. 1, 226, figure 27; 233, figure 28.

114: Douglas A. Irwin, "Exports and Imports of Merchandise, Gold, and Silver: 1790–2002," in Carter et al., eds., *Historical Statistics of the United States*, table Ee362-375.

117: Meinig, *Shaping of America*, vol. 1, 365, figure 63.

121: Joseph Van Fenstermaker, *The Development of American Commercial Banking: 1782–1837* (Kent, Ohio: Kent State University, 1965), 66–7, table 10.

155: D. W. Meinig, *The Shaping of America: A Geographical Perspective on 500 Years of History*, vol. 2, *Continental America, 1800–1867* (New Haven, Conn.: Yale University Press, 1993), 290, figure 39.

156: Meinig, *The Shaping of America*, vol. 2, 294, figure 40.

176: Meinig, *The Shaping of America*, vol. 2, 452, figure 77.

178: Meinig, *The Shaping of America*, vol. 2, 329, figure 46.

185: Charles W. Calomiris and Jonathan Pritchett, "Betting on Secession: Quantifying Political Events Surrounding Slavery and the Civil War," *American Economic Review* 106, no. 1 (2016): 13, figure 2.

212: Irwin, "Exports and imports," in Carter et al., eds., *Historical Statistics of the United States*.

225: Christopher Cotter, "Railroad Defaults, Land Grants, and the Panic of 1873," mimeo (2015), 7, figure 2; 8, figure 3.

226: National Bureau of Economic Research, Index of the General Price Level for United States [M04051USM324NNBR], retrieved from FRED Economic Data, Economic Research Federal Reserve Bank of St. Louis.

239: Gavin Wright, "Mining, Energy, Fisheries, and Forestry," in Carter et al., eds., *Historical Statistics of the United States.*

240: Christopher Jones, *Routes of Power: Energy and Modern America* (Cambridge, Mass.: Harvard University Press, 2014), 80, map 2.1.

244: D. W. Meinig, *The Shaping of America: A Geographical Perspective on 500 Years of History,* vol. 3, *Transcontinental America, 1850–1915* (New Haven, Conn.: Yale University Press, 1998), 241, figure 46.

278: Joshua L. Rosenbloom, "Work Stoppages, Workers Involved, Average Duration, and Person-Days Idle: 1881–1998," in Carter et al., eds., *Historical Statistics of the United States,* table Ba4954-4964.

293: The twenty-one cities are: St. Louis; Boston; San Francisco; Milwaukee; Denver; Lowell, Massachusetts; Charleston; Des Moines; Portland, Oregon; Peoria, Illinois; Galveston; Little Rock; Burlington, Vermont; Brookline, Massachusetts; Leadville, Colorado; Adrian, Michigan; Bath, Maine; Bowling Green, Kentucky; Perkin, Illinois; Junction City, Kansas; and Boise, Idaho. Colin B. Burk, "Voluntary and Nonprofit Associations per Capita, by Region and Type of Association, and in Selected Cities: 1840–1990," in Carter et al., eds., *Historical Statistics of the United States,* table Bg1-14.

305: Michael R. Haines, "Wholesale Prices of Selected Commodities: 1784–1998," in Carter et al., eds. *Historical Statistics of the United States,* table Cc205-266

306: Meinig, *The Shaping of America,* vol. 3, 254, figure 48; 257, figure 51.

362: S&P Dow Jones Indices LLC, Dow Jones Industrial Average [DJIA], retrieved from FRED.

400: Gauti B. Eggertsson, "Great Expectations and the End of the Depression," *American Economic Review,* 98, no, 4 (2008): 1478, figure 1.

410: The Mapping History Project, James Mohr and John Nicols, eds., Department of History, University of Oregon (1997), https://mappinghistory.uoregon.edu/.

429: Federal Reserve Bank of St. Louis and U.S. Office of Management and Budget, Federal Surplus or Deficit [-] as Percent of Gross Domestic Product [FYFSGDA188S], retrieved from FRED.

430: U.S. Bureau of Economic Analysis, Private Nonresidential Fixed Investment [PNFI], retrieved from FRED.

451: *Report on War Aid Furnished by the United States to the USSR* (Washington, D.C.: 1945).

478: Daniel Immerwahr, *How to Hide an Empire: A History of the Greater United States* (New York: Farrar, Straus and Giroux, 2019), 344; Foreign bases, David Vine, www.basenation.us/maps; Domestic/territorial bases, www.data.gov.

480: Irwin, "Exports and imports," in Carter et al., eds., *Historical Statistics of the United States.*

497: American Automobile Association, *The National System of Interstate and Defense Highways: As of June, 1958* (Washington, D.C.: 1958).

514: U.S. Bureau of Economic Analysis, Personal Consumption Expenditures [PCE], retrieved from FRED.

514: Organization for Economic Co-operation and Development, Consumer Opinion Surveys: Confidence Indicators: Composite Indicators: OECD Indicator for the United States [CSCICP03USM665S], retrieved from FRED.

520: Federal Reserve Bank of St. Louis and U.S. Office of Management and Budget, Federal Surplus or Deficit [-] as Percent of Gross Domestic Product [FYFSGDA188S], retrieved from FRED.

547: Economic Policy Institute Analysis of Unpublished Total Economy Productivity Data from Bureau of Labor Statistics (BLS) Labor Productivity and Costs Program, Wage Data from the BLS Current Employment Statistics, BLS Employment Cost Trends, BLS Consumer

Price Index, and Bureau of Economic Analysis National Income and Product Accounts, https://www.epi.org/productivity-pay-gap/.

549: U.S. Bureau of Labor Statistics, Labor Force Participation Rate—Men [LNS11300001], retrieved from FRED.

561: U.S. Bureau of Economic Analysis, Real Gross Private Domestic Investment [GPDIC1], retrieved from FRED.

563: James Oakes, Michael McGerr, Jan Ellen Lewis, Nick Cullather, and Jeanne Boydston, *Of the People: A History of the United States, Volume II: Since 1945* (New York: Oxford University Press, 2011).

598: Board of Governors of the Federal Reserve System (US), Effective Federal Funds Rate [FEDFUNDS], retrieved from FRED.

599: University of Michigan, University of Michigan: Inflation Expectation [MICH], retrieved from FRED.

601: Board of Governors of the Federal Reserve System (US), Trade Weighted U.S. Dollar Index: Major Currencies, Goods (DISCONTINUED) [TWEXMMTH], retrieved from FRED.

602: U.S. Bureau of Economic Analysis, Balance on Current Account, NIPA's [NETFI], retrieved from FRED.

611: U.S. Bureau of Economic Analysis, Shares of Gross Domestic Product: Gross Private Domestic Investment: Fixed Investment: Nonresidential [A008RE1Q156NBEA], retrieved from FRED.

612: U.S. Bureau of Economic Analysis, Shares of Gross Domestic Product: Personal Consumption Expenditures [DPCERE1Q156NBEA], retrieved from FRED.

613: Economic Policy Institute Analysis of Unpublished Total Economy Productivity Data from Bureau of Labor Statistics (BLS) Labor Productivity and Costs Program, Wage Data from the BLS Current Employment Statistics, BLS Employment Cost Trends, BLS Consumer Price Index, and Bureau of Economic Analysis National Income and Product Accounts, https://www.epi.org/productivity-pay-gap/.

614: Federal Reserve Bank of St. Louis and U.S. Office of Management and Budget, Federal Surplus or Deficit [-] as Percent of Gross Domestic Product [FYFSGDA188S], retrieved from FRED.

621: World Bank, Stock Market Capitalization to GDP for United States [DDDM01USA156NWDB], retrieved from FRED.

636: U.S. Bureau of Economic Analysis, Shares of Gross Domestic Product: Gross Private Domestic Investment: Fixed Investment: Nonresidential [A008RE1Q156NBEA], retrieved from FRED.

636: World Bank, Stock Market Capitalization to GDP for United States [DDDM01USA156NWDB], retrieved from FRED.

655: Federal Reserve Bank of St. Louis and U.S. Office of Management and Budget, Federal Surplus or Deficit [-] as Percent of Gross Domestic Product [FYFSGDA188S], retrieved from FRED.

656: Board of Governors of the Federal Reserve System (US), 10-Year Treasury Constant Maturity Rate [DGS10], retrieved from FRED.

658: Organization for Economic Co-operation and Development, Total Current Account Balance for the United States (DISCONTINUED) [BPBLTT01USQ188S], retrieved from FRED.

669: NASDAQ OMX Group, NASDAQ Composite Index [NASDAQCOM], retrieved from FRED.

671: U.S. Bureau of Economic Analysis, Corporate Profits After Tax with Inventory Valuation Adjustment (IVA) and Capital Consumption Adjustment (CCAdj) [CPATAX], retrieved from FRED.

671: U.S. Bureau of Labor Statistics, Nonfarm Business Sector: Labor Share [PRS85006173], retrieved from FRED.

674: Organization for Economic Co-operation and Development, Total Current Account Balance for the United States (DISCONTINUED) [BPBLTT01USQ188S], retrieved from FRED.

677: Board of Governors of the Federal Reserve System (US), Effective Federal Funds Rate [FEDFUNDS], retrieved from FRED.

686: David H. Autor, David Dorn, and Gordon H. Hanson, "The China Shock: Learning from Labor-Market Adjustment to Large Changes in Trade," *Annual Review of Economics* 8 (2016): 225, figure 6a.

687: U.S. Bureau of Labor Statistics, Labor Force Participation Rate—Men [LNS11300001], retrieved from FRED.

688: Robert G. Valletta, "Recent Flattening in the Higher Education Wage Premium: Polarization, Skill Downgrading, or Both?," NBER Working Paper, no. 22935 (2016): 35, figure 1.

693: Claudia Coulton, Kathryn W. Hexter, April Hirsh, Anne O'Shaughnessy, Francisca G. C. Richter, and Michael Schramm, "Facing the Foreclosure Crisis in Greater Cleveland: What Happened and How Communities are Responding," Urban Publications, paper 374 (2010).

695: Federal Deposit Insurance Corporation, RealityTrac Inc. S&P/Case-Shiller Home Price Index, retrieved from FRED.

699: Freddie Mac, 30-Year Fixed Rate Mortgage Average in the United States [MORTGAGE30US] and Federal Funds Target Rate (DISCONTINUED) [DFEDTAR], retrieved from FRED.

707: Federal Reserve Bank of St. Louis, TED Spread [TEDRATE], Board of Governors of the Federal Reserve System (US), 3-Month AA Financial Commercial Paper Rate [DCPF3M], and Federal Reserve Bank of St. Louis, Moody's Seasoned AAA Corporate Bond Yield Relative to Yield on 10-Year Treasury Constant Maturity [AAA10Y], retrieved from FRED.

712: Federal Funds Target Rate (DISCONTINUED) [DFEDTAR], retrieved from FRED.

716: Federal Reserve Bank of St. Louis, TED Spread [TEDRATE], Board of Governors of the Federal Reserve System (US), 3-Month AA Financial Commercial Paper Rate [DCPF3M], and Federal Reserve Bank of St. Louis, Moody's Seasoned AAA Corporate Bond Yield Relative to Yield on 10-Year Treasury Constant Maturity [AAA10Y], retrieved from FRED.

719: Paul Kiel and Dan Nguyen, "Bailout Tracker: Tracking Every Dollar and Every Recipient," ProPublica (2013), https://projects.propublica.org/bailout/list/simple.

720: Board of Governors of the Federal Reserve System (US), Assets: Total Assets: Total Assets (Less Eliminations from Consolidation): Wednesday Level [WALCL], Board of Governors of the Federal Reserve System (US), Currency in Circulation [CURRCIR], and Board of Governors of the Federal Reserve System (US), Commercial and Industrial Loans, All Commercial Banks [TOTCI], retrieved from FRED.

721: U.S. Bureau of Labor Statistics, Total Unemployed, Plus All Persons Marginally Attached to the Labor Force, Plus Total Employed Part Time for Economic Reasons, as a Percent of the Civilian Labor Force Plus All Persons Marginally Attached to the Labor Force (U-6) [U6RATE], retrieved from FRED.

730: Board of Governors of the Federal Reserve System (US), Assets: Total Assets: Total Assets (Less Eliminations from Consolidation): Wednesday Level [WALCL], retrieved from FRED.

NOTE ON SOURCES

———

I N ADDITION TO THE NECESSARY DOCUMENTATION OF SOURCES
in the endnotes, I have also referenced the works of scholarship that I
have relied on the most. But the endnotes do not begin to do justice to the
extensive bodies of literature that exist on the various topics covered. In a
work of synthesis like this one, a comprehensive bibliography was not
practical. For this reason, while I have cited older works of scholarship
when my arguments have directly drawn from their interpretations, in
general I have tried to reference recent works that for the reader are the
best paths into the scholarly literatures.

So that the endnotes did not become overly cumbersome, I have avoided
repetition by not including citations for many statistics. For these, I have
relied on two indispensable sources. First, there is Susan B. Carter, Scott
Sigmund Gartner, Michael R. Haines, Alan L. Olmstead, Richard Sutch,
and Gavin Wright, eds., *Historical Statistics of the United States: Millennial
Edition Online,* https://hsus.cambridge.org/HSUSWeb/toc/hsusHome.do.
For the twentieth and twenty-first centuries I have also relied upon FRED
Economic Data, Economic Research Federal Reserve Bank of St. Louis,
https://fred.stlouisfed.org/.

NOTES

═══

INTRODUCTION

1. Jonathan Levy, "Capital as Process and the History of Capitalism," *Business History Review* 91, no. 3 (2017): 483–510. On capital and uncertainty, see Jonathan Levy, "Radical Uncertainty," *Critical Quarterly* 62, no. 1 (2020): 15–28. On capital and psyche, see Jonathan Levy, "Primal Capital," *Critical Historical Studies* 6, no. 2 (2019): 161–93. On the concept of a capital asset, see Jonathan Levy, "Appreciating Assets: New Directions in the History of Political Economy," *American Historical Review* 122, no. 5 (2017): 1490–99. On capital and income, see Jonathan Levy, "Accounting for Profit and the History of Capital," *Critical Historical Studies* 1, no. 2 (2014): 171–214. On the relationship between the history of capitalism and economic history, see Jeremy Adelman and Jonathan Levy, "The Fall and Rise of Economic History," *Chronicle of Higher Education*, December 1, 2014.

2. Thorstein Veblen, "On the Nature of Capital II: Investment, Intangible Assets, and the Pecuniary Magnate," *Quarterly Journal of Economics* 23, no. 1 (1908): 104–36.

3. On capitalization, see Eli Cook, *The Pricing of Progress: Economic Indicators and the Capitalization of American Life* (Cambridge, Mass.: Harvard University Press, 2017); Fabian Muniesa et al., *Capitalization: A Cultural Guide* (Paris: Presses des Mines, 2017).

4. For a lucid account of this division, see Joseph Schumpeter, *History of Economic Analysis* (1954; New York: Oxford University Press, 1994), 276–78.

5. John Maynard Keynes, *The General Theory of Employment, Interest, and Money* (1936; New York: Harcourt, Brace & World, 1964), 264.

6. See Jens Beckert, *Imagined Futures: Fictional Expectations and Capitalist Dynamics* (Cambridge, Mass.: Harvard University Press, 2016).

7. Irving Fisher, *The Nature of Capital and Income* (New York: Macmillan, 1906), 328.

8. Thorstein B. Veblen, "On the Nature of Capital I: The Productivity of Capital Goods," *Quarterly Journal of Economics* 22, no. 4 (1908): 517–42.

9. See Katharina Pistor, *The Code of Capital: How the Law Creates Wealth and Inequality* (Princeton: Princeton University Press, 2019).

10. Andrew Carnegie, *The Autobiography of Andrew Carnegie* (1920; Philadelphia: PublicAffairs, 2011), 151.

11. Greg Grandin, *Fordlandia: The Rise and Fall of Henry Ford's Forgotten Jungle City* (New York: Metropolitan Books, 2009), 34.

12. John Arlidge, "I'm Doing 'God's Work'. Meet Mr Goldman Sachs," *Sunday Times*, November 8, 2009.

13. Albert O. Hirschman, *The Strategy of Economic Development* (New Haven: Yale University Press, 1964), 35–40.

14. Keynes, *General Theory,* 346.

15. Ibid., 165–74.

16. As Kaldor, in one of the best discussions of the issue, admitted, "it is very difficult to find satisfactory definition of what constitutes 'liquidity'—difficulty, I think, which is inherent in the concept itself." Nicholas Kaldor, "Speculation and Economic Stability," *Review of Economic Studies* 7, no. 1 (1938): 4. On liquidity, see also J. R. Hicks, "Liquidity," *Economic Journal* 72, no. 288 (1972): 787–802.

17. A recent article that emphasizes this point and is also an excellent guide to the debate about the definition of liquidity is M. G. Hayes, "The Liquidity of Money," *Cambridge Journal of Economics* 42, no. 5 (2018): 1205–18.

18. Of note, *liquidity, money,* and *perfect marketability* are often treated as synonymous. But they should not be. Stores of value—like land in early modern times—might not always be relatively marketable. The important point is that liquidity and illiquidity are relative qualities of all assets, on a spectrum and in relationship to one another. One of the defining features of capitalism is that it converges the two qualities of liquidity on the same assets.

19. Keynes associated illiquidity with both greater production and employment, which made sense in the 1930s, but does not always apply.

20. This formulation has a lineage in M. Kalecki, "Political Aspects of Full Employment," *Political Quarterly* 14, no. 4 (1943): 322–30.

CHAPTER 1: MERCANTILISM

1. Jacob Viner, "Power Versus Plenty as Objectives of Foreign Policy in the Seventeenth and Eighteenth Centuries," *World Politics* 1, no. 1 (1948): 15; Adam Smith, *An Inquiry into the Nature and Causes of the Wealth of Nations* (1776; Chicago: University of Chicago Press, 1976), 35.

2. David Ormrod, *The Rise of Commercial Empires: England and the Netherlands in the Age of Mercantilism, 1650–1770* (New York: Cambridge University Press, 2003).

3. See, for instance, George J. Stigler, introduction, in Smith, *Wealth of Nations,* xi–xv.

4. Emma Rothschild, *Economic Sentiments: Adam Smith, Condorcet, and the Enlightenment* (Cambridge, Mass.: Harvard University Press, 2001).

5. See, from neoclassical, Keynesian, and Marxist perspectives that all converge on a number of similar points: George J. Stigler, "The Division of Labor Is Limited by the Extent of the Market," *Journal of Political Economy* 59, no. 3 (1951): 185–93; John Hicks, *A Theory of Economic History* (Oxford: Clarendon Press, 1969), 25–41; Robert Brenner, "Property and Progress: Where Adam Smith Went Wrong," in Chris Wickham, ed., *Marxist History-Writing for the Twenty-First Century* (New York: Oxford University Press, 2007), 49–111.

6. Allyn A. Young, "Increasing Returns and Economic Progress," *Economic Journal* 38, no. 152 (1928): 527–42.

7. Morgan Kelly, "The Dynamics of Smithian Growth," *Quarterly Journal of Economics* 112, no. 3 (1997): 939–64.

8. Philip J. Stern and Carl Wennerlind, eds., *Mercantilism Reimagined: Political Economy in Early Modern Britain and Its Empire* (New York: Oxford University Press, 2014), 4.

9. Viner, "Power Versus Plenty," 15.

10. Beckert suggestively calls it an era of "war capitalism." Sven Beckert, *Empire of Cotton: A Global History* (New York: Knopf, 2014), 29–55.

11.   Kathleen Donegan, *Seasons of Misery: Catastrophe and Colonial Settlement in Early America* (Philadelphia: University of Pennsylvania Press, 2013).

12.   George Louis Beer, *The Old Colonial System, 1660–1754. Part I: The Establishment of the System, 1660–1688* (New York: Macmillan, 1912).

13.   On Shaftesbury, see Kenneth Harold Dobson Haley, *The First Earl of Shaftesbury* (Oxford: Clarendon, 1968); John Spurr, ed., *Anthony Ashley Cooper, First Earl of Shaftesbury, 1621–1683* (New York: Routledge, 2011); and William Appleman Williams, *The Contours of American History* (New York: Norton, 1989), 50–53, from which I drew inspiration for this chapter.

14.   William Dougal Christie, *A Life of Anthony Ashley Cooper: First Earl of Shaftesbury, 1621–1683*, 2 vols. (London: Macmillan, 1871), 1:183.

15.   *Gentlemen capitalist* is the term of P. J. Cain and A. G. Hopkins, *British Imperialism, 1688–2015* (New York: Routledge, 2016).

16.   Karen Ordahl Kupperman, *Providence Island, 1630–1641: The Other Puritan Colony* (New York: Cambridge University Press, 1993), 352.

17.   E. E. Rich, "The First Earl of Shaftesbury's Colonial Policy," *Transactions of the Royal Historical Society* 7 (1957): 51.

18.   Simply read through Shaftesbury's papers. South Carolina Historical Society, *The Shaftesbury Papers* (Charleston, S.C.: Arcadia, 1999).

19.   Thomas D. Wilson, *The Ashley Cooper Plan: The Founding of Carolina and the Origins of Southern Political Culture* (Chapel Hill: University of North Carolina Press, 2016).

20.   John Locke, *Two Treatises of Government*, ed. Peter Laslett (1689; New York: Cambridge University Press, 1988), 99.

21.   Paul Slack, "Material Progress and the Challenge of Affluence in Seventeenth-Century England," *Economic History Review* 62, no. 3 (2009): 576–603; Fredrik Albritton Jonsson, "The Origins of Cornucopianism: A Preliminary Genealogy," *Critical Historical Studies* 1, no. 1 (2014): 151–68.

22.   Thomas Leng, *Benjamin Worsley: Trade, Interest and the Spirit in Revolutionary England* (Suffolk, U.K.: Boydell Press, 2008), 154.

23.   B. E. Supple, *Commercial Crisis and Change in England, 1600–1642* (New York: Cambridge University Press, 1959).

24.   Keith Wrightson, *Earthly Necessities: Economic Lives in Early Modern Britain* (New Haven: Yale University Press, 2000), 150.

25.   Aristotle, *Aristotle: The Politics and the Constitution of Athens*, ed. Stephen Everson (New York: Cambridge University Press, 2011), 24.

26.   Thomas Hobbes, *Leviathan*, ed. Edwin Curley (1651; Indianapolis: Hackett, 1994), 58.

27.   William Cronon, *Changes in the Land: Indians, Colonists, and the Ecology of New England* (New York: Hill & Wang, 1983).

28.   Irving Rouse, *The Tainos: Rise and Decline of the People Who Greeted Columbus* (New Haven: Yale University Press, 1992), 9–12.

29.   Alan Taylor, *American Colonies* (New York: Viking, 2001), 22.

30.   Carl N. Degler, *Out of Our Past: The Forces That Shaped Modern America* (New York: Harper, 1959), 1.

31.   Harry S. Stout, *The New England Soul: Preaching and Religious Culture in Colonial New England* (New York: Oxford University Press, 1986), 22.

32.   Jack P. Greene, *Pursuits of Happiness: The Social Development of Early Modern British Colonies and the Formation of American Culture* (Chapel Hill: University of North Carolina Press, 1988), 10.

33.   John Winthrop, *The Journal of John Winthrop, 1630–1649*, ed. James Savage, Richard S. Dunn, and Laetitia Yeandle (Cambridge, Mass.: Belknap Press, 1996), 1–12.

34.   Ibid., 308.

35. Eli Heckscher, *Mercantilism*, trans. Mendel Shapiro (London: G. Allen & Unwin, 1935).

36. Keith Tribe, *The Economy of the Word: Language, History, and Economics* (New York: Oxford University Press, 2015).

37. Smith, *Wealth of Nations*, 449.

38. Rich, "Shaftesbury's Colonial Policy," 61.

39. Jeremy Adelman, "Mimesis and Rivalry: European Empires and Global Regimes," *Journal of Global History* 10, no. 1 (2015): 77–98; Sophus A. Reinert, *Translating Empire: Emulation and the Origins of Political Economy* (Cambridge, Mass.: Harvard University Press, 2011).

40. John Shovlin, "War and Peace: Trade, International Competition, and Political Economy," in Stern and Wennerlind, *Mercantilism Reimagined*, 311.

41. Carla G. Pestana, *The English Conquest of Jamaica: Oliver Cromwell's Bid for Empire* (Cambridge, Mass.: Belknap Press, 2017).

42. Ormrod, *Rise of Commercial Empires*, 1–59.

43. Steve Pincus, "Neither Machiavellian Moment nor Possessive Individualism: Commercial Society and the Defenders of the English Commonwealth," *American Historical Review* 103, no. 3 (1998): 705–36. My account of the transformation of political economy at this time draws heavily from Pincus's writings on the subject. See also Steve Pincus, "Rethinking Mercantilism: Political Economy, the British Empire, and the Atlantic World in the Seventeenth and Eighteenth Centuries," *William and Mary Quarterly* 69, no. 1 (2012): 3–34.

44. Christie, *Life of Anthony Ashley Cooper*, 2:ix–x.

45. Istvan Hont, *Jealousy of Trade: International Competition and the Nation-State in Historical Perspective* (Cambridge, Mass.: Harvard University Press, 2005).

46. Joel Kaye, *A History of Balance, 1250–1375: The Emergence of a New Model of Equilibrium and Its Impact on Thought* (New York: Cambridge University Press, 2014), 1–75.

47. Francis Bacon, *The Works of Lord Bacon*, ed. Benno Loewy (London: Henry G. Bohn, 1854), 519.

48. Carl Wennerlind, *Casualties of Credit: The English Financial Revolution, 1620–1720* (Cambridge, Mass.: Harvard University Press, 2011).

49. The most famous economic argument that ex post investment leads to savings, not the other way around, is John Maynard Keynes, *The General Theory of Employment, Interest and Money* (1936; New York: Harcourt, Brace & World, 1964).

50. Wennerlind, *Casualties of Credit*, 17–122.

51. Hobbes, *Leviathan*, 164.

52. On the growth of credit money in the English context, see Christine Desan, *Making Money: Coin, Currency, and the Coming of Capitalism* (New York: Oxford University Press, 2015).

53. Smith, *Wealth of Nations*, 351–71.

54. Among works of classical political economists, the most incisive treatment of these themes was Richard Cantillon, *Essay on the Nature of Trade in General*, trans. Antoin E. Murphy (1712; Carmel, Ind.: Liberty Fund, 2005).

55. Keynes, *General Theory*, 343.

56. Josiah Child, *Brief Observations Concerning Trade and Interest of Money* (London, 1668), http://avalon.law.yale.edu/17th_century/trade.asp.

57. Sidney Homer and Richard Sylla, *A History of Interest Rates* (Hoboken, N.J.: Wiley, 2005), 64.

58. Ibid., 124–26.

59. R. F. Harrod, *International Economics* (London: Macmillan, 1933), 104–36.

Under certain conditions, adjustment between exports and imports may occur at a higher level of output for the exporting country.

60. Steve Hindle, "Imagining Insurrection in Seventeenth-Century England: Representations of the Midland Rising of 1607," *History Workshop Journal*, no. 66 (Autumn 2008): 37.

61. Heckscher, *Mercantilism*.

62. Lauren Benton, *A Search for Sovereignty: Law and Geography in European Empires, 1400–1900* (New York: Cambridge University Press, 2009); Michael J. Braddick, *State Formation in Early Modern England* (New York: Cambridge University Press, 2000).

63. On the corporation as a governing entity, see Hendrik Hartog, *Public Property and Private Power: The Corporation of the City of New York in American Law, 1730–1870* (Chapel Hill: University of North Carolina Press, 1993); Christopher Tomlins, *Freedom Bound: Law, Labor, and Civic Identity in Colonizing English America, 1580–1865* (New York: Cambridge University Press, 2010), 67–132.

64. Hobbes, *Leviathan*, 218; Noel Malcolm, "Hobbes, Sandys, and the Virginia Company," *Historical Journal* 24, no. 2 (1981): 297–321.

65. Joshua L. Reid, *The Sea Is My Country: The Maritime World of the Makahs, an Indigenous Borderlands People* (New Haven: Yale University Press, 2015); Jean M. O'Brien, *Firsting and Lasting: Writing Indians Out of Existence in New England* (Minneapolis: University of Minnesota Press, 2010).

66. Patricia Seed, *Ceremonies of Possession in Europe's Conquest of the New World, 1492–1640* (New York: Cambridge University Press, 1995).

67. Bernard Bailyn, *The Barbarous Years: The Peopling of British North America: The Conflict of Civilizations, 1600–1675* (New York: Knopf, 2012).

68. Daniel K. Richter, *The Ordeal of the Longhouse: The Peoples of the Iroquois League in the Era of European Colonization* (Chapel Hill: University of North Carolina Press, 1992).

69. Pekka Hämäläinen, "The Shapes of Power: Indians, Europeans, and North American Worlds from the Seventeenth Century to the Nineteenth Century," in Juliana Barr and Edward Countryman, eds., *Contested Spaces of Early America* (Philadelphia: University of Pennsylvania Press, 2014), 31–68.

70. Carla Gardina Pestana, *The English Atlantic in an Age of Revolution, 1640–1661* (Cambridge, Mass.: Harvard University Press, 2004).

71. Taylor, *American Colonies*, 257.

72. Margaret Ellen Newell, *From Dependency to Independence: Economic Revolution in Colonial New England* (Ithaca, N.Y.: Cornell University Press, 1998).

73. Beer, *Old Colonial System*, 47.

74. "Charles II, 1663: An Act for the Encouragement of Trade," in *Statutes of the Realm*, vol. 5, *1628–80*, ed. John Raithby (s.l.: Great Britain Record Commission, 1819), 449–52, *British History Online*, accessed January 14, 2019, http://www.british-history .ac.uk/statutes-realm/vol5/pp449-452.

75. Abigail L. Swingen, *Competing Visions of Empire: Labor, Slavery, and the Origins of the British Atlantic Empire* (New Haven: Yale University Press, 2015).

76. Christie, *Anthony Ashley Cooper*, 2:ix–x.

77. *Journal of the Council for Foreign Plantations*, August 3, 1670, to September 20, 1672; and Council for Trade and Plantations, October 13, 1672, to December 22, 1674, both in Box 10, Sir Thomas Phillipps Collection, Library of Congress.

78. Rich, "Shaftesbury's Colonial Policy," 62.

79. Andrea Finkelstein, *Harmony and the Balance: An Intellectual History of Seventeenth-Century English Economic Thought* (Ann Arbor: University of Michigan Press, 2000), 179.

80. Rich, "Shaftesbury's Colonial Policy," 64.

81. Mark G. Hanna, *Pirate Nests and the Rise of the British Empire, 1570–1740* (Chapel Hill: University of North Carolina Press, 2015). On imperial governance, see Daniel J. Hulsebosch, *Constituting Empire: New York and the Transformation of Constitutionalism in the Atlantic World, 1664–1830* (Chapel Hill: University of North Carolina Press, 2005), 75–144.

82. Edmund Burke, *On Empire, Liberty, and Reform: Speeches and Letters*, ed. David Bromwich (New Haven: Yale University Press, 2000), 79.

83. Nuala Zahedieh, *The Capital and the Colonies: London and the Atlantic Economy, 1660–1700* (New York: Cambridge University Press, 2010); Trevor Burnard, "Making a Whig Empire Work: Transatlantic Politics and the Imperial Economy in Britain and British America," *William and Mary Quarterly* 69, no. 1 (2012): 51–56.

84. Pincus, "Rethinking Mercantilism."

85. Steve Pincus, *1688: The First Modern Revolution* (New Haven: Yale University Press, 2009).

86. Desan, *Making Money*; Wennerlind, *Casualties of Credit*.

87. Smith, *Wealth of Nations*, 21.

88. Young, "Increasing Returns and Economic Progress."

89. See Rothschild, *Economic Sentiments*.

90. On this point, the most incisive treatment is Gavin Wright, *Slavery and American Economic Development* (Baton Rouge: Louisiana State University Press, 2013).

91. Abigail Swingen, "Labor: Employment, Colonial Servitude, and Slavery in the Seventeenth-Century Atlantic," in Stern and Wennerlind, *Mercantilism Reimagined*, 57.

92. Even Locke was skeptical. Holly Brewer, "Slavery, Sovereignty, and 'Inheritable Blood': Reconsidering John Locke and the Origins of American Slavery," *American Historical Review* 122, no. 4 (2017): 1038–78; Christopher Leslie Brown, *Moral Capital: Foundations of British Abolitionism* (Chapel Hill: University of North Carolina Press, 2012).

93. Alan Gallay, *The Indian Slave Trade: The Rise of the English Empire in the American South, 1670–1717* (New Haven: Yale University Press, 2002), 299.

94. Joseph E. Inikori, *Africans and the Industrial Revolution in England: A Study in International Trade and Economic Development* (New York: Cambridge University Press, 2002), 187.

95. Thomas C. Holt, *Children of Fire: A History of African Americans* (New York: Hill & Wang, 2010), 3–52.

96. Edward B. Rugemer, "The Development of Mastery and Race in the Comprehensive Slave Codes of the Greater Caribbean During the Seventeenth Century," *William and Mary Quarterly* 70, no. 3 (2013): 429–58.

97. Simon P. Newman, *A New World of Labor: The Development of Plantation Slavery in the British Atlantic* (Philadelphia: University of Pennsylvania Press, 2013).

98. Richard S. Dunn, *Sugar and Slaves: The Rise of the Planter Class in the English West Indies, 1624–1713* (1972; Chapel Hill: University of North Carolina Press, 2000), 85.

99. On black slaves as capital assets, see Cedric J. Robinson, *Black Marxism: The Making of the Black Radical Tradition* (Chapel Hill: University of North Carolina Press, 2000), 109–11.

100. Caitlin Rosenthal, *Accounting for Slavery: Masters and Management* (Cambridge, Mass.: Harvard University Press, 2018).

101. Eric Kimball, "New Englanders and the Slave Economies of the West Indies," in Sven Beckert and Seth Rockman, eds., *Slavery's Capitalism: A New History of American Economic Development* (Philadelphia: University of Pennsylvania Press, 2016), 181–94; Wendy Warren, *New England Bound: Slavery and Colonization in Early America* (New York: Liveright, 2016).

102. Newell, *From Dependency to Independence*, 3.

103. David Eltis et al., *Atlas of the Transatlantic Slave Trade* (New Haven: Yale University Press, 2010), 200–203, table 6.

104. S. Max Edelson, *Plantation Enterprise in Colonial South Carolina* (Cambridge, Mass.: Harvard University Press, 2006).

105. Peter Wood, *Black Majority: Negroes in Colonial South Carolina from 1670 Through the Stono Rebellion* (New York: Knopf, 1974).

106. Jane Burbank and Frederick Cooper, *Empires in World History: Power and the Politics of Difference* (Princeton: Princeton University Press, 2010), 181–84.

107. David Armitage, "John Locke, Carolina, and the 'Two Treatises of Government,'" *Political Theory* 32, no. 5 (2004): 602–27.

108. Kathryn E. Holland Braund, *Deerskins and Duffels: The Creek Indian Trade with Anglo-America, 1685–1815* (Lincoln: University of Nebraska Press, 1993).

109. John J. McCusker and Russell R. Menard, *The Economy of British America, 1607–1789* (Chapel Hill: University of North Carolina Press, 1991), 174, table 8.2.

110. Lorena Seebach Walsh, *Motives of Honor, Pleasure, and Profit: Plantation Management in the Colonial Chesapeake, 1607–1763* (Chapel Hill: University of North Carolina Press, 2010).

111. Peter C. Mancall, "Tales Tobacco Told in Sixteenth-Century Europe," *Environmental History* 9, no. 4 (2004): 648–78.

112. Peter H. Lindert and Jeffrey G. Williamson, *Unequal Gains: American Growth and Inequality Since 1700* (Princeton: Princeton University Press, 2016), 52, table 32.

113. Matthew Kruer, "Bloody Minds and Peoples Undone: Emotion, Family, and Political Order in the Susquehannock-Virginia War," *William and Mary Quarterly* 74, no. 3 (2017): 401–36; Edmund S. Morgan, *American Slavery, American Freedom* (1975; New York: Norton, 2003).

114. David W. Galenson, *White Servitude in Colonial America: An Economic Analysis* (New York: Cambridge University Press, 1982).

115. Anthony S. Parent, *Foul Means: The Formation of a Slave Society in Virginia, 1660–1740* (Chapel Hill: University of North Carolina Press, 2003).

116. Zara Anishanslin, "Producing Empire: The British Empire in Theory and Practice," in Andrew Shankman, ed., *The World of the Revolutionary American Republic: Land, Labor, and the Conflict for a Continent* (New York: Routledge, 2014), 31.

117. Emma Hart, "From Field to Plate: The Colonial Livestock Trade and the Development of an American Economic Culture," *William and Mary Quarterly* 73, no. 1 (2016).

118. McCusker and Menard, *Economy of British America*, 91–117.

119. Ibid., 108, table 5.2; Phyllis Whitman Hunter, *Purchasing Identity in the Atlantic World: Massachusetts Merchants, 1670–1780* (Ithaca, N.Y.: Cornell University Press, 2001).

120. Cathy Matson, *Merchants and Empire: Trading in Colonial New York* (Baltimore: Johns Hopkins University Press, 2002); Thomas M. Doerflinger, *A Vigorous Spirit of Enterprise: Merchants and Economic Development in Revolutionary Philadelphia* (Chapel Hill: University of North Carolina Press, 1986).

121. Stanley Engerman et al., *Economic Development in the Americas Since 1500: Endowments and Institutions* (New York: Cambridge University Press, 2011).

122. T. H. Breen, *The Marketplace of Revolution: How Consumer Politics Shaped American Independence* (New York: Oxford University Press, 2004), 93 94, 120–30.

123. See Rothschild, *Economic Sentiments*.

124. Smith, *Wealth of Nations*, 26.

125. S. D. Smith, "British Exports to Colonial North America and the Mercantilist Fallacy," *Business History* 37, no. 1 (1995): 45–48; Zara Anishanslin, *Portrait of a*

Woman in Silk: Hidden Histories of the British Atlantic World (New Haven: Yale University Press, 2016).

126. Richard Lyman Bushman, *The Refinement of America: Persons, Houses, Cities* (New York: Knopf, 1992).

127. Kenneth Silverman, *The Life and Times of Cotton Mather* (New York: Harper-Collins, 1984).

128. Joseph Dorfman, *The Economic Mind in American Civilization, 1606–1865* (1949; New York: Augustus M. Kelley, 1966), 1:120. See also Mark Valeri, *Heavenly Merchandize: How Religion Shaped Commerce in Puritan America* (Princeton: Princeton University Press, 2010); Mark Peterson, *The Price of Redemption: The Spiritual Economy of Puritan New England* (Palo Alto, Calif.: Stanford University Press, 1997).

129. Thomas D. Eliot, "The Relations Between Adam Smith and Benjamin Franklin Before 1776," *Political Science Quarterly* 39, no. 1 (1924): 67–96.

130. Jacob M. Price, *Overseas Trade and Traders: Essays on Some Commercial, Financial and Political Challenges Facing British Atlantic Merchants, 1600–1775* (London: CRC Press, 1996).

131. Claire Priest, "Creating an American Property Law: Alienability and Its Limits in American History," *Harvard Law Review* 120, no. 2 (2006): 385–459.

132. David Hancock, *Citizens of the World: London Merchants and the Integration of the British Atlantic Community, 1735–1785* (New York: Cambridge University Press, 1995).

133. Gautham Rao, *National Duties: Custom Houses and the Making of the American State* (Chicago: University of Chicago Press, 2016), 19–44; Thomas M. Truxes, *Defying Empire: Trading with the Enemy in Colonial New York* (New Haven: Yale University Press, 2008).

134. Steve Pincus, *The Heart of the Declaration: The Founders' Case for an Activist Government* (New Haven: Yale University Press, 2016).

135. McCusker and Menard, *Economy of British America*, 331–50.

136. Engerman et al., *Economic Development in the Americas*, 11, fig. 1.1.

137. Lindert and Williamson, *Unequal Gains*, 43. For a critique of these estimates, see Thomas Weiss, review of *Unequal Gains*, *Journal of Economic History* 77, no. 3 (September 2017): 952–54.

138. Smith, "British Exports to Colonial North America."

139. Patrick K. O'Brien, "Mercantilism and Imperialism in the Rise and Decline of the Dutch and British Economies, 1585–1815," *De Economist* 148, no. 4 (2000): 469–501; Stanley L. Engerman, "British Imperialism in a Mercantilist Age, 1492–1849: Conceptual Issues and Empirical Problems," *Revista de Historia Económica* 16, no. 1 (1998): 195–231.

140. See, in favor of the contribution, Barbara L. Solow, *The Economic Consequences of the Atlantic Slave Trade* (Lanham, Md.: Lexington Books, 2014); and against, David Eltis and Stanley L. Engerman, "The Importance of Slavery and the Slave Trade to Industrializing Britain," *Journal of Economic History* 60, no. 1 (2000): 123–44.

141. R. Bin Wong, *China Transformed: Historical Change and the Limits of European Experience* (Ithaca, N.Y.: Cornell University Press, 1998).

142. John Gallagher and Ronald Robinson, "The Imperialism of Free Trade," *Economic History Review* 6, no. 1 (1953): 1–15.

143. See Hart, "From Field to Plate," 131.

144. Paul Hammond and David Hopkins eds., *Dryden: Selected Poems* (Harlow, UK: Pearson Education Limited, 2007), 190.

CHAPTER 2: ORGANIC ECONOMY, HOUSEHOLD ECONOMY

1. E. A. Wrigley, *Energy and the English Industrial Revolution* (New York: Cambridge University Press, 2010).

2. Christopher F. Jones, *Routes of Power: Energy and Modern America* (Cambridge, Mass.: Harvard University Press, 2014), 15.

3. As was the case in the northern Europe harvests of 1601–3. Bruce M. S. Campbell, "Nature as Historical Protagonist: Environment and Society in Pre-Industrial England," *Economic History Review* 63, no. 2 (2010): 314.

4. T. R. Malthus, *An Essay on the Principle of Population*, ed. Donald Winch (1798; New York: Cambridge University Press, 1992), 42, 43. In the second edition, Malthus distinguished "positive" from "preventive" checks, *preventive* meaning interventions by societies that reduced population size, so as to maintain the level of wealth and well-being.

5. Thomas Carlyle, *Latter-Day Pamphlets* (London: Chapman & Hall, 1850), 53.

6. Jack A. Goldstone, "Efflorescences and Economic Growth in World History: Rethinking the 'Rise of the West' and the Industrial Revolution," *Journal of World History* 13, no. 2 (2002): 323–89.

7. Adam Smith, *An Inquiry into the Nature and Causes of the Wealth of Nations* (1776; Chicago: University of Chicago Press, 1976), 71, 91.

8. Keith Pluymers, "Atlantic Iron: Wood Scarcity and the Political Ecology of Early English Expansion," *William and Mary Quarterly* 73, no. 3 (2016): 389–426.

9. Bruce M. S. Campbell, "Factor Markets in England Before the Black Death," *Continuity and Change* 24, special issue 1 (2009): 79–106.

10. Henry Vaughan, *Selected Poems*, ed. Robert B. Shaw (1640; Cheadle, U.K.: Littlehampton Book Services, 1976).

11. Brian Fagan, *The Little Ice Age: How Climate Made History, 1300–1850* (New York: Basic Books, 2000); William Chester Jordan, *The Great Famine* (Princeton: Princeton University Press, 1996).

12. Karen Ordahl Kupperman, "Apathy and Death in Early Jamestown," *Journal of American History* 66, no. 1 (1979): 24.

13. Douglas H. Ubelaker, "North American Indian Population Size: Changing Perspectives," in John W. Verano and Douglas H. Ubelaker, eds., *Disease and Demography in the Americas* (Washington, D.C.: Smithsonian Institution Press, 1992).

14. On "ghost acreage," see Eric Jones, *The European Miracle: Environments, Economies and Geopolitics in the History of Europe and Asia* (New York: Cambridge University Press, 2003); Kenneth Pomeranz, "Political Economy and Ecology on the Eve of Industrialization: Europe, China, and the Global Conjuncture," *American Historical Review* 107, no. 2 (April 2002): 425–46.

15. John Komlos, *The Biological Standard of Living in Europe and America, 1700–1900: Studies in Anthropometric History* (Aldershot, U.K.: Routledge, 1995).

16. Malthus, *Essay on Population*, 23.

17. By far the best economic analysis of the household in this period, although its focus is on Europe, is Jan de Vries, *The Industrious Revolution: Consumer Behavior and the Household Economy, 1650 to the Present* (New York: Cambridge University Press, 2008). On early American households more broadly, see Christopher Tomlins, *Freedom Bound: Law, Labor, and Civic Identity in Colonizing English America, 1580–1865* (New York: Cambridge University Press, 2010); Christopher Clark, *Social Change in America: From the Revolution Through the Civil War* (Chicago: Ivan R. Dee, 2006); Carole Shammas, *A History of Household Government in America* (Charlottesville: University of Virginia Press, 2002).

18. Janet Halley, "What Is Family Law? A Genealogy Part I," *Yale Journal of Law and the Humanities* 23, no. 1 (2013), 8.

19. Nancy Folbre and Barnet Wagman, "Counting Housework: New Estimates of Real Product in the United States, 1800–1860," *Journal of Economic History* 53, no. 2 (1993): 275–88.

20. Allan Greer, *Property and Dispossession: Natives, Empires and Land in Early Modern North America* (New York: Cambridge University Press, 2018), 27–55.

21. John C. Weaver, *The Great Land Rush and the Making of the Modern World, 1650–1900* (Montreal: McGill-Queen's University Press, 2003).

22. Donald Worster, *Nature's Economy: A History of Ecological Ideas* (New York: Cambridge University Press, 1985), 27.

23. Peter Birks, "Roman Law Concept of Dominium and the Idea of Absolute Ownership," *Acta Juridica* 7 (1985): 31.

24. James J. Sheehan, "The Problem of Sovereignty in European History," *American Historical Review* 111, no. 1 (February 2006): 5.

25. On English distinctiveness with respect to private property over land, see Tomlins, *Freedom Bound*, 133.

26. David J. Seipp, "The Concept of Property in the Early Common Law," *Law and History Review* 12, no. 1 (1994): 29–91.

27. Weaver, *Great Land Rush*, 49.

28. Robert Brenner, "Property Relations and the Growth of Agricultural Productivity in Late Medieval and Early Modern Europe," in A. Bhaduri and Rune Skarstein, eds., *Economic Development and Agricultural Productivity* (Cheltenham, U.K.: Edward Elgar, 1997). On enclosure, see Robert C. Allen, "Community and Market in England: Open Fields and Enclosures Revisited," in M. Aoki and Y. Hayami, eds., *Communities and Markets in Economic Development* (New York: Oxford University Press, 2001), 42–69.

29. Allan Kulikoff, *From British Peasants to Colonial American Farmers* (Chapel Hill: University of North Carolina Press, 2000).

30. Greer, *Property and Dispossession*, 18.

31. John Brewer and Susan Staves, eds., *Early Modern Conceptions of Property* (New York: Routledge, 1995).

32. Brian Donahue, *The Great Meadow: Farmers and the Land in Colonial Concord* (New Haven: Yale University Press, 2004).

33. Emma Hart, "From Field to Plate: The Colonial Livestock Trade and the Development of an American Economic Culture," *William and Mary Quarterly* 73, no. 1 (2016): 107–40; Claire Priest, "Creating an American Property Law: Alienability and Its Limits in American History," *Harvard Law Review* 120, no. 2 (2006): 385–459.

34. James A. Henretta, *The Evolution of American Society, 1700–1815* (Lexington, Mass.: Heath, 1973), 7.

35. Gordon S. Wood, *The Radicalism of the American Revolution* (New York: Knopf, 1991), 114.

36. Greer, *Property and Dispossession*, 4.

37. William Cronon, *Changes in the Land: Indians, Colonists, and the Ecology of New England* (New York: Hill & Wang, 1983).

38. Greer, *Property and Dispossession*, 42.

39. Kathleen Bragdon, *Native People of Southern New England, 1650–1775* (Norman: University of Oklahoma Press, 2009), 113.

40. The best account of Locke's defense of private property I know of, which stresses Locke's first emphasis on "common ownership," is Seana Valentine Shiffrin, "Lockean Arguments for Intellectual Property," in Stephen R. Munzer, ed., *New Essays in the Political Theory of Property* (New York: Cambridge University Press, 2001): 138–67.

41. John Locke, *Two Treatises of Government*, ed. Peter Laslett (New York: Cambridge University Press, 1988), 146.

42. Locke's library contained books he read on Native American agricultural practices. Vicki Hsueh, "Cultivating and Challenging the Common: Lockean Property, Indigenous Traditionalisms, and the Problem of Exclusion," *Contemporary Political Theory* 5 (2006): 193–214.

43. Tomlins, *Freedom Bound*, 150, 148.

44. Anya Zilberstein, *A Temperate Empire: Making Climate Change in Early America* (New York: Oxford University Press, 2016).

45. Robert Nozick, *Anarchy, State, and Utopia* (New York: Basic Books, 1974).

46. Virginia DeJohn Anderson, *Creatures of Empire: How Domestic Animals Transformed Early America* (New York: Oxford University Press, 2004), 171.

47. Joseph Conrad, *Heart of Darkness*, ed. Ross C. Murfin (1899; Boston: Bedford/St. Martin's: 2011), 21.

48. Pekka Hämäläinen, *The Comanche Empire* (New Haven: Yale University Press, 2008).

49. Stephen Innes, *Creating the Commonwealth: The Economic Culture of Puritan New England* (New York: Norton, 1995), 287.

50. Bernard Bailyn, *The Peopling of British North America: An Introduction* (New York: Random House, 2011).

51. Russell R. Menard, "Colonial America's Mestizo Agriculture," in Cathy D. Matson, ed., *The Economy of Early America: Historical Perspectives and New Directions* (University Park: Pennsylvania State University Press, 2006), 107–23.

52. Eric Sloane, *A Museum of Early American Tools* (New York: W. Funk, 1964).

53. Captain John Smith, *Writings with Other Narratives of Roanoke, Jamestown, and the First English Settlement of America* (New York: Library of America, 2007), 804.

54. Miguel León-Portilla, "Men of Maize," in Alvin M. Josephy, Jr., ed., *America in 1492: The World of the Indian Peoples Before the Arrival of Columbus* (New York: Vintage, 1992), 147–75.

55. This section draws heavily from William Nelson Parker, *Europe, America, and the Wider World: Essays on the Economic History of Western Capitalism*, vol. 2, *America and the Wider World* (New York: Cambridge University Press, 1984), 161–82, and also David Freeman Hawke, *Everyday Life in Early America* (New York: Harper & Row, 1988).

56. Alfred W. Crosby, Jr., *The Columbian Exchange: Biological and Cultural Consequences of 1492* (Westport, Conn.: Praeger, 2003).

57. J. R. McNeill, *Something New Under the Sun: An Environmental History of the Twentieth-Century World* (New York: Norton, 2000), 12.

58. Joyce E. Chaplin, *An Anxious Pursuit: Agricultural Innovation and Modernity in the Lower South, 1730–1815* (Chapel Hill: University of North Carolina Press, 1993).

59. John Demos, *Circles and Lines: The Shape of Life in Early America* (Cambridge, Mass.: Harvard University Press, 2004).

60. Peter H. Lindert and Jeffrey G. Williamson, *Unequal Gains: American Growth and Inequality Since 1700* (Princeton: Princeton University Press, 2016), 58, fig. 3-2.

61. Drew R. McCoy, *The Elusive Republic: Political Economy in Jeffersonian America* (Chapel Hill: University of North Carolina Press, 1980), 51.

62. Alan Taylor, *American Revolutions: A Continental History, 1750–1804* (New York: Norton, 2016), 33.

63. U.S. Bureau of the Census, *Century of Population Growth, 1790–1900* (Washington, D.C.: Government Printing Office, 1909), 96.

64. Lindert and Williamson, *Unequal Gains*, 55.

65. Shammas, *History of Household Government*, 33, table 1.

66. Anthony S. Parent, *Foul Means: The Formation of a Slave Society in Virginia, 1660–1740* (Chapel Hill: University of North Carolina Press, 2003), Byrd quote at 201.

67. William Blackstone, *Commentaries on the Laws of England*, book 1, *Of the Rights of Persons*, ed. David Lemmings (1765; New York: Oxford University Press, 2016), 272.

68. Ibid., 284–85.

69. Ibid., 300.

70. Laurel Thatcher Ulrich, *Good Wives: Image and Reality in the Lives of Women in Northern New England, 1650–1750* (New York: Knopf, 1980), 70.

71. Ellen Hartigan-O'Connor, *The Ties That Buy: Women and Commerce in Revolutionary America* (Philadelphia: University of Pennsylvania Press, 2011); Laurel Thatcher Ulrich, *A Midwife's Tale: The Life of Martha Ballard, Based on Her Diary, 1785–1812* (New York: Knopf, 1990).

72. Tomlins, *Freedom Bound*, 35.

73. Susan E. Klepp and Billy G. Smith, eds., *The Infortunate: The Voyage and Adventures of William Moraley, an Indentured Servant* (University Park: Pennsylvania State University Press, 1992), 46.

74. Robert J. Steinfeld, *Coercion, Contract, and Free Labor in the Nineteenth Century* (New York: Cambridge University Press, 2001).

75. Halley, "What Is Family Law?," 8.

76. Geoffrey Guest, "The Boarding of the Dependent Poor in Colonial America," *Social Service Review* 63, no. 1 (1989): 92–112.

77. Clark, *Social Change in America*, 7.

78. Thomas D. Morris, *Southern Slavery and the Law, 1619–1860* (Chapel Hill: University of North Carolina Press, 1996).

79. Priest, "Creating an American Property Law."

80. Klepp and Smith, *Infortunate*, 58.

81. David Brion Davis, *The Problem of Slavery in the Age of Emancipation* (New York: Knopf, 2014).

82. Bertram Wyatt-Brown, *Yankee Saints and Southern Sinners* (Baton Rouge: Louisiana State University Press, 1986), 162.

83. Willie Lee Rose, *Slavery and Freedom* (New York: Oxford University Press, 1982), 25.

84. Thomas C. Holt, *Children of Fire: A History of African Americans* (New York: Hill & Wang, 2010), 53–88.

85. Jennifer Morgan, *Laboring Women: Reproduction and Gender in New World Slavery* (Philadelphia: University of Pennsylvania Press, 2004).

86. Daron Acemoglu, Simon Johnson, and James A. Robinson, "Reversal of Fortune: Geography and Institutions in the Making of the Modern World Income Distribution," *Quarterly Journal of Economics* 117, no. 4 (2002): 1231–94; Stanley L. Engerman et al., *Economic Development in the Americas Since 1500: Endowments and Institutions* (New York: Cambridge University Press, 2011).

87. Anthony B. Atkinson, Thomas Piketty, and Emmanuel Saez, "Top Incomes in the Long Run of History," *Journal of Economic Literature* 49, no. 1 (2011), 31, table 5; Lindert and Williamson, *Unequal Gains*, 36.

88. Lindert and Williamson, *Unequal Gains*, 37.

89. This debate is intelligently summarized and cited thoroughly in Naomi R. Lamoreaux, "Rethinking the Transition to Capitalism in the Early American Northeast," *Journal of American History* 90, no. 2 (2003): 437–61, which also significantly advances it.

90. William Nelson Parker, "The True History of the Northern Farmer," in Parker, *Europe, America, and Wider World*.

91. Greer, *Property and Dispossession*, 99.

92. John Frederick Martin, *Profits in the Wilderness: Entrepreneurship and the Founding of New England Towns in the Seventeenth Century* (Chapel Hill: University of North Carolina Press, 1991).

93. Stuart Banner, *How the Indians Lost Their Land: Law and Power on the Frontier* (Cambridge, Mass.: Harvard University Press, 2009), 100.

94. Weaver, *Great Land Rush*, 88, 154.

95. Winifred Barr Rothenberg, *From Market-Places to a Market Economy: The Transformation of Rural Massachusetts, 1750–1850* (Chicago: University of Chicago Press, 1992).

96. De Vries, *Industrious Revolution.*

97. Priest, "Creating an American Property Law."

98. Colin G. Calloway, *The Scratch of a Pen: 1763 and the Transformation of North America* (New York: Oxford University Press, 2006).

99. This point is incisively made by Robert Brenner, "Property and Progress: Where Adam Smith Went Wrong," in Chris Wickham, ed., *Marxist History-Writing for the Twenty-First Century* (New York: Oxford University Press, 2011), 49–111.

100. Thomas Jefferson, *Writings: Autobiography / Notes on the State of Virginia / Public and Private Papers / Addresses / Letters,* ed. Merrill D. Peterson (New York: Library of America, 1984), 290.

101. "Safety-first" comes from Gavin Wright and Howard Kunreuther, "Cotton, Corn and Risk in the Nineteenth Century," *Journal of Economic History* 35, no. 3 (1975): 526–51. See also Richard Lyman Bushman, "Markets and Composite Farms in Early America," *William and Mary Quarterly* 55, no. 3 (1998): 351–74; Lorena Seebach Walsh, *Motives of Honor, Pleasure, and Profit: Plantation Management in the Colonial Chesapeake, 1607–1763* (Chapel Hill: University of North Carolina Press, 2010).

102. John J. McCusker and Russell R. Menard, *The Economy of British America, 1607–1789, with Supplementary Bibliography* (Chapel Hill: University of North Carolina Press, 1991), 132, table 6.

103. James T. Lemon, *The Best Poor Man's Country: A Geographical Study of Early Southeastern Pennsylvania* (Baltimore: Johns Hopkins University Press, 1972), 180–83.

CHAPTER 3: REPUBLICAN POLITICAL ECONOMY

1. Jonathan Israel, *The Expanding Blaze: How the American Revolution Ignited the World, 1775–1848* (Princeton: Princeton University Press, 2017).

2. Alan Taylor, *American Revolutions: A Continental History, 1750–1804* (New York: Norton, 2016), 211–50.

3. Stanley Elkins and Eric McKitrick, *The Age of Federalism: The Early American Republic, 1788–1800* (New York: Oxford University Press, 1993), 77.

4. Sarah Knott, *Sensibility and the American Revolution* (Chapel Hill: University of North Carolina Press, 2009).

5. Gautham Rao, *National Duties: Custom Houses and the Making of the American State* (Chicago: University of Chicago Press, 2016), 11.

6. James R. Fichter, *So Great a Proffit: How the East Indies Trade Transformed Anglo-American Capitalism* (Cambridge, Mass.: Harvard University Press, 2010).

7. Allan Kulikoff, " 'Such Things Ought Not to Be': The American Revolution and the First National Great Depression," in Andrew Shankman, ed., *The World of the Revolutionary American Republic: Land, Labor, and the Conflict for a Continent* (New York: Routledge, 2014), 134–64.

8. Peter H. Lindert and Jeffrey G. Williamson, *Unequal Gains: American Growth and Inequality Since 1700* (Princeton: Princeton University Press, 2016), 79. Twenty percent is the figure for 1770 and 1800. There were likely income gains between 1790 and 1800.

9. Joanne B. Freeman, *Affairs of Honor: National Politics in the New Republic* (New Haven: Yale University Press, 2001).

10. This point, made brilliantly, is the basis of the best political history of this decade, Elkins and McKitrick, *Age of Federalism.*

11. Jeffrey Sklansky, *Sovereign of the Market: The Money Question in Early America* (Chicago: University of Chicago Press, 2017), 21–92.

12. Farley Grubb, "Is Paper Money Just Paper Money? Experimentation and Variation in the Paper Monies Issued by the American Colonies from 1690 to 1775," in Christopher Hanes and Susan Wolcott, eds., *Research in Economic History* (Bingley, U.K.: Emerald Group, 2016), 32:147–224.

13. Andrew David Edwards, "Grenville's Silver Hammer: The Problem of Money in the Stamp Act Crisis," *Journal of American History* 104, no. 2 (2017): 337–62.

14. Curtis P. Nettels, *The Emergence of a National Economy* (New York: Holt, Rinehart, 1962), 43–44.

15. Ibid., 56.

16. Max M. Edling, *A Revolution in Favor of Government: Origins of the U.S. Constitution and the Making of the American State* (New York: Oxford University Press, 2003), 84.

17. Cathy D. Matson and Peter Onuf, *A Union of Interests: Political and Economic Thought in Revolutionary America* (Lawrence: University Press of Kansas, 1990), 31–49.

18. Irving Fisher, "The Debt-Deflation Theory of Great Depressions," *Econometrica* 1, no. 4 (1933): 337–57.

19. Andrew Shankman, *Crucible of American Democracy: The Struggle to Fuse Egalitarianism and Capitalism in Jeffersonian Pennsylvania* (Lawrence: University Press of Kansas, 2004).

20. Terry Bouton, *Taming Democracy: "The People," the Founders, and the Troubled Ending of the American Revolution* (New York: Oxford University Press, 2007).

21. Woody Holton, *Unruly Americans and the Origins of the Constitution* (New York: Hill & Wang, 2007), 145.

22. Sidney Homer and Richard Sylla, *A History of Interest Rates* (Hoboken, N.J.: Wiley, 2005), 275.

23. Justin du Rivage, *Revolution Against Empire: Taxes, Politics, and the Origins of American Independence* (New Haven: Yale University Press, 2017).

24. On the concerns of foreign investors, see Daniel J. Hulsebosch, "Being Seen Like a State: How Americans (and Britons) Built the Constitutional Infrastructure of a Developing Nation," *William and Mary Law Review* 58, no. 4 (2018): 1239–318.

25. Pauline Maier, *Ratification: The People Debate the Constitution, 1787–1788* (New York: Simon & Schuster, 2010).

26. Elkins and McKitrick, *Age of Federalism*, 114.

27. Thomas K. McCraw, *The Founders and Finance: How Hamilton, Gallatin, and Other Immigrants Forged a New Economy* (Cambridge, Mass.: Belknap Press, 2012), 94–96.

28. These were most prominently "Report on the Public Credit, January 9, 1790," "Report on a National Bank, December 13, 1790," and "Report on the Subject of Manufactures, December 5, 1791." See Alexander Hamilton, *Writings*, ed. Joanne B. Freeman (New York: Library of America, 2001), 531–613, 647–735.

29. Lindert and Williamson, *Unequal Gains*, 77–95; Holton, *Unruly Americans*, 37; Kulikoff, " 'Such Things Ought Not to Be,' " 152–53; Robert E. Wright, *One Nation Under Debt: Hamilton, Jefferson, and the History of What We Owe* (New York: McGraw-Hill, 2008).

30. On money and sovereignty, see Christine Desan, *Making Money: Coin, Currency, and the Coming of Capitalism* (New York: Oxford University Press, 2015); Andrew David Edwards, "The American Revolution and Christine Desan's New History of Money," *Law and Social Inquiry* 42, no. 1 (2017): 252–78.

31. Elkins and McKitrick, *Age of Federalism*, 155.

32. John Brewer, *The Sinews of Power: War, Money and the English State, 1688–1783* (London: Routledge, 1989).

33. Ron Chernow, *Alexander Hamilton* (New York: Penguin Press, 2004).

34. Gordon S. Wood, *Revolutionary Characters: What Made the Founders Different* (New York: Penguin Press, 2006), 127.

35. Gerald Stourzh, *Alexander Hamilton and the Idea of Republican Government* (Stanford, Calif.: Stanford University Press, 1970).

36. Alexander Hamilton, *The Papers of Alexander Hamilton*, vol. 5, *June 1788–November 1789*, ed. Harold C. Syrett (New York: Columbia University Press, 1962), 80–86.

37. Alexander Hamilton, James Madison, and John Jay, *The Federalist Papers*, ed. Isaac Kramnick (New York: Penguin Classics, 1987), 134.

38. Matson and Onuf, *Union of Interests*, 29.

39. Elkins and McKitrick, *Age of Federalism*, 109.

40. Robert Eric Wright, *Hamilton Unbound: Finance and the Creation of the American Republic* (Westport, Conn.: Greenwood Press, 2002); McCraw, *Founders and Finance*.

41. Hamilton, *Writings*, ed. Freeman, 164.

42. Gordon S. Wood, *The Radicalism of the American Revolution* (New York: Knopf, 1991), 276.

43. Gary J. Kornblith and John M. Murrin, "The Making and Unmaking of an American Ruling Class," in Alfred E. Young, ed., *Beyond the American Revolution: Explorations in the History of American Radicalism* (DeKalb: Northern Illinois University Press, 1993), 27–79.

44. Rao, *National Duties*, 131.

45. Hamilton, *Writings*, ed. Freeman, 578, 579.

46. Robert E. Wright, *Corporation Nation* (Philadelphia: University of Pennsylvania Press, 2013), 49–79; Hanna A. Farber, "Underwritten States: Marine Insurance and the Making of Bodies Politic in America, 1622–1815" (PhD diss., University of California, Berkeley, 2014).

47. Pauline Maier, "The Revolutionary Origins of the American Corporation," *William and Mary Quarterly* 50, no. 1 (1993): 51–84.

48. Elkins and McKitrick, *Age of Federalism*, 243.

49. On divisions between "radical" and "moderate" republicans during the Age of Revolution, see Israel, *Expanding Blaze*, 11–14. For a different framing that underscores likeness, see James T. Kloppenberg, *Toward Democracy: Struggle for Self-Rule in European and American Thought* (New York: Oxford University Press, 2016), 409–54.

50. On Jefferson's life, see John B. Boles, *Jefferson: Architect of American Liberty* (New York: Basic Books, 2017); Annette Gordon-Reed and Peter S. Onuf, *"Most Blessed of the Patriarchs": Thomas Jefferson and the Empire of the Imagination* (New York: Liveright, 2016).

51. Thomas Jefferson, *Writings: Autobiography / Notes on the State of Virginia / Public and Private Papers / Addresses / Letters*, ed. Merrill D. Peterson (New York: Library of America, 1984).

52. John Joseph Wallis, "The Concept of Systematic Corruption in American History," in Edward L. Glaeser and Claudia Goldin, eds., *Corruption and Reform: Lessons from America's Economic History* (Chicago: University of Chicago Press, 2006), 23–62.

53. J. G. A. Pocock, *Virtue, Commerce, and History: Essays on Political Thought and History, Chiefly in the Eighteenth Century* (New York: Cambridge University Press, 1985), 103–24.

54. John M. Murrin, "The Great Inversion, or Court Versus Country: A Comparison of the Revolution Settlements in England (1688–1721) and America (1776–1816)," in J. G. A. Pocock, ed., *Three British Revolutions: 1641, 1688, 1776* (Princeton: Princeton University Press, 1980), 368–453; Bernard Bailyn, *The Ideological Origins of the American Revolution*, 15th ed. (Cambridge, Mass.: Belknap Press, 2017).

55. Hamilton, *Writings*, ed. Freeman, 977.

56. Gordon-Reed and Onuf, *"Most Blessed of the Patriarchs."*

57. Gavin Wright, "The Role of Nationhood in the Economic Development of the

USA," in Alice Teichova and Herbert Matis, eds., *Nation, State, and the Economy in History* (New York: Cambridge University Press, 2003), 392.

58. Douglas R. Egerton, *Death or Liberty: African Americans and Revolutionary America* (New York: Oxford University Press. 2009), 78–79, 122–47. See also Alan Taylor, *The Internal Enemy: Slavery and War in Virginia, 1772–1832* (New York: Norton, 2013), 13–54.

59. Drew R. McCoy, *The Elusive Republic: Political Economy in Jeffersonian America* (Chapel Hill: University of North Carolina Press, 1980).

60. Thomas Jefferson, *The Papers of Thomas Jefferson*, vol. 13, *March to 7 October 1788*, ed. Julian P. Boyd (Princeton: Princeton University Press, 1956), 430–32.

61. Craige quoted in Joseph Stancliffe Davis, *Essays in the Earlier History of American Corporations* (Cambridge, Mass.: Harvard University Press, 1917), 1:186.

62. Kulikoff, " 'Such Things Ought Not to Be,' " 152.

63. Jefferson quoted in Elkins and McKitrick, *Age of Federalism*, 243.

64. Joyce Oldham Appleby, *Thomas Jefferson* (New York: Times Books, 2003), 19.

65. Bradford Perkins, *The Cambridge History of American Foreign Relations*, vol. 1, *The Creation of a Republican Empire, 1776–1865* (New York: Cambridge University Press, 1995), 22.

66. Nettels, *Emergence of a National Economy*, 231.

67. Hamilton, *Writings*, ed. Freeman, 671, 681.

68. Elkins and McKitrick, *Age of Federalism*, 263.

69. Richard Sylla, Robert E. Wright, and David J. Cowen, "Alexander Hamilton, Central Banker: Crisis Management During the U.S. Financial Panic of 1792," *Business History Review* 83, no. 1 (2009): 61–86.

70. James Madison, *The Papers of James Madison*, vol. 14, *6 April 1791—16 March 1793*, ed. Robert A. Rutland and Thomas A. Mason (Charlottesville: University Press of Virginia, 1983), 370–72.

71. Hamilton, *Papers*, ed. Syrett, 12:347–50.

72. Thomas Jefferson, *The Papers of Thomas Jefferson*, vol. 24, *1 June to 31 December 1792*, ed. John Catanzariti (Princeton: Princeton University Press, 1990), 351–60.

73. Richard Sylla, "Financial Foundations: Public Credit, the National Bank, and Securities Markets," in Douglas A. Irwin and Richard Sylla, eds., *Founding Choices: American Economic Policy in the 1790s* (Chicago: University of Chicago Press, 2011), 59–88.

74. Bouton, *Taming Democracy*, 216–43.

75. Kathleen DuVal, *Independence Lost: Lives on the Edge of the American Revolution* (New York: Random House, 2015), 223–91.

76. Rao, *National Duties*, 2, table 1.

77. Hamilton, *Papers*, ed. Syrett, 17: 428–29.

78. Peter L. Rousseau and Richard Sylla, "Emerging Financial Markets and Early U.S. Growth," *Explorations in Economic History* 42, no. 1 (2005): 5.

79. Hulsebosch, "Being Seen Like a State," 1303–13.

80. Rousseau and Sylla, "Emerging Financial Markets"; Richard Sylla, Jack W. Wilson, and Robert E. Wright, "Integration of Trans-Atlantic Capital Markets, 1790–1845," *Review of Finance* 10, no. 4 (2006): 613–44.

81. David R. Meyer, *The Roots of American Industrialization* (Baltimore: Johns Hopkins University Press, 2003), 13–86. Meyer emphasizes urban-rural exchange rather than Hamilton's reforms.

82. U.S. reexports of goods—overwhelmingly from the West Indies—to Europe valued $539,000 in 1790. By 1806, reexports valued over $60 million—exceeding the value of all domestically produced exports by some $11 million. Freight earnings increased from $6.2 million in 1791 to $42.1 million in 1807, and the value of overseas trade per capita, roughly in 1790 what it was in 1776, tripled between 1790 and 1807

(the highest rate ever in U.S. history). Nettels, *Emergence of a National Economy*, 396, table 17, 235–36; Douglass C. North, *The Economic Growth of the United States, 1790–1860* (New York: Norton, 1966), 249, table A-III, 25.

83.   Elkins and McKitrick, *Age of Federalism*, 441.

84.   Christopher H. Achen and Larry M. Bartels, *Democracy for Realists: Why Elections Do Not Produce Responsive Government* (Princeton: Princeton University Press, 2016), 157, table 6.5.

85.   Sean Wilentz, *The Rise of American Democracy: Jefferson to Lincoln* (New York: Norton, 2005), 40–98.

86.   Kulikoff, " 'Such Things Ought Not to Be,' " 149–51.

87.   Joyce Appleby, *Capitalism and a New Social Order: The Republican Version of the 1790s* (New York: New York University Press, 1984), 26–51.

88.   One member of the Electoral College mistakenly cast a vote for Aaron Burr, and so Burr and Jefferson tied. The House of Representatives ultimately elected Jefferson.

89.   "Letter from Alexander Hamilton, Concerning the Public Conduct and Character of John Adams, Esq. President of the United States, October 24, 1800," in Hamilton, *Writings*, ed. Freeman, 934–71.

90.   Thomas Jefferson, *The Papers of Thomas Jefferson*, vol. 38, *1 July to 12 November 1802*, ed. Barbara B. Oberg (Princeton: Princeton University Press, 2011), 565–67.

91.   Hamilton, *Writings*, ed. Freeman, 986.

92.   Ibid., 1022.

93.   McCraw, *Founders and Finance*, 232.

94.   François Furstenberg, "The Significance of the Trans-Appalachian Frontier in Atlantic History," *American Historical Review* 113, no. 3 (2008): 647–77.

95.   Taylor, *American Revolutions*, 267.

96.   Jefferson, First Inaugural Address, March 4, 1801, in *The Papers of Thomas Jefferson Digital Edition*, ed. Barbara B. Oberg and Jefferson Looney (Charlottesville: University of Virginia Press, 2008).

97.   Richard White, "The Louisiana Purchase and the Fictions of Empire," in Peter J. Kastor and François Weil, eds., *Empires of the Imagination: Transatlantic Histories of the Louisiana Purchase* (Charlottesville: University of Virginia Press, 2009), 37.

98.   D. W. Meinig, *The Shaping of America: A Geographical Perspective on 500 Years of History*, vol. 2, *Continental America, 1800–1867* (New Haven: Yale University Press, 1993), 242–43; Malcolm J. Rohrbough, *The Land Office Business: The Settlement and Administration of American Public Lands, 1789–1837* (New York: Oxford University Press, 1968), 3–50.

99.   Stanley Lebergott, *The Americans: An Economic Record* (New York: Norton, 1984), 83.

100.   Peter S. Onuf, *Jefferson's Empire: The Language of American Nationhood* (Charlottesville: University of Virginia Press, 2000), 55–76.

101.   Jonathan Atkins, *From Confederation to Nation: The Early American Republic, 1789–1848* (New York: Routledge, 2016), 56.

102.   Rashauna Johnson, *Slavery's Metropolis: Unfree Labor in New Orleans During the Age of Revolutions* (New York: Cambridge University Press, 2016); Adam Rothman, *Slave Country: American Expansion and the Origins of the Deep South* (Cambridge, Mass.: Harvard University Press, 2005), 1–36.

103.   Douglass North famously argued that transregional trade linkages because of cotton launched U.S. economic growth. North, *Economic Growth of the United States*. So strongly stated, this view is no longer viable. Subsequent research demonstrated the vitality of more local commerce. See Gavin Wright, "The Antebellum U.S. Economy," in Claude Diebolt and Michael Haupert, eds., *Handbook of Cliometrics* (Berlin: Springer, 2018), 1–23.

104. Meyer, *Roots of American Industrialization*, 13–86.

105. Wood, *Radicalism of the Revolution*, 326.

106. Richard Lyman Bushman, *The Refinement of America: Persons, Houses, Cities* (New York: Knopf, 1992), 400–25.

107. Elizabeth A. Bohls and Ian Duncan, eds., *Travel Writing 1700–1830: An Anthology* (New York: Oxford University Press, 2005), 393.

108. Burton Spivak, *Jefferson's English Crisis: Commerce, Embargo, and the Republican Revolution* (Charlottesville: University Press of Virginia, 1979), 9.

109. U.S. exports plummeted from $108 million to $22 million, and U.S. freight earnings dropped from $42 million to $23 million. Nettels, *Emergence of a National Economy*, 396, table 17, 235–36; North, *Economic Growth of the United States*, table A-III, 25. Custom rates fell from $16.4 million to $7.3 million. Rao, *National Duties*, 2, table 1.

110. As well as negotiating his authority with merchants. See Rao, *National Duties*, 132–65.

111. Spivak, *Jefferson's English Crisis*, 207.

112. Joseph H. Davis and Douglas A. Irwin, "Trade Disruptions and America's Early Industrialization," National Bureau of Economic Research, Working Paper No. 9944 (2003).

113. Alan Taylor, *The Civil War of 1812: American Citizens, British Subjects, Irish Rebels, and Indian Allies* (New York: Vintage Books, 2011), 428.

114. Jeremy Adelman and Stephen Aron, "From Borderlands to Borders: Empires, Nation-States, and the Peoples in Between in North American History," *American Historical Review* 104, no. 3 (1999): 814–41.

115. Richard White, *The Middle Ground: Indians, Empires, and Republics in the Great Lakes Region, 1650–1815* (New York: Cambridge University Press, 2010), 413–524.

116. J. M. Opal, *Avenging the People: Andrew Jackson, the Rule of Law, and the American Nation* (New York: Oxford University Press, 2017).

117. Robert V. Remini, *Andrew Jackson: A Biography* (New York: St. Martin's Press, 2008), 76.

118. John Joseph Wallis and Barry R. Weingast, "Equilibrium Federal Impotence: Why the States and Not the American National Government Financed Economic Development in the Antebellum Era," *Journal of Public Finance and Public Choice* 33, no. 1 (2018): 19–44.

119. John M. Murrin, "The Jeffersonian Triumph and American Exceptionalism," *Journal of the Early Republic* 20, no. 1 (2000): 1–25.

120. James Madison, "Seventh Annual Message," December 5, 1815, American Presidency Project, https://www.presidency.ucsb.edu/documents/seventh-annual -message-0.

121. John Lauritz Larson, *Internal Improvement: National Public Works and the Promise of Popular Government in the Early United States* (Chapel Hill: University of North Carolina Press, 2001), 65.

CHAPTER 4: CAPITALISM AND THE DEMOCRACY

1. Sean Wilentz, *The Rise of American Democracy: Jefferson to Lincoln* (New York: Norton, 2005), 181–520. See also Daniel Walker Howe, *What Hath God Wrought: The Transformation of America, 1815–1848* (New York: Oxford University Press, 2007).

2. Alexander Keyssar, *The Right to Vote: The Contested History of Democracy in the United States* (New York: Basic Books, 2000), 26–76.

3. Some historians have argued for a veritable "market revolution." See John Lauritz Larson, *The Market Revolution in America: Liberty, Ambition, and the Eclipse of the Common Good* (New York: Cambridge University Press, 2009); Charles Sellers, *The Mar-*

ket Revolution: Jacksonian America, 1815–1846 (New York: Oxford University Press, 1992). The view here is more in line with an older one, which focuses on the role of politics in the increasing extent of markets. See George Rogers Taylor, *The Transportation Revolution, 1815–1860* (New York: Rinehart, 1951).

4. For two brilliant accounts of that ethos in the midst of capitalism's and democracy's joint rise, see Michael Zakim, *Accounting for Capitalism: The World the Clerk Made* (Chicago: University of Chicago Press, 2018); Michael Zakim, *Ready-Made Democracy: A History of Men's Dress in the American Republic, 1760–1860* (Chicago: University of Chicago Press, 2003).

5. Fanny Trollope, *Domestic Manners of the Americans* (1832; New York: Penguin Classics, 1997), 38.

6. Peter L. Rousseau and Richard Sylla, "Emerging Financial Markets and Early U.S. Growth," *Explorations in Economic History* 42, no. 1 (2005): 1–26. For the North, see Naomi R. Lamoreaux, *Insider Lending: Banks, Personal Connections, and Economic Development in Industrial New England* (New York: Cambridge University Press, 1994). For the South, see Richard Holcombe Kilbourne, Jr., *Debt, Investment, Slaves: Credit Relations in East Feliciana Parish, Louisiana, 1825–1885* (Tuscaloosa: University of Alabama Press, 1995); Edward E. Baptist, *The Half Has Never Been Told: Slavery and the Making of American Capitalism* (New York: Basic Books, 2014), 75–111.

7. Peter H. Lindert and Jeffrey G. Williamson, *Unequal Gains: American Growth and Inequality Since 1700* (Princeton: Princeton University Press, 2016), 96–141.

8. Ibid.

9. Andrew Jackson, "Farewell Address," March 4, 1837, American Presidency Project, https://www.presidency.ucsb.edu/documents/farewell-address-0.

10. Gautham Rao, *National Duties: Custom Houses and the Making of the American State* (Chicago: University of Chicago Press, 2016); Harry N. Scheiber, "Private Rights and Public Power: American Law, Capitalism, and the Republican Polity in Nineteenth-Century America," *Yale Law Journal* 107, no. 3 (1997): 823–61. Sphering did not mean that public authority, in its proper sphere, could not be robust. See William J. Novak, *The People's Welfare: Law and Regulation in Nineteenth-Century America* (Chapel Hill: University of North Carolina Press, 1996).

11. James Willard Hurst, *Law and the Conditions of Freedom in the Nineteenth-Century United States* (Madison: University of Wisconsin Press, 1956), 1.

12. Naomi R. Lamoreaux and William J. Novak, eds., *Corporations and American Democracy* (Cambridge, Mass.: Harvard University Press, 2017); Naomi R. Lamoreaux and John Joseph Wallis, "States, Not Nation: The Sources of Political and Economic Development in the Early United States," Working Paper (New Haven: Yale University, 2015).

13. Lindert and Williamson, *Unequal Gains*, 103–4. On the continental U.S. as a free-trade zone, see Kevin H. O'Rourke and Jeffrey G. Williamson, *Globalization and History: The Evolution of a Nineteenth-Century Atlantic Economy* (Cambridge, Mass.: MIT Press, 1999), 29–56.

14. A classic account remains, Douglass C. North, *The Economic Growth of the United States, 1790–1860* (New York: Prentice-Hall, 1961), 122–34, 177–88.

15. Robert Lipsey, "U.S. Foreign Trade and the Balance of Payments, 1800–1913," National Bureau of Economic Research, Working Paper no. 4710 (April 1994), 22.

16. Stuart Bruchey, *Cotton and the Growth of the American Economy: 1790–1860: Sources and Readings* (New York: Harcourt, Brace & World, 1967), 23, table A-L, "Value of Leading Domestic Exports, United States: 1815–60."

17. Sven Beckert, *Empire of Cotton: A Global History* (New York: Knopf, 2014), 98–135.

18. Alan L. Olmstead and Paul W. Rhode, *Creating Abundance: Biological Innovation*

and American Agricultural Development (New York: Cambridge University Press, 2008), 104; Angela Lakwete, *Inventing the Cotton Gin: Machine and Myth in Antebellum America* (Baltimore: Johns Hopkins University Press, 2003).

19.   Paul Frymer, *Building an American Empire: The Era of Territorial and Political Expansion* (Princeton: Princeton University Press, 2017), 77–83.

20.   Reeve Huston, "Land Conflict and Land Policy, 1785–1841," in Andrew Shankman, ed., *The World of the Revolutionary American Republic: Land, Labor, and the Conflict for a Continent* (New York: Routledge, 2014), 334.

21.   Howe, *What Hath God Wrought*, 125–63.

22.   On labor systems in the lower Mississippi Valley, see Baptist, *Half Has Never Been Told*, 111–44; Walter Johnson, *River of Dark Dreams: Slavery and Empire in the Cotton Kingdom* (Cambridge, Mass.: Belknap Press, 2013).

23.   Paul Finkelman, *Slavery and the Founders: Race and Liberty in the Age of Jefferson* (New York: Routledge, 2014); Gavin Wright, "Slavery and American Agricultural History," *Agricultural History* 77, no. 4 (2003): 527–52.

24.   Harry L. Watson, *Liberty and Power: The Politics of Jacksonian America* (New York: Hill & Wang, 1990), 24.

25.   David R. Meyer, *The Roots of American Industrialization* (Baltimore: Johns Hopkins University Press, 2003); Diane Lindstrom, *Economic Development in the Philadelphia Region, 1810–1850* (New York: Columbia University Press, 1978).

26.   J. M. Opal, "Natural Rights and National Greatness," in Shankman, *World of Revolutionary Republic*, 306.

27.   Bray Hammond, *Banks and Politics in America from the Revolution to the Civil War* (Princeton: Princeton University Press, 1957), 251–85; Howard Bodenhorn, *State Banking in Early America: A New Economic History* (New York: Oxford University Press, 2002).

28.   Mathew Carey, *Essays on Political Economy; or, The Most Certain Means of Promoting the Wealth, Power, Resources, and Happiness of Nations, Applied Particularly to the United States* (Philadelphia: H. C. Carey & I. Lea, 1822), 419.

29.   Larson, *Market Revolution in America*, 39.

30.   See Wilentz, *Rise of American Democracy*, 181–217.

31.   J. M. Opal, *Avenging the People: Andrew Jackson, the Rule of Law, and the American Nation* (New York: Oxford University Press, 2017), 183–86; Murray N. Rothbard, *The Panic of 1819: Reactions and Policies* (Auburn, Ala.: Ludwig von Mises Institute, 2007), 37–80.

32.   Rothbard, *Panic of 1819*, 11.

33.   Opal, "Natural Rights and National Greatness," 308–9.

34.   *Annals of the Congress of the United States*, vol. 42 (1856), 1983.

35.   Henry L. Watson, *Andrew Jackson vs. Henry Clay: Democracy and Development in Antebellum America* (New York: Bedford/St. Martin's, 1998), 146. Clay had at his fingertips the works of two early U.S. political economists. The Philadelphian Mathew Carey's *Essays on Political Economy* (1822) was a neomercantilist critique of free trade. The Baltimore writer Daniel Raymond instructed that a citizen must "forgo his own private advantages for the public good." Daniel Raymond, *Thoughts on Political Economy: In Two Parts* (Baltimore: F. Lucas, 1820), 326.

36.   Andrew Shankman, "Capitalism, Slavery, and the New Epoch," in Sven Beckert and Seth Rockman, eds., *Slavery's Capitalism: A New History of American Economic Development* (Philadelphia: University of Pennsylvania Press, 2016), 252.

37.   John Lauritz Larson, *Internal Improvement: National Public Works and the Promise of Popular Government in the Early United States* (Chapel Hill: University of North Carolina Press, 2001), 39–71.

38.   Herman Melville, *Moby-Dick; or, The Whale* (1851; New York: Random House, 1994), 127.

39. Tyehimba Jess, *Olio* (Seattle: Wave Books, 2016), 102.

40. Andrew Jackson to James Gadsen, August 1, 1819, in Jackson, *The Papers of Andrew Jackson: 1816–1820*, ed. Harold D. Moser et al. (Knoxville: University of Tennessee Press, 1994), 307.

41. Opal, "Natural Rights and National Greatness," 310.

42. See Wilentz, *Rise of American Democracy*, 281–311; Watson, *Liberty and Power*, 42–72.

43. Rothbard, *Panic of 1819*, 34–55.

44. James L. Huston, "Virtue Besieged: Virtue, Equality, and the General Welfare in the Tariff Debates of the 1820s," *Journal of the Early Republic* 14, no. 4 (1994): 523–47.

45. John Taylor, *Tyranny Unmasked* (Washington, D.C.: Davis & Force, 1822), 27.

46. Opal, *Avenging the People*, 172–205.

47. Opal, "Natural Rights and Natural Greatness," 313.

48. Watson, *Liberty and Power*, 94.

49. Watson, *Andrew Jackson vs. Henry Clay*, 15.

50. Frymer, *Building an American Empire*, 113–27.

51. Anne F. Hyde, *Empires, Nations, and Families: A History of the North American West, 1800–1860* (Lincoln: University of Nebraska Press, 2011), 225.

52. Larson, *Internal Improvement*.

53. Watson, *Liberty and Power*, 137.

54. Richard R. John, *Spreading the News: The American Postal System from Franklin to Morse* (Cambridge, Mass.: Harvard University Press, 1995).

55. Wilentz, *Rise of American Democracy*, 372, 369.

56. Ibid., 365; Jane Ellen Knodell, *The Second Bank of the United States: "Central" Banker in an Era of Nation-Building, 1816–1836* (New York: Routledge, 2016), 56–64, 129, table 5.6.

57. Richard Holcombe Kilbourne, Jr., *Slave Agriculture and Financial Markets in Antebellum America: The Bank of the United States in Mississippi, 1831–1852* (New York: Routledge, 2006), 25–38.

58. Wilentz, *Rise of American Democracy*, 366.

59. Watson, *Liberty and Power*, 141.

60. Andrew Jackson and Daniel Webster, *Veto Message of President Andrew Jackson, on Returning the Bank Bill to the Senate with His Objections, July, 1832; Together with the Speech of the Hon. Daniel Webster, Relative to the Same* (Lowell: National Republican Central Committee Journal Press, 1832), 3.

61. Ibid., 20, 5, 11, 25.

62. Wilentz, *Rise of American Democracy*, 371.

63. Watson, *Liberty and Power*, 151.

64. Robert Vincent Remini, *The Age of Jackson* (Columbia: University of South Carolina Press, 1972), xvi.

65. William Leggett, *A Collection of the Political Writings of William Leggett*, ed. Theodore Sedgwick (New York: Taylor & Dodd, 1840), 2:39. On Leggett's thought, see Jeffrey Sklansky, *Sovereign of the Market: The Money Question in Early America* (Chicago: University of Chicago Press, 2017), 93–130.

66. Wilfred M. McClay, *The Masterless: Self and Society in Modern America* (Chapel Hill: University of North Carolina Press, 1994), 55.

67. Howard Gillman, *The Constitution Besieged: The Rise and Demise of Lochner Era Police Powers Jurisprudence* (Durham, N.C.: Duke University Press, 1993), 33–44; Scheiber, "Private Rights and Public Power."

68. Rao, *National Duties*, 180–202; Nicholas R. Parrillo, *Against the Profit Motive: The Salary Revolution in American Government, 1780–1940* (New Haven: Yale University Press, 2013).

69.   Gergely Baics, *Feeding Gotham: The Political Economy and Geography of Food in New York, 1790–1860* (Princeton: Princeton University Press, 2016), 20–56; Hendrik Hartog, *Public Property and Private Power: The Corporation of the City of New York in American Law, 1730–1870* (Chapel Hill: University of North Carolina Press, 1983), 158–76.

70.   Meyer, *Roots of American Industrialization*, 5, table 1.2.

71.   Robert E. Gallman, "Economic Growth and Structural Change in the Long Nineteenth Century," in Stanley L. Engerman and Robert E. Gallman, eds., *The Cambridge Economic History of the United States*, vol. 2, *The Long Nineteenth Century* (New York: Cambridge University Press, 2000), 43, table 1.13.

72.   Taylor, *Transportation Revolution*.

73.   Albert Fishlow, "Antebellum Interregional Trade Reconsidered," *American Economic Review* 54, no. 3 (1964): 352–64; Lindstrom, *Economic Development in Philadelphia Region*, 5–8.

74.   Lindert and Williamson, *Unequal Gains*, 102, table 5-3, 130.

75.   John Joseph Wallis and Barry R. Weingast, "Equilibrium Federal Impotence: Why the States and Not the American National Government Financed Economic Development in the Antebellum Era," *Journal of Public Finance and Public Choice* 33, no. 1 (2018): 19.

76.   Dan Bogart and John Majewski, "Two Roads to the Transportation Revolution: Early Corporations in the United Kingdom and the United States," in Dora L. Costa and Naomi R. Lamoreaux, eds., *Understanding Long-Run Economic Growth: Geography, Institutions, and the Knowledge Economy* (Chicago: University of Chicago Press, 2011), 177–204; Daniel B. Klein and John Majewski, "Economy, Community, and Law: The Turnpike Movement in New York, 1797–1845," *Law and Society Review* 26, no. 3 (1992): 469–512.

77.   Meyer, *Roots of American Industrialization*, 177.

78.   Stephen Minicucci, "Internal Improvements and the Union, 1790–1860," *Studies in American Political Development* 18, no. 2 (2004), 172; Larson, *Internal Improvement*, 71–108.

79.   Harry N. Scheiber, *Ohio Canal Era: A Case Study of Government and the Economy, 1820–1861* (Athens: Ohio University Press, 1969).

80.   Namsuk Kim and John Joseph Wallis, "The Market for American State Government Bonds in Britain and the United States, 1830–43," *Economic History Review* 58, no. 4 (2005): 736–64; Richard Sylla, Jack W. Wilson, and Robert E. Wright, "Integration of Trans-Atlantic Capital Markets, 1790–1845," *Review of Finance* 10, no. 4 (2006): 628, fig. 4.

81.   Edward E. Baptist, "Toxic Debt, Liar Loans, Collateralized and Securitized Human Bondage, and the Panic of 1837," in Michael Zakim and Gary J. Kornblith, eds., *Capitalism Takes Command: The Social Transformation of Nineteenth-Century America* (Chicago: University of Chicago Press, 2012), 69–92.

82.   Peter L. Rousseau and Richard Sylla, "Emerging Financial Markets and Early U.S. Growth," *Explorations in Economic History* 42, no. 1 (2005): 1–26.

83.   Ibid., 12, fig. 4, computed by subtracting consumption, net foreign investment, and government expenditure from an estimate of U.S. gross national product.

84.   Richard Sylla, "U.S. Securities Markets and the Banking System, 1790–1840," *Federal Reserve Bank of St. Louis Review* (May–June 1998), 93. See also Lamoreaux, *Insider Lending*; Bodenhorn, *State Banking in Early America*; Howard Bodenhorn, *A History of Banking in Antebellum America: Financial Markets and Economic Development in an Era of Nation-Building* (New York: Cambridge University Press, 2000).

85.   Lamoreaux, *Insider Lending*, 11–30.

86.   Rousseau and Sylla, "Emerging Financial Markets," 10.

87. Robert V. Remini, *Andrew Jackson and the Bank War* (New York: Norton, 1967).

88. Wilentz, *Rise of American Democracy*, 359–455.

89. Jane Knodell, "Rethinking the Jacksonian Economy: The Impact of the 1832 Bank Veto on Commercial Banking," *Journal of Economic History* 66, no. 3 (2006): 541–74.

90. Peter Temin, *The Jacksonian Economy* (New York: Norton, 1969); Beckert, *Empire of Cotton*, 230–33. This silver did not flow to Britain to finance imports of British manufactures because of British capital investments in American state public debts and state-chartered banks.

91. Stanley L. Engerman, "A Note on the Economic Consequences of the Second Bank of the United States," *Journal of Political Economy* 78, no. 4 (1970): 725–28.

92. Peter L. Rousseau, "Jacksonian Monetary Policy, Specie Flows, and the Panic of 1837," *Journal of Economic History* 62, no. 2 (2002): 457–88.

93. Hammond, *Banks and Politics in America*, 500–48.

94. Kim and Wallis, "Market for American State Government Bonds"; John J. Wallis, Richard E. Sylla, and Arthur Grinath III, "Sovereign Debt and Repudiation: The Emerging Market Debt Crisis in the U.S. States, 1839–1843," National Bureau of Economic Research, Working Paper no. 10753 (September 2004).

95. Howe, *What Hath God Wrought*, 570–612.

96. See Lamoreaux and Wallis, "States, Not Nation."

97. Theodore Sedgwick, *What Is a Monopoly?; or, Some Considerations upon the Subject of Corporations and Currency* (New York: G. P. Scott, 1835); Eric Hilt, "Early American Corporations and the State," in Lamoreaux and Novak, eds., *Corporations and American Democracy*, 39.

98. Stanley I. Kutler, *Privilege and Creative Destruction: The Charles River Bridge Case* (Baltimore: Johns Hopkins University Press, 1989).

99. Hilt, "Early American Corporations and the State," 66.

100. John Joseph Wallis, "Constitutions, Corporations, and Corruption: American States and Constitutional Change, 1842 to 1852," *Journal of Economic History* 65, no. 1 (2005): 211–56; Susan Pace Hamill, "From Special Privilege to General Utility: A Continuation of Willard Hurst's Study of Corporations," *American University Law Review* 49, no. 1 (1999): 81–180.

101. Robert E. Wright, *Corporation Nation* (Philadelphia: University of Pennsylvania Press, 2013), 49–80.

102. Pauline Maier, "The Revolutionary Origins of the American Corporation," *William and Mary Quarterly* 50, no. 1 (1993): 51–84. A classic account still worth reading is John Dewey, "The Historic Background of Corporate Legal Personality," *Yale Law Journal* 35, no. 6 (1926): 655–73.

103. Carter Goodrich, "The Revulsion Against Internal Improvements," *Journal of Economic History* 10, no. 2 (1950): 145–69; Lamoreaux and Wallis, "States, not Nation."

104. Colleen A. Dunlavy, "From Citizens to Plutocrats: Nineteenth-Century Shareholder Voting Rights and Theories of the Corporation," in Kenneth Lipartito and David B. Sicilia, eds., *Constructing Corporate America: History, Politics, Culture* (New York: Oxford University Press, 2004), 66–93; Maier, "Revolutionary Origins of the American Corporation."

105. Jonathan Levy, "Altruism and the Origins of Nonprofit Philanthropy," in Rob Reich, Lucy Bernholz, and Chiara Cordelli, eds., *Philanthropy in Democratic Societies: History, Institutions, Values* (Chicago: University of Chicago Press, 2016), 19–43.

106. Kenneth Lipartito, "The Utopian Corporation," in Lipartito and Sicilia, *Constructing Corporate America*, 94–119.

CHAPTER 5: CONFIDENCE GAMES

1.   Henry David Thoreau, *Civil Disobedience, Solitude and Life Without Principle* (Amherst, N.Y.: Prometheus Books, 1998), 64.

2.   Ralph Waldo Emerson, *Essays and Lectures: Nature: Addresses and Lectures / Essays: First and Second Series / Representative Men / English Traits / The Conduct of Life* (New York: Library of America, 1983), 465.

3.   Deirdre N. McCloskey, *The Bourgeois Virtues: Ethics for an Age of Commerce* (Chicago: University of Chicago Press, 2006).

4.   Nicholas Phillipson, *Adam Smith: An Enlightened Life* (New Haven: Yale University Press, 2010), 40–60.

5.   Albert O. Hirschman, *The Passions and the Interests: Political Arguments for Capitalism Before Its Triumph* (Princeton: Princeton University Press, 1977).

6.   Emma Rothschild, *Economic Sentiments: Adam Smith, Condorcet, and the Enlightenment* (Cambridge, Mass.: Harvard University Press, 2001).

7.   Benjamin Franklin, *Autobiography, Poor Richard, and Later Writings*, ed. J. A. Leo Lemay (New York: Library of America, 2005).

8.   Michael Zakim, *Accounting for Capitalism: The World the Clerk Made* (Chicago: University of Chicago Press, 2018).

9.   John Frost, *The Young Merchant* (Boston: G. W. Light, 1839), 36–37.

10.   Barbara Novak, *American Painting of the Nineteenth Century: Realism, Idealism, and the American Experience* (New York: Oxford University Press, 2007), 71–88.

11.   Herman Melville, *The Confidence-Man: His Masquerade* (1857; New York: Oxford University Press, 1999), 4.

12.   Jessica M. Lepler, *The Many Panics of 1837: People, Politics, and the Creation of a Transatlantic Financial Crisis* (New York: Cambridge University Press, 2013).

13.   F. O. Matthiessen, *American Renaissance: Art and Expression in the Age of Emerson and Whitman* (New York: Oxford University Press, 1968); David S. Reynolds, *Beneath the American Renaissance: The Subversive Imagination in the Age of Emerson and Melville* (New York: Knopf, 1988).

14.   James W. Cook, *The Arts of Deception: Playing with Fraud in the Age of Barnum* (Cambridge, Mass.: Harvard University Press, 2001), 225. This section draws heavily on Cook's brilliant account of Barnum, as well as Neil Harris, *Humbug: The Art of P. T. Barnum* (Boston: Little, Brown, 1973).

15.   Phineas Taylor Barnum, *The Life of P. T. Barnum, Written by Himself* (New York: Sampson Low, 1855), 13.

16.   Ibid., 396.

17.   Cook, *Arts of Deception*, 67.

18.   Allan R. Pred, *Urban Growth and City-Systems in the United States, 1840–1860* (Cambridge, Mass.: Harvard University Press, 1980), 11–37.

19.   "Introduction," *The Merchant's Magazine and Commercial Review* (July 1839), 1. See Stuart Mack Blumin, *The Emergence of the Middle Class: Social Experience in the American City, 1760–1900* (New York: Cambridge University Press, 1989), 66–107, 230–57.

20.   Rowena Olegario, *A Culture of Credit: Embedding Trust and Transparency in American Business* (Cambridge, Mass.: Harvard University Press, 2006), 36–118; Scott A. Sandage, *Born Losers: A History of Failure in America* (Cambridge, Mass.: Harvard University Press, 2005), 99–128.

21.   Cook, *Arts of Deception*, 100.

22.   Mark A. Noll, ed., *God and Mammon: Protestants, Money, and the Market, 1790–1860* (New York: Oxford University Press, 2001); Paul E. Johnson, *A Shopkeeper's Millennium: Society and Revivals in Rochester, New York, 1815–1837* (New York: Hill & Wang, 2004).

23. Harris, *Humbug*.

24. Cook, *Arts of Deception*, 76.

25. Laura Dassow Walls, *Henry David Thoreau: A Life* (Chicago: University of Chicago Press, 2017).

26. Jean-Jacques Rousseau, *Emile; or, On Education*, trans. Allan Bloom (1762; New York: Basic Books, 1979), 189.

27. Jean-Jacques Rousseau, *"The Discourses" and Other Early Political Writings*, ed. Victor Gourevitch (New York: Cambridge University Press, 1997); Mario Einaudi, *The Early Rousseau* (Ithaca, N.Y.: Cornell University Press, 1967).

28. Jean-Jacques Rousseau, *The Reveries of the Solitary Walker*, trans. Charles E. Butterworth (1782; Indianapolis: Hackett, 1992).

29. See Rahel Jaeggi, *Alienation*, ed. Frederick Neuhouser, trans. Alan Smith (New York: Columbia University Press, 2014).

30. Thomas Carlyle, *Past and Present* (London: Chapman & Hall, 1843), 212.

31. Joseph A. Schumpeter, *Capitalism, Socialism and Democracy* (1942; New York: HarperCollins, 1975), 143–55.

32. Emerson, *Essays and Lectures*, 217.

33. Ibid., 850.

34. See Rothschild, *Economic Sentiments*, on the conservative appropriation of Smith.

35. Robert A. Gross, "Culture and Cultivation: Agriculture and Society in Thoreau's Concord," *Journal of American History* 69, no. 1 (1982): 42–61.

36. Henry David Thoreau, *A Week on the Concord and Merrimack Rivers / Walden; or, Life in the Woods / The Maine Woods / Cape Cod* (New York: Library of America, 1985), 327.

37. Ibid., 366, 359.

38. See George Kateb, *The Inner Ocean: Individualism and Democratic Culture* (Ithaca, N.Y.: Cornell University Press, 1992); Stanley Cavell, *The Senses of Walden: An Expanded Edition* (Chicago: University of Chicago Press, 1992).

39. Thoreau, *Civil Disobedience, Solitude and Life Without Principle*, 67, 79.

40. Ibid., 63, 86, 68, 88.

41. Barnum, *Life of Barnum*, 399.

42. Thoreau, *Civil Disobedience, Solitude and Life Without Principle*, 85.

43. Herman Melville, *Complete Shorter Fiction* (New York: Everyman's Library, 1997), 222; "View of the Barnum Property," *Yankee Doodle* (July 31, 1847), 168.

44. See Tony Tanner, "Introduction," Melville, *Confidence-Man*, xi.

45. Robert S. Levine, ed., *The New Cambridge Companion to Herman Melville* (New York: Cambridge University Press, 2013), 114.

46. Adam Smith, *An Inquiry into the Nature and Causes of the Wealth of Nations* (1776; Chicago: University of Chicago Press, 1976), 26.

47. Melville, *Confidence-Man*, 7.

48. Ibid., 1.

49. Ibid., 7, 22.

50. Ibid., 56.

51. Ibid., 95–96.

52. Karl Marx, *Capital: A Critique of Political Economy*, vol. 1, trans. Ben Fowkes (1867; New York: Penguin Classics, 1992), 254, 255.

53. John Maynard Keynes, *The General Theory of Employment, Interest, and Money* (1936; New York: Harcourt, Brace & World, 1964).

54. Ibid., 166.

55. Henry David Thoreau, *Collected Essays and Poems*, ed. Elizabeth Hall Witherell (New York: Library of America, 2001), 510.

56. Melville, *Confidence-Man,* 97.

57. Ibid., 268–78.

58. See Viviana A. Zelizer, *Economic Lives: How Culture Shapes the Economy* (Princeton: Princeton University Press, 2010), esp. 363–82.

59. Melville, *Confidence-Man,* 268–78.

60. On this point in a different context, see Jonathan Lear, *Radical Hope: Ethics in the Face of Cultural Devastation* (Cambridge, Mass.: Harvard University Press, 2006).

61. Melville, *Confidence-Man,* 268–78.

62. Laurie Robertson-Lorant et al., *Hawthorne and Melville: Writing a Relationship,* ed. Jana Argersinger and Leland Person (Athens: University of Georgia Press, 2008), 46, 47.

CHAPTER 6: BETWEEN SLAVERY AND FREEDOM

1. On steamboats, see Walter Johnson, *River of Dark Dreams: Slavery and Empire in the Cotton Kingdom* (Cambridge, Mass.: Belknap Press, 2013), 73–96. On biological innovation, see Alan L. Olmstead and Paul W. Rhode, *Creating Abundance: Biological Innovation and American Agricultural Development* (New York: Cambridge University Press, 2008), 98–154.

2. Matthew Karp, *This Vast Southern Empire: Slaveholders at the Helm of American Foreign Policy* (Cambridge, Mass.: Harvard University Press, 2016).

3. Gavin Wright, *Slavery and American Economic Development* (Baton Rouge: Louisiana State University Press, 2013), 74, 93.

4. Johnson, *River of Dark Dreams,* 14.

5. Stuart Bruchey, *Cotton and the Growth of the American Economy: 1790–1860: Sources and Readings* (New York: Harcourt, Brace & World, 1967), 23, table 3-L, 10, table 2-B.

6. A. G. Hopkins, *American Empire: A Global History* (Princeton: Princeton University Press, 2018), 142–238.

7. Stanley L. Engerman et al., *Economic Development in the Americas Since 1500: Endowments and Institutions* (New York: Cambridge University Press, 2011).

8. Sean Wilentz, *The Rise of American Democracy: Jefferson to Lincoln* (New York: Norton, 2005), 521–796. My account of the two distinct capitalisms that emerged in the North and South after 1840 draws from and parallels Wilentz's argument that during this same time two distinct democracies emerged. On the politics of the 1850s, see also another classic account, David M. Potter, *The Impending Crisis, 1848–1861* (New York: Joanna Cotler Books, 1976).

9. An insightful retrospective from a participant observer is Robert William Fogel, *The Slavery Debates, 1952–1990: A Retrospective* (Baton Rouge: Louisiana State University Press, 2003). On the contemporary revival of debate, see Gavin Wright's review of Sven Beckert and Seth Rockman, eds., *Slavery's Capitalism: A New History of American Economic Development* (Philadelphia: University of Pennsylvania Press, 2016), available at https://eh.net/book_reviews/slaverys-capitalism-a-new-history-of-american -economic-development/.

10. Orlando Patterson, *Slavery and Social Death: A Comparative Study* (Cambridge, Mass.: Harvard University Press, 1982); David Brion Davis, *The Problem of Slavery in the Age of Emancipation* (New York: Knopf, 2014), 15–44.

11. Ralph V. Anderson and Robert E. Gallman, "Slaves as Fixed Capital: Slave Labor and Southern Economic Development," *Journal of American History* 64, no. 1 (1977): 24–46.

12. Karl Marx, *Capital: A Critique of Political Economy,* vol. 3, trans. David Fernbach (1894; New York: Penguin Classics, 1993), 945.

13.   Walter Johnson, *Soul by Soul: Life Inside the Antebellum Slave Market* (Cambridge, Mass.: Harvard University Press, 1999).

14.   Michael Tadman, *Speculators and Slaves: Masters, Traders, and Slaves in the Old South* (Madison: University of Wisconsin Press, 1990).

15.   Steven Deyle, *Carry Me Back: The Domestic Slave Trade in American Life* (New York: Oxford University Press, 2005), 42.

16.   Slave masters were "laborlords," not "landlords." Gavin Wright, *Old South, New South: Revolutions in the Southern Economy Since the Civil War* (New York: Basic Books, 1986), 3–50.

17.   Roger Ransom and Richard Sutch, "Capitalists Without Capital: The Burden of Slavery and the Impact of Emancipation," *Agricultural History* 62, no. 3 (1988): 133–60.

18.   Peter H. Lindert and Jeffrey G. Williamson, *Unequal Gains: American Growth and Inequality Since 1700* (Princeton: Princeton University Press, 2016), 139.

19.   W. E. B. Du Bois, *Black Reconstruction in America, 1860–1880* (New York: Free Press, 1998), 5.

20.   Wright, *Slavery and American Economic Development*.

21.   Carville Earle, "Beyond the Appalachians, 1815–1860," in Thomas F. McIlwraith and Edward K. Muller, *North America: The Historical Geography of a Changing Continent*, 2nd ed. (Lanham, Md.: Rowman & Littlefield, 2001), 165–88.

22.   Felipe González, Guillermo Marshall, and Suresh Naidu, "Start-up Nation? Slave Wealth and Entrepreneurship in Civil War Maryland," *Journal of Economic History* 77, no. 2 (2017): 373–405; Harold Woodman, *King Cotton and His Retainers: Financing and Marketing the Cotton Crop of the South* (Lexington: University of Kentucky Press, 1968).

23.   Tadman, *Speculators and Slaves*, 12.

24.   Deyle, *Carry Me Back*, 44.

25.   Johnson, *Soul by Soul*.

26.   *Slave Narratives: A Folk History of Slavery in the United States from Interviews with Former Slaves* (Washington, D.C., 1941), 7:38.

27.   Ibid., vol. 11, pt. 2, p. 13. I have modified the orginal vernacular of this transcription.

28.   Robert William Fogel, *Without Consent or Contract: The Rise and Fall of American Slavery* (New York: Norton, 1989), 61–80. For a critique, see Wright, *Slavery and American Economic Development*.

29.   Mark M. Smith, *Mastered by the Clock: Time, Slavery, and Freedom in the American South* (Chapel Hill: University of North Carolina Press, 1997), 106.

30.   Caitlin Rosenthal, *Accounting for Slavery: Masters and Management* (Cambridge, Mass.: Harvard University Press, 2018)

31.   Olmstead and Rhode, *Creating Abundance*, 98–154.

32.   Gavin Wright, "The Industrious Revolution in America," in Laura Cruz and Joel Mokyr, eds., *The Birth of Modern Europe: Culture and Economy, 1400–1800, Essays in Honor of Jan de Vries* (Leiden: Brill, 2010), 231.

33.   Wright, *Slavery and American Economic Development*, 89–99.

34.   Daniel B. Rood, *The Reinvention of Atlantic Slavery: Technology, Labor, Race, and Capitalism in the Greater Caribbean* (New York: Oxford University Press, 2017), 148–202.

35.   John D. Majewski, *Modernizing a Slave Economy: The Economic Vision of the Confederate Nation* (Chapel Hill: University of North Carolina Press, 2009).

36.   Deyle, *Carry Me Back*, 46.

37.   Albert O. Hirschman, *The Strategy of Economic Development* (New Haven: Yale University Press, 1964).

38.   Steven Hahn, *The Roots of Southern Populism: Yeoman Farmers and the Transfor-*

mation of the Georgia Upcountry, 1850–1890 (New York: Oxford University Press, 1983), 15–85.

39. Fogel, *Without Consent or Contract*, 71–87.

40. Drew Gilpin Faust, *James Henry Hammond and the Old South: A Design for Mastery* (Baton Rouge: Louisiana State University Press, 1982), 346.

41. Eugene Genovese, " 'Our Family, White and Black': Family and Household in the Southern Slaveholders' World View," in Carol Bleser, ed., *In Joy and in Sorrow: Women, Family, and Marriage in the Victorian South, 1830–1900* (New York: Oxford University Press, 1991), 73.

42. Faust, *Hammond and Old South,* 87. On the issue of slave breeding and family life, see Amy Dru Stanley, "Slave Breeding and Free Love: An Antebellum Argument over Slavery, Capitalism, and Personhood," in Michael Zakim and Gary J. Kornblith, eds., *Capitalism Takes Command: The Social Transformation of Nineteenth-Century America* (Chicago: University of Chicago Press, 2012), 119–44.

43. On the plantation household, see Thavolia Glymph, *Out of the House of Bondage: The Transformation of the Plantation Household* (New York: Cambridge University Press, 2008), 1–98.

44. Lacy K. Ford, *Deliver Us from Evil: The Slavery Question in the Old South* (Oxford: Oxford University Press, 2009).

45. James Henley Thornwell, "National Sins . . . ," *Southern Presbyterian Review* 13, no. 4 (1861): 649–88.

46. Elizabeth Fox-Genovese and Eugene D. Genovese, *The Mind of the Master Class: History and Faith in the Southern Slaveholders' Worldview* (New York: Cambridge University Press, 2005).

47. William Andrew Smith, *Lectures on the Philosophy and Practice of Slavery* (Nashville, Tenn.: Stevenson & Evans, 1856), 39.

48. Herbert S. Klein, *A Population History of the United States* (New York: Cambridge University Press, 2004), 85.

49. Daina Ramey Berry, *The Price for Their Pound of Flesh: The Value of the Enslaved, from Womb to Grave, in the Building of a Nation* (Boston: Beacon Press, 2017).

50. Jenny Bourne Wahl, *The Bondsman's Burden: An Economic Analysis of the Common Law of Southern Slavery* (New York: Cambridge University Press, 1997), 49–77.

51. Fogel, *Without Consent or Contract,* 70, 45, 53.

52. Wright, *Slavery and American Economic Development,* 100.

53. Dylan C. Penningroth, *The Claims of Kinfolk: African American Property and Community in the Nineteenth-Century South* (Chapel Hill: University of North Carolina Press, 2003).

54. Anderson and Gallman, "Slaves as Fixed Capital."

55. Michael O'Brien, *Conjectures of Order: Intellectual Life and the American South, 1810–1860* (Chapel Hill: University of North Carolina Press, 2004).

56. Albert Taylor Bledsoe et al., *Cotton Is King, and Pro-Slavery Arguments: Comprising the Writings of Hammond, Harper, Christy, Stringfellow, Hodge, Bledsoe, and Cartwright, on This Important Subject* (Augusta, Ga.: Pritchard, Abbott & Loomis, 1860), vii.

57. Eugene D. Genovese, *Roll, Jordan, Roll: The World the Slaves Made* (New York: Vintage Books, 1976), 317.

58. James Buchanan, "First Annual Message to Congress on the State of the Union," December 8, 1857, American Presidency Project, https://www.presidency.ucsb.edu/documents/first-annual-message-congress-the-state-the-union.

59. Lindert and Williamson, *Unequal Gains,* 96–141.

60. Stephanie McCurry, *Masters of Small Worlds: Yeoman Households, Gender Relations, and the Political Culture of the Antebellum South Carolina Low Country* (New York: Oxford University Press, 1995); Hahn, *Roots of Southern Populism,* 86–136.

61. Ford, *Deliver Us from Evil*, 508.

62. Wilentz, *Rise of American Democracy*, 577–744.

63. David R. Meyer, *The Roots of American Industrialization* (Baltimore: Johns Hopkins University Press, 2003), 129.

64. Thomas Weiss, "U.S. Labor Force Estimates and Economic Growth, 1800–1860," in Robert E. Gallman and John Joseph Wallis, eds., *American Economic Growth and Standards of Living Before the Civil War* (Chicago: University of Chicago Press, 1992), 22, table 1.1.

65. Thomas C. Cochran, *Frontiers of Change: Early Industrialism in America* (New York: Oxford University Press, 1981), 53.

66. Meyer, *Roots of American Industrialization*, 129.

67. Joseph Davis and Marc D. Weidenmier, "America's First Great Moderation," *Journal of Economic History* 77, no. 4 (2017): 1116–43.

68. Louis C. Hunter, *A History of Industrial Power in the United States, 1780–1930*, vol. 2, *Steam Power* (Charlottesville: University of Virginia Press, 1979).

69. Anthony F. C. Wallace, *Rockdale: The Growth of an American Village in the Early Industrial Revolution* (New York: Knopf, 1978).

70. Christopher Clark, *Social Change in America: From the Revolution Through the Civil War* (Chicago: Ivan R. Dee, 2006), 180.

71. Charles Cist, *Cincinnati in 1841: Its Early Annals and Future Prospects* (Cincinnati: n.p., 1841), 238.

72. Bruce Laurie, *Artisans into Workers: Labor in Nineteenth-Century America* (New York: Hill & Wang, 1989), 15–47.

73. Joshua L. Rosenbloom, "Path Dependence and the Origins of Cotton Textile Manufacturing in New England," in Douglas A. Farnie and David J. Jeremy, eds., *The Fibre That Changed the World: The Cotton Industry in International Perspective, 1600–1990s* (New York: Oxford University Press, 2004), 365–91.

74. Mathew Carey, *Essays on Political Economy; or, The Most Certain Means of Promoting the Wealth, Power, Resources, and Happiness of Nations, Applied Particularly to the United States* (Philadelphia: H.C. Carey & I. Lea, 1822), 478.

75. Robert F. Dalzell, *Enterprising Elite: The Boston Associates and the World They Made* (Cambridge, Mass.: Harvard University Press, 1987); Thomas Dublin, *Women at Work: The Transformation of Work and Community in Lowell, Massachusetts, 1826–1860* (New York: Columbia University Press, 1979).

76. Claudia Goldin and Kenneth Sokoloff, "Women, Children, and Industrialization in the Early Republic: Evidence from the Manufacturing Censuses," *Journal of Economic History* 42, no. 4 (1982): 753, table 3.

77. Ibid.

78. Jeremy Atack, Fred Bateman, and Thomas Weiss, *National Samples from the Census of Manufacturing: 1850, 1860, and 1870* (Ann Arbor, Mich.: Inter-university Consortium for Political and Social Research [distributor], 2006-03-30), https://doi.org/10.3886/ICPSR04048.v1.

79. Kenneth L. Sokoloff, "Investment in Fixed and Working Capital During Early Industrialization: Evidence from U.S. Manufacturing Firms," *Journal of Economic History* 44, no. 2 (1984): 545–56; Jeremy Atack, "Returns to Scale in Antebellum United States Manufacturing," *Explorations in Economic History* 14, no. 4 (1977): 337–59.

80. Weiss, "U.S. Labor Force Estimates," 22, table 1.1; Meyer, *Roots of American Industrialization*, 3, table 1.1; Robert E. Gallman, "Commodity Output, 1839–1899," in National Bureau of Economic Research, *Trends in the American Economy in the Nineteenth Century, Studies in Income and Wealth* (Princeton: Princeton University Press, 1960), 4:43, table A–1.

81. Clark, *Social Change in America*, 180.

82.   Kenneth L. Sokoloff and Georgia C. Villaflor, "The Market for Manufacturing Workers During Early Industrialization: The American Northeast, 1820 to 1860," in Claudia Goldin and Hugh Rockoff, eds., *Strategic Factors in Nineteenth Century American Economic History: A Volume to Honor Robert W. Fogel* (Chicago: University of Chicago Press, 1992), 29–65; Kevin H. O'Rourke and Jeffrey G. Williamson, *Globalization and History: The Evolution of a Nineteenth-Century Atlantic Economy* (Cambridge, Mass.: MIT Press, 1999), 119–94.

83.   Louis C. Hunter and Lynwood Bryant, *A History of Industrial Power in the United States, 1780–1930*, vol. 3, *The Transmission of Power* (Cambridge, Mass.: MIT Press, 1991), 12–13, 61.

84.   Lindert and Williamson, *Unequal Gains*, 104.

85.   Rolla Milton Tryon, *Household Manufactures in the United States, 1640–1860* (1917; A.M. Kelley, 1966), 308–9, table 1.7.

86.   Meyer, *Roots of American Industrialization*, 272.

87.   Nathan Rosenberg, "Technical Change in the Machine Tool Industry, 1840–1910," *Journal of Economic History* 23, no. 4 (1963): 414–43; David R. Meyer, *Networked Machinists: High-Technology Industries in Antebellum America* (Baltimore: Johns Hopkins University Press, 2006).

88.   Kenneth L. Sokoloff and B. Zorina Khan, "The Democratization of Invention During Early Industrialization: Evidence from the United States, 1790–1846," *Journal of Economic History* 50, no. 2 (1990): 363–78.

89.   Gary J. Kornblith, "The Craftsman as Industrialist: Jonas Chickering and the Transformation of American Piano Making," *Business History Review* 59, no. 3 (1985): 349–69.

90.   Wright, *Slavery and American Economic Development*, 52, 54.

91.   Joanne Pope Melish, *Disowning Slavery: Gradual Emancipation and "Race" in New England, 1780–1860* (Ithaca, N.Y.: Cornell University Press, 1998).

92.   Pennsylvania and New York passed gradual emancipation laws in 1780 and 1799 respectively, but final emancipation was achieved only in 1847 and 1827. New Jersey passed a gradual emancipation law in 1804 but did not legislate complete abolition until 1846. Hendrik Hartog, *The Trouble with Minna: A Case of Slavery and Emancipation in the Antebellum North* (Chapel Hill: University of North Carolina Press, 2018); Sarah L. H. Gronningsater, " 'Expressly Recognized by Our Election Laws': Certificates of Freedom and the Multiple Fates of Black Citizenship in the Early Republic," *William and Mary Quarterly* 75, no. 3 (2018): 465–506.

93.   Robert J. Steinfeld, *The Invention of Free Labor: The Employment Relation in English and American Law and Culture, 1350–1870* (Chapel Hill: University of North Carolina Press, 1991), 137–43.

94.   Ibid., 144–72.

95.   George Fitzhugh, *Cannibals All; or, Slaves Without Masters*, ed. C. Vann Woodward (1857; Cambridge, Mass.: Belknap Press, 1966).

96.   Dalzell, *Enterprising Elite*, 113–64.

97.   Amy Dru Stanley, "Home Life and the Morality of the Market," in Melvin Stokes and Stephen Conway, eds., *The Market Revolution in America: Social, Political, and Religious Expressions, 1800–1880* (Charlottesville: University Press of Virginia, 1996), 86. My account of the importance of household transformation at this time draws heavily from Stanley's brilliant and influential formulation.

98.   Kenneth Severens, *Southern Architecture: 350 Years of Distinctive American Buildings* (New York: Dutton Adult, 1981), 30–90.

99.   Frederick Law Olmsted, *The Cotton Kingdom: A Traveller's Observations on Cotton and Slavery in the American Slave States*, ed. Arthur Schlesinger (New York: Modern Library, 1969), 280.

100.   Clifford Edward Clark, *The American Family Home, 1800–1960* (Chapel Hill: University of North Carolina Press, 1986), 3–36.

101.   Andrew Jackson Downing, *Cottage Residences; or, A Series of Designs for Rural Cottages and Cottage Villas, and Their Gardens and Grounds. Adapted to North America* (New York: Wiley & Putnam, 1842), iii.

102.   Catharine Esther Beecher and Harriet Beecher Stowe, *The American Woman's Home; or, Principles of Domestic Science: Being a Guide to the Formation and Maintenance of Economical, Healthful, Beautiful, and Christian Homes* (Boston: J. B. Ford, 1869), 85.

103.   "The Sphere of Woman," *Symbol* (June 1844), 146.

104.   Nancy F. Cott, *The Bonds of Womanhood: "Woman's Sphere" in New England, 1780–1835* (New Haven: Yale University Press, 1997); Mary P. Ryan, *Cradle of the Middle Class: The Family in Oneida County, New York, 1790–1865* (New York: Cambridge University Press, 1981).

105.   For the farm wife/field hand estimate, see Lee Craig, *To Sow One More Acre* (Baltimore: Johns Hopkins University Press, 1993), 80. A similar subsidy argument, in relation to manufacture, has been made by Jeanne Boydston, *Home and Work: Housework, Wages, and the Ideology of Labor in the Early Republic* (New York: Oxford University Press, 1990). On working women, see Christine Stansell, *City of Women: Sex and Class in New York, 1789–1860* (New York: Knopf, 1986). On gender wage differentials, see Claudia Dale Goldin, *Understanding the Gender Gap: An Economic History of American Women* (New York: Oxford University Press, 1990), 59–62.

106.   Stanley, "Home Life"; Nancy Folbre, "The Unproductive Housewife: Her Evolution in Nineteenth-Century Economic Thought," *Signs* 16, no. 3 (1991): 463–84.

107.   Clark, *Social Change in America*, 140.

108.   John Majewski, "Why Did Northerners Oppose the Expansion of Slavery? Economic Development and Education in the Limestone South," in Sven Beckert and Seth Rockman, eds., *Slavery's Capitalism: A New History of American Economic Development* (Philadelphia: University of Pennsylvania Press, 2016), 277–98; Engerman et al., *Economic Development in the Americas Since 1500*, 121–68.

109.   Lindert and Williamson, *Unequal Gains*, 97. This was one reason why inequality increased in the South, following the prediction of Piketty that inequality will increase when capital income increases, since capital assets are owned by the well-off. Thomas Piketty, *Capital in the Twenty-First Century*, trans. Arthur Goldhammer (Cambridge, Mass.: Belknap Press, 2014), 1–38, 140–63.

110.   Marc Egnal, *Clash of Extremes: The Economic Origins of the Civil War* (New York: Hill & Wang, 2009), 101–22. I have followed Egnal's argument closely in my account of the political significance of this shift in trade patterns.

111.   James Oakes, *Freedom National: The Destruction of Slavery in the United States, 1861–1865* (New York: Norton, 2012).

112.   Michael F. Holt, *The Fate of Their Country: Politicians, Slavery Extension, and the Coming of the Civil War* (New York: Hill & Wang, 2004).

113.   See the figures for 1860 in Robert E. Gallman, "Self-Sufficiency in the Cotton Economy of the Antebellum South," *Agricultural History* 44, no. 1 (1970): 5–23.

114.   Egnal, *Clash of Extremes*, 102–6.

115.   Calvin Schermerhorn, "The Coastwise Slave Trade and a Mercantile Community of Interest," in Beckert and Rockman, *Slavery's Capitalism*, 209–24.

116.   O'Rourke and Williamson, *Globalization and History*, 77–92.

117.   Paul Frymer, *Building an American Empire: The Era of Territorial and Political Expansion* (Princeton: Princeton University Press, 2017), 142, fig. 4.3.

118.   On this point, see Wright, *Slavery and American Economic Development*, 48–82.

119.   D. W. Meinig, *Imperial Texas: An Interpretive Essay in Cultural Geography* (Austin: University of Texas Press, 1969), 34.

120. David R. Meyer, "Midwestern Industrialization and the American Manufacturing Belt in the Nineteenth Century," *Journal of Economic History* 49, no. 4 (1989): 921–37.

121. Lindert and Williamson, *Unequal Gains*, 102, table 5-3.

122. Ibid., 103–4. In 1860 British GDP per capita was $149 compared to $171 in the United States. British growth rates were in the neighborhood of 1 percent.

123. John Komlos, "Shrinking in a Growing Economy? The Mystery of Physical Stature During the Industrial Revolution," *Journal of Economic History* 58, no. 3 (1998): 779–802.

124. On this process, see Simon Kuznets, "Economic Growth and Income Inequality," *American Economic Review* 45, no. 1 (1955): 1–28.

125. Lindert and Williamson, *Unequal Gains*, 127–29.

126. Fogel, *Without Consent or Contract*, 320–88.

127. Ibid., 311.

128. Lawrence F. Katz and Robert A. Margo, "Technical Change and the Relative Demand for Skilled Labor: The United States in Historical Perspective," in Leah Platt Boustan, Carola Frydman, and Robert A. Margo, eds., *Human Capital in History: The American Record* (Chicago: University of Chicago Press, 2014).

129. Eric Foner, *Free Soil, Free Labor, Free Men: The Ideology of the Republican Party Before the Civil War* (1970; New York: Oxford University Press, 1995).

130. Joseph P. Ferrie, *Yankeys Now: Immigrants in the Antebellum United States, 1840–1860* (New York: Oxford University Press, 1999).

131. Harriet Beecher Stowe, *A Key to Uncle Tom's Cabin* (Boston, 1853), 257. In general, see Stanley, "Home Life."

132. Manisha Sinha, *The Slave's Cause: A History of Abolition* (New Haven: Yale University Press, 2016), 461–99.

133. Foner, *Free Soil, Free Labor, Free Men*, 27.

134. Nicole Etcheson, *Bleeding Kansas: Contested Liberty in the Civil War Era* (Lawrence: University Press of Kansas, 2004).

135. On Lincoln, see Eric Foner, *The Fiery Trial: Abraham Lincoln and American Slavery* (New York: Norton, 2010).

136. Abraham Lincoln and Stephen Arnold Douglas, *The Lincoln-Douglas Debates: The First Complete, Unexpurgated Text*, ed. Harold Holzer (New York: HarperCollins, 1993), 76.

137. Abraham Lincoln, "Address to the Wisconsin State Agricultural Society, September 30, 1859," in Michael P. Johnson, *Abraham Lincoln, Slavery, and the Civil War: Selected Writing and Speeches* (Boston: Bedford/St. Martin's, 2010), 33–36.

138. Sean Wilentz, *No Property in Man: Slavery and Antislavery at the Nation's Founding* (Cambridge, Mass.: Harvard University Press, 2018).

139. Lincoln and Douglas, *Lincoln-Douglas Debates*, 76.

140. Charles W. Calomiris and Jonathan Pritchett, "Betting on Secession: Quantifying Political Events Surrounding Slavery and the Civil War," *American Economic Review* 106, no. 1 (2016): 1–23.

141. Johnson, *Lincoln, Slavery, and the Civil War*, 63.

142. Lincoln and Douglas, *Lincoln-Douglas Debates*, 51, 116, 55.

143. Paul Finkelman, "Almost a Free State: The Indiana Constitution of 1816 and the Problem of Slavery," *Indiana Magazine of History* 111, no. 1 (2015): 64–95, https://doi.org/10.5378/indimagahist.111.1.0064.

144. Earle, "Beyond the Appalachians," 185.

145. Wilentz, *Rise of American Democracy*, 745–68.

146. John Craig Hammond, "The 'High-Road to a Slave Empire': Conflict and the Growth and Expansion of Slavery on the North American Continent," in Andrew

Shankman, ed., *The World of the Revolutionary American Republic: Land, Labor, and the Conflict for a Continent* (New York: Routledge, 2014), 346–69.

147. Peter S. Onuf, "The Empire of Liberty: Land of the Free and Home of the Slave," in Shankman, *World of Revolutionary Republic,* 212.

148. Calomiris and Pritchett, "Betting on Secession," 1.

CHAPTER 7: CIVIL WAR AND THE RECONSTRUCTION OF CAPITAL

1. Drew Gilpin Faust, *This Republic of Suffering: Death and the American Civil War* (New York: Knopf, 2008).

2. Michael Geyer and Charles Bright, "Global Violence and Nationalizing Wars in Eurasia and America: The Geopolitics of War in the Mid-Nineteenth Century," *Comparative Studies in Society and History* 38, no. 4 (1996): 619–57.

3. James Oakes, *Freedom National: The Destruction of Slavery in the United States, 1861–1865* (New York: Norton, 2012).

4. Thomas C. Holt, *Children of Fire: A History of African Americans* (New York: Hill & Wang, 2010), 133–84.

5. Roger Ransom and Richard Sutch, "Capitalists Without Capital: The Burden of Slavery and the Impact of Emancipation," *Agricultural History* 62, no. 3 (1988): 133–60.

6. Charles Beard and Mary Beard, *The Rise of American Civilization* (New York: Macmillan, 1927), 2:100.

7. Richard White, *Railroaded: The Transcontinentals and the Making of Modern America* (New York: Norton, 2011), 9. On decline of industry, see Claudia D. Goldin and Frank D. Lewis, "The Economic Cost of the American Civil War: Estimates and Implications," *Journal of Economic History* 35, no. 2 (1975): 299–326; Stanley Engerman, "The Economic Impact of the Civil War," *Explorations in Economic History* 3 (Fall 1966): 176–99.

8. Richard Franklin Bensel, *Yankee Leviathan: The Origins of Central State Authority in America, 1859–1877* (New York: Cambridge University Press, 1990), 238–302.

9. John A. James, "Public Debt Management Policy and Nineteenth-Century American Economic Growth," *Explorations in Economic History* 21, no. 2 (1984): 192–217; Jeffrey G. Williamson, "Watersheds and Turning Points: Conjectures on the Long-Term Impact of Civil War Financing," *Journal of Economic History* 34, no. 3 (1974): 636–61; Richard Eugene Sylla, *The American Capital Market, 1846–1914: A Study of the Effects of Public Policy on Economic Development* (New York: Arno Press, 1975), 40–80.

10. Nicolas Barreyre, *Gold and Freedom: The Political Economy of Reconstruction,* trans. Arthur Goldhammer (Charlottesville: University of Virginia Press, 2015). My emphasis in this chapter on the return to the gold standard draws heavily from Barreyre's excellent account.

11. Elliott West, "Reconstructing Race," *Western Historical Quarterly* 34, no. 1 (2003): 6–26. See also Jeffrey Ostler, *The Plains Sioux and U.S. Colonialism from Lewis and Clark to Wounded Knee* (New York: Cambridge University Press, 2004), 40–62; Ari Kelman, *A Misplaced Massacre: Struggling over the Memory of Sand Creek* (Cambridge, Mass.: Harvard University Press, 2013).

12. Robert Hass, *Time and Materials: Poems 1997–2005* (New York: Ecco, 2007), 5.

13. James M. McPherson, *Battle Cry of Freedom: The Civil War Era* (New York: Oxford University Press, 1988).

14. Bensel, *Yankee Leviathan,* 187.

15. Heather Cox Richardson, *The Greatest Nation of the Earth: Republican Economic Policies During the Civil War* (Cambridge, Mass.: Harvard University Press, 1997).

16.   Douglas A. Irwin, "Tariff Incidence in America's Gilded Age," *Journal of Economic History* 67, no. 3 (2007): 582–607.

17.   F. W. Taussig, *The Tariff History of the United States* (New York: G. P. Putnam's Sons, 1914), 160.

18.   Richard Edwards, Jacob K. Friefeld, and Rebecca S. Wingo, *Homesteading the Plains: Toward a New History* (Lincoln: University of Nebraska Press, 2017), 12.

19.   White, *Railroaded,* 22.

20.   Mark Wilson, *The Business of Civil War: Military Mobilization and the State, 1861–1865* (Baltimore: Johns Hopkins University Press, 2006), 1.

21.   Ibid., 75, 118.

22.   Bensel, *Yankee Leviathan,* 187.

23.   Thomas Weber, *The Northern Railroads in the Civil War, 1861–1865* (Bloomington: Indiana University Press, 1999).

24.   Samuel Richey Kamm, "The Civil War Career of Thomas A. Scott" (PhD diss., University of Pennsylvania, 1940).

25.   D. W. Meinig, *The Shaping of America: A Geographical Perspective on 500 Years of History,* vol. 3, *Transcontinental America, 1850–1915* (New Haven: Yale University Press, 2000), 4–32.

26.   Kamm, "Civil War Career of Thomas A. Scott."

27.   Goldin and Lewis, "Economic Cost of the American Civil War," 304, table 1. Another $485,673,000 was expended by state and local governments.

28.   Jay Sexton, *Debtor Diplomacy: Finance and American Foreign Relations in the Civil War Era, 1837–1873* (Oxford: Clarendon Press, 2005), 82–133.

29.   Henrietta M. Larson, *Jay Cooke, Private Banker* (Cambridge, Mass.: Harvard University Press, 1936).

30.   Ibid.

31.   David F. Weiman and John A. James, "The Political Economy of the U.S. Monetary Union: The Civil War Era as a Watershed," *American Economic Review* 97, no. 2 (2007): 271–75.

32.   Roger Ransom, "Economics of the Civil War," EH.net, August 24, 2001, available at http://eh.net/encyclopedia/the-economics-of-the-civil-war/.

33.   Maury Klein, *The Life and Legend of Jay Gould* (Baltimore: Johns Hopkins University Press, 1986), 69.

34.   Robert P. Sharkey, *Money, Class, and Party: An Economic Study of Civil War and Reconstruction* (Baltimore: Johns Hopkins University Press, 1959), 15–55.

35.   Klein, *Life and Legend of Gould,* 69.

36.   Ransom, "Economics of Civil War."

37.   Joseph A. Hill, "The Civil War Income Tax," *Quarterly Journal of Economics* 8, no. 4 (1894): 416–52.

38.   Ransom, "Economics of Civil War."

39.   Roger L. Ransom, *Conflict and Compromise: The Political Economy of Slavery, Emancipation, and the American Civil War* (New York: Cambridge University Press, 1989), 172–215.

40.   Sexton, *Debtor Diplomacy,* 134–89; Marc D. Weidenmier, "The Market for Confederate Cotton Bonds," *Explorations in Economic History* 37, no. 1 (2000): 76–97.

41.   Richard C. K. Burdekin and Farrokh K. Langdana, "War Finance in the Southern Confederacy, 1861–1865," *Explorations in Economic History* 30, no. 3 (1993): 352–76.

42.   Scott Reynolds Nelson, *Iron Confederacies: Southern Railways, Klan Violence, and Reconstruction* (Chapel Hill: University of North Carolina Press, 1999), 27–46.

43.   Sven Beckert, *Empire of Cotton: A Global History* (New York: Knopf, 2014), 242–73.

44. Stephanie McCurry, *Confederate Reckoning: Power and Politics in the Civil War South* (Cambridge, Mass.: Harvard University Press, 2010), 180, 167, 196.

45. Michael Brem Bonner, *Confederate Political Economy: Creating and Managing a Southern Corporatist Nation* (Baton Rouge: Louisiana State University Press, 2016).

46. Bensel, *Yankee Leviathan*, 94–237.

47. McCurry, *Confederate Reckoning*, 284.

48. Ibid., 263–309; Chandra Manning, *Troubled Refuge: Struggling for Freedom in the Civil War* (New York: Knopf, 2016).

49. James M. McPherson, "Could the South Have Won?," *New York Review of Books* (June 13, 2002).

50. Phillip S. Paludan, *A People's Contest: The Union and Civil War, 1861–1865* (New York: Harper & Row, 1988), 170–97, 231–62; Peter H. Lindert and Jeffrey G. Williamson, *Unequal Gains: American Growth and Inequality Since 1700* (Princeton: Princeton University Press, 2016), 156.

51. Richard White, *The Republic for Which It Stands: The United States During Reconstruction and the Gilded Age, 1865–1896* (New York: Oxford University Press, 2017), 23–63; Eric Foner, *Reconstruction,* updated ed., *America's Unfinished Revolution, 1863–1877* (New York: HarperPerennial Modern Classics, 2014), 176–227.

52. Gavin Wright, *Old South, New South: Revolutions in the Southern Economy Since the Civil War* (New York: Basic Books, 1986), 17–50.

53. Julie Saville, *The Work of Reconstruction: From Slave to Wage Laborer in South Carolina, 1860–1870* (New York: Cambridge University Press, 1994), 32–101; Willie Lee Rose, *Rehearsal for Reconstruction: The Port Royal Experiment* (New York: Oxford University Press, 1976).

54. Whitelaw Reid, *After the War: A Southern Tour: May 1, 1865, to May 1, 1866* (New York: Moore, Wilstach & Baldwin, 1866), 59.

55. Foner, *Reconstruction,* 160.

56. Amy Dru Stanley, *From Bondage to Contract: Wage Labor, Marriage, and the Market in the Age of Slave Emancipation* (New York: Cambridge University Press, 1998), 1–59.

57. Foner, *Reconstruction,* 160.

58. Gerald David Jaynes, *Branches Without Roots: Genesis of the Black Working Class in the American South, 1862–1882* (New York: Oxford University Press, 1986), 1–60.

59. Eric L. McKitrick, *Andrew Johnson and Reconstruction* (New York: Oxford University Press, 1988), 370.

60. Barreyre, *Gold and Freedom.*

61. Hugh McCulloch, *Men and Measures of Half a Century: Sketches and Comments* (New York: C. Scribner's Sons, 1889), 201.

62. Bensel, *Yankee Leviathan*, 238–302.

63. Stephen N. Broadberry and Douglas A. Irwin, "Labor Productivity in the United States and the United Kingdom During the Nineteenth Century," *Explorations in Economic History* 43, no. 2 (2006): 257–79.

64. Lance E. Davis and Robert E. Gallman, *Evolving Financial Markets and International Capital Flows: Britain, the Americas, and Australia, 1865–1914* (New York: Cambridge University Press, 2001).

65. *Report of a Select Committee of the Chamber of Commerce of the State of New-York: On the Subject of a Return to Specie Payments: November, 1867* (Washington, D.C., 1867), 4.

66. Herbert Ronald Ferleger, *David A. Wells and the American Revenue System, 1865–1870* (New York: Columbia University Press, 1942); Nancy Cohen, *The Reconstruction of American Liberalism, 1865–1914* (Chapel Hill: University of North Carolina Press, 2002), 23–60.

67. Bensel, *Yankee Leviathan*, 290.

68. Maurice Obstfeld and Alan M. Taylor, "Sovereign Risk, Credibility and the Gold Standard: 1870–1913 Versus 1925–31," *Economic Journal* 113, no. 487 (2003): 241–75.

69. Jonathan Levy, *Freaks of Fortune: The Emerging World of Capitalism and Risk in America* (Cambridge, Mass.: Harvard University Press, 2012), 121.

70. Paul H. Bergeron, ed., *The Papers of Andrew Johnson*, vol. 9, *September 1865–January 1866* (Knoxville: University of Tennessee Press, 1967), 478.

71. Barreyre, *Gold and Freedom*, 147–52; Jeffry A. Frieden, *Currency Politics: The Political Economy of Exchange Rate Policy* (Princeton: Princeton University Press, 2015), 49–103.

72. Gretchen Ritter, *Goldbugs and Greenbacks: The Antimonopoly Tradition and the Politics of Finance in America, 1865–1896* (New York: Cambridge University Press, 1997), 101.

73. Frieden, *Currency Politics*, 64.

74. Ibid., 65.

75. David Montgomery, *Beyond Equality: Labor and the Radical Republicans, 1862–1872* (New York: Vintage Books, 1967), 342–57.

76. Milton Friedman and Anna J. Schwartz, *A Monetary History of the United States, 1867–1960* (Princeton: Princeton University Press, 1963), 30, chart 3.

77. White, *Republic for Which It Stands*, 64–102.

78. Steven Hahn, *A Nation Under Our Feet: Black Political Struggles in the Rural South from Slavery to the Great Migration* (Cambridge, Mass.: Belknap Press, 2003), 163–316.

79. Bensel, *Yankee Leviathan*, 353.

80. Barreyre, *Gold and Freedom*, 194–234.

81. Taussig, *Tariff History of the United States*, 229, 191.

82. Bensel, *Yankee Leviathan*, 340–65.

83. Irwin, "Tariff Incidence in America's Gilded Age."

84. Ritter, *Goldbugs and Greenbacks*, 92.

85. Sharkey, *Money, Class, and Party*, 95; Richard H. Timberlake, "Ideological Factors in Specie Resumption and Treasury Policy," *Journal of Economic History* 24, no. 1 (1964): 29–52.

86. Frieden, *Currency Politics*, 49–103.

87. Ransom and Sutch, "Capitalists Without Capital."

88. Roger L. Ransom and Richard Sutch, *One Kind of Freedom: The Economic Consequences of Emancipation* (New York: Cambridge University Press, 1977), 109–10.

89. Harold D. Woodman, *New South, New Law: The Legal Foundations of Credit and Labor Relations in the Postbellum Agricultural South* (Baton Rouge: Louisiana State University Press, 1995).

90. Susan Eva O'Donovan, *Becoming Free in the Cotton South* (Cambridge, Mass.: Harvard University Press, 2007), 111–61; Saville, *Work of Reconstruction*, 102–42.

91. Thavolia Glymph, *Out of the House of Bondage: The Transformation of the Plantation Household* (New York: Cambridge University Press, 2008), 137–203; O'Donovan, *Becoming Free in the Cotton South*, 162–207; Tera W. Hunter, *To "Joy My Freedom": Southern Black Women's Lives and Labors After the Civil War* (Cambridge, Mass.: Harvard University Press, 1997), 21–43; Leslie A. Schwalm, *A Hard Fight for We: Women's Transition from Slavery to Freedom in South Carolina* (Urbana: University of Illinois Press, 1997), 147–233.

92. Lindert and Williamson, *Unequal Gains*, 161.

93. Wright, *Old South, New South*, 17–52.

94. Francis William Loring and Charles Follen Atkinson, *Cotton Culture and the South Considered with Reference to Emigration* (Boston: A. Williams, 1869), 32.

95. Ransom and Sutch, *One Kind of Freedom*, 83.

96. Ibid., 4.

97. Lindert and Williamson, *Unequal Gains*, 146.

98. On the economic irrationality of Jim Crow, see Gavin Wright, *Sharing the Prize: The Economics of the Civil Rights Revolution in the American South* (Cambridge, Mass.: Belknap Press, 2013).

99. Ransom and Sutch, *One Kind of Freedom*, 187–88.

100. John J. Clegg, "From Slavery to Jim Crow: Essays on the Political Economy of Racial Capitalism" (PhD diss., New York University, 2018).

101. Hahn, *Nation Under Our Feet*, 163–316; Thomas C. Holt, *Black over White: Negro Political Leadership in South Carolina During Reconstruction* (Urbana: University of Illinois Press, 1977).

102. James Oakes, "The Present Becomes the Past: The Planter Class in the Postbellum South," in Robert H. Abzug and Stephen E. Maizlish, eds., *New Perspectives on Race and Slavery in America: Essays in Honor of Kenneth M. Stampp* (Lexington: University Press of Kentucky, 1986), 149–63; Lee J. Alston and Joseph P. Ferrie, *Southern Paternalism and the American Welfare State: Economics, Politics, and Institutions in the South, 1865–1965* (New York: Cambridge University Press, 1999), 13–48.

103. Nate Shaw and Theodore Rosengarten, *All God's Dangers: The Life of Nate Shaw* (New York: Knopf, 1974), 27.

104. Jonathan M. Wiener, "Class Structure and Economic Development in the American South, 1865–1955," *American Historical Review* 84, no. 4 (1979): 970–92.

105. Ransom and Sutch, *One Kind of Freedom*, 80.

106. John A. James, "Financial Underdevelopment in the Postbellum South," *Journal of Interdisciplinary History* 11, no. 3 (1981): 443–54.

107. Richard White, "Information, Markets, and Corruption: Transcontinental Railroads in the Gilded Age," *Journal of American History* 90, no. 1 (2003): 19–43.

108. Klein, *Life and Legend of Gould*, 76–89.

109. Williamson, "Watersheds and Turning Points."

110. Elmus Wicker, *Banking Panics of the Gilded Age* (New York: Cambridge University Press, 2000), 133; Christopher Hanes and Paul W. Rhode, "Harvests and Financial Crises in Gold Standard America," *Journal of Economic History* 73, no. 1 (2013): 201–46.

111. Sidney Homer and Richard Sylla, *History of Interest Rates* (Hoboken, N.J.: Wiley, 2005), 284, table 44.

112. Klein, *Life and Legend of Gould*, 84; T. J. Stiles, *The First Tycoon: The Epic Life of Cornelius Vanderbilt* (New York: Knopf, 2009), 465.

113. Eli Cook, *The Pricing of Progress: Economic Indicators and the Capitalization of American Life* (Cambridge, Mass.: Harvard University Press, 2017), 173–82.

114. Alfred D. Chandler, *The Visible Hand: The Managerial Revolution in American Business* (Cambridge, Mass.: Belknap Press, 1977); Steven W. Usselman, *Regulating Railroad Innovation: Business, Technology, and Politics in America, 1840–1920* (New York: Cambridge University Press, 2002).

115. John F. Stover, *American Railroads* (Chicago: University of Chicago Press, 2008), 161.

116. David R. Meyer, "The National Integration of Regional Economies, 1860–1920," in Thomas F. McIlwraith and Edward K. Muller, eds., *North America: The Historical Geography of a Changing Continent* (Lanham, Md.: Rowman & Littlefield, 2001), 311, table 14.1.

117. Dave Donaldson and Richard Hornbeck, "Railroads and American Economic Growth: A 'Market Access' Approach," *Quarterly Journal of Economics* 131, no. 2 (2016): 799–858.

118. Homer and Sylla, *History of Interest Rates*, 284, table 38.

119. Lindert and Williamson, *Unequal Gains*, 167.

120. Klein, *Life and Legend of Gould*, 88–98.

121. Ibid., 116, 3.

122. Richard R. John, "Robber Barons Redux: Antimonopoly Reconsidered," *Enterprise and Society* 13, no. 1 (2012): 1–38.

123. Charles F. Adams, Jr., and Henry Adams, *Chapters of Erie, and Other Essays* (Boston: James R. Osgood, 1871), 12.

124. John, "Robber Barons Redux," 3.

125. Stiles, *First Tycoon*, 3–334.

126. Mark Wahlgren Summers, *The Era of Good Stealings* (New York: Oxford University Press, 1993), 46–54.

127. Wright, *Railroaded*, 28.

128. Charles W. McCurdy, "Justice Field and the Jurisprudence of Government-Business Relations: Some Parameters of Laissez-Faire Constitutionalism, 1863–1897," *Journal of American History* 61, no. 4 (1975): 981.

129. See Field's famous dissent in *The Slaughter-House Cases* 83 U.S. 36 (1873); see also Howard Gillman, *The Constitution Besieged: The Rise and Demise of Lochner Era Police Powers Jurisprudence* (Durham, N.C.: Duke University Press, 1993), 64–75. The culmination of "freedom of contract" jurisprudence would be *Lochner v. New York* 198 U.S. 45 (1905).

130. *The People ex. rel. v. Salem*, 20 Mich. 447 (1870).

131. Meinig, *Shaping of America*, 3:260.

132. On this history, see Richard R. John, *Network Nation: Inventing American Telecommunications* (Cambridge, Mass.: Belknap Press, 2010), 24–199.

133. Rachel St. John, *Line in the Sand: A History of the Western U.S.-Mexico Border* (Princeton: Princeton University Press, 2011), 57–63.

134. Francis Paul Prucha, *The Great Father: The United States Government and the American Indians* (Lincoln: University of Nebraska Press, 1995), 560.

135. White, *Republic for Which It Stands*, 103–35, 288–321; Steven Hahn, *A Nation Without Borders: The United States and Its World in an Age of Civil Wars, 1830–1910* (New York: Penguin, 2017), 270–316.

136. Anne F. Hyde, *Empires, Nations, and Families: A History of the North American West, 1800–1860* (Lincoln: University of Nebraska Press, 2011).

137. White, *Railroaded*, 28–29.

138. Robert William Fogel, *The Union Pacific Railroad: A Case in Premature Enterprise* (Baltimore: Johns Hopkins University Press, 1960), 70–73.

139. Nelson, *Iron Confederacies*, 71–94.

140. Meyer, "National Integration of Regional Economies," 311, table 14.1. See C. Vann Woodward, *Origins of the New South, 1877–1913: A History of the South* (Baton Rouge: Louisiana State University Press, 1951), 1–50.

141. Wright, *Old South, New South*, 52–60. Steven Hahn, *The Roots of Southern Populism: Yeoman Farmers and the Transformation of the Georgia Upcountry, 1850–1890* (New York: Oxford University Press, 2006), 137–268.

142. Gold reparations paid by France to Germany after the Franco-Prussian War had contributed to a momentary boom in Austria.

143. See Hannah Catherine Davies, *Transatlantic Speculations: Globalization and the Panics of 1873* (New York: Columbia University Press, 2018).

144. White, *Railroaded*, 68.

145. Homer and Sylla, *History of Interest Rates*, 284, table 38; 315, table 44.

146. In the antebellum period, railroads were built between cities. Jeremy Atack et al., "Did Railroads Induce or Follow Economic Growth? Urbanization and Population Growth in the American Midwest, 1850–1860," *Social Science History* 34, no. 2 (2010): 171–97. On building ahead of demand after the Civil War, see White, *Railroaded*, xxvii, 208, 462.

147. Levy, *Freaks of Fortune*, 143–49.

148. Homer and Sylla, *History of Interest Rates*, 315, table 44.

149. Mira Wilkins, *The History of Foreign Investment in the United States to 1914* (Cambridge, Mass.: Harvard University Press, 1989), 201, table 6.5.

150. White, *Republic for Which It Stands*, 253–87.

151. Arthur Hadley, *Railroad Transportation, Its History and Its Laws* (New York: G. P. Putnam's Sons, 1885), 63–81.

152. There might have been a slump in industrial output of as much as 10 percent. Agricultural output, however, likely held steady. Joseph H. Davis, "An Annual Index of U.S. Industrial Production, 1790–1915," *Quarterly Journal of Economics* 119, no. 4 (2004): 1177–215.

153. Samuel Rezneck, "Distress, Relief, and Discontent in the United States During the Depression of 1873–78," *Journal of Political Economy* 58, no. 6 (1950): 494–512.

154. White, *Railroaded*, 83–84.

155. Elliott West, *The Last Indian War: The Nez Perce Story* (New York: Oxford University Press, 2009).

156. Gregory P. Downs, "The Mexicanization of American Politics: The United States' Transnational Path from Civil War to Stabilization," *American Historical Review* 117, no. 2 (2012): 387–409.

157. C. Vann Woodward, *Reunion and Reaction: The Compromise of 1877 and the End of Reconstruction* (1951; New York: Oxford University Press, 1966), 101–21.

158. White, *Railroaded*, 109–33.

159. Holt, *Black over White*, 173–224.

160. Barreyre, *Gold and Freedom*, 194–234.

161. "U.S. Business Cycle Expansions and Contractions," National Bureau of Economic Research, http://www.nber.org/cycles.html.

CHAPTER 8: INDUSTRIALIZATION

1. Andrew Carnegie, *The Autobiography of Andrew Carnegie* (1920; Philadelphia: PublicAffairs, 2011), 141.

2. David Nasaw, *Andrew Carnegie* (New York: Penguin Press, 2006).

3. Alfred D. Chandler, *The Visible Hand: The Managerial Revolution in American Business* (Cambridge, Mass.: Belknap Press, 1977), 79–206.

4. Carnegie, *Autobiography*, 80.

5. Aristotle, *Aristotle: The Politics and The Constitution of Athens*, ed., Stephen Everson (New York: Cambridge University Press Press, 2011), 25.

6. Maury Klein, *The Genesis of Industrial America, 1870–1920* (New York: Cambridge University Press, 2007), 155.

7. Harold C. Livesay, *Andrew Carnegie and the Rise of Big Business*, 3rd ed. (New York: Pearson Longman, 2007), 74.

8. Nasaw, *Andrew Carnegie*, 113, 114.

9. Livesay, *Carnegie and the Rise of Business*, 78.

10. Carnegie, *Autobiography*, 151.

11. On Carnegie and the role of railroads in the early U.S. steel industry, see Thomas J. Misa, *A Nation of Steel: The Making of Modern America, 1865–1925* (Baltimore: Johns Hopkins University Press, 1995), 1–44.

12. Nasaw, *Andrew Carnegie*, 154.

13. Carnegie, *Autobiography*, 135.

14. Jonathan Levy, "Accounting for Profit and the History of Capital," *Critical Historical Studies* 1, no. 2 (2014): 171–214.

15. Livesay, *Carnegie and the Rise of Business*, 112.

16. Arthur Moore and Samuel Taylor Pound, eds., *They Told Barron: The Notes of Clarence W. Barron* (New York: Harper, 1930), 85.

17. Livesay, *Carnegie and the Rise of Business*, 120.

18. Ibid., 171.

19. Burton Jesse Hendrick, *The Life of Andrew Carnegie* (New York: Harper & Row, 1969), 1:202.

20. Livesay, *Carnegie and the Rise of Business*, 116. See also James Howard Bridge, *The Inside History of the Carnegie Steel Company: A Romance of Millions* (New York: Aldine, 1903).

21. Robert C. Allen, "American Exceptionalism as a Problem in Global History," *Journal of Economic History* 74, no. 2 (2014): 309–50. Richard Franklin Bensel, *The Political Economy of American Industrialization, 1877–1900* (New York: Cambridge University Press, 2000).

22. Dave Donaldson and Richard Hornbeck, "Railroads and American Economic Growth: A 'Market Access' Approach," *Quarterly Journal of Economics* 131, no. 2 (2016): 799–858.

23. David Ames Wells, *Recent Economic Changes: And Their Effect on the Production and Distribution of Wealth and the Well-Being of Society* (New York: D. Appleton, 1889), 60.

24. William Cronon, *Nature's Metropolis: Chicago and the Great West* (New York: Norton, 1991), 75–82; Wolfgang Schivelbusch, *The Railway Journey: The Industrialization of Time and Space in the Nineteenth Century* (1977; Berkeley: University of California Press, 2014).

25. The terminology and analysis of "backward and forward linkages" in the sequence of industrial development comes from Albert O. Hirschman, *The Strategy of Economic Development* (New Haven: Yale University Press, 1958), 98–103.

26. Arnold Toynbee, *Lectures on the Industrial Revolution of the 18th Century in England* (London, 1884).

27. J. B. Clark, "Capital and Its Earnings," *Publications of the American Economic Association* 3, no. 2 (1888): 9–69.

28. On the surge in growth, from an antebellum rate of 1.79 per annum 1870–1910 compared to an 1800–60 trend of 1.43 percent, although the 1850–60 rate was 1.79, see Peter H. Lindert and Jeffrey G. Williamson, *Unequal Gains: American Growth and Inequality Since 1700* (Princeton: Princeton University Press, 2016), 102, 169. Capital-labor ratios increased in manufacturing by 75 percent or more already between 1850 and 1870, implying capital deepening. Jeremy Atack, Fred Bateman, and Robert A. Margo, "Capital Deepening and the Rise of the Factory: The American Experience During the Nineteenth Century," *Economic History Review* 58, no. 3 (2005): 586. On the 1880s, see John A. James, "Structural Change in American Manufacturing, 1850–1890," *Journal of Economic History* 43, no. 2 (1983): 433–59. On the rate of capital formation and investment, see Jeffrey G. Williamson, "Watersheds and Turning Points: Conjectures on the Long-Term Impact of Civil War Financing," *Journal of Economic History* 34, no. 3 (1974): 636–61. On the rate of industrial production, see Joseph H. Davis, "An Annual Index of U.S. Industrial Production, 1790–1915," *Quarterly Journal of Economics* 119, no. 4 (2004): 1177–215; and Williamson, "Watersheds and Turning Points." See also Robert Gallman, "The United States Capital Stock in the Nineteenth Century," in Stanley L. Engerman and Robert E. Gallman, *Long-Term Factors in American Economic Growth* (Chicago: University of Chicago Press, 1986), 165–213.

29. Lewis Mumford, *Technics and Civilization* (1934; Chicago: University of Chicago Press, 2010), 163.

30. For a recent review of the literature, see Fredrik Albritton Jonsson, "The Industrial Revolution in the Anthropocene," *Journal of Modern History* 84, no. 3 (2012): 679–96. For the U.S. case in comparative perspective, see Allen, "American Exceptionalism."

31.   On "circular cumulative causation," see Gunnar Myrdal, *Economic Theory and Underdeveloped Regions* (London: Methuen, 1957).

32.   E. A. Wrigley, *Continuity, Chance and Change: The Character of the Industrial Revolution in England* (New York: Cambridge University Press, 1988).

33.   The resonance between depleting stocks of capital and energy has persisted. See Emma Rothschild, "Maintaining (Environmental) Capital Intact," *Modern Intellectual History* 8, no. 1 (2011): 193–212.

34.   Rolf Peter Sieferle, *The Subterranean Forest: Energy Systems and the Industrial Revolution,* trans. Michael Osmann (Cambridge, Mass.: White Horse Press, 2001), 197.

35.   Wrigley, *Continuity, Chance and Change,* 28.

36.   J. R. McNeill, *Something New Under the Sun: An Environmental History of the Twentieth-Century World* (New York: Norton, 2000), 12.

37.   Wrigley, *Continuity, Chance and Change,* 76.

38.   Alfred Marshall, *The Principles of Economics* (Cambridge, Mass.: Macmillan, 1890), 332–34.

39.   David R. Meyer, *Networked Machinists: High-Technology Industries in Antebellum America* (Baltimore: Johns Hopkins University Press, 2006); Catherine L. Fisk, *Working Knowledge: Employee Innovation and the Rise of Corporate Intellectual Property, 1800–1930* (Chapel Hill: University of North Carolina Press, 2009); Nathan Rosenberg, "Technical Change in the Machine Tool Industry, 1840–1910," *Journal of Economic History* 23, no. 4 (1963): 414–43; Philip Scranton, *Endless Novelty: Specialty Production and American Industrialization, 1865–1925* (Princeton: Princeton University Press, 1997); Philip Scranton, *Proprietary Capitalism: The Textile Manufacture at Philadelphia, 1800–1885* (New York: Cambridge University Press, 1984).

40.   Louis C. Hunter and Lynwood Bryant, *A History of Industrial Power in the United States, 1780–1930,* vol. 3, *The Transmission of Power* (Charlottesville: University Press of Virginia, 1991), 430.

41.   Richard G. Healey, *The Pennsylvania Anthracite Coal Industry, 1860–1902* (Scranton: University of Scranton Press, 2007).

42.   Barbara Freese, *Coal: A Human History* (Cambridge, Mass.: Perseus, 2003).

43.   Christopher F. Jones, *Routes of Power: Energy and Modern America* (Cambridge, Mass.: Harvard University Press, 2014), 59–88; Alfred D. Chandler, "Anthracite Coal and the Beginnings of the Industrial Revolution in the United States," *Business History Review* 46, no. 2 (1972): 141–81.

44.   Anthony F. C. Wallace, *Rockdale: The Growth of an American Village in the Early Industrial Revolution* (New York: Knopf, 1978).

45.   Jones, *Routes of Power,* 67.

46.   Nathan Rosenberg and Manuel Trajtenberg, "A General-Purpose Technology at Work: The Corliss Steam Engine in the Late-Nineteenth-Century United States," *Journal of Economic History* 64, no. 1 (2004): 61–99.

47.   David E. Nye, *Consuming Power: A Social History of American Energies* (Cambridge, Mass.: MIT Press, 1997), 75.

48.   Brian Black, "Oil Creek as Industrial Apparatus: Re-Creating the Industrial Process Through the Landscape of Pennsylvania's Oil Boom," *Environmental History* 3, no. 2 (1998): 210–29.

49.   Rosenberg and Trajtenberg, "General-Purpose Technology."

50.   Hunter and Bryant, *History of Industrial Power,* 3:340.

51.   Jeremy Atack, Fred Bateman, and Robert A. Margo, "Steam Power, Establishment Size, and Labor Productivity Growth in Nineteenth Century American Manufacturing," *Explorations in Economic History* 45, no. 2 (2008): 185–98.

52.   National Museum of History and Technology, *1876: A Centennial Exhibition: A*

Treatise upon Selected Aspects. . . . (1876; Washington, D.C.: Smithsonian Institution, 1976), 29.

53. Jones, *Routes of Power,* 10, 12.

54. D. W. Meinig, *The Shaping of America: A Geographical Perspective on 500 Years of History,* vol. 2, *Continental America, 1800–1867* (New Haven: Yale University Press, 1986), 397.

55. Hunter and Bryant, *History of Industrial Power,* 3:430.

56. Gordon M. Winder, "The North American Manufacturing Belt in 1880: A Cluster of Regional Industrial Systems or One Large Industrial District?," *Economic Geography* 75, no. 1 (1999): 71.

57. Nicholas Crafts and Alexander Klein, "Making Sense of the Manufacturing Belt: Determinants of U.S. Industrial Location, 1880–1920," *Journal of Economic Geography* 12, no. 4 (2012): 775–807.

58. Ibid., 2, 3.

59. Harvey S. Perloff et al., *Regions, Resources, and Economic Growth* (Baltimore: Johns Hopkins University Press, 1960), 115.

60. David R. Meyer, "Emergence of the American Manufacturing Belt: An Interpretation," *Journal of Historical Geography* 9, no. 2 (1983): 145–74.

61. Louis Ferleger, "Capital Goods and Southern Economic Development," *Journal of Economic History* 45, no. 2 (1985): 411–17; Gavin Wright, *Old South, New South: Revolutions in the Southern Economy Since the Civil War* (New York: Basic Books, 1986), 60–64.

62. David R. Meyer, "Midwestern Industrialization and the American Manufacturing Belt in the Nineteenth Century," *Journal of Economic History* 49, no. 4 (1989): 921–37.

63. Richard White, *Railroaded: The Transcontinentals and the Making of Modern America* (New York: Norton, 2011).

64. Glenn Porter and Harold C. Livesay, *Merchants and Manufacturers: Studies in the Changing Structure of Nineteenth Century Marketing* (Chicago: Ivan R. Dee, 1989); Charles W. McCurdy, "American Law and the Marketing Structure of the Large Corporation, 1875–1890," *Journal of Economic History* 38, no. 3 (1978): 631–34.

65. Ron Chernow, *Titan: The Life of John D. Rockefeller, Sr.* (New York: Random House, 1998).

66. Walter Licht, *Industrializing America: The Nineteenth Century* (Baltimore: Johns Hopkins University Press, 1995), 102–32.

67. For regional shares of value added, see Perloff, *Regions, Resources, and Economic Growth,* 152, 153, 158, tables 44, 46, 49,

68. Ibid. In 1870 the Midwest was responsible for 18 percent of value added in national manufacturing. In 1890, passing New England, it was responsible for 24 percent.

69. Perhaps Manchester, England's preeminent industrial city. Harold L. Platt, *Shock Cities: The Environmental Transformation and Reform of Manchester and Chicago* (Chicago: University of Chicago Press, 2005).

70. Cronon, *Nature's Metropolis,* 23–54.

71. Meyer, "Midwestern Industrialization"; Louis P. Cain, "From Mud to Metropolis: Chicago Before the Fire," *Research in Economic History* 10 (1986), 93–129.

72. Cronon, *Nature's Metropolis,* 55–96.

73. Michael P. Conzen, "The Maturing Urban System in the United States, 1840–1910," *Annals of the Association of American Geographers* 67, no. 1 (1977): 88–108.

74. John B. Jentz and Richard Schneirov, *Chicago in the Age of Capital: Class, Politics, and Democracy During the Civil War and Reconstruction* (Urbana: University of Illinois Press, 2012), 38.

75. See Carol E. Heim, "Structural Changes: Regional and Urban," in Stanley L. Engerman and Robert E. Gallman, eds., *The Cambridge Economic History of the United States*, vol. 2, *The Long Nineteenth Century* (New York: Cambridge University Press, 2000), 163–71.

76. Ann Norton Greene, *Horses at Work: Harnessing Power in Industrial America* (Cambridge, Mass.: Harvard University Press, 2008), 284.

77. Adam Mack, *Sensing Chicago: Noisemakers, Strikebreakers, and Muckrakers* (Urbana: University of Illinois Press, 2015).

78. Platt, *Shock Cities*, 215.

79. James Macfarlane, *The Coal-Regions of America: Their Topography, Geology, and Development* (New York: D. Appleton, 1873), 434.

80. Platt, *Shock Cities*, 141.

81. Rudyard Kipling, *The City of Dreadful Night: American Notes* (New York: H. M. Caldwell, 1899), 91, 92.

82. Horace Greeley, *The Great Industries of the United States: Being an Historical Summary of the Origin, Growth, and Perfection of the Chief Industrial Arts of This Country* (New York and Hartford: J. B. Burr & Hyde, 1872).

83. Mack, *Sensing Chicago*, 11.

84. Kipling, *City of Dreadful Night*, 93.

85. On this theme, see in general Platt, *Shock Cities*.

86. Kipling, *City of Dreadful Night*, 91.

87. Carl Sandburg, *Chicago Poems* (1916; New York: Dover, 1994), 1.

88. James Belich, *Replenishing the Earth: The Settler Revolution and the Rise of the Angloworld, 1783–1939* (New York: Oxford University Press, 2009), 335.

89. Robert J. Gordon, *The Rise and Fall of American Growth: The U.S. Standard of Living Since the Civil War* (Princeton: Princeton University Press, 2016), 53, table 2-3.

90. Thomas G. Andrews, *Killing for Coal: America's Deadliest Labor War* (Cambridge, Mass.: Harvard University Press, 2008), 1–19.

91. Lance E. Davis and Robert E. Gallman, *Evolving Financial Markets and International Capital Flows: Britain, the Americas, and Australia, 1865–1914* (New York: Cambridge University Press, 2001), 235, table 3:1-1. On the movement of capital west, see Noam Maggor, *Brahmin Capitalism: Frontiers of Wealth and Populism in America's First Gilded Age* (Cambridge, Mass.: Harvard University Press, 2017).

92. Belich, *Replenishing the Earth*, 32.

93. Wells, *Recent Economic Changes*, 170.

94. Jonathan Levy, *Freaks of Fortune: The Emerging World of Capitalism and Risk in America* (Cambridge, Mass.: Harvard University Press, 2012), 156.

95. Richard White, *"It's Your Misfortune and None of My Own": A History of the American West* (Norman: University of Oklahoma Press, 1991), 271.

96. William S. Greever, *The Bonanza West: The Story of the Mining Rushes, 1848–1900* (Norman: University of Oklahoma Press, 1968).

97. A. Paul David and Gavin Wright, "Increasing Returns and the Genesis of American Resource Abundance," *Industrial and Corporate Change* 6, no. 2 (1997): 211.

98. Carl J. Mayer and George A. Riley, *Public Domain, Private Dominion: A History of Public Mineral Policy in America* (San Francisco: Sierra Club Books, 1985).

99. David and Wright, "Increasing Returns," 223.

100. Bronson C. Keeler, *Where to Go to Become Rich* (Chicago: Belford, Clark, 1890).

101. White, *"It's Your Misfortune and None of My Own,"* 235.

102. Gavin Wright, "American Agriculture and the Labor Market: What Happened to Proletarianization?," *Agricultural History* 62, no. 3 (1988): 182–209.

103. See Levy, *Freaks of Fortune*, 150–90.

104. Keeler, *Where to Go to Become Rich*, 430.

105. Levy, *Freaks of Fortune*, 150–90.

106. Sigfried Giedion, *Mechanization Takes Command: A Contribution to Anonymous History* (1948; Minneapolis: University of Minnesota Press, 2014), 145.

107. Cronon, *Nature's Metropolis*, 181.

108. Daniel B. Rood, *The Reinvention of Atlantic Slavery: Technology, Labor, Race, and Capitalism in the Greater Caribbean* (New York: Oxford University Press, 2017), 174–96.

109. Giedion, *Mechanization Takes Command*, 155.

110. Wells, *Recent Economic Changes*, 51.

111. Alan L. Olmstead and Paul W. Rhode, *Creating Abundance: Biological Innovation and American Agricultural Development* (New York: Cambridge University Press, 2008), 17–63.

112. Wells, *Recent Economic Changes*, 90.

113. Steven C. Topik and Allen Wells, "Commodity Chains in a Global Economy," in Emily S. Rosenberg, ed., *A World Connecting: 1870–1945* (Cambridge, Mass.: Belknap Press, 2012), 718–20, 631.

114. Kevin H. O'Rourke, "The European Grain Invasion, 1870–1913," *Journal of Economic History* 57, no. 4 (1997): 775–801.

115. Gordon, *Rise and Fall of American Growth*, 74.

116. Ronald Findlay and Kevin H. O'Rourke, *Power and Plenty: Trade, War, and the World Economy in the Second Millennium* (Princeton: Princeton University Press, 2009), 382.

117. Levy, *Freaks of Fortune*, 231–63.

118. Joshua Specht, *Red Meat Republic: A Hoof-to-Table History of How Beef Changed America* (Princeton: Princeton University Press, 2019); Richard White, "Animals and Enterprise," in Clyde A. Milner, Carol A. O'Connor, and Martha A. Sandweiss, eds., *The Oxford History of the American West* (New York: Oxford University Press, 1994), 237–74.

119. David Igler, *Industrial Cowboys: Miller and Lux and the Transformation of the Far West, 1850–1920* (Berkeley: University of California Press, 2001); Donald Worster, *Under Western Skies: Nature and History in the American West* (New York: Oxford University Press, 1992).

120. Andrew C. Isenberg, *The Destruction of the Bison: An Environmental History, 1750–1920* (New York: Cambridge University Press, 2000), 93–122.

121. Worster, *Under Western Skies*, 41. M. Scott Taylor, "Buffalo Hunt: International Trade and the Virtual Extinction of the North American Bison," *American Economic Review* 101, no. 7 (2011): 3162–95.

122. Reviel Netz, *Barbed Wire: An Ecology of Modernity* (Middletown, Conn.: Wesleyan University Press, 2004).

123. Richard Hornbeck, "Barbed Wire: Property Rights and Agricultural Development," *Quarterly Journal of Economics* 125, no. 2 (2010): 767–810.

124. Worster, *Under Western Skies*, 40.

125. James Sanks Brisbin, *The Beef Bonanza; or, How to Get Rich on the Plains* (Philadelphia: J. B. Lippincott, 1885), 13, 146.

126. Netz, *Barbed Wire*, 32.

127. Specht, *Red Meat Republic*, 67–169.

128. Cronon, *Nature's Metropolis*, 225.

129. Giedion, *Mechanization Takes Command*, 212, 229–46.

130. Belich, *Replenishing the Earth*, 341.

131. Kipling quoted in Cronon, *Nature's Metropolis*, 208.

132. Michael Osman, "Preserved Assets," in Aggregate, *Governing by Design: Architecture, Economy, and Politics in the Twentieth Century* (Pittsburgh: University of Pittsburgh Press, 2012), 1–20.

133. Wells, *Recent Economic Changes*, 159.

134. Levy, *Freaks of Fortune*, 150–90.

135. Leonard A. Carlson, *Indians, Bureaucrats, and Land: The Dawes Act and the Decline of Indian Farming* (Westport, Conn.: Praeger, 1981).

136. Emily Greenwald, *Reconfiguring the Reservation: The Nez Perce, Jicarilla Apaches, and the Dawes Act* (Albuquerque: University of New Mexico Press, 2002).

137. Karl Jacoby, *Crimes Against Nature: Squatters, Poachers, Thieves, and the Hidden History of American Conservation* (Berkeley: University of California Press, 2001), 121.

138. Sarah Deutsch, *No Separate Refuge: Culture, Class, and Gender on an Anglo-Hispanic Frontier in the American Southwest, 1880–1940* (New York: Oxford University Press, 1987), 13–40.

139. Richard White, *The Roots of Dependency: Subsistence, Environment, and Social Change Among the Choctaws, Pawnees, and Navajos* (Lincoln: University of Nebraska Press, 1983), 220–314.

140. Topik and Wells, "Commodity Chains," 723.

141. Kenneth Warren, *Triumphant Capitalism: Henry Clay Frick and the Industrial Transformation of America* (Pittsburgh: University of Pittsburgh Press, 1996), 56–112.

142. David Montgomery, *The Fall of the House of Labor: The Workplace, the State, and American Labor Activism, 1865–1925* (New York: Cambridge University Press, 1987), 9–57.

143. Nasaw, *Andrew Carnegie*, 183.

144. Ibid., 371.

145. Joseph Frazier Wall, *Andrew Carnegie* (New York: Oxford University Press, 1970), 553.

146. Nasaw, *Andrew Carnegie*, 409.

CHAPTER 9: CLASS WAR AND HOME LIFE

1. Kenneth Warren, *Triumphant Capitalism: Henry Clay Frick and the Industrial Transformation of America* (Pittsburgh: University of Pittsburgh Press, 1996), 56–112; Paul Kahan, *The Homestead Strike: Labor, Violence, and American Industry* (New York: Routledge, 2013); Les Standiford, *Meet You in Hell: Andrew Carnegie, Henry Clay Frick, and the Bitter Partnership That Transformed America* (New York: Crown, 2005).

2. David Montgomery, *The Fall of the House of Labor: The Workplace, the State, and American Labor Activism, 1865–1925* (New York: Cambridge University Press, 1987), 41.

3. Ibid., 9–57.

4. Alice Kessler-Harris, *Out to Work: A History of Wage-Earning Women in the United States* (New York: Oxford University Press, 1982), 109, 122.

5. On profits, see James Howard Bridge, *The Inside History of the Carnegie Steel Company: A Romance of Millions* (New York: Aldine, 1903), 295. On wage reduction, see Warren, *Triumphant Capitalism*, 83.

6. Drew Keeling, *The Business of Transatlantic Migration Between Europe and the United States, 1900–1914: Mass Migration as a Transnational Business in Long Distance Travel* (Zurich: Chronos, 2013).

7. Warren, *Triumphant Capitalism*, 72.

8. Standiford, *Meet You in Hell*, 141.

9. Alexander Berkman, *Prison Memoirs of an Anarchist* (New York: Mother Earth, 1912).

10. Kahan, *Homestead Strike*, 346.

11. Standiford, *Meet You in Hell*, 15.

12. David P. Demarest, ed., *The River Ran Red: Homestead 1892* (Pittsburgh: University of Pittsburgh Press, 1992).

13. On the Great Railroad Strike of 1877, see Richard White, *The Republic for Which*

It Stands: The United States During Reconstruction and the Gilded Age, 1865–1896 (New York: Oxford University Press, 2017), 345–67; David O. Stowell, *The Great Strikes of 1877* (Urbana: University of Illinois Press, 2008).

14. So were mines. See Kevin Kenny, *Making Sense of the Molly Maguires* (New York: Oxford University Press, 1998).

15. Stowell, *Great Strikes of 1877*, 4–8.

16. Michael Kazin, "The July Days in San Francisco, 1877: Prelude to Kearneyism," in Stowell, *Great Strikes of 1877*, 136–63.

17. Richard Schneirov, "Chicago's Great Upheaval of 1877: Class Polarization and Democratic Politics," in Stowell, *Great Strikes of 1877*, 85, 91, 89; John B. Jentz and Richard Schneirov, *Chicago in the Age of Capital Class, Politics, and Democracy During the Civil War and Reconstruction* (Urbana: University of Illinois Press, 2012).

18. Michael Bellesiles, *1877: America's Year of Living Violently* (New York: New Press, 2010), 150.

19. John Hay, *The Bread-Winners: A Social Study* (New York: Frederick Warne, 1883).

20. William E. Forbath, *Law and the Shaping of the American Labor Movement* (Cambridge, Mass.: Harvard University Press, 1991), 19–36.

21. Karl Marx, *Capital: A Critique of Political Economy*, vol. 1, trans. Ben Fowkes (1867; New York: Penguin Classics, 1992)

22. Ibid., 1:932.

23. On the theme of time in *Capital*, see Moishe Postone, *Time, Labor, and Social Domination: A Reinterpretation of Marx's Critical Theory* (New York: Cambridge University Press, 1993).

24. Karl Marx, *The Eighteenth Brumaire of Louis Bonaparte*, trans. Eden Paul and Cedar Paul (1852; New York: International Publishers, 1994). On Marx and finance, see Karl Marx, *Capital: A Critique of Political Economy*, vol. 3, trans. David Fernbach (1894; New York: Penguin Classics, 1993).

25. Jeanne Lafortune, José Tessada, and Ethan Lewis, "People and Machines: A Look at the Evolving Relationship Between Capital and Skill in Manufacturing 1860–1930 Using Immigration Shocks," National Bureau of Economic Research, Working Paper no. 21435 (July 2015); Lawrence F. Katz and Robert A. Margo, "Technical Change and the Relative Demand for Skilled Labor: The United States in Historical Perspective," in Leah Platt Boustan, Carola Frydman, and Robert A. Margo, eds., *Human Capital in History: The American Record* (Chicago: University of Chicago Press, 2014), 15–57.

26. Milton Friedman and Anna Jacobson Schwartz, *A Monetary History of the United States, 1867–1960* (Princeton: Princeton University Press, 1963), 89–134; Eric J. Hobsbawm, *The Age of Empire, 1875–1914* (New York: Pantheon, 1987), 34–55.

27. Jeremy Atack and Fred Bateman, "How Long Was the Workday in 1880?," *Journal of Economic History* 52, no. 1 (1992): 129–60.

28. Peter H. Lindert and Jeffrey G. Williamson, *Unequal Gains: American Growth and Inequality Since 1700* (Princeton: Princeton University Press, 2016), 166–93.

29. Henry George, *Progress and Poverty: An Enquiry into the Cause of Industrial Depressions, and of Increase of Want with Increase of Wealth* (New York: K. Paul, Trench, 1879). On the debate at the time, see James L. Huston, *Securing the Fruits of Labor: The American Concept of Wealth Distribution, 1765–1900* (Baton Rouge: Louisiana State University Press, 2015).

30. Robert J. Gordon, *The Rise and Fall of American Growth: The U.S. Standard of Living Since the Civil War* (Princeton: Princeton University Press, 2016), 36.

31. White, *Republic for Which It Stands*, 477–517; Dora L. Costa, "Health and the Economy in the United States from 1750 to the Present," *Journal of Economic Literature* 53, no. 3 (2015): 503–70; Robert William Fogel, *The Escape from Hunger and Premature*

Death, 1700–2100: Europe, America, and the Third World (New York: Cambridge University Press, 2004); Richard H. Steckel, "Biological Measures of the Standard of Living," *Journal of Economic Perspectives* 22, no. 1 (2008): 129–52.

32. Gordon, *Rise and Fall of American Growth.*

33. Rosanne Currarino, *The Labor Question in America: Economic Democracy in the Gilded Age* (Urbana: University of Illinois Press, 2011), 40.

34. Gavin Wright, "The Industrious Revolution in America," in L. Cruz and J. Mokyr, eds., *The Birth of Modern Europe: Culture and Economy, 1400–1800. Essays in Honor of Jan de Vries* (Boston: Brill, 2011), 215–48; Martha Ellen Shiells, "Collective Choice of Working Conditions: Hours in British and U.S. Iron and Steel, 1890–1923," *Journal of Economic History* 50, no. 2 (1990): 379–92.

35. Susan B. Carter and Richard Sutch, "Historical Background to Current Immigration Issues," in James P. Smith and Barry Edmonston, eds., *The Immigration Debates* (Washington, D.C.: National Academy Press, 1998), 305. Tara Zahra, *The Great Departure: Mass Migration from Eastern Europe and the Making of the Free World* (New York: Norton, 2016).

36. Philip Scranton, *Endless Novelty: Specialty Production and American Industrialization, 1865–1925* (Princeton: Princeton University Press, 1997).

37. Katz and Margo, "Technical Change," 57, table 1.4, panel A.

38. Joshua Brown, "The Great Uprising and Pictorial Order in Gilded Age America," in Stowell, *Great Strikes of 1877*, 15–54.

39. Alexander Gourevitch, *From Slavery to the Cooperative Commonwealth: Labor and Republican Liberty in the Nineteenth Century* (New York: Cambridge University Press, 2015).

40. Christopher L. Tomlins, *Law, Labor, and Ideology in the Early American Republic* (New York: Cambridge University Press, 1993).

41. David Montgomery, *Beyond Equality: Labor and the Radical Republicans, 1862–1872* (New York: Vintage Books, 1972).

42. On the Knights in general, see Leon Fink, *Workingmen's Democracy: The Knights of Labor and American Politics* (Urbana: University of Illinois Press, 1983); Kim Voss, *The Making of American Exceptionalism: The Knights of Labor and Class Formation in the Nineteenth Century* (Ithaca, N.Y.: Cornell University Press, 1994).

43. Joseph Gerteis, *Class and the Color Line: Interracial Class Coalition in the Knights of Labor and the Populist Movement* (Durham, N.C.: Duke University Press, 2007).

44. Robert E. Weir, *Beyond Labor's Veil: The Culture of the Knights of Labor* (University Park: Pennsylvania State University Press, 1996), 182.

45. On the enduring significance of antimonopoly, see White, *Republic for Which It Stands*; Richard R. John, "Robber Barons Redux: Antimonopoly Reconsidered," *Enterprise and Society* 13, no. 1 (2012): 1–38.

46. Matthew Hild, *Greenbackers, Knights of Labor, and Populists: Farmer-Labor Insurgency in the Late-Nineteenth-Century South* (Athens: University of Georgia Press, 2007).

47. Beth Lew-Williams, *The Chinese Must Go: Racial Violence and the Making of the Alien in America* (Cambridge, Mass.: Harvard University Press, 2018); Currarino, *Labor Question in America*, 36–59.

48. Elizabeth Sinn, *Pacific Crossing: California Gold, Chinese Migration, and the Making of Hong Kong* (Hong Kong: Hong Kong University Press, 2013); Mae M. Ngai, "Chinese Gold Miners and the 'Chinese Question' in Nineteenth-Century California and Victoria," *Journal of American History* 101, no. 4 (2015): 1082–105.

49. Currarino, *Labor Question in America*, 45.

50. Lew-Williams, *Chinese Must Go.*

51. Gourevitch, *From Slavery to Cooperative Commonwealth*, 97–137.

52. Ibid., 6.

53. Daniel T. Rodgers, *The Work Ethic in Industrial America, 1850–1920* (Chicago: University of Chicago Press, 1978), 42.

54. Gourevitch, *From Slavery to Cooperative Commonwealth*, 121.

55. Rodgers, *Work Ethic in Industrial America*, 40–62.

56. John Curl, *For All the People: Uncovering the Hidden History of Cooperation, Cooperative Movements, and Communalism in America* (Oakland, Calif.: PM Press, 2012), 87–110; Mary A. O'Sullivan, *Dividends of Development: Securities Markets in the History of U.S. Capitalism, 1865–1922* (Oxford: Oxford University Press, 2016).

57. Carole Turbin, *Working Women of Collar City: Gender, Class, and Community in Troy, 1864–1886* (Urbana: University of Illinois Press, 1992), 155–95.

58. Gordon, *Rise and Fall of American Growth*, 34, table 2-1.

59. Kessler-Harris, *Out to Work*, 108–41.

60. Rosalyn Fraad Baxandall and Linda Gordon, eds., *America's Working Women: A Documentary History, 1600 to the Present* (New York: Norton, 1995), 98.

61. Ibid., 101–3.

62. Melvyn Dubofsky and Joseph A. McCartin, *Labor in America: A History*, 9th ed. (Hoboken, N.J.: Wiley-Blackwell, 2017), 117.

63. Theresa A. Case, *The Great Southwest Railroad Strike and Free Labor* (College Station: Texas A&M University Press, 2010).

64. White, *Republic for Which It Stands*, 518. See 518–51 for a general account.

65. "The Union and Iron Company to Start Up in November," *New York Times*, September 5, 1885.

66. Paul Avrich, *The Haymarket Tragedy* (Princeton: Princeton University Press, 1984), 393; James Green, *Death in the Haymarket: A Story of Chicago, the First Labor Movement and the Bombing That Divided Gilded Age America* (New York: Pantheon, 2006).

67. Case, *Great Southwest Railroad Strike*, 203.

68. Frederick Cooper, Thomas Cleveland Holt, and Rebecca J. Scott, *Beyond Slavery: Explorations of Race, Labor, and Citizenship in Postemancipation Societies* (Chapel Hill: University of North Carolina Press, 2000), 76–80.

69. Sven Beckert, *The Monied Metropolis: New York City and the Consolidation of the American Bourgeoisie, 1850–1896* (New York: Cambridge University Press, 2001), 294.

70. On Gilded Age mansions, see Edward C. Kirkland, *Dream and Thought in the Business Community, 1860–1900* (Ithaca, N.Y.: Cornell University Press, 1956), 29–50.

71. Edward Atkinson, *Addresses upon the Labor Question* (Boston: Franklin Press, 1886), 22, 5.

72. Susie Pak, *Gentlemen Bankers: The World of J. P. Morgan* (Cambridge, Mass.: Harvard University Press, 2013).

73. Amy Dru Stanley, "Home Life and the Morality of the Market," in Melvin Stokes and Stephen Conway, eds., *The Market Revolution in America: Social, Political, and Religious Expressions, 1800–1880* (Charlottesville: University Press of Virginia, 1996), 86.

74. Amy Dru Stanley, *From Bondage to Contract: Wage Labor, Marriage, and the Market in the Age of Slave Emancipation* (New York: Cambridge University Press, 1998), 138–74.

75. Maury Klein, *The Life and Legend of Jay Gould* (Baltimore: Johns Hopkins University Press, 1986), 65–76, 211–19.

76. Lori D. Ginzberg, *Women and the Work of Benevolence: Morality, Politics, and Class in the Nineteenth-Century United States* (New Haven: Yale University Press, 1990).

77. Ian Tyrrell, *Woman's World/Woman's Empire: The Woman's Christian Temperance Union in International Perspective, 1880–1930* (Chapel Hill: University of North Carolina Press, 1991).

78. Kessler-Harris, *Out to Work*, 97; Ellen Carol DuBois, *Woman Suffrage and Women's Rights* (New York: New York University Press, 1998).

79. U.S. Bureau of Labor, *Working Women in Large Cities* (Washington, D.C.: U.S. Government Printing Office, 1889), 21.

80. Stanley, *From Bondage to Contract*, 218–63.

81. George Miller Beard, *American Nervousness, Its Causes and Consequences: A Supplement to Nervous Exhaustion* (New York: Putnam, 1881).

82. Charlotte Perkins Gilman, *The Yellow Wall-Paper, Herland, and Selected Writings*, ed. Denise D. Knight (New York: Penguin Classics, 2009).

83. Richard Hofstadter, *Social Darwinism in American Thought* (1944; Boston: Beacon Press, 1992); Robert C. Bannister, *Social Darwinism: Science and Myth in Anglo-American Social Thought* (Philadelphia: Temple University Press, 1979).

84. Hofstadter, *Social Darwinism*, 85.

85. James Allen Rogers, "Darwin and Social Darwinism," in John Offer, ed., *Herbert Spencer: Critical Assessments* (New York: Taylor & Francis, 2000), 2:159.

86. For a reassessment of Spencer's philosophy, see Robert J. Richards, *Darwin and the Emergence of Evolutionary Theories of Mind and Behavior* (Chicago: University of Chicago Press, 1989).

87. Jonathan Levy, "Accounting for Profit and the History of Capital," *Critical Historical Studies* 1, no. 2 (2014): 171–214.

88. Edward Bellamy, *Looking Backward, 2000–1887*, ed. Matthew Beaumont (New York: Oxford University Press, 2009), 144.

89. Hofstadter, *Social Darwinism*, 45.

90. Andrew Carnegie, *The Gospel of Wealth Essays and Other Writings*, ed. David Nasaw (New York: Penguin Classics, 2006), 3.

91. John White, "Andrew Carnegie and Herbert Spencer: A Special Relationship," *Journal of American Studies* 13, no. 1 (1979): 57–71.

92. Andrew Carnegie, *Autobiography of Andrew Carnegie* (1920; Philadelphia: PublicAffairs, 2011), 339.

93. White, "Carnegie and Spencer," 58.

94. Herbert Spencer, *An Autobiography* (New York: D. Appleton, 1904), 2:406.

95. Hofstadter, *Social Darwinism*, 57.

96. William Graham Sumner, *What Social Classes Owe to Each Other* (New York: Harper & Brothers, 1883), 13.

97. Stanley, *From Bondage to Contract*, 98–137.

98. Hofstadter, *Social Darwinism*, 47–48.

99. Ibid., 60.

100. Kirkland, *Dream and Thought*, 142.

101. Beckert, *Monied Metropolis*, 220–21.

102. David R. Roediger, *Working Toward Whiteness: How America's Immigrants Became White: The Strange Journey from Ellis Island to the Suburbs* (New York: Basic Books, 2006), 11, 52; Matthew Frye Jacobson, *Barbarian Virtues: The United States Encounters Foreign Peoples at Home and Abroad, 1876–1917* (New York: Hill & Wang, 2000); Gwendolyn Mink, *Old Labor and New Immigrants in American Political Development: Union, Party, and State, 1875–1920* (Ithaca, N.Y.: Cornell University Press, 1986).

103. Schneirov, "Chicago's Great Upheaval of 1877," 95.

104. Currarino, *Labor Question in America*, 86–113; Leon Fink, *In Search of the Working Class: Essays in American Labor History and Political Culture* (Urbana: University of Illinois Press, 1994), 15–33; Bruce Laurie, *Artisans into Workers: Labor in Nineteenth-Century America* (New York: Hill & Wang, 1989), 176–210.

105. Jeremy Atack and Fred Bateman, "How Long Was the Workday in 1880?," *Journal of Economic History* 52, no. 1 (1992): 129–60.

106. On Gompers, see Nick Salvatore, "Introduction," in Samuel Gompers, *70 Years of Life and Labor*, ed. Nick Salvatore (Ithaca, N.Y.: ILR Press, 1985), xi–1.

107. Baxandall and Gordon, *America's Working Women*, 87–91, which draws from Edith Abbott, *Women in Industry: A Study in American Economic History* (New York: Appleton, 1910).

108. Laurie, *Artisans into Workers*, 177.

109. Forbath, *Law and American Labor Movement*, 42.

110. Montgomery, *Fall of the House of Labor*, 25.

111. Laurie, *Artisans into Workers*, 183.

112. Kessler-Harris, *Out to Work*, 153.

113. Currarino, *Labor Question in America*, 93.

114. Roy Rosenzweig, *Eight Hours for What We Will: Workers and Leisure in an Industrial City, 1870–1920* (New York: Cambridge University Press, 1983).

115. Nancy Woloch, *A Class by Herself: Protective Laws for Women Workers, 1890s–1990s* (Princeton: Princeton University Press, 2015).

116. Peter R. Shergold, *Working-Class Life: The "American Standard" in Comparative Perspective, 1899–1913* (Pittsburgh: University of Pittsburgh Press, 1982).

117. Leon Fink, *The Long Gilded Age: American Capitalism and the Lessons of a New World Order* (Philadelphia: University of Pennsylvania Press, 2014).

118. Forbath, *Law and American Labor Movement*, 61.

119. David Nasaw, *Andrew Carnegie* (New York: Penguin Press, 2006), 155.

120. "Thomas A. Scott Professorship in Mathematics," Department of Mathematics, School of Arts and Sciences, University of Pennsylvania, https://www.math.upenn.edu/about/department-history/scott-professorship.

121. Jonathan Levy, "Altruism and the Origins of Nonprofit Philanthropy," in Rob Reich, Lucy Bernholz, and Chiara Cordelli, eds., *Philanthropy in Democratic Societies: History, Institutions, Values* (Chicago: University of Chicago Press, 2016), 19–43.

122. On the Penn Railroad, see Albert J. Churella, *The Pennsylvania Railroad*, vol. 1, *Building an Empire, 1846–1917* (Philadelphia: University of Pennsylvania Press, 2012), 371–73. On the Constitution of 1873, the General Incorporation Act of 1874, and more generally the many restrictions Pennsylvania still maintained on private corporate activity, see Naomi Lamareoux, "Revisiting American Exceptionalism: Democracy and the Regulation of Corporate Governance: The Case of Nineteenth-Century Pennsylvania in Comparative Context," in William J. Collins and Robert A. Margo, eds. *Enterprising America: Businesses, Banks, and Credit Markets in Historical Perspective* (Chicago: University of Chicago Press, 2015), 46n36.

123. Levy, "Altruism and Nonprofit Philanthropy"; Ginzberg, *Women and Work of Benevolence*.

124. Carnegie, *Gospel of Wealth*, 1, 2.

125. Ibid., 10, 5.

126. Ibid., 10, 16.

127. Olivier Zunz, *Philanthropy in America: A History* (Princeton: Princeton University Press, 2011), 8–43; Barry D. Karl and Stanley N. Katz, "The American Private Philanthropic Foundation and the Public Sphere 1890–1930," *Minerva* 19, no. 2 (1981): 236–70.

128. Carnegie, *Gospel of Wealth*, 9.

129. John Davison Rockefeller, *Random Reminiscences of Men and Events* (New York: Doubleday, Page, 1913), 177.

130. Neil Harris, *Cultural Excursions: Marketing Appetites and Cultural Tastes in Modern America* (Chicago: University of Chicago Press, 1990), 85.

131. Noam Maggor, *Brahmin Capitalism: Frontiers of Wealth and Populism in America's First Gilded Age* (Cambridge, Mass.: Harvard University Press, 2017).

132. Alan Trachtenberg, *Incorporation of America: Culture and Society, 1865–1893* (New York: Hill & Wang, 1982), 73.

133. See Lawrence Levine, *Highbrow/Lowbrow: The Emergence of Cultural Hierarchy in America* (Cambridge, Mass.: Harvard University Press, 1988).

CHAPTER 10: THE POPULIST REVOLT

1. Nicolas Barreyre, *Gold and Freedom: The Political Economy of Reconstruction* (Charlottesville: University of Virginia Press, 2015), 225.

2. Ibid.; Richard Franklin Bensel, *The Political Economy of American Industrialization, 1877–1900* (New York: Cambridge University Press, 2000).

3. Richard Franklin Bensel, *Passion and Preferences: William Jennings Bryan and the 1896 Democratic National Convention* (New York: Cambridge University Press, 2008).

4. William Jennings Bryan, *The Cross of Gold: Speech Delivered Before the National Democratic Convention at Chicago, July 9, 1896* (Lincoln: University of Nebraska Press, 1996).

5. On populism then and now, see Nadia Urbinati, *Me the People: How Populism Transforms Democracy* (Cambridge, Mass.: Harvard University Press, 2019); Jan-Werner Müller, *What Is Populism?* (Philadelphia: University of Pennsylvania Press, 2016).

6. Michael Kazin, *A Godly Hero: The Life of William Jennings Bryan* (New York: Knopf, 2006), 62.

7. Bryan, *Cross of Gold,* 10–11.

8. Ibid.

9. Kazin, *Godly Hero,* 61.

10. Nell Irvin Painter, *Standing at Armageddon: United States, 1877–1919* (New York: Norton, 1987), 135.

11. Stephen Kantrowitz, *Ben Tillman and the Reconstruction of White Supremacy* (Chapel Hill: University of North Carolina Press, 2000).

12. Charles Postel, *The Populist Vision* (New York: Oxford University Press, 2007), 159.

13. Daniel T. Rodgers, *Atlantic Crossings: Social Politics in a Progressive Age* (Cambridge, Mass.: Belknap Press, 1998).

14. On the "modernity" of Populism, see Postel, *Populist Vision.* A less sympathetic interpretation was Richard Hofstadter, *The Age of Reform: From Bryan to F.D.R.* (New York: Knopf, 1955).

15. Claudia Goldin and Lawrence F. Katz, "The Origins of Technology-Skill Complementarity," *Quarterly Journal of Economics* 113, no. 3 (1998): 693–732.

16. Alan L. Olmstead and Paul W. Rhode, "Farms—Number, Population, Land, and Value of Property: 1850–1997 [Census Years]," in Susan B. Carter et al., eds., *Historical Statistics of the United States, Earliest Times to the Present: Millennial Edition* (New York: Cambridge University Press, 2006), table Da14–27.

17. According to the "Prebisch Effect," a rise in productivity in primary production is passed on to the buyer in the form of lower prices, whereas in manufacturing, incomes from productivity gains remain with producers. Raul Prebisch, *The Economic Development of Latin America and Its Principal Problems* (New York: ECLA, 1950).

18. Robert C. McMath, *American Populism: A Social History, 1877–1898* (New York: Hill & Wang, 1993).

19. Elizabeth Sanders, *Roots of Reform: Farmers, Workers, and the American State, 1877–1917* (Chicago: University of Chicago Press, 1999), 119.

20. Brooke Speer, *The "People's Joan of Arc": Mary Elizabeth Lease, Gendered Politics and Populist Party Politics in Gilded-Age America* (New York: Peter Lang, 2014); Lawrence Goodwyn, *Democratic Promise: The Populist Moment in America* (New York: Oxford University Press, 1976).

21. Omar H. Ali, *In the Lion's Mouth: Black Populism in the New South, 1886–1900* (Jackson: University Press of Mississippi, 2010).

22. Jonathan Levy, *Freaks of Fortune: The Emerging World of Capitalism and Risk in America* (Cambridge, Mass.: Harvard University Press, 2012), 150–90.

23. Lee Benson, *Merchants, Farmers, and Railroads: Railroad Regulation and New York Politics, 1850–1887* (Cambridge, Mass.: Harvard University Press, 1955).

24. Henry C. Adams, "Relation of the State to Industrial Action," *Publications of the American Economic Association* 1 (1887): 465–549.

25. Nelson A. Dunning, *The Farmers' Alliance History and Agricultural Digest* (Washington, D.C.: Alliance, 1891), 49.

26. McMath, *American Populism,* 83–107; Postel, *Populist Vision,* 103–36.

27. Jeffrey Sklansky, *Sovereign of the Market: The Money Question in Early America* (Chicago: University of Chicago Press, 2017).

28. Mark W. Summers, *Party Games: Getting, Keeping, and Using Power in Gilded Age Politics* (Chapel Hill: University of North Carolina Press, 2004), 264.

29. Morton Keller, *Affairs of State: Public Life in Late Nineteenth Century America* (Cambridge, Mass.: Harvard University Press, 1977).

30. Bensel, *Political Economy of Industrialization,* 457–509.

31. Gerald Berk, *Alternative Tracks: The Constitution of American Industrial Order, 1865–1917* (Baltimore: Johns Hopkins University Press, 1994), 105.

32. Sanders, *Roots of Reform,* 101–47.

33. Postel, *Populist Vision,* 159.

34. They did, however, in the Pacific Northwest. See Robert D. Johnston, *The Radical Middle Class: Populist Democracy and the Question of Capitalism in Progressive Era Portland, Oregon* (Princeton: Princeton University Press, 2003).

35. C. Vann Woodward, *Tom Watson: Agrarian Rebel* (New York: Oxford University Press, 1963), 370.

36. Niall Ferguson and Moritz Schularick, "The Empire Effect: The Determinants of Country Risk in the First Age of Globalization, 1880–1913," *Journal of Economic History* 66, no. 2 (2006): 283–312.

37. Lance E. Davis and Robert E. Gallman, *Evolving Financial Markets and International Capital Flows: Britain, the Americas, and Australia, 1865–1914* (New York: Cambridge University Press, 2001); Tamim Bayoumi, Barry Eichengreen, and Mark P. Taylor, eds., *Modern Perspectives on the Gold Standard* (New York: Cambridge University Press, 1996).

38. Kevin H. O'Rourke and Jeffrey G. Williamson, *Globalization and History: The Evolution of a Nineteenth-Century Atlantic Economy* (Cambridge, Mass.: MIT Press, 1999).

39. Ferguson and Schularick, "Empire Effect."

40. Jeremy Adelman, *Frontier Development: Land, Labour, and Capital on the Wheatlands of Argentina and Canada, 1890–1914* (Oxford: Clarendon Press, 1994).

41. Scott Reynolds Nelson, *A Nation of Deadbeats: An Uncommon History of America's Financial Disasters* (New York: Knopf, 2012), 188–200.

42. Douglas Steeples and David O. Whitten, *Democracy in Desperation: The Depression of 1893* (Westport, Conn.: Praeger, 1998).

43. David O. Whitten, "The Depression of 1893," EH.net, https://eh.net/encyclopedia/the-depression-of–1893.

44. Ron Chernow, *The House of Morgan: An American Banking Dynasty and the Rise of Modern Finance* (New York: Atlantic Monthly Press, 1990), 74–78; Orr, *"People's Joan of Arc,"* 105.

45. For a counterargument see Goodwyn, *Democratic Promise.*

46. Kazin, *Godly Hero,* 60–80.

47. Samuel Gompers, *The Samuel Gompers Papers: A National Labor Movement Takes Shape, 1895–1898* (Urbana: University of Illinois Press, 1986), 105.

48. Samuel Gompers, *Seventy Years of Life and Labour: An Autobiography* (1925; New York: Augustus M. Kelley, 1967), 88.

49. Naomi R. Lamoreaux, Margaret Levenstein, and Kenneth L. Sokoloff, "Financing Invention During the Second Industrial Revolution: Cleveland, Ohio, 1870–1920," National Bureau of Economic Research, Working Paper no. 10923 (November 2004), http://www.nber.org/papers/w10923.

50. Goodwyn, *Democratic Promise*, 279.

51. On McKinley's strategy in 1896, see Karl Rove, *The Triumph of William McKinley: Why the Election of 1896 Still Matters* (New York: Simon & Schuster, 2015).

52. Edward Atkinson, "The Money of the Nation: Shall It Be Good Or Bad?," *Sound Currency* 3, no. 15 (1896).

53. Levy, *Freaks of Fortune*, 277.

54. Jeffry A. Frieden, *Global Capitalism: Its Fall and Rise in the Twentieth Century* (New York: Norton, 2006), 15.

55. Jeffry A. Frieden, *Currency Politics: The Political Economy of Exchange Rate Policy* (Princeton: Princeton University Press, 2015), 104–36.

56. Jacqueline Goldsby, *A Spectacular Secret: Lynching in American Life and Literature* (Chicago: University of Chicago Press, 2006).

57. Naomi R. Lamoreaux, *The Great Merger Movement in American Business, 1895–1904* (New York: Cambridge University Press, 1988), 2.

58. Chernow, *House of Morgan*, 71–94.

59. Bradley Hansen, "The People's Welfare and the Origins of Corporate Reorganization: The Wabash Receivership Reconsidered," *Business History Review* 74, no. 3 (2000): 377–405.

60. Herbert Hovenkamp, *The Opening of American Law: Neoclassical Legal Thought, 1870–1970* (New York: Oxford University Press, 2014), 162–69.

61. Berk, *Alternative Tracks*, 47–75.

62. Mary A. O'Sullivan, *Dividends of Development: Securities Markets in the History of U.S. Capitalism, 1865–1922* (Oxford: Oxford University Press, 2016).

63. Philip Scranton, *Endless Novelty: Specialty Production and American Industrialization, 1865–1925* (Princeton: Princeton University Press, 1997); Lamoreaux, Levenstein, and Sokoloff, "Financing Invention"; Naomi R. Lamoreaux and Kenneth L. Sokoloff, eds., *Financing Innovation in the United States, 1870 to Present* (Cambridge, Mass.: MIT Press, 2007).

64. *Addyston Pipe & Steel Co. v. United States* (1899) was the lead case.

65. Lamoreaux, *Great Merger Movement*, 46–85.

66. But see O'Sullivan, *Dividends of Development;* Kenneth Snowden, "Historical Returns and Security Market Development, 1872–1925," *Explorations in Economic History* 27, no. 4 (1990): 381–420; and Thomas R. Navin and Marian V. Sears, "The Rise of a Market for Industrial Securities, 1887–1902," *Business History Review* 29, no. 2 (1955): 105–38.

67. Vincent P. Carosso, *Investment Banking in America: A History* (Cambridge, Mass.: Harvard University Press, 1970). See also O'Sullivan, *Dividends of Development*, which is skeptical of large investment banker influence.

68. See "Modern Business Capital" in Thorstein Veblen, *The Theory of Business Enterprise* (New York: Scribner, 1904), 133–76.

69. Hovenkamp, *Opening of American Law*, 165.

70. Irving Fisher, *The Nature of Capital and Income* (New York, 1906), 328.

71. On this point, see Jens Beckert, *Imagined Futures: Fictional Expectations and Capitalist Dynamics* (Cambridge, Mass.: Harvard University Press, 2016).

72. Julia C. Ott, *When Wall Street Met Main Street: The Quest for an Investors' Democracy* (Cambridge, Mass.: Harvard University Press, 2011).

73.   On these networks of "social capital," see Susie Pak, *Gentlemen Bankers: The World of J. P. Morgan* (Cambridge, Mass.: Harvard University Press, 2013).

74.   Chernow, *House of Morgan*, 84.

75.   Levy, *Freaks of Fortune*, 291; James Livingston, *Origins of the Federal Reserve System: Money, Class, and Corporate Capitalism, 1890–1913* (Ithaca, N.Y.: Cornell University Press, 1986), 56.

76.   Levy, *Freaks of Fortune*, 291.

77.   Livingston, *Origins of the Federal Reserve System*, 56.

78.   Chernow, *House of Morgan*, 85.

79.   Rodgers, *Atlantic Crossings*.

80.   Sanders, *Roots of Reform*.

81.   Thomas C. Leonard, *Illiberal Reformers: Race, Eugenics, and American Economics in the Progressive Era* (Princeton: Princeton University Press, 2016); Molly Ladd-Taylor, *Fixing the Poor: Eugenic Sterilization and Child Welfare in the Twentieth Century* (Baltimore: Johns Hopkins University Press, 2017).

82.   Rexford Guy Tugwell, *The Economic Basis of Public Interest* (New York: G. Banta, 1922), 23.

83.   John Dewey, "The Historic Background of Corporate Legal Personality," *Yale Law Journal* 35, no. 6 (1926): 655–73.

84.   In 1894 a Democratic Congress bowed to agrarian pressure from the South and West and levied a 2 percent income tax on the richest 10 percent of households. The U.S. Supreme Court struck down the income tax as unconstitutional in *Pollock v. Farmers' Loan & Trust. Co.* (1895), as the tax was not levied in proportion to population.

85.   Monica Prasad, *The Land of Too Much: American Abundance and the Paradox of Poverty* (Cambridge, Mass.: Harvard University Press, 2012), 148–74.

86.   Ajay K. Mehrotra, *Making the Modern American Fiscal State: Law, Politics, and the Rise of Progressive Taxation, 1877–1929* (New York: Cambridge University Press, 2013), 110–43, 242–92.

87.   Ron Chernow, *Titan: The Life of John D. Rockefeller, Sr.* (New York: Random House, 1998), 160, 129–72.

88.   Gerald Berk, *Louis D. Brandeis and the Making of Regulated Competition, 1900–1932* (Cambridge, Mass.: Cambridge University Press, 2009), 37.

89.   Richard E. Caves, Michael Fortunato, and Pankaj Ghemawat, "The Decline of Dominant Firms, 1905–1929," *Quarterly Journal of Economics* 99, no. 3 (1984): 523–46; Thomas K. McCraw and Forest Reinhardt, "Losing to Win: U.S. Steel's Pricing, Investment Decisions, and Market Share, 1901–1938," *Journal of Economic History* 49, no. 3 (1989): 593–619.

90.   William J. Novak, "The Public Utility Idea and the Origins of Modern Business Regulation," in Naomi R. Lamoreaux et al., eds., *Corporations and American Democracy* (Cambridge, Mass.: Harvard University Press, 2017), 139–76.

91.   Rodgers, *Atlantic Crossings*, 112–59.

92.   Berk, *Alternative Tracks*, 155.

93.   Linda Gordon, *Pitied but Not Entitled: Single Mothers and the History of Welfare, 1890–1935* (New York: Free Press, 1994); Theda Skocpol, *Protecting Soldiers and Mothers: The Political Origins of Social Policy in United States* (Cambridge, Mass.: Belknap Press, 1992).

94.   Nancy F. Cott, *The Grounding of Modern Feminism* (New Haven: Yale University Press, 1987).

95.   Sonya Michel, *Children's Interests/Mothers' Rights: The Shaping of America's Child Care Policy* (New Haven: Yale University Press, 2000).

96.   John Fabian Witt, *The Accidental Republic: Crippled Workingmen, Destitute Wid-

ows, and the Remaking of American Law (Cambridge, Mass.: Harvard University Press, 2004); Skocpol, *Protecting Soldiers and Mothers.*

97. Cedric B. Cowing, *Populists, Plungers, and Progressives: A Social History of Stock and Commodity Speculation, 1868–1932* (Princeton: Princeton University Press, 2016); Peter Knight, *Reading the Market: Genres of Financial Capitalism in Gilded Age America* (Baltimore: Johns Hopkins University Press, 2016).

98. Levy, *Freaks of Fortune,* 268–73.

99. Livingston, *Origins of the Federal Reserve System,* 71–102.

100. Peter Conti-Brown, *The Power and Independence of the Federal Reserve* (Princeton: Princeton University Press, 2016).

101. Victoria Saker Woeste, *The Farmer's Benevolent Trust: Law and Agricultural Cooperation in Industrial America, 1865–1945* (Chapel Hill: University of North Carolina Press, 1998).

102. Sanders, *Roots of Reform,* 148–78.

103. Roger Lowenstein, *America's Bank: The Epic Struggle to Create the Federal Reserve* (New York: Penguin Press, 2015), 228.

CHAPTER II: FORDISM

1. Vincent Curcio, *Henry Ford* (New York: Oxford University Press, 2013), 69.

2. Stefan Link, *Forging Global Fordism: Nazi Germany, Soviet Russia, and the Contest over the Industrial Order* (Princeton: Princeton University Press, 2020), the best study of Fordism as a global phenomenon there is; Stephen Kotkin, "Modern Times: The Soviet Union and the Interwar Conjuncture," *Kritika: Explorations in Russian and Eurasion History* 2, no. 1 (2001): 111–64.

3. Curcio, *Henry Ford,* 45.

4. Greg Grandin, *Fordlandia: The Rise and Fall of Henry Ford's Forgotten Jungle City* (New York: Metropolitan Books, 2009), 57.

5. Henry Ford, *My Life and Work,* ed. Samuel Crowther (Garden City, N.Y.: Doubleday, Page, 1922), 1.

6. Ibid., 1; Grandin, *Forldlandia,* 20.

7. Beth Tompkins Bates, *The Making of Black Detroit in the Age of Henry Ford* (Chapel Hill: University of North Carolina Press, 2012), 44.

8. Neil Baldwin, *Henry Ford and the Jews: The Mass Production of Hate* (New York: PublicAffairs, 2001).

9. Link, *Forging Global Fordism;* Kotkin, "Modern Times"; David E. Nye, *America's Assembly Line* (Cambridge, Mass.: MIT Press, 2013).

10. On this point Link, *Forging Global Fordism,* is particularly insightful.

11. Julia Ott, "What Was the Great Bull Market? Value, Valuation, and Financial History," in Sven Beckert and Christine Desan, eds., *American Capitalism: New Histories* (New York: Columbia University Press, 2018), 63–95.

12. Richard Snow, *I Invented the Modern Age: The Rise of Henry Ford* (New York: Scribner, 2013).

13. Paul A. David and Gavin Wright, "Early Twentieth Century Productivity Growth Dynamics: An Inquiry into the Economic History of 'Our Ignorance,'" University of Oxford Discussion Papers in Economic and Social History, no. 33 (October 1999).

14. Warren D. Devine, "From Shafts to Wires: Historical Perspective on Electrification," *Journal of Economic History* 43, no. 2 (1983): 349.

15. Alexander J. Field, *A Great Leap Forward: 1930s Depression and U.S. Economic Growth* (New Haven: Yale University Press, 2011), 46.

16.   Lindy Biggs, *The Rational Factory: Architecture, Technology, and Work in America's Age of Mass Production* (Baltimore: Johns Hopkins University Press, 1996), 95–160.

17.   Douglas Brinkley, *Wheels for the World: Henry Ford, His Company, and a Century of Progress* (New York: Viking, 2003).

18.   Deborah Clarke, *Driving Women: Fiction and Automobile Culture in Twentieth-Century America* (Baltimore: Johns Hopkins University Press, 2007), 10.

19.   Robert J. Gordon, *The Rise and Fall of American Growth: The U.S. Standard of Living Since the Civil War* (Princeton: Princeton University Press, 2016), 131.

20.   David E. Nye, *Consuming Power: A Social History of American Energies* (Cambridge, Mass.: MIT Press, 1997). Christopher W. Wells, *Car Country: An Environmental History* (Seattle: University of Washington Press, 2013).

21.   Steven C. Topik and Allen Wells, "Commodity Chains in a Global Economy," in Emily S. Rosenberg, ed., *A World Connecting: 1870–1945* (Cambridge, Mass.: Belknap Press, 2012), 668; Gary D. Best, *The Dollar Decade: Mammon and the Machine in 1920s America* (Westport, Conn.: Praeger, 2003), 121.

22.   Grandin, *Fordlandia*, 34.

23.   Antonio Gramsci, *Selections from the Prison Notebooks of Antonio Gramsci* (New York: International Publishers, 1971).

24.   Adam Tooze, *The Deluge: The Great War, America and the Remaking of the Global Order, 1916–1931* (New York: Penguin, 2015), 334.

25.   Henry Ford, "Mass Production," *Encyclopaedia Britannica* (New York: 1926), 30:821–23.

26.   Thomas Parke Hughes, *American Genesis: A Century of Invention and Technological Enthusiasm, 1870–1970* (New York: Viking, 1989); Leonard S. Reich, *The Making of American Industrial Research: Science and Business at GE and Bell, 1876–1926* (New York: Cambridge University Press, 1985); David F. Noble, *America by Design: Science, Technology, and the Rise of Corporate Capitalism* (New York: Knopf, 1977).

27.   Kenneth J. Arrow, "The Economic Implications of Learning by Doing," *Review of Economic Studies* 29, no. 3 (1962): 155–73.

28.   Lewis Mumford, *Technics and Civilization* (1934; Chicago: University of Chicago Press, 2010), 14, 10.

29.   Biggs, *Rational Factory*, 128.

30.   Brian Page and Richard Walker, "From Settlement to Fordism: The Agro-Industrial Revolution in the American Midwest," *Economic Geography* 67, no. 4 (1991): 281–315.

31.   See in general "Introduction," in Naomi R. Lamoreaux and Kenneth L. Sokoloff, eds., *Financing Innovation in the United States, 1870 to Present* (Cambridge, Mass.: MIT Press, 2007).

32.   Hughes, *American Genesis*, 184–248.

33.   Steven Klepper, "The Organizing and Financing of Innovative Companies in the Evolution of the U.S. Automobile Industry," in Lamoreaux and Sokoloff, *Financing Innovation*, 87, 89.

34.   Robert G. Szudarek, *How Detroit Became the Automotive Capital* (Detroit: SAE International, 1996).

35.   Charles E. Sorensen and Samuel T. Williams, *My Forty Years with Ford* (1956; Detroit: Wayne State University Press, 2006), 45.

36.   David Hounshell, *From the American System to Mass Production, 1800–1932: The Development of Manufacturing Technology in the United States* (Baltimore: Johns Hopkins University Press, 1985), 217–62.

37.   Ford, *My Life and Work*, 87.

38.   Thomas K. McCraw, *American Business Since 1920: How It Worked* (Wheeling, Ill.: Wiley-Blackwell, 2008), 17.

39. Stephen Meyer III, *The Five Dollar Day: Labor Management and Social Control in the Ford Motor Company, 1908–1921* (Albany: State University of New York Press, 1981), 24.

40. Federico Bucci, *Albert Kahn: Architect of Ford* (New York: Princeton Architectural Press, 1993), 43.

41. Daniel Nelson, *Frederick W. Taylor and the Rise of Scientific Management* (Madison: University of Wisconsin Press, 1980).

42. Nye, *America's Assembly Line*, 23.

43. Thomas J. Misa, *A Nation of Steel: The Making of Modern America, 1865–1925* (Baltimore: Johns Hopkins University Press, 1995), 211–52.

44. Bucci, *Albert Kahn.*

45. Clarence Hooker, *Life in the Shadows of the Crystal Palace, 1910–1927: Ford Workers in the Model T Era* (Bowling Green, Ohio: Bowling Green State University Popular Press, 1997).

46. Ernest W. McMullen, "The Concrete Factory," *Architectural Forum*, July 1919, 7–12.

47. Hounshell, *American System to Mass Production*, 228.

48. Hughes, *American Genesis*, 184–294.

49. Sigfried Giedion, *Mechanization Takes Command, a Contribution to Anonymous History* (New York: Oxford University Press, 1948).

50. Horace Lucien Arnold and Fay Leone Faurote, *Ford Methods and the Ford Shops* (New York: Engineering Magazine, 1915), 139.

51. Sorensen and Williams, *My Forty Years with Ford*, 131.

52. Allan Nevins and Frank Ernest Hill, *Ford: The Times, the Man, the Company* (New York: Scribner, 1954), 488.

53. Mumford, *Technics and Civilization*, 92.

54. John Roderigo Dos Passos, *U.S.A.*, vol. 3, *The Big Money* (1933; Boston: Mariner Books, 2000), 44.

55. Jeanne Lafortune, José Tessada, and Ethan Lewis, "People and Machines: A Look at the Evolving Relationship Between Capital and Skill in Manufacturing, 1860–1930, Using Immigration Shocks," National Bureau of Economic Research, Working Paper no. 21435 (July 2015).

56. Meyer, *Five Dollar Day*, 37, 77, 56. On working-class ethnicity in Detroit, see Olivier Zunz, *The Changing Face of Inequality: Urbanization, Industrial Development, and Immigrants in Detroit, 1880–1920* (Chicago: University of Chicago Press, 1982), 218–40.

57. Meyer, *Five Dollar Day*, 82, 83, 85.

58. Ibid., 162.

59. Ford, *My Life and Work*, 26.

60. Nye, *America's Assembly Line*, 98.

61. Samuel M. Levin, "The Growth of the Plan," in John Cunningham Wood and Michael C. Wood, eds., *Henry Ford: Critical Evaluations in Business and Management* (New York: Routledge, 2003), 1:162.

62. Daniel M. G. Raff and Lawrence H. Summers, "Did Henry Ford Pay Efficiency Wages?," *Journal of Labor Economics* 5, no. 4 (1987): S57–S86.

63. Meyer, *Five Dollar Day*, 116–23.

64. Hounshell, *American System to Mass Production*, 259.

65. Ford, *My Life and Work*, 2.

66. Tooze, *Deluge*, 353–73.

67. Henry Ford, in *Automobile* 35 (September 7, 1916): 417.

68. Olivier Zunz, *Making America Corporate, 1870–1920* (Chicago: University of Chicago Press, 1990), 81.

69. Ford, *My Life and Work*, 156.

70. *Dodge v. Ford Motor Co.*, 204 Mich. 459 (1919).

71. Allan Nevins and Frank Ernest Hill, *Ford: Expansion and Challenge, 1915–1933* (New York: Charles Scribner's Sons, 1933), 111–12.

72. Ibid., 152.

73. David Montgomery, *The Fall of the House of Labor: The Workplace, the State, and American Labor Activism, 1865–1925* (New York: Cambridge University Press, 1987).

74. Beverly Gage, *The Day Wall Street Exploded: A Story of America in Its First Age of Terror* (New York: Oxford University Press, 2010).

75. Christina D. Romer, "World War I and the Postwar Depression: A Reinterpretation Based on Alternative Estimates of GNP," *Journal of Monetary Economics* 22, no. 1 (1988): 91–115; Nathan S. Balke and Robert J. Gordon, "The Estimation of Prewar Gross National Product: Methodology and New Evidence," *Journal of Political Economy* 97, no. 1 (1989): 38–92.

76. Bates, *Making of Black Detroit*, 45.

77. Nevins and Hill, *Ford: Expansion*, 157, 159.

78. Ibid., 163.

79. James J. Flink, *The Automobile Age* (Cambridge, Mass.: MIT Press, 1990), 230.

80. Allan Nevins and Frank Ernest Hill, *Ford: Decline and Rebirth, 1933–1962* (New York: Charles Scribner's Sons, 1963), appendix I.

81. Nevins and Hill, *Ford: Expansion*, 280.

82. On Brazil, see Grandin, *Fordlandia*.

83. *Michigan Manufacturer and Financial Record* (Pick Publications, 1925), 17.

84. Bucci, *Albert Kahn*, 76.

85. Nye, *America's Assembly Line*, 46.

86. John H. Van Deventer, "1—Links in a Complete Industrial Chain," *Industrial Management* 64, no. 3 (1922): 131–37, esp. 137.

87. Edmund Wilson, *The American Earthquake: A Documentary of the Twenties and Thirties* (Garden City, N.Y.: Anchor Books, 1964), 243, 232.

88. Mardges Bacon, *Le Corbusier in America: Travels in the Land of the Timid* (Cambridge, Mass.: MIT Press, 2001), 102; Gillian Darley, *Factory* (London: Reaktion Books, 2003), 155.

89. Best, *Dollar Decade*, xiii.

90. Jane Heap, "Machine-Age Exposition," *Little Review* 11, no. 1 (1925): 22–24.

91. Cecelia Tichi, *Shifting Gears: Technology, Literature, Culture in Modernist America* (Chapel Hill: University of North Carolina Press, 1987), 227, 230.

92. Giedion, *Mechanization Takes Command*, 106.

93. Siegfried Kracauer, *The Mass Ornament: Weimar Essays*, trans. Thomas Levin (Cambridge, Mass.: Harvard University Press, 1995).

94. Emily Ann Thompson, *The Soundscape of Modernity: Architectural Acoustics and the Culture of Listening in America, 1900–1933* (Cambridge, Mass.: MIT Press, 2002).

95. Karen Lucic, *Charles Sheeler and the Cult of the Machine* (Cambridge, Mass.: Harvard University Press, 1991), 92.

96. Detroit Institute of Arts, *The Rouge: The Image of Industry in the Art of Charles Sheeler and Diego Rivera* (Detroit: Detroit Institute of Arts, 1978), 11, 22.

97. Gene Smiley, "The U.S. Economy in the 1920s," EH.net, 2004, https://eh.net/encyclopedia/the-u-s-economy-in-the-1920s/.

98. David Brody, *Workers in Industrial America: Essays on the 20th Century Struggle* (New York: Oxford University Press, 1980), 48–81; Meyer, *Five Dollar Day*, 194.

99. Bates, *Making of Black Detroit*, 60. See also Christopher L. Foote, Warren C. Whatley, and Gavin Wright, "Arbitraging a Discriminatory Labor Market: Black Workers at the Ford Motor Company, 1918–1947," *Journal of Labor Economics* 21, no. 3 (2003): 493–532.

100. Joyce Shaw Peterson, *American Automobile Workers, 1900–1933* (Albany: SUNY Press, 1987), 110–20.

101. Henry Ford, *Ford Ideals: Being a Selection from "Mr. Ford's Page" in The Dearborn Independent* (Dearborn Mich.: Dearborn, 1922), 293.

102. Howard P. Segal, *Recasting the Machine Age: Henry Ford's Village Industries* (Amherst: University of Massachusetts Press, 2008), 25; D. W. Meinig, *The Shaping of America: A Geographical Perspective on 500 Years of History*, vol. 4, *Global America, 1915–2000* (New Haven: Yale University Press, 2004), 50.

103. Grandin, *Fordlandia*, 67.

104. Hounshell, *American System to Mass Production*, 263–302.

105. Charles R. Morris, *A Rabble of Dead Money: The Great Crash and the Global Depression: 1929–1939* (New York: PublicAffairs, 2017), 91.

106. Daniel M. G. Raff, "Making Cars and Making Money in the Interwar Automobile Industry: Economies of Scale and Scope and the Manufacturing Behind the Marketing," *Business History Review* 65, no. 4 (1991): 721–53.

107. Zunz, *Making America Corporate*, 88.

108. Robert F. Freeland, *The Struggle for Control of the Modern Corporation: Organizational Change at General Motors, 1924–1970* (New York: Cambridge University Press, 2000).

109. Alfred Dupont Chandler, Stephen Salisbury, and Adeline Cook Strange, *Pierre S. Du Pont and the Making of the Modern Corporation* (New York: Harper & Row, 1971).

110. Zunz, *Making America Corporate*, 11–36, 125–48.

111. Lafortune, Tessada, and Lewis, "People and Machines."

112. Ray Batchelor, *Henry Ford, Mass Production, Modernism, and Design* (Manchester, U.K.: Manchester University Press, 1994).

113. Daniel Nelson, ed., *A Mental Revolution: Scientific Management Since Taylor* (Columbus: Ohio State University Press, 1992).

114. Noble, *America by Design*, 110–66.

115. Jonathan Levy, "Accounting for Profit and the History of Capital," *Critical Historical Studies* 1, no. 2 (2014): 171–214.

116. William E. Akin, *Technocracy and the American Dream: The Technocrat Movement, 1900–1941* (Berkeley: University of California Press, 1977), 13.

CHAPTER 12: THE GREAT DEPRESSION

1. Nicholas Crafts and Peter Fearon, "Depression and Recovery in the 1930s: An Overview," in Crafts and Fearon, eds., *The Great Depression of the 1930s: Lessons for Today* (New York: Cambridge University Press, 2013), 3, 10, table 1.2.

2. Liaquat Ahamed, *Lords of Finance: The Bankers Who Broke the World* (New York: Penguin Press, 2009), 5.

3. Milton Friedman and Anna Jacobson Schwartz, *A Monetary History of the United States, 1867–1960* (Princeton: Princeton University Press, 1963), 299–428.

4. Keynes saw this point clearly, in real time. John Maynard Keynes, "An Economic Analysis of Unemployment, (1931)" in Donald Moggridge and Elizabeth Johnson, eds., *The Collected Writings of John Maynard Keynes*, vol. 13, *The General Theory and After. Part I: Preparation* (New York: Cambridge University Press, 2013), 349.

5. My treatment of the collapse of fixed investment is heavily indebted to Richard Sutch, "The Liquidity Trap, the Great Depression, and Unconventional Policy: Reading Keynes at the Zero Lower Bound," Berkeley Economic History Laboratory, Working Paper no. 2014-05 (October 2014).

6. Crafts and Fearon, *Great Depression*, 10.

7. Keynes, "Economic Analysis of Unemployment," 349.

8. Robert S. McElvaine, ed., *Down and Out in the Great Depression: Letters from the Forgotten Man* (Chapel Hill: University of North Carolina Press, 1983), 42.

9. Barry Eichengreen, *Golden Fetters: The Gold Standard and the Great Depression, 1919–1939* (New York: Oxford University Press, 1992), 29–221.

10. Adam Tooze, *The Deluge: The Great War, America, and the Remaking of the Global Order, 1916–1931* (New York: Penguin, 2015); Barry Eichengreen and Peter Temin, "The Gold Standard and the Great Depression," *Contemporary European History* 9, no. 2 (2000): 183–207.

11. Ahamed, *Lords of Finance*, 90–91.

12. Eichengreen and Temin, "Gold Standard and the Great Depression."

13. Peter Temin, *Lessons from the Great Depression: The Lionel Robbins Lectures for 1989* (Cambridge, Mass.: MIT Press, 1990), 17.

14. Ibid., 14.

15. Crafts and Fearon, *Great Depression*, 6.

16. Harold James, *The German Slump: Politics and Economics, 1924–1936* (New York: Oxford University Press, 1986).

17. Tooze, *Deluge*.

18. John Kenneth Galbraith, *The Great Crash, 1929* (1954; Boston: Mariner Books, 2009). A recent argument in favor of the opposite position is Tim Nichols, "Stock Market Swings and the Value of Innovation, 1908–1929," in Naomi R. Lamoreaux and Kenneth L. Sokoloff, eds., *Financing Innovation in the United States, 1870 to Present* (Cambridge, Mass.: MIT Press, 2007), 217–46. The best balanced assessment in the economic history literature is Eugene N. White, "The Stock Market Boom and Crash of 1929 Revisited," *Journal of Economic Perspectives* 4, no. 2 (1990): 67–83. See also J. Bradford De Long and Andrei Shleifer, "The Stock Market Bubble of 1929: Evidence from Closed-End Mutual Funds," *Journal of Economic History* 51, no. 3 (1991): 675–700.

19. Julia Ott, "What Was the Great Bull Market? Value, Valuation, and Financial History," in Sven Beckert and Christine Desan, eds., *American Capitalism: New Histories* (New York: Columbia University Press, 2018), 63–95. I have drawn heavily from Ott's excellent formulation and account.

20. Mary A. O'Sullivan, *Dividends of Development: Securities Markets in the History of U.S. Capitalism, 1865–1922* (Oxford: Oxford University Press, 2016).

21. Ott, "What Was the Great Bull Market?," 64, 72.

22. Ibid.

23. Ibid., 74.

24. Eichengreen, *Golden Fetters*, 165. There was a "gold-exchange" standard, in which currencies, dollars and also pounds, became acceptable as central bank reserves.

25. Allan H. Meltzer, *A History of the Federal Reserve*, vol. 1, *1913–1951* (Chicago: University of Chicago Press, 2003), 253.

26. Nichols, "Stock Market Swings."

27. Ahamed, *Lords of Finance*, 279.

28. Mary A. O'Sullivan, "Funding New Industries: A Historical Perspective on the Financing Role of the U.S. Stock Market in the Twentieth Century," in Lamoreaux and Sokoloff, *Financing Innovation*, 163–216; Alexander Field, "Asset Exchanges and the Transactions Demand for Money, 1919–29," *American Economic Review* 74, no. 1 (1984): 43–59.

29. Arthur Lewis, "World Production and Trade, 1870–1960," *Manchester School* 20, no. 2 (1952): 128. Due to speculative expectations inventories adjust, not prices. On this point, see Nicholas Kaldor, "Speculation and Economic Stability," *Review of Economic Studies* 7, no. 1 (1938): 1–27.

30. Ott, "What Was the Great Bull Market?," 77.

31.   John Maynard Keynes, *General Theory of Employment, Interest, and Money* (1936; New York: Harcourt, Brace & World, 1964), 159.

32.   Charles P. Kindleberger and Robert Z. Aliber, *Manias, Panics, and Crashes: A History of Financial Crises*, 7th ed. (1978; New York: Palgrave Macmillan, 2015).

33.   Gary D. Best, *The Dollar Decade: Mammon and the Machine in 1920s America* (Westport, Conn.: Praeger, 2003), 86, 9.

34.   Ibid., 121.

35.   Shelley Stamp, *Movie-Struck Girls: Women and Motion Picture Culture After the Nickelodeon* (Princeton: Princeton University Press, 2000).

36.   Marieke de Goede, *Virtue, Fortune, and Faith: A Genealogy of Finance* (Minneapolis: University of Minnesota Press, 2005).

37.   Hoover titled this chapter in his memoirs "We Attempt to Stop the Orgy of Speculation." Herbert Hoover, *The Memoirs of Herbert Hoover: The Great Depression, 1929–1941* (New York: Macmillan, 1952), 16.

38.   Ahamed, *Lords of Finance*, 274.

39.   Ibid., 276.

40.   Galbraith, *Great Crash, 1929*, 22.

41.   Thomas Piketty and Emmanuel Saez, "Income Inequality in the United States, 1913–1998," *Quarterly Journal of Economics* 118, no. 1 (2003), 1–39.

42.   Susan Porter Benson, *Household Accounts: Working-Class Family Economies in the Interwar United States* (Ithaca, N.Y.: Cornell University Press, 2007).

43.   Charles R. Morris, *A Rabble of Dead Money: The Great Crash and the Global Depression: 1929–1939* (New York: PublicAffairs, 2017), fig. 5.5.

44.   Harold Bierman, Jr., *The Causes of the 1929 Stock Market Crash: A Speculative Orgy or a New Era?* (Westport, Conn.: Praeger, 1998).

45.   Eddie Cantor, *Caught Short! A Saga of Wall Street Wailing* (New York: Simon & Schuster, 1929), 1.

46.   Christina D. Romer, "The Great Crash and the Onset of the Great Depression," *Quarterly Journal of Economics* 105, no. 3 (1990): 597–624; Crafts and Fearon, *Great Depression*, 10.

47.   Kindleberger and Aliber, *Manias, Panics, and Crashes*, 80.

48.   Steve Keen, *Can We Avoid Another Financial Crisis?* (Malden, Mass.: Polity, 2017), 114, fig. 19.

49.   Ben S. Bernanke, "Nonmonetary Effects of the Financial Crisis in the Propagation of the Great Depression," *American Economic Review* 73, no. 3 (1983): 257–76; Charles W. Calomiris and Joseph R. Mason, "Fundamentals, Panics, and Bank Distress During the Depression," *American Economic Review* 93, no. 5 (2003): 1615–47.

50.   Irving Fisher, "The Debt-Deflation Theory of Great Depressions," *Econometrica* 1, no. 4 (1933): 337–57.

51.   J. Peter Ferderer and David A. Zalewski, "Uncertainty as a Propagating Force in the Great Depression," *Journal of Economic History* 54, no. 4 (1994): 825–49.

52.   Peter Temin, *Did Monetary Forces Cause the Great Depression?* (New York: Norton, 1976); Martha L. Olney, "Avoiding Default: The Role of Credit in the Consumption Collapse of 1930," *Quarterly Journal of Economics* 114, no. 1 (1999): 319–35. A more general explanation of the Depression that underscores the change in manufacturing toward expensive consumer durables is Michael A. Bernstein, *The Great Depression: Delayed Recovery and Economic Change in America, 1929–1939* (New York: Cambridge University Press, 1987).

53.   David M. Kennedy, *Freedom from Fear: The American People in Depression and War, 1929–1945* (New York: Oxford University Press, 1999), 58.

54.   William J. Barber, *From New Era to New Deal: Herbert Hoover, the Economists, and American Economic Policy, 1921–1933* (New York: Cambridge University Press, 1985), 65.

55. William E. Leuchtenburg, *Herbert Hoover: The American Presidents Series: The 31st President, 1929–1933* (New York: Times Books, 2009).

56. Kennedy, *Freedom from Fear*, 46.

57. Barber, *New Era to New Deal*, 5.

58. Michael A. Bernstein, *A Perilous Progress: Economists and Public Purpose in Twentieth-Century America* (Princeton: Princeton University Press, 2001), 40–72; Barber, *New Era to New Deal*.

59. Herbert Hoover, *American Individualism* (New York: Doubleday, Page, 1922), 22.

60. Ibid., 26, 37, 18, 27, 42, 28.

61. Kennedy, *Freedom from Fear*, 48.

62. Ellis W. Hawley, "Herbert Hoover, the Commerce Secretariat, and the Vision of an 'Associative State,' 1921–1928," *Journal of American History* 61, no. 1 (1974): 116–40.

63. Hoover, *Memoirs*, 257.

64. Ibid., 31.

65. Barber, *New Era to New Deal*, 93, table 51.

66. Ibid., 44.

67. Jonathan D. Rose, "Hoover's Truce: Wage Rigidity in the Onset of the Great Depression," *Journal of Economic History* 70, no. 4 (2010): 843–70.

68. Hoover, *Memoirs*, 45.

69. Kennedy, *Freedom from Fear*, 53.

70. Barber, *New Era to New Deal*, 86.

71. Price Fishback, "U.S. Monetary and Fiscal Policy in the 1930s," *Oxford Review of Economic Policy* 26, no. 3 (2010): 401–2.

72. Barber, *New Era to New Deal*, 80.

73. On the debate, see Douglas A. Irwin, *Peddling Protectionism: Smoot-Hawley and the Great Depression* (Princeton: Princeton University Press, 2011).

74. Morris, *Rabble of Dead Money*, 141.

75. Hoover, *Memoirs*, 67.

76. Derek Howard Aldcroft and Steven Morewood, *The European Economy Since 1914* (1978; New York: Routledge, 2013), 80; Ahamed, *Lords of Finance*, 400.

77. Harold James, *The End of Globalization: Lessons from the Great Depression* (Cambridge, Mass.: Harvard University Press, 2001), 47–57.

78. Douglas A. Irwin, "Did France Cause the Great Depression?," National Bureau of Economic Research, Working Paper no. 16350 (September 2010).

79. Charles Kindleberger, *The World in Depression, 1929–1939* (Berkeley: University of California Press, 1973), 83–107; Paulo Drinot and Alan Knight, eds., *The Great Depression in Latin America* (Durham, N.C.: Duke University Press, 2014).

80. Crafts and Fearon, *Great Depression*, 19, table 1.5.

81. Diane B. Kunz, *The Battle for Britain's Gold Standard in 1931* (1987; New York: Routledge, 2017).

82. Ahamed, *Lords of Finance*, 431.

83. Richard N. Cooper, "Fettered to Gold? Economic Policy in the Interwar Period," *Journal of Economic Literature* 30, no. 4 (1992): 2128.

84. Crafts and Fearon, *Great Depression*, 19, table 1.5.

85. Kindleberger and Aliber, *Manias, Panics, and Crashes*, 246.

86. Charles W. Calomiris and Stephen H. Haber, *Fragile by Design: The Political Origins of Banking Crises and Scarce Credit* (Princeton: Princeton University Press, 2014).

87. William E. Leuchtenburg, *The Perils of Prosperity, 1914–1932* (1958; Chicago: University of Chicago Press, 2010), 254; Price Fishback, "U.S. Monetary and Fiscal Policy in the 1930s," in Crafts and Fearon, *Great Depression*, 267–68.

88. Ahamed, *Lords of Finance*, 385.

89. Leuchtenburg, *Perils of Prosperity*, 254; Fishback, "U.S. Monetary and Fiscal Policy," 268.

90. Charles W. Calomiris and Berry Wilson, "Bank Capital and Portfolio Management: The 1930s 'Capital Crunch' and the Scramble to Shed Risk," *Journal of Business* 77, no. 3 (2004): 421–55.

91. Bernanke, "Nonmonetary Effects of the Financial Crisis."

92. Calomiris and Mason, "Fundamentals, Panics, and Bank Distress," argue in favor of illiquidity. On insolvency, see Elmus Wicker, *The Banking Panics of the Great Depression* (New York: Cambridge University Press, 1996).

93. Gary Richardson and William Troost, "Monetary Intervention Mitigated Banking Panics During the Great Depression: Quasi-Experimental Evidence from a Federal Reserve District Border, 1929–1933," *Journal of Political Economy* 117, no. 6 (2009): 1031–73.

94. Ahamed, *Lords of Finance*, 435.

95. Friedman and Schwartz, *Monetary History of United States*, 801, table B–3.

96. Ibid., 362–89. This account of the Fed's failures remains essential but is too quick to explain a complicated series of events through one single cause, the quantity of money treated only from the supply side. In part through the channel of bank credit, demand in addition to supply may determine the level of spending and income, which feeds into the measureable supply of money.

97. Crafts and Fearon, *Great Depression*, 10.

98. Hoover, *Memoirs*, 225.

99. Ibid., 86.

100. Barber, *New Era to New Deal*, 132–38.

101. Kris James Mitchener and Joseph Mason, " 'Blood and Treasure': Exiting the Great Depression and Lessons for Today," *Oxford Review of Economic Policy* 26, no. 3 (2010): 510–39.

102. Peter F. Basile, John Landon-Lane, and Hugh Rockoff, "Money and Interest Rates in the United States During the Great Depression," National Bureau of Economic Research, Working Paper no. 16204 (July 2010). D. H. Robertson, *Essays in Monetary Theory* (London: P. S. King, 1940), 34–36. D. H. Robertson coined the phrase *liquidity trap.* However he advocated a loanable funds theory of the interest rate, which rose and fell around the "real" rate determined by the supply of savings and demand for investment. This is different from the liquidity preference theory of Keynes, in which the demand for money as a store of value determines the interest rate.

103. Sutch, "Liquidity Trap," 7, fig. 4.

104. Crafts and Fearon, *Great Depression*, 10.

105. Barry Eichengreen and Douglas A. Irwin, "The Slide to Protectionism in the Great Depression: Who Succumbed and Why?," *Journal of Economic History* 70, no. 4 (2010): 871–97.

106. Crafts and Fearon, *Great Depression*; Peter Temin, "The Great Depression," in Stanley L. Engerman and Robert E. Gallman, eds., *The Cambridge Economic History of the United States*, vol. 3, *The Twentieth Century* (New York: Cambridge University Press, 2000), 301–28.

107. Scott A. Sandage, *Born Losers: A History of Failure in America* (Cambridge, Mass.: Harvard University Press, 2005), 262–65.

108. Michele Landis Dauber, *The Sympathetic State: Disaster Relief and the Origins of the American Welfare State* (Chicago: University of Chicago Press, 2012).

109. Donald Worster, *Dust Bowl: The Southern Plains in the 1930s* (New York: Oxford University Press, 1979).

110. Kennedy, *Freedom from Fear*, 163.

111. Studs Terkel, *Hard Times: An Oral History of the Great Depression* (New York: Random House, 1970), 38, 2, 22.

112. Robert S. McElvaine, *The Great Depression: America, 1929–1941* (New York: Times Books, 1993), 180–82.

113. Terkel, *Hard Times*, 68.

114. Walter B. Rideout, *Sherwood Anderson: A Writer in America* (Madison: University of Wisconsin Press, 2007), 2:173 Sherwood Anderson, *Puzzled America* (New York: Charles Scribner's Sons, 1935).

115. Mirra Komarovsky, *The Unemployed Man and His Family: The Effect of Unemployment upon the Status of the Man in Fifty-Nine Families*, ed. Michael Kimmel (1940; Walnut Creek, Calif.: AltaMira Press, 2004), 117.

116. Lorena Hickok, *One Third of a Nation: Lorena Hickok Reports on the Great Depression*, ed. Richard Lowitt and Maurine H. Beasley (Urbana: University of Illinois Press, 1981), 205.

117. Anthony J. Badger, *The New Deal: The Depression Years, 1933–1940* (New York: Hill & Wang, 1989), 11.

118. Hickok, *One Third of a Nation*, 206.

119. McElvaine, *Down and Out in the Great Depression*, 42.

120. Ibid., 42, 43.

121. Ronald L. Heinemann, *Depression and New Deal in Virginia: The Enduring Dominion* (Charlottesville: University of Virginia Press, 1983), 122.

122. Terkel, *Hard Times*, 31, 14, 59.

123. Elisabeth S. Clemens, "In the Shadow of the New Deal: Reconfiguring the Roles of Government and Charity, 1928–1940," in Elisabeth S. Clemens and Doug Guthrie, eds., *Politics and Partnerships: The Role of Voluntary Associations in America's Political Past and Present* (Chicago: University of Chicago Press, 2011), 79–120.

124. T. H. Watkins, *The Hungry Years: A Narrative History of the Great Depression in America* (New York: Macmillan, 2000), 83.

125. David E. Kyvig, *Daily Life in the United States, 1920–1940: How Americans Lived Through the "Roaring Twenties" and the Great Depression* (Chicago: Ivan R. Dee, 2004), 190.

126. Irving Bernstein, *The Lean Years: A History of the American Worker, 1920–1933* (1960; Chicago: Haymarket Books, 2010), 467.

127. William C. Pratt, "Rethinking the Farm Revolt of the 1930s," *Great Plains Quarterly* 8, no. 3 (1988): 131–44.

128. Beth Tompkins Bates, *The Making of Black Detroit in the Age of Henry Ford* (Chapel Hill: University of North Carolina Press, 2012), 145.

129. Kennedy, *Freedom from Fear*, 92.

130. Terkel, *Hard Times*, 97, 77.

131. Ibid., 75.

132. Kennedy, *Freedom from Fear*, 92.

133. Ibid., 96, 90, 98.

134. Ibid., 131.

135. Ibid., 131, 100, 101.

136. Ibid., 109.

137. Eichengreen, *Golden Fetters*, 23.

138. Meltzer, *History of Federal Reserve*, 1:380, 381.

139. Ahamed, *Lords of Finance*, 448.

140. Kennedy, *Freedom from Fear*, 384.

141. Eric Rauchway, *The Money Makers: How Roosevelt and Keynes Ended the Depression, Defeated Fascism, and Secured a Prosperous Peace* (New York: Basic Books, 2015), 39–54.

142. Temin, *Lessons from the Great Depression*.

143. Rauchway, *Money Makers*, 66.

CHAPTER 13: NEW DEAL CAPITALISM

1. David Runciman, *The Confidence Trap: A History of Democracy in Crisis from World War I to the Present* (Princeton: Princeton University Press, 2013), 76–110.

2. MacGregor Knox, *To the Threshold of Power, 1922/3: Origins and Dynamics of the Fascist and National Socialist Dictatorships* (New York: Cambridge University Press, 2007), 1:364.

3. Ira Katznelson, *Fear Itself: The New Deal and the Origins of Our Time* (New York: Liveright, 2013), 119.

4. Wolfgang Schivelbusch, *Three New Deals: Reflections on Roosevelt's America, Mussolini's Italy, and Hitler's Germany, 1933–1939* (New York: Metropolitan Books, 2006).

5. Katznelson, *Fear Itself.*

6. Shawn Kantor, Price V. Fishback, and John Joseph Wallis, "Did the New Deal Solidify the 1932 Democratic Realignment?," *Explorations in Economic History* 50, no. 4 (2013): 620–33. The answer is yes.

7. Jean Edward Smith, *FDR* (New York: Random House, 2007), 374.

8. Alan Brinkley, *Liberalism and Its Discontents* (Cambridge, Mass.: Harvard University Press, 1998), 18.

9. Two elegant summaries of various views are Jason Scott Smith, *A Concise History of the New Deal* (New York: Cambridge University Press, 2014); and Eric Rauchway, *The Great Depression and New Deal: A Very Short Introduction* (New York: Oxford University Press, 2008). See also Jeff Manza, "Political Sociological Models of the U.S. New Deal," *Annual Review of Sociology* 26 (2000): 297–322.

10. Smith, *FDR*, 263.

11. Eric Rauchway, *The Money Makers: How Roosevelt and Keynes Ended the Depression, Defeated Fascism, and Secured a Prosperous Peace* (New York: Basic Books, 2015), 66; Herbert Stein, *The Fiscal Revolution in America* (1971; Washington, D.C.: AEI Press, 1990), 39.

12. Gauti B. Eggertsson, "Great Expectations and the End of the Depression," *American Economic Review* 98, no. 4 (2008): 1476–516; Peter Temin and Barrie A. Wigmore, "The End of One Big Deflation," *Explorations in Economic History* 27, no. 4 (1990): 483–502; Christina D. Romer, "What Ended the Great Depression?," *Journal of Economic History* 52, no. 4 (1992): 757–84.

13. Daniel T. Rodgers, *Atlantic Crossings: Social Politics in a Progressive Age* (Cambridge, Mass.: Belknap Press, 1998); Richard Hofstadter, *The Age of Reform: From Bryan to F.D.R.* (New York: Knopf, 1955).

14. David M. Kennedy, *Freedom from Fear: The American People in Depression and War, 1929–1945* (New York: Oxford University Press, 1999), 363–80.

15. Price Fishback, "US Monetary and Fiscal Policy in the 1930s," *Oxford Review of Economic Policy* 26, no. 3 (2010): 385–413.

16. Peter H. Lindert and Jeffrey G. Williamson, *Unequal Gains: American Growth and Inequality Since 1700* (Princeton: Princeton University Press, 2016), 194–218. Finance, insurance, and real estate accounted for 14.75 percent of national income in 1929, but 8.93 by 1941. Alexander J. Field, *A Great Leap Forward: 1930s Depression and U.S. Economic Growth* (New Haven: Yale University Press, 2011), 67.

17. Jason Scott Smith, *Building New Deal Liberalism: The Political Economy of Public Works, 1933–1956* (New York: Cambridge University Press, 2005); Otis L. Graham, Jr., "The Planning Ideal and American Reality: The 1930s," in Stanley Elkins and Eric McKitrick, eds., *The Hofstadter Aegis: A Memorial* (New York: Knopf, 1974), 257–89.

18. Monica Prasad, *The Land of Too Much: American Abundance and the Paradox of Poverty* (Cambridge, Mass.: Harvard University Press, 2012).

19. Smith, *Building New Deal Liberalism*; Field, *Great Leap Forward*.

20. A point brilliantly formulated by M. Kalecki, "Political Aspects of Full Employment," *Political Quarterly* 14, no. 4 (1943): 322–30. In history, see Kim Phillips-Fein, *Invisible Hands: The Businessman's Crusade Against the New Deal* (New York: Norton, 2009).

21. Adam Tooze, *The Wages of Destruction: The Making and Breaking of the Nazi Economy* (New York: Viking Penguin, 2007).

22. Katznelson, *Fear Itself,* 3–26.

23. Liaquat Ahamed, *Lords of Finance: The Bankers Who Broke the World* (New York: Penguin Press, 2009), 435.

24. Rauchway, *Great Depression and New Deal,* 59.

25. Douglas B. Craig, *Fireside Politics: Radio and Political Culture in the United States, 1920–1940* (Baltimore: Johns Hopkins University Press, 2000), 15, fig. 4.

26. Lorena Hickok, *One Third of a Nation: Lorena Hickok Reports on the Great Depression,* ed. Richard Lowitt and Maurine H. Beasley (Urbana: University of Illinois Press, 1981), 215.

27. Franklin Delano Roosevelt, *FDR's Fireside Chats* (Norman: University of Oklahoma Press, 1992), 13–15, 17.

28. Rauchway, *Money Makers,* 53.

29. Ibid., 66, 71.

30. Jonathan Quann, "Ships of State: Global Shipping, the Emergence Fleet Corporation, and the Business of American Government, 1870–1930" (PhD diss., Princeton University, 2019).

31. Jordan Schwarz, *The New Dealers: Power Politics in the Age of Roosevelt* (New York: Knopf, 1993), 77.

32. Ibid., 75.

33. James Stuart Olson, *Saving Capitalism: The Reconstruction Finance Corporation and the New Deal, 1933–1940* (Princeton: Princeton University Press, 1988), 82.

34. Kris James Mitchener and Joseph Mason, "'Blood and Treasure': Exiting the Great Depression and Lessons for Today," *Oxford Review of Economic Policy* 26, no. 3 (2010): 510–39; Olson, *Saving Capitalism,* 45.

35. Schwarz, *New Dealers,* 123–56.

36. William Lasser, *Benjamin V. Cohen: Architect of the New Deal* (New Haven: Yale University Press, 2002).

37. Barrie W. Wigmore, "A Comparison of Federal Financial Remediation in the Great Depression and 2008–9," *Research in Economic History* 27 (March 25, 2010): 255–303.

38. For a critique of Glass-Steagall, see Charles W. Calomiris, "The Political Lessons of Depression-era Banking Reform," in Nicholas Crafts and Peter Fearon, *The Great Depression of the 1930s: Lessons for Today* (Oxford: Oxford University Press, 2013), 165–87.

39. Kris James Mitchener and Gary Richardson, "Does 'Skin in the Game' Reduce Risk Taking? Leverage, Liability and the Long-Run Consequences of New Deal Banking Reforms," *Explorations in Economic History* 50, no. 4 (2013): 508–25.

40. Rauchway, *Money Makers,* 88.

41. John L. Shover, *Cornbelt Rebellion: The Farmers' Holiday Association* (Urbana: University of Illinois Press, 1965), 118.

42. Douglas R. Hurt, *Problems of Plenty: The American Farmer in the Twentieth Century* (Chicago: Ivan R. Dee, 2002), 67–98.

43. Gavin Wright, *Old South, New South: Revolutions in the Southern Economy Since the Civil War* (New York: Basic Books, 1986), 227.

44. Roosevelt, *FDR's Fireside Chats,* 42–43.

45. John Morton Blum, *From the Morgenthau Diaries* (Boston: Houghton Mifflin, 1959), 70.

46. Rauchway, *Money Makers*, 91.

47. Lee J. Alston, "Farm Foreclosure Moratorium Legislation: A Lesson from the Past," *American Economic Review* 74, no. 3 (1984): 445–57; Howard H. Preston, "Our Farm Credit System," *Journal of Farm Economics* 18, no. 4 (1936): 673–84.

48. Olson, *Saving Capitalism*, 45.

49. On agrarian movements, see Kiran Klaus Patel, *The New Deal: A Global History* (Princeton: Princeton University Press, 2016).

50. John Joseph Wallis, "Lessons from the Political Economy of the New Deal," *Oxford Review of Economic Policy* 26, no. 3 (2010): 442–62; Karen M. Tani, *States of Dependency: Welfare, Rights, and American Governance, 1935–1972* (New York: Cambridge University Press, 2016).

51. Martha H. Swain, *Ellen S. Woodward: New Deal Advocate for Women* (Oxford: University of Press of Mississippi, 1995), 66.

52. Grace Abbott, *The Child and the State; Select Documents* (Chicago: University of Chicago Press, 1938).

53. Laura Phillips Sawyer, *American Fair Trade: Proprietary Capitalism, Corporatism, and the "New Competition," 1890–1940* (New York: Cambridge University Press, 2018), 237–308; Ellis W. Hawley, *The New Deal and the Problem of Monopoly: A Study in Economic Ambivalence* (Princeton: Princeton University Press, 1966).

54. Rexford Guy Tugwell, "Design for Government," reprinted in Tugwell, *The Battle for Democracy* (1935; New York: Greenwood Press, 1969), 14.

55. Jeremiah D. Lambert, *The Power Brokers: The Struggle to Shape and Control the Electric Power Industry* (Cambridge, Mass.: MIT Press, 2015), 51–92.

56. Smith, *Building New Deal Liberalism*, 2.

57. Louis Hyman, *Debtor Nation: The History of America in Red Ink* (Princeton: Princeton University Press, 2011). I draw from Hyman's interpretation on the general importance of this mechanism to the New Deal.

58. Colin Gordon, *New Deals: Business, Labor, and Politics in America, 1920–1935* (New York: Cambridge University Press, 1994), 166–203.

59. Irving Bernstein, *The Turbulent Years: A History of the American Worker, 1933–1940* (1966; Chicago: Haymarket Books, 2010), 217–317.

60. Schwarz, *New Dealers*, 104.

61. Alan Brinkley, *Voices of Protest: Huey Long, Father Coughlin, and the Great Depression* (New York: Vintage Books, 1983).

62. Kennedy, *Freedom from Fear*, 223.

63. James MacGregor Burns, *Roosevelt: The Lion and the Fox, 1882–1940* (New York: Harcourt, Brace, 1956), 206.

64. Robert Fredrick Burk, *The Corporate State and the Broker State: The Du Ponts and American National Politics, 1925–1940* (Cambridge, Mass.: Harvard University Press, 1990), 143.

65. Schwarz, *New Dealers*, 137.

66. William E. Leuchtenburg, *The FDR Years: On Roosevelt and His Legacy* (New York: Columbia University Press, 1995), 11.

67. George J. Sanchez, *Becoming Mexican American: Ethnicity, Culture and Identity in Chicano Los Angeles, 1900–1945* (New York: Oxford University Press, 1993); Lizabeth Cohen, *Making a New Deal: Industrial Workers in Chicago, 1919–1939* (New York: Cambridge University Press, 1990).

68. Crafts and Fearon, *Great Depression*, tables 1.2 and 1.9.

69. Kennedy, *Freedom from Fear*, 217.

70. Franklin D. Roosevelt, "Annual Message to Congress," January 4, 1935, Ameri-

can Presidency Project, https://www.presidency.ucsb.edu/documents/annual-message -congress-3.

71.   Smith, *Building New Deal Liberalism*, 87.

72.   But New Deal relief did diminish death rates. Price V. Fishback, Michael R. Haines, and Shawn Kantor, "Births, Deaths, and New Deal Relief During the Great Depression," *Review of Economics and Statistics* 89, no. 1 (2007): 1–14.

73.   Mark Hugh Leff, *The Limits of Symbolic Reform: The New Deal and Taxation, 1933–1939* (New York: Cambridge University Press, 1984), 150.

74.   Bruce Ackerman, *We the People*, vol. 2, *Transformations* (Cambridge, Mass.: Harvard University Press, 1998), 279–311.

75.   Schwartz, *New Dealers*, 109.

76.   Burns, *Roosevelt: Lion and Fox*, 208.

77.   Leff, *Limits of Symbolic Reform*, 138, 142–45. See also Edwin Amenta, Kathleen Dunleavy, and Mary Bernstein, "Stolen Thunder? Huey Long's 'Share Our Wealth,' Political Mediation, and the Second New Deal," *American Sociological Review* 59, no. 5 (1994): 678–702.

78.   Prasad, *Land of Too Much*.

79.   Jonathan Levy, "From Fiscal Triangle to Passing Through: Rise of the Nonprofit Corporation," in Naomi R. Lamoreaux and William J. Novak, eds., *Corporations and American Democracy* (Cambridge, Mass.: Harvard University Press, 2017).

80.   Gordon, *New Deals*, 204–305.

81.   Phillips-Fein, *Invisible Hands*.

82.   Leff, *Limits of Symbolic Reform*, 162–64.

83.   Lambert, *Power Brokers*, 1–50.

84.   William J. Novak, "The Public Utility Idea and the Origins of Modern Business Regulation," in Lamoreaux and Novak, *Corporations and American Democracy*, 139–76.

85.   "Public Utility Holding Act of 1935," *United States Code* 15, title 1 (1935): 2–36, https://www.sec.gov/about/laws/puhca35.pdf.

86.   Rodgers, *Atlantic Crossings*, 441.

87.   Edward D. Berkowitz, *America's Welfare State: From Roosevelt to Reagan* (Baltimore: Johns Hopkins University Press, 1991), 13–38.

88.   Alice Kessler-Harris, *In Pursuit of Equity: Women, Men, and the Quest for Economic Citizenship in 20th-Century America* (New York: Oxford University Press, 2001); Gwendolyn Mink, *The Wages of Motherhood: Inequality in the Welfare State, 1917–1942* (Ithaca, N.Y.: Cornell University Press, 1995); Linda Gordon, *Pitied but Not Entitled: Single Mothers and the History of Welfare, 1890–1935* (New York: Free Press, 1994).

89.   Kessler-Harris, *In Pursuit of Equity*, 84.

90.   Margot Canaday, *The Straight State: Sexuality and Citizenship in Twentieth-Century America* (Princeton: Princeton University Press, 2009), 91–134.

91.   Peter Conti-Brown, *The Power and Independence of the Federal Reserve* (Princeton: Princeton University Press, 2016), 15–39.

92.   Nelson Lichtenstein, *State of the Union: A Century of American Labor* (Princeton: Princeton University Press, 2002), 20–53.

93.   Bernstein, *Turbulent Years*, 349.

94.   Ibid., 397.

95.   Lasser, *Benjamin Cohen*, 141.

96.   Kennedy, *Freedom from Fear*, 282.

97.   Gary Gerstle, *Liberty and Coercion: The Paradox of American Government from the Founding to the Present* (Princeton: Princeton University Press, 2015), 244.

98.   Michael Denning, *The Cultural Front: The Laboring of American Culture in the Twentieth Century* (London: Verso, 1997).

99.   Laura Hapke, *Labor's Canvas: American Working-Class History and the WPA Art of the 1930s* (Newcastle, U.K.: Cambridge Scholars, 2008); Denning, *Cultural Front*.

100.   William Stott, *Documentary Expression and Thirties America* (Chicago: University of Chicago Press, 1986), 119. See also Michael Szalay, *New Deal Modernism: American Literature and the Invention of the Welfare State* (Durham, N.C.: Duke University Press, 2000).

101.   Robert H. Zieger, *The CIO, 1935–1955* (Chapel Hill: University of North Carolina Press, 1995), 42–65.

102.   Bernstein, *Turbulent Years*, 473.

103.   John Barnard, *American Vanguard: The United Auto Workers During the Reuther Years, 1935–1970* (Detroit: Wayne State University Press, 2005).

104.   Sidney Fine, *Sit-down: The General Motors Strike of 1936–1937* (Ann Arbor: University of Michigan Press, 1969), 38.

105.   Barnard, *American Vanguard*, 105.

106.   At the same time, steelworkers suffered violent defeat attempting to organize the "Little Steel" companies, pushing FDR to frustration. See Ahmed White, *The Last Great Strike: Little Steel, the CIO, and the Struggle for Labor Rights in New Deal America* (Oakland: University of California Press, 2016).

107.   Steve Fraser, "The Labor Question," in Steve Fraser and Gary Gerstle, eds., *The Rise and Fall of the New Deal Order, 1930–1980* (Princeton: Princeton University Press, 1989), 55–84.

108.   Leslie Hannah and Peter Temin, "Long-Term Supply-Side Implications of the Great Depression," *Oxford Review of Economic Policy* 26, no. 3 (2010): 561–80.

109.   Fishback, "US Monetary and Fiscal Policy."

110.   Eggertsson, "Great Expectations and End of the Depression"; Temin and Wigmore, "End of One Big Deflation"; Romer, "What Ended the Great Depression?"

111.   Douglas A. Irwin, "Gold Sterilization and the Recession of 1937–38," National Bureau of Economic Research, Working Paper no. 17595 (November 2011).

112.   Meltzer, *History of Federal Reserve*, vol. 1.

113.   Gauti B. Eggertsson, "Was the New Deal Contractionary?," *American Economic Review* 102, no. 1 (2012): 524–55.

114.   Robert J. Gordon, *The Rise and Fall of American Growth: The U.S. Standard of Living Since the Civil War* (Princeton: Princeton University Press, 2016), 559.

115.   Field, *Great Leap Forward*, 42–78.

116.   Claudia Goldin, *Understanding the Gender Gap: An Economic History of American Women* (New York: Oxford University Press, 1990); Julia Kirk Blackwelder, *Now Hiring: The Feminization of Work in the United States, 1900–1995* (College Station: Texas A&M University Press, 1997), 97; Winifred D. Wandersee Bolin, "The Economics of Middle-Class Family Life: Working Women During the Great Depression," *Journal of American History* 65, no. 1 (1978): 70.

117.   Jason E. Taylor and Todd C. Neumann, "The Effect of Institutional Regime Change Within the New Deal on Industrial Output and Labor Markets," *Explorations in Economic History* 50, no. 4 (2013): 582–98.

118.   Temin and Wigmore, "End of One Big Deflation."

119.   Carolyn Dimitri, Anne Effland, and Neilson Conklin, "The 20th Century Transformation of U.S. Agriculture and Farm Policy," USDA, Economic Information Bulletin no. 3 (June 2005), fig. 3.

120.   Kennedy, *Freedom from Fear*, 207; William Winders, *The Politics of Food Supply: U.S. Agricultural Policy in the World Economy* (New Haven: Yale University Press, 2009), 59.

121.   Katznelson, *Fear Itself*, 133–222. In February 1935, pressed by white planters,

the AAA "purged" leftists critical of the injustices of sharecropping, many of whom had supported black sharecroppers' unions.

122.   Jess Gilbert, *Planning Democracy: Agrarian Intellectuals and the Intended New Deal* (New Haven: Yale University Press, 2015).

123.   Wright, *Old South, New South*, 232.

124.   Gavin Wright, "The New Deal and the Modernization of the South," Stanford Institute for Economic Policy research, Working Paper no. 08-042 (August 2009); Briggs Depew, Price V. Fishback, and Paul W. Rhode, "New Deal or No Deal in the Cotton South: The Effect of the AAA on the Agricultural Labor Structure," *Explorations in Economic History* 50, no. 4 (2013): 466–86; Warren C. Whatley, "Labor for the Picking: The New Deal in the South," *Journal of Economic History* 43, no. 4 (1983): 905–29.

125.   Hyman, *Debtor Nation*, 71.

126.   Richard White, *"It's Your Misfortune and None of My Own": A New History of the American West* (Norman: University of Oklahoma Press, 1991), 463–95. Price V. Fishback, William C. Horrace, and Shawn Kantor, "The Impact of New Deal Expenditures on Mobility During the Great Depression," *Explorations in Economic History* 43, no. 2 (2006): 179–222.

127.   Smith, *Building New Deal Liberalism*, 36, 88, 89.

128.   Joseph Maresca, *WPA Buildings: Architecture and Art of the New Deal* (Atglen, Pa.: Schiffer, 2017).

129.   Field, *Great Leap Forward*, 42–78.

130.   Smith, *Building New Deal Liberalism*, 162.

131.   Olson, *Saving Capitalism*, 45.

132.   Richard White, *The Organic Machine: The Remaking of the Columbia River* (New York: Hill & Wang, 1995).

133.   Smith, *Building New Deal Liberalism*, 8.

134.   Sarah Milov, "Promoting Agriculture: Farmers, the State, and Checkoff Marketing, 1935–2005," *Business History Review* 90, no. 3 (2016): 505–36.

135.   Katznelson, *Fear Itself*, 272.

136.   David L. Carlton and Peter A. Coclanis, eds., *Confronting Southern Poverty in the Great Depression: The Report on Economic Conditions of the South with Related Documents* (Boston: Bedford/St. Martin's, 1996).

137.   Zieger, *CIO*, 66–110.

138.   Crafts and Fearon, *Great Depression*, tables 1.2 and 1.9.

139.   Gauti B. Eggertsson and Benjamin Pugsley, "The Mistake of 1937: A General Equilibrium Analysis," *Monetary and Economic Studies* 24 (December 2006): 1–41.

140.   Joshua K. Hausman, "What Was Bad for General Motors Was Bad for America: The Automobile Industry and the 1937/38 Recession," *Journal of Economic History* 76, no. 2 (2016): 427–77.

141.   Eggertsson and Pugsley, "Mistake of 1937."

142.   Herman Krooss, *Executive Opinion—What Business Leaders Said and Thought 1920s–1960s* (New York: Doubleday, 1970), 200.

143.   Leff, *Limits of Symbolic Reform*, 235.

144.   Thurman Wesley Arnold, *The Folklore of Capitalism* (1937; New Haven: Yale University Press, 1962).

145.   Alan Brinkley, *The End of Reform: New Deal Liberalism in Recession and War* (New York: Knopf, 1995), 106–36.

146.   Brinkley, *End of Reform*, 55, see also 23–24 and 70–80.

147.   The first stated theory of the multiplier in this respect was R. F. Kahn, "The Relation of Home Investment to Unemployment," *Economic Journal* 41, no. 162 (1931): 173–98.

148. John Maynard Keynes, *The General Theory of Employment, Interest, and Money* (1936; New York: Harcourt, Brace & World, 1964), 320, 378.

149. Theodore Rosenof, *Economics in the Long Run: New Deal Theorists and Their Legacies, 1933–1993* (Chapel Hill: University of North Carolina Press, 1997).

150. Schwartz, *New Dealers*, 187, 188.

151. John Maynard Keynes, "Letter to the President" (1938), in Robert Skidelsky, ed., *The Essential Keynes* (New York: Penguin, 2016), 393.

152. Diane Coyle, *GDP: A Brief but Affectionate History* (Princeton: Princeton University Press, 2014), 7–40.

153. "Warm Springs Memorandum, April 1, 1938," in Beardsley Ruml, Papers, Box 6, Folder 26, Special Collections Research Center, University of Chicago Library.

154. Franklin D. Roosevelt, "Message to Congress on Stimulating Recovery," April 14, 1938, American Presidency Project, https://www.presidency.ucsb.edu/documents /message-congress-stimulating-recovery.

155. See Brinkley, *End of Reform*.

156. John Maynard Keynes, "The United States and the Keynes Plan," *New Republic*, July 29, 1940, 158.

CHAPTER 14: NEW WORLD HEGEMON

1. Michael Geyer and Adam Tooze, "Substance, Scale and Scope of Peoples' War," in Michael Geyer and Adam Tooze, eds., *The Cambridge History of the Second World War*, vol. 3, *Total War: Economy, Society and Culture* (New York: Cambridge University Press, 2015), 2.

2. James T. Sparrow, *Warfare State: World War II Americans and the Age of Big Government* (New York: Oxford University Press, 2011), 71.

3. Geyer and Tooze, *Cambridge History of Second World War*, 3:5.

4. Adam Tooze, *The Wages of Destruction: The Making and Breaking of the Nazi Economy* (New York: Viking Penguin, 2007).

5. J. R. McNeill and Peter Engelke, *The Great Acceleration: An Environmental History of the Anthropocene Since 1945* (Cambridge, Mass.: Belknap Press, 2014).

6. Jeffrey Fear, "War of the Factories," in Geyer and Tooze, *Cambridge History of Second World War*, 3:94–121.

7. Alexander J. Field, *A Great Leap Forward: 1930s Depression and U.S. Economic Growth* (New Haven: Yale University Press, 2011), 91.

8. Mark R. Wilson, *Destructive Creation: American Business and the Winning of World War II* (Philadelphia: University of Pennsylvania Press, 2016). My account draws heavily from Wilson's excellent study.

9. Bruce Cumings, *Dominion from Sea to Sea: Pacific Ascendancy and American Power* (New Haven: Yale University Press, 2009). On the consumption debate, see Michael Edelstein, "War and the American Economy in the Twentieth Century," in Stanley L. Engerman and Robert E. Gallman, eds., *The Cambridge Economic History of the United States*, vol. 3, *The Twentieth Century* (New York: Cambridge University Press, 2000), 400.

10. Odd Arne Westad, *The Cold War: A World History* (New York: Basic Books, 2017), 53, 54.

11. Hugh Rockoff, *Drastic Measures: A History of Wage and Price Controls in the United States* (New York: Cambridge University Press, 1984), 127–76.

12. Cumings, *Dominion from Sea to Sea*, 304.

13. Robert J. Gordon and Robert Krenn, "The End of the Great Depression, 1939–1941: Policy Contributions and Fiscal Multipliers," National Bureau of Economic Research, Working Paper no. 16380 (September 2010).

14. Tooze, *Wages of Destruction*, 10.

15. Ira Katznelson, *Fear Itself: The New Deal and the Origins of Our Time* (New York: Liveright, 2013), 282–83.

16. Paul A. Kramer, *The Blood of Government: Race, Empire, the United States, and the Philippines* (Chapel Hill: University of North Carolina Press, 2006).

17. Peter James Hudson, *Bankers and Empire: How Wall Street Colonized the Caribbean* (Chicago: University of Chicago Press, 2017); Cyrus Veeser, *A World Safe for Capitalism* (New York: Columbia University Press, 2002).

18. Daniel Immerwahr, *How to Hide an Empire: A History of the Greater United States* (New York: Farrar, Straus & Giroux, 2019).

19. Eric Helleiner, *Forgotten Foundations of Bretton Woods: International Development and the Making of the Postwar Order* (Ithaca, N.Y.: Cornell University Press, 2014), 29–51; Elizabeth Borgwardt, *New Deal for the World: America's Vision for Human Rights* (Cambridge, Mass.: Belknap Press, 2007).

20. William Appleman Williams, *The Tragedy of American Diplomacy* (1959; New York: Norton, 2009).

21. Helleiner, *Fo,rgotten Foundations of Bretton Woods*.

22. Adam Tooze, *The Deluge: The Great War and the Remaking of Global Order* (London: Allen Lane, 2014); David M. Kennedy, *Freedom from Fear: The American People in Depression and War, 1929–1945* (New York: Oxford University Press, 1999), 426–64.

23. Westad, *Cold War*, 40.

24. Wilson, *Destructive Creation*, 55–58.

25. Ibid., 59.

26. Maury Klein, *A Call to Arms: Mobilizing America for World War II* (New York: Bloomsbury, 2013), 107–32.

27. Wilson, *Destructive Creation*, 61.

28. John Morton Blum, *From the Morgenthau Diaries: Years of Urgency, 1938–1941* (New York: Houghton Mifflin, 1959), 118.

29. Barry Eichengreen, "U.S. Foreign Financial Relations in the Twentieth Century," in Engerman and Gallman, *Cambridge Economic History of United States*, 3:489.

30. Wilson, *Destructive Creation*, 74; Klein, *Call to Arms*, 133–288.

31. Ramon Hawley Myers and Mark R. Peattie, eds., *The Japanese Colonial Empire, 1895–1945* (Princeton: Princeton University Press, 1984).

32. Tooze, *Wages of Destruction*, 552–89.

33. Richard Bessel, "Death and Survival in the Second World War," in Geyer and Tooze, *Cambridge History of Second World War*, 3:252–76.

34. Sparrow, *Warfare State*, 53.

35. Charles S. Maier, *Among Empires: American Ascendancy and Its Predecessors* (Cambridge, Mass.: Harvard University Press, 2006), 196.

36. Bill Winders, *The Politics of Food Supply: U.S. Agricultural Policy in the World Economy* (New Haven: Yale University Press, 2009), 69–74.

37. Field, *Great Leap Forward*, 85.

38. Paul A. C. Koistinen, *Arsenal of World War II: The Political Economy of American Warfare, 1940–1945* (Lawrence: University Press of Kansas, 2004), 303–13.

39. Philipp Lepenies, *The Power of a Single Number: A Political History of GDP* (New York: Columbia University Press, 2016), 57–96.

40. Philip Mirowski, *Machine Dreams: Economics Becomes a Cyborg Science* (New York: Cambridge University Press, 2001).

41. Robert Higgs, *Depression, War, and Cold War: Challenging the Myths of Conflict and Prosperity* (Oakland, Calif.: Independent Institute, 2009), 85.

42. John Kenneth Galbraith, "How Keynes Came to America," in *The Essential Galbraith*, ed. Andrea D. Campbell (1971; Boston: Houghton Mifflin, 2001), 236–48.

43. Field, *Great Leap Forward*, 79–106.

44. Gerald D. Nash, *The American West Transformed: The Impact of the Second World War* (Bloomington: Indiana University Press, 1985). For a critique of the war's impact on Pacific economic development, see Paul Rhode, "The Nash Thesis Revisited: An Economic Historian's View," *Pacific Historical Review* 63, no. 3 (1994): 363–92.

45. Wilson, *Destructive Creation*, 64, table 2.

46. Cumings, *Dominion from Sea to Sea*, 308.

47. Nash, *American West Transformed*, 19–20.

48. Klein, *Call to Arms*, 165.

49. Stephen B. Adams, *Mr. Kaiser Goes to Washington: The Rise of a Government Entrepreneur* (Chapel Hill: University of North Carolina Press, 1997).

50. Mike Davis, *City of Quartz: Excavating the Future of Los Angeles* (New York: Verso, 1990), 373–90; Nash, *American West Transformed*, 26–29.

51. Cumings, *Dominion from Sea to Sea*, 327.

52. Nash, *American West Transformed*, 38.

53. Carey McWilliams, *Southern California: An Island on the Land* (Salt Lake City: Peregrine Smith, 1946), 374.

54. Lynn Dumenil, ed., *The Oxford Encyclopedia of American Social History* (New York: Oxford University Press, 2012), 542.

55. Koistinen, *Arsenal of World War II*, 390–401.

56. Douglas Flamming, *Bound for Freedom: Black Los Angeles in Jim Crow America* (Berkeley: University of California Press, 2005); Gavin Wright, *Old South, New South: Revolutions in the Southern Economy Since the Civil War* (New York: Basic Books, 1986), 249–57.

57. Shirley Ann Wilson Moore, *To Place Our Deeds: The African American Community in Richmond, California, 1910–1963* (Berkeley: University of California Press, 2001), 40.

58. Mae M. Ngai, *Impossible Subjects: Illegal Aliens and the Making of Modern America* (Princeton: Princeton University Press, 2004), 127–68.

59. Vernon W. Ruttan, *Is War Necessary for Economic Growth? Military Procurement and Technology Development* (New York: Oxford University Press, 2006).

60. Frederick Kagan, "The Evacuation of Soviet Industry in the Wake of 'Barbarossa': A Key to the Soviet Victory," *Journal of Slavic Military Studies* 8, no. 2 (1995): 387–414.

61. Yuma Totani, *Justice in Asia and the Pacific Region, 1945–1952* (New York: Cambridge University Press, 2015).

62. Robert J. Gordon, *The Rise and Fall of American Growth: The U.S. Standard of Living Since the Civil War* (Princeton: Princeton University Press, 2016), 553.

63. Ibid., 549.

64. Leonard Rapping, "Learning and World War II Production Functions," *Review of Economics and Statistics* 47, no. 1 (1965): 81–86; Kenneth J. Arrow, "The Economic Implications of Learning by Doing," *Review of Economic Studies* 29, no. 3 (1962): 155–73.

65. Paul Kennedy, *Engineers of Victory: The Problem Solvers Who Turned the Tide in the Second World War* (New York: Random House, 2013).

66. Michael Miller, "Sea Transport," in Geyer and Tooze, *Cambridge History of Second World War*, 3:176, 179–81.

67. Hugh Rockoff, *America's Economic Way of War: War and the U.S. Economy from the Spanish-American War to the First Gulf War* (New York: Cambridge University Press, 2012), 194, table 6.6.

68. Kennedy, *Freedom from Fear*, 798–851.

69. Cumings, *Dominion from Sea to Sea*, 313.

70. Wilson, *Destructive Creation*, 64, 84, table 2.

71. Cumings, *Dominion from Sea to Sea*, 329; Richard Rhodes, *The Making of the Atomic Bomb* (1986; New York: Simon & Schuster, 2012).

72. Barton J. Bernstein, "The Atomic Bombings Reconsidered," *Foreign Affairs* 74, no. 1 (1995), 135, 149.

73. This is the influential argument of Sparrow, *Warfare State*.

74. Gary Gerstle, *Liberty and Coercion: The Paradox of American Government from the Founding to the Present* (Princeton: Princeton University Press, 2015), 256.

75. Brian Masaru Hayashi, *Democratizing the Enemy: The Japanese American Internment* (Princeton: Princeton University Press, 2004).

76. Lary May, *The Big Tomorrow: Hollywood and the Politics of the American Way* (Chicago: University of Chicago Press, 2000), 177.

77. Meg Jacobs, *Pocketbook Politics: Economic Citizenship in Twentieth-Century America* (Princeton: Princeton University Press, 2005), 179–220; Joanna Grisinger, *The Unwieldy American State: Administrative Politics Since the New Deal* (New York: Cambridge University Press, 2012).

78. Rockoff, *America's Economic Way*, 171, table 6.1.

79. Wilson, *Destructive Creation*, 162.

80. Abba P. Lerner, "Functional Finance and the Federal Debt," *Social Research* 10, no. 1 (1943): 38–51.

81. Rockoff, *America's Economic Way*, 171, table 6.1.

82. Paul A. Samuelson, "The Effect of Interest Rate Increases on the Banking System," *American Economic Review* 35, no. 1 (1945): 26. "*It should have been a one-per-cent war*," Samuelson added.

83. Sparrow, *Warfare State*, 119–59.

84. Rockoff, *America's Economic Way*, 176, table 6.3.

85. Julian E. Zelizer, *Taxing America: Wilbur D. Mills, Congress, and the State, 1945–1975* (New York: Cambridge University Press, 1998), 85.

86. Wilson, *Destructive Creation*, 92–138.

87. Ibid., 241.

88. Nelson Lichtenstein, *Labor's War at Home: The CIO in World War II* (1982; Philadelphia: Temple University Press, 2010).

89. Gary Gerstle, "Interpreting the 'American Way': The Working Class Goes to War," in Lewis A. Erenberg and Susan E. Hirsch, eds., *The War in American Culture: Society and Consciousness During World War II* (Chicago: University of Chicago Press, 1996), 105–27.

90. Robert H. Zieger, *The CIO, 1935–1955* (Chapel Hill: University of North Carolina Press, 1995), 143–46.

91. Kennedy, *Freedom from Fear*, 775.

92. Daniel Kryder, *Divided Arsenal: Race and the American State During World War II* (New York: Cambridge University Press, 2000).

93. Nikhil Pal Singh, *Black Is a Country: Race and the Unfinished Struggle for Democracy* (Cambridge, Mass.: Harvard University Press, 2004).

94. Elaine Tyler May, *Homeward Bound: American Families in the Cold War Era* (New York: Basic Books, 2008), 66–67.

95. Martha J. Bailey and Thomas A. DiPrete, eds., *A Half Century of Change in the Lives of American Women* (New York: Russell Sage Foundation, 2016); Julia Kirk Blackwelder, *Now Hiring: The Feminization of Work in the United States, 1900–1995* (College Station: Texas A&M University Press, 1997).

96. Dorothy Sue Cobble, *The Other Women's Movement: Workplace Justice and Social Rights in Modern America* (Princeton: Princeton University Press, 2004), 32.

97. William Chafe, *The Paradox of Change: American Women in the 20th Century* (New York: Oxford University, 1991).

98. Martha J. Bailey and Thomas A. DiPrete, "Five Decades of Remarkable but Slowing Change in U.S. Women's Economic and Social Status and Political Participation," in Bailey and DiPrete, *Half Century of Change*, 12, fig. 6, 13, fig. 7.

99. Sparrow, *Warfare State*, 256.

100. Margot Canaday, *The Straight State: Sexuality and Citizenship in Twentieth-century America* (Princeton: Princeton University Press, 2009), 137–73.

101. Sparrow, *Warfare State*, 250.

102. See U.S. Senate, "Bibliography of Full Employment," *Report to the Committee on Banking and Currency*, Senate Committee Print no. 2 (Washington, D.C., 1945).

103. John Maynard Keynes, "National Self-Sufficiency," *Yale Review* 22, no. 4 (1933): 760–61.

104. Jerome Seymour Bruner, *Mandate from the People* (New York: Duell, Sloan & Pearce, 1944), 186.

CHAPTER 15: POSTWAR HINGE

1. Henry Luce, "The American Century," *Life*, February 1941.

2. Ian Buruma, *Year Zero: A History of 1945* (New York: Penguin Press, 2013).

3. Melvyn P. Leffler, "The Emergence of an American Grand Strategy, 1945–52," in Leffler and Odd Arne Westad, eds., *Cambridge History of the Cold War*, 3 vols. (New York: Cambridge University Press, 2010), 1:67.

4. Mark Philip Bradley, *The World Reimagined: Americans and Human Rights in the Twentieth Century* (New York: Cambridge University Press, 2016); Elizabeth Borgwardt, *A New Deal for the World: America's Vision for Human Rights* (Cambridge, Mass.: Belknap Press, 2005).

5. Melvyn Leffler, *A Preponderance of Power: National Security, the Truman Administration, and the Cold War* (Stanford, Calif.: Stanford University Press, 1992), 56–59.

6. Christopher J. Tassava, "The American Economy During World War II," 7, table 1, https://eh.net/encyclopedia/the-american-economy-during-world-war-ii/.

7. James T. Patterson, *Grand Expectations: The United States, 1945–1974* (New York: Oxford University Press, 1996).

8. My argument that the postwar hinge was the crucial moment for determing the content of New Deal liberalism, as opposed to the First New Deal, Second New Deal, or World War II, draws heavily from Ira Katznelson, *Fear Itself: The New Deal and the Origins of Our Time* (New York: Liveright, 2013).

9. In the capitalist "free world," many U.S. Cold War allies—in Europe, and in Japan—developed not only social-democratic welfare states but also "mixed economies," in which state planning and public investment figured greatly.

10. Alvin H. Hansen, *After the War—Full Employment* (Washington, D.C.: National Resource Planning Board, 1942), 1.

11. Benn Steil, *The Battle of Bretton Woods: John Maynard Keynes, Harry Dexter White, and the Making of a New World Order* (Princeton: Princeton University Press, 2013).

12. John Horsefield, ed., *The International Monetary Fund, 1945–1965: Twenty Years of International Voluntary Cooperation*, vol. 3, *Documents* (Washington, D.C.: International Monetary Fund, 1969), 66–67.

13. Eric Helleiner, *States and the Reemergence of Global Finance: From Bretton Woods to the 1990s* (Ithaca, N.Y.: Cornell University Press, 1994), 33, 35.

14. Eric Helleiner, *Forgotten Foundations of Bretton Woods: International Development and the Making of the Postwar Order* (Ithaca, N.Y.: Cornell University Press, 2014).

15. Robert Skidelsky, *John Maynard Keynes: Fighting for Britain, 1937–1946*, 3 vols. (London: Macmillan, 2000), 3:343–60.

16. "A Decade of American Foreign Policy 1941–1949: The Bretton Woods Agreements," Avalon Project: Documents in Law, History, and Diplomacy, http://avalon .law.yale.edu/20th_century/decad047.asp.

17. On this point, see Steil, *Battle of Bretton Woods*, 155–200.

18. Helleiner, *States and Reemergence of Global Finance*, 25, 41.

19. Stephen Kemp Bailey, *Congress Makes a Law: The Story Behind the Employment Act of 1946* (New York: Columbia University Press, 1950).

20. Mark R. Wilson, *Destructive Creation: American Business and the Winning of World War II* (Philadelphia: University of Pennsylvania Press, 2016), 253–54; Louis Cain and George Neumann, "Planning for Peace: The Surplus Property Act of 1944," *Journal of Economic History* 41, no. 1 (1981): 129–35.

21. Samir Sonti, "The Price of Prosperity: Inflation and the Limits of the New Deal Order" (PhD diss., University of California, Santa Barbara, 2017).

22. Bailey, *Congress Makes a Law*, 49, 245.

23. Robert Griffith, "Forging America's Postwar Order: Domestic Politics and Political Economy in the Age of Truman," in Michael James Lacey, ed., *The Truman Presidency* (New York: Cambridge University Press, 1989), 65.

24. Bailey, *Congress Makes a Law*, 49. On the general issue, see Kathleen Bawn et al., "A Theory of Political Parties: Groups, Policy Demands and Nominations in American Politics," *Perspectives on Politics* 10, no. 3 (2012): 571–97.

25. Bailey, *Congress Makes a Law*, 10.

26. George Lipsitz, *Rainbow at Midnight: Labor and Culture in the 1940s* (Urbana: University of Illinois Press, 1994), 99–156.

27. Robert H. Zieger, *The CIO, 1935–1955* (Chapel Hill: University of North Carolina Press, 1995), 213.

28. Dorothy Sue Cobble, *The Other Women's Movement: Workplace Justice and Social Rights in Modern America* (Princeton: Princeton University Press, 2004).

29. Lisa Kannenberg, "The Impact of the Cold War on Women's Trade Union Activism: The UE Experience," *Labor History* 34, no. 2–3 (1993): 309–23.

30. Robert F. Freeland, *The Struggle for Control of the Modern Corporation: Organizational Change at General Motors, 1924–1970* (New York: Cambridge University Press, 2001), 175–223.

31. Howell John Harris, *The Right to Manage: Industrial Relations Policies of American Business in the 1940s* (Madison: University of Wisconsin, 1982), 115.

32. Nelson Lichtenstein, *The Most Dangerous Man in Detroit: Walter Reuther and the Fate of American Labor* (New York: Basic Books, 1995), 238.

33. Irving Howe and B. J. Widick, *The UAW and Walter Reuther* (New York: Random House, 1949), 137.

34. Harry S. Truman, *Public Papers of the Presidents of the United States: Harry S. Truman, 1945* (New York: Best Books, 1961), 1:281.

35. Bailey, *Congress Makes a Law*, 229.

36. Zieger, *CIO*, 213.

37. Lichtenstein, *Most Dangerous Man in Detroit*, 132.

38. Zieger, *CIO*, 220–25.

39. Freeland, *Struggle for Control*, 206, 211.

40. Lichtenstein, *Most Dangerous Man in Detroit*, 278–80.

41. Allan H. Meltzer, *A History of the Federal Reserve*, vol. 1, *1913–1951* (Chicago: University of Chicago Press, 2003), 650–700.

42. Charles S. Maier, *Among Empires: American Ascendancy and Its Predecessors* (Cambridge, Mass.: Harvard University Press, 2007), 151–90.

43. Will Clayton, Memorandum by the Under Secretary of State for Economic Affairs, *Foreign Relations of the United States, 1947, The British Commonwealth; Europe,*

vol. 3, Office of the Historian, https://history.state.gov/historicaldocuments/frus1947 v03/d136. On the postwar European economic conversion, see Alan S. Milward, *The Reconstruction of Western Europe 1945–1951* (London: Methuen, 1984).

44. Anders Stephanson, "Fourteen Notes on the Very Concept of the Cold War," in Gearóid Ó Tuathail and Simon Dalby, eds., *Rethinking Geopolitics* (New York: Routledge, 1998), 62–85.

45. Leffler, *Preponderance of Power*.

46. Bruce Cumings, "The American Century and the Third World," *Diplomatic History* 23, no. 2 (1999): 360.

47. Michael J. Hogan, *A Cross of Iron: Harry S. Truman and the Origins of the National Security State, 1945–1954* (New York: Cambridge University Press, 1998).

48. Westad, *Cold War*, 17.

49. Michael J. Hogan, *The Marshall Plan: America, Britain and the Reconstruction of Western Europe, 1947–1952* (New York: Cambridge University Press, 1987).

50. Nelson Lichtenstein, *State of the Union: A Century of American Labor* (Princeton: Princeton University Press, 2002), 119–20.

51. Ken Fones-Wolf and Elizabeth A. Fones-Wolf, *Struggle for the Soul of the Postwar South: White Evangelical Protestants and Operation Dixie* (Urbana: University of Illinois Press, 2015).

52. Elizabeth Bishop, "Over 2,000 Illustrations and a Complete Concordance," in *Poems* (1955; New York: Farrar, Straus & Giroux, 2011), 58.

53. Thomas W. Zeiler, "Opening Doors in the World Economy," in Akira Iriye, ed., *Global Interdependence: The World After 1945* (Cambridge, Mass.: Belknap Press, 2014), 203–84.

54. David Ekbladh, *The Great American Mission: Modernization and the Construction of an American World Order* (Princeton: Princeton University Press, 2010); Maier, *Among Empires*, 52.

55. Peter A. Hall and David Soskice, eds., *Varieties of Capitalism: The Institutional Foundations of Comparative Advantage* (New York: Oxford University Press, 2001).

56. Jane Burbank and Frederick Cooper, *Empires in World History: Power and the Politics of Difference* (Princeton: Princeton University Press, 2010), 181–84. On divergence across postwar political economies, see Andrew Shonfield, *Modern Capitalism: The Changing Balance of Public and Private Power* (New York: Oxford University Press, 1969).

57. Monica Prasad, *The Politics of Free Markets: The Rise of Neoliberal Economic Policies in Britain, France, Germany, and the United States* (Chicago: University of Chicago Press, 2006).

58. Timothy Mitchell, *Carbon Democracy: Political Power in the Age of Oil* (London: Verso, 2011).

59. Stephen Kinzer, *Overthrow: America's Century of Regime Change from Hawaii to Iraq* (New York: Times Books, 2006).

60. Victoria de Grazia, *Irresistible Empire: America's Advance Through Twentieth-century Europe* (Cambridge, Mass.: Belknap Press, 2005); Geir Lundestad, "Empire by Invitation? The United States and Western Europe, 1945–1952," *Journal of Peace Research* 23, no. 3 (1986): 263–77.

61. Joseph Masco, *The Theater of Operations: National Security Affect from the Cold War to the War on Terror* (Durham, N.C.: Duke University Press, 2014).

62. Robert M. Collins, *More: The Politics of Economic Growth in Postwar America* (New York: Oxford University Press, 2000), 21. See also Craufurd D. Goodwin, "Attitudes Toward Industry in the Truman Administration: The Macroeconomic Origins of Microeconomic Policy," in Lacey, *Truman Presidency*, 89–127.

63. William Winders, *The Politics of Food Supply: U.S. Agricultural Policy in the World Economy* (New Haven: Yale University Press, 2009), 77.

64. Harry S. Truman, *Memoirs*, vol. 2, *Years of Trial and Hope, 1946–1952* (New York: Doubleday, 1956), 267.

65. David B. Truman, *The Governmental Process: Political Interests and Public Opinion* (New York: Knopf, 1951).

66. Alexander von Hoffman, "A Study in Contradictions: The Origins and Legacy of the Housing Act of 1949," *Housing Policy Debate* 11, no. 2 (2000): 299–326.

67. Dolores Hayden, *Building Suburbia: Green Fields and Urban Growth, 1820–2000* (New York: Pantheon, 2003), 130.

68. Kenneth T. Jackson, *Crabgrass Frontier: The Suburbanization of the United States* (New York: Oxford University Press, 1985), 232.

69. Elaine Tyler May, *Homeward Bound: American Families in the Cold War Era* (1998; New York: Basic Books, 2008).

70. Hoffman, "Study in Contradictions"; James Baldwin, *Conversations with James Baldwin*, ed. Fred R. Standley and Louis H. Pratt (Jackson: University Press of Mississippi, 1989), 42; Francesca Russello Ammon, *Bulldozer: Demolition and Clearance of the Postwar Landscape* (New Haven: Yale University Press, 2016); Keeanga-Yamahtta Taylor, *Race for Profit: How Banks and the Real Estate Industry Undermined Black Homeownership* (Chapel Hill: University of North Carolina Press, 2019).

71. Hyman, *Debtor Nation*, 132–72.

72. Hayden, *Building Suburbia*, 131.

73. D. Hamberg, "The Recession of 1948–49 in the United States," *Economic Journal* 62, no. 245 (1952): 1–14.

74. Herbert Stein, *The Fiscal Revolution in America* (Washington, D.C.: AEI Press, 1990), 197–240.

75. Collins, *More*, 40–67; Michael A. Bernstein, *A Perilous Progress: Economists and Public Purpose in Twentieth-Century America* (Princeton: Princeton University Press, 2004), 91–114.

76. Collins, *More*, 24, 25.

77. Bruce Cumings, *The Korean War: A History* (New York: Modern Library, 2010).

78. Cumings, "American Century and Third World," 362.

79. Collins, *More*, 24, 25.

80. Richard Hofstadter, "American Power: The Domestic Sources," *American Perspective* (Winter 1950): 35.

81. Ellen Schrecker, *Many Are the Crimes: McCarthyism in America* (New York: Little, Brown, 1998); David K. Johnson, *The Lavender Scare: The Cold War Persecution of Gays and Lesbians in the Federal Government* (Chicago: University of Chicago Press, 2004).

82. Wilson, *Destructive Creation*, 238–88.

83. Meltzer, *History of Federal Reserve*, 1:698–724.

CHAPTER 16: CONSUMERISM

1. Samuel Feinberg, *What Makes Shopping Centers Tick* (New York: Fairchild Publications, 1960), 1.

2. James T. Patterson, *Grand Expectations: The United States, 1945–1974* (New York: Oxford University Press, 1996), 71; "Two Thirds of US Homes Now Boast Television Sets," *Sales Management*, November 20, 1955, 32.

3. Jan de Vries, *The Industrious Revolution: Consumer Behavior and the Household Economy, 1650 to the Present* (New York: Cambridge University Press, 2008).

4. Zara Anishanslin, *Portrait of a Woman in Silk: Hidden Histories of the British Atlantic World* (New Haven: Yale University Press, 2016); T. H. Breen, *The Marketplace of Revolution: How Consumer Politics Shaped American Independence* (New York: Oxford University Press, 2004).

5. Walter Johnson, *Soul by Soul: Life Inside the Antebellum Slave Market* (Cambridge, Mass.: Harvard University Press, 1999).

6. Daniel J. Boorstin, *The Americans: The Democratic Experience* (1973; New York: Knopf Doubleday, 2010), 89–164.

7. William R. Leach, *Land of Desire: Merchants, Power, and the Rise of a New American Culture* (New York: Pantheon, 1993); Kathy Peiss, *Cheap Amusements: Working Women and Leisure in Turn-of-the-Century New York* (Philadelphia: Temple University Press, 1985).

8. Roland Marchand, *Advertising the American Dream: Making Way for Modernity, 1920–1940* (Berkeley: University of California Press, 1985).

9. Becky M. Nicolaides, *My Blue Heaven: Life and Politics in the Working-Class Suburbs of Los Angeles, 1920–1965* (Chicago: University of Chicago Press, 2002).

10. George J. Sanchez, *Becoming Mexican American: Ethnicity, Culture and Identity in Chicano Los Angeles, 1900–1945* (New York: Oxford University Press, 1993); Lizabeth Cohen, *Making a New Deal: Industrial Workers in Chicago, 1919–1939* (New York: Cambridge University Press, 1990).

11. Lizabeth Cohen, *A Consumers' Republic: The Politics of Mass Consumption in Postwar America* (New York: Vintage Books, 2003), 302.

12. Thomas Schatz, *Old Hollywood/New Hollywood: Ritual Art and Industry* (Ann Arbor: University of Michigan Press, 1983), 18.

13. Breen, *Marketplace of Revolution*, 195–234.

14. Joanna Cohen, *Luxurious Citizens: The Politics of Consumption in Nineteenth-century America* (Philadelphia: University of Pennsylvania Press, 2017).

15. Lawrence B. Glickman, *Buying Power: A History of Consumer Activism in America* (Chicago: University of Chicago Press, 2009).

16. Cohen, *A Consumers' Republic*; Meg Jacobs, *Pocketbook Politics: Economic Citizenship in Twentieth-Century America* (Princeton: Princeton University Press, 2005).

17. John Lewis and Michael D'Orso, *Walking with the Wind: A Memoir of the Movement* (New York: Simon & Schuster, 1998), 71. See also Traci Parker, *Department Stores and the Black Freedom Movement: Workers, Consumers, and Civil Rights from the 1930s to the 1980s* (Chapel Hill: University of North Carolina Press, 2019).

18. Glenda Elizabeth Gilmore, *Defying Dixie: The Radical Roots of Civil Rights: 1919–1950* (New York: Norton, 2008).

19. Robert Westbrook, " 'I Want a Girl, Just Like the Girl That Married Harry Janes': American Women and the Problem of Political Obligation in World War II," *American Quarterly* 42, no. 4 (1990): 587–614.

20. Andrea Tone, *Devices and Desires: A History of Contraceptives in America* (New York: Hill & Wang, 2001), 203–84.

21. Victoria de Grazia, *Irresistible Empire: America's Advance Through Twentieth-Century Europe* (Cambridge, Mass.: Belknap Press, 2005); Bruce Cumings, "The American Century and the Third World," *Diplomatic History* 23, no. 2 (1999): 355–70.

22. Jean Baudrillard, *America* (New York: Verso, 1988), 77.

23. Alexander von Hoffman, "A Study in Contradictions: The Origins and Legacy of the Housing Act of 1949," *Housing Policy Debate* 11, no. 2 (2000): 299–326.

24. Cohen, *Consumers' Republic*, 122, 123.

25. Adam Rome, *The Bulldozer in the Countryside: Suburban Sprawl and the Rise of American Environmentalism* (New York: Cambridge University Press, 2001).

26. Patterson, *Grand Expectations*, 333.

27. Richard Rothstein, *The Color of Law: A Forgotten History of How Our Government Segregated America* (New York: Liveright, 2017).

28. Hayden, *Building Suburbia*, 135.

29. Ibid., 133.

30. Martha J. Bailey and Thomas A. DiPrete, eds., *A Half Century of Change in the Lives of American Women* (New York: Russell Sage Foundation, 2016), 12, fig. 6.

31. Patterson, *Grand Expectations*, 73, 74.

32. Betty Friedan, *The Feminine Mystique* (1963; New York: Norton, 2013), 337.

33. Richard A. Easterlin, *Birth and Fortune: The Impact of Numbers on Personal Welfare* (Chicago: University of Chicago Press, 1987), 3–15.

34. Virginia Savage McAlester, *A Field Guide to American Houses* (New York: Knopf, 2015), 597–612.

35. Elizabeth A. T. Smith, *Case Study Houses* (New York: Taschen, 2016).

36. Gwendolyn Wright, *Building the Dream: A Social History of Housing in America* (New York: Pantheon, 1981), 251.

37. Kenneth T. Jackson, *Crabgrass Frontier: The Suburbanization of the United States* (New York: Oxford University Press, 1985), 214.

38. David Kushner, *Levittown: Two Families, One Tycoon, and the Fight for Civil Rights in America's Legendary Suburb* (New York: Bloomsbury, 2009).

39. Ibid., 190.

40. N. D. B. Connolly, *A World More Concrete: Real Estate and the Remaking of Jim Crow South Florida* (Chicago: University of Chicago Press, 2014); Keeanga-Yamahtta Taylor, *Race for Profit: How Banks and the Real Estate Industry Undermined Black Homeownership* (Chapel Hill: University of North Carolina Press, 2019).

41. Christopher W. Wells, *Car Country: An Environmental History* (Seattle: University of Washington Press, 2013), 254.

42. Jackson, *Crabgrass Frontier*, 259.

43. Alison Isenberg, *Downtown America: A History of the Place and the People Who Made It* (Chicago: University of Chicago Press, 2004); Cohen, *Consumers' Republic*, 251.

44. Caley Dawn Horan, *Insurance Era: Risk, Governance, and the Privatization of Security in Postwar America* (Chicago: University of Chicago Press, forthcoming).

45. Kushner, *Levittown*, 190.

46. M. Jeffrey Hardwick, *Mall Maker: Victor Gruen, Architect of an American Dream* (Philadelphia: University of Pennsylvania Press, 2010). This section draws heavily from Hardwick's excellent history.

47. Ibid., 125.

48. Ibid., 48.

49. Cohen, *Consumers' Republic*, 257–90.

50. Victor Gruen and Larry Smith, *Shopping Towns USA: The Planning of Shopping Centers* (New York: Reinhold, 1960).

51. Wright, *Building the Dream*, 215–81.

52. Hayden, *Building Suburbia*, 154–80.

53. Thomas Pynchon, *The Crying of Lot 49* (1965; New York: HarperPerennial, 2006), 13.

54. Neil Harris, *Cultural Excursions: Marketing Appetites and Cultural Tastes in Modern America* (Chicago: University of Chicago Press, 1990), 281.

55. Hardwick, *Mall Maker*, 218.

56. Thorstein Veblen, *The Theory of the Leisure Class* (1899; New York: Oxford University Press, 2009), 49.

57. David Riesman, Nathan Glazer, and Reuel Denney, *The Lonely Crowd: A Study of the Changing American Character* (New Haven: Yale University Press, 1950).

58. Lawrence B. Glickman, ed., *Consumer Society in American History: A Reader* (Ithaca, N.Y.: Cornell University Press, 1999), 52.

59. Cohen, *Consumers' Republic*, 292–344.

60. The best and most comprehensive account is Avner Offer, *The Challenge of Afflu-*

ence: Self-Control and Well-Being in the United States and Britain Since 1950 (New York: Oxford University Press, 2006).

61. Daniel Horowitz, *Vance Packard and American Social Criticism* (Chapel Hill: University of North Carolina Press, 1994), 123–24.

62. De Grazia, *Irresistible Empire*.

63. Aristotle, *Aristotle: The Politics and The Constitution of Athens*, ed., Stephen Everson (New York: Cambridge University Press Press, 2011), 24.

64. On these themes in the long history of consumption, see Colin Campbell, *The Romantic Ethic and the Spirit of Modern Consumerism* (New York: Blackwell Pub, 1987), from which I have drawn heavily.

65. James Thurber, *The Thurber Carnival* (New York: Harper & Row, 1945), 51.

66. Vance Oakley Packard, *The Hidden Persuaders* (New York: D. McKay, 1957).

67. Ernest Dichter, *The Strategy of Desire* (New York: Doubleday, 1960).

68. Sigmund Freud, "Formulations on the Two Principles of Mental Functioning," in Gabriela Legorreta and Lawrence J. Brown, eds., *On Freud's "Formulations on the Two Principles of Mental Functioning"* (New York: Routledge, 2016), 7.

69. Packard, *Hidden Persuaders*, 33.

70. *Popular Mechanics* 111, no. 1 (1959), 284.

71. Ibid., 258, 265, 12, 24, 16, and 30.

72. Sean H. Vanatta, *Plastic Capitalism: Credit Cards and the Making of Modern Consumer Finance* (New Haven: Yale University Press, forthcoming).

73. For terrific reflections by a German director of Hollywood melodramas, see Douglas Sirk and Jon Halliday, *Sirk on Sirk: Conversations with Jon Halliday* (New York: Viking, 1972).

74. Ted Steinberg, *Down to Earth: Nature's Role in American History* (New York: Oxford University Press, 2002), 234, 226, 228.

75. Rome, *Bulldozer in the Countryside*, 46.

76. Daniel Horowitz, *The Anxieties of Affluence: Critiques of American Consumer Culture, 1939–1979* (Amherst: University of Massachusetts Press, 2004).

77. Packard, *Hidden Persuaders*, 13.

78. John Kenneth Galbraith, *The Affluent Society* (1958; New York: Mariner Books, 1998), 130.

79. "A New, $10-Billion Power: the U.S. Teen-age Consumer," *Life*, August 31, 1959, 78.

80. Jean-Christophe Agnew, "Coming Up for Air: Consumer Culture in Historical Perspective," *Intellectual History Newsletter* 12 (1990): 3–21.

81. Hal Foster, *The First Pop Age: Painting and Subjectivity in the Art of Hamilton, Lichtenstein, Warhol, Richter, and Ruscha* (Princeton: Princeton University Press, 2012), 105.

82. Jackson Lears, *Fables of Abundance: A Cultural History of Advertising in America* (New York: Basic Books, 1994); Leach, *Land of Desire*.

83. Foster, *First Pop Age*, 210–48.

84. Paul Goodman, *Growing Up Absurd: Problems of Youth in the Organized Society* (1960; New York: NYRB Classics, 2012), 20, 193.

85. Thomas Frank, *The Conquest of Cool: Business Culture, Counterculture, and the Rise of Hip Consumerism* (Chicago: University of Chicago Press, 1997). I rely heavily on Frank's excellent account.

86. Ibid., 100.

87. Ibid., 95.

88. Ibid., 207, 114.

89. One particularly compelling account is Frank Trentmann, *Empire of Things: How We Became a World of Consumers, from the Fifteenth Century to the Twenty-First* (New York: Harper, 2016).

90. Angus Deaton, *The Great Escape: Health, Wealth, and the Origins of Inequality* (Princeton: Princeton University Press, 2013).

91. Robert J. Gordon, *The Rise and Fall of American Growth: The U.S. Standard of Living Since the Civil War* (Princeton: Princeton University Press, 2016).

92. Karl-Erik Wärneryd, "The Life and Work of George Katona," *Journal of Economic Psychology* 2, no. 1 (1982), 1–31. See also George Katona, *The Mass Consumption Society* (New York: McGraw-Hill, 1964).

93. George Katona, *The Powerful Consumer: Psychological Studies of the American Economy* (New York: McGraw-Hill, 1960), 161, 167.

94. See Offer, *The Challenge of Affluence*.

95. Annie Ernaux, *The Years*, trans. Alison L. Strayer (2008; New York: Seven Stories Press, 2017).

CHAPTER 17: ORDEAL OF A GOLDEN AGE

1. Claudia Goldin and Robert A. Margo, "The Great Compression: The Wage Structure in the United States at Mid-Century," *Quarterly Journal of Economics* 107, no. 1 (1992): 1–34. For more recent measurements, see Peter H. Lindert and Jeffrey G. Williamson, *Unequal Gains: American Growth and Inequality Since 1700* (Princeton: Princeton University Press, 2016); Thomas Piketty, *Capital in the Twenty-First Century*, trans. Arthur Goldhammer (Cambridge, Mass.: Belknap Press, 2014).

2. Elaine Tyler May, *Homeward Bound: American Families in the Cold War Era* (1998; New York: Basic Books, 2008).

3. Manfredo Tafuri and Francesco Dal Co, *002: Modern Architecture* (New York: Electa/Rizzoli, 1986), 312.

4. Sean H. Vanatta, *Plastic Capitalism: Credit Cards and the Making of Modern Consumer Finance* (New Haven: Yale University Press, forthcoming).

5. Matthew Frye Jacobson and Gaspar Gonzalez, *What Have They Built You to Do? The Manchurian Candidate and Cold War America* (Minneapolis: University of Minnesota Press, 2006).

6. Joel Isaac, *Working Knowledge: Making the Human Sciences from Parsons to Kuhn* (Cambridge, Mass.: Harvard University Press, 2012).

7. Jonathan Levy, "From Fiscal Triangle to Passing Through: Rise of the Nonprofit Corporation," in Naomi R. Lamoreaux and William J. Novak, eds., *Corporations and American Democracy* (Cambridge, Mass.: Harvard University Press, 2017), 213–44.

8. Walker Percy, *The Moviegoer* (New York: Knopf, 1961), 9.

9. John Rawls, *A Theory of Justice*, rev. ed. (1971; Cambridge, Mass.: Belknap Press, 1999). In *A Theory of Justice*, Rawls said "income" but also "wealth" were "all-purpose means," both being rational to want whatever else one wants. Later, he argued in favor of "property owning democracy." John Rawls, *Justice as Fairness: A Restatement*, ed. Erin Kelly (Cambridge, Mass.: Belknap Press, 2001). On Rawls and the political-philosophical project his work gave rise to, see Katrina Forrester, *In the Shadow of Justice: Postwar Liberalism and the Remaking of Political Philosophy* (Princeton: Princeton University Press, 2019).

10. The finest study linking U.S. economic developments at home and abroad is Daniel Immerwahr, *Thinking Small: The United States and the Lure of Community Development* (Cambridge, Mass.: Harvard University Press, 2015). On economic development as aspiration, see Adom Getachew, *Worldmaking After Empire: The Rise and Fall of Self-Determination* (Princeton: Princeton University Press, 2019). On economic development generally, see Stephen J. Macekura and Erez Manela, eds., *The Development Century: A Global History* (New York: Cambridge University Press, 2018).

11. In many national economies recovering from the war, genuine "economic mir-

acles" did occur. Barry Eichengreen, *The European Economy Since 1945: Coordinated Capitalism and Beyond* (Princeton: Princeton University Press, 2008).

12. William E. Leuchtenburg, *In the Shadow of FDR: From Harry Truman to Barack Obama* (Ithaca, N.Y.: Cornell University Press, 2009), 94; Dwight D. Eisenhower, *The White House Years: Waging Peace, 1956–1961* (Garden City, N.Y.: Doubleday, 1965), 465; Grant Madsen, "The International Origins of Dwight D. Eisenhower's Political Economy," *Journal of Policy History* 24, no. 4 (September 2012): 675–708.

13. Perry Mehrling, *The New Lombard Street: How the Fed Became the Dealer of Last Resort* (Princeton: Princeton University Press, 2010), 46–62; Allan H. Meltzer, *A History of the Federal Reserve*, vol. 2, bk. 1, 1951–1969 (Chicago: University of Chicago Press, 2019), 89–115.

14. Richard V. Damms, *The Eisenhower Presidency, 1953–1961* (London: Longman, 2002), 10.

15. Monica Prasad, *The Land of Too Much: American Abundance and the Paradox of Poverty* (Cambridge, Mass.: Harvard University Press, 2012).

16. Julian E. Zelizer, *Taxing America: Wilbur D. Mills, Congress, and the State, 1945–1975* (New York: Cambridge University Press, 1999), 93, 147–78.

17. Levy, "Fiscal Triangle"; Alice O'Connor, "The Ford Foundation and Philanthropic Activism in the 1960s," in Ellen Condliffe Lagemann, ed., *Philanthropic Foundations: New Scholarship, New Possibilities* (Bloomington: Indiana University Press, 1999), 171.

18. Edward D. Berkowitz, *America's Welfare State: From Roosevelt to Reagan* (Baltimore: Johns Hopkins University Press, 1991), 160–66.

19. William Winders, *The Politics of Food Supply: U.S. Agricultural Policy in the World Economy* (New Haven: Yale University Press, 2009), 129–58.

20. James T. Patterson, *Grand Expectations: The United States, 1945–1974* (New York: Oxford University Press, 1996), 272.

21. Christopher W. Wells, *Car Country: An Environmental History* (Seattle: University of Washington Press, 2013), 254.

22. Robert M. Collins, *More: The Politics of Economic Growth in Postwar America* (New York: Oxford University Press, 2000), 47–48.

23. Robert Griffith, "Dwight D. Eisenhower and the Corporate Commonwealth," *American Historical Review* 87, no. 1 (1982): 96.

24. Dwight D. Eisenhower, "Farewell Radio and Television Address to the American People," January 17, 1961, American Presidency Project, https://www.presidency.ucsb.edu/documents/farewell-radio-and-television-address-the-american-people.

25. Andrew Shonfield, *Modern Capitalism: The Changing Balance of Power of Public and Private Power* (New York: Oxford University Press, 1965).

26. Edward S. Mason, ed., *The Corporation in Modern Society* (Cambridge, Mass.: Harvard University Press, 1959).

27. Francis Xavier Sutton et al., *The American Business Creed* (Cambridge, Mass.: Harvard University Press, 1956), 64–65.

28. S. Samuel Arsht, "The Business Judgment Rule Revisited," 8, no. 1 *Hofstra Law Review* (1979): 93–134.

29. Adolf A. Berle, *20th Century Capitalist Revolution* (New York: Harcourt, Brace, 1954), 39.

30. Edward S. Mason, "The Apologetics of 'Managerialism,'" *Journal of Business* 31, no. 1 (1958): 7.

31. *Money and Credit: Their Influence on Jobs, Prices, and Growth*, A Report of the Commission on Money and Credit, created by Congress in 1957 (Englewood Cliffs, N.J.: Prentice-Hall, 1964).

32. Robert Aaron Gordon and James Edwin Howell, *Higher Education for Business* (New York: Columbia University Press, 1959).

33. On the rate, see Edward N. Wolff, *A Century of Wealth in America* (Cambridge, Mass.: Belknap Press, 2017), 26, fig. 1.10. On bureaucratic calculation, see Jonathan Levy, "Accounting for Profit and the History of Capital," *Critical Historical Studies* 1, no. 2 (2014): 171–214.

34. Levy, "Accounting for Profit," 192–95.

35. Ibid., 195.

36. Alfred D. Chandler and Takashi Hikino, *Scale and Scope: The Dynamics of Industrial Capitalism* (Cambridge, Mass.: Belknap Press, 1990). For the political interpretation, see Robert F. Freeland, *The Struggle for Control of the Modern Corporation* (New York: Cambridge University Press, 2005).

37. Neil Fligstein, *The Transformation of Corporate Control* (Cambridge, Mass.: Harvard University Press, 1990), 191–225; Louis Hyman, "Rethinking the Postwar Corporation: Management, Monopolies, and Markets," in Kim Phillips-Fein and Julian E. Zelizer, eds., *What's Good for Business: Business and American Politics Since World War II* (New York: Oxford University Press, 2012), 195–211.

38. Nelson Lichtenstein, *State of the Union: A Century of American Labor* (Princeton: Princeton University Press, 2002), 122–40.

39. Richard M. Cyert and James G. March, *Behavioral Theory of the Firm* (1963; New York: John Wiley & Sons, 1992).

40. *A. P. Smith Manufacturing Co. v. Barlow,* 13 N.J. 145 98 A. 2d 581 (1953); Archie B. Carroll et al., *Corporate Responsibility: The American Experience* (New York: Cambridge University Press, 2012).

41. *Fortune,* August 1959, 103.

42. Howard Brick, *Transcending Capitalism: Visions of a New Society in Modern American Thought* (Ithaca, N.Y.: Cornell University Press, 2006).

43. Cyert and March, *Behavioral Theory of the Firm.*

44. Herbert A. Simon, "A Behavioral Model of Rational Choice," *Quarterly Journal of Economics* 69, no. 1 (1955): 99–118.

45. Fligstein, *Transformation of Corporate Control,* 116–60.

46. Carl Kaysen, "The Social Significance of the Modern Corporation," *American Economic Review* 47, no. 2 (1957): 313, 319.

47. John Harwood, *The Interface: IBM and the Transformation of Corporate Design, 1945–1976* (Minneapolis: University of Minnesota Press, 2011); Reinhold Martin, *The Organizational Complex: Architecture, Media, and Corporate Space* (Cambridge, Mass.: MIT Press, 2003).

48. Henry-Russell Hitchcock, "The Architecture of Bureaucracy and the Architecture of Genius," *Architectural Review* 10 (January 1947), 4.

49. Tafuri and Dal Co, *002: Modern Architecture,* 310.

50. Ibid., 622.

51. Louise A. Mozingo, *Pastoral Capitalism: A History of Suburban Corporate Landscapes* (Cambridge, Mass.: MIT Press, 2011), 129.

52. Cynthia A. Williams and Peer Zumbansen, eds., *The Embedded Firm: Corporate Governance, Labor, and Finance Capitalism* (New York: Cambridge University Press, 2011).

53. C. Wright Mills, *White Collar: The American Middle Classes* (1951; New York: Oxford University Press, 2002), xvii.

54. William H. Whyte and Joseph Nocera, *The Organization Man,* rev. ed. (1956; Philadelphia: University of Pennsylvania Press, 2002).

55. Cyert and March, *Behavioral Theory of the Firm,* 41–44.

56. Charles Perrow, *Complex Organizations: A Critical Essay* (New York: McGraw-Hill, 1986), 93.

57. James Tucker, *The Therapeutic Corporation* (New York: Oxford University Press, 1999).

58. Julia Kirk Blackwelder, *Now Hiring: The Feminization of Work in the United States, 1900–1995* (College Station: Texas A&M University Press, 1997), 151, table 6.1; Rosabeth Moss Kanter, *Men and Women of the Corporation* (New York: Basic Books, 1993).

59. Julie Berebitsky, *Sex and the Office: A History of Gender, Power, and Desire* (New Haven: Yale University Press, 2012), 141.

60. Helen Gurley Brown, *Sex and the Office* (New York: Pocket Books, 1964), 183.

61. Ralph Ellison, *Invisible Man* (1952; New York: Vintage Books, 1995), 577, 580.

62. Mark Greif, *The Age of the Crisis of Man: Thought and Fiction in America, 1933–1973* (Princeton: Princeton University Press, 2015).

63. Saul Bellow, *Humboldt's Gift* (1975; New York: Penguin Classics, 2008), 133–34.

64. D. W. Meinig, *The Shaping of America: A Geographical Perspective on 500 Years of History*, vol. 4, *Global America, 1915–2000* (New Haven: Yale University Press, 2004), 151.

65. George M. Marsden, *The Twilight of the American Enlightenment: The 1950s and the Crisis of Liberal Belief* (New York: Basic Books, 2014).

66. Robert M. Solow, "A Contribution to the Theory of Economic Growth," *Quarterly Journal of Economics* 70, no. 1 (1956): 65. Solow's work discovered that investment in the fixed capital stock did not lead to growth. The bulk was explained by an exogenous "residual," unexplained by the inputs in his model. The dynamism was outside capital investment, if assuming that capital is a thing (a bad assumption).

67. Judith Stein, *Running Steel, Running America: Race, Economic Policy, and the Decline of Liberalism* (Chapel Hill: University of North Carolina Press, 1998), 28.

68. Immerwahr, *Thinking Small*; Alice O'Connor, *Poverty Knowledge: Social Science, Social Policy, and the Poor in Twentieth-Century U.S. History* (Princeton: Princeton University Press, 2001).

69. Shonfield, *Modern Capitalism*, 339–41.

70. Bruce J. Schulman, *From Cotton Belt to Sunbelt: Federal Policy, Economic Development, and the Transformation of the South, 1938–1980* (New York: Oxford University Press, 1991), 185.

71. Collins, *More*, 56.

72. Herbert Stein, *Fiscal Revolution in America* (Washington, D.C.: AEI Press, 1990), 411, 412.

73. Schulman, *From Cotton Belt to Sunbelt*, 139.

74. Lyndon B. Johnson, "Annual Message to the Congress on the State of the Union," January 8, 1964, American Presidency Project, https://www.presidency.ucsb.edu/documents/annual-message-the-congress-the-state-the-union-25.

75. Zelizer, *Taxing America*, 93, 191–207.

76. James J. Kenneally, *Women and American Trade Unions* (St. Albans, Vt.: Eden Press, 1978).

77. Katherine Turk, *Equality on Trial: Gender and Rights in the Modern American Workplace* (Philadelphia: University of Pennsylvania Press, 2016), 4.

78. James T. Patterson, *The Eve of Destruction: How 1965 Transformed America* (New York: Basic Books, 2012), 112.

79. Ira Katznelson, *When Affirmative Action Was White: An Untold History of Racial Inequality in Twentieth-Century America* (New York: Norton, 2005).

80. On the relationship between race and economy in liberalism, the finest account by far is Stein, *Running Steel, Running America*. On the economic possibilities of civil rights movements, see Risa L. Goluboff, *The Lost Promise of Civil Rights* (Cambridge, Mass.: Harvard University Press, 2007).

81. For a survey of this vast literature, see Samuel Zipp, "The Roots and Routes of Urban Renewal," *Journal of Urban History* 39, no. 3 (2012): 366–91.

82. Francesca Russello Ammon, *Bulldozer: Demolition and Clearance of the Postwar Landscape* (New Haven: Yale University Press, 2016).

83. Lily Geismer, *Don't Blame Us: Suburban Liberals and the Transformation of the Democratic Party* (Princeton: Princeton University Press, 2015).

84. Thomas J. Sugrue, *The Origins of the Urban Crisis: Race and Inequality in Postwar Detroit* (Princeton: Princeton University Press, 1996).

85. Elizabeth Tandy Shermer, *Sunbelt Capitalism: Phoenix and the Transformation of American Politics* (Philadelphia: University of Pennsylvania Press, 2013).

86. Gavin Wright, *Old South, New South: Revolutions in the Southern Economy Since the Civil War* (New York: Basic Books, 1986), 239–74.

87. On capital flight, see Beth English, *A Common Thread: Labor, Politics, and Capital Mobility in the Textile Industry* (Athens: University of Georgia Press, 2006); Jefferson R. Cowie, *Capital Moves: RCA's Seventy-Year Quest for Cheap Labor* (Ithaca, N.Y.: Cornell University Press, 1999).

88. Schulman, *From Cotton Belt to Sunbelt*, 158.

89. Leah Boustan, *Competition in the Promised Land: Black Migrants in Northern Cities and Labor Markets* (Princeton: Princeton University Press, 2016).

90. Douglas Massey and Nancy Denton, *American Apartheid: Segregation and the Making of the Underclass* (Cambridge, Mass.: Harvard University Press, 1993).

91. Schulman, *From Cotton Belt to Sunbelt*, 135–72.

92. Stein, *Running Steel, Running America*, 123.

93. Ibid., 71, 108.

94. Robert Fitzgerald, *The Rise of the Global Company: Multinationals and the Making of the Modern World* (New York: Cambridge University Press, 2016).

95. U.S. Congress, House Foreign Affairs Committee, *Foreign Investment in the United States: Hearings Before the Subcommittee on Foreign Economic Policy . . . , January 29, February 5, 21, 1974* (Washington, D.C., 1974), 188.

96. Vanessa Ogle, "Archipelago Capitalism: Tax Havens, Offshore Money, and the States, 1950s–1970s," *American Historical Review* 122, no. 5 (2017): 1431–58.

97. Julian E. Zelizer, *The Fierce Urgency of Now: Lyndon Johnson, Congress, and the Battle for the Great Society* (New York: Penguin Press, 2015).

98. Martha J. Bailey and Sheldon Danziger, eds., *Legacies of the War on Poverty* (New York: Russell Sage Foundation, 2013).

99. Levy, "Fiscal Triangle," 233.

100. Annelise Orleck and Lisa Hazirjian, eds., *The War on Poverty: A New Grassroots History, 1964–1980* (Athens: University of Georgia Press, 2011), 14.

101. Josh Sides, *L.A. City Limits: African American Los Angeles from the Great Depression to the Present* (Berkeley: University of California Press, 2006).

102. On the 1960s crime wave, which predated mass incarceration, and for the best explanation of how mass incarceration was the result of insufficient postwar liberal economic development programs, see John Clegg and Adaner Usmani, "The Economic Origins of Mass Incarceration," *Catalyst* 3, no. 3 (2019): 9–53.

103. Becky Pettit and Bruce Western, "Mass Incarceration and the Life Course: Race and Class Inequality in U.S. Incarceration," *American Sociological Review* 69, no. 2 (2004): 164.

104. Louis Hyman, *Debtor Nation: The History of America in Red Ink* (Princeton: Princeton University Press, 2011), 233.

105. "Induction Statistics," Selective Service System, https://www.sss.gov/About/History-And-Records/Induction-Statistics.

106. Doris Kearns Goodwin, *Lyndon Johnson and the American Dream* (New York: HarperCollins, 1976), 359.

107. See Immerwahr, *Thinking Small*.

CHAPTER 18: CRISIS OF INDUSTRIAL CAPITAL

1. Emma Rothschild, "Reagan and the Real America," *New York Review of Books,* February 5, 1981.

2. Gary Herrigel, *Manufacturing Possibilities: Creative Action and Industrial Recomposition in the United States, Germany, and Japan* (New York: Oxford University Press, 2010).

3. The classic work framing this moment in terms of "crisis" is Jürgen Habermas, *Legitimation Crisis* (New York: Beacon Press, 1975).

4. Antonio Sergio Bessa et al., *Gordon Matta-Clark: Anarchitect* (New Haven: Yale University Press, 2017).

5. Charles S. Maier, " 'Malaise': The Crisis of Capitalism in the 1970s," in Niall Ferguson et al., eds., *The Shock of the Global: The 1970s in Perspective* (Cambridge, Mass.: Belknap Press, 2010), 235–59.

6. Edward N. Wolff, *A Century of Wealth in America* (Cambridge, Mass.: Belknap Press, 2017), 27, fig. 1.11; Robert Brenner, *The Economics of Global Turbulence: The Advanced Capitalist Economies from Long Boom to Long Downturn, 1945–2005* (New York: Verso, 2006), 105.

7. Nicholas Kaldor, *Causes of Growth and Stagnation in the World Economy* (New York: Cambridge University Press, 1996).

8. William Nordhaus, "Retrospective on the 1970s Productivity Slowdown," National Bureau of Economic Research, Working Paper no. 10950 (December 2004), 23, table 6; Alan S. Blinder and Jeremy B. Rudd, "The Supply-Shock Explanation of the Great Stagflation Revisited," National Bureau of Economic Research, Working Paper no. 14563 (December 2008).

9. Robert J. Gordon, *The Rise and Fall of American Growth: The U.S. Standard of Living Since the Civil War* (Princeton: Princeton University Press, 2016), 326, fig. E-1.

10. Alison Lefkovitz, *Strange Bedfellows: Marriage in the Age of Women's Liberation* (Philadelphia: University of Pennsylvania Press, 2018); Nancy MacLean, "Postwar Women's History: The 'Second Wave' or the End of the Family Wage?," in Jean-Christophe Agnew and Roy Rosenzweig, eds., *A Companion to Post-1945 America* (Malden, Mass.: Blackwell, 2006).

11. Barbara Ehrenreich, *The Hearts of Men: American Dreams and the Flight from Commitment* (1983; New York: Knopf, 2011), 121.

12. Jefferson Cowie, *Stayin' Alive: The 1970s and the Last Days of the Working Class* (New York: New Press, 2010), 167–210.

13. For an excellent summary of the debate, see J. Bradford Delong, "America's Peacetime Inflation: The 1970s," in Christina D. Romer and David H. Romer, eds., *Reducing Inflation: Motivation and Strategy* (Chicago: University of Chicago Press, 1997), 247–80.

14. Leon N. Lindberg and Charles S. Maier, eds., *The Politics of Inflation and Economic Stagnation: Theoretical Approaches and International Case Studies* (Washington, D.C.: Brookings Institution Press, 1985).

15. Cowie, *Stayin' Alive*, xxxvi.

16. Elizabeth Lunbeck, *The Americanization of Narcissism* (Cambridge, Mass.: Harvard University Press, 2014); John Ashbery, *Self-Portrait in a Convex Mirror* (New York: Viking, 1975), 71; Joni Mitchell, *The Complete Poems and Lyrics* (New York: Crown, 1997), 65.

17. William Gaddis, *J R* (1975; Champaign, Ill.: Dalkey Archive Press, 2012), 20.

18. Arthur M. Okun, *The Political Economy of Prosperity* (Washington: Brookings Institution Press, 1970), 31.

19. Barry J. Eichengreen, *Globalizing Capital: A History of the International Monetary*

System (Princeton: Princeton University Press, 2008), 126–33; Harold James, *International Monetary Cooperation Since Bretton Woods* (New York: Oxford University Press, 1996), 205–27.

20. Robert M. Collins, *More: The Politics of Economic Growth in Postwar America* (New York: Oxford University Press, 2000), 112.

21. Cowie, *Stayin' Alive*, 144.

22. Wyatt C. Wells, *Economist in an Uncertain World: Arthur F. Burns and the Federal Reserve, 1970–78* (New York: Columbia University Press, 1994), 61.

23. See Daniel J. Sargent, *A Superpower Transformed: The Remaking of American Foreign Relations in the 1970s* (Oxford: Oxford University Press, 2015), 100–30. I have drawn heavily from Sargent's excellent account.

24. Ibid., 108.

25. Collins, *More*, 112.

26. William Winders, *The Politics of Food Supply: U.S. Agricultural Policy in the World Economy* (New Haven: Yale University Press, 2009), 129–59.

27. Sargent, *Superpower Transformed*, 120–30.

28. Collins, *More*, 121.

29. Cowie, *Stayin' Alive*, 89, 126.

30. David Vogel, *Fluctuating Fortunes: The Political Power of Business in America* (New York: Basic Books, 1989), 7.

31. Brenner, *Economics of Global Turbulence*, 113.

32. Emma Rothschild, *Paradise Lost: The Decline of the Auto-Industrial Age* (New York: Random House, 1973), 14, 50.

33. Ibid.; see also Studs Terkel, *Working: People Talk About What They Do All Day and How They Feel About What They Do* (New York: Pantheon, 1974).

34. Brenner, *Economics of Global Turbulence*, 114, 103.

35. Cowie, *Stayin' Alive*, 23–74.

36. Paul Frymer, *Black and Blue: African Americans, the Labor Movement, and the Decline of the Democratic Party* (Princeton: Princeton University Press, 2007), 70–98; Nancy MacLean, *Freedom Is Not Enough: The Opening of the American Workplace* (Cambridge, Mass.: Harvard University Press, 2006), 108.

37. Cowie, *Stayin' Alive*, 125–66.

38. U.S. Department of Education, Health, and Welfare, *Work in America: Report of a Special Task Force to the U.S. Department of Health, Education, and Welfare* (Cambridge, Mass.: MIT Press, 1973).

39. Cowie, *Stayin' Alive*, 127; Brian Steensland, *The Failed Welfare Revolution: America's Struggle over Guaranteed Income Policy* (Princeton: Princeton University Press, 2008), 120–57.

40. Sonya Michel, *Children's Interests/Mothers' Rights: The Shaping of America's Child Care Policy* (New Haven: Yale University Press, 1999), 236–52.

41. Robert O. Self, *All in the Family: The Realignment of American Democracy Since the 1960s* (New York: Hill & Wang, 2012), 276–318.

42. Hugh Rockoff, *Drastic Measures: A History of Wage and Price Controls in the United States* (New York: Cambridge University Press, 1984), 200–34.

43. Sargent, *Superpower Transformed*, 122.

44. Ibid., 123, 124, 119.

45. Eric Helleiner, *States and the Reemergence of Global Finance: From Bretton Woods to the 1990s* (1996; Ithaca, N.Y.: Cornell University Press, 2015), 101–22.

46. Paul A. Volcker and Toyoo Gyohten, *Changing Fortunes: The World's Money and the Threat to American Leadership* (New York: Times Books, 1992), 113.

47. Meg Jacobs, *Panic at the Pump: The Energy Crisis and the Transformation of American Politics in the 1970s* (New York: Hill & Wang, 2016), 4–10.

48. Olivier J. Blanchard and Jordi Gali, "The Macroeconomic Effects of Oil Shocks: Why Are the 2000s So Different from the 1970s?," National Bureau of Economic Research, Working Paper no. 13268 (September 2007); Nordhaus, "Retrospective on 1970s Productivity Slowdown."

49. Daniel Bell, *The Coming of Post-Industrial Society: A Venture in Social Forecasting* (New York: Basic Books, 1976).

50. An excellent study in general that also roots changes in postwar employment and the rise of flexibility in Houston is Louis Hyman, *Temp: How American Work, American Business, and the American Dream Became Temporary* (New York: Viking, 2018).

51. Robert Venturi, Denise Scott Brown, and Steven Izenour, *Learning from Las Vegas* (Cambridge, Mass.: MIT Press, 1972).

52. Richard Bach, *Jonathan Livingston Seagull* (1970; New York: Scribner, 2014), 25.

53. Bruce J. Schulman, *The Seventies: The Great Shift in American Culture, Society, and Politics* (New York: Free Press, 2001), 102–17.

54. Steven High, *Industrial Sunset: The Making of North America's Rust Belt, 1969–1984* (Toronto: University of Toronto Press, 2003), 26–29, 59.

55. Dale A. Hathaway, *Can Workers Have a Voice? The Politics of Deindustrialization in Pittsburgh* (University Park: Pennsylvania State University Press, 1993).

56. Felix G. Rohatyn, "Reconstructing America," *New York Review of Books*, March 5, 1981.

57. William Julius Wilson, *The Truly Disadvantaged: The Inner City, the Underclass, and Public Policy* (1987; Chicago: University of Chicago Press, 2012), 34.

58. Gregory D. Squires, Larry Bennett, and Kathleen McCourt, *Chicago: Race, Class, and the Response to Urban Decline* (Philadelphia: Temple University Press, 1989), 113.

59. Paul A. Jargowsky, *Poverty and Place: Ghettos, Barrios, and the American City* (New York: Russell Sage Foundation, 1997); Wilson, *Truly Disadvantaged*, 3.

60. James Forman, Jr., *Locking Up Our Own: Crime and Punishment in Black America* (New York: Farrar, Straus & Giroux, 2017), 12; Julilly Kohler-Hausman, *Getting Tough: Welfare and Imprisonment in 1970s America* (Princeton: Princeton University Press, 2017).

61. Kim Phillips-Fein, *Fear City: New York's Fiscal Crisis and the Rise of Austerity Politics* (New York: Metropolitan Books, 2017).

62. William K. Stevens, "Houston: A New Promised Land for Skilled Middle Class," *New York Times*, February 10, 1978.

63. For more on Houston, see my essays at "Houston," Center for History and Economics, Harvard University, http://histecon.fas.harvard.edu/climate-loss/houston/houston.html.

64. Joe R. Feagin, *Free Enterprise City: Houston in Political-Economic Perspective* (New Brunswick: Rutgers University Press, 1988), 121.

65. Feagin, *Free Enterprise City*, 77.

66. Martin V. Melosi and Joseph A. Pratt, eds., *Energy Metropolis: An Environmental History of Houston and the Gulf Coast* (Pittsburgh, Pa.: University of Pittsburgh Press, 2007).

67. Ibid., 46, 76, table 3.1.

68. Oliver Gillham, *The Limitless City: A Primer on the Urban Sprawl Debate* (Washington, D.C.: Island Press, 2002); John R. Logan and Harvey L. Molotch, *Urban Fortunes: The Political Economy of Place* (1987; Berkeley: University of California Press, 2007).

69. Peter G. Rowe, Barrie Scardino, and William F. Stern, eds., *Ephemeral City: Cite Looks at Houston* (Austin: University of Texas Press, 2003).

70. Joe Ely, "Imagine Houston," https://www.youtube.com/watch?v=2uDAtAToMh4.

71. Joe R. Feagin, "The Secondary Circuit of Capital: Office Construction in Houston, Texas," *International Journal of Urban and Regional Research* 11, no. 2 (1987): 172–92.

72. Fredric Jameson, "Postmodernism, or The Cultural Logic of Late Capitalism," *New Left Review* 1, no. 146 (1984): 53–92.

73. Feagin, *Free Enterprise City*, 186.

74. Ibid., 10.

75. Timothy J. Minchin, *Labor Under Fire: A History of the AFL-CIO Since 1979* (Chapel Hill: University of North Carolina Press, 2017), 108–12.

76. Judith Stein, *Running Steel, Running America: Race, Economic Policy, and the Decline of Liberalism* (Chapel Hill: University of North Carolina Press, 1998), 109.

77. Feagin, *Free Enterprise City*, 95.

78. Kyle Shelton, *Power Moves: Transportation, Politics, and Development in Houston* (Austin: University of Texas Press, 2018), 43.

79. Gavin Wright, *Sharing the Prize: The Economics of the Civil Rights Revolution in the American South* (Cambridge, Mass.: Belknap Press, 2013).

80. Martha J. Bailey and Thomas A. DiPrete, eds., *A Half Century of Change in the Lives of American Women* (New York: Russell Sage Foundation, 2016); MacLean, *Freedom Is Not Enough*; Katherine Turk, *Equality on Trial: Gender and Rights in the Modern American Workplace* (Philadelphia: University of Pennsylvania Press, 2016).

81. Lefkovitz, *Strange Bedfellows*, 80.

82. Ibid., 68, table 1.

83. Marjorie J. Spruill, *Divided We Stand: The Battle over Women's Rights and Family Values That Polarized American Politics* (New York: Bloomsbury, 2017).

84. Ibid.

85. John Lukacs, *A New Republic: A History of the United States in the Twentieth Century* (New Haven: Yale University Press, 2004), 174.

86. Phyllis Schlafly, *Phyllis Schlafly Report* (February 1972); Melinda Cooper, *Family Values: Between Neoliberalism and the New Social Conservatism* (New York: Zone Books, 2017).

87. Barbara Ehrenreich, *The Hearts of Men: American Dreams and the Flight from Commitment* (1983; New York: Knopf Doubleday, 2011), 121.

88. Robert Wuthnow, *Rough Country: How Texas Became America's Most Powerful Bible-Belt State* (Princeton: Princeton University Press, 2014).

89. Spruill, *Divided We Stand*, 295.

90. Self, *All in the Family*, 309–38.

91. Wuthnow, *Rough Country*, 344.

92. Jane Mansbridge, *Why We Lost the ERA* (Chicago: University of Chicago Press, 1986).

93. Julian E. Zelizer, *Jimmy Carter: The American Presidents Series: The 39th President, 1977–1981* (New York: Times Books, 2010).

94. Sean Wilentz, *The Age of Reagan: A History, 1974–2008* (New York: Harper, 2008), 73–89.

95. Benjamin C. Waterhouse, *Lobbying America: The Politics of Business from Nixon to NAFTA* (Princeton: Princeton University Press, 2014).

96. Vogel, *Fluctuating Fortunes*, 196.

97. Waterhouse, *Lobbying America*, 10; Vogel, *Fluctuating Fortunes*, 193.

98. William E. Simon, *A Time for Truth* (New York: McGraw-Hill, 1978); Alice O'Connor, "Financing the Counterrevolution," in Bruce J. Schulman and Julian E. Zelizer, eds., *Rightward Bound: Making America Conservative in the 1970s* (Cambridge, Mass.: Harvard University Press, 2008).

99. W. Carl Biven, *Jimmy Carter's Economy: Policy in an Age of Limits* (Chapel Hill: University of North Carolina Press, 2002), 39–94, 27.

100. Ibid., 46.

101. Charles L. Schultze, *The Public Use of Private Interest* (Washington, D.C.: Brookings Institution Press, 1977), 16.

102. Avner Offer and Gabriel Söderberg, *The Nobel Factor: The Prize in Economics, Social Democracy, and the Market Turn* (Princeton: Princeton University Press, 2016).

103. Milton Friedman, "Inflation: Causes and Consequences," *Asia Publishing House* (1963), 17.

104. Milton Friedman, "The Role of Monetary Policy," *American Economic Review* 58, no. 1 (1968): 1–17.

105. Daniel Rodgers, *Age of Fracture* (Cambridge, Mass.: Harvard University Press, 2011), 41–76.

106. Angus Burgin, *The Great Persuasion: Reinventing Free Markets Since the Depression* (Cambridge, Mass.: Harvard University Press, 2012), 152–85.

107. Milton Friedman, *Capitalism and Freedom* (1962; Chicago: University of Chicago Press, 2002).

108. George J. Stigler, "The Theory of Economic Regulation," *Bell Journal of Economics and Management Science* 2, no. 1 (1971): 3–21.

109. R. H. Coase, "The Nature of the Firm," *Economica* 4, no. 16 (1937): 386–405; Richard A. Posner, *Economic Analysis of Law* (Boston: Little, Brown, 1972), 395.

110. Robert H. Bork, *The Antitrust Paradox: A Policy at War with Itself* (New York: Free Press, 1978), 405.

111. Eugene F. Fama, "Efficient Capital Markets: A Review of Theory and Empirical Work," *Journal of Finance* 25, no. 2 (1970): 383–417.

112. Gary S. Becker, *The Economic Approach to Human Behavior* (Chicago: University of Chicago Press, 1977).

113. Gary Becker, *Human Capital: A Theoretical and Empirical Analysis, with Special Reference to Education* (New York: National Bureau of Economic Research, 1964).

114. Friedman had also made this point.

115. Robert Lucas, "Rules, Discretion, and the Role of the Economic Advisor," in Stanley Fischer, ed., *Rational Expectations and Economic Policy* (Chicago: University of Chicago Press, 1980), 189–210.

116. Robert Lucas, "The Death of Keynesian Economics," *Collected Papers on Monetary Theory* (Cambridge, Mass.: Harvard University Press, 2013), 502.

117. Arthur M. Okun, *Prices and Quantities: A Macroeconomic Analysis* (Washington, D.C.: Brookings Institution, 1981).

118. Lucas, "Rules, Discretion."

119. Beth Bailey and David Farber, eds., *America in the Seventies* (Lawrence: University Press of Kansas, 2004), 1–8.

120. Eduardo Canedo, "The Rise of the Deregulation Movement in Modern America, 1957–1980" (PhD diss., Columbia University, 2008).

121. Schultze, *Public Use of Private Interest*, 17.

122. Biven, *Jimmy Carter's Economy*, 220.

123. Jimmy Carter, "Trucking Industry Deregulation Message to the Congress Transmitting Proposed Legislation," June 21, 1979, American Presidency Project, https://www.presidency.ucsb.edu/documents/trucking-industry-deregulation-message-the-congress-transmitting-proposed-legislation; Jimmy Carter, "Executive Order 12044—Improving Government Regulations," March 23, 1978, American Presidency Project, https://www.presidency.ucsb.edu/documents/executive-order-12044-improving-government-regulations.

124. Biven, *Jimmy Carter's Economy*, 222.

125. Stein, *Running Steel, Running America*, 230–40.

126. Sargent, *Superpower Transformed*, 229–64.

127. Ibid.

128. Biven, *Jimmy Carter's Economy*, 221.

129. Jacobs, *Panic at the Pump*, 196–234.

130. Sargent, *Superpower Transformed*, 276.

131. Ibid., 290.

132. Christopher Lasch, *The Culture of Narcissism: American Life in an Age of Diminishing Expectations* (New York: Norton, 1979).

133. Kevin Mattson, *"What the Heck Are You Up To, Mr. President?": Jimmy Carter, America's "Malaise," and the Speech That Should Have Changed the Country* (New York: Bloomsbury USA, 2009); Sargent, *Superpower Transformed*, 281.

134. Mattson, *"What the Heck Are You Up To,"* 190.

135. William Greider, *Secrets of the Temple: How the Federal Reserve Runs the Country* (New York: Simon & Schuster, 1987), 47.

136. Paul A. Volcker and Toyoo Gyohten, *Changing Fortunes: The World's Money and the Threat to American Leadership* (New York: Times Books, 1992), 167.

137. Jimmy Carter, "Decontrol of Domestic Oil Prices Statement by the President," June 1, 1979, American Presidency Project, https://www.presidency.ucsb.edu/docu ments/decontrol-domestic-oil-prices-statement-the-president.

CHAPTER 19: MAGIC OF THE MARKET

1. Ronald Reagan, "Inaugural Address," January 20, 1981, at American Presidency Project, https://www.presidency.ucsb.edu/documents/inaugural-address-11.

2. Ronald Reagan, "Remarks at the annual meeting of the boards of governors of the World Bank Group and International Monetary Fund, delivered on September 29, 1981, Washington, D.C.," https://www.presidency.ucsb.edu/documents/remarks-the -annual-meeting-the-boards-governors-the-world-bank-group-and-international.

3. Daniel T. Rodgers, *Age of Fracture* (Cambridge, Mass.: Belknap Press, 2011), 10. On free market advocacy, see also Angus Burgin, *The Great Persuasion: Reinventing Free Markets Since the Depression* (Cambridge, Mass.: Harvard University Press, 2012); Jennifer Burns, *Goddess of the Market: Ayn Rand and the American Right* (New York: Oxford University Press, 2009). The best account linking market thinking to popular cultural change in this period is James Livingston, *The World Turned Inside Out: American Thought and Culture at the End of the 20th Century* (Plymouth, U.K.: Rowman & Littlefield, 2010).

4. See, in real time, the insightful Viviana A. Zelizer, "Beyond the Polemics on the Market: Establishing a Theoretical and Empirical Agenda," *Sociological Forum* 3, no. 4 (1988): 614–34.

5. J. Jeffery Auer, "Acting Like a President; or, What Has Ronald Reagan Done to Political Speaking?," in Michael Weiler and W. Barnett Pearce, *Reagan and Public Discourse in America* (Tuscaloosa: University of Alabama Press, 1992), 95.

6. Scott Campbell, "Interregional Migration of Defense Scientists and Engineers to the Gunbelt During the 1980s," *Economic Geography* 69, no. 2 (1993): 204–23.

7. George Gilder and Steve Forbes, *Wealth and Poverty* (1981; Washington, D.C.: Regnery, 2012).

8. "Interview with Paul Volcker," Commanding Heights, http://www.pbs.org /wgbh/commandingheights/shared/minitext/int_paulvolcker.html.

9. Ibid.

10. Ibid.

11. Ibid.

12. Thus, the era's move toward "privatization" did not reduce authority; it merely changed the normative terms of its exercise. For this interpretation, and an important

philosophical critique of privatization in general, see Chiara Cordelli, *The Privatized State* (Princeton: Princeton University Press, 2020).

13. Nitsan Chorev, *Remaking U.S. Trade Policy: From Protectionism to Globalization* (Ithaca, N.Y.: Cornell University Press, 2007), 195–209; Saskia Sassen, *Territory, Authority, Rights: From Medieval to Global Assemblages* (Princeton: Princeton University Press, 2006).

14. Peter Conti-Brown, *The Power and Independence of the Federal Reserve* (Princeton: Princeton University Press, 2016). See Robert J. Barro and David B. Gordon, "Rules, Discretion and Reputation in a Model of Monetary Policy," *Journal of Monetary Economics* 12, no. 1 (1983): 101–21.

15. "Interview with Paul Volcker," Commanding Heights.

16. Eswar Prasad, Raghuram Rajan, and Arvind Subramanian, "The Paradox of Capital," *Finance and Development* 44, no. 1 (2007): 1–8.

17. Giovanni Arrighi, *The Long Twentieth Century* (New York: Verso, 1994).

18. Charles S. Maier, *Among Empires: American Ascendancy and Its Predecessors* (Cambridge, Mass.: Harvard University Press, 2006), 208–14.

19. Barry Bluestone and Bennett Harrison, *The Deindustrialization of America: Plant Closings, Community Abandonment, and the Dismantling of Basic Industry* (New York: Basic Books, 1982), 35–41.

20. Edward N. Wolff, *A Century of Wealth in America* (Cambridge, Mass.: Harvard University Press, 2017), 27, fig. 1.11.

21. William Lazonick and Mary O'Sullivan, "Maximizing Shareholder Value: A New Ideology for Corporate Governance," *Economy and Society* 29, no. 1 (2000): 19–20.

22. Perry Mehrling, *Fischer Black and the Revolutionary Idea of Finance* (Hoboken, N.J.: Wiley, 2005), 131, 274.

23. Thomas E. Copeland and Fred J. Weston, *Financial Theory and Corporate Policy* (Boston: Addison Wesley, 1979).

24. Greta R. Krippner, *Capitalizing on Crisis: The Political Origins of the Rise of Finance* (Cambridge, Mass.: Harvard University Press, 2011), 36, fig. 5, 38, fig. 6. I have drawn heavily from Krippner's excellent study throughout this chapter.

25. Christine J. Walley, *Exit Zero: Family and Class in Postindustrial Chicago* (Chicago: University of Chicago Press, 2013), 1, 57.

26. Tracy Neumann, *Remaking the Rust Belt: The Postindustrial Transformation of North America* (Philadelphia: University of Pennsylvania Press, 2016), 86.

27. Milton Rogovin and Michael Frisch, *Portraits in Steel* (Ithaca, N.Y.: Cornell University Press, 1993), 93, 137.

28. Dale A. Hathaway, *Can Workers Have a Voice? The Politics of Deindustrialization in Pittsburgh* (University Park: Pennsylvania State University Press, 1993).

29. Rogovin and Frisch, *Portraits in Steel*, 111, 104.

30. Timothy J. Minchin, *Labor Under Fire: A History of the AFL-CIO Since 1979* (Chapel Hill: University of North Carolina Press, 2017), 58, 70.

31. Joseph A. McCarty, *Collision Course: Ronald Reagan, the Air Traffic Controllers, and the Strike That Changed America* (New York: Oxford University Press, 2011).

32. Robert Brenner, *The Economics of Global Turbulence: The Advanced Capitalist Economies from Long Boom to Long Downturn, 1945–2005* (London: Verso, 2006), 200, fig. 12.1.

33. Jefferson Cowie, *Stayin' Alive: The 1970s and the Last Days of the Working Class* (New York: New Press, 2010), 357–71.

34. Diana B. Henriques, *A First-Class Catastrophe: The Road to Black Monday, the Worst Day in Wall Street History* (New York: Henry Holt, 2017), 81.

35. *FDIC Securities Proposal and Related Issues: Hearings Before the Subcommittee on Telecommunications, Consumer Protection, and Finance of the Committee on Energy and Commerce, House of Representatives*, 98th Cong., 1st sess., June 16 and 28, 1983 (Wash-

ington, D.C.: U.S. Government Printing Office, 1983), 3.

36. Robert Devlin, *Debt and Crisis in Latin America: The Supply Side of the Story* (Princeton: Princeton University Press, 1989), 63.

37. "International Finance: An Interview with Walter B. Wriston," *Fletcher Forum of World Affairs* 8, no. 2 (1984): 249.

38. Board of Governors of the Federal Reserve, "Transcript—Federal Open Market Committee Meeting, June 30–July 1, 1982," 28, 30.

39. Kei-Mu Yi and Jing Zhang, "Understanding Global Trends in Long-run Real Interest Rates," *Economic Perspectives* 41, no. 2 (2017), 1–21.

40. On the 1981 tax cut, see Monica Prasad, *Starving the Beast: Ronald Reagan and the Tax Cut Revolution* (New York: Russell Sage Foundation, 2018).

41. Michael J. Boskin, "Taxation, Saving, and the Rate of Interest," *Journal of Political Economy* 86, no. 2, pt. 2 (1978): S3–27.

42. Joseph White and Aaron Wildavsky, *The Deficit and the Public Interest: The Search for Responsible Budgeting in the 1980s* (Berkeley: University of California Press, 1989), 166, 112; Monica Prasad, *The Politics of Free Markets: The Rise of Neoliberal Economic Policies in Britain, France, Germany, and the United States* (Chicago: University of Chicago Press, 2006), 45–61.

43. Emma Rothschild, "Reagan and the Real America," *New York Review of Books*, February 5, 1981. This essay and others by Rothschild during the 1980s remain the most insightful series of reflections on the Reagan economy—then or since.

44. John O'Connor, "U.S. Social Welfare Policy: The Reagan Record and Legacy," *Journal of Social Policy* 27, no. 1 (1998): 40, 43.

45. Julilly Kohler-Hausmann, *Getting Tough: Welfare and Imprisonment in 1970s America* (Princeton: Princeton University Press, 2017), 164.

46. Loïc Wacquant, *Punishing the Poor: The Neoliberal Government of Social Insecurity* (Durham, N.C.: Duke University Press, 2009).

47. Ronald Reagan, "Executive Order 12329—President's Task Force on Private Sector Initiatives," American Presidency Project, https://www.presidency.ucsb.edu/documents/executive-order-12329-presidents-task-force-private-sector-initiatives. See also Cordelli, *The Privatized State.*

48. Jonathan Levy, "From Fiscal Triangle to Passing Through: Rise of the Nonprofit Corporation," in Naomi R. Lamoreaux and William J. Novak, eds., *Corporations and American Democracy* (Cambridge, Mass.: Harvard University Press, 2017), 213–44.

49. Robert Fitzgerald, *The Rise of the Global Company: Multinationals and the Making of the Modern World* (Cambridge, U.K.: Cambridge University Press, 2015), 482.

50. Emma Rothschild, "The Reagan Economic Legacy," *New York Review of Books*, July 21, 1988.

51. Krippner, *Capitalizing on Crisis*, 39, fig. 7.

52. Maurizio Franzini and Mario Pianta, *Explaining Inequality* (New York: Routledge, 2015), 64–67; William Lazonick, "Labor in the 21st Century: The Top 0.1 Percent and the Disappearing Middle Class," in Christian E. Weller, ed., *Inequality, Uncertainty, and Opportunity: The Varied and Growing Role of Finance in Labor Relations* (Ithaca, N.Y.: Cornell University Press, 2015), 143–94.

53. Rachel E. Dwyer, "The Care Economy? Gender, Economic Restructuring, and Job Polarization in the U.S. Labor Market," *American Sociological Review* 78 (May 2013): 390–416.

54. Rowena Olegario, *The Engine of Enterprise: Credit in America* (Cambridge, Mass.: Harvard University Press, 2016), 183; Wolfgang Streek, *How Will Capitalism End? Essays on a Failing System* (New York: Verso, 2017).

55. Louis Hyman, *Debtor Nation: The History of America in Red Ink* (Princeton: Princeton University Press, 2011), 281–87, fig. 7.3.

56. R. Taggart Murphy, *The Weight of the Yen: How Denial Imperils America's Future and Ruins an Alliance* (New York: Norton, 1996), 88–89.

57. Martin Feldstein, "The Dollar Exchange Rate," Remarks Before the World Affairs Council of Philadelphia, February 29, 1984.

58. Krippner, *Capitalizing on Crisis*, 105–6.

59. The only 1980s qualification to the postwar "business judgment rule" was the "Revlon doctrine," or that when selling corporations, boards of directors have fiduciary duties to sell to the highest bidder. William T. Allen, "Engaging Corporate Boards: The Limits of Liability Rules in Modern Corporate Governance," in Cynthia A. Williams and Peer Zumbansen, eds., *The Embedded Firm: Corporate Governance, Labor, and Finance Capitalism* (New York: Cambridge University Press, 2011), 98.

60. Johan Heilbron, Jochem Verheul, and Sander Quak, "The Origins and Early Diffusion of 'Shareholder Value' in the United States," *Theory and Society* 43, no. 1 (2014): 12.

61. Rita Kosnik, "Greenmail: A Study of Board Performance in Corporate Governance," *Administrative Science Quarterly* 32 (June 1987): 163–85.

62. In 1979 the Department of Labor, interpreting the Employment Retirement Income Security Act (ERISA) of 1974, applied the "Prudent Man Rule" to pensions' investment portfolios, making greater equity investments possible.

63. Henriques, *First-Class Catastrophe*, 173, 202, 102–20.

64. Heilbron, Verheul, and Quak, "Origins and Early Diffusion," 15; Frank Dobbin and Jiwook Jung, "Finance and Institutional Investors," in Karin Knorr Cetina and Alex Preda, eds., *The Oxford Handbook of the Sociology of Finance* (New York: Oxford University Press, 2012), 52–74.

65. Lina M. Khan, "Amazon's Antitrust Paradox," *Yale Law Journal* 126, no. 3 (2017): 721.

66. Marc Allen Eisner, *Antitrust and the Triumph of Economics: Institutions, Expertise, and Policy Change* (Chapel Hill: University of North Carolina Press, 1991).

67. Neil Fligstein, *The Architecture of Markets: An Economic Sociology of Twenty-First-Century Capitalist Societies* (Princeton: Princeton University Press, 2001), 154.

68. George Anders, *Merchants of Debt: KKR and the Mortgaging of American Business* (New York: Basic Books, 1992).

69. Frank Dobbin and Dirk Zorn, "Corporate Malfeasance and the Myth of Shareholder Value," in Diane E. Davis, ed., *Political Power and Social Theory* (Bingley, U.K.: Emerald Group, 2005), 179–98.

70. Fligstein, *Architecture of Markets*, 167.

71. Robert A. Taggart, Jr., "The Growth of the 'Junk' Bond Market and Its Role in Financing Takeovers," in Alan J. Auerbach, ed., *Mergers and Acquisitions* (Chicago: University of Chicago Press, 1988), 5–24.

72. Bryan Burrough and John Helyar, *Barbarians at the Gate: The Fall of RJR Nabisco* (1989; New York: HarperBusiness Essentials, 2009).

73. Ibid., 87, 505.

74. Wage dispersion among workers with the same education, for instance, explained more of the variance in labor income inequality than education levels. Franzini and Pianta, *Explaining Inequality*, 36.

75. Jeffrey G. Madrick, *Age of Greed: The Triumph of Finance, and the Decline of America, 1970 to the Present* (New York: Knopf, 2011), 89.

76. Bret Easton Ellis, *American Psycho* (New York: Vintage, 1991).

77. Marion Fourcade and Rakesh Khurana, "The Social Trajectory of a Finance Professor and the Common Sense of Capital," *History of Political Economy* 49, no. 2 (2017): 347–81.

78. Michael C. Jensen and William H. Meckling, "Theory of the Firm: Managerial

Behavior, Agency Costs, and Ownership Structure," *Journal of Financial Economics* 3, no. 4 (1976): 305–60.

79. Krippner, *Capitalizing on Crisis*, 56.

80. Donald MacKenzie, *An Engine, Not a Camera: How Financial Models Shape Markets* (Cambridge, Mass.: MIT Press, 2006).

81. Michael C. Jensen, "Takeovers: Their Causes and Consequences," *Journal of Economic Perspectives* 2, no. 1 (1988): 21–48.

82. Wolff, *Century of Wealth in America*, 27, fig. 1.11.

83. Lazonick and O'Sullivan, "Maximizing Shareholder Value," 23, 25.

84. Lawrence H. Summers, "Does the Stock Market Rationally Reflect Fundamental Values?," *Journal of Finance* 41, no. 3 (1986): 591–601.

85. Krippner, *Capitalizing on Crisis*, 33, fig. 3, 36, fig. 5.

86. Fredric Jameson, "Postmodernism, or the Cultural Logic of Late Capitalism," *New Left Review* 1, no. 146 (1984): 53–92.

87. Jonathan Levy, "Accounting for Profit and the History of Capital," *Critical Historical Studies* 1, no. 2 (2014): 171–214.

88. Mackenzie, *Engine, Not Camera*.

89. Leatrice Eiseman and Keith Recker, *Pantone: The Twentieth Century in Color* (San Francisco: Chronicle Books, 2011), 152–71.

90. Rothschild, "Reagan Economic Legacy."

91. Robert J. Gordon, *The Rise and Fall of American Growth: The U.S. Standard of Living Since the Civil War* (Princeton: Princeton University Press, 2016), 547, fig. 16-5.

92. Murphy, *Weight of the Yen*, 258–62.

93. Joe Feagin, *Free Enterprise City: Houston in Political-Economic Perspective* (New Brunswick, N.J.: Rutgers University Press, 1988).

94. Michael Kranish and Marc Fisher, *Trump Revealed: An American Journey of Ambition, Ego, Money, and Power* (New York: Scribner, 2016), 193.

95. Donald Trump and Tony Schwartz, *Trump: The Art of the Deal* (New York: Random House, 1987), 58.

96. David Geltner, "Commercial Real Estate and the 1990–1 Recession in the United States," Korea Development Institute, 2013, https://mitcre.mit.edu/wp-content/uploads/2013/10/Commercial_Real_Estate_and_the_1990–91_Recession_in_the_US.pdf.

97. C. Eugene Steuerle, *Tax Decade: How Taxes Came to Dominate the Public Agenda* (Washington, D.C.: Urban Institute Press, 1992), 39–56.

98. Aaron Major, "The New Capitalist Rich: Corporate Organizational Form and the Political Economy of U.S. Income Inequality," *Critical Historical Studies* 5, no. 2 (2018): 209–36.

99. Robert McIntyre, *Money for Nothing: The Failure of Corporate Tax Incentives 1981–1984* (Washington, D.C.: Citizens for Tax Justice, 1986).

100. Kitty Calavita, Henry N. Pontell, and Robert Tillman, *Big Money Crime: Fraud and Politics in the Savings and Loan Crisis* (Berkeley: University of California Press, 1997), 10–12.

101. Geltner, "Commercial Real Estate," 24.

102. Calavita, Pontell, and Tillman, *Big Money Crime*, 26.

103. Ibid., 43.

104. William J. Collins and Robert A. Margo, "The Economic Aftermath of the 1960s Riots in American Cities: Evidence from Property Values," *Journal of Economic History* 67, no. 4 (2007): 849–83.

105. William Julius Wilson, *When Work Disappears: The World of the New Urban Poor* (New York: Knopf, 1996).

106. John Clegg and Adaner Usmani, "The Economic Origins of Mass Incarcera-

tion," *Catalyst* 3, no. 3 (2019): 9–53.

107. Wacquant, *Punishing the Poor,* 65.

108. Levy, "From Fiscal Triangle," 237–38.

109. Loïc J. D. Wacquant, *Urban Outcasts: A Comparative Sociology of Advanced Marginality* (New York: Polity, 2008).

110. Clegg and Usmani, "The Economic Origins of Mass Incarceration," 11.

111. Rogovin and Frisch, *Portraits in Steel,* 191.

112. Keith Wailoo, *Pain: A Political History* (Baltimore: Johns Hopkins University Press, 2014), 98–100, 122.

113. Gabriel Winant, *Crucible of Care: The Rise of Healthcare and the Origins of a New Working Class* (Cambridge, Mass.: Harvard University Press, forthcoming 2021).

114. Bethany Moreton, *To Serve God and Wal-Mart: The Making of Christian Free Enterprise* (Cambridge, Mass.: Harvard University Press, 2009); Arlie Russell Hochschild, *The Managed Heart: Commercialization of Human Feeling* (1983; Berkeley: University of California Press, 2003); Viviana A. Zelizer, *Economic Lives: How Culture Shapes the Economy* (Princeton: Princeton University Press, 2010), 275–87.

115. Ruth Milkman, *Farewell to the Factory: Auto Workers in the Late Twentieth Century* (Berkeley: University of California Press, 1997), 3, 119.

116. Claudia Goldin and Lawrence F. Katz, *The Race Between Education and Technology* (Cambridge, Mass.: Belknap Press, 2008), 119–21.

117. Eileen Boris and Jennifer Klein, *Caring for America: Home Health Workers in the Shadow of the Welfare State* (New York: Oxford University Press, 2012), 86–87.

118. Ruth Milkman, *On Gender, Labor, and Inequality* (Urbana: University of Illinois Press, 2016), 199, 200.

119. Hal Foster, *Bad New Days: Art, Criticism, Emergency* (New York: Verso, 2015).

120. Jeffrey Frankel, "The Plaza Accord, 30 Years Later," National Bureau of Economic Research, Working Paper no. 21813 (December 2015), 2, 11.

121. Brenner, *Economics of Global Turbulence,* 206.

122. Nicholas Foster, " 'Green Corn Gleaming': Free Markets, Agrarian Myths, Agriculture, and American Political Economy in the 1980s" (master's thesis, University of Chicago, 2017).

123. Henriques, *First-Class Catastrophe,* 179.

124. "A Study of the Effects on the Economy of Trading in Futures Options," Board of Governors of the Federal Reserve System, the Commodity Futures Trading Commission, and the Securities and Exchange Commission (1984), I2.

125. Henriques, *First-Class Catastrophe,* 179, 239–40, 255.

126. Calavita, Pontell, and Tillman, *Big Money Crime,* 147.

127. Ben Bernanke and Cara S. Lown, "The Credit Crunch," *Brookings Papers on Economic Activity* 22, no. 2 (1991): 205–48; Olivier Blanchard, "Consumption and the Recession of 1990–1991," *American Economic Review* 83, no. 2 (1993): 270–74.

128. Stephen Kotkin, "The Kiss of Debt: The East Bloc Goes Borrowing," in Niall Ferguson et al., eds., *The Shock of the Global: The 1970s in Perspective* (Cambridge, Mass.: Harvard University Press, 2010), 80–96.

129. Claudia Goldin, "A Grand Gender Convergence: Its Last Chapter," *American Economic Review* 104, no. 4 (2014): 1091–119.

130. Chang-Tai Hsieh, Erik Hurst, Charles I. Jones, and Peter J. Klenow, "The Allocation of Talent and U.S. Economic Growth," *Econometrica* 87, no. 5 (2019): 1439–74.

131. Gordon, *Rise and Fall of American Growth,* 547, fig. 16-5.

132. Thomas Philippon, *The Great Reversal: How America Gave Up on Free Markets* (Cambridge, Mass.: Belknap Press, 2019), 207–22.

133. The tightening of labor markets during the macroeconomic expansion halted the rise in pay inequality in 1984, but just for a few years, before succumbing to the

era's general trend. Peter H. Lindert and Jeffrey G. Williamson, *Unequal Gains: American Growth and Inequality Since 1700* (Princeton: Princeton University Press, 2016), 220; Thomas Piketty, *Capital in the Twenty-First Century*, trans. Arthur Goldhammer (Cambridge, Mass.: Harvard University Press, 2014). But the post-1982 macroeconomic expansion featured the greatest sudden run-up in wealth inequality in all of U.S. history. The lever was asset price appreciation, or capital gains, which accounted for an estimated 80 percent of the new distribution. See James K. Galbraith, *Inequality and Instability: A Study of the World Economy Just Before the Great Crisis* (New York: Oxford University Press, 2012), 124; Wolff, *Century of Wealth in America*, 661.

134.   Milkman, *Farewell to Factory*, 121, 130, 197.

135.   Rogovin and Frisch, *Portraits in Steel*, 97.

CHAPTER 20: THE NEW ECONOMY

1.   Francis Fukuyama, *The End of History and the Last Man* (1992; New York: Free Press, 2006).

2.   James Champy, *Reengineering Management: The Mandate for New Leadership* (New York: HarperBusiness, 1995), 9.

3.   Alan Greenspan, "An Update on Economic Conditions in the United States," testimony before the Joint Economic Committee, U.S. Congress, June 10, 1998, https://www.federalreserve.gov/boarddocs/testimony/1998/19980610.htm.

4.   Lawrence H. Summers, "The New Wealth of Nations: Lessons from the 1990s," *Bulletin of the American Academy of Arts and Sciences* 53, no. 2 (1999): 32.

5.   William J. Clinton, "Remarks to the COMDEX 2000 Spring Conference in Chicago, Illinois," April 18, 2000, American Presidency Project, https://www.presidency.ucsb.edu/documents/remarks-the-comdex-2000-spring-conference-chicago-illinois.

6.   David Friend, *The Naughty Nineties: The Triumph of the American Libido* (New York: Twelve, 2017), 533.

7.   Daniel T. Rodgers, *Age of Fracture* (Cambridge, Mass.: Belknap Press, 2011).

8.   Douglas S. Massey, Jorge Durand, and Nolan J. Malone, *Beyond Smoke and Mirrors: Mexican Immigration in an Era of Economic Integration* (New York: Russell Sage Foundation, 2002).

9.   Greenspan, "Update on Economic Conditions."

10.   Robert J. Gordon, *The Rise and Fall of American Growth: The U.S. Standard of Living Since the Civil War* (Princeton: Princeton University Press, 2016), 547, fig. 16-5.

11.   John Clegg and Adaner Usmani, "The Economic Origins of Mass Incarceration," *Catalyst* 3, no. 3 (2019): 9–53.

12.   Alan Greenspan, "Remarks at the Annual Dinner and Francis Boyer Lecture of the American Enterprise Institute for Public Policy Research," Washington, D.C., December 5, 1996, https://www.federalreserve.gov/boarddocs/speeches/1996/19961205.htm.

13.   Bruce Cumings, *Dominion from Sea to Sea: Pacific Ascendancy and American Power* (New Haven: Yale University Press, 2009), 471–76, 424–27.

14.   Margaret O'Mara, *The Code: Silicon Valley and the Remaking of America* (New York: Penguin Press, 2019).

15.   John Padgett and Walter Powell, *The Emergence of Organizations and Markets* (Princeton: Princeton University Press, 2012), 376.

16.   Leslie Berlin, *Troublemakers: Silicon Valley's Coming of Age* (New York: Simon & Schuster, 2017), 147, 294.

17.   Ibid., 7–10.

18.   Janet Abbate, *Inventing the Internet* (Cambridge, Mass.: MIT Press, 1999), 56.

19.   Michael A. Hiltzik, *Dealers of Lightning: Xerox PARC and the Dawn of the Com-*

puter Age (New York: HarperBusiness, 1999), 48–51.

20. Leslie Berlin, *The Man Behind the Microchip: Robert Noyce and the Invention of Silicon Valley* (New York: Oxford University Press, 2005), 82–93, 164.

21. Cyrus C. M. Mody, *The Long Arm of Moore's Law: Microelectronics and American Science* (Cambridge, Mass.: MIT Press, 2016).

22. Hiltzik, *Dealers of Lightning*, 163–77, 273.

23. Walter Isaacson, *Steve Jobs* (New York: Simon & Schuster, 2011), 21–28, 81; Cumings, *Dominion from Sea to Sea*, 449.

24. Andy Hertzfeld, *Revolution in the Valley: The Insanely Great Story of How the Mac Was Made* (Sebastopol, Calif.: O'Reilly Media, 2004), 192.

25. Isaacson, *Steve Jobs*, 102–4.

26. Berlin, *Troublemakers*, 198–202, 255, 366.

27. Cumings, *Dominion from Sea to Sea*, 450.

28. Berlin, *Troublemakers*, 258.

29. Abbate, *Inventing the Internet*, 214–17; Manuel Castells, *The Internet Galaxy: Reflections on the Internet, Business, and Society* (New York: Oxford University Press, 2001), 9–65.

30. Michael Lewis, *The New New Thing: A Silicon Valley Story* (New York: Norton, 1999), 44, 81, 83, 112, 84.

31. Jim Clark and Owen Edwards, *Netscape Time: The Making of the Billion-Dollar Start-Up That Took On Microsoft* (New York: St. Martin's Press, 1999), 251.

32. Loïc Wacquant, *Punishing the Poor: The Neoliberal Government of Social Insecurity* (Durham, N.C.: Duke University Press, 2009), 57–67.

33. Jeff Pellin, "Yahoo Tempers Investor Euphoria," CNET, May 16, 1997.

34. Joan A. Rigdon, "Yahoo! IPO Soars in First Day, but Honeymoon May Not Last," *Wall Street Journal*, April 15, 1996.

35. An insider's account is David A. Vise and Mark Malseed, *The Google Story* (New York: Delacorte Press, 2005).

36. Berlin, *Troublemakers*, xv.

37. Friend, *Naughty Nineties*, 175.

38. Ibid., 185. Amazon.com Annual Report, 2000, 20, https://ir.aboutamazon.com/static-files/49b9a96d-f5ce-4695-a9a1-70eb8ffd3b87.

39. Ibid., 174; Michael Wolff, *Net Guide: Your Complete Guide to the Internet and Online Services* (New York: Random House, 1995).

40. Nitin Nohria, Davis Dyer, and Frederick Dalzell, *Changing Fortunes: Remaking the Industrial Corporation* (New York: Wiley, 2002), 23.

41. Walter Powell, "Neither Market Nor Hierarchy: Network Forms of Organization," *Research in Organizational Behavior* 12 (January 1990): 295–336.

42. Naomi R. Lamoreaux, Daniel M.G. Raff, and Peter Temin, "Beyond Markets and Hierarchies: Towards a New Synthesis of American Business History," *American Historical Review* 108, no. 2 (2003): 404–33.

43. Castells, *Internet Galaxy*, 70.

44. Paul Schreyer, "Computer Price Indices and International Growth and Productivity Comparisons," *Review of Income and Wealth* 48, no. 1 (2002): 15–31.

45. Castells, *Internet Galaxy*, 74–75.

46. Paul DiMaggio, ed., *The Twenty-First-Century Firm: Changing Economic Organization in International Perspective* (Princeton: Princeton University Press, 2001).

47. Richard Applebaum, "Big Suppliers in Greater China: A Growing Counterweight to the Power of Giant Retailers," in Ho-fung Hung, ed., *China and the Transformation of Global Capitalism* (Baltimore: Johns Hopkins University Press, 2009), 65–85.

48. Bethany Moreton, *To Serve God and Wal-Mart: The Making of Christian Free Enterprise* (Cambridge, Mass.: Harvard University Press, 2009).

49. Thomas J. Adams, "Making the New Shop Floor: Wal-Mart, Labor Control, and the History of the Postwar Discount Retail Industry in America," in Nelson Lichtenstein, ed., *Wal-Mart: The Face of Twenty-First-Century Capitalism* (New York: New Press, 2006), 213–29.

50. Nelson Lichtenstein, *The Retail Revolution: How Wal-Mart Created a Brave New World of Business* (New York: Henry Holt, 2009), 5–6.

51. Susanto Basu, John Fernald, Nicholas Oulton, and S. Srinivasan, "The Case of Missing Productivity Growth; or, Does Information Technology Explain Why Productivity Accelerated in the US but Not in the UK?," National Bureau of Economic Research, Working Paper no. 10010 (October 2003).

52. On temp work in general, see Louis Hyman, *Temp: How American Work, American Business, and the American Dream Became Temporary* (New York: Viking, 2018).

53. Castells, *Internet Galaxy*, 95–96.

54. "Don't Go Away Mad, Just Go Away," *New York Times*, February 13, 1996.

55. T. C. Melewar and S. F. Syed Alwi, eds., *Corporate Branding: Areas, Arenas and Approaches* (London: Routledge, 2015), 37.

56. Nohria, Dyer, and Dalzell, *Changing Fortunes*, 208, 217–18.

57. Nikil Saval, *Cubed: A Secret History of the Workplace* (New York: Doubleday, 2014), 183–255.

58. Alexandra Lange, *The Dot-Com City: Silicon Valley Urbanism* (Moscow: Strelka Press, 2014); Hal Foster, *The Art-Architecture Complex* (New York: Verso, 2013).

59. John P. Kotter, *The New Rules: How to Succeed in Today's Post-Corporate World* (New York: Free Press, 1995), 81, 181.

60. Gina Neff, *Venture Labor: Work and the Burden of Risk in Innovative Industries* (Cambridge, Mass.: MIT Press, 2012), 35.

61. Michel Feher, "Self-Appreciation; or, The Aspirations of Human Capital," *Public Culture* 21, no. 1 (2009): 21–41.

62. Studs Terkel, *Working: People Talk About What They Do All Day and How They Feel About What They Do* (New York: Pantheon, 1974), 2.

63. Ben Mezrich, *The Accidental Billionaires: The Founding of Facebook* (New York: Anchor, 2010), 249.

64. Barbara Ehrenreich and Arlie Russell Hochshild, eds., *Global Woman: Nannies, Maids, and Sex Workers in the New Economy* (New York: Owl Books, 2002), 90, 262; Erin Hatton, *The Temp Economy: From Kelly Girls to Permatemps in Postwar America* (Philadelphia: Temple University Press, 2011).

65. Nelson Lichtenstein, *State of the Union: A Century of American Labor* (Princeton: Princeton University Press, 2002), 246–76.

66. Preston Rudy, " 'Justice for Janitors,' not 'Compensation for Custodians': The Political Context and Organizing in San Jose and Sacramento," in Ruth Milkman and Kim Voss, eds., *Rebuilding Labor: Organizing and Organizers in the New Union Movement* (Ithaca, N.Y.: Cornell University Press, 2004), 138–41.

67. Sean Wilentz, *The Age of Reagan: A History, 1974–2008* (New York: Harper, 2008), 323–54.

68. Robert E. Rubin and Jacob Weisberg, *In an Uncertain World: Tough Choices from Wall Street to Washington* (New York: Random House, 2003).

69. Bob Woodward, *The Agenda: Inside the Clinton White House* (New York: Simon & Schuster, 1994), 139.

70. Joseph E. Stiglitz, *The Roaring Nineties: A New History of the World's Most Prosperous Decade* (New York: Norton, 2003), 3–55.

71. Kei-Mu Yi and Jing Zhang, "Real Interest Rates over the Long Run," Federal Reserve Bank of Minneapolis, Economic Policy Paper no. 16–10 (September 19, 2016),

https://www.minneapolisfed.org/research/economic-policy-papers/real-interest-rates
-over-the-long-run.

72. On the Fed as an institution larger than any one personality, see Peter Conti-Brown, *The Power and Independence of the Federal Reserve* (Princeton: Princeton University Press, 2016).

73. Nitsan Chorev, *Remaking U.S. Trade Policy: From Protectionism to Globalization* (Ithaca, N.Y.: Cornell University Press, 2007).

74. Massey, Durand, and Malone, *Beyond Smoke and Mirrors*, 20.

75. Rubin and Weisberg, *In an Uncertain World*, 216.

76. Sebastian Edwards and Miguel A. Savastano, "The Mexican Peso in the Aftermath of the 1994 Currency Crisis," in Paul Krugman, ed., *Currency Crises* (Chicago: University of Chicago Press, 2000), 183–240.

77. Robert Brenner, *The Economics of Global Turbulence: The Advanced Capitalist Economies from Long Boom to Long Downturn, 1945–2005* (London: Verso, 2006), 261.

78. Germany was still economically achieving post–Cold War reunification, while the Japanese economy was in a post-real-estate-and-financial-bubble liquidity trap.

79. Rubin and Weisberg, *In an Uncertain World*, 183.

80. William J. Clinton, "Address Before a Joint Session of the Congress on the State of the Union," January 23, 1996, American Presidency Project, https://www.presidency
.ucsb.edu/documents/address-before-joint-session-the-congress-the-state-the-union-10.

81. Felicia Kornbluh and Gwendolyn Mink, *Ensuring Poverty: Welfare Reform in Feminist Perspective* (Philadelphia: University of Pennsylvania Press, 2019), x, 130, 113.

82. Tim Wu, *The Master Switch: The Rise and Fall of Information Empires* (New York: Knopf, 2010), 243–48.

83. Steven Olley and Ariel Pakes, "The Dynamics of Productivity in the Telecommunications Equipment Industry," *Econometrica* 64, no. 6 (1996): 1263.

84. Lina M. Khan, "Amazon's Antitrust Paradox," *Yale Law Journal* 126, no. 3 (2017): 717–36.

85. Telecommunications Act of 1996, Pub. LA. No. 104–104, 110 Stat. 56 (1996), https://www.fcc.gov/general/telecommunications-act-1996.

86. Timothy J. Yeager, Fred C. Yeager, and Ellen Harshman, "The Financial Services Modernization Act: Evolution or Revolution?," *Journal of Economics and Business* 4, no. 59 (2007): 313–39.

87. Stanley Fischer, "Capital Account Liberalization and the Role of the IMF," IMF Seminar, September 19, 1997.

88. Sven Beckert, "American Danger: United States Empire, Euroafrica, and the Territorialization of Industrial Capitalism, 1870–1950," *American Historical Review* 122, no. 4 (2017): 1137–70.

89. Saskia Sassen, *The Global City: New York, London, Tokyo* (Princeton: Princeton University Press, 1991).

90. Saskia Sassen, *Territory, Authority, Rights: From Medieval to Global Assemblages* (Princeton: Princeton University Press, 2006), 234–36.

91. Branko Milanovic, *Global Inequality: A New Approach for the Age of Globalization* (Cambridge, Mass.: Belknap Press, 2016).

92. See M. Ayhan Kose et al., "Financial Globalization: A Reappraisal," *IMF Staff Papers* 56, no. 1 (2009): 10; Dani Rodrik and Arvind Subramanian, "Why Did Financial Globalization Disappoint?," *IMF Staff Papers* 56, no. 1 (2009): 112–38.

93. Paul R. Krugman, "It's Baaack: Japan's Slump and the Return of the Liquidity Trap," *Brookings Papers on Economic Activity* 2 (1998): 137–205.

94. Andrew Sheng, *From Asian to Global Financial Crisis: An Asian Regulator's View*

of Unfettered Finance in the 1990s and 2000s (New York: Cambridge University Press, 2009), 51, 62.

95. Ibid., 21–22.

96. Ibid., 7, 24, 31, 35–36, 41–43; Manuela Moschella, *Governing Risk: The IMF and Global Financial Crises* (New York: Palgrave Macmillan, 2010), 111, 101.

97. Axel Leijonhufvud and Earlene Craver, "Reform and the Fate of Russia," Documents de Travail de l'OFCE 2001-03, Observatoire français des conjonctures économiques, 2001.

98. Roger Lowenstein, *When Genius Failed: The Rise and Fall of Long-Term Capital Management* (New York: Random House, 2000), 153.

99. Ibid., 37, 4.

100. Fischer Black and Myron Scholes, "The Pricing of Options and Corporate Liabilities," *Journal of Political Economy* 81, no. 3 (1973): 637–54.

101. Lowenstein, *When Genius Failed*, 39.

102. Donald MacKenzie, *An Engine, Not a Camera: How Financial Models Shape Markets* (Cambridge, Mass.: MIT Press, 2006).

103. Lowenstein, *When Genius Failed*, 75.

104. Ibid., 195–207.

105. John Cassidy, *Dot.Con: The Greatest Story Ever Sold* (New York: Harper, 2002), 188.

106. Rawi Abdelal, *Capital Rules: The Construction of Global Finance* (Cambridge, Mass.: Harvard University Press, 2007), 123–61.

107. Richard C. Koo, *Balance Sheet Recession: Japan's Struggle with Uncharted Economics and Its Global Implications* (New York: Wiley, 2003).

108. Richard Duncan, *The Dollar Crisis: Causes, Consequences, Cures* (Hoboken: Wiley, 2005), 47, tables 3.1, 3.2.

109. James Glassman and Kevin Hassett, *Dow 36,000: The New Strategy for Profiting from the Coming Rise in the Stock Market* (New York: Times Books, 1999), 9.

110. Roger Lowenstein, *Origins of the Crash: The Great Bubble and Its Undoing* (New York: Penguin, 2004), 115.

111. Cassidy, *Dot.Con*, 222.

112. Alan Greenspan, "New Challenges for Monetary Policy," remarks before a symposium sponsored by the Federal Reserve Bank of Kansas City, Jackson Hole, Wyo., August 27, 1999.

113. Alan Greenspan, "High-tech Industry in the U.S. Economy," testimony before the Joint Economic Committee, U.S. Congress, June 14, 1999.

CHAPTER 21: THE GREAT MODERATION

1. Ben Bernanke, "Remarks at the Meetings of the Eastern Economic Association," Washington, D.C., February 20, 2004, https://www.federalreserve.gov/boarddocs/speeches/2004/20040220/.

2. Thomas Piketty, Emmanuel Saez, and Gabriel Zucman, "Distributional National Accounts: Methods and Estimates for the United States," *Quarterly Journal of Economics* 133, no. 2 (2018): 553–609.

3. Gilbert Cette, John Fernald, and Benoît Mojon, "The Pre–Great Recession Slowdown in Productivity," *European Economic Review* 88 (September 2016): 3–20.

4. Thomas Philippon, *The Great Reversal: How America Gave Up on Free Markets* (Cambridge, Mass.: Belknap Press, 2019), 63–64.

5. Adam Tooze, *Crashed: How a Decade of Financial Crises Changed the World* (New York: Penguin, 2018).

6. Branko Milanovic, *Global Inequality: A New Approach for the Age of Globalization* (Cambridge, Mass.: Belknap Press, 2016).

7. Tooze, *Crashed*.

8. Paul R. Krugman, "It's Baaack: Japan's Slump and the Return of the Liquidity Trap," *Brookings Papers on Economic Activity* 2 (1998): 137–205.

9. Raghuram G. Rajan, *Fault Lines: How Hidden Fractures Still Threaten the World Economy* (Princeton: Princeton University Press, 2010), 219.

10. Ben S. Bernanke, "The Global Saving Glut and the U.S. Current Account Deficit," remarks at the Sandridge Lecture, Virginia Association of Economists, Richmond, Va., March 10, 2005, https://www.federalreserve.gov/boarddocs/speeches/2005/200503102/default.htm.

11. Raghuram G. Rajan, "Investment Restraint, the Liquidity Glut, and Global Imbalances," remarks at the conference on Global Imbalances organized by the Bank of Indonesia, Bali, November 16, 2006, https://www.imf.org/en/News/Articles/2015/09/28/04/53/sp111506.

12. Robert Brenner, "New Boom or New Bubble?," *New Left Review* 25 (January–February 2004): 57.

13. Ibid., 65.

14. P. Lenain and S. Paltridge, "After the Telecommunications Bubble," OECD Economics Department, Working Papers no. 361 (2003), http://dx.doi.org/10.1787/311813664474.

15. Robert Brenner, "Towards the Precipice," *London Review of Books* 25, no. 3 (2003): 18–23. Brenner's article is the most insightful and prescient piece of economic analysis in the run-up to the Great Recession of which I am aware.

16. Robert Brenner, *The Boom and the Bubble: The U.S. in the World Economy* (New York: Verso, 2002), 292.

17. Robert W. Crandall, *Competition and Chaos: U.S. Telecommunications Since the 1996 Telecom Act* (Washington, D.C.: Brookings, 2005).

18. On Enron, see Gavin Benke, *Risk and Ruin: Enron and the Culture of American Capitalism* (Philadelphia: University of Pennsylvania Press, 2018); Bethany McLean and Peter Elkind, *Smartest Guys in the Room: The Amazing Rise and Scandalous Fall of Enron* (New York: Portfolio, 2003).

19. Benke, *Risk and Ruin*, 29, 51–58, 23, 89, 125–30.

20. Bethany McLean, "Is Enron Overpriced? It's in a Bunch of Complex Businesses. Its Financial Statements Are Nearly Impenetrable. So Why Is Enron Trading at Such a Huge Multiple?," *Fortune*, March 5, 2001.

21. Benke, *Risk and Ruin*, 180.

22. Ibid., 173.

23. Jesse Eisinger, *The Chickenshit Club: Why the Justice Department Fails to Prosecute Executives* (New York: Simon & Schuster, 2017).

24. Ron Suskind, *The Price of Loyalty: George W. Bush, the White House, and the Education of Paul O'Neill* (New York: Simon & Schuster, 2004), 291.

25. For a brilliant philosophical account of privatization, see Chiara Cordelli, *The Privatized State* (Princeton: Princeton University Press, 2020).

26. Linda J. Bilmes and Joseph E. Stiglitz, *The Three Trillion Dollar War: The True Cost of the Iraq Conflict* (New York: Norton, 2008).

27. Thomas L. Friedman, *The World Is Flat: A Brief History of the Twenty-First Century* (New York: Farrar, Straus & Giroux, 2005).

28. Enrico Moretti, *The New Geography of Jobs* (Boston: Houghton Mifflin Harcourt, 2012), 50–61.

29. Howard Wial, Susan Helper, and Timothy Krueger, "Locating American Manufacturing: Trends in the Geography of Production," *Brookings Report* (April 2012), 10.

30. Philippon, *Great Reversal*, 43.

31. Lina M. Khan, "Amazon's Antitrust Paradox," *Yale Law Journal* 126, no. 3

(2017): 564–907; Brad Stone, *The Everything Store: Jeff Bezos and the Age of Amazon* (New York: Little, Brown, 2013).

32. Shoshana Zuboff, *The Age of Surveillance Capitalism: The Fight for a Human Future at the New Frontier of Power* (New York: PublicAffairs, 2019), 63–127.

33. Ibid., 87.

34. For a positive take, see Jorge Guzman and Scott Stern, "The State of American Entrepreneurship: New Estimates of the Quality and Quantity of Entrepreneurship for 32 US States, 1988–2014," National Bureau of Economic Research, Working Paper no. 22095 (March 2016). For a negative, see Philippon, *Great Reversal*, 82.

35. Philippon, *Great Reversal*, 75.

36. Antonio García Martínez, *Chaos Monkeys: Obscene Fortune and Random Failure in Silicon Valley* (New York: HarperCollins, 2016).

37. See William H. Page and John E. Lopatka, *The Microsoft Case: Antitrust, High Technology, and Consumer Welfare* (Chicago: University of Chicago Press, 2007).

38. Tim Wu, *The Master Switch: The Rise and Fall of Information Empires* (New York: Knopf, 2010).

39. Khan, "Amazon's Antitrust Paradox."

40. Philippon, *Great Reversal*, 9, 56.

41. Efraim Benmelech, Nittai Bergman, and Hyunseob Kim, "Strong Employers and Weak Employees: How Does Employer Concentration Affect Wages?," National Bureau of Economic Research, Working Paper no. 24307 (February 2018).

42. Luigi Zingales, "Towards a Political Theory of the Firm," *Journal of Economic Perspectives* 31, no. 3 (2017): 113–30.

43. Daron Acemoglu et al., "Import Competition and the Great U.S. Employment Sag of the 2000s," *Journal of Labor Economics* 34, no. S1 (2016): S142–43.

44. Matias Covarrubias, Germán Gutiérrez, and Thomas Philippon, "From Good to Bad Concentration? U.S. Industries over the Past 30 Years," National Bureau of Economic Research, Working Paper no. 25983 (June 2019).

45. Ching Kwan Lee, *Against the Law: Labor Protests in China's Rustbelt and Sunbelt* (Berkeley: University of California Press, 2007).

46. David H. Autor, David Dorn, and Gordon H. Hanson, "The China Shock: Learning from Labor-Market Adjustment to Large Changes in Trade," *Annual Review of Economics* 8, no. 1 (2016): 228, 225, fig. 6.

47. Wial, Helper, and Krueger, "Locating American Manufacturing."

48. Fatih Guvenen, Greg Kaplan, Jae Song, and Justin Weidner, "Lifetime Incomes in the United States over Six Decades," National Bureau of Economic Research, Working Paper no. 23371 (April 2017).

49. Anne Case and Angus Deaton, *Deaths of Despair and the Future of Capitalism* (Princeton: Princeton University Press, 2020), 32, 64–66.

50. John Clegg and Adaner Usmani, "The Economic Origins of Mass Incarceration," *Catalyst* 3, no. 3 (2019): 14.

51. Hanna Rosin, *The End of Men: And the Rise of Women* (New York: Riverhead Books, 2012).

52. Ellen Willis, "Our Mobsters, Ourselves," *Nation*, March 15, 2001.

53. Bill Bishop, *The Big Sort: Why the Clustering of Like-Minded America Is Tearing Us Apart* (Boston: Houghton Mifflin Harcourt, 2008).

54. Bill Taylor, "Great People Are Overrated," *Harvard Business Review*, June 20, 2011.

55. Alexandra Lange, *The Dot-Com City: Silicon Valley Urbanism* (Moscow: Strelka Press, 2014).

56. George Saunders, "Jon," *New Yorker*, January 27, 2003.

57. Financial Crisis Inquiry Commission, *The Financial Crisis Inquiry Report: Final*

Report of the National Commission on the Causes of the Financial and Economic Crisis in the United States (Illinois: BN Publishing, 2011), 53.

58. On consolidation in finance, see Robert DeYoung, Douglas Evanoff, and Philip Molyneaux, "Mergers and Acquisitions of Financial Institutions: A Review of the Post-2000 Literature," *Journal of Financial Services Research* 36, no. 2 (2009): 87–110.

59. John V. Duca, John Muellbauer, and Anthony Murphy, "Housing Markets and the Financial Crisis of 2007–2009: Lessons for the Future," *Journal of Financial Stability* 6, no. 4 (2010): 203–17.

60. Chris Mayer, "Housing Bubbles: A Survey," *Annual Review of Economics* 3, no. 1 (2011): 559–77.

61. Alan Greenspan, "The Economic Outlook," testimony before the Joint Economic Committee, U.S. Congress, November 13, 2002.

62. Commission, *Financial Crisis Inquiry Report*, 86, 87.

63. Atif Mian and Amir Sufi, *House of Debt: How They (and You) Caused the Great Recession, and How We Can Prevent It from Happening Again* (Chicago: University of Chicago Press, 2014), 79.

64. R. Martin, "The Local Geographies of the Financial Crisis: From the Housing Bubble to Economic Recession and Beyond," *Journal of Economic Geography* 11, no. 4 (2011): 587–618.

65. Kerwin Kofi Charles, Erik Hurst, and Matthew J. Notowidigdo, "The Masking of the Decline in Manufacturing Employment by the Housing Bubble," *Journal of Economic Perspectives* 30, no. 2 (2016): 179–200.

66. In this account, I have drawn most heavily from the extraordinary resource library of the Financial Crisis Inquiry Commission, https://fcic.law.stanford.edu /resource.

67. Commission, *Financial Crisis Inquiry Report*, 12.

68. Ibid., 113, 71.

69. Ibid., 84, 104, 129.

70. Gillian Tett, *Fool's Gold: How the Bold Dream of a Small Tribe at J. P. Morgan Was Corrupted by Wall Street Greed and Unleashed a Catastrophe* (New York: Free Press, 2009), 96, 61–62.

71. Commission, *Financial Crisis Inquiry Report*, 141, 115, 251.

72. Ibid., 140, 115, 251.

73. Ibid., 140, 141, 132.

74. Melinda Cooper, *Family Values: Between Neoliberalism and the New Social Conservatism* (New York: Zone/Near Futures, 2017).

75. George Packer, *The Unwinding: An Inner History of the New America* (New York: Farrar, Straus & Giroux, 2013), 193.

76. Commission, *Financial Crisis Inquiry Report*, 10.

77. George W. Bush, "Remarks to the National Association of Home Builders in Columbus, Ohio," October 2, 2004, American Presidency Project, https://www.presidency .ucsb.edu/documents/remarks-the-national-association-home-builders-columbus-ohio.

78. Edward N. Wolff, *A Century of Wealth in America* (Cambridge, Mass.: Harvard University Press, 2017), 651–54.

79. Raghuram G. Rajan, "Has Financial Development Made the World Riskier?," presentation at "The Greenspan Era: Lessons for the Future," a symposium sponsored by the Federal Reserve Bank of Kansas City, Jackson Hole, Wyo., August 25–27, 2005 (Federal Reserve Bank of Kansas City, 2005), 313–69.

80. Alan Greenspan, "Federal Reserve Board's Semiannual Monetary Policy Report to the Congress," testimony before the Committee on Banking, Housing, and Urban Affairs, U.S. Senate, February 16, 2005, https://www.federalreserve.gov/boarddocs /hh/2005/february/testimony.htm.

81. Ricardo J. Caballero and Arvind Krishnamurthy, "Global Imbalances and Financial Fragility," *American Economic Review* 99, no. 2 (2009): 584–88.

82. Commission, *Financial Crisis Inquiry Report*, 83.

83. Ben S. Bernanke, Carol Bertaut, Laurie DeMarco, and Steven Kamin, "International Capital Flows and the Returns to Safe Assets in the United States, 2003–2007," *Banque de France Financial Stability Review* 15 (February 2011): 13–26.

84. Branko Milanovic, *Global Inequality: A New Approach for the Age of Globalization* (Cambridge, Mass.: Harvard University Press, 2016).

85. "Has Financial Development Made the World Riskier?," general discussion at "The Greenspan Era: Lessons for the Future," a symposium sponsored by the Federal Reserve Bank of Kansas City, Jackson Hole, Wyo., August 25–27, 2005 (Federal Reserve Bank of Kansas City, 2005), 388.

86. Philippon, *Great Reversal*, 207–22.

87. George Saunders, "My Flamboyant Grandson," *New Yorker*, January 28, 2002.

88. Commission, *Financial Crisis Inquiry Report*, 203.

89. Ibid., xx, 498, 200.

90. Ibid., 217, 18, 221.

91. Michiyo Nakamoto and David Wighton, "Citigroup Chief Stays Bullish on Buy-Outs," *Financial Times*, July 9, 2007.

CHAPTER 22: THE GREAT RECESSION

1. Financial Crisis Inquiry Commission, *The Financial Crisis Inquiry Report: Final Report of the National Commission on the Causes of the Financial and Economic Crisis in the United States* (Illinois: BN Publishing, 2011), xix.

2. Matt Egan, "Ex–Lehman CEO Dick Fuld: At Least My Mom Still Loves Me," CNNMoney, May 28, 2015, https://money.cnn.com/2015/05/28/investing/lehman-brothers-ceo-dick-fuld-comeback-attempt/index.html.

3. Diana Elizabeth Kendall, *Framing Class: Media Representations of Wealth and Poverty in America* (Oxford, U.K.: Rowman & Littlefield, 2005), 79.

4. "Skilling Claims He Knew Nothing," CNNMoney, February 7, 2002, https://money.cnn.com/2002/02/07/news/enron_roundup/.

5. "Greenspan Calls Financial Crisis a 'Credit Tsunami,'" *NPR*, October 23, 2008.

6. Robert E. Lucas, Jr., "Macroeconomic Priorities," *American Economic Review* 93, no. 1 (2003): 1.

7. Brilliantly making this point is Massimo Amato and Luca Fantacci, *The End of Finance* (New York: Polity, 2011).

8. Commission, *Financial Crisis Inquiry Report*, 227.

9. Ibid., 250–51.

10. Neil Irwin, *The Alchemists: Three Central Bankers and a World on Fire* (New York: Penguin, 2013), 2.

11. "FOMC Statement: The Federal Reserve Is Providing Liquidity to Facilitate the Orderly Functioning of Financial Markets," August 10, 2007, https://www.federalreserve.gov/newsevents/pressreleases/monetary20070810a.htm.

12. Commission, *Financial Crisis Inquiry Report*, 424.

13. Tao Wu, "The U.S. Money Market and the Term Auction Facility in the Financial Crisis of 2007–2009," *Review of Economics and Statistics* 93, no. 2 (2011): 619; Stephen G. Cecchetti, "Crisis and Responses: The Federal Reserve in the Early Stages of the Financial Crisis," *Journal of Economic Perspectives* 23, no. 1 (2009): 51–76.

14. Craig Torres and Scott Lanman, "Fed Emergency Borrowers Ranged from GE to McDonald's," *Bloomberg*, December 1, 2010.

15. Irwin, *Alchemists*, 153.

16. The share of dollar-denominated "cross border holdings" increased after 2008. Matteo Maggiori, Brent Neiman, and Jesse Schreger, "International Currencies and Capital Allocation," National Bureau of Economic Research, Working Paper no. 24673 (April 2019).

17. Perry Mehrling, *The New Lombard Street: How the Fed Became the Dealer of Last Resort* (Princeton: Princeton University Press, 2010).

18. Gary B. Gorton, *Slapped by the Invisible Hand: The Panic of 2007* (New York: Oxford University Press, 2010).

19. Michael J. Fleming, Warren B. Hrung, and Frank M. Keane, "Repo Market Effects of the Term Securities Lending Facility," *American Economic Review* 100, no. 2 (2010): 591.

20. On the legality of the Fed's use of Section 13(3), see Eric A. Posner, *Last Resort: The Financial Crisis and the Future of Bailouts* (Chicago: University of Chicago Press, 2018), 55–74.

21. Commission, *Financial Crisis Inquiry Report*, 281.

22. Ibid., 290.

23. Simon Johnson and James Kwak, *13 Bankers: The Wall Street Takeover and the Next Financial Meltdown* (New York: Pantheon, 2010), 208.

24. Andrew Ross Sorkin, *Too Big to Fail: The Inside Story of How Wall Street and Washington Fought to Save the Financial System—and Themselves* (New York: Penguin, 2010), 480.

25. Cecchetti, "Crisis and Responses," 65.

26. Mehrling, *New Lombard Street*, 134.

27. Sorkin, *Too Big to Fail*, 96–98, 210.

28. Bethany McLean, *Shaky Ground: The Strange Saga of the U.S. Mortgage Giants* (New York: Columbia Global Reports, 2015).

29. Commission, *Financial Crisis Inquiry Report*, 321.

30. Ibid., 321, 326, 327, 330.

31. Sorkin, *Too Big to Fail*, 268.

32. Commission, *Financial Crisis Inquiry Report*, 334.

33. Ibid., 335, 337.

34. Sorkin, *Too Big to Fail*, 360.

35. Commission, *Financial Crisis Inquiry Report*, 339.

36. For their own accounts of these events, see Ben S. Bernanke, *The Courage to Act: A Memoir of a Crisis and Its Aftermath* (New York: Norton, 2015), 248–69; Timothy F. Geithner, *Stress Test: Reflections on Financial Crises* (New York: Crown, 2014), 207–10; Henry M. Paulson, *On the Brink: Inside the Race to Stop the Collapse of the Global Financial System* (New York: Business Plus, 2010), 206–28.

37. Commission, *Financial Crisis Inquiry Report*, 342.

38. Ibid., 343, 344–45; Sorkin, *Too Big to Fail*, 339.

39. Commission, *Financial Crisis Inquiry Report*, 345, 376.

40. Sorkin, *Too Big to Fail*, 239.

41. Commission, *Financial Crisis Inquiry Report*, 357–8. On money markets during the crisis, see William A. Birdthistle, "Breaking Bucks in Money Market Funds," *Wisconsin Law Review* 2010, no. 5 (2010): 1155–1201.

42. Ibid., 357.

43. Richard Sutch, "The Liquidity Trap, the Great Depression, and Unconventional Policy: Reading Keynes at the Zero Lower Bound," Berkeley Economic History Laboratory, Working Paper no. 2014-05 (October 2014).

44. Commission, *Financial Crisis Inquiry Report*, 361, 359, 363, 341, 365.

45. Henry M. Paulson, Jr., "Statement on Comprehensive Approach to Market Developments," September 19, 2008, U.S. Department of the Treasury, https://www.treasury.gov/press-center/pressreleases/Pages/hp1149.aspx.

46. Sorkin, *Too Big to Fail*, 443.

47. Paulson, *On the Brink*, 288–99.

48. Marcin Kacperczyk and Philipp Schnabl, "When Safe Proved Risky: Commercial Paper During the Financial Crisis of 2007–2009," *Journal of Economic Perspectives* 24, no. 1 (2010): 44.

49. Commission, *Financial Crisis Inquiry Report*, 373–75.

50. Ibid., 374.

51. Irwin, *Alchemists*, 154; Bradley Keoun and Hugh Son, "Fed May Be 'Central Bank of the World' After UBS, Barclays Aid," *Bloomberg*, December 2, 2010; Phil Kuntz and Bob Ivry, "Fed's Once-Secret Data Compiled by Bloomberg Released to Public," *Bloomberg*, December 23, 2011.

52. J. Lawrence Broz, "The Politics of Rescuing the World's Financial System: The Federal Reserve as a Global Lender of Last Resort," *Korean Journal of International Studies* 13, no. 2 (2015): 323–51.

53. Edward N. Wolff, *A Century of Wealth in America* (Cambridge, Mass.: Harvard University Press, 2017), 562.

54. Theda Skocpol and Lawrence R. Jacobs, eds., *Reaching for a New Deal: Ambitious Governance, Economic Meltdown, and Polarized Politics in Obama's First Two Years* (New York: Russell Sage Foundation, 2011).

55. Eric Rauchway, "Neither a Depression nor a New Deal: Bailout, Stimulus, and the Economy," in Julian E. Zelizer, ed., *The Presidency of Barack Obama: A First Historical Assessment* (Princeton: Princeton University Press, 2018), 30–44.

56. Ron Suskind, *Confidence Men: Wall Street, Washington, and the Education of a President* (New York: Harper, 2011), 27–28, 38–40.

57. Barack Obama, "Remarks in La Crosse, Wisconsin," October 1, 2008, American Presidency Project, https://www.presidency.ucsb.edu/documents/remarks-la-crosse-wisconsin-1.

58. Barack Obama, "Remarks in Columbus, Ohio," November 2, 2008, American Presidency Project, https://www.presidency.ucsb.edu/documents/remarks-columbus-ohio-6.

59. Obama, "Remarks in La Crosse, Wisconsin."

60. U. S. Office of Management and Budget, *A New Era of Responsibility: Renewing America's Promise: President Obama's First Budget* (Washington, D.C.: U.S. Government Printing Office, 2010).

61. Obama, "Remarks in Columbus, Ohio."

62. Suskind, *Confidence Men*; Noam Scheiber, *The Escape Artists: How Obama's Team Fumbled the Recovery* (New York: Simon & Schuster, 2011).

63. Daniel Carpenter, "The Contest of Lobbies and Disciplines: Financial Politics and Regulatory Reform," in Skocpol and Jacobs, *Reaching for a New Deal*, 144.

64. Ivaylo D. Petev, Luigi Pistaferri, and Itay Saporta-Eksten, "An Analysis of Trends, Perceptions, and Distributional Effects in Consumption," in David B. Grusky, Bruce Western, and Christopher Wimer, eds., *The Great Recession* (New York: Russell Sage Foundation, 2011), 161–95.

65. Atif Mian and Amir Sufi, *House of Debt: How They (and You) Caused the Great Recession, and How We Can Prevent It from Happening Again* (Chicago: University of Chicago Press, 2014).

66. See "An Open Letter to Ben Bernanke," *Wall Street Journal* (November 10, 2010).

67. Scheiber, *Escape Artists*, 138.

68. Greg Kaplan and Giovanni L. Violante, "A Tale of Two Stimulus Payments: 2001 Versus 2008," *American Economic Review* 104, no. 5 (2014): 116–21.

69. Tracy Gordon, *State and Local Budgets and the Great Recession* (Stanford, Calif.: Stanford Center on Poverty and Inequality, 2012).

70. Michael Grunwald, *The New New Deal: The Hidden Story of Change in the Obama Era* (New York: Simon & Schuster, 2012), 82, 239.

71. J. D. Connor, "The Trader's Voice: Rick Santelli's Tea Party Rant," *Journal of Visual Culture* 14, no. 2 (2015): 185.

72. Theda Skocpol and Vanessa Williamson, *The Tea Party and the Remaking of Republican Conservatism* (New York: Oxford University Press, 2012).

73. Richard W. Johnson, *Older Workers, Retirement and the Great Recession* (Stanford, Calif.: Stanford Center on Poverty and Inequality, 2012).

74. Skocpol and Williamson, *Tea Party*, 63, 68–74.

75. Robert A. Moffitt, *The Social Safety Net and the Great Recession* (Stanford, Calif.: Stanford Center on Poverty and Inequality, 2012), 1.

76. Isaac Martin and Christopher Niedt, *Foreclosed America* (Stanford, Calif.: Stanford Briefs, 2015), 63.

77. Michael Hout and Erin Cumberworth, *The Labor Force and the Great Recession* (Stanford, Calif.: Stanford Center on Poverty and Inequality, 2012), 1.

78. Moffitt, *Social Safety Net*, 4.

79. Douglas S. Massey, *Immigration and the Great Recession* (Stanford, Calif: Stanford Center on Poverty and Inequality, 2012), 1.

80. Skocpol and Williamson, *The Tea Party and the Remaking of Republican Conservatism*, 201–9.

81. For an important philosophical critique of privatization, see Chiara Cordelli, *The Privatized State* (Princeton: Princeton University Press, 2020).

82. Suzanne Mettler, *The Submerged State: How Invisible Government Policies Undermine American Democracy* (Chicago: University of Chicago Press, 2011).

83. Donald Trump, "Speech at the Conservative Political Action Conference," Democracy in Action, Orlando, Fla., February 10, 2011, http://www.p2012.org/photos11/cpac11/trump02101 1spt.html.

84. Commission, *Financial Crisis Inquiry Report*, 227.

85. Martin and Niedt, *Foreclosed America*, 5, 83.

86. Eisinger, *Chickenshit Club*, 164–330.

87. Lane Kenworthy and Lindsay A. Owens, "The Surprisingly Weak Effect of Recessions on Public Opinion," in Grusky, Western, and Wimer, *Great Recession*, 196–219.

88. Martin and Niedt, *Foreclosed America*, 64–65.

89. Rebecca Barrett-Fox et al., *The Great Recession in Fiction, Film, and Television: Twenty-First-Century Bust Culture* (Lanham, Md.: Lexington Books, 2013).

90. Elizabeth Gumport, "Fictional Capital," *n+1* 10 (Fall 2010).

91. Adam Ashcraft, Allan Malz, and Zoltan Pozsar, "The Federal Reserve's Term Asset-Backed Securities Loan Facility," *FRBNY Economic Policy Review* 18, no. 3 (2012), 29–57.

92. "Ben Bernanke's Greatest Challenge," 60 Minutes, March 12, 2009, https://www.cbsnews.com/news/ben-bernankes-greatest-challenge/.

93. Suskind, *Confidence Men*, 234.

94. Geithner, *Stress Test*, 23–74.

95. Wolff, *Century of Wealth*, 22–29.

96. Piketty, Saez, and Zucman, "Distributional National Accounts: Methods and Estimates for the United States"; Emmanuel Saez and Gabriel Zucman, "Wealth In-

equality in the United States Since 1913: Evidence from Capitalized Income Tax Data," *Quarterly Journal of Economics* 131, no. 2 (2016): 519–78.

97. Ann Owens and Robert Sampson, *Community Well-Being and the Great Recession* (Stanford, Calif.: Stanford Center on Poverty and Inequality, 2012).

98. Thomas Philippon, *The Great Reversal: How America Gave Up on Free Markets* (Cambridge, Mass.: Belknap Press, 2019), 45–51.

99. Anne Case and Angus Deaton, *Deaths of Despair and the Future of Capitalism* (Princeton: Princeton University Press, 2020).

100. Hout and Cumberworth, *Labor Force*, 2.

101. Moffitt, *Social Safety Net*, 5.

102. Paul Starr, "Achievement Without Credit: The Obama Presidency and Inequality," in Julian E. Zelizer, ed., *The Presidency of Barack Obama: A First Historical Assessment* (Princeton: Princeton University Press, 2018), 45.

103. Lawrence R. Jacobs and Theda Skocpol, "Hard-Fought Legacy: Obama, Congressional Democrats, and the Struggle for Comprehensive Health Care Reform," in Skocpol and Jacobs, *Reaching for a New Deal*, 86–87, 73–874.

104. Daniel Carpenter, "The Contest of Lobbies and Disciplines: Financial Politics and Regulatory Reform," in Skocpol and Jacobs, *Reaching for a New Deal*, 158.

105. Congressional Budget Office, "Estimated Impact of the American Recovery and Reinvestment Act on Employment and Economic Output in 2014," February 2015.

106. James Bullard, "President's Message: Quantitative Easing—Uncharted Waters for Monetary Policy," Federal Reserve Bank of St. Louis, January 1, 2010, https://www.stlouisfed.org/publications/regional-economist/january-2010/quantitative-easinguncharted-waters--for-monetary-policy.

107. Jim Flaherty, Minister of Finance, "G7 Chair's Summary," Iqaluit, Nunavut, Canada, February 6, 2010, http://www.g8.utoronto.ca/finance/fm100206.html.

108. Timothy Geithner, "Welcome to the Recovery," *New York Times*, August 3, 2010.

109. Commission, *Financial Crisis Inquiry Report*, 375, 382.

AFTERWORD

1. Donald Trump and Tony Schwartz, *Trump: The Art of the Deal* (New York: Random House, 1987), 58.

2. "How Trump's Election Shook Obama: 'What if We Were Wrong?'," *New York Times*, May 30, 2018.

3. John Maynard Keynes, "National Self-Sufficiency," *Yale Review* 22, no. 4 (1933): 760–61.

INDEX

JONATHAN LEVY is the author of *Freaks of Fortune: The Emerging World of Capitalism and Risk in America* (winner of the Organization of American Historians' Frederick Jackson Turner Award, among other prizes). He is a professor in the Department of History and the John U. Nef Committee on Social Thought at the University of Chicago, where he also directs the Law, Letters, and Society program.

ABOUT THE TYPE

This book was set in Photina, a typeface designed by José Mendoza in 1971. It is a very elegant design with high legibility, and its close character fit has made it a popular choice for use in quality magazines and art gallery publications.